TOPOGRAPHIC MAP OF THE UNITED STATES

P9-DOB-409

Lake Superior

Lake Michigan

Lake Huron

Mississippi River

Lake Ontario

Lake Erie

St. Lawrence River

Lake Champlain

Mt. Washington (6,288 ft.)

Connecticut R.

Hudson R.

CAPE COD

Illinois R.

CENTRAL

PLAINS

Wabash R.

Ohio R.

River

Allegheny R.

Monongahela R.

MOUNTAINS

Susquehanna R.

Delaware R.

Potomac R.

James R.

R.

Chesapeake Bay

ARK HILLS

LOWER

Cumberland River

Tennessee R.

MISSISSIPPI

APPALACHIAN

Mt. Mitchell (6,684 ft.)

PIEDMONT

COASTAL PLAIN

CAPE HATTERAS

A T L A N T I C   O C E A N

VALLEY

Mississippi River

Alabama R.

Savannah R.

ATLANTIC

PLAIN

COASTAL

MISSISSIPPI DELTA

FLORIDA PENINSULA

G U L F   O F   M E X I C O

| 0 | 100 | 200 | 300 | 400 |

Miles

45°

40°

35°

30°

25°

75°

70°

ATLANTIC OCEAN

PUERTO RICO

18°

65°

| 0 | 50 | 100 |

Miles

FLORIDA KEYS

90°

85°

80°

AMERICA'S HISTORY

R. JACKSON WILSON
Smith College
EDITOR

MICHAEL P. CONZEN
University of Chicago
ADVISORY EDITOR FOR CARTOGRAPHY

America's History

JAMES A. HENRETTA
University of Maryland

W. ELLIOT BROWNLEE
University of California, Santa Barbara

DAVID BRODY
University of California, Davis

SUSAN WARE
New York University

THE DORSEY PRESS
Chicago, Illinois 60604

Front cover: John Lewis Krimmel. *Election Day at the State House, 1816.* Historical Society of Pennsylvania

Printing press featured with New Technology essays, courtesy Les Feller, Printers Row Printing Museum, Chicago

Cartography by Mapping Specialists, Ltd.

© THE DORSEY PRESS, 1987

ISBN 0-256-03544-X

Library of Congress Catalog Card No. 86–71320

Printed in the United States of America

1 2 3 4 5 6 7 8 9 0 KR 4 3 2 1 0 9 8 7

FOR OUR FAMILIES

PREFACE

History—the way people think about their society's past—comes in many sizes and shapes. It has been carved in hieroglyphs in Egyptian tombs and temples. It has been told in the chants and legends of countless tribal societies. It has been tucked away in meticulous dynastic diaries kept by Chinese court scholars. It has been cynically revised by prudent kings and careless politicians, beautifully written by blind Greek poets and insightful Hebrew scribes.

But however it has been told, history has usually been about the deeds of the great and powerful. The main actors in the story have been gods and prophets, kings and princes, rulers and presidents. Occasionally, something else might intrude, like a flood, earthquake, or famine. Sometimes even the "people" appeared—usually as an invading "horde," or some sort of unruly "mass" at a moment of riot or revolution. But traditional history has treated such natural and human eruptions as temporary distractions from the main stories of wars and marriages, struggles and follies of great men—and, rarely, great women.

In our own time some of this has changed. No notion has more currency in the twentieth-century world than "democracy." No term carries more weight than "the people." In such a world it is inevitable that historians should look a little away from the thrones and offices of the mighty, and pay some attention to "ordinary" people. From the time of the French and American revolutions, scholars in Europe and America began to talk about a new history, one that would be about "simple" men and women. They also began to think of history not as the outcome of the actions of powerful individuals, but as the result of "forces." These social and economic forces were what made history move. Princes and prime ministers were merely swept along in the stream, under the vain illusion that they could steer the boat or even guide the current itself.

The democratic project of writing history about "the people" occurred wherever the idea—if not the fact—of popular government took root. But for a long time the results were disappointing. In most societies, the documentary evidence had been produced and preserved by the rich and the powerful, and most working historians remained tied to those documents. The discussion of forces usually remained abstract or did not really deliver what it promised: an improved understanding of the daily lives of ordinary men and women.

But historians are nothing if not stubborn. And the twentieth century has seen some real progress. Here and there, rich studies began to be produced on this English village or that French town. "Schools" of historians formed, with the definite and committed purpose of doing what came to be called "social history." Scholarly journals were founded. New kinds of evidence were brought into play. Historians began to look into odd places for radically new kinds of "documentation." They studied the records of the Vienna boys' choir, going back centuries, to find out when boys were moved from soprano to tenor, as a way of getting at an obscure but crucial question: how had the age of puberty changed during centuries of time? They compared military muster rolls to find how men's heights changed over time, and were able to infer the impact of urbanization and city work on the health of white laborers. Slave manifests yielded similar insights on the health and living conditions of black slaves. Slowly, but with a growing measure of sureness, the possibility of a genuine social history became real.

In the United States, this kind of change in the discipline of history reached a climax of sorts beginning in the 1960s. A generation of scholars set out to perfect what they called the "new social history." With energy, dedication, and often real brilliance, they tried to reconstruct the lives of the poor, the dispossessed, and the oppressed. They asked questions not about presidents but about shoemakers and butchers. They turned their attention from exclusively male affairs like treaties and wars to the experiences of women and children. They painstakingly tried to find out what slave families were like. They looked away from the literature of "high" culture—from the supposedly great writings of novelists and poets—to folk tales. The stories of "Br'er Rabbit" gained a significance equal to the novels of Henry James or the writings of Thomas Jefferson. Finding out the age at which most women had their first child became as significant as trying to explain a decision of President Andrew Jackson.

And so, in the past quarter of a century, the ways historians do their work have been deeply changed. The change was partly just a continuation of the democratic project that had been under way in the western world for two centuries. But it was hurried along by two other things. First, the historians themselves were different. More and more they were female or they came from families that were either poor or ethnically outside the cultural mainstream that had produced most of the scholars in American universities before World War II. They were interested in those aspects of the American past that had produced their own and their families' lives. Second, the ways many of them thought about history were shaped by the civil rights movement, the effort to stop the war in Vietnam, and the revival of feminism. They learned to regard the political state with greater skepticism. And when they did their work as historians, they turned their search for the real meanings of history away from politics and the state toward things that seemed to them more illuminating and more concrete.

These changes in the practice of history were profound and—we think—splendid. The question we have pondered most is how to take advantage of a generation's worth of such work in an introductory textbook. Some historians have decided to continue to produce textbooks that still focus mainly on presidents, politics, elections, and wars—the traditional subject matter that the "new" social history tried to displace. Social history could wait, they reasoned, until the student took some more "advanced" course. Other textbooks have sought to inject social history into their books, paring down on the space allotted to traditional political subjects. A few historians have even tried to write introductory texts in which political history is largely dismissed and simply replaced by new material on family, work, childhood, and the like.

It has seemed to us—and this is the conclusion that has shaped our work on *America's History* for several years—that all these solutions were wrongheaded. Continuing to present American history to beginning students as though the important changes in the ways historians work had not happened is just as bad as giving engineering or physics students a textbook that ignores three decades of new scientific and technical discoveries. On the other hand, an introductory text solely concerned with social history would leave out central parts of our nation's history. The existence of the state, the story of political parties, and the effects of presidential action or Supreme Court judgments are just as real as and perhaps more important than marriage customs or childrearing practices.

So we decided to look for ways to combine the new social history and the more traditional focus on politics. But this decision was much easier to make than it was to carry out. We hoped to find some guidance in what we thought might be the best of the new textbooks produced in recent years. But what we found in them was mainly an attempt to *insert* social history into an old framework. The traditional ways of dealing with political history were all still in place, unchanged. The social history had been pinned on, like the tail on the donkey in the old children's game. A chapter on the 1890s—mainly about the election of 1896 and the Spanish-American War of 1898—might include a biographical sketch of a coal-miner, say, or a farm wife, but the individual's life remained outside the major events. The effect, in general, was of two parallel histories—one social, the other political—connected to each other only by the accidental fact that they happened at the same time.

What we have attempted, in contrast, is to put social and political history together, and in ways that use each to make better sense of the other. We realized that the history of American life could be understood best if we could lay out the fundamental conditions that controlled *both* the social lives of ordinary people *and* the practice of politics. This meant moving beyond conventional ways of organizing the story around political events that historians like to think of as "turning points" or "watersheds." Social change might have a pace and rhythm of its own. And understanding this pace and rhythm might even enable us to see political changes in a new light.

We searched for a way of understanding American history as a sequence of long phases of development. We finally decided on a unique chronological division of American history into three periods, each with its own defining characteristics. We have called these periods, first, Preindustrial America, running from the beginning of the sixteenth century down into the second or third decade of the nineteenth century; second, Industrializing America, lasting about a century, from the 1820s to the 1920s; and, third, State and Society, running from about 1920 to the present. Each of these periods had its own logic and its own special kinds of human relationships. Each period produced its own distinctive social *and* political history.

In fact, we realized as we worked that the very distinction between social and political history was a bit of an illusion. Every human action, no matter how trivial or how grandiose, has dimensions that have to be recognized as political and social. Political choices always expressed fundamentally *social* choices, shaped by human relationships like family, village, ethnicity, or class. On the other hand, every human experience—like marriage or employment—is also *political*. Every social action assumes that there are certain kinds of legitimate power, and is part of the same web of history that shapes "political" concepts like the idea of kingship, or election, or legislation.

In the end, we reminded ourselves that there is only *history*. Historians may use categories like economic history or diplomatic history as convenient ways of saying what kind of work they do. But such distinctions are only the devices of scholars, not the reality of human experience. And so we decided to drop the subtitle we had chosen earlier: "The Political and Social History of the United States." We believe we have found ways to fuse the best work of political and social historians into one understandable story. *America's History* is the result of our own effort to reach a coherent understanding of the nation's past, an understanding that speaks to us of both social and political facts: farm wives as well as presidents, social customs as well as acts of Congress, the ways people eat and keep warm as well as the ways they make wars or found governments.

Features

Our text contains a variety of special features that highlight and amplify upon key points in each period:

- Over 110 detailed maps in full color provide geographical context for events in the text. These maps illustrate the nation's history in both conventional and unusual ways, showing major territorial conflicts and military campaigns, the changing shapes and political importance of the states, as well as changes in ethnic and religious distribution, cultural patterns, industrial concentration, the shift from rural to urban life, and much more. Explanatory captions tell the story of each map and link it to the text.

- Each chapter includes a Time Line that graphically summarizes the key events in the chapter, giving students a quick reference for review.

- Scores of primary documents, averaging two per chapter, give students a rich and immediate sense of the past.

- Within each period, essays on New Technology describe revolutionary changes in technology that were central to the economic and cultural life of that period.

- Six photo essays explore the visual worlds and cultural milieu of each major period.

- Over 300 photographs in color and black and white provide visual documents of each chapter's main actors and events, as well as showing contemporary life and culture. Like the maps, all photographs have extensive informative captions that tell students the significance of each illustration.

- Forty-five graphs and tables present data that support arguments in the text, covering topics that range from demographic changes to changes in the national economy.

- Each chapter concludes with an extensive annotated bibliography to guide students' further reading and research.

Finally, our text comes with an *Instructors Manual*, student *Study Guide*, and a companion reader entitled *The Course of United States History*. This reader contains outstanding scholarly articles and innovative essays that teach students how to read primary documents.

Acknowledgments

We wish to thank R. Jackson Wilson for conceiving this project and for sharing with us the trials and thrills of bringing it to fruition. His close attention to the manuscript through its many drafts and his collegial support have meant a great deal to us.

We also thank the editors and the production staff of The Dorsey Press for their invaluable assistance; James Shacter and John Sturman for their masterful copy editing; and the following scholars, who read the manuscript with great care, saved us from many mistakes, and helped us develop a coherent and compelling portrait of the history of the American people: John K. Alexander, University of Cincinnati; Genevieve Berkhofer, University of Michigan; John D. Born, Jr., Wichita State University; Anne Boylan, University of Delaware; Jerry M. Cooper, University of Missouri–St. Louis; Alan Dawley, Trenton State; Robert R. Dykstra, SUNY Albany; Thomas R. Frazier, Baruch College, The City University of New York; James Gilbert, University of Maryland; Maurine Greenwald, University of Pittsburgh; Carl V. Harris, University of California, Santa Barbara; Mary Kelley, Dartmouth College; Bruce Laurie, University of Massachusetts; Russell Menard, University of Minnesota; John Murrin, Princeton University; Jerome Mushkat, University of Akron; David Nasaw, The College of Staten Island; John Schneider, University of Nebraska, Lincoln; Herb Shapiro, University of Cincinnati; James E. Sherwood; Kathryn Kish Sklar, University of California, Los Angeles; Judith E. Smith, Boston College; Emory Thomas, University of Georgia; Robert Weir, University of South Carolina; William Bruce Wheeler, University of Tennessee, Knoxville; John Scott Wilson, University of South Carolina; Nancy Woloch; and Virginia Yans, Rutgers University.

We as authors are listed on the title page in the order in which we have contributed to the text. James A. Henretta wrote chapters 1–10, W. Elliot Brownlee chapters 11–16, David Brody chapters 17–21, and Susan Ware chapters 22–31. Each of us, of course, read and criticized the chapters of the others, and we accept joint responsibility for the book as a whole.

JAMES A. HENRETTA
W. ELLIOT BROWNLEE
DAVID BRODY
SUSAN WARE

CONTENTS

xi

31 *A Proud but Troubled People* 954

A Time of Troubles 954

Lowered Expectations and New Challenges 963

ILLUSTRATIONS

MAPS

FIGURES

TABLES

PART ONE

𝒫REINDUSTRIAL

1607-1820

The past is like a foreign country. Like a strange land, the historic landscape is filled with unfamiliar things and people. Its political system, economic rules, social customs, and religious values appear alien to the eyes of the modern observer. To understand early American history, we must realize that the men and women who settled in North America were not members of a modern society. Their institutions, values, and personalities reflected the way of life of the traditional society of preindustrial Europe.

The first ten chapters of this book explore the character of preindustrial America. Our travels begin in Europe but take place primarily in the English colonies that became the United States. As in

AMERICA

any guidebook, these chapters contain hundreds of interesting facts and striking details. They describe the lives of ordinary as well as important people. And they explain the momentous political, social, and economic events that shaped people's experiences and gave their lives a larger historical significance.

The plot of the tale is complex. It is best understood in terms of certain central themes. These themes run through—and unite—the individual experiences of millions of men, women, and children, dozens of political and social institutions, and two centuries of history. Like the subplots of a long novel, the themes interweave continually with one another. Taken together, they reveal the growing complexity and diversity of life in preindustrial America.

Six themes give form and meaning to this historical drama. The first theme comprises a human tragedy of epic proportions. Millions of native Americans had occupied the land of the Western Hemisphere for centuries but, following the arrival of Europeans, they nearly vanished as a result of exploitation and disease.

The second theme is more inspiring. The Europeans who migrated to the New World came from impoverished agricultural societies wracked by periodic famines. Settling in the bountiful natural environment of North America, they created prosperous farming communities. Gradually, abun-

dance replaced poverty as the prime fact of economic life.

Every economic change has social causes and consequences. Destitute peasants formed the base of preindustrial Europe. In America, social class took a different form. The New World became both "the best poor man's country" for Europeans and a land of oppressive captivity for Africans. This simultaneous, and paradoxical, expansion of white freedom and black slavery is a third theme of the American drama.

The emergence of an increasingly free and competitive political system in America is a fourth theme. The first European settlers brought their traditional elitist customs and authoritarian doctrines to the new colonies. Aristocratic forms of government persisted, in weakened form, until the American War of Independence began in 1776. The revolutionary ideas of republicanism hastened the creation of more open, egalitarian systems of government.

The fifth theme involves the transformation of the American family, the basic social unit. English settlers lived in patriarchal, ancestral families. The father exercised supreme authority, both by custom and by law. Gradually, the traditional family declined in internal cohesion and social importance. By the end of the preindustrial period, the American family was evolving into a conjugal unit. This new family system had more equal emotional and legal relationships among husbands, wives, and children.

The changing character of religious institutions and values forms the final theme of this historical drama. Spiritual beliefs shaped the lives of many migrants to the New World. The societies they created became increasingly religious between 1607 and 1820, but theological dogma and religious authority changed as well. Many Americans rejected hierarchical forms of religious authority and rigid, pessimistic spiritual doctrines. In the United States, Protestant Christianity became increasingly tolerant, democratic, and optimistic.

These six themes, interwoven, tell an exciting and at times tragic story. They point to the emergence of a new and distinctively American preindustrial society. The new social order excluded native Americans and condemned Africans to bondage even as it offered Europeans rich opportunities for spiritual satisfaction, economic security, and political freedom.

1

THE EXPANSION OF PREINDUSTRIAL EUROPE

*D*uring the early Middle Ages, the period from about A.D. 400 to 1100, most Europeans lived in poor and highly stratified societies. Their feudal political institutions served the interests of a small class of armed nobles. These feudal states lacked the potential for sustained economic or geographic expansion.

Then, between 1100 and 1400, merchants in the city-states of Italy won political freedom from their feudal overlords. They quickly ousted Moslem middlemen from the lucrative Mediterranean trade in Oriental goods. The merchants' political success and commercial enterprise laid the basis for the Renaissance, a major revival of learning and culture. During the Renaissance, from about 1250 to 1400, Europeans greatly expanded their intellectual, artistic, and geographic horizons.

Influenced by the "new learning" of the Renaissance and by Italian maritime exploits, the Portuguese sought a new route to the Orient. Their mariners sailed boldly along the western coast of Africa and then across the Indian Ocean to Asia. Not to be outdone, Spanish adventurers explored and conquered vast areas in the Western Hemisphere.

Oriental riches poured into Europe, as did gold and silver from the mines of Middle America. These treasures increased prices and expanded economic activity, sparking 120 years of European prosperity. This expansive period is known as the "long" sixteenth century, from 1500 to 1620. It was an era of sustained economic and political development that led directly to the English colonization of North America.

Traditional Agricultural Society

From the Middle Ages to the Industrial Revolution, which began about 1750, most Europeans lived on the land, farming it with primitive tools, and consuming its meager produce. Their lives were hard and at the mercy of forces beyond their control. Bandits threatened their safety. Droughts destroyed their crops. Plagues killed their husbands, wives, and children. Amid this physical danger, the Christian church offered peasants emotional comfort and spiritual support during their earthly lives and the hope of eternal salvation after death.

The World of the Peasant

Preindustrial Europe consisted of a multitude of rural communities. A great mass of rural families, the peasantry, cultivated the soil. They built their own rude huts and produced most of the goods they needed to survive. Families exchanged surplus grain or meat with their relatives and neighbors and bartered these goods for the specialized services of such artisans as weavers, blacksmiths, and roof thatchers. Each village was nearly self-sufficient. There were few merchants, and commercial transactions were limited. "Variations in money hardly interest the greater part of the peasants," noted one French observer as late as 1713, for they "do not possess currency."

The primitive state of transport made extensive trade or travel difficult. Peasant villages were isolated, linked only by rough paths or dirt roads. Heavy rain or deep snow made these crude trails virtually impassable. Even in good weather, travel on oxen-drawn carts was slow and uncomfortable. Isolation limited people's horizons and aspirations. On rare occasions, a man might seek work (or a wife) in a nearby village, fight as an unwilling conscript in a distant war, or visit a major city. A woman would only leave her village to marry or to work as a domestic servant, to sell homespun textiles at a regional fair, or to make a pilgrimage to a famous religious shrine. All these events were exceptional. They amounted to brief and exciting forays into the wider world—momentary departures from the tightly restricted character of village life.

For most peasants, mere survival required heavy labor. Except for water- or wind-powered mills for grinding grain, the people had no engines and few labor-saving devices or machines. Raw muscle power was the major source of energy. Horses and oxen strained to break the soil with primitive wooden plows, while men pushed from behind. At harvest time, peasants cut hay, wheat, rye, and barley by hand. Swinging their small sickles, they moved through the fields at the agonizingly slow rate of about half an acre per person per day. Even when fine weather brought a good harvest, their labor yielded a meager return. Poor seed quality, lack of fertilizer, and inadequate plows kept output low—ten bushels of grain per acre at most. The margin of existence was thin.

Geography and climate determined the pattern of rural existence. Peasants in the hot Mediterranean region stopped work during the heat of the summer day. Their midday siesta became a highly prized custom in Spain, and migrants took it to the subtropical colonies in Middle America. For the peoples of northwestern Europe, dramatic seasonal changes in the weather established the basic rhythm of existence. The agricultural year held greater meaning for English country folk than the calendar year. Heavy farm labor did not begin in January. It started at the end of March, when the spring sun melted the snow and thawed the ground. As the soil dried, villagers plowed their land and prepared to plant. Lady Day—March 25—marked the symbolic advent of the English farming year. On that sacred day, commemorating the annunciation of the impending birth of Jesus Christ, peasants prayed to the Virgin Mary for a fertile crop. With less enthusiasm, they paid the first quarterly installment of their rent to their landlords.

Once the agricultural year began, the pace of life quickened. Peasants sowed their fields in April and May. They harvested the first crop of hay in June, dried it in the fields under the hot sun, and stored it as winter fodder for their livestock. During these busy spring months, men sheared the thick winter coats of sheep. Women washed the wool and began to spin it into yarn and weave it into cloth. Families often bartered their wool or a young lamb for flour to replenish depleted food supplies. Merchants and neighbors drove hard bargains because their own stocks of cereal always stayed low during the late spring and early summer months. Grain prices always increased greatly at these lean times.

Peak periods of mortality accompanied the seasonal variations in climate and food supply. Rural folk died in large numbers in January and February, unfortunate victims of freezing winter temperatures and virus diseases. High death rates occurred again in August and September, when the very young and the very old succumbed to fly-borne epidemics of infectious dysentery. The pattern of births likewise followed a seasonal rhythm. For hundreds of years in the villages of preindustrial Europe, and later in America, the greatest number of children were born in February and March. A smaller peak in

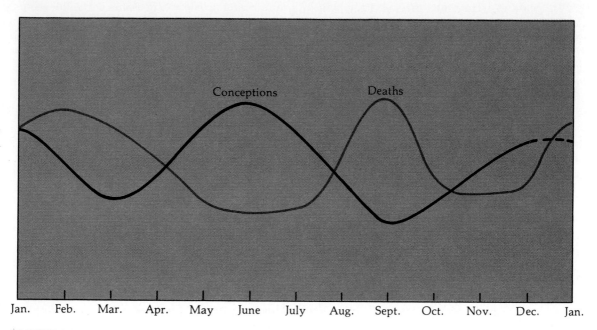

Conceptions   Deaths

Jan.   Feb.   Mar.   Apr.   May   June   July   Aug.   Sept.   Oct.   Nov.   Dec.   Jan.

FIGURE 1.1 THE YEARLY RHYTHM OF AGRICULTURAL LIFE

the birth rate came in September and October. The precise causes of this remarkable pattern remain a mystery. Seasonal variations in nutrition possibly affected the fertility of the husband's sperm or the wife's eggs. Perhaps changes in temperature, food supply, or female work patterns altered the rate of spontaneous abortions from month to month. Cultural and religious practices, such as the strict observance of Lent by Christians, may have diminished sexual activity at certain times of the year. One thing is certain. The seasonal pattern of births reflected life in the preindustrial world; it does not exist in modern urban societies.

The seasons affected both the definition of "work" and the character of "play." Preindustrial labor was task oriented. Spring planting and summer haymaking had to be done quickly, and these intense efforts pushed workers to the limit of their endurance. Peasants worked slowly between bouts of hard labor, mending fences, barns, and houses. Then, following the strenuous fall harvest, they celebrated in prolonged and often riotous bouts of merrymaking. As winter approached, the peasants slaughtered their excess livestock, preserved the meat with

salt or smoke, and began the time-consuming tasks of threshing grain and weaving textiles. Finally, just before the rigorous labor of spring, they staged festive carnivals. In emotional outbursts of dance and drink, they celebrated the end of the long winter night and prepared for the tasks of the agricultural year.

Over the generations, this pattern of concentrated effort and exuberant release became part of the mental outlook of rural folk. "There is nothing more frequent than for an Englishman to work till he has got his pockets full of money, and then go and be idle or perhaps drunk till this is all gone," the novelist Daniel Defoe complained in the early eighteenth century. "He'll drink as long as it lasts and then go to work for more." A German migrant to Pennsylvania likewise cherished the enforced leisure of a "real winter" and refused to move farther south. Without cold and snow, he argued, "people must work year in, year out, and that was not his fancy; winter, with a warm stove and sluggish days being indispensable to his happiness." Like peasants everywhere, men took their pleasures where they could find them.

The forces of nature and the power of human

MEDIEVAL PEASANT AGRICULTURE
European peasants plowed their fields in the autumn and harrowed them before spring planting. They worked hardest during the summer harvest, but spent much of the autumn and winter threshing their grain with hand flails. The lord's miller often had the exclusive right to grind grain into flour, and charged exorbitant fees. (The British Library)

EUROPEAN SOCIAL DISTINCTIONS
Two mounted and armed knights receive due respect from the peasantry. As Sir Thomas Smith described the English social order in the 1560s: "1. The first part of the Gentlemen of England . . . the nobility or aristocracy proper. 2. The second sort of Gentlemen . . . the gentry of Knights, Esquires and gentlemen. 3. Citizens, Burgesses and Yeomen. 4. The fourth sort of men which do not rule . . . day labourers, poor husbandmen, and all artisans . . . have no voice nor authority in our commonwealth and no account is made of them, but only to be ruled and not to rule others."(*Massacre of the Innocents* from the *Jerusalem Triptych*. Museum Narodowe, Warsaw; Polish State Institute of Art)

institutions made people's lives hard and short. As in all agricultural societies, owning land meant wealth, power, and security. Yet European peasants owned only a small part of the land on which they toiled. In the Beauvais region of France, for example, the aristocracy, along with the Roman Catholic church and absentee merchants, controlled nearly 60 percent of the land. In eastern Europe, peasants owned even less property. A visiting Englishman noted,

The truth is that the nobles are the only land-owners there, and the peasants are slaves, and the nobles, in order to maintain themselves, appropriate the toil and products of the workers, who form at least seven-eighths of the popula-

tion and are reduced to eating bread made from barley and oats.

In England, peasants lived better but gradually lost control of the land. Between 1500 and 1800, nobles and gentry seized possession of this vital resource, leasing small plots to tenant farmers or hiring landless peasants to work on their large estates.

These landed classes dominated rural society. Nobles and gentry served as the political agents of the princes and kings of Europe. Their powers as judges, magistrates, and militia officers neatly complemented the authority commanded by their economic resources and social status. Indeed, aristocrats occupied a special place in the social and legal order. Most nobles owned large estates and enjoyed legal privileges that were passed down, by birth, from one generation to the next. Nobles controlled their own legislative institutions, such as the French *parlements* and the English House of Lords. If accused of a crime, they could demand a trial before a jury composed of their own noble peers. They also had the right, by law or custom, to demand goods, services, and pledges of loyalty from their peasants.

The privileged elites lived very differently from the mass of rural folk. They wore carefully tailored garments of tightly woven cloth, rather than ill-cut breeches and blouses of rough homespun wool or linen. Their hands were as smooth as their clothes, not calloused and torn by the tasks of manual labor. However, noble lineage did not protect the aristocracy from the ravages of disease, such as measles or smallpox, and so their faces were as pockmarked as those of the peasants. Yet wealth and status meant comfort, leisure, and education. Many nobles and gentry had narrow, provincial outlooks, but they also had access to the wider world. They could travel, read books and religious tracts, and participate in affairs of state.

Their privileged existence rested ultimately on their armed might and political power—the ability to appropriate the surplus goods produced by the peasantry. Whether as east European serfs, small French proprietors, or English tenant farmers, peasants formed the agricultural foundation of the civilizations of Europe, but enjoyed few of the benefits. Exploited and downcast, many of these suffering men and women simply accepted their way of life. "Here is an admirable arrangement of nature," thought one French priest. "If she causes men to be born in misery she gives them the disposition that makes them able to endure it and even to forget it." But many could not forget. They hoped for a better life for themselves and their children. The ranks of the deprived peasants of Europe supplied the majority of the migrants to North America during the centuries to come.

The Religious Ethos

During the early Middle Ages, the Roman Catholic church converted the pagan peoples of Europe. By A.D. 1000, its spiritual jurisdiction embraced most of the continent and a score of peoples—Latins, Germans, Celts, Anglo-Saxons, and Slavs. The pope, as head of the Catholic church, ruled a vast institutional hierarchy of cardinals, bishops, and priests. He contested with princes and kings for wealth and power. Pope Boniface VIII tried to prohibit civil rulers from taxing the substantial lands owned by clergy. And, in 1302, he declared in the famous bull *Unam Sanctam* that "every human creature" was "subject to the Roman pontiff." Although few rulers accepted these claims, the Roman church stood as one of the great unifying institutions in European society. Its priests and monks preserved and extended learning in the common language of Latin. Its dogma provided a common understanding of God, the world, and human history.

Christian dogma penetrated all aspects of life. The church fathers linked the calendar of the religious year to the agricultural cycle, compressing most rituals into the cold months. The church celebrated the birth of Jesus Christ, the founder of Christianity, in December, the month with the fewest daylight hours. Three months later, as the spring sun revived the natural world, the major feast of Easter Sunday marked Christ's resurrection. This celebration combined Catholic doctrine with older pagan beliefs and folk customs. Easter took its name from the goddess of spring in the religion of ancient Rome. Pagan practices likewise accounted for the use of eggs, the symbol of new life. These traditions merged again in the rituals of the autumn

months. Pagan harvest celebrations gradually evolved into holy days of thanksgiving in the Christian calendar.

The merger of the sacred and the agricultural cycles endowed all wordly events with a supernatural meaning. Few Christians believed that events occurred by chance or as a result of natural causes. Rather, they happened because God willed them to happen. Did crops rot in the ground or wither under a hot sun? If so, the Lord must be displeased with his people. The Christian Bible stated as much. "The earth is defiled under its inhabitants' feet," read the Book of Isaiah, Chapter 24, "for they have transgressed the law." To avert divinely inspired calamities, pious peasants turned to their priests and begged forgiveness for their sins. Every village had a church or chapel, and a multitude of holy sites and wayside shrines dotted the map of Europe. These sacred places, with their statues of Christ and his saintly followers, were tangible points of contact between the material and spiritual worlds. By offering prayers to such images, Christians hoped to stave off worldly disaster and to assure themselves heavenly salvation.

God's presence in the world received constant emphasis. When he was a child in a peasant village, the eminent French theologian Jean Gerson recalled, his father stood before him with outstretched arms, saying "Thus, child, was your God crucified, who made and saved you." The ceremony of the mass continually reinforced the image of an ever-present God. According to Roman Catholic doctrine, priests had access to great spiritual powers as they conducted this ritual. They could actually transform ordinary bread and wine into the flesh and blood of Christ. On completing this miracle of transubstantiation, pastors in thousands of village churches placed the transformed (but still ordinary-looking) food on the tongues of the faithful. As the people consumed it, the body and blood of Christ mingled with that of human beings. Through this sacrament of Holy Communion, ordinary peasants—as well as priests, aristocrats, and kings—partook of the divine.

Fortified by God's presence, Christians confronted a world divided between the forces of good and those of evil. Indeed, the beginning of the heavenly millenium, the much-predicted thousand-year period of Christ's peaceful rule on

THE POWER OF RELIGIOUS IMAGERY
The graphic portrayal of the crucifixion of Jesus Christ had a powerful impact on ordinary peasants, for their own lives were filled with misery, pain, and the constant prospect of death. Similar images of tortured religious martyrs filled the churches of Catholic Europe. Protestants believed these visual symbols interfered with genuine worship. To create a "pure" spiritual faith, they usually gathered in plain, sparsely furnished churches. (Matthias Grünewald. *The Crucifixion* from the *Isenheim Altarpiece.* Musee Unterlinden, Colmar [Giraudon/Art Resource])

the earth, depended on God's triumph over his archenemy, Satan. Human beings played a pivotal role in this titanic battle. Satan was the fallen angel Lucifer. He had become the devil, who challenged the majesty of God, the creator of all things. Banished by God from the heavenly skies to the underworld of hell, Satan sought desperately to corrupt people and to win their allegiance. His ways were wily and treacherous. If false prophets spread suspicious doctrines and heresies, they were surely the tools of Satan. If a devout Christian fell mysteriously ill, the sickness might be the result of an evil spell, cast by a pagan conjurer or a witch with Satan's aid.

Popes and priests urged Christians to resist Satan's temptations and to crush his followers. Religious zeal prompted the princes and peoples of Europe to undertake a series of armed Crusades. Backed by Italian merchants seeking commercial gain, these expeditions sought to expel Moslem "infidels" from the holy lands of ancient Christianity. In Europe itself, the church hierarchy mobilized loyal followers to suppress those who challenged official dogma. In 1415, John Huss, the patriot reformer of Bohemia, was burned as a heretic for invoking the authority of

the Bible against that of the church, and his movement destroyed by military force. The specter of Satan loomed especially large after 1519, following Martin Luther's denial of the pope's spiritual authority and the revolt of various Protestant sects. Civil and religious authorities in Catholic and Protestant states alike accused thousands of men and women of heresy or witchcraft and put them to death.

Zealous Christian religions thus stood at the center of the spiritual and emotional consciousness of the European preindustrial world. As Europeans migrated to the Western Hemisphere, they took their religious heritage with them. Christian culture and the conflicts among Christian sects profoundly shaped the course of American history.

The Price of Survival

Life was always precarious in preindustrial Europe. About half the population died before the age of twenty-one. The survivors found hunger, cold, disease, and violence to be constant companions. A French doctor reported as famine and plague struck,

I have seen the latest epoch of misery. I have seen hunger transformed into passion, the inhabitants of a region without a harvest wander, led astray by suffering and deprived of everything, envy the fate of domestic animals, lie down in a meadow to eat grass, and share the food of wild beasts.

As two-hundred thousand landless vagrants roamed the French countryside during much of the seventeenth century, reports of robbery and rape by bands of brigands sent waves of panic across the land. Fearful peasants armed themselves with clubs or knives when they left the protection of their villages. Merchants safeguarded their goods with barred windows and heavy oak doors and feared for the lives of their families. "When they have pillaged the markets and the bakers' shops," wrote one worried German gentleman amidst a revolt of half-starved peasants, "they can pillage our houses and slit our throats. They are beginning to ransack the farms, why not ransack the castles." To defend their ancestral estates, nobles mobilized and armed their tenants and servants.

Violence and death stood forth as natural conditions of life. They prompted a fearful, suspicious, and pessimistic outlook. When rapid population growth and political upheaval disrupted English society, the philosopher Thomas Hobbes wrote the *Leviathan* (1651). This famous political treatise advocated a strong authoritarian government to restore order and stability. With scores of "sturdy beggars" and "swarmes of idle persons" searching for something to steal, Hobbes argued, "every man is enemy to every man." There was "continual fear and the danger of violent death; and the life of every man, solitary, poor, nasty, brutish, and short."

To survive in this uncertain world, peasants organized their lives and their communities in a hierarchical manner. Within the family, patriarchal beliefs clearly established the husband as the head of the household. God and nature "having created woman imperfect, and weak and feeble both in body and mind," a French gentleman declared, "has subjected her to the power of man." Legal rules and social customs ensured strict female subordination. Upon marriage, English women lost most of their property, including their clothes; they retained only

the right to "use" them. Their personal identities changed as well, for a married woman assumed the family name of her husband and usually moved to his village.

Males who owned property controlled the family's scarce agricultural resources in an equally patriarchal and authoritarian fashion. Normally they retained ownership of their farms until their physical strength ebbed, at age fifty to sixty. Only then, when their eldest children were nearly thirty years old, did they allow them to marry, providing land to sons and doweries to daughters. Parents arranged most marriages, choosing partners of adequate wealth and status. Their prime goals were the preservation of family property and old-age security for themselves, not the happiness of their heirs. This marriage system guarded the family's economic security, but at a high emotional and financial cost. Young adults endured years of forced sexual deprivation and close parental supervision. Between 10 and 20 percent never married at all, because neither peasants nor nobles could provide all their children with land and goods.

Within the family, as in society as a whole, hierarchy reigned supreme. The seating of family members around the dinner table was determined by sex and age. Many fathers wrote wills to preserve the family through a single male "line," bestowing most of their property on the eldest son and making him responsible for his siblings. Some landless brothers and sisters remained at home and worked on the farm in return for food and shelter. Others joined the ranks of the roaming poor, condemned by the accident of birth order to desperate lives on the margins of society. Impelled by scarcity to rule as patriarchal despots, many fathers suffered a cruel fate. An old man was often "a stranger in his children's houses," one observer noted, until "at last he dies, but it is well for him to make haste, for greed is there, and greed nerves the arm of hidden parricide."

The thin margin of material existence affected all aspects of social life. Influenced by folk beliefs that breast milk was whitened blood, malnourished mothers fed their hungry babies sparingly, calling them "greedy and gluttonous" little beasts. Infanticide occurred frequently. Newborn infants, especially females, were "helped to die" so that older brothers might live. Children seven

POVERTY, FAMINE, AND DEATH IN PREINDUSTRIAL EUROPE

There was a family in Beauvais in the parish of Saint-Etienne in the year 1693 named Cocu: Jean Cocu, weaver of serges, and his wife with three daughters, all four spinning wool for him, since the youngest daughter was already nine years old.

The family earned 108 sols a week, but they ate 70 pounds of bread between them. With bread up to ½ sol a pound, their livelihood was secure. With bread at 1 sol a pound, it began to get difficult. With bread at 2 sols, then at 3 sols—as it was in 1649, in 1652, in 1662, in 1694, in 1710—it was misery. Crisis in agriculture was nearly always followed by crisis in manufacturing: it certainly was in 1693, so work began to fall off, then income. They went without; perhaps they were able to lay their hands on a coin or two saved up for a rainy day; they pawned their things; they began to eat unwholesome food, bran bread, cooked nettles, mouldy cereals, entrails of animals picked up outside the slaughter-houses.

The "contagion" manifested itself in various ways. After hunger came lassitude, starvation, "pernicious and mortifying fevers." The family was registered at the Office of the Poor in December, 1693. In March, 1694, the youngest daughter died; in May the eldest daughter and the father. All that remained of a particularly fortunate family, fortunate because everyone in it worked, was a widow and an orphan. Because of the price of bread.

Source: Pierre Goubert, *Beauvais et le Beauvaisis* (Paris, 1960), p. 76–77.

---

and eight years old commonly lived in other households as servants, to relieve overcrowding at home and instill discipline. Communities regulated marriages to restrict population growth and maintain living standards. If young German couples did not have enough land, equipment, and household goods to create a farmstead, magistrates denied them permission to marry. In English "common field" villages, the male heads of families assembled regularly to order the cultivation of certain crops and limit the number of livestock that each household could graze on the common pasture. Fearful of change, village elders condemned economic innovation and social ambition. In their eyes, change threatened to upset the precariously balanced social equilibrium and destroy the community. Tradition became the measure of all existence. "After a thing had been practiced for so long that it becomes a Custom," an English clergyman proclaimed, "that Custom is Law."

The system of patriarchal and communal control shaped personal character. Most men and women born into preindustrial society achieved only a weak sense of individual identity and ambition. Even among the privileged class, individualism did not exist as a distinct cultural value.

Aristocrats trained their children not to act for themselves, but in the best interest of the lineage. Before 1500, artists rarely signed their paintings and frescos, implicitly acknowledging that the religious subjects depicted in their works were far more important than their own creative talents. In art as in life, figures of authority in the family and the community shaped identity and demanded submission. Most Europeans, including the majority of those who migrated to America, assumed that social survival depended on strict control by family heads and community leaders. These authoritarian and hierarchical attitudes shaped the character of American social and political development for more than a century.

Commerce and Conquest

Beginning around 1000, communities of merchants grew up in the small towns that dotted the rivers and seacoasts of Europe. These traders organized strong guilds and won political privileges from kings and feudal lords. In Italy, they created strong republican city-states. Merchants grew rich by stimulating European trade and manufacturing, and by distributing scarce and expensive spices, jewels, textiles, and ceramics imported from the Orient. Their patronage of the arts sparked a Renaissance of European culture and learning. Inspired by religious fervor and Italian prosperity, the monarchs of Portugal and Spain sought direct access to the spices and manufactures of Asia. Portuguese ships traded along the coast of Africa and, by 1500, had established commercial factories in India. Spanish explorers and adventurers looked westward, across the Atlantic Ocean. They discovered and conquered the native American civilizations of Mexico and Peru. Their oppressive rule, together with diseases brought from Europe, virtually exterminated the Indian peoples of Middle America.

War and Trade

During the ninth century, Christian kingdoms in Denmark and Sweden pioneered in the construction of strong seagoing vessels. For the next two centuries, Norse adventurers ranged widely

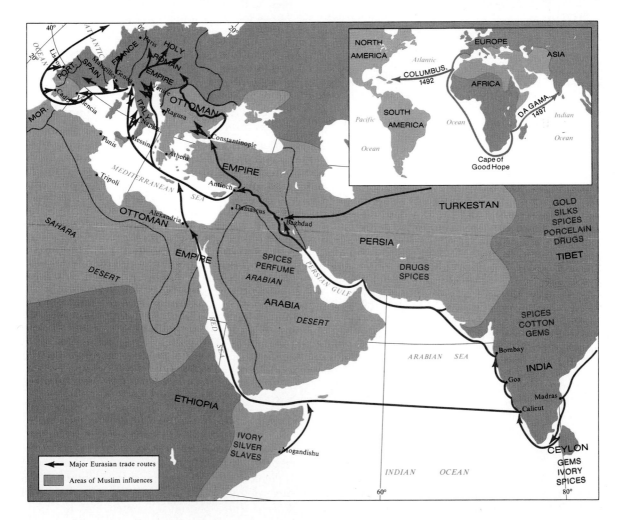

MAP 1.1 THE EXPANSION OF RENAISSANCE EUROPE
For centuries the Mediterranean Sea stood at the center of the trade routes of Europe, northern Africa, and southern Asia. Since 700 A.D., Muslim traders controlled this commerce, and Arab civilization flourished in Alexandria and Constantinople. Beginning the 1490s, Spanish, Portuguese, and Dutch adventurers and merchants opened up new trade routes and changed the pattern of world commerce.

over the lands touched by the Baltic Sea and the Atlantic Ocean. They established a kingdom in Russia, conquered Normandy in France, and invaded England in force. They braved the cold North Atlantic to discover and colonize Iceland and Greenland. Around 1000, these hardy European pioneers landed on Vinland, the eastern coast of North America. The Norse did not settle the distant continent. Instead, they plundered and conquered more accessible and populous territories along the western coast of Europe.

The center of military dynamism in Europe later shifted to the south. Between 1095 and 1300, armies of Christian Crusaders repelled Moslem advances into southern Europe and invaded Palestine. Motivated by religious zeal or perhaps the hope for adventure, plunder, or fame, the Knights of Saint John, of Malta, and of the Teutonic Order sought to capture the Holy Land in which Christ had lived and died.

War and trade went hand in hand. These military expeditions sparked shipbuilding and commercial expansion in the Italian cities of Venice, Genoa, and Pisa. By exposing European aristocrats to Oriental goods, they encouraged trade in luxury items. Italian merchants established trading houses in Cairo, Antioch, and other Mediterranean ports. They purchased goods from China, India, Persia, and Arabia and distributed them throughout Europe. Pepper, nutmeg, ginger, and cloves commanded high prices because of the great demand for spices to flavor and preserve meat and other perishable foods. The privileged classes in European feudal society supported a brisk market for smooth Chinese silks; bright Indian cottons; and sparkling emeralds, rubies, and sapphires from the mines of Ceylon and Tibet. Italian merchants profited handsomely from this trade, as did their partners in the Hanseatic League of cities in northern Europe. These German merchants distributed Oriental goods and Italian and Flemish textiles to markets in England, Russia, Scandinavia, and Poland, as well as Germany.

War and trade introduced the advanced knowledge and technology of Moslem and Oriental civilizations to the isolated and insular peoples of medieval Europe. During the twelfth century, Europeans learned to make and use magnetic compasses, water-powered mills, and mechanical clocks. From the Chinese they discovered the properties and uses of gunpowder. From Arab books and treatises, they rediscovered the great intellectual achievements of the Greeks and Romans in religion, philosophy, mathematics, astronomy, and geography.

The stimulus provided by this "new learning" sparked a period of immense cultural energy and activity, the Italian Renaissance, from about 1300 to 1550. The new commercial aristocracies in the city-states of Florence, Venice, Lucca, Pisa, and Bologna provided a crucial impetus to this era of thought and feeling. Wealthy merchants subsidized a remarkable array of artistic and intellectual projects. Michaelangelo, Vincenzo Bellini, and Filippo Brunelleschi designed and built great architectural masterpieces. Leonardo da Vinci and Raphael created magnificent religious paintings. Reflecting a new emphasis on human ability, these works depicted real individuals, with complex personalities, as well as more abstract and traditional symbols of God and salvation. Niccolo Machiavelli wrote *The Prince* (1513), a realistic, cynical treatise on political behavior that became a handbook of statecraft for rulers throughout Europe.

Italian merchants, bankers, and textile manufacturers achieved equal eminence. The family firms of the Bardi, the Alberti, and the Medici conducted trade, loaned vast sums of money, and spurred technological innovation throughout the continent. For the privileged classes of European society, the Renaissance proclaimed a new and more optimistic definition of human nature and ability. Renaissance man was not a prisoner of blind fate and natural forces but a many-sided personality with the power to change the world.

Machiavelli's heroes in *The Prince* were the ambitious monarchs of northwestern Europe—Louis XI of France, Henry VII of England, and Ferdinand of Aragon in Spain. To counteract the power of the nobility and to build strong national states, these kings formed alliances with merchants in the growing urban centers. Monarchs granted political privileges to guilds and towns and permitted merchants to trade throughout their realms. In return, they extracted taxes and loans to support royal armies. For the first time, an expansive commercial outlook challenged agrarian conservatism in the courts of western Europe.

A DUTCH MERCHANT FAMILY
Between 1550 and 1700, Dutch merchants dominated the carrying trade of Europe. Wealth poured into the Netherlands, creating the magnificent cities of Antwerp and Amsterdam. Yet Dutch culture had an austere, serious tone because of the strong influence of Calvinism. This prosperous family is attired almost completely in black and seems almost oblivious to the bountiful table spread before them. (Cornelis de Zeeuw. *Pieter de Moucheron and his Family.* Rijksmuseum, Amsterdam)

Portugal and Spain emerged as major centers of military, commercial, and religious dynamism. Beginning in 1400, the monarchs of the Iberian Peninsula used military force to subdue the feudal nobility and create unified kingdoms. Religious zeal played a crucial role in this process of nation-building because Christian kings gained power and status through Crusades against the Moors. These Arab Moslems had invaded southern Europe centuries before and still occupied large regions of Spain and Portugal. As Portuguese rulers recaptured Moorish lands, their ambitions expanded to include commerce as well as conquest. To bypass the Italian traders who controlled Oriental commerce, the Portuguese monarchy sought new routes to the wealth of Asia.

Prince Henry the Navigator emerged as the key individual in this maritime adventure. The prince was a complex man. A deeply pious Christian, he hoped to undermine Moslem power on the sea as well as on land. Yet Henry also patronized the "new learning" and drew upon Italy for the latest geographical and technical knowledge. In the spirit of the Renaissance, he sought to fulfill the predictions of his horoscope: "to engage in great and noble conquests and to attempt the discovery of things hidden from other men." Beginning in the 1420s, the prince sent Portuguese sailors into the Atlantic Ocean, where they rediscovered the Madeira and Azores islands. By 1435, Portuguese sea captains had moved beyond their traditional trade in salt, wine, and fish. Now they roamed along the west coast of Africa, seeking slaves, ivory, and gold. With strong monarchical support, Portuguese navigators probed for a direct ocean connection to Asia. In 1488, Bartholomew

Diaz rounded the Cape of Good Hope at the southern tip of Africa. Ten years later, Vasco Da Gama reached India itself and returned with a valuable cargo of pepper and cinnamon.

The Portuguese success marked an important point in world history. For centuries, Moslem peoples had controlled the trade routes between Asia and Europe. Through commerce and conquest they had spread the Islamic faith and Arab civilization beyond the Mediterranean to sub-Saharan Africa, parts of India, and Indonesia. They had marched into Europe and maintained a strong presence in its southeastern flank, the Balkans, for three centuries. But now the terms of the struggle between Christian and Moslem had shifted. The Portuguese had redirected the old Mediterranean war against Moors and Turks into a worldwide commercial and military contest. Square-rigged Portuguese ships and caravels, mounted with heavy cannon, outmaneuvered and outgunned Arab fleets off the coast of India. Backed by armed force, Portuguese and Dutch merchants established trading posts at key points around the great Indian ocean—Goa in India, Hormuz in Arabia, and Malacca in the East Indies. Soon these emergent Atlantic nation-states traded from Africa to Indonesia and up the coast of Asia to China and Japan. Portuguese and Dutch Christians replaced Arab Moslems as the leaders in world commerce.

Spain quickly followed. Portuguese success in the east prompted King Ferdinand of Aragon and Queen Isabella of Castille to seek a western route to the Indies. Married in their teens in an arranged match, the young monarchs combined their kingdoms. Their armies expelled the Moors from Granada, the last Moslem stronghold in western Europe, in 1492. Then, like Prince Henry, they turned their attention to maritime affairs and to the expertise of Italian geographers and sailors. During the Renaissance, Europeans rediscovered the maps and calculations of the ancient Greek geographers Strabo and Ptolemy. As mistakenly interpreted by Christopher Columbus, these maps suggested that Europe, Africa, and Asia covered more than half the earth's surface. The Atlantic Ocean, long feared by Arabs as the "green sea of darkness," appeared as a narrow strip of water separating Europe from the Orient. Repressing their skepticism to match Portuguese exploits, the monarchs and merchants of Spain commissioned Columbus "to discover and acquire islands and mainland in the Ocean Sea."

Columbus set sail in the early summer of 1492. Described by his son as "a man of noble and lofty ambitions," the Genoese sea captain now had the hereditary titles and offices of admiral, viceroy, and governor. He drove the crews of his three small ships and quieted their fears. After six weeks and three thousand miles, Columbus "discovered" the lands of the Western Hemisphere for Europeans. He left forty men on the island of Hispaniola and returned triumphantly with several natives to display to Queen Isabella. A mystical yet determined mariner, Columbus made three more voyages across the Atlantic before 1504. He explored various islands in the Caribbean Sea and the adjacent continental shore but still maintained that he had reached the Far East. He identified Cuba as Cipangu (Japan), the realm of the Great Khan, during his first voyage and maintained that illusion until his death in 1506. By that time, the Florentine merchant and geographer Amerigo Vespucci had explored the coast of South America, also in the service of Spain, and had graphically described it as a *neuvo mundo*, a New World. German geographers named it America in his honor.

The discovery and the naming of the new American world capped two centuries of military and commercial expansion by the peoples of southern Europe—first in the Mediterranean, then in the Indian Ocean, and finally in the Western Hemisphere. Renaissance learning and Christian zeal had lifted the ambitions of European monarchs, and mercantile dynamism had laid the foundations for the expansion of their influence to the far corners of the world.

The Conquest of the Native American Civilizations

Beginning about seventy-five thousand years before the birth of Christ, the ancestors of the native American peoples migrated from Eastern Asia across a land bridge to Alaska. Sixty thousand years later, the rising waters of the Pacific Ocean submerged this route under the Bering Strait. For fifteen thousand years, or about five hundred human generations, the new inhabitants of the Western Hemisphere had no contact with the rest of the world. These tribes of hunters slowly moved to warmer regions and adapted their economic and cultural lives to many climates.

Native American history changed dramatically with the transition from a hunting to an agricultural economy. This momentous change occurred most completely in Mexico and Peru. Beginning about 2000 B.C., the people of these highland regions domesticated maize, or Indian corn. They started with a wild grass; its ear, the edible fruit, was the size of an acorn. Through the centuries, these tribal peoples bred corn into an extremely large and nutritious plant. It was much hardier than wheat, the staple cereal of

Europe, and had more varieties and a higher yield per acre. By cultivating corn, they achieved an agricultural surplus. By 700 B.C., native Americans in the central highlands of Mexico had developed a complex civilization with a sophisticated cultural life.

Semi-nomadic tribes of hunters continually invaded these rich agricultural settlements. Over hundreds of years, the Teotihuacan tribe, then the Toltecs, and finally the Aztecs imposed political control over the peoples of the spacious Valley of Mexico. The conquerers adopted the settled way of life of these peoples and learned to manage their complex irrigation systems. They assimilated traditional spiritual beliefs and built new stone temples of great size and maj-

TENOCHTITLAN: THE AZTEC CAPITAL
This scale model suggests the magnificence of the Aztec capital. Huge temples (for worship and human sacrifice) dominated the city's central square. Food for its 100,000 residents came from artificial islands built on surrounding lakes, and goods from the entire empire filled the marketplace. Its magnificence overwhelmed Bernal Diaz del Castillo, who accompanied Cortes: "Some of the soldiers among us who had been in many parts of the world, in Constantinople, and all over Italy, and in Rome, said that so large a marketplace and so full of people, and so well-regulated and arranged, they had never beheld before." (American Museum of Natural History, New York)

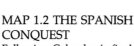

MAP 1.2 THE SPANISH CONQUEST
Following Columbus's final voyages, the Spaniards settled on Hispaniola. Rumors of a magnificent golden civilization led to Cortes's invasion of the Aztec Empire in 1519. By 1535, other Spanish *conquistadors* had conquered the Mayan temple cities and the Inca Empire in Peru. Soon American silver and gold poured into Europe, helping to spark the great price revolution of the sixteenth century.

esty at long-established religious sites. Gradually the invaders extended their control over adjacent valleys and tribes. Under the harsh military rule of the Aztecs, economic tribute from a score of subject peoples poured into the magnificent capital city of Tenochtitlan. Furs, gold, textiles, and food from a vast empire supported Aztec priests and warriors in a style comparable to the most lavish courts of Europe.

Mayan tribes in southeastern Mexico created a civilization of equal splendor and even greater artistic and intellectual sophistication. The Mayans built large religious centers in the rain forests where the flat Yucatan Peninsula rises slowly to the highlands of Guatemala. Skilled artists decorated massive stone temples with magnificent friezes and paintings. Mayan priests perfected a mathematically based calendar of great complexity. It not only told peasants when to plant their crops, but also predicted eclipses of the sun and the moon with great accuracy— and made these forecasts centuries in advance.

After A.D. 700, Mayan civilization fell into slow decline. Internal social struggles sapped its creative and intellectual energies. Peasants re-

volted against the privileged elite of priests and deserted long-established temple cities. Exploiting this weakness, neighboring tribes invaded the Mayan heartland and occupied outlying settlements. By the time of Columbus' voyages, Mayan society had become weak and divided.

When the Spaniards first arrived, they settled on Cuba, Hispaniola, and other Caribbean islands, easily subduing the Indian inhabitants. Then the soldiers and adventurers quickly penetrated the continent in search of gold and plunder. Vasco Nunez de Balboa crossed the Isthmus of Darien (Panama) in 1513 and became the first European to see the Pacific Ocean. Ponce de Leon explored the coasts of Florida. Rumors of the golden splendor of the Aztec empire drew Spanish attention to the Mexican highlands. In 1519, Hernando Cortes, the first of the great Spanish *conquistadors* (conquerors), landed on the coast near Vera Cruz. Leading a force of only about six hundred Spanish soldiers, he marched bravely into the interior. Within two years he had conquered the Aztec empire.

Cortes and his men mounted one of the most impressive conquests in world history. They were aided by various superstitious Aztec writings that predicted defeat by white-skinned, bearded strangers from the east. Horses, steel swords, and primitive muskets gave the Spaniards a great advantage over the native Americans. Despite impressive accomplishments in agriculture, art, and religion, the Indians had not developed an advanced technology. They smelted gold for jewelry but not iron for tools or weapons. They transported crops and goods on their backs, not on wheeled carts. And they had few beasts of burden and no cavalry, for there had been no oxen or horses in the Western Hemisphere. Consequently, Aztec warriors fought on foot, launching flint-tipped spears and arrows. Seated high on their horses, swinging heavy steel swords and protected by heavy armor, the Spanish soldiers cut their way through the best Indian troops.

These technological advantages, though formidable, were not overwhelming. With only about six hundred men and sixteen horses, Cortes was extraordinarily vulnerable. United resistance by the native Americans could easily have crushed the outnumbered European invaders. Like many successful conquerors, Cortes employed a strategy of divide-and-rule. His subtle diplomacy exploited existing divisions between the Aztecs and their subjects. Many Indian peoples resented the arrogant rule of the Aztecs because of an oppressive tribute system. Each year, the Aztec lords demanded the best products of the people's fields and workshops. They seized their finest clothes, furs, and craft goods. Most cruelly of all, the Aztecs took thousands of people to be killed as human sacrifices to the sun god. At the urging of Cortes, the subject tribes rebelled. The people of Tlaxcala in particular provided him with information, supplies, and thousands of soldiers. In the end, the Aztec empire collapsed not from Spanish military strength but from the revolt of subject Indian tribes.

The conquistadors deposed the Aztec emperor Montezuma and took over his centralized political system. Using this established administrative hierarchy, Spanish officials soon dominated their native American allies and extended their rule over the entire Valley of Mexico. Cortes' lieutenants systematically conquered the rest of the highland peoples and then moved against the Mayans in the Yucatan. Simultaneously,

INDIAN VIEWS OF THE SPANISH CONQUEST
The Indians of Middle America had developed a rich visual culture (but not a phonetic alphabet) and wrote in pictograms. These illustrations, from the 1540s, offer the Indians' impressions of Cortes's invasion. His forces included American Indians who rebelled against Aztec rule. (Top, Photo by O. Bauer & J. Beckett. Both, American Museum of Natural History, New York)

Francisco Pizarro mounted an expedition against the rich and powerful Inca empire in Peru. By the 1550s, the Spaniards stood as masters of Middle America, in firm control of centers of native American civilization.

The devastating impact of European diseases played a crucial role in the Spanish military victories. Native Americans had been isolated from the sicknesses of Europe and Asia for thousands of years. As a result, they lacked immunity or resistance to such common European diseases as smallpox, influenza, and measles. Epidemics spread like wildfire among the native Americans, including their soldiers. About half the Inca population may have died from European

WHAT WAS THE TRUTH ABOUT THE SPANISH CONQUEST?

A Franciscan monk tries to refute Bartolome de las Casas's condemnation of the Spanish conquest, 1555.

I saw and read a treatise that Las Casas composed on the subject of the Indians enslaved here in New Spain and on the islands, and another one concerning the opinion he rendered on putting the Indians in encomiendas....

No human being of whatever nation, law or status could read them without feeling abhorrence and mortal hate and considering all the residents of New Spain as the most cruel, abominable and detestable people there are under the sun....

May God pardon Las Casas for so gravely dishonoring and defaming, so terribly insulting and affronting these communities and the Spanish nation, its prince, councils, and all those who administer justice in your majesty's name in these realms....

First I must tell your majesty that when the Spaniards entered New Spain here, it had not been ruled for very long from Mexico City, nor by the Mexica [Aztecs], and the Mexica themselves had won and usurped dominion through war....

People suffered the cruelest of deaths, and our adversary the demon was very pleased with the greatest idolatries and most cruel homicides there ever were, because the predecessor of Moctezuma, lord of Mexico, called Ahuitzotzin, offered to the idols in a single temple and in one sacrifice that lasted three or four days, 80,400 men, whom they brought along four streets, in four lines, until they reached the sacrificial block before the idols. And at the time when the Christians entered New Spain, more than ever before there was sacrificing and killing of men before the idols in all the towns and provinces....

Now these and many other abominations, sins, and offenses made publicly to God and neighbors have been prevented and removed, our holy Catholic faith implanted, the cross of Jesus Christ and the confession of his holy name raised everywhere, and God has brought about a great conversion of people, in which many souls have been saved and are being saved every day; and many churches and monasteries have been built, with more than fifty monasteries inhabited by Franciscan friars alone....

During the last ten years the natives of this land have diminished greatly in number. The reason for it has not been bad treatment, rather the cause has been the great diseases and plagues that New Spain has had, so that the natives continue to decrease each day. God knows the cause; his judgements are many and hidden from us.

Source: Original published in Madrid, 1864; this translation from James Lockhart and Enrique Otte, eds., *Letters and People of the Spanish Indies: Sixteenth Century* (Cambridge University Press, 1976), pp. 220–222, 236, 239.

---

diseases even before Pizarro reached Peru. This abrupt population decline weakened the military strength and psychological strength of the tribes and guaranteed the success of the conquistadors.

European diseases not only destroyed the biological foundations of native American society, but they also greatly changed the history of the Western Hemisphere. Although estimates vary, probably twenty million Indians lived in Mexico and Guatemala at the time of the first Spanish invasion in 1519. Disastrous epidemics in 1521, 1545, and 1575 took millions of lives. By 1650, only three million native Americans remained.

The smaller and more scattered Indian tribes of North America later experienced a similar fate. Their numbers fell from five to seven million in 1650 to only one million by 1890.

Brutal economic exploitation accelerated this unrelenting decline of population. The Spanish government quickly dispatched royal governors, bureaucrats, and Catholic priests to administer its vast new dominion and to protect its new subjects. But conquistadors and other aspiring aristocrats already controlled the old Aztec tribute system, and the crown confirmed their rights to use Indian labor on their vast plantations. To raise livestock for export, the Spaniards destroyed the traditional agricultural system. Imported horses, cattle, and sheep now grazed the land once tilled by men and women. The livestock soon numbered in the millions, while native Americans faced virtual extinction.

This gigantic social disaster made the European triumph complete—and permanent. Unlike the peoples of Asia, Africa, and India, who endured similar European invasions, the native Americans could not perpetuate themselves as a people. Some intermarried with the Spaniards, eventually creating a large *mestizo* population with a predominately Spanish cultural outlook. Other Indians retreated into the mountains and preserved their traditional tribal cultures. In the centuries to come, their descendants lacked the numerical strength or the power—economic, political, or military—to regain control of their lands. For the tribes of the Western Hemisphere, the consequences of their discovery by Columbus in 1492 were tragic and irreversible.

The New World of Sixteenth-Century England

During the "long" sixteenth century of economic expansion, from 1500 to 1620, Europeans transformed the financial, political, and religious structures of their society. Following the Spanish conquest, American gold and silver flowed into Europe. The enormous influx of bullion sparked a great rise in prices that dramatically altered the balance of economic and political power. Simultaneously, a major schism divided the Christian church. Passionate debates over doctrine and practice led to the formation of Catholic and Protestant states, scores of new sects, and bloody religious wars.

These events took a particularly striking form in England. Monetary inflation, together with population growth, created a mobile population of landless peasants, powerful classes of wealthy merchants and rural gentry, and a crisis within the aristocracy. The Tudor and Stuart kings exploited these conditions to increase the power of the royal government. In alliance with the merchant community, they proposed policies of national economic development, beginning the age of mercantilism. By stressing their "divine right"

to rule without Parliament, the kings also advanced the new doctrine of monarchical absolutism. Strident demands by Presbyterians and Puritans for a total reformation of the Church of England increased the political tensions stemming from these social changes and institutional innovations. By 1640, England stood on the brink of civil war.

Prices and Population

American wealth made Spain the dominant nation in Europe. Gold and silver poured out of the rich mines of Zacatecas and Guanajuato in Mexico and Potosi in Bolivia. Between 1570 and 1630 it flowed into Spanish counting houses at the rate of five million pesos per year. About a fifth of this immense treasure went directly into the royal coffers. Philip II became the most powerful ruler in Europe. From the Escorial, his massive administrative palace outside Madrid, this zealous monarch presided over a vast empire. His dominions included The Netherlands, the wealthiest sections of Italy, and, after 1580, Portugal and all its possessions in America and the East Indies. Drawing on these overseas resources, Philip sought to impose Spanish power and Catholicism on all of Europe. His fleets defeated the Ottoman Turks in the battle of Lepanto in 1571, assuring Christian control of the western Mediterranean. He dispatched large armies to fight dynastic wars in Italy and to repress Protestantism in The Netherlands. In 1588, this proud and passionate monarch launched the 130 ships of the Spanish Armada in an unsuccessful invasion of Protestant England.

To finance his enterprises, Philip spent American bullion lavishly. He purchased arms, supplies, and ships from manufacturers in northern and central Europe. Spanish merchants imported textiles and metal wares from England and Germany, and the finest craft goods from France and Holland. German bankers, such as the famous Fugger family, grew rich from war loans to the increasingly ambitious Spanish monarch. Spain, its financial and psychological energies exhausted by continual war, gradually lost its preeminent position in Europe. Holland, France, and England, stimulated economically by Spanish gold, seized the initiative in commerce, manufacturing, and diplomacy.

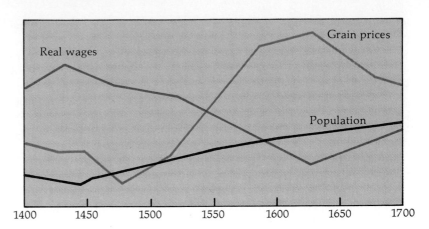

FIGURE 1.2 INFLATION IN
SIXTEENTH-CENTURY
EUROPE

Financial disruption accompanied this economic advance. Precious metals from America doubled the money supply of Europe. Twice as much money now "chased" the limited supplies of food and handmade goods available in preindustrial society. Prices rose sharply. As the population of England increased from three to five million between 1500 and 1620, the demand for scarce goods increased. The shortage of goods and the abundance of money produced massive inflation. During the course of a century, the price of a bushel of wheat soared from one to three shillings.

This "price revolution" had momentous social consequences. In the first place, inflation shifted the balance of economic power among the landowning classes in English society—aristocracy, gentry, and yeomen. Aristocrats had customarily rented out their estates on long leases for fixed rents. These agreements often lasted for "three lives," spanning the lifetimes of several generations of tenants. Such arrangements provided aristocrats with a secure income and a dominant place in the social order. "We eat and drink and rise up to play and this is to live like a gentleman," Viscount Conway affirmed. Lord Berkeley of Gloucester demonstrated his preeminence by visiting London accompanied by 150 servants. Then inflation struck. As grain prices tripled, the nobility's income from rents remained the same. By 1590, the actual income of many English aristocrats had fallen by half, undermining their political power and social status.

Well-established gentry families and rising yeoman farmers improved their relative position in landed society. The gentry had traditionally maintained closer supervision over their small estates. They quickly increased their rental income through flexible short-term leases. Yeomen also benefited from rising prices. Described as "middle people of a condition between gentlemen and cottagers or peasants," these landowners commonly worked their land with family labor. Now they used grain profits to build and furnish substantial houses, a revolution in domestic architecture known as the "great rebuilding" of rural England. Many tenants on noble estates became landowners. They paid the customary fixed rent to their aristocratic landlords, sold their surplus grain at inflated prices, and used the profits to buy small plots of land. Ultimately, this shift in agricultural fortunes altered the balance of political power. Supported by yeoman voters, members of the rising gentry entered the House of Commons and demanded new rights and powers for that representative body of freeholders.

The price revolution had a second, equally significant, impact on the common people of England. Peasants, laborers, and cottage workers accounted for three-fourths of the population. Before 1500, most of these rural folk lived in "open-field" villages. Their compact settlements consisted of small dwellings, each of which housed one family, and tiny plots for raising vegetables. Each family owned, or had a customary right to farm, several plots or long strips of land in the large fields surrounding the village. Since these fields were "open"—that is, not enclosed or divided by fences or hedges—cooperative farming was a necessity. The patriarchs of the village met every year to coordinate the plowing, planting, and harvesting of each field. This assembly also decided how many cows and sheep each family could graze on the commonly owned meadows. Communal cooperation was the price of economic security.

Such collective institutions reflected medieval social conditions and values. The rise in population disrupted this traditional way of life because the number of residents grew faster than agricultural output. As living standards declined, a growing demand for wool raised a new threat. Profit-minded landlords and woolen merchants used political influence in Parliament to annul the customary rights of open-field villagers. During the reigns of the major Tudor monarchs, Henry VII (1485–1509), Henry VIII (1509–1547), and Elizabeth I (1588–1603), Enclosure Acts reorganized these ancients common lands. Owners with firm legal deeds received consolidated parcels of land that they promptly enclosed as sheep pastures. Other residents were simply pushed off the land.

Enclosure destroyed the collective institutions and the way of life of a significant portion of the English peasantry. In 1500, open-field villagers tilled about 75 percent of the arable land of England; a century later, they cultivated only 60 percent. Displaced peasants lost their social identity as members of a village collectivity. Equally important, they no longer controlled the means of production—land, livestock, and farm equipment. "They take our hoiuses over our heads; they buy our grounds out of handes, they reyse our rents," one half-literate peasant complained, and 'they levey great, yea, unreasonable fines." Dispossessed families now lived in small rural cottages. Constantly on the brink of poverty, they spun and wove the wool of the sheep that had taken their place on the land. Or they worked as wage laborers on large agricultural estates owned by lawyers, government officials, merchants, or gentry. Gentlemen had taken "farms into their hands," a concerned observer noted in 1600, "and rented them to those that will give most, whereby the yeomanry of England is decayed and become servants to gentlemen." These impoverished peasants—and their sons and daughters—would eagerly migrate to America as humble indentured servants. Without land or hope at home, they looked across the ocean for a better life in the New World.

Mercantilism and Colonization

As the price revolution undermined the position of the landed aristocracy, the merchant community rose in importance. Merchants maintained the exchange systems of the preindustrial world and organized the long-distance trade in luxury goods from Asia. They moved bulky food products within smaller geographic areas, purchasing surplus grain, cheese, and meat from peasants and selling them in towns or regions where crops had failed. These wealthy middlemen became bankers, loaning money to ambitious kings, spendthrift nobles, and struggling yeomen. They also organized domestic and foreign markets for raw materials and finished goods. Beginning around 1350, English merchants sold high-quality wool to manufacturers in Flanders and shipped fine, tightly woven textiles back to England.

After 1500, English merchant capitalists created a new system of rural household manufacturing. This "putting-out" system mobilized the labor of thousands of rural families who had lost their land because of population growth or the enclosure movement. These men and women lived and worked in the small "cots," or cottages, that now dotted the countryside. They—and their children—took raw materials supplied by merchants and fabricated them into shoes, household goods, and textiles. The manufacture of woolens became a major occupation among "cotters" in Yorkshire, East Anglia, and the West Country. Merchants provided families with raw wool, often sheared from sheep on newly enclosed estates. Women and children washed and combed the wool and spun it into thread; male weavers turned it into cloth. Merchant entrepreneurs then gave the cloth to other wage laborers to dye and shape before selling the finished product in English and foreign markets.

The Crown assisted merchants in expanding the putting-out system of manufacturing. The Statute of Artificers of 1563 gave justices of the peace the authority to fix wages and threatened imprisonment for people who paid or received higher amounts. A new Poor Law in 1601 forced destitute people to work if they wished to receive alms. As these measures increased domestic production, the monarchs helped merchant capitalists sell their manufactures in foreign markets. The crown paid bounties on exported goods, negotiated commercial treaties with foreign states, and awarded special privileges to merchant groups. In 1555, the king gave a royal charter to the Muscovy Company, providing it with a monopoly on the export of English cloth to Russia. Commercial success prompted an explosion of chartered enterprises, the Levant Company in Turkey in 1581, the Guinea Company in Africa in 1588, and the East India Company in 1600.

Because monarchs used merchants to expand national wealth, this new system of production and trade became known as *mercantilism*. The kings hoped the policies would decrease foreign imports and poverty by boosting domestic manufacturing. Monarchical power would increase as well, because an expanding economy would swell the royal coffers with duties on trade and tax revenues. A strong and wealthy merchant community would provide the crown with effective political allies at home and the financial resources for foreign adventures.

The union between English kings and merchants created the wealth, shipping, and national purpose required to challenge Spanish dominance in the Western Hemisphere. As early as 1497, John Cabot explored the coasts of Newfoundland and Nova Scotia in the service of King Henry VII. But England sent only fishing expeditions to American waters for the next half-century. During the reign of Elizabeth I, from 1558 to 1603, the lure of Spanish gold drew English adventurers to the Western Hemisphere. Sir John Hawkins and other "sea dogs" plundered Spanish possessions in the Caribbean in the 1560s. In 1578, Sir Francis Drake returned from a privateering voyage against the Spanish bullion fleet with the immense fortune of £600,000, twenty times the yearly income of the wealthiest aristocrat. Yet England's merchant fleet—and naval power—remained too weak to support conquest and colonization in America.

The expansion of the English woolen trade after 1550 finally laid a firm foundation for a colonization movement. As merchants grew in wealth and numbers, they devised new forms of economic organization. The joint-stock company was a crucial innovation. By selling shares of stock to many investors, including the landed gentry and aristocracy, merchants mobilized substantial amounts of capital for commercial investment. Aided by royal charters, the joint-stock companies exported English woolens throughout the world, bolstering national wealth and pride.

Nevertheless, England's initial attempts to colonize America ended in failure. In the 1580s, Sir Humphrey Gilbert led an attempt to settle Newfoundland that collapsed for lack of colonists and sufficient financial backing. Sir Walter Raleigh dispatched three unsuccessful expeditions to North Carolina. One settlement, the famous "lost" colony of Roanoke, vanished without a trace or any apparent cause. Ferdinando Gorges likewise failed to establish a permanent settlement along the coast of Maine, again because of inadequate economic support and administrative planning.

These failures deeply impressed the leaders of the Virginia Company of London. As the company planned a new venture shortly after 1600, it carefully mobilized private resources and state support. Its merchant leaders received a charter from the crown that awarded the company exclusive rights of settlement and trade over the entire southern region of North America. Aided by this monopoly, the Virginia Company raised funds from no fewer than 56 London commercial firms and 659 individual investors. It sent settlers to Jamestown in 1607 and furnished the struggling colony with new recruits and fresh supplies for nearly two decades. Jamestown became the first permanent English settlement in America, the final product of a century of mercantile development.

Protestants and Puritans

English colonization in America stemmed from religious fervor as well as merchant power. Beginning in 1519, the Reformation divided Christian Europe into antagonistic sects and warring states. This schism began as a protest against corruption in the Roman Catholic church. Through the centuries, the church had become a wealthy institution; its ranks were now full of worldly men and women as well as potential saints. At the top of the ecclesiastical hierarchy, Pope Leo X, a member of the powerful Medici family, received five hundred thousand ducats a year from the sale of religious offices. Cardinal

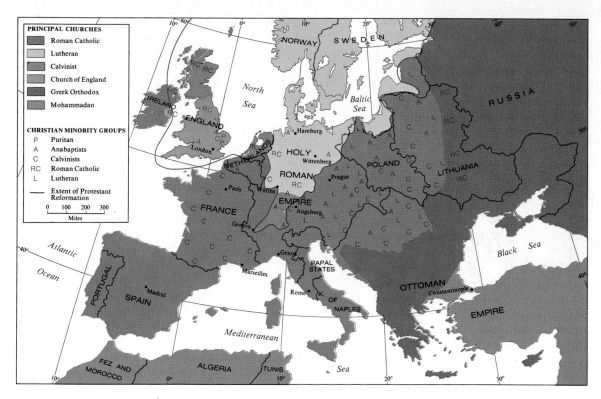

PRINCIPAL CHURCHES

- Roman Catholic
- Lutheran
- Calvinist
- Church of England
- Greek Orthodox
- Mohammadan

CHRISTIAN MINORITY GROUPS

- P   Puritan
- A   Anabaptists
- C   Calvinists
- RC   Roman Catholic
- L   Lutheran
- ——   Extent of Protestant Reformation

0 100 200 300
Miles

MAP 1.3 RELIGIOUS DIVERSITY IN EUROPE

By 1600, Europe was permanently divided into Protestant and Catholic countries. Lutheran princes and monarchs ruled northern Europe, and Calvinism had strongholds in Switzerland, Holland, and Scotland. Communities of Anabaptists and religious minorities dotted the map of Europe. Like the Puritans who challenged the legally established Protestant Church of England, such radical sects were often persecuted, as were Catholics who lived in predominantly Protestant countries. These religious divisions profoundly affected the settlement of British America.

Thomas Wolsey of England bestowed church positions on an illegitimate son, providing him with an income equal to that of 250 country priests. In church courts, serious crimes against morality could be absolved by paying fines. "The Lord desireth not the death of a sinner," one papal official explained, "but rather that he should pay and live." These abuses ignited a smoldering anticlericalism. Even a highly placed church official thought the clergy were a "gang of scoundrels" who should be "rid of their vices or stripped of their authority."

Inspired by Martin Luther, a resourceful German priest and theologian, hundreds of thousands of Christians deserted their traditional leaders and practices. Slowly they developed their own institutions and dogma. These Protestant churches differed profoundly from the Roman Catholic church in two crucial ways. First,

they reduced the authority of the clerical hierarchy and limited its spiritual powers. Many Protestant sects eliminated bishops completely; others severely restricted the bishops' control over pastors and laity. The reformers also denied that priests could perform miracles such as transubstantiation, the changing of bread and wine into the body and blood of Christ.

Instead, Protestants elevated the importance of the laity, the ordinary male and female church members. Following Luther, they stressed the "priesthood" of all believers. "Our baptism consecrates us all without exception," Luther argued, "and makes us all priests." To make the Bible accessible to everyone, reformers translated the sacred Book from Latin, known only to priests, into the vernacular, or common people's, languages of German, French, and English. They also gave greater financial and spiritual authority to the lay members of congregations. Protestant churches were less hierarchical and more democratic than those of Roman Catholicism.

Protestants also proclaimed different theological principles. This fundamental difference between the Catholic and the Protestant churches hinged on the interpretation of "free will." According to the great philosophical synthesis of the medieval theologian Thomas Aquinas, Christians had the power or free will to affect their own salvation. By their faith in God or by their "works" on the earth, people could achieve holiness and enter into heaven when they died. Luther rejected this basic Catholic premise. He denied that men and women could earn redemption by praying, receiving the sacraments, or doing good works. Rather, human beings were justified and saved only by the infusion of God's grace. Luther himself had been

JOHN CALVIN
This painting of the great Protestant theologian conveys the somber nature of his religious doctrines. The artist's depiction of Calvin's powerful and penetrating gaze likewise suggests the intensity of his spirit and intellect. (The New York Public Library; Astor, Lenox & Tilden Foundations)

strangely moved as he read the words of Saint Paul: "The just shall live by faith." "I felt," he wrote, "that I was altogether born again and had entered paradise through open gates." Salvation came as a gift from God, not as a result of human action: "For by grace are ye saved by faith; and that not of yourselves; it is the gift of God: not of works, lest any man should boast."

John Calvin, the great French Protestant theologian, was even more impressed by the majesty and power of God. Writing in exact, lucid, and elegant Latin and French, Calvin exalted the omnipotence of God and the weakness of ordinary mortals. His masterful *Institutes of the Christian Religion,* as definitively revised in 1559, propounded a pessimistic view of human ability and destiny. God was an awesome and absolute sovereign; man a depraved and pitiful person. Works and even preparation for grace were useless, for the divine will dominated all people and events. God governs the "wills of men," Calvin argued, "so as to move precisely to that end directed by him." Logically and remorselessly, he pursued this train of thought to its ultimate conclusion. God had "predestined" certain individuals, a small and privileged spiritual "elect," for salvation and condemned the great majority of men and women to the eternal miseries of hell.

The Protestant revolt against the authority and doctrines of the Roman church threw European society into utter turmoil. Who was to know which church practices or beliefs were correct? Many princes and kings in northern Europe embraced Protestantism, either out of principle or to free their kingdoms from papal taxation. Even Catholic monarchs exploited the upheaval to appoint bishops, tax church lands, and weaken the power of the pope. In England, Henry VIII initially was an important "defender of the true faith," but then he quarreled with the Spanish-controlled papacy over his divorce. Declaring his independence from Roman control, Henry established a national Church of England. He seized its rich lands and monastaries and sold about two-thirds of them, mostly to members of the gentry. Establishing himself as head of the church, the king took control of the appointment of bishops and parish priests.

Even as Henry VIII consolidated religious power in his own hands, he made few changes in dogma, organization, or ritual. Spiritual authority still flowed downward—from king to

TIME LINE
THE EXPANSION OF PREINDUSTRIAL EUROPE

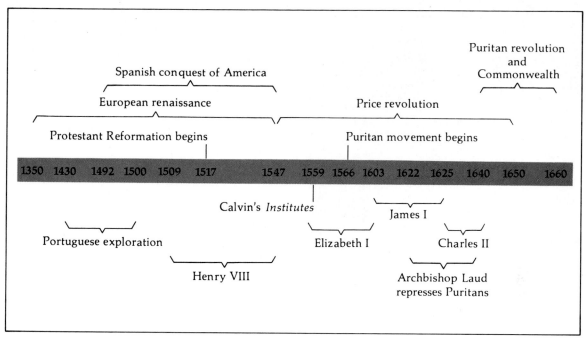

bishops to priests and, finally, to the laity. The king did allow an English translation of the Bible, but he rejected the Lutheran doctrine of the priesthood of the believer. Priests and sacraments remained important parts of the liturgy. Elizabeth I continued this moderate course. She tolerated Catholicism itself in the northern reaches of England and approved an ambiguous statement of dogma for the Church of England. The Thirty-Nine Articles were framed to allow belief either in traditional "free will" or in reformed doctrines of "faith" and predestination.

Many English Christians called for a radical reformation, a fundamental change in the organization of the Church of England. Ministers and congregations alike condemned the church's hierarchical structure. "It was anti-Christian and devilish and contrary to Scriptures," they maintained, to leave power in the hands of bishops. Reformers strongly preferred the Presbyterian system devised by John Knox for the Church of Scotland. In Knox's ecclesiastical structure, each local congregation elected lay elders. These "presbyters" assisted ministers in running the church. Equally important, they represented the laity in clerical synods that formulated dogma,

ordained new ministers, and enforced church discipline. By 1600, at least five hundred ministers within the Church of England advocated a presbyterian form of church organization.

Many English Protestants likewise demanded major changes in ritual and dogma. In 1566, "Puritans or unspotted lambs of the Lord" appeared in London. As their name implied, these Christians wished to purify the church of what they considered its false trappings and doctrines. Four major themes or principles shaped their teachings. First, Puritans, like Presbyterians, opposed an episcopal, or bishop-run, church structure. They preferred a congregational system that vested spiritual and financial authority in the hands of the laity. Second, these reformers insisted on the right, indeed the necessity, for individual Christians to read and interpret the Bible. Third, they stood strongly against a mystical interpretation of the sacrament of Communion, preferring simple religious exercises to the miraculous rituals led by priests.

Finally, Puritans condemned most Catholic ceremonies as idolatrous. They pointed out that churches had become palaces of pleasure rather than places of worship. Filled with beautiful stat-

KING JAMES I OF ENGLAND
This portrait captures the sharp intelligence of James I.
The King's consciously regal pose emphasizes his claim to
rule by "divine right." Yet James lacked firmness of
character and wise political judgement. As one
contemporary put it, "He could criticize a theory, but he
could not judge a man." (Attributed to Jan De Critz. *James
I.* National Maritime Museum, London)

ues and paintings, the sweet smell of incense,
and the magnificent robes of priests, the
churches distracted the senses and corrupted the
simple message of the Gospel. As the influential
Puritan minister William Perkins argued in the
pamphlet *Warning Against the Idolatrie of the Last
Times,* even a sacred object "feigned in the mind
by the imagination is an idol." Perkins stressed
the acquisition of spiritual knowledge through
the mind by Bible reading and by careful attention to finely argued sermons. Catholics made
God "earthy and fleshy," according to the great
Puritan poet John Milton, "because they could
not make themselves heavenly and spiritual."

The clerical hierarchy and the new Stuart
kings strongly resisted the demands for reform.
James I, who ruled from 1603 to 1625, favored
authoritarian religious institutions because he realized they bolstered monarchical power. The representative institutions of Presbyterianism, he
jokingly remarked, "agreeth as well with a monarchy as God with the Devil." In his anonymously published book, *The True Laws of Free
Monarchy* (1598), James argued that kings drew
their authority directly from God. Therefore,
they had a "divine right" to rule their realms as
they wished. As for the Puritans, James declared
after exchanging insults with their representatives, "I shall make them conform themselves or
I will harry them out of the land, or else do
worse."

As James suppressed dissent within the
Church of England, Puritans and other reformed
Christians sought refuge in Protestant states in
Europe. The Pilgrims, a sect that had separated
completely from the Church of England, settled
in Leiden in Holland. Soon, some Pilgrims migrated to America to preserve both their "pure"
Christian faith and their English way of life. Led
by William Bradford, these religious refugees
landed on the rocky shores of Massachusetts in
1620 and founded the Plymouth Colony. Thousands of nonseparating Puritans followed them
to "New" England over the next two decades,
driven from their homeland by the repressive
policies of Charles I, who reigned from 1625 to
1640.

Charles, like his brother James, stressed the
link between ecclesiastical hierarchy and absolute monarchy. As he put it simply, "No bishop,
No king." Charles also personally repudiated the
Calvinist doctrines of justification by faith and
predestination favored by the Puritans. Instead,
he adopted the position of the Dutch Protestant
theologian Jacobus Arminius. Arminius suggested that men and women might "choose" to
believe, thus recalling the Catholic doctrine of
free will, and that salvation was not limited to a
privileged elect. Puritans and Presbyterians in
Parliament bitterly attacked the king for his religious stand. In a direct challenge to his authority, they passed a resolution condemning all
those who perpetuated "popery or Arminianism."

English society was divided along political as
well as religious lines. In 1629, Charles dissolved
Parliament, which represented both the aristocracy, in the House of Lords; and the gentry,
merchants, and yeomen, in the House of Com-

CAMBRIDGE, MASSACHUSETTS PLATFORM FOR ADMISSION INTO THE CHURCH

In America, as in England, Puritans limited full membership in their churches to "visible saints" who made "a profession of faith and holiness." This document justifies this policy and emphasizes the importance of the clerical assistance and collective religious practices (or "ordinances") in assisting weak Christians to grow in grace.

The Doors of the Churches of Christ upon Earth do not by God's appointment stand so wide open, that all sorts of people, good or bad, may freely enter therein at their pleasure, but such as are admitted thereto, as members, ought to be examined and tried first, whether they be fit and meet to be received into church society, or not. The officers are charged with the keeping of the Doors of the Church. Twelve angels are set at the Gates of the Temple, lest such as were ceremonially unclean should enter thereinto.

The things which are requisite to be found in all church members are repentance from sin, and faith in Jesus Christ.

The weakest measure of faith is to be accepted in those that desire to be admitted into the Church, because weak Christians, if sincere, have the substance of that faith, repentance, and holiness which is required in church members; and such have most need of the ordinances for their confirmation and growth in grace.

---

mons. For a decade he ruled without the support of a representative body. By raising money through royal edicts, higher customs duties, and the sale of monopolies, Charles offended both the landed gentry and the merchant community, a stronghold of Puritanism. With the appointment of William Laud as Archbishop of Canterbury in 1633, religious and political strife came together and intensified. A passionate idealist, Laud was determined to preserve the structure and doctrines of the Church of England.

Within a few years of his appointment, Laud banished hundreds of Puritan ministers from their pulpits and forced their congregations to conform to Anglican ritual. In 1639, the zealous archbishop overreached himself by imposing a new Prayer Book on Presbyterian Scotland. This arbitrary action ignited riots and then armed resistance. A Scottish Presbyterian army marched on England, forcing Charles to call Parliament into session to vote funds to support his "Bishops War." Even as thousands of Puritans embarked for America, tens of thousands more prepared to take up arms against the king and his oppressive archbishop. These people, no less than those who migrated, wished to create a "New" England.

In religion as in other realms of life, the events of the "long" sixteenth century determined the character of the English colonization of North America. The relative decline of the aristocracy diminished its role and, as a result, the colonies would not have a legally privileged elite. Conversely, the rise of the merchant community gave traders a crucial role in the colonization movement. Peasants played a major part as well, for their lives had been endangered by the rise of population, prices, and enclosures. Many more men and women migrated to America from England than from Spain, and they sought land to farm rather than natives to conquer. Finally, as a result of the Protestant and Puritan reformations, these English migrants carried new and diverse forms of Christianity to the Western Hemisphere.

The legacy was rich and complex. As products of preindustrial Europe, these settlers transplanted to American soil hierarchical principles of family and political life, of economic and religious institutions, and of social identity. Yet these traditional authoritarian institutions and values had already been challenged and modified by a century and a half of major historical change. Settled by a society in transition, the English colonies in America embodied both traditional and more modern forms of political organization, religious institutions, and economic values.

*T*he Europeans who settled America came from a traditional agricultural society. For centuries in Europe, a privileged landed elite of nobles and gentry had presided over a vast mass of poor peasants. Rich and poor alike subscribed to the doctrines of the Christian church, which gave emotional richness and meaning to their lives. Both religious and worldly officials endorsed a hierarchical vision of the world, and the institutions of church and state demanded that individuals submit to authority as the price of social peace and survival.

The exploits of Italian merchants introduced new wealth and new learning into this traditional society. Adventurous monarchs allied themselves with merchants and bankers to capture the commerce of the Orient and undermine the power of the landed nobility. This alliance led to Portuguese commercial expansion and Spanish conquest of the culturally sophisticated and wealthy civilizations of Middle America.

England lacked the resources to settle America until the end of the "long" sixteenth century. By that time, English society had been disrupted by the price revolution, the Protestant Reformation, and the absolutist claims of the Stuart monarchs. Royal policies encouraged a colonization movement led by merchants and persecuted Puritans. As a result, the English colonies in America contained both traditional authoritarian institutions and more modern values and forms of authority.

Suggestions for Further Reading

Traditional Agricultural Society

Barbara W. Tuchman, *A Distant Mirror: The Calamitous 14th Century* (1978), presents a vivid portrait of political and religious life in the late medieval world. Johan Huizinga, *The Waning of the Middle Ages* (1924), is a masterful interpretation of the world view of traditional Europeans. Huizinga's intellectually oriented account should be complemented by Pierre Goubert, *The Ancient Regime* (1968), an incisive analysis of social structures and values. Goubert's *Louis XIV and Twenty Million Frenchmen* (1970) examines the relationship between the French people and the power of their monarch.

Other path-breaking studies in the social and political history of early modern Europe include Marc Bloch, *Feudal Society* (1940); Philippe Aries, *Centuries of Childhood* (1962); Norman Cohn, *The Pursuit of the Millennium* (1957); B. H. Slicher Van Bath, *The Agrarian History of Western Europe* A.D. *500–1850* (1963); Emanuel Le Roy Ladurie, *The Peasants of Languedoc* (1974); and Robert Mandrou, *Introduction to Modern France, 1500–1640: An Essay in Historical Psychology* (1976).

Commerce and Conquest

W. H. McNeil, *The Rise of the West* (1963), offers an incisive description of European political and cultural development, while economic expansion is treated in Robert R. Reynolds, *Europe Emerges: Transition Toward an Industrial World-Wide Society, 600–1750* (1961). For the development of southern Europe, read selectively in Fernand Braudel's massive and stimulating *The Mediterranean and the Mediterranean World in the Age of Philip II* (1949).

Boise Penrose, *Travel and Discovery in the Renaissance, 1420–1620* (1952), illuminates the growth of geographical knowledge, and J. H. Parry, *The Age of Reconnaissance* (1963), surveys European expansion around the world. Samuel Eliot Morrison offers an exciting biography of Columbus and his world in *Admiral of the Ocean Sea* (1942). See also Elaine Sanceau, *The Land of Prester John, A Chronical of Portuguese Exploration* (1944), and Charles Gibson, *Spain in America* (1966).

The native American civilizations of Middle America and their fate are succinctly described in Eric Wolf, *Sons of the Shaking Earth* (1957). More extended analyses appear in John S. Henderson, *The World of the Ancient Maya* (1981), and Nigel Davies, *The Aztecs: A History* (1973). The Spanish conquest is graphically portrayed in R. C. Padden, *The Hummingbird and the Hawk* (1962), and M. Leon Portilla, *The Broken Spears: The Aztec Account of the Conquest of Mexico* (1962). The important biological consequences produced by the interaction of the peoples of Europe and America are explored in A. W. Crosby, Jr.'s *The Columbian Exchange: Biological and Cultural Consequences of 1492* (1958) Classic accounts of the Spanish conquest include the memorable first-hand report by Bernal Diaz del Castillo, *The Discovery and Conquest of Mexico* (edited by I. A. Leonard, 1956), and William H. Prescott, *History of the Conquest of Mexico* (3 vols, 1843).

The New World of Sixteenth-Century England

Earl J. Hamilton, *American Treasure and the Price Revolution in Spain, 1501–1650* (1934), first outlined the impact of American gold and silver on the European economy. For the effect of population, see David Glass and D. E. Eversley, eds., *Population in History* (1965). For a general analysis of the "crisis of the sixteenth century," see the essays in T. A. Ashton, ed., *Crisis in Europe* (1965).

A brilliant and forceful portrait of English preindustrial society is offered by Peter Laslett, *The World We Have Lost* (1971). Other important surveys are Wallace Notestein, *The English People on the Eve of Colonization* (1951), and Carl Bridenbaugh, *Vexed and Troubled Englishmen, 1500–1642* (1968). Patrick Collinson, *The Elizabethan Puritan Movement* (1967), provides a good account of early Puritanism; Michael Walzer, *The Revolution of the Saints* (1965); Katherine George, *The Protestant Mind of the English Reformation* (1961); and Christopher Hill, *The Century of Revolution, 1603–1714* (1961), continue the story. For various social groups, see Lawrence Stone, *The Crisis of the Aristocracy* (1965); Mildred Campbell, *The English Yeoman* (1942); and W. G. Hoskins, *The Midland Peasant* (1957).

For accounts of early English colonization, see A. L. Rowse, *Sir Walter Raleigh* (1962), and *The Expansion of Elizabethan England*. See also David B. Quinn, *England and the Discovery of America, 1481–1620* (1974).

2

A CENTURY OF CONFLICT

1600-1700

*T*he expansion of preindustrial Europe touched off a century of conflict in America. Beginning in 1600, northern Europeans challenged the dominance of Spain and Portugal in the Western Hemisphere. The Spaniards already controlled Mexico and Peru, and the Portuguese ruled Brazil. In 1607, the English established a permanent settlement at Jamestown, Virginia. The French moved into Quebec in 1608, and the Dutch settled New Amsterdam in 1624. Warfare over these rival territorial claims quickly followed, as did successful Dutch attacks against the Spanish bullion fleet and Portuguese sugar plantations. America became a European battleground.

Colonization brought racial conflict as well. The Indian peoples of North America had not created densely populated civilizations like those of the Inca, Aztec, or Maya. Nor did their lands contain fabulous deposits of gold and silver. Yet millions of Indians inhabited North America in 1600. They controlled rich resources of land, furs, and labor that were eagerly sought by the European invaders. Brutal military strife soon warped the character of European and native American existence.

Religious and social conflicts broke out within the English settlements in North America. Strong-minded Puritan magistrates wanted a holy commonwealth in the New England region. To achieve this goal, they rigorously expelled individuals or groups who challenged their view of the ideal society. Conflict in Virginia resulted from economic and political inequality, not from enforced religious control. Thousands of aspiring migrants who expected to grow rich planting tobacco, died from disease or remained poor. Roused by a war with the Indians, oppressed freemen and servants rejected established authority. They seized control, though only for a short time, from the oligarchic government controlled by a few wealthy planters and political leaders.

These struggles underlined the fact that North America lay on the far margins of European civilization. In this rough, untamed arena, the limits of action were wide—and they were determined more by raw will than by traditional standards of behavior. Religious sects attempted radical social and political experiments. Profit-minded planters forcefully imposed their demands on rootless indentured servants. Dissatisfied groups threatened governments lacking the legitimacy brought by time and experience. Most dramatic of all, European Christians fought with one another and with tawny-skinned pagan aboriginals for control of the land and its natural resources.

The Invasion of North America

Northern Europeans embarked for the Western Hemisphere as adventurers, fur traders, or settlers. But to the native Americans, they all

32

seemed to be dangerous invaders. Cultural confrontation produced various results. French fur traders and Jesuit priests mingled peacefully with the Indians. Spanish monks converted the native Americans to Christianity. Dutch and English settlers seized their lands, igniting years of bloody warfare. As early as 1620, one Indian tribe called the English *wotowquenange* (stabbers and cutthroats). For the rest of the century, the newcomers battled tribal peoples for control of the eastern seacoast of North America.

The Native Americans

When Europeans first came to North America, five to seven million Indians may have inhabited the vast continent. These aboriginal peoples lived in hundreds of relatively small tribes and spoke about two thousand dialects. Each tribe occupied a distinct territory, and its members married among themselves. Tribes also belonged to one of twelve language groups, four of which dominated the eastern region. Europeans who settled between the Saint Lawrence River and Chesapeake Bay met tribes who spoke various Algonquin dialects. The eight thousand Delaware spoke the Algonquin dialect, as did the Pequot and Narragansett of New England. Dutch fur traders who moved inland along the Hudson River met aggressive Iroquois-speaking tribes—the Mohawk, Cayuga, Onondaga, Oneida, and Seneca. Adventurous traders who penetrated the far backcountry of the Chesapeake River Valley encountered peoples who spoke Sioux dialects. Europeans who landed on the coast between Carolina and Florida met

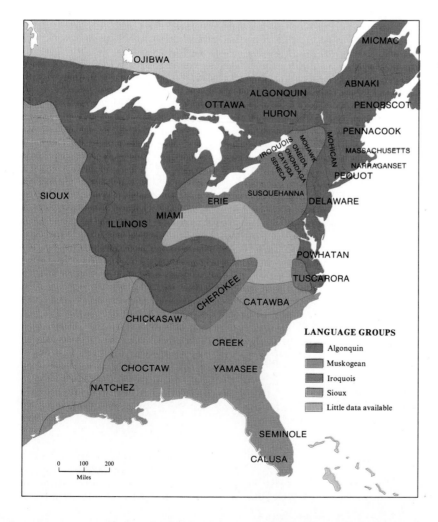

MAP 2.1 NATIVE-AMERICAN CULTURAL DIVERSITY
The Indians of eastern North America spoke four major languages—Algonquin, Muskogean, Iroquois, and Sioux. Each language group consisted of many separate tribes, ranging in size from two thousand to twenty thousand persons. The members of each tribe spoke a distinct dialect and married among themselves. Tribal rivalries and linguistic diversity often hindered united Indian resistance to the English invaders.

members of the Muskhogean language groups, including the twenty thousand members of the Creek tribe.

Native Americans differed in their activities as well as in language. Along the Saint Lawrence River, the short growing season made agriculture risky. Northern Algonquin tribes—the Abnaki and Penobscot—lived by hunting wild animals, fishing, and gathering wild grasses, nuts, and berries. In contrast, southern Algonquin peoples, such as the Pequot, Delaware, and Susquehannah, obtained most of their food from farming done by women. They supplemented these crops of corn, beans, and squash with fish or game killed by male hunters.

Favorable climatic conditions encouraged agricultural development, but the spread of technology from the Indian civilizations of Middle America was equally significant. Around A.D. 700, internal revolts and external wars disrupted the Mayan and Toltec empires, prompting migration across the Gulf of Mexico to the lower Mississippi River valley. Like later settlers from Europe, these Middle American peoples transplanted the advanced technology, social institutions, and religious beliefs of their traditional cultures.

Indians from Middle America either imposed a settled way of life on the tribes of North America or came in sufficient numbers to recreate their own social order. Archaeological excavations and historical records testify to the impact of their culture. As farmers, these migrants lived in the fertile valleys of the Mississippi region, rather than in its forests. They constructed large, permanent settlements with heavily fortified centers designed to resist attack. To perform religious ceremonies, the Middle Americans built huge earthen mounds, similar in design to the magnificent stone platforms in their homelands. One mound, near Emerald, Mississippi, stands thirty-five feet high and covers seven acres; it required years of labor to build. Surrounding these new temple sites were substantial cities in which artisans shaped clay, stone, and copper into pottery, tools, and jewelry with striking shapes and elaborate designs. As in Middle America, a privileged priest and warrior class dominated these complex societies. This elite group organized worship of the sun god, commanded military forces, and lived in comfort on the agricultural surplus taken from a lower class of peasant families.

By A.D. 1300, Mississippian civilization was in rapid decline. For some reason, the Middle American migrants could not sustain the sophistication of their traditional culture. Yet their influence lingered for centuries. About 1700, French explorers came upon the Natchez people of Mississippi. They found a highly stratified social order, not the usual tribal structure of equal clans. A monarch claiming descent from the sun god ruled the Natchez, assisted by an upper class of nobles and honored people. This distinct, arrogant religious and military elite married within its own ranks, strictly excluding the mass of the peasant population. Similar class divisions and religious practices existed, though to a much lesser extent, among the Muskhogean-speaking peoples of southeastern North America—the Creek, Chickasaw, Choctaw, Seminole, and Cherokee.

The agriculture of the Mississippi settlers became their most important cultural legacy. They introduced the flint hoe to the tribes of North America and provided them with superior strains of corn and other vegetables. As new agricultural technology and advanced pottery-making techniques spread northward, they changed the character of economic and social life. Corn and beans replaced wild game and fruits as the main foods. With a higher and more regular level of nutrition, the Indian population lived longer and grew in size. Prospering tribes built permanent villages of domed wigwams near their cornfields and lived there from April to October. They marked the yearly agricultural cycle with new religious ceremonies, such as the green corn and strawberry festivals among the Iroquois. Warriors continued to hunt wild animals, especially during the autumn and winter, but the tribes were no longer nomadic. The spread of agriculture made their lives more settled and secure. By the time Europeans invaded eastern North America, most of the Indians had cultivated and hunted their lands for generations.

European–Indian Interaction

When Richard Hakluyt, an English clergyman and geographer, advocated settlement in Virginia in 1585, he mentioned three "Inducements," or goals: "1. To plant the Christian religion, 2. to traffic in goods, 3. to conquer."

A PARADOXICAL VISION
To Europeans, the Indians were a new and unknown race. In the works of some artists, America appeared as a biblical Eden, overflowing with bountiful harvests and populated by a highly civilized and gentle people. As news of Indian massacres reached Europe, other artists pictured it as a demonic hell, inhabited by primitive and ruthless warriors. (Top, Jacques Le Moyne de Morgues. *Ahore shows Laudonnière The Marker Column set up by Ribault.* The New York Public Library; Astor, Lenox & Tilden Foundations. Bottom, The New York Public Library; Astor, Lenox & Tilden Foundations.)

In varying degrees, these religious, commercial, and imperialist aspirations motivated all Europeans who came to North America. The goals of the Europeans also influenced their perceptions of what they found there. Ambitious conquistidors often envisioned Indians as "wild beasts, unreasonable creatures, and brutish savages" who had to be ruled with an iron hand. Missionaries and merchants disagreed, viewing native Americans as "most gentle, loving, and faithful." They hoped trade would improve the Indians' living standards while instruction imparted "knowledge and obedience of the only true God and Savior of mankind." Depending on their goals, prejudices, and numbers, the various European invaders developed distinct patterns of cultural interaction with the tribes.

Spanish explorers penetrated the heart of North America as early as the 1540s. Searching for the fabled golden cities of the mythical seven cities of Cibola, Francisco de Coronado led an expedition northward from Mexico. He crossed the plains of what is now Texas and reached the grassy lands of central Kansas before turning back in failure. Hernando de Soto, fresh from the conquest of the Inca empire in Peru, started a similar enterprise between 1539 and 1542. He crossed Florida and parts of Georgia, North

Carolina, Tennessee, Arkansas, and Oklahoma before returning to Mexico via the Mississippi River. These military ventures resulted in the permanent establishment of a Spanish fort at Saint Augustine in Florida in 1565.

The Spaniards later spread Roman Catholicism among native American tribes in the Southwest. Spanish priests founded settlements in Arizona and New Mexico. Then, after 1700, monks of the Order of Saint Francis established a string of missions up the coast of California and in parts of Florida and Georgia. These religious emissaries tried to convert native Americans to the European way of life. Diligent and pious Franciscans closely supervised the Indians in the settlements. They taught them the basic doctrines of Catholicism but also strongly urged them to adopt European forms of agriculture. For the Spanish Franciscans, religious conversion and cultural assimilation went hand in hand.

Catholic explorers and missionaries from France dealt with the native Americans in a strikingly different way. During the 1530s, Jacques Cartier asserted French control over all the lands bordering on the Gulf of Saint Lawrence. Reasserting this claim in 1608, Samuel de Champlain founded Quebec and then marched far into the interior. Jacques Marquette, a priest of the Society of Jesus, or Jesuits, traveled down the upper reaches of the Mississippi River with the fur trader Louis Joliet in 1673. Nine years later, Robert de La Salle completed exploration of the majestic inland river. On the basis of these journeys, France claimed sovereignty over the entire region drained by the Great Lakes and the Mississippi River system.

French Jesuits gave spiritual substance to this claim. Beginning in 1625 and continuing for a century and a half, hundreds of priests spread the Catholic faith among the tribes of the interior. These highly trained and intellectually inclined missionaries lived mostly among the Huron, the prime fur suppliers to French traders, but also among the Iroquois and other southern tribes. In keeping with Jesuit practice in other parts of the world, the priests shared the Indians' way of life and sought to understand their customs. The Iroquois, reported Father Paul Ragueneau in a typically detailed and penetrating Jesuit document, believed that "our souls have

desires which are inborn and concealed, yet are made known by means of dreams. If it be not granted what it desires, the soul becomes angry and often it revolts against the body, causing various diseases and even death."

The Jesuits looked for points of correspondence between such native American beliefs and Catholic doctrines. They did not force the Indians to abandon their traditional culture, and so the tribes accepted these inquisitive, resourceful missionaries. The Jesuits slowly merged Catholic teachings into Indian culture. In New France, religious and cultural contact was much less coercive than in the Spanish missions.

The French colonial system likewise preserved continuity within native American society. Despite strenuous efforts by Cardinal Richelieu, the government minister who founded the Company of New France in 1628, only about two thousand French settlers came to North America by 1660. Aristocrats and other French landlords resisted colonization because they feared the loss of their work force. Even destitute peasants hesitated to move to Quebec because of the short growing season and the bitterly cold winters. Military men and the powerful bureaucracy also discouraged large-scale migration. They had other uses for the nation's human and financial resources. King Louis XIV expended the wealth and energies of his subjects in a series of great European wars. By the end of his reign in 1715, he had made France the dominant military power in western Europe.

Therefore, New France developed not as a settler-colony but as a vast fur-trading enterprise. The legendary French *coureurs de bois* (wood-runners) carried manufactured goods to tribes deep in the interior and traded them for deer skins and beaver pelts. They took these partially tanned furs by canoe and packhorse hundreds of miles to Montreal. Specialized merchant firms then shipped the pelts to Europe to be made into felt hats or fur coats and rugs.

The fur trade benefited almost everyone. Furs enabled the Europeans to dress more warmly and stylishly, and the native Americans obtained the manufactured products of a more advanced economy. In addition, this exchange system enabled tribal peoples to choose the goods they wished to buy. Indians eagerly adopted some European products, such as wool blankets, steel

MAP 2.2 A SATELLITE VIEW OF NORTH AMERICA IN 1650
Europeans had explored only a tiny fraction of the vast North American continent by 1650 and had settled even less. English colonies and Dutch trading posts dotted the eastern seaboard, while French priests and fur traders moved along the great inland waterways. From their strong base in New Spain, Spanish adventurers and missionaries probed northward into the western half of the continent.

knives, firearms, and iron utensils. These goods fitted easily into their traditional economic activities and way of life. On the other hand, the tribes rejected European tools that threatened their social and cultural values. Native American warriors wished to hunt and fight, not farm. They refused to buy the heavy plows used to cultivate small grains, such as wheat, barley, and rye. Out of necessity and self-interest, Indian women remained in control of crop production. But now they used iron hoes rather than flint ones to dig the fields of corn, squash, and beans.

At first, the French thought they would profoundly alter the life-styles of the native Americans. Government officials instructed the settlers "to civilize the Algonquins, live with them, and bring up their children in our manners and cus-

toms." But just the opposite occurred. Some French fur traders married Indian women (while engaging in sexual relations with many more), but the children of these unions grew up as Indians. Moreover, the small population of French peasants and traders adopted many Indian practices, as Peter Kalm, a Swedish traveler, observed in 1749.

The French in Canada in many respects follow the customs of the Indians, with whom they have constant relations. They use the tobacco pipes, shoes, gaiters, and girdles of the Indians. They follow the Indian way of waging war exactly and have adopted many other Indian fashions.

Like the French, the first Dutch settlers in North America placed their major emphasis on commerce rather than conquest. Henry Hudson, an Englishman in the service of the Dutch East India Company, sailed along the Atlantic coast in 1609 and discovered the Hudson River. By 1624, the newly founded Dutch West India Company had established fur-trading posts at Fort Nassau on the Delaware River near Philadelphia and at New Amsterdam (New York) and Fort Orange (Albany) along the Hudson. These wilderness outposts attracted few Dutch migrants. Unlike England, the Dutch provinces did not have a surplus agricultural population hungry for new land. Living in a solidly and devoutly Protestant land, Dutch men and women did not need to flee from religious persecution. Also, the booming state of Dutch commerce, both in Europe and the East Indies, provided employment for seamen and artisans.

Fearing an invasion from New England or New France, the Dutch West India Company tried to increase migration to its rich and unsettled American lands. To finance rapid settlement, the company granted huge estates, called *patroonships,* to wealthy Dutchmen. It stipulated that each patroon had to settle at least fifty tenants on his land within four years, or the estate would revert to the company. As had happened in New France, this Dutch attempt to create an agricultural colony failed. Of all the patroons, only the diamond merchant Kiliaen Van Rensselaer transported enough peasant-tenants to New Amsterdam. Even so, Governor Wilhelm Kieft's seizure of prime agricultural lands from neighboring tribes brought on three years of devastating war. By the end of "Kieft's War" (1643–1646), more than two hundred Dutchmen and a thousand Algonquin had been killed, many in bloody massacres of children, women, and elderly men.

The Dutch West India Company largely ignored its crippled North American settlement. The profit-seeking directors increased their investments in Africa, Brazil, and the Caribbean. Company ships had already captured the entire Spanish bullion fleet in 1628, providing shareholders with a massive dividend. Dutch adventurers now seized profitable Portuguese sugar estates in Brazil, providing new markets for the company's growing trade in African slaves. Lacking new Dutch capital and settlers, New Amsterdam remained a fur-trading colony with a small and diverse population of Dutch, English, and Swedes. These people were ruled in an authoritarian manner by a company-appointed governor, and they grew increasingly restive. English military forces captured New Amsterdam easily in 1664, and most of the Dutch residents peacefully accepted English rule. Like Montreal, Albany remained a center of the fur trade, a small and peaceful Dutch-English economic outpost in a region of native Americans.

NOVA BRITANNIA.

OFFERING MOST

Excellent fruites by Planting in VIRGINIA.

Exciting all such as be well affected to further the same.

LONDON

Printed for SAMVEL MACHAM, and are to be sold at his Shop in Pauls Church-yard, at the Signe of the Bul-head.

1 6 0 9.

ADVERTISING AMERICA, 1609
Printed broadsides encouraged wealthy Englishmen to invest in the Virginia Company and enticed potential settlers to seek their fortunes in this "new" and uncorrupted Britain. (The New York Public Library; Astor, Lenox & Tilden Foundations)

JAMESTOWN, VIRGINIA, IN 1607
Jamestown began as a military colony in an alien land. This artist's reconstruction accurately depicts the town as a fortified settlement. It is perched close by the river, the route of supply and escape. Outside the palisade, a group of settlers are engaged in military maneuvers. (Colonial Williamsburg Foundation)

From the beginning, English adventurers at Jamestown in Virginia had the goal of conquest as well as commerce. Powhatan, the chief of the Powhatan tribe, told the newcomers, "You have come here not to trade but to invade my people and possess my country." Few of the original band of 120 men were farmers. Many were gentlemen adventurers who owned stock in the Virginia Company. As one uncharitable observer noted, they were "unruly Sparks, packed off by their Friends to escape worse Destinies at home." These adventurers hoped to find Indians with hoards of gold, valuable goods to trade for English manufactured products, and densely settled towns with ample supplies of food and labor. Arriving at Jamestown in 1607, they found small tribes with few material possessions and largely reluctant workers. Unwilling or unable to plant crops for themselves, the adventurers died quickly from inadequate food and from disease. Only thirty-eight remained alive after nine

months in America. The strong dictatorial measures of Governor John Smith, an aggressive soldier of fortune, saved the infant colony from complete collapse.

Soon the new settlement confronted a hostile Indian population. Bolstered by fresh supplies and new recruits from England, Governor Thomas West raided Indian villages for food and demanded that the neighboring tribes acknowledge the sovereignty of the English king. Powhatan rejected these terms. The chief, whom Smith described as a man with "a grave majestical countenance," proposed instead that the English assist him against his enemies. In return, he would grant them settlement privileges. To cement this agreement, Powhatan permitted his daughter Pocahontas to marry the adventurer John Rolfe.

Within a decade, the agreement lay in ruins. The rapid expansion of white settlement alarmed Opechancanough, Powhatan's successor and cousin. Newly arrived migrants were not unruly aristocratic adventurers but *yeomen* (small planters) and peasants who coveted cleared Indian farmland for their own crops. Opechancanough realized that the new invaders were too numerous and too intent on settlement to be stopped by small-scale raids. Coordinating the movements of several tribes, he launched a surprise attack in 1622. The Indians killed 347 settlers, nearly a third of the white population, and vowed to drive the invaders back across the ocean. To preserve their foothold in Virginia, the English resorted to a "scorched earth" policy, burning cornfields to deprive the Indians of food. By the end of the year, the English triumphed; but some fighting continued until 1634, when the two sides made a peace agreement. Opechancanough attacked again in 1644, but the English quickly defeated him.

The cost of the war was high for both sides. The Indians killed, or wounded, or burned the property of about a fourth of the white population. However, the native Americans suffered even greater losses. More importantly, the two

THE INDIAN VILLAGE OF POMEIOCK
Artist John White accompanied Sir Walter Raleigh to Carolina in 1585 and returned to England with a magnificent series of watercolors. Many eastern tribes lived in similar semi-permanent villages set in the midst of cultivated fields. Several families lived in each domed wigwam, which was covered with woven mats and tree bark. (John White. *Indian Village of Pomeiock, 1585*. The British Museum)

peoples were locked in irreconcilable conflict. Now, as one English militiaman put it, the invaders could

> by right of Warre, and law of Nations, invade the Country, and destroy them who sought to destroy us; whereby wee shall enjoy their cultivated places, turning the laborious Mattock into the victorious Sword (wherein there is more ease, benefit and glory) and possessing the fruits of others labours.

Because the English came to America primarily as conquerors and settlers rather than as missionaries and fur traders, they faced many years of bloody fighting with the Indians for control of the land.

The Conquest of New England

At the same time that brutal warfare broke out in Virginia, thousands of English men and women sought refuge from religious persecution in New England. Led by William Bradford and John Winthrop, about ten thousand Pilgrims and Puritans braved the long, dangerous voyage across the Atlantic. Accompanying these religious dissenters were another ten thousand non-Puritans—peasants, indentured servants, and artisans fleeing from economic hardship and grinding poverty. Coming quickly and in such great numbers, these determined migrants represented an immediate threat to the Algonquin tribes of the northeastern region, the Massachusett, Narragansett, Pequot, Nipmuck, and Wampanoag.

Pious Puritans viewed themselves as a chosen people, with a responsibility to explain their actions to God and to their fellow men and women. "By what right or warrant can we enter into the land of the Savages," they asked themselves while still in England, "and take away their rightfull inheritance from them and plant ourselves in their places?" This compulsive self-examination continued as the Puritans occupied the land they called "New England." When a smallpox epidemic devastated the Indian population in 1633, John Winthrop interpreted the disaster as a mark of divine favor. "If God were not pleased with our inheriting these parts, why did he drive the natives before us?" the stern Puritan magistrate asked. "And why doth he still make roome for us by diminishing them as we increase?"

To justify the seizure of Indian lands, Puritan leaders advanced various legal arguments. They claimed, for example, that most land in America was *vacuum domicilium* (empty of habitation) because it had not been "subdued" by tilling or grazing. The Book of Genesis provided them with an appropriate text: "Be fruitful, and multiply, and replenish the earth, and subdue it." Thus, the Massachusetts General Court solemnly declared in 1652, "Indians within this jurisdiction have just right there to" only those lands they have "by possession or improvement, by subduing the same according to that in Genesis 1 and 28, chap 9:1 and Psalmes 115:6." Most Puritans considered this Bible-based policy not only divinely inspired, but also just and fair. "If we leave them sufficient for their own use," Winthrop commented, "we may lawfully take the rest, there being more than enough for them and us."

The Pequot disputed these arguments by force of arms. Like many other Algonquin tribes, they had been severely weakened by an epidemic in 1621. European diseases, probably carried by visiting English fishermen, swept through Indian villages, leaving the lands of the Massachusetts tribe littered with "bones and skulls." Despite these losses, the Pequot remained the strongest tribe in southern New England and a threat to their weaker neighbors. By the 1630s, Puritan settlements stretched deep into Pequot territory, especially along the broad plains of the Connecticut River valley. Pequot raids on frontier farms brought Puritan retaliation against Indian towns, and soon the two peoples were at war. Following a surprise attack on a Pequot village, Puritan militiamen massacred about five hundred men, women, and children. "God laughed at the Enemies of his People," one soldier boasted, "filling the Place with Dead Bodies." Puritan military forces ruthlessly tracked down the survivors, enslaving some and selling others to the West Indies. The Pequot tribe was virtually exterminated.

Such brutality reflected both the passion of war and the grim reality of interracial conflict.

TRIBAL CUSTOMS OF THE MOHAWKS

The Mohawks won control of the fur trade through warfare, but lost many warriors. A Dutch clergyman describes the common Indian practice of "adopting" captives to maintain kin networks and tribal strength, 1644.

The principal nation of all the savages and Indians hereabouts with which we have the most intercourse, is the Mohawks....

[They] are like us Dutchmen in body and stature; some of them have well formed features, bodies and limbs; they all have black hair and eyes, but their skin is yellow. In summer they go naked, having only their private parts covered with a patch. The children and young folks to ten, twelve and fourteen years of age go stark naked. In winter, they hang about them simply an undressed deer or bear or panther skin; or they take some beaver and otter skins, wild cat, raccoon, martin, otter, mink, squirrel or such like skins, which are plenty in this country, and sew some of them to others....

Our Mohawks carry on great wars against the Indians of Canada, on the River Saint Lawrence, and take many captives.... They spare all the children from ten to twelve years old, and all the women whom they take in war, unless the women are very old, and then they kill them too. Though they are so very cruel to their enemies, they are very friendly to us, and we have no dread of them....

The chiefs are generally the poorest among them, for instead of their receiving from the common people as among Christians, they are obliged to give to the mob; especially when any one is killed in war, they give great presents to the next of kin of the deceased; and if they take any prisoners they present them to that family of which one has been killed, and the prisoner is then adopted by the family into the place of the deceased person.

Like most Europeans, the Puritans viewed the Indians as culturally inferior people who did not deserve civilized treatment. Yet the English migrants were not "racist" in the modern sense of the term, because they did not regard native Americans as genetically inferior. They believed that aboriginals were white people with sun-darkened skins and degenerate customs. The Reverend John Eliot placed Indians squarely within the Biblical scheme of history. They were "Hebrews," he thought, "retrograde descendants of the Biblical patriarchy and the Ten Lost Tribes of Israel." Sin, not race, accounted for their condition. The Reverend Cotton Mather suggested that "probably the devil" delivered these "miserable savages" to America, "in hopes that the gospel of the Lord Jesus Christ would never come here to destroy or disturb his absolute empire over them."

This interpretation of Indian history inspired conversion as well as conquest. John Eliot, a missionary, translated the Protestant Bible into Algonquin and sought converts among the tribal peoples. He had less success than the Jesuits in New France because Puritan standards were high and rigid. Puritan ministers and congregations demanded that the Indians understand complex theological issues and undergo a prescribed conversion experience. Few native Americans passed these rigorous tests. By 1674, however, more than a thousand "praying Indians" lived in fourteen special towns and received regular religious instruction.

By this time, Puritan-dominated communities stretched for about fifty miles along the Massachusetts coast and throughout the Connecticut River valley. White demands for Indian lands increased as an extraordinarily high birthrate raised the English population to fifty-five thousand. These developments frightened Metacom (or King Philip), the leader of the Wampanoag tribe. To preserve the Wampanoag's ancestral homelands, Philip forged a military alliance with the Narragansett and Nipmuck peoples. Like Opechancanough in Virginia, he concluded that only united resistance could stem the relentless advance of English settlement.

Following the execution of three Wampanoag by Massachusetts Bay courts, the young warriors of the tribe demanded war. In 1675, Philip attacked white farms and villages throughout New England and was soon joined by his Narragansett allies. Bitter fighting continued for two years. By the end of "King Philip's War," as the English called it, the tribes had destroyed or forced the abandonment of about 20 percent of the towns in Massachusetts and Rhode Island and killed 5 percent of the adult white males. Puritan militiamen caused even greater bloodshed. About five thousand Indians, or 30 percent of the native American population of southeastern New England, died in the fighting or from the famine and disease that followed.

The brutal warfare in the forests and clearings of New England and Virginia lowered the moral standards of both peoples. Following the English invasion, native Americans renounced limited and symbolic forms of combat. Previously they had made sporadic and small-scale raids to maintain territorial boundaries and to demonstrate the skills of their warriors. Now the Indians adopted more destructive military ethics and goals. The tribes sought complete victory over their white enemies and, with increasing frequency, roasted male captives from other tribes to death in public spectacles of torture and celebration.

The English also adopted total warfare and called for the complete annihilation of their tribal enemies. The ordeal of conquest corrupted the high moral standards of the Puritans. Fishermen from Marblehead, Massachusetts, captured two Indians in the aftermath of King Philip's War and carried them into port. One of the captors recalled that "the women surrounded them, drove us by force from them, and then with stones, billets of wood, and what else they might, they made an end of these Indians. We found them with their heads off and gone, and their flesh in a manner pulled from their bones." Once roused, racial hatred did not die easily. Beginning in 1694, the Massachusetts General Court passed an act each year setting a bounty for the capture or killing of an enemy Indian.

The Indian Decline in the East

By 1700, the English conquest of the Atlantic seaboard was assured. Small groups of Indians, stripped of their lands and tribal identities, accepted a subservient status on the margins of

SEAL OF THE MASSACHUSETTS BAY COLONY, 1676
Even as the Massachusetts colonists fought native Americans in bloody battles, they placed an Indian on the official colony seal. Most Puritans no longer expected to carry the true religion back to England; as the seal suggested, they embraced their new home and were in America to stay. (American Antiquarian Society)

white society. Shattered tribes withdrew beyond the settled limits of New England and Virginia, but they could not escape the long reach of the invaders. Merchants carried on a flourishing trade in Indian slaves, especially in the frontier colony of Carolina. They sold hundreds of Indians to settlers in New York and New England, and thousands to planters in the West Indies. There were about fifty-three hundred whites in the infant Carolina Colony in 1708, and nearly as many slaves—twenty-nine hundred Africans and fourteen hundred native Americans. Coastal tribes experienced a double tragedy. They failed not only to repel the English invasion but also to maintain a vital cultural identity. European attacks and diseases continually reduced their number, and dislocation and despair prevented the creation of cohesive Indian communities. Many tribes faced virtual extinction.

The Indian tribes in the interior of North America survived, but their traditional way of life did not. White fur traders brought rum and European diseases as well as useful manufactured goods, and drunkenness and epidemics sapped the vitality of many tribes. Even European products hurt Indian society. The Cherokee, Huron, and Iroquois replaced their flint tools and clay pots with sturdy English and French ironware, but they lost their artisan skills. They became dependent on the fur trade for basic goods and could not return to a self-sufficient existence. Few Indians got rich from the lucrative commerce in furs, because European middlemen set the terms of trade and native American cultural values discouraged the accumulation of material possessions.

Nevertheless, intense competition for beaver pelts and deerskins introduced a new source of conflict into tribal life. Hard-pressed or calculating Indian families and villages claimed exclusive territorial hunting and trapping rights, undermining clan unity and tribal bonds. Armed with European guns, tribal warriors set out to control the fur trade. The aggressive, well-organized Iroquois seized pelts bound for Montreal and subdued the Huron and Erie peoples by force. They later extended their dominion to include the Delaware and the Susquehannah. As native Americans became more militant and expansionist, the internal tribal balance of power shifted. Elders lost authority to headstrong young braves, and male hunters and warriors became more important than female cultivators. As in all societies, a commitment to warfare increased the importance of those who made war.

In addition, the fur trade transformed the relationship between the native American tribes and the world of nature. Traditionally, Indians held animistic religious beliefs. Like many pagan peoples, they thought that everything in nature—the land, trees, rocks, and animals—contained living spirits. These animating forces demanded care and respect. Most of the clans within each tribe used an animal as their *totem* or symbol. This familiar animal—a fox, turkey, beaver, turtle, or deer, for example—stood as the mythical biological ancestor of the clan's members. To hunt these animals was a holy as well as a necessary activity, governed by complex religious rules and taboos. As hunters skinned beavers or butchered deer, they thanked the spirits of the animals for providing fur clothing

and rich venison. Then they respectfully disposed of the carcass and entrails. To throw the bones into a fire or a river was sacrilegious, a taboo that might bring misfortune upon the tribe.

The demands of the European fur trade destroyed these spiritual bonds to nature. Warriors now hunted to trade, not to fulfill clan obligations and subsistence needs. By 1700, the Carolina tribes provided white merchants in Charleston not only with captured Indian slaves, but also with about fifty-four thousand deerskins a year. Within a few decades, merchants handled 150,000 skins annually. By the 1760s, the fur trade throughout the continent involved the annual export of hundreds of thousands of pelts. An Indian hunter killed as many as twenty or thirty animals a year, and he sensed the displeasure of the spirits in nature. Epidemics seemed to confirm the anger of the animal spirits and to justify the slaughter of the forest creatures. The Micmac tribe of Nova Scotia had always killed beavers for fur clothing, but now it made "war upon these animals." As the warriors explained, they no longer knew "whether the beavers are among our friends or our enemies."

By becoming professional hunters, the native Americans adapted to the European invasion of their continent. The use of European manufactured products probably improved certain aspects of their standard of living, but at an extremely high cost. The fur trade brought disease, drunkenness, economic dependence, warrior predominance, and spiritual upheaval. Tribal membership dwindled and cultural creativity ebbed. The European fur trade, no less than military conquest and religious conversion, drastically altered the character of native American society.

Social Conflict in the Chesapeake Colonies

The Chesapeake colonies of Virginia and Maryland quickly developed a booming export-oriented tobacco economy. Entrepreneurs flocked to the new settlements and imported thousands of poor indentured servants to labor in their fields. However, social upheaval threatened as young male migrants sought land and advance-

THE TOBACCO ECONOMY
Tobacco was a "poor man's" crop. It grew well in small fields and was easy to process. The planter hung the tobacco stalk in a well-ventilated shed to cure for several months. Then he stripped the leaves and packed them tightly into large barrels, or "hogsheads." Yeomen and tenant farm families often exchanged their tobacco for English goods, imported by local planter–merchants. These entrepreneurs grew wealthy by providing credit, goods, and commercial services. (Colonial Williamsburg Foundation)

ment in the face of epidemics and falling tobacco prices. To preserve order and their own power, a small number of corrupt political officials seized control of the system of representative government. Economic inequality, a disastrous population loss, and political conflict brought Virginia to the verge of disintegration.

Tobacco and Disease

The London merchants and adventurers who owned stock in the Virginia Company established the Jamestown settlement along the lines of a business corporation. The company owned all the land. It appointed the governor and gave him, and a small council, complete control over settlers who were its employees or "servants." Poor management plagued the new colony. Of the approximately 1,200 servants sent over by the company in 1610, only 350 remained alive in Virginia by 1616. Many died from disease. Others returned to England because they were unwilling to work for the company for seven years in order to receive a grant of land.

To encourage migration, the Virginia Company altered the corporate structure of the Jamestown enterprise and granted land to indi-

vidual settlers. This action had momentous political consequences. The royal charter granted to the company specified that its settlers in America would retain all the "rights and liberties" of Englishmen. Under English law, property ownership implied voting privileges in representative political institutions. Following a company directive, Governor George Yeardley of the Virginia Colony convened the House of Burgesses, the first legislative assembly in North America, in 1619. Voters chose the members of the legislature, using the procedures of English town boroughs (or *burgs*, hence the name *Bur-gesses*). The House had the authority to make laws and levy taxes. However, legislative acts could be vetoed by the governor or nullified by the company in London. These attractive incentives of land ownership and local self-government spurred settlement, and about forty-five hundred new recruits embarked for Virginia within five years.

Following the Indian uprising of 1622, the Crown dissolved the Virginia Company and instituted royal government. Under this more effective administrative system, King James I assumed direct responsibility for the colony and its settlers. The monarch and his advisers chose the governor and the members of a small advisory council. They gave these appointed officials the power to veto legislation enacted by the elected House of Burgesses. To bolster his authority, the king brought about the legal establishment of the Church of England in Virginia, requiring all property owners to pay taxes to support the parish clergy. Not until 1639, when his absolutist rule was under severe attack in England, did King Charles I recognize the legitimacy of the House of Burgesses. Even then, Virginia laws required final ratification by the king's Privy Council in London. This edict guaranteed that sovereignty remained in royal hands.

Political institutions in the adjoining colony of Maryland, founded in 1632, took a different form. Charles made Cecilius Calvert, Lord Baltimore, the proprietor of Maryland. Baltimore owned all the land in the colony, and he could sell or give it away as he wished. As proprietor, Baltimore appointed the governor and all public officials. Yet the Maryland charter limited his power in two important respects. It specified both that Baltimore rule with the consent of the people, which led to the creation of a representative assembly as in Virginia, and that legislation be ratified by the Privy Council. In proprietary Maryland, as in royal Virginia, local self-government was firmly balanced by the authority of appointed governors and supervision by English officials.

The "discovery" of tobacco by the Europeans brought economic prosperity to the Chesapeake colonies. The Indians had long cultivated the tobacco plant and used its leaves as a medicine and a stimulant. King James I condemned the use of this "vile Weed" and warned that its "black stinking fumes" were "baleful to the nose, harmful to the brain, and dangerous to the lungs." Nevertheless, an almost insatiable European demand for tobacco began in the 1620s, setting off a forty-year economic boom. People ingested tobacco by breathing its smoke, chewing its leaves, or inhaling it as powdered snuff. American producers reaped healthy profits from this craze for nicotine, and planted more and more tobacco seedlings. "All our riches for the present do consist in tobacco," a happy planter remarked in 1630. The Chesapeake colonies exported about three million pounds of tobacco leaves in 1640 and ten million pounds a year by 1660. The historically new crop commanded high prices in the markets of Europe, and thousands of profit-hungry migrants flocked to the mild Chesapeake climate to plant it.

Disease took a frightful toll among these settlers. About five thousand English men and women came to Virginia before the Indian uprising of 1622. Most died within a year of their arrival, weakened by the hard Atlantic voyage and by food shortages. Migrants attracted by the tobacco boom fared no better. More than fifteen thousand settlers arrived in Virginia between 1622 and 1640, but the population rose only from fifteen hundred to eight thousand. Malaria was now the main culprit. Mosquitoes bred quickly in the warm, humid climate, and they spread malaria by biting (actually stabbing through the victim's skin). Malaria caused people to lose strength and their ability to resist other diseases. It struck pregnant women especially hard, and many never recovered from the ordeal of childbirth. The deadly "fevers and agues" held down the population for the rest of the century. Not until 1680 did the white population begin to increase by reproduction rather than through immigration.

Disease struck down many prominent men and government officials during the first decades of European settlement in America, and others returned to England in shock and dismay. As a result, only seven descendants of the pre-1635 leaders of Virginia were among the 110 most influential members of the House of Burgesses in the eighteenth century. The tobacco boom attracted a new wave of influential Englishmen, the sons of merchants and landed gentleman. But high death rates again delayed the formation of a stable ruling class. Only forty-nine of their descendants became powerful political leaders in later years. Maryland likewise lacked political stability and governmental continuity. Only six of the fifty-six men who sat in the governor's council before 1689 had sons who attained provincial office. Throughout the Chesapeake colonies, government leaders were "new men" who did not have deep roots in the social order.

Reports of the population disaster and the resulting political situation quickly reached England, but they did not halt the flow of migrants. The lure of land and tobacco was too great. Between 1640 and 1700, at least eighty thousand English settlers moved to Virginia and

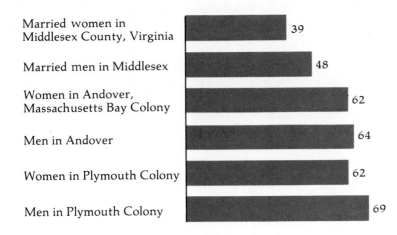

Married women in
Middlesex County, Virginia   39

Married men in Middlesex   48

Women in Andover,
Massachusetts Bay Colony   62

Men in Andover   64

Women in Plymouth Colony   62

Men in Plymouth Colony   69

FIGURE 2.1 AVERAGE LIFE
EXPECTANCY AT AGE
TWENTY IN NEW ENGLAND
AND THE CHESAPEAKE,
1640–1700

thousands more sought their fortunes in Maryland. About five thousand indentured servants sailed for the Chesapeake colonies from the port of Bristol. Shipping registers provide a composite portrait of these migrants. Most were under twenty-five years old and about three-fourths of them were male. Many of these rootless youths, lacking land or work in their villages, had traveled hundreds of miles to Bristol. Destitute and with no prospects, they set off for America with nothing to lose except their freedom.

Economic Power and Political Privilege

To pay for their passage to the Chesapeake colonies, penniless migrants relinquished their personal liberty by signing labor contracts called *indentures*. Merchants and sea captains negotiated these labor agreements on the docks of Bristol or London. Upon reaching Virginia or Maryland, captains assigned the contracts to local planters in return for cash or tobacco. Indentures bound the migrants to labor for a period of four or five years. Those under sixteen were obligated to work until the age of twenty-one. The planter-master provided food, clothing, and shelter for his indentured servants. In return, he received the products of their labor. Planters made handsome profits, especially in the early boom decades. With the price of tobacco at six pence a pound, each indentured servant produced an annual income of about five times the total cost of his labor contract.

Indentured servitude was both a financial bonanza and a system of social discipline. The planter strictly regulated his servants' lives. He had the legal right to beat them for disobedience or poor work and to grant or withhold permission to marry. If his servants ran away or became pregnant, he went into court to increase their terms of service. About a fifth of the female servants in Maryland were prosecuted for "bastardy," many under suspicious circumstances. As a Virginia law of 1692 explained, "dissolute masters have gotten their maids with child; and yet claim the benefit of their service." Uncooperative servants, both females and males were sold, their labor contracts transferred to other masters. In Virginia, one observer remarked in disgust that "servants were sold up and down like horses."

The system of indentured servitude exploited the young and the poor in favor of the old and the wealthy. In addition to labor and sexual favors, masters received a "headright" grant of fifty acres of land for each settler or servant brought into the colony. Before 1660, however, many servants benefited from these labor contracts. Female servants bore heavy burdens, but they enjoyed special opportunities as well. The scarcity of women caused men in Virginia to "grow very sensible of the Misfortune of Wanting Wives." Newly freed female servants married quickly, and many chose older men with substantial resources. Those who outlived their husbands often inherited control of the man's property and married again. During these boom years, many male servants also rose in the world. Hundreds of Maryland servants died from disease or overwork before their indentures expired, but at least half the survivors acquired land of their own. By migrating to America, they escaped a life of landless poverty.

Succeeding generations of indentured servants were less fortunate. By 1660, the tobacco boom had collapsed. European demand slackened and the market price fell to one penny a pound. New "mercantilist" legislation accentuated the impact of these economic forces. Beginning in 1651, the English Parliament restricted American trade to English- or colonial-owned ships. Other "Acts of Trade and Navigation" re-

quired the colonists to ship certain products, including tobacco, only to England. Chesapeake planters could no longer trade legally with Dutch merchants, who traditionally paid the highest prices for tobacco and offered European goods at the best rates. By placing a high customs duty on imported tobacco, the home government depressed the demand for Chesapeake exports even further. Planters increased their exports from about twenty million pounds of tobacco annually in the 1670s to forty-one million pounds between 1690 and 1720, but their profit margins were thin.

Economic stagnation hit especially hard at yeoman planters, tenant farmers, and indentured servants. With tobacco at one penny a pound, yeomen's families earned just enough to scrape by. Part of their annual crop of about two thousand pounds was usually substandard. Taxes took the earnings from perhaps two hundred pounds of tobacco a year, and clothes cost the money earned by another eight hundred pounds. Only about a thousand pounds of the crop remained for the purchase of supplies, equipment, or additional land. Tenant farmers had even less disposable income, because their rent consumed another six hundred pounds of tobacco. Under these circumstances, newly freed servants found it nearly impossible to become property owners. When their indentures expired, these freemen had the legal right to *patent* (be granted) fifty acres of uncleared land. To obtain a clear title, however, they had to pay the fees of clerks and surveyors. And to grow food and tobacco, the aspiring planters also needed tools, seed, and livestock. Most freemen had no choice but to sell their labor to wealthy planters or landlords once again. No longer indentured servants, they now worked as sharecroppers, tenants, and wage laborers. Fewer than a fourth of the freed indentured servants in Maryland between 1670 and 1705 became property owners. The rest labored for others, ending their working lives in much the same way as they had begun.

Established planters weathered the decline in the tobacco trade with greater success. Some had accumulated large landholdings through the headright system, and others used political influence to build up substantial estates. As tobacco profits fell, these aggressive, calculating entrepreneurs sold some land and leased the rest to

AN EARLY VIRGINIA ARISTOCRAT
William Byrd II (1674–1744) was born in America and educated in England and Holland. This portrait from 1704 captures Byrd's arrogance and his love of worldly pleasures. His diaries, written in a secret code, reveal his intelligence, personal compulsions, and a tense married life. "I rose at 6 o'clock," Byrd began the entry for October 31, 1709, "and read two chapters in Hebrew and some Greek in Lucian." Three days later: "I played ... with Mrs. Chiswell and kissed her on the bed till she was angry and my wife also was uneasy about it, and cried as soon as the company was gone." (Virginia Historical Society)

the growing army of tenant farmers. They lent money to hard-pressed yeomen, charging high rates of interest, and set up small stores that supplied manufactured goods to the growing population. Assuming the role of middlemen, the planters drew commissions for storing and selling the tobacco of their poorer neighbors to English merchants. Eventually, this elite of planter-merchants dominated the economic life of the Chesapeake colonies. Through indentures, wealthy planters in Charles County, Maryland, owned about 40 percent of the entire labor force. In Virginia, they owned nearly half the patented land.

Economic recession intensified social divisions and class conflicts. Even in boom times, the Chesapeake region had never been a utopia; too many people had died from disease. As the colonies became healthier, a tough, aggressive planter elite confronted a growing mass of young, single, landless laborers. Social conflict lay just below the surface.

Political corruption raised the tensions in the Chesapeake to the breaking point. In 1660, William Berkeley, a renowned Indian fighter, became governor of Virginia. Berkeley commanded great respect at first, but controversy arose as he used the powers of his office to give large land grants to himself and the members of his council. Soon his "Green Spring" faction, named after Berkeley's country estate, became a corrupt oligarchy. Council members used their political power and influence to exempt their own lands from taxation and to appoint friends and clients as county judges and local magistrates. To suppress dissent in the House of Burgesses, Berkeley resorted to similar tactics. The governor made land grants to friendly Burgesses and appointed their relatives to powerful and profitable offices as sheriffs, tax collectors, and justices of the peace.

Berkeley dominated the political system of Virginia for fifteen years. Once his favorites were in place, the governor refused to call new elections. As demands for legislative elections grew, the Burgesses changed the voting system to exclude propertyless freemen. With a stroke of a pen, they disenfranchised half the adult white males. Freeholding yeomen retained the vote, but they had such grievances as falling tobacco prices, rising taxes, and political corruption. Virginia stood on the brink of civil war.

Bacon's Rebellion

Racial warfare ignited the explosive social mixture. By 1675, Virginians and native Americans had lived at peace for thirty years. Following a major uprising in 1644, the Doeg and Pamukey tribes accepted English dominance. They lived north of the York River, on lands guaranteed by treaty, and pursued their traditional mode of existence. Tobacco planters had gradually encroached on these reserved Indian lands from the south and east. The Susquehannah tribe then migrated from the north and settled on the upper reaches of the Potomac River valley. Before the arrival of the Susquehannah, the tribes had been powerless. Their members had dwindled drastically in number from about thirty thousand in 1607 to only two thousand in 1669. The proud northern tribe bolstered Indian resistance to further white expansion.

As frontier skirmishes threatened the peace, the forty thousand whites in Virginia were divided among themselves. English settlers in the western regions demanded a policy of armed expansion, but planters in the coastal districts advised restraint. This geographic division followed class lines. Only a few wealthy planters, such as Nathaniel Bacon, a newly arrived Englishman, lived in the interior. Poor freeholders and aspiring tenant farmers made up the bulk of the western population. Having moved to the frontier for cheap land, they demanded the expulsion or extermination of the Indians.

Aggressive frontiersmen precipitated a new Indian war. To avenge the death of an Englishman in a livestock dispute, Virginia militiamen marched up the Potomac River into Maryland in the summer of 1675. First they indiscriminately murdered thirty Indians. Then, defying orders from Governor Berkeley, a force of about a thousand militiamen surrounded a fortified Susquehannah village. They lured four chiefs out of the stockade under a flag of truce and killed them on the spot. The outraged Susquehannah retaliated, taking eighty white lives in battles and raids on outlying plantations.

Speaking for coastal planters and fur traders, Berkeley recommended peace and a defensive military policy. In March 1676, the governor asked the House of Burgesses for funds to build and arm a series of frontier forts. Western settlers condemned this strategy as useless against mobile Indian bands and as a new drain on the limited resources of the colonists. Berkeley's plan, one freeholder argued, was simply "a design of the grandees [political leaders] to engross all our tobacco in their own hands." To demonstrate their purpose, about three hundred frontiersmen chose Nathaniel Bacon to lead them in battle. When Berkeley refused to grant Bacon a military commission, they marched against the Indians anyway. Unable to find the Susquehannah, Bacon and his men massacred the members of a peaceful tribe.

The military conflict led to a major political upheaval. At first, Berkeley condemned Bacon's army as "rebels and mutineers." But then, recognizing its power, the governor reversed himself and reinstated Bacon as a member of the Virginia council. Now on the defensive, he also gave in to the demand for legislative elections and accepted the far-reaching political reforms enacted by the new House of Burgesses. The Burgesses curbed the powers of the governor and the council. New legislation prohibited individuals from holding more than one government office and eliminated special land grants and tax exemptions. To cut the patronage powers of the Green Spring faction, the Burgesses made many local offices into elective posts. These laws benefited yeomen freeholders by cutting taxes and helped local and county officials increase their political influence. The legislature also restored the voting rights of propertyless freemen, who now made up a majority of the population.

These long-delayed reforms did not end the conflict, because Bacon and Berkeley had become personal enemies. Bacon had wealth and education, and friends in high places in England; he grew angry when Berkeley treated him as a young upstart. Moreover, the yeomen, tenants, and servants in Bacon's army resented decades of exploitation by the "grandees" and proudly flaunted their newfound power. Backed by about four hundred armed men, Bacon forced the Burgesses to commission him "General of Virginia" and then seized control of the colony. In August 1676, he proclaimed the goals of his men in a moving "Manifesto and Declaration of the People." This document demanded the death or removal of all native Americans and an end to the rule of wealthy "parasites." "The poverty of the country," Bacon proclaimed, "is

STRANGE NEWS
FROM
VIRGINIA;
Being a full and true
ACCOUNT
OF THE
LIFE and DEATH
OF
Nathanael Bacon Efquire,

Who was the only Caufe and Original of all the late Troubles in that COUNTRY.

With a full Relation of all the Accidents which have happened in the late War there between the Chriftians and Indians.

LONDON,
Printed for William Harris, next door to the Turn-Stile without Moor-gate. 1677.

AN ACCOUNT OF BACON'S REBELLION
Cheap pamphlets, even more than newspapers, provided English readers with political news and exciting stories of faraway lands. This title page hints at the consciousness of the times; it depicts the war not as a racial but as a religious struggle—between English Christians and pagan Indians. (Alderman Library, University of Virginia)

such that all the power and sway is got into the hands of the rich, who by extorious advantages, having the common people in their debt, have always curbed and oppressed them in all manner of ways."

Bacon's seizure of power brought civil war to Virginia. Berkeley fled to the eastern shore of Chesapeake Bay, urgently requested royal troops from England, and captured Jamestown with about five hundred armed supporters. Bacon's army promptly recaptured the capital, burned it to the ground, and plundered the plantations of Berkeley's allies. Only the sudden death of the rebel leader from dysentery gave the governor the upper hand. After his forces dispersed Bacon's army of frontiersmen and servants, Berkeley took his vengeance. The governor seized the estates of wealthy rebels and hanged twenty-three men.

Neither the killing nor the looting, nor even the reforms enacted by the House of Burgesses, altered the structure of Virginia society. A small planter-merchant elite still dominated the economic system after Bacon's Rebellion. The political leadership had changed its perspective. Its members realized the folly of a rigid, corrupt oligarchy that divided the property-owning class against itself. In the future, they found government positions for all substantial property owners with political ambitions. The budding "aristocrats" of the Chesapeake colonies also acted to contain the fury of their white servants, tenants, and freeholding neighbors. Following the rebellion, political leaders supported an expansionist military policy; they bought white votes and support with Indian lands.

To avoid new revolts by unruly indentured servants, the grandees used African slaves on their plantations. In the prime tobacco-growing region of All Hallows Parish in Maryland, Africans made up only about 10 percent of the population in 1675, but 35 percent by 1700. The transition to slavery stemmed partly from the declining availability of English indentured servants and from a major expansion in the African slave trade. It also reflected the fear of white rebellion and the search for a labor force that could be bound for life. To maintain their privileged class position, the leaders of Virginia and Maryland committed themselves (and their descendants) to a life based on the exploitation of black slaves.

Puritan New England

As seventeenth-century Virginians survived social and political chaos, Puritans in New England created a healthy, well-ordered, and stable society. The history of early New England has an epic quality. Devout Puritan migrants pictured themselves as fighting against impossible odds to preserve the "pure" Christian faith in the American wilderness. To fulfill this holy mission, Puritan ministers and magistrates suppressed dissent and imposed religious orthodoxy. The tide of human events complicated their

efforts, and by 1700 most reflective Puritans thought their religious experiment had failed. Nevertheless, these isolated Puritan communities stood forth as examples of a remarkably successful and just social order.

The Puritan Covenant

New England Puritans did not regard themselves as poor outcasts, thrown on the barren shore of a dangerous continent. Rather, they were central actors in a great historical drama. Religion and society had grown corrupt in England, John Winthrop explained, so that "all arts and trades are carried on in a deceitful manner and unrighteous course." The migrants constituted a "saving remnant," chosen by God to preserve the true faith. The Lord "has sifted a whole nation," the Reverend William Staughton declared, "that he might send choice grain over into this Wilderness." In time, God would summon colonists back to England to restore a pristine church. Thus, the Puritan experiment was vital to all Christendom. "We must consider that we shall be as a City upon a Hill," Winthrop told his fellow passengers aboard the ship *Arbella* in 1630. "The eyes of all people are upon us." Winthrop's words echoed through the centuries. Long after the Puritan experiment vanished, they gave Americans a vision of their special destiny as a people and a nation.

The Puritans carried a royal charter establishing the Massachusetts Bay Company. Issued by Charles I in 1629, this document created the body of stockholders who financed the migration. In taking the charter to America, Puritans transformed the financial corporation into a political institution. Stockholders in England relinquished rights to monetary dividends. Those who migrated became members of the General Court, empowered to enact laws for the new colony of Massachusetts Bay. Soon the migrating shareholders (or freemen) enacted rules that expanded political participation. An act of 1631 extended the right to vote and hold office to men who were members of an approved Puritan church. By the mid-1630s, the General Court had become a representative assembly, elected by the Puritan congregations in the various towns. Together with the governor and his assistants, who were elected by the freemen as a whole, the

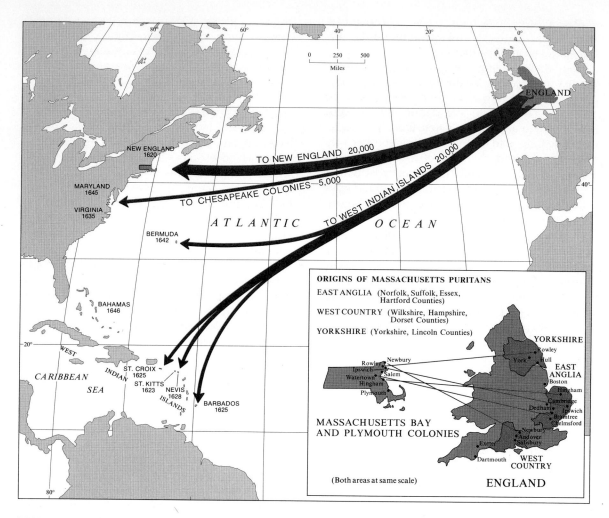

MAP 2.3 PURITANISM IN ENGLAND AND AMERICA

Nearly fifty thousand Puritans migrated to New England and the West Indies between 1620 and 1640. In New England, Puritan Saints dominated the institutions of church and state, creating "Holy Commonwealths" in Plymouth, Massachusetts Bay, and Connecticut. Migrants from the three major areas of English Puritanism—Yorkshire, East Anglia, and the West Country—commonly settled together. They named many new American communities after their English towns of origin and reestablished traditional regional customs, such as the field agriculture practiced in Rowley in Yorkshire and Rowley in Massachusetts Bay.

court sought to create a religious commonwealth. In 1636, it advised the magistrates to rule "according to the law now established, and where there is no Law, then as near the law of God as they can."

Puritan religious institutions reflected the influence of the Reformation and of English experience. As Protestants, the migrants to New England rejected the spiritual authority of the pope. As Puritans, they attacked the episcopal structure of the Church of England. They denied the power of bishops to ordain ministers, determine dogma, and regulate the affairs of the various churches. Following the example of the first Christians, they proposed a simple church structure centered on the lay congregation. Members had the power to decide dogma and appoint ministers. Because Puritans gave extensive powers to this lay body, they came to be known as Congregationalists.

The Puritans of the Massachusetts Bay Colony were avowed Calvinists. Following the teachings of the great French philosopher, John Calvin, they believed that God was all-powerful. Conversely, human beings were weak, helpless sinners who deserved eternal damnation. Yet God in his majesty had chosen to extend salvation to a few "elect" men and women, presumably the devout membership of Puritan churches. He had "predestined" this elect for heaven even before they were born.

The doctrines of election and predestination had bleak and harsh implications. They condemned the nonelect, who comprised a majority of the population even in New England, to a subordinate status on the earth and to eternal suffering in hell. Elected *Saints* (members of any Puritan church) themselves lived in great anxiety. They could never be certain that they were predestined for salvation. Puritan deathbeds became scenes of doubt and agony. "I have seen Persons Quaking on their Death Beds," the influential minister Cotton Mather reported, "and their very Beds therewith Shaking under them; From whence their first Shriek unto me, has been, 'O! The wrath of a Dreadful God, Makes me Tremble; I Tremble, I Tremble, at that wrath.' "

Puritans dealt with the uncertainties of election in different ways. Some New England congregations emphasized the importance of conversion, the magic moment at which God infused the sinner's soul with saving grace. Following this experience, the person enjoyed a special spiritual relationship with God and the assurance of salvation. Other Puritans stressed the necessity of ministerial assistance and church discipline to prepare the sinner's heart to receive God's grace. For them, conversion was the end of a long process of preparation. Because these Puritans seemed to say that individuals could choose to prepare themselves for grace, their position resembled that of the Dutch theologian Jacob Arminius. The Arminian God was more reasonable and merciful than the avenging God described by Calvin. If a person expressed "the merest desire to be saved," declared an English Puritan, William Perkins, God would bestow his saving grace.

Many New England Puritans embraced a collective "covenant" version of Arminianism. As ministers pondered the significance of their "errand into the Wilderness" of America, they detected an implicit contract with God. Their task was to preserve the pure faith and order their lives according to God's laws. In return, they would have his blessings as a divinely "chosen people." Let Christ "be your judge," thundered the Reverend John Eliot in *The Christian Commonwealth* (1655), "Let him be your law-giver, Let him be your king."

The Suppression of Dissent

Certain Puritans were particularly conscious of living at the center of a divinely ordered scheme. These "millenialists" believed that Christ's return to the earth was imminent. Some migrants thought the New England settlements would begin the thousand years of God's rule on the earth predicted in the Biblical Book of Revelations. "The ordinary means of the faithful propagating his gospel" would begin the millenium, the Puritan minister John Cotton argued in powerful sermons and pamphlets. If every believer participated personally in God's work, Cotton told his Boston congregation,

> an unprecedented and sustained religious revival will occur and at the end of the thousand years Satan will be released. Then wicked men will triumph for a season, Catholicism will revive, persecution will flourish. But Christ's coming will soon follow and with it the resurrection of the dead and the last judgement.

According to Cotton, preaching in the early 1630s, these events would begin "about the year 1655."

Most Puritan leaders feared the unsettling consequences of millennialism and all forms of religious "enthusiasm." As governor of the Massachusetts Bay Colony during the 1630s, John Winthrop used the authority of his office to suppress religious radicalism. Winthrop was a well-educated country squire. Troubled by the corrupt condition of English religion and society, he sold his estate and led a contingent of kin and neighbors to New England. The governor, a man of forceful character, mature judgment, and aristocratic temper, imposed authoritarian rule on the new settlement. Twice during the 1630s, he and his fellow magistrates banished Puritan radicals from the colony to preserve religous orthodoxy.

The first dispute involved the independence of church congregations. In 1620, the Pilgrims had established the Plymouth Colony. Lacking a royal charter, their leaders had agreed in the famous Mayflower Compact to create a civil society and enact laws by the vote of freemen. As in the Massachusetts Bay Colony, the voting franchise was limited to a minority of the population, but the General Court of Plymouth ruled without interference from authority-minded governors and magistrates. Equally significant, the church congregations of Plymouth were self-governing entities, unrestrained by elected magistrates. This autonomy reflected the Pilgrims' separatist ideology. Before fleeing to Holland, they had repudiated all ties to the Church of England and committed themselves to the separation of church and state.

Roger Williams, the minister of the Puritan Congregational Church in Salem, urged the migrants of the Massachusetts Bay Colony to follow the Pilgrim example. He advocated that Puritans proclaim independence from the Church of England, rather than reform it from within. Williams also condemned the legal establishment of religion in Massachusetts Bay. He thought political magistrates had authority only over the "bodies, goods, and outward estates of men," not over their spiritual lives. In addition, the resolute Salem minister questioned the moral and legal justification for the seizure of Indian lands. When Williams refused to stop his verbal attacks on the government's religious and territorial policies, the Puritan magistrates banished him from the colony. Accompanied by many of his followers, Williams founded the town of Providence, Rhode Island, in 1636. They obtained a corporate charter, which granted self-government, from Charles I and created political institutions that respected the liberty of conscience of the individual and the autonomy of separatist churches.

Stern Puritan magistrates in Massachusetts Bay soon detected another threat to their holy commonwealth. Anne Hutchinson, an accomplished midwife and the middle-aged wife of a merchant, had begun to hold weekly prayer meetings in her house. These discussions of scriptures and sermons drew as many as sixty women and attracted considerable attention. Rumors circulated that Hutchinson had attacked the teachings of many Boston clergymen. She intimated that the ministers placed too much emphasis on obedience to church laws and community standards. By suggesting that good behavior was a sign of salvation, they had endorsed the Covenant of Works. Instead, Hutchinson stressed the overriding importance of a direct spiritual relationship between God and the individual. Going beyond traditional interpretations of the Covenant of Faith, this forceful woman focused on the mystical aspects of God's grace and the freedom it conferred on a saint.

Hutchinson's activities greatly alarmed the authorities. By stressing a direct mystical relationship with God, she threatened the role of the ministers. Many of her most ardent supporters were merchants and other affluent migrants who resented clerical control. The magistrates also resented Hutchinson because of her sex. Like other Christians, Puritans believed in equality of souls; both women and men could achieve intimacy with God and heavenly salvation. At the same time, women were not equal on the earth. As one English pastor put it, "The woman is a weak creature not embued with like strength and constancy of mind." In matters of church and of state, they should be subordinate to men. "As for women," the Pilgrim minister John Robinson asserted, "they are debarred by their sex from ordinary prophesying, and from any other dealing in the church wherein they take authority over the man." They could never be ministers or even lay preachers, but only nonvoting members of the church.

These patriarchal values surfaced in Hutchinson's trial for heresy. The magistrates accused her of being an *antinomian,* a person who looks inward for grace and asserts freedom from the divine law embodied in the institutions of church and state. Described by Winthrop as "a woman of fierce and haughty courage," Hutchinson defended her beliefs with great skill and tenacity. But the odds against her were too great. Her judges extracted an admission of a direct relationship with God, which they considered a presumptuous heresy, and found her guilty of exceeding her proper station in life. "If

THE PURITAN VISION OF AN IDEAL SOCIETY

John Winthrop defines the Puritan mission in The Modell of Christian Charity, *1630.*

We must be knit together in this work as one man, we must entertain each other in brotherly affection, we must be willing to abridge ourselves of our superfluities for the supply of others' necessities, we must uphold ... our community as members of the same body. So shall we keep the unity of the spirit in the bond of peace. The Lord will be our God and delight to dwell among us His own people, and will command a blessing upon us in all our ways, so that we shall see much more of his wisdom, power, goodness and truth than formerly we have been acquainted with. We shall find that the God of Israel is among us, when ten of us shall be able to resist a thousand of our enemies, when He shall make us a praise and glory, that men shall say of succeeding plantations, the Lord make it like that of New England. For we must consider that we shall be as a city upon a hill, the eyes of all people are upon us.

Anne Hutchinson matches wits with Governor Winthrop at her trial for heresy, 1637.

Mr. Winthrop, Governor: Mrs. Hutchinson, you are called here as one of those that have troubled the peace of the commonwealth and the churches here.... You have maintained a meeting and an assembly in your house that hath been condemned by the General Assembly as a thing not tolerable nor comely in the sight of God nor fitting for your sex.... By what warrant do you continue such a course?

Mrs. H.: I conceive there lyes a clear rule in Titus, that the elder women should instruct the younger and then I must have a time wherein I must do it.

Gov.: You know that there is no rule that crosses another, but this rule crosses that in the Corinthians. But you must take it in this sense that elder women must instruct the younger about their business and to love their husbands and not to make them to clash.

Mrs. H.: I do not conceive but that it is meant for some publick times.

Gov.: Well, have you no more to say but this?

Mrs. H.: I have said sufficient for my practice.

---

she had attended her household affairs, and such things as belong to women," Winthrop proclaimed, she might have lived "usefully and honorably in the place God had set her." Her merchant supporters lacked sufficient political power to protect her. Condemned as a religious deviant by the General Court and banished from the Massachusetts Bay Colony, she followed Roger Williams into exile in Rhode Island.

Acting with speed and determination, the Puritan magistrates had defined and preserved religious orthodoxy. Political power in Massachusetts Bay, and in the other Puritan colonies in Plymouth and New Haven in Connecticut, rested firmly in the hands of religious realists. Their highest goals were the stability and survival of their holy commonwealths and the preservation of a "pure" Protestant faith. Nevertheless, the spectrum of Puritan belief and practice remained wide. Millenialism and religious enthusiasm continued to play an important role in New England, as did the traditions of anticlericalism and lay control.

These antihierarchical values gained increasing importance in Puritan communities. As the settlements evolved past the first decade of crisis, lay members of the churches claimed authority over most spiritual matters. Meeting as a congregation, they decided matters of doctrine, chose their ministers, and admitted new converts. In the Cambridge Platform of 1648, the laity won a written guarantee that each church was independent and equal. The churches were "distinct," the platform stated, "and therefore may not be confounded one with another; and equal, and therefore have not dominion one over another." Magistrates and ministers resisted lay control and local autonomy, and they won some concessions in the Cambridge Platform. It specified that "consociations" composed of ministers and leading laymen might meet to discuss church dogma and discipline. However, their decisions would not bind individual congregations. Dissatisfied with this compromise, ministers in Connecticut won additional authority in the Saybrook Platform of 1708. Yet throughout New England, the lay congregation remained the dominant institutional force. It used its control over church finances to control ambitious ministers and frequently forced them from their pulpits.

As Puritan laymen and clerics debated these issues, they expressed troubling doubts about the success of their historic mission. By 1660, the original migrants were growing old and millennial hopes had dimmed. A violent Puritan-led revolution in England during the 1640s had executed King Charles I, installed a representative republican regime, and sought to reform the Church of England by force. Leading New England Puritans returned to participate in this struggle, but they could not prevent the slow collapse of the revolutionary regime. By the 1650s, Oliver Cromwell, a zealous Puritan military leader, had taken dictatorial control of the English government and popular support for saintly rule quickly declined. In 1660, King Charles II restored the Stuart monarchy and reestablished episcopal rule in the Church of England.

These setbacks in England prompted American Puritans to reevaluate the meaning of their "errand into the wilderness." The outlook was grim. In many congregations, the second generation had not sustained an intense religious spirit. Perhaps awed by their parents' fervor, a few young adults had experienced conversion and been accepted into full communion. Their "deadness of soul" threatened the Puritan experiment. Church members had never numbered more than a bare majority of the population; they might become a small minority. To avert spiritual and political decline, a group of ministers advocated new criteria for church membership. Known as the Halfway Covenant of 1662,

RICHARD MATHER
Richard Mather (1596–1669) began an intellectual tradition that extended over three Puritan generations. Stripped of his pulpit by Archbishop Laud, Mather migrated to New England in 1635. His son, Increase Mather (1639–1723), was a leading Boston clergyman and theologian. His grandson, Cotton Mather (1663–1723), wrote *Magnalia Christi Americana*, an epic account of the Puritan religious adventure in New England. (American Antiquarian Society)

these proposals would bestow partial church membership on the descendants of the elect. As they awaited conversion, Halfway members could be baptized, participate in church affairs, and even have their own children baptized.

The Halfway Covenant altered Calvinist theology by making salvation more predictable. As Increase Mather, a leading Puritan minister explained, "God has seen meet [fit] to cast the line of election so that generally elect Children are cast upon elect Parents." Many lay members of the elect refused to accept this novel doctrine. They had personally experienced the influx of God's saving grace and demanded that their children face the same emotional and spiritual test. Many congregations refused for years, or even for decades, to adopt the Halfway Covenant. The church in Dedham, Massachusetts, did not accept the new doctrine until 1692, following the deaths of most of the original migrants.

The Halfway Covenant increased the Puritans' sense of "tribalism." Seeing themselves as a chosen people, New England Puritans had never been dedicated evangelists, intent upon converting others. By stressing the hereditary nature of election, the Halfway Covenant confirmed this inward-looking vision. In future generations, those born into the elect would dominate the membership of the Congregational churches. For example, the First Church of Milford, Connecticut, had 962 members between its founding in 1639 and 1770. No fewer than 693, or 72 percent, of these Puritan Saints were the biological descendants of the thirty-six families who established the original congregation.

The Puritans had come to America with high expectations. Some thought their migration signaled the beginning of the millennium of Christ's rule on the earth. Others believed they would be called back to Europe as the saviors of Christendom. When the course of earthly events dashed these sacred missions, their ministers laid out a new set of goals. They told the Puritans to maintain their identity as a chosen people and to create in the American wilderness a new society based on high moral and intellectual principles. One epic had ended, but another had just begun.

A Freeholding Society

While serving God, the Puritans built settlements that resembled the most prosperous and independent peasant communities in Europe. The New England migrants consciously avoided the worst features of the old agricultural society, such as harsh landlords and an abusive aristocracy, oppressive taxes, and impoverished landless laborers. Instead, the Puritans created a society composed of landowning farm families. The families lived in tightly knit towns and had a firm sense of communal responsibility and identity.

The New England governments implemented these social values through their land-distribution policies. They conveyed land to individuals in *fee simple*. This form of property title placed almost no restrictions on the use of land. In England, most land was held under lease or was subject to restrictive tenures or feudal dues. Some migrants had owned land in England under *copyhold* tenure, which limited its use to the ancient *custom of the manor*. Others had paid an annual *quitrent,* a token sum of money or goods that signified that the land was "quitted" of other feudal dues. Quitrents symbolized the continuing subordinate status of the landowner to a local aristocrat or to the king. By granting land in fee simple, the New England governments repudiated the legal legacy of feudal hierarchy. Their leaders wanted a society of independent freeholders.

The Puritan governments also encouraged the formation of organized communities. The General Court of Massachusetts Bay did not normally grant land to individuals. Instead, it bestowed the title to a township, usually measuring six miles by ten miles, on a group of settlers. These settlers, called *proprietors,* owned the land collectively, admitted other families to their ranks, and distributed the township among themselves. Subsequently, they (and nonproprietors who purchased land in the community) controlled the institutions of local government. Town meetings composed of the male heads of families elected selectmen to manage affairs. They also levied taxes; enacted ordinances regarding fencing, lot sizes, and roadbuilding; and regulated the use of the common fields used for grazing livestock and cutting firewood. Widespread participation and extensive powers made these New England towns very different from most peasant communities in Europe, which were dominated by resident nobles, royal bureaucrats, or absentee landlords.

The political power of the towns determined the structure of the colonywide government. Beginning in 1634, each town in the Massachusetts Bay Colony elected its own representatives to the General Court. Increasingly, power came from below rather than from the governor and the assistant magistrates, who were selected by the voters. Even the prestige of a powerful defender of orthodoxy, such as John Winthrop, did not overawe the residents of most towns. When Winthrop intervened in a dispute over the selection of militia officers in Hingham, he met stout resistance. As one Hingham militiaman put it,

MAP 2.4 SETTLEMENT PATTERNS IN NEW ENGLAND

By 1700, the Puritans had spread along the Atlantic coast and far up the broad plains of the Connecticut River valley. Initially most towns were compact settlements, such as Wethersfield, Connecticut; families lived close to one another in the "nucleated" village center and traveled daily to the surrounding fields. The rugged geography of eastern Massachusetts encouraged a more dispersed form of settlement. The migrants who settled in Andover, Massachusetts, preferred to live on their own farms, connected by roads that stretched far into the countryside.

he would "die at the sword's point, if he might not have the choice of his own officers."

The political autonomy of the towns encouraged cultural diversity. Migrants from the various agricultural regions of England often congregated in separate towns. Most of the settlers of Rowley, Massachusetts, came from one of the "drowsy corners" of northern England, the East Riding of Yorkshire. Not surprisingly, they introduced Yorkshire manorial customs, such as communally regulated open-field agriculture. In contrast, the proprietors of Watertown hailed primarily from the economically dynamic region of East Anglia. They quickly duplicated its system of separate family farmsteads. The common circumstances of life in New England gradually diminished the significance of these local customs, as did the similar Puritan beliefs of many settlers. By 1700, a fairly uniform and distinctive culture had appeared throughout the region. It was founded on the principles of Puritan religious values, local political autonomy, and the nearly universal ownership of freehold property by farm families.

Widespread ownership did not imply equality of wealth or status. Hierarchy still prevailed in this transplanted European society. Migrants from privileged backgrounds transferred their social identity to America. Before Edward Johnson came to New England, he was a substantial landowner in Kent, a man of "rank and quality." Johnson became well known on both sides of the Atlantic as the author of the *Wonder-Working Providence of Zion's Saviour*, a prophetic tract published in 1650. But he prospered in the Massachusetts Bay Colony primarily because his social status won him a large land grant as a proprietor of the town of Woburn.

A similar pattern prevailed in most New England towns. About 10 pecent of the proprietors of Windsor, Connecticut, received 40 percent of the land distributed in 1640, while the bottom 20 percent of the proprietary families received only 4 percent. Farther up the Connecticut River at Springfield, Massachusetts, John Pynchon owned thousands of acres. The General Court had rewarded him handsomely for his exploits as an Indian fighter. In 1685, Pynchon rented land or housing to 49 of the 120 male adults in Springfield. Because of his economic power, he dominated the political life of the town.

Puritan leaders justified these economic distinctions, just as they defended the restriction of voting privileges to the spiritual elect. "In all times," John Winthrop declared, "some must be rich, some poor, some high and eminent in power and dignities, others mean and in subjection." "God hath Ordained different degrees and orders of men," concurred the wealthy Boston merchant John Saffin, "some to be High and Honorable, Masters and Commanders, others to be Subjects, and to be commanded." Otherwise, Saffin noted with disdain, "there would be a meer parity among men."

In many settlements, economic inequality increased through the years. Initially, most proprietors owned sizable farms, ranging in area from one hundred to six hundred acres. They owned enough property to establish most of their sons within the community. In 1685, about three-fourths of the taxpayers in Andover, Massachusetts, were either settlers who had founded the town in the 1640s, or their sons. The security of these proprietary families came at the expense of newcomers. Nonproprietors had to buy land from established residents or, if they lacked financial resources, work on their farms as tenants or laborers. By 1702, in Windsor, Connecticut, about 30 percent of the adult male taxpayers were landless. It took years of saving, or migration to a new town, for these men and their families to become freeholders.

However, New England settlers had the opportunity to acquire property, unlike most English laborers. Even those at the bottom of the American social scale had some economic security. Nathaniel Fish was one of the poorest men whose estate underwent probate in Barnstable, Massachusetts, in the 1690s. The assessors evaluated his possessions at less than a tenth of the value of the wealthiest estates in the town. Yet Fish owned a two-room cottage, eight acres of land, an ox, and a cow. For him, and thousands of other migrants in New England, America was the promised land. Whatever doubts the Puritans had about the success of their religious mission, they could justly applaud the political stability and economic security of their society. Amid the rocky soils and harsh climate of New England, they had created strong communities and a resilient culture.

By 1700, Englishmen and women had created

TIME LINE
A CENTURY OF CONFLICT

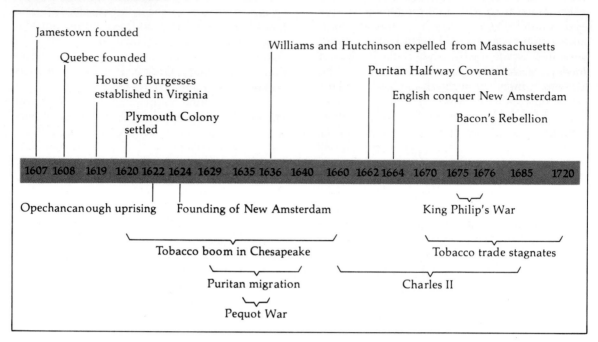

large, vigorous colonies in New England and the Chesapeake Bay region. They had vanquished a score of native American tribes and established two distinct social and cultural systems. The New England colonies exhibited many authoritarian features, but they also had transplanted some of the antihierarchical tendencies of English society. Their institutions increased the power of the religious laity, ensured economic security and independence for most families, and bolstered local political autonomy and power. The Chesapeake colonies embodied a different set of English traditions. Hierarchy and authority characterized their religious, economic, and political institutions and values. These divergent seventeenth-century origins profoundly influenced the development of American society throughout its preindustrial history and beyond.

Four types of conflict appeared in seventeenth-century America.

The expansionist nation-states of Europe competed with one another for territory. Spain claimed the southern half of North America, and French fur traders roamed the northern half. English settlers and armies conquered Dutch trading outposts along the eastern seaboard.

English men and women fought even more bitterly with the native American tribes. The Indians nearly wiped out the Virginia Colony in 1622, and they dealt New England a devastating blow in 1675–1676. By the end of King Philip's War and Bacon's Rebellion, the English invaders had prevailed. The defeated seacoast tribes never again threatened white dominance.

Internal strife was equally important. During Governor Berkeley's reign, from 1660 to 1681, the proud, powerful leaders of Virginia ruled in their own self-interest. With the collapse of the tobacco boom after 1660, freed servants and yeomen farmers faced hard times. During Bacon's Rebellion in 1675–1676, they joined with prominent county families to attack the corrupt provincial oligarchy. Following this white insurrection, Chesapeake planters turned to the use of a black enslaved labor force.

Strife within the Puritan commonwealths of New England usually took a legal form. The magistracy continually used its political power to suppress dissent, as in the banishment of Roger Williams and Anne Hutchinson. These theological battles continued in the struggle over the Halfway Covenant of 1662. In New England, as throughout North America, conflict was the keynote of seventeenth-century life.

Suggestions for Further Reading

The Invasion of North America

Wilcomb B. Washburn, *The Indian in America* (1975), presents a good overview of native American culture. Francis Jennings, *The Invasion of America* (1975), weighs the impact of European settlement from a critical perspective, as does W. R. Jacobs, *Dispossessing the American Indian: Indians and Whites on the Colonial Frontier* (1972). Gary B. Nash, *Red, White, and Black: The Peoples of Early America* (1982), provides a compact analysis of differing patterns of cultural interaction.

For the story of early settlement from the English point of view, see Alden Vaughan, *American Genesis: Captain John Smith and the Founding of Virginia* (1975), and *New England Frontier: Puritans and Indians, 1620–1675* (1965). See also A. W. Trelease, *Indian Affairs in Colonial New York: The Seventeenth Century* (1960); W. F. Craven, *White, Red and Black: The Seventeenth-Century Virginian* (1971); and Verner Crane, *The Southern Frontier, 1670–1732* (1956).

The most recent scholarship in this field has used an anthropological approach to present a synthesis of Indian and European experience. See James Axtell, *The European and the Indian: Essays in the Ethnohistory of Colonial North America* (1981); Karen Ordahl Kupperman, *Settling with the Indians: The Meeting of English and Indian Cultures in America, 1580–1640* (1981); and Neal Salisbury, *Manitou and Providence: Indians, Europeans, and the Making of New England, 1500–1643* (1982).

Social Conflict in the Chesapeake Colonies

W. F. Craven, *The Dissolution of the Virginia Company* (1932), traces the fate of the company in England, while Edmund S. Morgan, *American Slavery, American Freedom* (1975), brilliantly evokes the character of life in the new colony. A fine analytic study of a single community is Carville Earle, *The Evolution of a Tidewater Settlement Pattern: All Hallows Parish, Maryland 1650–1783* (1975), while Gloria L. Main offers a detailed presentation in *Tobacco Colony: Life in Early Maryland, 1650–1720* (1982). For a discussion of political institutions, see W. F. Craven, *The Southern Colonies in the Seventeenth Century, 1607–1689* (1949), and Aubrey C. Land, *Colonial Maryland: A History* (1981).

Two contrasting accounts of Bacon's Rebellion are T. J. Wertenbaker, *Torchbearer of the Revolution* (1940), and Wilcomb B. Washburn, *The Governor and the Rebel* (1958). Exciting scholarship on the seventeenth-century Chesapeake appears in Thad W. Tate and David L. Ammerman, eds, *The Chesapeake in the Seventeenth Century: Essays on Anglo-American Society* (1979).

Puritan New England

The intellectual history of Puritanism is best explored in the many works of Perry Miller. See his *The New England Mind: The Seventeenth Century* (1939) and the shorter treatment in *Orthodoxy in Massachusetts, 1630–1650* (1933). For church affairs, see Edmund S. Morgan, *Visible Saints* (1963), and David Hall, *The Faithful Shephard* (1972). Two biographies that convey the shifting currents of orthodoxy are Edmund S. Morgan, *The Puritan Dilemma: The Story of John Winthrop* (1958), and Robert Middlekauff, *The Mathers: Three Generations of Puritan Intellectuals, 1596–1728* (1971). Samuel Eliot Morison, *Builders of the Bay Colony* (1930), vividly conveys the early history of Massachusetts Bay, and Governor William Bradford's history *Of Plymouth Plantation* (1952) does the same for the Pilgrim colony.

For a discussion of dissent in early New England, see Ola Winslow, *Master Roger Williams* (1957); Emery Battis, *Saints and Sectaries: Anne Hutchinson and the Antinomian Controversy* (1962); and the controversial analysis by Lyle Kohler, *A Search for Power: The Weaker Sex in Seventeenth Century New England* (1980).

Among the more interesting community studies that reveal the character of the lives of ordinary New England men and women are John Demos, *The Little Commonwealth: Family Life in Plymouth Colony* (1971); Kenneth A. Lockridge, *A New England Town: Dedham, Massachusetts, 1636–1737* (1970); and Philip J. Greven, Jr., *Four Generations: Population, Land and Family in Colonial Andover, Massachusetts* (1970). See also Edmund S. Morgan, *The Puritan Family* (1944); David G. Allen, *In English Ways: The Movement of Societies to Massachusetts Bay in the Seventeenth Century* (1980); and Paul Boyer and Steven Nissenbaum, *Salem Possessed: The Social Origins of Witchcraft* (1974).

3

THE CREATION
OF AN AMERICAN
POLITICAL SYSTEM
AND ECONOMY

For a generation following Bacon's Rebellion, the English colonies in America remained a group of small, isolated settlements. They had a total population of 175,000 in 1675 and barely 250,000 in 1700. By the middle of the eighteenth century, a dramatic growth in population and trade elevated the colonies to a position of considerable economic and strategic importance. More than 1.2 million people lived in the colonies that stretched along the Atlantic coast from Massachusetts to Georgia. They consumed about 10 percent of all British exports. These settlements also provided thousands of military recruits. Colonial soldiers fought to prevent French expansion in Canada and the West Indies, and to curtail Spanish influence in Florida and the Gulf of Mexico. The French foreign minister, the Count of Vergennes, predicted, "It is possessions in America that will in future form the balance of power in Europe."

As the English colonies matured into "provinces" within a transatlantic imperial system, they developed stable and distinct political organizations. Until 1715, English officials attempted to bring the American settlements under direct administrative control. Then, because of colonial resistance and new commercial priorities, the English government adopted a policy of "salutary neglect." Freed from close direction from abroad, the colonies copied English models and created strong, flexible institutions of representative government. American politics reflected the interests and priorities of colonial groups, but became more dependent on the political language and ideologies current in England.

A similar paradox arose in economic life. By the early decades of the eighteenth century, the settlements were firmly integrated into the South Atlantic system of commerce. Trading through European middlemen, American planters imported thousands of enslaved African laborers. They forced them to grow sugar, tobacco, or rice and exported these crops for consumption in Europe. This transatlantic system of trade tied colonial producers to foreign labor supplies and markets. At the same time, it assisted the rapid development of a strong American economy. In financial as in political life, the American settlers created increasingly independent institutions that were tightly integrated into the European world of politics and commerce.

The Transformation of American Politics

At the end of the seventeenth century, a series of crises shook the English and American political systems. Administrative centralization by the Stuart kings prompted the Glorious Revolution of 1688 in England and revolts in three American colonies. Colonial political instability continued until 1715. Then the rise of Whig aristocrats in England and the decline of powerful oligarchies in Ameria created a stable governmental order that lasted for two generations. Members of elite social groups continued to dominate provincial public life, but they—and many of their policies—won the voluntary allegiance of most of the white population.

The New Mercantilism

By 1650, the monarchs of Europe had long pursued policies designed to increase the wealth of their nations. They used the mercantile classes to achieve this goal, and so the system of state-instigated economic growth became known as mercantilism. Queen Elizabeth I of England, who reigned from 1558 to 1601, awarded commercial monopolies to various groups of traders, and King James I (1601–1625) and Charles I

A WEST INDIAN SUGAR PLANTATION
Sugar was the most profitable—and the most deadly—of all American crops. Africans toiled and died by the thousands on West Indian plantations; their British owners lived a life of luxury, as absentee planters, in London. The planters sold their sugar in England. American merchants purchased West Indian molasses, a by-product of the refining process, to be distilled into rum at mainland American seaports. (Both, West India Committee)

(1625–1649) granted charters to promote the settlement of America. The Crown eventually imposed royal government on Virginia to safeguard the economic profits of the tobacco trade. It also strongly supported the creation of slave plantations in its Caribbean island colonies. English merchant–planters turned Barbadoes into a major sugar-producing center after 1650, and English naval forces conquered the Spanish sugar island of Jamaica. A century of state economic and military activity created a flourishing commercial system.

As the mainland settlements and the West Indian islands prospered, English mercantilism entered a second phase. The state now stressed the regulation of colonial trade. In 1651, Parliament passed the first Navigation Act, which restricted English and colonial commerce to ships registered in England, Ireland, and the American plantations. Upon their restoration to the throne in 1660, the Stuart kings extended these mercantilist regulations. Charles II (1660–85) immediately reenacted the Navigation Act banning foreign shipping from English and colonial ports. In 1661, additional legislation required that all European exports to America be shipped though the mother country. This measure assisted English manufacturers by cutting the volume of non-English goods flowing to the colonies, and it guaranteed profits to English merchants for handling these exports.

Then, in 1663, the Staple Act specified that certain colonial products, primarily the valuable staple crops of sugar, tobacco, indigo, and logwood, could be exported only to England. Two subsequent laws closed loopholes in these regulations and ensured their enforcement. The Revenue Act of 1673 imposed a special "plantation duty" on specific articles exported to another colony and created a staff of customs officials in American ports to collect the levy. The Navigation Act of 1696 increased the legal powers of the customs agents and required all American governors to enforce these trade regulations under penalty of dismissal.

English merchants and manufacturers strongly supported these commercial regulations, for they faced serious competition from Dutch traders. Sailing from New Amsterdam and the island of Saint Eustatius in the West Indies, Dutch merchants supplied the American colonies with imported goods and carried their crops of sugar and tobacco directly to European markets. When the Dutch refused to stop this lucrative trade, England upheld the Navigation Acts by force. The English and Dutch fought commercial wars from 1652 to 1654, in 1664, and again in 1673. English troops captured the fur-trading settlement of New Amsterdam, and the increasingly powerful English navy won control of the seas. Henceforth, the English merchant marine dominated American commerce.

The Stuart monarchs promoted colonial settlement by creating new proprietary colonies. In 1663, Charles II bestowed Carolina on eight aristocrats who had supported his return to power. In 1664, he granted the colony of New Jersey to his brother James, the Duke of York. James promptly relinquished control of New Jersey to Lords Carteret and Berkeley, who were also proprietors of Carolina. James took possession of the newly captured Dutch territory of New Amsterdam and renamed it New York, after his aristocratic title. In 1681, Charles II granted William Penn the colony of Pennsylvania, in payment of a large debt and in respect for Penn's father, an influential admiral.

In less than two decades, the king had given most of the unclaimed land in eastern North America to a small group of aristocrats. These English nobles had title to millions of acres of land, to sell, lease or settle as they pleased. They had the right to appoint governors and other officials in their colonies and to veto legislation passed by any assembly of residents. Within broad limits they were free to shape the social and political character of their settlements—and they did so. The Carolina proprietors temporarily imposed an aristocratic form of government on their colony in a document entitled "The Fundamental Constitutions of Carolina" (1669). William Penn designed his colony as a refuge for Quakers and other victims of religious persecution. Whatever the outcome, the new proprietors were lords of the land.

As the king relinquished control of these unsettled American lands, royal bureaucrats set out to enforce the Acts of Trade and Navigation in the colonies. They immediately confronted stout resistance. Edward Randolph, a royal administrator, reported that Massachusetts authorities took "no notice of the laws of trade." They

MAP 3.1 BOSTON IN 1676
The social geography of Boston reflected the city's position as the main American seaport. Boston's urban core consisted of a well-developed waterfront area of docks and warehouses and, along King Street, a separate area of government buildings and of residences owned by wealthy merchants. Artisans and laborers lived along the other streets and side lanes, and grew some of their food in backgardens and nearby fields.

claimed that the corporate charter granted to their founding company by Charles I took precedence over this legislation and exempted the colony from most of the regulations. The Puritans' arrogant attitude outraged Randolph, and he urged his superiors to use English troops to "reduce Massachusetts to obedience."

At the urging of Randolph and other officials, the English government embarked upon a policy of administrative centralization. The Lords of Trade, a committee of the king's Privy Council, had charge of commercial and colonial affairs. In 1679, the lords denied the claim of the Massachusetts Bay Colony to the adjoining frontier province of New Hampshire. Instead, the lords created a separate colony with a royal governor. Two years later, the committee clarified and lim-

ited the privileges of proprietors. The lords required William Penn to submit all legislation enacted in Pennsylvania to the Privy Council for approval. Then, in 1684, the Lords of Trade won a major legal victory. The English Court of Chancery annulled the charter of Massachusetts Bay, thus undermining the Puritan colony's bid for political autonomy.

When James, Duke of York, became king in 1685, he strongly supported the increase of royal authority. Backed by the new monarch, the Lords of Trade obtained the revocation of the corporate charters of Connecticut and Rhode Island. They promptly joined these settlements with the Massachusetts Bay Colony and the king's own proprietary colony of New York. The result was a vast new colony, the Dominion of

New England, a model of colonial administration. The king dispatched a former military officer, Sir Edmund Andros, to Boston armed with a long list of coercive instructions. Following James' orders, Andros abolished the existing legislative assemblies and ruled in the king's name without representative institutions of government. As the name implied, New England was to be the king's own "dominion."

The centralized administrative structure of the dominion was the logical culmination of the second, or regulatory, phase of English mercantilism. Since 1651, the royal government had enacted a series of stringent laws controlling trade. It had gone to war three times to protect its maritime interests, and it had used strong legal weapons to attack the autonomy of the Puritan colonies. Even Charles II's lavish grants to proprietors had certain regulatory features because they placed these American settlements in the hands of the king's closest associates. Assisted at first by Parliament, the Stuart monarchs had greatly extended their personal power over the imperial system. With the establishment of the Dominion of New England, James II struck directly at the autonomy of government institutions in America and at the political power of the oligarchs who controlled them. He imposed mercantilist rules and royal edicts by administrative decree.

The Glorious Revolution

A political *coup d'etat*, the so-called Glorious Revolution of 1688, arrested the trend toward absolute monarchical rule in England and America. By annulling corporate charters and ruling without parliamentary support, James II had offended influential English political leaders. Whig merchants, Tory aristocrats, and independent country gentlemen all opposed the king's policies. Equally important, James II's Catholic sympathies aroused the English people, most of whom were devout Protestants. When the king's second wife, a Spanish Catholic princess, gave birth to a son and heir in 1688, protests occurred throughout England. Assured of the people's support, parliamentary leaders staged a quick and bloodless rebellion. They forced James II into exile and placed his Protestant daughter

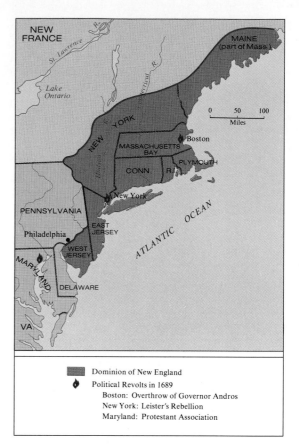

MAP 3.2 THE DOMINION OF NEW ENGLAND
James II created the Dominion in 1686 to strengthen royal control of the colonies. Revolts in Boston and New York City ousted royal officials in 1689, effectively ending the Dominion. In Maryland, a Protestant Association led a third revolt, deposing the Roman Catholic proprietary governor.

(by his first wife) on the throne. England's new monarchs, Queen Mary II and her Dutch husband, William of Orange, agreed to respect the traditional powers of Parliament.

The Glorious Revolution led to minor rebellions in three colonies, Massachusetts, Maryland, and New York in 1689. Each of these upheavals reflected serious local conflicts, but they all reflected growing colonial opposition to the new imperial administrative policies. As the first governor of the Dominion of New England, Sir Edmund Andros quickly attacked all the major institutions of New England society. He lent his support and prestige to the Church of England, thus alienating Congregational clergy and laity. Andros banned town meetings, rousing resistance in scores of rural villages accustomed to political autonomy. He imposed arbitrary taxes, creating enemies among members of the now-extinct General Court. The governor charged that all the land titles granted under the original Massachusetts charter were invalid. He demanded quit-rents on new patents issued by his office, repudiating the principle of freehold tenure. After a year in office, the gruff military man had few friends and many enemies.

News of the accession of William and Mary touched off an uprising in Boston. A printed "Manifesto" called on the townspeople to oust the appointees of James II and to "seize the vile persons who oppressed us." The "rabble" responded, according to customs official Edward Randolph, "acted & managed by the preachers." The town militia seized the governor and forced him to return to England. A Council for the Safety and Conservation of the Peace ruled the colony until the election of a new General Court.

Meanwhile, in London, the eminent Puritan minister Increase Mather petitioned for the restoration of the old charter of 1629. William and Mary agreed to break up the Dominion of New England and restore representative assemblies in the various colonies. Following the advice of the Lords of Trade, the new monarchs named a royal governor for the Massachusetts Bay Colony and allowed voting rights for property owners who were not members of Puritan congregations. This political compromise worked successfully for seventy years. The new charter of 1692 gave Massachusetts considerable autonomy while increasing royal control over the vital areas of trade and military defense.

The rebellion in Maryland stemmed from long-standing religious and economic conflicts. Following the Glorious Revolution, a "Protestant Association" forcibly seized power. The association issued a "Declaration of Reasons and Motives" accusing the deposed officials of "Popish Idolatry and Superstition." Many of these men were Catholics who had been appointed to positions of power and profit in Maryland because of their ties to Lord Baltimore, the Catholic proprietor. Small freeholders and tenant farmers supported the revolt for economic as well as religious reasons. Like Nathaniel Bacon's followers in Virginia, they had suffered from falling tobacco prices, rising taxes, and the high fees collected by proprietary officials.

To restore order to the religiously divided colony, the Lords of Trade sent a royal governor and exercised direct control over Maryland until 1715. Then Benedict Calvert, the fourth Lord Baltimore, converted to Protestantism, and the Crown restored his proprietary rights. Political tensions decreased after the religious issue had been resolved. A rising demand for tobacco after 1720 brought greater prosperity. Like Virginia, Maryland remained a society with sharp class and racial divisions, but with an increasingly stable and united governing class.

Unlike the uprisings in Maryland and Massachusetts, the New York revolt of 1689 was not quick, bloodless, or easily resolved. Ethnic antagonisms led to political executions and decades of social strife. When England conquered New Amsterdam in 1664, most of the Dutch inhabitants had remained in the colony. About 67 percent of the taxpayers in the city of New York in 1677 had Dutch names, and in 1695, 58 percent were Dutch. Artisans and small shopkeepers made up most of the city's Dutch population, and communities of Dutch farmers dotted the countryside. Many resented the English merchants, and their wealthy Dutch commercial allies, who dominated the economy. As proud Protestants from Holland, Dutch freeholders and artisans welcomed the accession of Mary and William of Orange to the English throne. They joined with Puritan farmers on Long Island in attacking the "Popish Doggs & Divells" appointed by James II to administer the Dominion of New England.

The city militia ousted Francis Nicholson, the "pretended Protestant" lieutenant governor of the dominion, and replaced him with their own leader, Jacob Leisler, a German migrant who had married into an English merchant family. Leisler, a militia captain, at first had the support of all ethnic and class groups, but this solidarity quickly disintegrated. Dutch artisans in the city of New York challenged the wealthy merchants who had dominated its government. They elected six of their own number—a bricklayer,

A PROSPEROUS DUTCH FARMSTEAD
By the 1730s many Americans enjoyed a rising standard of living. Dutch settlers in the Hudson River
Valley were especially prosperous, because of their location and the widespread use of black slaves.
To record his success, Marten Van Bergen of Leeds, New York, had this mural painted over his
mantelpiece. (John Deaton. Detail of *Van Bergen Overmantel (Homestead)*. New York State Historical
Association, Cooperstown)

baker, innkeeper, artist, carpenter, and mariner—to the ten-member Board of Aldermen.

Leisler himself freed debtors from prison and
urged the creation of a more democratic town-
meeting form of government. To protect their
political power, the merchants attacked him and
the legitimacy of his rule. A pamphlet written by
Nicholas Bayard accused Leisler of being a
"Mansaniello," the peasant fishmonger who in
1647 had led a popular revolt in Naples, Italy. In
the eyes of the merchant establishment, the rebellion against the dominion had become a social
revolution.

The arrival of a new royal governor, Henry
Sloughter, in 1691 restored merchant rule.
Backed by Sloughter, merchant aldermen passed
ordinances that reduced artisan wages. The new
government also indicted Leisler and seven of
his associates for treason. A jury composed
solely of Englishmen convicted Leisler and his
brother-in-law, Jacob Milburne, and the two
men were hanged and then decapitated. This
stern reprisal broke the political power of the
Dutch artisans and intensified underlying class
and ethnic antagonisms. When Leisler and Milburne were reburied in a Dutch churchyard in
1698, about twelve hundred people, or a fourth
of the city's population, honored their memory
by marching in the funeral procession. Political
instability continued in New York until the
1710s, when Governor Robert Hunter settled
most of the disputes between the Leislerian and
anti-Leislerian factions.

The events of 1689 represented a major turning point in the political and administrative history of the American colonies. The uprisings in
New York and Boston toppled the authoritarian
institutions of the Dominion of New England.
This decisively reversed the trend toward strict
mercantilist regulation of the colonies. The Navigation Acts remained in force and, despite some
smuggling, channeled colonial trade through England. However, the purposeful administrative
control undertaken by the Lords of Trade and
James II came to an end. The restoration of representative assemblies diminished royal control
and permitted the development of American political autonomy.

During the reigns of William and Mary (1689–1701) and Queen Anne (1702–1713), English officials groped indecisively for a new colonial policy. Parliament created a new Board of Trade in 1696. The first appointees consisted of rising politicians and experienced bureaucrats. Nevertheless, the board failed to muster political support for its program of placing all colonial governments under direct control of the Crown. New York, New Jersey, and Massachusetts became provinces with royal governors, but Connecticut and Rhode Island continued to elect all their own officials under the terms of the corporate charters granted by Charles I. Despite the board's efforts to eliminate the proprietary colonies created by Charles II, the Calvert and Penn families retained ownership and political authority in Maryland and Pennsylvania. In the 1720s, however, the board ended proprietary rule in North and South Carolina, because poor management had aroused popular unrest and led to disastrous Indian wars.

During this period, the Board of Trade won widespread backing only for its policy of resisting the expansion of other European nations in North America. With the end of the Dutch maritime threat, English officials concentrated on French activities in Canada and Europe. England provided large financial subsidies to various German states to resist the military forces of King Louis XIV of France and encouraged the American colonial governments to oppose French encroachments in America. In King William's War (1689–1697), provincial militiamen fought with French troops in the wide belt of Indian territory separating New France from New England and New York. During Queen Anne's War (1702–1713), the French mobilized Algonquin tribes to attack outlying English settlements. Warriors destroyed the Massachusetts town of Deerfield in 1704 and massacred many of its people. With considerable royal assistance, New England volunteers captured the French fort at Port Royal in Nova Scotia, but then failed in two expeditions against the French stronghold at Quebec.

The stakes of these confrontations between England and France were high in Europe but limited in America. Few troops fought in the engagements, and the New York frontier remained quiet. Both English and French fur traders persuaded their governments to refrain from military expeditions that would disrupt their lu-crative trade with the Indians. Equally important, the powerful Iroquois tribes pursued a policy of "aggressive neutrality," refusing to assist either European nation. The Treaty of Utrecht in 1713 ended the series of wars and did not alter territorial boundaries in America. For the next generation, England and France lived in peace, enabling colonial development to proceed under favorable conditions.

Society and Politics

Before 1700, authoritarian economic and religious elites dominated colonial political life. Governor William Berkeley and his Green Spring faction ruled Virginia with an iron hand. Lord Baltimore appointed wealthy fellow Catholics to high positions in Maryland. Puritan magistrates banished dissidents, and New York merchants executed Leislerians for treason. Ruling political oligarchies denounced opposition to their policies as seditious. They condemned groups that resisted them as illegitimate "factions."

This political behavior reflected a set of hierarchical philosophical assumptions. Men and women were not free by nature to do as they wished, according to Governor John Winthrop of the Massachusetts Bay Colony, and they had the "liberty to that only which is good, just, and honest." The ruling magistrates would decide what was proper. "The greatest part of mankind are but as tools and Instruments for others to work by," the Reverend William Hubbard of Boston reminded his flock in 1676. As another minister put it, the best political system was one in which a "speaking Aristocracy" exercised firm control over a "silent Democracy." The laws of God and nature ordained that power should come from above, not below. "I think it most Natural," an English political philosopher proclaimed, "that Authority should Descend from *Kings* and *Fathers* to *Sons* and *Servants*."

The Glorious Revolution challenged the precepts and institutions of authoritarian politics. In England, the Whig political faction grew increasingly powerful. Whigs stood for a constitutionally limited monarchy rather than an absolute one. They insisted on a "mixed government" that divided power among the three social orders of monarchy, aristocracy, and the commons. Beginning with the reign of William and Mary, Whig aristocrats and politicians slowly

FIGURE 3.1 FAMILY
CONNECTIONS AND
POLITICAL POWER

strengthened the powers of Parliament in relation to those of the Crown.

The leaders of the American representative assemblies sought to duplicate the Whig victories. To increase the authority of the elected assemblies and decrease the powers of the appointed councils and royal governors, provincial assemblymen modeled the procedures of their institutions on those of the English House of Commons. They established the same committees, guarded the authority to levy taxes, and claimed a position of constitutional equality with the royal or proprietary governor. "The people in power in America," William Penn protested during a struggle with the Pennsylvania Assembly, "think nothing taller than themselves but the Trees."

Changes in the structure of American society laid the foundations for this rise in the power of the assemblies. A key factor was the emergence of cohesive social units in colonial towns and countries. In the Chesapeake Bay colonies, a sharp decline in white death rates after 1690 led to the creation of stable families and the transmission of political influence from one generation to the next. In New England, the intermarried grandchildren of the original migrants had already formed communities with a strong sense of identity. In the long-settled town of Andover, Massachusetts, for example, thirty-one adult male members of the Abbot family appeared on the tax list of 1755, all descendants of George Abbot I.

The ties of family and kinship formed the social basis of political power. Family connections enabled young men to win appointment to a low-level office in a town government or county militia. Individual ability, combined with kinship ties, then determined the rate and height of their ascent up the political ladder. During the middle decades of the eighteenth century in Concord, Massachusetts, members of the Barrett clan won about a third of the elections for the positions of town selectman and provincial assemblyman. In New Brunswick, New Jersey, a European traveler noted that the "principal personages" were "General White, Colonel Bayard, and Judge Patterson—all these families are related and live in close contact." John Adams commented, "Go into every village in New England, and you will find that the office of justice of the peace, and even the place of representative, have generally descended from generation to generation, in three or four families at most."

The appearance of scores of capable local leaders shifted the center of political power. Men elected to provincial assemblies in the eighteenth century had strong roots in their locality or kinship group. They had served for years as a town selectman, county justice of the peace, church vestryman, or officer in the county militia. As assemblymen, they opposed governors and policies that did not address the needs of their communities. Governors, proprietors, and colonial oligarchies found it difficult to control the assemblies through patronage, and the number of representatives grew continually because of population increases and westward expansion. Reluctantly, the political leaders accepted the existence (but still not the legitimacy) of political dissent and opposition factions.

Eventually, this process of socio-political evolution created colonywide kinship networks. Seven members of the Lee family sat in the Virginia House of Burgesses in the 1750s, representing five counties. More than half the committee leaders of the legislature were members by blood or marriage of the great Virginia families, the Lees, Byrds, Washingtons, and Carters. In New York, family rivalries crystalized into competitive factional politics. The Delancy family led a legislative faction composed of members of the Church of England, and the Livingston family stood at the head of a coalition of Hudson River Valley landlords and dissenting religious sects.

This new system of American politics had democratic and elitist features. Political authority came increasingly from below. The elected representatives of towns and counties slowly increased the powers of the assemblies in relation to those of appointed governors and councils. Yet the social composition of local governments and provincial legislatures gave a hierarchical cast to the political system. Most selectman, justices of the peace, and assemblymen ranked among the wealthiest 10 percent of the taxable population in the Chesapeake colonies and the Carolinas and among the richest 30 percent in the northern colonies. Most white adult males owned enough property to qualify for the vote, but they usually voted for their social "betters."

In the aftermath of the revolts of the late seventeenth century, however, political leaders took increased notice of the potential power of the people—with good reason. There were no police or military forces leaders could use to impose arbitrary or unpopular laws. In 1737, when officials implemented controversial regulations governing the public market in Boston, rioters destroyed the market building and defied the authorities to arrest them. "If you touch One you shall touch All," an anonymous letter warned Sheriff Edward Winslow, "and we will show you a Hundred Men where you can show one."

That letter said it in a nutshell. Popular resistance and organization on a number of levels—

in town meetings, county courts, and provincial assemblies, as well as in crowd actions—had undermined the authoritarian political system of the seventeenth century. Local elites now avoided policies that threatened the vital interests of the mass of the white population. At the same time, they struggled among themselves, and against proprietors and royal governors, for power on the colonial level. American social development and political maturity had created a system of authority that was broadly responsive to popular pressure and increasingly immune from British control.

"Salutary Neglect"

Provincial political autonomy also resulted from British policies during the reigns of the first two Hanoverian monarchs, George I (1714–1727) and George II (1727–1760). The government relaxed its supervision of the American settlements, and British ministers restricted their efforts to the military defense of the colonies and the encouragement of trade with Great Britain. The dramatic increase in colonial wealth and population testified to their success. In 1770, the eminent political philosopher Edmund Burke praised this administrative strategy as one of "salutary neglect." Other British political leaders thought the relaxation of imperial control had been a disaster. As Charles Townshend of the Board of Trade argued as early as 1754, the American assemblies had used this opportunity to usurp nearly all "the ancient and established prerogatives wisely preserved in the Crown."

Whether salutary or not, British neglect resulted from the political system that was developed by Sir Robert Walpole. Between 1720 and 1742, Walpole served simultaneously as the king's chief adviser and the leader of the Whig majority in the House of Commons. As prime minister, Sir Robert transformed the once-antagonistic relationship between king and Parliament into harmonious cooperation. He used astute political alliances and patronage appointments to assure parliamentary majorities for the policies of the king's ministers. Walpole governed in the monarch's name but with Parliament's consent.

This political technique had its costs. A small

PRIME MINISTER SIR ROBERT WALPOLE
Walpole (left) is talking to the Speaker of the House of
Commons. A brilliant tactical politician, Walpole used
patronage to command a majority of votes in the
Commons. By looking out for the financial interests of
George I and George II, the German-speaking monarchs,
he won their support as well. Walpole's personal motto,
"let sleeping dogs lie," partly explains the colonial policy
of "salutary neglect." (William Hogarth/Sir James
Thornehill. *House of Commons, 1730*. Clandon Park, The
National Trust)

but vocal parliamentary opposition attacked Walpole for using places, pensions, and other gifts
to create a "Court" party. These "Dissenting"
or "Real" Whigs argued that such "corruption"
undermined the independence of Parliament.
They condemned Walpole's creation of a large
national debt as the cause of high taxes and political intrigue. They warned that the expansion
of the royal bureaucracy threatened the liberties of the people. The Real Whigs maintained
that they were the true heirs of the Glorious
Revolutionaries of 1688. Many landed gentlemen
with *Tory* (conservative Royalist) principles likewise opposed Walpole's financial and administrative innovations. They favored a "Country"
ideology that celebrated the independence of the

members of Parliament. As country gentlemen,
they feared the power wielded by a central bureaucracy or a standing army.

The principles of the Real Whig and Country
party factions attracted considerable attention in
America. The attacks on Walpole provided a
compelling interpretation of struggles between
the provincial assemblies and royal governors.
Like Walpole and his ministers, the governors
had formidable powers. They could call and dissolve assemblies at their pleasure. They could
veto legislation and grant land. They could appoint judges, justices of the peace, and other
officials. Using this power and patronage, governors tried to ensure majority support in the
assemblies for the king's policies. Influenced by
Real Whig and Country party ideologies, some
Americans interpreted these normal political maneuvers in more sinister terms. "An ill [evil] governor not only enslaves the present generation,
but makes slavery hereditary to latest posterity,"
a pamphleteer declared during a dispute in 1734
over freedom of the press in New York. Governors achieved this goal, a writer in the Boston
Weekly Newsletter explained during another dispute, by "increasing the number of officers dependent on the Crown and thereby influencing
elections and destroying the liberties of the people." Walpole's policies thus had the strange and
unexpected effect of adding an ideological dimension to the colonial assemblies' quest for
power.

The political maneuvers of Walpole and his
ministers undermined the royal administrative
system in an even more direct way. Few zealous, reform-minded officials came to the American colonies. Rather, colonial posts were filled
with office seekers who had good political connections and mediocre talents. In 1731, William
Cosby became governor of New York because
his wife was related to Lord Halifax. He saw his
office as a road to wealth. Cosby's salary demands, land grants, and sale of offices threw the
province into political chaos for a decade. His
successor, George Clinton, was little better. Clinton owed his appointment to a family connection to the Duke of Newcastle, who was
Walpole's chief political manager. He was a
weak governor and failed to uphold the traditional powers of his office.

Patronage appointments also sapped the vi-

THE GOVERNOR LOSES CONTROL

Salutary neglect and weak British officials opened the way for colonial assemblies to assert their will. Here, Governor George Clinton writes Parliament confessing his inability to control the provincial New York assembly.

My Lords,

I have in my former letters inform'd Your Lordships what Incroachments the Assemblys of this province have from time to time made on His Majesty's Prerogative & Authority in this Province in drawing an absolute dependence of all the Officers upon them for their Saleries & Reward of their services, & by their taking in effect the Nomination to all Officers....

1stly, That the Assembly refuse to admit of any amendment to any money bill, in any part of the Bill; so that the Bill must pass as it comes from the Assembly, or all the Supplies granted for the support of Government, & the most urgent services must be lost.

2ndly, It appears that they take the Payment of the [military] Forces, passing of Muster Rolls into their own hands by naming the Commissaries for those purposes in the Act.

3rdly, They by granting the Saleries to the Officers personally by name & not to the Officer for the time being, intimate that if any person be appointed to any Office his Salery must depend upon their approbation of the Appointment....

I must now referr it to Your Lordships consideration whether it be not high time to put a stop to these usurpations of the Assembly on His Majesty's Authority in this Province and for that purpose may it not be proper that His Majesty signify his Disallowance of the Act at least for the payment of Saleries.

---

tality of the Board of Trade. Walpole, and especially Newcastle, turned the board into a repository for ministerial "placemen." In return for supporting the ministry in Parliament, these second- and third-rate politicians received a seat on the board and a comfortable yearly payment. The lack of a purposeful board undermined the morale of capable colonial appointees. "I imagined like most young beginners that I should be able to make a mighty change in the face of affairs," Governor Gabriel Johnson wrote to his patron after three years in North Carolina, "but a little experience of the people, and reflection on the situation of things at home, has absolutely cured me of this mistake." He concluded, "I now confine my care entirely to do nothing which can be reasonably blamed, and leave the rest to time, and a new set of inhabitants."

A commercial war with Spain in the West Indies in 1739 focused new attention on America. The governors of the northern colonies raised hundreds of volunteers for a successful but costly assault on the Spanish town of Cartagena in Panama. Troops commanded by General James Oglethorpe defended the new British colony of Georgia, founded in 1733, against Spanish attack, but failed to capture Saint Augustine in Florida. A general European war broke out in 1740, and New England militiamen captured the powerful French fortress of Louisbourg. These modest contributions to the British war effort bolstered provincial self-esteem, as did the growth of the American colonial population. In another century, Governor William Shirley of Massachusetts predicted in 1745, the colonies would "vye for Numbers with the subjects of France, and lay a foundation for a Superiority of British power upon the continent of Europe."

As America became a prize in European diplomacy, British ministers revived plans for administrative reform. These proposals received little enthusiasm from a demoralized and mediocre colonial bureaucracy. In 1744, Governor Clinton of New York heard rumors of a "proposal for Establishment by Act of Parliament dutys upon Stamp Papers." He immediately cautioned his superiors against such action. "The people in North America," Clinton warned, "are quite strangers to any Duty but such as they raise themselves and was such a Scheme to take place without their Knowledge It might prove a dangerous consequence to his Majesty's Interest."

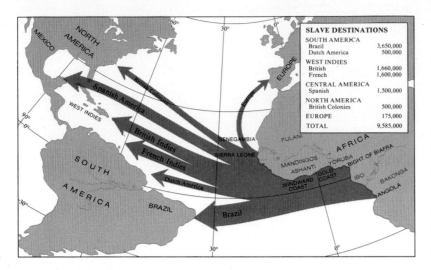

SLAVE DESTINATIONS	
SOUTH AMERICA	
Brazil	3,650,000
Dutch America	500,000
WEST INDIES	
British	1,660,000
French	1,600,000
CENTRAL AMERICA	
Spanish	1,500,000
NORTH AMERICA	
British Colonies	500,000
EUROPE	175,000
TOTAL	9,585,000

MAP 3.3 THE TRANSATLANTIC SLAVE TRADE
Between 1520 and 1810, European slave traders brought nearly ten million Africans to the Western Hemisphere. Another two million died en route. Most slaves labored in the sugar industry of Brazil and the Caribbean islands. Between 1700 and 1810, sugar planters imported about sixty thousand slaves each year; most of the blacks died within five years from disease or overwork.

The decades of salutary neglect had taken their toll. The royal bureaucracy in colonial America was in shambles, filled with inadequate political appointees and lacking a coherent policy. Exploiting this opportunity, the American assemblies sucessfully confronted royal governors. They established the practice of levying all taxes and bent many governors to their will by refusing to appropriate funds for their salaries. By the 1750s, the "rise of the assembly" had become an established fact.

The South Atlantic Slave Economy

During the seventeenth century, Euopeans created a remarkable new agricultural system in the Western Hemisphere. European merchants seized or bought millions of Africans and transported them across the Atlantic Ocean. They sold the captives to European planters who kept them in slavery on land taken from native Americans. The planters forced their African slaves to produce sugar and other valuable crops, which merchants then sold in Europe. This South Atlantic System profoundly affected the historical development of four continents. It set off a commercial revolution in Europe from 1650 to 1750 that vastly increased the wealth and power of the merchant classes there and in the American colonies. At the same time, the massive trade in slaves sapped the economic resources of Africa, beginning a long-term process of underdevelopment. This transatlantic system of production and commerce created a score of racially divided colonies. Most of them were in South America or the West Indies, but they included the English colonies on the North American mainland.

The South Atlantic System

By the end of the seventeenth century, England began to profit substantially from products of its New World settlements. The chief products included sugar from the West Indies and tobacco from the Chesapeake Bay colonies. During the following century, tobacco production doubled and the sugar crop tripled in size. Of all the major staple crops produced on American plantations, such as tobacco, rice, indigo, and coffee, sugar was by far the most valuable. England continually expanded its sugar plantations, first in Barbadoes, then in the Leeward Islands, and finally in Jamaica.

Sugar was the most complex and expensive agricultural product in the entire preindustrial world. The high cost of running a sugar plantation included the land, slave labor, and mill equipment. Only wealthy merchants or landowners had the necessary capital, and so a small planter-merchant oligarchy dominated the sugar industry. At the height of its prosperity in 1774, the island colony of Jamaica had about 680 sugar plantations and a labor force of 105,000 African slaves. Successful planters earned from 8 to 10 percent annually on their invested capital. This was a high rate of return, for government bonds usually paid only 4 percent in interest. "The profits of a sugar plantation in any of our West Indian colonies are generally much greater than those of any other cultivation that is known either in Europe or America," the English economist Adam Smith declared in his important book *The Wealth of Nations* (1776).

Great Britain's participation in the South Atlantic System helped make it one of the most powerful nations in Europe. This economic stimulus worked in various ways. In the first place, capital resources that yielded low rates of return at home were diverted to the West Indies. Because most West Indian planters lived as "absentees" in London, their annual profits continually bolstered the domestic economy. Secondly, the export of sugar, tobacco, and other crops to Eur-

opean nations bolstered the British balance of trade. The Acts of Trade and Navigation specified that American planters had to ship their staple crops to Britain. They were then "reexported" to Europe in return for gold or needed manufactures. These reexports of American commodities amounted to about a third of the total British export trade in 1710 and increased to half by 1750.

In addition, the South Atlantic System made Britain the leading European maritime and naval power. British and American shipyards built hundreds of ships to bring machinery, supplies, and settlers to the colonies. Additional vessels transported slaves from Africa to the Western Hemisphere and carried staple crops back to Europe. Thousands of men found employment building the port facilities, warehouses, and dwellings of Liverpool, London, and Glasgow, the commercial centers of the trade in slaves, sugar, and tobacco. Others worked as sugar or

SEA CAPTAINS IN SURINAM
Despite the English Navigation Acts, New England merchants conducted a flourishing trade with the Dutch West Indian island of Surinam. This tavern scene, painted by Boston artist John Greenwood in the 1750s, suggests some of the pleasures of the seafaring life. (John Greenwood. *Sea Captains Carousing in Surinam*. The Saint Louis Art Museum)

A SLAVE COFFLE
Some European merchants specialized in "human commerce." They raided West African coastal villages for sturdy young men and women, or they purchased captives taken in war or slave raids from African traders. Slaves marched to waiting ships in coffles, tied or chained to each other. (Library of Congress)

tobacco refiners and rum distillers, and as manufacturers for growing markets in America and Europe. By 1750, British exports no longer depended on the wool trade. The economy was on the brink of the Industrial Revolution. As an ardent imperialist declared in 1745, the British Empire "was a magnificent superstructure of American commerce and naval power on an African foundation."

Although the South Atlantic System increased the prosperity of Europeans, it undermined the vitality of West African societies. Between 1570 and 1870, the transatlantic slave trade uprooted about ten million Africans from their homeland, six million during the eighteenth century alone. This continual drain of young males and females lowered the output of the African economy. And because Europeans took most of the profits of the trade in slaves and their labor, the export of human resources brought few benefits in return. In the 1680s, the Royal African Company, an English firm, sold male slaves in the West Indies for five or six times as much as it had paid for them in Africa. Before dying of disease, overwork, or old age, these slaves produced sugar worth two to three times their purchase price. Europeans used a slave to produce goods worth ten times the value of the rum, tinware, or cloth that the African economy received in return. The underdevelopment of Africa assisted the development of Europe.

The spiritual distress produced by the South Atlantic System was no less profound. The European demand for slaves made kidnapping common along the coast of West Africa and for hundreds of miles inland. It encouraged an increase in the number and severity of wars among the tribes of the region. This growth of violence, in turn, brought a transformation in the political structure of African societies. Powerful centralized slave-trading states replaced loose tribal federations in much of West Africa. Class divisions hardened as well and people of noble birth sold men and women of lesser status into slavery.

In Africa, as on the plantations of the Western Hemisphere, slavery depreciated the dignity of human life. "A man becomes the standard of prices," an English traveler in Africa observed. "A slave is a note of hand that may be discounted or pawned; he is a bill of exchange that carries himself to the destination and pays a debt; he is a tax that walks corporately into the chieftain's treasury." The slave trade lowered the moral tone as well as the economic potential of African society.

THE BRUTAL "MIDDLE PASSAGE," 1735

Olaudah Equiano, also known as Gustavus Vasa, was sold into slavery by a conquering tribe. He bought his freedom from his American master and later published a memoir of his experiences.

The first object which saluted my eyes when I arrived on the coast was the sea, and a slave ship which was then riding at anchor, and waiting for its cargo....

I now saw myself deprived of all chance of returning to my native country, or even the least glimpse of hope of gaining the shore, which I now considered as friendly; and I even wished for my former slavery in preference to my present situation, which was filled with horrors of every kind, still heightened by my ignorance of what I was to undergo. I was not long suffered to indulge my grief; I was soon put down under the decks, and there I received such a salutation in my nostrils as I had never experienced in my life: so that with the loathsomeness of the stench, and crying together, I became so sick and low that I was not able to eat, nor had I the least desire to taste any thing. I now wished for the last friend, death, to relieve me; but soon, to my grief, two of the white men offered me eatables; and, on my refusing to eat, one of them held me fast by the hands, and laid me across, I think the windlass, and tied by feet, while the other flogged me severely. I had never experienced any thing of this kind before: and, although not being used to the water, I naturally feared that element the first time I saw it, yet, nevertheless, if could I have got over the nettings, I would have jumped over the side, but I could not; and, besides, the crew used to watch us very closely who were not chained down to the decks, lest we should leap into the water: and I have seen some of these poor African prisoners most severely cut for attempting to do so, and hourly whipped for not eating.

Virginia's Decision for Slavery

Africans first arrived in the English mainland colonies in 1619, when a Dutch sea captain sold twenty black laborers to settlers in Jamestown. Many of these Africans had Spanish names. They probably had served as slaves on one of the West Indian islands or in Brazil, where sugar production had already begun. Whatever their previous social status, these Africans were not legally enslaved once they arrived in Virginia. The medieval serfdom that had tied English peasants to the land or a master had long since died out. English common law acknowledged various degrees of "unfree" status, such as indentured servitude, but it made no provision for lifetime or hereditary bondage. The concept of chattel slavery—that is, the ownership of one human being by another—was alien to English law.

Nor did the history or customs of England allow the treatment of individuals as property. When an African chief offered to sell slaves to Richard Jolison, the Englishman replied that his people "did not deal in such commodities; neither did we buy or sell one another, or any that had our own human shapes." This belief in personal liberty had become ingrained in the common people of England. The manager of a Jamaican sugar plantation slapped a newly arrived English overseer who returned the blow, declaring that he had "not come hither to slave it."

English colonists responded in various ways to the slavery on Spanish, Portuguese, and Dutch plantations. In the West Indies, the exploitation of African labor promised great profits. Therefore, many English planters began to practice slavery. Others migrated to the American mainland in search of societies composed primarily of free farm families. In New England, ministers and magistrates used Biblical precedent to justify enslavement. They maintained that Africans were descended from the "dark-skinned sons of Ham" and deserved an inferior social status because of Ham's sin. However, the Puritans owned few Africans because slavery did not go well with their system of economic production and their social values.

PASSAGE ON A SLAVE SHIP

This drawing (by a naval officer on board) and architect's plan for a slave ship graphically indicate the crowded and unsanitary conditions that normally took the lives of 10–20 percent of the passengers. Disease was the main culprit, but despair took its toll as well. "We found a great deal of Discontent among the Slaves, particularly the men ..." a white sailor wrote in his journal, "to our great Amazement about an hundred Men Slaves jump'd overboard ... who would not endeavor to save themselves, but resolv'd to die, and sunk directly down." (Top, National Maritime Museum, London; Bottom, Library of Congress)

Nor did planters in Maryland and Virginia immediately import large numbers of Africans. For most of the seventeenth century, white indentured servants were readily available. White servants also cost less, an important consideration because of the high death rates for both races. Only three or four hundred Africans lived in the Chesapeake colonies in 1649, a mere 2 percent of the population. Even in 1670, blacks made up only about 5 percent of the people there, and some of them lived more like indentured servants than slaves.

Records indicate that until 1660 a few Africans received their freedom after a period of sevice. In fact, some of these African freemen purchased black slaves and the labor contracts of white servants. However, even in those early years, most Chesapeake planters treated Africans more harshly than white laborers and held them to longer terms of service. In discriminating against their African workers, the English migrants laid the social and psychological foundations for the legalization of slavery.

From the beginning, the English regarded themselves as different from Africans. In private letters and official documents, they mentioned such factors as skin color, facial and body structure, language, and place of origin. They referred to some of their workers as "Negroes" to differentiate them from white indentured servants. But in a European world dominated by passionate theological controversy and warfare, religious identity was a primary point of contrast. Africans were pagans, not Christians. For some English settlers, this distinction justified slavery. For others, it explained who could be a slave. "All servants imported or brought into this country by sea or land who were not Christians in their native country shall be accounted and be slaves," proclaimed a Virginia statute of 1705.

By this time, a series of laws had gradually debased the status of Africans. In the 1660s, judges in the Chesapeake colonies imposed heavier penalties on African runaways than on English servants guilty of the same offense. New legislation forbade Africans to own firearms or to join the militia. It also abridged some of their property rights. "No negroe or Indian," the Virginia House of Burgesses stated in 1670, "tho

baptized and enjoying their own Freedom, shall be capable of any such purchase of Christians, but yet not debarred from buying any of their own nation."

Race had become as important as religion in defining social status. The carefully worded law allowed Christian Africans and Indians to own servants, but not white servants. Race also emerged as a permanent mark of identity. Laws enacted between 1667 and 1671 specified that Christian conversion did not qualify an African servant for eventual freedom. Beginning in the 1680s, Virginia statutes referred to people of English descent as "white" rather than as "Christian." A law of 1692 prohibited sexual intercourse between English and African. It condemned the offspring of such unions as "that abominable mixture and spurious issue."

Deprived of one right after another, African laborers found that their own servitude was permanent. As their children grew to maturity, this subordinate status applied to them as well. By the 1670s, English planters and legislators had drawn a tight net of lifelong and hereditary servitude around the African population. This process had been slow and uncertain, for slavery was neither economically necessary nor culturally familiar. Then, in the aftermath of Bacon's Rebellion, the planter elite made slavery the preferred form of labor and defined it clearly in colonial law. A South Carolina statute of 1692 declared that black slaves belonged to the land owned by their masters. Virginia legislation of 1705 defined those of African origin or born to African mothers as the personal property, or chattel, of their masters. In each case, the English colonists had created a new legal status and reserved this inferior condition only for those whose skin was not white.

The Slave Economy

During the eighteenth century, the major era of the African slave trade, European merchants and sea captains brought more than six million Africans to the Western Hemisphere. From 85 to 90 percent of the captives survived the "middle passage," the harsh transatlantic voyage on crowded, disease-ridden slave ships. The main agony still awaited them.

INDIAN AND AFRICAN AGRICULTURE

Native Americans and Africans had mastered the art of growing rice, corn, and tobacco by the time of their first contact with Europeans. By appropriating this knowledge, English settlers brought about the first major technological breakthroughs in American history.

Neither rice nor corn nor tobacco was originally an English crop, yet they quickly became crucial to the colonial economy. In 1770, Chesapeake tobacco formed 27 percent of all American commodity exports, while the rice raised in Georgia and South Carolina accounted for another 10 percent. Corn was the most widely grown of all American crops. The poor subsisted on corn—as bread, mush, or porridge—and middling and well-to-do farmers fed corn ears and stalks to their livestock. Yet without the transfer of native American and African crop technologies, even this modest standard of living would not have been possible for the English settlers.

Corn production shaped the very consciousness of many native American peoples. The Agawam Indians of Massachusetts, for example, began their year with the month of Squannikesas, a word that meant "when they set Indian corn." Subsequent months had names prescribing the weeding, hilling, and ripening of corn. To appease the spirit forces in nature and ensure a bountiful harvest, the Seneca Indians of New York held a corn-planting ceremony. After soaking the corn seeds, they asked the Thunderers, "our grandfathers," to water the crops, and beseeched "our older brother," the sun, not to burn them.

Growing corn was women's work. Indian women prepared the ground with wooden hoes tipped with bone, flint, or clamshells. Making "heaps like molehills, each about two and a half feet from the others," a Dutch traveler reported, they carefully planted "in each heap five or six grains." As the tall slender plants appeared, the women heaped more dirt to support the roots. They also "put in each hill three or four Brazilian [kidney] beans. When they grow up, they interlace with the corn, which reaches to a height of from five to six feet; and they keep the ground free of weeds."

The double planting of corn and beans represented a major technological advance. It dramatically increased the total yield from an acre of cleared land. The beans also fixed nitrogen in the soil and conserved moisture, preventing erosion and preserving soil fertility. Finally, beans and corn provided a diet rich in vegetable proteins. By raising sixty bushels of corn on two acres, Indian women provided half the calories required by five persons for a year.

Their economic contribution gave Seneca women considerable political power, including the right to choose a clan chieftain. They jealously guarded their productive role. "If a man took hold of a hoe to use it," a Quaker missionary reported as late as 1809, "the Women would get down his gun by way of derision & and laugh and say such a Warrior is a timid woman."

English farmers appropriated Indian corn technology and assimilated it into their own culture. Protestant ministers prayed to the Christian God for a bountiful harvest. Men, not women, planted, tended, and harvested the crop. They also adapted corn production to their horse-and-plow technology. After clearing their fields of tree stumps, farm-

Most of the Africans lived short, brutal lives on the sugar plantations of Brazil or the West Indies. Sugar was a killer crop under the best of circumstances. The planting and harvesting of sugar required intense periods of hard work, much of it under a hot subtropical sun. The economics of the South Atlantic System made the circumstances far from ideal. Sugar prices were high and the cost of slaves was low. Therefore, many European planters simply worked their slaves to death and then imported more from Africa. Slaveowners did not encourage the for-mation of a stable work force of families and their natural reproduction. Instead, planters purchased six males for every female and forced pregnant women to work in the fields. The waste of human life was staggering and indefensible. Between 1708 and 1735, British sugar planters on Barbados imported about eighty-five thousand African slaves. But during that period, the black population of the island increased only from forty-two thousand to forty-six thousand. Weakened by inadequate nutrition, oppressive labor, and crowded living conditions, thousands ers plowed furrows at three-foot intervals from north to south. Then they cut new east-west furrows, heaping up the soil into Indian-style cornhills at the intersecting points.

English methods were less labor-intensive than Indian planting techniques, and less productive. Yields averaged from ten to fifteen bushels per acre, not thirty, and the fertility of the soil diminished much more quickly. Nevertheless, corn became the premier American crop, "which grain," a Welsh migrant to Pennsylvania noted, "produced more increase than any other Graine whatsoever." Corn served as a dietary staple for poor people in the northern colonies, and for white tenant farmers and black slaves in the South.

Some of these Africans played a major role in the transfer of rice technology to South Carolina. Settled by the English in the 1670s, the colony initially languished for want of a staple crop. A few English colonists planted rice during the 1670s and 1680s, but without great success. "The people being unacquainted with the manner of cultivating rice," a white planter later recalled, "many difficulties attended the

first planting and preparing it, as a vendable commodity."

Unlike Europeans, West Africans had a thorough knowledge of rice planting. Along the Windward Coast of Africa, an English traveller noted, rice "forms the chief part of the African's sustenance." "The rice fields or *lugars* are prepared during the dry season," he explained, "and the seed sown in the tornado season, requiring about four or five months growth to bring it to perfection." Enslaved blacks brought their skills to Carolina. In 1690, an Englishman named John Stewart actively promoted rice production, both as an export crop and to "throw by Indian corn to feed slaves with rice as cheaper." Slaves welcomed the cultivation of a familiar food and their knowledge was crucial to its success.

At first, English planters searched for machines, such as a "rice mill," to separate the tough husk of the rice seed from the nutritious grain inside. In 1691, the government awarded Peter Jacob Guerard a two-year patent on "A Pendulum Engine, which doth much better, and in lesse time and labour, huske rice." Neither Guerard's invention

nor any other machine proved equal to the task, leaving English planters dependent on African technology. Throughout the eighteenth century, slave women used traditional mortar and pestle methods to process rice. They placed the grain in a large wooden mortar hollowed from the trunk of a pine or cypress tree. Then they beat it with long wooden pestles, quickly removing the husks and whitening the grains. By 1700, a royal official informed the English Board of Trade that the settlers had "now found out the true way of raising and husking Rice."

Technology always has cultural significance. Few English farmers adopted African rice technology for their own use. Rather, a few hundred Carolina planters imported thousands of African slaves and developed large rice plantations. Their use of African rice technology created a racially divided society dominated by a white planter-merchant aristocracy. The transfer of native American corn technology had a more democratic outcome. It provided a reliable and abundant crop for generations of white pioneer farmers.

---

of Africans died in epidemics of yellow fever, smallpox, and measles.

In the mainland colonies, the situation was less tragic. Between 1619 and 1770, British tobacco and rice planters imported about 250,000 Africans. Many—perhaps most—of the slaves in the Chesapeake settlements lived relatively long lives. Tobacco cultivation required less demanding physical labor than sugar. Equally important, Chesapeake tobacco plantations were small, dispersed enterprises; the low concentration of slaves inhibited the spread of epidemic diseases.

Moreover, the proportion of female slaves was much higher than in the West Indies. Women made up about a third of the African population of Maryland before 1720, and many of them bore children. By the 1720s, the Chesapeake slave population was increasing through reproduction. Virginia and Maryland planters continued to import new slaves—at least fifty thousand between 1730 and 1750—but many Chesapeake counties had as many American-born as African-born slaves by the 1760s.

The success of these blacks in increasing their

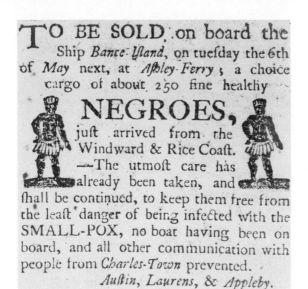

TO BE SOLD on board the Ship *Bance-Iſland*, on tueſday the 6th of *May* next, at *Aſhley-Ferry*; a choice cargo of about 250 fine healthy NEGROES, juſt arrived from the Windward & Rice Coaſt. —The utmoſt care has already been taken, and ſhall be continued, to keep them free from the leaſt danger of being infected with the SMALL-POX, no boat having been on board, and all other communication with people from *Charles-Town* prevented.

Auſtin, Laurens, & Appleby.

N. B. Full one Half of the above Negroes have had the SMALL-POX in their own Country.

SLAVERY AND DISEASE

The inter-mixture of Europeans, Africans, and Indians in America created a new and unhealthy environment, for each race lacked immunities to common diseases found on the other continents. South Carolina merchants used this printed broadside to assure potential customers that their cargo of slaves had not been exposed to a small-pox epidemic in Charleston. (Library of Congress)

numbers by reproduction was unequaled by enslaved Africans in any other region of the Western Hemisphere. At first, their white owners did not plan the natural increase among slaves. Gradually, Chesapeake planters began to appreciate the economic benefits of a naturally increasing work force. They continued to import a significant number of African women and encouraged large families among their slaves. An absentee owner instructed his plantation agent in 1759,

> The breeding wenches particularly, you must instruct the overseers to be kind and indulgent to, and not to force them when with child upon any service or hardship that will be injurious to them . . . and the children to be well looked after that none of them suffer in time of sickness for want of proper care.

High African survival rates encouraged the

transition to a black labor force on the plantations of the Chesapeake colonies. Beginning in the 1680s, wealthy planters replaced their servants with slaves. After 1720, following rises in the European prices and demand for tobacco, they increased the size of their labor forces. By the 1740s, a typical plantation in All Hallows Parish in Maryland had nine or ten slaves. Thousands of small landowners now became slaveowners. They used their higher tobacco profits to purchase one or two blacks to assist them with the work of their farms and to increase their profits further. Slave ownership by the middling class of whites, composed of yeomen and artisans, was a new development. It made African bondage increasingly common in Chesapeake society. In Talbot County in Maryland in 1745, most white property owners, and some white tenant farmers, owned at least one slave. By 1775, almost 60 percent of the white families in the southern colonies held a black in bondage.

Slavery increased because it was profitable. African laborers in South Carolina brought especially handsome financial returns to their owners. Land-hungry whites from the small island of Barbados settled Carolina in the 1680s, but the new colony grew slowly because it lacked an export crop. The English failed in their attempts to grow rice in the wet coastal lowlands. Then, about 1700, African slaves who had grown rice in their homelands began to plant it to feed themselves. Their success yielded a bitter legacy. White planters organized rice-producing plant-

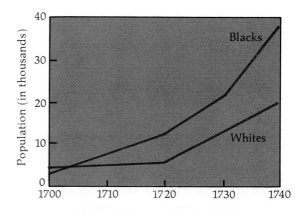

FIGURE 3.2 THE GROWTH OF SLAVERY IN SOUTH CAROLINA

CHARLESTON IN 1739
The rice trade made Charleston into a prosperous seaport. Small sailing vessels transported the rice from lowland plantations to the town's wharfs for shipment to ports in the West Indies and southern Europe. South Carolina merchants, such as Henry Laurens, gradually won control of this trade from British firms. (Bishop Roberts. *Charlestown Harbor*. Colonial Williamsburg Foundation)

ations and exported their new crop to continually growing European markets.

By 1730, Charleston merchants shipped about seventeen million pounds of rice to Europe annually. By the 1770s, the yearly export crop of Carolina and Georgia planters reached seventy-five million tons. To grow this lucrative crop, white planters and merchants imported tens of thousands of African slaves. Blacks composed a majority of the South Carolina population by 1730 and formed about 80 percent of the people in the rice-growing lowlands. A wealthy elite of planter-merchants owned most of these slaves and dominated the new agricultural system. From their lavish mansions in Charleston, they controlled the economic and political life of the colony and its black work force.

The South Atlantic System drastically changed the racial composition of the American colonies. In 1776, about five hundred thousand blacks lived in the colonies that declared their independence as the United States. People of African birth or descent numbered about a third of the population of the southern colonies and a fifth of the entire colonial population. This percentage was the highest in American history.

The trade in slaves and the profits of their labor brought great wealth to some English settlers and their descendants. Many white farm families attained smaller financial rewards from this exploitative labor system. For most Africans, slavery meant misery and deprivation for generations. Ultimately, the creation of a racially divided slave economy represented a tragedy for the entire population. In any society with slaves, everyone is less free because the masters must create authoritarian institutions and use brutal force to control the subject people. "Let the lands of the Western Hemisphere lie fallow," the French philosopher Abbé Raynal proclaimed in his *Historie des deux Indies* (1781), "if it means that to make these lands productive, man must be reduced to brutishness, whether he be the man who buys, or he who sells, or he who is sold."

The Northern Commercial Economy

The South Atlantic System provided a major stimulus to the British economy and to that of the northern colonies. Before 1740, neither New England nor the middle colonies of New York, New Jersey, and Pennsylvania produced a staple crop for export to Europe. They had few slaves, but these colonies were deeply involved in the sugar trade. "Men are so intent upon planting sugar," a West Indian planter wrote Governor John Winthrop of the Massachusetts Bay Colony as early as 1647, "that they had rather buy food at very dear rates than produce it by labour, so infinite is the profit of sugar works." Responding to this challenge, New England merchants and farmers shipped bread, lumber, fish, meat, and other necessities to the English sugar islands.

By 1700, the economic systems of the West Indies and New England were tightly intermeshed. This commerce prompted the creation of new occupations and raised the standard of living of the New England population. As Thomas Bannister explained in "An Essay on the Trade of New England" (1714), trade with the sugar islands "imploys a great number of Ships and sailors. The tradesmen feel the Benefit by the Merchandise of Soap, Candles, Beer, the building of Ships, and the great Number of Casks this Trade imploys." Farmers and fishermen benefited as well, Bannister pointed out, for "the landed Interest" exported "very much Hay, Oats, Onions, Apples, Pork, Beef, Staves, bread, butter, and Flour. The Fishery by a great Export of Mackerel and refuse cod."

West Indian goods received in return for these commodities increased the complexity and productivity of the New England economy. Merchants established distilleries in the port cities to make rum from West Indian molasses. Traders exchanged the rum for tanned furs produced by native Americans. Rhode Island merchants bartered it along the African coast for slaves. The West Indian trade also brought much-needed gold and silver coins to the mainland colonies. Some of this coinage provided a domestic money supply, but merchants used most of it to purchase manufactured goods from England.

Americans used West Indian bills of exchange for the same purpose. These bills were basically a private form of money that London merchant houses gave to West Indian planters as payment for their sugar. The planters used the bills of exchange to pay New England merchants for their commodities. The merchants then exchanged or sold them for British products, completing the cycle.

A complex net of private trading agreements thus tied the interdependent regions of the British empire together. The English government realized the mutually beneficial results of this system of economic exchange. Therefore, in 1698 it began to support the export of food from the mainland colonies to the sugar islands. If the West Indies grew foodstuffs "instead of sugar-canes, cotton, ginger, and indigo," a parliamentary committee declared, this would be "greatly prejudicial to England, in respect of its navigation and riches."

The participation of the northern colonies in the South Atlantic System was broadly consistent with British economic goals. Yet this trade had unforeseen implications for the mercantilist system. Mercantilist writers generally insisted that colonial regions should produce only agricultural goods or other raw materials. They should not manufacture goods or provide commercial services; these tasks were reserved for the artisans and merchants of the mother country. However, the Acts of Trade and Navigation allowed the colonists to own ships and transport goods within the empire.

Merchants from Boston, Newport, New York City, and Philadelphia used their geographic position to take control of the trade along the coast of North America. More surprisingly, they ousted British merchants from the commerce between the mainland and the West Indies. By 1740, colonial merchants controlled about 95 percent of this trade. They also carried a substantial portion of the manufactured goods imported into the northern port cities from London and Bristol. Quite unexpectedly, the Navigation Acts had led to the creation of a strong provincial mercantile community.

American merchant ships, built mostly in colonial shipyards, roamed the Atlantic in search of trade and profit. The voyage of the schooner *Jolly Robin* in 1754 was typical. The captain of this small ship took on a cargo of fish and lumber in New England and sold it at Bilboa in northern Spain. There the *Jolly Robin* picked up a cargo of salt, which

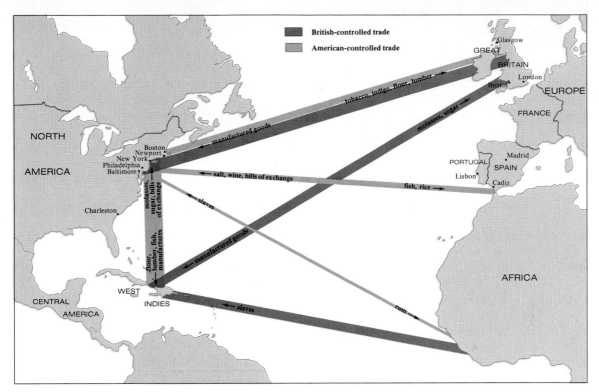

MAP 3.4 THE RISE OF THE AMERICAN MERCHANT

Mercantilist doctrine specified that the colonies should produce agricultural goods, leaving manufacturing and commerce in British hands. British merchants controlled most of the transatlantic trade in manufactures, sugar, tobacco, and slaves. However, a wealthy and powerful merchant community developed in the mainland colonies. Merchants in Boston, New York, and Philadelphia dominated the commerce in molasses and provisions with the West Indies. Newport merchants traded with Africa, and Charleston merchants carried rice to southern Europe.

eventually was sold in America. This payment covered the cost of the fish and lumber and of the voyage itself. A handsome profit was still to come. At Bilboa, the captain received salt, cash, and bills of exchange. He took the financial notes to London and exchanged them for manufactured goods, and his merchant backers sold them in America at a profit. By putting together dozens of such ventures, provincial traders gave employment to hundreds of seamen, financed a large shipbuilding industry, and created thriving commercial establishments with significant capital resources.

American enterprise eventually ran up against powerful British economic interests. By 1720, more than 250,000 people lived in New England and the rapidly growing middle colonies. These farmers, fishermen, and artisans produced a substantial amount of goods for export. The sugar plantations of the British West Indies

could not absorb all the surplus production of the mainland. Therefore, colonial merchants expanded their trade with the French sugar islands. The French planters needed far more food and supplies than could be produced in the small French settlement in Louisiana. Using abundant imports from the English colonies— food, lumber, horses, and casks, for example— French sugar planters rapidly expanded their output. Because their sugar cane grew on rich virgin land, the French producers undercut the British in the competitive European market. By the 1730s, the British sugar industry was near collapse. It could not match French prices in Europe and depended for survival on its monopoly of the English and Irish markets.

A powerful group of absentee plantation owners and sugar merchants petitioned Parliament and won passage of the Molasses Act of

TIME LINE
THE CREATION OF AN AMERICAN POLITICAL SYSTEM AND ECONOMY

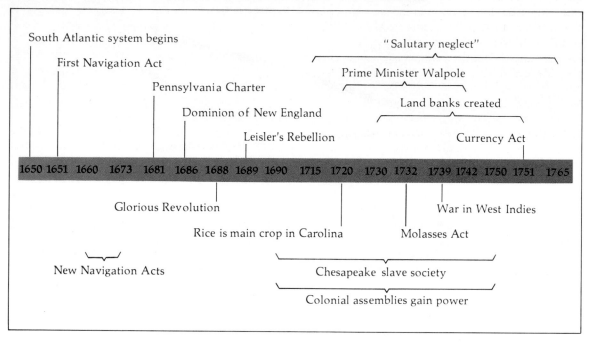

1732. This legislation was designed to raise the production cost for French planters and thus restore the competitive position of British sugar. The Molasses Act permitted colonial merchants to sell agricultural goods to French planters, because the English government realized the importance of this trade to the northern colonies. But the act put a high tax on French molasses to prevent it from being imported into America. The government expected this legislation to increase the profits of British planters because colonial distillers would have to buy more molasses from them. The government also maintained that the French would still purchase food and other necessities from Americans, for they had no other source of supply.

Colonial merchants and public officials strongly disagreed. They protested that the Molasses Act would destroy their trade with the French islands and cripple their distilling industry. They also argued that the act, by cutting the supply of gold and silver from the French trade, would undermine their ability to purchase British manufactured products.

American penetration of the South Atlantic System thus created a major conflict between British and colonial interest groups. The royal government responded by enacting legislation favorable to British merchants and sugar producers. Government officials insisted that the colonies assume the subordinate economic position dictated by mercantilist principles. American merchants replied by refusing to obey the Molasses Act. By bribing customs officials or by smuggling, they continued to import hundreds of thousands of gallons of French molasses while avoiding the tax. The Royal Customs Service collected little in molasses duties in 1733 and even less in succeeding years. Fortunately for the northern colonies, the British government never demanded strict enforcement of the act. An abrupt rise in sugar prices in the protected British market raised the profits of merchants and producers and quieted their protests.

The struggle over molasses symbolized the maturity of the American economy and the inevitability of future confrontations with the Crown. Colonial assemblies and British merchants had already battled over monetary policy. An inadequate supply of gold and silver coins had long stifled financial transactions in the colonies. Merchants used most of the coins from the British and French West Indies trade to pay for English manufactures. To create a domestic money supply, the assemblies of ten colonies established land banks between 1712 and 1737. These banks lent money, in the form of paper currency, to farmers and other landowners. The banks secured these loans by mortgages on their landed property (hence the term *land bank*). They used the interest charged on these loans to cover their expenses and to support public projects. This imaginative system of finance provided governments with funds without raising taxes. It also provided a respected medium of exchange and thereby increased trade.

These monetary policies led to conflicts with British merchants. Most of the colonies ran their land banks in a fiscally conservative and responsible way. They issued small amounts of paper currency, insisted that borrowers provide adequate collateral, and demanded strict repayment. An exception was Rhode Island where the representatives of farmers and small towns dominated the assembly. Between 1715 and 1750, at their urging, Rhode Island issued far more in paper currency than any other province. This vast supply of paper money produced a depreciated currency. As more and more bills were printed, it took more money to buy the same amount of goods.

British—and American—merchants protested against this inflationary fiscal policy. Merchants were usually creditors rather than debtors; they lent more money, in the form of credit, than they borrowed. They pointed out that a rapidly depreciating currency harmed them financially, for Rhode Island residents paid for their debts with newly printed money that was worth less. Because Rhode Island was a small colony with a corporate charter, and hence no royal governor, British officials tolerated this fiscal abuse. But when Massachusetts began to create a land bank in 1740, merchants raised the specter of a massive inflation and the British prohibited the bank. Parliament then passed a Currency Act in 1751. This law prevented all the New England colonies from establishing new land banks and from allowing public bills of credit to be used as legal tender to pay private debts. In 1764, a new Currency Act extended these prohibitions to all the American colonies.

Many British merchants and government officials thought such decisive intervention into colonial economic affairs was long overdue. American merchants, farmers, and assemblies had taken advantage of the liberal provisions of the Navigation Acts. They had developed trade routes and monetary policies that threatened to undermine the British mercantilist system. Little had been done to curb these actions during the period of salutary neglect. The royal bureaucracy had been too weak and demoralized to uphold the primacy of British financial or political interests. As a result, in the structure of their economic life as in the powers of their representative assemblies, the American colonies had become increasingly autonomous and self-sufficient.

A distinctive political system and a vigorous economy emerged in the American colonies during the century from 1650 to 1750.

The Glorious Revolution of 1689 marked a crucial turning point in colonial political affairs. Previously, Parliament had enacted a series of Navigation Laws regulating colonial trade, and King James II had eliminated many political privileges in the Dominion of New England. The colonial revolts of 1689 reversed this trend toward imperial centralization and preserved representative government in America. Between 1714 and 1754 the British policy of salutary neglect permitted American merchants to violate the spirit—and often the letter—of the Navigation Acts. Lax administration and patronage appointments allowed capable, aggressive American politicians to strengthen the powers and influence of the colonial assemblies.

The expansion of the South Atlantic System of trade likewise created an increasingly strong colonial economy. This system forced millions of Africans into slavery and took a vast toll in human life. By the 1680s, planters in the Chesapeake colonies had established a slave regime.

The black population increased rapidly through both importation and reproduction. The expansion of slavery after 1700 brought great profits to tobacco and rice planters in the American colonies, and to sugar planters in the West Indies. By trading with the British and French sugar islands, northern merchants and farmers shared in the commercial revolution and economic prosperity generated by the South Atlantic System.

Suggestions for Further Reading

The Transformation of American Politics

For a general discussion of mercantilism see Eli Hecksher, *Mercantilism* (1935). Klaus Knorr, *British Colonial Theories, 1570–1850* (1944), traces the shifting application of mercantilist principles.

Institutional studies include George L. Beer, *The Origins of the British Colonial System* (1908); Lawrence A. Harper, *The English Navigation Laws* (1939); and Charles M. Andrews, *The Colonial Period of American History*, vol. IV (1938).

Later scholarship has focused less on the institutional structure and more on political activity. See Michael Kammen, *Empire and Interest* (1970); Alison G. Olson, *Anglo-American Politics, 1660–1775* (1973); and Jack M. Sosin, *English America and the Restoration Monarchy of Charles II: Transatlantic Politics, Commerce, and Kinship* (1980).

Wesley Frank Craven, *The Colonies in Transition, 1660–1713*, provides a sound introduction to the history of the colonies founded during the Restoration. More detailed accounts are available in C. M. Andrews, *The Colonial Period of American History*, vols. II and III (1936,1937); T. J. Wertenbaker, *The Founding of American Civilization: The Middle Colonies* (1938); and M. Eugene Sirmans, *Colonial South Carolina* (1966).

The background of the Glorious Revolution is covered in Michael Hall, *Edward Randolph and the American Colonies, 1676–1703* (1960), and Viola Barnes, *The Dominion of New England* (1923). Jerome R. Reich, *Leisler's Rebellion: A Study of Democracy in New York, 1664–1720* (1953), should be supplemented by David S. Lovejoy, *The Glorious Revolution in America* (1972), a fine general treatment of the uprisings of 1688. M. G. Hall, et al, *The Glorious Revolution in America* (1972), provides a useful set of contemporary documents.

The appearance of a distinctive American polity is traced by Jack P. Greene, *The Quest for Power: The Lower Houses of Assembly in the Southern Royal Colonies, 1689–1776* (1963), and Bernard Bailyn, *The Origins of American Politics* (1968). The decline of English administrative power is told in Leonard W. Labaree, *Royal Government in America* (1935), while John Schutz, *William Shirley* (1961), shows how a competent colonial governor wielded power. Stanley N. Katz, *Newcastle's New York* (1968), and Patricia U. Bonomi, *A Factious People,* (1971), discuss the creation of a more open government in New York.

The South Atlantic Slave Economy

Philip Curtin, *The Atlantic Slave Trade: A Census* (1969), provides a careful estimate of the size of the trade in African slaves. For the effect on African society, see Walter Rodney, *West Africa and the Atlantic Slave Trade* (1969), and Basil Davidson, *The African Slave Trade* (1961). Davidson's *The African Genius* (1970) is a good introduction to African history.

T. H. Breen and Stephen Innes, *"Myne Owne Ground"* (1980), offer a close look at the lives of some of the first American slaves and free blacks. Winthrop D. Jordan, *White Over Black* (1968), and Edmund Morgan, *American Slavery, American Freedom* (1975), provide contrasting interpretations of the decision for slavery in Virginia.

Excellent comparative studies of slave societies include Herbert Klein, *Slavery in the Americas* (1967); Carl Degler, *Neither Black Nor White* (1971); and Richard S. Dunn, *Sugar and Slaves* (1972).

The intimate relationship between northern commercial development and the South Atlantic System is explored in Bernard Bailyn, *The New England Merchants in the Seventeenth Century* (1955); J. R. Hedges, *The Browns of Providence Plantation* (1962); and Richard Pares, *Creole and Yankee* (1957).

4

THE CULTURES OF PREINDUSTRIAL AMERICA

By the middle of the eighteenth century, the population of British North America consisted of a diverse assortment of peoples. Migrants from various European countries had flocked to the colonies, bringing new languages, religious practices, and social values. The institutions and customs established by English migrants during the seventeenth century influenced this complex mixture of cultures, as did regional patterns of economic development. Broadly speaking, three distinct cultural orders appeared: the English- and Puritan-dominated settlements in New England, the racially divided colonies of Chesapeake Bay and the Carolinas, and the ethnically varied middle colonies in between.

Each of these societies had features that resembled those of Great Britain or western Europe, but each also had a distinct American character. The farming communities of New England reproduced the forms of agriculture, family life, and gender roles of the peasant villages of England. Yet the widespread ownership of land, continual geographic expansion, and a freehold spirit gave New England a special cultural tone of its own.

In the Chesapeake colonies, the planter elite copied the style of living of the landed gentry and aristocracy of England. Yet the culture of this emerging upper class was raw and boister-

ous; it lacked refinement. The physical coercion inherent in slavery complicated the planters' quest for civility and elegance. This contradiction produced a culture characterized by both patriarchal hospitality and aggressive violence. As the slaves raised successive generations of children, they created a non-European cultural tradition in North America. Their Afro-American culture blended various West African customs with the social norms and language of the English settlers.

Because of their ethnic and religious diversity, the middle colonies—Pennsylvania, New York, and New Jersey—had the widest variety of cultures. These cultural differences gave the region its distinctive character and resulted in new patterns of social interaction. The people of the middle colonies developed especially strong loyalties to their own ethnic or religious groups. The region had less sense of community than New England and less prominent class divisions than the Chesapeake. Its political and religious institutions were more diverse and less coercive than those of Europe or the other American regions.

Whatever the differences among them, these preindustrial American societies shared a common provincial character. Generations of social development on an isolated continent produced cultures that were simpler in form and substance than those of Europe or Africa. The migrants and their descendants were unable to reproduce the level of material existence, intellectual activity, and cultural sophistication of their metropolitan homelands.

Northern Freehold Society

During the eighteenth century, New England and the middle colonies developed regional variations of a freeholding agricultural society. The farm family formed the basic social unit in both regions. This family had a special character that came from the lineal ties binding parents and children together as economic and emotional units. Women occupied an important but subordinate place in their families and in their societies, although the cultural norms governing women's lives varied somewhat between the regions. Changing economic conditions threatened the freehold ideals of the farming population, especially in New England, and prompted a series of creative responses.

The Lineal Farm Family

In 1750, freeholders cultivated about 30 percent of the land in England. The nobility and gentry owned the remaining 70 percent and leased it to tenants. In the northern regions of North America, the proportions were reversed and freeholding farm families controlled 70 percent of the settled land. These families, whose prime goals were landed independence and family continuity, set the cultural norms of rural society. "The hope of having land of their own & becoming independent of Landlords is what chiefly induces people into America," a New York official reported in the 1730s. "The desire of leaving a certain estate to their children overcomes all other considerations."

The acquisition of a freehold estate was neither easy nor automatic. In 1786, an "Honest Farmer" recounted his life story to the readers of the *Pennsylvania Packet*.

My parents were poor, and they put me at twelve years of age to a farmer, with whom I lived till I was twenty one. I married me a

THE CHARACTER OF FAMILY LIFE
This mid-eighteenth century portrait shows a husband and a wife, seated to the left, and their ten children. The wife's face shows the rigors of childbearing. Her eldest son and daughter are already in their mid-20's, and the youngest is still in her arms. Children grew up with much older (or younger) siblings in these families, and childrearing occupied much of the parents' lives.
(Artist Unknown. *The Cheney Family*. National Gallery of Art, Washington. Gift of Edgar William and Bernice Chrysler Garbisch)

LETTER FROM AN AMERICAN FARMER

Hector St. John de Crevecoeur, a French immigrant to America, published a series of letters in the late eighteenth century. Here he describes northern freeholding society in glowing but essentially accurate terms.

We are a people of cultivators, scattered over an immense territory, communicating with each other by means of good roads and navigable rivers, united by the silken bands of mild government, all respecting the laws, without dreading their power, because they are equitable. We are all animated with the spirit of an industry which is unfettered and unrestrained, because each person works for himself. If he travels through our rural districts he views not the hostile castle, and the haughty mansion, contrasted with the clay-built hut and miserable cabbin, where cattle and men help to keep each other warm, and dwell in meanness, smoke, and indigence. A pleasing uniformity of decent competence appears throughout our habitations. The meanest of our log-houses is a dry and comfortable habitation. Lawyer or merchant are the fairest titles our towns afford; that of a farmer is the only appellation of the rural inhabitants of our country. It must take some time ere he can reconcile himself to our dictionary which is but short in words of dignity and names of honor. There on a Sunday he sees a congregation of respectable farmers and their wives, all clad in neat homespun well mounted or riding in their own humble waggons. There is not among them an esquire, saving the unfettered magistrate. There he sees a parson as simple as his flock, a farmer who does not riot on the labour of others. We have no princes for whom we toil starve, and bleed: we are the most perfect society now existing in the world. Here man is free as he ought to be....

---

wife—and a very working young woman she was—and we took a farm of forty acres on rent. In ten years I was able to buy me a farm of sixty acres, and soon added another sixty acres, with which I am content. I bought several lots of outland for my children, which amounted to seven when I was forty-five years old.

At each stage of his life, the Honest Farmer confronted problems faced by many others. These children of poor parents often worked as indentured servants in return for room, board, and farming instruction. Large numbers of them ended their indentures without land and then struggled for one or two decades as farm laborers or tenants to save enough to buy a few acres of their own. Their economic trials had just begun, however. Unless they acquired enough property to leave a landed estate to their children, they condemned the next generation to relive their own slow climb from servant, to laborer, to tenant, to freeholder.

Generations of bitter experience in European villages had confirmed the importance of a landed estate. Most migrants who became property owners in America assumed the responsibility for the economic fate of their children. As their sons and daughters reached the age of twenty-three to twenty-five, the parents provided each with the land, livestock, and household goods needed to create a new farmstead. This assistance repaid children for their labor on the parents' farm and ensured their future loyalty. Parents knew they would need help during old age from their children. To guarantee this assistance, many farmers delayed the final award of a landed inheritance until their own death.

In the meantime, the Honest Farmer and other freeholders used financial leverage to arrange their children's marriages. Experienced in matters of the heart and the pocketbook, they allowed their offspring only a right of veto. This system of arranged marriages reflected economic reality. At the time of marriage, each generation began to transfer its hard-earned land and goods to the next. The family's future prosperity depended on the wise choice of marriage partners for the children.

Farm parents in newly settled communities

could provide all their children with a landed inheritance. But high birth rates strained the resources of even prosperous families, and poorer parents were able to give land to only some of their heirs. The average number of children born in farm families fell from six or seven around 1700 to five or six a century later. However, this decline did not erase the demand for inherited property. The Reverend Samuel Chandler of Andover, Massachusetts, recalled that he had "been much distressed for land, for his children," seven of whom were males. Dispersing the accumulated capital resources of the family among so many heirs often brought a decline in living standards. In the mid-eighteenth century, in Concord, Massachusetts, about 60 percent of the sons of farmers owned less land than their fathers.

To preserve the ideals of a freehold society and the continuity of the family line, American farmers followed a number of strategies. Some fathers used the legal device of *entail* to keep their lands from being divided. They simply willed the entire family farmstead to the eldest or youngest male and specified that this pattern should continue forever. For example, Ebenezer Perry of Barnstable, Massachusetts, gave all his land to his son Ebenezer, Jr. He directed that it devolve in turn on Ebenezer's "eldest son sur-

viving and so on to the male heirs of his body lawfully begotten forever."

In Guilford, Connecticut, a "stem family" system of residence and inheritance achieved the same goal. Parents chose a married son or son-in-law to live with them and to inherit the farm. They provided other offspring with money, apprenticeship contracts, or frontier land tracts to encourage them to migrate to less densely settled communities. German settlers in Pennsylvania developed another plan from their customs, which authorized community leaders to distribute property equally among all heirs. They now wrote legally binding wills giving the family property to the eldest son, but requiring him to pay money or goods to the younger children. These farm parents favored one of their offspring in order to preserve and perpetuate the family's freehold estate.

Many family farmers in New England tried to achieve the same goal while treating all their children equally. If a man died without a will, the laws of Massachusetts and Connecticut directed that the family property be distributed equally to all heirs except the eldest sons, who, according to Biblical custom, received a double portion. These values of equality were so important to parents in Chebacco, Massachusetts, that they stretched their dwindling supply of

LADY UNDRESSING FOR A BATH
This delightful painting captures a moment of intimacy between an unknown upper-class American woman and her husband. Many marriages were "arranged" by parents and only gradually grew into love-matches. Others began with a strong emotional bond. "Our Hearts have been united from the first, in so firm, so strong, so sweet an Affection," Sally Logan Fisher of Philadelphia wrote to her husband, "that words are incapable of setting it forth." (Artist Unknown. *Lady Undressing for a Bath.* National Gallery of Art, Washington. Gift of Edgar William and Bernice Chrysler Garbisch)

A MARYLAND WHEAT HARVEST, 1738

Beginning in the 1730s, wheat became a major export crop in Maryland and Virginia. This engraving probably depicts a German farm in western Maryland, for the harvesters use oxen (not horses) and because German women (unlike English) commonly worked in the fields. English slaveowning planters in the Tidewater region likewise turned to wheat production. (Maryland Historical Society)

land to the limit. About 90 percent of Chebacco's fathers divided their land rather than bequeath their small farms to a single heir. Other equality minded parents moved their families to frontier regions where land was cheap and abundant. "The Squire's House stands on the Bank of the Susquehannah," the traveler Philip Fithian reported from the Pennsylvania backcountry in the 1770s. "He tells me that he will be able to settle all his Sons and his fair Daughter Betsy on the Fat of the Earth."

The cultural values embodied in these lineal farm families ensured the continuance of a freehold agricultural society. Family members created productive capital together and shared the profits of their collective labor. Parents raised, educated, and assisted their children financially, and the offspring provided labor and old-age security. The central goal, impressed continually on the minds of both young and old, was the extension of the family line across the generations on a freehold estate. The great historic accomplishment of these men and women was the achievement of this worthy goal. They created societies of small property owners with a sense of personal worth and dignity. A French visitor

found that the rural world of New England and the middle colonies contrasted sharply with European peasant life. In America, he found "men and women whose features are not marked by poverty, by lifelong deprivation of the necessities of life, or by a feeling that they are insignificant subjects and subservient members of society."

Women's Place

In Europe and America, legal and cultural standards gave men greater importance than women. Whatever their social status or personal abilities, colonial women remained in a subordinate position. Males asserted a firm claim not only to political power, but also to domestic authority. As the Reverend Benjamin Wadsworth advised female readers of *The Well-Ordered Family* (1712), "Tho possibly thou has greater abilities of mind than he has, art of some high birth, and he of a more mean extract, or didst bring more Estate to Marriage than he did; yet since he is thy Husband, God has made him the head and set him above thee." Therefore, Wadsworth concluded, it is "thy duty to love and reverence him."

Such religious teachings and cultural norms restricted the behavior of colonial women and influenced them throughout life. Small girls watched their mothers defer to their fathers. As they grew to adulthood, young women learned they would receive smaller inheritances than their brothers. In a typical will, Ebenezer Chittendon of Guilford, Connecticut, bequeathed all his land to his sons. Then he decreed that "Each Daughter have half so much as Each Son, one half in money and the other half in Cattle."

Lineal family values gave preference to the husband and the children at the expense of the wife. Upon marriage, the bride gave up legal ownership of all her personal property—money, household goods, and even clothes—to her husband. In addition, the laws of most colonies required her to relinquish use-rights to any land she might own, first to her husband and, upon his death, to their children. Only upon her own death could the widow dispose of the land as she wished. In compensation, a widow received certain "dower rights." These normally consisted of the use of a third of the family estate during her lifetime. Depending on her husband's will, the widow might lose her dower rights if she remarried. In any event, she could not sell such family land without the permission of the courts. The wife's rights were subordinate to those of the family as a whole. They also ranked behind those of the male "line" that stretched across the generations. If a father died, his male relatives could take legal control of his children from his widow—and in some cases did so. In case of divorce, which occurred rarely in the eighteenth century, the father had the undisputed right to custody of the children. In law as in life, men exercised predominant authority.

A woman's place in the social order was as a dutiful daughter to her father and a helpmeet to her husband. Some women fulfilled these roles better than others did. Because of personal ability, family training, or sheer determination, they excelled at the tasks of farm life. Many expertly spun thread from flax and wool and wove it into shirts and gowns. Others adeptly knit sweaters and stockings, preserved food, made candles and soap, churned butter, and mastered dozens of other productive tasks required to maintain a rural household. The community lavished praise on these talented women. "I have a great and longing desire to be very notable," a Virginia woman wrote upon her marriage. Ezra Stiles, the president of Yale College, educated his

SELF-PORTRAIT OF AN ARTIST AT WORK
Eighteenth-century American women took great pride in their textile-making skills. They spun and wove wool into cloth and fashioned it into clothes. As time permitted, they created beautifully designed quilts and embroidery. Executed by a self-conscious woman, this masterpiece of needlework exhibits the tools of her craft and symbols of her mortality. (Connecticut Historical Society)

BRIDES TO VIRGINIA

A letter from the Virginia Company in 1623 indicates how the shortage of women worked to improve their social and legal status in the seventeenth-century Chesapeake colonies.

We send you in this ship one widow and eleven maids for wives for the people in Virginia: there hath been especial care had in the choice of them; for there hath not any one of them been received but upon good commendations. We pray you all ... to take them into your care....

There are nearly fifty more which are shortly to come, are sent by certain worthy gentlemen, who taking into their consideration that the plantation can never flourish till families be planted, and the respect of wives and children fix the people on the soil. Therefore have given this fair beginning: for the reimbursing of whose charges it is ordered that every man that marries them give 120 weight of the best leaf tobacco for each of them, and in case any of them die, that proportion must be advanced to it upon those that survive. That marriage be free according to the law of nature, yet would we not have these maids deceived and married to servants, but only to such free men or tenants as have means to maintain them. We pray you therefore to be fathers to them in this business, not enforcing them to marry against their wills; neither send we them to be servants, save in case of extremity, for we would have their condition so much bettered as multitudes may be allured thereby to come unto you.

---

daughter to be a "notable Woman." "I'm the picture of bustling notability," exclaimed one wife. Women with fewer accomplishments felt the sting of their shortcomings. As Abigail Hyde confessed to her parents, "the conviction of my deficiencies as a mother is overwhelming."

The demands of bearing and raising a family were indeed arduous. Most women in New England and the middle colonies married in their early twenties; their husbands were usually two to four years older. The great majority of wives survived multiple childbirths—without pain-killing drugs, which did not yet exist. A typical colonial woman bore five to seven children before the onset of menopause in her early 40s. For about twenty of their most active years, most wives were either pregnant or breastfeeding a baby. "The care of my Babes takes up so large a portion of my time and attention," Sarah Ripley Stearns explained, that she had no time for religious activities. Her experience was normal. Large families sapped the physical strength and emotional stamina of most women and focused their energy on domestic activities.

Ethnic background as well as childbearing shaped the character of women's lives. Travelers in colonial America often remarked that German and French-Canadian women "are always in the fields, meadows, stables, etc. and do not dislike any work whatsoever." Similarly, among the Scotch-Irish in Pennsylvania, women did "all the Drudgery of a family as well as any German woman." Males of English descent—at least those in the Puritan settlements—were more reluctant to have their wives work in the fields. "Women in New England," Timothy Dwight reported approvingly, "are employed only in and about the house and in the proper business of the sex."

The size of farms and families gradually decreased through the years, and women devoted more time to tasks other than childbearing. After 1750, parents in Andover, Massachusetts, and many other long-settled communities had an average of only four children. Wealthier women, such as Susan Huntington of Boston, spent more time in "the ordering of domestic affairs, the regulation of servants, the care & culture of children, and the perusal of necessary books, including the scriptures." Poorer farm women gave greater attention to the tasks of economic production. They made yarn, cloth, shoes, or cheese for sale in the expanding market economy.

However, strict cultural rules still limited the extent of women's participation in the wider community. Although Quakers in Pennsylvania believed "that women can be called to the ministry as well as men," a French visitor noted, and

Baptists in Rhode Island permitted women to vote on church affairs, most religious groups insisted that females assume an inferior position in the church. Throughout New England, in "the Congregational Churches I never knew or read of the Sisters voting," Ezra Stiles wrote in his journal. "They often stay with the brethren & see & hear what is transacted, but don't even speak in Church."

In women's activities as in other aspects of life, the freehold agricultural society of New England differed somewhat from that in the middle colonies. For example, women who grew up in the Puritan culture learned to read and write. About 60 percent of white New England women signed their names to legal documents in the mid-1700s, twice as many as in the Chesapeake colonies. On the other hand, New England women assumed fewer roles in the religious institutions of their society than Pennsylvania Quaker women, and they also performed a smaller variety of agricultural tasks than German and Scotch-Irish females. These regional and ethnic differences were only variations on the general theme of female subordination. Despite their increasing freedom from childraising, women remained bound to an inferior social status by an intricate web of legal rules, cultural norms, and religious restrictions.

Malthus and America

In his famous *Essay on the Principle of Population*, published in 1798, the English clergyman Thomas Malthus reached a startling conclusion. His research indicated that the population of the Atlantic world was growing faster than the food supply. Malthus predicted that the growing gap between population size and food supply would produce increasing poverty, famine, and death. To prevent this disaster, he urged policies of late marriage and birth control (through abstinence from sexual intercourse); such practices would cut the rate of population growth. Americans, Malthus observed, had the additional option of westward expansion to increase their supply of food.

The New England experience shows both the validity and limitations of Malthus' brilliant insight into the process of change in preindustrial agricultural society. The population of New En-

TABLE 4.1 DIMINISHING PROPERTY IN THE FULLER FAMILY, KENT, CONNECTICUT

	Date of Birth	Highest Assessment on Tax List
First Generation		
Joseph Fuller	1699	203 pounds
Second Generation		
Joseph Jr.	1723	42
Zachariah	1725	103
Jeremiah	1728	147
Nathaniel	?	67
Adijah	?	46
Simeon	?	49
Abraham	1737	136
Jacob	1738	59
Isaac	1741	7
	Average:	72 pounds
Third Generation		
Abel	?	40
Abraham, Jr.	?	50
Oliver	1747	50
Daniel	1749	65
Howard	1750	28
Benejah	1757	32
Ephraim	1760	100
John	1760	?
Asahel	1770	48
James	1770	40
Revilo	1770	35
Samuel	?	14
	Average:	40 pounds

gland grew in classic Malthusian fashion, doubling each generation. The Puritan colonies had slightly fewer than a hundred thousand people in 1700, but two hundred thousand in 1725 and almost four hundred thousand by 1750. Under the stimulus of this population pressure, settlers continually moved inland from the Massachusetts coast and up the Connecticut River valley into the far inner areas of New England. Every year, they hacked new farms out of the forest to provide capital resources for the growing population.

Rapid population increase nevertheless threatened long-settled areas with agricultural decline and social instability. By 1750, the ample lands distributed to the original migrant families had been divided and then subdivided. Generations of use had depleted the fertility of even the richest bottom lands. Lacking farms or resources to bequeath to their children, parents lost some control over young people's labor and marriages. With little prospect of an inheritance, young men refused to stay on the family farm and migrated to newly settled regions. Young women entered into sexual relationships and used the resulting pregnancies to get their parents' consent to marry men with little property and few prospects. The number of first-born children conceived before marriage rose steadily and spectacularly throughout New England—from about 10 percent in the 1710s to 30 percent in the 1740s and then, in some communities, to 40 percent. "If they were again in the same circumstances," one Anglican minister commented, these youths "would do the same again, because otherwise they could not obtain their parents' consent to marry."

Westward expansion was just one response to population growth. New Englanders altered their crops and diets, beginning around 1700. The original migrants planted fields of wheat and barley to provide bread and beer. They supplemented these traditional staples of the English diet with wild game or fish and seasonal vegetables. Adapting to environmental conditions and the demands of the West Indian market, New England farmers gradually replaced this mixed-crop agriculture with a grazing economy based on corn, cattle, and hogs. They gave up wheat because it grew poorly in the thin soil and instead sowed rye for bread. They planted apple orchards to provide cider and turned their barley plots into cornfields. Corn provided a hardy food for the settlers, and the abundant leaves of the corn plant furnished feed for livestock. The cattle and hogs were butchered and preserved as salt beef and salt pork. "The general subsistence of the poor people," the physician William Douglass observed in the 1720s, "is salt pork and Indian beans, with bread of Indian corn meal, and pottage of this meal with milk for breakfast and supper." Agricultural adaptation had produced a diet based on stored and preserved foods.

In the middle of the eighteenth century, the need to feed more people led to a second series of changes. New England farmers now planted nutritious potatoes, whose high yields offset the effect of the shrinking farms. They introduced English grasses, such as red clover, cowpea, and timothy, to provide summer forage for their livestock and also nitrogen for the depleted soil. As a result, they continued to produce surplus salted and pickled meat for export to the West Indies. In 1770, the meat shipped by New England farmers—and, to a lesser extent, by those in the middle colonies—accounted for about 5 percent of the value of all exports from the mainland colonies. The creative adaptation of the agricultural economy not only prevented a food shortage, but also generated surplus food for export.

Cultural traditions likewise helped the people of New England adapt to population pressure. Close family and community ties brought the creation of a three-level system of economic exchange that increased the region's productive capacity. First, members of kinship groups continually assisted one another. Men exchanged tools, draft animals, and grazing land. Women and children worked together, spinning yarn, sewing quilts, or shucking corn. Each family unit gave or received labor as its needs or resources required. This sharing of labor and goods permitted every farm to achieve maximum output at the lowest cost. Second, men and women with special skills developed a similar exchange system. Farmers plowed the fields of neighbors who were artisans and then took pots, plows, and furniture to them for repair.

These transactions were given a monetary value, but no money changed hands. Rather, debts and credits were recorded in personal account books. After a number of years, the accounts were balanced and then settled with the exchange of small amounts of cash. This exchange system could work only in a closely knit society with shared cultural values. New England farmers thus produced a surplus that they sold in the commercial exchange system of the market economy.

In the middle colonies, the European demand for wheat was more important than cultural traditions in averting a Malthusian subsistence crisis. The population of this region rose at a phenominal rate—from 50,000 in 1700 to 125,000 in 1730 to 300,000 by 1760—but the supply of fertile land was much greater than that in New England. Moreover, a gently rolling countryside and a frost-free growing season of about 120 days aided the cultivation of wheat, which was much in demand. Wheat prices in the Atlantic world doubled between 1720 and 1770, bringing

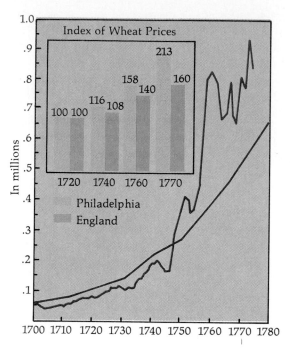

Index of Wheat Prices

1720	1740	1760	1770
100 100	116 108	158 140	213 160

Philadelphia
England

━━ Population

━━ English imports (in £)

FIGURE 4.1 RATES OF POPULATION GROWTH AND ENGLISH IMPORTS IN THE MIDDLE COLONIES

prosperity to farmers of the middle colonies. By 1770, the value of wheat, bread, and flour shipped from these settlements, and the adjoining colonies of Maryland and Virginia, amounted to about 20 percent of all colonial exports.

Many families prospered from growing grain, but few grew rich. Preindustrial technology greatly limited output. If the ripe grain was not cut promptly, it sprouted. Yet a worker with a hand sickle could reap only a half-acre a day. A family could harvest only about ten acres of wheat each year, from which it threshed perhaps 120 bushels of grain. During the 1750s, farmers began to use a *cradle*, a long-handled scythe with wooden fingers above the cutting blade. This tool doubled the productivity of a harvest worker to an acre a day. Some farm families now planted more acres yearly and had a greater surplus to sell. Most earned a modest cash income and had ample wheat and corn for their own families and livestock. "In this prov-

ince," the German minister Gottlieb Mittelburger reported from Pennsylvania, "even in the humblest or poorest houses, no meals are served without a meat course; and no one eats bread without butter or cheese."

Agricultural exports introduced new social divisions into rural communities. During the first decades of settlement in Chester County, Pennsylvania, there was remarkably little economic inequality. In 1693, the poorest 30 percent of the county's taxpayers owned a substantial 17 percent of the assessed wealth, and the top 10 percent controlled 23 percent. Most houses had one or two rooms and a minimal amount of furniture, such as a few benches or stools plus a bed in a loft. Only the wealthiest families ate with pewter utensils on ceramic plates. The great majority consumed their simple fare from wooden *trenchers* (platters) and drank from wooden *noggins* (cups).

Two generations later, the general standard of living had risen significantly but the life-styles were much less uniform. Estate inventories of wealthy farmers describe spacious houses filled with couches, mahogany tables, four-poster beds, table linen, silver serving bowls, and imported Dutch dinnerware. This gracious style of life testified to the growth of economic inequality. By 1760, the richest 10 percent of the families in Chester County owned about 30 percent of the community's assessed wealth. In another generation they controlled 40 percent. The social spectrum was now much wider and more difficult to traverse because the poorest 30 percent of the property owners held a mere 6 percent of the society's assets. These men and women lived only a little better than the first migrants and had fewer prospects for advancement.

Both affluence and poverty stemmed from population growth in a booming agricultural economy. Only 257 taxpayers and their families lived in Chester County in 1693, but their number grew to nearly 4,300 by 1760. New settlers needed land, equipment, and goods, and middlemen supplied such essentials. These entrepreneurs gradually formed a new class of land speculators, storekeepers, gristmill operators, and rural landlords. As the commercial and agricultural capitalists reaped handsome profits, they rose to the top of the social scale, joining the small group of farmers who hired servants or had slave labor. Wealthy families lived very different lives than the small-scale freehold farmers who formed the majority of property owners.

A new landless class also appeared at the bottom of rural society in the middle colonies. By 1765, nearly half the adult males in Chester County did not own land. Some young males were the sons of property owners and eventually inherited at least part of their father's estate. But just as many were "inmates," who were not of English descent. As the assessor in the predominately Scotch-Irish township of Londonderry explained, inmates were single men or families "such as live in small cottages and have no taxable property, except a cow, very few of them have a horse." Known in England as "cotters," many of these men and women lived in poverty. They were scattered in the hilly areas of the countryside or concentrated in certain districts in small trading and manufacturing towns.

An "abundance of Poor people live on Wolfes hill and in Adams Town" in the mostly German settlement of Lancaster, Pennsylvania, William Shippen noted in 1773. They "maintain their Families with great difficulty by day Labour," scratching out a bare subsistence from "their garden truck, as they call it, and a cow, which every one of them is not able to purchase." Many of these men hoped to become tenants and then landowners. This was a difficult but realistic goal, for the Penn family sought to create a freehold society in their proprietary colony by selling plots of land at reasonable prices.

German and Scotch-Irish migrants in New York had a harder time climbing the agricultural ladder. The Dutch West India Company had created vast patroonships in the fertile Hudson River valley, and some of these quasi-feudal estates still existed. In addition, the first English governors had bestowed large tracts of land on some families. For decades, few migrants took up residence on these estates despite the rich soil and prime river location. In 1714, the Manor of Rensselaerwyck had only eighty-two tenants on its hundreds of thousands of acres. Population growth gradually caused a scarcity of freehold land, forcing more families to accept tenancy leases. There were 345 Rensselaerwyck tenants in 1752 and nearly 1,000 in 1779. Many of these families had recently arrived from Europe and were "too poor to be farmers, having

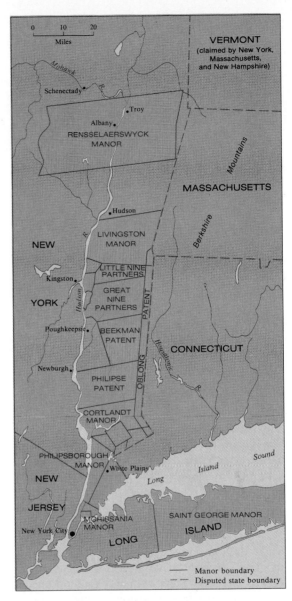

MAP 4.1 THE HUDSON RIVER MANORS
Wealthy Dutch and English manorial lords owned most of the fertile eastern bank of the Hudson River valley. They leased their lands to German tenant families and refused to sell farms to migrants from New England. Consequently, boundary disputes and tenant uprisings occurred continually in New York.

not the wherewithal to buy Cattle to stock a farm." To dissuade potential tenants from migrating to the frontier, or to Pennsylvania, the manor lords offered attractive terms. They gave settlers long leases and the right to sell the next tenant any improvements made on the property.

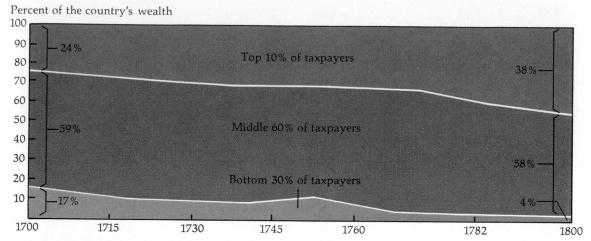

FIGURE 4.2 INCREASING SOCIAL INEQUALITY IN CHESTER COUNTY, PENNSYLVANIA

With determination, luck and wheat profits, some tenants saved enough to buy freehold property. Yet much of the Hudson River Valley remained a world of tenant farmers, distinct from the freehold agricultural cultures of New England and Pennsylvania.

Even the communities of freeholders had become more complex agricultural societies. In Pennsylvania, wealthy gentlemen farmers and commercial middlemen owned a substantial proportion of the taxable property. German tenants and Scotch–Irish inmates struggled for subsistence and land. In grain-poor New England, creative agricultural adaptation could generate only a limited surplus. Many small-scale freehold farmers fell on hard times. As the most numerous class, these farm families had considerable political leverage. Their demands for land banks and ample supplies of paper money sparked sharp confrontations not only with British merchants, but also with wealthy provincial creditors. "The Popular or *Democratick* part of the Constitution," the pro-creditor physician William Douglass complained in 1739, "are generally in Debt, and by their too great Weight or Influence in Elections, have made a depreciating Currency." The community stood divided by economic interest and class position. Freehold farmers had turned to political action to maintain the economic basis of their cultural ideal of landed independence. As Malthus noted, Americans escaped a subsistence crisis. But he failed to realize

that they feared a return to the depressed status of the European peasantry. This threat profoundly shaped their actions during the era of the American Revolution.

Masters and Slaves

Racial slavery in the southern colonies shaped the character of both white and black culture. Slave ownership provided wealth and status to a ruling class with aristocratic pretensions. This planter elite dominated the white yeomen farmers and tenants of the Chesapeake colonies and backcountry settlers in the Carolinas. To deter political revolts, slaveowners emphasized racial solidarity among whites. To assert their mastery over their African workforce, planters used physical violence. The black population adapted as well as it could to life under slavery and created a new Afro–American culture.

The Traditional Social Order Restored

Life in the seventeenth-century Chesapeake colonies fulfilled the worst vision of the English philosopher Thomas Hobbes. For most migrants, it was truly "solitary, poor, nasty, brutish, and short." Disease struck down migrants like flies, and death continually destroyed the social bonds of family, friendship, and community. Most men never married because there were few female settlers or indentured servants. Early deaths disrupted most marriages that did take place. Rarely did both parents survive to see their children grow to adulthood. The family system broke into fragments—unmarried young men, widowed older women, and orphaned children.

This erosion of the basic social unit altered some aspects of traditional male authority. Because their male relatives and friends died so early, husbands in the Chesapeake gave greater legal authority to their wives by naming them to execute their wills. These men also gave less importance to the family "line" in the distribution of property. Their wills commonly bestowed more than the normal one-third dower rights on widows and frequently permitted them to retain this legacy if they remarried. Women used their scarcity and the high death rates to good advantage. Through marriage, most white women rose on the social scale and enjoyed greater legal privileges.

However, this change in cultural norms was short-lived. Disease and death struck less frequently by the early eighteenth century. In the more stable families and communities, males restored their authority and traditional patterns of inheritance. By 1750, most Chesapeake husbands who wrote wills named male kin rather than wives as the executors of their estates and the legal guardians of the children. Most of them restricted their widow's estate to the customary one-third.

These changes within the family signaled the general restoration of traditional forms of hierarchy. Between 1680 and 1720, tens of thousands of African slaves began to work on the plantations of the planter elite. The use of slaves solidified the economic predominance of the wealthy planters. They created self-sufficient plantations by using blacks to grow food as well as tobacco; to build houses, wagons, and tobacco casks; and to make shoes, clothes, and other necessities. This strategy of self-sufficiency helped the planters survive depressed prices and cyclical fluctuations in the tobacco market. But small-scale planters fared poorly during this period. Their incomes declined and they fell increasingly into debt to planter-merchant creditors.

The Virginia gentry encouraged these yeomen to accept their subordinate economic position by increasing their political rights. When Alexander Spotswood, the royal governor of Virginia from 1710 to 1722, tried to raise property qualifications for voting, the Council of Burgesses strongly opposed him. To win popular support, the council progressively reduced the annual poll tax paid by every free man. Before Bacon's Rebellion, this levy amounted to forty-five pounds of tobacco. It fell to eleven pounds by 1700 and to only five pounds between 1701 and 1750. As Spotswood complained, the Burgesses "have declared their resolution to raise no Tax on the people, let the occasion be what it will."

The leaders of Chesapeake society had created a new political culture. It united, rather than divided, the white population. Yeomen planters elected their wealthy neighbors to political office and deferred to their authority. In return, the planter elite lowered taxes, reduced political corruption, and curried the favor of voters at election time, treating them to rum, food, and money. This compromise had its basis in the common culture of the white population. Poor and wealthy planters enjoyed many of the same amusements. They both drank lots of liquor, bet aggressively on horse races and cockfights, and boasted of their manly prowess. The gentry were still a boisterous class, worldly in outlook and capable of patriarchal hospitality and aggressive violence.

As time passed, the planter elite gave their social power a tangible form. Unlike the absentee sugar producers of the West Indies, the tobacco planters in the Chesapeake were committed to life in America. Between 1725 and 1750, they replaced their modest wooden houses with mansions of brick and mortar. They sought elegance and refinement, modeling themselves after the English aristocracy. Virginia planters avidly read English newspapers and pamphlets, imported English clothes and eating fashions, and sent their sons to be educated as gentlemen in London. Hundreds of aspiring Virginians passed a few years at the Inns of Court, the gathering place and training ground for young English lawyers. From the social chaos of the seventeenth century, slaveowning planters formed a stable ruling class. They began to transform their rough, boisterous culture into one of great elegance and learning by the period of the American Revolution.

Oppression and Resistance

The moral and human cost of creating the Virginia aristocracy, and the ruling class in South Carolina, was high. The learning and civility of these families rested on the repression of their African slaves, and the century between 1675 and 1775 stands out as the most brutal period of American slavery. The Europeans who migrated to the Western Hemisphere during the seventeenth century came from societies scarred by bloody religious wars, systematic oppression of the poor, and mortal punishments for minor crimes. It took no great act of will for English planters to exploit their white indentured servants. The relatively few cultural barriers against physical violence vanished in the face of racial difference. The Puritans virtually exterminated the Pequot Indians. English slaveowners in the West Indies routinely branded their Africans with hot silver irons. Chesapeake planters resorted to castration; nose slitting; and cutting off fingers, toes, and ears to keep their slaves in submission. The worst aspects of human nature found ample expression in the legal and moral vacuum of slavery.

The extent of violence and, more broadly, of social control varied according to the size and density of the slave population. As cattle raising gave way to rice production in South Carolina, the number of Africans increased dramatically. By 1726, about two-thirds of the blacks in one South Carolina parish (county) lived on only eighteen plantations, with slave populations ranging from twenty-five to ninety-four. The masters of these large enterprises exerted severe control over their slaves. Previously, blacks had provided their own subsistence, but now owners generally agreed that "the Slaves shall be fed and provided for by the master." They forbade their black workers to leave the plantation without special passes and, to enforce these regulations, installed special night watches and rural patrols. Beatings and whippings became regular features of plantation life, and penalties for resistance—disobedience, refusal to work, running away—increased in severity.

The slave regime affected whites as well as blacks. "The whole commerce between master and slave is a perpetual exercise of the most boisterous passions, the most unremitting despotism on the one part, and degrading submissions on the other," Thomas Jefferson observed on the basis of personal experience. "Our children see this, and learn to imitate it." Each successive generation of whites was "nursed, educated, and daily exercised in tyranny." Whites who grew up in this society were conditioned to use terror to maintain their privileged social position.

Slaves dealt with repression in a variety of individual and collective ways. Some cooperated with their masters. They made implicit bargains over work and living conditions and hoped to avoid their masters' wrath. Other slaves expressed their discontent by working slowly or carelessly, or they stole plantation goods and exchanged them with one another. Goaded beyond endurance, individual Africans attacked their owners or overseers. In the northern as well as the southern colonies, whites took brutal vengeance for such acts of black violence. In 1712, two dozen slaves set fire to a building in New York City and killed nine whites. New York authorities deported fifty blacks to the West Indies, hanged thirteen, and starved another to death in chains. They burned four other slaves to death, one over a slow fire "that he may continue in torment for eight or ten hours," and broke the body of another rebel on a medieval torture wheel.

Most blacks realized the impossiblity of a successful revolt. They lived in an alien land surrounded by an armed white majority. Therefore, Africans searched for paths of escape. During the 1730s, the Spanish governor of Florida tried to rouse slaves in the Carolinas in order to weaken those English settlements. He promised blacks freedom and land if they fled to Florida. In November 1738, whites reported that sixty-nine blacks had gone to Saint Augustine. The following February, rumors circulated "that a Conspiracy was formed by Negroes in Carolina to rise and make their way out of the province." When war between England and Spain broke out in 1739, the conspirators acted. Seventy-five slaves banded together near the Stono River, killed a number of whites, and marched south toward Florida "with Colours displayed and two Drums beating." Unrest swept the countryside. The white militia eventually killed many of the rebels, dispersed the rest, and prevented a general rebellion.

Fear of slave revolts swept the colonies in the

MAP 4.2 THE DIVERSITY OF SLAVERY
In 1775 slavery existed in every colony, but took dramatically different forms. Black majorities in South Carolina and parts of Virginia prompted whites to enforce rigorous slave codes. Yet these blacks created strong cultural communities and maintained their African heritage. Slaves who lived in predominantely white regions suffered less repression but lost more of their traditional culture.

wake of the Stono uprising. Following several unexplained fires and robberies in 1741, New York City authorities embarked upon a bloody inquisition. They hanged or burned to death twenty blacks and four whites—alleged accomplices in the uprising—and transported eighty slaves to the West Indies.

Such repressive meaures prevented collective black rebellions against slavery for more than a generation. Then, during the American War of Independence, thousands of blacks deserted southern plantations to seek freedom behind the

British lines. Whatever the political and intellectual accomplishments of the Virginia and Carolina planter aristocracies, they had not convinced blacks to accept enslavement.

The Creation of an Afro-American Society

African slaves came from diverse tribal backgrounds and spoke about a hundred languages or dialects. The buying strategies of white planters encouraged this cultural intermixture. "The safety of the Plantations," declared a widely read English pamphlet of 1694, "depends upon having Negroes from all parts of *Guiny*, who not understanding each others languages and Customs do not, and cannot, agree to Rebel." Chesapeake planters imported slaves from all parts of western Africa—Senegambia, the Gold Coast, Nigeria, and Angola. South Carolina slaveowners preferred Angolan laborers and took nearly 40 percent of their work force from that country. In no colony, however, did any African tribe or language group become numerically dominant. Even the "Babel of Languages" spoken by Africans from different tribes could not prevent plots, Governor Spotswood of Virginia remarked during one uprising, "for freedom Wears a Cap which Can Without a Tongue, Call Together all those who Long to Shake off the Fetters of Slavery."

Nonetheless, this diversity made it difficult for slaves to talk to one another or feel a common identity. Tribal distinctions were strong and prominent. Africans used ritual scars and other marks to show their tribal status. "He is marked in the manner of his country with dots under both eyes," stated a Virginia advertisement for a runaway slave. Other newspaper notices revealed that four "new Gambia men" had run off together, as had four slaves from the "Fullah Country." Such runaways usually took their hoes, bedding, and other equipment with them. Occasionally they succeeded in establishing a tribal community in Indian territory. Most Africans who remained in captivity also maintained their tribal or linguistic identity, through both marriage and friendship.

The pressure of time and circumstance gradually broke down these tribal barriers. Many slaves on small Virginia plantations gave up

AFRICAN CULTURE ENDURES
Slaves dance on an eighteenth-century South Carolina plantation. According to modern research, the dance and the musical instruments are of Yoruba origin. Shipping records indicate that one sixth of South Carolina slaves came from the Niger River–Gold Coast region, the homeland of the Yoruba tribe, which lends support to this identification. (Artist Unknown. *The Old Plantation.* The Abby Aldrich Rockefeller Folk Art Center, Williamsburg, Va.)

their native tongues for English. "I noticed that all blacks spoke very good English," a European visitor noted with some surprise. Perhaps, he thought, their "American masters speak and communicate with them." In the predominately black South Carolina lowlands, slaves continued to use their African languages. Slowly, through a complicated process of linguistic invention, they created a new Gullah dialect that incorporated some English and many African words into an African grammatical structure. The dialect could be understood by a wide variety of tribes, and these Africans eventually became bilingual or even trilingual. They spoke in their native tongue to members of their tribal or language group, conversed in Gullah with other slaves and knowledgeable white overseers, and talked in broken English to their owners.

In the West Indies, black society retained a strong African character. Slaves died quickly on the sugar islands and were continually replaced by new arrivals. A West Indian-born black community developed only after the abolition of British slavery in 1833. However, an Afro-American culture developed on the mainland a full century earlier. By the 1730s, mainland slaves spoke English or Gullah and raised enough children to re-

produce their numbers. This new generation of blacks had no direct experience of life in Africa. The Afro-American population grew in size and confidence, and its members married among themselves. They encouraged newcomers from Africa to conform to their language and cultural ways.

As generations of whites and blacks lived in close proximity, their cultures converged. For example, African musical rhythms became part of the white experience. "Betwixt the Country dances," Nicholas Creswell, an Englishman, reported in the 1770s, Virginians "have what I call everlasting jigs. A Couple gets up and begins to dance a jig (to some Negro tune)." Yet slavery severely limited Afro-American creativity. In North America, slavery took an especially rigid social and cultural form, and racial categories were sharply defined. Whites strongly discouraged racial assimilation. They outlawed *miscegenation* (sexual union between the races) and enslaved the children of slave mothers even if the fathers were free white men. A person was either white and free or black and enslaved.

A more graded social hierarchy developed in the British West Indies and in Portuguese and Spanish colonies, where status reflected the degree of racial intermixture and cultural assimilation. Some mainland slaveowners freed their offspring by black women, but the number of free mulattoes was relatively small. Whites did not encourage them to improve their economic position and social status by adopting English cultural values and Christian religious beliefs.

Thus, successive generations of Afro-Americans retained a cultural identity that differed from that of the white majority. They lived hard lives, with few material comforts to show for decades of labor. "We entered the huts of the Blacks," a well-traveled European wrote in the late eighteenth century, and

> they are .more miserable than the most miserable of the cottages of our peasants. The husband and wife sleep on a mean pallet, the children on the ground; a very bad fireplace, some utensils for cooking, but in the middle of this poverty some cups and a teapot. . . .They work all week, not having a single day for themselves except for holidays.

"One sees," he concluded, "that the condition of our peasants is infinitely happier."

The comparison between slaves and peasants was logical. European peasants migrated to America to escape oppressive economic and social conditions, and most succeeded. Africans were forced into slavery and a rigid, narrow way of life that strongly resembled that of an exploited peasant community. Slaves, like peasants, fell back on the ties of family and community—and eventually religion—to create a more satisfying existence. A traveler in the southern backcountry encountered an Afro-American who had been taken prisoner by native Americans. The Indians, the traveler reported, "had given him a wife, a mother, and plenty of land to cultivate if he chose it, and the liberty of doing everything but making his escape." Nevertheless, the black intended "to render himself up a voluntary slave to his former master, that he might there once more embrace those friends and relatives from whom he had been so long separated." The incident reflected the emergence of an Afro-American society. To this slave, as to many others, escape was a mixed blessing. It meant physical freedom but the loss of cultural identity.

Toward a New Social Order

The society of the middle colonies lacked both the rigidity of class and race of the southern provinces and the cultural and religious uniformity of New England. These colonies did not seem to have strong institutional forms and a distinct social identity. They had no established churches, for example, and were populated by a diverse mixture of Europeans. Yet the middle colonies had more order and purpose than appeared at first glance. Strong ethnic ties united German and Scotch-Irish settlers, as did deep religious loyalties among Quakers, Presbyterians, and members of other churches and sects. This voluntary allegiance to distinct social groups, and their peaceful interaction with one another, offered a glimpse of the future. Cultural pluralism and an open social and political order characterized much of American society in the nineteenth century.

Ethnic Diversity

The most striking quality of the middle colonies was their mixture of ethnic and religious communities. When the Swedish traveler Peter Kalm visited Philadelphia in 1748, he found twelve churches representing diverse theological and ethnic traditions. There were Anglicans, Quakers, Swedish and German Lutherans, Scotch-Irish Presbyterians, and even a Roman Catholic congregation. William Penn was largely responsible for this variety. The Quaker proprietor personally recruited settlers from Wales and had his *Brief Account of the Province of Pennsylvania* translated into Dutch and German to attract Protestants from those countries. Moreover, the Frames of Government written by Penn and his associates guaranteed freedom of worship to all religious groups. "No man, nor number of men upon earth," Penn declared, "hath power or authority to rule over men's consciences in religious matters." Pennsylvania had no established church or religious taxes, and all Christians could vote and hold office.

Thousands of Europeans migrated to Pennsylvania, and to New York and New Jersey, after 1700. They had been pushed out of Europe by wars, religious disputes, and worsening economic conditions. The Scotch-Irish made up the

MAP 4.3 ETHNIC DIVERSITY
By 1775, the populations of many mainland colonies were no longer primarily English. The influx of thousands of German and Scotch-Irish migrants made the Middle Colonies and the southern backcountry one of the most ethnically and religiously diverse regions in the entire western world.

largest group. These Presbyterians were descended from the Scots sent to northern Ireland as a Protestant garrison following the English conquest in the seventeenth century. In Ireland, the Scots faced nearly as much discrimination as the Catholic majority. The Test Act of 1704 excluded both Catholics and Presbyterians from public office in Ireland. It reserved this privilege to members of the Church of England. In addition, British mercantilist regulations placed heavy import duties on the woolen goods produced by Scotch-Irish weavers.

During the 1720s, rising taxes and poor harvests sparked a major Scotch-Irish migration to America. "Read this letter, Rev. Baptist Boyd," one settler wrote back to his minister, "and look and tell all the poor folk of ye place that God has opened a door for their deliverance." In New York, he explained, "all that a man works for is his own; and there are no revenue hounds to take it from us here; there is no one to take away yer Corn, yer Potatoes, yer Lint or yer Eggs." Most Scotch-Irish settled in the middle colonies and in the Carolina backcountry, but some sought cheap land in New Hampshire and the Maine district of Massachusetts.

Gemans flooded into the middle colonies in a series of waves. Early in the eighteenth century, Penn convinced persecuted German religious sects to settle in his colony. Later, boatloads of German peasants from the war-torn Palatine region became tenants on the manors of the Hudson River valley in New York. By the 1720s, the population of southwestern Germany and Switzerland was growing rapidly. Declining economic conditions stimulated interest in America among thousands of peasants and artisans. In 1729, Heinrich Schneebeli of Zurich made an exploratory trip to Pennsylvania. "Wages were far better than here," he told his relatives and neighbors upon his return, and "one also enjoyed there a free unhindered Exercitium Religiones." Thirty people immediately asked the local bailiff for permission to emigrate. Ten years later, Martin Thommen made a similar request to the magistrates of Basel. "His estate was heavily mortgaged," this artisan explained, and he "could not save enough for the Interest" because "his craft of saddler was becoming overcrowded." By selling his property, Thommen planned to pay his debts and the cost of passage to America for himself and his wife and seven children. Other German-speaking migrants could pay only part of their transportation; they went to Pennsylvania as *redemptioners*, a kind of indentured servant. Hans Buser departed in this manner, along with his wife and five children, because in his district "there was not much work available for a day laborer."

Whatever their motivation or resources, Germans came in large numbers. More than twenty-five thousand German-speaking Swiss migrated to America, and another hundred thousand settlers journeyed from various German states and principalities. The major influx began in 1732 and 1733, when seventeen shiploads of settlers arrived in Pennsylvania, and lasted for twenty years. In 1749, twenty-four ships deposited over six thousand Germans on the docks of Philadel-

THE PERILS OF EMIGRATION

Gottlieb Mittelberger emigrated from his native Germany to Pennsylvania in 1750. His description of the rigors faced by German emigrants makes an interesting comparison with the slave's account in Chapter 3.

[The journey from Germany to Pennsylvania, via Holland and England] lasts from the beginning of May to the end of October, fully half a year, amid such hardships as no one is able to describe adequately with their misery....

Both in Rotterdam and in Amsterdam the people are packed densely, like herrings so to say, in the large sea-vessels. One person receives a place of scarcely 2 feet width and 6 feet length in the bedstead, while many a ship carries four to six hundred souls; not to mention the innumerable implements, tools, provisions, water-barrels and other things which likewise occupy much space....

When the ships have for the last time weighed their anchors near the city of Cowes in England, the real misery begins with the long voyage. For from there the ships, unless they have good wind, must often sail 8, 9, 10 to 12 weeks before they reach Philadelphia. But even with the best wind the voyage lasts 7 weeks.

But during the voyage there is on board these ships terrible misery, stench, fumes, horror, vomitting, many kinds of seasickness, fever, dysentery, headache, heat, constipation, boils, scurvy, cancer, mouthrot, and the like, all of which come from old and sharply salted food and meat, also from very bad and foul water, so that many die miserably.

Children from 1 to 7 years rarely survive the voyage; and many a time parents are compelled to see their children miserably suffer and die from hunger, thirst and sickness, and then to see them cast into the water. I witnessed such misery in no less than 32 children in our ship, all of whom were thrown into the sea. The parents grieve all the more since their children find no resting-place in the earth, but are devoured by the monsters of the sea.

---

phia. Some remained in the city, completing the terms of their indentured servitude. Other redemptioners worked as family units on farms to pay the cost of the voyage and earn money to acquire land of their own. Thousands of these so-called Pennsylvania Dutch migrants came with considerable goods or financial resources. They began farming in the rich Lancaster Valley and quickly became prosperous from the booming export trade in wheat. Additional groups of Germans moved down the Shenandoah Valley into the western districts of Maryland, Virginia, and the Carolinas.

These European migrants formed exclusive linguistic and cultural communities in the middle colonies and the southern backcountry. More than fifteen thousand settlers from the Highlands of Scotland lived in North Carolina by the 1770s. Most proudly wore their tartan plaids and spoke their native Gaelic tongue. The 150,000 Scotch-Irish who came to America spoke English. Many, intent on practicing their Presbyterian faith, migrated in congregations led by ministers. Most of these ethnic and religious migrants maintained close ties with members of their own culture. For example, all the customers of storekeeper Henry King in the village of Second River, New Jersey, were of Dutch origin. In Chester County, Pennsylvania, about 70 percent of the children of Welsh Quaker migrants married other Welsh Quakers, and so did 60 percent of the next generation's children.

Germans formed particularly cohesive communities because of their language. About 75 percent of the migrants who settled in Lancaster, Pennsylvania, during the 1740s spoke German. Smaller, more remote German communities jealously guarded their traditional culture. One German minister in North Carolina admonished his congregation "not to contract any marriages with the English or Irish. We owe it to our native country to do our part that German blood and the German language be preserved and more and more disseminated in America." Many German settlements achieved this goal. Most American-born Germans took marriage partners of

TAVERN CULTURE
Women emerged as prominent tavern-keepers in the eighteenth century, frequently working alone after their husbands' death. Some taverns catered to genteel guests and travellers; others to ordinary farmers or poor sailors. In all taverns, thought John Adams, "the money, health, modesty of most that are young and of many old are wasted; here diseases, vicious habits, bastards, and legislators are frequently begotten." (Connecticut Historical Society)

their own ancestry, read German-language newspapers, and attended church services conducted in their native tongue. "The intercourse of Germans with each other is kept chiefly in their own language," the eminent Pennsylvania physician and statesman Benjamin Rush remarked in the late eighteenth century. The main exception, Rush noted, were the leading men "who visit the capital and trading or country towns, and speak English." European migration to the middle colonies had produced a society of distinct linguistic, cultural, and religious communities.

Quakers and Political Pluralism

Migrants who ventured into the New England colonies often aroused considerable resentment. During the 1720s, this prejudice against "foreign-ers" resulted in mob violence in Boston "to prevent ye landing of Irish." A Connecticut town raised a similar protest against a Scotch-Irish Presbyterian minister "because he is a stranger." "And we are informed," the town selectmen continued, "that he came out of Ireland; and we do observe that since he has been in town that the Irish do flock into town; and we are informed that the Irish are not wholesome Inhabitants."

Ethnic prejudice existed in the middle colonies as well. The struggle in New York over the regime of Captain Jacob Leisler pitted Dutch against English settlers. Yet political compromises in these colonies diminished cultural conflict. The laws of New York required all adults to pay taxes for the support of religion. However, each settlement could choose its own pastor and church. Even this "multiple establishment" was too restrictive for the Quaker migrants who dominated the early political life of Pennsylvania. They devised a policy of complete religious toleration.

The Quakers were a radical English Protestant sect, known formally as the Society of Friends. Like the Puritan migrants to New England, Quakers wanted to restore the simplicity and spirituality of the primitive Christian church. There the similarities ended. The theology of the Society of Friends differed greatly from the Calvinist doctrines of New England Congregationalism. Following the teachings of their founder, George Fox, Quakers believed that all men and women, not just a small Elect, could achieve salvation. The Friends designed their prime religious institution—the weekly meeting—to assist their members to be moved by the inner light of grace and understanding that God had instilled in each person. Since spiritual enlightenment came from within, the society did not endorse a highly trained ministry, adept in the theological analysis of Biblical texts. Rather, Quakers encouraged anyone, male or female, who felt the promptings of the inner light to speak at the meeting. "Nearest the front by the wall are two benches," Peter Kalm reported following his visit to a Philadelphia meetinghouse. "In these pews sit those of both sexes who either are already accustomed to preach or expect to be inspired by the Holy Ghost."

WILLIAM PENN'S CHARTER OF PRIVILEGES, 1701

Because no People can be truly happy, though under the greatest Enjoyment of Civil Liberties, if abridged of the Freedom of their Consciences, as to their Religious Profession and Worship . . ., I do hereby grant and declare, That no Person or Persons, inhabiting in this province or Territories, who shall confess and acknowledge *One* Almighty God, the Creator, Upholder and Ruler of the World; and profess him or themselves obliged to live quietly under the Civil Government, shall be in any Case molested or prejudiced, in his or their Person or Estate, because of his or their conscientious Persuasion or Practice, nor be compelled to frequent or maintain any religious Worship, Place or Ministry, contrary to his or their Mind, or to do or suffer any other Act or Thing, contrary to their religious Persuasion.

And that all Persons who also profess to believe in *Jesus Christ*, the Saviour of the World, shall be capable (notwithstanding their other Persuasions and Practices in Point of Conscience and Religion) to serve this Government in any Capacity, both legislatively and executively.

English Quakers repudiated fundamental principles of the social and political order during the seventeenth century. They refused to pay religious taxes, take oaths in legal proceedings, serve in the army, or remove their hats to those of superior rank. This rejection of the traditional social hierarchy extended to the dress and language of everyday life. To emphasize their belief in religious equality, Quakers usually wore plain attire without elaborate decorations. They also used terms of familiarity, such as "thee" and "thou" instead of the more formal "you." Responding to this radical attack on their authority, the English government and the Church of England persecuted the sect and welcomed the departure of thousands of its members to a far-off colony.

In Pennsylvania, the Quakers gave political and institutional form to their religious principles. They were pacifists, and so they avoided warfare with native Americans. They negotiated formal treaties with the various tribes and purchased Indian land rather than seizing it by force. These policies irritated non-Quaker settlers on the frontier and did not completely eliminate conflict with the Indians. However, there was no major Indian war in Pennsylvania from the time of its first settlement in the 1680s until the 1750s, a record unmatched elsewhere in the colonies.

Because of its policy of religious toleration, the Quaker colony at first avoided many theological conflicts as well. The proprietary governor and the assembly of Pennsylvania welcomed all Christian sects and refused to give political or legal or financial support to any church. These liberal policies attracted a dozen radical German religious sects, such as the Moravian Brethren, as well as thousands of more orthodox Lutheran and Reformed Protestants.

Most of the congregations prospered, but some European-trained ministers doubted that religion could survive without the authority of the government behind it. "Throughout Pennsylvania the preachers do not have the power to punish anyone, or to force anyone to go to church," complained Gottlieb Mittelburger, a German minister, in his *Journal of a Trip through Pennsylvania* (1750). "Sunday is very badly kept," he reported, "especially in the rural districts, where most country folk pay little attention to it. Apostle-days and holydays are not observed at all. Many other people plough, reap, thresh, hew or split wood and the like." The minister concluded that "Liberty in Pennsylvania does more harm than good to many people, both in soul and body."

Mittelburger's analysis was perceptive but wrong. He correctly called attention to the lack of political support for religious discipline. However, he neglected to mention that government

A QUAKER MEETING FOR WORSHIP
Like other Protestants, Quakers in England and America worshipped in plain, unadorned buildings. Surprisingly, only men sit on the raised front bench in this (slightly damaged) 1670 painting of an English meeting; in England and among Quaker migrants to America, women took a prominent role in religious worship and affairs. A Dove, the Christian symbol for the Holy Spirit, hovers over the meeting, signifying the worshippers' search for the "inner light" within themselves. (Egbert van Heemskerk, *The Quaker Meeting*, c. 1690. Quaker Collection, Haverford College)

coercion was often ineffective. Many Europeans and Americans who lived in societies with established churches paid religious taxes reluctantly— and avoided them if they could—and defied laws requiring church attendance. More importantly, Mittelburger failed to appreciate the power of communal self-discipline. The various religious sects in Pennsylvania enforced proper moral behavior on their own members. Each Quaker family, for example, belonged to a weekly meeting that met regularly for religious worship. A monthly meeting attended to matters of discipline, and one of its committees visited each family four times a year. The committee made certain that children received proper religious instruction, and it also reported on the moral and social behavior of the parents. Acting on such a report, the Chester men's monthly meeting disciplined one of its members "to reclaim him from his evil conversation, as drinking to excess and keeping vain company."

Quaker monthly meetings watched over the marriage arrangements of their members with special care. They continually warned against marriages with non-Quakers and used strong communal sanctions to deter such unions. During the early eighteenth century, Quaker meetings in Chester County disowned about two-thirds of those who married outside the faith. They barred these young men and women from religious services and urged their families and friends to treat them as outcasts. The monthly meetings also regulated marriages between Quakers. They functioned like the formal marriage courts in many European towns. The meetings granted permission to marry only to couples with sufficient land, livestock, and equipment to support themselves and their future children.

Over a few generations, this strict system of marriage rules shaped the character of the Quaker community. Parents of wealthy or middling status provided their sons with ample land, and their daughters with substantial dowries. Their children married within the meeting. Many offspring of poorer Quaker parents lacked the required resources and could not obtain the meeting's permission. Quakers thus encouraged their poor to remain unmarried or *disowned* (expelled) them for disobedience. They acted through their own institutions to uphold the ideal of a prosperous society of freeholding families. The communal self-discipline of the Quakers demonstrated that religious freedom did not lead to social chaos.

The Pennsylvania experience also revealed the tensions inherent in a political society composed of distinct ethnic and religious groups. By the middle of the eighteenth century, Pennsylvania politics were sharply divided along cultural lines. German settlers in the western counties wanted representation in the assembly in proportion to their numbers. Scotch-Irish migrants on the frontier demanded a more aggressive policy against the Indians. Soon, one observer noted, Scotch-Irish Presbyterians, German Baptists, and German Lutherans had combined in "a general confederacy of the three societies" against the "ruling party" of Quakers.

Given the nonauthoritarian and representative political institutions of eighteenth-century America, such political alliances were to be expected. Yet religious zeal and ethnic prejudice added a dangerous dimension to these conflicts over issues and prevented their resolution. The middle colonies as a whole were "composed of people of different nations, different manners, different religions and different languages," an English traveler remarked. They lived in peace and yet, he warned, "they have a mutual jealousy, for religious zeal is secretly burning." These latent passions became evident during the American Revolution and nearly destroyed the fabric of the political order.

Regional Provincialism

By 1750, most Pennsylvania whites and many who lived in the Chesapeake colonies could trace their American ancestry back for three generations. In New England, the fourth- or fifth-generation descendants of the original settlers were reaching adulthood. Where did their cultural loyalties lie? These men and women were of English descent, but they lived three thousand miles from England. They had never participated directly in English political or social life. Nor had their parents or, in many cases, their grandparents. Because of the passage of time, plus the influence of African and non-English European migrants, their culture was not quite

English. Yet, for two reasons, it was not American either. First, the settlers lived in regionally based cultures. Second, these cultures were pale copies of English, German, or African models. They lacked a sense of a distinct American identity.

American regionalism found expression in the houses, farms, and stores built by the settlers. During the seventeenth century, the English migrants modified the design and appearance of their houses because of the abundance of wood. They made few roofs of thatch, the bundled straw often used in England, because lighter wood shingles were readily available. Likewise, the abundance of heavy framing timber allowed carpenters to run single posts from the foundations to the roofs of two-story buildings. These timbers increased the strength of the houses and simplified the construction process. Carpenters also used long wooden rafters to attach convenient lean-tos to the backs of colonial houses for cooking and storage.

Distinct regional building styles evolved in response to environmental conditions and the impact of new cultural traditions. New Englanders preferred English housing styles with the chimney in the middle of the building to conserve heat during the long, cold winters. On the other hand, southerners chose designs with fireplaces in the end walls. This arrangement spread the warmth from cooking fires during the months of high heat and humidity. Welsh and German migrants to the middle colonies disregarded the abundant supply of wood and duplicated the stone housing styles of their ancestors. In 1798, more than 80 percent of the 480 houses in Germantown, Pennsylvania, were stone buildings.

In all regions, most houses were small and as in Europe, had one or two small rooms. In 1798, about a third of Germantown's residents lived in single-story cottages of fewer than four hundred square feet. Small farm dwellings dotted the rural landscape. "I looked out on some countryside," noted a European visitor to New Jersey and Delaware, and "I saw hamlets as miserable as the huts of our peasants." Philip Fithian, a graduate of the College of New Jersey (now Princeton University) and the resident tutor in the mansion of a Virginia planter, graphically described the crowded social intercourse in the humble cottages.

EUROPEAN ARCHITECTURAL INFLUENCE

The first generations of English colonists lived in simple wooden houses. Beginning in the 1720s, wealthy Americans copied formal English architectural styles, constructing huge and elaborately decorated mansions in the Georgian style, like the Longfellow House at the right. German settlers usually built in stone, reflecting traditional practices in the Rhineland. Peter Troxell, Sr. built the unusually large dwelling at the left in 1756 to house his own family and that of his newly married eldest son, Peter Troxell, Jr. (Left, Lehigh County Historical Society; Right, Longfellow National Historic Site, National Park Service)

In almost all these rural Cots I am under the Necessity of sleeping in the same Room with all the Family. It seems indelicate, at least new, to strip, surrounded by different Ages & Sexes, & rise in the Morning, in the Blaze of Day, with the Eyes of, at least, one blinking Irish female, searching out Subjects for Remark.

Actually, crowded living conditions were normal in preindustrial Europe and America, and Fithian's privileged existence was not. Depending on the time of day or the season of the year, each room in the cottages served a different purpose—eating, craft production, cooking, or sleeping. The modern concept of privacy was unknown, and the lack of eating utensils encouraged communal habits. A well-educated English traveler was astonished by what he saw in a backcountry German settlement.

I was witness to a kind of meal I had never before experienced. Some sour milk was warmed up and placed on the table. The whole family (of which there were seven or eight) partook of it, all of us sitting round *one* large bowl, and dipping our spoons in one after another. A dish of stewed pork was then served up, accompanied with some hot pickled cabbage. This was devoured in the same hoggish manner, two or three eating off the same plate, and all in the midst of filth and dirt.

As southern planters, northern farmers, and urban artisans and merchants acquired greater wealth, they built larger houses and furnished them with elegant objects and utensils. The additional space and personal possessions encouraged a new code of manners. The new houses had separate rooms for cooking, working, sleeping, and entertaining. Living in large, subdivided interior areas, parents and children became accustomed to some privacy. They now had rooms and possessions of their own. More comfortable material conditions thus enhanced the notion of individuality—the sense of an autonomous self—among the families of privileged social groups.

Domestic buildings and furnishings reflected wealth as well as cultural preferences and environmental conditions. The cottages of the poor in all regions of America were copies of the dwellings of the people's ancestors—in England, Scotland, Germany, or Africa. These families could not afford elaborate dwellings and had no knowledge of new architectural forms. They built in traditional ways and often with traditional materials. At the other end of the social scale, the process of architectural design was completely different. Wealthy Americans returned from visits to England impressed by the grandeur of the new Georgian architectural style. Most Georgian houses were two stories high and had four rooms, with a central hall and a completely symmetrical floor plan and facade. Families of wealth and status imported design books from England and instructed local builders to duplicate this style. As a result, Georgian architecture, with its emphasis on balance and order, appeared in all regions of colonial America. It typified the basic provincialism of upper-class American culture, the dependence on imported forms and fashions.

Other architectural traditions developed in each of the three main colonial regions as carpenters adapted high-style Georgian designs for middling farmers and artisans. In the Carolinas, many of these farmers lived in one-story houses with two rooms and symmetrical facades. Their homes had a steep roof, unlike the Georgian

style, to lessen the summer heat. In Pennsylvania, builders kept the low Georgian roof and the balanced exterior appearance. However, they divided the interior into three rooms, as was common in the Rhineland region of Germany.

English fashions and manners also affected various aspects of American material culture. During the first generations of settlement, the migrants used jugs, plates, and other ceramics brought from England. Beginning about 1680, people of New England and the Chesapeake colonies bought locally produced ceramics. Their purchases of pots, mugs, and containers supported a substantial number of potters. In the mid-eighteenth century, English manufacturers recaptured this market. New techniques of production enabled them to export thousands of pieces of durable, low-priced pottery to the colonies. At the same time, new English fashions altered American drinking habits. Before the 1740s, only a few families in Maryland drank tea or owned tea sets. Then the English rage for tea drinking spread to the colonies. Within twenty years, tea-service items—cups, teapots, and sugar bowls—appeared on more than half the probate inventories of colonists' estates.

TIME LINE
THE CULTURES OF PREINDUSTRIAL AMERICA

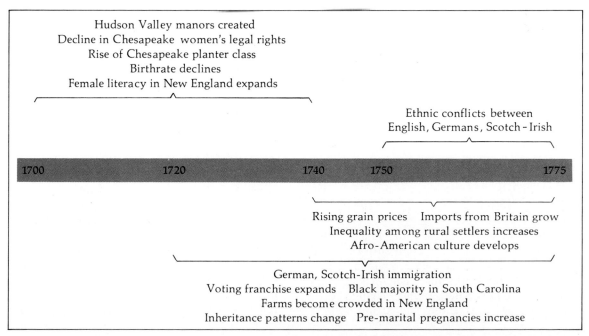

Hudson Valley manors created
Decline in Chesapeake women's legal rights
Rise of Chesapeake planter class
Birthrate declines
Female literacy in New England expands

Ethnic conflicts between
English, Germans, Scotch-Irish

| 1700 | 1720 | 1740 | 1750 | 1775 |

Rising grain prices   Imports from Britain grow
Inequality among rural settlers increases
Afro-American culture develops

German, Scotch-Irish immigration
Voting franchise expands   Black majority in South Carolina
Farms become crowded in New England
Inheritance patterns change   Pre-marital pregnancies increase

AMERICAN AND GERMAN FOLK ART
Shem Drowne, a Boston tinsmith, executed this gilded copper Indian weathervane for the residence of the Royal Governor in 1716. German migrants carried their artistic traditions to Pennsylvania, as indicated by the decoration on this eighteenth-century wooden box. By that time, the third generation of New England settlers had created a new folk tradition, using American symbols.
(Left, Shem Drowne, artisan. American Antiquarian Society; Right, Museum of New Mexico)

The seventeenth-century American colonies became "provinces" by the middle of the eighteenth century. The spread of English architectural styles, ceramics, and cultural fashions, and political ideologies drew the once-isolated settlements back into the orbit of the English metropolis. Wealthy Americans were most affected by this process. For example, southern aristocrats sent their sons to London for legal training and built large Georgian mansions on their slave-based plantations. Lawyers in Massachusetts wore English-style gowns and wigs.

Other colonists viewed such cultural and material English imports suspiciously. Craftsmen in port cities complained that imported manufactures destroyed their livelihoods. Conservatively inclined rural farmers feared new fashions and manners as threats to their traditional way of life. The intrusion of English culture threatened to separate the colonial social elite from the mass of the population. Yet it also provided a common set of values and practices. It thereby counteracted a century of regional cultural development and the effect of the diverse European migrations. In 1750, however, British North America remained a society of diverse racial and ethnic groups living in three regional cultures. It was not yet distinctly "American" in either condition or consciousness.

---

*I*n 1750, an "American" identity did not yet exist. The colonists lived in one of three distinct regional cultures.

In the northern colonies, the lineal family farm was the cultural ideal. High birth rates and limited arable land threatened yeoman farm society in New England, but creative adaptation averted economic decline. Families changed their inheritance practices, eating habits, and farming methods to maintain farm ownership and other traditional values.

In the middle colonies, rising wheat prices brought prosperity to family farmers. Hudson Valley landlords and their tenants also benefited, but most European migrants preferred the liberal land policies of Pennsylvania. A great influx of German and Scotch-Irish settlers increased that region's ethnic and religious diversity. New forms of religious authority emerged in Pennsylvania, as did the prospect of ethnic political strife.

The growth of racial slavery shaped the character of southern culture. Blacks outnumbered whites in some areas. Despite their diverse tribal backgrounds and harsh living conditions, slaves created families and began to form an Afro-American society. Wealthy slave-owning planters made up an intermarried elite and solidified their authority by granting political privileges to white yeomen and tenant farmers.

Well-educated southerners, like wealthy merchants and landowners in the other regions, adopted English architectural styles, political ideals, and social values. This imported "high culture" coexisted with strong regional American cultures.

Suggestions for Further Reading

Northern Freehold Society

Richard Hofstadter's *America at 1750* (1971) offers a comprehensive yet incisive overview. James T. Lemon, *The Best Poor Man's Country* (1972), and H. R. Merrens, *Colonial North Carolina in the Eighteenth Century* (1964), explore the development of American farming from a geographical perspective. For the emergence of tenancy, see Gregory A. Stiverson, *Poverty in the Land of Plenty: Tenancy in Eighteenth-Century Maryland* (1978), and the more optimistic interpretation in Sung Bok Kim, *Landlord and Tenant in Colonial New York* (1978).

Nancy Woloch, *Women and the American Experience* (1984), is an excellent survey. The English background can be traced in Sheila Rowbotham, *Hidden From History* (1976), and Lawrence Stone, *Family, Sex and Marriage in England, 1500–1800* (1979). See also Laurel Thatcher Ulrich, *Good Wives: Image and Reality in the Lives of Women of Northern New England, 1650–1750* (1982). Older but still valuable studies include Alice Clark, *Working Life of Women in the Seventeenth Century* (1919), and Julia C. Spruill, *Women's Life and Work in the Southern Colonies* (1938).

The problems of a mature economy and diverse society are explored in Richard L. Bushman, *From Puritan to Yankee: Character and the Social Order to Connecticut, 1690–1775* (1967); Charles Grant, *Democracy in the Frontier Town of Kent* (1961); and Stephanie G. Wolf, *Urban Village: Germantown, Pennsylvania, 1683–1800* (1977).

Masters and Slaves

Rhys Isaac, *The Transformation of Virginia, 1740–1790* (1983), graphically evokes the character of Chesapeake life. Daniel Black Smith, *Inside the Great House* (1980), explores family life among the elite, while Paul G. E. Clemens, *The Atlantic Economy and Maryland's Eastern Shore* (1980), depicts important shifts in the Chesapeake economy. Carl Bridenbaugh, *Myths and Realities: Societies of the Colonial South* (1952), surveys regional variations within the South.

The development of American slavery is traced in Peter H. Wood, *Black Majority: Negroes in Colonial South Carolina* (1974); Gerald W. Mullin, *Flight and Rebellion: Slave Resistance in Eighteenth-Century Virginia* (1972); and A. Leon Higginbotham, Jr., *In the Matter of Color: Race and the American Legal Process* (1978). See also Edgar J. Mcmanus, *Black Bondage in the North* (1973), and Richard Price, ed., *Maroon Societies: Rebel Slave Communities in the Americas* (1973).

Toward a New Social Order

David Galenson, *White Servitude in Colonial America* (1981), offers a statistical analysis of English indentured servants; it complements the classic study of Abbot E. Smith, *Colonists in Bondage* (1947). For studies of other migrants, see R. J. Dickson, *Ulster Emigration to Colonial America, 1718–1775* (1966); Jon Butler, *The Hugenots in America* (1983); and James H. Kettner, *The Development of American Citizenship, 1608–1870* (1978). Other valuable works include Frederick Klees, *Pennsylvania Dutch* (1951); C. C. Graham, *Colonists from Scotland* (1956); and James G. Leyburn, *The Scotch Irish* (1962).

For the Quaker experience in Pennsylvania, see Edwin B. Bronner, *William Penn's "Holy Experiment"* (1962); Frederick B. Tolles, *Metting House and Counting House* (1948) and *Quakers and Atlantic Culture* (1960); and J. William Frost, *The Quaker Family in America* (1973). Good discussions of Pennsylvania politics include Gary B. Nash, *Quakers and Politics, 1681–1726* (1968), and Alan Tully, *William Penn's Legacy: Politics and Social Structure in Provincial Pennsylvania, 1726–1755* (1978).

Abbott Lowell Cummings, *The Framed Houses of Massachusetts Bay* (1979), is a detailed study of surviving houses. Additional material can be found in Thomas Waterman, *The Dwellings of Colonial America* (1950), and Hugh S. Morrison, *Early American Architecture* (1952). The "material culture" of early America has become a subject for serious scholarly work. A fine introduction to the subject is James B. Deetz, *In Small Things Forgotten* (1977).

PRINT CULTURE AND POPULAR IMAGINATION

Most preindustrial Americans read books printed only in black and white. Therefore, this photographic essay contains no pictures of illustrated manuscripts, no brilliantly colored paintings, and no richly toned watercolors or engravings. To capture the essence of the visual world of early Americans, everything here appears in black and white, as the people of the time would have seen it.

But not quite; for we perceive these pictures differently than their original audience did. Pictures exist in people's minds as well as on the pages of books, and the mental world of early American men and women differed greatly from our own. Their world was filled with strange supernatural powers and astonishing demons (plate 1) that took on color and force in the imagination. To recapture their universe of thought and belief will strain our imaginations considerably.

Samuel Sewall will help us. Sewall was born in England in 1652 and educated at Harvard College in Massachusetts. He married the daughter of John Hull, the leading merchant of the colony, and enjoyed a long and distinguished life as a merchant, politician, and judge. Sewall was also a devout Puritan. From 1674 until his death in 1730, he kept a detailed diary.* Through this rich

*This essay is indebted to David D. Hall, "The Mental World of Samuel Sewall." The *Proceedings* of the Massachusetts Historical Society 92 (1980): 21–44.

PLATE 1
The woodcuts that illustrated editions of *The Divine Comedy* by Dante Alighieri (1265–1321) shaped European conceptions of Hell for centuries. This Florentine engraving from *Monte Sancto di Dio* (circa 1491) shows a variety of demons persecuting Christians condemned to Hell for eternity because of their earthly sins. (Antonio Bettini. The Metropolitan Museum of Art. Harris Brisbane Dick Fund, 1925)

historical source, we can enter his mind and glimpse the imagination of his age.

The Christian Bible shaped Sewall's view of the world. When a woman choked on a piece of meat and died, Sewall immediately thought of a verse in the first Book of Corinthians: "Whether therefore ye eat, or drink, or whatsoever ye do, do all to the glory of God." More significantly, he interpreted ordinary bits of news from Europe in terms of the Biblical prophecies in the Book of Revelation. Reading of the Marquis de Langalerie's project to found a new Protestant colony, Sewall quickly concluded "that he is the person God will [use] for pulling down the Throne of Antichrist, [as] is so designed in the Revelation."

Sewall's pattern of thought reflected the religious sensibility depicted in Albrecht Dürer's woodcut of the Four Horsemen of the Apocalypse (plate 2). The movement of earthly events was not random, Sewall wrote, but was part of a larger rhythm of life and of time, "GOD's time." So, too, with the happenings of everyday life. Sewell was perplexed and troubled when Joseph Dudley received exactly 666 votes in an election, for such a repetitive number could not be accidental. Likewise the sudden crash of a glass on the floor: "How suddenly and with surprise can God destroy." The natural world was especially revelatory of the Divine Will. "At Boston upon the Lord's Day. . . . about 6 P.M.," Sewell wrote in his diary,

PLATE 2
The Black Death of the 1340s killed millions of Europeans, and famines in subsequent centuries took the lives of millions more. Many Christians believed these events prefigured the "Last Things" predicted in The Revelation of John in the Bible. This woodcut by the famous German artist Albrecht Durer (1471–1528) shows the Four Horsemen of the Apocalypse— pestilence, war, famine, and death—trampling princes and peasants alike. Similar woodcuts illustrated Martin Luther's German translations of the Bible and later English editions as well. (The New York Public Library Picture Collection)

PLATE 3
A wave of religiously inspired violence swept over Europe between 1500 and 1650. Catholic and Protestant princes and peoples fought bitter wars against each other and killed thousands of alleged wizards and witches. This woodcut of 1555 shows three witches being burned at the stake. Reflecting popular belief, it depicts the devil as a grotesque animal with the power to possess the souls of his followers. (The New York Public Library Picture Collection)

a Noble *Rainbow* was seen in the Cloud, after great Thundering, and Darkness, and Rain. . . . I hope this is a sure Token that CHRIST Remembers his Covenant for his beloved *Jews* [the Puritans] under their Captivity and Dispersion; and that He will make haste to prepare for them a City that has foundations, whose Builder and Maker is GOD.

This optimistic outcome was not assured. Like most religious men and women in Europe and America, Sewell interpreted events as the outcome of a titanic struggle between God and the devil (plate 3). Satan was both powerful and pervasive, as Sew-

all's friend Cotton Mather had demonstrated in an influential book on witchcraft. God's ways were themselves mysterious. Sewell spent an evening intently listening to Mather "mentioning that more Ministers Houses than others proportionably had been smitten with Lightning; inquiring what the meaning of God should be in it."

Sewell's reading provided hints of the possible supernatural meaning of natural events. In *The Day of Doom* (plate 4), which Sewell read, the New England pastor Michael Wigglesworth vividly evoked Christ's return to the earth amid the crashing thunder and blaring trumpets mentioned in the Book of Revelation. Henceforth, Sewell was alive to

the significance of sounds. When a great earthquake shook New England in 1720, he reported that someone in Portsmouth had "heard a fine musical sound, like the sound of a Trumpet at a distance." Perhaps the Day of Doom was at hand.

As a devout Christian, Sewall tried to convince Massachusetts legislators to replace the pagan day-names "Tuesday, Thursday, and Satterday" with the numbers "Third, fifth and seventh," because "the Week [was] a memorial of the Creation perfected in so many distinct days." Yet, Sewall shared the pagan belief in a world full of invisible spiritual forces that affected human lives and history (plate 5). Before building an addition to his

The Day of Doom:
OR, A
DESCRIPTION
Of the Great and Laſt
Judgment.
WITH
A SHORT DISCOURSE
ABOUT
ETERNITY.

Eccleſ. 12. 14.
For God ſhall bring every work into Judgment,
with every ſecret thing, whether it be good,
or whether it be evil.

LONDON,
Printed by *W G.* for *John Sims,* at the *Kings-*
Head at *Sweetings-Alley-end* in *Cornhill,*
next Houſe to the *Royal-Exchange,* 1673.

PLATE 4
Michael Wiggleworth's *Day of Doom* was first printed in Cambridge, Massachusetts, in 1662 and immediately struck a popular nerve. The first edition of 1,800 copies sold out within a year, and Wiggleworth's poetic reflections on the prospect of death and damnation were reprinted in many American and English editions. Only a few copies survive, probably because these books were read so intensively that they simply disintegrated from use. (The New York Public Library)

---

1 6 7 8.

The Dominion of the Moon in Man's Body
(according to Aſtronomers)

The *Head* and *Face* the *Ram* doth crave,
The *Neck* and *Throat,* the Bull will have,
The loving *Twins* do rule the *Hands,*
The *Breſt* and *Sides* in *Cancer* bands,
The *Heart* and *Back* the *Lyon* claims,
Bowels and *Belly Virgo* gains;
The *Reyns* and *Loyns* are *Libra's* part,
The *Secrets Scorpio's* are by Art;

PLATE 5
Almanacs, read by tens of thousands of Americans each year, contained pagan as well as Christian symbolism. This picture of the Man of Signs appeared in John Foster's Almanac of 1678. The accompanying poem explains the impact of the astrological signs of the zodaic on various parts of the human body. (American Antiquarian Society)

house, Sewell consulted with a minister to see if the times were propitious. He subsequently drove a pin into the floor of the new dwelling, a ritual act rooted in pagan folklore. Years later, he placed two wooden carvings of "cherubims heads" on his gate-posts to signify the presence of protecting spiritual forces. Like most colonial Americans, Sewall lived in an enchanted world.

Religious imagery and belief in supernatural forces pervaded the popular culture of New England for another century. It found expression in newspaper and privately published reports of physical miracles, such as the "remarkable Recovery of Mrs. Mary Read" (plate 6), and in political imagery during the American Revolution (plate 7).

By this time, however, many educated colonists no longer accepted a supernatural world view. Around 1700, the culture of well-read Europeans and Americans diverged from that of the common people. The "New

PLATE 6
Even in the 1760s, many Americans believed that the world was filled by supernatural forces, controlled by the Devil or by God. Accounts of spectacular celestial events or of miraculous recoveries, such as that of Mrs. Mary Read, commanded a wide readership. The final sentence of this account refers to Dr. Watt's hymnbook, a bestselling collection of sacred songs that greatly influenced popular religious culture. (American Antiquarian Society)

An Account of the remarkable Recovery of Mrs. MARY READ, of *Rehoboth*, to the Ufe of her Limbs, of which fhe had been deprived Three Years.

MARY READ having been confined to her Bed Three Years fuccefsively, namely, from June, 1766, to June, 1769, and never walked a Step; on the 24th Day of July, 1769, as fhe lay meditating, thefe Words came to her like a Voice audibly fpoken, " Daughter be of good Cheer, thy Sins are forgiven thee, arife and walk :" They were repeated Three Times over, which caufed her to think it was the Voice of God fpeaking to her by his Word and Spirit. But this Queftion was put in her Mind, How do you know it is the Voice of God ? With this Suggeftion, It is not the Voice of God. Then fhe doubted whether it was God's Voice or not ; upon which thefe Words came unto her,---" It is I the Lord that fpeaketh unto thee,---fear not." She ftill hefitating about the Matter, faid, I truft that God fpoke to me by Way of Command. The Words were repeated the Second Time,---" It is I, the Lord of Hofts, that fpeaketh unto thee, arife and walk, fear not."---As fhe was greatly folicitous to know whether it was the Voice of God or not, the Words were repeated over the Third Time,---" It is the Lord of Hofts, the God of Ifrael that commandeth thee,---Arife and walk, fear not." This was backed with the Words of Samuel, " Behold, to obey is better than Sacrifice, and to hearken than the Fat of Rams." This confirmed her that it was the Voice of God, and his almighty Power. Now fo ... Power of God ! For while the Words were repeating, the Ufe of her Limbs were reftored to her again ; the Cords and Sinews on one Side of her, which had been fhrunk up fix or feven Inches, for fo long a Time, were then ftretched out, and fhe became ftraight, and received Strength, and immediately rofe up from her Bed and walked ! And now fhe defires that all People would praife GOD for this miraculous and glorious Deliverance vouchfafed unto her. Afterward the 55th Hymn of Doctor Watts's, in the firft Book, was brought fweetly to her Mind.

120

Learning" of the European Enlightenment had appeared not only in learned scientific treatises, but also in widely read almanacs (plate 8). Sometimes the worlds of Enlightenment thought and of popular religious belief appeared on the same page, in apparent harmony (plate 9 on page 122).

The social reality showed a more pronounced change. By the time of Sewall's death in 1730, educated English and American men and women had detached themselves from the old popular culture. They stopped believing in witchcraft, so public prosecution of conjurers and woman healers stopped. They no longer participated in popular fairs and carnivals because, as one French writer explained, "all these diversions show a folly and a coarseness which makes the taste for them resemble that of pigs." Instead, wealthy and well-educated people in Europe and its colonies created a social world defined by class, marked by symmetry and

PLATE 7
The cover of this almanac from 1774 suggests the continuing evocative power of traditional religious imagery. Death takes the life of "the wicked Stateman, or the Traitor to his Country," (probably Thomas Hutchinson, the much-vilified American-born Governor of Massachusetts), while a demon displays a list of his crimes. (American Antiquarian Society)

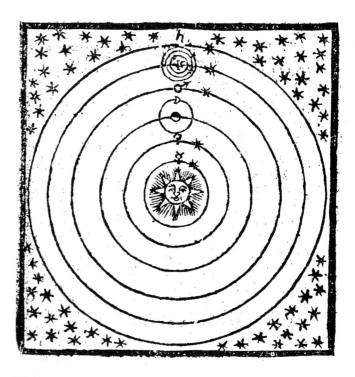

PLATE 8
John Foster's almanac of 1675 contained this picture of the Copernican System. Confuting the medieval Christian world view, it pictures the sun rather than the earth at the center of the universe. The text presents a detailed scientific summary of the annual orbits of the planets, anticipating Isaac Newton's gravitional explanation of celestial movements in his *Mathematical Principles of Natural Philosophy* (London, 1687). (American Antiquarian Society)

order in architecture and by cultivation and grace in religious belief and personal relations (plate 10).

Most important of all, educated people embraced a scientific view of the world. Benjamin Franklin had much less formal education than Samuel Sewall, but he read widely in enlightened political and scientific literature, and his own works were praised by European intellectuals. Unlike Cotton Mather, Franklin did not conceive of lightning as a supernatural sign of God's displeasure but as a natural force that could be rendered harmless by human ingenuity (plate 11). The Christian Bible did not shape his imagination. In fact, as Franklin explained in his *Autobiography*, "from the different books I read, I began to doubt of Revelation itself." An enchanted religious world view was no longer central to the print culture of Franklin and other educated Americans, or to their imaginations. The sound of trumpets no longer announced the end of the world.

PLATE 9
By the 1720s, evidence of the European scientific enlightenment had reached America. This extract from Nathaniel Bowen's almanac uses mathematical reasoning to explain why London experienced a "Great Eclipse" of the sun in November 1722, while Boston was only partially darkened. As Bowen's concluding spiritual verse indicates, the new scientific outlook coexisted with an older, religiously based understanding of the world. (American Antiquarian Society)

you see A, Represents the Center of the Earth, B, the Body of the Moon, C, the Center of the Sun, D, that part of the Earth which we Inhabit : here we see, he that has the Sun right over head, (or in his Zenith,) has the Sun wholly hid by the dark body of the Moon at B, When at the same time he that stands at D, injoys the whole body of the Sun above the top of the Moon. *As for instance*, in the Great Eclipse in *November* 1722. in the City of *London*, but about 6 Digits, or the Lower, or South-half of the Sun is darkned, when at *Boston* above Eleven Digits & half of the Upper or North side of the Sun is darkned, leaving only a small Glimmer of Light on the Lower or Southerly Rim of the Sun ; and if our Lover of the Mathamaticks had been Master of Knowledge enough to have Calculated that Eclipse, I dare ingage he would not have contented himself with so senseless a Reduction.

THE weary Pilgrim oft doth Ask & Know,
How far he's come, how far he has to go.
His way is Tedious, and his Heart's opprest,
And his desire is to be at Rest.
Our Life's a Journey, yet fond Man Delays,
T' enquire out the Number of his Days.
He cares, not he, how slow his Hours spend,
His Journey's better than his Journeys End.

Another Year, (if GOD preserve my Life) you shall hear further from, Yours,

From my House at Marblehead, *the 20th of Septemb.* 1722. N. BOWEN.

PLATE 10
This well-ordered scene from George Bickman's *Universal Penman* (London, 1733) symbolizes the emergence of a distinct upper-class culture. Accomplished, genteel musicians perform for a wealthy family at their country estate. The house in the background has a perfectly symmetrical facade, underlining the desire of members of the upper class for an ordered existence. Similar scenes, perhaps less lavish, typified the amusements of wealthy colonial Americans. (The Newberry Library, Chicago)

PLATE 11
Franklin's *Experiments and Observations on Electricity* (1751) and his kite experiments won international acclaim. A French nobleman devised this elaborate apparatus for safely drawing "electrical fire" from the clouds, while the English scientist Joseph Priestly praised Franklin's demonstration of the identity of lightning and electricity as the greatest scientific discovery since the time of Newton. (American Philosophical Society)

5

THE CONVERGENCE OF EUROPE AND AMERICA

*B*eginning in 1740, a series of dramatic changes shook the American colonies. Within two decades, these upheavals greatly altered the colonists' religious, economic, and political lives. First, the intellectual and spiritual environment underwent dramatic change. Many educated Americans adopted political and philosophical principles advanced by European thinkers associated with a period called the Enlightenment, or the Age of Reason. These men and women took an increasingly secular, rather than a religious, view of human society. Simultaneously, thousands of Americans joined a great religious revival that made Protestant Christianity a more vital force in colonial life. Second, the American economy changed in character. A boom in exports and imports increased the importance of merchants and of commercial agricultural production in seaboard areas. At the same time, the rapid settlement of isolated frontier regions created large districts whose production did not exceed subsistence levels. Third, the movement into the interior sparked political confrontation and armed violence. Westward expansion led to new battles with native Americans; rebellions by frontier settlers against eastern colonial governments; and a major military conflict, the French and Indian War (1754–63).

These events added a new complexity to American life. On the surface, they appear dis-similar and even contradictory. Yet they have in common a European source or connection. Enlightenment thought and religious revivalism spread from Europe to America. Likewise, the easy availability of British manufactured products and credit greatly assisted the expansion of colonial trade. It also subsidized westward settlement, especially in the Chesapeake colonies. In addition, the French and Indian War tied the future of the colonies to the diplomatic struggles of Europe. By 1765, the American settlements were no longer isolated colonies. They had become dynamic, active participants in the social and political life of the larger European world.

The Enlightenment and Pietistic Religion

Ideas never exist in a social vacuum. They reflect the conditions or values of individuals or groups. Wealthy planters and merchants, the ministers who preached to them, and some urban artisans adopted the outlook of educated men and women in Europe. These beliefs included the Enlightenment's emphasis on the power of human reason to shape the character of the world. Most ministers and farmers were more receptive to the ideas of the current religious revival, which stressed the dependence of human beings on God and the necessity for devout, pious submission to his will. These two opposite conceptions of the world, and the social groups that adopted them, came into conflict during the generation-long series of religious revivals known as the Great Awakening.

Magic and Science

When a measles epidemic struck Boston in the 1710s, the eminent Puritan minister Cotton Mather sought a religious remedy. The disease could be avoided, Mather suggested, "by getting the Blood of the Great Passover sprinkled on our Houses." Two decades earlier, his father, Increase Mather, had argued that God's power gave some men supernatural sight on Tuesdays and Fridays. The Deity's intervention also explained the mystery of the "inchanted pin," which could penetrate the skin without drawing blood. Like most Christians in the preindustrial world, the Mathers believed in a God who intervened directly in the world.

Most Americans were also influenced by astrological interpretations of events. As farmers planted their crops, they consulted almanacs that contained elaborate charts. These charts, along with diagrams and pictures, correlated the movements of the planets and the stars with the signs of the zodiac. By deciphering the charts, farmers determined the best times to plant crops, to get their children married, or to make other important decisions. Astrology had its source in pagan interpretations of the world. According to these views, the natural world was filled with spirits and powers that could be used for good or evil. Swedish settlers in Pennsylvania ascribed magical powers to the great white mulleen, a common wild plant. When they had a fever, the visiting Swedish naturalist Peter Kalm reported, they "tie the leaves around their feet and arms."

Organized Christian churches tolerated this magical and partly pagan view of the world because their own doctrines included similar beliefs. For example, Catholics believed in *transubstantiation*, a priest's ability to change bread and wine into Christ's body and blood. Protestants received many celestial warnings from God, such as blazing stars, monstrous births, and rainstorms of blood. Yet there were also many points of tension between the Christian and pagan viewpoints. Ordinary men and women occasionally claimed special powers as

ENLIGHTENMENT SCIENCE
Denis Diderot published this illustration of a chemical laboratory in his famous *Encyclopedia* (1751). The great French *philosophe* sought to "collect all the knowledge scattered over the face of the earth." Enlightenment thinkers hoped this knowledge would yield general scientific laws and the true principles of social organization. (Giraudon/Art Resource)

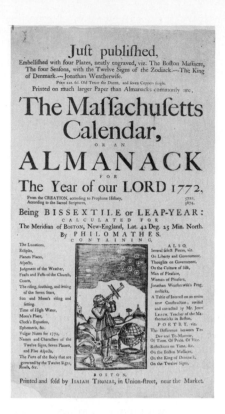

Just published,

Embellished with four Plates, neatly engraved, viz. The Boston Massacre, The four Seasons, with the Twelve Signs of the Zodiack.---The King of Denmark.--- Jonathan Weatherwife.

Price 22s. 6d. Old Tenor the Dozen, and seven Coppers single.

Printed on much larger Paper than Almanacks commonly are,

The Massachusetts Calendar,

OR AN

ALMANACK

FOR

The Year of our LORD 1772,

From the CREATION, according to Prophane History,
According to the Sacred Scriptures,

Being BISSEXTILE or LEAP-YEAR:

CALCULATED FOR

The Meridian of BOSTON, New-England, Lat. 42 Deg. 25 Min. North.

By PHILOMATHES.

CONTAINING,

BOSTON:

Printed and sold by ISAIAH THOMAS, in Union-street, near the Market.

THE PAGAN SYMBOLIC UNIVERSE

Next to the Bible, almanacs were the most widely purchased and widely read books in colonial America. In addition to information on the seasons and farming practices, they usually contained elaborate pagan astrological charts, "the Twelve Signs, Seven Planets, and Five Aspects," mentioned at the lower left of the almanac cover. Like the man "sighting" the stars, many Americans subscribed to the pagan belief that the movement of celestial bodies directly affected human events. (American Antiquarian Society)

diviners or healers. Their alleged ability to influence events through incantations, spells, or elaborate rituals earned respect in some places and hatred in others. Fearful of challenges to their own spiritual authority, New England ministers attacked these people as "wise" or "cunning." They branded them as witches or as consorts of the devil, the evil spirit of Christianity. Civil authorities hanged fourteen people as witches in Massachusetts and Connecticut between 1647 and 1662, and the belief in witchcraft remained strong for another generation. In 1692, a religious group dominated by poor farmers in Salem, Massachusetts, used charges of witchcraft to attack fellow church members who were more

successful economically. Massachusetts authorities arrested 175 men and women, and executed 22 of them as wizards or witches. Fear and suspicion spread into the neighboring village of Andover. Its people "were much addicted to sorcery," claimed one observer, for "there were forty men in it that could raise the Devil as well as any astrologer."

Gradually, a more rational and scientific view of the world supplanted the spiritual perspective. This change first occurred among educated Americans. By the 1720s, Cotton Mather joined with Zabdiel Boylston, a prominent Boston physician, in supporting the new technique of inoculation as a deterrent to smallpox. Ministers and lay people with more traditionalist views opposed inoculation. They argued that only God had the power to decide life and death; human interference was both presumptuous and useless. The medical community was also divided. At first, William Douglass, another Boston physician, feared that inoculation would spread the disease rather than contain it. He was soon dissuaded by factual, scientific evidence. Few of the inoculated people had died, Douglass now reassured the suspicious Boston population, whereas "an exact scrutiny" revealed that 6,000 others "have now had the small Pox and of these 844 died."

Both inoculation and Douglass' mode of factual reasoning reflected the impact of the "new learning" of the European Enlightenment. The Enlightenment was a complex, many-sided intellectual movement, but it was based on a few fundamental principles. The most important of these were a belief in the power of human reason, the existence of laws in nature, and the progressive improvement of society. For example, the English scientist Isaac Newton explained the movement of the planets around the sun in mathematical terms. Newton's laws and principles, such as that of gravity, described how the world could operate without the constant intervention of a God. Other philosophers of the Enlightenment looked for natural causes for disease and various worldly events. In his *Two Treatises of Government* (1689), the English philosopher John Locke argued that political authority did not result from divine powers given to monarchs, but from "social compacts" among people. Likewise, Locke's influential *An Essay Concerning Human Understanding* (1690) proposed that ideas themselves were not innate or God given; they came from experience. The mind at birth was a *tabula rasa* (blank sheet), according to Locke. This sheet was gradually filled by the data conveyed by the senses and arranged by the mind. Many educated American colonists adopted these natural or environmental explanations of disease, political institutions, and human development. "I am sensible much is dependent on education," Elizabeth Smith, an upper-class American mother, wrote in 1750, for "the Infant Mind, I believe, is a blank, that easily receives my impression."

This "new learning" prompted some ministers to revise the intellectual foundations of their religious principles. Jonathan Edwards, a Congregational minister in Northampton, Massachusetts, emerged as America's first major philosopher. Edwards, an effective revivalist preacher and an extraordinarily learned man, was familiar not only with Locke, but also with the French philosopher René Descartes and other European thinkers. Edwards feared that Locke's empirical psychology—the importance given to material facts—threatened religious orthodoxy. Repudiating this aspect of Locke's thought, Edwards argued that the universe consisted of God's ideas; the world existed only because it existed in God's mind. However, Edwards did use Locke's emphasis on the data conveyed by the senses to explain and justify emotional preaching. By stimulating the passions of his audience, he argued, a minister could make individuals more receptive to God's grace.

Other New England ministers used Enlightenment modes of thought to discuss many aspects of life. In the 1720s, John Wise of Ipswich, Massachusetts, defended New England Congregationalism by using Locke's principles. Just as the "social compact" formed the basis of civil society, Wise argued, so the covenant among the members of a congregation established the legitimacy of a religious community. In 1761, Ezra Stiles, the president of Yale College, maintained that the "laws of human increase" were "as properly a subject of systematical Science as botony." In strikingly modern language, Stiles advocated "the classing and generalizing of experiments or facts, and pursuing their obvious inductions to certain general Laws; with which we may be prepared for useful and interesting applications."

JONATHAN EDWARDS (1703–1758)
Edwards was America's first major philosopher. As a devout Christian conscious of his intellectual gifts, he struggled to achieve true humility. "I have greatly longed of late, for a broken heart, and to lie low before God," he wrote in 1739. "I cannot bear the thought of being no more humble than other christians. . . . I am greatly afflicted with a proud and self-righteous spirit." (Joseph Badger. *Jonathan Edwards*. Yale University Art Gallery. Bequest of Eugene Phelps Edwards)

Implicit in Stiles's remarks was the Enlightenment belief in the improvement of society through purposeful human thought and action. In 1751, Quaker and Anglican merchants in Philadelphia had used private donations and public funds to found the Hospital for the Sick Poor. In 1767, leading residents built the Bettering House to shelter the aged and disabled and to offer employment to the poor. The founders intended these institutions to reduce taxes paid for relief for the poor, and so their establishment reflected the interests of wealthy Philadelphians. But the hospital and the Bettering House also stood as symbols of Enlightenment reform. They testified to the growing confidence among the educated classes of their ability to control the social environment.

The growing cultural presence of the colonial elite manifested itself in a variety of clubs, schools, and publications. Beginning in the

1740s, wealthy men subscribed to a variety of journals, including the *General*, the *New York*, and the *Massachusetts* magazines. By 1765, nearly every colony had a regularly published newspaper. Private schools and public libraries spread, and the efforts of various religious sects more than doubled the number of American colleges. Presbyterians founded the College of New Jersey (Princeton) in 1747, and New York Anglicans followed with King's College (Columbia) in 1754. Baptists established the College of Rhode Island (Brown) in 1764, and members of the Dutch Reformed Church founded Queen's College (Rutgers), in New Jersey two years later. Other educational innovators created a medical college in Philadelphia in 1765 and one at King's College in 1767.

Educated Americans familiar with the "new learning" often played a leading role in the founding of church-related colleges. They believed that Enlightenment thought was compatible with their religious values. Actually, it was, given their conception of God and the world. Many merchants and urban artisans were deists, who maintained that God had created the world but allowed it to operate according to the laws of nature. In their view, human reason could establish the principles of natural religion; mankind was not depraved but possessed the capacity for righteousness as well as for sin. These well-to-do Americans and their ministers were solidly established in a number of urban congregations. They stood proud and confident, but also isolated. Most of the population still adhered to older, less scientific views of God and the universe.

Pietism

European *pietism* greatly strengthened traditional American congregations. This eighteenth-century religious movement placed little stress on theological dogma. Pietist preachers emphasized the moral reformation of society, emotional religious services, and a mystical union with God. They appealed to the hearts, not the minds, of their listeners. These teachings attracted peasants, artisans, and laborers, who joined churches by the thousands. Pietistic sects were well established in many German states by the 1720s. The forceful leadership of John Wesley, who advocated disciplined "methods" of worship, later

EVANGELIST GEORGE WHITEFIELD
No painting ever captured Whitefield's magic. When he spoke to a crowd near Philadelphia, his sermon "was sharper than a two-edged sword. The bitter crys and groans were enough to pierce the hardest heart. Some of the people were pale as death; others were wringing their hands; others lying on the ground; . . . and most lifting their eyes to heaven and crying to God for mercy." (John Wollaston. *George Whitefield*. National Portrait Gallery, London)

created a large body of pietistic Methodists within the Church of England.

German migrants brought pietism to America. Attracted by the guarantee of religious freedom, hundreds of German sectarians settled in Pennsylvania. Inspired by their example and his own European experience, the migrant Dutch minister Jacob Frelinghuysen led a revival in the Dutch Reformed Church in New Jersey during the 1720s. He stressed the necessity of a conversion "crisis" to assure salvation. Frelinghuysen encouraged private prayer meetings among the converted, and lay preaching by members of the congregation. During the 1730s, two other clergymen, William Tennent and his son Gilbert, copied his innovations. The brothers led a series of revivals among the Scotch-Irish Presbyterians of New Jersey and Pennsylvania.

THE RELIGIOUS TRAVAIL OF NATHAN COLE, CONNECTICUT FARMER

When I saw Mr. Whitfield come upon the Scaffold he lookt almost Angelical; a young, Slim, slender Youth before some thousands of people with a bold undaunted Countenance, and my hearing how God was with him every where as he came along it Solemnized my mind; and put me into a trembling fear before he began to preach; for he looked as if he was Cloathed with Authority from the Great God; . . . and a sweet solleme solemnity sat upon his brow and my hearing him preach, gave me a heart wound; By Gods blessing: my old Foundation was broken up, and I saw that my righteousness would not save me; then I was convinced of the doctrine of Election: and went right to quarrelling with God about it; because that all I could do would not save me; and he had decreed from Eternity who should be saved and who not: I began to think I was not Elected, and that God made some for heaven and me for hell. And I thought God was not Just in so doing, I thought I did not stand on even Ground with others, if as I thought; I was made to be damned; My heart then rose against God exceedingly, for his making me for hell; Now this distress lasted Almost two years—Poor—Me—Miserable me. . . .

Hell fire was most always in my mind; and I have hundreds of times put my fingers into my pipe when I have been smoking to feel how fire felt: And to see how my Body could bear to lye in Hell fire for ever and ever. . . .

And while these thoughts were in my mind God appeared unto me and made me Skringe: before whose face the heavens and the earth fled away; and I was Shrinked into nothing; I knew not whether I was in the body or out, I seemed to hang in open Air before God, and he seemed to Speak to me in an angry and Sovereign way what won't you trust your Soul with God; My heart answered Oh yes, yes, yes; . . .

I was set free, my distress was gone, and I was filled with a pineing desire to see Christs own words in the bible; . . .

I saw was the 15th Chap: John—on Christs own words and they spake to my very heart and every doubt and scriple that rose in my heart about the truth of Gods word was took right off; . . .

I got the bible up under my Chin and hugged it; it was sweet and lovely; the word was nigh me in my hand, then I began to pray and to praise God; . . .

In New England, the revival of religious enthusiasm stemmed from the strong regional tradition of Calvinist Puritanism, rather than a European influence. Beginning in the late seventeenth century, ministers developed a new type of sermon called the *jeremiad*. Named after the angry Biblical prophet Jeremiah, these sermons warned that God would punish Christians who lacked fervor. Cotton Mather created youth societies to encourage early piety. Hundreds of young people joined the revivals led by Jonathan Edwards in the Connecticut River Valley during the 1730s. Like the revivals in New Jersey, these spiritual awakenings were primarily regional events with diverse social and theological roots.

Then, beginning in 1740, the young English evangelist George Whitefield induced a massive outpouring of religious enthusiasm throughout the colonies. Huge crowds greeted Whitefield as he traveled from Georgia to Massachusetts. "Religion is become the Subject of most Conversations," the Pennsylvania *Gazette* reported in June 1740. "No books are in Request but those of Piety and Devotion; and instead of idle Songs and Ballads, the People are everywhere entertaining themselves with Psalms, Hymns and Spiritual Songs." By the time Whitefield reached Boston, the Reverend Benjamin Coleman noted, the people were "ready to receive him as an angel of God."

Whitefield's life symbolized the international scope of the religious revival. A disciple of Wesley in England, Whitefield experienced conversion after reading German pietistic literature. His greatest success came in America. "He looked almost Angelical—a young, slim, slender youth," according to one Connecticut farmer. Whitefield spoke magnificently and, like most evangelical ministers, did not read his sermons from carefully composed notes. He spoke vividly from memory, raising his voice to emphasize important points. He evoked an emotional response by the use of striking Biblical metaphors and sharp gestures. As an unsympathetic observer described the performance of Daniel Bliss, one of Whitefield's followers:

> Toward the Close of his Sermon he began to raise his Voice and to use many extravagant Gestures; and then began a considerable groaning and then the Congregation were in the utmost Confusion, some crying out, some laughing, and Bliss still roaring to them to come to Christ, they answering, *I will, I will, I'm coming, I'm coming.*

Whitefield's sermons moved thousands to tears and remorse. Hearing the great evangelist preach, said Nathan Cole, a Connecticut farmer, "gave my heart a wound, by God's blessing. I was made to be damned. My heart then rose against God exceedingly for his making me for hell. This distress lasted almost two years."

Like Cole, hundreds of men and women made religion a major part of their lives. New England ministers told packed congregations that they were "undone, helpless, and hopeless creatures" who had to renounce their pride and humble themselves before an omnipotent God. As Jonathan Edwards proclaimed in his famous printed sermon, *Sinners in the Hands of An Angry God* (1742), God held them "by a thin thread over the abyss of *hell.*" This fear of damnation drove the revival forward in Calvinist New England. In the middle colonies, influenced by the more optimistic message of European pietism, the hope of heaven swelled the size of congregations. Whitefield's "New Light" tours transformed the regional revivals into the Great Awakening, a vast upheaval that permanently altered the character of American religion.

FIGURE 5.1 CHURCH GROWTH BY DENOMINATION, 1700–1780

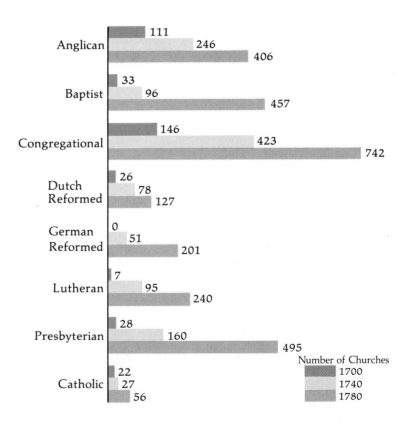

Like all cultural explosions, the Great Awakening had severe critics. "Old Light" Christians condemned the "cryings out, faintings and convulsions" produced by emotional preaching. Influential urban theologians, such as Charles Chauncey of Boston, accused the "New Lights" of interpreting the scriptures "by impulses and impressions," rather than through careful reading. Many ministers resented the New Light laity who invaded their parishes. Inspired by Whitefield's example, dozens of farmers, devout mothers, and untutored artisans roamed the countryside, preaching to all who would listen. The Connecticut assembly heeded these Old Light protests and prohibited itinerant preachers from speaking to established congregations without the minister's permission. When Whitefield returned to the colony in 1744, he found many pulpits closed to him.

These religious divisions shattered church institutions. The Dutch Reformed Church split apart. New Light congregations in the Hackensack Valley of New Jersey and in New York fiercely resisted conservative Dutch groups who looked for support to church authorities in Holland. New Light followers of Gilbert Tennent established a "log cabin" college in Princeton, New Jersey, but conservative Presbyterians used their power in regional synods to refuse ordination to the new graduates. New Lights in New England established 125 "separatist" churches by 1754. Most of these new congregations reaffirmed the authority of the laity over doctrine and made new members testify to a conversion experience. Many of these New Light Congregational churches then split over the issue of infant versus adult baptism. Members who believed in adult baptism—as a symbol that followed the conversion experience—joined Baptist churches.

The religious institutions and ethnic diversity of the middle colonies had long encouraged toleration. The Great Awakening strengthened the trend toward liberty of conscience and extended it to New England. New Lights stoutly resisted attempts by civil and church authorities to preserve a single "orthodox" standard of belief and behavior. "I shall bring glory to God in my bonds," a dissident preacher wrote from a Massachusetts jail, "the Lord hath made those bonds

A BLACKSMITH TURNED PREACHER
Inspired by Whitefield, hundreds of untrained men and women became preachers. Established ministers branded them "illiterate men of ordinary abilities," both to preserve religious orthodoxy and their own social status. As a Virginia Old Light put it, "We are often by birth, and always by education and profession, gentlemen." (Benjamin Henry Latrobe. Maryland Historical Society)

my liberty." In 1750, New Lights won repeal of a Connecticut law curtailing itinerant preachers and then questioned all government control of religion. According to the influential Baptist preacher Isaac Backus, "God never allowed any civil state upon earth to impose religious taxes." Such political debate and agitation had an effect. By 1760, though Congregationalism remained the legally established religion of New England, members of New Light and Baptist congregations could assign their religious taxes to support their own ministers.

The Great Awakening thus strengthened religious institutions while altering their character. Church membership became more of a voluntary act, and ministers lost some of their traditional authority. In his influential pamphlet *The Dangers of an Unconverted Ministry* (1740), Gilbert Tennent maintained that the conversion experience, not theological training, qualified ministers to hold their office. Such pietistic attacks on authority, together with their emphasis on the equality of all men and women before God, frightened many Americans who had wealth and high social status. Charles Chauncey warned of "strong attempts to destroy all property, to make all things common, wives as well as goods." Another conservative charged that the New Lights were "Turners of the World upside down." These fears were exaggerated. Only a few New Lights, such as the fiery radical minister James Davenport of New Haven, Connecticut, directly attacked the rich and powerful. Davenport called on his audiences to "Pull them down, turn them out, and put others in their places." Yet the Great Awakening contained a strong democratic thrust. "Does not the course of all this difficulty lie in this," asked the Baptist preacher Isaac Backus, "that the common people claim as good a right to judge and act for themselves in matters of religion as civil rulers or the learned clergy?"

Equally important, the pietist revivals reinforced the strong community values held by rural people. Most white American men and women had grown up in closely knit farming villages. They felt their traditional way of life was threatened by the pressure of increased population on their natural resources, by the consequent migration from their villages, and by new commercial forces. Through the Great Awakening, these farm families reaffirmed their commitment to the cooperative ethic of rural life. "In any truly Christian society," Gilbert Tennent explained, "mutual *Love* is the *Band* and *Cement*." Many pietist leaders were suspicious of what they regarded as the calculating, competitive temperament of merchants and land speculators. Jonathan Edwards spoke for most of his congregation when he condemned a "private niggardly spirit" as more suitable "for wolves and other beasts of prey, than for human beings." For many New Lights, the world was full of hostile social and economic forces. They sought security by falling back on their communities and on their belief in an activist God who would intervene directly in their lives. "All nature is full of God," concluded one revivalist minister, "full of his perpetual, moving, guiding, and over-ruling influence."

This vision of the world contrasted sharply with that held by Americans influenced by Enlightenment thought. They saw the world as safe and predictable, run by laws. These wealthy merchants and educated planters had more confidence in human abilities. They expressed impatience with communal standards that inhibited economic innovation and social change. Their spokesmen began to develop a new ideology that redefined the good of society as the pursuit of individual self-interest. As the Reverend Jonathan Mayhew of Boston put it, "the publick happiness is nothing but the happiness of a *number of individuals* united in society."

The Great Awakening had raised fundamental questions about the nature of God, religious and political authority, and economic behavior. It also had sharpened the conflicts between social groups that held different views on these issues.

Conflict in Virginia

These struggles were particularly intense in Virginia. The Church of England was the legally established religious institution and was supported by public taxes. Yet it had never ministered to most of Virginia's people. Blacks made up about 40 percent of the population, but they were generally excluded from church membership. Their owners feared that Christianization of the slaves would lead to demands for emancipation. Virginia's laws required all whites to attend Sunday religious services, but many landless families—another 20 percent of the population—avoided this obligation or came irregularly. Middling white freeholders, who composed 35 percent of the people, formed the core of most Anglican congregations, but they had little power over church affairs. Small groups of prominent planters dominated the parish vestries, the lay organizations that helped ministers manage church affairs.

The wealthy vestrymen used their control over parish finances to keep migrant Anglican ministers in a subordinate position. As the Bishop of London explained in 1751, most Virginia clergymen were "Scotch or Irish, who can get no employment at home and enter into the service more out of necessity than choice." The vestrymen used the ministers' poverty and the lack of a bishop in America to protect their own interests. One minister complained that the wealthy planters dismissed any preacher who "had the courage and resolution to preach against any Vices taken into favor by the leading Men of his Parish."

To maintain their dominant position, the

DIVERSITY ALONG THE SOUTHERN FRONTIER

An Anglican minister laments ethnic and religious diversity in his territory.

You must understand that all (or greatest Part) of this Part of the Province where I am, has been settled within these 5 Years by Irish Presbyterians from Belfast, or Pennsylvania and they imagin'd that they could secure this large Tract of fine Country to themselves and their Sect. Hereon, they built Meeting Houses, and got Pastors from Ireland, and Scotland. But with these there has also a Great Number of New Lights and Independants come here from New England, and many Baptists. . . .

'Tis these roving Teachers that stir up the Minds of the People against the Establish'd Church, and her Ministers—and make the Situation of any Gentleman extremely uneasy, vexatious, and disagreeable. . . .

These Sects are eternally jarring among themselves—The Presbyterians hate the Baptists far more than they do the Episcopalians, and so of the Rest—But (as in England), they will unite altogether—in a Body to distress or injure the Church establish'd.

---

planters denied even popular and successful pastors a full measure of status. In 1754, the Virginia council removed the Reverend John Moncure from the Commission of the Peace for Stafford County. It claimed that "every Clergyman has enough to do, to discharge his Duty as a Minister without engaging himself in Civil Affairs." Forty-six Anglican ministers promptly protested Moncure's dismissal and asked for higher salaries. The Virginia House of Burgesses responded angrily by cutting the ministers' pay. The Twopenny Acts of 1755 and 1758 forced the clergymen to accept only two pence a pound for the sixteen thousand pounds of tobacco they received as a salary, rather than the higher market price. This action to "oppress the Clergy" brought the intervention of the Bishop of London, who had jurisdiction over the church in America. At his urging, British authorities canceled the Twopenny Acts, reviving the Burgesses' fear of control by the English government.

This dispute culminated a decade of unrest in America within the Church of England. Inspired by readings from George Whitefield's sermons, a Virginia bricklayer named Samuel Morris led a group of Hanover County Anglicans out of the established church in 1743. Morris and his followers desired a more vital religious experience. They invited New Light Presbyterian ministers from Scotch-Irish settlements in southwestern Virginia to lead mass prayer meetings. Local revivals soon spread across the countryside.

These events created a dilemma for the political leadership of Virginia. For decades, public officials had encouraged Scotch-Irish migration to the frontier to provide a buffer against Indian attacks. The House of Burgesses had passed a Toleration Act that gave these Presbyterians the right to practice their own religion and use taxes to support their ministers. Yet the Anglican gentry feared that a pietist invasion of the Tidewater region along the Atlantic coast would undermine the established church and their own social position. Every Sunday, gentry families displayed their fine clothes, well-bred horses, and elaborate carriages to the assembled community. Vestrymen often gathered outside the church, waited until the minister started the service, and then marched in a body to their front-row seats. These opportunities for a symbolic display of the gentry's authority would vanish if small freeholders deserted the Church of England for the Presbyterians.

To revitalize the established church, the planter elite reproached the Anglican clergy for their "immoral and almost scandalous Lives." "Secure the Virtue and Decency of the Ministry," the influential planter Langdon Carter advised the Bishop of London, and "you will then see the wandering Flocks gathering to their former folds." To restrain the Presbyterian New Lights, Governor William Gooch denounced their "false teachings" that "lead the innocent and ignorant people into all kinds of delusion." Using their control of the county courts, Anglican planters rescinded licenses for Presbyterian meetinghouses and harassed Samuel Davies, a popular New Light preacher. These actions kept most of the small freeholders of eastern Virginia within the Church of England. The strictness of the Presbyterians' dogma and practice—even their New Light ministers were trained in Greek and Latin—discouraged mass conversions among the landless white and black populations.

During the 1760s, evangelical Baptists converted the poorer classes of the Chesapeake colonies. Thousands of yeomen and tenant farm families eagerly flocked to revivalist meetings. In vivid, emotional language, unlearned Baptist preachers spoke to them as equals and organized them into congregations. Hundreds of black slaves joined the new church groups, for many Baptists stressed the equality before God of all men and women. This recruitment of poor whites and blacks brought a violent response from the ruling gentry. Led by sheriffs and justices of the peace, armed bands of Anglican planters broke up Baptist services by force. In Caroline County, one Baptist reported, the "Parson of the Parish" attacked "Brother Waller, running the end of his horsewhip in his mouth and laying his whip across the hymn book." When Waller attempted to pray, "he was violently jerked off the stage; they caught him by the back part of his neck, beat his head against the ground, and a gentleman gave him twenty lashes with his horsewhip."

THE ARCHITECTURE OF WORSHIP
Baptist meeting houses were rough and cramped, but worshippers touched one another—in flesh and spirit—as they prayed together. In Anglican churches, the minister's pulpit (and sermon) dominated the proceedings, and wooden barriers separated families from one another. Anglican architecture was formal and hierarchical; that of the Baptists, intimate and egalitarian. (Both, Yale University Library)

The intensity of the gentry's response was the product of several factors—class antagonism, loyalty to the Anglican church, and the Baptists' challenge to their traditional culture. Baptist ministers condemned as vices such customary pleasures of Chesapeake males as horse racing, gambling, drinking, whoring, and cockfighting. To replace the aggressive, boisterous planter lifestyle, they proposed a puritanical, cooperative Christian community. Baptist preachers urged their followers to adopt a serious moral outlook, to instill order and discipline into their lives, and to call one another "brother" and "sister." They rejected the formal, hierarchical rituals of Anglican worship and led emotional services of shared fellowship. One Sunday, "about 2000 people came together," a Baptist minister recorded in his journal in June 1771,

> we went to a field and making a circle in the center, there laid hands on the persons baptized. The multitude stood around weeping, but when we sang *Come we that love the lord* they were so affected that they lifted up their hands and faces towards heaven and discovered such cheerful countenances in the midst of flowing tears as I have never seen before.

The appeal of Baptist dogma and ritual was overwhelming. Despite fierce resistance from the gentry, Baptist congregations soon included about 20 percent of Virginia's white population.

The pietist revival changed the cultural tone of Chesapeake society but did not transform its structure. Most Baptists sought to withdraw from an immoral world, not to conquer it. They wanted the freedom to conduct church services and seek converts. Like most eighteenth-century pietists, they did not attack the social or political power of the elite. Yet the Anglican planters correctly sensed a threat to their privileged position, for three reasons. First, the revival spread democratic principles of church organization and egalitarian values among white yeomen and tenant farmers. Moreover, a deep belief in a living God gave meaning to the lives of poor families and better prepared them to defend their economic interests. Second, Baptist—and, later, Methodist—ministers began the Christianization of the slaves. These conversions lessened the cultural differences between the two races, thus weakening the practice of slavery, and gave blacks a new sense of religious identity. Third, the pietists forced the Anglican ruling class to accept religious pluralism. To gain Baptist support during the American War of Independence, the Virginia gentry eliminated compulsory religious taxes and made all churches equal before the law. The planter elite still controlled the economic resources and political institutions, but its religious and cultural values were no longer dominant. Pietism gave cultural form to the class divisions of the Chesapeake colonies and left a legacy of conflicting value systems.

Economic Expansion and Social Structure

Between 1740 and 1765, the colonies became an important market for the manufactured goods produced by the rapidly developing British economy. To pay for these imports, Americans increased the productivity of their own economy. They increased the amount and diversity of their agricultural exports, expanded their commercial enterprises, and invested in new shipyards and domestic industries. Under this economic stimulus, the seaport cities grew quickly and developed complex occupational and social structures. These developments created an increasingly mature preindustrial economy.

Transatlantic Trade

By the middle of the eighteenth century, the Industrial Revolution was well underway in Great Britain. Craftsmen had devised and built various water- and steam-driven machines. These machines powered lathes for shaping wood, jennies and looms for fabricating textiles, and hammers for forging iron. Such mechanical devices produced goods far faster than human labor could. The entrepreneurs who established workshops and factories drove their employees harder than most traditional masters. They forced the workers to labor long hours and to keep pace with the relentlessly moving machines. These changes in technology and work discipline greatly increased the supply of manufactured goods. British producers now could sell more linen and woolen textiles, iron utensils, paper, chinaware, gunpowder, and glass than ever before—often at lower prices.

English and Scottish merchants launched aggressive campaigns to sell these products, and the colonies were a prime market. Transatlantic freight rates dropped steadily after 1720 because of a decline in piracy, along with better port facilities. In addition, the rapid growth of the colonial population created an expanding demand for manufactured goods. By 1770, the mainland colonies bought about 13 percent of all British exports and rivaled the West Indian sugar islands in economic importance within the empire.

These American purchases dramatically altered the character of transatlantic finance. Before 1750, American settlers dealt with their British suppliers on a pay-as-you-go basis. Chesapeake planters calculated the value of their tobacco exports to London or Glasgow and ordered manufactured goods, or slaves, of comparable value. Northern merchants likewise maintained a balance between their imports and their export sales of grain, fish, furs, and timber. Their contracts with British mercantile houses left them little choice. The British called for payment within six months of shipment, a severe requirement because of the four to six weeks required for each trip across the Atlantic. As part of their aggressive marketing strategy, British merchants extended the payment period to twelve months. Colonial traders and shopkeepers took advantage of these liberal terms of credit. They expanded their inventories of manufactured goods and increased their sales to distant backcountry farmers.

American consumption rose faster than the colonists' ability to pay the British for imported products. During the 1750s and 1760s, they paid for only a little more than 80 percent of the British goods that they imported. The colonies built up a substantial debt to the British by 1770. Yet it was relatively small in view of the magnitude of the transatlantic trade. Indeed, it was less significant than the colonists' success in paying for most of their imported manufactured products.

The expansion of agricultural exports provided a major source of American income. Tobacco remained the most important export, accounting for about 25 percent of all earnings. Growers in the Chesapeake colonies sent thirty-two million pounds of tobacco abroad in 1700, fifty-two million in 1740, and eighty-three million in 1770. Scottish entrepreneurs financed the expansion of American production. Glasgow merchants captured control of the French tobacco market in the 1720s, and expanded their distribution network throughout Europe. By the 1760s, they bought nearly half of the annual Chesapeake tobacco crop, offering settlers in the newly opened Piedmont region ample credit for the purchase of African slaves and British manufactures.

Agricultural exports brought even greater prosperity to the white slaveowners of South

FIGURE 5.2 POPULATION, BRITISH IMPORTS, AND THE AMERICAN BALANCE OF PAYMENTS

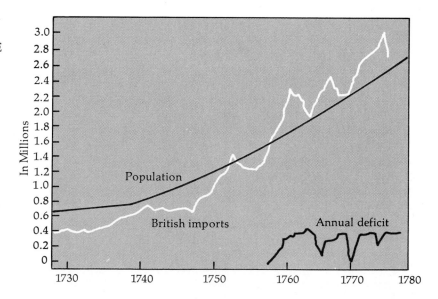

PROCESSING INDIGO IN SOUTH CAROLINA

Eliza Lucas (Pinckney) was born in the West Indies in 1722 and moved to South Carolina in 1738. Supervising the family's plantations in her father's absence, she introduced indigo production to the colony in 1741 and perfected it by 1744. Carolina planters became the major suppliers of this valuable purple-blue dye to the British textile industry, exporting 100,000 lbs. each year. (Charleston Library Foundation)

Carolina. A subsidy from the British government encouraged the production of indigo, a plant that yielded a deep violet-blue dye used in textiles. In 1770, planters in the South Carolina uplands sent large shipments of indigo to England. That same year, lowland plantations produced about seventy-five million pounds of rice for export.

Meanwhile, a booming export trade in wheat, flour, and bread strengthened the northern agricultural economy. Before 1740, the nations of western Europe produced just enough grain to feed themselves. They imported only luxury goods, such as sugar, coffee, cotton, and spices, from the semitropical region of the Western Hemisphere. Then a rapid and sustained growth in the European population created an increased demand for food. However, agricultural production remained static, and the growth of the manufacturing work force reduced the relative size of the peasant population. The increased use of horses for transportation and warfare placed additional strain on the limited agricultural output. Unable to produce enough grain themselves, Europeans bought wheat from America—in years of poor harvests at first, and then regularly. By the late 1760s, England had become a grain-importing country. Four of its American colonies—New York, Pennsylvania, Maryland, and Virginia—became the breadbasket of the Atlantic world.

The demand for wheat brought high profits to American producers. Wheat prices jumped about 30 percent between 1740 and 1770 in Amsterdam and London, and prices in the Philadelphia market nearly doubled. Colonial merchants, who had markets in both Europe and the West Indies, bid fiercely for grain. Rising agricultural prices shifted the terms of transatlantic trade in favor of American producers. During the 1740s, the sale of a hundred bushels of wheat bought 150 yards of English woolen cloth; two decades later, a hundred bushels purchased 250 yards. Thus, a rising demand for American tobacco, rice, indigo, and wheat, together with rising prices for these commodities, enabled the colonies to import vast quantities of British manufactures without going deeply into debt.

The creation of new American manufacturing enterprises was equally important. New England merchants returned from the West Indies not only with specie and bills of credit but also with molasses and partially refined sugar. New Englanders distilled the imported molasses into rum and sold great quantities of it at home and abroad. By the 1760s, Boston distillers exported more than half a million gallons of rum yearly. Other entrepreneurs built sugar factories for the production of refined sugar, which previously had been imported from England.

The West India trade also created a strong fishing industry and merchant marine. In 1770, the northern colonies exported fish valued at about 15 percent of all colonial exports. The New England fishing fleet had more than six hundred

TABLE 5.1 AMERICAN EXPORTS OF GOODS AND SERVICES, 1770

Product	Estimated Value
Tobacco	760,000
Shipping Earnings	610,000
Bread and Flour	412,000
Rice	312,000
Fish	287,000
Financial services	220,000
Indigo	117,000
Sale of ships	75,000

ships, and they provided employment for over four thousand sailors. The merchant fleet was even larger. By the 1760s, merchants of Boston, Newport, New York City, Philadelphia, and Charleston dominated American coastal trade and the commerce between the mainland and the sugar islands. In addition, ships owned by colonists carried 75 percent of the goods shipped between American cities and European ports. British mercantile houses remained dominant only in the tobacco and sugar trades. Their ships shuttled these crops to Europe and supplied the plantation colonies with manufactured goods and African slaves.

The expansion of American and British commerce financed a major expansion of the colonial shipbuilding industry. Seventy sawmills dotted the Piscataqua River in New Hampshire as early as 1720, providing lumber for homes, warehouses, and ships. Artisans in small coastal villages built scores of fishing boats and vessels for the coastal trade, and shipyards near the major port cities produced oceangoing vessels. Boston shipyards launched about six thousand tons of freighters annually during the 1730s, and Philadelphia yards doubled that tonnage by the 1760s. The ready availability of inexpensive timber enabled American builders to compete successfully with English shipyards. By 1770, colonial-built ships made up about a third of the British merchant marine.

The domestic manufacture of goods—ships, rum, iron, furniture, and many other products—had become a major factor in the American economy. The relative growth of domestic production was more important than the rising

transatlantic trade. In 1700, the colonies exported nearly 18 percent of all the commodities they produced, and they imported many of the basic necessities of life. By 1770, the proportion of exports had fallen to about 12 percent of total production. In addition, the colonists now had most of the craft skills needed to maintain a mature preindustrial economy. Around 30 percent of their export earnings came from the sale of nonagricultural products, such as ships, rum, iron, and commercial services. Except in the important area of low-priced manufactured goods, the American economy was on the verge of independence.

Urban Growth and Social Diversity

The American port cities grew rapidly as a result of their commercial activity and manufacturing enterprise. By the late 1760s, Newport, Baltimore, and Charleston each had more than ten thousand people. Boston had fifteen thousand and New York twenty-one thousand. Philadelphia, with nearly thirty thousand, had a population equal to that of most European provincial centers.

The volume of trade was the crucial factor in the size of these cities. For example, Boston owed its early prominence to its merchant fleet. In the early decades of the eighteenth century, Boston merchants owned about 40 percent of the colonial shipping capacity. Philadelphia grew initially as the port of entry for manufactured goods for the Chesapeake Bay and the expanding population of Pennsylvania. Then the Quaker City surpassed Boston as it became the export center of the American grain trade. The bustling export trade in wheat likewise transformed nearby Baltimore from a sleepy village to a major port within a few decades. Charleston owed its size to the shipment abroad of deerskins, indigo, and rice. All of these port cities developed important trade-related industries as well. Philadelphia shipyards employed hundreds of shipwrights and laborers, and the Boston rum industry provided work for scores of coopers. Legislation requiring all Hudson Valley wheat to be inspected and processed in New York City made that port a flour-milling center.

This commercial activity consisted of four separate operations—shipping goods, distributing

TABLE 5.2 POPULATION OF MAJOR
AMERICAN TOWNS, 1775

Philadelphia	30,000
New York	22,000
Boston	16,000
Charleston	12,000
Newport	11,000
Baltimore	10,000
New Haven, Conn.	7,000
Norwich, Conn.	7,000
Norfolk, Vir.	6,000
New London, Conn.	5,000
Salem, Mass.	5,000
Lancaster, Pa.	5,000

imports, marketing exports, and manufacturing trade-related items. Each of these enterprises created different occupational groups. As shipping centers, the port cities served as the transfer points for thousands of tons of goods. There were no motor-driven cranes or machines to lift or move agricultural commodities and manufactured products; so hundreds of men worked on the docks of Boston, Philadelphia, and New York. They unloaded goods from ocean-going vessels and stored them in warehouses or stacked them on smaller coastal freighters. These laborers lived in small houses or tenements in the back alleys of crowded waterfront districts, and drank cheap New England rum in nearby taverns.

Free white workers avoided such jobs because of the low pay and heavy labor, and so employers recruited slaves and indentured servants. Afro-American slaves made up about 10 percent of Boston's population around 1750, and 20 percent of the people of New York City. In Philadelphia, slaves and indentured German migrants totaled 20 percent of the city's residents and held nearly half the laboring jobs. Whether enslaved, indentured, or merely poor, these men and their families formed an economically indispensable laboring class in every port city.

The transport of imports and exports created more mobile and prosperous groups of workers. During the 1760s, a small fleet of trading vessels sailed back and forth between Philadelphia and scores of villages along Delaware Bay and its tributaries. Their crews carried European goods and news into the backcountry, and piled heavy barrels of flour and wheat on the decks for the

return voyage. An extensive land-based transport system provided jobs for hundreds of professional teamsters. It took at least ten thousand wagon trips to move the 370,000 bushels of wheat and corn and the 16,000 barrels of flour exported yearly from the eastern shore of Maryland. Entrepreneurs and artisans established taverns, livery stables, wagon works, and wheel repair shops at key locations along the wagon routes, providing additional employment.

These interior trading centers extended the economic and social diversity of the port cities into the agricultural backcountry. In the 1760s, ten small towns of three hundred to five hundred people dotted the rural districts of Pennsylvania. They served as centers of commerce and small-scale artisan production. "Rather than go farther back into the country where lands are cheap or undertake the arduous task of clearing new lands," a traveler reported in 1773, hundreds of Pennsylvanians had turned "to manufacturing, and live upon a small farm, as in many parts of England." Censuses and tax records indicate that artisans numbered about a fourth of the taxable population of Germantown, Pennsylvania. More than two hundred craftsmen pursued their trades in the interior town of Lancaster.

This trade-related manufacturing developed furthest in the port cities. Scores of shipwrights built ocean-going and coastal vessels. Hundreds of other artisans made the ropes, sails, and metal fittings for the new fleet and renovated many other fishing boats and merchant freighters. Coopers turned out thousands of barrels to hold rum, molasses, flour, fish, pickled meat, and other commodities. All these workers needed housing, food, and clothing, providing employment for additional storekeepers and craftsmen. By the 1760s, nearly half the workers of Philadelphia and other seaports were artisans—butchers, shoemakers, weavers, glaziers, bakers, carpenters, masons, and dozens of other specialists. Many owned their own tools and shops. Together with retail shopkeepers and clerical workers, the craftsmen and their families formed a substantial middling group in the diverse urban environment.

A small group of wealthy merchants stood at the top of urban society. Their commercial ventures formed the foundation of the productive

MAP 5.1 URBAN GROWTH
IN PENNSYLVANIA,
1730–1765
In 1730, Philadelphia anchored a
string of market towns along the
lower Delaware River. Then the
rapid expansion of farming
prompted the growth of western
trading centers and county seats,
such as Lancaster and York. This
new urban network was most
developed some distance from
Philadelphia, beyond the farming
districts in the city's shadow.

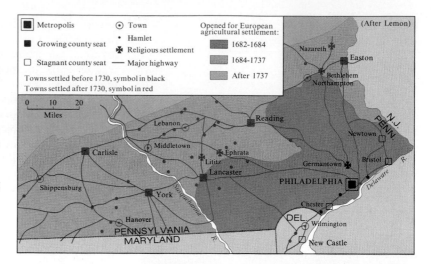

system and brought handsome profits. About
150 merchants controlled 70 percent of Philadelphia's trade in 1770. The taxable assets of Anglican merchants averaged £3,100, and Quaker
merchants had an average assessment of £2,900.
These were immense sums, comparable to capital resources of $400,000 to $500,000 in the
United States during the 1980s. They dwarfed
the £30 in property owned by tailors or the £250-
350 accumulated by well-to-do artisans. The
wealthiest 10 percent of Philadelphia's population controlled 60 to 65 percent of the city's
taxable resources. This distribution of wealth resembled that in European commercial towns,
and it represented another indication of the maturity of the American economy. The share of
wealth held by the urban elite remained steady
for the rest of the preindustrial period and increased dramatically only after the Industrial
Revolution began.

Merchants used their substantial capital resources to invest in trade-related industries, such
as shipbuilding. They also set up small factories
to process the goods that they carried. In the
1760s, the Brown brothers of Providence, Rhode
Island, manufactured candles made from whale
oil. Other merchants built distilleries or invested
in urban real estate. Many reaped substantial
profits as the population growth pushed land
values higher. In 1763, a Philadelphia city lot
measuring twenty-seven feet by forty-five feet
had a value four times as high as in 1756. As
property owners, many artisans shared this
prosperity.

A PROSPEROUS BACKCOUNTRY MERCHANT
Moses Marcy of Southbridge, Massachusetts stands in
front of his large gambrel-roofed house, surrounded by
ships and account books—symbols of his lucrative, but
controversial, calling. "The Business of a Merchant, *as a
Merchant,* is to find . . . the greatest Profit" complained
one Massachusetts moralist, "and it never enteres into his
Mind *when two legal Branches of Trade* lie open befor him,
which of them is for the greatest good of the Country."
(Artist Unknown. *Moses Marcy.* Old Sturbridge Village,
Sturbridge, Mass. [Henry E. Peach])

DEBATE OVER COLONIAL PRICE CONTROLS

A letter to a New York newspaper demands price controls in times of scarcity, 1763.

There was perhaps never a more just or necessary law passed in this province, than the late by-law for regulating the prices of provisions sold in our markets. For the impositions of the butchers, and the extravagant demands of some of our country people, have loudly called for redress, and must soon have proved to the poorer sort absolutely ruinous.

For we have really been imposed upon by one of the most impudent combinations that was ever suffered among a free and thinking people. Was it not astonishing, and beyond all human tolerance, that beef should be sold from 7d. to 8d. per lb., when it might be offered for 3d. and 4d., and yield a sufficient profit!

A Friend "to the liberty of Englishmen" advocates market-determined prices.

Whereas the gentlemen of the City of New York have been pleased to make a law, and prefix a certain price upon country produce, such as eatables or provisions, brought to the City of New York; and lay a certain fine upon all persons that give a greater or larger price for what they buy. But they forgot to insert in their laws, that no lesser prices should be offered, or given, under the same fine. We thought we were born free Englishmen, and had the liberty, as such, to sell our own effects at our own liberty.

Urban life remained hard for day laborers, merchant seamen, and other wage earners. Few members of this sizable group, which comprised about 30 percent of the workers of Philadelphia and the other ports, owned a house or a garden. As land values and wheat prices went up, so did their rent and food expenses. Many scraped by on household budgets that left no margin for sickness, accidents, or unemployment. Only men who were lucky enough to find steady year-round work earned enough to meet the basic living expenses of a married couple with two children. A single man could get along on a laborer's or a seaman's wage, but most families could not. To make ends meet, wives took in washing and sewing, and parents sent their children out to work as soon as possible. To save enough money to buy a house, families shared their crowded rooms with boarders. In good economic times, such personal sacrifices brought many wage-earning families the economic security they desperately desired. Periods of commercial depression meant irregular work, which led to hunger and reliance on charity.

Dependence on commerce made urban life more uncertain than farm life. Trade generally increased in the decades after 1740, but it followed unpredictable cyclical patterns. During periods of recession, merchants looked anxiously at overstocked warehouses and feared bankruptcy. "I think we have a gloomy prospect before us," a public official reported from Philadelphia in 1765, "as there are of late some Personas failed, who were in no way suspected, and a probability of some others, as the whisper goes."

Some port cities did not share in the expansion of transatlantic trade and domestic manufacturing. Boston's population, for example, remained at about fifteen thousand from 1740 until the American War of Independence. Hard times sharpened social divisions in Boston. Many "good and honest housekeepers" were "willing to pay their Debts," the Reverend Benjamin Colman argued in a pamphlet during one commercial slump, "but can't raise the Money, unless they will Sell their Houses at half value." They were "Squeezed and Oppress'd to Maintain a few Lawyers," he charged, "while the great part of the Town can hardly get Bread to satisfie Nature." Colman exaggerated, but he accurately reflected the social divisions and competing economic interests in commercial port cities. As America developed a mature preindustrial economy, new tensions appeared among increasingly diverse occupational groups and social classes.

The Struggle for the American Land

During the 1750s and 1760s, political upheavals disrupted life in many agricultural regions. The main issue was control of the land. British aristocrats revived old proprietary claims to vast tracts of American territory. Migrants from the seaboard colonies fought for settlement rights in the West. Westward expansion ended a half-century of relatively peaceful relations with the Indian tribes and with the French in Canada. Following the French and Indian War in 1754–1763, western settlers clashed with eastern colonial governments over a variety of financial and political matters. For two decades, ethnic rivalries, legal disputes, and armed violence stretched the effectiveness of existing political systems to the breaking point.

Who Owns the Land?

By 1750, the density of settlement in some American agricultural regions resembled that in preindustrial Europe. "Improved" farms with well-cultivated and fenced fields drew high prices, and forested frontier tracts were in great demand. Ownership of the land—by yeomen families, enterprising speculators, aristocratic proprietors, and rival colonial governments— suddenly emerged as a burning issue.

New England faced the worst pressures of population growth and westward migration. In 1738, most of the founders of the new town of Kent, Connecticut, traced their American ancestry back four generations. Their families had been moving slowly north and west for a century; now they had reached the generally accepted boundary of the colony. Refusing to accept these legal limits, Connecticut farmers formed the Susquehannah Company. In the early 1750s, the company petitioned the Connecticut legislature to revive the sea-to-sea boundaries described in the colony's original seventeenth-century charter. Specifically, the company urged the legislature to claim jurisdiction over the Wyoming Valley in northeast Pennsylvania, and it sold land titles to Connecticut migrants who settled there. However, with the full support of the Pennsylvania assembly, the Penn family affirmed its proprietary rights over the Wyoming Valley and issued land patents to its own settlers. Soon the rival groups of land claimants burned each other's houses. To avert further violence, the two colonial governments referred the dispute over Connecticut's western boundary to English authorities in London.

Armed conflict also broke out along the unmarked border separating Massachusetts and New Hampshire from New York. Seeking flat fertile land, New England farmers left the hilly uplands and moved into disputed territory in the Hudson River Valley. Their cultural values brought them into immediate conflict with New York authorities and landowners. Coming from a freehold society, the New England migrants refused to accept the tenancy leaseholds customary on the great manors owned by the Cortland, Philipse, Van Rensselaer, and Livingston families. Instead, they purchased titles from Massachusetts speculators and encouraged Dutch and German tenants on the manors to repudiate their leases and demand ownership rights. When the manorial lords took legal action, migrants and tenant farmers rose in rebellion in Westchester, Dutchess, and Albany counties in 1766. At the direction of the royal governor, General Thomas Gage led two British regiments to assist local sheriffs and manorial bailiffs. The troops evicted many New England squatters and speculators from the disputed territory and suppressed the tenant uprising.

Proprietors with large territorial claims won convincing legal and political battles in other colonies as well. The Penn family successfully defended its ownership of all unsettled lands in Pennsylvania against a challenge from the legislature. In New Jersey, large landowners used seventeenth-century proprietary legal titles to oust yeomen farmers from disputed properties. Throughout the southern colonies, English aristocrats revived long-inactive land grants from King Charles II. They asserted ownership of millions of acres of undeveloped land and the right to collect yearly quit-rents in regions already settled. A legal suit gave Lord Fairfax ownership of the northern neck of Virginia, along the Potomac River, providing him with a substantial income from rents and leases. Lord Granville, an heir of one of the original Carolina proprietors, had kept his land ownership rights when the colony reverted to royal control in 1729. Now he enforced the collection of rents in the Granville district of North Carolina. Long-established proprietary families also profited from the increased demand for land. By the 1760s, the American income of Lord Baltimore, proprietor of Maryland, made him one of the richest men in England. A decade later, the Penn family took in almost as much annually from land sales in Pennsylvania and from rents.

The proprietors' ability to uphold quasi-feudal land claims underscored the growing resemblance between rural society in Europe and America. Freehold property was in short supply in settled areas of the colonies, and long-vacant manors filled up with reluctant tenant farmers. Moreover, the legal and administrative systems of the colonial governments had become powerful and effective. Proprietors now turned to these established institutions to oust squatters or to impose fines or jail terms on farmers who refused to pay their annual rents.

The American land had never been completely free for the taking by yeomen farmers, but now it was even less so. Population pressure made it expensive, manorial and proprietary rights limited its freehold status, and the legal system upheld the property claims of English aristocrats and wealthy American landlords. As in Virginia on the eve of Bacon's Rebellion, the future appeared bleak for landless tenants and threatening to yeomen farm families.

The Great War for Empire

Despite land shortages in the east, migration into the fertile lands west of the Appalachian Mountains progressed slowly. In New York, the Iroquois tribes formed a powerful confederation and used military strength and astute diplomacy to deter white settlement. Exploiting their geographic location, the Iroquois played off the French in Canada against their British rivals. The Delaware leader Teedyuscung explained the situation to his tribe as he deciphered a pictorial message from his Iroquois allies: "You see a Square in the Middle, meaning the Lands of the

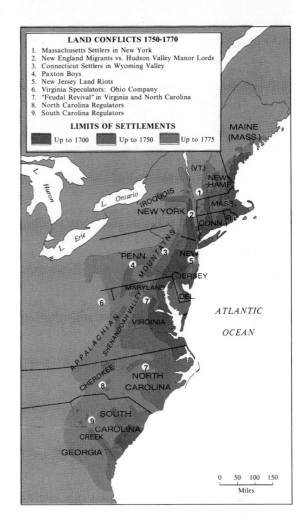

MAP 5.2 WESTWARD EXPANSION AND ARMED CONFLICT
The American population more than doubled from 1.2 to 2.5 million between 1750 and 1775, sparking legal battles and armed struggles over the ownership of eastern farms and western lands. Violence became an important factor in political life, as backcountry settlers fought with Indians, rival land claimants, and eastern governments.

Indians; and at one End the Figure of a Man, indicating the English; and at the other End another, meaning the French. Let us join together to defend our land against both."

The Iroquois and their allies followed this strategy successfully. They traded with both the English and the French for guns and supplies and threatened military retaliation against unauthorized settlement in their territory. William

Johnson, the Indian agent for the British government in the early 1750s, bargained with the Mohawk, one of the Iroquois tribes. He wanted to settle Scottish migrants on the rich lands of the Mohawk Valley, west of Albany, New York. To get permission from the Mohawk, Johnson had to give them a vast supply of manufactured goods.

In the South, westward migration led to war with French Canada. Land speculators, rather than restless settlers, touched off this conflict. In 1747, a group of prominent Virginia aristocrats led by the royal governor, Robert Dinwiddie, organized the Ohio Company. With the assistance of John Hanbury and other politically powerful London merchants, the company obtained a grant of two hundred thousand acres of land along the Ohio River and the promise of another three hundred thousand acres. To complete this lucrative land grab, Dinwiddie sent Colonel George Washington of the Virginia militia to the Ohio region. Asserting Virginia's claim to these Indian lands, the young and ambitious Washington built a sturdy fort at the point where the Monongahela and Allegheny rivers joined to form the Ohio. The French controlled the fur trade in this region and sensed a larger threat to their claims of sovereignty over the interior of the North American continent. They replied to Dinwiddie's initiative by capturing Washington and his garrison at the fort and renaming it Fort Duquesne. By July 1754, Virginia was at war with France in the American backcountry, and the French and Indian War had begun.

When news of the fighting reached London, the British ministry searched for a firm but inexpensive response. A protracted European war against France had just ended in 1749, and the British treasury was depleted. Country gentlemen in Parliament strongly opposed aggressive military action that would increase the land tax. Prime Minister Henry Pelham agreed. "There is such load of debt, and such heavy taxes already laid upon the people," Pelham argued, "that nothing but an absolute necessity can justifie our engaging in a new War." Yet Lord Halifax, the new and energetic head of the Board of Trade, and the rising statesman William Pitt demanded an expansionist colonial policy. The Board of Trade proposed a political "Union between ye Royal, Proprietary, & Charter Governments"

and the appointment of a high-ranking military officer as governor-general of all the colonies. Acting independently, delegates from most of the northern colonial governments met at Albany, New York, and hammered out a similar scheme. This Albany "Plan of Union" was designed primarily by Benjamin Franklin of Pennsylvania. It proposed that each colony would send delegates to an American continental assembly presided over by a royal governor-general. The assembly would assume responsibility for all western affairs—trade, Indian policy, and defense.

These innovative proposals generated little enthusiasm in America or in Britain. Most colonial leaders feared that the Albany Plan would lead to greater British control and higher taxes. In Britain, the Duke of Newcastle warned that "Uniting too closely the Northern Colonies" might lead to a dangerous movement for "An independency from this Country." However, the French presence in the Ohio region necessitated immediate action. In 1755, therefore, the British government sent General Edward Braddock to America with two regiments of British troops.

As the French and Indian War began, Britain held a strong physical advantage. Its two million American colonists outnumbered the French settlers of Canada by fourteen to one. Once the British government mobilized the colonies for war, victory was almost assured. However, wilderness conditions limited the military action for two years.

Braddock led a force of 1,400 regulars, accompanied by 450 Virginia militiamen, against Fort Duquesne in 1755. French and Indian forces launched a surprise attack on his forces and dealt a crushing defeat to the Anglo-American army. They killed Braddock and half his men as they retreated in disorder through the forest. New England troops captured Fort Beausejour in French Nova Scotia (Arcadia) that same year. To eliminate French influence in this region, they deported six thousand Arcadian inhabitants, sending them primarily to Louisiana and South Carolina. New England militiamen also mounted an unsuccessful assault on the French fortress at Louisbourg. The French retaliated by capturing Fort Oswego on Lake Ontario and by supplying their native American allies in the Ohio Valley with goods and military supplies. French and In-

	French Claims
	British Claims
	Spanish Claims
	Disputed British-French Claims
	Disputed British-Spanish Claims
♟	Fort

MAP 5.3 EUROPEAN SPHERES OF INFLUENCE, 1754

Native Americans used the struggle among Britain, France, and Spain to maintain control over most of the interior of eastern North America. As a British official commented, "To preserve the Ballance between us & and French is the great ruling Principle of Modern Indian Politics." The Great War for Empire disrupted this delicate balance. By 1763, the British had ousted the French from Canada. Anglo-American settlers moved steadily westward, occupying native American lands and unleashing a new series of Indian wars.

dian raids pushed back the perimeter of Anglo-American influence in frontier regions, but they did not seriously threaten densely settled areas.

Two years of fighting in America led to a major military confrontation in Europe. France renewed its traditional alliance with Spain, bolstering its naval power. France also, in a startling diplomatic reversal, made a pact with Austria, Britain's longtime partner. By 1756, French and Austrian armies threatened to invade the duchy of Hanover, the homeland of King George II of England; and the territories of Britain's new ally, Frederick the Great of Prussia.

At this crucial juncture, William Pitt became the principal British secretary of state. Like previous English statesmen, Pitt wanted to keep the French forces pinned down in Europe. He therefore sent funds to Frederick the Great to sustain thousands of Prussian troops in the field. Then Pitt embarked upon a new maritime strategy. He mobilized Britain's naval and military forces for combat against the French in America, India, and throughout the world. Participation in the South Atlantic System had greatly expanded British trade and wealth; the growth of manufacturing and industrial enterprise at home had increased its financial and material resources. Britain was now a major power and, for the first time, the equal of France. It had enough resources to preserve the balance of power in Europe *and* to build a worldwide maritime empire. Pitt's strategy turned the French and Indian War into Britain's Great War for Empire.

To win the American part of this contest, Pitt pursued three interrelated policies. First, he sought vigorous military leadership. He gave top commands to three young but impressive officers—James Wolfe, Jeffrey Amherst, and William Howe. Second, Pitt provided generous military subsidies to the colonies. He agreed to pay half the cost of the troops raised in the colonies and to supply them with arms and equipment. Third, Pitt committed main units of the British navy and thousands of British regulars to the American conflict.

By 1759, British commanders had sufficient resources to launch a coordinated three-pronged attack on Quebec, the heart of French Canada. One force led by General John Stanwix moved northward from Fort Duquesne, which had been

recaptured in 1758 and renamed Fort Pitt. The goal of this expeditionary force was to sever French ties to the west. General Amherst led a second Anglo-American army northward from New York. This overland invasion of New France was designed to draw the attention of French forces and their Indian allies. Meanwhile, a third British force—the major one—of fifty warships, two hundred transport and supply vessels, and eighty-five hundred troops sailed up the Saint Lawrence River in June 1759. Its objective was the main French army stationed at the capital of Quebec. General Wolfe, the British commander, probed the city's strong defenses for two months but without success. Then, in a dramatic predawn attack in early September, about four thousand British troops scaled the two-hundred foot cliffs at Foulon Bay and took up positions on the flat plains before the city. Led by General Louis Montcalm, French troops advanced against Wolfe's army but faltered in the face of superior British firepower. Quebec fell to the British assault, and this battle effectively decided the entire conflict. The British navy dominated the Atlantic Ocean and prevented French reinforcements from reaching the beleaguered colony. In 1760, British forces captured Montreal and completed the conquest of Canada.

The Great War for Empire continued for three more years, but the fighting switched to other parts of the world. In a series of well-executed and disciplined offensives, Frederick the Great's Prussian armies fought off much larger French and Austrian forces. With government assistance, the British East India Company captured French commercial outposts in India and became a major force in the affairs of that region. In 1762, British naval and military forces seized the French sugar island of Martinique and the Spanish colonies of Cuba and the Phillipine Islands. When the war ended, Pitt was no longer in office. But his maritime strategy had extended British power throughout the world and gave his successors the opportunity to make an advantageous peace.

The Treaty of Paris in 1763 confirmed the triumph of British arms. The pact awarded Britain the French province of Canada, all French territory east of the Mississippi River, and the

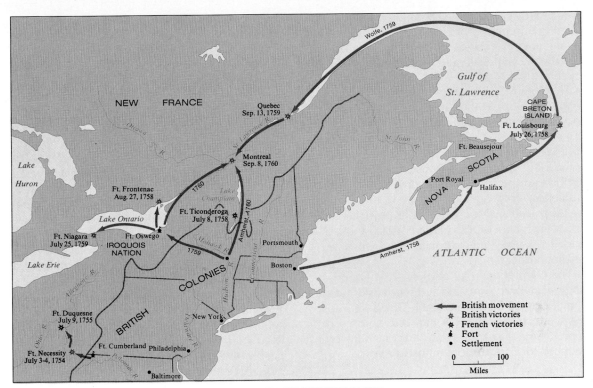

MAP 5.4 THE ANGLO-AMERICAN CONQUEST OF NEW FRANCE

In 1759, British and American troops overwhelmed French forces and captured Quebec, prompting "public rejoicing" throughout the colonies. "The Illuminations and Fireworks exceeded any that had been exhibited before," the South Carolina *Gazette* reported. However, the celebrations failed to impress British military leaders. Provincial soldiers were "the dirtiest, most contemptible, cowardly dogs you can conceive," General James Wolfe told a friend. "There is no depending on them in action." This viewpoint influenced Britain's decision in 1775 to crush the colonial rebellion with military force.

Spanish province of Florida. In return for this sovereignty over eastern North America, Britain restored the sugar islands of Martinique and Guadeloupe to France, and Cuba and the Phillipines to Spain. These terms aroused controversy in Britain. Some politicians wanted to retain the captured sugar islands, because of their great value and their capacity to absorb agricultural goods exported from the mainland. They warned that the expulsion of the French from Canada would encourage American designs for independence. However, other economic and political interests prevailed. West Indian planters, fearing competition from highly productive plantations, urged Parliament to keep Canada rather than the French islands. British fur traders also favored Canada, as did manufac-

turers who supplied the mainland market. In addition, the British feared a vehement protest from the colonies if it returned Canada to their traditional French Catholic enemy.

The Great War for Empire revealed the divergent interests of Britain and America. American speculators and public officials had stirred up the war, but the colonial assemblies were slow to support it. Before raising troops, they demanded the right to appoint officers and control military operations. They used the wartime emergency to augment their powers at the expense of the royal governors. Also, American merchants conducted illicit trade with the French West Indies throughout the war. It was absurd, declared one outraged British politician, that French armies attempting "to Destroy one English province, are actually supported by Bread raised in another." Pitt himself charged that this blatant and extensive American trade allowed the French "to sustain and protract this long and expensive war."

The colonial assemblies resented the British demands because the Americans had virtually no voice in determining wartime policy or the terms for peace. In 1763, for example, the Ottawa leader Pontiac led a major Indian uprising in the Ohio Valley. In response, the British ministry issued the Proclamation of 1763. This edict prohibited white settlement west of the crest of the Appalachian Mountains. The proclamation, an intelligent attempt to prevent Indian wars, offended colonial land speculators and westward-looking farmers.

The celebrations that marked the triumph of Anglo-American arms in the French and Indian War, followed by the favorable Treaty of Paris, obscured these tensions but did not resolve them. They appeared again, and in more pronounced forms, during the postwar years.

Western Settlers and Eastern Interests

The French and Indian War focused attention on the western frontier. In the aftermath of the fighting, settlers in the western regions of Pennsylvania and North and South Carolina challenged the policies of colonial authorities. Their protests stemmed from a variety of causes, including Indian conflicts, political inequality, and farm bankruptcies. But these issues reflected a common opposition to the power of eastern political and economic interests.

As long as Quakers dominated Pennsylvania politics, relations with native American tribes remained peaceful. The colonial assembly discouraged rapid westward migration and carefully negotiated white access to Indian lands. As Scotch-Irish migrants settled along the Pennsylvania frontier, they demanded an expansionist policy backed, if necessary, by military force. When Quaker and other eastern politicians refused to enact an aggressive Indian policy, the westerners reacted with violence. An armed band of Scotch-Irish farmers, known as the Pax-

ton Boys, massacred twenty members of a peaceful Indian tribe in 1763. Scotch-Irish settlers actively resisted Governor John Penn's attempts to protect the rest of the tribe and bring the murderers to justice. About 250 men marched on Philadelphia, and colonial authorities mobilized the militia to defend the city. Intercepting the Paxton Boys at Lancaster, Benjamin Franklin calmed the angry mob and negotiated a compromise. Provincial authorities stopped the prosecution of the men, and the Scotch-Irish tempered their demands for the expulsion of the Indians.

In South Carolina, an intense wartime struggle between whites and the powerful Cherokee tribe produced social and political chaos. Local government collapsed in many backcountry districts, and outlaw bands roamed unchallenged across the countryside. To restore order, slave-owning planters and yeomen farmers organized a vigilante group called the Regulators, which suppressed the outlaw communities. Then the Regulators imposed moral discipline on the "low people"—the hunters, squatters, vagrants, and propertyless laborers who lived an irregular existence along the fringes of respectable society. They whipped those suspected of poaching, stealing, or immoral behavior. The Regulators even instituted a forced-work program for all "idle persons without a visible way of getting an honest living."

The South Carolina government accepted Regulator rule, despite its arbitrary and illegal character. Eastern authorities feared that an armed confrontation between the militia and the Regulators would create an opportunity for slave revolts on the lowland rice plantations. The colonial assembly therefore compromised with the backcountry insurgents by removing some long-standing grievances. The assembly created locally controlled courts in the west and reduced fees for legal documents. But lowland planters and merchants refused to reapportion the legislature to provide western settlers with representation equal to their growing numbers. The assembly likewise continued to tax the thin soil of the upland region at the same rate as the fertile lands of the low country. As in Pennsylvania, eastern political and economic factions compromised with westerners on specific issues but maintained their dominant position.

TIME LINE
THE CONVERGENCE OF EUROPE AND AMERICA

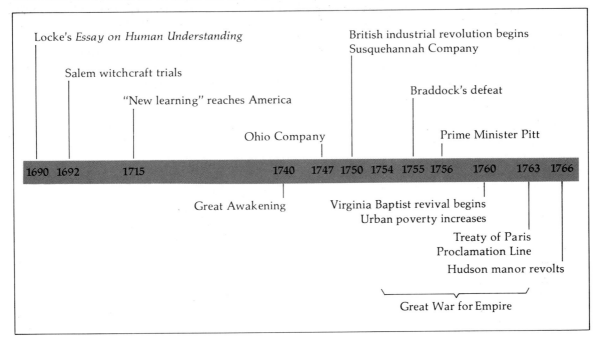

Locke's *Essay on Human Understanding*

Salem witchcraft trials

"New learning" reaches America

Ohio Company

British industrial revolution begins
Susquehannah Company

Braddock's defeat

Prime Minister Pitt

1690 1692   1715   1740   1747 1750 1754 1755 1756   1760   1763 1766

Great Awakening

Virginia Baptist revival begins
Urban poverty increases

Treaty of Paris
Proclamation Line

Hudson manor revolts

Great War for Empire

The Regulators could not continue the struggle because they lacked legitimate authority within their own region. Ordinary settlers and well-to-do people resented their arbitrary assumption of power. Vowing to end Regulator rule, former justices of the peace organized a "Moderator" movement. In March 1769, about six hundred armed supporters of each backcountry group confronted each other near the Saluda River. They exchanged angry words and then gunshots. Only a day of hard negotiations and an agreement to end Regulator rule averted wholesale violence. The Regulators restored order and won greater political autonomy for the west, but they failed to alter the balance of regional power.

In North Carolina, eastern and western social groups struggled over legislative power and commercial credit. By the 1760s, the credit economy of the transatlantic market system extended into the backcountry. English and Scottish merchant firms set up small stores where their agents exchanged manufactured goods for locally produced tobacco, wheat, and hides. Many backcountry farmers lacked enough money to expand production or provide farmsteads for their children without going into debt to these merchant firms. Others fell into debt by purchasing slaves. The number of blacks in Orange County, North Carolina, jumped from 45 in 1754 to 729 by 1767. As debt obligations increased, so did the number of defaults. In one three-year period, the merchants of Granville County brought 350 debt suits to local courts. The courts directed sheriffs to seize the property of bankrupt farmers and sell it at auction to pay merchant creditors and court costs.

This extensive use of the legal system to collect debts violated the customs of the subsistence-oriented economy of the North Carolina backcountry. As in rural communities in New England, loans were based on personal trust and often ran on for years. Creditors frequently accepted repayment in the form of labor rather than cash or goods. Legal action was used only as a last resort, not as a normal business procedure. Backcountry farmers reacted angrily to the new system and the occupational groups that ran it. "Mark any Clerk, Lawyer, or Scotch merchant," warned Herman Husband, a farmer, "We must make these men subject to the laws or they will enslave the whole community."

Actually, the merchants usually had the law on their side, regardless of community traditions. To prevent the seizure and sale of their lands, livestock, or equipment, yeomen debtors banded together in another Regulator movement. The North Carolina Regulators did not suppress outlaws or "low people" but challenged the colonial governments. They intimidated judges, closed courts by force, and broke into jails to free their arrested leaders. The Regulators also sought to win political power and change public policies. Their leader, Herman Husband, urged the election of planters and farmers to the legislature rather than "Lawyers, Clerks, and others connected with them." The Regulators asked for tax payments in the "produce of the country," rather than in hard-to-get cash; the reduction of legal costs and sheriff's fees in debt cases; and an equitable distribution of the costs of government. Insurgents in Anson County argued in 1769 that each person should pay taxes "in proportion to the profits arising from his Estate."

The North Carolina Regulators developed a far-reaching democratic ideology, but they lacked the power to succeed against the colonial government. In 1771, Governor William Tyron mobilized the militia, defeated a large Regulator force in the battle of the Alamance River, and tracked down and hanged seven insurgent leaders. Not since Bacon's and Leisler's uprisings in the late seventeenth century had political conflict in America resulted in such bloodshed. In far-off Connecticut, the Reverend Ezra Stiles wrote approvingly of the Regulators. "What shall an injured & oppressed people do when their Petitions, Remonstrances & Supplications are unheard & rejected," he asked, "and Oppression and tyranny (under the name of Government) continued with Rigor & Egyptian Austerity?"

Stiles wrote with the emerging struggle for American independence from Britain in mind, but his remarks covered a generation of disputes within the colonies as well. There had been more conflict and violence among whites between 1740 and 1765 than in the previous half-century. New Lights condemned Old Lights and Enlightenment deists; poor Virginia Baptists challenged the Anglican elite; proprietors and manorial lords evicted squatters and suppressed tenants; migrant yeomen families fought over land claims; and British and American soldiers fought a major war. America had become a diverse, conflict-ridden society.

These events were as much signs of strength as of weakness. They testified to the complexity and vitality of the American colonies and the potential for an independent existence.

---

*B*etween 1740 and 1765, Europe exerted a new and significant influence on the British colonies in North America.

The "new learning" of the European Enlightenment spread among educated merchants, planters, and clergymen. At the same time, such European migrants and preachers as George Whitefield brought pietism to America. These contrasting intellectual and emotional systems of thought and behavior sharpened existing social divisions. In Virginia, they led to a cultural confrontation between Anglican gentry and Baptist farmers.

The expansion of transatlantic trade likewise brought more Americans into the international market economy. Colonial exports increased, but imports from Great Britain rose even faster. As a result, the colonists fell deeply into debt to their British suppliers. The seaport cities grew rapidly during these years, and merchants became increasingly wealthy and powerful.

Rural population growth encouraged conflicts over land rights. Manorial lords, absentee proprietors, and speculators claimed large tracts of land. New England migrants contested their ownership by force in New York and Pennsylvania and other backcountry settlers demanded greater representation in colonial legislatures. Westward movement generated new conflicts with the French in Canada and with native Americans wishing to preserve their lands. These struggles—over religious principles, economic development, and land rights—reflected the growing complexity of American colonial society.

Suggestions for Further Reading

The Enlightenment and Pietistic Religion

Studies of witchcraft include Marion Starkey, *Devil in Massachusetts* (1969), and John Demos, *Entertaining Satan* (1982). The growth of medical knowledge is covered in Richard Shryock, *Medicine and Society in America, 1660–1860* (1960). For the impact of European intellectual currents, see Henry May, *The Enlightenment in America* (1976), and Louis B. Wright, *The Cultural Life of the American Colonies* (1957).

Bernard Bailyn, *Education in the Forming of American Society* (1960), is a stimulating introduction to the subject, while Lawrence A. Cremin, *American Education: The Colonial Experience* (1970), offers a comprehensive study. Richard Warch captures the spiritual tenor of higher education in *School of the Prophets: Yale College, 1701–1740* (1973). See also James Axtell, *The School upon a Hill* (1974). Russell B. Nye provides a useful survey of *American Literary History, 1607–1830* (1970).

Richard Hofstadter, *America at 1750* (1971), presents a superb overview of the First Great Awakening. More specialized studies include E. S. Gaustad, *The Great Awakening in New England* (1957), and Alan Heimart, *Religion and the American Mind* (1966). Two good biographies of revivalists are Patricia Tracy, *Jonathan Edward, Pastor* (1979), and Christopher Jedrey, *The World of John Cleaveland* (1979). Richard Bushman, ed., *The Great Awakening* (1970), conveys the spirit of the revivals in an excellent anthology of primary materials.

Wesley M. Gewehr, *The Great Awakening in Virginia* (1930), outlines the scope of the revivals, and Rhys Isaac, *The Transformation of Virginia* (1982), captures the emotions of ordinary participants. W. G. McLoughlin, *Isaac Backus and American Pietistic Tradition* (1957), discusses the Baptist experience in New England, as does C. C. Goen, *Revivalism and Separatism in New England* (1962). Sidney E. Ahlstrom, *A Religious History of the American People* (1972), can be consulted for the revival in the Middle Colonies.

Economic Expansion and Social Structure

Gary M. Walton and James F. Shepherd, *The Economic Rise of Early America* (1979), trace the growing importance of commerce. Stuart Bruchey, *The Roots of American Economic Growth, 1607–1861* (1965), is useful. Studies of important topics include Harold Innes, *The Cod Fisheries* (1940), and Joseph Ernst, *Money and Politics in America, 1755–1775* (1973). Jackson T. Main, *The Social Structure of Revolutionary America* (1975) is comprehensive and interesting. On life in the cities, see Gary B. Nash, *The Urban Crucible* (1979); John K. Alexander, *Render Them Submissive; Responses to Poverty in Philadelphia* (1980); and Douglas Greenberg, *Crime and Law Enforcement in Colonial New York* (1976).

The Struggle for the American Land

Robert Gross, *The Minutemen and Their World* (1976), analyzes the growing shortage of land and the farmers' response. John Shy, *Toward Lexington: The Role of the British Army in the Coming of the American Revolution* (1965), deals with border wars along the New York frontier. The speculative activities of Virginia gentlemen are discussed in Charles Sydnor's entertaining *Gentlemen Freeholders: Political Practices in Washington's Virginia* (1956).

Anthony Wallace, *The Death and Rebirth of the Seneca* (1970), offers an outstanding anthropological discussion of the Iroquois and traces their military and diplomatic strategies. Edward P. Hamilton, *The French and Indian Wars* (1962), provides a more conventional treatment. The concluding chapter of Clarence Ver Steeg, *The Formative Years* (1964), lucidly discusses the Great War for Empire. Backcountry political agitation forms the focus of Richard M. Brown, *The South Carolina Regulators* (1963), and some of the essays in Alfred Young, ed., *The American Revolution: Essays in the History of American Radicalism* (1976).

6

TOWARD
INDEPENDENCE:
A DECADE
OF DECISIONS

In 1765, The American colonists were relatively prosperous, loyal subjects of Great Britain. Ten years later, they stood on the brink of civil war. They were angry, armed, and prepared to secede from the British Empire. What caused this rapid and largely unexpected change? The events that led to the American decision for independence occurred at such a bewildering pace that few people understood them clearly at the time. They knew only that the traditional imperial system had collapsed and that they had been caught up in a process of unpredictable change.

In retrospect, it is clear that the movement toward American independence, like all great historical events, stemmed from a complex and interrelated series of causes. For purposes of analysis, these factors are best treated in three separate categories.

First, there were immediate causes of this upheaval in American political life. The Great War for Empire had severely strained the British treasury, and the colonists' behavior during the conflict raised troubling administrative issues. Therefore, British ministers embarked upon a sustained campaign for imperial political and economic reform. Their actions brought vigorous American resistance based on a tradition of self-

government and collective action. The climax of these immediate causes came with the Stamp Act controversy of 1765.

The Stamp Act crisis itself was a second cause of the American movement for independence. The events of 1765 transformed British and colonial politics. Outraged by colonial resistance to the Stamp Act, British ministers sought constitutional supremacy rather than compromise. In the colonies, this initial confrontation produced resistance by American patriots. The patriots, who were now extremely suspicious of British intentions, mobilized resistance to new imperial measures. The intensity of the Stamp Act crisis thus began a dynamic process of escalation that drove the British government and its American colonies further and further apart.

Third, the character of American preindustrial society profoundly shaped the final outcome of the struggle. The nature of economic and intellectual life in the seaport cities prompted people there to take a leading role in the early stages of the independence movement. Similarly, the structures of agricultural life allowed the rural population to ignore the imperial crisis at first and then actively to support the demands of patriot leaders for political independence.

Reform and Resistance

Most administrative reforms in government produce political protest but not a violent crisis. However, specific factors in Great Britain and America transformed an attempted reform of the imperial system into an all-out confrontation. Prime Minister George Grenville wanted not only to tax Americans, but also to reduce their political and economic power. Convinced patriots such as Samuel Adams urged colonial political leaders and ordinary citizens to follow radical programs of resistance. Yet these and all the other actors in the drama were caught up in larger forces of change. By the early 1760s, all British officials favored imperial reform, and most American colonists strongly opposed any curtailment of their traditional rights and privileges. There was little room for maneuver.

Background for Revolution

The French and Indian War revealed the weakness of British imperial administration. In Massachusetts, the Board of Trade complained, "almost every act of executive and legislative power is ordered and directed by votes and resolves of the General Court." Nearly every colonial assembly appropriated funds for troops and supplies only if it had some control over military appointments and operations. In Virginia, the House of Burgesses refused to levy taxes to support the war effort. Instead, it resorted to deficit financing and printed a substantial amount of paper currency. As the Virginia government bought military supplies and paid its troops with this money, the value of the currency fell by nearly 20 percent. Yet Virginia law required creditors to accept the currency at its face value.

When the Burgesses twice refused to amend the law, British merchants appealed to Parliament for relief. In 1751, Parliament had prohibited the New England colonies from using government bills of credit as legal tender. Now it passed the Currency Act of 1764, banning this practice in all the American colonies. The result was financial distress and dislocation, for the colonists lacked sufficient specie both to pay for British manufactured products and to maintain domestic trade.

Parliament's intrusion into the colonial credit system followed other measures of imperial control. For twenty-five years, colonial customs officials had failed to enforce the Molasses Act of 1733. Provincial merchants bribed low-paid customs agents to underreport the quantity of French molasses they imported. Shocked by the extent of illegal trade with the French islands during the French and Indian War, the British ministry ordered strict enforcement. "Since you sailed from here," Timothy Orne, a Salem merchant, wrote to one of his ship captains in 1758, incoming vessels "have been permitted to Enter about One Eighth or Tenth part of their Cargo paying 6d Sterling p. gall. Duty for what is entered—which is more than twice as much as was given before." To ensure full compliance with the Molasses Act and the other Navigation Acts, the British government ordered the navy to prevent illegal trade with the French islands and enacted the Revenue Act of 1762. This measure eliminated the widespread practice of leasing offices to deputies who accepted bribes to augment their income. The era of "salutary neglect" had ended.

British officials then undertook a fundamental review of the entire West Indian trade. The resulting Sugar Act, passed by Parliament in 1764, again levied duties on imported French molasses. However, this new legislation balanced the interests of American merchants and farmers with those of British sugar planters to a greater extent than did the Molasses Act. Its architects were treasury officials Thomas Whately and Charles Jenkinson. They knew that the American colonists had to market their goods in the French islands in order to earn specie to buy manufactured goods from Britain. The treasury officials therefore resisted demands from British planters for a prohibitive tax on foreign molasses and proposed a smaller duty instead. Whately and Jenkinson argued that this tax would make British molasses competitive with the cheaper French product but would not destroy the American export trade or the provincial distilling industry.

American merchants and manufacturers rejected the revision of the Molasses Act. Distillers in Rhode Island and Massachusetts protested in public that even the proposed smaller tax would wipe out the trade with the French islands. They

SOCIETY AND ARCHITECTURE IN NEW YORK CITY
By the 1760s New York was a booming seaport with a diverse population and a complex architectural tradition. Well-proportioned buildings of Dutch design (far left) easily blended in with the English church topped by a prominent cupola. A newly constructed, large, and austere Methodist chapel challenged these established architectural styles, just as its artisan members questioned the dominance of the traditional political elites. (Joseph Beekman Smith. *Wesley Chapel, 1768.* John Street United Methodist Church, New York)

vowed privately to evade the new legislation through smuggling or bribery. More significantly, colonial political leaders raised constitutional objections to the Sugar Act. Thomas Cushing, the Speaker of the Massachusetts House of Representatives, argued that the duties constituted a tax. As a revenue measure, he maintained, the act was "contrary to a fundamental Principall of our Constitution: That all Taxes ought to originate with the people." A House committee went further. It declared that such parliamentary acts "have a tendency to deprive the colonies of some of their most essential Rights as British subjects."

The committee's concern was justified. In addition to levying duties, the Sugar Act of 1764 extended the jurisdiction of Vice-Admiralty Courts. These courts operated without the procedures and protections of English common law. There was no trial by jury; rather, a judge heard arguments and decided cases solely on the basis of parliamentary legislation. Americans had opposed these courts since they were established in 1697. To limit their power, colonial legislatures extended the jurisdiction of their own courts to cover all customs offenses occurring in coastal waters or American seaports. As a result, friendly American judges and common-law juries often freed merchants charged with violating the Navigation Acts.

The Sugar Act reaffirmed the jurisdiction of the Vice-Admiralty Courts regarding all customs offenses, reviving old colonial fears and raising new constitutional objections. Richard Bland, an influential Virginia planter, condemned these courts as discriminatory. He charged that they unjustly singled out British subjects living in America and this, Bland declared, "constituted an unnatural Difference between Men under the same Allegiance, born equally free, and entitled to the same civil rights." He concluded that "*Rights* imply *Equality*" because the colonists "were not sent out to be the Slaves but to be the Equals of those that remained behind." Bland's logic was compelling, but his premises were wrong. The Vice-Admiralty Courts played a major role in British commercial life. The new legislation was not discriminatory but only extended British practice to America.

The real issue was the growing power of the British government, first at home and now in America. Mercantile legislation required a bureaucracy and administrative tribunals to enforce it. Both the size and the powers of the British Customs Service and other government agencies expanded continually. Between 1750 and 1780, the number of royal bureaucrats jumped from about five thousand to fourteen thousand. The extension of vice-admiralty jurisdiction alerted Americans to the growth of the British government and the threat it posed to what they called the traditional "rights of Englishmen."

"Here is the contrast that stares us in the face," proclaimed John Adams, a young Boston lawyer defending the merchant John Hancock on a charge of smuggling:

> The Parliament in one Clause guarding the People of the Realm, and securing to them the benefit of a Tryal by the Law of the Land, and by the next Clause, depriving all Americans of that Privilege. What shall we say to this Distinction? Is there not in this Clause a Brand of Infamy, or Degradation, and Disgrace, fixed upon every American? Is he not degraded below the Rank of an Englishman?

Confronted by a purposeful British movement for imperial reform, Adams and other Americans searched for firm legal grounds on which to stand. Lawyer and statesman James Otis, whom Adams described as a "flame of fire," denied that Parliament had the constitutional right to authorize the use of writs of assistance, or search warrants, because they violated traditional English rights. Instead, American patriots felt the ground giving way beneath them. When Governor Francis Bernard of Massachusetts heard that the House had objected to the Sugar Act on the grounds of no taxation without

representation, he asked whether people in America had any constitutional rights. "The rule that a *British* subject shall not be bound by laws or liable to taxes, but what he has consented to by his representatives," Bernard suggested, "must be confined to the inhabitants of Great Britain only."

Policy makers in London shared this narrow definition of American rights, and they acted deliberately to increase British control over colonial affairs. In 1763, the government assigned fifteen infantry regiments—about ten thousand men—to peacetime service in North America. Three motives influenced this sizable commitment of military forces. First, Britain needed most of the troops to occupy captured territories in Canada and Florida and to prevent revolts by their French and Spanish residents. Second, experienced officials in London, including Lord Halifax, the former head of the Board of Trade, and Henry Knox, a former treasury official in Georgia, feared an Indian war. They instructed military commanders to enforce the Proclamation Line of 1763, which banned white migration into Indian lands west of the Appalachian Mountains. For some of these officials, the third motive was the most important. "The main purpose of Stationing a large Body of Troops in America," Knox wrote in a memorandum to policy

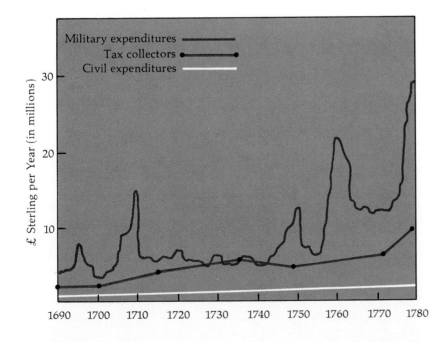

FIGURE 6.1 THE GROWING POWER OF THE BRITISH STATE

makers, was "to secure the Dependence of the Colonys on Great Britain."

How was this to be accomplished? Knox did not elaborate how infantry regiments might deter demands for American political autonomy. Governor Jonathan Belcher of New Jersey had considered this question when riots disrupted his colony in the 1740s. The mere presence of British troops, he told royal authorities, would not "drive Assemblies or people from their Obstinate ways of Thinking, into reasonable measures." To be effective, military power had to be used, not just displayed. In sending a large number of troops to America, the British ministry showed that it was prepared to use force to carry through a reform of the imperial system.

The Stamp Act

The deployment of ten thousand troops in North America precipitated a major financial decision in Britain and a constitutional crisis in the colonies. The ministry lacked the £200,000 per year needed to clothe, house, feed, and pay the soldiers. Military expenditures during the Great War for Empire had increased the national debt from £75 million to £133 million. Treasury officials refused to impose additional domestic levies because the land tax had reached an all-time high. Since the total public debt of the American colonies amounted to less than £1 million, they looked to the colonists for the funds to support the troops.

George Grenville, chancellor of the exchequer and prime minister, had a scheme to raise the necessary funds. As he introduced the Sugar Bill in Parliament early in 1764, Grenville announced his intention to seek a colonial stamp tax the following year. Such a tax would impose levies on court documents, land titles, contracts, newspapers, and other printed items. These taxes had been levied in England since 1694. By the 1760s, they yielded an annual revenue of £290,000. Grenville anticipated that Americans might object to the taxes on constitutional grounds. So he asked if any member of the House of Commons doubted "the power and sovereignty of Parliament over every part of the British dominions, for the purpose of raising or collecting any tax?" No one rose.

Grenville promptly informed the American assemblies that a stamp tax would be voted in 1765 unless they could "among themselves and in modes best suited to their circumstances, raise a sum adequate to their defence." This challenge threw the London representatives of the colonial legislatures into confusion. Some, including Richard Jackson, were English merchants or lawyers; others, such as Benjamin Franklin, were American public leaders. They all agreed that the colonies could not apportion the defense budget among themselves. The British refused to coordinate such an effort, and there were no intercolonial political institutions to assume the task.

Believing that passage of the Stamp Act was inevitable, Jackson suggested that the colonial assemblies "signify their Assent and Desire to that Tax" to prevent "a Precedent from internal Taxes being imposed without their Consent." Franklin countered with a proposal for American representation in the British Parliament. "If you chuse to tax us," the imaginative American suggested, "give us Members in your Legislature, and let us be one People." With the exception of William Pitt, British politicians rejected this radical notion, and so did most colonial leaders. Influential Philadelphia merchants warned Franklin "to beware of any measure that might extend to us seats in the Commons." They feared that a handful of colonial delegates could not prevent the passage of harmful legislation. For these reasons, the Pennsylvania assembly declared, the colonies "neither are nor can be represented, under the present Circumstances." At this point, American leaders had no satisfactory alternatives to the constitutional and economic positions taken by the British prime minister.

Grenville was anxious to assert the constitutional supremacy of Parliament. As the House of Commons met in 1765, his chief assistant observed that the Stamp Act was "the great measure of the Sessions on account of the important point it establishes, the Right of Parliament to lay an internal Tax upon the Colonies." The ministry's plan worked smoothly. The House of Commons refused to accept American petitions opposing the new legislation. Then it approved the Stamp Act by the overwhelming vote of 205 to 49. The act not only levied duties on a wide range of legal documents and printed matter, but it also specified that the proceeds be used in America for military supplies. Parliament decreed further that violations of the act could be tried in Vice-Admiralty courts as well as in courts of common law. In addition, at the request of General Thomas Gage, commander of the British military forces in America, Parliament passed a Quartering Act. This legislation required the colonial assemblies to provide barracks and supplies for British troops who were dispatched to the seaboard colonies. Grenville's design was complete. He had forced a constitutional confrontation not only on the crucial issue of taxes, but also on the right to a trial by jury and on compulsory support of a standing army.

The Crowd Rebels

The response from the colonies was far stronger than the British had predicted. In the Virginia assembly, the eloquent young firebrand Patrick Henry introduced a series of resolutions sharply objecting to the Stamp Act. As approved by the House of Burgesses in May 1765, these Virginia Resolves claimed for Americans "all Liberties, Privileges, Franchises, and Immunities" ever held by the "People of Great Britain." Any attempt to tax the colonists without the consent of their elected representatives, the resolutions warned, "has a manifest Tendency to Destroy AMERICAN FREEDOM." The Massachusetts House of Representatives, in a letter to all the assemblies, proposed a meeting in New York City in October to prepare a united response to the Stamp Act.

Before this Stamp Act Congress could meet, popular protests erupted in nearly every colony. Disciplined urban mobs, usually calling themselves Sons of Liberty, demanded the resignation of the men appointed to collect the new taxes. In August, the Boston Sons of Liberty carried an effigy of Andrew Oliver, the Massachusetts stamp tax collector, through the streets. Then they beheaded it and burned it on a large bonfire. Spurred on by these acts of violence, the crowd destroyed a new brick building owned by Oliver and broke down the doors to his house. Town authorities were helpless because most of the Massachusetts militia had joined the mob. Boston merchants also opposed the Stamp Act. Some of their leaders advised Oliver to resign; otherwise "his House would be immediately Destroyed and his Life in Continual Danger."

Two weeks later, a mob attacked the house of Lieutenant Governor Thomas Hutchinson. The crowd plundered his wine cellar, burned his library, and began to dismantle the house itself. Hutchinson had many enemies, for he had long defended social privilege, creditor interests, and imperial authority. Now, in the heat of crisis, the common people of Boston took their revenge.

The exploits of the Boston Sons of Liberty sparked intimidation of royal officials throughout the colonies. Protest marches in Annapolis and Baltimore prompted the Maryland stamp tax collector, Zachariah Hood, to flee to New York City. There, the local Sons of Liberty forced him to resign his office. In Connecticut, a disciplined crowd humiliated collector Jared Ingersoll. Born to a prominent family, Ingersoll had served as the assembly's agent in London. He worked actively against the Stamp Act but, accepting its inevitability, sought appointment as a collector.

Ingersoll paid dearly for this decision. About five hundred farmers and artisans confronted him near Wethersfield. They refused to be swayed by his social status and commanding personal presence. "They lookt upon this as the Cause of the People," one rioter shouted, and "did not intend to take Directions about it from any Body." After hours of debate Ingersoll capitulated. At the command of the mob, he gave three cheers for "Liberty and Property," tossed his hat into the air, and resigned his office.

The size and number of the Sons of Liberty mobs was surprising, but not their existence. Crowd actions formed an integral part of political life in both Britain and America. Every November 5, for example, Protestant crowds celebrated the failure of a conspiracy led by the Catholic Guy Fawkes in 1605. Colonists poured into the streets on three other types of occasions as well. Crowds often functioned as a semilegal *posse commitatus* (power of the country) when local authorities refused to act on an issue. These mobs closed houses of prostitution, expelled people with infectious diseases, and enforced the social standards of the community.

Other crowds mobilized to defend the economic interests of particular social groups. During King William's War (1689–1697), Boston artisans rioted to prevent merchants from exporting scarce grain from the town. In New Jersey during the 1740s, farmers closed the courts by force to prevent the legal seizure of their property. These crowds also claimed moral justification for their behavior. Their "Violence and unlawful Actions" were legitimate, not criminal, one New Jersey rioter explained, because an uprising indicated that the people had been "wronged and oppressed, or else they would never *rebell agt. the Laws.*"

The third form of popular protest anticipated the Stamp Act riots, for it was directed against British officials. Lumbermen and sawmill workers occasionally attacked officials called surveyors of the woods when they prevented the illegal cutting of tall and straight pine trees reserved for the British navy. From time to time, merchants provoked reprisals against overzealous customs agents. And in 1747, Boston crowds rioted for three days to protest the impressment of merchant seamen for forced service in the British navy. A young Harvard graduate, Samuel Adams, offered a forceful intellectual defense of these mobs. In his *Two Treatises on Government,* John Locke had argued that government derived legitimacy from its protection of people and property. Adams used Locke's premises to good

effect. When seamen and other people "are suddenly attack'd without the least Warning," Adams maintained, "they are treated as in a State of Nature, and have a Natural Right to repel those Mischiefs against which they can derive no Security from the Government."

The Stamp Act riots thus evolved from American historical experience and English political ideology. In beheading the effigy of Andrew Oliver, the Boston crowd emulated the ritual killing of the pope on Guy Fawkes Day. The cry of "Liberty and Property" that a mob forced from Jared Ingersoll harked back to the Whig and republican ideologies that motivated the English revolutions of the seventeenth century. These rich traditions gave the crowds a sense of identity and purpose, and their social composition made them a formidable political force.

Most mobs were not formed by random individuals but by men and women who knew one another in jobs, churches, or neighborhoods. Of the thirty-six young men in the Sons of Liberty in Albany, New York in 1765, twenty belonged to the same firefighters' club and twelve had pews in the balcony of the Dutch Reformed Church. These social connections ensured that the Sons of Liberty would continue as a political force from month to month and crisis to crisis. The Stamp Act riots gave institutional identity and an ideological quality to existing groups of artisans and laborers in American cities.

THE GREEN DRAGON CONSPIRACY

Three Sons of Liberty proudly proclaim their role in planning the Boston Tea Party. Paul Revere's Masonic "Lodge of St. Andrew" owned the Green Dragon Tavern; its symbols appear in the top left corner. A secret society with hundreds of lodges in Europe and America, the Masons were firm advocates of republican political principles. (John Johnston. *Green Dragon Tavern.* American Antiquarian Society)

SONS OF LIBERTY FROM A LOYALIST'S PERSPECTIVE

In the morning of the 27th Inst. between five and six a Mob Assembled and Erected a Gallows near the Town House and then Dispers'd, and about Ten A Clock Reassembled and took The Effigys of the Above Men and the Stamp Master and Carted them up Thames Street, then up King Street to the said Gallows where they was hung up by the Neck and Suspended near 15 feet in the Air, And on the Breast of the Stamp Master, was this Inscription THE STAMP MAN . . . and upon the Breast of the Doct'r was write, THAT INFAMOUS, MISCREATED, LEERING JACOBITE DOCT'R MURFY. . . . And about five A Clock in the Afternoon they made a Fire under the Gallows which Consum'd the Effigy's, Gallows and all, to Ashes. I forgot to tell you that a Boot hung over the Doctor's Shoulder with the Devil Peeping out of it . . . we thought it was all over. But last Night about Dusk they all Muster'd Again, and first they went to Martin Howard's, and Broke Every Window in his house Frames and all, likewise Chairs Tables, Pictures and every thing they cou'd come across. . . . this Moment I'v Rec'd a Peace of News which Effects me so Much that I Cant write any More, which is the Demolition of your worthy Daddy's house and Furniture etc. But I must just let you know that the Stamp Master has Resign'd. . . .

A Political Legacy

As crowds challenged royal authority in the streets, elected officials worked diligently to obtain repeal of the new legislation. Most of the colonies sent representatives to the Stamp Act Congress in New York City in October 1765. The delegates adopted a moderate stance. As politicians trained in the arts of conciliation and compromise, they did not threaten a political revolt. Nor did they directly contest the constitutionality of the Stamp and Sugar acts. Rather, they protested the abridgement of the "invaluable rights and liberties" of Americans, especially the "two privileges essential to freedom," trial by jury and taxation by consent. Then they humbly petitioned for repeal of the Stamp Act, reassuring Parliament that Americans "glory in being subjects of the best of Kings having been born under the most perfect form of government."

An angry populace demanded more drastic and more immediate action. The Stamp Act officially went into effect on November 1, 1765. The day before, about two hundred New York City merchants proclaimed a boycott on English imports. Shopkeepers and tradesmen promised their suppport and joined artisans, laborers, and seamen in a mass protest meeting. Late into the night, the crowd marched through the streets, crying "Liberty" and breaking streetlamps and windows. The next night, three thousand New Yorkers surrounded the fort where the tax stamps were stored and plundered the house of an unpopular British officer.

As November 5, Guy Fawkes Day, approached, Lieutenant Governor Cadwallader Colden feared an open assault on the fort. He called on General Gage to use force against the crowd, but the small military contingent was greatly outnumbered and the prudent British commander refused. "Fire from the Fort might disperse the Mob," he told Colden, "but it would not quell them; and the consequence would in all appearance be an Insurrection, the commencement of Civil War." In New York, as in virtually every major urban area in America, popular resistance nullified the Stamp Act.

These uprisings produced an important political legacy. For the first time since the Albany Conference of 1754, representatives from the various colonial assemblies had met together and had agreed upon a common course of action. The Stamp Act Congress laid a firm foundation for future intercolonial cooperation. The merchant community likewise developed a sense of unity, for Boston and Philadelphia merchants soon joined New York traders in boycotting British goods. Following the military effort by all the colonies during the French and Indian War, the Stamp Act crisis created a sense of "American" identity. It also gave a sharp popular, even democratic, ideological tone to this emerging sense of unity. "Nothing is wanting but your own Resolution," a New York Son of Liberty declared during the upheaval, "for great is the Authority and Power of the People." A New York pamphleteer warned against the designs of traditional political leaders who protested only against the Stamp Act, for they "would have us be at the mercy of the British Parliament in every article but taxation."

Americans had cherished their political autonomy and representative institutions before 1765, but they were equally proud of their ties to Great Britain. Political conflicts during the French and Indian War and the British reform movement disrupted this delicate balance. When Prime Minister Grenville forced a constitutional confrontation, many colonists responded by questioning all British authority. A majority of Americans would no longer display the unthinking obedience that had assured the stability of royal rule for the previous three generations.

"The truth of the matter is the hands of the Government are not strong enough to oppose the numerous body of people," the Philadelphia customs collector concluded in 1770. "What can a Governor do without the assistance of the Governed? What can the magistrates do, unless they are supported by their Fellow citizens?" The Stamp Act crisis had eroded the emotional foundations of power. After 1765, the British government was on the defensive in America.

The Growing Confrontation

The violent events of 1765 put Great Britain and its American colonies on a collison course. There was room for compromise, for careful statesmanship could still protect the vital interests of each side. Ultimately, however, British ministers preferred confrontation to conciliation. And the willingness—even the obsession—of Massachusetts patriots to sharpen the constitutional con-

flict diminished the chances for a peaceful solution. Political rivalries in Britain and the economic self-interest and ideological rigidity of both sides brought a gradual escalation of the conflict. By 1771, the lines were clearly drawn and the possibility of a compromise solution had virtually vanished.

The Constitutional Debate

Ministerial instability at home prevented a firm British response to the Stamp Act riots. When George III took the throne in 1760, he reasserted the constitutional powers of the monarchy. He demanded that the Whig aristocratic oligarchy relinquish some of the governmental authority it had appropriated since the 1720s. In particular, the king insisted on the choice of the prime minister regardless of his nominee's support in the House of Commons.

George's activism produced a decade of ministerial upheaval—and a disastrous lack of continuity in British policy toward America. In 1761, the king forced William Pitt to resign as prime minister—in the middle of a military victory—and installed his own favorite, Lord Bute. When lack of parliamentary support undermined Bute's position in 1763, George reluctantly turned to Grenville, who commanded a majority in the House of Commons. Just as American agitation against the Stamp Act reached a climax, the king lost confidence in Grenville over unrelated issues and dismissed him. The governmental crisis with the colonies became the responsibility of the new prime minister, Lord Rockingham, and his "Old Whig" supporters.

From the American point of view, Rockingham was an ideal prime minister. He was young, inexperienced, and open to persuasion. He and his colleagues bitterly opposed Grenville and were anxious to question his policies. Most important of all, the Rockingham Whigs stood for the imperial policy of "salutary neglect." They believed that America was important for the "flourishing and increasing trade" that had given Britain commercial supremacy in the Atlantic, not as a source of tax revenues. In fact, many Old Whigs doubted the constitutionality of taxing the colonists without their consent. General Henry Conway, the new secretary of state, had questioned the extent of parliamentary power during the Stamp Act debates. The Duke of Newcastle, the patron of many American royal governors, told the House of Lords that he was "much against Taxation."

British merchants likewise campaigned vigorously for conciliation. Many traders and manufacturers had large inventories of goods in 1765, and the Stamp Act crisis caused a drastic fall in sales. Most American mercantile houses supported New York's call for halting the import of British products. In addition, many colonial firms could not pay for British goods already received on credit. Following the Currency Act of 1764, gold and silver were in short supply and payment in paper currency was prohibited. Hundreds of British companies faced bankruptcy because of cash-flow problems. "The Avenues of Trade are all shut up," a Bristol merchant complained, "We have no Remittances and are at our Witts End for Want of Money to fulfill our Engagements with our Tradesmen." In January 1766, the leading commercial centers of London, Liverpool, Bristol, and Glasgow deluged Parliament with a flood of petitions. Organized by Rockingham's followers, this petition campaign emphasized the great value of the American trade and also stressed the harm to British prosperity inflicted by the Stamp Act.

Nevertheless, the uprisings in America generated intense anger in Britain. Speaking as a member of the opposition faction, Grenville asked Parliament to declare its "just resentment and indignation at the outrageous tumults and insurrections" in the colonies. Public officials demanded that Americans submit on the constitutional issue. "The British legislature," Chief Justice Sir James Mansfield declared, "has authority to bind every part and every subject without the least distraction, whether such subjects have a right to vote or not." Even William Pitt, long known for his pro-American views, took a guarded position. Pitt questioned the wisdom of taxing the colonists and called for the repeal of the Stamp Act "absolutely, totally, and immediately." However, he maintained that British authority over the colonies was "sovereign and supreme, in every circumstance of government and legislation whatsoever."

Rockingham tried to reconcile the conflicting constitutional positions, economic interests, and political factions. Swayed by the merchant community and the arguments of the colonial agents, the British government decided to repeal, rather than revise, the Stamp Act. Equally important, it chose not to transfer British troops from Canadian and frontier garrisons to the rebellious seaport cities. The government also mollified the colonists by revising the Sugar Act, reducing the duty on French molasses by a third. However, Parliament insisted that the duty be collected and extended it to apply to previously untaxed molasses from the British islands. This action threatened to create another constitutional deadlock. The revised Sugar Act not only regulated foreign trade, which most American public officials accepted as a valid exercise of parliamentary authority, but it also raised a revenue. Some colonists challenged this as an unconstitutional tax. Parliament sharpened the constitutional issues with the Declaratory Act that accompanied the repeal of the Stamp Act in 1766. It reaffirmed the "full power and authority" of Parliament to "bind the colonies and people of America in all cases whatsoever."

Despite this strong statement of parliamentary supremacy, the constitutional issues remained blurred. The Declaratory Act did not explicitly mention taxation. Moreover, the act closely resembled a statute binding the British dependency of Ireland; yet the Irish Parliament voted its own taxes. The limits of Parliament's power remained open to negotiation.

A few British leaders, such as Lord Camden, believed that "taxation and representation are inseparably united" and ruled out taxation of the colonies. Others replied that America was "virtually" represented in Parliament. They argued that the British merchants in the House of Commons could defend colonial interests. Still other British public leaders seized on the distinction made by Daniel Dulany, a conservative Maryland lawyer. Dulany suggested that Americans opposed "internal" duties but accepted "external" taxes on trade. Benjamin Franklin heightened this impression. Testifying before the House of Commons in 1766, Franklin seemed to say that Americans accepted Dulany's distinction.

In fact, colonial opinion was less divided than opinion in Britain. Most American public officials maintained that the colonists had all the rights and privileges of British subjects, including taxation by consent. They rejected "virtual representation" because, as the events leading up to the Currency Acts of 1751 and 1764 demonstrated, the interests of British merchants and American consumers were far from identical. Following the Stamp Act crisis, most American leaders opposed any British measure that infringed on the powers of the American assemblies. Like the Old Whigs in Britain, they yearned for the autonomy they had enjoyed during the era of salutary neglect: "It is easy to propose a plan of conciliation," Franklin declared, "Mine may be expressed in a few words: *repeal* the laws, *renounce* the right, *recall* the troops, *refund* the money, and *return* to the old method of requisition."

The Townshend Duties

The clock of history could not be turned back. A reform-minded and assertive British Parliament rejected the old methods as unsuited to new realities. Early in 1767, Rockingham's Old Whig ministry collapsed. William Pitt, the wartime hero who now sat in the House of Lords as the Earl of Chatham, headed the new government as prime minister. The great statesman was in decline, chronically ill with bouts of gout. Because of Pitt's frequent absence from Parliament, Chancellor of the Exchequer Charles Townshend assumed command. Since his service on the Board of Trade in the 1750s, Townshend had fa-

vored imperial reform. Only Pitt's pro-American sentiments kept Townshend from acting immediately. Then, as Parliament debated the military budget in 1767, Grenville demanded that the colonists pay for the British troops in America and that the savings be used to reduce the English Land Tax. Townshend, convinced of the necessity for reform, committed the government to find a new source of revenue in America.

The result was the Townshend Act of 1767, which put duties on paper, paint, glass, tea, and other goods imported into the colonies. Townshend allocated the expected revenue partly for military expenses and partly for "the Charge of the Administration of Justice and the Support of Civil Government." He intended to pay the salaries of governors, judges, and other officials, thus depriving the colonial assemblies of control over their livelihoods. To increase the power of the royal bureaucracy still further, Townshend reorganized the Customs Service. A new Revenue Act of 1767 created a Board of American Customs Commissioners in Boston and four Vice-Admiralty Courts in Halifax, Boston, Philadelphia, and Charleston. These administrative innovations represented a greater threat to colonial autonomy than the duties themselves.

Most American public officials condemned the new legislation. In his widely read *Letters from a Farmer in Pennsylvania*, John Dickinson argued that the Townshend duties were not designed to regulate trade but to bring in revenue.

FIGURE 6.2 THE COINCIDENCE OF TRADE AND POLITICS, 1763–1776

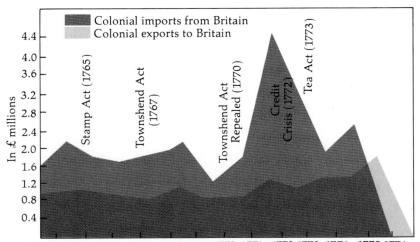

As such, they were taxes imposed without consent. In February 1768, the Massachusetts House of Representatives sent a letter to other assemblies condemning the Townshend Act as an infringement of the colonists' "natural & constitutional Rights." Boston and New York merchants called for stopping British imports for 1769, but Philadelphia mercantile houses refused to go along. Acting through the Pennsylvania assembly, they petitioned the king for repeal of the Townshend duties. Some merchant seamen also protested that a year-long boycott meant no work and financial disaster. However, the residents of seaport towns in New England and New York generally favored a halt to British imports. The Sons of Liberty backed up these sentiments with intimidation. They published names of noncompliers in newspapers, stoned their store windows, and harassed their employees.

Gradually, this popular pressure built widespread support for nonimportation. In New England, Puritan injunctions against "luxury and dissipation" still carried weight. Ministers and public officials condemned the use of "foreign superfluities." They encouraged the domestic manufacture of such necessities as textiles and paper. In Charleston, South Carolina, influential merchant Christopher Gadsden joined with artisans to support nonimportation. Finally, in March 1769, Philadelphia merchants joined the movement. Two months later, the members of the Virginia House of Burgesses agreed privately among themselves not to import dutied articles, British luxuries, and slaves.

"The whole continent from New England to Georgia seems firmly fixed," the Massachusetts *Gazette* proudly announced in November 1769, "like a strong, well-constructed arch, the more weight there is laid upon it, the firmer it stands; and thus with Americans, the more we are loaded, the more we are united." The seed of national unity planted at Albany and watered at the Stamp Act Congress had begun to bloom.

Nonimportation brought a sharp improvement in the American balance of trade with Great Britain. The colonies incurred a deficit of only £230,000 in 1768, compared with £500,000 in a normal year, and accumulated a massive surplus of £816,000 during the nonimportation year of 1769. This financial pressure achieved its goal. British merchants and manu-

facturers petitioned Parliament for repeal of the controversial legislation, although with less enthusiasm than at the time of the Stamp Act. Once again the American colonies and the British ministry were locked in an economic and political battle with high constitutional stakes.

The Threat of Coercion

By 1769, a series of incidents had stretched the imperial system to the breaking point. In New York, the assembly had refused to comply with the Quartering Act of 1765. Fearing a forced drain on its treasury, the assembly initially rebuffed General Gage's requests for accommodations and supplies for his troops. Later, it limited assistance to two infantry battalions and one artillery company. The financial struggle intensified when Townshend transferred frontier garrisons to seaboard settlements to avert political agitation. The responsibility for defense against Indian attacks rested once again wih the assembly. Pitt demanded that New York raise the needed funds, and members of Parliament proposed that an extra port duty be imposed by the British. Secretary of State Shelburne took an even harder line. He suggested a military governor for New York, armed with authority to seize funds from the colonial treasury to quarter troops. The governor also would have instructions "to act with Force or Gentleness as circumstances might make necessary." In the end, the British government adopted Townshend's plan for a "Restraining Act." Passed by Parliament in June 1767, this legislation suspended the New York assembly until it obeyed the Quartering Act. The coercive measure finally cowed the stubborn colonial assemblymen. They appropriated funds to support the resident military garrison and to provide for Indian defense.

The Restraining Act was an important precedent. In the past, the British Privy Council had monitored the actions of the colonial assemblies. Through the years, it had invalidated about 5 percent of all colonial laws as contrary to British practice or policy. The Restraining Act was a much more powerful administrative weapon. It threatened the actual existence of American representative institutions, not just the specific laws that they enacted. British ministers quickly used this weapon again. A copy of the Massachusetts

House letter opposing the Townshend Duties reached London in April 1768. Lord Hillsborough, the new secretary of state, promptly branded it as "an unjustifiable opposition to the constitutional authority of Parliament." He told Govenor Francis Bernard to threaten the immediate dissolution of the assembly to force the House to rescind its action.

Hillsborough backed up these strong words with a show of force. Since early in 1768, the American customs commissioners in Boston had reported widespread and defiant smuggling activities in New England. "Our Officers were resisted and defeated in almost every Attempt to do their duty," they reported. In response to their plea to strengthen the "Hand of Government," Hillsborough now ordered two regiments of troops to Boston from Britain. When a belligerent crowd forced the customs officials to seek refuge on a navy warship, he instructed General Gage to dispatch two additional regiments from Halifax. Soon about a thousand British regulars were encamped in Boston. Gage accused Massachusetts public leaders of "Treasonable and desperate Resolves," and Parliament threatened a special commission to hear evidence of treason.

Boston merchants added new fuel to the fire when they advocated a nonimportation agreement for all the colonies. With King George's support, Hillsborough suggested a plan to isolate the agitators in Massachusetts. He proposed repeal of the Townshend duties in the other provinces, and the use of the British army to bring the rebellious New Englanders to their knees. The prospect of military coercion was real.

At this critical point, the British ministry's resolve faltered. England ran short of food in 1768; throughout the countryside, rioters protested against rising food prices and seized grain and bread. Troops killed seven demonstrators in the highly publicized "Massacre of Saint George Fields." Exploiting these serious domestic problems, opposition politicians demanded a change of ministers. John Wilkes led a radical reform movement that demanded the end of government corruption and administrative coercion. American patriots identified their own cause with that of Wilkes. They watched apprehensively as the British denied the popular leader his elected seat in Parliament on four separate occasions. Political protests and riots in Ireland over the growing military budget there added to the ministry's difficulties.

By late 1769, the danger of civil war within the empire had passed. The king no longer supported Hillsborough's scheme to coerce Massachusetts, and merchant petitions against the Townshend duties began to have an effect. When Lord North, Townshend's successor, formed a new ministry early in 1770, he sought a face-saving compromise. With some justification, North declared that it was "contrary to the true principles of commerce" for Britain to tax its own exports to America; the objective of mercantilism was to increase the consumption of British goods in its colonies. The prime minister there-

THE BOSTON "TEA PARTY" Disguised as Mohawk Indians, the Sons of Liberty boarded the *Dartmouth* under strict discipline. One participant who hid some tea in his pockets was "stripped of his booty and his clothes together, and sent home naked." Because of this judicious behavior, radical patriots claimed that they had acted "constitutionally." (Library of Congress)

WHAT EXTENT PARLIAMENT'S AUTHORITY?

Governor Thomas Hutchinson and the Massachusetts General Assembly debate the nature of sovereign power, January 1773.

The Governor's Address:

When our predecessors first took possession of this plantation, or colony, under a grant and charter from the Crown of England, it was their sense, and it was the sense of the kingdom, that they were to remain subject to the supreme authority of Parliament. This appears from the charter itself, and from other irresistible evidence. This supreme authority has, from time to time, been exercised by Parliament, and submitted to by the Legislature. . . . At length the constitution has been called in question, and the authority of the Parliament of Great Britain to make and establish laws for the inhabitants of this province has been, by many, denied. . . . I know of no arguments, founded in reason, which will be sufficient to support these principles, or to justify the measures taken in consequence of them. It has been urged, that the sole power of making laws is granted, by charter, to a Legislature established in the province. . . . I do not find, gentlemen, in the charter, such an expression as sole power, or any words which import it. . . . I know of no line that can be drawn between the supreme authority of Parliament and the total independence of the colonies: it is impossible there should be two independent Legislatures in one and the same state; for although there may be but one head, the King, yet the two Legislative bodies will make two governments as distinct as the kingdoms of England and Scotland before the union. . . .

The Representatives' Reply:

Your Excellency tells us, "you know of no line that can be drawn between the supreme authority of Parliament and the total independence of the colonies." If there be no such line, the consequence is, either that the colonies are the vassals of the Parliament, or that they are totally independent. As it cannot be supposed to have been the intention of the parties in the compact, that we should be reduced to a state of vassalage, the conclusion is, that it was their sense, that we were thus independent. "It is impossible," your Excellency says, "that there should be two independent Legislatures in one and the same state." May we not then further conclude, that it was their sense, that the colonies were, by their charters, made distinct states from the mother country? . . . Notwithstanding all the terrors which your Excellency has pictured to us as the effects of a total independence, there is more reason to dread the consequences of absolute uncontrolled power, whether of a nation or a monarch, than those of a total independence.

---

fore repealed the duties on glass, paper, paint, and most other items. However, North insisted on retaining the tax on tea as a symbol of parliamentary supremacy. These decisions were important but anticlimatic. The crucial turning point had come in 1769 when the ministry failed to follow the New York Restraining Act with support for Hillsborough's firm American policy.

Five years of conflict had ended in a stalemate, and the struggle over taxes and constitutional principles had left a residue of ill will. Even William Pitt thought the American merchants and assemblies had carried "their notions of freedom too far" and would "not be subject to the laws of this country." Benjamin Franklin also recognized that the colonies had repudiated the authority of Parliament. He concluded that they were now "so many distinct and separate states" but "having the same Head, or Sovereign, the King." Thomas Hutchinson, the American-born royal governor of Massachusetts, disputed Franklin's logic. He denied that there could "be two independent legislatures in one and the same state." To Hutchinson, sovereignty was indivisible; it was all or nothing. "I know of no line," he told the Massachusetts House, "that can be drawn between the supreme authority of Parliament and the total independence of the colonies." Not so, replied a House committee. If Britain and the colonies were united by the king as "one head and common sovereign," they could "live happily in that connection."

In 1765, American public leaders had accepted Parliament's authority and opposed only certain "unconstitutional" legislation. By the early 1770s, the most outspoken patriots repudiated Parliament and claimed equality for their own assemblies under the king. Nor did they flinch when reminded that George III condemned their agitation. As the Massachusetts House advised Hutchinson, "There is more reason to dread the consequences of absolute uncontrolled supreme power, whether of a nation or a monarch, than those of total independence."

There the matter rested with little room for compromise. If Parliament insisted on exercising its claim to sovereignty, it would have to subdue at least some Americans by force. Sensing this awful alternative, the British ministry hesitated to take the final fateful step. For the time being, it would not seek another trial of strength with the Americans and the increasingly self-conscious and well-organized patriot movement.

Roots of Resistance

What motivated the American patriots who first opposed British policies? What circumstances in their own lives prompted other men and women to accept their vision of the world and their political goals? The questions are simple, but the answers are complex. Political decisions take place in a social world filled with economic self-interest, ideological bias, and deeply held traditional values. The intellectual roots of the American patriot movement extended deep into the political theory of Britain and Europe. The conditions and social values that encouraged broad colonial resistance were the products of the diverse and contradictory evolution of American preindustrial society.

Urbanism and Ideology

Political upheaval took two forms in America during the 1760s and 1770s. In the backcountry, *rebellions* sought to preserve traditional ways of life against outside pressures. As patriots in the seaport cities fought British administrative reform, they at first shared this backward-looking mentality. Gradually, however, the urban patriots defined their goals in forward-looking and

revolutionary terms. The diversity of urban life encouraged sharp intellectual controversy. Royal officials, merchants, and the Sons of Liberty vigorously debated political and constitutional issues in public meetings, pamphlets, and newspapers. This urban agitation continually pushed the colonial assemblies, which were dominated numerically by rural representatives, to make a firm defense of American rights.

Merchants led the opposition to imperial reform because it directly affected their economic lives. The Sugar Act and customs reform raised the cost of molasses from the French West Indies and made smuggling more difficult. The Stamp Act and the Townshend duties increased merchants' costs, while the Currency Act complicated their financial transactions. Moreover, increased competition from British traders cut merchant profits. By selling their goods directly to colonial shopkeepers at special "auction" sales, British firms bypassed American mercantile houses. As a result of the new controls, taxes, and competition, the customs collector in Rhode Island reported, the interests of Britain and the colonies were "deemed by the People almost altogether incompatible in a Commercial View."

The emerging American legal profession also played a prominent role in the imperial crisis. Before 1725, lawyers worked at the margins of American society. Merchants and planters feared them as potential political rivals or as dangerous manipulators who could upset land titles or commercial contracts. Farmers shunned lawyers as the unscrupulous agents of creditors or as expensive intermediaries. As the number of real estate transactions, civil suits, and mercantile documents multiplied, the size and status of the legal profession increased. During the 1750s, as many Harvard graduates entered the law as became ministers. In the following decade, William Livingston founded a law society in New York, modeling it after the famous Grey's Inns of Court in London. In Massachusetts, members of a new bar association sought to raise professional standards by refusing to appear in court cases with nonaccredited "pettifoggers."

Because of their education and skills, lawyers found themselves at the center of the imperial debate. Merchants hired them to prevent seizure of their ships by zealous customs officials or Vice-Admiralty judges. Lawyers who sat in the colonial assemblies contested the legality of various measures, often in defense of their own professional interests. They protested when the Board of Trade changed the terms of appointments for colonial judges. Previously they had served during "good behavior." Now judges served only at the "pleasure" of the royal governor. The lawyers contended that this procedure compromised the independence of the judiciary. Because most American lawyers had been trained in the tradition of English common law, they opposed Vice-Admiralty Courts that tried cases without a jury.

As the imperial crisis intensified, the Americal legal profession divided. Most older lawyers adopted a neutral position or remained loyal to the Crown. Years of legal practice had given them a deep respect for the law; they found it emotionally impossible to repudiate established institutions of authority. Their younger colleagues had greater revolutionary potential. "The lawyers are the Source from whence the Clamours have flowed in every Province," General Gage commented during the Stamp Act controversy. In 1776, twenty-five lawyers were among the fifty-six men who signed the Declaration of Independence.

Lawyers and other educated colonists drew on three intellectual traditions to fashion a defense of American rights. In his learned *Dissertation on the Canon and Feudal Law* (1765), John Adams sought precedents in English common law. Adams invoked this venerable tradition to protest the denial of a jury trial for John Hancock, an influential Boston merchant accused of smuggling. "This 29th Chap. of Magna Charta" respecting jury trials, he argued, "has for many Centuries been esteemed by Englishmen, as one of the noblest Monuments, one of the firmest Bulwarks of their Liberties." Four years earlier, in the famous Writs of Assistance case, James Otis had disputed the legality of search warrants on similar grounds. These colonial lawyers maintained that customary or common-law rights and privileges could not be abridged by parliamentary statutes. This older view of the British Constitution was no longer held by legal experts in the mother country. For John Adams, the colonists' "essential rights as British subjects" justified their resistance.

Rationalism stemming from the Enlightenment was a second major intellectual resource for educated provincials. Unlike common-law attorneys, Enlightenment philosophers questioned the authority of past precedent. They began from the premise that all individuals possessed certain "natural rights." With these in mind, they evaluated the legitimacy of existing laws and customs. Enlightenment assumptions appeared in the master's thesis that Samuel Adams wrote at Harvard. Adams, an older cousin of John Adams, emerged during the 1760s as a leading patriot politician in Boston and one of the first advocates of American independence. His master's thesis was a step toward his political career. It examined the legitimacy of constituted authority and had the provocative title "Whether it be lawful to resist the Supreme Magistrate, if the Commonwealth cannot be otherwise preserved?" Adams drew heavily upon the political philosophy of John Locke and other Enlightenment theorists. Using "natural rights" as a standard, he justified both the Boston anti-impressment riots of 1747 and the Stamp Act uprising. Thomas Jefferson subsequently enshrined Enlightenment principles in the Declaration of Independence. He justified separation from Great Britain because it had infringed the "unalienable rights" guaranteed to all men and women.

The English political tradition provided the third ideological source for the American patriot movement. Whig principles had long focused attention on the dangers of unlimited royal power. "Real Whig" and "Country Party" attacks on the political and financial policies of Sir Robert Walpole, the first British prime minister, and his successors warned of oppressive laws enacted by a corrupt Parliament. Viewed from the Real Whig perspective, the ministry's program of imperial reform assumed a sinister meaning. Joseph Warren, a Boston physician and ardent patriot, noted that many townspeople thought the Stamp Act was intended "to force the colonies into rebellion," whereupon the ministry could use "military power to reduce them to servitude." A like-minded pamphleteer claimed that the administrative posts created by the Revenue Act of 1767 would be filled by "lazy, proud, worthless *pensioners* and *placemen*" who would corrupt the American political system. These conspiratorial charges reached a climax following the so-called Boston Massacre in March 1770. British troops in Boston fired on an unruly

DR. JOSEPH WARREN'S BOSTON MASSACRE ORATION

The ruinous consequences of standing armies to free communities may be seen in the histories of Syracuse, Rome, and many other once flourishing states. . . . And this will be more especially the case when the troops are informed that the intention of their being stationed in any city is to overawe the inhabitants. That this was the avowed design of stationing an armed force in this town is sufficiently known; and we, my fellow citizens, have seen, we have felt the tragical effects! *The fatal fifth of March 1770, can never be forgotten.* The horrors of *that dreadful night* are but too deeply impressed in our hearts. Language is too feeble to paint the emotion of our souls when our streets were stained with the blood of our brethren—when our ears were wounded by the groans of the dying, and our eyes were tormented with the sight of the mangled bodies of the dead. . . .

I am confident that you never will betray the least want of spirit when called upon to guard your freedom. . . . Your illustrious fathers were her zealous votaries. When the blasting frowns of tyranny drove her from public view they clasped her in their arms; they brought her safe over the rough ocean and fixed her seat in this then dreary wilderness. . . . You surely cannot, with such examples before your eyes, as every page of the history of this country affords, suffer your liberties to be ravished from you by lawless force, or cajoled away by flattery and fraud. . . . If you perform your part, you must have the strongest confidence that the same Almighty Being who protected your pious and venerable forefathers—who enabled them to turn a barren wilderness into a fruitful field, who so often made bare his arm for their salvation will still be mindful of you, their offspring.

---

crowd that was protesting soldiers' taking civilian jobs, killing five civilians and wounding others. The Boston town meeting issued a resolution that warned of a "deep-laid and desperate plan of imperial despotism" aimed at the "extinction of all civil liberty."

This rhetoric was exaggerated, but the charges had a solid basis. British administrative reform did threaten the interests of a variety of American groups. The Proclamation Line of 1763 curbed the acquisitive appetites of land speculators and westward migrants. The Restraining Act undermined the corporate powers of the New York assembly and threatened all American representative institutions. In addition, there was the British economic presence—in new taxation measures, increased imports of manufactured goods, and the growing commercial debt. As one pamphleteer put it, Americans were being compelled to give the British "our money, as oft and in what quantity they please to demand it."

Americans could—and did—respond to these events in narrow terms, as threats to their self-interest. But common-law lawyers, natural-rights theorists, and Real Whig politicians also stated American objections in the broader terms of political philosophy. By so doing, they added new dimensions to the struggle. These ideological statements provided a common vocabulary of dissent. They related one British action to another, demonstrating an overall ministerial intent and underlining the need for a common response. These statements also endowed resistance with a higher moral meaning, the defense of English or natural rights from tyranny. Ultimately, they transformed a series of colonial rebellions into a united revolutionary movement.

The Tea Act

With the repeal of most of the Townshend duties, a peaceful solution of the crisis had seemed possible. Merchants in New York and Philadelphia rejected appeals from Boston to extend the nonimportation agreements. In a spirit of compromise, they accepted the symbolic tax on tea and the revenue duties on wine, molasses, and textiles in the revised Sugar Act. Trade soon surpassed its former levels. In England, the political philosopher Edmund Burke advised Parliament to "leave the Americans as they anciently stood and do not burthen them by taxes."

Colonial politicians remained wary. The Virginia House of Burgesses created a Committee of Correspondence "to obtain the most early and authentic intelligence" of British actions affecting America, "and to keep up and maintain a correspondence and communication with our sister colonies." With each successive crisis, the patriots had developed closer ties, a sense of shared identity, and an increasing suspicion of British motives.

Parliament's passage of the Tea Act in May 1773 confirmed American fears. The Tea Act provided financial relief to the British East India Company. This royally chartered firm had fallen deeply into debt because of military expeditions that extended British trade and influence in India. The new legislation offered the company a loan and reduced the duties on the tea it imported into England. The company also received a special license to export surplus tea to America. Lord North realized that many colonists would react angrily to these provisions, but he accepted the risk. Like Grenville and Townshend before him, North was not content to declare the supremacy of Parliament. Given an appropriate occasion, he would demonstrate it.

North's insensitivity to the fragility of the imperial system was costly. The Tea Act began a series of events that led directly—and almost inescapably—to the American War of Independence. News that the East India Company planned to establish warehouses in Boston, New York, Charleston, and Philadelphia shocked many American merchants. "The Fear of an Introduction of a Monopoly in this Country," General James Haldimand, the commander of British troops in New York, warned the ministry, "has induced the mercantile part of the Inhabitants to be very industrious in opposing this Step and added Strength to a Spirit of Independence already too prevalent." When the Massachusetts Committee of Correspondence called on patriots to prevent the landing of tea by the East India Company, it received strong support. In most port cities, the local Sons of Liberty forced ship captains to take the tea back to England or made officials store it in public warehouses.

Events in Boston predictably took a different turn. For decades, the Massachusetts House of Representatives had bitterly resisted British authority. Boston mounted the first and most violent crowd actions against the Stamp Act, and its merchants led the opposition to the Townshend duties. The Boston Massacre took place there, and its citizens had long condemned the tax on tea. "The passion for TEA has grown so universal and strong," a letter to the Boston *Gazette* warned in 1768, "the politicians who planned our ruin, I mean the placemen and pensioners who expect to be supported by it, selected this article as a bait to allure us to their snare." It was Boston's destiny to spark the eventual bloody conflict.

Chance also figured in these events. Tea of the East India Company arrived aboard the *Dartmouth* in November 1773. It was consigned to Elisha and Thomas Hutchinson, Jr., the sons of Governor Thomas Hutchinson. Once an advocate of American autonomy, the governor bitterly opposed the Massachusetts patriots, and with good reason. Stamp Act rioters had destroyed his house. Patriots had stolen his private correspondence, and Benjamin Franklin had published it to smear Hutchinson's reputation. The Massachusetts House had condemned his defense of parliamentary power and petitioned for his removal from office. Hutchinson was determined to uphold the Tea Act. His desire for revenue, his family's financial interests, and his deeply held constitutional principles left him no choice.

Hutchinson and the patriots were soon locked in a fateful struggle. To prevent the Sons of Liberty from forcing the *Dartmouth* to return the tea to England, Hutchinson had his sons pass the ship through customs. Now the *Dartmouth* could not depart without a pass from the governor, and time was on his side. If the tea duty were not paid within twenty days, customs officials could legally seize the cargo, land it with the support of the British army and navy, and sell it at auction. The Massachusetts patriots met the governor's challenge. The Boston Committee of Correspondence assigned Paul Revere, William Molineaux, and Thomas Young to lead a group of artisans aboard the *Dartmouth*. Disguised as Indians, they boarded the ship on a cold December night, broke open the 342 chests of tea, and threw them into the harbor. John Adams described the event, which became known as the Boston Tea Party, in his diary the next

THE COERCIVE ACTS AND "SLAVERY"
This powerful image of enslavement is a metaphor for the fate of Boston following the Coercive Acts of 1774. Ten residents are trapped in a cage similar to those used to punish black slaves. British troops and cannon guard the city. Because white Americans lived in a slave-owning society, they were especially sensitive to the threat of absolute power. (Library of Congress)

day: "This Destruction of the Tea is so bold, so daring, so firm, intrepid & inflexible, and it must have so important Consequences and so lasting that I cannot but consider it as an Epocha in History."

Adams did not exaggerate. Frustrated and outraged, the British Privy Council declared that the time had finally come to "secure the Dependence of the Colonies on the Mother Country." "Concessions had made matters worse," the king added, "the time had come for compulsion." Parliament decisively rejected a proposal to repeal the duty on tea. Instead, in the spring of 1774, it enacted four "Coercive Acts," also known as the "Intolerable Acts," to force Massachusetts into submission. A Port Bill closed Bos-

ton Harbor until the East India Company received payment for the destroyed tea. A second parliamentary edict restricted the powers of local town meetings and the Massachusetts House, while vesting the royal governor with greater authority. Other legislation provided for the quartering of troops and threatened the patriot leadership. It gave the governor authority to move trials for capital offenses, including treason, to other colonies or even to Great Britain.

Hillsborough had originally proposed this "divide and rule" strategy in 1769. The policy of imposing heavy penalties on Massachusetts might have worked at that time. However, the success of nonimportation and the work of the colonial Committees of Correspondence had created a firm sense of unity among the seaboard colonies. "The cause of Boston, the despotick measures in respect to it, I mean," George Washington declared from Virginia, "now is and ever will be considered as the cause of America."

Parliament's passage of the Quebec Act in 1774 heightened the sense of common danger. This law extended the boundaries of Canada into the Ohio River valley, thus extinguishing the land claims of Virginia and several other colonies. Equally important, the Quebec Act gave legal recognition to Roman Catholicism. This concession to the French Catholic residents of Canada aroused old religious fears, especially in New England. The British had not intended the Quebec Act as a coercive measure, but it convinced many Americans that all the provinces faced Boston's fate.

The First Continental Congress met in Philadelphia in September 1774 to respond to the new British measures. All the colonies sent delegates except Georgia, which was controlled by pro-British leaders. The New England representatives advocated a political union among the colonies and immediate military preparations. Many southern leaders were also prepared to resist royal authority. They now believed there was a British plot "to overturn the constitution and introduce a system of arbitrary government."

Only the delegates from the middle colonies still hoped for a political compromise that would preserve American rights and liberties within the British Empire. These men of "loyal principles" seized the initiative. Joseph Galloway of Pennsylvania offered a scheme for reconciliation sim-

MAP 6.1 BRITISH WESTERN POLICY, 1763–1774
To prevent Indian wars, the Proclamation Line of 1763 restricted white settlement west of the Appalachian Mountains. Nevertheless, colonial land speculators planned the new colonies of Vandalia and Transylvania. The Quebec Act of 1774 designated these colonies as Indian Reserves and, by vastly increasing the boundaries of Quebec, eliminated the sea-to-sea land claims of many eastern colonies. The act angered American settlers and speculators and frightened colonial political leaders because it made no provision for a representative assembly in Quebec.

ilar to the abortive Albany Plan of Union of 1754. He called for an American government composed of a legislative council elected by all the colonial assemblies, and a President-General appointed by the king. The new government would have the power to veto parliamentary legislation affecting America. Galloway asked the Continental Congress to endorse his plan as the basis for a negotiated settlement. The delegates tabled this scheme, but only by the close vote of six colonies to five. With a British military force "occupying" Boston, the majority thought Galloway's plan was too conciliatory.

Instead, the First Continental Congress condemned the Coercive Acts and demanded their repeal. It proclaimed that the Declaratory Act of 1766 and all other parliamentary legislation af-

fecting American "life, liberty, and property" were "unconstitutional." The Congress threatened economic retaliation if its demands for political autonomy were not met. It warned the British that new nonimportation and nonconsumption agreements would go into effect in December 1774. The delegates voted to cut off colonial exports to Britain, Ireland, and the West Indies in September 1775 if the royal government still refused to repeal the acts. Ten years of imperial political and constitutional conflicts had led to all-out financial warfare.

The British response was firm and unyielding. The government branded the Continental Congress as an illegal assembly and reaffirmed its intention to enforce the Coercive Acts. Only William Pitt continued to hope for a peaceful compromise. In January 1775, he proposed the removal of British troops from Boston as part of a comprehensive constitutional settlement. Pitt asked Parliament to give up its claim to tax the colonies, eliminate the Vice-Admiralty Courts, suspend the Coercive Acts, and recognize the Continental Congress as a lawful representative body. In return for these and other concessions, he demanded that the Continental Congress acknowledge parliamentary supremacy and grant a perpetual revenue to cover part of the British national debt.

Pitt's dramatic intervention, like that of Galloway in Philadelphia, was doomed to failure. The British had twice backed down in the face of colonial violence and financial pressure. A third retreat was impossible; the honor of the nation was at stake. The government rejected Pitt's plan and also Colonial Secretary Lord Dartmouth's proposal to send commissioners to America to negotiate a settlement. Instead, Lord North demanded that the Americans pay the cost of their own defense and administration. They must also recognize Parliament's authority to tax them, but, North indicated, parliament would not exercise that right. To back up its strong stand, the British government sent a large military force to America, blockaded the trade between the colonies and foreign nations, and ordered General Gage to suppress illegal dissent in Massachusetts.

For ten years, British officials had tolerated colonial riots, political insubordination, and continual escalation of American demands—tax relief, legislative equality, and now virtual independence. "Now the case seemed desperate," Lord North told Governor Thomas Hutchinson of Massachusetts, living in exile in London. "Parliament would not—could not—concede. For aught he could see it must come to violence."

The Rising of the Countryside

Residents of the seaport cities started the patriot movement, but the predominantly rural population decided its fate. Most farm folk, because their lives were deeply rooted in the soil, initially had little interest in the imperial controversy. Many of them had left Europe to escape political and religious strife. The debates in the colonial assemblies over constitutional issues had little significance for them. Their prime allegiance was to their families, their neighbors, and their community. Like the force of gravity, the circumstances of daily life in preindustrial America pulled these men and women back to local events—the state of the harvest, a relative's illness, or their minister's sermon.

The French and Indian War awakened the political consciousness of the rural population, for it drew their sons off to war and raised taxes. In Newtown on Long Island, farmers paid an average tax of ten shillings per household before 1754. To pay New York's military expenses, the tax jumped to thirty shillings in 1756. Peace brought little relief; the costs imposed by the Quartering Act gave Newtown an average tax of twenty shillings in 1771. Even so, Newtown and other rural communities escaped much of the turmoil of the crisis. The Sugar and Stamp acts and the Townshend duties did not directly affect them. Moreover, a steady European demand for tobacco, rice, and wheat kept agricultural prices high between 1764 and 1775, bringing wealth to some planters and modest prosperity to many farmers.

Nevertheless, their social and political values drew many farmers and planters into the imperial debate. For some, the increasing importation of British manufactured products threatened the traditional rural values of thrift and frugality. New England ministers warned their congregations that they had been "of late years insensibly drawn into too great a degree of luxury and dissipation." They welcomed nonimportation as a remedy for the disease that was undermining America's moral health. Patriot leaders and crowds of spectators cheered when Daughters of Liberty, as women and girls throughout the colonies called themselves, publicly spun wool into thread for the domestic production of cloth. The rough homespun clothes of the farm folk became a badge of patriotism. This campaign against frivolous purchases reached a climax at the First Continental Congress. The delegates passed a third nonimportation agreement and then condemned Americans who continued the tradition of wearing expensive clothes at funerals. The Congress approved only "a black crape

TIME LINE
TOWARD INDEPENDENCE: A DECADE OF DECISIONS

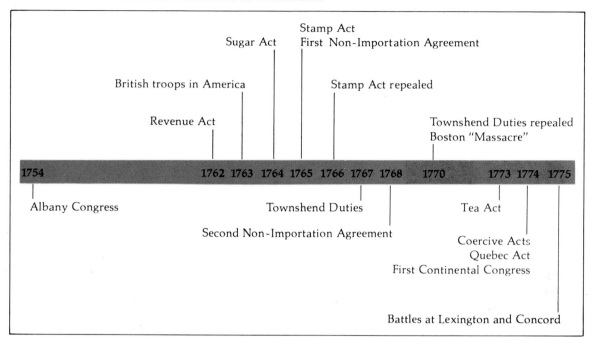

or ribbon on the arm or hat for gentlemen, and a black ribbon and necklace for ladies." John Adams hoped that if war came, its financial sacrifices "would cure Americans of their vicious and luxurious and effeminate Appetites, Passions and Habits."

These symbolic affirmations of older cultural values were often directed against British officials and military men. The majority of British army officers came from the upper ranks of society and were often haughty, arrogant, or immoral in their personal behavior. Most colonists resented their claims to social superiority and the corrupt behavior of many civilian officials. The image of the greedy British official seeking only the "gratification of his private Passions" loomed large in the pages of *The Independent Reflector,* a patriot newspaper in New York. As the town meeting of Petersham, Massachusetts, put it in a letter to Boston patriots, the royal army and bureaucracy would drain "this People of the Fruits of their Toil."

Rural discontent had its basis in economic reality. The yeoman tradition of agricultural independence was under attack everywhere. A shortage of arable land blunted the aspirations of farmers in long-settled regions. Newly assertive aristocratic proprietors imposed rents and controlled large tracts along the frontier. Merchants began legal proceedings when farmers could not pay their debts. If these burdens were compounded by new British taxes, many farmers feared the loss of their land, which would "bring us into a State of abject Slavery." The prospects were grim. "The duty on tea," declared one patriot pamphleteer, "was only a prelude to a window-tax, hearth-tax, land-tax, and poll-tax, and these were only paving the way for reducing the country to lordships." By the 1770s, many northern yeomen had become personally involved in the imperial controversy. British policies seemed to threaten their cultural ideal of landed independence.

Despite their much higher standard of living, many Chesapeake slaveowners came to a similar conclusion. British merchants had granted liberal credit beginning in the 1750s, and many planters went deeply into debt. An obligation of

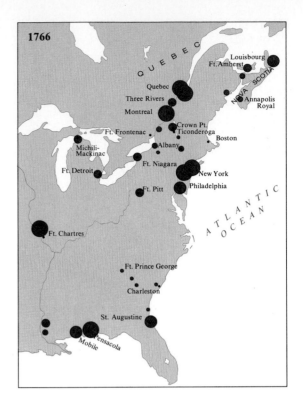

MAP 6.2 THE CHANGING DEPLOYMENT OF BRITISH TROOPS, 1763–1775
These maps reflect changes in British military priorities. In 1763, most British battalions (depicted by the large circles, representing 350 men) were stationed in Canada to deter Indian wars and French-Canadian revolts. Additional companies of troops (shown by smaller circles, approximately 40 men) were scattered among frontier forts. Following the Stamp Act riots of 1765, the British moved troops to garrisons in New York and Philadelphia. By 1775, eleven battalions of British troops occupied Boston, the center of the patriot independence movement.

£1,000 was once considered excessive, a Virginia planter observed in 1766, but

> ten times that sum is now spoke of with indifference and thought no great burthen on Some Estates. In 1740 I don't remember to have seen such a thing as a turkey carpet in the Country except a small thing in the bedchamber. Now nothing are so common as Turkey or Wilton Carpets, the whole furniture, Roomes, Elegant, and every appearance of opulence.

High living led either to financial disaster or economic anxiety. Many planters welcomed the nonimportation agreements as a check on their expensive habits. "The more I consider a scheme of this sort," George Washington told his neighbor George Mason in 1769, "the more ardently I wish success to it, because many families are reduced almost to penury and want, from the low ebb of their fortunes and estates daily selling for the discharge of debts." Nonimportation reduced some liabilities, but debt was inevitable in an expanding agricultural economy.

Debts to British merchants added a psychological quality to the debate over constitutional principles. Southern planters also felt the nagging sensation of economic dependence. To achieve greater self-sufficiency, Robert Carter joined the nonimportation movement and established a "Linnen and Woolen Factory" using the labor of his male and female slaves. The Coercive Acts raised the threat of political dependence; new British legislation might seize control of the county courts and the House of Burgesses from the planter elite. These concerns moved the southern gentry toward resistance. "The spark of liberty is not yet extinct among our people," one planter observed, "and if properly fanned by the Gentlemen of influence will, I make no doubt, burst out again into a flame."

In New England, at least, elite agitation was unnecessary. In the farming community of Concord, Massachusetts, about 80 percent of the male heads of families and a number of single women signed the Solemn League and Covenant supporting nonimportation. Following the passage of the Coercive Acts, most Massachusetts towns sent representatives to extralegal county conventions. In August 1774, more than 150 delegates from country towns met in Concord, for a Middlesex County Congress. The Congress advised the people to close the royally sanctioned courts and to transfer their allegiance to the colonial legislature. Crowds of armed men prevented the Court of General Sessions from meeting, and rural patriots began to harass supporters of the royal regime. The sup-

port in the countryside for the patriot cause limited Governor Thomas Gage's authority to Boston, where it rested primarily on the bayonets of his thirty-five hundred troops.

Civil war was imminent. On September 1, 1774, British troops marched out of Boston and seized colonial armories and storehouses at Charlestown and Cambridge. In response, about twenty thousand colonial militiamen mobilized hastily to safeguard depots of military supplies at Concord and Worcester. The Concord town meeting voted to raise two companies of troops to "Stand at a minutes warning in Case of alarm." These militiamen were called "minutemen" because they had been warned to mobilize at a minute's notice. Defying an order from Governor Gage, the Massachusetts assembly met on its own. It issued regulations for the collection of taxes and assumed the normal responsibilities of government. In April 1775, the Continental Congress began to raise an American army of eighteen thousand men.

Lord Dartmouth declared Massachusetts in a

THE BATTLE OF LEXINGTON

At dawn, seventy men—half the adult males in Lexington—confronted six companies of British regulars on the town's green. "Ye villans, ye Rebels, disperse" shouted several British officers. "Damn you, disperse." Then someone fired a shot. In a state of panic, British troops fired at will, killing eight "Minutemen" and wounding nine more. (Amos Doolittle. *The Battle of Lexington, April 19, 1775.* Museum of Art, Carnegie Institute, Pittsburgh. Howard N. Eavenson Americana Collection)

state of "open rebellion." He advised Gage that "force should be repelled by force" and urged the governor to march quickly against the "rude rabble." Gage dispatched troops to capture colonial leaders and supplies at Concord. However, Paul Revere and two other Boston patriots rode their horses across the countryside to warn the colonists. Local militiamen met the British at Lexington early on the morning of April 19. Shots rang out, and then a British volley killed eight militiamen and wounded others. Moving quickly on to Concord, the 700 British soldiers encountered 400 patriots. This time the British took the heavier losses, a dozen wounded and three dead. The worst was yet to come for the

British troops. As they retreated to Boston along narrow, winding country roads, more than 1,000 minutemen from neighboring towns ambushed them repeatedly. At the end of the day, 73 British soldiers lay dead, 174 were wounded, and 26 were missing. British fire had killed 49 militiamen and wounded 39.

Neither Governor Gage nor the Massachusetts assembly had anticipated such a bloody outcome, but the actions of both sides since the Tea Act led directly to it. Now too many men had died to enable a peaceful compromise to be reached. Ten years of conflict had led to war, and the extent of British authority in America would be decided by force.

---

*A*s the Great War for Empire ended, British officials began to reform the imperial system. George Grenville became prime minister in 1764 and imposed a direct tax on the colonies. The Stamp Act of 1765 produced a passionate defense of American rights by disciplined mobs,

colonial assemblies, and an extra-legal Stamp Act Congress.

Between 1765 and 1770, American and British politicians vigorously debated constitutional issues. Colonial spokesmen drew their arguments from English common law, Enlightenment thought, and the writings of dissenting Whigs. Parliament responded by repealing the Stamp Tax while declaring its complete authority over the colonies. Charles Townshend instituted a new tax on trade in 1767, and Americans responded with economic coercion. Two years later, the British government nearly adopted Lord Hillsborough's plan to crush American resistance movement by force; instead, it repealed most of the Townshend duties. By 1770, the two sides had reached a constitutional and political impasse. They had little room for compromise.

Lord North brought on the final crisis by passing the Tea Act of 1773. When Bostonians resisted the new law, the British used political and military force to uphold their supremacy. American political leaders met in the First Continental Congress in 1774. The Congress supported Massachusetts and announced a new program of economic warfare. Equally important, a majority of American farmers were now prepared to resist arbitrary British rule. The stage was set for the bloodshed at Lexington and Concord in April 1775.

Suggestions for Further Reading

Reform and Resistance

Lawrence Gipson stresses the legacy of the Seven-Years War in *The Coming of the Revolution, 1763–1775* (1954). Charles M. Andrews, *The Colonial Background of the American Revolution* (1924), remains valuable, while Merrill Jensen, *The Founding of a Nation* (1968), offers a detailed survey. Classic studies include George L. Beer, *British Colonial Policy, 1754–1763* (1907); A. M. Schlesinger, *The Colonial Merchants and the American Revolution* (1917); and Oliver Dickerson, *The Navigation Acts and the American Revolution* (1951). Later studies, among them Jack Sosin, *Agents and Merchants* (1965), and Michael Kammen, *A Rope of Sand* (1970), demonstrate the weakness of colonial agents in London and the determination of the British ministry.

Edmund S. and Helen M. Morgan, *The Stamp Act Crisis* (1953), offer a fine account of the events of 1765. Complementary works include Peter Shaw, *American Patriots and the Rituals of Revolution* (1981); Pauline Maier, *From Resistance to Revolution* (1972); and John C. Miller, *Sam Adams, Pioneer in Propaganda* (1936). For an understanding of British politics, see Louis B. Namier, *England in the Age of the American Revolution* (1930), and Herbert Butterfield, *George III and the Historians* (1957).

The Growing Confrontation

Studies of individual colonies capture the hostile mood of many Americans. See David Lovejoy, *Rhode Island Politics and the American Revolution* (1958); Ronald Hoffman, *A Spirit of Dissension: Economics, Politics and the Revolution in Maryland* (1973); Oscar Zeichner, *Con-necticut's Years of Controversy* (1950); and David C. Skaggs, *Roots of Maryland Democracy* (1973).

Good studies of patriot leaders include Page Smith, *John Adams* (1962); Richard Beeman, *Patrick Henry* (1982); and John C. Miller, *Sam Adams: Pioneer in Propaganda* (1936).

Roots of Resistance

The impact of Enlightenment thought on the revolutionary generation is emphasized by Carl Becker, *The Declaration of Independence* (1922), and Randolph G. Adams, *Political Ideas of the American Revolution* (1958). Two outstanding analyses of the radical and "Real Whig" traditions are Caroline Robbins, *The Eighteenth Century Commonwealthman* (1959), and Bernard Bailyn, *Ideological Origins of the American Revolution* (1967). For a discussion of the legal tradition, see Charles H. McIlwain, *The American Revolution: A Constitutional Interpretation* (1923), and Hiller B. Zobel, *The Boston Massacre* (1970).

Benjamin Labaree, *The Boston Tea Party* (1964), is comprehensive and stimulating. It should be read in conjunction with Bernard Donoughue, *British Politics and the American Revolution: The Path to War, 1773–1775* (1972); John Shy, *Toward Lexington* (1965); and David Ammerman, *In the Common Cause* (1974), a study of American response to the Coercive Acts. For a superb study of the roots of American resistance, competing social groups and ideologies, and the course of the revolution in New York, see Edward F. Countryman, *A People in Revolution* (1983).

7

WAR, REVOLUTION, AND THE NEW POLITICAL ORDER

In 1775, the American patriots were rebels who took up arms in a civil war against their British countrymen. They sought the restoration of their traditional colonial privileges, both economic and political. Their foe was the British government headed by Lord North, the prime minister. With the Declaration of Independence of July 4, 1776, the rebels became revolutionaries by severing their historic dependence on Great Britain. They also became republicans by repudiating the authority of King George III. The patriots gave their newly independent states republican constitutions by vesting ultimate political authority in the hands of the people, not a hereditary monarch. The new state governments would be radical experiments in self-rule.

Which individuals or social groups should exercise power in the new republican society, and for what purposes? How should general republican principles be translated into specific constitutional forms and legislative systems? Political philosophers had debated such questions for centuries. Americans had to answer them quickly while fighting for the very survival of their state governments. The long war against Great Britain nearly undermined the legitimacy of their republican institutions. Military destruction and economic hardship sharpened existing social divisions and tested the courage and will of the American people.

In 1783, peace brought independence and new problems to the United States. American political leaders struggled with the difficult issues of economic recovery, western settlement, and social conflict. Yeoman farmers, seeking to create a more democratic society, led a challenge to take control of state governments from merchants and slaveholders. Intense political and ideological struggles continued for a decade. The ratification of a federal Constitution in 1789 finally defined the character of the new institutions of republican government.

The Constitution was the creation of nationalists and economic conservatives. It increased the power of the central government in relation to that of the states. The new framework of government also bolstered the privileged economic and political position of traditional ruling elites. Nevertheless, the Constitution placed the final stamp of legitimacy on the revolution of 1776. It brought the most creative period in American political development to a close. And it bequeathed to subsequent generations a flexible, enduring system of republican government.

Toward Independence

The outbreak of fighting in Massachusetts roused patriot forces in all the colonies. British loyalists mustered their supporters as well, arguing vigorously for continued allegiance to the

Crown. When persuasion failed, they resorted to military force. Violent confrontations between loyalists and patriots took place in many colonies and induced patriot leaders to make a final break from Great Britain.

The Continental Congress issued a Declaration of Independence and prepared for war. Britain responded with a massive military invasion to crush the rebels. Major fighting raged for five years. Confronted by determined American resistance and French military intervention, the British finally sought a negotiated peace. The patriots, by the force of arms, thus won independence for their "States united".

Civil War

Loyalists, also called Tories, first appeared as a distinct political force at the First Continental Congress in 1774. These delegates had divided sympathies. They strongly defended American rights against imperial reformers but feared the consequences of active resistance. Most loyalists drew back in horror at the thought of American independence. This contradictory attitude undermined their political effectiveness. In 1774, Governor John Wentworth of New Hampshire tried to raise an armed loyalist force to combat the Sons of Liberty. But he could muster only one sheriff, two justices of the peace, four provincial councillors, and two of his personal secretaries. A month later, Wentworth's Tory Association had just fifty-nine members. Most of them were government officials or wealthy merchants who held lucrative supply contracts with the British army or navy. Leading Tories in other colonies came from the same occupational groups—royal officials, lawyers, and merchants with government contracts. Once drawn into the world of British power and prestige, they found it difficult to leave.

A second loyalist group consisted of wealthy, conservative Americans who were emotionally unprepared for sudden change or violent rebellion. Some, like Jared Ingersoll, a Connecticut lawyer, had endured personal humiliation by the Sons of Liberty. As staunch advocates of hierarchy, they dreaded a more democratic society. As men of wealth, they feared the economic consequences of a government elected and managed by the people at large. Another loyalist,

Governor Thomas Hutchinson of Massachusetts, worried that repudiation of Great Britain would unleash a mob and "must prove the ruin of the colony."

Ordinary farmers with distinct cultural or religious identities made up the largest group of Tories. For many, their loyalty to the Crown reflected long-standing conflicts with neighboring patriots. For example, New Lights in the Dutch Reformed Church in the Hackensack Valley of New Jersey actively supported the patriots, while their Old Light opponents favored the loyalists. In New York, economic position influenced political allegiance. The Livingston family and their landowner allies in the Hudson River Valley became ardent patriots; many of their unhappy tenants pledged support to Britain. In the Carolina backcountry, Highland Scotch migrants followed the lead of their clan chieftains and remained loyal to the Crown. Like the mass of Tories everywhere, these men and women had a distinct cultural or religious heritage—or old economic and political scores to settle with patriot-dominated governments or social groups.

The loyalists demonstrated their political strength at the Second Continental Congress in Philadelphia in May 1775. At the urging of patriot leaders, the Congress resolved to undertake "the defense of American liberty." It voted to raise a Continental army and appointed George Washington of Virginia to command the New England forces beseiging the British in Boston. Delegates with Tory sympathies strongly opposed all these measures, which were approved, as John Adams complained, only "by bare majorities." Led by John Dickinson of Pennsylvania, delegates favoring reconciliation with Britain won majority support for an "Olive Branch" petition expressing loyalty to King George III. It asked the king to obtain repeal of oppressive parliamentary legislation. The patriots in the Continental Congress responded with a strong declaration of the "Causes and Necessity" of taking up arms. While dreading the "calamities of civil war," they stated their resolve "to dye Freemen rather than live as Slaves."

The king failed to take advantage of these divisions in the Continental Congress and among the American people. He refused to accept the Olive Branch petition and instead, in August

1775, issued a Proclamation for Suppressing Rebellion and Sedition. The patriots then implemented a congressional edict cutting off all exports to Britain and its West Indian possessions. Parliament followed by passing a Prohibitory Act that outlawed commercial trade with the rebellious colonies. Each side used every economic weapon at its disposal.

Meanwhile, southern loyalists mobilized for war. Lord Dunmore, the royal governor of Virginia, fled to a British warship in June 1775. From there he organized a military force, the Queen's Own Loyal Virginians, and a regiment of black troops. After the king's proclamation condemning rebellion, Dunmore branded the patriots as "traitors" and declared martial law. He issued a controversial proclamation of his own, offering freedom to slaves and indentured servants who joined the loyalist cause. Lord Dunmore's proclamation jolted the leaders of Chesapeake society. With Dunmore's sending troops against their plantations and promising freedom to their slaves, many planters called for a final break with Great Britain.

Demands for independence came from North Carolina as well, also in response to a Tory military initiative. Early in 1776, the royal governor, Josiah Martin, raised a force of about fifteen hundred Scotch Highlanders to seize control of the colony. Patriot militia defeated Martin's army in the Battle of Moore's Creek Bridge and captured more than eight hundred of his troops. Subsequently, armed patriot artisans repelled a British naval assault on Charleston, South Carolina. As in Virginia, the taste of blood pushed the patriots toward independence. In April 1776, a Provincial Congress in North Carolina empowered its representatives "to concur with the Delegates of other Colonies in declaring Independency, and forming foreign alliances." Virginia quickly followed. Led by George Mason, James Madison, Edmund Pendleton, and Patrick Henry, Patriots called a special convention in Virginia. In May, this representative body resolved unanimously "to declare the United Colonies free and independent states."

A final break required repudiation of the king and of the monarchical system itself. This step was difficult, for most Americans retained a deep loyalty to the Crown. Patriot crowds had drank enthusiastically to the king's health during

the Stamp Act riots and virtually every other anti-imperial demonstration. They blamed Parliament, not their king. The psychological roots of this loyalty to George III extended deep into the structure of American society. Like many preindustrial peoples, the colonists used family metaphors to describe their system of authority. The "Elders" of the society commanded respect in town meetings and church congregations. The family was a "little commonwealth" ruled by its male head. The monarch was much more than a sovereign authority; he ruled as the "father of his people." To deny the power and legitimacy of the king threatened the order of society itself. To repudiate the monarchy was to question all hierarchy and all paternal authority.

The course of events prepared Americans for this radical action against their political "father." In their eyes, he had supported ministers who

PATRICK HENRY, A GREAT ORATOR
Henry's use of the language and gestures of evangelical preachers created a new mode of political oratory. "His figures of speech . . . were often borrowed from the Scriptures," Edmund Randolph recalled, and "his style . . . was vehement," transfusing "into the breasts of others the earnestness depicted in his own features." (Lawrence Sully. *Patrick Henry*. Mead Art Museum, Amherst College. Bequest of Herbert L. Pratt, class 1895)

THE KILLING OF THE KING
An angry New York crowd pulls down a statue of George III in 1776. Previously, patriots had accepted the fiction that the king could do no wrong and had attacked his ministers instead. The change in regard for the King was embodied in the Declaration of Independence, which repudiated Americans' symbolic father, accusing him of plotting "an absolute tyranny." (The New York Public Library; Astor, Lenox & Tilden Foundations)

passed oppressive legislation. He had ignored their Olive Branch petition. And he had condemned his "children" as traitors and ordered the use of military force against them. Thomas Paine crystallized these antimonarchical sentiments in his powerful pamphlet *Common Sense*, published in January 1776. Paine, a former corsetmaker, had been fired from the English Customs Service for agitating for higher wages. He migrated to Philadelphia in 1774 and mingled with artisans who shared his Enlightenment-inspired republican sentiments.

"Monarchy and hereditary succession have laid the world in blood and ashes," Paine proclaimed in *Common Sense*. Brilliantly mixing coarse insults with Biblical quotations, Paine blasted the British system of "mixed government." He denied that it guaranteed liberty, the argument advanced by the French philosopher Montesquieu in his well-known *The Spirit of the Laws* (1748). Rather, Paine declared, it yielded tyranny, "monarchical tyranny in the person of the King and aristocratical tyranny in the persons of the peers." Only the "republican materials" of the House of Commons gave Britain a measure of freedom. Paine's message was clear. The colonies should forsake the monarchical tyr-

anny of George III and create independent republican states. "A government of our own is our natural right," Paine concluded. "TIS TIME TO PART."

Published as Tory military forces took the offensive, *Common Sense* had a decisive effect on American political opinion. Twenty thousand copies were sold within a few months, providing patriot leaders with a convincing justification of independence. In June, Richard Henry Lee presented the Resolution of the Virginia Convention to the Continental Congress. It demanded complete repudiation of "all allegiance to the British Crown." Committed loyalists withdrew from the Congress, leaving staunch patriots to push the resolution forward. Thomas Jefferson devoted most of the Declaration of Independence to a detailed indictment of the king's conduct. The Congress approved it unanimously on July 4, 1776.

Almost overnight, reluctant American rebels became dedicated republican revolutionaries. Crowds celebrated the Declaration by burning effigies of George III and tearing down statues of the king. In these outbursts of frenzied destruction, the patriots broke their psychological ties to the monarchy and the mother country.

The Fortunes of War

As the Continental Congress declared independence in Philadelphia, a British army of about ten thousand men landed outside New York City. Its commander, General William Howe, had served in America during the French and Indian War and distinguished himself in the battle of Quebec. He had orders to capture New York City and seize control of the Hudson River, thus isolating the determined rebels in New England. By August, reinforcements swelled the invasion force to thirty-two thousand troops. Howe had a decided advantage over General Washington's ill-equipped, poorly-trained Continental army of twenty thousand men. The British defeated the Americans in the Battle of Long Island and then nearly trapped the patriot army on Manhattan Island. Outgunned and outmaneuvered, Washington retreated—first to Harlem Heights, then to White Plains, and finally across the Hudson River into New Jersey. By December, Howe had pushed the tired Continental troops across the Delaware River into Pennsylvania.

As the winter cold and snow ended the military campaign season, the patriot forces managed a few triumphs. On Christmas night, Washington· staged a surprise attack across the Delaware River at Trenton. He forced the surrender of about a thousand Hessians, German-speaking soldiers who were fighting as mercenaries for the British army. A few days

MAP 7.1 THE WAR IN THE NORTH
In 1776, the British drove Washington's army across New Jersey and into Pennsylvania. The Americans' counter-attacked at Trenton and Princeton, setting up winter quarters at Morristown. In 1777, Howe captured Philadelphia from the south, while Burgoyne and St. Leger launched invasions from Montreal. Aided by thousands of New England militia, General Horatio Gates defeated Burgoyne at Bennington and then at Saratoga, the military turning point of the war.

THE BATTLE OF TRENTON
General Washington told Congress that "on our Side the War should be defensive," but his bold attack across the Delaware River on December 26, 1776, gave Americans their first military victory. Nonetheless, Washington learned the art of guerilla warfare, constantly evading battles with larger British forces. (George Washington Parke Custis. *Battle of Trenton*. Dietrich American Foundation, Philadelphia [Will Brown])

later, the Continental army won a small engagement at Princeton, New Jersey. These victories were the only bright stars in a dark night. They raised sagging patriot morale but could not hide the British military superiority.

Yet the rebellion continued. The British successes did not crack the will of the rebels. Howe himself was partly responsible. He had opposed the Coercive Acts and hoped for a negotiated settlement. The British general did not follow up his early victories with a ruthless pursuit of the retreating American army. Howe's caution reflected military weakness as well. His troops were fighting on alien soil, three thousand miles from supplies and reinforcements. A major defeat meant disaster. Britain had few seasoned soldiers to send to America, and mercenaries were expensive. Under these circumstances,

Howe's deliberate tactics were understandable but costly. Despite continual defeats, the Continental army remained intact as a symbol and instrument of American resistance.

Howe's failure contrasted sharply with Washington's success. The American general managed to avoid defeat even though his army consisted of ragged recruits. Few yeomen farmers or trained militiamen joined the Continental army. These experienced men preferred to serve in local units near their crops and families. Two other groups provided most of the recruits. In the Continental units commanded by General William Smallwood of Maryland, for example, most of the soldiers were either poor, American-born youths or older foreign-born men who were former convicts or indentured servants. These recruits enlisted in order to receive bounties

THE HARDSHIPS OF SOLDIER LIFE

From the diary of a surgeon at Valley Forge.

December 14—Prisoners and deserters are continually coming in. The army, which has been surprisingly healthy hitherto, now begins to grow sickly from the continued fatigues they have suffered this campaign. Yet they still show a spirit of alacrity and contentment not to be expected from so young troops. I am sick—discontented—and out of humour. Poor food—hard lodging—cold weather—fatigue—nasty cloathes—nasty cookery—vomit half my time—smoaked out of my senses—the Devil's in't—I can't endure it—Why are we sent here to starve and freeze?—What sweet felicities have I left at home: A charming wife—pretty children—good beds —good food—good cookery—all agreeable—all harmonious! Here all confusion—smoke and cold—hunger and filthyness—a pox on my bad luck!

People who live at home in luxury and ease, quietly possessing their habitations, enjoying their wives and families in peace, have but a very faint idea of the unpleasing sensations and continual anxiety the man endures who is in a camp, and is the husband and parent of an agreeable family. These same people are willing we should suffer every thing for their benefit and advantage and yet are the first to condemn us for not doing more!!

General George Washington describes the conditions of the American army at winter quarters in Morristown, New Jersey.

The army is again reduced to an extremity of distress for want of provision. The greater part of it has been without meat from the 21st to 26th. To endeavor to obtain some relief, I moved down to this place, with a view of stripping the lower parts of the country of the remainder of its cattle. . . .

Military coercion is no longer of any avail, as nothing further can possibly be collected from the country in which we are obliged to take a position, without depriving the inhabitants of the last morsel. . . .

It has been no inconsiderable support of our cause, to have had it in our power to contrast the conduct of our army with that of the enemy, and to convince the inhabitants that, while their rights were wantonly violated by the British troops, by our they were respected. This distinction must, unhappily, now cease, and we must assume the odious character of the plunderers instead of the protectors of the people; the direct consequence of which must be, to alienate their minds from the army and insensibly from the cause. . . .

Without a speedy change of circumstances, this dilemma will be involved: either the army must disband, or what is, if possible, worse, subsist upon the plunder of the people. . . .

---

of a hundred acres of land and twenty dollars in cash for three years of service. They knew nothing about military tactics, and many of them panicked in the face of a British artillery bombardment or a flank attack. Others deserted, unwilling to accept the discipline, hardship, and danger of military life. Public support for the Continental army was also weak, for many patriots mistakenly believed that victory did not require a standing army. General Philip Schuyler, commander of New York's Continental forces, complained that his troops were "weak in numbers, dispirited, naked, destitute of provisions, without camp equipage, with little ammunition, and not a single piece of cannon." Given this situation, Washington's great achievement was to avoid an overwhelming defeat.

The British government now realized that the American rebellion was extensive and well organized. Unlike English food riots, it could not be contained and suppressed by a show of force. Victory in America would require a military commitment similar to that of the French and Indian War. Accepting the challenge, the government prepared a major campaign for 1777. The isolation of New England remained the primary goal. The British colonial secretary, Lord Germain, ordered General John Burgoyne to lead a large army down from Canada to Albany, New York. Germain also instructed a smaller British and Indian force to converge on Albany through the Mohawk Valley. He told Howe to send additional assistance to Burgoyne from forces commanded by Sir Henry Clinton in New York City.

Instead, Howe proposed an attack on Philadelphia, the home of the Continental Congress. He wanted to force Washington into a fixed battle and end the war with a single major victory. With Germain's apparent approval, Howe set his forces into motion—but very slowly. Rather than march through New Jersey, the British general transported thousands of troops by sea. They sailed up Chesapeake Bay to assault the Quaker City from the southwest. Howe's men easily outflanked the American fortifications at Brandywine Creek and marched triumphantly into Philadelphia in late September. The Continental Congress fled into the interior, first to Lancaster and then to York.

However, the British paid a high price for this victory. Howe's slow advance against Philadelphia exposed Burgoyne to defeat. Initially the Canadian expedition moved swiftly across Lake Champlain, through the American defenses at Fort Ticonderoga, and toward the upper reaches of the Hudson River. Then, in early August, patriot raiding parties cut Burgoyne's long, thin supply lines to Canada. About two thousand militiamen rallied to protect American military supplies at Bennington, Vermont, depriving the British of food and fresh horses and oxen. Moreover, Clinton refused to send aid to Burgoyne from New York City until some of Howe's troops returned from Philadelphia. Burgoyne's army of five thousand regulars and two thousand Tory and Indian auxiliaries was trapped in the wilderness. Thousands of patriot militiamen from nearby states joined the American army commanded by General Horatio Gates. They surrounded Burgoyne's troops at Saratoga, New York, and forced their surrender on October 17, 1777.

This stunning victory was the turning point of the war. It far outweighed Howe's capture of Philadelphia, for Saratoga cost the British more than five thousand seasoned troops and led to an American alliance with France. Since their expulsion from Canada in 1763, the French had worked to undermine the British in America. They invested heavily in Martinique and Guadeloupe and won complete control of the Euro-

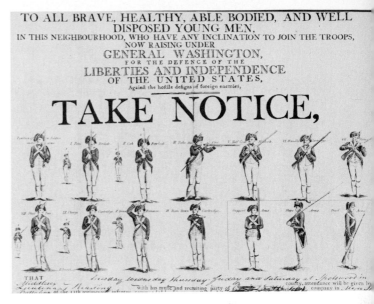

AN AMERICAN RECRUITING POSTER
"Although we were an outpost and had but six or eight men in town," wrote Jonathan Elkins of Peacham, New Hampshire, "we sent two of them—James Bailey and Moses Chamberlain—for we feared if the British were not going to be stopped, we shall all be ruined." (Library of Congress)

pean sugar trade. The French Foreign Minister, le comte de Vergennes, was a determined opponent of Britain and became an early supporter of American independence. He persuaded King Louis XVI to extend a secret loan to the rebellious colonies in 1776 and provide them with gunpowder. Following the American victory at Saratoga, Vergennes urged a formal alliance with the United States to prevent a negotiated end to the rebellion.

Even before Saratoga, opposition to the war was growing in Britain. To meet the military budget, the government increased the land tax in 1776; raised the stamp duty in 1777; and imposed new taxes on carriages, wine, and imported goods. "It seemed we were to be taxed and stamped ourselves instead of inflicting taxes and stamps on others," one politician complained. Yet the king still demanded that the rebellion be crushed, whatever the financial cost. If America achieved independence, he told Lord North, "the West Indies must follow them. Ireland would soon follow the same plan and be a separate state, then this island would be reduced to itself, and soon would be a poor island indeed."

Therefore, North sought a negotiated constitutional settlement. In March 1778, Parliament renounced its right to tax the American colonies, repealed the Tea and the Prohibitory acts, and appointed a commission headed by Lord Carlisle to discuss terms with the Continental Congress. To bring the colonies back into the empire, the commission was empowered to return their constitutional relationship to the "condition of 1763."

The British concessions came too late. By 1778, many Americans had decisively embraced both independence and republicanism. Furthermore, Benjamin Franklin and two other diplomats, Arthur Lee and Silas Deane, had just signed commercial and military treaties with France, the most powerful nation in Europe. Franklin and his associates used the threat of a negotiated settlement with Britain to win favorable terms for American merchants and French commitment to American independence. The Treaty of Alliance specified that after France entered the war against Great Britain, neither partner would sign a separate peace before the "liberty, sovereignty, and independence" of the United States was assured. In return, the American diplomats pledged that their government would recognize French conquests in the West Indies.

"There has been a great change in this state since the news from France," a patriot soldier reported from war-torn Pennsylvania. "The Tories have all turned Whigs," he explained. "They begin, mercenary wretches, to be as eager for Continental Money now as they were a few weeks ago for British gold." Decisive French intervention would have ended the war. The French navy now had secure American ports from which to operate. It could easily have cut British supply routes across the Atlantic and attacked the troops occupying Newport and New York City.

When France entered the war in June 1778, it had very different military priorities. France concentrated its naval forces in the Caribbean Sea, where it hoped to seize a rich sugar island. Spain entered the war on the French side in 1779, giving the allies clear naval superiority. But Spain wanted the war to continue until it had re-

captured Florida and the strategic garrison at Gibraltar. The treaties with France provided the United States with needed financial and military assistance. At the same time, they tied the destiny of the new American republic to an intricate web of European diplomatic alliances and territorial quarrels.

Victory at Yorktown

Britain had one more opportunity to end the rebellion by force. The government lacked the financial resources and parliamentary support to mount a major offensive. It therefore adopted a new strategy, the systematic conquest of the rich rice- and tobacco-growing southern states. The British knew that southern patriots lacked military manpower. Most planters refused to arm their slaves or allow black regiments. Many whites declined to join the Continental army; fearing slave uprisings, they served only in local militia units. These patriot weaknesses contrasted with Tory strength. Thousands of loyalists in Georgia and the Carolinas stood ready to join an invading British army or provide it with food and supplies.

To implement its southern strategy, the government ordered the main British army to evacuate Philadelphia and move to New York. This action drew major units of the Continental army to the north. Then a British force of about thirty-five hundred men captured Savannah, Georgia in December 1778. It mobilized hundreds of blacks to build barricades and unload military supplies in preparation for an offensive. By the end of 1779, the British forces numbered more than ten thousand troops. Led by Sir Henry Clinton, they advanced against Charleston, South Carolina. Clinton's soldiers took the city in May 1780, capturing General Benjamin Lincoln and five thousand American troops. By August, the British controlled most of the state. In the battle of Camden, Lord Cornwallis routed an understaffed patriot army commanded by General Horatio Gates, the hero of Saratoga. The British southern strategy seemed to be working. Local Tories assisted Cornwallis as he moved through South Carolina, while only about twelve hundred patriot militiamen aided Gates at Camden.

Then the tide turned. Patriot guerillas led by

the "Swamp Fox," General Francis Marion, harassed British forces occupying South Carolina. A force composed primarily of North Carolina farmers defeated a regiment of loyalist troops at King's Mountain in October 1780, taking about a thousand prisoners. General Daniel Morgan won a narrow victory over a Tory force at Cowpens, North Carolina, early in 1781. Then, in May 1781, Continental units commanded by General Nathaniel Greene fought Cornwallis' army to a draw at Guilford Court House. Bolstered by Virginia militiamen, patriot forces in the Carolinas had broken the back of the British offensive and slowly recaptured lost territory.

Cornwallis carried the battle to Virginia, the stronghold of American resistance in the South. Aided by reinforcements from Clinton in New York, the British general moved easily through the Tidewater region. He met only light opposition from a small American army commanded by the Marquis de Lafayette, a republican-minded Frenchman. Lafayette had volunteered his services to the American cause long before the alliance of 1778. He had returned to France early in 1780 to persuade King Louis XVI to change French military priorities. The king finally sent about five thousand troops under the command of General Comte de Rochambeau to Rhode Island, where they threatened the British army in New York. Now, as Lafayette dueled with Cornwallis in Virginia, the French monarch ordered the large fleet commanded by Admiral Francois de Grasse into American waters. When Cornwallis reached the York Peninsula of

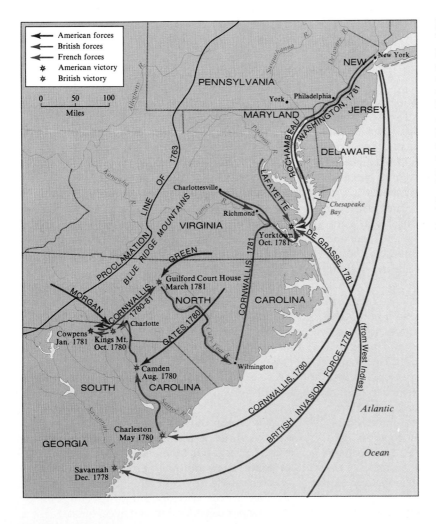

MAP 7.2 STALEMATE AND VICTORY IN THE SOUTH
British naval and military forces captured Savannah in 1778 and Charlestown in May, 1780. Brutal warfare raged in the Carolina backcountry over the next eighteen months, fought as much by small bands of irregulars as by disciplined armies. When Cornwallis carried this struggle into Virginia in late 1781, Washington and Lafayette surrounded his forces at Yorktown, aided by the French fleet under Admiral de Grasse.

RIFLEMEN AND GENTLEMEN
Backcountry Virginia riflemen wore hunting tunics of durable linen, and carried Indian tomahawks and long "Kentucky" rifles. Their rude dress contrasted with that of gentlemen who, like the soldier to the right, wore "a regular Uniform of Blue, turn'd up with Buff; with plain yellow metal Buttons, Buff Waist Coat & Breeches, and white Stockings." (Anne S. K. Brown Military Collection, Brown University Library)

Virginia, Washington launched a well-coordinated attack. Feinting an assault on New York City, Washington secretly transported General Rochambeau's French army to Virginia. Simultaneously, Admiral de Grasse positioned his fleet off the coast, establishing naval control of Chesapeake Bay. Cornwallis was surrounded at Yorktown, outnumbered three to one on land and cut off from reinforcement or retreat by sea. He surrendered his army of seven thousand men on October 19, 1781.

The Franco-American victory at Yorktown broke the will of the British government. The British lacked the financial resources to raise a new army. The combined fleets of France and Spain menaced the British West Indian islands. Dutch merchants took control of some British overseas trade. And a newly formed league of European states threatened to break the British commercial blockade of France by force. Britain was isolated diplomatically in Europe and stymied militarily in America. As 1781 ended, the government ended the active prosecution of the war in America and started negotiations for peace.

Why were the British defeated? Angry mem-

bers of Parliament blamed the military command. With some justification, they cited Howe's conciliatory tactics in 1776; Germain's failure to coordinate the movements of Howe's and Burgoyne's armies in 1777; and Cornwallis' decision to march deep into Virginia in 1781. Yet these tactical decisions might have worked out. Their failure testified primarily to the high odds against British success. In attempting to crush a major rebellion by force, the Crown had committed thousands of troops to a distant land. They faced a determined, well-manned rebel army and militia and, eventually, the well-equipped military forces of France, their traditional and powerful European enemy. A great general or a magnetic leader, such as William Pitt, might have suppressed the rebellion and restored British authority. But ordinary men were destined to fail.

Why were the Americans victorious? They had the strategic advantage of fighting on their own territory, but little else. They had to create an army from nothing, establish a command structure staffed by competent officers, and supply their forces with food and arms. Washington's inspired leadership achieved what a lesser commander might not have been able to accomplish. The American general deferred to civil authority and maintained the political and financial support of the Continental Congress and the state governments. He exercised firm yet tolerant control over his subordinates and recruited outstanding men, such as Baron Von Steuben of Germany, to instill order and discipline into the ranks of the Continental army. Washington understood what was needed to wage war in a preindustrial agricultural society. Even as he built up the Continental army into a respectable fighting force, he deftly deployed militia units of fighting farmers.

In addition to brilliance, Washington had a greater margin for error than the British generals who opposed him. The French desire for diplomatic and military revenge against Great Britain provided crucial material resources and helped assure a decisive American victory. Popular support gave the American general an equally important advantage. Although loyalists composed about 20 percent of the white population, and forty thousand Tories fought as regular troops in the British army between 1775 and 1783, there were twice as many avid patriots. They dominated all the state governments in New England and in the crucial southern state of Virginia. These ordinary men and women mobilized the local resources required to fight a long war, providing American troops with homespun clothing, shoes, and food. And they intervened decisively in the fighting. For example, thousands of militiamen beseiged General Gage in Boston in 1775, surrounded Burgoyne at Saratoga in 1778, and forced Cornwallis to relinquish the Carolinas in 1781. This warfare in the countryside deprived the British troops of safe areas and local supplies, offsetting their superior training, equipment, and military support. In the end, the allegiance of the American people decided the conflict. The British, lacking widespread popular support, achieved little with their many military victories, and their two major defeats proved catastrophic.

THE PASSIONS OF WAR
"Seize, Kill or Apprehend the Rebel Guards," read one Tory battle order in Westchester County, New York, the scene of bitter warfare between patriot and loyalist farmers. When American partisans captured Major Andre, a British officer, behind American lines and out of uniform, they hung him as a spy. (Library of Congress)

The Disruptions of War

The military conflict affected every aspect of American society. The fighting disrupted individual lives and the economy as a whole. The cost of the war destroyed the fiscal systems of the Continental Congress and the state governments. Various groups fought bitterly over the allocations of these financial burdens and for political power in the new states. A coalition of farmers and artisans created a constitution in Pennsylvania with many democratic features. Led by John Adams, more conservative republicans endorsed Whig theories of "mixed government" and set up institutions that enhanced the political power of wealthy merchants and planters. For a decade, Americans debated the proper constitutional framework for their new republican society.

War, Inflation, and Debt

"An army, even a friendly one, are a dreadful scourge to any people," Jedidiah Huntington of Connecticut wrote home from the Pennsylvania front in 1778. "You cannot imagine what devastation & distress mark their steps." As British and American armies marched back and forth between New York and Philadelphia, New Jersey became the hub of the revolution. Both armies posed a constant danger to life and property. Leading patriots and loyalists in the Hackensack Valley fled from their homes to escape certain arrest. Soldiers and partisans looted their farms, either for political revenge or for valuable livestock and supplies of scarce food. Poorly disciplined troops sexually harassed and raped women and girls. They beat imprisoned male partisans and burned their houses and barns.

Old ethnic and religious quarrels flared under the pressure of military strife. Many Scotch-Irish and Germans in the Hackensack valley joined the British cause, while those of English ancestry flocked to the patriot side. Economic self-interest created new animosities. Loyalists fought their way through patriot roadblocks to sell grain to General Howe's army in Philadelphia. In the Carolina backcountry, fierce battles between patriot and tory militiamen generated long-lasting hatred. After the war, the Sons of Liberty accosted William Rees, a former loyalist officer, and dealt fifty blows to his back with a hickory stick. When a group of Tories attempted to reclaim their former lands, a patriot mob killed eight and injured many more. "From a habit of putting the British to death," Judge Aedanus Burke of South Carolina observed, "our citizens have reconciled their minds to the killing of each other." "The rage of civil discord hath advanced among us with an astounding rapidity," the French migrant Michel-Guillaume Crevecoeur noted in his famous *Letters from an American Farmer* (1782). "The laws are no longer respected and all the social bonds are loosened." "What is man," he lamented as the bloodshed continued, "when no longer connected with society; or when he finds himself surrounded by a convulsed and a half dissolved one?"

The indirect effects of the fighting were less dramatic but no less important. British troops occupied all major American seaports at some point during the war, disrupting their commerce and causing thousands to flee. The population of New York City fell from about twenty-one thousand in 1775 to fewer than half that number at the end of the war. Ten years later, the urban economy had not recovered. In 1790, only 6 percent of the American people lived in towns of twenty-five hundred or more. This percentage was the lowest in peacetime in more than half a century.

The rural population suffered equally severe hardships. Taxes rose dramatically. In the small farm town of Windham, Connecticut, the annual prewar property tax was 1 percent of its assessed value; during the war, the tax rose to 6 percent. From time to time, military units or state governments seized livestock, grain, and other supplies. Many farm parents had difficulty feeding their families. Marriage rates dropped sharply because young people lacked the resources to establish new farmsteads. Families had fewer children, either because husbands were away in military service or because wives avoided pregnancy in a time of danger and uncertainty. The birth rate in Concord, Massachusetts, fell to 16.9 per 1,000 adult women. This was significantly below the annual rate of 24.5 per 1,000 both before and after the war.

The cost of the war overwhelmed the financial capacities of most of the state governments. Newly elected officials feared that large tax increases would undermine their fragile authority, and they sought other ways to raise money. They began by taking loans from wealthy individuals; this yielded about $18 million. These funds quickly ran out, and the states issued paper currency worth $260 million, using the money to pay soldiers and purchase supplies. The currency was not backed by specie reserves or tax revenues, and so its value quickly depreciated. The value of North Carolina's paper money fell so much that the state government itself refused to accept it in payment of taxes. Instead, the state ordered each taxpayer to provide one piece of clothing for the army.

The monetary system created by the Continental Congress also collapsed, threatening the entire war effort. The Congress had no authority to levy taxes, but relied on funds requisitioned from the

THE FLOOD OF PAPER CURRENCY

The Continental Congress issued this six dollar bill in November, 1776. It promised eventual payment in gold or silver. As Congress printed huge amounts of paper money in 1778 and 1779, the value of the dollar collapsed—giving rise to the phrase "not worth a Continental." (Library of Congress)

state governments. More often than not, states made their payments late or not at all. To obtain funds in 1778, the Congress pledged a French loan of $6 million in specie as security; wealthy Americans promptly purchased $27 million in Continental loan certificates. These funds were quickly exhausted, and the Congress, like the states, financed the war primarily with printed bills of credit. Between 1775 and 1779, it issued currency with a face value of $191 million. Tax revenues requisitioned from the states retired only $3 million of these bills from circulation.

Citizens refused to accept currency at its face value. In 1777, to buy goods worth $1 in gold or silver, a person needed $3 in Continental bills. The ratio increased to 7 to 1 in 1778, to 42 to 1 in 1779, and to 100 to 1 in 1780. When the rate of exchange between Continental currency and specie reached 146 to 1 in 1781, only speculators would accept the money. The army could neither purchase supplies nor pay its men, and General Washington called urgently for a national system of taxation. "Unless the Congress are vested with powers competent to the great purposes of war, our cause is lost," the commander-in-chief warned.

The Continental Congress acted decisively to restore financial order. It asked the states to increase their taxes and to purchase outstanding bills of credit at the rate of one silver dollar for every forty paper dollars. This devaluation program redeemed $120 million in Continental currency at a cost of $3 million in specie. Astute speculators and merchants reaped a substantial profit. They had accumulated Continental bills from thousands of ordinary citizens at rates of 80, 100, or 120 to 1. Now they cashed them in, doubling or tripling their investment. Some speculators held on to the remaining $71 million or bought it up. They hoped the currency would be redeemed at its face value at the end of the war.

The big losers in this financial game were soldiers, farmers, and artisans, who had received the bills as military pay or for supplies. Currency depreciated as it sat in their pockets or under their mattresses for a few weeks or months, and they got less for it than they gave. Individually, the financial sacrifices of these ordinary citizens were small; they paid a small "tax" every time depreciating currency passed through their hands. Collectively, these "currency taxes" paid the huge cost of the war.

The inflation—the worst in American history—created intense political conflicts. As prices rose, consumers condemned merchants and other traders as "enemies, extortioners, and monopolizers of everything which distress our country." In 1776, the New England states established price limits for domestic commodities and imported goods. A year later, a regional convention in New Haven, Connecticut, restricted prices and wages at a level 75 percent greater than those of 1774. At the same time, a North Carolina law limited the profit of storekeepers to 25 percent of the purchase price.

These political controls proved ineffective. They applied only to private transactions, not to public finance. An unlimited supply of paper currency made runaway prices inevitable because a growing supply of money was chasing a limited amount of goods. Farmers refused to sell grain at the established rates; they hoarded it until they found a willing buyer. In 1777, to prevent these illegal transactions, the Massachusetts legislature passed an "Act to prevent Monopoly and Oppression." Three years later, government officials admitted that the regulations had "Shut up our Granaries, discouraged Husbandry and

Commerce, and Starved our Sea Ports." There had been "such a stagnation of Business and such a withholding of Articles, as has obliged the People to give up its measure or submit to starving."

Wartime inflation hit soldiers especially hard. Many recruits enlisted for three years at a fixed rate of pay. Their money bought fewer goods each year for themselves and their families. Urban artisans and wage earners also suffered as the cost of their food and housing rose much faster than their incomes. Many of their creditors refused to accept paper money in payment for debts and insisted on silver or gold. "I would rather suspend the payment altogether for a Year or two," a landlord in Lancaster, Pennsylvania, wrote his rental agent in 1777, "you are not to press any of the people for payment" in currency.

As inflation continued, creditors guarded their economic position through political action. Between 1780 and 1782, they persuaded all the state legislatures to repeal "legal tender" laws. Thereafter, merchants, landlords, and other creditors could legally refuse to accept depreciated paper currency and could demand payment in specie. The long war had destroyed the American financial system. Debt cases swamped the courts, and political conflicts increased among farmers, artisans, merchants, and speculators. The war brought higher taxes, a relentless inflation, and a lower standard of living for most of the population.

Republicanism Debated

After 1776, Pennsylvania replaced Massachusetts as the center of revolutionary action and ideological debate. As the home of the Continental Congress, Philadelphia was the "capital" of the new American states. Events in Pennsylvania, moreover, dramatically raised the major social, economic, and constitutional issues of the American Revolution. Yeomen farmers, urban artisans, and wage earners created the most democratic political movement in the United States. Pennsylvania republicans quarreled bitterly but creatively over constitutional issues. And Philadelphia politics pitted advocates of the new economic ideology of *laissez-faire* against defenders of traditional mercantilist principles.

The movement for independence split Pennsylvania along the lines of class and ethnicity. Before 1755, wealthy Quaker merchants and landowners controlled Pennsylvania politics. Quakers refused to support an aggressive Indian policy or the war against the French. Governor John Penn built a strong proprietary party composed of Anglican merchants and Scotch-Irish Presbyterians. In response, the Quaker-dominated assembly sent Benjamin Franklin to London in 1764 to petition the king for a royal governor. To curry favor with the British, the assembly refused to condemn the Stamp Act.

In response, Philadelphia artisans questioned their traditional political alliance with the Quakers. Artisans comprised about half of the city's population and owned nearly 40 percent of its wealth. They feared that British imports would threaten their small-scale manufacturing enterprises. When Quaker merchants refused to support nonimportation following the Townshend duties, craftsmen formed a mechanics' association. Its members declared their intention to preserve "our just Rights and Privileges to us and our Posterity against every attempt to violate the same, either here or on the other side of the Atlantic." They quickly forged an alliance with rural Scotch-Irish Presbyterians and challenged the system of deferential politics dominated by rural landlords and urban merchants. First, the artisans demanded that "one or two Mechanics be elected to represent so large a body of inhabitants." Then, as pro-British merchants lost popular support, the artisans seized control of the independence movement. By February 1776, forty artisans sat with forty-seven merchants on the Philadelphia Committee of Resistance.

This open, turbulent atmosphere encouraged laborers, seamen, servants, and poor craftsmen to enter the political arena. These men and their families made up about 40 percent of the city's population but had little wealth and few social organizations. Their new political consciousness stemmed from participation in anti-imperial mobs. Beginning in 1776, they enlisted in the newly formed patriot militia and suddenly became a powerful political force. Inspired by the democratic aspects of Whig ideology, the militiamen claimed the right to elect their officers, "for annual election is so essentially necessary to the Liberty of Freemen." They also demanded the right to vote in elections, regardless of their age or wealth, since they were defending the state with their lives. In addition, the militiamen proposed compulsory military service for all white adult males. They asked for a graduated schedule of penalties, in "proportion to each man's property," for those who failed to serve.

This democratic-republicanism stemmed from three social and intellectual sources. First, craftsmen favored a "labor" theory of value. They believed that monetary reward should depend on the amount of work put into a product. Artisans disliked merchants, landlords, and middlemen who prospered through financial manipulations rather than manual labor. Second, evangelical religion prompted and justified these egalitarian sentiments. Gilbert Tennent, a leading New Light, served as pastor of Philadelphia's Second Presbyterian Church from 1744 to 1764. He told his Scoth-Irish congregation that all men and women were equal before God. During the prewar crisis with Great Britain, these Presbyterians shouted in street demonstrations that they had "No king but King Jesus." Third, a few key individuals provided intellectual leadership. Thomas Paine transmitted the republican radicalism of English artisans to Philadelphia, while David Rittenhouse, Charles Thomson, James Cannon, and Benjamin Rush were well read in Whig tracts and Enlightenment pamphlets.

In 1776, the coalition of farmers, artisans, and intellectuals took control of Pennsylvania politics. They implemented a constitution that created the most democratic system of government in Europe or America. Written primarily by Cannon and Rittenhouse, this document gave all free adult males the right to vote and hold office. It created a *unicameral* (or one-house) assembly that had complete legislative power. This institutional innovation guaranteed that the will of the legislative majority would become law. There was no council or upper house to represent the wealthy or aristocratic segment of society, and no powerful governor with the right to veto. The goal of the Pennsylvania Constitution was democratic-republicanism: a more egalitarian political and social order. The constitution mandated an extensive system of education, protected citizens from imprisonment for debt, and called for a society in which "every freeman, to preserve his independence, (if without a sufficient estate),

ought to have some profession, calling, trade or farm, whereby he may honestly subsist."

Quaker and Anglican merchants contested this shift in the balance of class power by covertly opposing the new republican regime. When General Howe invaded Pennsylvania and occupied Philadelphia in 1777, the Presbyterian-dominated assembly took extreme steps to safeguard the state. It required loyalty oaths of all the people, exiled suspected Tories, and executed two Quakers on charges of treason. These actions increased ethnic and class tensions, as did the Presbyterians' use of law to impose their religious principles. The Presbyterian-dominated assembly suppressed "Vice and Immorality" by outlawing gambling, horseracing, theatrical shows, and all "evil practices which tend to debauch the minds and corrupt the morals of the subjects of the Commonwealth."

The end of British occupation in 1778 brought a severe food shortage and soaring prices to Philadelphia. In May 1779, a crowd of artisans and laborers seized a merchant for illegally exporting flour. Calling a town meeting, they created a Committee on Prices. The committee imposed price controls, and this action began a major debate on economic policy. Led by the influential financier Robert Morris, Philadelphia merchants opposed such regulation of the economy. They wanted prices to be determined by supply and demand in an open market. Regulation only caused hoarding, they argued; conversely, higher prices would bring goods to the market and relieve scarcity.

Leading patriots gave an ideological tone to these arguments. Washington stated that price controls were "inconsistent with the very nature of things," and Franklin condemned them as "contrary to the nature of commerce." The ordinary citizens of Philadelphia disagreed. At a town meeting in August, 1779, 2,115 voters favored government regulation of the market and only 281 opposed it. However, tanners and shoemakers refused to accept the rates set by the Committee on Prices. Like farmers who wanted the highest market price for their products, these artisans protested that the regulations denied them a living wage.

The conflicts over economic policy finally undermined the democratic coalition that wrote the Pennsylvania Constitution of 1776. Wealthy

Whig patriots exploited the political inexperience and the mistakes of the Presbyterian-dominated assembly. Gradually, they won the support of artisans and Germans for a new Contitutional Convention to alter the basic framework of government. In 1790, a new constitution established a *bicameral* (two-house) legislature, thus providing an upper house that could be controlled by merchants and landowners. The democratic-republican institutional structure created in 1776 had been overturned in a counterrevolution led by the elite.

The course of events in Pennsylvania mirrored those in America as a whole. In the first rush of revolutionary fervor, democratic aspirations found expression in many states. The people of Mecklenburg County instructed their representatives to the North Carolina Constitutional Convention of 1776 to "oppose everything that leans to aristocracy or power in the hands of the rich and chief men exercised to the oppression of the poor." As middling western farmers and urban artisans entered the halls of government, politics became more democratic in style and substance. The new House of Burgesses, a Virginian remarked in 1776, was "composed of men not quite so well dressed, nor so politely educated, nor so highly born as some Assemblies I have formerly seen." But, he concluded, "they are the People's men (and the People in general are right)."

This democratic thrust produced an elitist response. From Boston, John Adams condemned the unicameral legislature proposed in Paine's *Common Sense* as "so democratical that it must produce confusion and every evil work." To counteract the influence of the Pennsylvania Constitution of 1776, Adams circulated manuscript copies of his own *Thoughts on Government*. In this political treatise, Adams ingeniously adapted the English Whig theory of "mixed government" for a republican society. *Thoughts on Government* outlined an institutional system in which the people elected a governor and a bicameral legislature. In addition, an appointed—not an elected—judiciary interpreted controversial legislation. Adams had divided state power into three parts—legislation, executive action, and adjudication—and assigned each function to different branches of the government. He thus sought to duplicate the "balance" among the so-

cial orders of monarchy, aristocracy, and commons in the English system.

This Whig (or "aristocratic") definition of American republicanism served the interests of the privileged classes. Adams wanted men of wealth and status to dominate the upper house of the legislature and to check the power of popular majorities. The Massachusetts statesman also intended that the appointed judiciary be staffed by men with extensive legal training, not by elected judges.

Adams' *Thoughts on Government* reflected the sentiments of the traditional aristocratic leaders of the southern states. For example, George Mason advised the Virginia Contitutional Convention to restrict membership in the upper house to men with estates of "at least two thousand value," a sum that would limit entry to the top 5 percent of the population. The South Carolina gentry wrote these class safeguards into law. The South Carolina Constitution of 1778 required candidates for governor to have a debt-free estate of £10,000; senators to be worth £2,000; and assemblymen to have property valued at £1,000. These stringent rules barred all blacks and about 90 percent of the white adult male population from these offices. And property qualifications restricted voting to a minority of the white males.

In 1776, most observers recognized that the creation of republican governments in America constituted both an independence movement and a revolution. Kings, queens, and princes ruled most of the nations of Europe, and merchant oligarchies or landed aristocracies dominated the rest. To vest political authority in the hands of the people and make elected representatives and governors responsible to them was a radical act. Or so it seemed. By 1800, the German political theorist Friedrich Gentz offered an alternative view. He argued that Americans had not carried through a radical revolution but only a conservative defense of their traditional society from British interference. Was Gentz correct?

The first constitutions of South Carolina and Pennsylvania offer complex and contradictory answers to such questions. These constitutions made America the first modern revolutionary nation because they created political institutions based on the popular will. Yet there were strong traditional and hierarchial elements in some of these documents and in the institutions they created. In South Carolina and throughout the South, independence brought few political changes. Wealthy planters and merchants led the revolt against British rule and subsequently consolidated their traditional position of dominance. Now they ruled through a Whig aristocratic-republican form of "mixed government." In the more egalitarian society of Pennsylvania and much of the North, republicanism assumed a radical and democratic cast. Previously powerless social groups achieved a stronger political presence and emphasized democratic aspects of republican ideology. They broadened the definition of republican equality to include economic and social, as well as political, rights. "An equality of property," the educator Noah Webster argued a few years later, "is the very *soul* of a republic." The American Revolution was both a traditional elitist revolt against outside control and an ideologically charged democratic political movement.

Property and the New Social and Political Order

By 1783, the American states' experiment in self-rule had just begun. As Americans debated major issues, they defined the character of their republican society. The respect for property rights inherent in eighteenth-century republicanism influenced the outcome of many of these controversies. It determined the handling of loyalists' estates and helped preserve slavery. During the 1780s, debates over rival conceptions of property rights divided legislators in most states into opposing factions. A desire to uphold the property rights of creditors prompted influential politicians to create a stronger national government in the federal Constitution of 1787.

Liberty and Property

The patriots fought the British not only for their lives and liberty, but also for the rights of private property. The three values were closely linked in republican theory. The Massachusetts Constitution of 1780 declared that every citizen should be protected "in the enjoyment of his life, liberty,

and property, according to the standing laws." The Virginia Bill of Rights went further by asserting that the "means of acquiring and possessing property" was an inherent right. This active definition of property rights had broad social and political implications. It meant that individuals and families should possess sufficient productive property to provide a livelihood and make them responsible members of the community. On the assumption that only individuals with enough property could act independently, most state constitutions restricted voting privileges to those with a freehold estate of a certain minimum value. Without property, liberty was impossible.

This deep regard for property rights affected the treatment of loyalists. More than a hundred thousand Tories emigrated to Canada, the West Indies, and Britain, abandoning considerable goods, lands, and buildings. Some patriots favored confiscation of the property of these "traitors," but most American public officials opposed the repudiation of property rights. The government of North Carolina initially rented out loyalist estates; it confiscated them only after the British invaded the South. Most loyalist property in Massachusetts was handled by the court system under a long-established "Act to Provide for the Payment of Debts." After creditors had been reimbursed, the rest of an estate reverted to resident wives or widows of departed Tories. Only the government of New York argued that public authorities could abridge the property rights of individuals. It confiscated loyalist estates by affirming the "sovereignty of the people of this state in respect to all property."

These policies limited the social and economic impact of the Tory departures. Most states seized only the property of leading Loyalists— and only to raise revenue. They did not break up large landed estates in order to create a more equal distribution of wealth. In fact, most states sold confiscated property to the highest bidder. Georgia seized about 128,000 acres of land from 166 Tories and sold it to 188 patriots; 12 of these purchasers acquired a total of 42,000 acres. Elsewhere, the sale of loyalist property produced a somewhat more democratic result. About half of the new owners in North Carolina were small-scale farmers. And the tenants on the Philipsburg estate in New York claimed preemption rights on lands they had previously leased. As a result, about 80 percent of this fertile tract was divided into small farms.

The loyalist emigration increased social mobility in the seaport cities but did not alter the structure of urban society. To fill the financial vacuum created by the departure of Tory merchants, the Lowell, Higginson, Jackson, and Cabot families moved their trading enterprises into Boston from neighboring Essex County. Likewise, newcomers to Philadelphia displaced some Quaker and Anglican mercantile firms. As in most rural areas, wealthy patriots replaced affluent Tories at the peak of society. The economic hierarchy inherited from the European and the colonial experience remained intact in the new republican society.

So did the social and political inferiority of women. The War strained the customary division of labor and status between the sexes. Thousands of women assumed increased responsibility for the business of farming while their husbands were away in military service. Some wives acquired a taste for decision making. "We have sow'd our oats as you desired," Sarah Cobb Paine wrote to her absent husband, "had I been master I should have planted it to Corn."

The extraordinary excitement of the war years also overwhelmed customs that restricted political discourse to men. Despite their husbands' reservations, upper-class women discussed political issues in letters, diaries, and daily conversations. "The men say we have no business" with politics, Eliza Wilkinson complained in 1783, "but I won't have it thought that because we are the weaker sex as to bodily strength we are capable of nothing more than domestic concerns. They won't even allow us liberty of thought, and that is all I want."

As Wilkinson's protest indicates, republican political principles challenged laws and customs that placed women in a subordinate legal position. "All men would be tyrants if they could," Abigail Adams chided her husband John in a famous exchange of letters regarding republican ideology and women's rights. "If particular care and attention is not paid to the ladies," she continued in a tone that was only half joking, "we will not hold ourselves bound by any laws in which we have no voice or representation."

Her prime concern was not voting rights for women, but their strictly subordinate position under the law. Even as her husband and other American political leaders were busy "emancipating all nations," Abigail Adams pointed out, "you insist upon retaining absolute power over Wives."

Slavery raised the identical issue. The American Revolution generated intense debate over the institution of slavery and revealed deep contradictions in republican ideology. Many white patriots who demanded liberty for themselves realized the inconsistency of holding blacks in perpetual bondage. "I wish most sincerely there was not a Slave in the province," Abigail Adams wrote her husband John in 1774. "It always appeared a most iniquitous Scheme to me—to fight ourselves for what we are daily robbing and plundering from those who have as good a right to freedom as we have." In 1775, the clergy and laity of the Scottish-dominated Saint Andrew parish in Georgia declared that slavery was an "unnatural practice founded in injustice and cruelty, debasing part of our fellow creatures below men, and laying the basis of that liberty we contend for upon a very wrong foundation."

The intense questioning of slavery was new, and it stemmed from several sources. Beginning in the 1750s with John Woolman, a writer, some Quakers questioned the morality of slavery and urged their coreligionists to free their slaves. Responding to the call of the yearly meeting of 1776 to "clear their hands" of slavery, many North Carolina Quakers manumitted (freed) their blacks. Other churches extended religious fellowship to the Afro-American population. Some pietistic religious sects, because they believed in universal salvation, welcomed both enslaved and free blacks into their congregations. Such actions diminished the cultural differences between the races and raised additional doubts about the moral legitimacy of slavery.

Enlightenment principles played an important role in the new debate over slavery. John Locke had argued that ideas stemmed from impressions and experience and were not innate. Following his lead, many Enlightenment thinkers emphasized the importance of the cultural environment in shaping human behavior and values. Hence, the oppressive conditions of slavery accounted for the debased situation of the black

THE MASSACHUSETTS COURTS RULE SLAVERY IS UNCONSTITUTIONAL

In 1783, Chief Justice William Cushing ruled that the natural right to freedom asserted in the Massachusetts constitution of 1780 had abolished African slavery.

As to the doctrine of Slavery and the right of Christians to hold Africans in perpetual servitude, and sell and treat them as we do our horses and cattle, that (it is true) has been heretofore countenanced by the Province Laws formerly, but nowhere is it expressly enacted or established. It has been a usage. . . .

A different idea has taken place with the people of America, more favorable to the natural rights of mankind, and to that natural innate desire of Liberty, which with Heaven (without regard to color, complexion, or shape of noses-features) has inspired all the human race. And upon this ground our Constitution of Government, by which the people of this Commonwealth have solemnly bound themselves, sets out with declaring that all men are born free and equal—and that every subject is entitled to liberty, and to have it guarded by the laws, as well as life and property—and in short is totally repugnant to the idea of being born slaves. This being the case, I think the idea of slavery is inconsistent with our own conduct and Constitution.

---

race, not some inherent inferiority in the people themselves. "A state of slavery has a mighty tendency to shrink and contract the minds of men," one American observer noted. Anthony Benezet, a philanthropist who funded a school for blacks in Philadelphia, declared that "the Negroes are generally sensible, humane and sociable, and as capable of improvement as White People." If blacks were freed from bondage, concluded Benjamin Rush, the Philadelphia republican, they could become active, responsible citizens.

Objections to slavery were diverse in their origins and underlying assumptions, but they mingled easily in the public mind. In 1784, a conference of Virginia Methodists used religious conviction, natural-rights philosophy, and revolutionary ideology to condemn slavery. The conference declared that slavery was "contrary to the Golden Law of God on which hang all the Law and Prophets, and the unalienable Rights of Mankind, as well as every Principle of Revolution."

The weight of this spiritual and intellectual testimony crushed the traditional religious and cultural arguments used to defend slavery. In the northern states, where there were relatively few slaves, it laid the basis for black emancipation. By 1784, four northern states—Massachusetts, Pennsylvania, Connecticut, and Rhode Island—had either abolished slavery or provided for its gradual end. Within another two decades, all states north of Delaware adopted similar legislation.

However, emancipation did not mean equality. Racial prejudice remained strong. A Massachusetts Act of 1786 prohibited whites from marrying blacks, Indians, or mulattoes. Emancipation itself was slow, selective, and incomplete. The New York Emancipation Edict of 1799, for example, did not grant freedom to enslaved blacks but only to their children—and then only when they reached their twenty-fifth birthday. As late as 1810, more than thirty thousand slaves still served white masters in the northern states, nearly a fourth of the total black population of those states. The slow process reflected white fears of a large community of free blacks, plus resistance by northern slaveowners to legislation that would free their black chattels without compensation, thus violating their property rights.

The contradiction between the republican values of liberty and property reached an acute stage in the South. Blacks made up from 30 to 60 percent of the people of those states and represented a huge financial investment. Most political leaders were slaveowners, and they used the power of the state to deter emancipation. In 1776, the North Carolina legislature condemned Quaker manumissions as "highly criminal and reprehensible." It directed the imprisonment of freed blacks and their sale at public auction. Even the British invasion did not shake white determination to keep slaves in a completely subordinate position. When merchant John Laurens of South Carolina suggested in 1779 that the state raise three thousand black troops to assist the outnumbered patriots, the assembly rejected his proposal overwhelmingly. Of all the southern states, only Maryland recruited a large number of slaves and freed them in return for their military service.

Understandably, southern blacks sought freedom on their own. Hundreds of Georgia slaves fled to Spanish Florida following the British invasion. Two neighbors of Richard Henry Lee, a prominent Virginia patriot, lost "every slave they had in the world," as did nearly "all of those who were near the enemy." Eight mothers and their children were among the fifty-three blacks who fled from John Ball's Virginia plantations and sought refuge behind the British lines. When the British army left Charleston, more than five thousand blacks accompanied the sol-

JAMES LAFAYETTE
James was a slave owned by William Armistead of Virginia. In 1781, he served as a spy for the American army commanded by the Marquis de Lafayette, who noted that "his intelligence from the enemy's camp was industriously collected and most faithfully delivered." The Virginia Assembly rewarded James by purchasing his freedom. The former slave adopted Lafayette's surname and, when the famous French general returned to the United States in 1824, had the honor of meeting with him in Richmond. (Virginia Historical Society)

diers; another thirty-five hundred fled from Savannah.

Many slaves bargained wartime loyalty to their masters for a promise of liberty. Using a Manumission Act passed in 1782, Virginia planters granted freedom to more than ten thousand slaves within a decade. Some whites acted out of gratitude for past service. Others were influenced by republican principles or the sermons of Methodist and Baptist preachers. A third group of slaveowners combined altruism with economic self-interest; they required blacks to purchase their freedom through paid work as artisans or laborers. By 1810, manumission and self-purchase raised the number of freed men and women in Maryland to about a third of the black population. In Delaware, freed blacks outnumbered slaves three to one.

Yet a movement for general emancipation did not develop in the Chesapeake colonies despite black activism and antislavery agitation in the northern states. Few whites wanted a society filled with freed blacks. They also soon realized that private manumissions threatened the existence of slavery. "Henny will try to pass for a free woman, as several have lately been set free in this neighborhood," a slaveowner warned his friends regarding a runaway black. Alarmed by the loss of control over slaves, the Virginia legislature in 1792 made it more difficult for whites to free them. Following Thomas Jefferson, many Chesapeake planters now argued that slavery was a "necessary evil" required to maintain their life-styles and to deter a black challenge to white supremacy. To calm their troubled consciences, they treated their blacks more kindly and freed a few favorites—but remained slaveowners for the rest of their lives.

Thus, the tide turned against emancipation even before the expansion of cotton production gave slavery a new economic rationale. The rice planters of Georgia and the Carolinas adamantly opposed emancipation throughout the revolutionary era. They resisted legislation to outlaw the transatlantic slave trade and imported thousands of new slaves from Africa. A final argument against peaceful emancipation came in 1800 when Virginia authorities prevented a slave uprising planned by a slave, Gabriel Prosser. They arrested and hanged Prosser and about thirty of his followers. Virginia thus reaffirmed

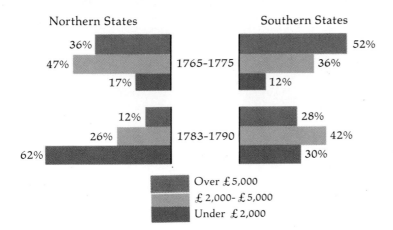

Northern States   Southern States

36%   52%
47%   1765-1775   36%
17%   12%

12%   28%
26%   1783-1790   42%
62%   30%

■ Over £5,000
■ £2,000- £5,000
■ Under £2,000

FIGURE 7.1 THE REVOLUTION
AND POLITICAL
DEMOCRACY:
CHANGE IN THE WEALTH OF
ELECTED OFFICIALS

the South's commitment to slavery and white property rights, whatever the cost to republican principles. "Liberty and equality have brought the evil upon us," a letter to the Virginia *Herald* proclaimed in the aftermath of the rebellion, for such doctrines are "dangerous and extremely wicked in this country, where every white man is a master, and every black man is a slave."

Property and Politics

The 1780s were a critical period for the new states. A stubborn recession gripped their economies, wartime debts undermined their financial stability, and widespread political discontent threatened their legitimacy. Peace did not bring a return of prewar prosperity. The war destroyed much of the American merchant fleet, disrupted trade connections, and eliminated lucrative markets. British laws excluded northern producers from the sugar islands. And without the assistance of Glasgow merchants, Chesapeake planters could not increase their tobacco exports to Europe. The decline of the export trade lowered the American standard of living. The population grew from 2.4 to 3.6 million between 1775 and 1787, but exports increased only slightly, from $10.7 to $11.6 million. As a result, Americans had fewer resources per capita to buy imported manufactured products. Nevertheless, low-priced British goods flooded urban markets. Responding to artisan protests, New York, Rhode Island, Pennsylvania, and Massachusetts imposed tariffs on imported manufactures.

The financial legacy of the war compounded the economic distress. Most state governments entered the 1780s with worthless currencies and sizable debts. North Carolina owed its creditors $1.7 million, while Virginia had unredeemed securities worth $2.7 million. Speculating merchants and landowners had purchased many of these debt certificates for less than their face value. Now they advocated high taxes, so that the states could redeem their bonds quickly and at full worth.

Major political battles broke out in many states. Before the war, wealthy merchants, lawyers, and landowners had generally dominated the institutions of representative government. Their poorer neighbors elected them to office and usually deferred to their political judgment. But widespread mobilization during the war eroded this deferential system of politics and encouraged many men to express their own views. Lower property qualifications for voting gave artisans greater political power, and reapportionment of the legislatures increased the representation from western agricultural regions. Middling farmers and artisans now formed a majority of the lower houses of most northern legislatures and a sizeable minority in the southern legislative bodies. Demonstrating their new political consciousness and power, they successfully opposed the collection of back taxes and the rapid redemption of the public debt.

The representatives of backcountry planters and yeomen farm families often took the offensive. For example, they persuaded the South

THE REBELS OF 1786
This woodcut shows Daniel Shays and Jacob Shattuck in their Continental Army uniforms. "Liberty is still the object I have in view" wrote one Shaysite; but, replied the one-time radical patriot Samual Adams, "the man who dares to rebel against the laws of a republic ought to suffer death." Shattuck was convicted of treason and hanged. Shays fled to New York State where he died, a poor farmer, in 1821. (National Portrait Gallery, Washington)

Carolina legislature to move the state capital from the merchant-dominated seaport of Charleston to Columbia, an inland city. They also won passage of a law that prevented sheriffs from selling seized farm lands to repay debts; instead, creditors had to accept installment payments over a three-year period. The legislators assisted debtors by increasing the supply of paper currency. The Maryland House of Delegates enacted a similar profarmer and prodebtor program in 1785 and again in 1786, only to have it rejected by a creditor majority in the more conservative state senate.

As James Madison pointed out, these political struggles were not between "the Class with, and the Class without, property." Those who lacked property—slaves, indentured servants, laborers, and tenant farmers—played only a minor role. Wealthy mercantile leaders and landed property owners battled with a larger coalition of less affluent farmers, traders, and artisans for control of the state governments.

The depressed economic conditions of the 1780s increased the stakes of these struggles. David Ramsey, a physician and member of the

South Carolina legislature and the future author of the well-known *History of the American Revolution* (1789), assailed his colleagues for undermining the "just rights of creditors." Another procreditor legislator, John Lloyd, condemned laws preventing the prompt collection of debts as an unwarranted "interference of the legislature in private contracts." Although unpopular among creditors, these measures eased the financial strain on hard-pressed yeomen and tenant farmers and prevented a major social upheaval.

The absence of such legislation in Massachusetts produced an armed uprising. Beginning in 1781, eastern merchants and creditors lobbied successfully for high taxes and against paper money. These procreditor policies facilitated rapid repayment of the state's war debt but undermined the fragile financial structure of many newly settled areas. Such regions produced few surplus goods that could be sold to pay high taxes and cover private debts. Creditors and sheriffs hauled delinquent farmers into court, saddled them with high legal fees, and threatened them with imprisonment for debt or with the loss of their property. Led by Daniel Shays, a former captain in the Continental army, hundreds of western and central Massachusetts farmers revolted in 1785 and 1786. They closed the courts by force; freed their supporters from jail; and called county conventions to protest against high taxes, eastern creditors, and legislative inaction.

As a movement against outside economic forces, Shays' Rebellion resembled the North Carolina Regulator movement. As a struggle against high taxes and outside political control, it was similar to the American fight for independence. Wealthy Whig patriots found themselves in a contradictory position. They supported the principle of popular resistance but deplored its implications for their property rights. "The people have turned against their teachers the doctrines which were inculcated to effect the late revolution," complained the archconservative Massachusetts political leader Fisher Ames. To preserve its authority, the Massachusetts legislature passed a Riot Act that outlawed illegal gatherings and Governor James Bowdoin mobilized the state militia. The troops quickly dispersed Shays's supporters and ended the revolt.

The Whig Constitutional Triumph

The political impact of Shays' Rebellion was more important than the uprising itself. Previously, conservative Whigs had protested against prodebtor legislation primarily at the state level; now they increased their demands for a stronger central government. Between 1777 and 1781, the states had ratified the Articles of Confederation, which established a permanent central government with limited legislative and fiscal powers. The wartime achievements of the Confederation Congress, as the Continental Congress was often called after 1781, were remarkable. It raised and supported the Continental army, established the alliance with France, arranged foreign loans, and negotiated favorable terms of peace with Great Britain. However, the central government lacked the power to regulate commerce or affect the internal financial affairs of the states. Therefore, it could do little to influence events during the economic recession that occurred during the 1780s. Indeed, the government's own debts grew steadily—to $39 million by 1787—because it could not impose taxes itself and the hard-pressed states refused to honor its requisitions for funds. By increasing the Confederation government's delegated powers, merchants and creditors hoped to counteract the inflationary fiscal policies of the state legislatures and bolster foreign commerce.

A second nationalist political faction also favored a stronger central government. It consisted of military officers, diplomats, and officials

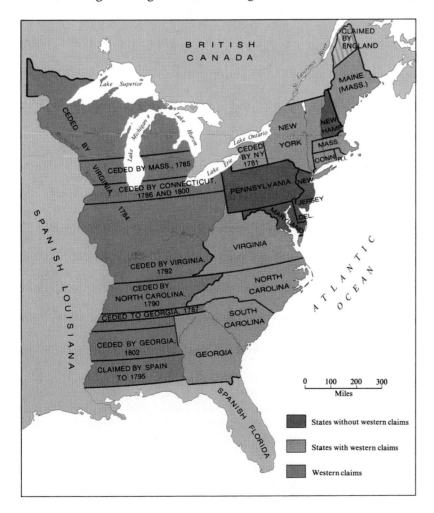

MAP 7.3 THE CONFEDERATION AND WESTERN LAND CLAIMS
The Confederation government devised a brilliantly successful solution to the conflicting land claims of the several states. Beginning in 1781, the states ceded their claims to the Confederation, thus ending a generation of legal disputes and violent conflicts among rival groups of settlers. By 1802, a vast "national domain" stretched from the Appalachian Mountains to the Mississippi River and was open to settlement by citizens of all the states.

who had served in the Continental Congress during the war. These men had acquired a national, rather than a state or local, outlook. They advocated strong nationwide policies on issues controlled by the states, such as western settlement, tariffs, and tax revenue. The Articles of Confederation had reserved these matters to the states unless the state legislatures agreed unanimously to delegate them to the central government. Even less controversial legislation in Congress required the approval of nine of the thirteen states.

The nationalist faction struggled with some success to overcome the formidable obstacles created by the Articles of Confederation. In 1784 and 1785, the Congress confirmed its authority over the western lands ceded by the states or obtained from the British through the Treaty of Paris. It designed a comprehensive settlement policy for these lands and assigned the revenue from western land sales to the support of the central government and the reduction of the national debt. The Northwest Ordinance of 1787 provided for the creation of three to five states— eventually Ohio, Indiana, Illinois, Michigan, and Wisconsin—and prohibited slavery within their boundaries. The ordinance specified that each new "territory" would be ruled initially by a governor appointed by Congress. Then, as the number of people in these territories increased, they would elect their own legislatures. Eventually, they could apply for admission to the Union and receive all the rights and privileges of the existing states. This enlightened settlement policy prevented the establishment of separate "colonies" by the eastern states and enhanced the concept of an American nation.

The nationalist faction advocated further increases in the revenue of the central government. In 1781, it won passage by Congress of a 5 percent tax on imports. Rhode Island, invoking its rights under the Articles of Confederation, rejected this grant of taxing power to the government. New York exercised a similar veto when Congress enacted such a tax in 1783, because that state's own tariff yielded substantial revenue. Unwilling to accept defeat, the nationalists called a Commercial Convention in Annapolis, Maryland, in 1786 to discuss tariff and taxation policies. When only twelve delegates from five states showed up, the convention proposed a new meeting in Philadelphia to undertake a board review and revision of the Articles. In February 1787, Congress passed a resolution supporting the plan to revise the Articles and make them "adequate to the exigencies of government and the preservation of the Union."

The constitutional convention began in May 1787. Fifty-five delegates attended, representing every state except Rhode Island, whose legislature opposed increased central authority. The deliberations took place behind closed doors. Many of the delegates, including George Washington, Benjamin Franklin, Robert Morris, John Dickinson, William Livingston, and Charles Pinckney, had distinguished careers during the war for independence. Most of them had nationalist sympathies. As the historian Charles A. Beard pointed out in *An Economic Interpretation of the Constitution of the United States* (1913), most delegates also were identified with procreditor Whig republican factions in their own states. As individuals and as a group, they were committed to a stronger and fiscally conservative central government. They differed only regarding the means by which to accomplish these goals.

As the convention began its business, the delegates elected Washington as the presiding officer. They agreed that each state would have one vote and that a majority would decide an issue. Then the delegates split into two camps over the nature of the proposed national government. Those from the smaller states favored a plan devised by William Patterson, the former attorney general of New Jersey. This "New Jersey Plan" gave the existing central government the power to raise revenue, control commerce, and make requisitions from the states. While increasing national authority, it did not substantially infringe on the guarantees of state sovereignty in the Articles of Confederation. Hence it appealed to small states, which feared domination by their larger neighbors in a stronger central government.

After a month of debate, a bare majority of the states rejected Patterson's plan. Instead, the delegates agreed to use a revolutionary proposal from the Virginia delegation as the basis for their deliberations. This "Virginia Plan" for a truly national government was the brainchild of James Madison. Madison, who was only thirty-six years old, had grown up on an estate in Vir-

THE ANTI-FEDERALIST ARGUMENT AGAINST THE CONSTITUTION OF 1787

James Winthrop of Massachusetts and Melancton Smith of New York advance Democratic and Localist arguments against the proposed constitution.

Winthrop:

I shall be asked what is meant by the *natural aristocracy*, and told that no such distinction of classes of men exists among us. It is true, it is our singular felicity that we have no legal or hereditary distinctions of this kind; but still there are real differences. Every society naturally divides itself into classes. . . . In every society, men of this class will command a superior degree of respect; and if the government is so constituted as to admit but few to exercise to the powers of it, it will, according to the natural course of things, be in their hands. . . .

This will be a government of oppression. . . . A few years ago, we fought for liberty; we framed a general government on free principles; we placed the state legislatures, in whom the people have a full and a fair representation, between Congress and the people. . . . Now it is proposed to go into the contrary, and a more dangerous extreme—to remove all barriers, to give the new government free access to our pockets, and ample command of our persons, and that without providing for a genuine and fair representation of the people.

Smith:

. . . It is the opinion of the ablest writers on the subject, that no extensive empire can be governed upon republican principles, and that such a government will degenerate to a despotism, unless it be made up of a confederacy of smaller states, each having the full powers of internal regulation. This is precisely the principle which has hitherto preserved our freedom. . . . It is impossible for one code of laws to suit Georgia and Massachusetts. They must, therefore, legislate for themselves.

This new system is, therefore, a consolidation of all the states into one large mass, however diverse the parts may be of which it is to be composed. . . . The attempt made by Great Britain to introduce such a system, struck us with horrour, and when it was proposed by some theorist that we should be represented in parliament, we uniformly declared that one legislature could not represent so many different interests for the purposes of legislation and taxation.

---

ginia. He had graduated from Princeton, where he read deeply in classical and modern political theory, and served in the Confederation Congress for three years. A convinced nationalist at this time, Madison sought to circumvent state authority. "Instead of operating on the States," his new central government would "operate without their intervention on the individuals composing them." He wanted the "due supremacy of national authority" while leaving local institutions intact "so far as they can be subordinately useful." In adopting the Virginia Plan, the delegates exceeded their mandate to revise the Articles of Confederation. They embarked instead upon the creation of a new national system of republican government.

During the hot summer of 1787, the delegates debated the details of the new constitutional framework. As political realists, these experienced American politicians drafted a document that would be accepted by as many existing factions and interest groups as possible. To reconcile the interests of all the states, both large and small, they proposed a national legislature with two chambers. This was a familiar idea in view of the colonial experience and the legislative institutions created by the state constitutions. In the upper house, called the Senate, each state would have two members regardless of its size, wealth, or population. But in the lower chamber, the House of Representatives, seats would be apportioned on the basis of population. The population of each state would be determined by a census every ten years.

The delegates responded to the concerns of the states in other ways as well. They created an office of president, the equivalent of a colonial governor-general in terms of power, and made it independent of the legislature. The selection of the president rested in the hands of an electoral college composed of delegates elected on a state-by-state basis. The constitutional convention also gave the state governments the authority to determine property qualifications for voting. Moreover, they specified that the state legislatures, not the voters at large, would elect the members of the Senate. By giving the existing state legislatures important roles in the new central government, the convention hoped to win their support.

The constitutional convention was well aware of sectional divisions within American society, and it acted accordingly. To mollify planters in Georgia and the Carolinas, the delegates gave constitutional protection to the African slave trade for twenty years. Bowing to northern anti-slavery sentiment, they decreed that the slave trade could be abolished after that period of time by legislative action. A second sectional compromise resolved the controversial and slavery-related issues of taxation and representation. Southern delegates wanted to include slaves in a state's population when determining representation in the lower house of the national legislature. Northern delegates objected, on the republican grounds that propertyless slaves were not full members of the political system. The convention finally agreed that a slave would count as three-fifths of a white person for purposes of representation. Slaves would be included in the same fashion if Congress apportioned direct taxes on the basis of population.

With these difficult state and sectional issues resolved, the convention bestowed extensive authority on the proposed national government. The final document was agreed to by all but three of the delegates on September 17, 1787. It declared the Constitution and all legislation and treaties made under its authority to be the supreme law of the land. It gave the national government control over the armed forces, taxation, and external commerce. Furthermore, the Constitution authorized the national legislature to make all laws "necessary and proper" to implement the provisions of the document. Other clauses in the Constitution met the goals of the procreditor delegates. It deprived the states of the power to issue money or to enact any "Law impairing the Obligation of Contracts." To establish the credit of the United States, the document mandated that the new government would honor the existing national debt. Thus, the members of the Philadelphia convention translated into constitutional form their vision of a strong national state committed to the defense of established property rights.

The procedures for ratifying the new Constitution were as controversial as the document itself. The convention feared, with good reason, that its scheme of government would not receive the unanimous consent of the state legislatures. It therefore specified that the Constitution would go into effect upon ratification by special conventions in at least nine of the thirteen states. As with the adoption of the Virginia Plan, such a provision constituted a clear violation of the Articles of Confederation. Nevertheless, both the Confederation Congress and the state legislatures accepted this procedure. The Congress transmitted the new Constitution to the states, which called elections for delegates to conventions to ratify it, and a great national debate began.

The proponents of the new Constitution called themselves Federalists, even though they advocated a "national" rather than a "federal" governmental framework. They seized the initiative and argued that the document written at Philadelphia would remedy the acknowledged defects of the Articles of Confederation and create a strong and prosperous Union. The anti-Federalists who opposed the Constitution drew popular support primarily from areas with subsistence-agricultural economies, but their leaders came from all regions and classes. Some, like Governor George Clinton of New York, were state politicians. They pointed out that the proposed Constitution violated the Articles and undermined the sovereignty of the states. Other anti-Federalists were motivated by economic self-interest. In Maryland, for example, debt-ridden lawyers and merchants opposed ratification to preserve their financial position. But many—perhaps most—anti-Federalist leaders were moved by ideological reservations. They warned that the Philadelphia document lacked a Bill of Rights to protect the individual from the state. They also argued that it concentrated political power in the hands of a few national legislators. With considerable foresight, the anti-Federalists suggested that most of these legislators would be wealthy or famous men. Thus, the Constitution would remove the government from the control of the people. Adopting an argument ad-

TIME LINE
WAR, REVOLUTION, AND THE NEW POLITICAL ORDER

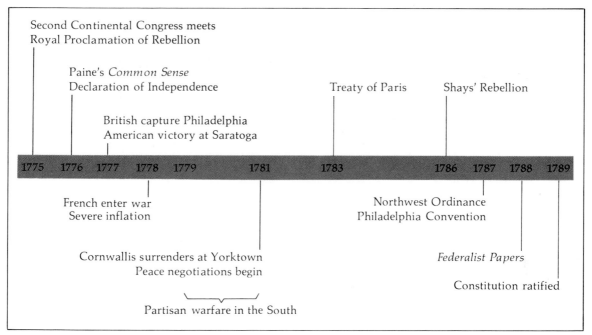

vanced by Baron Montesquieu, the French political philosopher, the anti-Federalists maintained that republican institutions were suited only for cities or small states.

These arguments were weighty. To counter their impact in the hotly contested New York ratification convention, James Madison, John Jay, and Alexander Hamilton wrote a series of newspaper articles called *The Federalist Papers*. These nationalists stressed the need for a strong government to conduct foreign affairs and denied that it would foster domestic tyranny. They pointed out that power within the national government was divided among a president, a bicameral legislature, and a judiciary. Following John Adams in his *Thoughts on Government*, they maintained that each branch of government would "check and balance" the others, thus preserving liberty. Madison composed an original and brilliant rebuttal of Montesquieu. The rising Virginia politician suggested that the great size and social diversity of the United States would safeguard republican government rather than destroy it. He argued that the great number of interest groups would diffuse power and prevent tyranny.

The Federalist Papers persuaded some delegates to the state ratifying conventions, especially in the crucial large states of New York and Virginia. To sway others, Federalist politicians promised that the new constitution would be immediately amended to include a Bill of Rights. The constitutions of most of the states contained declarations of basic individual rights, such as the liberty of conscience in religious matters and the right to a jury trial, and many citizens favored similar protection from the proposed national government. The expectation that George Washington would be the first president prompted other Americans to support ratification. In addition, the many positive features of the Constitution won the support of influential merchants, urban artisans, and market-oriented farmers.

Conventions in the small and economically vulnerable states of Delaware, New Jersey, Georgia, and Maryland voted nearly unanimously in favor of ratification; they strongly preferred the new Constitution to the Articles of Confederation. Delegates in Pennsylvania, Connecticut, and South Carolina approved it by two-to-one margins. Elsewhere, such political tactics

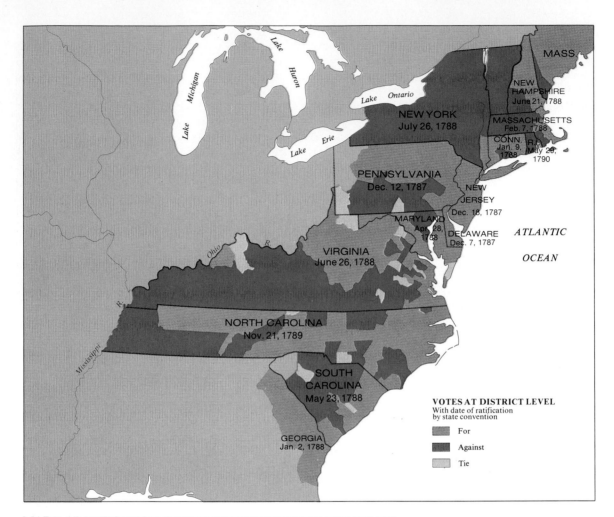

MAP 7.4 RATIFICATION OF THE CONSTITUTION IN THE STATES

In 1907, the geographer Owen Libby offered a socioeconomic interpretation of the ratification of the Constitution. Plotting the voting results on a map, he observed that most delegates from seaboard or commercial-farming districts favored the Constitution, while those from backcountry agricultural areas opposed it. Subsequent research has confirmed Libby's argument for certain regions, such as North and South Carolina and Massachusetts. However, other factors influenced delegates in some states, such as Georgia, where delegates voted unanimously for ratification.

as fraud, intimidation, and misrepresentation led to narrow majorities—57 to 47 in New Hampshire, 187 to 168 in Massachusetts, 89 to 79 in Virginia, and 30 to 27 in New York.

Given the political atmosphere of the 1780s, few Federalists expected a wider victory. Working against great odds, they had gained a fundamental change in the American system of government. Their triumph had ideological and social as well as constitutional implications. The United States Constitution symbolized the resurgence of the traditional American political elite and the decline of its artisan and yeomen opponents. The new Constitution firmly established the Whig definition of republicanism in the basic framework of government. At least temporarily, it consigned democratic-republican principles and politicians to a secondary place in the American political order. The Revolutionary era had come to an end.

$\mathscr{A}$merican independence became a pressing political issue in 1774. Loyalists sought reconciliation unsuccessfully through the Olive Branch petition and then organized for war. Fighting between loyalists and patriots prepared many Americans to accept Thomas Paine's arguments in *Common Sense* and to declare independence in 1776.

General William Howe failed to crush George Washington's continental forces in 1776, and British strategy led to a major American victory at Saratoga in 1777. The French alliance of 1778 helped the American forces counter the British southern offensive and to corner Lord Cornwallis's troops at Yorktown. Military mistakes played a prominent role in Britain's loss of the war. The American victory also resulted from French assistance, Washington's leadership, and—most importantly—popular support for the patriot cause.

By financing the war with paper money, the state and Confederation governments produced devastating inflation and two decades of social conflict. State legislatures assisted debtors during the 1780s, and wealthy creditors sought a strong national government safe from popular control. Pennsylvanians waged the first debate over "democratic" and "aristocratic" republicanism. Most states adopted "Whig" constitutions, designed to diffuse government power and protect property rights. Property in slaves was abolished in the northern states but upheld in the South.

In Philadelphia, men of property and a national vision drafted a new Constitution to replace the Articles of Confederation. After a tense struggle between Federalists and anti-Federalists, representatives of the American people ratified the Constitution, creating a new national government.

Suggestions for Further Reading

Toward Independence

Robert M. Calhoon, *The Loyalists in Revolutionary America* (1973), provides a comprehensive overview. In *The American Tory* (1962), William H. Nelson illuminates the cultural roots of Loyalism, while Wallace Brown, *The King's Friends* (1965), discusses their class status. For Tory military activities, see Paul H. Smith, *Loyalists and Redcoats* (1964). Fine biographies of Loyalists include L. H. Gipson, *Jared Ingersoll* (1920), and Bernard Bailyn, *The Ordeal of Thomas Hutchinson* (1974).

John R. Alden, *A History of the American Revolution* (1969), is a general military history, as is Howard Peckham, *The War for Independence* (1958). For a British perspective, see Piers Mackesy, *The War for America* (1964). Two fine critical studies of wartime strategy are Eric Robson, *The American Revolution in Its Political and Military Aspects* (1954), and John Shy, *A People Numerous and Armed: Reflections on the Military Struggle for American Independence* (1976). Charles Royster, *A Revolutionary People at War* (1979), uses military mobilization to discuss American ideology and social character.

James T. Flexner, *George Washington in the American Revolution* (1968), illuminates his contribution to the war effort. Samuel E. Morison, *John Paul Jones* (1959), is a lively biography, while William M. Fowler, *Rebels Under Sail* (1976), offers a broader account of the American navy. Samuel F. Bemis, *The Diplomacy of the American Revolution* (1935), is still authoritative, but also see Richard W. Van Alstyne, *Empire and Independence* (1965). Richard B. Morris, *The Peacemakers* (1965), provides an absorbing treatment of the peace negotiations. Morris and Henry S. Commager, eds., *The*

Spirit of Seventy-Six (1958), offer a dramatic anthology of eye-witness accounts of wartime events.

The Disruptions of War

For good discussions of the fiscal problems created by the war, see E. James Ferguson, *The Power of the Purse: A History of American Public Finance* (1961), and Clarence L. Ver Steeg, *Robert Morris, Revolutionary Financier* (1954).

Elisha P. Douglass, *Rebels and Democrats* (1955), documents the struggle for equal political rights and majority rule during the war. Eric Foner, *Tom Paine and Revolutionary America* (1975), provides a discussion of this conflict in Pennsylvania, while David Hawke, *In the Midst of a Revolution* (1961), gives a more extended and equally absorbing account. Jackson T. Main, *The Upper House in Revolutionary America* (1967), finds a modest movement toward democratic representation. For statements of Whig republicanism, see Bernard Bailyn, *The Ideological Origins of the American Revolution* (1967), and Willi Paul Adams, *The First American Constitutions* (1982). J. F. Jameson, *The American Revolution Considered as a Social Movement* (1926), remains a good summary of the social changes of the revolutionary era.

Property and the New Social and Political Order

Two good discussions of the political aspects of slavery are Donald Robinson, *Slavery in the Structure of American Politics, 1765–1820* (1971), and Duncan J. MacLeod, *Slavery, Race, and the American Revolution* (1974). Benjamin Quarles, *The Negro in the American Revolution*

(1961), outlines the dimensions of black military and political activities during the war, as do various essays in Ira Berlin and Ronald Hoffman, eds., *Slavery in the Revolutionary Era* (1982). For abolitionist thought and action, see David B. Davis, *The Problems of Slavery in the Era of Revolution* (1975), and Arthur Zilversmit, *The First Emancipation: The Abolition of Slavery in the North* (1967).

In 1883, John Fiske called the decade of the 1780s *The Critical Period of American History*. Merrill Jensen's *The Articles of Confederation* (1940) provides a good corrective; his study of *The New Nation* (1950) is a balanced overview of the decade. Later accounts of the political and social struggles of this period include Richard P. McCormick, *Experiment in Independence: New Jersey in the Critical Period* (1950); Staughton Lynd, *Class Conflict, Slavery, and the United States Constitution* (1968); Jackson T. Main, *Political Parties Before the Constitution* (1973); and David Szatmary, *Shays' Rebellion: The Making of an Agrarian Insurrection* (1980). For a general overview of scholarship, see Ronald Hoffman and Peter J. Albert, eds., *The Sovereign States in an Era of Uncertainty* (1982).

Discussion of the Constitutional Convention must begin with Charles Beard, *An Economic Interpretation of the Constitution of the United States* (1913). Critics of Beard include Robert Brown, *Charles Beard and the Constitution* (1956), and Forrest McDonald, *We the People* (1956) and *E Pluribus Unum* (1965). Gordon S. Wood, *The Creation of the American Republic* (1969), provides support for the Beardian perspective while offering an impressive treatment of American political theory and intellectual history. Max Farrand, *The Framing of the Constitution* (1913), gives a good account of the convention, as does Clinton Rossiter, *The Grand Convention* (1966). For the ratification struggle, see Robert A. Rutland, *The Ordeal of the Constitution* (1966); Jackson T. Main, *The Anti-Federalists* (1974); and Linda Grant De-Pauw, *The Eleventh Pillar: New York State and the Federal Constitution* (1966). Selective reading in *The Federalist Papers* written by Madison, Hamilton, and Jay provides valuable insight into the discourse and political science of the revolutionary era.

8

THE POLITICAL WORLD: COMMERCIAL ENTERPRISE AND WESTWARD EXPANSION

*B*y creating national political institutions elected by the people, the Constitution added a new dimension to American life. Now the debates that took place on the national level were directly related to political alignments in states and local electoral districts. They reflected social and economic interest groups as well. As secretary of the treasury in the new national government under President George Washington, Alexander Hamilton, a Federalist, supported legislation favorable to merchants and creditors. In response, James Madison and Thomas Jefferson broke away from their Federalist allies. The two Virginia statesmen founded the rival Democratic–Republican party, which defended the interests of southern planters and western farmers. The Democratic–Republican party was usually called the Republican party (but it had no connection with the Republican party of today, which was only established in 1854).

The Federalists and Republicans fought for power for a generation. Because this struggle involved two well-organized political factions, historians refer to it as the First Party System. During the 1790s, Federalists and Republicans battled first over the financial legislation favored

by Hamilton. Then, mobilizing popular support, they took opposite sides on the ideological issues raised by the French Revolution. Finally, following the outbreak of war between Britain and France, the two parties advocated radically different foreign policies to defend American commerce.

This political rivalry left a rich intellectual legacy, because Federalist and Republican leaders proclaimed contrasting definitions of republican government and of the American future. Hamilton favored a hierarchical system of government and a mercantilist economic policy. His policies promoted the political dominance of a wealthy mercantile elite and the development of large-scale manufacturing enterprises. Jefferson supported a more democratic and egalitarian ideology. He defended the moral and political superiority of an agricultural society filled with prosperous, independent artisans and yeomen farm families.

Jefferson's election to the presidency in 1800 began a new series of political conflicts. The Republicans encouraged rapid settlement of the West. But expansion into the interior threatened Federalist political power in the East and native

American land rights along the frontier. More-over, the renewal of war in Europe brought British and French attacks on American ships. Federalists and Republicans revived their bitter debate over commercial policy. They also clashed over British military assistance to western Indian tribes. Eventually, Madison and western Republicans led the United States into a second war with Great Britain. In response, New England Federalists threatened to secede from the Union.

The years between 1789 and 1815 were crucial to the development of the American political tradition. The political struggles of those years reflect the character of the entire society. To trace the fortunes of the Federalists and the Republicans is to understand the development of a new governmental system, the social groups that influenced public policy, and the economic and ideological forces that shaped the future of the nation.

The Political Crisis of the 1790s

The 1790s were years of economic prosperity and political crisis. War in Europe brought substantial profits to American farmers and spectacular fortunes to American merchants. Soon after the ratification of the Constitution, however, the Federalists split into two irreconcilable factions. The ideological issues raised by the French Revolution sharpened these political divisions. Pro-French Republicans and pro-British Federalists bitterly attacked each other. By the end of the decade, the American republican experiment faced grave danger as an undeclared foreign war prompted a policy of domestic political repression.

Hamilton Versus Jefferson

In the first national elections, in 1789, the Federalists who had supported ratification of the Constitution swept into office. The anti-Federalists elected only eight of their leaders to the new House of Representatives and vanished as a coherent political force. The electoral college selected George Washington of Virginia as the first president. John Adams of Massachusetts received the second highest number of electoral

WASHINGTON'S FINAL CHALLENGE
"In the name of America, of mankind at large, and your own fame," the Marquis de Lafayette urged Washington to become the first President of the United States. "You only can settle that political machine." Washington himself felt like "a culprit who is going to the place of his execution . . . without that competency of political skill, abilities, and inclination which is necessary" to the task. (Amos Doolittle. Washington's Inauguration. The New York Public Library, Stoke's Collection)

votes and became vice-president. Washington, once the military savior of his country, now became its political father. At fifty-seven years of age, he was a man of great personal dignity and prestige. Instinctively cautious, the new president established executive departments similar to those in the old Confederation government. To head the Department of State, Washington chose Thomas Jefferson, a fellow Virginian and an experienced diplomat. As secretary of the treasury, he turned to Alexander Hamilton. Still in his early 30s, Hamilton was a bright, ambitious, and vigorous lawyer and political journalist. He had served as Washington's aide-de-camp during the War of Independence.

Hamilton's political philosophy and financial policies immediately disrupted Washington's administration. The treasury secretary was a self-made man. The son of a Scotch overseer in the West Indies, Hamilton was raised by his mother's family. He moved to New York in 1773 to attend King's College. His wit, charm, and military bravery immediately impressed the New York elite, as did his political outlook. At the constitutional convention, Hamilton condemned the "amazing violence and turbulence of the democratic spirit" and called for an authoritarian government headed by a president with nearly monarchical powers.

By marrying into the wealthy Schuyler family, Hamilton became—in practice as well as principle—a member of the wealthy merchant class. "The people are turbulent and changing," he argued, and so "they seldom judge or determine right." As treasury secretary, Hamilton strongly favored the mercantile elite and linked their interests and power with those of the national government.

To achieve this end, Hamilton presented an ambitious legislative program to Congress. His recommendations to the Senate and the House of Representatives took the form of three major documents: "Report on Public Credit" (January 1790), "Report on a National Bank" (December 1790), and "Report on Manufactures" (December 1791). Hamilton's policy on public credit reassured foreign and domestic creditors by promising compensation for wartime debts. He proposed the redemption at face value of the millions of dollars of securities issued by the Confederation government.

The redemption proposal had enormous implications. It would bolster faith in the government's credit, but only by creating a powerful new group of public financiers. During the 1780s, financial speculators had purchased vast quantities of confederation bills at low prices. In December 1784, for example, the Burrells of Boston, a major merchant house, purchased £2,500 in continental notes, paying three to five shillings on the pound. If these depreciated notes were paid off at their face value of twenty shillings per pound, the Burrells and other speculators would reap an enormous profit.

In addition, Hamilton wanted to institutionalize this wealthy class of financiers. By paying creditors with new securities, rather than with

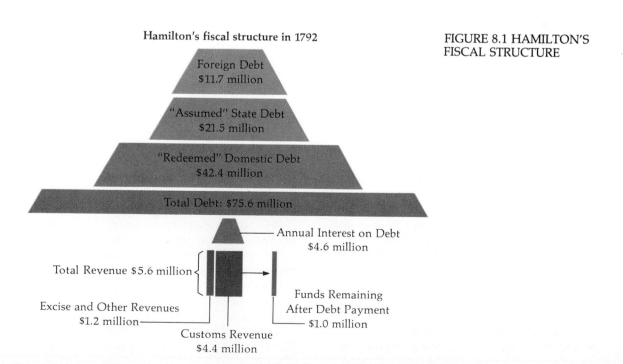

Hamilton's fiscal structure in 1792

Foreign Debt
$11.7 million

"Assumed" State Debt
$21.5 million

"Redeemed" Domestic Debt
$42.4 million

Total Debt: $75.6 million

Annual Interest on Debt
$4.6 million

Total Revenue $5.6 million

Excise and Other Revenues
$1.2 million

Customs Revenue
$4.4 million

Funds Remaining
After Debt Payment
$1.0 million

FIGURE 8.1 HAMILTON'S FISCAL STRUCTURE

specie, the treasury secretary planned to create a permanent national debt. This scheme would tie the interests of the new financial elite to the national government. Patrick Henry, speaking for the Virginia legislature, objected strongly. "In an agricultural country like this," he protested, "to erect, and concentrate, and perpetuate a large monied interest must prove fatal to the existence of American liberty."

Hamilton quickly advanced a second proposal that favored wealthy creditors and speculators. Under the terms of his "assumption" plan, the government would pay all the remaining war debts of the states. This imaginative scheme unleashed a flurry of speculation and even corruption. For example, Assistant Treasury Secretary William Duer used his inside knowledge for personal profit. Before news of Hamilton's proposal became public, Duer bought up the debt certificates of North and South Carolina. When he resold them to northern financiers, other speculators entered the market. By the end of 1790, residents of northern states owned more than half the combined debts of Virginia, South Carolina, and North Carolina. About a dozen speculators in New York City held nearly $2 million of these securities.

Jefferson and other southern politicians condemned such financial intrigues and the "corrupt squadron of paper dealers" who arranged them. Most southern congressmen supported the assumption of state debts in principle because they agreed with Hamilton that the struggle for independence was a national affair. However, they questioned the terms of his legislation. Some states, such as Virginia, had already levied high taxes and paid most of their war debts. Now their citizens would have to pay the debts of other states as well—and mostly for the benefit of northern speculators. To win support for his controversial plan, Hamilton made a deal with the large and powerful congressional delegation from Virginia. He agreed to support the transfer of the national capital from Philadelphia, its temporary home, to a new federal district across the Potomac River from Virginia.

This political bargain did not eliminate the fears of many Americans. As a Virginia congressman, James Madison questioned the wisdom and morality of Hamilton's redemption and assumption proposals. He reminded his colleagues that shopkeepers, hard-pressed farmers,

and dedicated soldiers had accepted Continental bills during the dark days of the war. Many of these citizens had sold their certificates as the value of the bills dropped. Despite their valiant support for the war effort, they would get nothing under Hamilton's plan. Madison therefore presented Congress with legislation that gave holders of Continental certificates "the highest price which has prevailed in the market"; the remaining funds would go to the original purchasers. "This will not do perfect justice," Madison admitted, "but it will do more real justice . . . than any other expedient."

Joined by Thomas Jefferson, Madison also warned of the danger of a permanent debt. Pointing to the British experience, the two Virginians argued that financiers would speculate in public funds, influence government policies, and corrupt elected officials. As John Taylor, another Virginian, put it, "Money in a state of civilization is power." These protests, no matter how valid, failed. Nearly half the members of the House of Representatives, twenty-nine of the sixty-four congressmen, owned Continental securities, many through purchase. They defeated Madison's proposal by the convincing margin of thirty-six to thirteen. In reply, an angry poet composed an ode called "On the rejection of Mr. Madison's motion:"

A soldier's pay are rags and fame,
A wooden leg—a deathless name.
To specs, both *in* and *out* of Cong.
The four and six per cents belong!

Madison protested again in 1791 when Congress chartered a national financial institution, the First Bank of the United States. Both individuals and the government would own the bank's stock. Its prime functions would be to handle government funds and to issue bank notes, providing a respected paper currency for the specie-starved American economy.

The bank's charter prompted a major debate on constitutional principles. In private discussions with President Washington, Jefferson argued that Congress lacked the authority to establish a national bank. His strict view of the Constitution rested on the assumption that the government had only the powers explicitly stated in the document. Hamilton disagreed. "If the *end* be clearly comprehended within any of the specified powers," Hamilton reasoned, ". . . and if the measure is not forbidden by any particular provision of the Constitution, it may safely be deemed to come within the compass of national authority." This loose interpretation of the Constitution hinged on the so-called "elastic clause" that empowered Congress to make "all Laws which shall be necessary and proper." On this issue, as on most, Washington agreed with Hamilton rather than Jefferson, and he signed the legislation creating the bank.

When Washington was elected to a second term as president in 1792, his administration split into irreconcilable factions. "Mr. Madison, co-operating with Mr. Jefferson," Hamilton complained, "is at the head of a faction decidedly hostile to me . . . and actuated by views . . . subversive of good government." Soon thereafter, Jefferson resigned as secretary of state in order to mobilize opposition to the government's economic policies.

Meanwhile, Hamilton enacted the final element of his financial system, a revised schedule of tariffs. In 1789, Congress had imposed a tax of fifty cents a ton on foreign ships entering American ports and a duty of 5 to 15 percent on imported goods. At the treasury secretary's request, Congress increased these rates to provide funds to pay the interest on the national debt.

Customs revenues rose steadily, totaling $45 million between 1801 and 1805 and providing about 90 percent of the government's income from 1790 to 1820. These duties ensured the political and financial success of Hamilton's redemption and assumption programs.

Hamilton defended tariffs for revenue purposes. However, he did not advocate higher duties to protect American manufacturers from foreign competition. The treasury secretary feared that protective tariffs would hurt his merchant allies, whose livelihood depended on foreign trade, and might cut the revenues needed to fund the national debt. Nevertheless, Hamilton had a vision of America as a self-sufficient manufacturing nation. In 1790, he appointed Tench Coxe, the secretary of the Pennsylvania Manufacturing Society, as an assistant secretary of the treasury. With Coxe's assistance, Hamilton prepared his famous "Report on Manufactures," which provided the first comprehensive survey of American manufacturing capacity.

More fundamentally, Hamilton's report presented a coherent, intellectual rationale for American mercantilism. In his influential treatise *The Wealth of Nations* (1776), the English economist Adam Smith had advanced a set of new *laissez-faire* economic policies. Smith argued that traditional state-directed mercantilist regulations,

TWO YOUNG MEN OF THE REVOLUTION
Thomas Jefferson and Alexander Hamilton here confront each other, as they did through much of their political lives. A comparison of their principles defines the world of political discourse in the new American republic. Jefferson favored farmers and artisans; he had a vision of westward expansion; he sought a broad, democratic franchise, with rule by legislative majorities; held a "strict" view of the Constitution; and supported pro-French foreign policy. Hamilton favored aid to merchants and financiers; he wanted a nation of "manufacturers"; fought for property qualifications for voting; sought judicial control of legislative "tyranny"; argued for all "necessary and proper" powers for the Executive branch; and supported pro-British diplomacy. (Left, John Trumbull. Detail of *The Declaration of Independence*; Right, John Trumbull. *Alexander Hamilton*; Both, Yale University Art Gallery)

subsidies, and duties restricted rather than expanded production. He advocated a free market in which the laws of supply and demand would allocate goods. Following this logic, Smith suggested that the United States should remain an agricultural society. It should raise farm products, where it held a comparative advantage, and exchange them for European manufactures.

Hamilton opposed Smith's reasoning. He pointed out that production costs are never fixed, but can be altered by technological innovation or public policies. If American manufacturers were given the "patronage of government," the treasury secretary thought they could compete successfully with European producers. To encourage merchants to invest in technologically innovative factories, Hamilton and Coxe incorporated a private Society for Establishing Useful Manufactures. Having protected the financial investments and commercial interests of the mercantile class, Hamilton hoped to turn the United States into a society of wealthy capitalist entrepreneurs and bustling factory workers.

Few southern planters, western farmers, or northern artisans endorsed Hamilton's vision of the American future. Speaking both from ideological conviction and personal observation, Jefferson condemned this path of economic development. In England, he pointed out, manufacturing regions had masses of propertyless wage earners. Poor and economically dependent on their employers, these laborers did not have the political freedom required to sustain a republican society.

Jefferson himself came from an aristocratic background. He grew up as a privileged and well-educated member of the Virginia planter elite. Like many other wealthy slaveowners in the late eighteenth century, Jefferson pursued a quiet life-style. Rather than hunting and gambling, he preferred reading about architecture, natural history, and scientific farming. More than most privileged Americans, Jefferson embraced a democratic political philosophy. Like Hamilton, who spoke of "the ordinary depravity of the human race," the Virginian recognized the difficulty of preserving private morality and public virtue. Yet, in the spirit of the Enlightenment, Jefferson was firmly convinced of the "improvability of the human race."

Jefferson devoted his political career to this goal. In the Declaration of Independence, he announced the primacy of "life, liberty, and the pursuit of happiness." In his *Notes on Virginia* (1785) and other writings, he gave form and substance to this vision. "Those who labor in the earth are the chosen people of God," Jefferson declared. It was therefore in the nation's interest to develop a strong agricultural economy, raising "raw materials" and throwing "open the doors of commerce" to the world. To this end, he drafted the Ordinance of 1784 for the Confederation government. To encourage westward migration, it provided for the rapid admission of new states into the Union on the basis of political equality. Following Jefferson's draft, the Northwest Ordinance of 1787 prohibited slavery, life-leases, and quitrents in the future states of Ohio, Indiana, Illinois, Michigan, and Wisconsin. If yeomen owned fertile western farms, rather than working for landlords on leased or rented land, Jefferson argued that they would produce bountiful harvests. This grain and meat would feed European nations "who in return would manufacture and send us in exchange our clothes and other comforts." In Jefferson's view, westward expansion and foreign commerce would eliminate the worst features of eighteenth-century agriculture—widespread tenancy in the South and subdivided farms in New England—while preserving its best features. America would become a vigorous, uncorruptable society of independent yeoman farm families.

Madison shared this commitment to an agricultural society but worried about its future. As early as 1788, he predicted rapid population growth in the West and a surplus work force. To avoid agricultural stagnation and the growth of factories, Madison sought to increase farm exports. As a member of Congress, he promoted American shipping and commercial treaties with foreign nations. Hamilton dreamed of an economically self-sufficient United States dominated by merchants and manufacturers. In contrast, Madison and Jefferson stressed commercial interdependence with Europe in order to maintain and expand a society based on family farmers and independent artisans.

Both visions were realistic, for the mature American pre-industrial economy of the 1790s had both a prosperous agricultural base and a dynamic commercial sector. And both views came to pass. During the nineteenth century, the United States experienced an agricultural as well as an industrial revolution. The number of small-scale family farms grew by the millions as Americans settled the West, but large-scale manufacturing enterprises owned by a wealthy elite also became more important. As prophets, Jefferson and Hamilton predicted the future. As political statemen, they helped bring it about.

War and Politics

Events in Europe pulled the American economy out of the recession of the 1780s. The French Revolution began in 1789 when the peasant and bourgeois classes rebelled against the aristocracy and an oppressive monarchical state. The rebels set up a constitutional monarchy at first, but a more radical republican regime took power in 1792. To protect the revolution from domestic subversion and foreign attack, the new French government went to war in 1793 against a British-led coalition of monarchical states. Revolution and war disrupted European society. Grain prices rose sharply, and the continuing population growth sustained high prices. In England, the price of wheat jumped from five shillings a bushel before 1790 to eight or nine shillings during the next twenty-five years. Farmers in the Chesapeake and the Middle Atlantic states quickly increased their exports to Europe, earning ample profits.

A boom in cotton exports simultaneously revived the agricultural economy of the southern states. Americans had expanded cotton production during the War of Independence in order to make their own textiles. Subsequently, the mechanization of English cloth production created an ever-expanding export market. In 1793, Eli Whitney's invention of a gin to comb seeds from cotton fibres gave a final boost to production and promoted the expansion of slavery. By 1800, cotton exports totaled 15 million pounds a year; in 1810, 93 million pounds. The annual value of cotton exports, $7 million, far outstripped that of tobacco, the traditional southern staple crop, at $4.5 million. The total value of American agricultural exports more than doubled between 1790 and 1810, rising from $19.9 to $42.3 million yearly. As Jefferson had hoped, European markets provided many American farm communities with unparalleled prosperity.

American merchants profited even more handsomely following the outbreak of war between France and Britain. President Washington immediately issued a Proclamation of Neutrality, enabling United States citizens to trade legally with both belligerents. As neutral carriers, American merchant ships could pass through the British naval blockade of French ports. They quickly took over the lucrative trade between France and its West Indian sugar islands. The American merchant fleet became one of the largest in the world, with about 355,000 tons of shipping in 1790, and more than 1.1 million tons by 1808. Commercial earnings rose spectacularly, averaging $20 million annually in the 1790s and $30 million during the following decade. In 1810, Europeans paid $39.5 million to American merchants for shipping services, more than five times the value of United States cotton exports.

Stimulated by this commercial renaissance, American port cities came alive after two decades of stagnation. Shipowners invested part of their profits in new vessels, providing work for thousands of shipbuilders, sailmakers, seamen, and laborers. To display their new wealth, many merchants built elegant federal-style town houses, giving employment to hundreds of carpenters and masons. This massive rebuilding of commercial and residential districts restored the prewar prominence of the seaport cities and added a new splendor. In New York City, the assessed value of property jumped dramatically—from $5.8 to $20.7 million—between 1790 and 1800.

Philadelphia was filled with new buildings, a European visitor reported in 1799, "chiefly of red brick, and in general three stories high. A great number of private houses have marble steps to the street door, and in other respects are finished in a style of elegance." The remarkable surge in agricultural exports and mercantile enterprise raised the American standard of living above its pre-1775 level, finally erasing the impact of two decades of war, revolution, and depression.

The price of economic prosperity was bitter political conflict. The naval policies of the belligerent European powers greatly affected American citizens, as did their ideologies. Most politically aware Americans welcomed the French Revolution of 1789 because it endorsed republican principles and institutions. The French

TECHNOLOGY AND REPUBLICAN VALUES

In 1805, the young American scientist Benjamin Sillman visited the indusrial city of Manchester, England. He was impressed by the great factories, which he called "the wonder of the world, and the pride of England," but deeply depressed by the condition of the workers. They appeared to him "at best, but an imbecile people," degraded by the conditions in which they worked and lived. "Heaps of dung, rubble from buildings, putrid, stagnant pools are found here and there among the houses," another visitor to Manchester reported, and

> a sort of black smoke covers the city. The sun seen through it is a disc without rays. Under this half daylight 300,000 human beings are ceaselessly at work . . . the crunching wheels of machinery, the shriek of steam from boilers, the regular beat of the looms, the heavy rumble of the carts, these are the noises from which you can never escape in the sombre half-light of these streets.

Revolted by this dismal scene, Sillman recalled a peaceful image of American "fields and forests, in which pure air . . . and simple manners, give vigour to the limbs, and a healthful aspect to the face." Were the wonders of English technology, he asked, worth "the physical and . . . moral evils which they produce?"

Sillman's question was that of an entire generation of Americans. Their republican polity depended upon the moral virtue and independent habits of freeholding farmers and propertied artisans. How could these values be sustained by oppressed operatives, mere "imbecile people"? Technological advance seemed incompatible with republican civilization.

No American struggled harder with this issue than Thomas Jefferson. "Those who labour in the earth are the chosen people of God," Jefferson wrote in his *Notes on the State of Virginia* (1785), and he remained committed to the moral superiority of a society of yeoman farm families. Yet Jefferson, like Benjamin Rush of Philadelphia, knew that "a people who are *entirely* dependent upon foreigners for food or clothes, must always be subject to them." Even before the Embargo of 1807 and the War of 1812 convinced him of the necessity of American manufacturing, Jefferson advocated the use of advanced farm technology. He introduced cast-iron plows and improved threshing machines on his Monticello, Virginia plantation, and rotated crops according to the latest scientific formulas.

Jefferson championed domestic manufacturing as well. As early as 1796 he bought an iron-cutting machine to make nails and, by employing a dozen young male slaves, achieved an output of ten thousand nails a day. By 1812, Jefferson had built two water-powered mills at another plantation and equipped his Monticello slaves for the manufacture of textiles. He and other Americans, he boasted to a European friend,

> have reduced the large and expensive machinery for most things to the compass of a private family, and every family . . . is now getting machines on a small scale for their household purposes. . . . I need 2,000 yards of linen, cotton and woolen yearly, to clothe my family, which this machinery, costing $150 only, and worked by two women and two girls, will more than furnish.

Here, then, was Jefferson's solution to the problem of the "dark satanic mills" of Manchester. Each American household would become a small factory, a decentralization of production that would use the labor of "women, children, and invalids" and enhance the economic independence of American freeholders. In Jefferson's mind, the key was democratic ownership of the means of production.

Jefferson's vision was noble and realistic. Between 1790 and 1820, America became a nation of household producers. Hundreds of rural families made nails; thousands manufactured shoes and textiles for their own use and market sale. Yet Jefferson's vision was flawed by internal contradictions and was limited in scope. In terms of social power, how different was his nail-making facility from a Manchester factory? Was slave labor really more moral or republican than wage labor? And, over the long run, could household producers compete successfully with the water- and steam-driven efficiency of large-scale factories owned by wealthy capitalists? A candid observer must answer "no" to both questions. Jefferson had addressed the crucial issue of the social organization of production, but he left unresolved the question of the compatibility of technological advance with republican values. The question remains unresolved to this day.

abolished many feudal customs and established a constitutional monarchy that divided power among the king, nobility, and bourgeoisie. However, the creation of the more democratic First French Republic in 1792 and the execution of King Louis XVI the next year divided American political opinion. Many American artisans celebrated the new French republican regime. They founded Democratic-Republican clubs modeled on the radical Jacobin artisan organizations in Paris. And they praised the egalitarian social reforms of the French republicans. In Philadelphia, some Americans celebrated the beheading of the king at a dinner at which "the head of a roasted pig was severed from its body, and being recognized as an emblem of the murdered King of France, was carried round to the guests. Each one placing the cap of liberty upon its head, pronounced the word 'tyrant.' "

These pro-French activities altered the character of American politics. Jefferson's followers welcomed Edmund Genêt, the French minister to the United States, with triumphal parades. They applauded his efforts to enlist American warships in France's war against Great Britain. "The cause of France is the cause of man, and neutrality is desertion," proclaimed the novelist Hugh Henry Breckenridge, an influential Pennsylvania Democratic-Republican. Using the ideologically charged language of the French Revolution, Democratic-Republicans addressed one another as "citizen" as a symbol of equality. They condemned Hamilton's economic policies as "aristocratic" and attacked the pro-British views of many leading Federalists.

The French-inspired resurgence of the democratic-republicanism of the Revolutionary era frightened many Americans. Most of these men

THE BUSTLING PORT OF NEW YORK
Following independence, New York City quickly became the largest American seaport. Prosperous merchants built new warehouses and stone dwellings of three and four stories along the waterfront. These imposing structures dominated the smaller, wooden buildings of the eighteenth century, such as the Tontine Coffee House (center). (Francis Guy. *The Tontine Coffee House.* The New-York Historical Society)

and women were people of wealth, conservative religious convictions, or Federalist sympathies. Some denounced the French republic for the executions of Louis XVI and his aristocratic supporters. Others repudiated its policies of social equality. Still others condemned the French regime's abandonment of Christianity in favor of a new religion of Reason. Leading Federalists denounced Genêt for violating Washington's Proclamation of Neutrality and persuaded the president to demand his recall. Then, in 1794, the Federalist-dominated Congress passed a Neutrality Act. It prohibited Americans from fighting in the war between France and Britain and barred the belligerents' naval forces from American ports. The French Revolution had transformed American debate over Hamilton's economic policies into a major ideological and political confrontation.

British policies accentuated these divisions. Following an Order in Council in November 1793, the Royal Navy seized 250 American ships bound for France from the West Indies. The British confiscated their cargoes of sugar as wartime contraband. The ministry justified these seizures by invoking the Rule of 1756. This controversial principle of international law restricted the wartime commerce of neutral states to that conducted during peace. Most Federalist merchants, despite substantial losses, did not demand retaliatory measures. They feared that war against Great Britain would throw the United States into the arms of radical French republicans, cripple American commerce, and undermine Hamilton's system of public finance.

President Washington sent John Jay, an ardent New York Federalist, to Britain. He instructed Jay to resolve the maritime issues as well as territorial and financial disputes dating back to the War of Independence. Jay returned with a comprehensive agreement that included significant British concessions. The Jay treaty, signed in 1794, called for the withdrawal of British garrisons from six forts in the American Northwest, the end of British support to western Indian tribes, and the arbitration of American commercial claims. However, the treaty required the United States to make "full and complete compensation" to British creditors for all prewar debts owed by its citizens. It also acknowledged Britain's right to remove French property from

neutral ships, thus abandoning the American claim that "free ships make free goods."

Jefferson and his Democratic-Republican followers denounced the concessions to America's former enemy, the leading defender of monarchical principles. The Jay treaty narrowly escaped defeat. The Senate ratified it by a vote of twenty to ten in June 1795, just meeting the two-thirds majority required by the Constitution. Yet the treaty's significance was clear. As long as Hamilton and his Federalist allies were in power, the United States government would have a pro-British foreign policy.

The First Party System

The debate over foreign policy dominated the presidential election of 1796. This contest marked a new era in American history, for it featured the appearance of organized political parties. Beginning in the early 1790s, first Hamilton and then Madison formed political alliances in Congress to support their legislative programs. At first, these factions followed sectional lines. Northern congressmen supported the Bank of the United States by a margin of thirty-three to one, for example, while southern representatives opposed it, nineteen to six. By the elections of 1794, these sectional factions had acquired names—Federalists and Democratic-Republicans—and distinct ideological identities. Now both groups recruited supporters in each state. To prepare for the 1796 election, the parties called legislative caucuses of elected supporters. These informal conventions prepared lists of candidates and mobilized voter support.

Neither past experience nor the state or national Constitutions provided for political parties. Most of the Founding Fathers deeply regretted their appearance. "If I could not go to heaven but with a party, I would not go there at all," Jefferson declared. In common with most American political theorists, Jefferson believed that representative institutions adequately expressed the will of the people. Other political aggregations—Shaysite mobs, factions in state legislatures, ideological parties—were unnecessary and dangerous. "Decency and Respect are due to Constitutional Authority," proclaimed the one-time radical Samuel Adams, "and those Men, who under any Pretence or by any Means whatever, would lessen the Weight of Government lawfully exercised must be Enemies to our happy Revolution and Common Liberty."

As president, Washington tried to stand above parties, but his pro-Hamiltonian beliefs exposed him to partisan attack. The bitterness of party strife contributed to Washington's decision not to seek a third presidential term in 1796. Of all the Founding Fathers, only Madison accepted the inevitability of political parties. In *The Federalist Papers*, the young statesman suggested that the impulse to differ was founded in human nature and would inevitably find expression in a free state. Yet even Madison, a supreme political realist, did not envision permanent political parties. He assumed that temporary coalitions would contest a specific issue and then disappear.

Like other members of his generation, Madison failed to realize that the American Revolution had begun a fundamental transformation of the political system. The trials of war clarified the distinct interests of various social groups and classes. Simultaneously, the new ideology of popular sovereignty encouraged citizens to mobilize politically. At first, political labels changed frequently. In Virginia, for example, most of the anti-Federalist delegates who opposed ratification of the Constitution in 1788 became Republicans after 1793, as did many of the yeoman farmers who elected them. Similarly, many leaders of the Federalist party in New York had been conservative Whig patriots during the struggle for independence.

These class and regional divisions became more apparent—and persistent—following the appearance of organized political parties. Merchants and creditors in the northwestern states joined the Federalist party, as did wheat-exporting slaveowners in the Tidewater districts of the Chesapeake states. The Republican coalition was more diverse. It included mechanics and artisans in seaport cities, southern tobacco planters, northeastern traders, German and Scotch-Irish migrants, and subsistence farmers throughout the country. Republican policies appealed to a much larger constituency, but the Federalists' prestige, wealth, and experience made them a potent political force.

Federalist candidates won a majority of seats in the electoral college in 1796 and selected John

Adams as president. Surprisingly, Thomas Jefferson, a Republican, received the second highest total when some Federalist electors refused to vote for Charles Pinckney of South Carolina, Adams's running mate. Jefferson became vice-president in a divided administration.

As chief executive, Adams favored a strongly pro-British foreign policy. He condemned French seizures of American merchant ships and accused France of meddling in United States domestic politics. When three agents of Prince Talleyrand, the French foreign minister, solicited a loan and a bribe from three American peace commissioners. Adams urged Congress to prepare for war. To overcome Republican objections, he charged that Talleyrand's agents, whom he dubbed X, Y, and Z, had insulted American honor. Many congressmen agreed. The Federalist-controlled Congress cut off trade with France and authorized American privateers to seize French ships. Between 1798 and 1800, the United States became an unofficial ally of Great Britain, a monarchy and its one-time enemy. It fought an undeclared war against France, a republic and its savior during the War of Independence.

As always, the passions of war inflamed domestic politics. To discourage political activity by pro-French immigrants, the Adams administration passed an Alien Act in 1798, authorizing the deportation of foreigners. A few Federalist supporters favored even harsher treatment. "Were I president," volunteered William Cobbett, a British pamphleteer writing in Philadelphia under the pen name "Peter Porcupine," "I would hang them or they would murder me." To meet these exaggerated concerns, the Naturalization Act of 1798 increased the residence requirement for citizenship and voting from five to fourteen years. The Federalist Congress also enacted a harsh Sedition Act in 1798 to curb Republican criticism. This law prohibited the publication of false or malicious attacks against the president, Congress, or the nation. "He that is not for us is against us," thundered the Federalist *Gazette of the United States*. Using these new powers, Federalist prosecutors arrested more than twenty Republican newspaper editors, charged them with sedition, and sent some of them to prison. For the first—but not the last—time in the history of the United States, a controversial foreign war had prompted domestic protest and government repression.

Republicans assailed the Sedition Act as contrary to the Constitution. To meet anti-Federalist criticisms raised during the debate over ratification, the first Congress had proposed a dozen amendments to the new Constitution. By 1791, voters in the various states had ratified ten amendments, known as the Bill of Rights. Most of these amendments protected individuals from the power of the national government. For example, they affirmed the right to a trial by jury, protected citizens from "unreasonable searches," and guaranteed that people would not be deprived of "life, liberty, or property, without due process of law." The First Amendment pertained directly to the Sedition Act. This amendment prohibited the government from interfering with the free exercise of religion or "abridging the freedom of speech, or of the press." Given these guarantees, the constitutionality of the Sedition Act was open to serious question.

Republican leaders did not turn to the Supreme Court with their objections to the Sedition Act. The Court's powers were still vague, and the Constitution did not define its authority. Nor did the Judiciary Act of 1789, which established the court system of the national government. Moreover, the Supreme Court was an appointive, not an elected, body, and was filled with Federalists.

Madison and Jefferson therefore took their case to representative institutions elected by the people. At their request, the Kentucky legislature passed a resolution in November 1798, declaring the Alien and Sedition Acts to be "unauthoritative, void, and of no force." Even more significantly, the Kentucky resolution, written by John Breckinridge, asserted that the national government consisted of a compact of states. "As in all other cases of compact among parties having no common Judge," it declared, "each party has an equal right to judge for itself." A similar resolution, drafted for the Virginia legislature by Madison, claimed less extensive powers and rights for the various states. This resolution noted, however, that the Tenth Amendment to the Constitution reserved to the states and the people all powers not expressly delegated to the national government.

Nevertheless, it was clear that Madison and Jefferson were reconsidering their political positions. At the Philadelphia convention, Madison had advocated a strong national government, created by and responsible to the people. In the heat of partisan politics, he now supported the dubious argument that the Constitution resulted from a compact among the states. Similarly, Jefferson modified his ideological opposition to political parties. "In every free and deliberating society there must, from the nature of man, be opposite parties," he wrote in 1798. He thought these political organizations were valuable as well, "to watch and relate to the people" the activities of the government and the opposing party.

As Jefferson campaigned for the presidency in 1800, Republicans condemned the Sedition Act and championed the rights of the states. President Adams responded by negotiating with France to end the undeclared war at sea. Often vain, thin skinned, and dogmatic, Adams possessed great personal strength and determination as well. He rejected the advice of Hamilton and other Federalist leaders to extend the war and to benefit politically from nationalist fervor. Adam's supporters depicted Jefferson as a pro-French radical, "the archapostle of irreligion and free thought."

However, the Republicans won a resounding victory. Voters protested against the war with France—and a national tax on land and houses to pay for it—by giving the Republicans a majority in both houses of Congress. Thanks to the influence of Aaron Burr of New York, their vice-presidential candidate, the Republicans carried that state and won a clear majority in the electoral college.

Burr and Jefferson received the same number of electoral votes and so each had a claim to the presidency. In the event of such a tie vote, the Constitution specified that the House of Representatives select the president. On the thirty-sixth ballot, the Federalists in the House gave up their effort to block Jefferson's election. Alexander Hamilton played a crucial role in this political drama. Calling Burr an "embryo Caesar" and the "most unfit man in the United States for the office of president," the former treasury secretary persuaded key Federalists to permit the selection of Jefferson, his long-time rival. "This step was not taken," Senator James Bayard of Delaware recalled, "until it was admitted on all hands that we must risk the Constitution and a Civil War or take Mr. Jefferson."

Jefferson called the election the "Revolution of 1800," and justifiably so. With the peaceful transfer of power between parties, the national government had survived domestic conflict and external war. Slowly and grudgingly, Americans accepted the legitimacy of an opposition party. Thus, the Adams administration prosecuted Republican journalists, but it did not threaten the Republican party itself. The Republicans remained committed to the Union. "We are completely under the saddle of Massachusetts and Connecticut, and they ride us very hard," Jefferson complained to a friend in 1798, "but if on a temporary superiority of one party, the other is to resort to a secession from the Union, no federal government can ever survive."

In his inaugural address, Jefferson downplayed partisan quarrels. The new president reminded Americans of their common political heritage of representative government, popular sovereignty, and peaceful dissent. "We are all Republicans, we are all Federalists," he proclaimed as he asked his audience

to bear in mind this sacred principle, that though the will of the majority is in all cases to prevail, that will to be rightful must be reasonable; that the minority possess their equal rights, which equal laws must protect, and to violate would be oppression.

A new American political tradition was in the making. The election of 1800 demonstrated that governments elected by the people could be changed by them—even in times of bitter partisan conflict—in an orderly and peaceful fashion.

Westward Expansion

As statesmen of the new nation developed a political tradition, a vast popular migration took place toward the interior of North America. In 1789, about two-thirds of the 3.9 million American people lived within fifty miles of the Atlantic Ocean. Only 200,000 made their homes west of the Appalachian Mountains. By 1820, the population had more than doubled, to 9.6 million. But now 2 million Americans inhabited nine new states and several territories west of the Appalachians. This massive migration encouraged

A NEW WESTERN FARM
Western farmers first settled next to rivers, to ensure easy transport and access to market. They felled and split trees to make houses and fences and planted hills of Indian corn among the stumps. Many lived among native Americans, who only slowly and grudgingly moved from their ancestral lands. (Library of Congress)

innovation in eastern agriculture. It generated demands for liberal land policies and for transportation links. And, like previous westward movements, it brought whites into violent confrontations with native Americans.

Migration and Agricultural Change

Two streams of migrants poured into the fertile, well-watered lands between the Appalachians and the Mississippi River. Thousands of white tenant farmers, poor yeomen, and young couples deserted the hierarchical rural economy of the Chesapeake states. They sought social freedom and land of their own. "Boundless settlements," a letter in the Maryland *Gazette* warned as early as 1785, will open "a door for our citizens to run off and leave us, depreciating all our landed property and disabling us from paying taxes."

By 1790, more than a hundred thousand southerners had ignored such pleas from the dominant planting class. They moved through the Cumberland Gap into Kentucky or along the Knoxville Road into Tennessee. Those states joined the Union in 1792 and 1796, respectively. As the price of cotton rose to 18 cents a pound after 1800, thousands of new settlers flocked across the mountains. By 1820, the two states had a total population of nearly a million.

A second wave of migrants flowed out of New England. They moved less to escape a dominant gentry class than to find arable land. The tax list for Kent, Connecticut, in 1796 re-

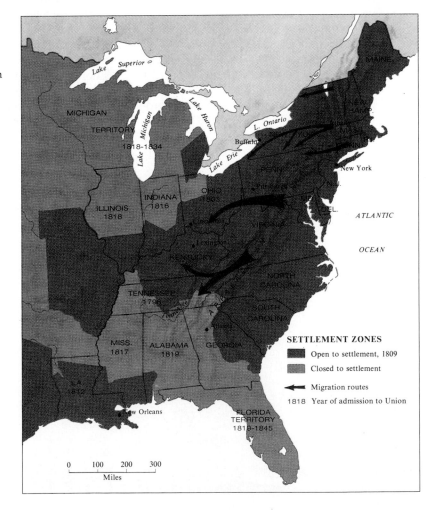

MAP 8.1 THE APPALACHIAN BARRIER
Only a few Americans settled west of the Appalachian Mountains before the 1780s. Then thousands of migrants from Pennsylvania and the Chesapeake states moved down the Shenendoah Valley into Kentucky and Tennessee, while others settled in southern Ohio. A second stream of migrants flowed out of New England across New York and into northern Ohio.

SETTLEMENT ZONES

Open to settlement, 1809

Closed to settlement

Migration routes

1818   Year of admission to Union

vealed the seriousness of the problem. It listed 103 farmsteads, inhabited by 100 fathers and 109 adult sons. All the other adult sons, and most of the daughters, had moved away. Previous generations of Kent parents had subdivided their lands to provide for their children; now the small farms would support only one heir. Ten Kent families moved to Amenia, New York. By selling their small but well-established farms for $20 to $30 an acre, parents could buy enough uncleared western land—at $2 or $3 an acre—for themselves and all their children.

By 1820, more than eight hundred thousand migrants had settled in the upstate counties of New York. Thousands more New Englanders had gone to Ohio, which entered the Union in 1803. To ease the emotional burdens of migration, many settlers moved in cohesive groups. "The town of Herkimer is entirely populated by families come from Connecticut," an astonished traveler reported from central New York. "We stayed at Mr. Snows who came from New London with about ten male and female cousins."

The massive exodus drained labor and capital from settled agricultural communities. To compensate for these losses, many eastern farmers adopted new crops and methods of cultivation. In New England, they planted potatoes, a high-yielding and nutritious food that stored well. In the wheat-growing Middle Atlantic states, enterprising farmers replaced their inefficient wooden plows. In 1810, nearly half the estates probated in Ulster County, New York, listed an improved cast-iron model. These superior plows dug a deeper furrow and required only one yoke of oxen rather than two or three. By saving on livestock and labor, cast-iron plows enabled poor and middling farmers to maintain production even though their sons and daughters moved west.

Wealthier farmers adopted many improvements advocated by European agricultural reformers. In the James River region of Virginia, for example, slaveowning planters completed a long-term transition from tobacco to wheat as their major crop. Progressive planters adopted a four-field system of rotation to increase soil fertility by raising the nitrogen content. Their workers planted clover and followed it with wheat, corn, wheat, and clover once again. Farmers using this clover rotation system in Easton,

Pennsylvania, more than doubled their average annual wheat yield, from twelve to twenty-five bushels an acre.

Northern yeoman farmers also adopted crop rotation, but they produced dairy goods for urban markets. These farmers planted corn in spring and used its stalks and ears to feed their milk cows in winter. During the fall, they spread manure and planted their fields with winter wheat. This intensive system of production required year-round labor, but it raised farm output and income significantly. The westward migration thus reduced the surplus population in eastern farming areas and stimulated agricultural innovation.

The Transportation Bottleneck

As American farmers moved west, they found they could not ship their crops back east. As in all preindustrial societies, poor land transportation severely limited the access to markets. Roads remained primitive even in long-settled regions. Narrow dirt wagon trails meandered from one country town to another, turning into impassable mudholes following the spring thaw or a heavy rain. Ox-driven carts moved slowly, carried small loads, and had high operating expenses. In 1816, Pennsylvania wheat farmers paid 30 cents a ton-mile to move their grain. At this rate, it cost as much to send wheat 30 miles to Philadelphia as to transport it by sea to London. As a result, more than 80 percent of northern farm production in 1820 was consumed within the local community. Only farmers who lived near rivers or canals, with shipping rates of 5 or 6 cents a ton-mile, coordinated their production with an outside market. Even southern planters, with relatively lightweight and valuable crops of tobacco and cotton, complained about land transportation costs.

To remedy the deplorable state of inland transport, the new state governments actively encouraged road-building ventures. Pennsylvania granted corporate charters to fifty-five private turnpike companies between 1793 and 1812. New York chartered fifty-seven similar enterprises and Massachusetts over a hundred. Turnpikes, which had contoured and graveled surfaces, cut travel time but not high costs, and they did nothing to increase capacity. Therefore, the states and entrepreneurs began to build inland waterways. They dredged rivers to make them passable and constructed short canals to bypass waterfalls and rapids. Yet in 1816, there were only about a hundred miles of canals in the entire United States, and only three canals extended more than two miles.

The glaring limitations of preindustrial transportation shaped the character of western settlement. Migrants paid premium prices for land along navigable streams in the vast area drained by the Ohio, Tennessee, and Mississippi rivers. To market their surplus grain, meat, and cotton, they built shallow barges and floated down the Mississippi to the ocean port of New Orleans. By 1815, New Orleans received about $5 million in agricultural products yearly. These shipments remained small—roughly $15 in goods from each farm family west of the Appalachians—because of the distance and the difficulties of up-stream navigation. Until the development of the steamboat, inland settlers could not easily receive manufactured goods or other supplies in return for their produce.

New England migrants in upper New York faced even greater transportation problems. The first section of the Erie Canal, connecting the central counties of New York with the Hudson River, opened in 1819. No outside market had existed there previously, and so settlers developed the region in a "bootstrap" fashion. They carried tools, plows, livestock, and household necessities across the Appalachians and into the flat plains and rolling hills of New York. These settlers exchanged their first crops and newly born livestock for the cash and manufactured goods brought by the next wave of migrants. As one pioneer recalled,

> In the early years, there was none but a home market, and that was mostly barter—it was so many bushels of wheat for a cow; so many bushels for a yoke of oxen. The price of a common pair of cowhide boots would be $7, payable in wheat at 62 cents per bushel.

This creative system of exchange had narrow limits. It did not yield sufficient profits to purchase land, and most migrants had meager savings. Yet congressional land policies made a western farm relatively expensive to buy. The Northwest Ordinances of 1785 and 1787 divided the Northwest Territory into uniform sections or townships. These townships measured six miles square and were divided into thirty-six sections of 640 acres, or one square mile. Each section had to be sold as a whole, at a minimum price of $1 per acre. Thus, a person needed at least $640 in cash to acquire land in the public domain, and usually considerably more.

Poor migrants demanded better terms, but the Federalist-dominated Congresses of the 1790s refused to comply. The Land Act of 1796 allowed a year's credit on half the purchase price but doubled the minimum cost to $2 per acre. Federalist politicians had no desire to encourage the movement of voters and resources to what was regarded as the Republican West. As Republican political power increased, new legislation promoted western settlement. New laws in 1800 and 1804 reduced the minimum allotment to 320 and then to 160 acres, and allowed payment over four years. Westward-bound farmers finally achieved major assistance in the Land Act of 1820. This law eliminated the credit system but reduced the minimum purchase to eighty acres and the price to $1.25 per acre. Now $100 in cash could buy a western farm at a government auction.

Few settlers purchased farmsteads at such a favorable price, however, because fertile lands and those near streams cost more. Speculators also boosted the cost of farmland. To raise funds quickly, the government sold millions of acres in the Northwest Territory to the Ohio and Scioto land companies, often for a few cents an acre. These private firms resold the land to migrants, charging as much as the market would bear. They had to offset their purchase and administrative expenses and provide ample profits for their investors.

State governments also sold land rights to private companies, sometimes to avoid administrative costs but more often as a result of dubious political deals. Robert Morris, a Philadelphia merchant known as the "financier of the Revolution," acquired 1.3 million acres of land in the Genesee region of New York for $75,000. He reaped a quick profit, selling the land for $275,000 to a group of English investors headed by Sir William Pulteney. Pulteney and his associates took their profits over a longer period. By 1829, their land agents in New York had received $1.2 million from sales to migrant farmers. Elsewhere in New York, the Dutch-owned

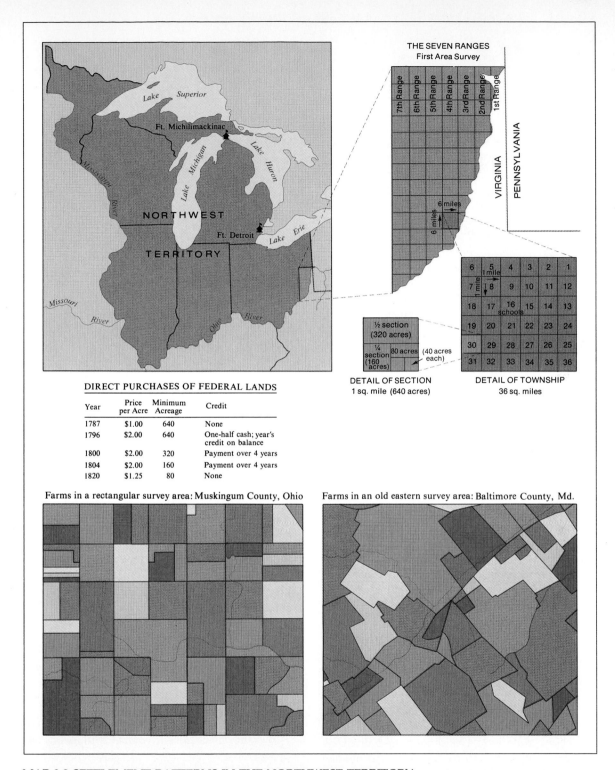

THE SEVEN RANGES
First Area Survey

7th Range | 6th Range | 5th Range | 4th Range | 3rd Range | 2nd Range | 1st Range

VIRGINIA

PENNSYLVANIA

6 miles

DETAIL OF SECTION
1 sq. mile (640 acres)

½ section (320 acres)
¼ section (160 acres)
80 acres
(40 acres each)

DETAIL OF TOWNSHIP
36 sq. miles

6	5	4	3	2	1
7	8	9	10	11	12
18	17	16 schools	15	14	13
19	20	21	22	23	24
30	29	28	27	26	25
31	32	33	34	35	36

1 mile

DIRECT PURCHASES OF FEDERAL LANDS

Year	Price per Acre	Minimum Acreage	Credit
1787	$1.00	640	None
1796	$2.00	640	One-half cash; year's credit on balance
1800	$2.00	320	Payment over 4 years
1804	$2.00	160	Payment over 4 years
1820	$1.25	80	None

Farms in a rectangular survey area: Muskingum County, Ohio

Farms in an old eastern survey area: Baltimore County, Md.

MAP 8.2 SETTLEMENT PATTERNS IN THE NORTHWEST TERRITORY

The property lines of eastern farms were usually irregular, following the contours of the land, as in the survey of Baltimore County, Maryland (lower right). In Muskingum County, Ohio, and throughout the Northwest Territory, surveyors imposed a rectangular grid on the landscape in advance of settlement. Farmers purchased neatly defined blocks of land either directly from the federal government or from land speculators, such as the Seven Ranges Company, that had bought large sections of the National Domain.

Holland Land Company acquired millions of acres of land. South of the Ohio River, the Transylvania and Vandalia companies promoted the settlement of vast tracts.

Local land entrepreneurs were equally active and successful. The influential Wadworth family in the Genesee region of New York created leasehold estates similar to the manors of the Hudson River Valley. The Wadworths retained ownership of this prime farm-land but leased it rent-free for seven years to attract cash-poor migrants. Because of their cultural ideal of freehold ownership, many New England migrants shunned these attractive terms. They preferred to sign lease-purchase contracts with the Holland Land Company. They could then work their own land while accumulating money to buy it. The lack of outside markets made payment difficult, and the company charged 7 percent interest, so some farmers fell deeper into debt. By 1819, the landed debt of farmers in counties west of the Genesee River amounted to $5 million. In the ten New York counties dominated by the Holland Land Company, there were more tenant farmers with land-purchase contracts than there were freeholders.

Had these American farmers fled declining prospects in the East, only to submit to a new system of tenancy and economic hierarchy in the West? In one sense, the answer was yes. In any new settlement, it took the labor of a generation to clear land; to build houses, barns, and roads; and to plant orchards. This process of capital accumulation was extremely difficult without low-cost access to markets. Many migrants remained in debt to landlords or land companies for decades. Lacking the cash to buy manufactures, they made their own clothes and repaired old tools. On the whole, their standard of living declined. As late as 1840, per capita income west of the Appalachians amounted to only about 70 percent of the national average.

Yet migrants continued to move west—and in ever-growing numbers. Whatever the backbreaking labor, crude living conditions, and financial burdens, a western farmstead would eventually provide a secure, independent livelihood for the settlers and their children. Overcoming numerous obstacles, thousands of Americans succeeded in this modest quest. "A noble field of Indian corn stretched away into the forest on

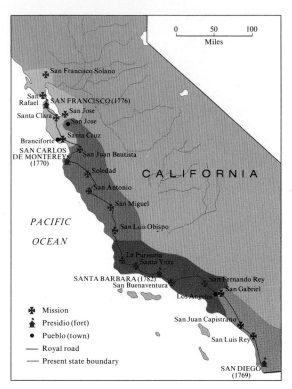

MAP 8.3 THE SETTLEMENT OF SPANISH CALIFORNIA, 1769–1823
While Britain and the United States struggled for control of the trans-Appalachian west, Spain established a dominant position in California. Spanish officials ruled vast administrative domains from *praesidios*. Monks of the Society of St. Francis (Francisians) built Indian missions along the coast, and a few thousand migrants from New Spain lived in pueblos or on scattered cattle ranches.

one side," an English visitor to an Ohio farm observed in the 1820s,

> and immediately before the house was a small potato garden, with a few peach and apple trees. The woman told me that they spun and wove all the cotton and woollen garments of the family, and knit all the stockings; her husband, though not a shoemaker by trade, made all the shoes. She manufactured all the soap and candles they used. All she wanted with money, she said, was to buy coffee, tea, and whiskey, and she could 'get enough any day by sending a batch of butter and chickens to market.'

This bootstrap method of settlement testified to the vigor of American preindustrial society. A century of agricultural development in the seaboard states had produced enough surplus population and capital goods to begin the conquest of the vast North American continent. But the fate of this great enterprise lay in doubt. The success of the yeoman farm society envisioned by Madison and Jefferson depended on major advances in transportation. The constraints of the preindustrial economy limited prosperity in the West.

The Native American Challenge

Before the land west of the Appalachians could be settled, it had to be conquered. Until the War of Independence, native American tribes controlled the entire region. The main tribes of the south—the Catawba, Chickasaw, Choctaw,

Creek, and Cherokee—actively resisted Anglo-American settlement far to the east of the mountains. The six Iroquois nations of New York used military strength and astute diplomacy to negotiate as near-equals with the advancing whites. Most Indian tribes, their lands threatened by migrants from the seaboard settlements, allied themselves with the British against the Americans.

This strategy failed to preserve the native American lands. The Delaware tribe joined with Tory forces to destroy frontier settlements in the Wyoming Valley of Pennsylvania. Iroquois warriors sacked farms in the Cherry Valley of New York. Cherokee tribemen disrupted life in the Carolina backcountry. By the end of the war, however, Continental troops and local militiamen had repulsed the Cherokee in the South.

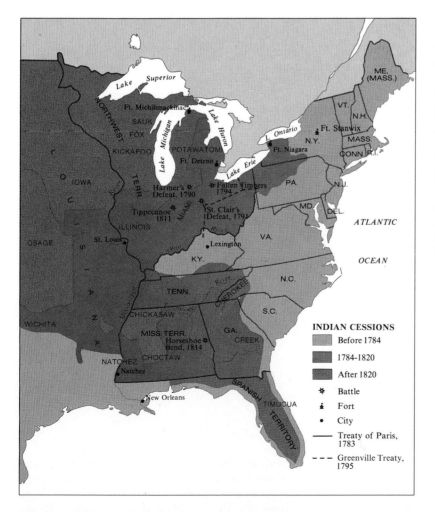

MAP 8.4 THE DIPLOMACY OF CONQUEST
The United States claimed ownership of the trans-Appalachian west by right of conquest over Great Britain. Most Indian tribes contested the legitimacy of this claim and the cessions made to the U.S. government in the treaty of Fort Stanwix in 1784. The American government sent armies into the west in the 1790s and during the War of 1812 to extract new treaties from the western tribes. This armed diplomacy forced the cession of most Indian lands east of the Mississippi River.

TREATY NEGOTATIONS
AT GREENVILLE
In 1785 the Shawnee, Chippewa,
Ottawa, Miami and other tribes
formed the Western Confederation to
stop white settlement at the Ohio
River. The American victory at the
Battle of Fallen Timbers (1794)
opened up the region, but the Treaty
of Greenville (1795) explicitly
recognized many Indian rights.
(Unidentified Artist. Detail of *Treaty
of Greenville*. Chicago Historical
Society)

Equally significant, American soldiers had destroyed dozens of settlements and thousands of bushels of wheat in the Iroquois heartland. The once-powerful Iroquois Confederacy now lacked the military power to resist white advance, and its British ally offered little diplomatic support. The governor of Quebec proposed a separate Indian state between the United States and Canada, but Britain did not insist on this buffer zone. In the Treaty of Paris, which ended the war in 1783, the British relinquished all claims of sovereignty to the lands east of the Mississippi River and south of the Great Lakes. The new American republic asserted ownership of these Indian lands by right of treaty and of conquest.

Americans soon found that it was easier to claim Indian territory than to occupy it. The Iroquois and the undefeated tribes west of the Ohio River refused to accept the Treaty of Paris. The Confederation Congress therefore appointed commissioners to negotiate separate treaties with the various tribes. In the Treaty of Fort Stanwix in 1784, the Iroquois ceded all tribal lands west of New York and Pennsylvania to the United States. Moreover, they accepted confinement on relatively small reservations in New York. In 1785, the American commissioners used threats of armed force to extract agreements from western tribes. The Chippewa, Delaware, Ottawa, and Wyandot relinquished their claims to most of the future state of Ohio.

Within two years, the tribes repudiated these agreements. They claimed, with some justification, that the treaties had been signed under duress. To open central and western New York to white settlement, land speculators and the state government used liquor and bribes to reach new agreements. However, western tribes stood firm in their resistance. Led by the Shawnee, the tribes of the Ohio Valley mobilized for war. In 1790 and 1791 they dealt crushing defeats to American expeditionary forces commanded by General Josiah Harmar and General Arthur St. Clair.

Aggressive military expansion divided political opinion in the new republic. Critics warned of immoral attempts to exterminate native Americans and of the possible use of a permanent army to suppress political dissent. Yet many southern congressmen feared an alliance among such western frontier tribes as the Shawnee, Chippewa, Ottawa, and Potawatomi. They strongly supported President Washington's decision to double the army to five thousand men. In 1794, bolstered by new recruits, General "Mad Anthony" Wayne defeated the Western Indian Confederacy in the Battle of Fallen Timbers, forcing the tribes to the bargaining table.

In the Treaty of Greenville in 1795, the United States renounced its claim to the ownership of Indian lands in the Northwest Territory. In return, the Indian chiefs made specific "cessions and relinquishments" of large tracts of land. They also acknowledged American sovereignty over the entire region. The Indians agreed to place themselves "under the protection of the United States, and no other Power whatever." This agreement complemented the Jay Treaty with Great Britain because it increased the likelihood that the British would withdraw their garrisons from American territory.

Rapid westward migration quickly undermined the territorial agreements. Ohio entered the Union in 1803 and two years later had more than a hundred thousand people. Thousands of new migrants moved into Indiana and Illinois. Governor William Henry Harrison of the Indiana Territory used threats, bribes, and trickery to "purchase" millions of acres of Indian land. State officials and land speculators in Georgia, Tennessee, and the Mississippi Territory made similar deals.

These agreements threatened thousands of native Americans with imminent eviction from their ancestral lands. Sensing the prospect of an Indian uprising, Governor-General James Craig of Canada quietly renewed British military assistance to tribes in the Ohio River Valley. Simultaneously, the Shawnee chief Tecumseh, assisted by his brother, the Prophet Tenskwatawa, revived the Western Indian Confederacy. They vowed to push white settlement back to the eastern side of the Ohio River. Southern tribes quickly added their support, and the prospect of war loomed once again along the entire western frontier.

Tecumseh's success reflected long-standing Indian fears and his own appeal as a religious leader. Christian missionaries had penetrated deep into Indian territory and won many native American converts. But most Indian leaders deeply resented the intrusion of Christian beliefs and demanded a return to traditional religious values and social customs. A number of tribes repudiated white migration and cultural influence by staging revivals of traditional spiritual beliefs. These religious movements added political focus to their anger against the whites.

Tenskwatawa used his considerable spiritual powers to encourage diplomatic alliances among the western tribes. His religious message suggested that devoted warriors would emerge unscathed from battle. To symbolize the religious roots of Indian military resistance, Tecumseh centered his confederacy at a sacred town located at the junction of Tippecanoe Creek and the Wabash River. Governor Harrison burned the town after his troops defeated the Indians in the Battle of Tippecanoe in 1811 (see the account of the battle on page 230). Harrison thus unleashed a religious war as well as a territorial resistance movement. Soon the entire frontier was in turmoil. As always in American history, warfare with native Americans was the price paid for white western expansion.

The Republicans in Power

Between 1800 and 1824, three Republicans from Virginia—Thomas Jefferson, James Madison, and James Monroe—each served two terms as president. Supported by strong majorities in Congress, they reversed many Federalist policies, thus completing what Jefferson called the Revolution of 1800. The "Virginia Dynasty" of presidents vigorously supported the acquisition and settlement of the West. Territorial expansion and maritime disputes led to a new and unpopular conflict with Great Britain, the War of 1812. By the end of that war, the Federalists no longer existed as a national political force. The First Party System was over.

Jefferson as President

Thomas Jefferson was a brilliant man, perhaps the most accomplished and versatile statesman in the history of the United States. An astute diplomat and an insightful political philosopher, he was also a superb politician. Upon entering the presidency in 1801, Jefferson immediately courted New England by appointing three men from that Federalist stronghold to major government posts. Levi Lincoln became attorney general, Henry Dearborn the secretary of war, and Gideon Granger the postmaster general. Through careful use of patronage, Jefferson quickly bolstered Republican organizations in New England as well. His efforts succeeded. In the election of 1804, he carried every New England state except Connecticut.

Jefferson inherited a government dominated by Federalist appointees. In addition to the bureaucrats who managed the affairs of state, the outgoing Federalists had packed the judiciary. Early in 1801, President Adams appointed John

A POTTAWATOMIE CHIEF
ON THE BATTLE OF TIPPECANOE

His mind sharpened by the experience of defeat, Chief Shabonee offers a penetrating view of reality: the unfaithfulness of friends and allies, the intensity of determined men and women, and the false hopes raised by those who lead their nations into war.

It was fully believed among the Indians that we should defeat General Harrison, and that we should hold the line of the Wabash and dictate terms to the whites. The great cause of our failure, was the Miamies, whose principal country was south of the river, and they wanted to treat with the whites so as to retain their land, and they played false to their red brethren and yet lost all. They are now surrounded and will be crushed. The whites will shortly have all their lands and they will be driven away. . . .

Our young men said: We are ten to their one. If they stay upon the other side, we will let them alone. If they cross the Wabash, we will take their scalps or drive them into the river. They cannot swim. Their powder will be wet. The fish will eat their bodies. The bones of the white men will lie upon every sand bar. Their flesh will fatten buzzards. These white soldiers are not warriors. Their hands are soft. Their faces are white. One half of them are calico peddlers. The other half can only shoot squirrels. They cannot stand before men. They will all run when we make a noise in the night like wild cats fighting for their young. . . .

Such were the opinions and arguments of our warriors. They did not appreciate the great strength of the white men. I knew their great war chief, and some of his young men. He was a good man, very soft in his words to his red children, as he called us; and that made some of our men with hot heads mad. I listened to his soft words, but I looked into his eyes. They were full of fire. I knew that they would be among his men like coals of fire in the dry grass. The first wind would raise a great flame. I feared for the red men that might be sleeping in its way.

. . . Our women and children were in the town only a mile from the battle-field waiting for victory and its spoils. They wanted white prisoners. The Prophet had promised that every squaw of any note should have one of the white warriors to use as her slave, or to treat as she pleased.

Oh how these women were disappointed! Instead of slaves and spoils of the white men coming into town with the rising sun, their town was in flames and women and children were hunted like wolves and killed by hundreds or driven into the river and swamps to hide.

With the smoke of that town and the loss of that battle I lost all hope of the red men being able to stop the whites. . . .

Marshall, an ardent Virginia Federalist, as chief justice of the Supreme Court, a position he held until 1835. Then the Federalist-controlled Congress enacted a new Judiciary Act. It created sixteen new judgeships, six additional circuit courts, and an array of posts for marshals and clerks. As he left office, Adams filled these positions in a series of last-minute "midnight appointments." The Federalists "have retired into the judiciary as a stronghold," Jefferson complained, ". . . and from that battery all the works of Republicanism are to be beaten down and destroyed." The Republican Congress promptly repealed the controversial Judiciary Act, thereby eliminating many of the Federalist-held positions. In addition, James Madison, Jefferson's secretary of state, refused to accept the legality of the commission of one midnight appointee, William Marbury.

Madison's action led to the celebrated Supreme Court case of *Marbury v. Madison*. Chief Justice Marshall's decision in this case, handed down in 1803, established the basis for judicial review of the Constitution and of congressional legislation. Marshall ruled that Marbury had a right to his commission. But he also declared that the Supreme Court lacked the authority to order Madison to deliver it.

Marshall's decision was politically astute. In the first place, he avoided a direct confrontation between the Federalist justices and the Republican administration. At the same time, Marshall laid a claim to extensive powers for the Supreme Court. He argued that it was "emphatically the province and duty of the judicial department to say what the law is." Marshall had made a political—as well as a legal—statement, for his decision challenged Madison and Jefferson's position in the Virginia and Kentucky resolutions of 1798. It repudiated their argument that the state legislatures had the sole authority to judge the constitutionality of national laws.

The Republican-controlled Congress was nearly as adept at using the Constitution for political purposes. The Constitution empowered the House of Representatives to bring impeachment charges against officials for "high crimes and misdemeanors." The Senate then would judge the accused official in a formal trial. Using these provisions, Republicans punished Federalist judges for their past political activities. First, they impeached a mentally unstable judge, John Pickering of New Hampshire, and won his removal from office. Next, they attacked Supreme Court Justice Samuel Chase in retaliation for his vigorous enforcement of the Sedition Act. Chase escaped impeachment by only a narrow vote.

President Jefferson followed a more conciliatory policy. While supporting repeal of the Judiciary Act, he kept most Federalist bureaucrats in their offices. Jefferson judged these officials on ability, not party loyalty. During his eight years as chief executive, he removed only 109 of 433 presidential appointees—and 40 of these were controversial midnight appointees of Adams.

Yet Jefferson was determined to carry through the Revolution of 1800 by reversing what he considered dangerous Federalist innovations. Congress refused to renew the politically motivated Alien and Sedition Acts. It amended the Naturalization Act to permit resident aliens to become citizens after five years. Jefferson likewise modified many financial policies devised by Alexander Hamilton. To pay for his redemption and assumption programs, Hamilton had imposed a variety of internal taxes. His excise tax on whiskey had led to a rebellion in western Pennsylvania in 1794. Inspired by both the North Carolina Regulators and the Jacobins of France, the so-called Whiskey Rebels waved banners proclaiming Liberty, Equality, and Fraternity. To put down this rebellion, President Washington had raised fifteen thousand troops, creating Republican fears of political oppression by a standing army.

The Jefferson administration abolished all internal taxes and reduced the size of the permanent army. It pursued a policy of fiscal economy as well. Jefferson appointed Albert Gallatin, a brilliant Swiss-born Republican, as secretary of the treasury. Gallatin instituted a fiscally conservative regime, carefully controlling government expenditures. Believing the national debt to be "an evil of the first magnitude," he used ample customs revenues to reduce it from $83 million in 1801 to $45 million in 1808. By the end of his second term, Jefferson had changed the government's economic priorities. The nation was no longer run in the interests of northeastern creditors and merchants.

Equally important, Jefferson turned the eyes of the nation away from Europe and toward the American West. In 1795, he had strongly supported the Pinckney treaty, an agreement with Spain negotiated by the Federalist diplomat Thomas Pinckney. This pact safeguarded the interests of Americans west of the Appalachians. It gave western settlers the right to ship farm products down the Mississippi River, the boundary between the United States and Spanish Louisiana. The treaty also allowed Americans to store commodities at the Spanish port of New Orleans prior to export. When Spanish officials revoked this transshipment right in 1802, Jefferson became greatly alarmed.

Events in Europe prompted the crisis. Napoleon Bonaparte, a brilliant and daring 30-year-old general, had seized power in France in 1799. Almost immediately, Napoleon began a fantastic career of imperial conquest. He invaded Egypt, only to be defeated by British troops and naval forces. The young general then dreamed of a new French Empire in America. First, in a secret treaty, he forced Spain to return Louisiana to France, overturning the Treaty of Paris of 1763. Then he mobilized an expeditionary force to invade the rich sugar island of Santo Domingo. White planters on the island had declared independence from the First French Republic in 1793, but their regime had been overthrown by black rebels led by Toussaint L'Overture. Napoleon planned to recapture Santo Domingo and to join it with Guadeloupe, Martinique, and Louisiana in a new, economically integrated American empire.

To preserve the trade guaranteed by the Pinckney treaty, Jefferson reversed the pro-French foreign policy of the Republican party.

Any nation that denied Americans access to New Orleans, he remarked, must be "our natural and habitual enemy." To avoid conflict with Napoleon, Jefferson instructed Robert R. Livingston, the United States minister in Paris, to purchase the port of New Orleans. The president sent James Monroe, a former congressman and governor of Virginia, to Britain to seek its assistance if France refused to sell or to open the Mississippi to American commerce. Meanwhile, Secretary of State Madison encouraged American merchants to help the black government of Santo Domingo resist the French invasion.

Jefferson's determined diplomacy yielded a magnificent prize. Military resistance and yellow fever crippled the French forces in Santo Domingo, and the threat of a new war against Britain in Europe prevented France from sending reinforcements. Napoleon now feared a possible invasion of Louisiana by American settlers or troops. Acting with characteristic decisiveness, the French general gave up his dream of an empire in America. In April 1803, he offered to sell Louisiana as well as New Orleans, and the American diplomats quickly agreed to what became known as the Louisiana Purchase. "We have lived long," Livingston remarked to Monroe, who had joined him in Paris, "but this is the

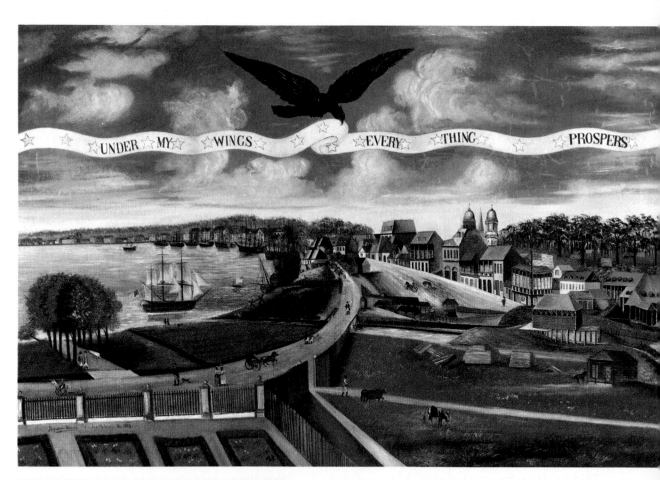

THE AMERICAN EAGLE OVER NEW ORLEANS
Jefferson's dramatic purchase of Louisiana made New Orleans an American city, but only in name. The culture of the French colonists (or Creoles) remained strong for decades. "The great enmity existing between the Creoles . . . & the Americans," a traveler noted, produced "fights and Challenges—there are some of both sides in jail." (Boqueto de Woieseri. *A View of New Orleans Taken From the Plantation of Marigny, November 1803.* Chicago Historical Society)

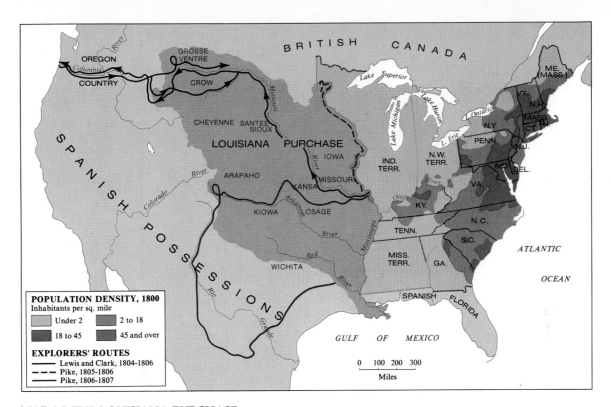

MAP 8.5 THE LOUISIANA PURCHASE

In 1802, Jefferson predicted that the lands of the great Mississippi Valley "from its fertility . . . will ere long yield half of our whole produce, and contain more than half of our whole population." "The day that France takes possession of New Orleans," the President warned, "we must marry ourselves to the British fleet and nation." To prevent this outcome, he purchased Louisiana from Napoleon I for $15 million.

noblest work of our lives." For about $15 million, they had purchased the vast territory between the Mississippi River and the Rocky Mountains.

The sheer magnitude of the Louisiana Purchase overwhelmed Jefferson's reservations about its constitutionality. In the debate over the Bank of the United States in 1791, he had argued that the government was limited to "expressly" delegated powers. Yet the Constitution failed to specify if, or how, new territories could be acquired. To fulfill his goal of westward expansion, Jefferson pragmatically compromised his strict views and used the treaty-making powers in the Constitution for the Louisiana Purchase. Federalists roundly criticized Jefferson's inconsistency, but they largely accepted his diplomatic triumph.

Jefferson was a competent scientist who wanted to expand knowledge of the American environment. He assigned his personal secretary, Meriweather Lewis, to explore the Louisiana Territory. Lewis and William Clark, an army officer, traveled up the Missouri River, across the Rocky Mountains, and down the Columbia River to the Pacific Ocean. After two years, Lewis and Clark returned with maps of this vast wilderness and striking accounts of its natural resources and native American inhabitants.

Despite its great importance to the United States, the Louisiana Purchase threatened the Union. New England Federalists had long feared limitless westward expansion. Now, some Connecticut Federalists, including Timothy Pickering, Roger Griswold, and Jedediah Morse, talked openly of secession. When Alexander Hamilton refused to support their plan for a separate Northern Confederacy, they courted Aaron Burr, the ambitious Republican vice-president.

As Burr campaigned for the governorship of New York in 1804, Hamilton accused him of plotting to dismember the nation. In response, Burr challenged his long-time enemy to a duel, the aristocratic method of settling personal disputes. Hamilton died from gunshot wounds, and state courts in New York and in New Jersey, where the illegal duel took place, indicted Burr for murder.

These events led to another secessionist scheme. Burr completed his term as vice-president in early 1805 and then moved west to avoid prosecution. There he conspired with General James Wilkinson, the American military governor of the Louisiana Territory. The precise details of their plan are not known. It involved either the capture of Spanish land in Mexico or a rebellion to establish Louisiana as a separate nation, headed by Burr. When the former vice-president led an armed force down the Ohio River, Wilkinson betrayed his ally and arrested him on a charge of treason. Chief Justice Marshall, sitting as a circuit judge, presided over an intensely political trial. To thwart Jefferson's efforts to convict Burr, Marshall intervened repeatedly from the bench and assured his acquittal.

The ultimate decision was less important than the sensational events that preceded it. Jefferson's expansionist policies had increased sectional tension and party conflict. They created new diplomatic problems as well, both with the Spaniards in Florida and Mexico and with the British in Canada. Western expansion had become a major factor in the foreign and domestic politics of the United States.

Crisis at Sea

The outbreak of the Napoleonic Wars (1802–1815) between France and Great Britain, temporarily eclipsed the growing importance of the American West. As in the 1790s, the belligerent powers boarded United States ships and confiscated their cargoes. Following Admiral Horatio Nelson's resounding victory over the French navy in the Battle of Trafalgar in 1805, the British tightened their naval blockade. The Royal Navy seized the American ship *Essex* for carrying sugar and molasses from the West Indies to France. A British vice-admiralty judge refused to consider these products as American "re-exports," although the *Essex* had intentionally stopped at a United States port in order to make that claim. Instead, the judge ruled that the sugar and molasses were French, since there had been a "continuous voyage," and therefore were subject to seizure. This new British restriction on neutral trade threatened the profits of American merchants and revived anti-British sentiment.

Napoleon replied to the British blockade with his own declaration of economic warfare. He implemented the Continental System, a blockade plan designed to destroy the British export trade. The system began with the Berlin and Milan decrees of 1806 and 1807. These edicts banned British ships, and neutral vessels that stopped at British ports, from European ports under French control. In response, the British required neutral shippers to obtain special licenses to pass through their naval blockade. American merchants were trapped. If their ships stopped at a British port for goods or a license, they faced seizure by France and its allies. But if they refused to carry British goods or permits, their cargoes might be condemned as contraband by the Royal Navy. American traders feared the British blockade more than French customs officials. They took out about ten thousand licenses in 1809 and eighteen thousand in 1810.

The American traders' response preserved profits but not pride. Both Federalists and Republicans resented what they considered British arrogance. The Royal Navy's impressment of American seamen further ruffled national pride. The phenomenal expansion of commerce provided about four thousand new jobs for sailors each year on merchant ships. Hundreds of men fled from harsh British naval discipline and low pay to fill these positions. To catch the deserters, the Royal Navy stopped American merchant ships and seized British-born seamen. Some of these sailors were naturalized citizens of the United States, and others carried forged American identity papers. Still others were Americans impressed by accident—and increasingly by design. During the 1790s, British warships seized about twenty-four hundred sailors from American ships; between 1802 and 1811, they impressed nearly eight thousand.

The American resentment erupted into anger

TIME LINE
THE POLITICAL WORLD: COMMERCIAL ENTERPRISE AND WESTWARD EXPANSION

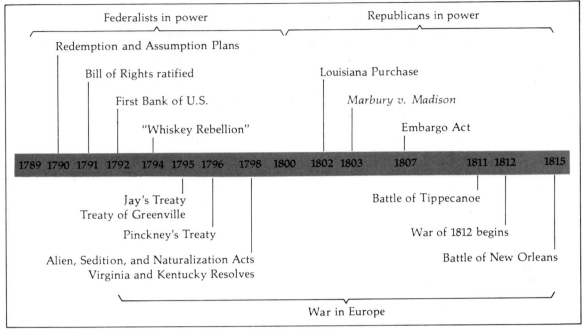

in 1807. The British warship *Leopard* opened fire on the *U.S.S. Chesapeake*, killing or wounding twenty-one men and taking four alleged deserters. "Never since the battle of Lexington have I seen this country in such a state of exasperation as at present," Jefferson declared.

Like most Republicans, Jefferson had little desire to be pulled into war over commercial issues. He appreciated the importance of foreign trade, since the export of agricultural goods was a key aspect of his vision of American economic development. The president knew military action would increase domestic political conflict. It also would require the expansion of the army and navy and involve an increase in taxes or in the national debt. These considerations had determined his action in an earlier commercial dispute. Federalist administrations had made tribute payments to the Barbary States of North Africa to prevent pirate-like attacks on American merchant ships in the Mediterranean Sea. Jefferson ended these bribes in 1801 and responded slowly when city-states of Tunis, Morocco, Tripoli, and Algiers renewed their assaults. Not until

1805 did United States naval squadrons force a revision of the tribute system.

Jefferson responded just as cautiously to the British attack on the *Chesapeake*. He rejected demands for revenge and instead closed American territorial waters to British warships. The president requested reparations for damages and demanded an end to impressment. The diplomatically astute British government apologized for the attack. It promised eventual compensation but firmly defended its blockade and impressment policies.

Working closely with Secretary of State Madison, Jefferson embarked on a new policy of "peaceful coercion." With the Embargo Act of 1807, the American leaders hoped to end both the Continental System and the British naval blockade. This legislation prohibited American ships from transporting cargo to any nation until France and Britain repealed their restrictions on American trade.

The diplomatic initiative was imaginative but naive because Jefferson and Madison exaggerated the commercial power of the United States.

Neither Britain nor France depended completely on the American merchant marine. Furthermore, the two European powers were determined to continue the war, regardless of the commercial cost. The American leaders also underestimated the cunning of Federalist merchants, who ordered their captains to sail between foreign ports until the embargo was lifted. Trade was their lifeblood. To reap wartime profits, merchants were prepared to take their chances with the British navy and Napoleon's officials.

As the American export trade fell from $108 million in 1806 to $22 million in 1808, the merchants' representatives in Congress charged the Republicans with crippling their interests and jeopardizing the economic health of the nation. In reply, Congress passed the Force Act to prevent smuggling between New England and Canada. It gave customs officials extraordinary and arbitrary enforcement powers. "Would to God," exclaimed one Federalist, "that the Embargo had done as little evil to ourselves as it has done to foreign nations."

Despite public discontent with the embargo, the voters elected Madison to the presidency in 1808. Madison was a brilliant political philosopher and an effective congressman, but he had performed poorly as secretary of state. As John Beckley, a loyal Republican activist, observed in 1806, "Madison is deemed by many too timid and indecisive as a statesman." Beckley tried to convince James Monroe to fight for the Republican presidential nomination, contrasting "the known energy and decision of your character" with Madison's timidity. Unfortunately for the Republicans—and the nation—Monroe declined. Instead, at a crucial juncture in foreign affairs, a weak and vacillating man became president.

Madison's diplomatic policy reflected his indecisiveness as a statesman. At his request, the Republican-controlled Congress repealed the embargo in 1809 and replaced it with the Non-intercourse Act. This legislation permitted trade with all nations except France and Britain. It promised the resumption of normal commerce once the belligerents respected America's neutral rights. When this second attempt at peaceful coercion failed, Madison tried another tactic. A measure introduced by Congressman Nathaniel Macon, called Macon's Bill No. 2, reopened legal trade with Britain and France in 1810. It authorized the president to invoke new sanctions if either nation interfered with American commerce. Napoleon astutely exploited this poorly conceived legislation. In public statements, he exempted American commerce from the Berlin and Milan decrees; privately, the French emperor instructed customs officials to enforce the Continental System. The British ministry refused to alter its policies. "The Devil himself could not tell which government, England or France, is the most wicked," the exasperated Macon declared.

Other Republicans thought they knew. Since 1809, such eastern party leaders as Vice-President George Clinton, the former governor of New York, and Senator Robert Smith of Maryland had condemned British policies. By 1810, Republican congressmen from the South and West voiced similar sentiments. With some justification, they accused Britain of aiding Tecumseh and the Western Indian Confederation. Some southern representatives wanted an excuse to seize Florida from Spain, Britain's ally in Europe. In fact, armed Americans took control of western Florida and sought its annexation to the United States.

Southern planters campaigned for the annexation of eastern Florida as well. They wished to prevent slaves from taking refuge among the Seminole Indians. "I wish you would authorize the President to take possession of East Florida immediately," Thomas Jefferson wrote his son-in-law, John W. Epps of Virginia, in the House of Representatives. "The militia of Georgia will do it in a fortnight." Republican politicians in the West predicted an equally rapid conquest of British Canada. Henry Clay, an avowed "war hawk" from Kentucky and the new Speaker of the House of Representatives, pushed Madison toward war with Great Britain. John Calhoun, a rising young congressman from South Carolina, likewise endorsed an aggressive military stance.

To unify his party and win renomination for president in 1812, Madison now abandoned the policy of peaceful coercion. He demanded respect for American territorial sovereignty in the West and neutral rights in the Atlantic. When the British failed to respond quickly, Madison asked Congress to declare war. In June 1812, a closely divided Senate voted nineteen to thirteen

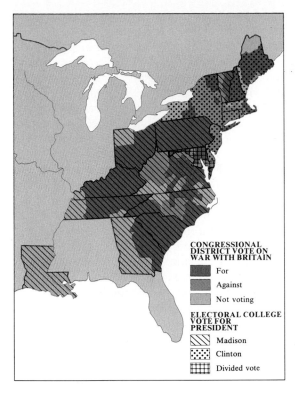

MAP 8.6 WAR AND POLITICS IN 1812
Most congressmen who voted for war with Great Britain in June 1812 came from districts that supported Republican James Madison in the subsequent presidential election. Conversely, most congressmen who opposed the war represented Federalist districts. Thus, the decision for war reflected partisan politics rather than a national consensus.

for war, and the House of Representatives concurred, seventy-nine to forty-nine. A rush of patriotic fervor helped Madison win reelection in 1812. He amassed 128 electoral votes, mostly from the South and West. His Federalist opponent, Dewitt Clinton of New York, received 89 votes largely from the New England and Middle Atlantic states.

The voting pattern indicated that the War of 1812 would be a "western war with eastern labels." The conflict ostensibly arose over the commercial issues of impressment and neutral rights. However, Federalist merchants and seamen vigorously opposed the declaration of war, as did a majority of voters in the Atlantic Coast states. Conversely, about twenty-eight Republi-

can congressmen, "war hawks" from the frontier political districts of the South and West, strongly supported it. These congressmen acted from a variety of motives. Some thought the British blockade had cut agricultural prices. Others wanted territorial spoils in Florida and the final defeat of the Western Indian Confederacy. A few politicians dreamed of annexing British Canada. Beyond these motives, many Republicans thought war was the only way to preserve American honor. As President Madison proclaimed in his second inaugural address, "national honor is national property of the highest value."

The War of 1812

Republican hopes for a series of rapid military victories quickly collapsed. American privateers captured scores of merchant vessels during the first months of the war, but then the Royal Navy redeployed its fleet and British commerce moved in relative safety. By 1813, the British had seized the maritime initiative. A flotilla of British warships moved up and down the American coastline, harassing shipping and threatening seaport cities. In 1814, this fleet sailed up Chesapeake Bay. British forces stormed ashore and set fire to most of the government buildings in the District of Columbia, the new United States capital. The British then advanced on Baltimore but were repulsed by courageous American resistance at Fort McHenry, inspiring Francis Scott Key, a Washington attorney, to compose "The Star-Spangled Banner." After two years of sporadic warfare, United States forces stood on the defensive in the East.

In the West, the United States failed to exploit its geographic advantage. Republican politicians had predicted an easy military advance into Canada, but they underestimated the difficulties of transportation and supply. General William Hull, the governor of the Michigan Territory, invaded western Canada in the summer of 1812. He quickly retreated because of a lack of reinforcements. By quickly building ships, the United States won naval superiority on the Great Lakes. Commodore Oliver Perry defeated a small British flotilla on Lake Erie, permitting General William Henry Harrison to launch an

POKING FUN AT THE FEDERALISTS
A Republican cartoon of 1812 portrays a Federalist
congressman as King of New England and Grand Master
of the "cod-fish aristocracy" of merchants. By making
Quincy look like a fish, the artist humorously but
effectively disputed the Federalists' claims to social
superiority. (Library of Congress)

attack on British and Indian forces near Detroit.
Harrison killed his old rival Tecumseh, now an
officer in the British army. Another American expedition captured and burned the Canadian capital of York (now Toronto).

These minor victories were poor substitutes
for a major invasion of Canada. Political opposition in the northeastern states prevented such a
military stroke. New England governors prohibited state militiamen from fighting outside the
United States. Boston merchants and banks
declined to lend money to the national government; they invested in British funds instead. Ordinary citizens likewise refused to buy American
bonds. New England Federalists actively opposed the war effort in other ways as well. Led
by Daniel Webster, a young, dynamic congress-

man from New Hampshire, they voted against
the higher taxes and tariffs needed to finance the
fighting. To force a negotiated peace, Webster
and his Federalist colleagues discouraged army
enlistments and prevented the conscription of
state militiamen into the American army.

Sectional opposition to the war reached its
height in 1814. The Massachusetts legislature
called for a convention "to lay the foundation for
a radical reform in the National Compact." In
December, Federalists from all the New England
states gathered in Hartford, Connecticut. Some
delegates to the Hartford convention proposed
secession from the Union, but the majority
called for revision of the Constitution. Their goal
was to reverse the declining role of their party—
and of New England—in an expanding nation.
To end the "Virginia Dynasty" of presidents,
delegates proposed a constitutional amendment
limiting the presidency to one four-year term
and rotating the office among citizens from different states. Other Federalists suggested
amendments restricting commercial embargoes
to sixty days and requiring two-thirds majorities
in Congress to declare war, prohibit commerce,
and admit new states to the Union.

During the winter of 1814, the United States
government faced the threat of internal secession
and external invasion. In the north, the Hartford
convention called for substantial revision of the
Constitution. Far to the south, British transports
landed thousands of seasoned veterans for an attack on New Orleans. A single ray of hope broke
the darkness. Britain had finally defeated Napoleon in Europe. To end its war with the United
States as well, the British entered negotiations
with an American delegation at Ghent in Belgium. The American commissioners—John
Quincy Adams, Albert Gallatin, and Henry
Clay—initially demanded an end to British impressment and territorial gains in Canada and
Florida. The British insisted on a native American buffer state between the United States and
Canada. In the end, neither side won significant
concessions. The Treaty of Ghent, signed on
Christmas Eve of 1814, required both nations to
give up their territorial gains and to decide the
Canadian-American boundary in subsequent ne-
gotiations.

The result of the war hardly justified three
years of costly fighting and a sharply divided na-

tion. It confirmed the judgment of contemporary critics and later historians that the War of 1812 was unnecessary, undertaken at the wrong time and for partisan reasons. But a final victory in combat lifted American morale and seemed to justify the fighting. Before news of the Treaty of Ghent reached the United States, newspaper headlines proclaimed an "ALMOST INCREDIBLE VICTORY!! GLORIOUS NEWS." Troops commanded by General Andrew Jackson had dealt a crushing defeat to the British force attacking New Orleans.

Whatever its other results, the war had created a new group of political leaders—Henry Clay, Daniel Webster, and John Calhoun—and, in Andrew Jackson, a national hero. Jackson, a rugged slaveowning planter from Tennessee, came to public attention as a controversial Indian-fighter and expansionist. In 1814, he led a troop of militia against the Creek Indians. After defeating them in the Battle of Horseshoe Bend, his men mercilessly slaughtered the women and children of the tribe. Jackson then ordered his troops into Spanish Florida, overwhelming a Creek settlement near Pensacola.

At New Orleans, Jackson commanded a mixed force of regular troops, city militiamen, and frontier fighters. They fought behind carefully constructed breastworks and were amply supplied with cannon. "Our artillery fired upon their whole columns . . . with grapeshot and cannister bombs," reported one American

THE BATTLE OF NEW ORLEANS
British troops advance from right to left along the riverbank (foreground) in an unsuccessful attempt to outflank the American defenders. Secure behind their battlements, Jackson's troops easily repelled the main British frontal assault, inflicting hundreds of casualties. (Jean Hyacinthe de Laclotte. Detail of *Battle of New Orleans*. New Orleans Museum of Art. Gift of Edgar William and Bernice Chrysler Garbisch)

observer. "The slaughter must have been great." The British lost thousands of their finest troops, suffering about seven hundred killed and ten thousand wounded or captured. American casualties totaled only thirteen killed and fifty-eight wounded.

Jackson's triumph was the only significant victory of the entire war for either side. The Battle of New Orleans seemed to testify, as one headline put it, to the "RISING GLORY OF THE AMERICAN REPUBLIC!" It redeemed the nation's battered pride and, along with the coming of peace, undercut Federalist demands for a revision of the Constitution. The political institutions of the republic had survived a generation of strife.

---

*D*uring the 1790s, Alexander Hamilton and Thomas Jefferson created opposing political parties based on distinct philosophical principles. The Federalist economic policies of Hamilton favored northern merchants and financiers, and so Jefferson and James Madison organized farmers, planters, and artisans into the Democratic-Republican party. The French Revolution added an ideological factor to the American party conflict, and the seizure of United States merchant ships led to an undeclared war with France. The Federalists passed the harsh Alien and Sedition Acts to suppress wartime opposition, and the Republicans challenged national authority in the Kentucky and Virginia resolutions. The political crisis of the 1790s threatened the existence of the new American republic.

Jefferson won election as president in 1800. The Republican Congress attacked the Federalist-dominated judiciary and repealed various Federalist innovations. With the Louisiana Purchase, Jefferson pursued his vision of America as a land of independent farmers. Faced with new British seizures of American merchant ships, he and Madison enacted the controversial embargo of 1807 and other restrictions on commerce.

President Madison, influenced by western Republican "war hawks" and his own concern for national honor, led the United States into war against Britain in 1812. New England Federalists, who bitterly opposed westward expansion and the embargo, refused financial and military support for the war. They also demanded various revisions in the Constitution. As in the 1790s, domestic economic and ideological conflicts and foreign entanglements divided the American people and almost led to disastrous consequences.

Suggestions for Further Reading

The Political Crisis of the 1790s

John C. Miller, *The Federalist Era* (1960), is an overview of the decade. For biographies that convey its political flavor and conflicts, see Marcus Cunliffe, *George Washington: Man and Monument* (1958); John C. Miller, *Alexander Hamilton: Portrait in Paradox* (1958); and Broadus Mitchell, *Alexander Hamilton* (1962). For Jefferson, see Merrill Peterson's excellent study, *Thomas Jefferson and the New Nation* (1970). Claude G. Bowers, *Jefferson and Hamilton* (1925) vividly portrays the conflicts between the two great statesmen.

L. M. Sears, *George Washington and the French Revolution* (1960), and Paul A. Varg, *The Foreign Policy of the Founding Fathers* (1963), set the stage for the diplomatic conflicts of the era. E. P. Link, *Democratic-Republican Societies, 1790–1800* (1942), and Harry Ammon, *The Genet Mission* (1973), trace the increasingly bitter domestic results. Two exhaustive studies of important treaties are Samuel F. Bemis, *Jay's Treaty* (1923), and *Pinckney's Treaty* (1960).

The literature on the first party system is ample and interesting. Richard Hofstader, *The Idea of a Party System* (1969), is a wide-ranging and insightful overview. Joseph Charles, *The Origins of the American Party System* (1956), and W. N. Chambers, *Political Parties in a New Nation* (1963), offer more detailed accounts. Morton Borden, *Parties and Politics* (1967), is short and perceptive. Noble Cunningham, *The Jeffersonian Republicans* (1957), discusses party organization, while Alfred F. Young, *The Democratic Republicans of New York* (1967), and Paul Goodman, *The Democratic Republicans of Mas-*

sachusetts (1964), are excellent discussions of state politics. For studies of the second president, see Stephen Kurtz, *The Presidency of John Adams* (1957), and Peter Shaw, *The Character of John Adams* (1976). Leonard W. Levy, *Legacy of Suppression* (1960), and J. M. Smith, *Freedom's Fetters* deal with the political and constitutional issues raised by the Alien and Sedition Acts.

Westward Expansion

Ray Allen Billington provides a general overview in *Westward Expansion* (1964), while F. S. Philbrick, *The Rise of the West, 1754–1830* (1964) is more detailed. Malcolm J. Rohrbough, *The Land Office Business* (1968), discusses the disposal of public lands in the West, and his *The Trans-Appalachian Frontier* (1975) provides a general analysis of social and political change. George Rogers Taylor, *The Transportation Revolution, 1815–1860* (1951), graphically portrays the limitations of the preindustrial transportation system, as does L. D. Baldwin, *The Keelboat Age on Western Waters* (1941). Nathan Miller, *The Enterprise of a Free People* (1962), and Richard Ellis, *Farmers and Landlords* (1958), examine the development of upstate New York during this period.

Reginald Horsman, *Expansion and American Indian Policy, 1783–1812* (1967) and *The Frontier in the Formative Years* (1970) are excellent surveys of military conflicts between whites and native Americans. The assault on Indian culture is described by Bernard W. Sheehan, *Seeds of Extinction* (1973). An interesting interpretation of the formation of American national identity in terms of these conflicts is Richard Slotkin, *Regeneration through Violence: The Mythology of the American Frontier* (1973). For the native American perspective, see A. F. C. Wallace, *The Death and Rebirth of the Seneca* (1970), and Glenn Tucker, *Tecumseh: Vision of Glory* (1956).

The Republicans in Power

Marshall Smelser, *The Democratic Republic, 1801–1815* (1968), surveys the period in some depth, while John R. Howe, *From the Revolution to the Age of Jackson* (1973), has a briefer treatment. Dumas Malone, *Jefferson the President* (2 vols., 1970 and 1974), is a masterful treatment, and Leonard D. White, *The Jeffersonians* (1951), outlines Republican administrative innovations. Raymond Waters, Jr., *Albert Gallatin* (1957), is a good study of the Jeffersonian financial wizard. Adrienne

Koch, *The Philosophy of Thomas Jefferson* (1943), and Merrill D. Peterson, *The Jeffersonian Image in the American Mind* (1960), study the creation and influence of Jefferson's political philosophy.

E. W. Lyon, *Louisiana in French Diplomacy, 1759–1804* (1934), and A. P. Whitaker, *The Mississippi Question* (1934), treat the background of the Louisiana Purchase. Bernard De Voto, ed., *The Journals of Lewis and Clark* (1953), and Donald Jackson, *The Letters of the Lewis and Clark Expedition* (1963), convey the difficulties and excitement of the great expedition. For Aaron Burr, see the contrasting interpretations presented by Nathan Schachner, *Aaron Burr* (1937), and Thomas P. Abernethy, *The Burr Conspiracy* (1954). Another account is Gore Vidal, *Burr*.

Bradford Perkins, *Prologue to War* (1961), explains the international roots of the crisis at sea, as does A. L. Burt, *The United States, Great Britain, and British North America* (1940). Jefferson's naval policy is treated in R. W. Irwin, *Diplomatic Relations of the United States and the Barbary Pirates* (1931), and his attempt at commercial coercion in L. M. Sears, *Jefferson and the Embargo* (1927). For Madison, see Irving Brant, *James Madison: Secretary of State* (1953), and Ralph Ketcham, *James Madison* (1971). Julius W. Pratt, *The Expansionists of 1812* (1925), stresses western and southern agitation for war; Reginald Horsman, *The Causes of the War of 1812* (1962), presents the case for impressment and neutral rights; and R. H. Brown, *The Republic in Peril: 1812* (1964), emphasizes the defense of national honor and republican institutions.

F. F. Beirne, *The War of 1812* (1949), and H. L. Coles, *The War of 1812* (1965), deal with military events, while S. F. Bemis, *John Quincy Adams and the Foundations of American Foreign Policy* (1949), and Bradford Perkins, *Castlereagh and Adams* (1964), cover the peace negotiations. See also Fred L. Engleman, *The Peace of Christmas Eve* (1962). A lively and perceptive analysis of the Battle of New Orleans appears in John William Ward, *Andrew Jackson: Symbol for an Age* (1963). James M. Banner, *To the Hartford Convention* (1970), examines the decline of the Federalists. Other good studies of Federalists and their policies include David H. Fischer, *The Revolution of American Conservatism: The Federalist Party in the Era of Jeffersonian Democracy* (1965); S. E. Morison, *Harrison Gray Otis* (1969); and Shaw Livermore, *Twilight of Federalism* (1962).

9

A MATURE PREINDUSTRIAL SOCIETY

By the 1820s, whites had lived in North America for two hundred years. The population of the newly independent United States had grown to 9.6 million. By most standards of the preindustrial world, American society represented a remarkable achievement. Its people lived free of an arbitrary government that imposed high taxes and of a clergy that inflicted rigid dogmas. A majority of its white citizens lived in tightly knit families and enjoyed economic security in a pleasant and bountiful natural environment. "Of the twenty millions of people in France," Thomas Jefferson remarked while serving as American minister in Paris, "there are nineteen million more wretched, more accursed in every circumstance of human existence than the most conspicuously wretched individual of the whole United States."

Like most whites, Jefferson ignored the plight of black Americans, who lived in slavery. By 1820, those of African descent numbered 1.8 million, nearly 20 percent of the population. He also forgot about hundreds of thousands of native Americans who lived on the geographic and social fringes of the United States. The presence of Afro-Americans and Indians made America very different from the nations of Europe. After two centuries of war and slavery, white Americans lived as a "master race," with substantial control over blacks and Indians. Future relations among

the three races remained unclear. "Next to the case of the black race within our bosom," James Madison remarked as he left the presidency in 1816, "that of the red race on our borders is the problem most baffling to the policy of our country."

Two centuries of white population growth and cultural development also produced an increasingly diverse and complex social order. By the early nineteenth century, white Americans had created three distinct regional cultures— southern, New England, and Middle Atlantic. Whites also belonged to various religious cultures, and each sect or denomination had its own set of beliefs and rituals. Some religions drew most of their members from a certain region, as did New England Congregationalism. Others had strong ethnic or class identities. These social identities of region and religion— and of class—shaped the character of the emerging system of American education.

In addition to race and social identity, a set of economic and legal institutions affected the lives and behavior of the American people. Beginning with the War of Independence, merchant capitalists financed the expansion of domestic manufacturing. Thousands of men and women shifted their economic energies from farming to handicraft production. Americans in all occupations also participated more intensively in the market economy. Between 1790 and 1820, state governments assisted the emergence of this mature pre-industrial economy through financial subsidies and innovative legislation. Diversity and complexity—in racial composition, cultural life, and economic affairs—characterized American life as the preindustrial era ended in the 1820s.

The Subject Races

Between 1776 and 1820, white Americans used the power of the state and national governments to establish new racial policies. These legal rules and cultural norms shaped racial interaction until the Civil War broke out in 1861. In the South, whites expanded slavery; in the North, they freed blacks but confined them to socially inferior positions. In the West, migrating farmers and government policies exerted increasing pressure on the native American tribes. Missionaries tried to convert the Indians to Christianity and destroy their tribal identities. Native Americans and Afro-Americans both resisted white domination. They created cultures that reflected white values but retained a distinct character of their own.

The Fate of the Native Americans

European civilizations colonized much of the world during the nineteenth century. In Africa, the Americas, Asia, and Australia they used military power to crush resistance by tribal peoples and seize their lands. The Indians of North America were among the first to suffer this fate. Following the War of Independence, white Americans determinedly pushed hundreds of native American tribes westward or confined them to small eastern reservations.

To justify these policies, whites condemned the Indian way of life and glorified their own. "The savage must ever recede before the man of civilization," proclaimed one southerner. "The square mile which furnished game to a single family of hunters, will support a thousand families by agriculture and the mechanic arts." For many educated whites, the conquest of the vast American West represented a repetition of the historical evolution of mankind—replacing primitive savagery with higher cultural forms. As the

Appropriations Committee of the House of Representatives bluntly declared in 1818, "those sons of the forest should be moralized or exterminated."

Government officials translated these intellectual assumptions into specific policies. Their goal was the destruction of the traditional native American social order. In 1785, for example, Secretary of War Henry Knox urged the breakup of commonly owned tribal lands. Reflecting his European cultural heritage, Knox advocated the distribution of farming plots to individual Indian families as their private property.

In the early nineteenth century, white leaders attacked the political integrity of the tribes. They demanded that Indians abandon political allegiance to tribal governments and submit to the jurisdiction of state and national laws. In 1819, to encourage native Americans to accept such white institutions, Congress established an annual Civilization Fund of ten thousand dollars. Public officials welcomed the efforts of religious missionaries to change Indian values. A Kentucky preacher, Isaac McCoy, explained that his goal was to make the Indian "a farmer, a citizen of the United States, and a Christian."

If the goal was clear, the process was not. Ministers from Quaker, Congregationalist, and Presbyterian churches generally argued that civilization must precede Christianity. They knew their religious teachings represented a distinct world view and were intellectually demanding. Therefore, they argued that Indians would understand the Christian gospel only after adopting white social customs and agricultural methods. Evangelical preachers, many of them from Moravian, Baptist, and Methodist churches, thought God's word had greater power. They believed the Christian message itself would "be the most successful means of civilizing" the Indians. Actually, the missionaries challenged the entire native American way of life, material as well as spiritual. As one missionary remarked, he had been "entirely unable to separate religion and civilization" and therefore spread "Christian civilization."

Few tribes accepted this viewpoint peacefully. Politically independent tribes expelled white missionaries and forced Christianized Indians to practice traditional rites. To justify their values, Indian leaders devised theories of cultural and religious dualism. They argued that the Great

A CHIEF'S UNDERSTANDING OF RELIGION

Seneca Chief Red Jacket rejects the primacy of Christianity and endorses religious dualism, 1805.

Brother: Continue to listen. You say that you are sent to instruct us how to worship the Great Spirit agreeably to his mind; and, if we do not take hold of the religion which you white people teach, we shall be unhappy hereafter. You say that you are right, and we are lost. How do we know this to be true? We understand that your religion is written in a book. If it was intended for us as well as you, why has not the Great Spirit given to us, and not only to us, but why did He not give to our forefathers, the knowledge of the book, with the means of understanding it rightly? . . .

Brother: The Great Spirit has made us all, but he has made a great difference between his white and red children. He has given us different complexions and different customs. To you He has given the arts. To these He has not opened our eyes. We know these things to be true. Since He has made a great difference between us in other things, why may we not conclude that He has given us different religion according to our understanding? The Great Spirit does right. He knows what is best for his children; we are satisfied.

Spirit made the two races different and intended them to follow distinct ways of life. Nevertheless, missionary pressure and military defeat undermined tribal solidarity. Many tribes split into hostile religious factions. Among the Seneca of New York, for example, the prophet Handsome Lake persuaded his followers to combine Christian precepts with traditional beliefs. Led by Red Jacket, a more conservative group of Seneca remained loyal to the old animistic agricultural ceremonies—the green-corn dance, the strawberry festival, and the false-face pageant.

Even Christianized Indians clung tenaciously to the central core of their tribal identity. They continued to view themselves as members of a clan, the basic unit of native American society. They paid reverence to the totem animal—a deer, turtle, fox, or bear—that was the symbol and mythical founder of the clan. They also gave new Christian identities to familiar clan spirits.

Strong clan loyalties likewise prevented missionaries from introducing European agricultural methods. White farm families lived according to a set of male-dominated cultural values relating to sex roles, property rights, and marriage rules. Many eastern tribes depended on hoe agriculture, conducted by women, for their basic food supply and had very different social values. In these tribes—the Iroquois, Delaware, Creek, and many others—individuals took their identity from their mother's clan. The right to cultivate or hunt on certain lands passed from mother to daughter. A boy did not receive property rights from his father, but through his female relatives—from the clan of his mother or his wife. This matrilineal inheritance system reflected the economic importance of women, who provided corn, squash, beans, and other basic foods.

As in all societies, those who controlled the economic resources commanded social respect and personal power. To preserve their authority, Indian women resisted the missionaries' attempts to dislodge them from the corn and squash fields. For their own reasons, few native American males wished to be farmers. They preferred manly roles as hunters and warriors. Clan leaders likeswise opposed the European custom of male-led families owning separate farmsteads. This system of property rights would undermine their authority to allocate use-rights on tribal lands and to mediate clan disputes. Moreover, the elaborate system of native American marriage rules depended on clan identity. It strictly prohibited sexual relations between members of the same clan. To accept white family values would be to repudiate clan identity and the essence of Indian life.

The great disparity between the native American and European social systems discouraged cultural assimilation. Indians adopted white ways only under special circumstances. The Cherokee tribes of Georgia and the Carolinas, for example, fought the advancing white settlers throughout the eighteenth century. This military effort resulted in an unusually centralized political system. By 1794, the Cherokee had established a national council headed by two prominent chiefs. Unlike the clans, the traditional political units of Indian society, the council oversaw certain activities of all thirteen thousand members of the tribe. By 1808, the national council maintained a mounted police force and had assumed some of the order-keeping responsibilities of the clans. Two years later, the council abolished clan revenge for murder and established a limited patrilineal inheritance system.

A small faction of Christian Cherokee mixed-bloods devised most of these innovations. The majority of mixed-bloods were the offspring of white fur traders and Indian women. Growing up in a bicultural world, they learned the language and political ways of the dominant white Americans. When whites attempted to oust the Cherokee from their ancestral lands from 1806 to 1809 and from 1817 to 1819, Christian mixed-bloods promoted the creation of a strong tribal identity. Sequoyah, a well-educated mixed-blood, designed a written script for the Cherokee language in 1821, and the tribe began to publish a newspaper. In 1827, the Cherokee introduced a new charter of tribal government modeled directly on the United States Constitution. By this time, many mixed-bloods had abandoned their traditional tribal ways. They dressed, thought, and behaved much like white planters. James Vann, a Georgia Cherokee, owned more than twenty black slaves, two trading posts, a grist mill, and a ferry. By the early 1830s, forty-two prominent mixed-blood Cherokee families held a total of 1,013 slaves. At least one member of each of these families could read both the English and Cherokee languages.

Caught between two cultures, Christianized mixed-bloods were fully accepted by neither.

THE "CIVILIZED" CHEROKEE
Mixed-blood Cherokee adopted many white ways. In 1821, Sequoyah invented a written script for the Cherokee language. The tribe's newspaper was printed in both Cherokee and English. Few full-blooded Cherokee could read either language; they retained their ancestral customs and traditional oral culture. (Thomas McKenney. *Se-Quo-Yah*. Philadelphia Museum of Art. Gift of Miss Willian Adger)

Whites wanted to push them westward, and full-blooded Cherokee condemned their economic values and cultural innovations. Full-bloods seized political power in communities in the Great Smoky Mountains, where they made up about 90 percent of the people, and gradually took control of the national council. They strongly preferred the culture and religious values of their ancestors to those of the whites. Like most native Americans west of the Appalachians, the full-bloods wanted to remain on their lands. "We would not receive money for land in which our father and friends are buried," a Creek chief declared. "We love our land; it is our mother." In the coming decades, full-blooded Creek and Cherokee and members of most other tribes resisted both cultural assimilation and forced removal.

The Expansion of Slavery

By 1820, there were about 250,000 free blacks in the United States, 13 percent of the Afro-American population. In the northern states, blacks took advantage of their freedom to create a variety of institutions. Led by the Reverend Richard Allen, Philadelphia blacks established an independent Christian sect, the African Methodist Episcopal church, in 1794. AME churches soon appeared in all northern cities, along with black schools, mutual assistance societies, and fraternal clubs. Free blacks in the South lived a more precarious existence, because they always faced the threat of reenslavement. They congregated in such organizations as the Charleston Brown Fellowship Society, a group composed of people of mixed ancestry. Relatively few free blacks moved to the West, where white settlers passed restrictive laws to deter such migration. "The natural difference between them and ourselves," an Illinois state senator declared in 1827, "forbids the idea that they should ever be permitted to participate with us in the political affairs of our government."

The institution of slavery remained strong as well. To make up for their losses during the War of Independence, rice planters in Georgia and South Carolina quickly reestablished the trade in African slaves. As a result of their political power, the Constitution exempted this trade from control for twenty years. When the time limit expired in 1808, northern antislavery reformers persuaded Congress to ban the importation of slaves. By then, planters in the lower South had purchased 250,000 new Africans, a number equal to all slave importations during the entire colonial period. Furthermore, even under the oppressive conditions of slavery, more blacks were born each year than died. Between 1775 and 1820, the black population grew from 0.5 million to 1.8 million. Two-thirds of this remarkable increase resulted from reproduction rather than importation.

By 1820, forced internal migration represented a new threat to black families and communities. After the Revolution, the Chesapeake tobacco industry stagnated. Tobacco production did not reach levels of the 1770s until the 1820s, when cultivation expanded into North Carolina, Kentucky, and Tennessee. Searching for new economic opportunities, hundreds—and then thousands—of white planters migrated to cotton-growing lands in the Southwest. Alabama entered the Union in 1817 and Mississippi followed in 1819.

INTERNAL SLAVE TRADE
Mounted white traders escort a convoy of slaves from Virginia to Tennessee. "I am Sold to a man by the name of Peterson a trader," lamented one Georgia slave, "My Dear wife for you and my Children my pen cannot Express the griffe I feel to be parted from you all. . . . if we Shall not meet in this world I hope to meet in heaven." (Lewis Miller. *Slave Trader, Sold to Tennessee.* Abby Aldrich Rockefeller Folk Art Center, Williamsburg, Va. Gift of Dr. and Mrs. Richard M. Kain in memory of George Hay Kain)

In the boom year of 1818, a government land office in Huntsville, Alabama, took in $7 million. The expression "doing a land office business" soon entered the American language as a metaphor for fantastic expansion and commercial activity. Its meaning for blacks was more ominous because migrating whites forced some or all of their slaves to move with them. Blacks soon formed half the populations of the southwestern states. Before this migration ended, whites moved more than 835,000 slaves from their American birthplaces to the booming cotton belt. By 1850, about 75 percent of the slaves in the United States labored on the new cotton plantations.

The population history of the Cedar Vale estate in Virginia graphically illustrates the effects of white plantation-building on black life. Between 1815 and 1835, John Cowper Cahoon, Jr., created a labor force at Cedar Vale. He purchased twenty-eight slaves from twelve owners, forcibly separating the men and women from their families. The blacks bore and raised a new generation of workers on Cahoon's estate. This second Cedar Vale generation, in turn, formed new families, but then the splintering process began again.

Like most white planters, Cahoon gave some slaves to his sons and daughters as part of their marriage settlements. He sold others to pay debts. The results were equally tragic for the blacks. Transported to new plantations by Cahoon's children or through sale, the Cedar Vale slaves had to begin life anew under oppressive conditions. Laboring "from day clean to first dark" on frontier plantations, they slowly rebuilt their shattered personal lives and emotional ties.

The expansion of slavery destroyed the hopes of antislavery advocates. Both northern and southern whites supported the American Colonization Society, founded in 1817. This organization worked not only to end slavery, but also to remove blacks from the United States. By arranging for the immediate transportation of freed blacks to Africa, the society hoped to encourage voluntary manumission. Few white planters responded, however, because they could sell their slaves at increasingly higher prices. Many northern blacks opposed the society as well. They wanted to gain equal rights and social dignity in the land of their birth. By 1830, the society had settled only a few thousand freed men and women in its newly created African republic of Liberia.

In the North, antislavery reformers shifted their emphasis. They reluctantly accepted the reality of slavery in the South but sought to end the illegal importation of new slaves from Africa. At their urging, many northern states passed "personal liberty" laws. These laws protected free blacks from being kidnapped or illegally seized under the terms of the Fugitive Slave Act of 1793.

Most significant of all, reformers urged northern politicians to oppose the territorial extension of slavery. During the 1810s, Louisiana, Mississippi, and Alabama joined the Union with state constitutions permitting slavery. When Missouri applied for admission on a similar basis in 1819, antislavery forces seized the political initiative. Congressman James Tallmadge of New York proposed a ban on the importation of slaves into Missouri and the gradual emancipation of its black inhabitants. Missouri rejected these conditions, and the northern majority in the House of Representatives blocked its admission to the Union. In response, southerners used their power in the Senate, which was equally divided between thirteen free and thirteen slave states, to refuse statehood to Maine. Tempers frayed in the heat of debate. "You have kindled a fire which all the waters of the ocean cannot put out," Senator Thomas W. Cobb of Georgia warned Tallmadge, and "which seas of blood can only extinguish."

After two years of controversy, Congress finally resolved the stalemate. Representative Henry Clay of Kentucky and other skilled politicians devised a series of agreements known collectively as the Missouri Compromise. Maine entered the Union as a free state in 1820, and Missouri followed as a slave state in 1821. This bargain preserved the existing sectional balance in the Senate and set a precedent for future admissions of states. To mollify anti-slavery sentiment in the House of Representatives, southern congressmen agreed to the territorial restriction of slavery. The Missouri Compromise prohibited slavery in the Louisiana Territory north of latitude 36° 30', the southern boundary of Missouri, while permitting it south of that line.

This pragmatic compromise continued the

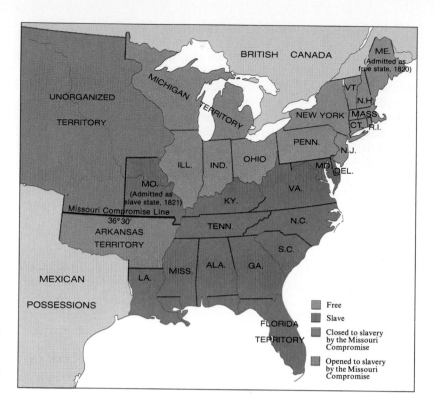

MAP 9.1 THE MISSOURI COMPROMISE
The Missouri Compromise Line resolved the issue of slavery in the territory of the Louisiana Purchase until the 1850s. Slavery was forbidden north of the line, with the exception of the state of Missouri. To maintain an equal number of free and slave states in the U.S. Senate, the compromise also provided for the nearly simultaneous admission of Maine and Missouri.

tradition begun at the Philadelphia Constitutional Convention. In 1821, as in 1787, northern and southern political leaders gave highest priority to the Union. They found complex but workable ways to reach agreement on the different economic interests and moral principles of their societies. However, new and more difficult political tensions arose continually. The Philadelphia delegates resolved their sectional differences in two months; Congress took two years to work out the Missouri Compromise. Americans now realized that future power in the national government would depend on the westward movement of the competing systems of free and slave labor. The fate of the West, of the Union, and of the black race were inextricably intertwined.

Afro-American Society and Culture

Two events encouraged the development of a cohesive Afro-American culture in the United States. First, the end of the legal slave trade in 1808 reduced the flow of imports to a trickle. As a result, African practices and beliefs gradually diminished as important aspects of black life.

Second, the westward movement diminished regional differences within the slave culture. As Afro-Americans from the Chesapeake region and the Carolinas mingled in the southwestern states, they created a more unified culture. For example, the black Gullah dialect of the Carolinas gradually faded away in the cotton belt because slaves born in the Chesapeake preferred to use English.

This new Afro-American culture contained many elements of African origin. As the traveler Isaac Holmes reported in 1821.

> In Louisiana, and the state of Mississippi, the slaves . . . dance for several hours during Sunday afternoon. The general movement is in what they call the Congo dance; their music often consists of nothing more than an excavated piece of wood . . . one end of which is a piece of parchment.

Similar descriptions of blacks who "danced the Congo and sang a purely African song to the accompaniment of . . . a drum made by stretching a skin over a flour barrell" appeared as late as 1890. Some slaves also followed West African models in building their rude wooden cabins. They designed the structures in an "I" shape, with rooms one after another from front to back. In contrast, most European dwellings extended sideways, with two rooms in the front.

African customs probably led to black incest taboos in America as well. Even on relatively self-contained plantations, slaves shunned marriages between cousins. About 175 slave children were born on the Good Hope Plantation in South Carolina between 1800 and 1857. Forty percent of the infants were related by blood to three slaves from Africa who helped establish this black community and who were still alive in 1857. Despite the elaborate tangle of kinship, only one marriage between cousins took place during this period. Cultural norms among white South Carolina slaveowners were quite different. Many of their sons and daughters married cousins. They did so in order to keep inherited property within an extended family and to maintain an intermarried ruling elite.

Masters and slaves also had distinct marriage ceremonies. Whites insisted on legally binding marriage contracts among themselves, both to regulate morals and to establish the ownership of property. But slaveowners denied legal marriage to blacks. They wanted to be able to sell their slaves without breaking a marriage bond. A concern for property rights overrode their moral principles.

To sanctify their sexual unions and to affirm them before the community, slaves devised their own marriage rituals. Young men and women asked their parents' consent to marry. Then they sought their owner's permission to have a wedding ceremony and to live together in a separate cabin. Following African custom, many couples signified their union by jumping over a broomstick together on this public occasion. If their owners permitted, Christian brides and grooms had a religious ceremony performed by a white or black preacher. Unlike the exchange of vows among whites, these rites never ended with the phrase "Till death do you part." Everyone knew that the sale of slaves regularly disrupted black marriages.

After marriage, most slave couples who were not separated by sale lived in stable sexual unions. On the Good Hope Plantation in South Carolina, about 70 percent of the black mothers had all their children in a stable married union. Most other mothers had their first child with one man, a so-called "outside" birth before marriage. Then they bore all their other children with their husbands. Likewise, 40 percent of the women on the large Stirling sugar plantation in Louisiana had all their children with one man. Yet black family life was less stable there, probably because heavy work in the sugarfields took the lives of many men. Thirty percent of the adult slave women on the Stirling plantation lived alone, raising their children of several fathers.

The oppressive conditions of slavery thus partially undermined black efforts to create a satisfying family life. Yet slaves struggled constantly to control their own lives. A few gave their children names with African roots, such as Cuffee, to denote a male born on Friday. The majority of slaves chose names of British origin but did so with great care. Many free Afro-America mothers named one of their daughters

A SYMBOL OF SLAVERY—AND FREEDOM
The prominent scar on the forehead of this black woman, widely known as "Mumbet," symbolized the cruelty of slavery. When she won emancipation through a court suit, she chose a name befitting her new legal status: Elizabeth Freeman. (Artist Unknown. *Elizabeth Freeman [Mumbet].* Massachusetts Historical Society)

TABLE 9.1 AFRO-AMERICAN NAMING PATTERNS

Good Hope Plantation Slaves Orangebury, South Carolina			
Date of Birth	Baby's Name	Parents' Names	Source of Baby's Name
1793	Hector	Bess, Hector	Father
1806	Clarinda	Patty, Primus	Mother's mother
1811	Sambo	Affy, Jacob	Mother's father
1813	Primus	Patty, Primus	Father
1824	Sarah	Phoebe, Jack	Mother's mother
1828	Major	Clarinda, Abram	Father's father

after themselves. Like many whites, they wished to establish a symbolic tie between the generations. Few slave mothers made such a choice, however. The law decreed that slave status passed through the mother's womb, irrespective of the legal status of the father. The refusal of slave women to give their first names to their daughters thus had a wider significance. It was their way of protesting against the legal doctrine of uterine descent. Slave men followed the opposite strategy. Because whites refused to acknowledge the blacks' legal status as fathers, many enslaved black males named their sons after themselves.

These symbolic gestures by blacks were small but important. By naming children after fathers, aunts, uncles, and cousins, slaves gave cultural significance to the biological ties of kinship. Like the establishment of incest rules and marriage ceremonies, the naming patterns created order in a harsh, arbitrary world.

The creation of a black cultural community gradually improved the quality of slave life. During the eighteenth century, the diverse tribal origins and languages of African-born slaves slowed the creation of a cohesive black society with strong family ties. White males exploited unattached African women. Their raping of female slaves resulted in a significant mulatto population. Some white fathers freed their mulatto offspring, but most of these mulattoes remained slaves and married black men and women. Each generation of Afro-American marriages broadened the genetic impact of the first racial intermixture. More than a third of the nine thousand Mississippi blacks who registered their slave marriages after the Civil War acknowledged ancestry containing some degree of intermixture. Their family histories stood as graphic testimony to the brutal nature of eighteenth century slavery.

After 1800, sexual exploitation and other forms of physical violence against blacks decreased. Following the Revolution, political leaders condemned forced miscegnation as an aristocratic vice, ill suited to life in a republican society. The increasing importance of Christian pietism also prompted many whites to free their slaves or treat them more humanely. In addition, the end of the African slave trade caused planters to act differently. They now promoted the growth of black families—to increase the supply of workers—and used incentives of food and housing to increase output. Public opinion in the North helped lessen the number of whippings, beatings, and rapes. Slavery was no longer a national institution or even a morally defensible one. "The moral power of the world is against us," Congressman Francis W. Pickens of South Carolina admitted in the early 1830s. "It is idle to disguise it."

Leading southern planters attempted to reform their own society. As gentlemen of wealth and status, they turned their backs on the greediness and brutality of their past. Through state legislation, the planter elite revised the legal basis of slave discipline. New laws forbade the castration of slaves and made masters responsible for the mistreatment or death of their blacks. Only a few owners were ever prosecuted under these statutes, but the laws proclaimed a new code of social conduct. Equally important, they signified a decline in legally approved violence against blacks. The number of slaves legally executed for rebellion, arson, murder, or other crimes dropped significantly. They averaged twelve a year in Virginia between 1780 and 1815, but only six a year thereafter in the equally populous state of South Carolina.

As leading white slaveowners altered their values and behavior, they evolved a new conception of blacks. In the eighteenth century, planters referred to imported Africans as "pagans," "savages," or "beasts". Now they had owned Afro-American slave families for decades, or even generations. As a result, many male slaveowners began to depict themselves as the "fathers" of their dependent black "children." George Tucker's novel *The Valley of the Shenandoah* (1824) offered the first prominent literary expression of slaveowners as the paternalistic guardians of their black laborers.

Afro-Americans themselves played a significant role in the evolution of slavery from a tyrannical to a supposedly paternalist system. By creating stable families and coherent cultural communities, they placed themselves in a position to bargain successfully with their owners for various rights. In 1811, David Ross of Oxford, Virginia, advertised his iron works for lease. He informed prospective purchasers that "the male Laborers are all allowed a double Quantity of Bread and an equal quantity of meat as the Common rations allowed to a Soldier or Sailor." When the threat of bankruptcy loomed two years later, Ross complained that his slaves considered these ample rations "as their legal right" and refused to accept a reduction. "How does it happen," he asked, "that we are servants of servants, disgraced, involved in distress? Our ruin is that the labourers do not labor."

Blacks in the lowlands of South Carolina likewise gained some control over their working lives. During the eighteenth century, slaves had persuaded their masters to accept a "task" system. Each day, a slave had to complete a precisely defined task—turning up a quarter acre of rice land, hoeing a half acre, or pounding seven mortars of rice. "Once a slave has completed his task," an observer noted in 1806, "his master feels no right to call upon him." Often finishing their task "by one or two o'clock in the afternoon," a Methodist preacher reported, slaves

> have the rest of the day for themselves, which they spend in working in their own private fields, consisting of 5 or 6 acres of ground . . . planting rice, corn, potatoes, tobacco &c. for their own use and profit.

Afro-Americans jealously guarded these hard-won rights. "Should any owner increase the work beyond what is customary," a South Carolina planter admitted, "he subjects himself . . . to such discontent amongst his slaves as to make

them of but little use to him." Like iron producer David Ross in Virginia, these planters had the legal power of tyrants; they could use brutal punishment to extract more labor from their slaves. But most nineteenth century slaveowners chose not to do so. They now confronted an interrelated slave community that stubbornly resisted new demands or arbitrary orders. Like Ross, they adopted a more paternalistic approach. The result, on the whole, was a more flexible and humane slave system.

Although paternalism introduced humanity into slavery, it did not fundamentally alter the distribution of power. Whites still controlled all the economic resources and remained in political command. Moreover, southern planters turned paternalism to their own advantage. Beginning in the 1830s, they began to justify slavery not as a "necessary evil" but as a "positive good." They pictured themselves as benevolent masters ruling inherently inferior slaves. "The Negro races stand at the lowest point in the scale of human beings," wrote one southerner, "and we know no moral or physical agencies which can redeem them from their degradation." The racist doctrine of genetic inferiority had always lurked in the shadows of American slavery. Now it moved to center stage. This false doctrine would outlive the slave system and poison relations between whites and blacks well past the middle of the twentieth century.

Slaves resisted the new paternalism just as they had fought the old tyranny. Some blacks, such as Gabriel Prosser of Virginia, replied to white coercion by plotting mass uprisings and murders. Denmark Vesey, a free black married to a slave woman, planned a rebellion in Charleston, South Carolina, in 1822, only to have it discovered and crushed at the last moment. Nat Turner, a field slave, led a major revolt in Southampton County, Virginia in 1831. He led his followers on a murderous rampage that left fifty-five whites dead. Battles with local militiamen and federal troops took Turner's life and those of forty of his followers.

Most blacks realized that white military superiority ruled out a successful revolt for freedom. Flight was equally futile. Their African homeland was too far away, and the northern and western states were hotbeds of racial prejudice. Slaves had to build the best possible lives for themselves where they were. As the black abolitionist

LEMUEL HAYNES (1753–1833)
Born a slave in Massachusetts,
Haynes fought in the Revolutionary
War and was ordained as a
Congregational minister in 1785. He
served as minister of a predominately
white parish in Rutland, Vermont,
for thirty years. (*Rev. Lemuel Haynes
in the Pulpit.* Museum of Art, Rhode
Island School of Design, Gift of Miss
Lucy T. Aldrich)

Frederick Douglass wisely observed, slave communities were "pegged down to a single spot" and must "take root there or nowhere."

And so enslaved blacks developed a peasant-like culture. Like the poor peasants of Europe, they worked as dependent agricultural laborers. Also like European peasants, they built close-knit communities based on family, kinship, and religion. Next to the family, the Christian religious community gradually became the center of black life.

Slaves gave their own interpretation to the Protestant gospel. Black theology generally ignored the doctrines of original sin and predestination. It also paid little attention to the New Testament's view of God as a lawgiver and symbol of authority. Instead, most black Christians envisioned God as the liberating warrior of the Old Testament who saved his chosen people. "Their cause was similar to the 'Israelites'," Martin Prosser told his fellow slave conspirators during his brother Gabriel's thwarted rebellion in Virginia in 1800.

> I have read in my Bible where God says, if we worship him, we should have peace in all our land and five of you shall conquer a hundred, and a hundred of you a hundred-thousand of our enemies.

As the *Charleston Mercury* observed in 1831, "Slaves who profess to be followers of Christ are generally the most negligent in their duty and the most difficult to manage."

The Christian message promoted spiritual endurance as well as physical resistance. Many slaves identified with the persecuted Christ. They recalled that Christ had accepted torture and death so his followers might attain peace and justice in heaven. Amid the manifest injustice of their own world, these Afro-Americans used Christian principles to affirm their equality with whites in the eyes of God. Slaves thus accepted the names, language, and religion of their masters but adapted them for their own ends. Imprisoned in a bicultural world, they learned from whites but lived as blacks.

The Formation of Social Identity

Few Europeans migrated to the United States between 1775 and 1815. By the 1820s, therefore, nearly the entire white population had been born in the United States. American birth did not imply a common national identity, for the distinct regional cultures of the colonial period remained strong. To offset social diversity, state authorities strengthened the system of public education. Schools became important instruments for the creation of common cultural values as well as the transmission of knowledge. American Protestantism remained divided into scores of competing sects. However, institutional differences among the sects narrowed as legislators devised a new set of legal relationships between religious organizations and the political state. Diversity, not unity, was the central cultural reality in most aspects of life.

Regional Cultures

Generations of travelers had contrasted the racially and class-divided South with the more unified farming societies of New England and the Middle Atlantic regions. The national union of the states accentuated these regional distinctions. "When I was in Congress," Timothy Bloodworth of North Carolina recalled in 1789, "the Southern and Northern Interests divided at the Susquehanna River." During the 1790's, Charles Pinckney of South Carolina, the Federalist vice-presidential candidate and diplomat, called attention to regional "habits and manners," and these differences found vivid expression in popular speech. "Yankee," a foreign traveler learned, was "a name given derisively, or merely jestingly," to the residents of New England because of their sharp commercial practices. Moreover, "the name of 'Buckskin' is given to the inhabitants of Virginia, because their ancestors were hunters and sold buck, or rather deer skins."

European visitors agreed that these popular stereotypes reflected genuine cultural differences. In 1800, an Englishman detected an intense religious "fanaticism" in New England, but he also found "a great strain of industry among all ranks of people." Compared with the South, he thought "the lower order of citizens have a better education, are more intelligent, and better informed." This judgment mirrored those of earlier observers, who also perceived an unsettled way of life in the southern states. "The state of poverty in which a great number of white people live in Virginia" surprised the Marquis de Chastellux, an aristocratic French

military officer, in the 1780s. Other visitors commented on the rude manners and heavy drinking of white tenant farmers and small freeholders. Like the boisterous gentry class of the early eighteenth century, they had a "passion for gaming at the billiard table, a cock-fight or cards."

Actually, the rural culture of New England had high educational standards. The Puritan legacy included strong traditions of primary schooling and Bible reading. As a result, about 90 percent of the adult males and more than half the adult females in 1790 had at least a minimal ability to read and write. In Virginia, on the other hand, more than a third of the adult white males and most of the white women could not write their names. They signed legal documents, such as wills and marriage licenses, with an "X" or some other mark.

TOWN MEETING DEMOCRACY
Local democracy took a special form in New England. Town meetings disdained rule by "a mere majority." Instead, they often debated (and even fought) until an issue was settled "by a full and united consent of the whole." Their democratic tradition had a more collective character than the rough-and-tumble democratic politics of the Middle Atlantic region. (Library of Congress)

PURITAN CULTURE PERSISTS
Reflecting their cultural heritage, this prosperous New England couple wear plainly cut clothes and hold symbols of literacy—a book and a pen. The artist was their son. He shows his mother looking directly at him, suggesting a more personal relationship than with his stern-faced father, a traditional New England patriarch. (Old Sturbridge Village, Sturbridge Mass. [Henry E. Peach])

This disparity in literacy reflected different social values and financial priorities. In 1800, the four thousand white inhabitants of Essex County in Virginia spent about $1,000 for local government, including schooling and relief of the poor. That same year, the small township of Acton, Massachusetts, with only about nine hundred residents, spent $950 for local public purposes, including $550 on education alone. Migrants carried these educational traditions into the western territories and states. By the 1840s, New England settlers in Indiana had set up a broad system of public primary education. But they did so only after a bitter twenty-year battle with tax-shy yeoman migrants from the South.

Regional identity surfaced again in the observance of holidays. In Virginia and other states with an Anglican religious heritage, Christmas was an occasion for feasts and celebrations. However, the people of Puritan New England condemned these ceremonies as superstitious. Most New England churches did not celebrate the birth of Christ until the middle of the nineteenth century. They focused their festive energies on Thanksgiving Day, commemorating the trials and triumphs of the first Pilgrim and Puritan settlers. New England customs received national attention during the War of Independence, for Congress frequently declared days of fasting and thanksgiving. As with schooling, migration remained the prime path of cultural diffusion. As New England farmers moved westward across the Hudson River, they took their holidays with them. New York adopted an annual Thanksgiving Day in 1817, and other northern states followed suit.

Regional variety reflected the distinct historical experiences of Americans living in certain geographic areas. By 1820 in New England, many men and women could trace their American roots back six or seven generations. Their communities—and the region itself—overflowed with kinfolk. The Lynn, Massachusetts, *Directory* of 1830 listed 281 members of the Newhall family as residents of the town. There were also 259 Breeds, 195 Alleys, and 162 Johnsons. A list of only twelve family names covered a total of 1,660 persons and comprised 27 percent of the town's population.

Geography alone did not produce a unified regional culture. In Pennsylvania and the other Middle Atlantic states, each migrant group retained its own cultural characteristics. Quakers, Germans, Scotch-Irish, and, to a lesser extent, Dutch married within their own ethnic group. Citizens of German ancestry maintained their language as well as their customs in small agricultural villages from Pennsylvania to North Carolina. "The inhabitants are practically all German," a visitor to Hanover, Maryland, noted in the early nineteenth century. "Habits, speech, newspapers, cooking—all German." Even more strikingly, "by dress and way of life," he identified the residents of nearby Frederick Town "as Germans of the 16th century. Old women, with coifs tied under their chins, wear on top of them large white hats without crowns like huge flat plates. The men have long wide linen trousers." In the Lutheran church in Frederick Town, German remained the language for church services, Sunday school instruction, and record keeping until 1820.

Ethnic clannishness hindered the development of a cohesive Middle Atlantic culture. From a wider perspective, the distinct customs of each region inhibited the development of an American national identity. In most ways of life, the people of New England, the South, and the Middle Atlantic states followed the traditional ways of their ancestors. Only certain events, such as national elections and wars, reminded people that they were citizens of the United States. Thus, the term "Uncle Sam" came into use during the War of 1812. "This cant name for our government has got almost as common as John Bull" for the British, a newspaper in Troy, New York, explained. "The letters U.S. on government waggons &c are supposed to have given rise to it."

In an essay called "The Significance of the West In American History" (1893), the historian Frederick Jackson Turner suggested that a national identity developed first in the western territories and states. He assumed that western migrants gave prime allegiance to the national government, since it created these political units,

Frontier zones by 1810
Directions of cultural diffusion
Cultural core (pre-1725)
Secondary area (1740-1775)
Tertiary area (1780-1820)

0   100   200   300
Miles

(After Mitchell)

Southern New England

Southeastern Pennsylvania

Chesapeake

South Carolina Coast

MAP 9.2 THE TRANSPLANTATION OF REGIONAL CULTURES
By 1725, four distinct cultures had developed along the Atlantic coast, ranging from homogeneous Puritan New England to the racially divided plantation society of South Carolina. Beginning in the 1740s, migrants from the ethnically diverse Middle Colonies and from the Chesapeake region moved into the backcountry. Then, between 1780 and 1820, settlers carried all four regional cultures into different areas west of the Applachians. Extensive cultural intermixture—and conflict— occurred only in southern Ohio and in Kentucky and Tennessee.

and that the frontier experience created a common "American" character. Turner underestimated the force of regional self-interest and of cultural tradition. When 176 residents of Granville, Massachusetts, decided to move west, they carefully selected a site in Ohio whose "peculiar blending of hill and valley" resembled the landscape of their New England community. They transplanted their Congregational church, complete with minister and elders, as well as their system of freehold agriculture. Throughout the region west of the Appalachians, most migrants reproduced the eastern or southern communities from which they had come.

Subsequently, the settlers' lives revolved primarily around the affairs of their new western region, not those of the nation as a whole. When Jedidiah Morse published his *American Geography* in 1793, he listed three "grand divisions of the United States"—northern, middle, and southern. A new edition appeared in 1819, and Morse added "Western States and Territories" as a separate section with a distinct character and interest of its own.

The sources of national identity and common cultural values lay elsewhere—in cities and elite social and political groups. An analysis of the images carved on gravestones shows how urban ideas and cultural styles achieved wide circulation. In the early eighteenth century, many New England gravestones presented graphic images of distress, such as skulls with blank eyes and grinning faces. These images expressed the Puritans' fascination with the inevitability of death and the prospect of eternal damnation. Beginning in the 1730s, tombstone carvers in urban seaports copied images of death that were fashionable among the English upper classes. They inscribed stones with optimistic symbols of resurrection and salvation, such as winged cherubs. This new visual representation of death spread slowly along the routes of commerce. Carvers in river valleys copied the imported "high style" form. Then craftsmen from neighboring towns brought the new style to outlying settlements.

In the 1790s, a new death image quickly achieved wide use, reflecting the increasing speed of commerce and communication. Wealthy merchants in American port cities again copied English fashions. They ordered gravestones inscribed with a willow tree overhanging an urn on a pedestal. This image represented a sentimental lament about the tragedy of death. By the 1820s, this new image could be seen in graveyards in all major inland cities. The carvings even appeared in a small cluster of Appalachian hill towns in western Virginia.

By this time, "print culture" had begun to play an important part in American life. Thirty daily newspapers were published in the growing cities of the United States. Nearly a thousand local newspapers, mostly four-page weeklies, carried news, market information, and advertisements to people in small towns and rural areas. Political parties subsidized some of these newspapers and thereby hastened the emergence of a national political culture. Likewise, the influential *Niles Weekly Register*, established in Baltimore in 1811, and the *North American Review*, founded in Boston 1815, carried important state and national news to every region.

Nevertheless, at the end of the preindustrial era, the United States remained a nation of regional cultures. Only members of certain elite groups participated in a national culture. A dramatic transformation in transportation, print technology, and education would be necessary to create an American culture and social identity.

Education and Society

Formal education played a minor role in the lives of most Americans before 1800. Locally funded public schools provided many children in New England with basic instruction in reading and writing. Boys and girls in other regions received similar training mostly in private schools. Compared with European preindustrial societies, the literacy rate was high, especially in New England. At higher educational levels, the new republic lagged far behind most European nations. It lacked a strong heritage of educational achievement, and only a small fraction of young men—and almost no women—went to high school. Only about 1 percent of the adult males in New England, and an even smaller number in other regions, graduated from college.

The United States had yet to develop a strong intellectual culture. Joel Barlow, a Yale graduate

CHANGING IMAGES OF DEATH

Death—sudden, arbitrary, and painful—was a constant presence in the preindustrial world. Pre-1700 New England gravestones often depicted death as a frightening skull, crowned with a laurel to signify its inevitable victory. Bats of hell lurk in the bottom corners, warning Christians of the punishments to come, while Angels hold out the hope of heavenly salvation. By the 1740s, a smiling cherub adorned many gravestones, welcoming the dead into a more peaceful spiritual world. In the 1790s, this angelic image gave way to the naturalistic symbol of the willow tree and urn. Death had lost its sting and its Christian imagery. (Left, Allan Ludwig; Center and right, Essex Institute, Salem, Mass.)

and an ardent Jeffersonian patriot, called for an epic literature that would celebrate American greatness. His epic poem *The Columbiad* (1807) was ambitious but undistinguished. Charles Brockton Brown of Philadelphia wrote six interesting novels between 1798 and 1801, but his preoccupation with the psychological depths of human experience attracted few readers. Mercy Otis Warren's *History of the Revolution* (1805) contained stirring memories of leading American patriots, as did the best-selling *Life of Washington*, written about 1800 by "Parson" Mason Weems, an Episcopal minister. Yet neither work was particularly accomplished from a historical or literary point of view.

Of all the American writers in the early years of the republic, only Washington Irving achieved fame in Europe. His essays and histories, including *Salamagundi* (1807), *Diederick Knickerbocker's History of New York* (1809), and *The Sketch Book* (1819), had substantial American sales. Irving lived abroad for seventeen years, fascinated by the more intense European intellectual world. "Literature is not yet a distinct profession with us," Thomas Jefferson explained to an English correspondent. "Now and then a strong mind arises, and at its intervals from business emits a flash of light. But the first object of young societies is bread and covering."

This environment challenged the ingenuity of American educators. "America must be as independent in *literature* as she is in politics," proclaimed Noah Webster. In his *Dissertation on the English Language* (1789), Webster "Americanized" the spelling of various words, such as *labor* instead of the British *labour*. His *Blue-Book Speller*, which was first published in 1783 and used illustrations of correct grammar to instill moral principles, sold millions of copies. "Vir-tue ex-alt-eth a na-tion," one example of correct pronunciation by syllables began, "but sin is a re-proach to a-ny peo-ple." In other writings, Webster called on his fellow citizens to detach themselves "from the dependence on foreign opinions and manners, which is fatal to the efforts of genius in this country."

Jefferson and Benjamin Rush, a Philadelphia physician, responded with ambitious proposals for national intellectual independence. They mapped out plans for a comprehensive system of primary and secondary education. This broad-based institutional structure would be capped by colleges to educate young men in the liberal arts. There would also be a university, where distinguished scholars would offer lectures in law, medicine, divinity, and political economy.

The pleas of these educational planners fell on deaf ears. So did the call of Caleb Bingham, an influential Boston author of school textbooks, for "an equal distribution of knowledge to make us emphatically a 'republic of letters.' " In fact, many Americans questioned whether they should support higher education. "Let anybody show what advantage the poor man receives from colleges," an "Old Soldier" wrote to the Maryland *Gazette*. "Why should they support them, unless it is to serve those who are in affluent circumstances, whose children can be spared from labor, and receive the benefits." These arguments were well taken, for Jefferson's educational scheme assumed that most Americans would receive only a minimal education. "The mass of our citizens may be divided into two groups, the laboring and the learned," he wrote.

Similar elitist assumptions pervaded the thinking of a new generation of educational promoters in the 1820s. In many eastern states, merchants and manufacturers campaigned successfully for the expansion of public elementary schools. They raised standards through the legal certification of qualified teachers and the appointment of state superintendents of education. Self-interest as well as public virtue motivated these gentlemen-reformers. Many of them came from Federalist backgrounds and feared the popular will. They intended to use the schools to shape the characters of children from the laboring classes. In particular, they wanted to instill the virtues of self-discipline and individual enterprise. School textbooks therefore stressed the importance of useful knowledge that would help students make their way in the world. They praised honesty and hard work, while condemning gambling, drinking, and laziness.

Educational reformers likewise campaigned for laws requiring schools to teach American history. They thought instruction in patriotism would foster a set of shared cultural ideals and social values. The experience of Thomas Low Nichols, a New Hampshire schoolboy of the 1820s, fulfilled their most optimistic hopes:

We were taught every day and in every way that ours was the freest, the happiest, and soon to be the greatest and most powerful country in the world. This is the religious faith of every American. He learns it in his infancy and can never forget it.

In the past, the task of educators had been to transmit widely accepted knowledge and values from one generation to the next. Now they were also assigned the mission of instilling patriotism and overcoming social divisions.

This purposeful use of the school system received a mixed response. Wealthy Americans with worldy tastes and aristocratic values deplored the education of the laboring classes and the emphasis on practical knowledge. They preferred an elitist educational system that encouraged the European customs of leisurely reading and appreciation of the arts.

Farmers, artisans, and laborers were equally critical, but for different reasons. As working people, they valued schools as sources of basic instruction in reading, writing, and arithmetic. They supported public funding for primary schools, but not for secondary schools or colleges. By the age of twelve, most of their children worked on a full-time basis as apprentices, domestic servants, or farm laborers. They could not take advantage of secondary education. In Massachusetts towns with public high schools, for example, only about 20 percent of the eligible children were enrolled as late as 1860. Their parents' wealth permitted this fortunate minority to receive advanced intellectual training. As with other aspects of life in early nineteenth century America, educational institutions reflected the growth of social diversity.

Religion Versus Reforms

The War of Independence brought major reforms in the institutional structure of American religion. Throughout the southern states, the Church of England lost its privileged legal status. Anglican churches renounced their allegiance to the king of England and reorganized themselves as the Protestant Episcopal Church of America. To win popular support for the war, patriot leaders in Virginia ended their harassment of dissident Presbyterian and Baptist sects. In 1776, the Virginia Convention issued a Declaration of Rights that, thanks to James Madison, guaranteed "the free exercise of religion." Later that year, the legislature passed an act exempting dissenters from taxes for the support of the established Anglican church. Subsequently, the lawmakers rejected a bill supported by George Washington and Patrick Henry that would have imposed a "general assessment" tax to provide funds for all religious groups. Instead, heeding Baptist objections to publicly supported churches, the legislature in 1786 enacted Thomas Jefferson's Bill for Establishing Religious Freedom. This bill made all churches equal before the law and gave direct financial support to none. Equally significant, it endorsed the principle of individual liberty of conscience in religious matters.

Most public leaders accepted religious freedom and the end of an established church with great reluctance. Many still favored a single religious institution backed by the authority of the political state. Proclaiming traditional principles brought from Europe, they argued that a firm union of church and state promoted morality and respect for authority. "Pure religion and civil liberty are inseparable companions," one group of North Carolinians advised their minister. "It is your particular duty to enlighten mankind, to inculcate from the pulpit the unerring principles of truth and justice, the main props of all civil government."

These traditional assumptions prompted constitutional conventions in many states to bestow full political rights only on Protestant Christians. For example, the North Carolina Constitution of 1776 established religious qualifications for holding public office. It disqualified any citizen "who shall deny the being of God, or the Truth of the Protestant Religion, or the Divine Authority of the Old or New Testament." Similar provisions appeared in the Mississippi Constitution of 1817 and the constitutions of other states.

The commitment to the creation of a Protestant Christian culture led to political battles in many states. In New England, Congregational churches maintained their privileged legal position until the 1830s. However, they no longer attempted to suppress Baptist and Methodist churches. Equally important, dissenting Christians could use their religious taxes to support their own ministers. In the Middle Atlantic states, the sheer number of sects—Anglican, Presbyteri-

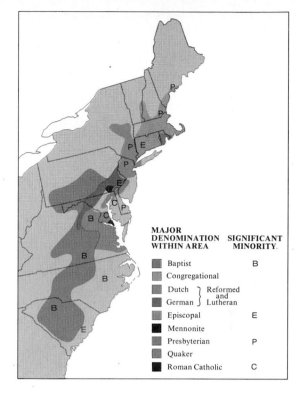

MAP 9.3 SOCIAL DIVERSITY AND RELIGIOUS INSTITUTIONS
Ethnic and religious diversity undermined the concept of a legally established church. During the 1780s, legislatures in the Middle Atlantic and southern states eliminated religious taxes and made all churches equal before the law, primarily because religious diversity left them no politically feasible alternative. In New England, the predominance of English settlers (and the relatively small number of Episcopalians and Presbyterians) preserved the established Congregational Church until the 1830s.

an, Dutch Reformed, German Lutheran, and Quaker, among others—prevented legislative agreement on an established church or compulsory religious taxes.

Yet state governments continued to assist religious institutions in a variety of ways. They enforced religious tests for voting and office-holding, offered tax exemptions on church property, and penalized individuals who questioned the doctrines of Protestant Christianity. The First Amendment to the United States Constitution did not cover these activities. It only prohibited the national government from establishing a state church or interfering with religious freedom. Similar constitutional limitations did not apply to state governments until the adoption of the Fourteenth Amendment in 1868.

Moreover, Americans of the early nineteenth century defined religious freedom very narrowly. Judges in state courts usually gave preference to community values rather than to individual rights. In 1811, Chancellor James Kent of the New York Supreme Court confirmed the conviction of Timothy Ruggles for blasphemy. While drunk, Ruggles had publicly and disrespectfully shouted the names of God, Christ, and the Holy Spirit. Local authorities could have prosecuted Ruggles for disorderly conduct, an offense against society. Instead, they tried him for blasphemy, a crime against the religious order.

A jury found Ruggles guilty and he appealed his conviction, arguing that the charge of blasphemy infringed his liberty of conscience. This was a weighty defense. Even Chancellor Kent admitted that the New York Constitution of 1778 guaranteed "the free, equal and undisturbed enjoyment of religious opinion." Nevertheless, Kent declared, "the people of this State profess the general doctrines of Christianity." For Ruggles "to scandalize the author of these doctrines" was "to strike at the root of moral obligation and weaken the security of social ties."

Rationalist freethinkers condemned such legal and political interference in religious matters. These advocates of "natural religion" believed that God had given human beings the power of reason so they could determine moral truths for themselves. Ethan Allen, the leader of the Green Mountain Boys of Vermont during the War, wrote a widely circulated pamphlet called *Reason the Only Oracle of Man* (1784). In their rational search for truth, freethinkers questioned many doctrines and rituals of Christianity. Thomas Paine, the famous pamphleteer of the Revolution, attacked churches as "no other than human inventions set up to terrify and enslave mankind, and monopolize power and profit."

In reply, Christians accused rationalists of being atheists, though most freethinkers were deists. Like Thomas Jefferson, they thought God had made the world like a watchmaker fashions a clock. "God Almighty is himself a Mechanic," proclaimed Thomas Cooper, an emigrant English scientist and president of the College of South Carolina. Once set in motion, the world ran according to natural laws. Philip Freneau, an ardent patriot poet and deist, thought that in "Nature" one could

see, with most exact design,
The world revolve, the planets shine.
The nicest order, all things meet,
A structure in itself complete.

To protect society from what they charged was "ecclesiastical tyranny," freethinkers demanded the complete separation of church and state.

Many Baptists also favored the constitutional separation of church and state, but for entirely different reasons. They wished to protect their churches from state control. Isaac Backus, a leading New England Baptist, warned his followers not to incorporate their churches in order to receive tax funds under the "general assessment" laws of Massachusetts. Legal incorporation might expose them to public control. Instead, Backus urged a voluntary system of church support.

Other American Protestants also endorsed the principle of voluntary support of churches, since it increased the power of the laity over the clergy. A devout Connecticut Congregationalist opposed legislation to appropriate funds for religious purposes. He maintained that it would encourage "a clerical hierarchy inconsistent with the spirit of toleration, or the principles of republicanism." Despite these protests, state governments continued to assist Protestant churches. The American Revolution ended the legal establishment of religion, except in New England, but it did not result in the complete separation of church and state.

Following independence, Americans also confronted the fact that some Protestant churches seemed more suited than others to a republican society. The hierarchical structure of the Episcopal church offered the most dramatic contrast with American political institutions. In the Episcopal church, as in the Roman Catholic church, authority flowed down from bishops to ministers and then to the congregation. Presbyterianism conformed more closely to the republican principle of popular sovereignty, because church members elected laymen to its ruling synods.

Quakers, Baptists, and Congregationalists had the most democratic forms of church government. The lay members of these churches controlled the appointment of ministers and decided doctrinal issues. In addition, the churches functioned without bishops or a religious hierarchy that stood apart from, and above, the local congregations. Methodism represented a blend of authoritarian and democratic features. As an offshoot of the Church of England, Methodism had an episcopal structure. Bishops took the lead on theological issues and enforced order in the church. Yet the evangelical fervor of early Methodism produced a democratic religious culture. Most Methodists encouraged lay preaching and the active participation of the entire congregation in church life.

Thousands of Americans joined Methodist and Baptist congregations, partly because of the democratic attitudes of these churches. Republicanism undermined the hierarchical religious institutions in other ways as well. To prevent the defection of its members, the Episcopal church in Dedham, Massachusetts, gave voting rights on nontheological issues to the entire congregation.

As Isaac Backus had warned, the legal incorporation of churches exposed them to supervision by society as a whole. In the case of *Robertson v. Bullion* (1854), the New York Supreme Court decided that a Presybterian congregation, not the synod, was the legal owner of the church's buildings and other property. Even more importantly, the court ruled that the congregation had the right to select the minister by a majority vote, regardless of the synod's orders. This republican principle of majority control, the decision stated, was "what the public sentiment of the country would seem to demand." Substantial religious diversity remained, but American Protestant Christianity was slowly becoming republican in structure and spirit.

The Mature Preindustrial Economy

The American economic system changed in two significant ways between 1780 and 1820. First, the production of manufactured goods increased greatly, permitting a higher standard of living while reducing dependence on European imports. Enterprising merchants organized the leap in domestic production by financing a rural-based handicraft system. This capitalist outwork system integrated tens of thousands of handicraft workers, many of them women, into the market economy. Second, the state governments actively promoted economic development. Their legislative activism created a new system of political economy and encouraged a fundamental change in the legal definition of property rights.

Merchant Capitalism

Through their trading activities, merchants had dominated the life of the colonial port cities. With the departure of British officials, American businessmen set the social and cultural tone as well. "It is a Nation of Merchants," an English visitor reported from Philadelphia in 1798, "always alive to their interest; and keen in the pursuit of wealth in all the various modes of acquiring it." Commercial opportunities provided by European wars from 1792 to 1815 brought rising profits to established merchant houses and fortunes to daring entrepreneurs.

The exceptional success stories of two immigrants illustrate the rewards of commercial ingenuity in a booming maritime economy. Robert Oliver arrived in Baltimore in 1783 as the American agent for a group of traders in Belfast, Ireland. Two years later, he entered a mercantile partnership. Oliver contributed £2,000 to the enterprise and watched his investment grow slowly during the recession of the 1780s; it amounted to £3,300 by 1789. Then, with the spectacular wartime shipping boom, the firm's assets jumped to £110,000. In a restless pursuit of gain, Oliver began to trade on his own. He reaped spectacular profits from the Santo Domingo coffee trade and speculation in Mexican gold and silver. By 1807, Oliver had become a millionaire.

The rise of John Jacob Astor was equally remarkable. He migrated from Germany to New York City in 1784 and found his way into the fur trade in the Pacific Northwest. Soon Astor emerged as the leading New York merchant trading with China. Investing his commercial profits in real estate, Astor became the largest landowner in the rapidly growing port of New York.

A new banking system financed this expansion of mercantile enterprise. During the colonial period, Americans lacked reliable and ample supplies of credit. Government-sponsored land banks made small loans to farmers, taking mortgages on their land as security. Merchants relied on partnerships, personal loans, or the credit extended by British suppliers. In 1781, during the War of Independence, Philadelphia merchants established the Bank of North America to provide short-term commercial loans. Traders in Boston and New York founded similar institutions in 1784.

At the urging of Alexander Hamilton, Congress chartered the Bank of the United States in 1791. The government owned 20 percent of the bank's stock. The bank had the power to issue notes, payable upon demand in gold or silver, and to make commercial loans. The demand for credit prompted the bank's managers to establish branches in eight major cities by 1805. They limited loans to three times the value of the bank's holdings in specie, but profits still averaged a handsome 8 percent annually. When the bank's charter expired in 1811, merchants in about twenty cities organized local banks, using state charters. They desperately needed credit institutions to finance their commercial transactions.

Using their capital and credit, the merchants developed a new manufacturing system. American artisans had always made a wide variety of goods, selling or exchanging them within the local community. In 1784, for example, John Hoff, a clockmaker of Lancaster, Pennsylvania, sold some of his fine wooden-cased clocks for money and traded others with his neighbors. In return, he received a dining table, a bedstead, women's shoes, pine boards, and even labor for his small farm.

This system of local barter created a prosperous and diversified rural society in New England and the Middle Atlantic regions, but it did not encourage the specialization of manufacturing. Weavers were the largest group of artisans in Newtown, Long Island, during the 1780s, but they made up only 7 percent of the adult male population. Communities of artisans appeared in only a few places, including seacoast shipbuilding towns, iron-smelting works in Pennsylvania and Maryland, and the shoe-producing center of Lynn, Massachusetts.

During the War of Independence, merchants helped increase the production of manufactured goods. Using their financial resources and organizational talents, they helped rural artisans make paper, gunpowder, cheese, and textiles. When the Marquis de Chastellux, a French military officer, visited a farmstead in Farmington, Connecticut in 1781, he found the residents "making a sort of camblet, as well as another woolen stuff with blue and white stripes for women's dress. . . . The sons and grandsons of the family were at work; one workman can make five yards a day."

Subsequently, nationalist pride prompted calls for the expansion of these enterprises. "Until we manufacture more," the *Boston Gazette* declared in 1788, "it is absurd to celebrate the Fourth of July as the birthday of our independence." However, the pace of domestic manufacturing slackened between 1792 and 1815. Low-priced British goods, especially textiles, flooded the market. Equally important, major American mercantile houses found it more profitable to invest their resources in commerce.

Yet some merchants, particularly those in inland areas, began systematically to organize rural households for market production. At first, they simply marketed goods traditionally produced for local consumption. In Brookfield, Massachusetts, "as along the whole road from Boston," a Polish visitor reported in 1798, "we saw women engaged in making cheese." Traveling through Berlin, New Hampshire in 1797, the Connecticut minister and author Timothy Dwight recorded a capsule history of Yankee commercial enterprise. Before the War of Independence, he was told, peddlers had sold locally made tinware with "a horse and two baskets." After the war, he reported, merchants encouraged local artisans to increase their output. Then they furnished young men "with a horse and a cart covered with a box or with a wagon; and . . . these young men direct themselves to the Southern States."

Gradually, merchants invested directly in the productive process. Entrepreneurial capitalists in Lynn, Massachusetts, extended the shoe-production network deep into the countryside of Massachusetts and New Hampshire. They bought leather, thread, and awls for thousands of households, and farm women and children stitched together the thin leather upper sections of shoes. Merchant wagons then carried the shoe sections back to Lynn for final assembly and shipment to markets, at first in the South

THE SLATER MILL, 1790
Slater's Mill, in Pawtucket, Rhode Island, used water power to spin cotton onto seventy-two bobbins.
The machines worked much faster than household spinning wheels, and only required the labor of a
dozen women and children. Outwork weavers then wove the cotton into fabrics on handpowered
household looms. (Anonymous Artist. *Pawtucket Bridge and Falls [Slater Mill].* The Rhode Island
Historical Society)

and then throughout the nation. By the end of
the 1820s, household workers produced more
than a hundred thousand pairs of boots and
shoes a year in thirty different Massachusetts
towns.

Merchants invested even greater resources in
the growing textile industry. For generations,
farm women and their daughters had clothed
their own families. Governor Sir Henry Moore of
New York reported in 1767 that

> the custom of making Coarse Cloths in pri-
> vate families prevails throughout the entire
> province, and almost in every house a sufficient
> quantity is manufactured for the use of the fam-
> ily. Every house swarms with children who are
> set to work as soon as they are able to Spin and
> Card; and as every family is furnished with a
> loom, the Itinerant weavers who travel about the
> country, put the finishing hand to the work.

Beginning in the 1780s, merchants built hundreds of small mills along the creeks and rivers
of New England and the Middle Atlantic states.
Mill workers used water-powered machines to
card and comb wool—and later cotton—and to

pound woven cloth into shape. Now working as
wage laborers, farm women and children spun
the wool into thread and yarn. Some women or
their husbands wove finished cloth as well.
Otherwise, the merchants distributed it to male
weavers in other rural families. In his *Letter on
Manufactures* (1810), Secretary of the Treasury
Albert Gallatin reported about twenty-five
hundred outwork weavers in New England.
Household weaving reached its peak in 1820,
when more than twelve thousand outworkers
produced cloth in New England.

The merchant-led expansion of rural manufacturing transformed the character of the agricultural economy. To supply artisans with raw
materials, enterprising farmers switched from
mixed-crop agriculture to raising livestock. The
booming shoe business consumed thousands
of cattle hides each year, and cheesemakers
needed the milk of large herds of cattle. Textile
producers purchased the wool sheared from tens
of thousands of sheep. The demand for farm
products revived the economies of many eastern
agricultural communities. Concord, Massachusetts, had one slaughterhouse and five small

tanneries in 1792. A decade later, there were eleven slaughterhouses and six flourishing tanning houses in the town. Foul odors drifted over Concord, but the townspeople were more prosperous than ever before.

The outwork system likewise altered the lives of many rural folk. Families now combined livestock farming with the production of manufactured goods for market sale. In 1794, Tench Coxe, secretary of the Pennsylvania Manufacturing Society, pointed out that "the union of manufactures and farming is more convenient on the grazing and grass farms. Parts of every day, and a great part of the year, can be spared from the business of the farm, and employed in some mechanical, handicraft, or manufacturing business." When the French republican political leader and author Brissot de Warville visited Worcester County, Massachusetts, the next year, he found "almost all these houses . . . inhabited by men who are both cultivators and artisans; one is a tanner, another a shoemaker, another sells goods; but all are farmers."

This union of rural producers and merchant capitalists began the market revolution in the United States. As farm families joined the outwork system, they no longer produced all their own food, made most of their clothes and bedding, or bartered their surplus for other necessities. Instead, they concentrated their productive energies on activities rewarded by merchants. They used the cash from the sale of farm products or the credit earned as wages to buy goods in local stores.

Increasingly, the rural population became an integral part of the commercial economy centered in the seaport cities and eastern towns. "Straw hats and Bonnets are manufactured by many families," noted a Maine official of the 1820 Census of Manufacturing, "and females make better wages than spinners, weavers, or seamstresses." A decade later, another observer estimated that "probably 8,000 females" in the vicinity of Foxborough, Massachusetts, braided and sewed rye straw into hats for market sale.

The expansion of household production made manufacturing a basic component of the national economy. Domestic manufacturing required both the commercial skills and capital resources of the merchant community, and the labor and raw materials provided by the rural population.

With this advance in artisan and outwork production, the United States achieved a significant degree of self-sufficiency and a new prosperity. Beginning around 1800, the per capita income of Americans rose at an annual rate of more than 1 percent and more than 30 percent each generation. By the 1820s, this extraordinary expansion of wealth laid the basis for the American Industrial Revolution. After a half-century of political freedom, the republic had achieved economic independence.

A Transformation in the Law

State governments played a vital role in the process of economic change. They dominated political and administrative affairs throughout the nineteenth century. State governments abolished slavery in the North and passed legislation that ensured its existence in the South. State legislators set voting requirements, controlled city governments, and established the taxation system. They delegated administrative authority to county and town officials and supervised their actions. As a result, the state governments affected the day-to-day lives of most Americans much more than did national political institutions.

Beginning in the 1790s, state governments developed a new American system of mercantilism. Following traditional European models, the legislatures used the political system to stimulate commerce and create wealth. State mercantilism took form in charters granted to private business corporations. Chartered companies were not new; English investors had used them to establish the first settlements in North America. Yet few of these business organizations existed during the colonial period. English law prohibited a chartered corporation, such as a colonial government, from granting its own charters. Therefore, American merchants and investors financed mills, shipyards, and trading ventures through private partnerships. These business arrangements worked well enough, but they lacked some of the legal and economic advantages of state-chartered corporations.

Following independence, Americans quickly remedied this institutional deficiency. By 1800, state governments had granted more than three hundred charters to private business corporations. Legislators used the legal power of incorporation primarily to promote investment in roads, bridges, and other transportation facilities. Republican ideology provided ample justification for these charters. By increasing trade, legislators argued, new roads would increase the general welfare. In 1794, the Lancaster Turnpike Company opened a graded gravel road between Lancaster and Philadelphia. Its success touched off a turnpike construction spree that connected dozens of inland market centers to one another and to seaport cities.

Legal incorporation assisted the private companies in a variety of ways. Some charters limited the liability of merchants to the amount of their investments, thus protecting other assets in the event of business failure. More importantly, most transportation charters included the power of *eminent domain.* This legal device gave bridge, turnpike, and canal corporations the authority to force the sale of land along their right-of-ways. They could use the legal system to take land from a property owner for a reasonable price, even if the owner did not wish to sell.

Once the transportation projects were underway, state legislatures assisted the establishment of banks and manufacturing enterprises. During the decade following the embargo of 1807, New England governments awarded special charters to more than two hundred mining, manufacturing, and banking companies. By 1816, there were 246 state banks in the United States. Always alert to new opportunities for economic expansion, states now invested government funds in a variety of private and public ventures. Between 1820 and 1824, state legislators issued $13 million in bonds to finance expensive canal-building projects.

The result of these innovative policies was a new system of political economy. Americans no longer conceived of government as a passive institution, limited to the enforcement of existing laws and social arrangements. Citizens now assumed that state governments would intervene actively in the economy. When Missouri lawmakers wrote their first constitution in 1820, they specified that "internal improvements shall forever be encouraged by the government of this State."

The burst of state legislative activity began a new legal era as well. During the colonial period,

English common law had shaped American thinking about legal issues. When deciding cases, judges relied on precedents established in previous court cases. Beyond doing this, they assumed that the law contained the ultimate principles of religious and political authority. As Daniel Dulany, Sr., a leading Maryland lawyer and politician, declared in 1728, "The Common Law takes in the Law of Nature, the Law of Reason and the Revealed Law of God."

Republican ideology undermined the intellectual foundations of this old legal order. As Americans debated constitutional principles, they recognized that the law was a product of the political process, not a sacred body of immutable truths. Then, during the 1790s, the leaders of the Republican party mounted a direct attack on the common law. They maintained that "judge-made law" was inferior to the "statute law" enacted by the elected representatives of the people.

Republican-minded jurists defended the primacy of statute law. In his treatise on *American Jurisprudence* (1819), Judge John Milton Goodenow asserted that judges should not interpret or "create" the law by their decisions. Rather, a magistrate in a republic "should be *governed* himself by *positive* law, and executes and enforces the will of the supreme power, which is the will of THE PEOPLE." Other judges agreed that legislatures could use the law as an instrument of social or economic policy. However, they insisted that judges retain a crucial role in the legal and political systems. Legislative statutes could only "establish a general unbending rule," the jurist Zephanial Swift argued in 1810, so judges had to interpret the law and shape it "to every possible variety of circumstance."

The judicial career of John Marshall revolved around these debates over judicial activism and legal instrumentalism. The great Virginia Federalist served as Chief Justice of the United States from 1801 to 1835. Three principles shaped Marshall's philosophy of the law: the supremacy of national over state legislation, a traditional concept of property rights, and an attitude of judicial activism. The celebrated case of *Marbury v. Madison* revealed Marshall's activism. He ruled that the Supreme Court had the authority to decide the constitutionality of congressional legislation. This case also revealed Marshall's nationalism, for his opinion repudiated the

Republican position that state legislatures could decide constitutional issues.

Marshall's nationalism—and his Federalist bias—surfaced again in the controversial case of *McCulloch v. Maryland* (1819). In 1816, Congress had chartered the Second Bank of the United States and given it certain powers over state banks. To preserve the independence and competitive position of state-chartered banks, the Maryland legislature imposed an annual tax of fifteen thousand dollars on the Baltimore branch of the Second Bank and limited its authority to issue notes. The bank resisted this legislation through legal action. When the case reached the Supreme Court, lawyers representing Maryland adopted Thomas Jefferson's argument against the First Bank of the United States. They claimed that Congress lacked the constitutional authority to charter a national bank. Even if the bank were constitutional, they maintained that Maryland had a right to tax the branch offices within its boundaries.

Marshall rejected both arguments. The Second Bank was constitutional, the chief justice stated, because its establishment was "necessary and proper," given the national responsibility to control currency and credit. Marshall stressed the powers implied by, but not specifically mentioned in, the Constitution. "Let the end be legitimate, let it be within the scope of the Constitution," he wrote, "and all means which are appropriate . . . are constitutional." Not surprisingly, Marshall's words were almost identical to those of Alexander Hamilton during the debate on the First Bank in 1791.

On the issue of taxation, Marshall embraced the argument advanced by Daniel Webster, another Federalist and the Second Bank's legal counsel. Following Webster, Marshall asserted that "the power to tax involves the power to destroy." If Maryland could tax the Second Bank, he maintained, the national government would be rendered "dependent on the States." This result, Marshall argued with less than completely convincing logic, "was not intended by the American people" when their representatives ratified the Constitution. In 1821, the chief justice used similar reasoning to declare the supremacy of national courts over state courts. In the case of *Cohens v. Virginia*, Marshall proclaimed that the Constitution diminished state sovereignty.

Therefore, state court decisions could be appealed to the national judiciary.

Marshall's traditional conception of property rights also reflected his Federalist viewpoint. The Constitution prohibited the states from passing any "law impairing the obligation of contracts." The delegates to the Philadelphia convention inserted this clause to protect merchants and other creditors. Prompted by the economic conflicts of the 1780s, it was intended primarily to prevent states from enacting laws delaying the payment of debts.

Marshall used the contract clause to defend all vested property against legislative challenge. His decisions eventually hindered the efforts of state governments to foster economic growth and social progress. For example, the case of *Fletcher v.*

THE GREAT DANIEL WEBSTER
Webster (1782–1852) was a brilliant constitutional lawyer, an adept practical politician, and a great orator. Born in rural New Hampshire, he became a leading spokesman for American business. As a Federalist during the War of 1812, Webster strongly defended the rights of the states. Becoming a strong nationalist during the 1820s, he composed the famous phrase, "Liberty and Union, now and for ever, one and inseparable." (Joseph Goodhue Chandler. *Daniel Webster at Bunker Hill*. Hood Museum of Art, Dartmouth College. Julia L. Whittier Fund)

OPINION OF CHIEF JUSTICE JOHN MARSHALL IN *FLETCHER V. PECK*

In this case, the Supreme Court declared a state law unconstitutional for the first time. The ruling established the precedence of the United States Constitution over state laws.

The principle asserted is, that one legislature is competent to repeal any act which a former legislature was competent to pass; and that one legislature cannot abridge the powers of a succeeding legislature. The correctness of this principle, so far as respects general legislation, can never be controverted. But if an act be done under a law, a succeeding legislature cannot undo it. The past cannot be recalled by the most absolute power.

Conveyances have been made, those conveyances have vested legal estates, and, if those estates may be seized by the sovereign authority, still, that they originally vested is a fact, and cannot cease to be a fact. When, then, a law is in its nature a contract, when absolute rights have vested under that contract, a repeal of the law cannot divest those rights.

Peck (1810) involved a large grant of land made by the Georgia legislature to the Yazoo Land Company. A newly elected state legislature cancelled the grant, alleging that it had been obtained through fraud and bribery. Investors who had purchased Yazoo lands appealed to the Supreme Court to uphold their titles. Speaking for his colleagues on the Court, Marshall ruled that the original legislative grant constituted a contract and could not be repudiated.

The Court used similar logic in the case of *Dartmouth College v. Woodward* (1819). The college was a private institution, established by a charter granted by King George III in 1769. In the early nineteenth century, the Republican-dominated legislature of New Hampshire tried to convert the college into a public university. The Dartmouth trustees resisted this plan and engaged Daniel Webster to plead their case before the Supreme Court. The Federalist lawyer based his argument directly on the Court's decision in *Fletcher v. Peck*. The royal charter had bestowed "corporate powers and privileges" on the college, Webster maintained. It therefore constituted a contract and could not be changed by the New Hampshire legislature.

Marshall convinced his colleagues to accept this argument, but only with great difficulty. Many Supreme Court justices had been appointed by Republican presidents. They hesitated to restrict the powers of state legislatures or to endorse the conservative definition of property rights set forth in the Dartmouth case. After months of deliberation, the justices followed Marshall and ruled in favor of the college.

Marshall's difficulties in the Dartmouth case reflected more than partisan politics. A rival concept of property rights commanded increasing respect among legislators, jurists, and the public. The expansion of manufacturing prompted this rethinking of legal principles. As merchants and other capitalist entrepreneurs built dams to provide waterpower for mills, they often flooded adjacent agricultural lands. Farmers took legal action to protect their property. They accused the dam builders of trespassing and sought damages. The farmers won many of these cases because the common law gave preference to the use of land for agricultural purposes. In 1795, for example, a New Jersey court ruled that interference with the natural flow of a river for nonfarming purposes was illegal "without the consent of all who have an interest in it."

These decisions threatened to stifle economic development, and so state legislatures passed laws that limited the legal remedies available to farm owners. The Massachusetts Milldam Act of 1795 allowed mill proprietors to flood adjacent agricultural lands. It forced farmers to accept fair compensation for their lost acreage and prevented them from blocking the construction of mills or seeking damages. When farm owners contested the constitutionality of these laws, judges generally supported the state legislatures.

TIME LINE
A MATURE PREINDUSTRIAL SOCIETY

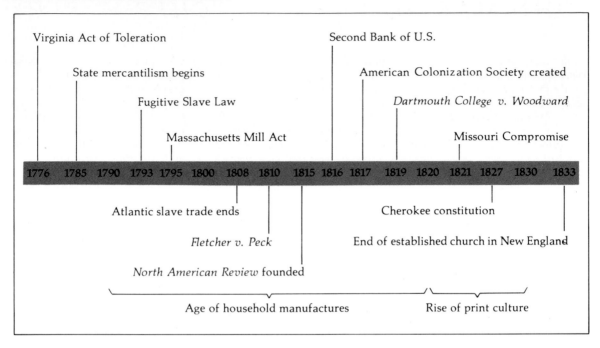

They gave preference to a "dynamic" rather than a "static" use of property.

Judges likewise upheld state laws granting the power of eminent domain to private turnpike and canal corporations. A New Jersey court declared that "the opening of good and easy internal communications is one of the highest duties of government." The Massachusetts Superior Court added that a "turnpike road is a public highway, established for a public use, and is to be regarded as a public easement, and not as private property." To these judges, social utility justified the legal takeover of private property.

The rulings shocked Daniel Webster and other traditionalists. In the eyes of the Federalist politician, they constituted no less than a "revolution against the foundations on which property rests." Actually, the judges—like the state legislatures—were giving property rights a new definition. The case of *Palmer v. Mulligan* (1805) revealed the important principles at the heart of the legal transformation. This case involved a New York dam owner who sought to prevent the

construction of a new milldam elsewhere on a river. He maintained that his "first use" of the waterway bestowed exclusive rights. The New York Supreme Court rejected this argument, ruling that "competition and rivalry," not monopoly, would best serve the public interest. The judges' decision reflected the growing importance of competition as an American social value. It also indicated that expansion and growth had become the prime goals of economic policy.

Only after John Marshall left the Supreme Court in 1835 did the new conception of property rights become firmly imbedded in the laws of the United States. By the early 1820s, however, the direction of legal and social change was clear. For more than a generation, the state legislatures had purposefully used the law as an instrument of social and economic policy. State judges had formulated new legal principles to assist the development of transportation and manufacturing. The United States had become a mature pre-industrial society, and a larger number of citizens were more innovative and enterprising then ever before.

*B*etween 1780 and 1820, the United States became a mature, complex preindustrial society. White Americans encouraged native Americans and Afro-Americans to adopt the whites' culture and institutions. They confined Indians on reservations in an attempt to Christianize them, but without great success. Following the end of the slave trade in 1808, blacks were cut off from their African roots. They adopted the English language, Protestant Christianity, and other white practices, but adapted them to their own needs. By creating strong communities based on family and religion, blacks prompted their white masters to devise a paternalistic, rather than a tyrannical, slave system.

White Americans developed social identities based on region and religion. Those who lived in New England, the Middle Atlantic states, and the southern and western regions each saw themselves as a distinct people, the product of unique historical experiences. A national sense of identity appeared only gradually, as the result of political union, the teaching of patriotism in schools, and the spread of books and newspapers from major cities. The United States remained religiously diverse as well. However, most churches became more "American" and "republican" in structure and doctrine.

The American economic system developed rapidly following independence. Merchant capitalists created a flourishing outwork system of rural manufacturing. State governments awarded corporate charters to assist transportation companies, manufacturers, and banks. The Supreme Court initially upheld traditional concepts of ownership, but the increasingly competitive economic system gradually encouraged a more dynamic legal perception of property rights.

Suggestions for Further Reading

The Subject Races

F. P. Prucha, *American Indian Policy in the Formative Years* (1962), surveys federal legislation, while William Brandon, *The Last Americans: The Indians in American Culture* (1974), traces the interaction between whites and native Americans. Angie Debo, *A History of the Indians of the United States* (1970), is a comprehensive study. For more detailed cultural analyses, see Wilcomb B. Washburn, *The Indian in America* (1974); A. H. De Rosier, Jr., *The Removal of the Choctaw Indians* (1971); and Donald Jackson, ed., *Black Hawk: An Autobiography* (1955).

Ira Berlin, *Slaves Without Masters: The Free Negro in the Antebellum South* (1974), is comprehensive and stimulating, as is Leon Litwack, *North of Slavery: The Negro in the Free States, 1790–1860* (1961). David Brion Davis, *The Problem of Slavery in the Age of Revolution* (1974), traces the origins of American anti-slavery thought, while Arthur Zilversmit, *The First Emancipation* (1967), outlines its first results. G. M. Frederickson, *The Black Image in the White Mind* (1971), explores the persistence of racism, as does William Stanton, *The Leopard's Spots: Scientific Attitudes Toward Race in America* (1960). D. L. Robinson, *Slavery in the Structure of American Politics, 1765–1820* (1970), is a fine study of early sectional compromises regarding slavery; Glover Moore, *The Missouri Compromise* (1953), provides a detailed analysis of that crisis.

Later literature on Afro-American society is ample and stimulating. John Blassingame, *The Slave Community* (1972), offers a convenient overview, designed in part to refute the arguments of Stanley Elkins, *Slavery:* *A Problem in American Institutional and Intellectual Life* (2d ed., 1968). By concentrating on the black experience, Eugene D. Genovese, *Roll Jordan Roll: The World the Slaves Made* (1974), and Herbert G. Gutman, *The Black Family* (1976), have altered the terms of the debate. Albert Raboteau, *Slave Religion* (1968), is also useful.

The Formation of Social Identity

Regional identity provides the focus for studies of the South, such as Clement Eaton, *The Growth of Southern Civilization* (1961); Monroe Billington, *The American South* (1971); and William R. Taylor, *Cavalier and Yankee: The Old South and American National Character* (1961). The character of New England has to be approached more indirectly, through such studies as Stanley K. Schultz, *The Culture Factory: Boston Public Schools, 1789–1860* (1973); Carl Bode, *The American Lyceum* (1956); and Van Wyck Brooks, *The Flowering of New England* (1936). Frederick Jackson Turner, *The Frontier in American History* (1920), discusses the creation of a distinct western identity, while Ray Allen Billington, *America's Frontier Heritage* (1967), demonstrates the complexity of the process of cultural transmission. Frank L. Mott, *American Journalism* (1950) and *A History of American Magazines* (2 vols., 1930 and 1938), traces the emergence of print culture.

Robert Spiller, et al., *Literary History of the United States* (1948), discusses the rise of American literature, as does Van Wyck Brooks, *The World of Washington Irving* (1944); Neil Harris, *The Artist in American Society, 1790–1860* (1966); and Richard Ellis, *After the Revolution:*

Studies in American Culture (1975). See also Richard B. Lewis, *The American Adam* (1955). On the growth of American education, see Merle Curti, *The Social Ideas of American Educators* (1935); Rush Welter, *Popular Education and Democratic Thought* (1962); and Lawrence Cremin, *The American Common School* (1951). Michael B. Katz, *The Irony of Early School Reform* (1968), is an indispensable critical analysis.

Henry F. May, *The Enlightenment in America* (1976), provides a comprehensive overview of religious thought in the early republic. Perry Miller, *The Life of the Mind in America: From the Revolution to the Civil War* (1966), is incisive and stimulating. H. M. Morais, *Deism in Eighteenth Century America* (1934), remain useful, as does Ralph H. Gabriel, *The Course of American Democratic Thought* (1956). Sydney Ahlstrom, *A Religious History of the American People* (1972), is comprehensive. A shorter overview is Sidney E. Mead, *The Lively Experiment: The Shaping of Christianity in America* (1963). For a discussion of church-state relations, see Mark DeWolfe Howe, *The Garden and the Wilderness* (1967); Anson P. Stokes, *Church and State in the United States* (1950); and William G. McLoughlin, *New England Dissent, 1630–1833: The Baptists and the Separation of Church and State* (1971).

The Mature Preindustrial Economy

Stuart Bruchey, *The Roots of American Economic Growth, 1607–1861* (1965), and Douglass C. North, *The Economic Growth of the United States, 1790–1860* (1961), are fine conceptual overviews. Curtis R. Nettles, *The Emergence of a National Economy, 1775–1815* (1962), is a comprehensive and sound survey. Constance M. Green, *Eli Whitney and the Birth of American Technology* (1956), traces the rise of technical innovation; Bray Hammond, *Banks and Politics in America* (1957), details the appearance of new credit institutions and instruments; and Stuart Bruchey, *Robert Oliver* (1956), explores the increased scope of the merchant capitalist. A. H. Cole, *The American Wool Manufacture* (1926); Percy Bidwell, *The Rural Economy of New England* (1916); and Rolla S. Tryon, *Household Manufactures in the United States* (1916), describe the growth of household production in rich detail. The first volume of Victor S. Clark, *History of Manufactures in the United States* (1928), is also valuable, as is Paul W. Gates, *The Farmers's Age* (1960), which explores related changes in agricultural production.

The classic study of state assistance to economic development is Oscar and Mary Handlin, *Commonwealth: A Study of the Role of Government in the American Economy: Massachusetts 1774–1861* (1947). Other important studies include Louis Hartz, *Economic Policy and Democratic Thought, Pennsylvania 1776–1860* (1948); Milton S. Heath, *Constructive Liberalism* (1954); and E. M. Dodd, *American Business Corporations Until 1860* (1954).

A pathbreaking analysis by Morton Horwitz, *The Transformation of the American Law, 1780–1860* (1976), relates economic development to legal history and provides a new framework for the study of John Marshall and the Supreme Court. A. J. Beveridge, *The Life of John Marshall* (4 vols., 1916–1919), is a classic biography. Other studies include R. K. Faulkner, *The Jurisprudence of John Marshall* (1968); C. G. Haines, *John Marshall: A Life in Law* (1974); and Richard E. Ellis, *The Jeffersonian Crisis: Courts and Politics in the New Republic* (1971). Gerald Dunne, *Justice Joseph Story and the Rise of the Supreme Court* (1970), probes the thought of another brilliant Supreme Court justice. Other important legal studies include J. Williard Hurst, *Law and the Conditions of Freedom* (1956); William Nelson, *The Americanization of the Common Law* (1976); and Lawrence M. Friedman, *A History of American Law* (1973). For good biographies of significant state judges, see Leonard Levy, *The Law of the Commonwealth and Chief Justice Shaw* (1967), and John Horton, *James Kent* (1939). Two excellent collections of documents are Charles M. Haar, ed., *The Golden Age of American Law* (1965), and Perry Miller, *The Legal Mind in America* (1962).

$\mathcal{S}$OCIAL DISTINCTIONS IN THE NEW REPUBLIC

The images in this essay reflect the problem of social distinctions in a republican government. Most eighteenth-century political thinkers believed a republican polity would flourish only in a society composed of morally virtuous and relatively equal citizens. "To this species of Government," remarked Carter Braxton of Virginia, "everything that looks like elegance and refinement is inimical." The radical English republican Richard Price had great hopes for America, because its society seemed to consist "of only a body of yeomanry supported by agriculture, and all independent, and nearly upon a level." Visual images of humble log cabins inhabited by proud, independent pioneers (plate 1) reinforced this European notion of American republican simplicity.

Americans shared this view for the most part, but they also knew their society was rife with aristocratic European vices. They hoped that republicanism would

PLATE 1
Primitive conditions on the American frontier enforced a life of republican simplicity. The woman in this French engraving stands proudly at the door of a typical hut, described by one pioneer as "a barbarous rectangle of unhewed and unbarked logs." The menacing pine trees hint at the artist's reservations about the isolation and difficulties of life in the wilderness. (The Newberry Library, Chicago)

271

banish "the syren LUXURY with all her train of fascinating pleasures, idle dissipation, and expensive amusements from our borders." They longed for a society based on "honest industry, sober frugality, simplicity of manners, plain hospitality and christian benevolence." Through a sympathetic depiction of deeply religious, Bible-reading cotters (plate 2), the New England artist Eunice Pinney offered a striking image of Samuel Adam's Calvinistic vision of America as "the *Christian Sparta*." In a more festive but equally republican spirit, George Lehman portrayed ordinary people enjoying life in the friendly, wholesome atmosphere of a country tavern in Pennsylvania (plate 3).

Yet most artists were well aware that merchants, planters, and wealthy gentry dominated American society. Some painters embraced the aristocratic viewpoint of these social groups or recognized their own dependence on wealthy patrons. They produced striking views of federalist Boston and complimentary portraits of well-born leaders, showing them as rich but upright and virtuous men and women (plates 4 and 5). Some American

PLATE 2

The dress of these cotters (so called because they live in a humble cottage or "cot") is much too grand for their economic condition. Yet Eunice Pinney has accurately captured the importance of Bible-reading in the lives of many poor artisans. After a long day's work, this family gathers to hear the familiar, inspiring biblical stories, to take stock of their spiritual lives and—at least for one boy—to take a nap, or pray. (*The Cotter's Saturday Night.* National Gallery of Art, Washington. Gift of Edgar William and Bernice Chrysler Garbisch)

PLATE 3

The stylishly dressed dancers command the attention of the onlookers, but the artist suggests the relative social equality of rural communities and the simple, spontaneous character of leisure-time activities. (George Lehman, *Dance in a Country Tavern*, The Historical Society of Pennsylvania)

PLATE 4
Boston in the 1760s was the home of the Sons of Liberty and of revolutionary republicanism. A generation later the city was the bastion of aristocratic New England federalism. This impressive view of State Street and the Old State House, painted by James B. Marsten in 1801, underlines the change. Fancy carriages and modishly dressed men and women, not radical mobs, now fill the streets. (Massachusetts Historical Society)

PLATE 5
The commanding pose struck by Chief Justice Oliver Ellsworth reflects his aristocratic self-esteem and his dominant position in Connecticut politics and society. Abigail Wolcott, his satin-attired wife, was the daughter of a former Governor. Ralph Earl, the talented artist who painted this portrait, has emphasized the family's aristocratic status by showing a large mansion (presumably theirs) through the window. (Wadsworth Atheneum, Hartford. Gift of Ellsworth heirs)

273

artists hoped republicanism would mean a leveling of "that exuberance of pride which has produced an insolent domination in a few, a very few, opulent, monopolizing families." The sketches of Pennsylvania artist Benjamin Henry Latrobe take a decidedly critical view of the dominance southern planters exerted over their black slaves (plate 6) and poor white neighbors.

The art of the new republic was not the exclusive province of professional artists. A strong European folk art tradition survived and flourished in German settlements in Pennsylvania, Maryland, and North Carolina (plate 7). A new native folk art blossomed in New England, in the extraordinarily beautiful samplers stitched by hundreds of schoolgirls (plate 8). Other young women depicted the life they saw around them in simple portraits using the pinprick technique (plate 9 on page 276). Folk art had deep roots in German culture or in the sewing skills of generations of New England women, and much of it had great

PLATE 6
Republicanism was a complex ideology, founded on liberty but compatible with slavery. As later southern apologists for slavery correctly pointed out, the Roman Republic was a slave-owning society. This watercolor sketch from the Virginia Journals of Benjamin Henry Latrobe nonetheless conveys the artist's discomfort with the haughty power a white slaveowner exercises over his barefoot black female property. (Maryland Historical Society)

PLATE 7
This delightful watercolor depicts a gentleman in traditional dress walking among giant tulips, a familiar motif in Pennsylvania German folkart. The lace cuffs, white stockings, and walking stick suggest the man's high social status, as does the artist's delicate treatment of the hand holding the long pipe. (Rare Book Department, Free Library of Philadelphia [Arthur Soll])

PLATE 8

Between 1780 and 1830 young American women made thousands of elaborately hand-stitched samplers, similar to this product of Mary Balch's famous school in Providence, Rhode Island. Samplers often reflected republican values, such as faith in education, and testified to the spread of institutions that provided basic intellectual skills and cultural refinement to girls from wealthy and middling families. (Museum of Art, Rhode Island School of Design)

PLATE 9
The influence of French urban culture created a distinct Afro-American community in New Orleans, as the dignified bearing and dress of this slave woman suggest. The young amateur artist, "Miss M. Brook," created the textured surface on this watercolor by pricking the paper repeatedly with a pin, a commonly used technique around 1800. (America Hurrah Antiques, New York)

visual power. Yet this art, like most works created by untutored amateurs, presented reality in a straightforward, realistic fashion. The goal of the artist was to depict the world, not render a verdict on it.

Self-styled "republican" artists assumed the broader mandate of providing their fellow citizens with inspiring republican images. In 1782, Congress placed the eagle on the Great Seal of the United States, and this aggressive masculine symbol of power soon appeared everywhere. Eagles were stamped on spoons,

inlaid on furniture, sewed into coverlets, and painted on ceramic plates. The birds also appeared in hundreds of engravings, often in company with a beautiful young Goddess of Liberty. This dual imagery had strong sexual overtones, reflecting a long literary tradition that identified power with men and freedom with women. As one author put it, "freedom is a virgin, that everyone seeks to deflower." If liberty were not adequately protected, he continued, the overwhelming desire for dominion in mankind would bring "a rape" of

freedom "upon the first opportunity." By combining these antagonistic male and female images, Abijah Canfield celebrated the apparent success of American republicanism in reconciling governmental power with individual freedom (plate 10).

Other artists conveyed republican values in more subtle and mundane ways. The strong presence of Mrs. Sargent in *The Sargent Family* exalts the newly defined role of American women as "republican mothers" who commanded the household and raised their children as virtuous

PLATE 10

After the Revolution, American artists used patriotic national symbols to inspire their fellow citizens to act morally. Like Abijah Canfield in his painting of *Liberty as a Goddess of Youth* (circa 1800), they depicted figures dressed in the garb of Republican Rome. Only a few American women, and no men, actually dressed in the flowing robes of the neo-classical artistic style. The costume was a conscious allusion to the Roman republican tradition. (Library of Congress) citizens (plate 11). The young artist Deborah Goldsmith took a strong ideological stance in *The Talcott Family* (plate 12). The composition of the painting implicitly praised marriages based on the relative equality of husband and wife. Goldsmith's own historical understanding is translated in this picture into an evocative image of republican social ideals. Goldsmith's painting proclaims the belief that, as John Smilie of Pennsylvania commented in another context, a "democratic government like ours admits of no superiority."

PLATE 11

This anonymous painting of the Sargent family (1800) depicts the new emphasis on the domestic duties and authority of women. The mother's position, firmly seated in the center of the room, shows her control over the household domain. The father enters from the outside, indicating that his prime concerns now lie elsewhere, in the field of business. (National Gallery of Art, Washington. Gift of Edgar William and Bernice Chrysler Garbisch)

PLATE 12

The Talcotts of central New York state blended old and new family values. The married couple sit side by side, a visual mark of equality, and the husband touches his wife and delicately holds his child, indicating the close emotional attachments of the new, more republican conjugal family. The aging mother-in-law sits at a slight distance, perhaps as a reminder of the older, more formal relations between family members in public. (Abby Aldrich Rockefeller Folk Art Center, Williamsburg, Va.)

10

TOWARD
A NEW CULTURE

As the United States celebrated the fiftieth anniversary of its declaration of independence from Britain, Americans had cause for sadness as well as joy. On July 4, 1826, John Adams and Thomas Jefferson died within a few hours of each other. The death of two former presidents on Independence Day made a profound impression on many Americans. They took it as what seemed to be a clear sign that God looked with favor on their experiment in self-government. The Founding Fathers had died, but the republic lived on.

The 1820s marked another—and more important—milestone in the nation's history. Few people noted it at the time, but this decade brought the passing of the "old America." For two centuries, colonists and then citizens had lived within the confines of tightly knit farm communities. Now, in a mature and increasingly dynamic preindustrial society, a new culture took shape.

The new American culture is best examined from three perspectives. First, an analysis of the public culture reveals new political and ideological systems. A fresh generation of political leaders had come to maturity during the War of 1812. Trained as lawyers and skilled in the art of compromise, these professional politicians created a more open and democratic system of government. At the same time, an articulate business class became an important force in American life. Its capitalist ideology embodied a new set of assumptions regarding the sources of human action and the proper organization of society.

Second, a survey of private identity discloses a fundamental shift in American institutions and values. The family, the basic unit of social organization, lost its old patriarchal structure and assumed a conjugal character. Young men and women rejected the traditional lineal rules governing courtship, marriage, and family life. Influenced by sentimentalism, they married for love. They had fewer children, but their families were more child centered. The activities and outlook of women changed as well. Prompted by republican ideology and religious fervor, women took an increasingly prominent part in family life and public affairs.

Third, a discussion of the national character indicates a new and powerful sense of personal ability. A series of evangelical Protestant revivals brought millions of Americans into Christian churches. Many ministers proclaimed an optimistic theology that stressed human ability and universal salvation. Secular spokesmen likewise celebrated the power of the individual to tame nature and create a new and better world. "The temperate zone of North America," Chief Justice George Robertson of the Kentucky Supreme Court declared in a July 4 oration, "already exhibits many signs that it is the promised land of civil liberty, and of institutions designed to liberate and exalt the human race."

The Dimensions of Public Culture

During the Revolutionary era, men of affairs controlled American political life. Like George Washington, they combined the role of statesman with that of planter, merchant, or gentleman farmer. The First Party System produced a new breed of political leaders, men who specialized in law and government. The expansion of commerce and manufacturing likewise created distinct social groups. Capitalists and craftsmen now voiced different ideologies and economic goals, as did the growing class of propertyless laborers. The social order became less unified, even as public institutions grew in power and authority. The result was a more complex public culture.

A New Political Spirit

The struggle between Republicans and Federalists came to an end after the War of 1812. And peace in Europe ended two decades of conflict in America over foreign policy. The passionate ideological conflicts of the 1790s gradually faded away. Similarly, the Federalist party's eastern-oriented policies and elitism received little support in an expanding, westward-looking nation. "No federal character can run with success," the New York Federalist statesman Gouverneur Morris lamented, and the election results of 1818 confirmed his pessimism. Following the voting, Republicans outnumbered Federalists in the Senate, 37 to 7, and in the House of Representatives, 156 to 27.

The overwhelming Republican majorities ended the First Party System. Federalism, as the

ELECTION DAY, 1816
Passionate conflicts between Federalists and Republicans made American politics more democratic than ever before. As this painting by John Lewis Krimmel of a vivid Philadelphia election scene suggests, political campaigns became a major aspect of the public culture of the United States. American flags wave over the scene, linking each party with patriotism, while the date (over the door to the right) recalls the writing of the already-sacred Constitution of 1787. (John Lewis Krimmel. *Election Day 1816.* Historical Society of Pennsylvania)

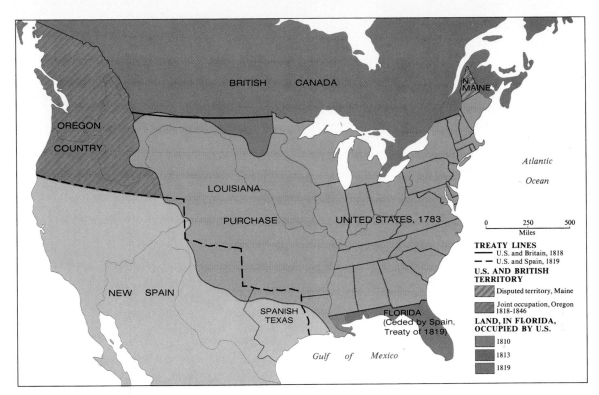

MAP 10.1 DEFINING THE NATIONAL BOUNDARIES

At the end of the Napoleonic Wars, American statesmen quickly concluded treaties with Great Britain and Spain. The agreements defined the boundary with Canada in the north and New Spain in the west. They eliminated the threat of war until the 1840s and provided the young American nation with a much-needed period of peace and security.

great historian Henry Adams put it, was "a half-way house between the European past and the American future." Now that the future had come, most Federalists joined various factions of the Republican party. The lack of more than one party prompted contemporary observers—and some historians—to call the two terms of President James Monroe, from 1817 to 1825, the Era of Good Feeling. Actually, national political harmony was more apparent than real, for the dominant Republican party was divided into increasingly vocal factions.

The career of John Quincy Adams illustrates the triumph of the Republican party and its policies. Adams was the son of the John Adams and, in his dour and suspicious manner, greatly resembled the Federalist president. Wary of British motives, John Quincy joined the Republicans prior to the War of 1812 because he preferred their foreign policy.

As secretary of state under Monroe, the younger Adams pursued an expansionist western policy that would have astounded his father. In 1817, General Andrew Jackson led an expedition into East Florida and seized two Spanish forts. He then executed two British subjects, accusing them of promoting Indian raids into the United States. Despite strong reservations about Jackson's aggressive personality and provocative conduct, Adams defended the general.

Adams also used this opportunity to annex East Florida, which Spain ceded to the United States in a treaty signed in 1819. In return, the United States accepted responsibility for financial claims against Spain, renounced its dubious title to Spanish Texas, and agreed on a boundary between New Spain (now Mexico) and the Louisiana Territory. Adams also negotiated agreements with Great Britain. The Rush-Bagot treaty of 1817 and the Webster-Ashburton agreement of 1819 removed armed vessels from the Great Lakes and established boundaries separating Maine and the Louisiana Territory from Canada. As a result of Adams's efforts, the United States gained undisputed possession of nearly all the land south of the 45th parallel and east of the Rocky Mountains.

With this continental empire in mind, President Monroe outlined a new foreign policy for the United States. In his farewell address to the nation in 1796, President Washington had warned against "entangling alliances" with European powers. Monroe, prompted by Secretary of State Adams, picked up this theme in his annual address to Congress in 1823. He announced that the United States would not interfere in the internal affairs or the external rivalries of European powers. More significantly, the president declared that the American continents were no longer "subject for further colonization" by the nations of Europe.

Thirty years later, Monroe's declaration became known as the Monroe Doctrine. In 1823, John Quincy Adams intended it as a warning to Spain. He had extended diplomatic recognition two years earlier to the Latin American republics that revolted from Spain during the Napoleonic Wars. Now Adams warned Spain not to try to reconquer its former colonies. He hoped as well to restrict Russian influence to Alaska and away from the Pacific Coast of the United States. The former Federalist had embraced the westward vision of Jefferson and the Republicans.

Even as Adams and Monroe looked to the future, they retained a traditional conception of republican government. The Founding Fathers had placed their hopes for the preservation of liberty on the virtue of the American people. Monroe echoed these beliefs. He wrote in 1822,

> We are about to make the experiment, whether there is sufficient virtue in the people to support our free republican system of government. Surely our government may go on and prosper without the existence of parties.

However, the passionate controversies during the First Party System had fundamentally altered the character of American politics. To compete with the rising Republicans, such young Federalist lawyers as Harrison Gray Otis of Massachu-

setts and James Kent of New York modified the staunch elitism of their elders. Federalists remained aristocratic in their dress and behavior, a Massachusetts Republican noted with disdain, decked out in "powder and queues..., white top-boots, breeches, and shoe buckles," but they also worked to "court public favor." They supported popular causes, organized parades and barbecues, and created a party organization to bring out the vote on election day. Their strenuous efforts resulted in hotly contested elections in which nearly 80 percent of the voters took part.

This new democratic spirit sparked a wave of constitutional revision in the states. In 1807, New Jersey abolished property-holding requirements for voting, and Maryland did so in 1810. Constitutions for the new states of Indiana, admitted in 1816, Illinois in 1818, and Alabama in 1819 were equally democratic. Connecticut, Massachusetts, and New York revised their constitutions between 1818 and 1821. They reapportioned their legislatures on a geographic basis and established more democratic forms of local government. Like Thurlow Weed of New York, most Federalist leaders opposed these innovations because they "dreaded the effect of extending and cheapening suffrage." But they could not hold back the democratic tide. Except in Rhode Island, Virginia, Florida, and Louisiana, universal white male suffrage was enacted by the 1820s. If such "democratic doctrines" had been advanced ten years earlier, Chancellor James Kent of New York protested, they "would have struck the public mind with astonishment and terror."

This political revolution was the work of a new breed of public leaders, many of them lawyers. During the Revolutionary era, American attorneys had raised the standards of their profession. They established bar associations and worked successfully for legislation that prevented untrained lawyers from practicing law. By 1800, most of the sixteen states required lawyers to have three to seven years of formal or apprenticeship training. Harvard, Columbia, and William and Mary offered lectures on legal issues. In 1784, Judge Tapping Reeve began to train lawyers in Litchfield, Connecticut, creating the first law school with a national reputation. Assisted by Judge James Gould, Reeves gave

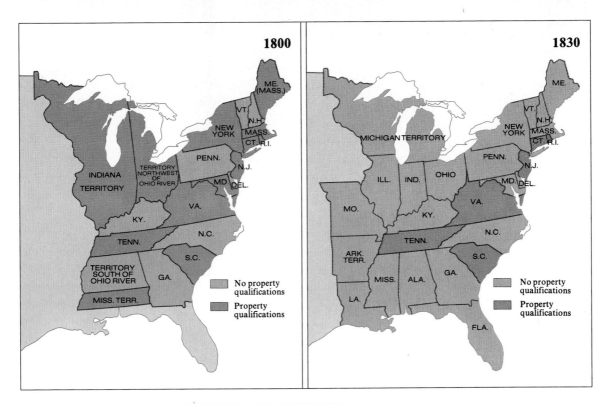

MAP 10.2 THE EXPANSION OF WHITE MALE SUFFRAGE
Between 1800 and 1830 the United States became a political democracy. Existing states revised their
constitutions to grant the vote to all taxpaying white males, and most western states joined the union
with constitutions providing for universal white male suffrage. Only a few states retained traditional
qualifications limiting the vote to property owners.

students a thorough grounding in the technical
elements of private law—contracts, torts, mercantile law. In its half-century of existence, the
Litchfield law school graduated more than a
thousand lawyers, including three future supreme court justices and two vice-presidents,
Aaron Burr of New York and John C. Calhoun
of South Carolina.

As the legal system became more important,
republican-minded reformers attacked what they
called the "professional aristocracy" that controlled it. They demanded far-reaching changes,
as they had done in the political system. These
reforms included the regulation of lawyers' fees,
the election—rather than the appointment—of
judges, and the creation of small-claims courts in
which ordinary citizens could represent themselves. Supported by ambitious men from middling backgrounds, reformers also won lower

standards for admission to the bar. By the 1820s,
only eleven of the twenty-six states required definite periods of legal instruction.

The intellectual quality of the legal profession
declined as a result of these reforms, but the bar
became more democratic in composition and
spirit. Legal prestige, especially in newly established communities, depended on hard work
and achievement rather than established wealth
and family connections. Lawyers emerged as excellent and democratic politicians. Through eloquent orations in local courtrooms, they became
popular heroes and won election to state and national legislatures in increasing numbers. Their
ranks produced the professional politicians who
now displaced patrician men of affairs from the
center of American political life.

Henry Clay, the Speaker of the House of
Representatives from 1811 to 1824, was a good

example of such a man. Clay came from a well-to-do, but undistinguished, slaveowning family in Virginia. He trained for the law first with the eminent legal authority George Wythe, a signer of the Declaration of Independence, and then with former governor Robert Brooke. Leaving these connections behind, Clay moved to the new state of Kentucky. In 1797, at the age of twenty, he established a law practice in the thriving town of Lexington. The ambitious young lawyer married into a well-established family and quickly won election to the state legislature. A master of eloquent speech, Clay rose rapidly and received appointments to unexpired terms in the United States Senate in 1806 and again in 1810. Elected to the House of Representatives in 1811 at the age of thirty-four, he was immediately chosen as its speaker. Clay made this office a position of great influence by using his political skills and bold oratory.

A committed Jeffersonian, Clay nonetheless challenged the elder statesmen of the Republican party. As the chief "war hawk," he helped push President Madison into the War of 1812. Clay later became the leader of a group of "new Republicans." He did not fear the nationalist innovations of the early Federalists, having been only a youngster during the 1790s. Indeed, their policies were so appealing that Clay became an economic nationalist. In 1816, he supported the creation of the Second Bank of the United States. The following year, he won passage of the "Bonus Bill," sponsored by Representative John C. Calhoun of South Carolina, which provided government funds for roads and other internal improvements.

Just as John Quincy Adams had abandoned Federalism to establish an American continental empire, so Henry Clay forged a blend of Federalist economic principles and Republican political ideology. Yet "Harry of the West," as Clay was popularly known, stood more for the American future than did his fellow Republican from New England. As Adams himself noted, Clay was one of a new generation of public leaders, a man who had risen "upon the broadest shoulders of democracy." The end of the First Party System produced both diversity within the dominant Republican party and a more open political culture.

The Business Class

In 1800, whatever their political outlook, most whites in rural America shared a common culture. Gentlemen farmers talked easily to yeomen about crop yields, livestock breeds, and the unpredictability of the weather. Poor southern whites and aristocratic slaveowners shared the same forms of amusement—gambling, cockfighting, and horseracing. Poor and rich Quakers attended the same meeting house, as did Presbyterians, Anglicans, and Congregationalists of different economic groups. "Almost everyone eats, drinks, and dresses in the same way," a European visitor reported from Hartford, Connecticut, in 1798, "and one can see the most obvious inequality only in the dwellings." Social hierarchies existed in these farming towns and villages, but the various groups shared many cultural and religious values.

Public events, such as milita musters, affirmed this cultural unity, as did popular festivals and other amusements. When a middle-aged man married a young widow or girl, young men from all economic ranks protested their loss. Frequently they treated the newly married couple to a *skimeton*, or *charivari*, a noisy ritual of English origin.

In Delaware County, New York, thirty or forty young men gathered to harass a bride and groom and nearly caused a riot. "About sunset the Skimetonians assembled together with their instruments of music which had been preparing for about three days," an eyewitness reported. They surrounded the house where the wedding feast was taking place and began to play. "During this music there was a dish of gunpowder, feathers, and Brimestone set on fire." When a wedding guest went outside with a lantern, "it was dashed out of his hands and he was thrown in the mud and his hat was took by someone and was cut in pieces." The "Skimeton boys" finally departed at dawn, leaving twenty-five broken windows and a subdued couple.

Popular rituals frequently gave symbolic expression to social divisions. Men and women of the lower classes used these devices to poke fun at, or to get favors from, their social superiors. On the wedding night of local aristocrat John Glenville, three hundred revelers in Ohio shook

BENJAMIN FRANKLIN'S TRIUMPH

Like most men and women of genius, Franklin was ahead of his time. After 1800, business class moralists elevated his pithy sayings in "Poor Richard's Almanac" to a popular creed. This illustration shows a page from *Bowle's Moral Pictures or Poor Richard Illustrated: Lessons for Young and Old Industry*, which was published after Franklin's death. (*Bowle's Moral Pictures.* Yale University Art Gallery. The Mabel Brady Garvan Collection)

cowbells, beat on washtubs, and blew whistles as they descended on the newlyweds' house. When Glenville refused their demands for wine, the crowd hoisted a fifty-pound pig through the window of the honeymoon chamber.

Once a year in Boston, free blacks also mocked the upper classes. The Massachusetts General Court began its annual session on the last Wednesday of May. On this festive occasion, blacks conducted mock elections. Poking fun at white political leaders and institutions, they filled public offices from their own ranks in a satiric Negro Election Day ritual. Then, joined by hundreds of whites, they led a racuous celebration that lasted far into the night.

This unified social order broke into fragments in the early nineteenth century. Most significantly, merchants and manufacturers set themselves off as a separate social group. Occasionally, contemporaries referred to this group as the "middle class," a term first used in England in 1811. However, the newly selfconscious elite drew many of its members from wealthy mercantile families. For this reason, it is best described as the "business class."

The members of the business class began to create a historically new way of life. They started by redefining traditional Christian moral injunc-tions regarding work. In the past, Protestant ministers had counseled their congregations to "be diligent in the business of your lawful calling." They warned that "a man *lothful in Business* is not a man *Serving the Lord.*" For these moralists, however, the pursuit of gain was not an end in itself. It was merely a means of serving God or evidence of divine grace.

In the expanding capitalist economy of the early nineteenth century, prosperity became a goal pursued for its own sake. Moreover, human aspirations were no longer limited to the satisfactory performance of a traditional set of expectations suggested by the term "calling." Men were no longer "called" to be mere lawyers, ministers, or merchants. Instead, they were expected to excel and to have boundless ambitions. As Governor Lewis Cass of the Michigan Territory proclaimed in 1827,

> A principle of progressive improvement seems almost inherent in human nature. We are all striving in the career of life to acquire riches, or honor, or power, or some other object, whose possession is to realize the day dreams of our imagination.

Cass articulated new assumptions regarding the sources of human action and the goals of life. But spokesmen of the business class soon transformed them into accepted matters of fact. The editor of the *Lancaster* (Pennsylvania) *Examiner and Herald* told his readers that it was "as strange as it was unnatural" for men and women to lack "individual enterprise."

The new business-class mentality broke sharply from the past in many ways. In eighteenth-century America, for example, all social classes freely drank alcoholic beverages as part of their daily routine. John C. Warrren, a Boston physician, remembered that in New England in 1800 most men indulged "the general and pernicious habit of a morning draught" of wine or rum. "A conversation under such circumstances was not likely to be brief," he noted, "so that no small part of the morning was wasted in this relaxation." Warren himself took a hostile view toward the old habits of drink and conviviality. He welcomed such new organizations as the Society for the Promotion of Industry, Frugality, and Temperance. Like others with business-class values, Warren favored a reformation in emotional attitudes and social behavior. He wanted men and women to impose rigid self-discipline on themselves and to give the highest priority to economic achievement.

The impact of business-, or middle-, class morality split the social order. Many artisans of modest financial status joined wealthier merchants and manufacturers in the temperance movement. These craftsmen and their wives also prized an ordered existence and a life filled with labor. "Up, brother, to your toil to-day," began one workingmen's song,

> Let purse proud, bloated sluggards preach
> Of labor as a curse!
> Their rotten health and morals teach
> That idleness is worse.

However, many other independent craftworkers followed their traditional habits. The employees in one Lynn, Massachusetts, shoe shop sent an apprentice to a neighborhood rum store every day at 11 A.M. and again at 4 P.M. He brought back a two-quart jug of "black strap," a popular drink made from rum and molasses. On the other hand, some wage earners had temperance imposed on them by their employers. George Logan, a prosperous Pennsylvania farmer, had always "during Harvest allowed each Man one pint of Rum per day." Influenced by the temperance crusade, he switched this ration to the much weaker malt beer. When other Pennsylvania farm owners eliminated the customary alcohol allowance in the 1830s, many laborers refused to work for them.

Temperance advocates sometimes used their political influence to change public policy. In 1816, the town council of Columbia, Pennsylvania, refused to license fairs. The councilmen claimed that these popular summer events encouraged drinking and violent behavior. Boston authorities used similar arguments in 1831 to ban the century-old celebration of Negro Election Day. The property-owning and working classes no longer enjoyed the same cultural pleasures and pastimes.

New social distinctions appeared in thousands of households as well. Wealthy families had always kept servants—slaves, indentured workers, or the children of poorer neighbors. Many middling farmers also provided room and board for young men and women in return for their labor. Among the business class, however, the nature of dependent service changed dramatically. Few servants now produced goods. Instead, merchants, manufacturers, lawyers, and shopkeepers hired live-in maids, cooks, nannies, and cleaners. Domestic service became a female occupation, a major new source of employment for young women of the working class. In 1800, there were about 40,000 free domestic servants in the United States and 755,000 white families, an approximate ratio of one servant to every twenty households. Forty years later, the nation had more than 240,000 nonslave servants and 2.5 million white families, a ratio of about one to ten.

The business class made up only about 5 percent of the white population, but these families exercised power through their wealth, status, and exclusive voluntary organizations. In Cincinnati, Ohio, for example, 270 influential businessmen formed a Chamber of Commerce. By giving institutional form to their emerging collective identity, these merchants set themselves apart from less affluent traders and shopkeepers.

Marriages cemented social and economic ties. Beginning in the late eighteenth century, New England merchant families used two types of marriage alliances to create a closely defined elite. Some merchant parents encouraged their children to marry cousins—the sons and daughters of their own brothers and sisters. As among South Carolina slaveowners who developed similar practices, these marriages kept inherited wealth within an extended family. In other cases, previously unrelated parents "exchanged" several of their children. In a striking example, four daughters of the Cabot merchant family of Salem, Massachusetts married four sons of the Higginsons, another prominent commercial family. These marriages formed the genetic and legal identity of the so-called Boston Brahmins. This wealthy, cultured, intermarried elite dominated the social and intellectual life of nineteenth-century New England.

The Boston Brahmins devised ingenious ways to maintain their financial resources and cultural identity. Many merchants set up private trust funds for their children and grandchildren. In this way they passed wealth on to succeeding generations while keeping it intact as capital for large-scale investments. With a similar end in mind, Brahmins created capital endowments for charitable, educational, and cultural establishments, including Harvard College; Massachusetts General Hospital; and the Boston Athenaeum, a private library. These private or quasi-public institutions controlled sizable amounts of investment capital. They also provided the sons of the elite with training and professional employment.

In addition, Boston merchants founded new types of private financial corporations, such as the Massachusetts Hospital Life Insurance Company. Created in 1817, Massachusetts Life accumulated funds from insurance premiums. Its board of directors invested some of this capital in government bonds and banking stocks. The directors channeled the rest of these funds, through favorable loans to themselves, into the development of textile mills and the transportation network of New England.

Thoughtful members of the business class sensed a contradiction between their wealth and their ideology. They urged all Americans to adopt the virtues of industry and temperance and to rise in the world. At the same time, they recognized that an expanding capitalist society widened economic divisions. A yeoman society filled with independent families of farmers and

A BUSINESS-CLASS DINNER PARTY
By 1820 the Boston "Brahmins" were an intermarried aristocracy of capitalist families. Their wealth and patronage helped create a vital intellectual and artistic culture. Henry Sargent, who painted this exclusive event, was himself a member of an important Boston family, one that is still influential today. (Henry Sargent. Detail of *The Dinner Party*. The Museum of Fine Arts, Boston. Gift of Mrs. Horatio Lamb in memory of Mr. & Mrs. Winthrop Sargent)

artisans no longer seemed possible. "Entire independence ought not to be wished for," Ithamar A. Beard, the paymaster of the Hamilton Manufacturing Company, told a mechanics' association in 1827. "In large manufacturing towns, many more must fill subordinate stations and must be under the immediate direction and control of a master or superintendent, than in the farming towns."

The message was clear. Business-class values were democratic, but the economic system that supported them was not. Merchants, manufacturers, and bankers had ample incomes, but clerical workers, artisans, and shopkeepers did not. No matter how hard they worked or how thrifty they were, most urban families could accumulate only modest savings. Emotional tension and insecurity spread through their lives. An economic recession, sickness, or simple bad luck could quickly dash their hopes of rising in the world.

The contradiction between the democratic values of the business class and its privileged financial position became a persistent factor in American history. Its implications were all too obvious, especially to politicians being pressed for democratic political reforms. Daniel Webster warned the Massachusetts constitutional convention of 1820, "There is not a more dangerous experiment than to place property in the hands of one class, and political power in those of another." As Webster sensed, both the democratization of politics and the emergence of the new business-class elite were just beginning. But in the coming decades, both these tendencies would gather force, completing the break with the traditional preindustrial order.

Mechanics and Workers

The growing identity of the business class hastened the formation of group consciousness throughout American society. Among artisans, craft identity had existed for more than a generation. In Philadelphia in 1788, carpenters, shoemakers, bakers, shipbuilders and a score of other craft groups marched proudly in parades celebrating the ratification of the Constitution. Flags and banners symbolized their strong sense of occupational allegiance. "May the government protect us," proclaimed the green flag of the weavers, depicting a lion holding a shuttle in its paw. The bricklayers assumed a more republican air. Their flag reminded onlookers that "both buildings and rulers are the works of our hands."

After 1800, the artisans developed a wider sense of social identity. Craftsmen now referred to themselves both as practitioners with a specific skill and as members of a "mechanic" group. By the 1820s, Massachusetts artisans supported a newspaper, the *Lynn Mirror*; the Mechanics Bank; the Mechanics Rifle Company; and the Mechanics Mutual Fire and Insurance Company.

At the same time, artisans divided along class lines. With the expansion of the outwork system, many master craftsmen became commercial middlemen. They no longer worked with their hands, making boots, furniture, or cloth. Instead, they turned into capitalist entre-

AN ARTISAN BANNER
Like most American artisans, members of the Society of Pewterers had a strong craft identity and political ideology. They supported the Constitution of 1787 because its provisions protected their wares from British competition. Later most Pewterers endorsed Jefferson's vision of a nation of "producers." They demanded that government—like their carefully shaped metal plates and pots—be "Solid and Pure." (*The Flag of the Society of Pewterers.* The New-York Historical Society)

FIGURE 10.1 THE HUMAN COST OF URBAN CAPITALISM: HEIGHTS OF WHITE MALE FARMERS AND URBAN LABORERS

preneurs, hiring scores of rural women and urban journeymen to make such products under their direction. As master craftsmen became employers—and thus members of the new business class—their journeyman workers organized craft unions to protect their own interests. "The real object . . . of this association," stated the constitution of the Mechanics Union of Philadelphia in 1828, is "to assist in establishing a just balance of power . . . between all the various classes and individuals which constitute society at large." In such eastern cities as Philadelphia, New York, and Baltimore, printers and other artisans attempted to force their employers to adopt a common wage scale, but with only limited success.

The expansion of capitalist enterprise also increased the size of the propertyless working class. These men and women had a distinct set of cultural values. Raised in rural areas, they were accustomed to the seasonal and task-oriented work regime of agricultural society. They resented the strict, year-round labor schedule in urban jobs. These wage earners often did not report to their jobs on time, and they skipped whole days of work when their pocketbooks permitted. Many laborers flocked to minstrel shows and saloons. The motto of the Four Alls tavern in Moyamensing, Pennsylvania, captured the sentiments of its customers:

THE FOUR ALLS

1. *King*—I govern all.
2. *General*—I fight for all.
3. *Minister*—I pray for all.
4. *Laborer*—And I pay for all.

Whatever their jobs, laborers and semiskilled workers earned about six dollars a week. This pay provided only a bare level of subsistence for their families. Sporadic employment and low living standards undermined their morale and physical well-being. In Massachusetts, shoemakers died at an average age of forty-three, while farmers lived to sixty-four.

Many young wage earners joined volunteer fire companies where they found congenial companions and drinking partners as well as additional income. Property owners paid cash bonuses to fire fighters who saved their goods and buildings. The young volunteers gathered on festive occasions for the traditional rituals of merrymaking. In Baltimore, a group of rowdies called themselves the Callithumpians. They celebrated the Fourth of July by wearing grotesque clothing and making a racket with tin pans and rattles. As young workers moved from region to region searching for jobs, Callithumpians appeared in most eastern cities and in many rural areas in the West. In New York, a group of Callithumpians ushered in the New Year, an amused eyewitness reported, "with the darndest racket you'd ever wish to hear. There was more than ten thousand fellers with whistles, penny trumpets, tin pails, shovels, and tongs. Why, they made more noise than a concert of cats."

Beneath the noise, the social makeup of these groups of merrymakers had changed. Young men from business-class or property-owning farm families no longer joined in skimetons or other noisy celebrations. Consequently, the victims stopped accepting these rituals as good fun and condemned them as "a survival of semibarbaric times." In urban areas, many festive events turned into violent confrontations between racial, religious, and economic groups.

The increasingly dissimilar American people no longer shared common values and rituals. By the 1820s, they stood divided into distinct cultures, though tied to one another by economic necessity and an increasingly democratic political system. As the customs and values of the traditional preindustrial society faded away, a new public culture had come into being.

Changing Private Identities

As the culture of the United States changed, so did life within the families that composed its basic units. Influenced by economic circumstances and cultural sentimentalism, Americans began to create a new set of marriage rules. Young men and women from urban and well-to-do backgrounds developed a conjugal system of family relationships. They started raising their children in new ways. Large numbers of American women began to strive to create a more active and respected identity for themselves. Many women found outlets for their energy and ambition in religious and educational institutions.

The Conjugal Family

During most of the preindustrial period, American families had a patriarchal, lineal form. The husband dominated his wife, and both parents arranged the marriages of their children. They chose marriage partners carefully to ensure the social status of the family line and the financial well-being of their offspring. "I rely on you to see the property settlement properly drawn etc. *before the marriage*," a Virginia planter wrote to a lawyer on behalf of his orphaned niece, "for I by no means consent that Polly shall be left to the Vicissitudes of Life."

Shifting economic conditions undermined this parent-controlled marriage system. As land holdings shrank in long-settled rural areas, parents could no longer provide all their children with substantial farms in the community. As a result, parents had much less control over marriages, and sons and daughters chose their own partners.

Cultural sentimentalism likewise encouraged a new marriage system. Sentimentalism represented a new way of perceiving the world. It glorified the importance of "feeling"—that is, the emotional understanding of life's experiences. Those influenced by this new sensibility sought a physical, sensuous, poetic appreciation of nature, God, and human relationships.

Beginning about 1800, sentimentalism affected all classes of American society. It appeared, for example, in the German and English literary works read by highly educated Americans. The most popular plays were melodramas, in which playwrights and actors evoked a surplus of emotion from audiences by playing on their hopes and fears. William Dunlap, an innovative theatrical entrepreneur, drew packed audiences to his productions of the German melodramatist August von Kotzebue. Religious revivalism also emphasized the emotional commitment of the believer rather than an intellectual comprehension of theology. The passionate stirrings of the heart were a more valid form of experience than the clear logic of the brain.

Sentimentalism prompted marriages based on love—and justified their legitimacy. Parents had always considered physical attraction and emotional compatibility when arranging marriages for their children, but these romantic factors did not have a high cultural value. Mothers and fathers placed greater emphasis on personal character and financial resources. One eighteenth-century Virginia mother argued that young women should remain single "till they were old enough to form a proper *judgement* of mankind" and not be deceived by their emotions.

The testimony of couples seeking divorces suggests the impact of sentimentalism on traditional cultural expectations. Only a few men and women requested legal separations in preindustrial America, but court petitions in divorce cases changed significantly through the years. Before 1765, most petitions in Massachusetts charged the spouse with neglect, abandonment, or adultery. Such failings represented serious offenses against the moral order of society as well as private conflicts between husbands and wives. By 1800, personal emotional complaints predominated in divorce petitions. Women and men now cited the absence of conjugal affection as a justification for divorce. One women complained that her husband "ceased to cherish her," and a male petitioner lamented that his wife had "almost broke his heart."

The new marriage system gave young adults greater freedom but had shortcomings of its own. Like Eliza Southgate of Maine, most young men and women sought spouses who were "calculated to promote my happiness." Yet some of them lacked the maturity and experience to choose wisely. They married for love, only to suffer bitter disappointment when their spouses failed them as financial providers or helpful companions. Other men and women never married because sentiment distorted their expectations of courtship.

Couples who found lasting happiness in marriage had to work out new family relationships. As lineal ties crumbled and children migrated to different communities, parents played a smaller role in their married lives. As a result, wives could not rely as much on their parents for emotional support and became more dependent on their husbands. The marriage contract "is so much more important in its consequences to females than to males," George Cutler astutely noted in his journal while studying law with Judge Tapping Reeve in 1820 in Litchfield, Connecticut:

> for besides leaving everything else to unite themselves to one man, they subject themselves to his authority. He is their all—their only relative—their only hope. As for him, it is upon his employment that he depends almost entirely for the happiness of his life.

Patterns of Child Raising

These white Americans had smaller families than their parents or grandparents. In the farm village of Sturbridge, Massachusetts, women who married between 1730 and 1760 bore an average of 8.8 children. As Sturbridge farms grew smaller and handicraft production increased, parents had fewer children. Sturbridge women who started having children between 1800 and 1820 averaged only 6.0 offspring.

By the 1820s, in urban areas of Massachusetts, native-born white women gave birth to an average of only four children. This birthrate

THE NEW CONJUGAL FAMILY

In this painting Grace and Philip Schuyler regard one another with true affection, suggesting the new emotional bonds between husbands and wives. They likewise show affection for their children by encouraging their individual musical and literary talents. The dramatic contrast with earlier family portraits (pp. 15 and 90) reveals the new character of family life. (Ambrose Andrews. *The Schuyler Family*. The New-York Historical Society)

barely maintained a stable population. About a third of the children raised in urban areas in the United States died before the age of twenty-one from such diseases as measles, diptheria, or smallpox. In addition, thousands of young men migrated to the West, depriving young women of marriage partners. By the 1820s, spinsters made up about 13 percent of the adult females in Massachusetts and nearly 10 percent in other eastern states.

The relative abundance of women was one reason for the decline in family size. Because there were few eligible men, women took longer to find suitable partners. Most of them now married between the ages of twenty-four and twenty-six rather than at twenty to twenty-two. The delay of two to four years had important results. These women had fewer children because they were married for a shorter period during their most fertile years.

Equally important, many women did not want large families. Beginning around 1800,

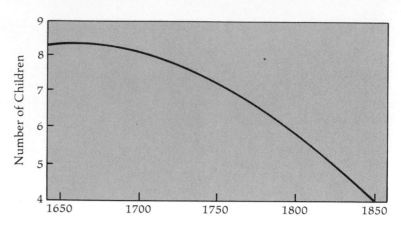

FIGURE 10.2 FAMILY SIZE IN
NEW ENGLAND

many parents deliberately limited the size of their families. After having four or five children, these women and their husbands avoided conception. Many couples abstained from sexual intercourse, and others used various methods of birth control. Some mothers extended their period of breast-feeding. They did not know that milk production inhibits the release of viable eggs, but folk wisdom assured them of the result. In 1799, after thirty-nine-year-old Sally Downing had her sixth child, her mother consoled her. "This might be the last trial of this sort," she told her daughter, if Sally "could suckle the baby for two years" and reach menopause. Because parents limited births once their families had reached a desired size, women stopped childbearing earlier. In Sturbridge, for example, mothers bore their last child at an average age of 38.7 years in 1750, but at 35.4 in 1840.

As American parents had fewer children, they began to practice new forms of raising them. The historical character of child-raising practices, like many aspects of private behavior, is difficult to document. Most foreign visitors to the United States thought parents indulged their children and did not discipline them. "Mr. Schuyler's second son is a spoiled, little child, as are all American children," the Marquis de Chastellux observed in 1780, "very willful, mischievous, and likeable." Brissot de Warville, another French observer, noted that outdoor privies had "a lower seat for children," which he interpreted as "a mark of parental solicitude." Writing in 1797, a Polish aristocrat agreed that American children were "spoiled" and showed "scant respect" for their parents. He suggested that this behavior stemmed from the "general ideas of

Liberty and Equality engraved on all their hearts."

Some Americans used republican ideology to justify the results of noncoercive childraising. A British visitor was dumbfounded when an American father excused his son's "resolute disobedience" with a smile and the remark, "A sturdy republican, sir." Foreigners thought parents in the United States encouraged their children to be independent rather than subordinate, so that youths would be able to "go their own way."

An analysis of the child-rearing literature read by American parents supports this interpretation—but also modifies it. Ministers wrote most of the pamphlets, sermons, and advice books dealing with children. Therefore, the changing content of this literature mirrors the evolution of religious thought and probably of actual practice as well.

Reflecting the dominant influence of Calvinist theology, most seventeenth-century authors had taken a grim view of the condition and treatment of children. "The newborn babe is full of the stains and pollution of sin, which it inherits from our first parents though our loins," proclaimed a widely circulated English pamphlet of 1676. Since this original sin was "bound up in the heart of a child," ministers emphasized the need for stern discipline. "The stubborness and stoutness of mind arising from natural pride," an early New England minister asserted, had to "be broken and beaten down." Many American parents accepted these doctrines of innate infant depravity and strict discipline throughout the eighteenth century.

Meanwhile, a more optimistic view of children commanded increasing respect. In his *Thoughts on Education* (1692), the English philosopher John Locke argued that children were "rational creatures." They should be encouraged to act correctly by reasoned restraint, advice, and praise. As Locke put it, parents had to "keep up a child's spirit, easy, active, and free, and yet at the same time to restrain him from many things he has a mind to do and to draw him to things that are uneasy to him." John Wesley, the founder of the Methodist church, incorporated these Lockian principles into the teachings of English Methodism. The writings of the eminent Boston minister Cotton Mather circulated them widely in America. In such essays as "A Family Well-Ordered," Mather told his readers to instill in their children "a high opinion of their father's love" and to obtain obedience by threatening the withdrawal of parental affection. "To be chased

CONTRASTING MODES OF EDUCATION
This delightful painting pokes fun at a strict teacher and, indirectly, at the approach evangelicals advocated for raising children by harsh discipline. The children's faces reflect the rationalist outlook of the artist. To borrow words from a minister of the time, we can see in their eyes "the first dawn of reason, beaming forth its immortal rays." (Frick Art Reference Library)

for a while out of my presence," Mather concluded on a personal note, was "looked upon as the sorest punishment in the family."

These two traditions of advice—the authoritarian Calvinist and the affection-oriented rationalist—appealed to different social groups in the United States. Educated or wealthy Americans, especially members of the Anglican church, which became the Episcopal church in 1789, usually treated their children kindly, even indulgently. Foreign travelers often intermingled with these well-to-do Americans and viewed their customs as the national norm. Actually, most yeomen and tenant farmers, and other workers, were much stricter. In particular, families in Calvinist churches practiced authoritarian ways of raising children.

Both these traditions changed significantly during the early nineteenth century. Evangelical Calvinist ministers still insisted on the need to create humble, self-denying men and women whose wills were subordinate to God. In his essay "On the Mother's Role in Education" (1833), John Abbott defended "fear" as a "useful and necessary principle in family government." Children "should submit to your authority," he advised parents, not to "your arguments and persuasions." Yet Abbott cautioned that it was "ruinous to the disposition of a child, exclusively to control him by this motive." Other Calvinists also adopted a less authoritarian position.

Rationalist authors placed increasing emphasis on children's capacity for education. The goal of infant discipline, they suggested, should be the early and thorough development of the child's conscience. Young children could then police their own behavior.

Parents who married for love followed affection-oriented practices in raising their children. The names they gave the youngsters indicated a new stress on the unique individuality of each child. Before 1800, most white Americans gave their own first names to one of their sons and daughters. Fathers and mothers thus symbolically stamped their own identities on their offspring. In the 1660s, Joseph and Mary White Rowlandson of Lancaster, Massachusetts, named two of their children Joseph and Mary. Through future generations, this family tradition populated the countryside around Lancaster with Josephs and Marys. After 1800, however, fewer parents named their offspring after themselves. When they did, they also gave the child a distinctive middle name. For example, Jonathan Bolton Lincoln of Hingham, Massachusetts, shared his father's first and last names and, as his middle name, the family name of his mother.

As the children of the early nineteenth century grew up, their parents sought to develop the consciences of the youngsters. They read fictional stories to their children that stressed self-discipline and orderly personal habits. They encouraged the young people to accept the burdens of independence—of thinking, talking, and acting for themselves. As foreign observers noted, American children had greater freedom than those in Europe. However, the youthful Americans had to assume greater responsibilities for self-development as well.

Gradually, the American conjugal family evolved into a child-centered institution in which the mother had considerable authority. Before 1800, when the lineal family system ruled by the father was the norm, judges commonly gave him custody of the children in divorce cases. Later, judges in Connecticut, Pennsylvania, and New York overturned such traditional procedures. In 1813, for example, Chief Justice Thompson of the Pennsylvania Superior Court declared that custody was "not a matter of right which the father can claim at the hands of the court. It is the benefit and welfare of the infant to which the attention of the Court ought principally to be directed."

Then, in 1830, the Maine Supreme Judicial Court awarded custody of the children to the mother in a divorce case. The judges stated that the "parental feelings of the mother toward her children are naturally as strong, and generally stronger than those of the father."

These and other legal decisions reflected the beginnings of fundamental changes in the private identities of many Americans. The judges' concern with people's feelings reflected the rise of sentimentalism. The legal emphasis on maternal love and children's welfare underlined the emergence of the child-centered conjugal family. This new system of family relationships appeared as a coherent unit primarily among urban, business-class, and well-educated Americans. Yet many others were beginning to adopt

one or more of the new values. These ordinary men and women defined new personal identities for themselves and helped to establish the first outlines of a new American middle-class culture. This new culture would not become dominant until the 1830s and 1840s. But the shape it would take was already becoming clear.

Women's "Sphere"

The growing complexity of American preindustrial society raised fundamental questions regarding the "place" and legal status of women. In the predominately agricultural society of the colonial period, the wife's role was taken for granted. Men simply assumed that she was a subordinate helpmate for her husband. Law or custom excluded married women and their daughters from political office, legal independence, and family authority. Unmarried women and widows had greater legal autonomy, but most of them lacked the economic resources required to be truly independent. Many women accepted their inferior position, depreciating themselves as "weaker vessels" and "helpless females."

The nature of farm life obscured—and, to some extent, offset—the subordinate position of women. Farm tasks of men and women overlapped. Wives and daughters labored in the barn, garden, and workshop, and sometimes in the field, while fathers took a day-to-day role in raising the children. However, if the work roles were complementary and nearly equal, the division of power was not. The wife and children worked *for* the father as well as with him.

The definition of sex roles was even sharper in the families of slaveowning planters, gentlemen farmers, and urban residents. The wives of most merchants, lawyers, and wealthy landlords rarely shared their husbands' work. Elizabeth Murray Smith, a successful Boston dry-goods store owner, was an exception. She migrated from Scotland in 1749 at the age of twenty-three and eventually married three wealthy merchants. Despite her business success, Smith recognized that "domestic economy . . . is the female dignity, & praise." As a Virginian lady explained a few decades later, she had learned that "within the sphere of domestic life

THE DILEMMAS OF WOMANHOOD, 1801

Eliza Southgate was born into a wealthy Maine family in 1783. At school in Boston, she discovered both radical doctrines of sexual equality and the reality of female subordination. In letters to a male cousin, this sensitive young woman tried to resolve these contradictory messages and to define her own stance toward the male world.

But every being who has contemplated human nature on a large scale will certainly justify me when I declare that the inequality of privilege between the sexes is very sensibly felt by us females, and in no instance is it greater than in the liberty of choosing a partner in marriage; true, we have the liberty of refusing those we don't like, but not of selecting those we do. This is undoubtedly as it should be....

I never was of opinion that the pursuits of the sexes ought to be the same; on the contrary, I believe it would be destructive to happiness, there would a degree of rivalry exist, incompatible with each should have a separate sphere of action,—in such a case there could be no clashing unless one or the other should leap their respective bounds. Yet to cultivate the qualities with which we are endowed can never be called infringing the prerogatives of man....

The cultivation of the power we possess, I have ever thought a privilege (or I may say duty) that belonged to the human species, and not man's exclusive prerogative. Far from destroying the harmony that ought to subsist, it would fix it on a foundation that would not totter at every jar. Women would be under the same degree of subordination that they now are; enlighten and expand their minds, and they would perceive the necessity of such a regulation to preserve the order and happiness of society....

It does not follow (O what a pen!) that every female who vindicates the capacity of the sex is a disciple of Mary Wolstoncraft. Though I allow her to have said many things which I cannot but approve, I confess I admire many of her sentiments...

Woman's chief glory & happiness ought to exist." Some women proudly accepted this role and "the duties that are annex'd to my Station." Others complained that they were confined to a "narrow sphere." A few clearly voiced their resentment at being "Chain'd down to domestic Dutiys" that "Stagnate the Blood and Stupefie the Senses."

The Revolutionary fervor in America and Europe in the late eighteenth century prompted some women to challenge the inferior status of their sex. Judith Sargent Murray, the daughter of a wealthy New England merchant, wrote an essay called "On the Equality of the Sexes" in 1779 and published it in 1790. In her treatise, Murray took issue with the widely accepted view of Lord Halifax, a prominent English statesman and essayist, in his *Advice to a Daughter*, first published in 1688. Halifax wrote that "in the economy of the world, the men . . . had the larger share of reason bestowed upon them." To refute his statement, Murray systematically compared the intellectual faculties of males and females. The young New England author argued that women had memories equal to those of men, and imaginations that were superior. Murray conceded that most women were inferior to males in judgment and in reasoning powers, but simply because of a lack of training. "We can only reason from what we know," she pointed out, emphasizing that most women had been denied the "opportunity of acquiring knowledge."

An English woman, Mary Wollstonecraft, stated this feminist viewpoint forcefully in a pathbreaking book, *A Vindication of the Rights of Women* (1792). Many American women condemned Wollstonecraft's sexually adventurous personal life, but her arguments in the book commanded the attention of educated men and women. Reasoning from republican principles of civic equality, she asserted that women deserved equal status with men in all political and social activities.

Most American men read *The Rights of Women* with disdain or a lack of understanding. Wollstonecraft's statements bore little resemblance to the traditional division of power between the sexes. In the political arena, for example, the majority of American men strongly supported the extension of the vote to all taxpayers; many advocated universal male suffrage. But, as events in New Jersey clearly demonstrated, few men envisioned a political role for women. Following the Revolution, New Jersey gave the vote to qualified property owners, without regard to gender. But when a large number of women exercised this right in a series of fierce battles between Republicans and Federalists, the New Jersey legislature revoked their vote in 1807. As an anonymous male wrote to a newspaper at the height of the controversy, "Women, generally, are neither by nature, nor habit, nor education, nor by their necessary condition in society fitted to perform this duty with credit to themselves or advantage to the public."

A few American public leaders responded more positively to female demands for greater equality, but they usually did so with male needs in mind. In his *Thoughts on Female Education* (1787), the physician Benjamin Rush advocated the intellectual training of women so they would "be an agreeable companion for a sensible man." Rush and other republican-minded men of affairs likewise welcomed the appearance of loyal "republican mothers" who would instruct "their sons in the principles of liberty and government." Suggested Rush, "Let the ladies of a country be educated properly, and they will form its manner and character."

Ministers emphasized the role that women could assume in moral and religious education. "Preserving virtue and instructing the young are not the fancied, but the real 'Rights of Women,'" the Reverend Thomas Bernard told the Female Charitable Society of Salem, Massachusetts, in 1803. He urged his audience to forget about the public roles advocated by Mary Wollstonecraft and other feminists. Instead, women should remain content with the care of children, for this gave them "an extensive power over the fortunes of man in every generation." In Bernard's view, women should stay in their "sphere," but the powers and status of this sphere should be publically acknowledged and considerably enhanced. "We look to you ladies to raise the standard of character in our own

sex," the Reverend Joseph Buckminister of Portsmouth, New Hampshire, echoed in 1810.

This limited redefinition of women's sphere appealed to many American women because it bolstered their social identity. "She is still *woman*," Mary Van Schalkyck, a young New Englander, wrote in 1803, with "duties prescribed her by the God of Nature essentially different form those of *man*." Van Schalkyck and other educated, upper-class women accepted that each gender "should have a separate sphere of action," but they insisted on the equality of the male and female worlds. "I will never consent to have our sex considered in an inferior point of light," Abigail Adams, the wife of President John Adams, proclaimed in 1799. "Let each planet shine in their own orbit. God and nature design'd it so—if man in *Lord*, woman is *Lordess*."

In becoming the "guardians of virtue" suggested by Thomas Bernard, women assumed a new social role. Previously, religious authorities had considered the moral capabilities of men and women to be equal. If anything, English and American moralists viewed women as more susceptible to the devil's wiles, either as sexual temptresses or as dangerous witches. Clerical authors reversed this image after 1750, and by 1800, they ascribed sexual promiscuity to male aristocratic manners rather than female voluptuousness. They also claimed that modesty and purity were inherent parts of women's nature. Thus, women had unique qualifications for the tasks of spiritual uplift. Thomas Grimké, a South Carolina minister and social reformer, asserted,

> Give me a host of educated pious mothers and sisters, and I will do more to revolutionize a country, in moral and religious taste, in manners and in intellectual cultivation than I can possibly do in double or triple the time, with a similar host of men.

Women themselves took new religious initiatives in the late eighteenth century. Mother Ann Lee founded the Shaker sect in England in 1758 and, with scores of followers, migrated in 1774 to America, where she quickly attracted hundreds more. During the following decade, Jemima Wilkinson, another powerful female revivalist, won dozens of converts to her own sect. Women in traditional churches were equally

JOHN AND ABIGAIL ADAMS

Both Adamses had strong personalities and pursued their goals with determination. In 1794, John fondly accused his wife of being a "Disciple of Wollstonecraft," but Abigail's commitment to legal equality for women long predated the publication of Wollstonecraft's treatise, *A Vindication of the Rights of Woman* (1792). (Left, Mather Brown. *John Adams.* Boston Athenaem; Right, Artist Unidentified. Portrait Traditionally said that to be of *Abigail Adams.* New York State Historical Association, Cooperstown)

active. In 1797, Isabella Graham organized the New York Society for the Relief of Widows with Small Children, using church resources to address a persistent female concern. Boston women, led by Mary Webb, created the Female Society for Missionary Purposes in 1800.

The social composition of American churches encouraged the mobilization of female energy. Women composed about 60 percent of the members admitted into New England Congregational churches in the late eighteenth century; this proportion rose to 70 percent after 1800. Strongly supported by male ministers, activist women in local congregations followed the examples set by Webb, Graham, and other leaders. In 1810, a Massachusetts woman reported that "there is a female society in almost every town in the region, who meet at stated seasons for prayer." In New Hampshire, women managed more than fifty local "cent" societies that raised funds for the Society for Promoting Christian Knowledge.

Female activism brought changes in religious practice. Traditionally, many Protestant sects, including Congregationalists, Presbyterians, Quakers, and Lutherans, seated men and women on different sides of the church during regular Sunday services; and ministers often conducted separate prayer meetings for each sex. Now Methodist and Baptist preachers encouraged mixed praying, which people referred to as "promiscuous" assemblies. Even Presbyterian and Congregational churches adopted this innovation in frontier areas, and with impressive results. "Our prayer meetings have been one of

the greatest means of the conversion of souls," a minister in central New York related in the 1820s, "especially those in which brothers and sisters have prayed together. If God has honoured any meetings amongst us, it has been these."

Many laymen resented the emphasis on women's moral superiority and the activism that resulted. "Women have a different *calling*," one man argued in the *Dedham* (Massachusetts) *Gazette* in 1816. "They are neither required nor permitted to be exhorters or leaders in public assemblies." "That they *be chaste, keepers at home* is the Apostle's direction," this traditionalist concluded.

Ministers nevertheless promoted female religious groups, and women became increasingly conscious of their new social power. By the 1820s, mothers throughout the United States founded local maternal associations to encourage Christian child raising. Newsletters, such as *Mothers' Magazine* and *Mothers' Assistant*, were widely read in hundreds of small towns and villages. The organizations and publications created a sense of shared purpose and a new feeling of gender identity among women. By the 1830s, one foreign observer announced that she "never saw, or read, of any country where religion had so strong a hold upon the women."

The moral expansion of women's sphere affected American society in important ways. Many young women and their male escorts upheld female virtue by postponing sexual intercourse until marriage. Their self-restraint represented a major change from the eighteenth-century, when many couples had sexual union during courtship. In Bristol, Rhode Island, for example, about half the women who married between 1740 and 1760 bore a child within eight months of their wedding day. In Hingham, Massachusetts, the proportion of premarital conceptions increased from 10 percent before 1710 to more than 30 percent between 1750 and 1800. Then they declined sharply. By 1830, only 15 percent of the newly married parents in Hingham had conceived a child before marriage. The new emphasis on female virtue, combined with other social changes, encouraged premarital chastity.

The widespread participation of females in religious life also helped begin a new era in the history of women. Never before had so many women belonged to groups or institutions with an interest in social affairs. Churches supported scores of seminaries that gave girls a sound religious education. Emma Willard, the first American woman who publicly advocated higher education for women, opened the Middlebury (Vermont) Female Seminary in 1814. She later founded a school for girls in Waterford, New York, that moved to nearby Troy in 1821. Catharine Beecher, another important educator and author, established a female academy in Hartford, Connecticut, and later in Cincinnati.

Women's educational institutions produced a host of educated women. Within a few decades, they began to displace men from their traditional roles as teachers. In the 1820s, women taught summer sessions in many schools. By the following decade, they worked during the more demanding winter sessions as well. However, female teachers earned far less than their male colleagues because of women's inferior social status. Their monthly pay of twelve to fourteen dollars with room and board was slightly below that of farm laborers.

Nevertheless, these women had significant moral and intellectual responsibilities. Their opportunities to participate in the affairs of society far outstripped those open to women during the Revolutionary era. As Catharine Beecher said in 1827, "A lady should study not to *shine* but to *act*." The change in women's private identities had important public effects and began to alter the character of American culture.

The Creation of the American National Character

Americans created a distinct national character during the half-century following the War of Independence. The United States also became a fervently Protestant nation for the first time. This change resulted from the Second Great Awakening, the largest and most sustained religious revival in American history. Religious organizations and beliefs played a major role in unifying an otherwise diverse society. In addition, the theological doctrines of the Second Great Awakening confirmed the value placed on individual effort. Many European observers regarded white Americans as individualists pursuing their destinies in a unique social order that lacked hierarchy and honored economic achievement. The United States was no longer a traditional society.

The Second Great Awakening

Between 1790 and 1830, every decade brought a major upsurge of Protestantism in some region of the new nation. First, Baptists and Shakers evangelized the backcountry of New England, as did Universalists. Universalism, repudiating Calvinist doctrines of eternal damnation, taught that ultimate salvation was guaranteed to all. This optimistic message attracted thousands of converts in northern New England.

After 1800, camp meeting revivals swept the frontier regions of South Carolina, Kentucky, Tennessee, and Ohio with thundering intensity. James McGready, a Scotch-Irish Presbyterian preacher, "could so array hell before the wicked," an eyewitness reported, "that they would tremble and quake, imagining a lake of fire and brimstone yawning to overwhelm them." In combination, these frontier preachers created an awesome scene. James Finley, a future Methodist minister, attended the Cane Ridge, Kentucky, revival of 1801 as a lad of twenty, and it left a lasting impression:

> The noise was like the roar of Niagara. The vast sea of human beings seemed to be agitated as if by a storm. I counted seven ministers, all preaching at one time, some on stumps, others

WOMEN IN THE AWAKENING
The preacher is male, but women fill the audience. By creating new religious organizations, women emerged from the Second Great Awakening with enhanced moral and social power. The Awakening remains one of the most far-reaching women's movements in American history. (Kenneth Lucas. *Camp Meeting.* The New-York Historical Society)

on wagons. . . . Some of the people were singing, others praying, some crying for mercy. A peculiarly strange sensation came over me. My heart beat tumultuously, my knees trembled, my lips quivered, and I felt as though I must fall to the ground.

Through revivals, Baptist and Methodist preachers reshaped the spiritual landscape of the southern and southeastern states. They eventually won the allegiance of most of the white population and firmly implanted evangelical Protestant Christianity among Afro-Americans.

The revivals had a lasting effect because they generated new religious institutions. The appearance of active women's groups in New England and the Middle Atlantic states doubled the amount of organized religious energy. In the South and West, Baptist and Methodist preachers devised new church structures. Ordinarily, these ministers did not settle among a congregation. A Methodist circuit-rider, "riding a hardy pony or a horse . . . with his Bible, hymnbook, and Discipline," moved about continually, establishing new churches. Traveling "through storms, wind, hail, snow, and swamps, wet, weary, and hungry," he searched

for devout families and brought them together for worship. The minister then appointed lay elders to lead the new congregation and enforce moral discipline until he returned.

These missionary efforts shifted the base of American religion. The leading denominations of the Revolutionary era—the Congregationalists, Episcopalians, and Quakers—declined in relative importance. For the most part, they were content to maintain existing congregations or to grow slowly through the natural increase and migration of their members. New evangelical churches—the Baptists, Methodists, and Presbyterians—grew much more rapidly because they actively sought converts.

To impart their message, evangelical ministers copied the techniques of George Whitefield and other eighteenth-century revivalists. They translated the intuitive genius of the New Light preachers into a prescribed method. Manuals on "practical preaching" advised emphasis on piety, not on learning. They particularly stressed the power of the spoken word rather than the written sermon. "Preach without papers," advised one minister, "seem earnest & serious; & you will be listened to with Patience, & Wonder; both your hands will be seized, & almost shook off as soon as you are out of the Church." This vigorous type of preaching imparted a sense of direction and purpose to hundreds of local revivals.

A second burst of innovation solidified the Second Great Awakening and extended its cultural impact. Religious leaders founded new theological seminaries, such as Andover in Massachusetts and Lane in Ohio. Like Harvard, Yale, Princeton, and other colleges that had long trained men for the ministry, these institutions increased cohesion and cooperation among clergymen. Equally important, they fostered loyalty to nationwide denominations composed of a multitude of local congregations. Yet growing self-identity among individual denominations did not lead to competition and bitter theological debates. Instead, American Protestant churches became less dogmatic. Many congregations abandoned books and pamphlets, such as the orthodox *Watts Hymnal*, that contained controversial interpretations. They replaced them, one layman explained, with publications that would not give "offense to the serious christians of any denomination."

The founding of five interdenominational societies between 1815 and 1826 created a national religious movement. These new organizations—the American Education Society (1815), the Bible Society (1816), the Sunday School Union (1824), the Tract Society (1825), and the Home Missionary Society (1826)—were centered in New York, Boston, and Philadelphia.

Organization on a national scale gave an impressive sense of destiny to the Second Great Awakening. National institutions united the individual energies of thousands of church members in a great collective undertaking. "I want to see our State evangelized," declared one pious layman:

> Suppose the great State of New York in all its physical, political, moral, commercial and pecuniary resources should come over to the Lord's side. Why it would turn the scale and could convert the world. I shall have no rest until it is done.

This intense emphasis on human ability and on universal salvation made the Second Great Awakening very different from the revivals of the 1740s. In New England, the leaders of the First Awakening had stressed the Calvinist doctrine of election—that is, they implied that God

selected only a distinct minority for heavenly salvation. Even in Virginia, where the Baptist revival of the 1760s conveyed a more optimistic theology, the old Calvinist beliefs continued to raise fears. "Election, Election, Election! O this Election & Reprobation," complained one man in the backcountry. "I am much troubled with these doctrines."

Following Independence, religion in America became more humanistic and democratic. Many highly educated and economically secure Congregationalists became deists. They devised a new Unitarian philosophy that repudiated the concept of the Trinity, a God composed of Father, Son, and Holy Spirit. Instead, Unitarians proposed an indivisible and "united" God and stressed the power of human reason. "The ultimate reliance of a human being is, and must be, on his own mind," argued the famous Unitarian minister William Ellery Channing, "for the idea of God is the idea of our own spiritual nature, purified and enlarged to infinity."

The theology of Samuel Hopkins commanded a larger following. Reflecting an older, eighteenth-century understanding of "virtue," Hopkins contended that moral depravity consisted of self-love. The New England clergyman then imparted a new and more purposeful thrust to this doctrine. Hopkins maintained that individuals who received God's sanctifying grace were obliged to act in a benevolent fashion, assisting others to seek God.

Lyman Beecher, the leading New England clergyman of the early nineteenth century, endorsed the doctrine of benevolent action. He also raised the prospect of universal salvation. Although Beecher insisted, as did his Calvinist predecessors, that human beings had a natural tendency to sin, he declared that all men and women had the capacity to choose God. In his sermons, redemption took the form of a self-induced spiritual awakening, not an arbitrary summons from a stern God. Beecher's softening of Calvinism would soon seem conservative, however, as new evangelicals began to preach even more open and emotional ideas about conversion.

The success of the Second Great Awakening threatened to undermine its original spiritual mission. By the 1820s, some church leaders complained that religious benevolence had prompted the creation of organizations that placed primary

TIME LINE
TOWARD A NEW CULTURE

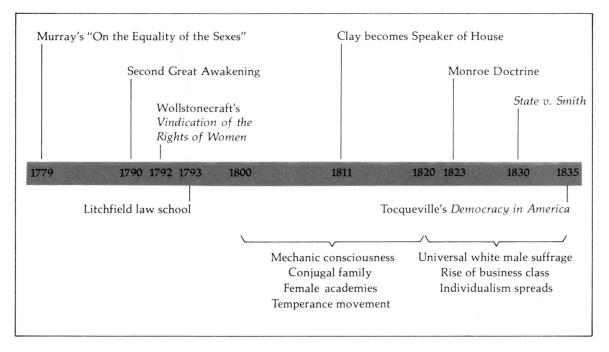

Murray's "On the Equality of the Sexes"   Clay becomes Speaker of House

Second Great Awakening   Monroe Doctrine

Wollstonecraft's
*Vindication of the
Rights of Women*   *State v. Smith*

| 1779 | 1790 | 1792 | 1793 | 1800 | 1811 | 1820 | 1823 | 1830 | 1835 |

Litchfield law school   Tocqueville's *Democracy in America*

Mechanic consciousness   Universal white male suffrage
Conjugal family   Rise of business class
Female academies   Individualism spreads
Temperance movement

---

emphasis on reforming society. They warned Christians to concentrate on spiritual goals and not "to substitute their own projects for the humble use of scriptural means." Yet the revival movement itself stressed the power of human will to change the world. As religion became a dynamic force in American life, it inevitably became involved in earthly affairs.

It was not surprising, therefore, that on July 4, 1827, the Reverend Ezra Stiles Ely called on the members of the Seventh Presbyterian Church in Philadelphia to begin a "Christian party in politics." Ely entitled his sermon "The Duty of Christian Freemen to Elect Christian Rulers." It asserted a new goal for the American republic that Thomas Jefferson and John Adams would have found strange and perhaps troubling. The two Founding Fathers, who had been in their graves less than a year, believed America's mission was to spread political republicanism. But Ely urged the United States to become an evangelical Christian nation, dedicated to the task of religious conversion at home and abroad. "All our rulers ought in their official capacity to serve the Lord Jesus Christ," Ely declared.

The National Character

As foreign travelers observed the changing flow of life in the new American republic, they recorded vivid impressions of the nation's culture. These visitors came from European countries that were now more traditional than the United States. The foreigners were accustomed to social orders characterized by political hierarchy, limited economic opportunity, religious orthodoxy, patriarchial families, and profound social inequality. The French-born essayist Michel-Guillaume Jean de Crevecoeur, who wrote under the name of Hector St. John de Crevecoeur, compared the two societies in his famous *Letters from an American Farmer* (1782). He wrote that his European homeland was ruled by "great lords who possess everything, and a herd of people who have nothing." In America, he continued, there "are no aristocratical families, no courts, no kings, no bishops. . . ."

In the minds of most Europeans, the distinctiveness of American culture stemmed from the economic opportunities open to a broad segment of the white population. "A consciousness of

FIRST IMPRESSIONS OF NEW YORK CITY, 1820

A Swiss-German immigrant ponders the confused cultural reality of republican America: educated tailors, degraded blacks, and ill-mannered families of wealth.

It is impossible for Europeans to imagine rightly the activity and energy, or rather the reality and life, of America. It is the dream of a high fever made real. One hour you exult in the good fortune of becoming a citizen of this happy land under such a just and wise constitution and government, being able to live among such unprejudiced, moral, and educated people; the next hour you would like to flee to an uninhabited desert. The principle of an eternal anarchy is reflected in the Constitution. The laws seem to benefit only scoundrels. The people seem to be a mob of vagabonds, haphazardly come together, from whom all feeling for tradition, order, and propriety has vanished. You no longer find a pleasing, gentle education, but only materialistic self-interest.

You step into a workshop and find a fine, pleasing, well-educated shoemaker or tailor, one who could indeed pass for a personage in Europe who had completed several schools. You come into the house of a prominent citizen, who has perhaps a million dollars; the rooms are fitted with the most costly furnishings and the floors, beginning by the front door, are covered with Turkish rugs. Mother and daughter sit on sofas made of mahogany or ebony, the upholstery supported by steel coils; they dress themselves in clothing which would not shame a princess, and you are greeted with the words, "Well, whaddya think of this country? You got a wife and child?" If a person is given a polite invitation to dinner, it is offered with the formula, "Well, canya eat with us?"

When you go down a street you see attractive houses to the left and right; wherever a door opens a gorgeously dressed person emerges. But then you come to the street where mostly Negroes live; horrible faces wound about with kerchiefs meet you; everything indicates the deepest degradation.

---

independence forms the character of the Americans," an Englishman explained in 1796, because "the means of subsistence being so easy in this country, and their dependence on each other consequently so trifling, the spirit of servility to those above them so prevalent in European manners, is wholly unknown to them."

Foreign visitors also recognized the importance of the republican ideology of the American Revolution. By emphasizing the sense of personal dignity produced by economic independence, republicanism further undermined traditional hierarchical authority. "The law is the same for everyone both as it protects and as it punishes," one European noted. "In the course of daily life everyone is on the most perfect footing of equality."

European travelers were well aware that economic prosperity and legal equality had not prevented the formation of class divisions in the United States. "Wealth, power and higher education rule over need and ignorance" in America as elsewhere, one visitor declared bluntly. Visitors agreed, however, that class divisions in America differed from those in Europe. The United States had always lacked—and the Constitution prohibited—a legally defined and privileged class of nobles. The absence of an aristocracy of birth encouraged Americans to seek upward social mobility and to create class divisions based on achievement. "In Europe to say of someone that he rose from nothing is a disgrace and a reproach," an aristocratic Polish visitor explained in 1798. "It is the opposite here. To be the architect of your own fortune is honorable. It is the highest recommendation." A generation later, Frances Trollope, the usually critical English author of *Domestic Manners of the Americans* (1832), agreed. "Any man's son may become the equal of any other man's son," she remarked, "and the consciousness of this is certainly a spur to exertion."

Alexis de Tocqueville, a French statesman, gave classic expression—and a new description, *individualism*—to the character of the American people. "Individualism is a novel expression," he noted in his famous book *Democracy in America* (1835). The French aristocrat devoted great energy to defining this striking aspect of American culture. In Europe, he pointed out, "aristocracy had made a chain of all the members of the community, from the peasant to the king." In America, on the other hand, "democracy breaks that chain and severs every link of it." Americans lacked the security and predictability of life in an established, hierarchical society, and the individual was thrown "back forever upon himself alone."

Tocqueville's verdict on the new society was mixed. In America, he declared, "I saw the freest and most enlightened men placed in the happiest condition that there is in the world." Yet he detected a peculiar unhappiness, "as if a kind of cloud habitually covered every visage." He traced this to the American "taste for material enjoyments" and to the "universal competition" in an open society.

> When all the prerogatives of birth and fortune are eliminated, an easy and unbounded career seems to open itself up to the ambition of men, and they readily suppose that they are called to destinies grand. But this is an erroneous view which experience corrects all the days of their lives.

"When men are almost alike and all follow the same route," he concluded on a pessimistic note, they must ever strive for superiority and can never achieve "an easy and tranquil existence."

Many Americans also saw the flaws in a culture that honored limitless ambition and individual self-achievement. As a Philadelphia journeyman argued,

> A conscientious man in these times, can scarcely expect to earn more than a *competency* [the money needed to maintain a decent standard of living]. If more than this is aimed for, man is apt to become the oppressor of his fellows—taking advantage of their necessities and obtaining the fruits of their labor without rendering a just recompense.

Men and women with inherited wealth and family status likewise questioned the moral legitimacy of a social order determined by financial achievement. "The Aristocracy of Kingston is more one of money than any village I have ever seen," complained Nathaniel Booth in 1825. His ancestors had once ruled Kingston, a rapidly growing New York town. Now, he lamented, "man is estimated by dollars—what he is worth determines his character and position at once."

Individualism thus had intrinsic flaws, and it had major limitations as a description of the American character. The behavior it depicted did not include the life experiences of Afro-Americans, native Americans, most white women, and even many white men. Legal rules or social customs severely limited their freedom of action. Yet individualism rapidly achieved mythical status. To Europeans, it seemed the opposite of the hierarchical patterns of life in their own societies. For Americans, individualism summed up the reality of their own quest for self-realization and social identity.

The myth drew life from the historical experiences of hundreds of thousands of white Americans between the 1770s and the 1820s. During this half-century, the citizens of the United States won a war for political independence and created republican governments. They began the process of massive westward migration and widespread domestic manufacturing, and many participated in intense religious revivals.

Amid these changes, Americans reevaluated a number of traditional certainties. Hierarchical social structures and religious institutions, lineal family relationships, strict child-raising practices, and authoritarian political practices no longer commanded unthinking allegiance. Slowly but surely, the American people established new institutions, values, and symbols that expressed the more expansive and democratic features of their own lives. They were no longer confined by traditional European institutions and values. They were creating a new American culture based on the principles of republicanism, capitalism, and Christianity. Within this new framework of life and thought, they struggled to work out their individual destinies.

By the 1820s, the United States had a new political culture. Following the War of 1812, the Federalist party declined, ending the First Party System. Groups within the dominant Republican party struggled for power during the so-called Era of Good Feeling. Politics became less aristocratic and more democratic, and the national, state, and local governments were dominated by lawyers and professional politicians rather than by well-established men of affairs.

Simultaneously, businessmen advanced a new "middle-class" morality based on industry and temperance. Some farmers and artisans favored this morality, but many others did not. Consequently, families from different social groups participated in a democratic political system but no longer shared similar cultural values.

Many Americans lived different private lives as well. Sentimentalism encouraged marriage for love as well as for economic security. Wives became more equal partners in these new conjugal families and they often used reason rather than authority in raising children. The English feminist Mary Wollstonecraft advocated complete equality for women, and American women assumed greater moral authority and a more significant role in religious affairs.

An American national character took shape by the 1820s. This image was complex and did not include many social groups. Nonetheless, most European observers regarded the United States as a democratic society, filled with men and women who had strong evangelical Christian principles and who were committed to individual ambition and self-achievement.

Suggestions for Further Reading

The Dimensions of Public Culture

George Dangerfield, *The Era of Good Feeling* (1952), is a good introduction but underestimates the extent of factional political struggles. Henry Ammon, *James Monroe: The Quest for National Identity* (1971), relates the president's struggle to restore harmony. Samuel F. Bemis, *John Quincy Adams and the Foundations of American Foreign Policy* (1949), describes the richly varied career of the great statesman. On the Monroe Doctrine, see A. P. Whitaker, *The United States and the Independence of Latin America* (1941), and Dexter Perkins, *The Monroe Doctrine* (1927).

Clement Eaton, *Henry Clay and the Art of American Politics* (1957), is a perceptive discussion of the rise of a new political outlook. Chilton Williamson, *American Suffrage from Property to Democracy* (1960), discusses the extension of the right to vote. For constitutional revision, see Fletcher C. Green, *Constitutional Development in the South Atlantic States, 1776–1860* (1930), and Merrill D. Peterson, ed., *Democracy, Liberty, and Property: The State Constitutional Conventions of the 1820s* (1966). Dixon Ryan Fox, *The Decline of Aristocracy in the Politics of New York* (1927), remains useful. Daniel Calhoun, *Professional Lives in America, 1750–1850* (1965), traces the new importance of lawyers in politics.

The emergence of the business class can be traced in Kenneth W. Porter, *The Jacksons and the Lees: Two Generations of Massachusetts Merchants* (1937); E. Digby Baltzell, *Puritan Boston and Quaker Philadelphia* (1978); and William Miller, ed., *Men in Business* (1962). For studies of urban development that outline the social impact of class formation, see Sam Bass Warner, *The Private City* (1968); Stuart Blumin, *The Urban Threshold* (1976); Thomas Bender, *Toward an Urban Vision* (1975); and Leonard L. Richard, *Gentlemen of Property and Standing* (1970). The character of early business class ideology is outlined in C. S. Griffin, *Their Brothers' Keepers: Moral Stewardship in the United States, 1800–1865* (1960), and David Rothman, *The Discovery of the Asylum* (1971).

The character of artisan culture is presented in Charles S. Olton, *Artisans for Independence* (1975); A. F. Davis and M. H. Haller, eds., *The Peoples of Philadelphia: A History of Ethnic Groups and Lower Class Life* (1973); and J. R. Commons, et al., *History of Labor in the United States* (4 vols., 1918–1935). Carl F. Kaestle, *The Evolution of an Urban School System: New York City, 1750–1850* (1973), and Roger Lane, *Policing the City* (1967) trace the emergence of separate cultural worlds.

Changing Private Identities

The appearance of a new cultural sensibility can be traced in Vernon L. Parrington, *The Romantic Revolution in America, 1800–1860* (1927); E. D. Branch, *The Sentimental Years* (1934); and Ann Douglas, *The Feminization of American Culture* (1977). See also Daniel Calhoun, *The Intelligence of a People* (1973) for shifting intellectual perceptions.

The emergence of the conjugal family in England is outlined by Lawrence Stone, *Family, Sex, and Marriage in England* (1979), and in America by Carl Degler, *At Odds: Women and the Family in America* (1980). See also Michael Gordon, ed., *The American Family in Social-Historical Perspective* (1973). Linda Gordon, *Woman's Body,*

Woman's Right: A History of Birth Control in America (1976) has some material on family limitation in preindustrial America. Philip Greven, *The Protestant Temperament: Patterns of Childrearing, Religious Experience, and the Self* (1977) is a path-breaking study. It should be supplemented by Daniel Blake Smith, *Inside the Great House: Planter Family Life in Eighteenth Century Chesapeake Society* (1980); Lloyd deMause, ed. *The History of Childhood* (1974); and Greven, ed., *Child-Rearing Concepts, 1628–1861* (1973). Other important studies include Bernard Wishy, *The Child and the Republic* (1970); Ann Kuhn, *The Mother's Role in Childhood Education* (1947); and Monica Kiefer, *American Children Through Their Books* (1948). Jamil Zainaldin, *Law in Antebellum Society* (1983) has some material on the legal aspects of family life.

Richard D. Morris, *Studies in the History of American Law* (1930) places emphasis on the legal rights of women in America. For important modifications of this view, see Carol Berkin and Mary Beth Norton, eds., *Women of America: A History* (1979) and Linda K. Kerber, *Women of the Republic* (1980). Lynne Withey, *Dearest Friend: A Life of Abigail Adams* (1981) is a good biography: other studies of Revolutionary era women include Linda Grant DePauw, *Founding Mothers* (1976); Paul Engle, *Women in the American Revolution* (1976); and Elizabeth Evans, ed., *Weathering the Storm* (1975).

Margaret George, *One Woman's "Situation": A Study of Mary Wollstonecraft* (1970), explores the dilemmas of early feminism. The gains and losses stemming from the redefinition of women's "sphere" are assessed in Nancy F. Cott, *The Bonds of Womanhood: "Women's Sphere" in New England, 1780–1835* (1977); Katherine Kish Sklar, *Catherine Beecher, A Study in American Domesticity* (1973); and various essays in Mary Hartman and Lois Banner, eds., *Clio's Consciousness Raised* (1974). For women's religious initiatives, see Mary P. Ryan, *Cradle of the Middle Class* (1981); Barbara Epstein, *The Politics of Domesticity: Women, Evangelism, and Temperance* (1978); and Keith Melder, *Beginnings of Sisterhood: The American Women's Rights Movement 1800–1850*

(1977). Anne Frior Scott, *The Southern Lady* (1970), and Catherine Clinton, *The Plantation Mistress* (1982), examine the experience of upper-class southern women. Eugene Genovese, *Roll, Jordan Roll* (1976), discusses the lives of slave women, as does Herbert Gutman, *The Black Family* (1976).

Thomas A. Woody, *A History of Women's Education in the United States* (1929), is still valuable. For woman writers, see Ann Douglas, *The Feminization of American Culture* (1978); Susan P. Conrad, *Intellectual Women in Romantic America* (1976); and Nina Baym, *Women's Fiction* (1978).

The Creation of the American National Character

Perry Miller, *The Life of the Mind in America* (1966), explores the impact of religion on American thought, while Russell B. Nye, *Society and Culture in America, 1830–1860* (1974), records its social impact. For revivalism, see C. A. Johnson, *The Frontier Camp Meeting* (1955); Bernard A. Weisberger, *They Gathered at the River* (1958); Wilbur D. Cross, *The Burned-Over District* (1950); and William G. McLoughlin, *Modern Revivalism* (1955). For the decline of New England Calvinism, see Conrad Wright, *The Beginnings of Unitarianism* (1955); D. P. Edgell, *William Ellery Channing* (1955); and Daniel W. Howe, *The Unitarian Conscience* (1970).

George Dangerfield, *The Awakening of American Nationalism, 1815–1828* (1965), points to a new sense of American identity. W. F. Craven, *The Legend of the Founding Fathers* (1956), and Paul C. Nagel, *One Nation Indivisible* (1964), explore this theme, as does Russell B. Nye, *The Cultural Life of the New Nation, 1776–1830* (1960). Warren S. Tryon, *A Mirror for Americans: Life and Manners in the United States, 1790-1870, as Recorded by American Travelers* (3 vols., 1952), is a convenient and useful collection. Perceptive accounts by foreign travelers include Michael Chevalier, *Society, Manners, and Politics in the United States* (1839); Frances Trollope, *Domestic Manners of the Americans* (1832); and Alexis de Tocqueville, *Democracy in America* (1835).

PART TWO

*I*NDUSTRIALIZING

1820–1920

In 1820, America was still a predominantly agricultural society. A century later it had become the world's most powerful industrial economy. This profound transformation in American life began slowly in the northeastern states and then, after the Civil War, quickly accelerated and spread across the entire nation. The impact of the Industrial Revolution was not random; rather, it acted in quite distinctive ways to bring about social and political change. Six *structural* features of the industrializing society shaped the character of American life over this period.

First, technological and organizational innovations stood at the heart of the Industrial Revolution. Water- and steam-powered machines and the

AMERICA

new factory system boosted production, while canals and railroads created a vast national market. Industry produced an ever-increasing share of the country's wealth—from a negligible amount in 1820, to a third in 1869, to more than a half in 1899. The nature of business enterprise also changed, as small companies and independent artisans gave way to nationally organized, bureaucratically run corporations.

Second, industrialization produced an ambitious and increasingly powerful business class that sought to assert its leadership over American society. The business class enlisted religion in its efforts, sometimes to bring about reform, and at other times to justify the new economic order. Business leaders also shaped American politics, especially through their dominating role in the antebellum Whig Party and in the Republican Party from the Civil War onward.

Third, rival social groups rose to challenge the power of the business class and its economic and cultural policies. Many workers proposed the reform of industrial society, first in the workingmen's parties of the 1830s, then in the Knights of Labor, and after 1900 in the Socialist party. They also organized collectively through trade unions, under the leadership of the American Federation of Labor. Farmers turned to political action to protect their interests. They supported Andrew Jackson's Democratic party before the Civil War and, during the 1890s, turned briefly to the Populist party to advance their political demands. Throughout this cen-

tury of social transformation, many immigrants—first from Ireland and Germany and later from south and central Europe—espoused social and religious values different from those of the business class.

Fourth, native-born Americans of middle-class status became increasingly powerful. Many shared the values of business leaders and, in effect, joined the business class. Some middle-class Americans joined an abolitionist movement that attacked southern slavery as a sinful expression of arbitrary personal power, and that eventually achieved its overthrow. Middle-class men and women also expressed reservations about the new industrial order. They formed a variety of religious and reform movements that sought to introduce social order into an economic world where change seemed the only rule. Middle-class reformers likewise played an important role in the Progressive movement between 1900 and 1920. The Progressives secured the passage of state and federal legislation that curbed the arbitrary power of the large corporations that now dominated American economic life.

Fifth, industrialization created sharp sectional divisions in American society and politics. During the 1840s and 1850s, both the industrializing North and the slave-holding South tried to impose their distinctive labor systems on the West, a struggle that led eventually to the Civil War. Then, during the 1880s and 1890s, western and southern farmers protested strongly against eastern railroads and market systems that adversely affected their agricultural economy. Sectional interests likewise played a role in foreign policy, most notably in the Mexican War, and in persistent disputes over protectionism and trade policy.

Sixth, and finally, industrialization spurred the creation of an urban society divided by class. Urban growth occurred initially in textile towns and commercial centers and, after the Civil War, in large industrial cities such as Cleveland, Pittsburgh, and Birmingham. Urban neighborhoods reflected the emerging class structure, with the poor concentrated in the factory districts, the middle class in the suburbs, and the rich in exclusive urban neighborhoods or on country estates.

The industrialization of the United States created a new social order and a set of economic, political, and cultural issues that were fundamentally different from those of the preindustrial era. Between 1820 and 1920, American people lived in a distinct universe of values, thought, and action, one from which our own modern age of the twentieth century springs.

11

THE INDUSTRIAL REVOLUTION

*I*n 1831–1832 Alexis de Tocqueville, a French aristocrat, observed Americans at work and remarked, "What most astonishes me ... is not so much the marvelous grandeur of some undertakings, as the innumerable magnitude of small ones." Tocqueville astutely identified a key feature of the American industrial revolution: it was the product of thousands of small innovations.

The term "industrial" points to the fact that innovations in manufacturing were central to the economic transformations that occurred between the 1820s and the late nineteenth century. And the term "revolution" captures the drama of those innovations and their spectacular effects. The development of more productive factories led to an era distinct from the preindustrial period, even though most Americans remained farmers and most manufacturing was done by craftsmen laboring in households or traditional shops until after the Civil War. By the 1820s, the remarkable impact of new factories had already changed the meaning of the term "manufacturing." Previously, Americans used this word to refer simply to the process of making things by hand. In the 1820s, they began to use the term to describe production carried on in factories by large numbers of workers who tended power-driven machinery.

Most of the essential ingredients for an industrial revolution were in place by the 1820s. The United States had an incredible abundance of natural resources. Its people were highly skilled in traditional crafts. In its mature preindustrial economy, agriculture, commerce, and finance were dynamic and efficient. The country's traders linked the nation to world markets. A business leadership had emerged, united by an entrepreneurial ideology that expressed a commitment to industry, frugality, independence, and self-help.

Throughout the preindustrial period in the United States, production of goods and services of all kinds had expanded rapidly. The population grew almost as rapidly, and consequently the standard of living of the average American increased very slowly. However, the innovations in manufacturing that were widely adopted during the 1820s enabled Americans to produce far more goods and services per person. These innovations triggered others—in manufacturing, agriculture, and transportation—that further increased productivity. Thus, during the 1820s, a new, more productive era began.

The Industrial Revolution and the economic growth it sparked first centered in the Northeast, where capitalists and laborers joined to manufacture goods in new ways. Soon, though, Americans in all walks of life, in all parts of the nation, found that the Industrial Revolution touched them in some concrete way. Most profoundly, new methods of production and expanding markets reshaped their working lives. Even people outside the industrial and mercantile centers of the nation experienced changes in how they supported themselves and their fami-

UPPER FALLS OF THE GENESEE RIVER, 1835
Like many early industrial sites, these prosperous flour mills at Rochester, New York were located to take advantage of natural resources. The Genesee River provided water to irrigate the wheat farms of the Genesee Valley, it offered transportation of grain to the mills, and the falls powered the mill machinery. (The New-York Historical Society)

lies. Farmers concentrated more heavily on production for urban markets, and western artisans often faced difficulty in competing with eastern manufacturers. These transformations of work, in turn, reshaped the ways people married and raised children, where they lived, what clothes they wore and foods they ate, and how they received information about the world beyond their hometowns.

For people with property or with skills that were in demand, the Industrial Revolution usually enhanced material opportunities and rewards, especially in urban areas. These people consumed more goods and services, had fewer but better-educated children, and read more books and newspapers. For those citizens who were on the margin of the new society, however, the Industrial Revolution often brought bewildering dislocation, loss of status, and economic insecurity.

The sweeping material transformations produced by industrialization led to deep changes in American politics, culture, religion, and intellectual life. In every realm of their social existence, Americans became preoccupied with the remark-able force of the Industrial Revolution. Some tried to deny, escape, or resist its power. Others sought to celebrate and reinforce its influence. Virtually no one could stand by dispassionately.

The force of industrialization continued to gain momentum after 1840 and played a central role in the coming of the Civil War. This chapter describes the origins of the Industrial Revolution during the 1820s and 1830s and discusses how it transformed material life during those decades. Later chapters will trace industrialization beyond 1840 and discuss its effects on other aspects of American society.

Northeastern Industrialization

In hundreds of factories, Americans developed innovations in the technology and organization of production. These innovations were of two types: the organization of workers into large, synchronized groups, and the replacement of hand tools by power-driven machines.

New ways of organizing work, even without any technological improvements, could make manufacturing more efficient. Some merchant capitalists reorganized the craft production of shoes, boots, and clothing. They expanded the "outwork" system and increased the specialization of labor in their shops. Other manufacturers increased the scale of production by introducing factory-type organization for the first time. The slaughterhouses of Cincinnati employed "disassembly" lines to butcher hogs during the 1830s. In these slaughterhouses, a simple system of overhead rails moved carcasses past stationary workers who were assigned specific tasks: splitting the animals, removing various organs, trimming, weighing, and, finally, hosing down the cleaned carcasses before packers pickled them and stuffed them in barrels. All of these tasks could be done slowly on any Ohio farm, but in the factory less than one minute was required for the entire process. By the 1840s, Cincinnati had become known as "Porkopolis."

Technological improvements alone could also increase productivity. As early as 1782, in Delaware, the prolific inventor Oliver Evans built a highly automated labor-saving flour mill driven by water power. His machinery lifted the grain to the top of the mill, cleaned the grain as it fell into hoppers, ground it into flour, conveyed the flour back to the top of the mill, and then cooled the flour during a second descent into barrels. Evans employed only six men to mill a hundred thousand bushels of grain a year.

During the 1820s and 1830s, manufacturers in a variety of industries, from cotton spinning to gun making, improved productivity by combining organizational and technological innovations. When manufacturers linked factory organization with high-speed power machinery, they achieved the dramatic productivity gains of the Industrial Revolution. Designing and fabricating machines that could produce goods at high speeds was the most difficult problem to face American manufacturers. Once they had solved these technological problems, the Industrial Revolution swept through virtually all of American manufacturing.

The Textile Industry

The economic transformation of the United States was part of an international industrial revolution that began in Great Britain in the mid-eighteenth century. British manufacturers made their first and most revolutionary advances in the textile industry. By the 1780s, their productivity enabled them to cut prices so dramatically that their exports threatened the livelihood of traditional producers in America. Desperate to recapture the domestic market and to win a share of the soaring profits made by their British competitors, American textile manufacturers copied the British technology.

American manufacturers received great assistance from skilled artisans who emigrated from Britain. These artisans provided the detailed and up-to-date information American manufacturers

PORK PACKING IN CINCINNATTI
This pork-packing plant in Cincinnati used little modern technology except an overhead moving pulley system that carried hog carcasses past the workers. The plant's efficiency was primarily organizational; each worker was assigned a specific task. Such plants pioneered the design of the moving assembly lines that reached their sophisticated development in the twentieth-century automobile factories of Henry Ford. (The Cincinnati Historical Society)

MAP 11.1 EARLY INDUSTRIAL ENTERPRISE IN NEW ENGLAND

As new and improved textile machinery spread across New England, modern textile factories sprang up and became concentrated at locations such as Waltham and Lowell in eastern Massachusetts. On the lower two maps, each circle is focused on a town with one or more textile factories. The area of each circle indicates the relative number of spindles or employees in that town, data sufficiently similar for historians to trace and compare the development of the industry over this period.

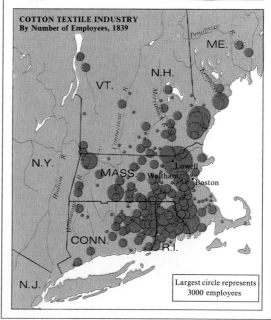

needed to reproduce British machines. Lured by high wages, and even offers of partnerships, large numbers of British artisans, including machine builders, sailed to the United States. Their actions violated British laws prohibiting both the export of textile machinery and the emigration of skilled laborers. To conceal their departure, many artisans disguised themselves as ordinary laborers. Others escaped by hiding in barrels. By 1812, more than three hundred skilled British textile workers had gathered in the Philadelphia area alone.

Samuel Slater, the most important of the British mechanics to arrive at this time, emigrated in 1789. In England's industrial district of Derbyshire he had served as an apprentice to Jedediah Strutt, a partner of Richard Arkwright, who invented and operated the most advanced machinery for spinning cotton. The young Slater memorized the design of Arkwright's machinery and, disguised by a beard, set sail for New York. There he met Moses Brown, a wealthy merchant who owned a failing cotton mill in Providence, Rhode Island. After taking over the management of Brown's mill, Slater duplicated the entire set of machines used by Arkwright's firm. Because Slater's mill was far more advanced than any in operation in the United States, the year 1790 is a convenient date to mark the introduction of industrial technology to the United States.

Even advanced mills like Slater's, however, had difficulty competing with British mills for the American market. Americans had one major advantage but a number of disadvantages. The nation's natural resources provided American manufacturers with cheap water power to run machinery and a rich agricultural base that spared textile manufacturers from having to import raw cotton or wool. The British, however, had the benefit of falling costs of transatlantic shipping and lower interest rates, which allowed them to build factories and finance marketing less expensively. And because British firms were better established, they could cut prices severely and endure short-run losses in order to drive competing American firms out of business.

Most important, British manufacturers could draw from a large pool of rural poor and underemployed urban laborers to recruit workers willing to perform simple, repetitive, low-paying factory jobs. To some extent the British advantage lay in the size of its population, which in 1810 numbered about 12.6 million, contrasted with 7.3 million Americans. More critically, however, unskilled American laborers received much better pay for work on farms or on construction projects than did their British counterparts. American farm workers—men, women, and children—could not be easily attracted to factory labor. And the federal government did little to protect the nation's high-wage workers and high-cost industries during the periods of most intense competition with the British. Congress did not pass significant tariffs against British manufactured goods until 1828. Then, in 1833, under pressure from southern planters and farmers who wanted to keep down the price of manufactured goods, Congress began to reduce even those tariffs.

As a consequence of these disadvantages, American textile manufacturers often failed.

Even those who did not fail made good profits only when wars cut off British competition. To overcome the British, American textile manufacturers had to address the central problem of low-cost British labor. They took their own steps to mobilize large groups of workers into factories. Manufacturers made their most ambitious efforts in New England, where they gathered workers into new towns adjacent to mill dams and waterfalls that could provide power for spinning machines and power looms.

The Boston Manufacturing Company was the leading innovator at this stage of the Industrial Revolution. Its machinery was the product of the industrial espionage of the Boston merchant Francis Cabot Lowell. In 1811, Lowell spent an apparently casual holiday touring English textile mills. A wealthy, well-educated, and charming young man, he flattered his hosts by asking thousands of questions. But his easy manner hid a serious purpose. He paid close attention to the answers he received, and later, in his hotel rooms, he secretly made detailed drawings of the machinery and mill construction. On returning to the United States, he and two other merchants, Nathan Appleton and Patrick Tracy Jackson, raised the capital to form the Boston Manufacturing Company. In 1814, they opened a plant in Waltham, Massachusetts, based on Lowell's drawings.

WOMEN WORKERS IN A TEXTILE MILL

These women, working in an English cotton factory that closely resembled those in America, tended spinning machines and looms driven by water power transmitted by a system of belts and wheels. The women here are probably knotting broken threads, while the man is most likely adjusting the machinery. (The Yale University Art Gallery. Mabel Brady Garvan Collection)

LUCY LARCOM ON HER EARLY DAYS AT LOWELL

I never cared much for machinery. The buzzing and hissing and whizzing of pulleys and rollers and spindles and flyers around me often grew tiresome. I could not see into their complications, or feel interested in them. But in a room below us we were sometimes allowed to peer in through a sort of blind door at the great waterwheel that carried the works of the whole mill. It was so huge that we could only watch a few of its spokes at a time, and part of its dripping rim, moving with a slow, measured strength through the darkness that shut it in. It impressed me with something of the awe which comes to us in thinking of the great Power which keeps the mechanism of the universe in motion.

. . . we did not call ourselves ladies. We did not forget that we were working-girls, wearing coarse aprons suitable to our work, and that there was some danger of our becoming drudges. I know that sometimes the confinement of the mill became very wearisome to me. In the sweet June weather I would lean far out of the window, and try not to hear the unceasing clash of sound inside. Looking away to the hills, my whole stifled being would cry out

Oh, that I had wings!

Still I was there from choice, and

The prison unto which we doom
    ourselves,
No prison is.

I regard it as one of the privileges of my youth that I was permitted to grow up among those active, interesting girls, whose lives were not mere echoes of other lives, but had principle and purpose distinctly their own. Their vigor of character was a natural development. The New Hampshire girls who came to Lowell were descendants of the sturdy backwoodsmen who settled that State scarcely a hundred years before. Their grandmothers had suffered the hardships of frontier life. . . . Those young women did justice to their inheritance. They were earnest and capable; ready to undertake anything that was worth doing. My dreamy, indolent nature was shamed into activity among them. They gave me a larger, firmer ideal of womanhood. . . .

Country girls were naturally independent, and the feeling that at this new work the few hours they had of every-day leisure were entirely their own was a satisfaction to them. They preferred it to going out as "hired help." It was like a young man's pleasure in entering upon business for himself. Girls had never tried that experiment before, and they liked it. It brought out in them a dormant strength of character which the world did not previously see.

The Boston Manufacturing Company pioneered what became known as the Waltham Plan. It employed large numbers of young, single women as operators of mass-production textile machinery. The manufacturers recruited these young women from farms by offering them higher wages than they could earn in the "outwork" system of shoe and broom production or in service as maids or cooks. In addition, manufacturers provided company-run boarding houses and cultural activities, such as evening lectures. And they reassured anxious parents by enforcing strict curfews, prohibiting alcoholic beverages, and requiring regular church attendance. In the 1820s and 1830s, other Boston-owned firms, such as the Hamilton, Suffolk, and Tremont corporations, adopted the Waltham Plan.

Some young women at Waltham banked their wages for later use. One wrote to a cousin in the 1830s that she wanted to attend Oberlin College (the first coeducational U.S. college, founded in 1833) "because I think it the best way of spending the money I have worked so hard to earn." Others supported their families and parents. A daughter might help her father to pay off a farm mortgage, a brother to acquire more schooling, or her family to accumulate a dowry for her own marriage. In 1835, at eleven years of age, Lucy Larcom of Lowell, Massachusetts, went to work in a textile mill. In *A New England Girlhood* (1889), she recalled that she started work "with a light heart" because the work meant that she "was not a trouble or burden or expense" to her widowed mother. Regardless of what the young

COTTON-SPINNING MACHINES

The industrial revolution in America began in the textile factories of New England. By 1800, an array of machines were in use to clean and fluff raw cotton fibers and to prepare the fibers for weaving. Carding machines, which consisted of two cylinders full of wire pins, combed the fibers into parallel strands. Roving machines rolled the carded cotton into a loose roll called a roving.

The real revolution in textile manufacture came with changes in spinning technology. Rates of production were severely limited by the slow process of spinning cotton fibers into thread. As late as the 1760s, all thread was spun by individuals at hand-turned spinning machines. In 1765, British inventor James Hargreaves invented the spinning jenny, also called the hand jenny. The key tool in spinning had always been the spindle, which twists together strands of fiber to make thread. Hargreaves's spinning jenny imitated the function of spinning wheels. The operator manually turned a wheel that spun a series of spindles, each of which simultaneously drew out the roving and twisted it into thread.

Jennies saved labor by spinning from twenty-four to more than a hundred spindles at once. However, a jenny required a skilled operator. The spinner placed bobbins (spools) with roving on the machine's frame and tied a bit of roving from each bobbin to a spindle, first passing the fibers through a carriage that moved back and forth on the frame. After drawing out the rovings by moving the carriage, the spinner clamped the rovings to the carriage and then turned the wheel to spin the spindles. When the thread had been given enough twist, the operator moved the carriage forward again while turning the spindles more slowly to wind the thread onto the bobbins. The jenny had to be stopped between the drawing and the twisting, and slowed before winding, and so it had to be driven by hand. Because of the labor costs required, relatively few jennies were adopted for cotton spinning in America.

Americans preferred the spinning frame, or water frame, a machine patented in England in 1769 by Richard Arkwright and brought to the United States by Samuel Slater. As its name implied, the water frame was powered by water. Its chief innovation was to separate the functions of drawing and twisting. After two pairs of rollers elongated the thread, it was passed down the arm of a flier, a device attached to a spindle. The flier twisted the thread and wound it onto a bobbin attached to the spindle.

The only skill needed to operate a water frame was the ability to knot a broken thread. The machine ran continuously on inexpensive water power. In addition to saving expensive labor, the frame worked much faster than the jenny. A single water frame produced as much thread as several hundred spinning wheels working together. Moreover, the water frame produced a thread that was coarse enough for the rugged cloth in great demand in America. Even more significantly, its thread was strong enough to be used on power looms for the warp, the vertical threads strung in tension through which the weft threads were woven to form the finished cloth.

American inventors quickly made significant improvements in the water frames. By 1830, virtually all the processes involved in the manufacture of cotton cloth had been mechanized in the United States, and most new mills had departments for carding, roving, spinning, and power-loom weaving. The enormous gains in textile productivity and profitability inspired a host of inventors and entrepreneurs to mechanize other kinds of industry. The industrial revolution had seized the American imagination.

women did with their wages, they enjoyed the greater degree of personal independence that their incomes provided. "Don't I feel independent!" one wrote to her sister in the 1840s. "The thought that I am living on no one is a happy one indeed to me."

Throughout the 1820s and 1830s, young women made up a majority of all workers in the cotton-textile industry and nearly half of the workers in woolen-textile manufacturing. By the early 1830s, more than forty thousand women worked in textile mills. Most of the remaining twenty thousand textile workers were children under the age of fourteen, and most of these were girls. Men comprised only a small fraction of the textile operatives. They worked primarily in Rhode Island, under the Fall River Plan, which offered unskilled factory work to entire families. The success of the Waltham and Fall River plans reflected the meager profitability of New England agriculture and the high birth rates of New England farm families. The region's poorer farms could not hold young people, who quickly took up factory work, even when it meant operating fast-moving machines, doing highly repetitive tasks, and disrupting traditional family life.

The Waltham and Fall River plans gave New England manufacturers a competitive edge over most American textile manufacturers. In New York and Pennsylvania, where agricultural employment was far more attractive than in New England, textile producers were slower to enter the Industrial Revolution. They concentrated their innovative efforts in producing higher-quality cloth than the British and New England mills manufactured. In the South, textile entrepreneurs almost always failed because they lacked a cheap supply of labor. When they attempted to bid slaves away from planters, they discovered that the price of slaves was prohibitively high because of the huge profits the planters could earn by producing cotton. The southern textile industry languished until after the Civil War.

But the Waltham and Fall River plans did not lower the costs of labor enough for New England manufacturers to compete with the British on equal terms. To do so, textile manufacturers throughout the United States had to do more than introduce British technology and attract large groups of workers to factories. They had to adapt British technology to produce cotton cloth with far fewer unskilled workers.

Again, the Boston Manufacturing Company was the leader. From the outset, its machinery was more advanced than the British equivalents. After Francis Lowell returned from England in 1811, he turned over his drawings to an experienced textile mechanic, Paul Moody. Moody improved on the best British techniques. When the Waltham plant opened in 1814, its power looms operated at even higher speeds than those which Lowell had sketched. Moreover, the Waltham factory was the first in the world to perform all the operations involved in converting cotton into cloth under one roof.

The Boston Manufacturing Company continued to improve its technology, and other New England firms quickly imitated its success during the 1820s, when the New Englanders finally established their competitive superiority over the British in American markets. As a result of technological innovations, the cost of labor per yard of cotton cloth to New England manufacturers declined from nearly four cents in the early 1820s to less than two cents a decade later. Meanwhile, the output of New England cotton mills increased about fivefold.

American manufacturers of woolen textiles joined the move to modify machines to reduce their labor costs. For example, they introduced the Goulding automatic roving machine. It fed wool automatically between carding rollers (devices with teeth that straightened and blended wool fibers) and formed a strand of wool that could be transferred to spinning machinery. With this machine, manufacturers eliminated the need to have small children pass wool from one machine to another. British producers, able to hire more poor children than their American counterparts, did not adopt this innovation for another twenty-five years.

In 1825, Thomas Jefferson observed, "Our manufacturers are now very nearly on a footing with those of England." He found that England "has not a single improvement which we do not possess, and many of them adopted by ourselves to our ordinary use." During the 1830s, the American iron and steel industry began to adopt the world's most modern industrial technology—large-scale blast furnaces (to melt iron ore into pig iron), puddling (the melting of pig iron to remove impurities), and rolling (the shaping of semimolten iron by rollers). By 1840, Americans had successfully copied and adapted British technology in every industry where the British had once led.

Manufacturers and Skilled Workers

The success of the Industrial Revolution in textile production in the 1820s and 1830s depended primarily on the contributions of numerous small manufacturers and skilled workers who merged capital with technical innovation. Only in Massachusetts did merchant capitalists—entrepreneurs such as Francis Cabot Lowell—invest in modern industry and amass great fortunes.

Manufacturers usually could not borrow, let alone accumulate, large amounts of capital. Because merchant capitalists failed so often, the wealthiest citizens avoided investing in manufacturing until well after the Civil War. Bankers made long-term investments in transportation, the bonds of state governments, or commercial banking itself. Nor did the emerging stock markets assist manufacturers. The New York Stock and Exchange Board, founded in 1817, listed only the stocks of transportation companies, banks, and insurance companies.

Thus, until the 1840s, individuals of modest wealth provided almost all the capital required to start new manufacturing firms. Small entrepreneurs and their families bravely took risks and invested their savings in these concerns. Skilled mechanics and small merchants commonly pooled their capital, often borrowing from family and friends, to start a small factory. Storekeepers invested in small mills with the expectation that the mills would expand their business. A mill could increase a storekeeper's ability to purchase supplies for his store and, by generating jobs and income, increase the local market for his goods.

The early history of industry in Rockdale, Pennsylvania, a small mill village in the Delaware Valley near Philadelphia, illustrates the role of small manufacturers, of their personal (often family) capital, and of the uncertainty of their ventures. In 1825, four manufacturers made cloth in Rockdale. William Martin, a young, modestly wealthy, Philadelphia merchant, purchased his mills in a sheriff's sale (a sale of bankrupted property) with his savings and those of his brother-in-law. He then expanded the mills with money borrowed from an uncle and a mortgage on the property. In 1829, cloth prices tumbled and forced him into bankruptcy. The second manufacturer was John Phillips, the son of a prominent Philadelphia merchant who had fallen on hard times. John had nevertheless married well and borrowed from his new brother-in-law to buy mills. Strong family support and prudent management enabled him to survive and, in 1835, to relocate his machinery in a new mill in Philadelphia. The third was John Crozer, a farmer and owner of a failing sawmill. He bought a mill at a sheriff's sale by mortgaging his farm and borrowing from a brother-in-law.

With enormous personal energy and sustained family assistance, he became one of the wealthiest men in Rockdale. The fourth manufacturer, John Carter, was an immigrant and was the only one with considerable experience in textiles, from his years as a mill manager in England. Because of his expertise, he was able to borrow extensively from local banks. Nonetheless, largely because he lacked relatives with capital, he became the first of the four to fail, suffering a devastating bankruptcy in 1826. The lesson was clear. Success was impossible without determination, skill, and family finances.

Small entrepreneurs like those in Rockdale had close relationships with skilled workers. In fact, during the 1820s and 1830s, the boundary between small manufacturers and craftsmen was easily crossed. Many craftsmen themselves started manufacturing firms or joined them as partners; they provided most of the technical knowledge for the Industrial Revolution. Literally thousands of modest craftsmen, a relatively large number by European standards, developed the simple inventions that, cumulatively, revolutionized American manufacturing. Few of these artisans had formal education, but they had learned much about machinery in small, traditional craft shops and, increasingly, in modern factories.

In Rockdale, Richard Garsed was one such inventor. At eight years of age, in 1827, he started working in a textile mill. Ten years later, after his father had bought a small mill in Rockdale, Garsed made experimental improvements in his father's power looms. In three years, he nearly doubled their speed. By 1842, he had invented a "cam and harness" device (patented in 1846), which allowed elaborately figured fabrics, such as damask, to be woven by machine.

By the 1820s, skilled American craftsmen had replaced British immigrants at the cutting edge of technological innovation. The most accomplished craftsmen usually based their successes on elaborate ties of family and friendship. In the Delaware Valley, the remarkable Sellars family dominated an interrelated group of inventors who transmitted their mechanical knowledge from one generation to the next. Samuel Sellars, Jr., invented a machine for twisting worsted woolen yarn. His son John harnessed water power for the efficient operation of the family's

A MACHINE SHOP
The skilled workers in this small shop in Shaftsbury, Vermont, used power-driven machine tools to fashion chisels and steel squares. This scene was probably painted during the 1850s, but such shops first appeared during the 1820s to make implements for use by factory workers, carpenters, building contractors, and farmers. (The New-York Historical Society. Bella C. Landauer Collection)

saw and grist mills and devised a machine that wove wire sieves. John's sons and grandsons, in turn, built machine shops that turned out a variety of new products—riveted leather fire hoses, paper-making equipment, and eventually locomotives.

In 1824, members of the Sellars family joined with other mechanics and small manufacturers to found the Franklin Institute in Philadelphia. Named after Benjamin Franklin, whom the mechanics admired for his scientific accomplishments and his friendship to their profession, the institute fostered a sense of professional identity for mechanics. It published a journal, provided instruction in the mechanical arts, and organized annual fairs for exhibiting the most advanced products and rewarding their designers. For example, at the 1842 fair the institute judges awarded a silver medal to Richard Garsed for "cotton and worsted damask table covers" that promised "successful competition with the imported." Skilled craftsmen in Ohio and other states soon established their own Mechanics In-

stitutes, offering all the programs that the Franklin Institute had pioneered.

American mechanics advanced the Industrial Revolution most forcefully by developing new machines and tools that could make other machines. Many of these innovative mechanics worked in the textile industry. They devised lathes, planers, and boring machines capable of making interchangeable textile-machine parts. These machine-tooled parts made it possible to manufacture textile machinery that was low in price and precise enough in design and construction to operate at higher speeds than British equipment.

Craftsmen who designed machine tools were even more important in industries producing goods made of iron or steel, such as plows, scythes, and axes. In 1832, David Hinman and Elisha K. Root, mechanics employed by Samuel W. Collins in his Connecticut axe-making company, built a vastly improved die-forging machine—a machine that pressed and hammered hot metal into dies, or cutting forms. Using this machine, a skilled worker increased his production of axe heads from twelve to three hundred a day. Manufacturers of steam engines for railroads and steamboats also improved their tools. When a Scottish engineer visited the Philadelphia locomotive works of Matthias Baldwin in 1837, he admired the results, "twelve locomotive carriages in different states of progress, and all of substantial and good workmanship." He emphasized that "Those parts of the engine, such as the cylinder, piston, valves, and slides, in which good fitting and fine workmanship are indispensable to the efficient action of the machine, were very highly finished."

Some of the most significant machine-building innovators worked in the firearms industry, and none was more influential than Eli Whitney. Throughout his life, Whitney consistently tried to bring technical insights to the manufacture of products for which there was an adequate market. When he was only fourteen, his fascination with tools, especially those that could be used to make other tools, convinced his father to install a forge on their Massachusetts farm so that the boy could produce nails and knife blades for local markets.

In 1792, after teaching school and graduating from Yale College, Whitney went to the South Carolina plantation of Catherine Greene, the young widow of Revolutionary War general Nathanael Greene. There he began to build a machine that could remove the seeds from upland, short-staple cotton—a process so laborious that it was prohibitively expensive, even with slave labor. Whitney succeeded in 1793 and returned to New Haven, Connecticut, where he tried to manufacture the "gins"—short for "engines"—in quantity. To do this, he had to develop special machine tools. Even with such machines, and with continuing financial support from Catherine Greene, he could not keep up with the demand of southern planters for cotton gins. Whitney hoped he could maintain a monopoly for his gin, which he had patented in 1794. But the federal patent law did not protect him from the planters who made their own gins or from manufacturers who made slight improvements on his design.

Disgusted and in debt, Whitney turned to the development of a product with a guaranteed market for his modern manufacturing techniques. In 1798, he obtained a federal contract to manufacture ten thousand muskets. He promised to produce the muskets in only twenty-eight months, based on his belief that he could design machine tools that would enable him to produce interchangeable parts for them. He would, he said, "form the tools so that the tools themselves shall fashion the work and give to every part its just proportion—which when once accomplished will give expedition, uniformity, and exactness to the whole." He devised improved forms and gigs to guide the hands of skilled workers; he crafted the first milling machine, which used sharp teeth on a gearlike wheel to cut metal; and he achieved a greater degree of interchangeability than anyone before him. But his success was incomplete. It took him ten years to fulfill his original contract, and, even so, he had to resort to much traditional handcrafted production. The federal government, however, largely because of Thomas Jefferson's interest, continued to issue contracts so that Whitney could perfect his technique.

Whitney died in 1825 without achieving his goal of complete mass production. Later in the 1820s, John H. Hall, an engineer at the federal armory at Harpers Ferry, Virginia, with whom Whitney had collaborated, developed all the basic machine tools required to produce modern arms—turret lathes, milling machines, and precision grinders.

By 1840, American mechanics had created the first modern machine-tool industry in the world. Consequently, manufacturers could produce complicated machinery at high speeds and in great quantity. Such machinery enabled the Industrial Revolution to spread relentlessly throughout American manufacturing during the next fifty years.

Market Expansion

During the 1820s and 1830s, the Industrial Revolution stimulated the rapid expansion of the American marketplace. Manufacturers and merchants in the industrializing Northeast promoted foreign trade, forged a true national market, and stimulated the growth of cities and towns.

Interregional exchanges of goods and people occurred in the United States long before the

Industrial Revolution took hold. But after 1820, the scope and intensity of such exchanges increased dramatically. The business leaders of the Northeast demanded the farm products of other regions; in return, they offered low-cost manufactured goods and mercantile services that increased farm productivity. They used the modern corporation and the technology of the Industrial Revolution to promote a massive, interregional transportation system. The South, too committed to cotton production for industrialization to develop there and trading chiefly with Great Britain, remained largely outside this economic network. But northeastern manufacturers and merchants bound together the Northeast and the Northwest with ties of mutual economic dependence.

Expanding Trade

During the 1820s and 1830s, Americans reduced their economic reliance on Europe. Even after political independence, northerners and southerners alike relied on the export of farm products to Europe. Between 1790 and 1810, Americans exported as much as 15 percent of their national product—roughly the same level as had prevailed a half-century earlier. By 1830, however, they had dramatically lowered their exports to only 6 percent of the national product, a level that remained constant until the mid-twentieth century.

As exports declined in significance, Americans developed their internal trade of both agricultural and manufacturing goods. Americans traded with each other in two ways. First, they exchanged goods *within* regions. Philadelphians, for example, traded locally manufactured textiles for a wide variety of farm products grown in the immediate vicinity. They bought dairy products, fruits and vegetables, hay for the horses that pulled carriages, coaches, and omnibuses, and wood for heating and cooking, as well as staples such as flour and corn. Second, Americans exchanged products *between* regions. Most important, merchants in the industrializing Northeast traded their textiles, clothing, boots and shoes, muskets, and farm equipment for wheat, corn, whiskey, and hogs from the farms of the Great Lakes basin and the Ohio Valley. Manufacturers and farmers in these regions specialized in pro-

duction for shipment to other regions. Because this interregional trade grew rapidly, they increased their scale of production, became more efficient, and enlarged their profits.

The South, meanwhile, traded heavily in international markets. Southerners made the United States the world's largest cotton producer by the 1820s. They exported most of the cotton to Britain and imported most of their manufactured goods from British suppliers. Southerners obtained most of their financing and mercantile services from British importing houses. Food did not figure in this trade. Southerners fed themselves almost entirely from nearly self-sufficient plantations or small farms on the fringe of the cotton economy. They did import some food from the Northwest, via the Mississippi, but for only a small fraction of their needs.

Thus, the South's economy remained tied, not to other parts of the United States, but to Europe. Its plantation economy resembled those of colonies like Brazil or Cuba. As in those areas, the earnings from exports went largely to Europeans and to local landlords. Like the landed classes of other plantation societies, southern planters reinvested their profits in expanding their slave labor force and in increasing the size of their estates.

Urban Growth

Northern industrialization and market expansion stimulated the economic life of cities and towns, which offered more and more opportunities. Urban places—defined as localities with more than twenty-five hundred people—grew rapidly, led by three distinct types of towns and cities: new industrial towns, the great Atlantic seaports, and new commercial cities and towns in the Northwest. Collectively, towns and cities began to boom during the 1820s; their population for the first time began to increase more rapidly than the population as a whole.

The most rapidly growing towns were those with the most modern industries. Such towns were usually located along the fall line—the line where the Appalachian foothills drop to the Atlantic coastal plain and rivers cascade downhill in falls and rapids. Towns along this line—such as Lowell, Massachusetts; Hartford, Connecticut; Trenton, New Jersey; and Wilmington,

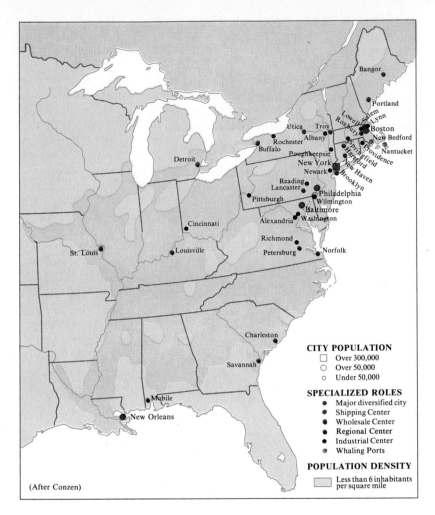

MAP 11.2 THE NATION'S MAJOR CITIES IN 1840
By 1840 American cities formed a national system, although there were relatively few cities in the south and the northwest. In this system, cities developed specialized roles—Cincinnati and Pittsburgh became industrial centers, Hartford and Lancaster grew as regional centers for farm communities, and Brooklyn and Buffalo developed as wholesaling centers. The oldest ports on the Atlantic seaboard remained the most diversified and played critical roles in managing and organizing the national economy.

CITY POPULATION
- ☐ Over 300,000
- ○ Over 50,000
- ○ Under 50,000

SPECIALIZED ROLES
- ● Major diversified city
- ● Shipping Center
- ● Wholesale Center
- ● Regional Center
- ● Industrial Center
- ◉ Whaling Ports

POPULATION DENSITY
- Less than 6 inhabitants per square mile

(After Conzen)

Delaware—provided falling water that could run machinery cheaply at high speeds. The populations of these towns escalated as manufacturers recruited an industrial labor force. Led by the modern industrial towns, the number of towns and cities with between 2,500 and 50,000 people more than doubled, from 58 in 1820 to 126 in 1840. The total population in such communities almost tripled, from 443,000 in 1820 to 1,141,000 in 1840.

The rise of industrial towns stimulated the growth of the great Atlantic seaports—Boston, New York, Philadelphia, and Baltimore. Manufacturers in the new towns depended on seaport merchants to market their finished goods and acquire raw materials in large quantities. The new manufacturers also relied on established bankers in the seaports to provide short-term credit. The new industries in turn stimulated the expansion of some traditional crafts in the older cities, especially those that involved the production of construction materials, such as glass, nails, bricks, and paint, and of expensive consumer goods, such as fashionable clothing, carriages, and furniture. Paper making also prospered because readers in the urban centers of the Middle Atlantic states demanded an ever-increasing supply of newspapers, pamphlets, and books. By 1840, paper making had become one of the largest industries in New York City.

While the old Atlantic seaports remained the largest of American cities, as a group they increased only at the same rate as the population as a whole. New York was the exception; its growth rate was phenomenal, twice that of the nation's overall rate during the 1820s and 1830s. It was emerging as the economic center of the nation.

New York boasted the best harbor in the United States. Ships had unobstructed, yet protected, access to the docks on Manhattan Island, and ocean vessels could sail or steam 150 miles up the Hudson River to Albany. No other Atlantic port provided such deep penetration of the interior. Moreover, New York merchants were unusually enterprising. They had made their city the smuggling center of British North America during the eighteenth century and had used their wits to survive British occupation during the Revolution. More than merchants in Boston or Philadelphia, they welcomed outsiders and their money.

The New York merchants aggressively sought to control trade. In the 1790s they accepted the auction sale of merchandise, a system favored by British exporters. These auctions allowed the British to sell their goods directly, in large lots, to American customers and thus to take part of the profit that American importers would otherwise earn. Philadelphia and Boston importers, worried that the auctions would ruin their own business, persuaded their city governments to deny licenses for auctions. But these merchants, like all merchants outside New York, soon discovered that they had to purchase British goods *through* New York, which had deftly won control of the British import trade.

In another brilliant stroke, New York merchants used the auction system to gain control of trade with the interior. In 1817, led by William Bayard, president of the New York City Chamber of Commerce, they convinced New York's state government to enact a law that earmarked tax revenues from auction sales to construct the Erie Canal from Albany to Buffalo and Lake Erie. Supported in part by these revenues, the Erie Canal was opened in 1825. It connected New York City and Albany with the burgeoning farming communities of upstate New York and with the entire Great Lakes region.

New York merchants applied their aggressiveness to foreign commerce as well. Four Quaker merchants founded the Black Ball Line in 1818 to carry goods between New York and Liverpool, London, Le Havre, and other European ports. This "packet service"—which carried persons, cargo, and mail on a regular schedule—was highly profitable for all exporters and importers interested in dependable transatlantic service. New York merchants also gained an insurmountable lead in trade with the newly independent Latin American nations of Brazil, Peru, and Venezuela. And they controlled a small but growing portion of the cotton trade. Their agents in southern ports offered finance, insurance, and shipping to cotton exporters and won for New York a dominant share of the cotton that passed through northern harbors. By

A NEW YORK CITY AUCTION
A merchant on Chatham Street hawks his wares in one of the public auctions that were common in New York City in the 1840s. The French painter of this scene, like so many European visitors, admired American prosperity but scorned its crassness. He was fascinated by the children shown here acquiring an early education in American material values. (E. Didier. Museum of the City of New York/The J. Clarence Davies Collection)

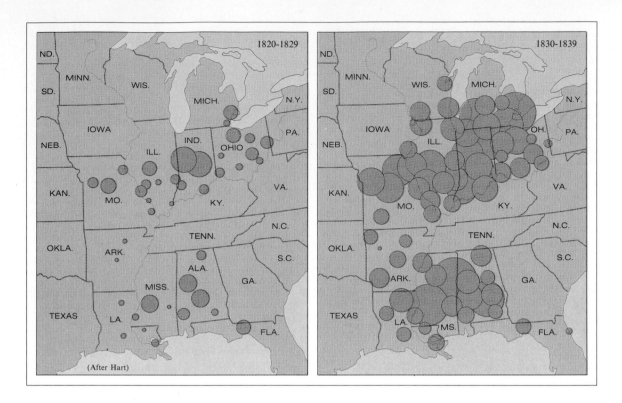

MAP 11.3 WESTERN LAND SALES, 1820–1862

Land offices opened up on the frontier to sell government land. Each of the circles in this series of maps centers on a land office, and the area of each circle depends upon the relative amount of land sold at that office. The maps show how settlement spread and intensified in farm lands of the Ohio Valley and the cotton plantations of the Southwest during the 1820s and the 1830s. In later decades the tide of settlement shifted westerly and northwesterly into Indiana, Michigan, Iowa, Wisconsin, and Minnesota.

1840, New York's mercantile community controlled almost two-thirds of the nation's foreign imports and almost half of all foreign trade, both imports and exports.

Western cities also grew rapidly. In 1830, New Orleans, Pittsburgh, Cincinnati, and Louisville accounted for almost three-quarters of the urban population in the West. Saint Louis joined this group by 1840, as a result of the swift growth of traffic to and from territory west of the Mississippi. Rochester, Buffalo, Cleveland, Detroit, and Chicago also grew rapidly during the 1830s. The initial expansion of all of these cities resulted from their location at critical junctions in the transportation system. They were places where goods had to be transferred from one mode of transport to another. Goods often came into these cities on canal boats or farmers' wagons and left on river steamboats or sailing ves-

sels. The merchants and bankers in such cities took advantage of their special location in the transportation system to develop the marketing, provisioning, and financial services that were essential to farmers and to small-town merchants in the hinterlands. These Western cities were commercially dynamic, but manufacturing in these communities remained almost entirely preindustrial. None of them yet challenged the industrial preeminence of the seaport cities to the east.

Farming New Land

The Industrial Revolution affected rural people in the United States in a far different way than it affected Europeans. Industrialization in Europe forced a massive reduction and relocation of rural populations. In the United States it promoted

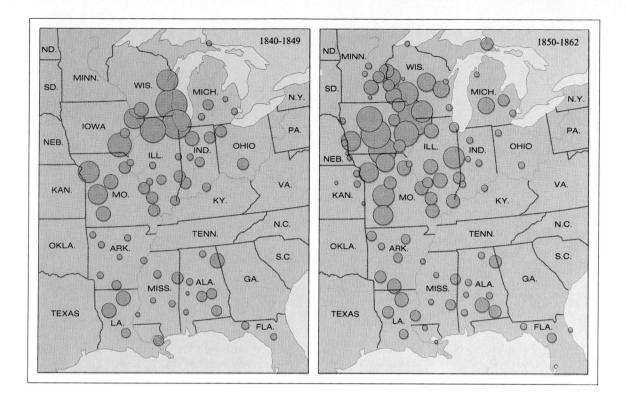

the rapid occupation of new lands by farmers and a huge increase in the rural population. The series of maps above illustrate the shifting patterns of land sales and settlement during this period. At the same time that the nation's industrial towns and seaport cities gained in size and importance, millions of farming families were moving west, across the Appalachian Mountains.

These pioneers migrated in three great streams, two from the South. Cotton producers continued the movement they had begun after the War of 1812, into the new states of Alabama (admitted to the Union in 1817) and Mississippi (1819), and on into Louisiana (1812), Missouri (1821), Arkansas (1836), and Texas (1845). In a second stream, farmers from the upper South, especially Virginia and Kentucky, followed westward routes they had established as early as the 1790s. They ferried their wagons across the Ohio River and introduced corn and hog farming in the southern parts of Ohio (1803), Indiana (1816), and Illinois (1818). Thus, southerners led the early settlement of the Old Northwest.

People from the Northeast made up the third stream of migrants. Settlers had poured into up-

state New York as early as the 1790s but did not reach the trans-Appalachian West in large numbers until the 1830s. Then settlers from New England and the Middle Atlantic states, particularly New York, traveled along the Erie Canal to establish wheat farms in the Great Lakes basin—northern Ohio, northern Illinois, Michigan (1837), and Wisconsin (1848).

These westward migrations significantly shifted the population center of American society. By 1830 about 3 million people—more than a fourth of the nation's population—lived west of the Appalachians. By 1840 this figure had risen to over 5 million, more than a third of all Americans. Western growth often meant the stagnation or decline of Eastern communities. Vast numbers of men and women left the seaboard states where they were born, taking with them their savings, personal property, and skills. During the 1820s and 1830s, the Carolinas, Vermont, and New Hampshire lost nearly as many people through migration as they gained through the excess of births over deaths. In New England, abandoned farms and homes dotted the countryside, their owners gone in search of better lands farther west.

Farmers moved west for complex and varying reasons. Some simply wanted to increase their profits. Others wanted to acquire enough land to maintain their sons and grandsons in traditional rural communities. However, all farmers appreciated the economic opportunities offered by the virgin soils of the West. A cotton planter from upland Georgia, a prosperous wheat farmer from the Connecticut Valley, and a hardscrabble subsistence farmer from Vermont might have very different values, but all could recognize the economic advantage of taking up farming on new land. Planters who moved to new lands in the Southwest were glad to leave behind soil depleted of nutrients by cotton cultivation. Farmers migrating to the prairies of the Northwest were relieved of the heavy labor required to clear forests. They soon discovered that sweat and toil expended on a patch of fresh prairie yielded a much larger crop than the same-sized plot in the East.

New and improved tools made farmers even more eager to occupy new lands. During the 1830s farmers throughout the North bought the new cast iron plow that Jethro Wood had patented in 1819. Wood's introduction of replaceable cast iron parts (including the easily worn-out edge of the share) made it impossible for village blacksmiths to compete with northeastern foundries, which could manufacture a lower-cost, higher-quality product. With this single device, farmers cut their plowing time in half and could till much larger fields. Western farmers purchased many other inexpensive, high-quality, mass-produced necessities: shovels and spades, which Alan Wood, at his Delaware Iron Works, began fabricating from rolled iron in 1826; axes, which the Collins Company of Connecticut began forging in the same year; and horseshoes, which Henry Burden of Troy, New York, began to make in 1835.

Cheap land prices made western settlement an even more practical choice. Congress reduced the price of federal land from $2.00 an acre to $1.25 in 1820. For $100, a farmer could buy eighty acres (the minimum required under federal law). This federal price set the basic market price of all undeveloped land. Developers and speculators were forced to follow the federal yardstick because settlers usually had the option of buying public land. The low price led to swift

settlement. During the 1820s and 1830s, the average American family saved $500 in ten years. Consequently, an investment of $100 or $200 in land was well within the means of most migrating people.

Western agriculture actually furthered the Industrial Revolution. Efficient western farms enabled eastern manufacturers to buy cotton, wool, leather, and other raw materials at low prices, thus helping them to compete with the British. Abundant, inexpensive supplies of grain, meat, fish, vegetables, and fruit helped to maintain the health and strength of factory workers. The growing urban populations of the Northeast increased the demand for, and prices of, all types of farm goods. Eastern factories provided cheaper clothing, tools, and household goods to western farmers, making it easier for them to continue the expansion of farming. And western markets were of growing importance to Eastern industry. During the 1830s, the production of farm implements such as horseshoes, plows, shovels, scythes, hoes, and axes accounted for fully half of the nation's consumption of pig iron. Westward expansion enabled industrializing America to take advantage of cheap land and to realize the economic advantages of regional specialization.

The Transportation Revolution

The dramatic territorial expansion during the Industrial Revolution required a transportation revolution. In 1820, the nation had no true road system, particularly in the West. Spring thaws, rainstorms, and snow made dirt roads impassable. Western settlers complained to the federal government that they lacked even roads to get their goods to market. To correct these inadequacies and to integrate great chunks of territory into their buoyant economy, Americans rapidly built a transportation system of unprecedented size, complexity, and expense.

Through the 1830s, in cooperation with state governments, the federal government built interregional roads for pedestrians, horses, herds of livestock, and heavily loaded wagons. The most significant feat was the National Road, which connected Cumberland, Maryland, with Wheeling, Virginia, in 1818, crossed the Ohio River in 1833, and reached Vandalia, Illinois, in 1850. By

CONSTRUCTION OF THE ERIE CANAL
Gangs of construction workers on the Erie Canal had to excavate deep cuts through rough land. The artist who sketched this scene, like the canal planners, was more interested in the scale of the project than the personalities of the faceless workers. Working conditions were even worse in the marshes near Syracuse where, in 1819, a thousand workers fell ill with fever and many died. (John William Hill. *Junction of Erie and Champlain Canals,* ca. 1832. The New-York Historical Society)

then, construction of major interregional roads ceased; their role had been taken over by canals and railroads. Local road building continued, but the quality of roads did not improve until automobiles were introduced in the early twentieth century.

Canal construction was the most important part of the transportation revolution. Americans began to build canals to connect inland areas along rivers and lakes with coastal cities and towns at the end of the War of 1812. Progress came slowly because of the great capital investments required and the lack of engineering expertise. When the New York legislature initiated the Erie Canal in 1817, no canal in the United States was longer than twenty-eight miles.

New Yorkers drove hard to complete the Erie Canal, the first water link between the Atlantic coast and the trans-Appalachian West. Three key advantages made this project possible. First,

ambitious New York City merchants vigorously supported the canal. Second, New York's powerful governor, De Witt Clinton, lent his full support to the enterprise. Third, most of the canal crossed gentle terrain. Consequently, even amateur surveyors—such as James Geddes and Benjamin Wright, who had been trained as lawyers—were able to design and construct much of the canal. The Erie Canal was an instant success. Even the first section, a stretch of 75 miles opened in 1819, immediately generated large profits. When the entire canal was completed, in 1825, a ribbon of water, complete with locks to raise and lower boats, reached 364 miles from Albany to Buffalo. Branch canals added 180 more miles to its reach.

The Erie Canal fulfilled every promise of its promoters. It moved settlers from New England and New York to the Old Northwest. It gave the new farmers of the Great Lakes basin, as well as those of upstate New York, cheap access to the port of New York. And it placed western communities within easy reach of eastern manufacturers and the merchants of New York City. After a trip on the Erie Canal in 1830, the novelist Nathaniel Hawthorne wrote:

> Surely the water of this canal must be the most fertilizing of all fluids, for it causes towns with the masses of brick and stone, their churches and theaters, their business and hubbub, their luxury and refinement, their gay dames and polished citizens, to spring up, till in time the wondrous stream may flow between two continuous lines of buildings, through one thronged street, from Buffalo to Albany.

The spectacular benefits and profits brought about by the Erie Canal prompted a national canal boom. Civic and business leaders in major cities and towns competed vigorously to build their own canals to capture trade with the West. These canal promoters took advantage of New York's experience by hiring the young men who had learned canal engineering while building the Erie. They also copied New York's fiscal innovations. They persuaded state governments to charter companies, to guarantee their credit, to invest directly or to force mutual savings banks to invest in them, and sometimes even to take over their ownership. Altogether, state govern-

ments provided or sponsored almost three-quarters of the $200 million invested in canals by 1840. By then, new canals had completed three critical links: (1) from the coastal plain to the up-country of the Atlantic seaboard states; (2) from the seaboard states to the Great Lakes basin and the Ohio Valley; and (3) from the Great Lakes to the Ohio and Mississippi rivers.

The steamboat, another product of the industrial age, ensured the success of this vast transportation system. The steamboat was invented in 1807, when Robert Fulton navigated his *Clermont* up the Hudson. Steamboats traveled faster, met tighter schedules, and carried more cargo than did sailing ships. Until the 1820s, however, their large consumption of wood or coal fuel made them very expensive to run and they could not navigate shallow western rivers. Then engineers broadened the hulls of the boats to increase their cargo capacity and, most important, to give them a shallower draft. They also reduced the weight of the boats by using lighter wood. Able to navigate in as little as three feet of water, these new steamboats could maneuver around tricky snags and sandbars. The wider, flat decks speeded the loading and unloading of cargo. The new steamboats greatly lowered the costs of river transport. During the 1820s alone, the steamboat at least halved the costs of upstream river transport. By 1830, steamboat travel

FIGURE 11.1 INLAND FREIGHT RATES

ROAD TRANSPORTATION, 1838
This coach has just passed over one of the best western thoroughfares, a "corduroy road" made of
tree trunks laid across a swamp. In 1842, the English author Charles Dickens traveled on such a road
and wrote: "The very slightest of the jolts with which the ponderous carriage fell from log to log was
enough . . . to have dislocated all the bones in the human body." (George Tattersall. *Highways and
Byeways of the Forest*. Museum of Fine Arts, Boston. M. & M. Karolik Collection of American
Watercolors and Drawings)

dominated the major rivers and lakes of the country.

The new water routes dramatically increased the flow of goods. In 1835, migrants to the Old Northwest sent back 268,000 barrels of flour on canal boats; just five years later they shipped more than a million. Water transport also allowed people to travel more cheaply and sped the exchange of news, technical information, and business advice, as illustrated in map 11.4 on page 328. In 1830, a traveler or a letter from New York could go by water to Boston in a day and a half, to Charleston in five days, to New Orleans in two weeks, and to Detroit in two weeks. Thirty years earlier, the same journeys, by road or sail, would have taken twice as long. Businesses and individuals communicated far more efficiently, and this in turn stimulated business enterprise.

The system of long-distance, interregional water travel was essentially complete by 1840. Another transportation era was about to dawn. Although the Baltimore and Ohio railroad had received its charter in 1828, railroads remained small, unconnected systems until 1840. They either carried only passengers or linked very limited areas in the interior to water routes. The great era of railroad building lay in the future; the magnificent system of canals and steamboats reigned for nearly twenty-five years.

The New Business Corporation

State governments used corporate charters to promote the development of the national transportation network and to forge a national market. These charters granted businesses various privileges, including monopoly powers, tax

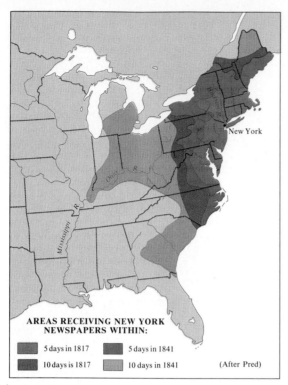

AREAS RECEIVING NEW YORK
NEWSPAPERS WITHIN:

5 days in 1817		5 days in 1841	
10 days is 1817		10 days in 1841	(After Pred)

MAP 11.4 THE SPEED OF BUSINESS NEWS
The transportation revolution and aggressive
entrepreneurs increased the speed of trade and
communication between the Atlantic seaboard and the
continental interior. The national circulation of
newspapers grew along with trade, and the New York
newspapers became the most important sources of
economic news. This map shows the dramatic
improvements in communication between 1817 and 1841.

exemptions, and, most important, limited liability—which restricts the amount an investor can lose to the value of his or her stock in the company. By extending such privileges to more transportation companies, states accelerated the accumulation of the large amounts of capital needed to build transportation systems. They also reduced the need to tax the public for that purpose. Banks also incorporated, but few mercantile firms and almost no manufacturers did. Until after the Civil War, manufacturers did not need huge accumulations of capital. They preferred to continue as partnerships or sole proprietorships to remain free from state regulations.

States gradually made the ability to incorporate a right rather than a privilege. During the 1820s, the states minimized the conditions neces-
sary for incorporation, and in the 1830s legislatures ceased granting corporate charters one by one with special acts. Instead, they established general incorporation acts that turned over the chartering process to administrators. As more businesses received charters, however, it became difficult to protect the monopoly privileges that corporate charters often guaranteed. Younger entrepreneurs often challenged the monopolies of established businesses as inconsistent with the ideals of a republic. The courts responded to these challenges by weakening the legal definition of corporate privilege and thus promoting more entrepreneurial use of property. The Supreme Court under John Marshall contributed to this trend. In *Gibbons v. Ogden* (1824), for example, the Court struck down a monopoly that the New York legislature had granted to Aaron Ogden for steamboat passenger service across the Hudson River between Manhattan and Elizabethport, New Jersey.

The ruling, however, did not clearly favor an instrumental view of property—one that was hostile to the granting of monopolies. The Court overturned the Ogden monopoly because the competitor, Thomas Gibbons, had a congressional charter, and the Court believed that the federal government had paramount authority over the regulation of interstate commerce. Only after John Marshall left the Court in 1835 did an entrepreneurial, instrumental view of property fully triumph. In the landmark case of *Charles River Bridge v. Warren Bridge* (1837), the new chief justice, Roger B. Taney, ruled in favor of the Warren Bridge Company, which in 1828 had received a charter from the Massachusetts legislature to collect tolls across the Charles River. He ruled against the Charles River Bridge Company, which had received an earlier charter that the company claimed granted an *exclusive* right to collect bridge tolls on the river. Taney did adhere to Marshall's doctrine that state governments had to respect charters, but he also argued that a legislature could not be *presumed* to have granted an exclusive, monopolistic right. His language affirmed wide access to the benefits of government: "while the rights of private property are sacredly guarded, we must not forget that the community also has rights, and the happiness and well-being of every citizen depends on their faithful preservation." In effect, he claimed that the destruction of monopoly and

MOVING DAY IN NEW YORK CITY
The quest for higher status and income became most visible in New York City on May 1, the
traditional day for moving. The crush included small merchants who took down their signs and
sought better locations. The artist, who included himself in the lower left corner of the picture, agreed
with the English observer who wrote that people jammed the streets "as if alarmed by some extensive
conflagration." (Mr. & Mrs. Screven Lorillard Collection [Photography by Eric Schaal, The *Life* History
of the United States/*The Sweep Westward* © 1963 Time-Life Books, Inc.])

the stimulation of competition were in the best
interest of the community.

The courts thus reconciled government-
granted privileges with the ideals of a republican
society. State governments could follow both
Marshall and Taney. Following Marshall, they
could protect the privileges granted in corporate
charters. Following Taney, they could diffuse
those privileges as widely as possible through
society. State governments could maintain privilege but reduce its significance. Widening access
to privilege increased the flow of capital to corporate enterprise and promoted the construction
of the national transportation system.

The Birth of Industrial Society

The Industrial Revolution transformed material
life in the United States by providing a bonanza
of goods and services. But the new affluence
had its costs. The economic system sharpened
and widened class distinctions that were based
on ownership and use of property. And industrialization, accompanied by the westward
movement, dramatically altered residential patterns and social relations in ways that many people disliked.

May Day in New York City most clearly showed the new affluence and mobility. By custom, the city's residents reserved this day for their moves to new dwellings. In the preindustrial era, possessions were plain and few, and the moves went smoothly. By the 1820s, the scene was more complicated. The streets were clogged with people hauling their belongings. Visitors to New York described running a gauntlet of feather beds, chairs, carpets, looking glasses, paintings, and baskets of crockery and cut glass. New Yorkers carried with them the trappings of comfort and status that the Industrial Revolution provided on an unprecedented scale.

New Yorkers who owned little or no property, however, were less visible on May Day. Yet they too moved often, shifting between crowded apartments, boarding houses, and rude shacks in working-class districts and slums. In fact, those without property moved continually. Unskilled workers toiled throughout New York—as laborers on docks and construction projects or as servants in hotels, restaurants, and upper-class homes—but they suffered high rates of unemployment. They and their families moved frequently in search of better work or cheaper housing. If they could afford it, they sometimes even moved West. But their mobility did not significantly improve their circumstances; they became even poorer relative to people with property than they had been before the onset of the Industrial Revolution.

The Concentration of Wealth

The Industrial Revolution brought substantial material benefits to most Americans. Increasing per capita incomes and falling prices of mass-produced goods allowed most Americans to improve their standards of living.

Higher standards of living were most obvious in American architecture. The wealthiest merchants and industrialists built increasingly expensive and elaborate homes and public buildings, creating urban landscapes that reflected their new prosperity. Walking the streets of New York in 1840, one could encounter, within the space of a few blocks, simple, utilitarian buildings housing foundries; P. T. Barnum's Broadway Museum, with a gigantic billboard displaying a threatening serpent; handsome new churches; banks and mercantile firms with the facades of Greek temples; and three-story brownstones with Greek porticoes. Much of this architecture had political as well as aesthetic significance. The Greek Revival style was popular because many Americans admired the republicanism of ancient Greece and supported the Greek rebellion of 1821 against Turkish rule. And American architects, attempting to liberate the nation's culture from British influences, turned elsewhere for aesthetic inspiration.

Middle-class homes also underwent significant change. Few middle-class people, even in the West, still lived in the cramped log cabins like the one on Broadway that presidential candidate William Henry Harrison used as part of his campaign headquarters in 1840. More typical were the homes around the Harrison headquarters. The most impressive of these were built of brick and stone. But wooden residences were much more numerous, and they were constructed very differently from log cabins or traditional frame buildings. In the 1830s, American carpenters devised a faster method to construct housing: the "balloon frame." Traditional wood construction had depended on the careful fitting together of heavy timbers; experienced housewrights fashioned a strong frame with mortise-and-tenon joints, while western farmers fitted trimmed logs together. The balloon frame, much lighter in weight (as its name implied) but almost as strong, formed a house with a vertical grid of thin wooden studs joined by nails to cross-pieces at top and bottom. Once the carpenter had thrown up the frame, he simply nailed wood sheathing to the studs as walls and then added a layer of clapboard siding.

Even an inexperienced carpenter could erect a balloon frame. The process saved enough labor to reduce the cost of housing by 40 percent—and it was quick. The balloon frame made it possible for Chicago, where it was first introduced, to spring up almost overnight. Everywhere, the balloon frame soon dominated construction of homes and other small buildings. During the 1830s, the four-room balloon-frame house became the standard residence, replacing the one- or two-room house that had prevailed in preindustrial society.

CONSTRUCTING A BALLOON FRAME HOUSE
The fragile-looking balloon frame shown on the left will provide a surprisingly strong skeleton for the substantial type of house on the right. Because people of modest means could build balloon frame houses with the labor of family members, friends, or low-skilled carpenters, they could afford houses that were available only to the very wealthy before the 1830s. (W. W. Wilson. *A Balloon Frame House*. The Metropolitan Museum of Art. Harris Brisbane Dick Fund, 1934)

Additional innovations quickly followed. Factories manufactured other prefabricated parts—doors, window frames, shutters, and hardware—that could be easily inserted into the balloon frame. Architects published self-help manuals with detailed plans of simple houses for carpenters and families building their own homes. Consequently, houses became cheaper but more standardized—built to common specifications with similar parts—than they had been previously.

Home ownership was not distributed equally among the different classes. Nor was any other aspect of the new abundance produced by the Industrial Revolution. At the end of the eighteenth century, the richest 10 percent of the nation's families owned between one-third and one-half of the nation's wealth. Their share became even larger during the 1820s and 1830s. By 1860, the wealthiest 10 percent owned more than two-thirds of the nation's wealth.

Wealthy elites dominated property ownership, especially in the major Atlantic seaports. In 1840 the richest 1 percent of the population in these cities owned as much as 10 percent of the population had owned fifty years before. This 1 percent owned more than 40 percent of all "tangible" property—land, ships, buildings, and household furnishings. In New York City, the richest 4 percent of the population owned more than three-quarters of the tangible property. Their concentration of holdings of "intangible" property—stocks, bonds, and mortgages—was even greater.

This growing inequality stemmed primarily from the opportunities created by industrial and commercial expansion. Hence, great concentrations of wealth were less common in smaller towns or agricultural areas. Yet similar trends existed there as well. Even in modest-sized, non-industrial Massachusetts towns, the richest 10 percent of families typically owned 50 percent or more of the tangible property by 1840.

The new manufacturers, like Francis Cabot Lowell, increased their fortunes most rapidly. More generally, the Americans whose incomes rose most were those who exploited the unevenly distributed technological changes brought on by the Industrial Revolution. Technical advances, concentrated in the textiles, machine tools, and firearms industries, particularly rewarded the owners and skilled workers in those areas. Those who promoted, designed, and adapted the most modern machinery, and those who mobilized and disciplined the labor needed to operate that machinery, enjoyed the most rapidly growing profits, salaries, or wages.

Merchants tended to amass their wealth more slowly. Large merchants in the Atlantic ports—New York's John Jacob Astor and Philadelphia's Stephen Girard, for example—had become wealthy through the traditional means of earning profits on trade. Nonetheless, their wealth grew substantially because growing populations and per capita levels of consumption stimulated trade. And these merchants also profited from shrewd investments in urban real estate. The steady growth of older fortunes meant that Astor, Girard, and the other large Eastern merchants remained the wealthiest Americans during the 1820s and 1830s.

The concentration of wealth in the hands of a few individuals intensified partly because the wealthy, often linked by business and family ties, could easily acquire the best information about new investment opportunities. Family fortunes thus often became self-perpetuating. Moreover, nineteenth century governments almost never taxed inheritances or intangible property and usually taxed real and personal property at extremely low rates. Therefore, wealthy manufacturing and mercantile families could retain their fortunes, and their economic power, into the second or third generation.

The very sluggish increase in the wages of unskilled workers sharpened the concentration of wealth. In Massachusetts in 1825, the daily wage of a common laborer—about 75 cents—was about two-thirds that of a skilled machinist. By the 1840s, the laborer's wage had increased to about $1 but was now less than half the typical machinist's. Consequently, the incomes of unskilled workers fell well behind those of people who had skills or owned property. Moreover, the cost of living was actually higher for unskilled than for skilled workers. The unskilled had to spend a larger share of their incomes simply to buy food and fuel at rising prices. So they had less money left to take advantage of the rapidly falling prices of manufactured goods. (In the 1830s, the poorest workers in the cities had to spend two dollars out of every three they earned just to feed their families; middle-class families fed themselves on less than a third of their earnings.) Thus, people who lacked skills or property were even worse off, in relative terms, than their low wages indicated during the early Industrial Revolution.

Access to Wealth

Before the Industrial Revolution, families often lost hard-earned assets through foolish investments, poor business sense, imprudent living, or simple bad luck. But the Industrial Revolution increased the rate at which fortunes, large and small, were dissipated. Financial panics, which increased in intensity, drove growing numbers of even cautious, calculating investors into bankruptcy. Jeremiah Thompson, New York's largest cotton trader and one of the organizers of the Black Ball Line, went bankrupt in 1827. Philip Hone, wealthy merchant and mayor of New York in the 1820s, never recovered from his losses and the bankruptcy of his son during the

Panic of 1837, the worst financial crisis before the Civil War. For modest property owners, the new techniques of production sometimes diminished wealth and status. For example, during the 1830s traditional house carpenters lost business and income to less skilled carpenters who threw up balloon-frame structures.

Far more people, however, improved their economic and social standing than lost ground. The middle class grew rapidly in both size and importance, despite the increasing concentration of property in the hands of the very wealthy. Craftsmen, engineers, and skilled machine operators found their skills in high demand and their wages rising. Likewise, building contractors, grocers, shopkeepers, and butchers in booming urban areas profited from an abundance of customers. Farmers discovered that the growing urban demand for meat, dairy products, and perishables, as well as for the staples of wheat, corn, and cotton, increased their income. Most Americans saved about 15 percent of their income, often placing their surplus funds in local banks and new savings institutions. Many eventually bought property with their savings. By 1840 about half of all free American men over the age of thirty had acquired at least moderate holdings of wealth—a house, furniture, a little land, and some savings. In agricultural communities an even higher percentage owned some land.

A few of the richest men in every community had grown up in poverty. Thomas Kempshall of Rochester, New York, was an example. Kempshall was born in England, but his father died after the family arrived in the United States, leaving Thomas's eldest brother, a carpenter, to raise nine siblings. Thomas began work by assisting his brother. Then he clerked in a dry-goods store. The owner of the store made Thomas a partner shortly before his own retirement. This gave Thomas enough status to marry the sister of a wealthy publisher and land speculator in 1824. Kempshall used the resources of his new family to expand the dry-goods store and open a large millstone factory. In 1827, he invested in the construction of the largest flour mill in the United States. In 1838, having become one of the richest men in Rochester, he turned to politics and won election to a seat in Congress.

Kempshall's rise from poverty was not typical. Most of the newly wealthy did not advance as far or as rapidly. Those who did usually had much in common with Kempshall. They were ambitious and shrewd in their business judgments, they were industrious and frugal, and they had a keen sense of the new opportunities that the Industrial Revolution created. Sometimes they made friendships that proved profitable, and they frequently made fortunate marriages. Usually their families and households provided an environment congenial to success and competition. What Kempshall lacked that most of the newly wealthy had was an initial advantage—modest property ownership, education, or a skill that allowed some savings. With some of these advantages, young men could plan their lives, learn useful skills, and move, if necessary, to a new town.

Social mobility was limited and difficult for most men of modest means. The surest route to property ownership was self-employment, but many young men could not pursue this course. By 1840, as many as half the nation's workers were laborers who worked for wages, rather than for their own profits. With the demand for skilled labor, some wage laborers could realistically hope to acquire skills or to own property. But ordinary laborers faced a high probability of a lifetime with little chance to buy a home or land.

The wage laborers with the slimmest chance of upward mobility were casual workers, who accounted for about 10 percent of the labor force. The day laborers who dug thirty feet deep in dirt and stone to build canals, who carried lumber and bricks for construction projects, who loaded and unloaded ships and wagons, and who hauled goods in and out of warehouses were most numerous. In 1840, nearly twenty-five thousand such workers were employed on the Erie Canal. Day laborers owned no property except the clothes they wore, and their work provided no economic security. In depressions they bore the brunt of unemployment, and even in the best of times their work was usually unpredictable and seasonal.

Casual labor was also dangerous. Serious injury was common and often meant that a worker could no longer support his family. Laborers building canals through swamps often contracted malaria and yellow fever. In 1831, the economist Mathew Carey reported that 5 percent of the canal workers returned to their families in the winter with their health broken "by fevers and agues."

Some wage laborers, particularly in the West, eased hardship by maintaining a garden or keeping a few animals to supplement the family diet. But this was of only slight assistance during the winter, when food was scarce and storms and frozen rivers and canals could shut down trade, ending work for longshoremen and draymen. For them and other casual workers, winter was often a season of appealing for charity and searching continuously, sometimes fruitlessly, for a little work chopping wood or cutting ice.

For wage earners who acquired no property, hope for mobility rested with their children. But these workers had few resources to pass on. In fact, most could not afford to educate their offspring, to apprentice them, or to accumulate small dowries so that their daughters could marry men with better prospects. Instead, their children had to work to help support their families. For most wage-earning families, the economic future was dim and uncertain. Only those who could sustain themselves without the wages their children earned could find much meaning in the nation's economic promise.

Mobility Versus Community

Industrialization and agricultural expansion shifted the distribution of economic activity and increased the rate of geographical mobility. Americans now moved from place to place at remarkable rates searching out economic opportunity. In Boston, one household in three moved each year. Many of these households simply moved from one neighborhood to another. But most Bostonians, like most Americans who moved, left for new, growing communities. A majority of the people living in the booming towns at any given time were likely to be merely passing through. Yet, in even the most rapidly growing towns, in both the East and West, well-established property owners tended to stay put. This stable core controlled much of the shape of industrial society and provided continuity and a sense of order to the local community.

The most geographically mobile Americans during the early Industrial Revolution were young people with low-income, low-security jobs, who owned little or no property. Unskilled workers moved most often because they rarely owned property or had stable, predictable employment. Nothing tied them down. Another sizable element in migration consisted of mature people who had owned property but had suffered economic reversals. The traditional manufacturers and artisans who found their livelihoods threatened by industrialization also migrated frequently. Household weavers, blacksmiths, and harness makers, for example, often left eastern towns as their customers turned to cheap goods produced in factories. These skilled craftsmen either turned to new types of employment or re-established their craft farther west, where they hoped to gain a competitive edge because of the high transportation costs for goods from Eastern industrial centers.

In contrast, families with property rarely moved to new communities. Typically, they moved only once or twice, most often when the head of the household was in his late thirties or early forties. In the mill towns and farming communities of Massachusetts before the Civil War, about a fourth of the families remained in place for at least ten years. These families were headed by men who were older, skilled, and propertied. They tied themselves closely to other established families. In training their children, they emphasized the virtues of geographical and social stability.

Propertied people who did move west recognized the risks. They knew that success in the West, as everywhere, depended heavily on the quality and strength of personal relationships. Prospective migrants preferred, when possible, to travel with or to seek out family or established friends. Often wives corresponded with sisters, cousins, and old friends to identify communities where their families would find support. As a result, migrants usually moved to communities founded by people of similar backgrounds. New Englanders, for example, largely avoided the towns of the Ohio Valley that southerners had established. And in new communities, migrants immediately sought out familiar churches, fraternal lodges, crafts, and professions to form their first friendships. When young middle-class men traveled alone to new communities, their families urged them to seek out respectable people

and to be wary of "confidence men." In 1828, a popular self-help manual warned young migrants that they would encounter men who, "instead of acting in open daylight, pursuing the direct and straight-forward path of rectitude and duty [put on] false appearances; working in the dark, and carrying their plans by stratagem and deceit."

In response to the need for building trustworthy relationships in the West, cores of more permanent citizens quickly formed in new communities from Rochester to Cincinnati, Nashville, and Saint Louis. The first residents with property and aspirations created networks among themselves. The first merchants, artisans, and professionals established loyal clienteles, sound reputations, and good credit ratings. From this core came the leaders and prime beneficiaries of the Industrial Revolution. They celebrated their success, becoming the greatest "boosters" of the new communities. From their perspective, their communities had prospered because of their own group efforts.

To maintain their power, the first generation of well-established community leaders became the patrons of new migrants. They backed young men who had some education, skill, or family connection and had embarked on a search for improvement. The community leaders helped these young men acquire skills or loaned them money to start new businesses. Often they supported their daughters' decisions to marry one of these industrious migrants. Many of the young men, in turn, scouted western opportunities for relatives who still lived in the East.

Success in the new communities usually required membership in the stable core of local property owners. There were exceptions, to be sure. Ichabod Washburn, for example, became one of the richest citizens of Worcester, Massachusetts, even though his family had virtually no property and he had moved nine times before he was twenty-one. He arrived in Worcester in 1819 and took advantage of some experience in the metal trades to establish himself as a successful manufacturer of wire. Highly successful individuals like Washburn were in a distinct minority among migrants, especially those without property, but were sufficiently numerous to establish the nineteenth-century myth that those who "got out, got ahead."

The Plight of the Urban Workers

The reorganization of work—the rapid spread of both factories and the "outwork" system—created strains on community leaders in their efforts to provide social stability. Local elites, particularly employers in large Atlantic seaports and eastern industrial towns, could no longer maintain close contact with and exert control over people who labored for wages. In the new northeastern workplaces, traditional family, religious, or communal authority became less effective in ordering work relationships. The story was different in the newer communities of the Northwest, where wage laborers and employers continued to maintain close on-the-job contact. Western manufacturing remained largely the province of households and small workshops that employed fewer than twenty people.

Even in industries in which the factory system did not yet flourish, employers separated themselves from the work of their wage earners. During the 1820s, for example, in response to growing demand for shoes, master shoemakers, or cordwainers, began to separate their lives from those of their employees. Many cordwainers expanded their shops to include a large number of journeymen and apprentices, usually moving them to a back room while using the front room to meet customers. In these back rooms the workers cut leather into soles and "uppers." Then the masters sent out the soles and uppers to "fitters," often women who worked at home and sewed the parts together into finished shoes. During the early 1830s, masters expanded their reliance on "outwork" even further. They moved everyone except a foreman out of the central shop and traded with journeyman shoemakers who now labored at home, often in boarding houses in the back streets of town. Later in the decade, merchant capitalists gained control of the shoemaking trade, from the purchase of raw materials to the marketing of the finished product. A new, more impersonal system of wage labor and large-scale production had replaced the small, intimate shops where masters, journeymen, and apprentices had worked side by side.

The separation of employers and wage earners affected residential patterns. Before the Industrial Revolution, most wage earners had lived close to their employers, often even in the same homes. By the 1830s, though, most employers in northeastern cities lived in different neighborhoods from their employees. The experience of Everard Peck, the foremost publisher in Rochester, was typical. When Peck established a small weekly newspaper in 1820, he followed the preindustrial tradition of boarding the young printers who worked for him in his own home; work and domestic life were closely interwoven. As Peck's employees increased in number, such living arrangements became impossible. By 1830, Peck operated a printing office, a daily paper, a bookstore, paper mill, and a warehouse. Only the most skilled and trusted of his printers now lived with him; the rest shifted for themselves. Continuity between the household and the workplace was disappearing.

By the 1830s, factory workers, journeymen, and unskilled casual laborers in northeastern towns and cities lived in well-defined neighborhoods. Certain blocks became dominated by large, congested boarding houses, where many single men and women lived crowded together under unhealthy conditions. Landlords converted houses, including basements and attics, into apartments and then used the profits from rentals to build more tenements. They often squeezed a number of buildings onto a single lot; these were interspersed with outhouses and connected by foul-smelling courtyards and dark alleys.

The lives of many wage earners deteriorated. They became anxious and tense over the breakdown of traditional order, over their loss of social status, and over their new working and living conditions. They significantly increased their consumption of alcohol. In the eighteenth century, Americans drank large quantities of inexpensive rum. Then they turned to "spirits," especially gin and whiskey, distilled by farmers as a convenient way to get their grain to market. Liquor was an integral and accepted fact of preindustrial life; it lubricated ceremonies, celebrations, work breaks, barn raisings, and games. During the 1820s, however, urban wage earners led Americans to new heights of alcoholic consumption. By 1830, per capita consumption of gin and whiskey had risen to more than five gallons a year, more than twice the rate of consumption during the 1980s. Drinking habits changed as well. At work, those who were not members of craft unions committed to abstinence began to drink more often than during the traditional 11 A.M. and 4 P.M. "refreshers." Journeymen used apprentices to smuggle whiskey into shops, and then, as a baker recalled, "One man was stationed at the window to watch, while the rest drank." And many workers who frequented saloons became less interested in casual camaraderie than in solitary and heavy drinking.

"Grog shops" and "tippling houses" appeared on almost every block in the working-class districts and became focal points for urban disorder and crime, including assaults, burglary, and vandalism. Fueled by unrestrained drinking, a fist fight among young men one night could turn into a brawl the second night and into a full-scale riot the third. The urban police forces, consisting of low-paid watchmen and amateur constables, could not contain the chaos.

The growing disorder was visible and disturbing to employers and substantial property owners like Philip Hone, a New York merchant who complained to his diary in 1840:

> Riot, disorder, and violence increase in our city, [so that] every night is marked by some outrage committed by gangs of young ruffians who prowl the streets insulting females, breaking into the houses of unoffending publicans, making night hideous by yells of disgusting inebriety, and—unchecked by the city authorities—committing every sort of enormity with apparent impunity.

Some of the more affluent families began to flee to residential communities on the urban fringe. But just as many of the wealthiest citizens maintained their residences close to the heart of the old seaport cities, and most middle-class housing remained within walking distance of cheap rooming houses and industry. Even though neighborhoods grew more distinct, no class dominated any large section of the city. People across the social spectrum retained a high degree of day-to-day physical proximity, even in the largest cities. These were cities where most people lived within walking distance of work, school, church, shops, and saloons. Transporta-

tion on the horse-drawn omnibus, although too expensive for all but the wealthier merchants and businesspeople, moved slowly through the late afternoon crowds. It could not protect the wealthy from the sight of disorderly, sometimes drunken crowds in the muddy cobblestone streets.

Such scenes left little doubt in the minds of the wealthy that they had lost much of their control over the poorer strata of society. When they began to ponder this reality during the 1830s, they tended to overlook the role of the Industrial Revolution. They did not consider how it had widened the gap between rich and poor and disrupted traditional social relations. Nor did the wealthy recognize that wage earners had become alienated and anxious because the actual effects of the Industrial Revolution on their lives failed to conform to the picture painted by the more successful classes. When the wealthy responded to social disorder, they did not seek to halt or reverse the Industrial Revolution but, instead, worked to eradicate its disturbing symptoms and to control the social disorder that industrialization had created.

The Business Cycle and Economic Instability

The Industrial Revolution produced not only social disorder but also growing economic instability—increasingly severe fluctuation in prices, production, employment, and incomes. The business cycle, now a very prominent part of American economic life, reinforced all the other disruptive forces of the Industrial Revolution. Economic instability had particularly harsh effects on people who lacked property or skills.

During much of the 1820s and 1830s, economic growth proceeded without significant interruption. After the Panic of 1819 and a depression that lasted through 1820, European demand for American agricultural goods triggered an upswing in the business cycle. This expansion—sustained by the rapid growth of internal markets, by continued British demand for American commodities, by European investment in American canals, and by favorable banking conditions—lasted until the Panic of 1837.

FOOD RIOT, AS DESCRIBED BY A WEALTHY NEW YORKER

From the diary of Philip Hone, 1837.

Monday, Feb. 13.—*Riots.* This city was disgraced this morning by a mob regularly convened by public notice in the park for the notable purpose of making bread cheaper by destroying the flour in the merchants' warehouses. The following notice was extensively published on Saturday by placards at the corners of the streets:

Bread, Meat, Rent, Fuel— Their Prices Must Come Down.

The Voice of the People Shall be Heard, and Will Prevail.

The People will meet in the Park, rain or shine, at four o'clock on Monday afternoon to inquire into the cause of the present unexampled distress, and devise a suitable remedy.

All friends of humanity, determined to resist Monopolists and Extortioners, are invited to attend.

Many thousands assembled on this call. The day was bitter cold and the wind blew a hurricane, but there was fire enough in the speeches of Messrs. Windt and Ming to inflame the passions of the populace. These two men . . . did not tell them in so many words to attack the stores of the flour merchants, but stigmatized them as monopolists and extortioners, who enriched themselves at the expense of the laboring poor. They said that Eli Hart & Co. had 50,000 barrels of flour in their store, which they held at an exorbitant price whilst the poor of the city were starving. This was a firebrand suddenly thrown into the combustible mass which surrounded the speaker, and away went the mob to Hart's store in Washington near Cortlandt Street, which they forced open, threw 400 or 500 barrels of flour and large quantities of wheat into the street, and committed all the extravagant acts which usually flow from the unlicensed fury of a mob. The mayor and other magistrates, with the police officers, repaired to the spot, and with the assistance of many well-disposed citizens, succeeded after a time in clearing and getting possession of the store. From thence the mob went to Herrick & Co. in Water Street, and destroyed about fifty barrels of flour. The mayor ordered out a military force, which with the other measures adopted, kept the rioters in check.

Source: Allan Nevins, ed., *The Diary of Philip Hone.* New York: Dodd, Mead, 1936, pp. 241–242.

The Panic of 1837 began in Britain. In late 1836, the Bank of England, convinced that it was losing too much specie (hard currency) to the United States, curtailed the flow of investment. Concurrently, the British demand for cotton declined sharply, causing the bankruptcy of British and American mercantile firms whose lending was based on cotton as security. These events set off a wave of bankruptcy and restriction of credit that affected merchants and bankers throughout the United States. Without adequate credit, American trade, manufacturing, and farming entered a depression.

Recovery was slow. The Bank of England continued to keep credit tight until the early 1840s. Bumper cotton crops in the late 1830s drove down cotton prices, hurting merchants in international trade. Many states, unable to raise taxes or to borrow in depressed conditions, defaulted on the bonds they had issued to finance canal building and thereby undermined British confidence in American investments. To protect themselves, American banks insisted on holding larger amounts of specie. But this policy reduced the money available to the general public. As a result, spending, investment, and prices declined even further.

The depression lasted until 1843. By that year prices had fallen, on the average, to almost half of their 1837 levels. Overall investment in the American economy fell almost 25 percent between 1837 and 1843, led by a 90 percent decline in canal construction. Investment in railroads and manufacturing also fell dramatically. Slumping investment and production forced workers out of jobs, and in 1838 unemployment rose to an unprecedented level of almost 10 percent; in seaports and industrial centers it approached 20 percent. Taken together with the bankruptcies of farms and businesses, massive unemployment shocked a broad spectrum of Americans. As Reverend Henry Ward Beecher put it:

> The world looked upon a continent of inexhaustible fertility (whose harvest had glutted the markets, and rotted in disuse), filled with lamentation, and its inhabitants wandering like bereaved citizens among the ruins of an earthquake, mourning for children, for houses crushed, and property buried forever.

Bleak pessimism sapped self-confidence and prolonged the depression. But by 1843, prices had fallen so low that consumers, both domestic and foreign, started buying the products of industry and agriculture, thus stimulating recovery. This new expansion lasted more than fifteen years.

Economic instability also stemmed from de-

MAP 11.5 ANATOMY OF A PANIC: BANK SUSPENSIONS IN MAY, 1837
Although the first bank failures occurred in Natchez and Tallahassee, the collapse of New York City banks several days later precipitated a chain reaction of national panic. Rivers, canals, and post roads carried news of the panic from New York to Saint Louis in just 12 days. The resulting pattern of bank failures provides a dramatic picture of the economic nerve system of the nation—a nerve system dominated by New York.

TIME LINE
THE INDUSTRIAL REVOLUTION

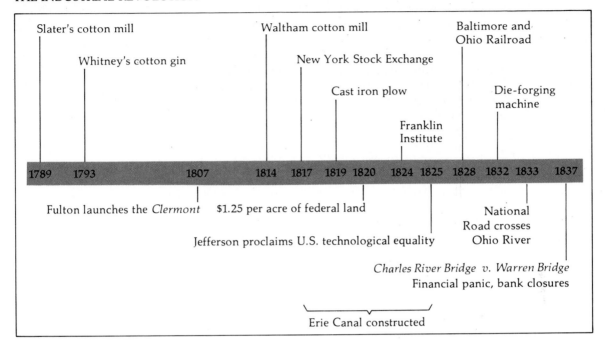

pendence on agricultural exports and lack of control over foreign markets. Sharp declines in agricultural prices, particularly cotton, periodically disrupted the lines of credit that extended from British merchants and bankers to American merchants, bankers, and planters. While American production for export was declining relative to production for domestic consumption—and while cotton exports were important primarily to the South—any disruption of credit flowing to the South often had severe ripple effects on the entire economy.

Industrialization made the economy more complex and its parts more interdependent. Disruptions in any sector, including international trade, had more serious effects on the entire economy than they had previously. The greater reliance of the industrial economy on capital meant that a sudden shortage of capital could devastate the entire economy. Furthermore, American industrialization and expansion depended on large amounts of long-term investment from Europe, primarily from Great Britain, to finance the construction of canals and rail-

roads. Whenever the flow of investment from Great Britain came to a halt, depression radiated throughout the economy.

By 1840, economic instability had become a persistent threat to the new industrial order in the United States. This problem, like the increasing concentration of wealth and income, loss of status for many workers, and disruptions of traditional social order, offset the benefits of increased productivity and income. For Americans who experienced or feared the unemployment and reduced incomes of industrial depressions, modern economic growth had not lived up to its promise.

Economic and political leaders found no solution to the problem of economic instability. And most Americans, encouraged by the material advantages they began to enjoy during the 1820s and 1830s, discounted the importance of instability and largely ignored its social costs. They became so deeply committed to the Industrial Revolution that the nation was unable to deal creatively with the sources of instability until the mid-twentieth century.

*I*nnovations in manufacturing technology during the 1820s enabled Americans to become more efficient and triggered advances in agriculture and transportation. These innovations launched the Industrial Revolution in the United States.

Northeastern manufacturers made the most dramatic advances. New England textile manufacturers led the way by copying the power-driven machines of British manufacturers, by mobilizing large groups of workers—primarily young, single women—into factories, and by adapting British machines to offset the higher price of labor in the United States. Sustaining the Industrial Revolution throughout the Northeast were the ideas and capital of small manufacturers and skilled workers. Most important, these people developed the machine tools required to produce complicated equipment capable of producing goods at high speeds and in great quantity.

The Industrial Revolution established the basis for a national market. Most Americans became more reliant on internal trade in agricultural and manufacturing goods, although

southerners remained dependent on the export of cotton, the import of British manufactured goods, and British commercial services. Urbanization accelerated, led by new industrial towns along the fall line and by New York City, which became the nation's leading trading center. Industrialization also stimulated the settlement of the Old Northwest, resulting in increasing agricultural production that helped to sustain the nation's economic growth. To integrate the national market, Americans built a transportation system, based heavily on waterways, that was unprecedented in size and complexity.

Economic growth meant that most Americans, especially those who were able to take advantage of the modern technological change, improved their standard of living. But industrialization widened distinctions among classes, disrupted residential patterns and working relations, and periodically increased unemployment. Networks of community leaders helped to stabilize life for mobile Americans who owned property, but for nonpropertied Americans, especially within the largest cities, the dislocations became severe.

Suggestions for Further Reading

Northeastern Industrialization

Books that provide insights with respect to the contribution of technological change to the Industrial Revolution include H. J. Habakkuk, *American and British Technology in the Nineteenth Century: The Search for Labour-Saving Inventions* (1962); David A. Hounshell, *From the American System to Mass Production, 1800–1932: The Development of Manufacturing Technology in the United States* (1984); Melvin Kranzberg and Carroll W. Pursell, Jr., *Technology in Western Civilization* (1967); and Nathan Rosenberg, *Perspectives on Technology* (1976). The relationship between technological change and the development of the textile industry is worked out in Paul F. McGouldrick, *New England Textiles in the Nineteenth Century* (1968).

Stanley Lebergott, *Manpower in Economic Growth: The United States Record since 1800* (1964) provides a useful survey of the contribution of labor to the Industrial Revolution. A study which provides an in-depth analysis of the situation of a critical group of women workers is Thomas Dublin, *Women at Work, The Transformation of Work and Community in Lowell, Massachusetts, 1826–1860* (1979). Tracing the history of early industrialization in another representative commu-

nity, but from an anthropological perspective, is Anthony F. C. Wallace, *Rockdale, The Growth of an American Village in the Early Industrial Revolution* (1978). Regional studies of the early Industrial Revolution include Peter J. Coleman, *The Transformation of Rhode Island* and Diane Lindstrom, *Economic Development in the Philadelphia Region, 1810–1850* (1978). Surveys of the Industrial Revolution that illuminate its economic dimensions include W. Elliot Brownlee, *Dynamics of Ascent: A History of the American Economy* (1974) and Douglas C. North, *The Economic Growth of the United States, 1790–1860* (1961).

Market Expansion

Urban development in this period is best explored through R. G. Albion, *The Rise of New York Port, 1815–1860* (1939); Eric E. Lampard, "The Evolving System of Cities in the United States: Urbanization and Economic Development," in Harvey S. Perloff and Lowdon Wingo, Jr. (eds.), *Issues in Urban Economics* (1968); Richard C. Wade, *The Urban Frontier: Pioneer Life in Early Pittsburgh, Cincinnati, Lexington, Louisville, and Saint Louis* (1964); and Alan R. Pred, *Urban Growth and the Circulation of Information: The United States System of Cities, 1790–1840* (1973). The best introductions to the agricultural expansion in this period are Paul W. Gates, *The Farmer's Age: Agriculture, 1815–1860* (1960) and Lewis C. Gray, *History of Agriculture in the Southern United States to 1860* (1933). The classic history of the role of transportation in the industrial revolution is George R. Taylor, *The Transportation Revolution, 1815–1860* (1951). For studying the role of canals, one should begin by consulting Carter Goodrich, *et al., Canals and American Economic Development* (1961). On the contribution of the law to early industrialization, see Oscar Handlin and Mary Flug Handlin, *Commonwealth: A Study in the Role of Government in the American Economy, Massachusetts, 1774–1861* (1947); Morton J. Horwitz, *The Transformation of American Law, 1780–1860* (1977); James Willard Hurst, *Law and the Conditions of Freedom in the Nineteenth Century United States* (1964).

The Birth of Industrial Society

The best introductions to the study of the distribution of wealth and income during the early industrialization are found in Frederick C. Jaher, *The Urban Establishment, Upper Strata in Boston, New York, Charleston, Chicago, and Los Angeles* (1982); Edward Pessen, *Riches, . Class, and Power Before the Civil War* (1973); Lee Soltow (ed.), *Six Papers on the Size Distribution of Wealth and Income* (1969); and Jeffrey G. Williamson and Peter H. Lindert, *American Inequality: A Macroeconomic History* (1980). Studies of wealth and income structure must be supplemented with analysis of social mobility such as presented by Robert Doherty, *Society and Power: Five New England Towns, 1800–1860* (1977); Don H. Doyle, *The Social Order of a Frontier Community: Jacksonville, Illinois, 1825–1870* (1978); Michael B. Katz et al., *The Social Organization of Early Industrial Capitalism* (1982); Peter R. Knights, *The Plain People of Boston, 1830–1860* (1971); and Stanley Lebergott, *The American Economy: Income, Wealth and Want* (1976). Some of the disruptive effects of mobility on urban life are addressed in Alan Dawley, *Class and Community, The Industrial Revolution in Lynn,* (1976); Karen Haltunen, *Confidence Men and Painted Women, A Study of Middle-class Culture in America, 1830–1870* (1982); Paul E. Johnson, *A Shopkeeper's Millennium: Society and Revivals in Rochester, New York, 1815–1837* (1978); Roger Lane, *Policing the City, Boston 1822–1885* (1967); W. J. Rorabaugh, *The Alcoholic Republic, An American Tradition* (1979); Ian R. Tyrell, *Sobering Up: From Temperance to Prohibition in Antebellum America, 1800–1860* (1979); and Sam Bass Warner, Jr., *The Private City* (1968).

12

THE POLITICAL CULTURE OF INDUSTRIALIZING AMERICA

The Industrial Revolution changed the lives of millions of American men and women in ways that raised basic social and political questions for them. In the 1820s and 1830s, it became increasingly clear that traditional social and political institutions could not cope with industrial development and a market economy. The institutions of the family, the village or urban neighborhood, the artisan's shop of masters and journeymen and apprentices, the religious congregation, the vestry and the town meeting, had all succeeded well in preindustrial society, where people lived and worked together in self-sufficient, close-knit communities. The new economy drew people into national, even international affairs. It created a world that was far less predictable, less personal, and more complicated than preindustrial society.

Not everyone was equally touched by the Industrial Revolution. Many people lived at its fringes and continued to think of their experience in traditional terms. But the changes made most Americans alter their ways of life to match the new economic and social realities. The new middle-class property owners and the business elite of manufacturers and merchants led the transformation. They promoted a vigorous movement of evangelical religion and moral re-

form. The goal of this movement was to train men and women to prize efficiency, industry, and moral discipline and to think of themselves as fundamentally different from people whose lives were not governed by these values. The result was the beginning of the formation of a new social class—a business class—with an increasingly clear sense of its own identity.

The Industrial Revolution also had a profound effect on American politics. The most important political phenomenon of the two decades after 1820 was the emergence of Andrew Jackson. With his vigorous personality, Jackson took political center stage when he first ran for the presidency in 1824. He and the Democratic party that he shaped dominated the scene until 1840, when the new Whig party defeated his hand-picked successor, Martin Van Buren.

Jackson defined himself as the political leader of the "producing class" of farmers and workers, committed to removing the "special privileges" of the rich and the business class. His Whig opponents gradually defined themselves as the party that would use the federal government actively to promote the development of business, transportation, and industry. The Whig challenge to Jackson's Democratic party initiated the Second Party System—the competition between the Democratic and Whig parties which structured politics until the rise of the Republican party in the 1850s.

Both the Democrats and the Whigs built coalitions of diverse groups and interests. They organized on a national scale and competed efficiently for the support of an expanding mass electorate. They were increasingly managed by professional politicians whose work was to create a political "product" that would satisfy as many different kinds of voters as possible. Together, evangelical moral reformers and party politicians molded a new political culture in America.

The Rise of the Business Class

In the 1820s and 1830s, a new social class took shape in the United States. It consisted mostly of prosperous property owners who were, in economic terms, literally "middle class"—a group that stood between the wealthier factory owners, merchants, and financiers at one extreme and the growing class of nonpropertied wage earners at the other. Its members were the families of the men who had accumulated enough money to live comfortably but not enough to become the capitalist owners of the factories, shipping lines, banks, and other large enterprises of the Industrial Revolution. They were the engineers and skilled mechanics, the foremen and contractors who served the manufacturers; they were prosperous farmers and well-to-do craftsmen; they were professional men of modest means; they were shopkeepers or manufacturers' clerks and agents; they owned small enterprises or worked in large banks, firms, or stores that they did not own. Typically, they had been able to buy their houses and perhaps a little land.

Such people dressed well. They could afford a carriage and a good horse or two. Their wives and daughters were literate, perhaps even educated, and could play the pianos that graced the carefully decorated front parlors of their well-built houses. There were books on their shelves, and usually a servant or two in the kitchen and stables. They attended church and sent their sons and daughters to good schools. They were most numerous in New England, but groups of these families lived in every American town, even in the agrarian South.

Middle-class men and women felt growing differences between themselves and the rapidly increasing number of people who owned nothing and had to struggle to earn enough just to survive. Instead, their education, material well-being, and aspirations gave the middle class a sense of identification with the wealthy families of the business elite. Together, the business elite and the middle class formed the new business class. There might be an enormous economic gulf between a truly wealthy factory owner and his foremen and clerks. But they were beginning to share the same moral and religious ideas. This would be an important key to the political culture of industrializing America.

The Benevolent Empire

When the members of the business elite and the middle class contemplated the social changes that were reshaping their society, they noticed primarily the potential for social dislocation and disorder, especially among the working poor. They did not denounce industrialization, however. To resolve conflicts of conscience, they focused instead on the excesses of industrialization. They attempted to introduce new forms of discipline, first into their own lives and then into the lives of ordinary farmers, laborers, and factory workers.

The effort of the business class to create a society marked by moral discipline began in the Northeast among members of the business elite who had strong Congregationalist or Presbyterian connections and traditions. Ministers in these churches, together with well-established merchants—and their wives—launched a program of social regulation. One of their leading spokesmen, Congregationalist minister Lyman Beecher of Boston, proclaimed their purpose: to restore "the moral government of God." Because of these people's aggressive quest for moral purity and their firm belief in charity, historians have labeled them the "Benevolent Empire."

The specific targets of the Benevolent Empire were familiar evils like drunkenness, prostitution, and crime. The method for conquering them was new. Instead of relying on traditional local solutions such as charity for the poor or church sermons, reformers established large-scale regional and even national organizations—for example, the Prison Discipline Society and the American Society for the Promotion of Temperance—to institutionalize charity and to combat evil systematically. Each of these organizations had its managing staff, its network of volunteers and chapters, its newspaper, and its published tracts. Together the groups set out to "rescue" prostitutes and save the abandoned children of the poor. They worked to have the insane taken from attics and cellars and put into well-ordered and disciplined asylums. They labored to reform the criminal justice system, to shift its emphasis from the public and physical punishment or humiliation of criminals to rehabilitation in prisons where moral self-discipline would be emphasized. By removing from their midst individuals whom they viewed as both incompetent and evil, the reformers claimed they would ensure the vitality and independence of the citizenry and consequently strengthen the republic.

Women were increasingly active in this effort. Since the 1790s, there had been a number of charitable organizations sponsored by upper-class women, such as the Society for the Relief of Poor Widows with Small Children, founded in 1797 in New York by Isabella Graham, a devout Presbyterian and a widow herself. The development of such organizations was spurred by the Benevolent Empire. By the 1820s, Graham's society was assisting hundreds of widows and their children in New York City. Graham's daughter, Joanna Bethune, set up other charitable institutions, including the Orphan Asylum Society and the Society for the Promotion of Industry, which gave subsidized employment to hundreds of poor women.

The deepest conviction of the men and women who founded the Benevolent Empire was that religion provided the answer to social problems. One of the greatest threats they saw to the "moral government of God" was the decline of the traditional Sabbath. During the 1820s, the conduct of business on Sunday became increasingly common, especially among merchants and shippers who did not want their goods and equipment to lie idle one day of every seven. Congress had even passed a law in 1810

that allowed mail to be transported—though not delivered—on Sunday.

In 1828, Lyman Beecher and other Congregationalist and Presbyterian ministers formed the General Union for Promoting the Observance of the Christian Sabbath. To the General Union, the question of the Sunday mail law was not important in itself. It was a symbolic issue chosen in the hope that it might stir Christians to take up the task of social purification. The General Union spread its chapters—usually with women's auxiliaries—from Maine to the Ohio Valley. It lobbied for local Sabbath regulations, collected funds, published tracts, organized rallies, and circulated petitions. It behaved, in short, very much like a political party.

Although the numerous societies, associations, unions, and leagues of the Benevolent Empire found support in every community, they also met resistance, especially with respect to keeping the Sabbath. Owners of barges on the Erie Canal, and of taverns and hotels, refused to close on Sundays. Working men, who labored twelve or fourteen hours a day, scorned the notion that they ought to spend their one day of recreation in meditation and prayer. Baptist and Methodist clergymen, whose congregations tended to be poorer than those of the Congregationalists or Presbyterians, objected to the patronizing tone of the General Union. And when the Benevolent Empire proposed to teach slaves Christianity, or to send missionaries among the Indians, white southerners were outraged.

Such resistance or indifference limited the success of the Benevolent Empire, whose purpose was all too obviously to regulate the behavior of others, by persuasion if possible but by law if necessary. A different kind of message was required if religious reformers were to do more than preach to the already converted and to discipline the already disciplined.

Business-Class Revivalism and Reform

Beginning in 1825, in towns stretching along the Erie Canal, a minister named Charles Grandison Finney had striking success with revival meetings. He was not part of a traditional religious elite. Born to poor farmers on the New York frontier in 1792, Finney determined to make

CHARLES FINNEY, EVANGELIST
Finney (1792–1875) had a long and influential career after his New York revivals. In 1835, he established a theology department at the newly founded Oberlin College, where he helped train a generation of ministers. Finney served as president of the college from 1851 to 1866. This daguerreotype was taken in 1850, while Finney and his second wife, Elizabeth Atkinson, were on an evangelistic tour of Great Britain. (Oberlin College Library)

himself part of the new middle class as a lawyer. But in 1823 he underwent a highly emotional conversion experience and was ordained as a Presbyterian preacher after two years of informal religious study.

Finney's religious message centered on the notion that God waited to welcome any sinner who truly wanted salvation and that only God's grace, poured into the heart of the believer, made a moral life possible. He rejected an emphasis on original sin and stressed that an exercise of free will—submission to the Holy Spirit—could lead to a Christian conversion. He believed that religious instruction in official church doctrine by a trained minister did not bring—and might even hinder—salvation. What counted, Finney proclaimed, was not a person's belief in the technical doctrines of a church, but the *will* to be saved. His was an emotional faith that refuted the intellectual basis of faith in many established Protestant churches.

Wherever he preached, Finney won converts. The conversions were dramatic, emotional, and often tearful. Although most of Finney's con-

verts were members of the middle class, he became famous for converting wealthy individuals and the poor, who seemed lost to drink, sloth, and misbehavior. The political theory of Finney's revivals was that religious conversion brought everyone, rich and poor, into the same moral community. The pride of the rich (if not their wealth) and the shame of the poor (if not their poverty) would give way to an exultant celebration of a new brotherhood in Christ. Conversion should change not only people's eternal fate, but also their moral standing in their towns—identifying them spiritually with an earnest, pious, middle-class respectability.

Finney's most spectacular triumph began in 1830 when he moved his revivals from small towns to Rochester, New York, a major Erie Canal city, at the invitation of local business and political leaders. For six months he preached every day. He also held group prayer meetings in family homes, in which women played an active role. Finney's wife, Lydia, took a highly visible part in his ministry. She and other pious, middle-class wives visited the homes of the unconverted, often while disapproving husbands were at work. Week after week, Rochester was saturated with the evangelical message. Schools and businesses stopped for prayer. Spontaneous religious meetings were held in houses and even in the streets.

Finney was initially successful with members of the business elite and their wives. Many of these people were nominal Christians and church members who had not experienced the emotional sense of salvation that Finney promoted. Finney soon claimed he had converted the "great mass of the most influential people" of Rochester—especially the manufacturers and merchants who shipped grain on the Erie Canal. As part of their conversion, these "influential people" often confessed that their lives had been overly governed by money and too little devoted to the moral well-being of their own souls and those of their employees. With this confession came a pledge to reform their own lives and to try to reform the lives of their workers. They would attend church, drink only water, work steady hours, and encourage their employees to follow suit. In 1831, one of Rochester's Presbyterian churches rewrote its covenant in a way that gave a new meaning to the concept of "business." Every member pledged to "renounce all the ways of sin, and to make it the business of our life to do good and promote the glory of God."

And so the business leaders of Rochester set out to reform their city. Their favorite target was alcohol, which seemed to them to be the most wasteful and damaging social habit of their workers and also the most obvious sign of a collapsing social order. But they also tried to meet what they thought were the workers' spiritual needs. In 1832, wealthy businessmen founded a new Free Presbyterian Church—called "free" because members did not have to pay for pew spaces. This church was specifically designed to serve canal workers, transients, and the settled poor. Soon two similar evangelical churches were founded in Rochester. To reinforce the work of these churches, Rochester's business elite founded other institutions—a savings bank to encourage thrift, Sunday schools for poor children, and the Female Charitable Society to provide relief for the families of the unemployed.

Within limits, the attempt to create a harmonious community of morally disciplined Christians was effective. Before the Panic of 1837 and the economic depression that followed, many workers—often led by their wives—became converts and church members. Workers tended to follow the example set by their employer. And employers who had been "saved" often sealed

converts' rspectability with raises, promotions, or bonuses.

Finney's revival seldom reached those who resisted conversion; nor did it move many poor people. Skilled workers who belonged to strong craft organizations—bootmakers, carpenters, stonemasons, and boat builders—also seemed immune to salvation. Some of them even supported newspapers opposing the revival, arguing that workers needed organization, higher wages, and schools more than sermons and prayers. But the very existence of these critics only heightened the converts' zeal for rebuilding society into an evangelically defined Christian order.

During the 1830s, revivals like Rochester's swept through cities and towns from New England to the Ohio Valley. Dozens of younger ministers—Baptists and Methodists as well as Congregationalists and Presbyterians—energetically adopted the evangelical message and its techniques. They succeeded wherever the middle class was large. In New York City, where Finney successfully established himself soon after he left Rochester, the wealthy silk merchants Arthur and Lewis Tappan founded a magazine, *The Christian Evangelist*, to promote his ideas. With the assistance of manufacturers and merchants, evangelists soon reached sinners the way the most progressive business reached cus-

A FAMILY'S MORNING DEVOTIONAL

This 1842 illustration from *Godey's Lady's Book*, a leading influence on the tastes of the emerging business class, portrays the kind of family Bible reading and prayer that the Finney revivals encouraged. Here, *Godey's* idealizes an affluent young mother and father who are attempting to set a good example for their child and two servants. (From *Godey's Lady's Book*. The Newberry Library, Chicago)

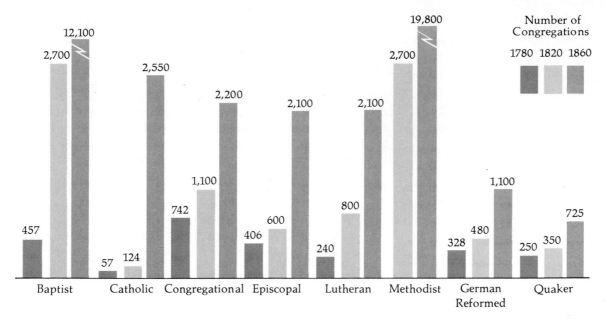

FIGURE 12.1 CHURCH GROWTH BY DENOMINATION, 1780–1860

tomers. They standardized and simplified their religious message, aimed it at masses of people, and measured their success in quantitative terms—by the number of converts.

The evangelicals organized most effectively on a national scale in the temperance movement. They gained control over the American Temperance Society, which had been organized in 1828. By the mid-1830s this society had two thousand chapters with more than two hundred thousand members. It adapted the methods that had worked so well in the revivals—group confession and prayer; singing; and sudden, emotional conversion—and took them into virtually every town and city in the North. These techniques worked best among the families of the business class, for whom drink was becoming a fearful mark of social disrepute. On one day in New York City in 1841, four thousand persons took the temperance "pledge." The average annual consumption of spirits fell from about five gallons for each person in 1830 to about two gallons in 1845. But temperance was mainly a habit of the business class.

Evangelical reformers also sought to revise the work ethic that had been so important to the American tradition. The founders of seventeenth-century New England had believed that hard work in an earthly "calling" was a duty that peo-

ple owed to God. They stopped short of believing that God would reward Christians with worldly riches. In the late eighteenth century, Benjamin Franklin expressed the secular ideal of work in his *Autobiography*, in which he implied that an industrious man could become a rich one. When Franklin's *Autobiography* was finally published in full in 1818, it found a huge audience, mostly young men, ready and willing to believe that if they worked hard, saved their money, and were temperate in their habits and honest in their dealings, success would be theirs. The same lessons were taught in countless magazines, children's books, manuals for young men, and novels. The idea of the "self-made man" became part of American popular culture.

The evangelical reformers put a religious twist on Franklin's notions. Laziness, drinking, and other wasteful habits could not, they preached, be cured simply by Franklin's patient methods of self-discipline. People had to undergo a profound change of heart, possible only with religious conversion. With God's grace would come the determination to put away drink, sloth, and sin. Then even the poorest family could look forward to a prosperous new life.

Only a minority of laboring men and women were actually inducted into the moral community of the evangelical movement. Most people

THE ECSTASY OF A CAMP MEETING
In isolated rural areas, especially those with many
Baptists and Methodists, the camp meeting was a more
common forum for evangelical revivals than were church
and prayer meetings. Such meetings, organized while
farm work was slack, attracted families who camped in
wagons and tents for as long as a week to join in the
intense religious excitement and social life. (The Whaling
Museum, New Bedford, Mass.)

who became religious converts, took the temperance pledge, or promoted the ideal of the self-
made man were already fairly prosperous and
enjoyed respectable standing in their communities. Evangelical religion reinforced the sense of
common identity within the business class and
this group's commitment to the concepts of individual enterprise, success, and moral discipline
that comprised the ethic of the Industrial Revolution.

The Labor Alternative

Many workers looked with deep suspicion on
the efforts of the business class to reform society.
To them, it seemed that the task was not to create harmony between owners and workers, but
to recognize the inevitable conflict between the
people who had to sell their labor and the people who bought it. Many believed the only hope
for individual workers to change industrial conditions was to organize themselves into societies,
associations, and unions.

The main successes of the early labor movement came among skilled workers. But even in
factories that employed unskilled women and
girls—the factories that were at the leading edge
of industrialization—there were some efforts to
resist the increasing demands of employers for
more work and less pay. Cotton-mill operatives,
who numbered around twelve thousand by
1820, engaged in sporadic strikes, usually to protest pay cuts or more stringent work rules. In
1828, women mill workers in Dover, New
Hampshire, struck against new rules that fined
them for lateness and provided certificates of
regular discharge only for "faithful" employees.
The strikers worried that disobedient workers
would be fired and then be unable to find jobs
because they lacked these certificates. In 1834,
more than eight hundred Dover women struck
again, protesting wage cuts. Two thousand
women in Lowell, Massachusetts, not only
struck, but also withdrew their savings from a
Lowell bank that their employers owned. The
Boston Transcript reported that "one of the leaders mounted a pump, and made a flaming . . .
speech on the rights of women and the iniquities
of the 'monied aristocracy.' " Almost invariably,
these strikes ended the way the one at Lowell
did: the employers fired the strike leaders, and
the rest of the workers returned to the mills.
Overpowered by the employers, and viewing
factory employment as temporary and rather
irrelevant to their futures, the woman mill
workers did not react to their defeats by forming
permanent organizations.

During the 1820s and 1830s, the union movement was carried forward primarily by workers
with preindustrial skills still needed in the industrial era. These skilled workers included great
numbers of traditionally trained tailors, carpenters, cordwainers, printers, coopers, shipwrights, and weavers. Such workers, however,
were seriously divided. Those who had skills
outside the areas of work revolutionized by technology—most workers in the building trades, for
example—viewed the Industrial Revolution as
beneficial and did not clash with the business
class in a fundamental way. They organized, but
largely to advance their incomes and prospects
for upward economic mobility. The shortage of
skilled labor strengthened their bargaining position. Workers whose skills were threatened by
industrialization, on the other hand, organized

primarily in self-defense. Their goals went beyond wages and sometimes involved a radical critique of the Industrial Revolution and the new class structure that was emerging.

The rapid urbanization of the 1820s triggered a strong, widespread demand for construction workers. They used their improved bargaining position to reduce their hours of work, which were usually "sun to sun," as with virtually all laborers. Since the preindustrial era, Americans had accepted such hours as normal, but the quickening of economic activity led employers to demand greater intensity of effort during working hours. For carpenters, house painters, stonecutters, nailers, and cabinetmakers, the pressure became most intense during the spring and summer, when construction was feverish and the working day increased to more than twelve hours.

Construction workers formed strong and stable labor unions to demand a shorter working day. In 1825, about six hundred carpenters in Boston struck against their contractor-employers, demanding a standard ten-hour day—6 A.M. to 6 P.M., with an hour each for breakfast and dinner. They failed, but a group of journeymen carpenters in Philadelphia had greater success in 1827. After a strike, several hundred of these workers won the ten-hour day and initiated coordinated action by groups of unions in the city. They then led building-trade workers in founding the Mechanics' Union of Trade Associations, the first effective citywide organization of wage earners in Philadelphia. They even founded a political party, the Working Men's party.

The Mechanics' Union emphasized the ten-hour day, while the party worked for a diverse program, including more equal taxation, abolition of banks, and universal education. The last goal was most important. Public schools would enable the children of workers to acquire skills that would not become obsolete and to advance more rapidly into the ranks of the propertied. So the party asked the city and state to provide all citizens with public education that would combine "one or more mechanical arts" with "literary and scientific instruction." Such training would "place the citizens of this extensive republic on an equality" and "bring the children of the poor and rich to mix together as a band of republican brethren" so that "united in youth in the acquisition of knowledge, they will grow up

together, jealous of naught but the republican character of their country."

The skilled workers who participated in the building-trade unions maintained their traditional values. They continued to take pride and find sustenance in their work, and they stressed the importance of the communal solidarity of their crafts. They found their pride and solidarity well rewarded in the growing urban economy of the 1820s and 1830s. They improved their relative economic position and expanded their holdings of property significantly. Consequently, they had little reason to challenge the new order and considerable reason to promote their own version of social harmony.

Other skilled workers were less conservative. The artisans who faced declining incomes, unemployment, and loss of status due to industrialization of their trades banded together and, within a framework of traditional values, criticized the business class. Hatters, printers, and weavers were among the most threatened workers, and they formed craft unions during the 1820s and 1830s. Leaders of these artisans formulated a "producer's" ideology that defined their position in relation to both the business class and unskilled wage earners. Like capitalist entrepreneurs, the artisans valued their position as independent, self-employed workers. They cast a critical eye on the new system of manufacturing and its effects on society. They advanced what they called a "labor theory of value," based on the idea that the price of a product should reflect the labor required to make it and that most of the income from its sale should be paid to the person who made it. Applying this theory, the artisans condemned the accumulation of wealth by capitalist employers and expressed disgust at "the gaudy palaces in which they reside." They feared being reduced to the status of nonpropertied wage earners and becoming, as they put it, "slaves to a monied aristocracy."

Prominent among the threatened artisans were journeyman shoemakers, who now either worked at routine tasks in central shops or fashioned the various parts of shoes at home under an "outwork" system. For these journeymen, the key to a viable social system was a system of production in which employers were master craftsmen who worked with their journeymen in household shops; the skill of the workers and their ownership of their tools would guarantee

DE TOCQUEVILLE ON THE USE OF PUBLIC ASSOCIATIONS IN AMERICAN LIFE

The political associations that exist in the United States are only a single feature in the midst of the immense assemblage of associations in that country. Americans of all ages, all conditions, and all dispositions constantly form associations. They had not only commercial and manufacturing companies, in which all take part, but associations of a thousand other kinds, religious, moral, serious, futile, general or restricted, enormous or diminutive. The Americans make associations to give entertainments, to found seminaries, to build inns, to construct churches, to diffuse books, to send missionaries to the antipodes; in this manner they found hospitals, prisons, and schools. If it is proposed to inculcate some truth or to foster some feeling by the encouragement of a great example, they form a society. Wherever at the head of some new undertaking you see the government in France, or a man of rank in England, in the United States you will be sure to find an association.

. . . In aristocratic societies men do not need to combine in order to act, because they are strongly held together. Every wealthy and powerful citizen constitutes the head of a permanent and compulsory association, composed of all those who are dependent upon him or whom he makes subservient to the execution of his designs.

Among democratic nations, on the contrary, all the citizens are independent and feeble; they can do hardly anything by themselves, and none of them can oblige his fellow men to lend him their assistance. They all, therefore, become powerless if they do not learn voluntarily to help one another. . . . As soon as several of the inhabitants of the United States have taken up an opinion or a feeling which they wish to promote in the world, they look out for mutual assistance: and as soon as they have found one another out, they combine. From that moment they are no longer isolated men, but a power seen from afar, whose actions serve for an example and whose language is listened to. The first time I heard in the United States that a hundred thousand men had bound themselves publicly to abstain from spiritous liquors, it appeared to me more like a joke than a serious engagement, and I did not at once perceive why these temperate citizens could not content themselves with drinking water by their own firesides. I at last understood that these hundred thousand Americans, alarmed by the progress of drunkenness around them, had made up their minds to patronize temperance. They acted in just the same way as a man of high rank who should dress very plainly in order to inspire the humbler orders with a contempt of luxury. It is probable that if these hundred thousand men had lived in France, each of them would singly have memorialized the government to watch the public houses all over the kingdom.

Source: Alexis de Tocqueville, *Democracy in America.* New York: Random House, 1981, pp. 403–408.

---

them a considerable control over wages and the pace of work. But the new system of production removed work from the household shop, made the master into a mere employer, and eroded the skilled worker's control of the pace and conditions of labor.

The journeymen of Lynn, Massachusetts, proclaimed their independence from the master craftsmen in 1830 by forming the Mutual Benefit Society of Journeymen Cordwainers. "The division of society into the producing and nonproducing classes," they explained, "and the fact of the unequal distribution of value between the two, introduced us at once to another distinction—that of capital and labor." The cordwainers, who made high-quality boots and shoes, declared, "Labor now becomes a commodity, wealth capital, and the natural order of things is entirely reversed." Therefore, "antagonism and opposition is introduced in the community; capital and labor stand opposed." In 1836, cordwainers and printers each set up national craft unions to coordinate the activities of various local unions.

Unions of threatened artisans evolved a political program designed to destroy concentrations of economic power and privilege and to restore their version of social harmony. In so doing, they appealed to the spirit of the American Revolution. The revolution had been necessary to destroy monopolies and special privileges created by the king, they said. Now another revolution was needed to destroy the monopolies created by capital. Such a revolution would, the artisans believed, allow individuals to regain the dignity and independence expected of the citizens of a republic. Artisan groups promoted antimonopoly legislation, antibanking regulations, the adoption by the states of universal suffrage for white males, and the abolition of imprisonment for debt. They also supported general property taxation, which they hoped would tax concentrations of wealth more heavily and reduce taxes on small property owners.

The force of artisan protest waned after the mid-1830s. Factory competition had already forced large numbers of artisans to abandon their crafts and consequently their movement. Meanwhile, business-class evangelism and appeals for cooperation between employer and employee had gained momentum. The unions gradually moved away from politics and concentrated on the issues of greatest interest to skilled workers—shorter working days and higher wages. For a time, favored by market conditions, they succeeded and refined tactics of strike and boycott.

Following the model of the Philadelphia building trades, unions formed coalitions and initiated scores of strikes throughout the Northeast. These strikes established the ten-hour day as the standard day's work for most skilled workers in the largest cities and for virtually all the skilled workers in the building trades. American skilled workers had won more from their employers than had their counterparts anywhere else in the industrializing world. With the ten-hour day a reality, the unions turned their energies to boosting wages. They organized more than fifty strikes during the twelve months before the Panic of 1837.

In response, employers from New York to Saint Louis mobilized against the unions. Manufacturers had organized before to regulate the quality of production or to fix prices, but never primarily to combat labor. A favorite antiunion tactic was that of the employers in New York City who, in 1836, blacklisted workers who belonged to the Union Trade Society of Journeymen Tailors. The employers also used the courts. Their suits focused on unions that insisted on closed shops, which hired only union members. During the 1830s, employers of carpet weavers in Thompsonville, Connecticut; shoemakers in Geneva and Hudson, New York; tailors in New York City; plasterers in Philadelphia; and cordwainers in Boston all charged unions with violation of either common law or, in New York state, statutes that prohibited such "conspiracies." In 1836, courts found the carpet weavers and the plasterers innocent. But the New York Supreme Court ruled that the Geneva shoemakers had violated the law. The closed shop, the New York court held, had caused "an industrious man" to be "driven out of employment" and trade to be restricted. "It is," the court held, "important to the best interests of society that the price of labor be left to regulate itself"—in other words, that individual workers be denied an opportunity to organize. Following this precedent, a lower court found the New York tailors guilty of conspiracy. Vocal union protest over this decision, including a rally of twenty-seven thousand demonstrators outside New York's City Hall, intimidated juries who heard similar cases. Later that year, juries acquitted the Hudson shoemakers, the Philadelphia plasterers, and the Thompsonville carpet makers.

The legal standing of closed shops improved most notably in 1842, when Chief Justice Lemuel Shaw of Massachusetts handed down an influential ruling in *Commonwealth v. Hunt*. The case began in 1840, when Hunt and other members of the Boston Bootmakers' Society had been brought into municipal court for trying to enforce a closed shop. Shaw made two critical rulings: (1) a union was a criminal organization only if its *objectives* were criminal; and (2) union members were within their rights in attempting to enforce closed shops, even through strikes. This decision discouraged courts, even outside

Massachusetts, from charging that unions were inherently criminal or from finding that the closed shop was socially harmful.

But economic conditions were far more important than the law in determining the fate of the labor unions of the 1830s. The depression that followed the Panic of 1837 and continued through 1843 increased unemployment among skilled workers and effectively halted the union movement. In 1837, the *New York Star* reported that six thousand masons, carpenters, and other building-trade workers had been discharged. Rising unemployment further demoralized artisans who already feared displacement or had lost status. Increasing numbers despaired over the possibility of organizing to oppose the forces of industrialization and simply dropped out of the labor movement. Most local unions and workers' assemblies and all the national labor organizations disappeared, along with their newspapers and other publications.

The organized skilled workers had been a considerable force during the 1820s and 1830s, but, internally divided and isolated from other workers, they had little ultimate effect on the Industrial Revolution. By 1840, the evangelical call for workers to embrace the values of the emerging business class was stronger than the plea of labor unions for workers to unite to break up concentrations of power and wealth. The concerted evangelism of the business class, along with the significant economic gains that the Industrial Revolution did in fact bring to many workers, discouraged laborers from forming an organized labor movement. Overwhelmed by a powerful message full of spiritual, democratic, and material promise, wage earners did not develop either the ideology or the organization necessary for a united labor movement. The most prosperous wage earners—skilled workers in the most mechanized industries—readily identified with the interests of the business class. Even the least prosperous unskilled workers believed in individual upward mobility or doubted that they could advance themselves through collective effort. In any case, unsteady, uncertain employment and the highest degree of geographic mobility of any segment of society precluded organized movement among unskilled workers.

The Challenge of Democratic Politics

The emerging business class faced a more serious challenge in the political arena. During the 1820s virtually all Americans, except some members of the most traditional elites, believed that democratization of the republic would fulfill the ideals of the revolution and would prove useful in advancing their own interests. The presidency of Andrew Jackson sharpened differences between social and economic groups in the country to an unprecedented degree. For the first time, in response to Jackson's policies, the northern business class found its interests threatened by opposition from farmers, laborers, and southern planters.

Political Parties in Industrial Society

The democratization of politics, under way since the 1780s, continued into the 1820s and 1830s. As western states joined the Union, they adopted constitutions that gave the right to vote and to hold office to all white males over twenty-one. In the 1820s, most eastern states followed suit by dropping property requirements for voting, some hoping this would persuade residents not to move west. By 1840, the electorate included more than 90 percent of the adult white male population. At the same time, most states established the direct popular election of governors, presidential electors, and some judges. Not only could more people vote; they could vote for more of their government officials.

The Industrial Revolution accelerated the pressures to expand participation in government. Many people saw the possibilities of using the powers of government either to resist or to promote the Industrial Revolution. The growing ease of communication affected politics as well as the economy, giving state and national issues more immediacy at the local level. The voting public became much larger and more complex in its composition, better informed, and more emotionally involved in politics.

Political parties reorganized in response to democratic pressures and helped promote this heightened participation. The new, more democratic parties that emerged in every state during the 1820s and 1830s had to be as concerned with organization and discipline as they were with increasing participation. Organization was necessary so that a wide diversity of interests could band together to appeal effectively to the electorate and to unite in shaping legislation. The new party organizations inculcated group discipline. They instilled party loyalty and persuaded party members to accept a candidate or position chosen by the party regardless of personal preferences. The New York Republican party and its leader, Martin Van Buren, pioneered in establishing party discipline in the 1820s. Once, after seventeen Republicans in the state legislature threatened to vote against the party line, Van Buren asked that they "magnanimously sacrifice individual preferences for the general good." They agreed and were rewarded with a banquet where, as one observer wrote, "Something approaching to divine honors were lavished on the Seventeen."

Nonetheless, the power of party leaders rested as much on the breadth of their support as on their ability to provide discipline. They needed the votes of economic elites as well as small property owners and even nonpropertied workers. Parties built loyalty by calling for programs of governmental action that would appeal to a wide spectrum of the electorate. At the national level, Andrew Jackson was the party leader most successful in reaching across sectional and class lines to establish a strong, loyal constituency.

Andrew Jackson first ran for president as a Republican in 1824. The Federalist party had virtually disappeared; the Republican party was fragmented; new party groupings were being organized and reorganized feverishly in many states; and five presidential candidates, all calling themselves Republicans, crowded the field. Jackson emerged as the candidate most in touch with the changing social environment.

In his first bid for the presidency, Jackson ran as a figure who would represent the entire nation. It was true that he was a southwesterner—a senator from Tennessee—and that his chief financial backers were wealthy friends from Nashville; he also spoke most clearly for the southerners who had moved west of the Appalachians and formed a majority of the population of the West. More important, people in all regions knew Jackson as the hero of the Battle of New Orleans in the War of 1812. And Jackson had the crucial support of Van Buren's New York party machinery.

Jackson advocated a democratic republic. His supporters criticized the practice, customary under the First Party System, of having a congressional caucus nominate the presidential candidate. They condemned the caucus system as aristocratic. They had especially harsh words for the congressional caucus that had chosen the "official" 1824 Republican candidate, Secretary of the Treasury William H. Crawford.

Jackson surprised most prominent political leaders by winning a plurality of both the popular and electoral votes in 1824. Crawford, stricken by a serious illness, received little support outside Georgia, his home state, and Virginia, where he was born. John Quincy Adams, the son of John Adams, had some national support, largely because of the role he had played in foreign affairs as secretary of state under James Monroe, but the public identified him as the candidate of New England. Speaker of the House Henry Clay campaigned vigorously, but his support was limited largely to his home state of Kentucky and the Ohio Valley. Secretary of War John C. Calhoun also campaigned, but his following was so small, almost exclusively from South Carolina, that he withdrew before the election.

Jackson won ninety-nine electoral votes. Adams received eighty-four, while Crawford won forty-one and Clay trailed with thirty-seven. No candidate had a majority, and so the election had to be decided by the House of Representatives, which had the constitutional responsibility to choose the president from among the three leading contenders. Clay, now out of the race, used his influence as Speaker of the House to build a New England–Ohio Valley coalition that threw the election to Adams. In return, Adams agreed to appoint Clay secretary of state. Jackson's supporters began almost at once to prepare for 1828, to overturn the "corrupt bargain" between Clay and Adams.

As president, John Quincy Adams attempted to implement the policies of the coalition that

JOHN QUINCY ADAMS
This famous photograph of John Quincy Adams
(1767–1848), taken near the end of his life, suggests the
tenacity and moral commitment that contributed to his
seventeen-year career as a congressman from
Massachusetts. Far more effective in Congress than he
had been as president, Adams became a vigorous
opponent of slavery as the leader of the "conscience
Whigs." (The Metropolitan Museum of Art. Gift of I. N.
Phelps Stokes, Edward S. Hawes, Alice Mary Hawes,
Marion Augusta Hawes, 1937)

had elected him, a program designed to advance
industrialization. He and his supporters presented it explicitly as the program of the business elite of the Northeast and Northwest.
Adams not only failed to implement the policies
but also contributed to increased enthusiasm for
Andrew Jackson.

President Adams hoped to enact measures
aimed at "promoting the improvement of agriculture, commerce, and manufactures, the cultivation of the mechanic and of the elegant arts,
the advancement of literature and the progress
of the sciences, ornamental and profound."
These lofty plans included the establishment of
a national university in Washington, extensive
scientific explorations of the Far West, and the
building of a national observatory. Most central

to Adams's plans was the enactment of a broad
set of economic policies that Henry Clay had labeled the "American System" and for which he
had campaigned in 1824. The American System
included a protective tariff to stimulate manufacturing and establish an enlarged domestic market for American agriculture; subsidies, financed
by tariff revenues, for internal improvements to
stimulate commerce; and a national bank that
would promote a uniform currency and expansive credit. The bank already existed; the Second
Bank of the United States had been founded in
1816 with a twenty-year charter. The great political question of the 1830s was whether to keep it.

Adams advocated expensive plans whose primary beneficiaries seemed to be the wealthiest
members of the business community. Combined
with his arrogant, superior manner, Adams's
budgetary plans provoked immediate and forceful opposition. On his deathbed in 1826, Thomas
Jefferson stirred up anti-Federalist fears, declaring that Adams sought to establish "a single and
splendid government of an aristocracy . . . riding and ruling over the plundered ploughman
and beggared yeomanry."

Facing massive opposition in Congress, Adams accomplished little. He could persuade a
hostile Congress to make only modest increases
in appropriations to improve navigation and begin extending the National Road from Wheeling,
Virginia, into Ohio. Congress did increase tariffs—in fact, it set them higher than Adams
wished. Representatives of a variety of manufacturing, mining, and farming interests banded together in 1828 to support each others' favorite
tariffs. The result became known as the "Tariff
of Abominations," which set rates on manufactured goods at about 50 percent and levied tariffs
on a host of raw materials, including flax, hemp,
iron, lead, molasses, and raw wool. Despite his
reservations, Adams signed the legislation.

The tariff provoked vigorous opposition in
the South, especially among the cotton planters.
The tariffs raised the cost of imported British
manufactured goods, increasing the cost of living in the South, and disrupting that section's
all-important cotton trade with Britain. Adams's
problems in the South, and increasingly in the
West, were aggravated by his apparent support
for the rights of native Americans. On moral
grounds, he refused to enforce an 1825 treaty in
which the Creek nation ceded to the state of

Georgia land they had occupied under an earlier federal treaty of 1791. Adams claimed Georgia had obtained the new treaty through fraud, and he ordered another one to be negotiated. When Georgia's governor, a backwoodsman named George M. Troup, defied Adams and threatened to take control of the Indian lands, Adams declared that it was the president's duty to uphold federal jurisdiction "by all the force committed for that purpose to his charge."

Adams did not seek to offset his waning popularity and power by building support within his party. In fact, he distrusted political parties and kept as appointees even hostile politicians if he believed they did their jobs competently. After deciding to run for reelection in 1828, he refused to pay any attention to his campaign. He confirmed his aloof, paternalistic image by telling supporters that he would not ask the American people to reelect him. "If my country wants my services," he said, "she must ask for them."

The Birth of the Democratic Party

As the president's problems mounted, Jackson became increasingly confident of victory in the election of 1828.

Jackson's campaign organization was brilliant. He assembled a broad, seemingly incongruous coalition to strengthen his support beyond the old Southwest. He successfully wooed the South Carolina supporters of John C. Calhoun, who ran as Jackson's vice-presidential candidate in 1828; the Virginians who had inherited power from Jefferson, Madison, and Monroe; former Pennsylvania Federalists who were drifting without a political home; and the skilled, disciplined leaders of Martin Van Buren's New York organization.

Jackson's message was as broad and mixed as his organization. He and the leaders of his coalition fashioned an appeal designed to attract voters from all regions and classes. The Jacksonians avoided concrete pledges that might alienate significant portions of the electorate. Thus, when Jackson implied that he would oppose high tariffs, he made no commitment to specific alternatives. He even remained vague on the question of how much support the government might give to westward expansion. However, Jackson's military and political record suggested that he would vigorously support the ambitions of Westerners and of all those, throughout the country, for whom the West symbolized opportunity.

Instead of dwelling on specific policies, the Jacksonians campaigned in 1828 on an emotionally charged political message. They attacked "special privilege" and emphasized, more than the Republicans ever had, that forceful democratic measures were necessary to root it out. Their changing party label suggested the emphasis on democracy within a republican system. Initially, they called themselves "Democratic Republicans," while the Adams forces took the name "National Republicans." As the campaign wore on, the Jackson forces simplified their name to "Democrats."

Jackson's supporters made their message as personal as possible, spreading it widely through rallies, newspapers, and pamphlets. On the one hand, they attacked President Adams by declaring that despite his upright demeanor, he personified the corrupt consequences of special privilege. They hammered the theme of the 1824 "corrupt bargain" with Clay and accused Adams of aristocratic extravagance and sinful behavior. Their most sensational charge was that as minister to Russia, Adams had tried to procure an American girl for the czar's pleasure. On the other hand, they praised Jackson's virtue, making much of his frontier origins and stressing his rise to wealth and fame without the benefit of formal education or association with a political faction. Jackson's image was that of a "natural" aristocrat, one who had achieved success by his own efforts.

The Jacksonians designed their message to attract Americans of all classes, including middle-class men who believed that further destruction of special privilege was necessary to increase economic opportunity. But the Jacksonians hoped to form a specific coalition when they criticized the American System. In the North, they sought backing from people who wished to resist the Industrial Revolution by preventing federal support for manufacturing, internal improvements, and banking. In the South, the Jacksonians courted planters and small farmers alike; both groups tended to oppose the American System. Most white southerners shared Jackson's hostility to native Americans and had applauded his slaughter of the Creek in 1814. Elites in the South, both planter and commercial,

FIGURE 12.2 CHANGES IN
AMERICAN VOTING
PATTERNS

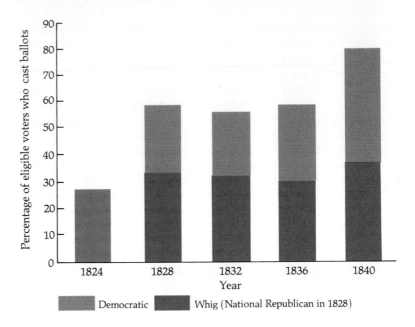

knew that Jackson did not threaten their interests and recognized him as one of their own.
Jackson's origins had been humble, but, due to
his military career and his marriage, which had
linked him with the most influential families in
Nashville, he had risen to become a prosperous
attorney, cotton planter, and slaveowner.

The Jacksonian strategy worked. Whereas
only about a fourth of the eligible electorate
voted in 1824, more than half voted in 1828,
overwhelmingly for Jackson. He and Calhoun
received 178 electoral votes to only 83 for Adams. Urban workers, both skilled and unskilled,
supported Jackson. Support from labor unions of
all kinds was important, as was the aid of frontier settlers throughout the West. Small, poorer
farmers in the Northeast supported Jackson. So
did southern planters.

Jackson's only area of weakness was New England. To the northern business elite, Jackson's
election was unsettling. After the election, Daniel Webster, an old Federalist, predicted to his
business friends in Boston that when Jackson
came to Washington, "he will bring a breeze
with him. Which way it will blow, I cannot
tell. . . . My *fear* is stronger than my *hope*." On
inauguration day, after watching an unruly
crowd climb over the elegant furniture in the
White House to shake the new president's hand,
Supreme Court Justice Joseph Story declared,
"The reign of King 'Mob' seemed triumphant."

The Jacksonian Presidency

Andrew Jackson emerged as the leader of a new
political party that produced a major, nationwide
realignment of voters. For the party to hold and
enlarge its constituency, Jackson had to implement its campaign message. In the process, he
expanded the powers of the presidency as an instrument of popular will and gave the party a
central role in his administration.

To implement the people's will as party
leader, Jackson reformed officeholding in the
federal government. He declared that long tenure in federal jobs encouraged officeholders to
view their positions as personal fiefdoms rather
than public obligations. He promised to root out
islands of corruption and to introduce rotation in
office, returning officials every four years "to
making a living as other people do." He dismissed the argument that this would deny the
government the valuable expertise of experienced officials. The duties of public service, Jackson said, were "so plain and simple that men of
intelligence may readily qualify themselves for
their performance." Other Democrats put it
more bluntly. As William L. Marcy, a Jackson
supporter from New York declared, "To the vic-
tors belong the spoils." In practice, Jackson acted
with some caution in dismissing public officials,
and he took care to avoid needless antagonisms.
But the policy of rotation allowed Jackson greater

flexibility in rewarding loyal Democrats with public office and thus strengthened his efforts to build a modern political party.

Jackson skillfully used his highest-level appointments to broaden and consolidate the power of his party. He selected cabinet officers purely for their ability to represent the various Democratic constituencies harmoniously. But this cabinet was window dressing. Jackson never called cabinet meetings, relying instead on an informal group of advisers whose opinions he valued. This "kitchen cabinet" included several newspaper editors, such as Francis Preston Blair of Kentucky, who edited the *Washington Globe;* Roger B. Taney of Maryland, who was to become attorney general and chief justice of the United States; several Treasury Department officials, including Amos Kendall, also from Kentucky, who collaborated with Jackson on many of his state papers; and, most influential of all, Secretary of State Martin Van Buren.

In developing programs for his administration, and in building a constituency for the Democratic party, Jackson sought to maintain a balance between the past and future. Presenting himself as defender of the republic, Jackson sought to smash obstacles that impeded an inde-

ANDREW JACKSON
This painting from 1837 displays the striking blend of romance and force of character that was Jackson's valuable public image. Other contemporary portraits showed Jackson in more rustic setting and dress, as befitted his role as "the people's president." Here, he is posed in the full regalia of the presidency. (*Andrew Jackson,* attributed to Ralph E. W. Earle. Ladies Hermitage Association)

pendent, responsible citizenry intent on self-improvement. His targets included Indians, the tariff, the rebellious state of South Carolina, and, most significantly, the Second Bank of the United States. He hoped his program would appeal to those who embraced the new economic transformations. To these people, he said he would destroy barriers to the creation of new opportunities. On the other hand, he responded to the needs of people who were alienated from the Industrial Revolution. To them, he promised to preserve traditional farms and crafts by promoting westward expansion and to restore social harmony by destroying special privilege—represented symbolically by the Second Bank.

Jackson and the Native Americans

Jackson quickly and effectively enlarged the western base of the Democratic party through his Indian policy—a policy approved by white westerners of all classes and occupations. Jackson's commitment to removal of native Americans was deep. He hated Indians and had massacred and defrauded them long before becoming president. After leading the Tennessee militia in defeat of the Creek in 1814, he forced them to cede more than twenty million acres of territory to the United States. Then he turned on the Cherokee, some of whom had helped him against the Creek, and compelled them to sell three million acres to the government at a token price. In 1817, he wrote to President Monroe, "I have long viewed treaties with the Indians an absurdity not to be reconciled to the principles of our government." In Jackson's view, Indians blocked the advance of citizen farmers and republican virtue. He believed they were barbaric and could not become part of American society. He was convinced that any means should be used to remove them from the path of civilization. Publicly, Jackson argued that federal removal of Indians was both efficient and humane; it simultaneously enhanced economic opportunity for American society and sheltered an inferior people. As president, he sought to complete his work of sweeping all tribes to lands west of the Mississippi.

The Five Civilized Tribes—the Cherokee and Creek in Georgia and Alabama; the Chickasaw and Chocktaw in Mississippi, Alabama, and Tennessee; and the Seminole in Florida—remained

JACKSON TO THE CHEROKEE AND THE CHEROKEE'S REPLY

From Andrew Jackson's speech to the Cherokee tribe, March 7, 1835:

Your fathers were well known to me, and the regard which I cherished for them has caused me to feel great solicitude for your situation. . . . Listen to me, therefore, as your fathers have listened . . .

You are now placed in the midst of a white population. Your peculiar customs . . . have been abrogated by the great political community among which you live; and you are now subject to the same laws which govern the other citizens of Georgia and Alabama. . . . Most of your people are uneducated, and are liable to be brought into collision at all times with their white neighbors. Your young men are acquiring habits of intoxication. With strong passions, and without those habits of restraint which our laws inculcate and render necessary, they are frequently driven to excesses which must eventually terminate in their ruin. The game has disappeared among you, and you must depend upon agriculture and the mechanic arts for support. And, yet, a large portion of your people have acquired little or no property in the soil itself, or in any article of personal property which can be useful to them. How, under these circumstances, can you live in the country you now occupy? Your condition must become worse and worse, and you will ultimately disappear, as so many tribes have done before you. . . .

I have no motive, my friends, to deceive you. I am sincerely desirous to promote your welfare. Listen to me, then, while I tell you that you cannot remain where you are now. Circumstances that cannot be controlled, and which are beyond the reach of human laws, render it impossible that you can flourish in the midst of a civilized community. You have but one remedy within your reach; and that is, to remove to the West and join your countrymen, who are already established there. And the sooner you do this, the sooner you will commence your career of improvement and prosperity. . . .

John Ross and fellow Cherokee reply to Congress:

Owing to the intelligence of the Cherokee people, they have a correct knowledge of their own rights, and they well know the illegality of those oppressive measures which have been adopted for their expulsion, by State authority. . . . For more than *seven long years* have the Cherokee people been driven into the necessity of contending for their just rights, and they have struggled against fearful odds. . . . Their resources and means of defence, have been seized and withheld. The treaties, laws, and constitution of the United States, their bulwark, and only citadel of refuge, put beyond their reach. . . . The judgments of the judiciary branch of the government, in support of their rights, have been disregarded and prostrated; and their petitions for relief, from time to time before Congress, been unheeded. . . .

[By the Treaty of New Echota] all the lands, rights, interests, and claims . . . of the Cherokee people east of the Mississippi are pretended to be ceded to the United States for the pittance of $5,600,000. . . . The Cherokee Territory, within the limits of North Carolina, Georgia, Tennessee and Alabama, is estimated to contain *ten millions of acres*. It embraces a large portion of the finest lands to be found in any of the States; and a salubrity of climate unsurpassed by any; possessing superior advantages in reference to water power. . . .

The entire country is covered with a dense forest of valuable timber, also abounding in inexhaustible quarries of marble and lime stone. Above all, it possesses the most extensive regions of the precious metals known in the United States. . . . Independent of all these natural advantages and invaluable resources, there are many extensive and valuable improvements made upon the lands by the native Cherokee inhabitants, and those adopted as Cherokee citizens, by intermarriages.

. . . Justice and equity demand, that in any final treaty for the adjustment of the Cherokee difficulties, that their rights, interests, and wishes should be consulted; and that the individual rights of the Cherokee citizens, in their possessions and claims, should be amply secured; and as freemen, they should be left at liberty to stay or remove where they please . . .

Sources: Andrew Jackson, "To the Cherokee Tribe of Indians East of the Mississippi River." Letter, March 16, 1835; John Ross and others, "Memorial of the Cherokee Representatives Submitting the protest of the Cherokee nation against the ratification, execution, and enforcement of the treaty negotiated at New Echota, in December, 1935." Letter, June 22 (1836).

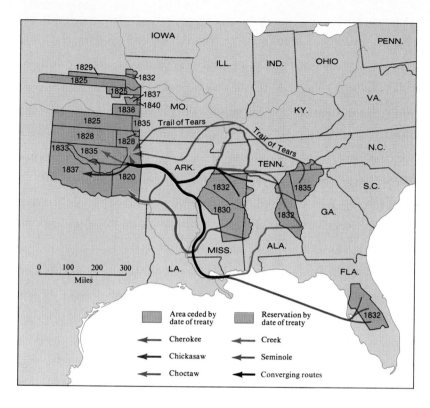

MAP 12.1 THE REMOVAL
OF NATIVE AMERICANS
This map shows the lands of the
southeastern tribes before and
after their removal during the
1820s and 1830s, and the routes
of their forced migrations. A
comparison of this map with the
land sales on page 322 shows that
the tribal lands ceded in Alabama
and Mississippi became those
most sought after by white
settlers during the 1830s. No
white settlers occupied land on
the new reservations before the
Civil War.

in the South. These tribes had successfully
retained control of tribal enclaves, often with
federal protection guaranteed by earlier treaties.
The Cherokee were particularly successful because they had a centralized political system,
a thriving agricultural economy, and leaders
who worked to gain white sympathy by adopting the trappings of plantation society. Tragically, the Five Tribes occupied high-quality
cotton land that was directly in the path of white
settlement.

Jackson's policy involved, first, withdrawal of
the federal troops who protected the tribal enclaves that were created in the southeastern
states after the War of 1812. He realized this
would leave the native Americans subject to
state law, which had a sharp anti-Indian edge.
Jackson knew, for example, that in 1825 and
again in 1827, Georgia had forced the Creek to
cede most of their territory to the state. In 1828,
Georgia went further, declaring that Cherokee
were not an Indian nation but a collection of individuals who were tenants on state-owned
land. Other states followed Georgia's example;
they restricted the tribal rights of native Ameri-

cans, thus opening the way for whites to acquire
Indian property.

Jackson also promoted the Indian Removal
Act of 1830. This legislation offered the tribes
land west of the Mississippi in exchange for their
eastern holdings. When Jackson sent agents to
negotiate with the Civilized Tribes, he instructed
the agents to tell the Indians "as friends and
brothers to listen to their father." The agents
should promise the tribes that in the West "their
white brothers will not trouble them"; their
brothers "will have no claim to the land," and
the Indians "can live upon it, they and all their
children, as long as grass grows and water
runs." Knowing that Jackson would send federal
troops to remove them if necessary, the tribes
negotiated almost a hundred treaties for such exchanges.

Jackson waged war on the native Americans
who would not leave for the trans-Mississippi
West. With an army of seven thousand men,
General Winfield Scott set out to drive all of the
southeastern tribes across the Mississippi. By
1837, all were gone except the Cherokee and a
minority of Florida's Seminole, who had refused

to accept removal. Aided by runaway slaves, many of whom had married into the tribe, the Seminole fought a guerrilla war into the 1840s against federal troops and the state militia. Jackson's Indian war extended even into the Northwest. In 1832, he sent regular army troops to Illinois to subdue Chief Black Hawk, the leader of the Sac and Fox tribes.

A treaty finally signed with the Cherokee in 1836 allowed them two years to leave their homeland. By the deadline, in 1838, only two thousand of the eighteen thousand Cherokee had left. During the summer of that year, under orders from President Martin Van Buren, General Scott rounded up fifteen thousand Cherokee and placed them in concentration camps. A few escaped to isolated Cherokee villages in the mountains of North Carolina. In the winter, the rest undertook a long and grueling march to the

BLACK HAWK
In 1833, Black Hawk, the chief of the Sac and Fox tribes, dictated his autobiography. He described how, facing hostile Sioux, he stubbornly led a thousand of his people west into Illinois in 1832 to grow corn on some of their old land. In the Black Hawk War, the army and Illinois militia chased Black Hawk into the Wisconsin Territory and then massacred women and children at Bad Axe as they tried to escape across the Mississippi River. (George Catlin. *Muk-a-tah-mish-o-kah-kaik, The Black Hawk*. The Thomas Gilcrease Institute, Tulsa)

new Indian Territory, in present-day Oklahoma—a route they remembered as the Trail of Tears. Only eleven thousand reached Oklahoma in 1838; as many as four thousand died on the journey, victims of racial prejudice and the ruthless hunger of whites for new land.

Jackson carried out this Indian policy in the face of two adverse rulings by the Supreme Court. In 1827, the Cherokee had adopted a constitution and proclaimed themselves a separate nation within the United States. After Georgia's 1828 declaration, the Cherokee Nation appealed to the Supreme Court. The Cherokee argued that Georgia's denial of their independence violated the U.S. Constitution. Chief Justice John Marshall supported their appeal. In *Cherokee Nation v. Georgia* (1831), speaking for a majority of the justices, he argued that the Indians were "domestic dependent nations" with a right to their land. In another case, *Worcester v. Georgia* (1832), Marshall held that the Indian nations were "distinct political communities, having territorial boundaries, within which their authority is exclusive . . . which is not only acknowledged, but guaranteed by the United States." Jackson reputedly responded, "John Marshall has made his decision; now let him enforce it." As a consequence of the wide popularity of Jackson's policy, no significant support emerged for the Court or its position, and Marshall's ruling was never enforced.

The Tariff and Nullification

Jackson's second attack against those who tried to block the destiny of the republic came during the South Carolina nullification controversy. This dispute stemmed from the chronic insecurity that plagued South Carolina's slaveholding elite. South Carolina was unusual for a slave state. Its sizable slave population—56 percent of the state's total in 1830—made it more similar to Haiti, Jamaica, or Barbados than to the South as a whole. Like their West Indian counterparts, South Carolina planters constantly and profoundly feared both slave rebellions and the power of outside governments to abolish slavery. (In the West Indies, the British began a massive program of gradual, compensated emancipation in 1831.)

The British program aggravated fears in South Carolina over the future course of America's policy toward slavery. In the fall of 1832, South Carolina's leaders decided to contest the limits of federal power, choosing the tariff as their target. They had good reasons to focus on tariffs. The planters had lost repeatedly on tariff questions, most recently in 1832, when Congress passed tariff legislation that left the 1828 rates of the "Tariff of Abominations" essentially unchanged. A South Carolina state convention, under planter leadership, took a bold step. It adopted an "ordinance of nullification," which declared null and void the tariff acts of 1828 and 1832 and forbade the collection of tariff duties within the state.

The act of nullification rested on the constitutional arguments of Jackson's vice president, John C. Calhoun, which he had articulated anonymously in the *South Carolina Exposition* (1828). These arguments would form the basis of "states'-rights" arguments even in the late twentieth century. Drawing on the Kentucky and Virginia Resolutions of 1798, Calhoun returned to the anti-Federalist argument that sovereignty lay not with the American people as a whole but with collections of people acting through their state governments. Only the "principals," acting through state-level constitutional conventions, just like those that had ratified the Constitution, could determine whether acts of Congress were constitutional. If any state decided that a federal law was unconstitutional, it could "interpose" by declaring the law null and void within its borders. Unless three-fourths of the other states ratified an amendment assigning Congress the power in question, the challenged law would be nullified. And, even if such an amendment were adopted, the dissident state still had the option of secession from the republic.

Calhoun did not immediately admit authorship of the *Exposition*, but he took a visible position on the issue of states' rights in 1830 following an extended debate in the Senate between Robert Y. Hayne of South Carolina and Daniel Webster of Massachusetts over the nature of the Union. That debate began in January 1830 when Hayne, protesting a resolution of Samuel A. Foot of Connecticut to restrict western land sales, suggested that the West should join forces with the South in opposition to the land and tariff policies of the Northeast. Webster, defending

JOHN C. CALHOUN
Calhoun (1782–1850) longed for a close alliance of businessmen and planters for protection against factory laborers and slaves. During Jackson's second term, Calhoun cooperated with leading Whigs, hoping that the new party might sponsor that alliance. But in 1837, when he decided that northern Whigs would not accept his ideas of state sovereignty and nullification, Calhoun abandoned his Whig allies and later rejoined the Democratic party. (The Bettmann Archive)

his section, turned from economic issues and challenged Hayne to debate the issue of states' rights. Hayne responded with the arguments of Calhoun's *Exposition.* while Calhoun looked on approvingly. Webster, often speaking directly to Calhoun, replied with a stirring defense of national power in which he concluded: "Liberty and Union, now and forever, one and inseparable." What became known as Webster's "Second Reply to Hayne" circulated more widely than had any other congressional speech. It received the implicit endorsement of Andrew Jackson in April 1830 when, at a dinner party to celebrate Jefferson's birthday, he looked squarely at Vice-President Calhoun and offered the toast: "Our Federal Union—it must be preserved." Calhoun immediately replied: "The Union—next to our liberty most dear! May we all remember that it can only be preserved by respecting the rights of the states and distributing equally the benefits and burdens of the Union."

In 1831, Calhoun admitted his authorship of the *Exposition* and elaborated his views further. Meanwhile, he faced mounting pressure to leave the administration—both from pro-slavery radicals in South Carolina and from Jackson. The differences between Calhoun and Jackson on the nature of Union had become too great, and Secretary of State Martin Van Buren, who wished to remove Calhoun as a rival for power, helped convince Jackson that Calhoun was an enemy. In December 1832 Calhoun resigned from the vice presidency (to be succeeded by Van Buren in 1833), became a U.S. Senator from South Carolina, and led the nullification movement.

Despite Calhoun's leadership, no other state supported South Carolina's effort to nullify federal tariffs in 1832. The state's leadership had been speaking, as it turned out, not for the South as a whole but only for their state. Other Southerners perceived no imminent threat to slavery. They recognized the value of Jackson's vigorous support of territorial expansion. Most held the Union in high regard and did not believe that restoring low tariffs warranted a challenge to either federal authority or to President Jackson, whom they generally supported.

Jackson appealed directly to the loyalty of his fellow slaveowners and expansionists. Publicly, he declared that nullification violated the Constitution, "unauthorized by its spirit, inconsistent with every principle on which it is founded, and destructive of the great object for which it was formed." Jackson also brandished federal power. He reinforced the federal forts in South Carolina by sending a warship and several armed boats to the port of Charleston to enforce tariff collections. He asked Congress to pass a "force bill," authorizing him to use the army and navy if necessary to compel obedience to acts of Congress. Privately, he declared that nullification was treason and threatened to hang Calhoun.

In Congress, Calhoun argued on behalf of his nullification theory, even though he recognized the weakness of his political position. With Henry Clay, he worked out a compromise. Calhoun and Clay proposed a new tariff bill that provided for an annual reduction of the tariff so that by 1842 rates would return to the levels set in 1816. The tariff bill passed, thus allowing the nullifiers to save face. That same day, March 1, 1833, Congress enacted the force bill as well.

Jackson signed both bills into law; he was satisfied to win on the principle of nullification's illegality, to have demonstrated that it was fruitless for an individual state to resist federal force, and to have augmented his party's base in the South. He had established that no state could nullify a law of the United States, either in theory or in practice. Secession was the only option, and Jackson made it clear that this action, as well as nullification, would be met with federal force. His declaration that nullification was inconsistent with a strong Union won support throughout the North and the South. Memories of the American Revolution and the War of 1812 were fresh enough for Americans of virtually all regions and classes to see clearly the need for a strong government to protect independence and promote expansion.

The Bank Veto

Jackson's most vigorous political offensive was his attack on the Second Bank of the United States, one of the essential elements of the American System. Using the vocabulary of the Revolution, he played on popular distrust of banking and finance and made the Bank the focus of resentment against the era's unsettling social and economic changes.

The Second Bank of the United States was a large commercial bank that the federal government had chartered for twenty years in 1816 and partially owned (to the extent of 20 percent of the bank's stock). Its most important role was the stabilization of the nation's money supply. Most American money consisted of notes—in effect, paper money—that state-chartered commercial banks issued with the promise to redeem the notes with gold or silver coin on demand. The Bank played its stabilizing role by regularly collecting these state bank notes, returning them to the banks that had issued them, and demanding that the banks convert them into gold and silver coin. With the threat of collection hanging over them, state banks had to be conservative in extending credit in the form of bank notes. The banks continued to issue more notes than they could redeem at any given time, thereby expanding the money supply. But, under the discipline imposed by the Second Bank, they had to do so cautiously. During the prosperous 1820s, the Second Bank performed especially well, maintaining steady, predictable increases in the money supply throughout the nation. By enhancing investors' confidence in the monetary stability of the developing West, the bank promoted increases in the supply of capital for new investment, a role especially appreciated by bankers and investors in Boston, New York, and Philadelphia.

Most people did not understand commercial banking, particularly its capacity to enlarge the money supply through the lending of bank notes. Nor did they appreciate the functions of the Second Bank. It was easy to believe that banking was a nonproductive, parasitic activity and that bankers earned their profits illegitimately through the exercise of special privilege. Some Americans had specific grievances against bankers. Wage earners, for example, sometimes received payment in highly depreciated notes issued by unstable state banks. In response, they often advocated the destruction of all banking to eliminate all money except specie, or "hard" money—coins minted from precious metals. Various interest groups played on popular prejudices for the purpose of killing the Second Bank. Wealthy New York bankers, including supporters of Martin Van Buren, wanted to see federal deposits in their banks, and some bankers in smaller cities, including Nashville supporters of Jackson, wanted to be free of regulation by the Second Bank.

In 1832, Jackson's opponents in Congress, led by Henry Clay and Daniel Webster, united to embarrass Jackson. Knowing that the president opposed the Second Bank, and realizing that many Democrats in Congress disagreed with him, Clay and Webster hoped to lure Jackson into the trap of a divisive and unpopular veto just before the 1832 elections. So they engineered passage of a bill to recharter the Bank.

Seeming to fall into the trap, Jackson vetoed the bill. But he accompanied his veto with a powerful message that gained wide circulation. He denounced the Second Bank as a nest of special privilege and of monopoly power that advanced the interests "of the few at the expense of the many," damaging the "humbler members of society—the farmers, the mechanics, and laborers—who have neither the time nor the means of securing like favors to themselves."

The corporate charter of the Second Bank had made "the rich richer and the potent more powerful." It was, Jackson declared, an example of "the means by whose silent and secret operation a control would be exercised by the few over the political conduct of the many by first acquiring . . . control over the labor and earnings of the great body of the people." The president singled out the monopolists who profited from special privilege and inside dealing. By inference, he attacked Webster, a director of the Boston branch of the Second Bank, for having drawn on the bank for loans and received fees from it for legal services. Finally, Jackson made a connection that was especially damning in republican patriots' eyes. He emphasized the heavy investment by British aristocrats in the Second Bank.

Following his veto, Jackson worked to destroy the power of the Bank even before its charter expired in 1836. In this "bank war," he replaced a secretary of the treasury who was loyal to the Second Bank with Robert B. Taney, whom he ordered to withdraw the federal government's deposits from the Second Bank. In 1833, Taney eagerly complied, moving the cash to state banks, called "pet banks" by Jackson's opponents. In 1836, after the death of John Marshall, Jackson rewarded Taney by appointing him Chief Justice of the Supreme Court, where he served until his death in 1864. Taney agreed with Marshall's belief in judicial supremacy, but he led his Court, composed of a majority of Jackson appointees, in a new direction. Through cases like *Charles River Bridge v. Warren Bridge* (1837), the Taney Court limited corporate privileges, thereby giving constitutional legitmacy to Jackson's antimonopoly hostility.

In his veto and subsequent "bank war," Jackson had a better sense of the public's anti-corporate mood than did the supporters of the Bank. His most fervent supporters came from a broad spectrum of people who resisted industrialization. But Jackson also won support for his position from some promoters of economic growth, such as state bankers who had originally supported the Second Bank but now believed its demise would open the way for more speculative investments by their banks. Thus, he managed to expand his coalition of groups, even though some held diametrically contradictory positions on the value of banking and even industrialization. The bank veto, however, stimulated significant organized opposition that culminated in the formation of the Whig party.

The Second Party System

Jackson's argument that the death of the Second Bank would increase economic opportunity did not satisfy most of the northern business class. Indeed, the bank veto, and the rest of Jackson's economic program, inspired the business elite to organize a new party—the Whig party. The two parties, Democratic and Whig, constituted the Second Party System, which survived until the rise of the Republican party in the mid-1850s.

Emergence of the Whigs

As early as Jackson's first term, his opponents in Congress began to form an alliance. They called themselves "Whigs" and referred to Jackson as "King Andrew I." These names conjured up associations with the American and English parties, also called Whigs, that had opposed the power of King George III. The Whigs meant to imply that Jackson had violated the Constitution through tyrannical abuses of executive power and that they were better defenders of the republic than were the Democrats. They attempted to turn Jackson's republican rhetoric against him.

Initially, little more than common opposition to Jackson united the congressional Whigs, who included Senators Webster of Massachusetts, Clay of Kentucky, and Calhoun of South Carolina. Webster and Clay had a bond of common economic interests. Webster spoke on behalf of New England's business elite, and Clay represented the commercial interests of the Ohio and Mississippi valleys. Calhoun, having broken with Jackson over nullification, represented the planter class of the lower South and had reservations about the economic ideas of his congressional allies. Supporting the popular Clay, who ran on the National Republican ticket against Jackson in 1832, the Whigs attacked Jackson for his abuses of patronage and the veto power, endorsed the American System, and called for rechartering the Second Bank.

Jackson and his new running mate, Martin Van Buren, won the 1832 election in a landslide.

A WHIG CARTOON
This political cartoon lampooned Andrew Jackson as a monarch fully equipped with the trappings of royalty and trampling on the Constitution. The caption emphasized Jackson's contempt for judges and criticizes many of his political appointments. It concluded by asking, "Shall he reign over us, or shall the PEOPLE RULE?" (The New-York Historical Society)

They carried a majority of the popular vote and overwhelmed Clay in the electoral vote, 219 to 49. The outcome deeply troubled the congressional Whigs. They explained Jackson's victory in terms of the popularity of his position on the Second Bank and his symbolic opposition to industrialization. Clay and Webster did not support government protection of monopolies, but they feared that Jackson had opened the door for the destruction of all privilege and the value of corporate charters. Even worse, they feared, Jacksonians such as the president's close adviser Amos Kendall might lead their followers to policies of drastic redistribution of wealth. They listened apprehensively in 1834 when Kendall, embracing a labor theory of value, declared that people "who produce all wealth are themselves left poor" and that "they see principalities extending and palaces built around them, without being aware that the entire expense is a tax upon themselves."

In response, the congressional Whigs began elaborating their own plan for the nation's future. By the 1836 election, they had formulated a well-defined alternative to the Democratic vision and had begun to popularize it among the northern middle class.

Whig Ideology

Whigs believed it was "natural" for a relatively few individuals to acquire a large share of the wealth, to represent the people in a republican government, and to use government power as they thought necessary for the welfare of all. They believed the increasing concentrations of power and wealth that accompanied the advance of modern banking, manufacturing, and transportation furthered the welfare of the entire community.

The Whigs attempted to reconcile their elitism with republican ideals in several ways. First, they asserted that American society was really classless because it did not ascribe permanent status to groups and individuals and because its institutions fostered upward mobility. Second, they argued that it was "natural" in a republic for wealthy individuals to represent other citizens. Constrained by a republican Constitution and by the moral influence of religion, elites would govern in the best interests of all. Third, the Whigs argued that the ruling class promoted industrialization and economic growth, which in turn strengthened the republic by creating a more prosperous citizenry and by merging the interests of labor and capital.

To the Whigs, even the most modern factories were sources of social harmony. In 1830, Edward Everett, a Whig congressman from Massachusetts and a leading Whig publicist, told a Fourth of July crowd in Lowell that "the alliance

which you have . . . established between labor and capital . . . may truly be called a *holy alliance*." He proclaimed that factories like those at Lowell "form a mutually beneficial connection between those who have nothing but their muscular power and those who are able to bring into the partnership . . . property which was itself, originally, the work of men's hands, but has been converted, by accumulation and thrift, from labor into capital." Everett concluded, "Woe to the land where labor and intelligence are at war! Happy the land whose various interests are united together by the bonds of mutual benefit and kind feeling!"

The Whigs criticized Jackson and the Democrats for underestimating possibilities for upward mobility, for pitting the poor against the rich, and for disrupting social harmony. They attacked Jackson's strong presidency by warning against strong, highly individualistic executives who pandered to the growing masses of voters. And they claimed that Democratic economic programs would turn back the clock, impoverishing and weakening the republic.

As an alternative, the Whigs offered legislative rule and a program of governmental intervention in the economy. They wanted to see a more vigorous national government, with Congress, rather than the president, exercising leadership. Whigs advocated the American System of Henry Clay and John Quincy Adams.

Among the congressional opponents of Andrew Jackson, only Calhoun and his southern followers had reservations about the full-blown Whig ideology and program. He had the greatest concern over the Whig objection to fixed classes, although he also disliked Whig nationalism and Clay's tariff. Calhoun argued that the Whig ideal of equal opportunity contradicted the realities of slavery and of industrial society. In 1837, he wrote, "There is and always has been in an advanced stage of wealth and civilization a conflict between labor and capital." He argued that southern slaveowners and northern factory owners belonged to the same privileged class and faced the same threat from below. He therefore urged northern capitalists to join a defensive alliance with the planters. In Calhoun's view, social harmony was possible only with recognition, acceptance, and reinforcement of existing, sharp distinctions of class. Whigs, he argued, ought to unite around a common defense of privilege and social order.

The other Whig leaders, however, did not accept Calhoun's critique. Daniel Webster admitted that Calhoun's description of "a clear and well-defined line between capital and labor" might fit the South or Europe. But in the North, Webster argued, "this distinction grows less and less definite as commerce advances." Pointing to Massachusetts, Webster declared, "I do not believe there is on earth, in a highly civilized society, a greater equality in the condition of men than exists there." Calhoun, Webster maintained, had neglected the growing importance of the northern middle class.

The Whig Triumph

Led by the congressional Whigs, a coalition of groups emerged to run candidates at the state and local levels in 1834 and 1836. The coalition was strongest in New England, New York, and in the new communities along the shores of the Great Lakes. Congregationalist traditions, economic needs, and Protestant revivalism laid the groundwork for the appeal of the Whig message and program. During the 1830s, business-class enthusiasts for moral reform and Whig politicians discovered that they had mutual interests. Government intervention along Whig lines could be part of a comprehensive program designed to restore community harmony and strengthen the Industrial Revolution.

The Whig message, conveyed by Henry Clay, also won support from people of southern origin in the Ohio and Mississippi valleys. In spite of their religious and cultural differences from northern Whigs, the farmers, bankers, and shopkeepers in the southern tier of Northwest states agreed that positive government action was needed for economic development. They found national banking and public investment in internal improvements especially attractive. They also supported the ideal of a classless society led by "natural" elites. They gradually formed alliances with the business class to the north.

In the South, support for the Whig party was less cohesive, resting more on the appeal of specific elements in the Whig program than on the force of the Whigs' social vision. Many non-slaveholding whites in the back country, especially in western Virginia and the deepest hill country of the other seaboard states, were Whigs because they advocated a positive federal program of banking and internal improvement to break the grip of planter elites in their region. There was also a significant Whig minority among wealthy planters who invested heavily in railroads, banks, and factories and who had close ties to northern markets and New York capitalists. Finally, some states' rights Democrats in Virginia and South Carolina who were upset with Jackson's threat of force to suppress nullification joined the Whigs.

Throughout most of the nation, however, the Whigs had great difficulty appealing to the poorest voters, and they had to compete sharply for middle-class voters. During the 1830s, most farmers and wage earners felt powerfully attracted to the Jacksonian economic program and values, which stressed freedom from coercion by social elites.

The Whigs achieved only modest success in the congressional elections of 1834. In the 1836 elections, they faced Van Buren, who ran on Jackson's record, which now included not only the bank veto but also the "bank war." The Whigs ran three presidential candidates hoping to maximize the opposition votes from the various sections and to force the election into the House of Representatives, which the Whigs now controlled. They lost. The total electoral votes collected by the Whigs—73 by William Henry Harrison of Ohio, 26 by Hugh L. White of Tennessee, and 14 by Daniel Webster—fell far short of Van Buren's 170 votes. Van Buren's base of electoral support in the populous states of New York, Pennsylvania, and Virginia proved decisive.

A Whig breakthrough finally came in 1840, after Van Buren's lackluster administration. Perhaps because Van Buren was known primarily as a professional politician and had neither ties with the Founding Fathers nor a record of military heroism, voters did not find him inspiring. Moreover, many people did not understand the overwhelming influence of international economic forces on the business cycle, and so blamed him for the depression that followed the Panic of 1837. Van Buren's administration accomplished

TIME LINE
THE POLITICAL CULTURE OF INDUSTRIALIZING AMERICA

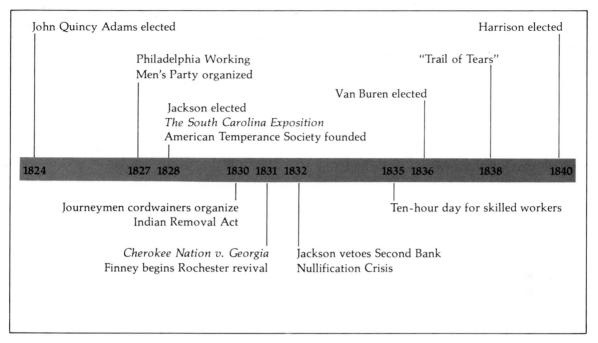

little beyond the passage of the Independent Treasury Act, in 1840, which required the federal government to keep its cash in government vaults rather than in banks. The chief objective of this legislation was to prevent the government from playing favorites among bankers, and from using federal deposits to expnd banking and the money supply.

In 1840, the Whigs decided that the economic depression's effect of discrediting and ruining the Democrats made it unnecesssary for the Whigs to take clear positions on the issues. They nominated for the presidency William Henry Harrison of Ohio, who was noted for his victories over native Americans at Tippecanoe and the British in the Battle of the Thames (Ontario) in the War of 1812. Harrison lacked political experience and was sixty-eight years old, but Clay and Webster cared little. They distrusted a strong president and planned to use Harrison as the rubber stamp for congressional enactment of the Whig program. Moreover, Harrison's military record, Virginia roots, and strong identification with western interests made him a Whig

version of Andrew Jackson. His candidacy strengthened the Whig appeal to Democratic voters who blamed Van Buren for the Panic of 1837.

The Whigs concentrated on organizing the electorate rather than developing issues. As a result, the Harrison campaign was the first to be conducted as an exuberant carnival. The Whigs turned pamphleteering, song fests, parades, and well-orchestrated mass meetings into a new political style. When a Democratic newspaper unwisely declared that Harrison would be happy to retire to a log cabin if he had a pension and an ample supply of hard cider, the Whigs quickly described their candidate as a simple man of the people who loved log cabins and cider. Although Harrison was actually a man of some wealth the 1840 election became the "log cabin" campaign.

The Whigs got the better of the contest over which candidate was closer to the people. Casting Harrison as a latter-day Andrew Jackson, and aided by the lingering depression, they won a narrow popular victory, an overwhelming electoral victory (including the votes of New York and Pennsylvania), and control of Congress. Popular interest in a presidential election had never been greater. Whereas about 60 percent of the eligible voters had taken part in 1832 and 1836, more than 80 percent voted in 1840.

Thus, by 1840, two national parties competed vigorously for the support of a mass electorate. Although the Whigs left their platform somewhat vague in 1840, the parties offered distinct visions of industrialization and the social and political orders. For the next decade competed on terms that were reasonably equal. The Democrats held edges in party discipline and mass loyalty. But the Whigs had an advantage in wealth and the cohesiveness of their leadership and support, based on the interests of the emerging business class.

A business class, consisting of middle-class property owners led by a business elite, coalesced in northern communities during the 1820s and 1830s. Its members publicly acknowledged the disorder that accompanied industrialization. They joined revivals led by evangelical clergymen such as Charles G. Finney, who believed that Christian conversions could mobilize free wills on behalf of worldly perfection. In Finney's revivals, business leaders and middle-class citizens pledged to attend church regularly, respect their families, abstain from alcohol, and urge others to embrace religion. A temperance pledge became an important badge of respectability.

Simultaneously, workers, particularly those who practiced traditional skills, sought to reform industrial conditions by forming labor unions to demand the ten-hour day and by establishing political parties to promote a more equitable society. Strikes increased and the unions made some gains, but the depression following the Panic of 1837 halted the labor movement. By 1840, the evangelical call for workers to embrace the values of the business class had become stronger than the pleas for workers to unite and break up concentrations of power and wealth.

The emerging business class faced its greatest challenges in politics. Andrew Jackson, the first president to regard himself as an instrument of democratic will, mobilized the support of laborers, farmers, and southern planters for the Democratic party. Jackson's veto of the rechartering of the Second Bank of the United States disturbed the emerging business class and stimulated the formation of the Whig party, marking the beginning of the Second Party System. Led by Henry Clay and Daniel Webster, the Whigs appealed to the emerging business class and designed an ideology to reconcile elitism with republican ideals. In the election of 1840, the Whigs blamed the Democrats for the Panic of 1837 and took control of the government.

Suggestions for Further Reading

The Rise of the Business Class

Elaboration of the concept of the business class can be found in Michael Katz et al., *The Social Organization of Early Industrial Capitalism* (1982). Surveys of reform movements closely linked to the Second Great Awakening include C. S. Griffen, *The Ferment of Reform, 1830–1860*; Alice F. Tyler, *Freedom's Ferment, Phases of American Social History from the Colonial Period to the Outbreak of the Civil War* (1944); and Ronald G. Walters, *American Reformers, 1815–1860* (1978). Studies of the relationship between religious evangelism and reform are particularly rich for communities in New York State. See Whitney R. Cross, *The Burned-Over District, The Social and Intellectual History of Enthusiastic Religion in Western New York, 1800–1850* (1950); Paul E. Johnson, *A Shopkeeper's Millennium: Society and Revivals in Rochester, New York, 1815–1837* (1978); and Mary Ryan, *Cradle of the Middle Class, The Family in Oneida County, New York, 1790–1865* (1981).

An earlier generation of historians of labor emphasized the organization of unions during early industrialization. See Norman Ware, *The Industrial Worker, 1840–1860* (1924) and John R. Commons, *History of La-*

bour in the United States, Vol. One (1918). More recently, historians have explored the political context of the labor movement. See Alan Dawley, *Class and Community, The Industrial Revolution in Lynn* (1976); Paul G. Faler, *Mechanics and Manufacturers in the Early Industrial Revolution, Lynn Massachusetts, 1780–1860* (1981); Susan E. Hirsch, *Roots of the American Working Class, The Industrialization of Crafts in Newark, 1800–1860* (1978); Bruce Laurie, *Working People of Philadelphia, 1800–1860* (1980); and Sean Wilentz, *Chants Democratic, New York City and the Rise of the American Working Class, 1788–1850* (1984).

The Challenge of Democratic Politics

Books exploring the democratic sources of Jacksonian politics include Lee Benson, *The Concept of Jacksonian Democracy: New York as a Test Case (1961);* Robert Kelley, *The Cultural Pattern in American Politics, The First Century* (1979); Richard P. McCormick, *The Second American Party System: Party Formation in the Jacksonian Era* (1966); Marvin Meyers, *The Jacksonian Persuasion, Politics and Belief* (1957); Edward Pessen, *Jacksonian America* (1970); Arthur M. Schlesinger, Jr., *The Age of Jackson* (1945); and John William Ward, *Andrew Jackson, Symbol for an Age* (1962). For introductions to the history of Indians and Indian policy during the Jackso-

nian era, consult D'Arcy McNickle, *Native American Tribalism, Indian Survivals and Renewals* (1973); Francis P. Prucha, *American Indian Policy in the Formative Years* (1962); R. N. Satz, *American Indian Policy in the Jacksonian Era* (1975); and Dale Van Every, *Disinherited: The Lost Birthright of the American Indian* (1966). The Nullification controversy receives close attention in Richard N. Current, *John C. Calhoun* (1963) and William W. Freehling, *Prelude to Civil War: The Nullification Controversy in South Carolina, 1810–1836* (1966). The most comprehensive survey of bank politics during this period is Bray Hammond, *Banks and Politics in America from the Revolution to the Civil War* (1957). For Jackson's bank war, see Robert V. Remini, *Andrew Jackson and the Bank War* (1967). Peter Temin's *The Jacksonian Economy* (1969) discounts Jackson's banking policies as having any significant effect on economic stability.

The Second Party System

The development of Whig politics receives particular attention in Richard N. Current, *Daniel Webster and the Rise of National Conservatism* (1955); Clement Eaton, *Henry Clay and the Art of American Politics* (1957); Daniel Walker Howe (ed.), *The American Whigs, An Anthology* (1973) and *The Political Culture of the American Whigs* (1979).

13

INDIVIDUALISM
AND REFORM

The economic transformations that occurred between 1820 and 1860 had contradictory effects on the ways Americans thought about themselves as individuals and as a society. The changes brought by expansion and industrialization seemed to liberate individuals, to make men and women more free to act on their own private choices. The bonds of traditional restraints on individual lives were being loosened. Men, and even women, could believe that each person could become the master of his or her own fate.

But there was another side to these changes. Industrialization and economic growth did not just promise liberation for the indivdual. They also demanded cohesive forms of social organization. They required that men and women submit to common disciplines of work. They brought about an increasing degree of standardization, not just of manufactured products but also of human behavior.

Alexis de Tocqueville observed the contest between the supremacy of the individual and the demands of social responsibility during his 1831–1832 tour of the United States. In *Democracy in America*, he described a tendency of Americans to be moved in opposite ways, by self-interest but also by devotion to the interests of the community. Americans, he said, seemed at one time to be "animated by the most selfish cupidity; at another by the most lively patriotism." These opposing passions were so powerful, he thought, that Americans must have them "united and mingled in some part of their character."

For writers and philosophers, for religious and social reformers, for reflective politicians—in fact, for everyone who thought seriously about the industrializing world—the main problem of the age was the reconciliation of the freedom of the individual with the legitimate demands of society. Writers explored the same issue and produced an outpouring of brilliant novels, essays, and poetry that constituted the first real American literature. Other writers, less gifted but more in touch with the minds and experiences of a mass audience, created a new popular ideology of women and the family. Some men and women approached the problem more directly and established a variety of utopian communities as experimental, collective havens from competitive society. But for many others, the problem was too practical to be dealt with in fiction or verse and too pervasive to be dealt with by withdrawing into an artificial, isolated community. Such people tried instead to reform some aspect of society that violated their idea of the correct moral relationship between the individual and the community.

Reformers embraced the ideal of individual freedom but, at the same time, accepted and urged others to accept an inner discipline. Where these Americans found others guilty of excessive individualism, they attempted to reform them, often by seeking a religious commitment from them. The most dramatic outlet for this reform enthusiasm was a new attack on slavery that began in the 1830s. Abolitionists, finding slavery to be the expression of the untrammeled individualism of slaveholders, as well as a denial of the individual freedom of slaves, launched a reform movement that attacked slavery with all the energies of religious evangelism.

Intellectual Ferment in American Literature

The American reading public remained enthusiastic about European—particularly British—writers throughout the nineteenth century. In the 1840s and 1850s, the most popular novelists in the nation were not Americans, but British writers like Sir Walter Scott and Charles Dickens. The American fiction that did become popular, such as Washington Irving's *The Sketch Book* (1819) and James Fenimore Cooper's *The Last of the Mohicans* (1823), were written by men who spent much of their mature lives in Europe. In fact, Irving and Cooper measured their success by the response of British or French audiences to their work.

Yet economic developments encouraged the emergence of a literature written by American authors, about American themes, and for American readers. In 1820, more than two-thirds of the books Americans bought were British. By 1850, American firms published more than two-thirds of the books purchased in the United States. The same kinds of changes that had transformed other economic activities were at work in publishing. Nine out of every ten Americans could read, and libraries were growing in both number and size. Publishers could tap this enormous market with increasing efficiency because of low-cost transportation and industrial technology. The Napier steam-driven press (1825) and the Hoe rotary press (1847) made it possible to mass-produce cheap books. Publishing houses emerged, primarily in New York, Philadelphia, and Boston. They competed vigorously with each other, using the same techniques that other manufacturers used. They offered discounts to booksellers, they advertised in magazines and newspapers, they sent sales agents into the field, and they recruited authors the way manufacturers recruited gifted engineers and designers. Between 1820 and 1850, American book publishers increased their sales from about $2.5 million to $12.5 million—a fivefold increase that was about double the increase in the population.

Responding in part to this revolution in the economics of authorship, American writers, led by Ralph Waldo Emerson, began to create a distinctively American literature. A number of the writers were extraordinarily talented, and their work was as distinguished as any literature being produced anywhere in the world. But the questions they pursued in their writing were uniquely American. They explored with unusual clarity and insight the conflicts that troubled many people, especially the members of the new business class. They produced a literature that was a uniquely American examination of the troubled relationship between society and the individual.

Unitarianism and Transcendentalism

Much of the groundwork for a distinctive American literature was laid within the religious reform movement that established a new Protestant denomination known as Unitarianism. The Unitarians' main strength lay in New England, where wealthy and educated men and women, usually former Congregationalists, founded Unitarian churches in almost every town during the 1820s. Gradually, Unitarians gained control of Harvard's divinity school, the most prestigious training institution for ministers. By the 1840s, Unitarianism had become an unofficial ideology for New England's intellectual elite.

The key doctrine of the Unitarians was suggested by their name. They believed in the "unity" of God—that is, that God was not a trinity of Father, Son, and Holy Spirit. But for the intellectuals who were so important to Unitarianism, this doctrine was only a minor aspect of the movement. They believed that God had not come into the world as Christ to save fallen mankind, because mankind was not so hopelessly fallen as to *need* such a miraculous salvation. Indeed, for William Ellery Channing, whose 1819 sermon on the "Liberal Christian" summarized Unitarian beliefs, mankind's virtue was the beginning of all true religion. Channing rejected the Calvinist idea that all men and women were fatally stained by original sin. He taught instead that in human beings lay "a great nature, the divine image, and vast capacities." It was the work of religion to liberate individuals to use their reason to discover this saving truth for themselves, in ways not confined to scripture and religious dogma.

Within a decade, Unitarianism had become one of the more important religious denominations for New England's social and economic elite. Yet a new generation of young Unitarian ministers almost immediately challenged the mild doctrines of their church and began to call for an even greater liberation of people's creative imaginations. This circle of young men—and a few of their women friends—focused on ideas they borrowed from philosopher Immanuel Kant and from German romanticism, as translated by the English poet Samuel Taylor Coleridge and Harvard professor Edward Everett, who had studied in Germany. These Unitarian radicals believed that behind the world that was available to the senses was another, ideal order of reality. This reality "transcended," or went beyond, the usual ways by which people know the world. This ideal reality could be known only by mysterious intuitive powers through which, at moments of inspiration, people could travel past the limits of their ordinary experience and gain a mystical knowledge of ultimate and eternal things.

Gradually, an intellectual movement called Transcendentalism took shape. The intellectual leader of the transcendentalists was a second-generation Unitarian minister, Ralph Waldo Emerson. Emerson resigned his Boston pulpit in 1832, at the age of twenty-nine, to become a writer and lecturer. His subject was what he called "the infinitude of the private man." Emerson's message, as he elaborated it in increasingly popular talks and essays, was centered on the idea of the radically free individual.

"Our age," Emerson's great complaint ran, "is retrospective." In their inherited institutions and societies, people were trapped just as surely as if they were buried in the "sepulchres of the

RALPH WALDO EMERSON
The threat which Emerson and transcendentalism posed to orthodox religion produced criticism and even ridicule. This cartoon appeared in *Illustrations of the New Philosophy* in 1844. It played upon Emerson's statement in *Nature* (1836): "Standing on the bare ground,—my head bathed by the blithe air, & uplifted into infinite space,—all mean egotism vanishes. I become a transparent Eyeball." (Top, Library of Congress; Bottom, Houghton Library, Harvard University)

fathers." They wore the ideas of people from earlier times as a kind of "faded masquerade." They needed to break free of the boundaries of tradition and custom. This could be done only if each individual discovered his or her own "original relation with Nature." Emerson celebrated individuality, self-reliance, dissent, and nonconformity as the only methods by which a person might become free to discover a private harmony with what he called, in almost mystical fashion, "currents of Universal Being." And for Emerson, the ideal setting for such a discovery was not society and its institutions, but solitude under an open sky, among nature's rocks and trees.

Emerson's genius was his capacity to translate these vague ideas into examples that made sense to ordinary middle-class Americans. His essays and lectures conveyed the idea that all of nature was saturated with the presence of God. For example, Emerson could say that if God was everywhere, then he was present in even the most routine sights of everyday life, a "bare common" or a railroad. Emerson's celebration of the possibilities of human achievement could be translated into a celebration of things that philosophers had traditionally ignored or scorned. He could even celebrate money itself. It was not "the root of all evil." Instead, it "represents the prose of life." It "is in its effects and laws, as beautiful as roses."

Emerson's message reached hundreds of thousands of people, primarily through his lectures. Public lectures were a spectacularly successful new enterprise in the 1820s and 1830s. In 1826, an organization known as the American Lyceum was founded to "promote the general diffusion of knowledge." It organized lecture tours by speakers of all sorts—poets, preachers, scientists, reformers—and soon had taken firm hold, especially in the North. In 1839, 137 local lyceum groups in Massachusetts invited slates of lecturers to their towns during the fall and winter "season" to speak to more than 33,000 subscribers. Of all the hundreds of lecturers on the circuit, Emerson was the most successful. Between 1833 and 1860, he gave fifteen hundred lectures in more than three hundred different towns in twenty states. And he was well rewarded. For seven lectures in Philadelphia in 1854, he was paid more than a thousand dollars—over twice the annual income of an average American family.

The Celebration of the Individual

Emerson's celebration of the liberated individual tapped currents of faith that already ran deep among his middle-class audiences. The publication of the autobiography of Benjamin Franklin in 1818 had given Americans a homely model of an individual determined to reach "moral perfection" by the solitary cultivation of private virtues. Charles Grandison Finney's account of his own conversion experience in 1823 pointed in Emersonian directions, too. Finney pictured his conversion as a mystical union of an individual, alone in the woods, with God.

Emerson's notion that the solitary individual in nature might transcend the constraining boundaries of society, and discover a new self, also had a familiar ring to millions of American readers. America's most successful writers of fiction of the 1820s—Washington Irving and James Fenimore Cooper—developed themes similar to Emerson's in their works. In *The Sketch Book*, Irving painted unforgettable portraits of two characters who became part of American folk culture, Ichabod Crane and Rip Van Winkle. As their stories begin, each of these characters is trapped by social circumstances. Rip is the prisoner of his poor farm, his domineering wife, and family obligations that he feels only as burdens. Ichabod, a poor schoolteacher, longs to marry the buxom and bedimpled Katrina Van Tassel, sell her father's fine farm, and leave for Kentucky. Ichabod and Rip escape into new lives as a result of solitary encounters with mysterious beings that they meet away from civilization. Ichabod meets a ghostly headless Hessian at night in Sleepy Hollow. Rip meets the ghosts of Henry Hudson's crew, who drug him into a twenty-year sleep. As a result of these encounters, Ichabod and Rip transcend their old lives. Ichabod is transformed from a poor village schoolteacher into a lawyer, a politician, a journalist, and a judge. Rip is liberated from wife and farm to do what he loves best—idle around the village spinning yarns.

An equally celebrated fictional character, and as deep a presence in middle-class culture, was the figure of the frontier scout Leatherstocking in the novels of Cooper. Beginning with *The Pioneers* (1823) and *The Last of the Mohicans* (1826) and ending with *The Deerslayer* (1841) Cooper built an enormously popular legend around his

GALLERY OF AMERICAN WRITERS: THOREAU, WHITMAN, POE, HAWTHORNE, LONGFELLOW, MELVILLE

The most popular writer in this gallery was Henry Wadsworth Longfellow (1807–1882), a professor of modern languages and literature at Smith and Harvard Colleges, who won fame for *Evangeline* (1847), *Hiawatha* (1855), *The Courtship of Miles Standish* (1858), and *Tales of a Wayside Inn* (1863–1874). Edgar Allan Poe (1809–1849) originated the detective story genre in America and was an influential literary critic, but he, too, was best known for his poetry, particularly *The Raven* (1845). (Left to right, Concord Free Public Library; The Walt Whitman Birthplace Association; The New-York Historical Society; Culver Pictures; Mathew Brady Studio, National Portrait Gallery, Washington, Meserve Collection; Joseph Oriel Eaton. *Herman Melville.* Houghton Library, Harvard University. Gift of Mrs. Henry K. Metcalf)

hero. The key fact about Leatherstocking—or "Hawkeye," "Natty Bumppo," or "Deerslayer," as he was also known—was his solitude in nature. His moral goodness grew directly out of his "original relation" with nature. He was a radically free individual, at odds with law and custom, comfortable only in the forest, a nearly perfect model of what Emerson considered the cardinal virtues of self-reliance and nonconformity. Cooper meant his hero to represent the nobility, innocence, and strength of frontier Americans. Preoccupied with defending American democracy to Europeans, Cooper struck a responsive chord in American readers.

Emerson did not so much imitate these earlier models as make their tentative suggestions into a systematic program for an American literature. In 1837, he delivered an address at Harvard entitled "The American Scholar." It was intended as a literary declaration of independence from what he called the "courtly muse" of old Europe. He called for a literature that would celebrate democracy and the ideal of individual freedom, that would find its inspiration not in the doings and sayings of aristocratic courts, but in the "familiar, the low . . . the milk in the pan; the bal-

lad in the street; the news of the boat; the glance of the eye; the form and gait of the body." In this spirit, a remarkable group of American writers burst onto the scene in the 1840s and 1850s— Henry David Thoreau, Walt Whitman, Nathaniel Hawthorne, and Herman Melville were among the most important—and explored Emerson's principal concerns, notably individual insight, nature, and the limiting constraints of society.

The writer who worked under Emerson's most direct influence was Henry David Thoreau, who lived near him in Concord, Massachusetts. Thoreau decided to take Emerson's notion of solitude in nature quite literally. He built a cabin at the edge of Walden Pond, near Concord, and lived there from 1845 to 1847. The result was *Walden, Or Life in the Woods* (1854). *Walden* was Thoreau's story of an "experiment" in practical self-reliance. It was also a story of his spiritual quest for meanings that went beyond the traps and artificialities of life in a "civilized" society. On the practical side, Thoreau included his list of accounts, a profit-and-loss statement that recorded his expenditures for a little sugar or a bit of string, and his income from the little surplus production he managed. On the spiritual side, he presented the record of a different kind of "commerce," with what he called the "Celestial Empire." It was this kind of venture in self-discovery, rather than hermitlike subsistence farming, that he was really promoting:

> If one advances confidently in the direction of his dreams, and endeavors to live the life which he had imagined, he will meet with a success unexpected in common hours. He will put some things behind, will pass an invisible boundary; new, universal, and more liberal laws will begin to establish themselves around and within him. . . . If a man does not keep pace with his companions, perhaps it is because he hears a different drummer.

An equally triumphant glorification of the possibilities of the liberated individual was made by another writer who was influenced by Emerson. Walt Whitman said that when he came to Emerson, he had been "simmering, simmering." Then Emerson "brought me to a boil." He had been a journalist, an editor of the *Brooklyn Eagle* and other newspapers. But it was poetry that had been the "direction of his dreams." *The Leaves of Grass*, first published in 1855 and constantly revised and expanded for almost four decades thereafter, was the record of his attempt to pass a number of "invisible boundaries": between solitude and community; between body and spirit; between prose and poetry; even between the living and the dead. It was a wild, exuberant poem in both form and content. It self-consciously violated every poetic rule and every canon of respectable taste, daring readers either to shut the book in revulsion or accept Whitman's idiosyncratic vision whole.

At the center of the *Leaves of Grass* is the figure of the poet, "I, Walt." He begins alone: "I celebrate myself, and sing myself," loafing in nature, "observing a spear of summer grass." But because he has what Emerson calls an "original relation" with nature, the poet claims not solitude, finally, but perfect communion with others: "And what I assume you shall assume,/ For every atom belonging to me as good belongs to you." Democracy was one of Whitman's favorite subjects. He argued militantly that a poet in a democracy could claim a profoundly intimate, mystical relationship with his mass audience.

This intimacy included sex. Emerson was always respectable. Thoreau worried about "an animal in us," a creature "reptile and sensual," that "awakens in proportion as our higher nature slumbers." Whitman would have none of this. If Emerson could make money out to be as beautiful as roses, Whitman would do the same with the human body:

> I sing the body electric.
> The armies of those I love engirth me and I engirth them.
> They will not let me off till I go with them, respond to them,
> And discorrupt them, and charge them full with the charge of the soul.

Emerson tried to persuade Whitman to drop the sections of the *Leaves of Grass* that dealt most explicitly with sex. But Whitman refused, explaining later that "if I had cut sex out I might just as well have cut everything out. . . . It would have been violated at its most sensitive spot."

Whitman took another dangerous step for an artist in the mid-nineteenth century. He condemned organized religion with its "creeds and priests." When democracy has done its work, he predicted in the preface to the *Leaves of Grass*

> There will soon be no more priests. Their work is done. They may wait awhile, perhaps a generation or two, dropping off by degrees. A superior breed shall take their place. A new order shall arise and they shall be the priests of man, and every man shall be his own priest.

For both Emerson and Thoreau, the individual had the spark of divinity. For Whitman, however, the individual had expanded to become divine, and had found Whitman as prophet.

The Limits of Individualism

Emerson, Thoreau, and Whitman were not naively or simple-mindedly optimistic about the cheerful possibilities of experience for liberated individuals. Whitman wrote of human suffering with as much passion as he wrote of everything else. Emerson's joyous accounts of the exhilarations that could come in nature were tinged with anxiety. "I am glad," he said, "to the brink of fear." Thoreau's gloomy judgment of everyday life was that "The mass of men lead lives of quiet desperation." Still, such dark murmurings were muted in their work, woven into their triumphant and expansive assertions that nothing was impossible for a man or woman who was able to break free of the limits of tradition, law, and other social restraints.

The two greatest American novelists of the period, Nathaniel Hawthorne and Herman Melville, addressed the same set of questions about the opposition between individual transcendence and the legitimate requirements of social order, discipline, and responsibility. Their answers were darker than those of Emerson, Thoreau, and Whitman. Hawthorne and Melville dwelt on the vanities, corruption, and excesses of individualism. They issued warnings that unfettered ego could destroy both individuals and their social arrangements.

Hawthorne's most brilliant exploration of the theme of individual transcendence was *The Scarlet Letter* (1850). It concerns two individuals, Hester Prynne and Arthur Dimmesdale, who challenge their seventeenth-century New England community in the most blatant way—by committing adultery, producing a child, and refusing to bend to the community's condemnation. But the result of this assertion of individual freedom against communal discipline is not exaltation at all, but tragedy. Wracked by guilt and unable to confess, Dimmesdale dies in anguish. Hester learns from the experience that a truly virtuous life can be found only by a person who is willing to do good within the social order. She works out a slow and quiet penance by patiently nursing the sick and performing other benevolent services to the community that had condemned and scorned her. As she does this, she gradually embroiders the scarlet "A" she has been forced to wear as a sign of her adultery until it becomes not a mark of sin but a work of art. Hawthorne's message was clear: Hester's real sin was pride; claiming to be a law unto herself led to defeat, pain, and personal disaster.

In *Moby Dick* (1851), Melville explored the same problem in even more extreme and tragic terms. The novel begins as a whaling captain, Ahab, embarks on an obsessive hunt for a white whale, Moby Dick, that severed Ahab's leg in an earlier expedition. Ahab is a version of Emerson's liberated individual with an intuitive grasp of hidden meanings in nature. He believes that the whale is pure, demonic evil. Ahab's form of "self-reliance" is to hunt the whale down, no matter what the cost. In the end, though, the relationship between Ahab and the whale is reversed. The captain becomes the demon, and the whale becomes the hunter.

The relationship between Ahab and the whale is a transcendental one. Ahab claims the power to see past the surface appearances of things, to know intuitively their hidden meaning. And he does this in an extreme moral solitude that separates him from other men. The trouble, as Melville tells the story, is that Ahab can only hunt the whale in a social way. Ahab's ship, the *Pequod*, is an industrial community. In fact, the novel is perhaps the most detailed description of an actual industry, whaling, ever written in the United States or in Britain. Ahab's transcendental adventure subverts the legitimate purposes of the whaling voyage. As a result, not only Ahab but the crew of workers have to die. Only one person, Ishmael, is left to tell the tale.

Moby Dick was a commercial failure. So was *Walden,* and so too was *Leaves of Grass.* The middle-class audience that was the primary target of American publishers was unwilling to follow Melville into the dark, exploring dangers of individualism gone mad. This audience was equally unimpressed by Thoreau's extreme and demanding version of transcendentalism and by Whitman's boundless claims for the mystical union between the man of genius and the democratic mass. What American readers emphatically preferred was the more modest examinations of individualism offered by Emerson and Hawthorne. They seemed to speak of patient, unthreatening kinds of self-improvement, in tones that were congenial to an audience that believed individual achievement could best come through hard work, discipline, and what the Declaration of Independence called "a decent respect to the opinions of mankind."

Perspectives from a "Separate Sphere"

Some writers who developed American themes worked outside the inspiration provided by Emerson. Among them was a group of women novelists. They, too, pondered the balance between individual and social responsibility, but they did so with a concern for the special situation of women. The growth of an American literature and publishing industry coincided with an important redefinition of the role of women in middle-class life. Women formed growing majorities in most religious congregations. Middle-class women were playing increasingly important roles in reform movements. They were marrying later—or not at all. They were having fewer children and employing more servants—two or three times as many servants by the 1860s as they had had at the end of the Revolution. They also constituted a majority of the reading public that bought the magazines and books that poured from American presses. In the 1850s, according to the estimate of *Harper's Magazine,* four out of five readers of books or magazines were women. And, increasingly, women were *writing* those books, editing and filling the pages of magazines with stories and poems.

Much of what women wrote and read was sentimental or superficial—as was much of what men were writing and reading during the period. Yet women's influence on middle-class culture was much greater than even Emerson's, let alone Thoreau's or Melville's. Novels by the leading women writers of the day often sold hundreds of thousands of copies. Catharine Maria Sedgwick gained this kind of enormous popularity in the 1820s; Caroline Howard Gilman and Caroline Lee Hentz in the 1830s; Harriet Beecher Stowe in the 1840s; and Sara Parton, Augusta Evans Wilson, and Susan Warner in the 1850s.

These novelists were interested in a particular aspect of the tension between individual liberation and the demands of society. Their "individual" was a woman, and their "society" was the family. Their stories explored the question of whether liberation for women implied a liberation *from* the constraints of marriage or a fulfillment *within* the family. Their sentimental melodramas, punctuated often by tearful domestic scenes, shared an assumption that had become increasingly popular in America since the 1790s: that women occupied a "separate sphere," with its own morality and its own possibilities.

The dominant message of women's novels, stories, and poems was that women could achieve their potential only within the sphere of marriage and family. For women, as Hentz wrote in *Ernest Linwood* (1856), "In the depth of the heart there is a lower deep, which is never sounded save by the hand that wears the *wedding-ring.*" In her last novel, *Married or Single* (1857), Sedgwick concluded that "God has appointed marriage" for woman; marriage is "the great circumstance" of a woman's life.

For these writers, marriage did not imply a submissive or passive role. In fact, they were claiming a superior status for women within the sphere of family life. Women, they suggested, were finally responsible for forming the character of their husbands and sons. In *Means and Ends* (1839), Sedgwick wrote that "By an unobtrusive and unseen process, are the characters of men formed, at home, by the mother . . . where the moral basis is fixed." Susan Warner, in her novel *Queechy* (1852), creates a romantic male figure, Guy Carleton. He is all that a man—without a woman—can be: "an uncommonly fine example of what nature alone can do for a man." But he is incomplete, because he lacks religion.

HARRIET BEECHER STOWE
Until the 1850s, Harriet Beecher Stowe (1811–1896) devoted most of her energies to the support of her husband and seven children. She was dissatisfied with her roles as housewife and mother but felt guilty when writing diverted her from family life. The reception that greeted *Uncle Tom's Cabin* convinced her that writing could have a powerful moral purpose. She produced thirty more novels, at the rate of nearly one per year. (Culver)

"A character of nature's building is at best a very ragged affair, without religion's finishing hand." What he needs, plainly, is the gentle religious influence of a woman. He is transformed by his bride, whom he describes as "by far the nobler creature—worth many such as I." Saved by his wife, he is able to become truly moral and to devote the rest of his life to helping the poor.

With her abolitionist *Uncle Tom's Cabin* (1852), Harriet Beecher Stowe became the most successful woman novelist of the period. The book was not merely an antislavery novel. It was also an extended discussion of women and the family. Time after time in the story, women and even little girls are shown to be morally more sensitive and superior to the men around them. In Stowe's picture of slave society, it is females who offer the best hope of eventual freedom for blacks and of salvation for both blacks and whites. Home and family held deeply religious meanings for Stowe. In *The Minister's Wooing*

(1859), she wrote that home was the "appointed sphere for woman, more holy than cloister, more saintly and pure than church and altar."

In this body of fiction, women's sphere centered on the home, but it did not end there. Female characters were often shown as active in church and community life, although they had to keep themselves unspotted by the sordid political, military, and economic sphere of men. As Sedgwick put it in *Means and Ends,* it was never "intended that women should lead armies, harangue in halls of legislation, bustle up to the ballot boxes, or sit on judicial tribunals." But if a woman's life could be centered on marriage and the home, then her influence might extend through religious and reform work into society at large. In *The Mother-in-Law* (1851), Sedgwick said that "The peace of families, the social welfare of the whole community" depended on marriage, "the most sacred tie on earth." But in *Married or Single* she made it clear that this "sacred tie" was not an end in itself, but "the central point, whence all the relations of life radiate, and the source of all political and social virtue."

The success of women novelists put an ironic twist on their celebration of the private sphere of marriage and family. These writers were actually engaged in a very public—and commercial—enterprise. They often began their careers writing under assumed names—almost always female names—but they eventually dropped their anonymity. Bargaining vigorously with their publishers, often making their own livings and even supporting their families, they were, in fact, among the first successful professional women in the United States. Their success seemed to support Caroline Lee Hentz's judgment that "Mind, we verily believe, is of no sex."

In a number of women's novels, the problem of the woman of intellect was taken up in ways that echoed Emerson's or Hawthorne's speculations on the relationship between the extraordinary individual and society. One common solution was to present a female character of strength and intelligence, but then to humble that character by making her admit that an active career could not bring "fulfillment" to a woman. In Sara Parton's autobiographical novel *Ruth Hall* (1855), the protagonist is a woman writer trying to support her family. She is forced to admit in the end that there is something unnatural about this. "No happy woman," she warns her daughter, "ever writes." The same strategy was followed by Augusta Evans Wilson in *Beulah* (1859). Again, the central character is an intellectually superior woman. She is humbled in the end by "brain fever." Left alone, finally, with God and her husband, Beulah wonders how she had ever been "so proud of my intellect."

There was an alternative solution to the problem of the talented woman, a solution that reflected the increasing real-life participation of women in religious congregations and reform organizations. If the talented and energetic heroine could find a way to place her unusual abilities to good use, then the contradiction between "domestic" and "public" life was softened. Given such a formula, women writers and their heroines could be seen as female versions of ministers. Stowe told her readers that she would make them feel "as if you had been hearing a sermon." Hentz could speak of her writing career as a legitimate calling, or "vocation . . . for which God has endowed me."

The vision of opportunity for women expressed by these novelists was, in its own way, as optimistic as Emerson's. However, the women's emphasis was on fulfillment through altruism and acceptance of the bonds of traditional marriage. In that sense, their acceptance of social constraints matched that of Hawthorne and Melville. In fact, these novelists went beyond Hawthorne and Melville by suggesting a specific solution to the imbalance between individual and communal responsibility: a reaffirmation of the moral role of women. Sharing the perspectives of the woman novelists, many middle-class women played a major role in attempting to reform both family life and American society at large.

Communal Experiments

Many Americans who were distressed over the difficulties of individual fulfillment within American society withdrew, at least for a time, into utopian communal experiments. These groups had diverse goals, ranging from the establishment of a separate, more rewarding society for like-minded people to the reform of American society as a whole by setting an inspiring example.

Brook Farm

Transcendentalist enthusiasm for individual potential often led to rejection of industrial society. At one time or another, virtually all transcendentalists, even the conservative Emerson, felt that American society could not accommodate their aspirations for individual realization and achievement. Many went further, withdrawing into insular communities. Often they aimed to reform by example; they hoped to uplift society through inspiration.

The most important communal experiment of the transcendentalists was Brook Farm, founded in 1841 by a Unitarian minister, George Ripley, in West Roxbury, Massachusetts. This community sought freedom from the tension and degradation of a competitive society, as well as a harmonious environment for the full development of mind and soul. Ripley explained that he "wished to prepare a society of liberal, intelligent and cultivated persons, whose relations with each other would permit a more wholesome and simple life than can be led amidst the pressure of our competitive institutions."

The intellectual life at Brook Farm was electric. Hawthorne lived there for a time. All of the major transcendentalists, including Emerson and Margaret Fuller, the editor of the foremost transcendentalist journal, the *Dial*, were residents or frequent visitors. One member recalled that the transcendentalists "inspired the young with a passion for study, and the middle-aged with deference and admiration, while we all breathed the intellectual grace that pervaded the atmosphere." Music, dancing, games, plays, parties, picnics, and dramatic readings filled leisure hours. Emerson wrote that Brook Farm meant "education" to most of its residents. It was, he said, "to many the most important period of their life . . . a French Revolution in small."

Brook Farm may have represented some moral progress, but it did not provide economic self-sufficiency. Many of its members in the initial years were ministers, teachers, writers, students. Relatively few families lived at Brook Farm; Ripley's message appealed mostly to young, single men and women who came from well-to-do Boston families, who were Unitarians, and who sought alternatives to careers devoted to the acquisition of wealth. There were few

COMMUNAL EXPERIMENT AT BISHOP HILL
This picture from Bishop Hill, a commune founded by a sect of Swedish pietists in Illinois in 1848, indicates that women as well as men toiled in the fields, and suggests that work there was highly organized. But the younger members of Bishop Hill were unwilling to accept community discipline, and the community dissolved in 1862. (Bishop Hill Historic Site/Illinois Historic Preservation Agency)

farmers or artisans. And, until 1844, Ripley and his individualistic followers paid little attention to the need for the efficient organization of their farming and crafts.

In 1844, however, the Brook Farmers adopted a constitution embracing the ideas of a contemporary French utopian, Charles Fourier, who envisioned cooperative work and living units ("phalanxes") in which those who labored would receive the largest portion of a community's earnings. Fourier's utopian vision stimulated educated farmers and craftsmen to start nearly 100 cooperative communities from Massachusetts to Michigan. Virtually all were short-lived; the reorganized Brook Farm was no exception.

Under their constitution, the Brook Farmers attracted some artisans and farmers. They organized themselves in a more disciplined fashion, particularly in organizing housekeeping to free women to produce handicrafts. However, the community made only marginal economic gains and did so at the cost of a factory-like regimentation that depressed many of the original members. One of the residents wrote that "the joyous spirit of youth was sobered." Finally, after a devastating fire in 1846, the organizers disbanded and sold the farm.

Brook Farm's failure demonstrated that communal experiments had to establish a high degree of group discipline in order to survive. Among the many such experiments undertaken during the Industrial Revolution, only a few provided as much latitude to individual members as did those of the transcendentalists. The other communal groups were typically motivated by religious doctrines that emphasized the necessity for constraining the individual in order to limit the opportunity for sin. And they usually attracted individuals of lesser property and standing—people with less to lose in submission to the group—than those who joined Brook Farm.

The Shakers

One of the experiments that put the strongest emphasis on regulating the sinful behavior of individuals was that of the Shakers. The Shakers first organized a church in America in 1787, following the death of Ann Lee Stanley, an English immigrant whom they believed to be the incarnation of Christ and thus the Second Coming. Her "testimony against the lustful gratifications of the flesh as the source and foundation of human corruption" led the Shakers to conclude that they must withdraw from the world in order to follow Christ. Beginning in New Lebanon, New York, the Shakers founded twenty communities, mostly in New England, New York, and Ohio. During the 1820s they entered their most vigorous period of community formation, and

during the 1830s they attracted more than three thousand converts. Shakers embraced the common ownership of property, accepted the government of the church, and pledged themselves to celibacy and to abstinence from alcohol, tobacco, politics, and war. Applicants had to declare themselves "sick of sin" and undertake a program of systematic confession that could last for years. To the Shakers, sin was wholly the product of a society that impeded a chaste and self-denying life.

The Shakers' beliefs that God was "a dual person, male and female" and that Ann Lee Stanley represented God's female element provided the underpinning for their attempt to banish distinctions between the sexes. In practice, they maintained a traditional division of labor between men and women, but they vested the authority for governing each community, in both

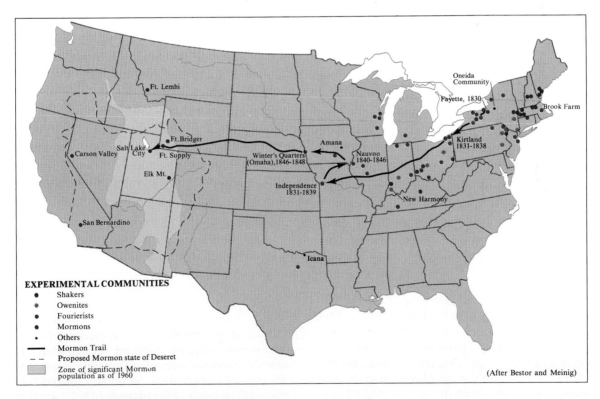

MAP 13.1 COMMUNAL EXPERIMENTS BEFORE 1860
Some experimental communities sought out frontier locations, but the vast majority simply looked for secluded areas in well-settled regions. The avoidance of the South by these groups is striking. The most successful experimenters by far were the Mormons, who ultimately sought extreme isolation and built an agrarian empire in Utah. Their proposed state of Deseret materialized to some extent—in the form of a large area of the United States where Mormon culture became influential.

its religious and economic spheres, in women and men alike; the Shaker communities commonly had twice as many women as men.

New members flowed steadily into the Shaker communities. They were drawn by the highly structured community life, by an opportunity to escape from the flux and stress of American life through the submersion of individual identity, by the chance offered to women for participation in community leadership, and by the economic success of the communities. Shaker agriculture and crafts, especially furniture making, acquired a reputation for quality that enabled most of the communities to become self-sustaining and even very comfortable. However, during the 1840s and 1850s the communities stopped growing, and some began to decline. Because they required celibacy, they had to rely on converts to replace those who died or returned to society. During the late nineteenth century almost all of the communities disappeared, although a few did survive into the twentieth century.

The Oneida Community

The Oneida Community fell somewhere between the transcendentalist and the Shaker communities. John Humphrey Noyes founded this community in his hometown of Putney, Vermont, in 1836. In 1848, he and his followers moved to Oneida, New York; Noyes left Putney under the threat of prosecution after he imposed the doctrine of "complex marriage," which meant that all the members of his community were married to each other. Like the Shakers, Noyes was attempting to gain community control over sexuality. His solution was love, usually expressed in sex without orgasm, between successive partners, with childbearing strictly regulated by the community. Closely related objectives were to free women from being regarded as the property of husbands and to free children, who were raised in community nurseries, from being regarded as the property of their parents. Of all the communities organized along socialist lines, Oneida presented the most radical alternative to traditional marriage and family life.

By the mid-1850s more than two hundred people lived in the Oneida Community, but it remained financially insecure. Fortunately, the inventor of what proved to be a highly success-

ful steel trap then joined. With the profits from the production of traps, the community diversified into the production of other products, notably silverware called Community Plate. Its quality provided the basis for an economic success that continued after 1879, when Noyes fled to Canada to avoid prosecution for adultery and the community abandoned complex marriage. In 1881, its members founded a joint-stock company, the Oneida Community, Ltd., which survived into the twentieth century.

The Mormon Experience

The most successful of all the insular experiments, in terms both of attracting followers and in protecting itself from the surrounding society, was that of the Mormons, the Church of Jesus Christ of Latter Day Saints.

Joseph Smith, the founder of the Mormon Church, was a vigorous, powerful individual. Born in Vermont in 1805, he moved at the age of ten with his rather poor farming and shopkeeping family to Palmyra, in western New York. His education was rudimentary, but, with his mother, he heard innumerable sermons and read the Bible constantly. In a series of religious experiences that began in 1820, Smith came to believe that God had singled him out for a special, immediate, and private revelation of divine truth. Smith felt that God had called him to be a prophet with a message for redeeming a sinful society fatally flawed by excessive individualism. Ultimately, he chose to stand apart from that society.

In 1830, Smith published his revelations as *The Book of Mormon*, which he claimed he had translated from ancient hieroglyphics on gold plates shown to him by an angel named Moroni. In the same year he organized a church. Smith's theology and leadership of his church addressed the growing tension between the claims of the individual—claims that his own career as prophet typified—and the need for social order. He offered a solution: a church that would assert control over all aspects of life. Smith encouraged people to adopt many of the patterns of behavior that were central to the Industrial Revolution—hard work, saving, and risk taking. At the same time, however, he imposed a communal framework that concentrated power in the church elders.

The success of Smith's message was phenom-

A MORMON MAN AND HIS WIVES
Mormon families, such as this one pictured during the late 1840s, achieved a degree of prosperity
that was unusual for pioneer farm families partly because of the labor of multiple wives. This
homesteader's cabin, although cramped for such a large family, is well built, with a brick chimney
and a luxury for any pioneer home—a glass window. (Culver)

enal. He began with a small congregation in western New York. By the early 1840s, he had attracted as many as thirty thousand followers to a new Mormon community in Nauvoo, Illinois. Smith's growing community was continually moving from state to state, seeking a refuge for its disciplined life. The Mormons found that they could prosper only in isolation. The demands of their order, their hostility to other sects, and their success in attracting converts provoked the resentment of their neighbors wherever they lived.

At Nauvoo, tensions heightened. Smith refused to abide by any Illinois law that he did not approve personally. He then had a new revelation, one that encouraged polygamy—the practice of taking more than one wife at the same time. This was typical of Smith's innovations: a radical reform designed to preserve a traditional institution—marriage. It also angered a large minority of the Mormon community. Internal dissension, violence, and outside intervention ensued, and Smith was arrested. In 1844, an anti-Mormon mob, led by members of the Illinois militia, stormed the Carthage jail, where Smith and his brother were being held, and murdered them both.

Now led by Brigham Young, an early convert of Smith's, the Mormon elders resolved that they could ensure their independence only by leaving the United States and seeking a home in the wilderness. In 1846, leaving the antipolygamy minority behind, Young began a phased migration of more than ten thousand people across the Great Plains. They reached Great Salt Lake, in what was still Mexican territory. Within a decade, Young and his theocracy transformed the desert landscape by building elaborate irrigation systems. The Mormons used communal labor and developed innovative principles of communal water rights that the federal government and all the states of the semiarid West later adopted. With these systems, the Mormons quickly spread planned agricultural communities along the base of the Wasatch Range, in present-day Utah.

During the 1850s, the Mormons faced challenges to their isolation, but none of these disrupted their society. Many of the westward migrants made detours from the Oregon and

California trails to purchase supplies from Mormon farmers, but this only contributed to Mormon prosperity. Potentially more serious was the effort of the federal government to assert authority over Utah. Congress rejected a Mormon petition to create a new state, Deseret, stretching all the way to Los Angeles and San Diego. Then, in 1850, Congress set up the Utah Territory with Young as territorial governor. In 1857–1858, Democratic President James Buchanan intervened, submitting to pressure from Protestant clergy, from concerned federal officials in Utah, and from his Republican challengers. He removed Young from the governorship and sent a small army to Salt Lake City. The "Mormon War," however, proved bloodless. Buchanan decided to negotiate, fearing that an attack on the "domestic institution" of polygamy might be used as a precedent to justify attacks on another "domestic institution," slavery. Ultimately, he withdrew the troops and accepted his failure to establish federal control in Utah.

Republicans were more eager than Buchanan and the Democrats to wipe out polygamy. In their 1856 platform they referred to polygamy and slavery as "relics of barbarism." But the administration of Abraham Lincoln became too absorbed in the Civil War to pay much attention to Utah. Consequently, the Mormons found themselves free to build their community, and Young ruled the territory through figurehead governors until his death in 1877. The Mormons did not formally abolish polygamy until 1890, six years before Utah became a state. They had succeeded where other social experiments and utopian communities had failed. They had devised the ideological and physical means to make their communal experiment prosper and expand.

The Antislavery Movement

Most Americans who sought to change society did not join experimental communal groups. They remained actively engaged in their communities and worked to reform American life through moral appeals and the restructuring of existing institutions. Their celebration of individual potential finally led these reformers to focus their energies on the need for the liberation of slaves.

By 1820, opposition to slavery—influenced by republican ideology and British antislavery advocates such as William Wilberforce—had already accomplished a good deal. Congress had outlawed the international slave trade in 1808 (the earliest date permitted by the Constitution). Most northern states had already abolished slavery. And the Missouri Compromise had prohibited slavery in most of the Louisiana Purchase. During the 1820s and 1830s, the most vocal opponents of slavery wanted to go much further. Three different approaches competed between 1820 and 1840: (1) gradual emancipation of the nation's slaves—1.5 million in 1820—and return of the freed slaves to Africa, with compensation paid to their former owners; (2) emancipation through slave flight or rebellion; and (3) emancipation through direct appeals to the conscience of slaveowners.

African Colonization

Proponents of compensated emancipation and African colonization founded the American Colonization Society in 1817. This society was led by prominent representatives of the upper South and the border states who wanted to eradicate slavery in order to promote economic and social development along northern lines. However, those supporters of colonization who were from New England and New York had a different emphasis. They wanted primarily to remove free blacks from the North.

Northern colonizationists regarded the North's 250,000 free blacks as "notoriously ignorant, degraded and miserable, mentally diseased, brokenspirited, acted upon by no motive to honourable exertions, scarcely reached in their debasement by the heavenly light," in the words of the American Colonization's Society 1829 report. Colonizationists often played key roles in maintaining the disenfranchisement and segregation of free blacks. By 1860, only five northern states (Maine, Massachusetts, New Hampshire, Rhode Island, and Vermont, which contained only 6 percent of the northern black population) had extended suffrage to all adult male blacks. New York imposed special property and residence requirements on black voters. Connecticut, New Jersey, and Pennsylvania denied the blacks' right to vote, as did every southern state.

DAVID WALKER'S APPEAL TO FREE BLACKS

Men of colour, who are also of sense, for you particularly is my APPEAL designed. . . . Look into our freedom and happiness, and see of what kind they are composed!! They are of the very lowest kind—they are the very *dregs*!—they are the most servile and abject kind, that ever a people was in possession of! If any of you wish to know how FREE you are, let one of you start and go through the southern and western States of this country, and unless you travel as a slave to a white man (a servant is a *slave* to the man whom he serves) or have your free papers (which if you are not careful they will get from you) if they do not take you up and put you in jail, and if you cannot give good evidence of your freedom, sell you into eternal slavery, I am not a living man. . . . we are so subjected under the whites, that we cannot obtain the comforts of life, but by cleaning their boots and shoes, old clothes, waiting on them, shaving them &c . . . Understand me, brethren, I do not mean to speak against the occupations by which we acquire enough and sometimes scarcely that, to render ourselves and families comfortable through life, I am subjected to the same inconvenience, as you all.—My objections are, to our *glorying* and being *happy* in such low employments. . . . your full glory and happiness, as well as all other coloured people under Heaven, shall never be fully consummated, but with the *entire emancipation of your enslaved brethren all over the world*. . . .

There is great work for you to do. . . . You have to prove to the Americans and the world, that we are MEN, and not *brutes*. . . .

Southern supporters of colonization likewise believed that blacks lacked the capacity to succeed in American society. Colonization, they thought, was necessary to prevent a destructive war between whites and blacks, who accounted for almost 40 percent of the southern population in 1820. Kentuckian Henry Clay, a supporter of the movement, wanted full emancipation but declared that emancipation without colonization "would be followed by instantaneous collisions between the two races, which would break out into a civil war that would end in the extermination or subjugation of the one race or the other." By 1830 the American Colonization Society, with money raised from individuals, state governments, and churches, had transported 1,400 blacks to a colony in Liberia, on the west coast of Africa. However, of these, only 200 had been emancipated as a consequence of the efforts of the society.

A Radical Approach

Most free blacks rejected colonization. In 1817, a meeting of three thousand free blacks in Philadelphia's Bethel Church informed "the humane and benevolent inhabitants of the city" that "we have no wish to separate from our present homes for any purpose whatever." They explained that they were "contented with our present situation and condition" and wanted only "the use of those opportunities . . . which the Constitution and the laws allow to all." At conventions and in pamphlets and newspapers, free blacks throughout the North seconded these sentiments and also called for an end to slavery. In 1827, two free blacks, John Russwurm and Samuel E. Cornish, began the first black newspaper, *Freedom's Journal*. The Boston agent for *Freedom's Journal* was David Walker, a free black from North Carolina who made a living selling second-hand clothes. In 1829, he published a vigorous pamphlet *Appeal . . . to the Colored Citizens*, which ridiculed the religious pretensions of slaveholders, justified slave rebellion, and warned that the slaves would revolt if justice were delayed. To white Americans he said, "We must and shall be free . . . in spite of you . . . And woe, woe, will be it to you if we have to obtain our freedom by fighting." He added: "I do declare that one good black man can put to death six white men." Within a year Walker's *Appeal* had gone through three printings and reached free blacks in the South. In 1830, Walker and other black abolitionists called a national convention in Philadelphia. Walker died under mysterious circumstances later that year, but the convention became an annual event. The delegates never adopted a position as radical as Walker's, but they regularly condemned slavery, colonization, and northern discriminatory legislation. They also urged free blacks to use every legal means to improve the condition of their race and asked for divine assistance in breaking "the shackles of slavery."

In 1831, the violence that David Walker had contemplated took concrete form when Nat Turner, a slave in Southampton County, Virginia, staged a bloody revolt. Turner had taught himself how to read as a child and had hoped to be emancipated, but a new master forced him into field work and another master separated him from his wife. Turner became deeply spiritual, seeing visions and concluding that he might carry Christ's burden of suffering in a race war. Taking an eclipse of the sun as an omen, Turner plotted with a handful of relatives and close friends to meet the masters' terror with terror of their own. They killed almost sixty slaveowners and members of their families, often dismembering and decapitating them. Turner had hoped that an army of slaves would join his liberation force, but he had mustered only sixty men by the time white militia formed to protect two large plantations and dispersed Turner's poorly armed and exhausted followers. In retaliation, whites killed blacks at random all over the county. One company of cavalry killed forty blacks in two days, putting the heads of fifteen on poles to warn "all those who should undertake a similar plot." Fifty slaves were tried formally, and twenty of these were hanged. After hiding for nearly two months, Turner too was captured and hanged, still identifying his mission with that of Christ.

Evangelical Abolitionism, to 1840

The threat of bloody revolution, coupled with the inspiring example of free blacks who sought to eradicate slavery, had a profound effect on some young white opponents of slavery. Many were evangelical ministers and their supporters. They became evangelists against slavery, appealing to the Christian conscience of individual

slaveowners for immediate emancipation. Gradual change or compromise had no place in this new campaign. The issue was absolute: slaveowners and their supporters were sinning by depriving slaves of their God-given status as free moral agents. If the slaveowners did not repent, the evangelical abolitionists believed, they inevitably faced the prospect of revolution in this world and damnation in the next.

The two most influential leaders of the antislavery movement of the 1830s were William Lloyd Garrison and Theodore Dwight Weld. Garrison was an early antislavery advocate and was less influenced by the evangelical revivals than were Weld and other white abolitionists. A Massachusetts-born printer, Garrison had collaborated in Baltimore during the 1820s with a Quaker, Benjamin Lundy, who published the *Genius of Universal Emancipation,* the leading antislavery newspaper of the decade. In 1830, Garrison went to jail, convicted of libeling a New England merchant engaged in the domestic slave trade. After seven weeks, through Lundy's intervention, Arthur Tappan, a wealthy New

WILLIAM LLOYD GARRISON
This picture captures the moral intensity that Garrison displayed in 1854 when he publicly burned the Constitution and declared: "So perish all compromises with tyranny." His self-righteous defiance of proslavery laws was part of a passionate quest to destroy all institutions that prevented individuals from discovering their full potential. (Culver)

York merchant, paid the fine necessary to release Garrison, enabling him to found his own antislavery weekly, *The Liberator*, in Boston in 1831. In the following year he spearheaded the formation of the New England Antislavery Society.

From the outset, *The Liberator* deplored gradual or compensated emancipation and demanded immediate abolition of slavery, without any reimbursement for slaveholders. Garrison condemned the American Colonization Society, charging that it was a group whose real aim was to strengthen slavery by removing troublesome blacks who were already free. He even attacked the Constitution for its recognition of slavery. It was, he pronounced, "a covenant with death, an agreement with Hell." Nothing was safe from Garrison's criticism. He denounced ministers and even the authenticity of Scripture itself whenever he felt slavery was sanctioned. Increasingly, Garrison concluded that slavery was a sign of deep corruption infesting *all* institutions, and called for comprehensive reform of American society as a whole.

Garrison attracted many avid followers, and to them he became a cultural hero on the scale of Ralph Waldo Emerson, Joseph Smith, or Charles Grandison Finney. Like these men, he made thundering assertions of his own identity. In the first number of *The Liberator*, he declared: "I *will* be harsh as truth and as uncompromising as justice. . . . I am in earnest—I will not equivocate—I will not excuse—I will not retreat a single inch—AND I WILL BE HEARD."

Theodore Dwight Weld, an active participant in the religious revivals of the 1830s, was a more restrained abolitionist. The son of a Congregationalist minister, Weld joined the ministry and made a commitment to reform after hearing Charles Grandison Finney preach in Utica, New York. Working within the churches of New York and the Northwest, he shifted his focus from temperance and educational reforms to abolitionism. In these churches, primarily Presbyterian and Congregationalist, Weld preached the moral responsibility of all Americans for the denial of liberty to the slaves. In 1834, Weld inspired a group of students at Lane Theological Seminary in Cincinnati to form an antislavery society. When Lane's president, Lyman Beecher, sought to repress the society, the "Lane rebels" left, enrolling at Oberlin College and joining Weld in

his evangelism. Weld's crusade gathered force, buttressed by theological arguments he advanced in *The Bible Against Slavery* (1837). Working closely with him were two abolitionists, Angelina Grimké, whom he married in 1838, and her sister, Sarah. They had left their father's South Carolina plantation, converted to Quakerism and abolitionism in Philadelphia, and had become antislavery lecturers.

With the assistance of the Grimké sisters, Weld provided the antislavery movement with a new base of evidence in a massive book, *American Slavery As It Is: Testimony of a Thousand Witnesses* (1839). Weld addressed the reader "as a juror to try a plain case and bring in an honest verdict." The question he posed was: "What is the actual condition of the slaves in the United States?" In answering, Weld presented evidence from southerners themselves, some of it from the more than twenty thousand editions of southern newspapers he had searched. Among the firsthand accounts were those of Angelina Grimké, who recalled her childhood in Charleston. She told, for example, of a treadmill that Charleston slave-owners used for punishment and of a prominent white woman who sent slaves there regularly: "One poor girl, whom she sent there to be flogged, and who was accordingly stripped *naked* and whipped, showed me the deep gashes on her back—I might have laid my whole finger in them—*large pieces of flesh had actually been cut out by the torturing lash.*" The book sold more than a hundred thousand copies during its first year alone. In 1833 Weld and Garrison joined forces to establish the American Antislavery Society. Funded by Arthur and Lewis Tappan, this organization aimed to reach the middle-class public.

The abolitionists used two approaches, one that addressed the public, and another aimed at politicians. First, they sought to create a moral climate so intense that slaveowners would have to accept programs of abolition. They used the tactics of the religious revivalists: public meetings led by stirring speakers, small gatherings sponsored by local antislavery chapters and their women's auxiliaries, and home visits by agents of the movement. The abolitionists also used new techniques of mass communication. Garrison's radical individualism did not stand in the way of attempts to reach a mass market.

Assisted by the new steam press, the American Antislavery Society was able to distribute more than 100,000 pieces of literature in 1834 and more than a million in 1835. Most dramatic was the "great postal campaign," begun in 1835, which flooded the nation, including the South, with abolitionist pamphlets. In July 1835 alone, abolitionists mailed more than 175,000 items through the New York City post office.

The abolitionists' second broad strategy was to mobilize public pressure on legislative bodies—in particular, on Congress. They wished to force the government to confront slavery. In 1835 the American Antislavery Society encouraged local chapters and members to bombard Congress with petitions for specific action: the abolition of slavery in the District of Columbia, abolition of the domestic slave trade, removal of the "three-fifths compromise" from the Constitution, and the denial of admission of new slave states to the Union. In 1836 alone more than thirty thousand such petitions reached Congress. By 1838, a total of nearly five hundred thousand signed petitions had arrived in Washington.

These activities drew increasing numbers of middle-class men and women to abolitionism. During the 1830s, local abolitionist societies grew swiftly, from about two hundred in 1835 to more than five hundred in 1836 and to nearly two thousand by 1840. Almost two hundred thousand people joined them. Meanwhile, the leadership of the movement broadened beyond the original core of free blacks, Quakers, and evangelical Christians. Some of the transcendentalists, for example, were moved by the stark contrast between their claims for individual potential and the reality of slavery. Thanks to their literary skills and, in some instances, their wealth, many became leaders of the movement in New England.

Women contributed in a crucial way. One of the first abolitionists was a black woman, Maria W. Stewart, who spoke out in Boston during the early 1830s. As the movement grew, thousands of women throughout the North followed her example. They condemned the immorality of slavery; they delivered lectures to audiences of both men and women; they supplied more than half of the signatures on the petitions that the American Antislavery Society sent to Congress; and they conducted home "visitations" to win converts among other women and their husbands. They also established their own abolitionist organizations, including the Philadelphia Female Antislavery Society, founded by Lucretia Mott in 1833; the Boston Female Antislavery Society, founded by Maria Weston Chapman and twelve other women; and the Antislavery Conventions of American Women, formed by a network of local societies during the late 1830s. The women's societies raised money for *The Liberator* and the American Antislavery Society, supported agents and speakers against slavery, distributed literature, and established schools for free blacks.

By the late 1830s abolitionism had mobilized and merged the reform ideas and energies of both religious revivalism and transcendentalism. What remained uncertain was the ability of the movement to develop practical strategies that would actually succeed in eradicating slavery.

Hostility to Abolitionism

In the South the conjunction of Nat Turner's rebellion and the beginnings of Garrison's *Liberator* touched off an intense effort to defend slavery. In 1831–1832, after Turner's rebellion, the Virginia legislature considered but rejected, by a vote of 73 to 58, gradual emancipation and colonization. This effectively ended discussion of the end of slavery in the South. Instead, in the 1830s, the southern states toughened their slave codes, the laws governing the behavior and treatment of slaves. They limited the movement of slaves and prohibited teaching slaves to read to prevent them from absorbing abolitionist literature. Southern legislatures banned abolitionism and passed resolutions demanding that northern states follow suit. The Georgia legislature even offered a $5,000 reward to anyone who would kidnap Garrison and bring him to the South to be tried for inciting rebellion. Public meetings routinely offered rewards for the capture of anyone distributing abolitionist literature. In Nashville, vigilantes whipped a northern college student for distributing abolitionist pamphlets. In Charleston, in 1835, a mob attacked the post office and destroyed sacks of abolitionist mail from the North. After that, southern postmasters generally refused to deliver mail of suspected abolitionist origins.

At the same time, southern leaders began to

JOHN C. CALHOUN DEFENDS SLAVERY

To maintain the existing relations between the two races. . . . is indispensable to the peace and happiness of both. It cannot be subverted without drenching the country in blood, and extirpating one or other of the races. Be it good or bad, it has grown up with our society and institutions, and is so interwoven with them, that to destroy it would be to destroy us as a people. But let me not be understood as admitting, even by implication, that the existing relations between the two races in the slaveholding States is an evil:—far otherwise; I hold it to be a good. . . . Never before has the black race of Central Africa, from the dawn of history to the present day, attained a condition so civilized and so improved, not only physically, but morally and intellectually. It came among us in a low, degraded, and savage condition, and in the course of a few generations it has grown up under the fostering care of our institutions,

reviled as they have been, to its present comparatively civilized condition.

. . . I may say with truth, that in few countries is so much left to the share of the laborer, and so little exacted from him, or where there is more kind attention paid to him in sickness or infirmities of age. Compare his condition with the tenants of the poor houses in the more civilized portions of Europe—look at the sick, and the old and infirm slave, on one hand, in the midst of his family and friends, under the kind superintending care of his master and mistress, and compare it with the forlorn and wretched condition of the pauper in the poor house. . . . I fearlessly assert that the existing relation between the two races in the South . . . forms the most solid and durable foundation on which to rear free and stable political institutions. . . . There is and always has been in an advanced stage of wealth and civilization, a

conflict between labor and capital. The condition of society in the South exempts us from the disorders and dangers resulting from this conflict; and which explains why it is that the political condition of the slaveholding states has been so much more stable and quiet than that of the North. . . . the experience of the next generation will fully test how vastly more favorable our condition of society is to that of other sections for free and stable institutions, provided we are not disturbed by the interference of others, or shall have sufficient intelligence and spirit to resist promptly and successfully such interference.

. . . One thing alarms me—the eager pursuit of gain which overspreads the land, and which absorbs every faculty of the mind and every feeling of the heart. Of all passions avarice is most blind and compromising.

---

develop a new intellectual defense of slavery. They argued that slavery provided the slave with protections against the evils of the industrial system; it promoted "harmony" in relations between the races; it provided for a more efficient, orderly labor supply than was available in the North; and it had a basis in Scripture. This last argument was particularly crucial to southerners who needed a rationalization for enslaving other Christians. Defenders of slavery, such as Thornton Stringfellow, a Baptist minister from Virginia, claimed that Saint Paul had recognized Christian churches that contained both masters and "servants." And Stringfellow cited Saint Paul's injunction: "Servants, obey your masters."

In this sharpening self-image of plantation society, only an exceptional person—the planter—deserved genuine freedom. He was seen as

surrounded by people who were incompetent and incapable of freedom. His task was to achieve a "disinterested benevolence" so that he could lead and manage. Only his exceptional willpower, reason, and self-control made society and order possible. Indeed, southern leaders, such as John C. Calhoun, advised the northern business elite that it could hold northern society together only by asserting the power that flowed from their own "natural superiority." Calhoun wanted northern business leaders to think and act more like planters.

The southern arguments won considerable support in the North. Some wealthy northerners sympathized with the South's appeal for unity among social elites. Traditional elites, and many members of the emerging business class, were troubled by the tactics of the abolitionists, who seemed to threaten the stability of the family by encouraging the active participation of women in the movement. Economic self-interest also provoked hostility to abolitionism. For example, some wealthy New York merchants and New England textile producers found reasons to support the arguments of their southern customers or suppliers. And, to some wage earners, abolitionism seemed to promise increased competition in northern labor markets from free blacks. Finally, only a small minority of any class of northerners believed in black equality; the rest were sympathetic to the racism of the planters. Within the North, the threats posed by abolitionism seemed particularly severe in the communities of the Ohio Valley, which southerners had founded and peopled, where fear of free blacks was especially intense, and where resentment of the extreme tone of the abolitionists' message ran high.

Some northern opponents of the abolitionists were as violent as those in the South. Mobs, sometimes led by people whom the abolitionists described as "gentlemen of property and standing," intimidated free blacks and abolitionists. They disrupted abolitionist meetings and routinely destroyed abolitionist printing presses. In 1833, fifteen hundred New Yorkers, the first antiabolitionist mob, stormed a church in a search for William Lloyd Garrison and Arthur Tappan. The next year, prominent New Yorkers cheered a mob of casual laborers who vandalized and set fire to Lewis Tappan's house, and a white mob swept through Philadelphia's black neighborhoods, clubbing and stoning residents, destroying homes and churches, and forcing hundreds to leave the city. In 1835, in Utica, New York, lawyers, local politicians, merchants, and bankers broke up an abolitionist convention and beat up several of the delegates. A mob burned the Philadelphia abolitionists' "temple of liberty" and started a bloody race riot. When Prudence Crandall undertook to admit black girls to her private school in Connecticut, local citizens had her arrested and threw filth in her well, forcing her to close the school. In 1835 a Boston mob dragged Garrision through the streets, threatening to hang him. In 1837, in Alton, Illinois, a mob shot and killed an abolitionist editor, Elijah P. Lovejoy.

President Andrew Jackson, swayed by these demonstrations of northern hostility to the abolitionists, privately approved South Carolina's censorship of the United States mails. Publicly, in his 1835 annual message to Congress, he called on northern states to suppress abolitionism, and he asked Congress to deny the use of the mails to abolitionist groups. Congress adopted the "gag rule" in 1836. Under it, antislavery petitions went unread. In the same year, Connecticut passed a "gag law" in an attempt to suppress abolitionist speakers, but no other northern state followed suit.

The violence and suppression surprised antislavery advocates and shocked many people who had not participated in abolitionism but had joined evangelical revivals. The disorder, destruction of property, and killing seemed additional symptoms of a society in need of order and cohesion. They redoubled their efforts to find the means for social harmony. Many, like Abraham Lincoln, reached the conclusion that Andrew Jackson had encouraged anarchy by promoting excessive individualism. In response, they worked to build the Whig party. Other abolitionists focused their efforts more specifically on slavery as a political question.

Antislavery After 1840: The Rise of Free-Soil

As assaults on the antislavery movement mounted, most abolitionists dissociated themselves from Garrison's broad attack on American institutions and searched for a new approach. These abolitionists were evangelical Christians, and, because they had been primarily responsible for managing the postal and petition campaigns of the 1830s, they were experienced in practical politics. They wished to attract Americans who neither supported nor opposed abolitionism, and to propose practical political solutions. They were no less radical than Garrison in terms of their commitment to abolitionism, but they were more willing to work within the existing political system.

Garrison and his supporters, however, became even more adamant that the American Antislavery Society retain a broad platform, which included equal participation for women in the society, pacifism, abolition of prisons and asylums, and, in 1843, expulsion of the slave states from the Union. The attacks on abolitionists had, in fact, made the Garrisonians even more radical. In 1837, Garrison came under the influence of John Humphrey Noyes and began to emphasize even more strongly his belief that institutions, rather than individuals, were the source of all sin and that virtually all American institutions were corrupt. Garrison gained support for his position even among some clergymen. Henry C. Wright, an evangelical Congregationalist minister with a background in reform movement, abandoned preaching to work with Garrison and declared that he was proud to be among the "poor, despised, obscure, untitled laymen" rather than among the pretentious clergy. As the violence grew, Wright wrote, "Eggs & Brick bats have done us more good than soft words of flattery."

This growing rift in the abolitionist movement fractured the American Antislavery Society in 1840. Most abolitionists left it to join the American and Foreign Anti-Slavery Society, with its leadership in New York and its major financial backing from Lewis Tappan. Others—such as Theodore Weld, who had left the organized movement along with the Grimkés in 1838—avoided both camps. Weld sought to avoid factional disputes within the movement and, in any case, found both camps lacking. He disliked Garrison's dilution of abolitionism in a broad-based reform effort but found distasteful what he described as the "anti-woman" attitude of the more conservative abolitionists.

In 1840 most of the abolitionists who had split with Garrison began to emphasize electoral politics as a means to eliminate slavery. They established the Liberty party and nominated Kentuckian James G. Birney, whom Weld had converted to abolitionism, as its presidential candidate in 1840 and 1844. The founders of this party decided to reduce the intensity of the moral demands placed on northern audiences and to de-emphasize the moral and political rights of slaves. They recast abolitionism in terms of republican ideals, defining the problem of slavery not as individual sin but as a threat to republican institutions. Thus, the Liberty party's platform charged that there was a tyrannical "Slave Power" conspiracy composed of southern planters and those northern businesspeople who depended on them. The conspiracy was said to draw its strength from an absolute control over human beings, which endangered the republic. The Liberty party founders pointed to Congres-

sional passage of the "gag rule" as evidence of this elite conspiracy. They warned that the "Slave Power" imperiled the rights of free speech, free assembly, and the free press, in the North as well as in the South.

The Liberty party did not campaign for outright abolition. It stood for a new program: "free-soil," meaning the prohibition of slavery in the western territories. The West, thought to be the key to the future of the republic, was to be kept pure of slavery and secure for freedom. The supporters of free-soil retained their enthusiasm for individual freedom, but they now expressed a greater interest in the freedom of whites occupying new lands than in freedom for slaves. This shift of emphasis led Garrison to denounce the party as "whitemanism," a racist effort to make the territories white.

Despite Garrison's hostility, the new political approach won the support of many women and free black abolitionists, who themselves were denied the political rights that white men enjoyed. Women in the American and Foreign Anti-Slavery Society established dozens of new female societies throughout the Great Lakes states and worked for free-soil. In Saint Cloud, Minnesota, Jane Swisshelm founded an antislavery newspaper, the *Visitor*, that commented vigorously on politics and won, she claimed, thousands of votes for free-soil candidates.

Many black abolitionists also supported the more conservative free-soil movement. They believed that the terror used to maintain slavery would ultimately require a violent solution. But they felt that the free-soil movement was the only practical way to provoke the necessary confrontation. However, they did urge white free-soilers to pay greater attention to emancipation within the South and to civil rights for blacks within the North. They pointed out, for example, that no state admitted to the Union after Maine in 1820 had extended the suffrage to blacks.

One supporter of free-soil was Frederick Douglass, who emerged during the 1840s as a leading antislavery strategist, the most electrifying of all abolitionist orators, and the foremost black abolitionist. Douglass had been born a slave in Maryland, but he escaped to Massachusetts in 1838, and in 1841 he joined Garrison as a lecturer. In 1847, he bought his freedom from his Maryland owner to ensure that he would not

FREDERICK DOUGLASS
Frederick Douglass (1817–1895) carried his abolitionist career into the Civil War, recruiting regiments of black soldiers for the Union cause and then promoting federal guarantees of black suffrage and civil rights. Later he advised Republican administrations on Caribbean affairs, held federal jobs in the District of Columbia, and served as U.S. consul general to Haiti. (Library of Congress)

be arrested as a fugitive. He and other black abolitionists established their independence from their white counterparts, including even the radical Garrisonians. In 1843, these black leaders called the Convention of the Free People of Color, at which they advocated slave rebellions. Douglass continued to plead for revolution, even after 1847, when he rejected Garrison's insistence on expulsion of the southern states—which Douglass believed would leave the slaves completely at the mercy of slaveowners. In that year, Douglass founded his own abolitionist newspaper, the *North Star*, but won few followers among northern whites. Disappointed but realistic, Douglass and the other black abolitionists decided that supporting the growing free-soil movement was their only sensible political choice.

During the 1840s and 1850s, the strategy of political abolitionism gained support. Birney's Liberty party received only about 7,000 votes in 1840 but more than 60,000—more than 2 percent of the total vote cast—in 1844. Then, in 1848, the new Free-Soil party, which inherited its platform from the Liberty party, received more than 290,000 votes, more than 10 percent of the total. Next, during the 1850s, the Republican party would form and embrace a free-soil policy. Although many Americans did not believe that slaveowning was sinful or that blacks deserved equality, they could be convinced that slavery threatened liberty and economic opportunity for white people in the West.

The Movement for Women's Rights

At first, celebration of self—of individual identity and liberation—was less important to the women's movement than to abolitionism. Before the Civil War, most of the participants in the women's movement concentrated on expanding women's power within their "separate sphere." But by the 1840s, heavily influenced by abolitionism, the women's movement did begin to develop a feminist ideology—an ideology arguing that women had social and political rights equal to those of men.

Origins of the Women's Movement

The Industrial Revolution shaped the movement for women's rights in complex ways. On the surface, the Industrial Revolution seemed to limit economic opportunities for women. It sharpened the lines of demarcation between the home and the workplace and accentuated the division of labor within the home. Women were now less involved in the production of goods (in a household workshop, for example) and more concerned with providing personal services in the home. Mothers, for example, became increasingly preoccupied with setting moral examples and providing solace and support for the "working" members of the family.

On a deeper level, however, the change in the roles of women within the family created a basis for greater independence and power. Drawing on the enhanced esteem attached to their family roles and reinforcing each other through intensified community and kinship ties, middle-class women fostered a common identity in "womanhood." They used it to enlarge their influence over decisions in all areas of family life, including the bearing of children and even their husbands' choice of work. For most middle-class women, greater influence over family life was enough. But some seized on the logic implicit in the emphasis on the moral role of women to increase their involvement outside of the home.

Young middle-class women in New York and New England entered the public arena through the religious revivals of the 1820s and 1830s. The revivals emphasized individual free will and provided a central role for women in the conversion process. They involved women more deeply in community life, enhanced their sense of self-esteem, and led them into other reform movements, such as temperance, moral reform, prison reform, and educational reform.

Women followed the injunctions of Charles Grandison Finney and the other evangelical leaders to do "good works." Moral reform was among the first of their efforts. They attempted to end prostitution, to punish those whose sexual behavior violated the Ten Commandments, to reform fallen women, and to protect single women from moral corruption. The movement began in 1834, when a group of middle-class women founded the New York Female Moral Reform Society and elected Lydia Finney, Charles's wife, as its president. By 1837, the New York society had fifteen thousand members and 250 chapters. In 1840 it organized a national association, the American Female Moral Reform Society, with 555 chapters located throughout the North.

Employing only women as its agents, book-keepers, and staff, this society concentrated on the problems of young women who worked and lived away from their families. They attempted to provide moral "government" for factory girls, seamstresses, clerks, and servants who were beyond the direct control of families and churches. The women reformers even went to brothels, where they sang hymns, offered prayers, searched for runaway daughters, and took down the names of clients. They founded homes of refuge for prostitutes, homeless girls, and migrant women. They sought state laws regulating sexual behavior, including making seduction a crime, and brought about the passage of such laws in Massachusetts, in 1846 and New York in 1848.

Women with backgrounds in evangelical re-

DOROTHEA DIX
Between 1841 and 1844, Dorothea Dix (1802–1887) visited 18 state penitentiaries, 300 county jails and houses of correction, and more than 500 almshouses, in addition to innumerable hospitals and houses of refuge. At the outbreak of the Civil War, she was appointed superintendent of women nurses. This put her in charge of hospital nursing for the Union forces and made her the highest-ranking woman in the federal government. (Brown Brothers)

form also turned their energies to social institutions. Almshouses, asylums, hospitals, and jails became the prime targets for improvement. Women first visited these places, which were growing in number during the 1830s and 1840s, to ease the condition of the residents. What they saw in such places inspired efforts toward institutional reform. The most accomplished reformer was Dorothea Dix. In 1841, she visited a jail in Cambridge, Massachusetts, as a Sunday school teacher for the women incarcerated there. Outraged that insane women were jailed with the general prison population, Dix began a two-year investigation of the treatment of the indigent insane in Massachusetts. Her report prompted Massachusetts to enlarge the state hospital in Worcester. Her success in Massachusetts led to a nationwide crusade on behalf of state hospitals for the insane. Between 1843 and 1854, she traveled more than thirty thousand miles, visited hundreds of institutions, and prepared dozens of reports and memorials to state legislatures. Her success in arousing public opinion forced many states to create or significantly expand their state hospitals. Although Dix persuaded Congress to pass a bill in 1854 that provided federal land grants for national hospitals, President Franklin Pierce vetoed the bill, saying it was unconstitutional and too expensive. Dix continued her work overseas, founding an international movement to improve treatment of the insane.

Education and Child Rearing

Educational reform attracted more women than any other movement for institutional reform. This was a movement with roots in republican ideology, evangelical Christianity, transcendentalism, and the demands of ordinary farmers and workers for the education required for success in an industrializing world. To school reformers, only well-educated people could make responsible, independent acts of will. Emerson argued that only with education could individuals respond to his injunction "Trust thyself." With education on behalf of self-realization, he said, "every heart" would vibrate to the same "iron string" of self-trust.

Educational reforms focused on the expansion and standardization of public elementary schools. Massachusetts was the most significant innovator in this drive, adopting a public school law that many other states imitated. With the support of many women, Massachusetts established a state board of education in 1837 and appointed Horace Mann, a transcendentalist and the brother-in-law of Nathaniel Hawthorne, as its first secretary. In his eleven years as secretary, Mann outlined the modern apparatus of public schools. His reforms included the founding of a state "normal" school to train teachers and the establishment of standards for instruction in reading, writing, and arithmetic; lengthening the school year; raising teachers' salaries to make careers in teaching attractive; organizing a state association of teachers; and improving instruction by replacing the untrained, highly mobile young men who had dominated the teaching profession with better-educated, more stable, and, in Mann's view, more moral young women.

During the 1840s and 1850s, in response to the reforms of Horace Mann and others, thousands of young middle-class women took advantage of this new opportunity. Their intellectual leader was Catharine Beecher, the daughter of Congregationalist minister Lyman Beecher. She founded academies for young women in Hartford and Cincinnati in the 1820s and 1830s in the belief that women should have a special commitment to education because they had a more general obligation to foster moral development. Since "to enlighten the understanding and to gain the affections is a teacher's business," and since "the mind is to be guided chiefly by means of the affections," she asked: "is not *woman* best fitted to accomplish these important objects?" To Beecher, "moral and religious education must be the foundation of national instruction," and education must be carried out by "energetic and benevolent women." By 1850, public elementary schools, staffed largely by women, had expanded greatly. No states made attendance compulsory, but demand for the new schools was so great that about half of the elementary school-age population attended on at least a part-time basis. About 59 percent of the white males, 53 percent of the white females, and 10 percent of free blacks, both male and female, attended. And children in school in 1850 received, on the average, more than four hundred days of schooling in their lives, in contrast with two hundred days in 1800.

Educational reform dwelt as heavily on the family as on the schools. Both the evangelical and transcendentalist movements called on parents to devote themselves to setting moral examples to counter the confusions and disruptions of industrialization. Some reformers, again led by Catharine Beecher, called for an elevation of family life. They wrote books on "domestic economy," urging Christians to infuse their homes with love and altruism, making them centers of morality. Without such reform, they argued, all other social improvements would achieve nothing.

Behind this moralizing was the theological movement among many Protestants away from the Calvinist presumption of original sin and toward a view of children as innocents whose characters depend on loving parental nurturing. Ministers still insisted on the need to create humble, self-denying men and women whose

THE GRIMKÉ SISTERS
Sarah Moore Grimké (1792–1873) and Angelina Emily Grimké (1805–1879) joined the Philadelphia Female Antislavery Society and began abolitionist lecturing in 1836. They drew crowds of thousands—and scathing criticism for having lost, as some Massachusetts clergymen put it, "that modesty and delicacy . . . which constitutes the true influence of women in society." The Grimké sisters responded with powerful statements protesting male domination of women. (Library of Congress)

wills were subordinate to God. But they began to soften the traditional Calvinist position, suggesting that parental restraint and discipline applied to infants would soon develop the child's own conscience. Transcendentalists took this positive view of children even further. Bronson Alcott, a member of Emerson's intimate circle, shaped the vision into a coherent theory. As he raised his four daughters—including Louisa May Alcott, the author of *Little Women*—Alcott formulated a philosophy of child-rearing based on the moral autonomy of the individual and the capacity for moral perfection. Influenced by religious traditions, he admitted that the infant was "selfish." Yet Alcott declared that this weakness could be overcome. "The *child* must be treated as a free, self-guiding, *self-controlling* being," he argued, for this would assist the youth in deliberately transcending selfish passions. "His will is the ready servant of his heart," Alcott concluded, "and under all conditions of his nature, yields itself to the declaration of conscience—the law of the spirit." For discipline, he advocated a withdrawal of parental love rather than physical punishment.

Women figured centrally in the new ideal of moral education. Catharine Beecher urged wives and mothers to devote their prime physical and emotional energies to their children. She led in the development of a popular self-help literature designed to reach middle-class wives and mothers. Her sister, Harriet Beecher Stowe, helped popularize the same ideas through her domestic novels. In manuals and magazines, such as *Godey's Lady's Book*, women were instructed on how to make their homes at once more efficient and more moral. Catharine Beecher's *Treatise on Domestic Economy* (1841) was reprinted almost every year during the 1840s and the 1850s, becoming the standard text on housekeeping and child-rearing. In it, mothers found both practical advice and fervent injunctions to create homes that would allow their husbands and children to lead more moral lives.

Abolitionism and Feminism

Under the influence of abolitionist ideas and politics, some women began to find Catharine Beecher too conservative. They rejected the implicit bargain she had made for enlarging the realm of women. They could not accept a restricted role in society in return for the meager reward of greater control over domestic life and their children's education.

Shaping the ideas of the radical wing of the women's movement were the two abolitionists Angelina and Sarah Grimké. In 1837, responding to the demand of some Congregationalist clergymen that she cease speaking to mixed male and female audiences, Sarah responded: "The Lord Jesus defines the duties of his followers in his Sermon on the Mount . . . without any reference to sex or condition. . . . Men and women are CREATED EQUAL! They are both moral and accountable beings and whatever is right for man to do is right for woman." The next year, Angelina debated Catharine Beecher, invoking the belief that gender should not affect the manner in which people shape society. She declared:

> It is a woman's right to have a voice in all the laws and regulations by which she is governed, whether in Church or State. . . . The present arrangements of society, on these points are a *violation of human rights, a rank usurpation of power,* a violent seizure and confiscation of what is sacredly and inalienably hers.

By 1840, the Grimkés were asserting that traditional roles within the family amounted to the "domestic slavery" of women.

Not all abolitionist women shared these views. But they all gained confidence outside the home and learned much about the organizational requirements for successful reform. Women with different concepts of women's proper "sphere" sought equality with men within the abolitionist movement. As their participation in the movement grew, many women demanded representation in antislavery societies equal to their numbers. At the same time, however, their activities, especially the vigorous antislavery lecturing by the Grimkés, aroused opposition from members of the abolitionist clergy who believed that their behavior was immoral. They also drew criticism from male abolitionists who feared that such visible departures from tradition would damage the political chances of the antislavery movement.

William Lloyd Garrison, however, argued that "our object is *universal* emancipation, to redeem women as well as men from a servile to an equal condition." In 1840, at the convention of the American Antislavery Society, he insisted on the right of women to participate equally in the organization. With the votes of several hundred New England women, Abby Kelley was elected to the organization's business committee. This event precipitated the split between the supporters of Garrison and those who founded the American and Foreign Anti-Slavery Society.

The Program of Seneca Falls

The split among abolitionists disrupted the link between the movement for women's equality and abolitionism. Nonetheless, some women abolitionists, like Abby Kelley, Lucretia Mott, and Elizabeth Cady Stanton, who had been radical-

ized by the discrimination they had encountered, remained with Garrison. They recruited new women agents, including Lucy Stone, to address hostile audiences on the common interests of slaves and women.

Supporting the growing feminism of the Garrisonians was Margaret Fuller, a transcendentalist who was not an abolitionist but powerfully asserted the rights of women in *Women in the Nineteenth Century,* published in the *Dial* in 1842 and as a book in 1844. She believed that women needed psychological and social independence—the ability "to grow, as an intellect to discern, as a soul to live freely and unimpeded." She declared, "We would have every arbitrary barrier thrown down" and "every path laid open to Woman as freely as to Man." If societies placed men and women, "the two sides of the great radical dualism" of human nature, on an equal footing, they could end all injustice. After 1845, Fuller gained visibility as the *New York Tribune's* literary critic and as a correspondent in Italy during that country's revolution of 1848. Her friends hoped that she would become a leader in the women's movement, but in 1850, returning to the United States at the age of forty, she drowned in a shipwreck.

During the 1840s, radical women gradually saw the need for a pragmatic course of action, one that remained within the existing social and political structures and did not directly threaten the existing division of labor within the family. They adopted the objective of strengthening women's legal position. In so doing, they won support from women abolitionists who had abandoned Garrison but never lost their passion for women's rights.

In 1848, the abolitionist women took a critical step. They called a convention in Seneca Falls, in upstate New York. Led by Elizabeth Cady Stanton and Lucretia Mott, who had met at the World's Anti-Slavery Convention in 1840, and joined by a few sympathetic male abolitionists like Frederick Douglass, the convention outlined, for the first time, a coherent program for women's equality. Like the free-soilers, the delegates at Seneca Falls based their program on republican ideology, adopting resolutions patterned directly on the Declaration of Independence. Among their declared principles was "that all men and women are created equal; that they are endowed by the Creator with certain in-

THE FEMINISM OF LUCY STONE (1855)

Lucy Stone (1818–1893) graduated from Oberlin College in 1847 and came to feminism through abolitionist lecturing. She delivered this speech extemporaneously at a national women's rights convention in Cincinnati in 1855.

The last speaker alluded to this movement as being that of a few disappointed women. From the first years to which my memory stretches, I have been a disappointed woman. When, with my brothers, I reached forth after the sources of knowledge, I was reproved with "It isn't fit for you; it doesn't belong to women." Then there was but one college in the world where women were admitted, and that was in Brazil. I would have found my way there, but by the time I was prepared to go, one was opened in the young state of Ohio—the first in the United States where women and negroes could enjoy opportunities with white men. I was disappointed when I came to seek a profession worthy an immortal being—every employment was closed to me, except those of the teacher, the seamstress, and the housekeeper. In education, in marriage, in religion, in everything, disappointment is the lot of woman. It shall be the business of my life to deepen this disappointment in every woman's heart until she bows down to it no longer. I wish that women, instead of being walking shoe-cases, instead of begging of their fathers and brothers the latest and gayest new bonnet, would ask of them their rights.

The question of Woman's Rights is a practical one. . . . The flour-merchant, the house-builder, and the postman charge us no less on account of our sex; but when we endeavor to earn money to pay all these, then, indeed, we find the difference. Man, if he have energy, may hew out for himself a path where no mortal has ever trod, held back by nothing but what is in himself; the world is all before him, where to choose; and we are glad for you, brothers, men, that it is so. But the same society that drives forth the young man, keeps woman at home—a dependent—working little cats on worsted, and little dogs on punctured paper; but if she goes heartily and bravely to give herself to some worthy purpose, she is out of her sphere and she loses caste. . . . I know not what you believe of God, but I believe He gave yearnings and longings to be filled, and that He did not mean all our time should be devoted to feeding and clothing the body. The present condition of woman causes a horrible perversion of the marriage relation. It is asked of a lady, "Has she married well?" "Oh, yes, her husband is rich." Woman must marry for a home, and you men are the sufferers by this; for a woman who loathes you may marry you because you have the means to get money which she cannot have. But when woman can enter the lists with you and make money for herself, she will marry you only for deep and earnest affection.

---

alienable rights: that among these are life, liberty and pursuit of happiness." They asserted, however, that "the history of mankind is a history of repeated injuries and usurpations on the part of man toward woman, having its direct object the establishment of an absolute tyranny over her." To educate the public as to this reality, they resolved to "use every instrumentality within our power. . . . We shall employ agents, circulate tracts, petition the State and national legislatures, and endeavor to enlist the pulpit and the press on our behalf."

During the 1850s, national women's rights conventions were held annually, and there were numerous local and regional meetings. The emphasis was on establishing the right of married women to control their own property and earnings; guaranteeing custody of children in the event of divorce; ensuring their right to sue or testify in court; revising concepts of female inferiority found in established religious theology; and winning the vote for women. The Seneca Falls convention had resolved that it was the "duty of women of this country to secure themselves their sacred right to the elective franchise."

By 1860, fourteen states, following New York's pioneering law of 1848, adopted laws protecting the property of married women in the event of the death or incapacitation of their husbands. In this effort, women reformers were joined by upper-class, conservative males. An important motive behind the passage of these laws was the desire to protect propertied men in

TIME LINE
INDIVIDUALISM AND REFORM

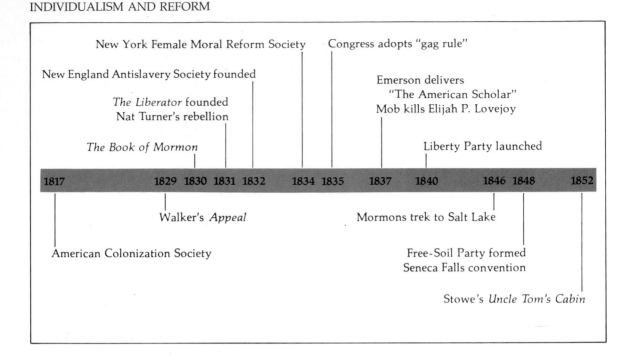

the event of bankruptcy (by preserving their spouses' assets intact) and to protect patriarchs with large estates who feared that dissolute or incompetent sons-in-law might lose or ruin their holdings; these men preferred to allow their daughters to hold assets independently.

The campaign for suffrage made little headway before the Civil War, although it became important to the ideology and organization of the women's movement. The 1851 national convention of women resolved that the right of suffrage was "the corner-stone of this enterprise, since we do not seek to protect woman, but rather to place her in a position to protect herself." A resolution passed by the 1856 national convention of women declared "that the main power of the woman's rights movement lies in this: that while always demanding for woman better education, better employment, and better laws, it has kept steadily in view the one cardinal demand for the right of suffrage: in a democracy, the symbol and guarantee of all other rights." Such resolutions, however, were dismissed by legislatures with comments like that of a New York representative: "It is well known that the object of these unsexed women is to overthrow [marriage], the most sacred of our institutions."

The accomplishment of the 1850s that proved most significant for women was their mastery of organization. Meetings and publicity widened the participation of women in feminist causes, and feminist leaders grew in number. Susan B. Anthony was the most important addition. While many women leaders of the 1830s and 1840s had been gifted lecturers, Anthony's foremost talents were organizational. She was a member of a Massachusetts Quaker family from near Rochester, New York. She had participated in moral reform and in a female antislavery society. She had lectured widely on antislavery and religion, bitterly resigned a teaching position over discrimination against women, and joined the temperance movement as a paid fundraiser. In 1851, when she was thirty-one, she joined the movement for women's rights and forged an enduring friendship with Elizabeth Cady Stanton. Her experience in the temperance movement proved valuable, especially because it had taught her "the great evil of woman's utter dependence on man for the necessary means to aid reform movements."

In promoting the cause of feminist reforms during the 1850s, Anthony created a network of political "captains," all women. Living in each of New York's counties, they could collect thousands of signatures on petitions in just a few days. She lobbied the state legislature relentlessly. In 1860, her efforts culminated when New York gave women the legal right to collect their own wages (which fathers or husbands previously could insist on collecting), to bring suit in court, and to enjoy, if widowed, full control of their own property.

The organizational and legislative successes of the women's rights movement during the 1850s provided the basis for the more aggressive reform attempts that followed the Civil War. During the 1850s, however, most Americans, even most abolitionists, did not regard the issues that the women's rights movement had raised to be of great concern. And virtually all feminists stressed a higher immediate priority: the abolition of slavery. Women as different as Susan B. Anthony and Harriet Beecher Stowe expressed evangelical outrage over slavery. Stowe never joined an antislavery society, but in her novel *Uncle Tom's Cabin*, which her sister Catharine Beecher helped her to write, she delivered an abolitionist message to more homes than any antislavery campaigner ever did. By charging that among the greatest moral failings of slavery was its destruction of the slave family and the degradation of slave women, Beecher reinforced the message of a real-life former slave, Sojourner Truth, who lectured to both antislavery and women's rights conventions. Truth hammered home the point that women slaves were denied not only their basic human rights but also the protected "sphere" enjoyed by free women. "I have ploughed and planted and gathered into barns, and no man could head me—and ain't I a woman?" she asked in 1851. "I have borne thirteen children, and seen most of 'em sold into slavery, and when I cried out with my mother's grief, none but Jesus heard me—and ain't I a woman?"

By the 1850s, free-soil enthusiasm and women's evangelical outrage over slavery dominated the antislavery movement. Although free-soil and women's evangelism accelerated the demise of slavery, they made American society more conservative. Stowe's condemnation of slavery, based on an affirmation of the purifying role of motherhood, delayed the development of the critique of traditional roles within the family that would be necessary for a fully developed feminist ideology. Free-soil, which became the centerpiece of the Republican party platform, allowed that party, building on Whig ideology, to celebrate economic opportunity in the North; the Republicans were thus able to divert attention almost completely from the costs and limitations of the Industrial Revolution. Consequently, reform energy, focused on the problem of slavery from the perspectives of women's evangelism and free-soil, reinforced both the traditional family and American industrialization.

---

*I*ndustrialization challenged Americans to reconcile claims for the supremacy of the individual with society's needs for cohesion. Among those who responded to the challenge were writers who produced a distinctive American literature, one that ranged from an embrace of individual potential to warnings of the dangers of individualism. A group of women authors suggested a solution to the imbalance between individual and communal responsibility—a reaffirmation of the moral role of women.

Many Americans deplored the changes in society that encouraged excessive individualism. Some of these critics created communal alternatives to industrial society. Others continued to embrace the ideal of individual freedom but, at the same time, accepted an inner discipline. When they found others guilty of excessive individualism, they often attempted to reform them through religious commitments.

The primary thrust of reform was an attack on slavery, inspired by radical actions by free blacks and slaves. In the 1830s, evangelical abolitionists, finding slavery the expression of the unrestrained individualism of slaveholders, appealed to Christian consciences by calling for immediate emancipation. These abolitionists encountered violent hostility in the South and North. In response, most abolitionists turned to political tactics, such as calling for the exclusion of slavery from the territories, that would attract middle-class Americans to their movement.

Some reformers sought to expand opportunities for women. Women had participated in the religious revivals of the 1820s and 1830s and had joined temperance, moral reform, and educational reform movements; many turned to abolitionism as well. Abolitionism, however, radical-ized some women; they turned from expanding the power of women within a "separate sphere" to developing a feminist ideology. During the 1840s they began to campaign for women's suffrage. Nonetheless, until the Civil War, reform-minded women concentrated primarily on eradicating slavery.

Suggestions for Further Reading

Intellectual Ferment and Communal Experiments

Recent studies of American literature which discuss themes of individualism and democracy include Ann Douglas, *The Feminization of American Culture* (1977); Mary Kelley, *Private Woman, Public Stage: Literary Domesticity in Nineteenth-Century America* (1984); Harold Kaplan, *Democratic Humanism and American Literature* (1972); and Larzar Ziff, *Literary Democracy, The Declaration of Cultural Independence in America* (1981). On transcendentalism, see Anne C. Rose, *Transcendentalism as a Social Movement, 1830–1850* (1981). On communitarian experiments, see Arthur Bestor, Jr., *Backwoods Utopias: The Sectarian and Owenite Phases of Communitarian Life in America*; Lawrence Foster, *Religion and Sexuality: Three American Communal Experiments of the Nineteenth Century* (1981); Klaus J. Hansen, *Mormonism and the American Experience* (1981); Louis J. Kern, *An Ordered Love: Sex Roles and Sexuality in Victorian Utopias—The Shakers, the Mormons, and the Oneida Community* (1981); Charles Nordhoff, *The Communistic Societies of the United States* (1875, reprinted 1960); Thomas F. O'Dea, *The Mormons* (1957).

The Antislavery Movement and Women's Rights

Surveys of reform that are useful in understanding the anti-slavery movement include the works by C. S. Griffen, Alice F. Tyler, and Ronald G. Walters for Chapter 12. Those that focus on anti-slavery include Robert H. Abzug, *Passionate Liberator, Theodore Dwight Weld and the Dilemma of Reform* (1980); Gilbert H. Barnes, *The Anti-Slavery Impulse, 1830-1844* (1933); David Brion Davis, *The Problems of Slavery in the Age of Revolution 1770–1823* (1975); Louis Filler, *The Crusade Against Slavery, 1830–1860* (1960); Leon F. Litwack, *North of Slavery: The Negro in the Free States, 1790–1860*; Stephen B. Oates, *To Purge this Land with Blood, A Biography of John Brown* (1970); Lewis Perry, *Childhood, Marriage, and Reform: Henry Clarke Wright, 1797–1870* (1980); Benjamin Quarles, *Black Abolitionists* (1969); James B. Stewart, *Holy Warriors, The Abolitionists and American Slavery* (1976); John Thomas, *The Liberator: William Lloyd Garrison* (1963); and Bertram Wyatt-Brown, *Lewis Tappan and the Evangelical War Against Slavery* (1959). For the role of women in the anti-slavery movement, consult Edmund Fuller, *Prudence Crandall, An Incident of Racism in Nineteenth Century America* (1971); Blanche Hersh, *The Slavery of Sex: Feminist Abolitionists in Nineteenth-Century America* (1978); Gerda Lerner, *The Grimke Sisters from South Carolina: Pioneers for Women's Rights and Abolition* (1967); and Alma Lutz, *Crusade for Freedom: Women of the Antislavery Movement* (1968).

The most comprehensive history of women in the United States is Nancy Woloch, *Women and the American Experience* (1984). On the social history of women, see W. Elliot Brownlee and Mary M. Brownlee, *Women in the American Economy, A Documentary History, 1675–1929* (1976); Nancy F. Cott, *The Bonds of Womanhood, "Women's Sphere" in New England, 1780–1835* (1977); Carl N. Degler, *At Odds: Women and the Family in America from the Revolution to the Present* (1980); Linda Gordon, *Woman's Body, Woman's Rights: A Social History of Birth Control in America* (1976); James Reed, *From Private Vice to Public Virtue: The Birth Control Movement and American Society since 1830* (1978); and Mary P. Ryan, *Cradle of the Middle Class, The Family in Oneida County, New York, 1790–1865* (1981). The most thorough description of the participation of women in benevolence and reform is Keith Melder, *Beginnings of Sisterhood: The American Women's Rights Movement, 1800–1850* (1977). For studies of more specific aspects of women's involvement in benevolence, see Barbara J. Berg, *The Remembered Gate: Origins of American Feminism, The Woman and the City, 1800–1860* (1978); Estelle B. Freedman, *Their Sister's Keepers: Women's Prison Reform in America, 1830–1930* (1981). On educational reform, see Lawrence A. Cremin, *American Education: The National Experience, 1783–1876* (1980); Linda A. Pollock, *Forgotten Children: Parent-Child Relations from 1500 to 1900* (1983); and Stanley K. Schultz, *The Culture Factory: Boston Public Schools, 1789–1860* (1973). The definitive biography of Catharine Beecher is Kathryn Kish Sklar, *Catharine Beecher, A Study in American Domesticity* (1973). The leading histories of feminists and the early women's rights movement include Paula Blanchard, *Margaret Fuller: From Transcendentalism to Revolution* (1978); Ellen Du Bois, *Feminism and Suffrage: The Emergence of an Independent Women's Movement, 1848–1869* (1978); and Eleanor Flexner, *Century of Struggle: The Woman's Rights Movement in the United States* (1959).

PRINTS, PAINTINGS, AND THE DEVELOPMENT OF DEMOCRATIC ART

PLATE 1

As early as the 1830s, political prints combined journalism and propaganda. They were virtually the only visual medium for conveying political news until the Civil War, when photography began to come into its own. (Chicago Historical Society)

PLATE 2

By the 1850s, the most popular Currier & Ives prints were those that showed idealized images of a prosperous, rural life. This verdant scene, one of several titled "Home, Sweet Home," dates from 1869. The apparently unscathed Union soldier returns to a perfect home, an orderly oasis in the woods. (Museum of the City of New York)

Pictorial art in the United States, like literature, developed uniquely American characteristics between the 1820s and the onset of the Civil War. American painters, printmakers, and writers remained under the powerful influence of European style and techniques but began to find in American experience new, fascinating material for their work. Their prints, paintings, and literature in a sense began to tell Americans about themselves and their nation.

In contrast to the black and white prints available to colonial Americans, the color prints that gained astonishing popularity in the 1830s were both more factual and more sensational. Publishers in the 1830s began to use steel and wood engravings and lithography to satisfy a newly literate, prosperous mass market that bought magazines, books, and prints as quickly as they were produced. Mass-produced lithographs, hand-colored by armies of employees, became immensely popular. Subsequent developments enabled printers to produce multicolored prints mechanically (plate 1). The first such print showed a victorious William Henry Harrison after the election of 1840.

Prints rapidly became an important means of disseminating national news. They also brought drama, fashion, and social commentary to all parts of the country. Because prints could be bought fairly cheaply, middle class families commonly acquired extensive collections. They bought prints depicting battles, fires, shipwrecks, notable personalities, new communities in the West, and the latest industrial technology—such as the steamboat and the McCormick reaper.

The leading printmaker of the day was the New York firm of Nathaniel Currier (to become Currier & Ives in 1857). Currier often commissioned prints from well-known artists. His prints of bucolic country scenes (plate 2),

401

urban events, and disasters (plate 3) reached consumers through a nationwide network of dealers. Currier & Ives, more than any other printing firm, gave Americans in all parts of the country common visual impressions of recent events.

Middle class families also relied on prints to follow changing styles of architecture and to keep abreast of the latest fashions "out East." *Godey's Lady's Book*, a magazine of literature and fashion for women, was published from 1830 to 1898. Women from Bangor to Charleston, New York to Cincinnati took pages from *Godey's* to their seamstresses as patterns for new dresses (plate 4). Businesses also used prints to advertise in new ways. Locomotive manufacturers, for example, commissioned prints not so much to reach the small market of locomotive buyers but to stimulate public interest in rail travel (plate 5).

Until the development of moving pictures and home photography in the early twentieth century, the print was the most popular form of pictorial art in the United States. Many of the leading painters in pre-Civil War America were trained as printmakers, and so were familiar with popular taste. Thomas Cole (1801–1848), the most influential landscape painter of the period, had worked as an apprentice wood engraver in his native England before studying drawing at the Pennsylvania Academy. Cole's first exhibition in New York in 1825 quickly attracted the interest of wealthy collectors. His early paintings, such as *View of the White Mountains* (plate 6), glorified the American wilderness of the Ohio Valley, northern New England, western New York, and, most especially, the Hudson Valley.

Asher B. Durand (1796–1886), Cole's successor in landscape

PLATE 5

This advertisement for the "Outside Connected Passenger Engine" was intended to impress viewers with the scale and novelty of industrialism. The original passenger cars were simply stagecoaches with railroad wheels, but by 1840 they were elongated and designed specifically for rail travel. (National Museum of History and Technology, Smithsonian Institution, Washington)

PLATE 6

Cole's early landscapes show a bold, theatrical wilderness in a style similar to the European romantic style. During the 1840s, Cole altered his style and painted subjects on dramatic moralistic themes to suit the tastes of his wealthy patrons. (*View of the White Mountains.* Wadsworth Atheneum, Hartford. Bequest of Daniel Wadsworth)

403

PLATE 7
Durand worked until the mid 1830s as a book illustrator. One of his projects
was a series of illustrations for James Fenimore Cooper's tremendously popular
book, *The Spy*. (*Kindred Spirits*. The New York Public Library)

painting, apprenticed as an engraver and worked as an illustrator until the 1830s. His landscapes are less passionate than
Cole's—a shift that parallels the
taming of the wilderness as more
and more Americans created
farms and settlements in western
territory. In *Kindred Spirits* (plate
7), the human figures are larger
in relationship to the landscape
than are any figures in Cole's
paintings. The belief in the unity
of humankind and nature, which
Durand shared with many
Americans, had attained a temporary equilibrium with the popular enthusiasm for the potential
of the individual.

Cole and Durand established
a national tradition of landscape
art. While they and their disciples, collectively known as the
Hudson River School, varied
their moral themes and their
treatment of the individual in nature, they all viewed painting as
a patriotic act—a visual expression of Manifest Destiny. Philip
Hone, one of Cole's patrons, remarked, "Every American is
bound to prove his love of country by admiring Cole."

Although few Americans of
the period actually saw these
landscapes first hand, the paintings had a tremendous impact on
American art, and so on the
shape and outlook of the nation's
culture. The Hudson River
School's reverence and awe toward natural beauty passed
along to the so-called Rocky
Mountain painters, of whom the
German immigrant Albert Bierstadt (1830–1902) was the most
celebrated. Bierstadt's *The Rocky
Mountains* (1863), for example,
was an enormous canvas that
used the mountains' towering
majesty as a symbol of the
nation's accomplishment and
promise (plate 8).

If these triumphant land-
scapes sprang from the pride of
patriotism, the domestic scenes

404

PLATE 8
Bierstadt, who had come to New Bedford, Massachusetts as a small child, returned to Germany to study at the Dusseldorf Academy in 1853 and then resumed his American career in 1857. His spectacular portraits of America's "manifest destiny" earned him wide popular acclaim and the largest commissions of his day. (*The Rocky Mountains*. The Metropolitan Museum of Art. Rogers Fund, 1907)

of so-called genre painting showed a profound respect for everyday life. *Power of Music*, painted by William Sidney Mount (1807–1868), treats blacks with a degree of realism and sympathy that was highly unusual for the day (plate 9).

The painter who first directly reached a mass American audience—and the mass imagina-

PLATE 9
Mount painted vignettes based on his experiences growing up on rural Long Island. Despite its gentle, wistful quality, this painting portrays the social barriers created by racism. Mount's agent urged him to paint black subjects because he believed they would sell well in Europe. (*The Power of Music*. The Century Association, New York)

PLATE 10
Bingham was the first major painter from the West. Largely self-taught, he began his career during the 1830s by painting portraits and designing political banners for Whig campaigns in Missouri. This painting was popular nationwide, and was distributed in a colored aquatint engraving to the ten thousand members of the American Art-Union. (*The Jolly Flatboatmen in Port*. The Saint Louis Art Museum)

PLATE 11
Bingham's political paintings did not portray anecdotes or address political issues. Like this one, they expressed a generic patriotism, with congenial crowds of good-natured citizens, usually men. Women would have been largely irrelevant to Bingham's subject matter. (*Verdict of the People*. The Boatmen's National Bank of St. Louis Art Collection)

tion—was George Caleb Bingham (1811–1879). His first major commercial success, *Jolly Flatboatmen in Port* (plate 10), sold 10,000 copies as a color engraving in 1857. More than any other genre painter, Bingham directly and enthusiastically showed the public worlds of work and politics. His series of election paintings (1850–1855) became famous. With lavish detail and bold figures, *The Verdict of the People* (plate 11) celebrates the openness and fairness of American democracy.

Another painter of the period, George Inness (1825–1894), showed the harmonious coexistence of industry, agriculture, and nature in *The Lackawanna Valley* (plate 12). But, as modern art critic Robert Hughes wrote of a much later period, there was trouble in paradise. Not all painters shared the uncritical enthusiasm of Durand, Bierstadt, and Bingham. David G. Blythe (1815–1865) was furious at what he saw as the hypocritical greed of the new middle class. In *Courtroom Scene* (plate 13) and other works, he caricatured ordinary Americans with bitter wit. As the Civil War approached, even Bingham's happy vision of America faltered; his paintings after 1856 are lifeless copies of his earlier themes.

The two most original and talented American painters of the pre-Civil War era sensed the destructive consequences of America's hectic growth and development. John James Audubon (1785–1851) and George Catlin (1796–1872) both became preoccupied with documenting the American wilderness they believed was doomed to extinction. In marked contrast to the emotional, moralistic art of other painters, Audubon and Catlin painted vanishing wildlife and Indians with scientific precision.

Audubon emigrated to the United States from France in 1803. After a failed career as a shopkeeper, in 1819 he began obsessively drawing the birds he saw along the Mississippi Valley flyway. Failing to find any interest in his paintings in America, Audubon returned to Europe. A

PLATE 12

At age nineteen, after being apprenticed to engravers in New York City, Inness began to paint landscapes in the style of the Hudson River School. *The Lackawanna Valley* expresses, more clearly than almost any other painting, the period's optimism over America's natural bounty and industrial promise. (National Gallery of Art, Washington. Gift of Mrs. Huttleston Rogers)

PLATE 13

Painting in obscurity and poverty in Pittsburgh, Blythe never found a market for his bleak representations of common Americans. Although his work was unique among American painters before the Civil War, it had a dark, pessimistic tone similar to that of Herman Melville's writing. (*Courtroom Scene.* The Screven Lorillard Collection)

407

PLATE 14
Audubon's engravers copied his watercolor paintings onto copper plates. Audubon hand-colored the first set of prints and supervised their subsequent production. A complete set of plates, *The Birds of America*, and accompanying text sold by subscription for a thousand dollars. In America, a smaller version, called the octavio edition, cost one hundred dollars, an enormous sum for a book at the time. (*Louisiana Heron*. The New-York Historical Society)

French lithographer agreed to print his collection of 435 hand-colored plates. Audubon painted wildlife as noble creatures. *Louisiana Heron* (plate 14) shows the bird dominating its surroundings like a hero of the wild.

George Catlin's portraits of American Indians lacked Audubon's flair. They are nearly as straightforward as photographs; in the later part of his career, in fact, Catlin often photographed his subjects before he painted them. In the 1830s, while Andrew Jackson was displacing Indians in the Southeast, Catlin traveled 2,000 miles up the Missouri River and spent nearly eight years painting and living among more than forty tribes. To our eyes, his painting of Four Bears, second chief (plate 15) has a rare dignity and the beauty of accurate description. But Catlin never gained a significant following. Depressed by the Indians' tragedy and his own lack of an audience, he moved on to South and Central America in the 1850s and then to self-imposed exile in Europe. Only much later—too late—would a substantial number of Americans come to share Catlin's concern for the people whom territorial expansion and industrialization had oppressed and victimized.

PLATE 15
Catlin's paintings have an unfinished quality due to wilderness conditions and the speed with which he worked, driven by his vision of the western Indians as a dying people. He assembled nearly 500 paintings and thousands of artifacts in an "Indian Gallery" and traveled America between 1837 and 1851, to intrigued but unsympathetic audiences. (*Four Bears, second chief*. National Museum of American Art, Smithsonian Institution. Gift of Mrs. Joseph Harrison, Jr.)

14

SOCIAL TENSION AND SECTIONAL CRISIS

fter 1840, the United States experienced increasingly rapid economic development. While the pace of the Industrial Revolution quickened in both America and western Europe, westward expansion in America brought particularly spectacular growth. Those who benefited from this growth had much to celebrate. Southern planters, notably cotton planters, watched their profits rise. The northern middle class could afford more goods with every passing year. And the northern business elite continued to acquire an increasing share of all forms of property.

However, economic development created a problem with tragic implications. The North and South developed in different ways. The North grew increasingly industrial. The fortunes of the South became increasingly tied to slavery. In effect, two different economic systems were evolving. The differences between them generated a cultural and social schism that threatened to rend the Union.

Gradually, the differences between North and South came to focus on the West and the future of slavery in the territories. For decades, most Whig and Democratic politicians, both northern and southern, had tried to keep slavery from becoming a threat to the unity of their parties or the Union itself. But in the presidential elections of 1844 and 1848, antislavery third parties held the balance of power. When the United States

acquired much of the territory of Mexico in a war of conquest, the problem of slavery in the West came to the center of American politics. In 1850, Whig and Democratic leaders hammered out a set of laws known as the Compromise of 1850 in a desperate effort to maintain party as well as national unity. Instead, this compromise set the stage for the disintegration of the Second Party System.

A Distinctive Society

Some southern planters regarded themselves as aristocrats, detached from the marketplace. But most behaved like northern capitalists, doing what they considered necessary to protect their investments and maximize their profits. Unlike northern capitalists, though, the most important investments of planters lay in slaves and land rather than in factories. During the decades before the Civil War, demand for cotton by British and American textile manufacturers grew so rapidly that more and more plantations grew cotton. Cotton was grown most profitably with slave labor; hence slavery became increasingly important to the South, and the planters exploited slaves more ruthlessly. To produce large profits, which would disappear if labor were no longer free, the system had to remain a vital means of social control by keeping blacks and nonslaveholding whites subservient to the will of the planters. To protect their power, the planters developed an elaborate defense of slavery and tried to cement the loyalty of nonslaveholding whites. Most important, they attempted to make the West secure for slavery. This, however, put the South on a fateful collision course with the industrial North.

The Slave Economy

The South's economy grew rapidly and generated high incomes, for both slaveowners and other whites. Between 1840 and 1860, per capita income, even taking the meager incomes of slaves into account, increased more rapidly in the South than in the United States as a whole. In 1860, only the Northeast, Great Britain, and Australia had higher per capita incomes than the South. Southern prosperity was based on dynamic agricultural production dominated by the export staples of tobacco, rice, sugar and, above all, cotton. By the 1850s, when the "cotton kingdom" had already swept across the Mississippi River into Texas, the South accounted for more than two-thirds of the world's cotton output. In 1860, southern cotton commanded enough money in European markets to account for almost two-thirds of the total export trade of the United States.

As in the North, agriculture in the South was highly productive. It generated large revenues compared with the investment of labor, capital, and land. But unlike northern agriculture, southern agriculture did not depend on domestic consumers or improvements in farm technology. Southern planters depended on three other fac-

SOUTHERN PLANTATION LIFE
Although this painting by Giroux idealizes life on the cotton plantation—much as the defenders of slavery did—it does suggest the importance of slavery and of self-sufficiency to the largest plantations in the South. Small farms in the South far outnumbered large plantations, but the plantations established economic and social styles that most white southerners tried to emulate. (C. Giroux. *Cotton Plantation*. Museum of Fine Arts, Boston. M. & M. Karolik Collection).

MAP 14.1 THE DISTRIBUTION OF SLAVE POPULATION, 1790–1860
The cotton boom was largely responsible for the westward shift of slave population. In 1790, slaves were concentrated most heavily on the tobacco plantations of the Chesapeake Bay and the rice and indigo areas of South Carolina. By 1860, slaves were most heavily concentrated on the cotton and sugar land of the lower Mississippi Valley, and along an arc of fertile cotton land—the "black belt"—sweeping from Mississippi through Georgia. No slaves lived in Pennsylvania, New Jersey, and New York by this date.

tors—British markets, fresh land, and slavery. The British connection was crucial. The buoyant demand of British textile mills drove up the export price of cotton, and British mercantile houses provided the major sources of capital for the southern planters. The acquisition of fresh land was equally significant to southern agriculture because cotton ruined the soil more quickly than did most other crops. In the early 1850s, one observer described Georgia's plantation belt as "red old hills stripped of their native growth and virgin soil, and washed with deep gullies, with here and there patches of Bermuda grass, and stunted pine shrubs, struggling for a scanty subsistence on what was one of the richest soils in America." Most important, southern planters depended on slave labor. Slavery allowed them to organize labor into large-scale specialized routines that resembled factory work but were far more demanding, intense, and brutal.

The South became increasingly committed to slave labor. Most migrants from the North and from Europe avoided the South, and the majority of those who did go there found jobs that did not force them to compete with cheap slave la-

bor. Few immigrants came even during the 1850s, when there were increased opportunities in southern cities. The South actually *lost* free workers because a significant portion of its white population, especially in the border states, migrated to the upper Ohio Valley and, during the 1850s, to Oregon and California. Few slaves arrived from Africa after 1808, when Congress banned international slave trading. But the high birth rate of the existing slave population provided the necessary labor force for the expansion of cotton production and the westward sweep of the cotton frontier.

Slavery enabled the planters to impose strict organization on labor, and they forced their slaves into intensely specialized and disciplined work. The owner or overseer assigned each slave specific tasks for every season and organized the hands into disciplined "gangs," which worked in the fields at a feverish pace. Overseers, most of whom were white, and drivers, who were themselves slaves, used the threat of the whip to force their gangs into tight, coordinated units for plowing, hoeing, and picking. A traveler in Mississippi in 1854 watched an army

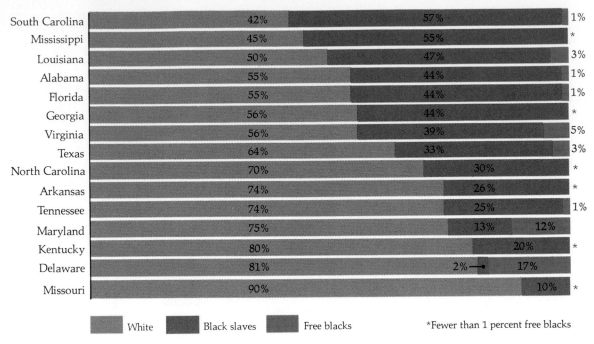

	White	Black slaves	Free blacks

*Fewer than 1 percent free blacks

FIGURE 14.1 PROPORTION OF BLACK AND WHITE POPULATION

of slaves return from the fields at the end of a summer day:

>First came, led by an old driver carrying a whip, forty of the largest and strongest women I ever saw together; they were all in a simple uniform dress of a bluish check stuff, the skirts reaching little below the knee; their legs and feet were bare; they carried themselves loftily, each having a hoe over the shoulder, and walking with a free, powerful swing.

Next marched the plowhands with their mules, "the cavalry, thirty strong, mostly men, but a few of them women." Finally, "a lean and vigilant white overseer, on a brisk pony, brought up the rear."

Plantation owners would have been unable to organize free farm workers under the discipline of slave gangs. On family farms, or on farms with only a few slaves, field workers insisted on a degree of independence and a variety of tasks. Throughout the country, whenever farm owners tried to organize free workers into gangs, the free laborers demanded wages that made their output unprofitable. Or they simply quit, preferring to find employment as sharecroppers, casual workers, or factory hands. There was a large difference between the high wages that free laborers would have received from cotton planters and the cost of rearing and maintaining slaves. The planters reaped this economic gain from slavery.

Because of the enormous demand for cotton, the availability of new land, and the gang labor system, investments in slaves were extremely profitable. All planters, except those with the poorest land, made profits that averaged about 10 percent a year on their investments in slaves during the 1840s and 1850s. Even the most successful New England textile firms rarely produced a higher rate of return.

The high profits from cotton production and slavery created two economic liabilities. First, high profits led southern investors to concentrate their resources in cotton and slaves, rather than in manufacturing. Consequently, the percentage of people who lived in towns and cities and worked in manufacturing was twice as high in the North as in the South. A more tragic liability was slavery's discouragement of investment in human beings. Planters made little or no effort to educate or train their slaves or poor whites. In fact, laws actually forbade education for slaves. Without large urban and industrial sectors, and lacking a large force of skilled, educated workers, the South faced severe difficulties in long-term economic development.

The northern business class used the threat of unemployment to discipline free workers. But it relied more on the appeals of evangelical Christianity and the promise of economic rewards. Southern planters, on the other hand, emphasized coercion, terror, and suppression of open communication to keep the slaves in line. Planters could use these tactics as long as they insulated their society from the rest of the nation. And, because the South relied heavily on foreign markets, it did enjoy a high degree of economic independence from the rest of the United States.

Ideals and Realities of the Planter Class

The planters made up a tiny minority of southern whites. In 1860, only about forty-six thousand individuals —little more than 0.5 percent of the white population of the South—owned twenty or more slaves. Only about eight thousand owned fifty or more. Nevertheless, this minority dominated southern society more completely than the business elite controlled the North.

The planters maintained their control in part by holding out to the majority of whites the possibility of entering their elite class. Most planters lived in relatively unpretentious farmhouses. However, the enormous profits of the 1840s and 1850s enabled the wealthiest planters to flaunt their wealth by building splendid plantations, indulge in displays of conspicuous consumption, and buy hordes of slaves. In the new cotton lands of the Mississippi Valley, many large cotton planters had risen from modest circumstances. Their prosperity whetted the appetites of all slaveowners—more than 380,000 individuals, belonging to about a fourth of white southern families—and the small farmers who aspired to own slaves. Like most farmers and other small property owners in the North, these southerners wanted greater wealth and status.

In the elaborate defense of slavery that southerners began to develop during the 1830s, especially after Nat Turner's rebellion and the rise of the abolitionist movement, the planters reinforced the message conveyed by their material

prosperity. They promoted descriptions of themselves as superior, noble beings whom other whites should admire or at least treat with deference. Sermons, novels, and tracts defending slavery pictured the planter as a born leader who acted with grace and restraint. The planters were, it was said, generous, hospitable, courageous, loyal, and—in the spirit of Sir Walter Scott's novels, which were popular in the South—they were chivalrous and treated women with respect. In his novel *George Balcombe* (1836), Nathaniel Beverley Tucker described the planters as descendants of "the ancient cavaliers of Virginia." They were "men in whom the spirit of freedom was so blended with loyalty as to render them alike incapable of servility and selfishness."

Idealized along with the planter was his wife—a glorification that went beyond even the northern middle-class view of pure womanhood. Defenders of southern culture believed the planter's wife had the exceptional qualities required to match those of her spouse. These virtues included sexual purity, which contrasted with what was described as the passionate sexuality of black women. Planters' wives thus became symbols of the moral superiority of whites over blacks.

The reality of plantation life for planters' wives was far more complex. Most of them ran the daily affairs of the plantation. They educated their children and cared for the sick. They managed complicated households and often entire plantations when their husbands were away, fell ill, or died. Northern men disapproved of a woman giving orders to any man, but southern white men did not object if white women directed the work of black men. However, southern white men drew a firm line that ruled out sexual intimacy between white women and black men. White men brutally punished any suspected black offenders and insisted that slavery was necessary to protect southern womanhood and prevent the mixing of the races.

This belief, and the strength of its appeal, in part reflected the guilt of planters who routinely had sex with their female slaves and fathered children by them. As one southern woman put it, "violations of the moral law made mulattoes as common as blackberries." Planters' wives generally kept quiet about this, perhaps doing nothing more than writing in their diaries. When

Mary Boykin Chesnut of South Carolina encountered a man who provided for his mulatto children in his will, she wrote in her diary: "His [white] wife and daughters, in their purity and innocence, are supposed never to dream of what is as plain before their eyes as the sunlight."

The planters relied heavily on a racist ideology to maintain the loyalty of nonslaveholders. Central to this ideology was the claim that blacks made up an inferior race—permanently unsuited for freedom and requiring rigid social control. Supporters of slavery also pictured the denial of freedom to blacks as having a highly positive result. It provided a "mudsill" class that freed whites from the most degrading kinds of work. Thus, southerners saw slavery as guaranteeing equality and freedom for whites and thereby protecting the highest values of the republic. As William Yancey of Alabama told a northern audience, "Your fathers and my fathers built this government on two ideas; the first is that the white race is the citizen and the master race, and the white man is the equal of every other white man. The second is that the Negro is the inferior race."

In maintaining the loyalty of nonslaveholders, the planters faced no significant competition. Manufacturers, merchants, lawyers, doctors, editors, and ministers comprised a far smaller proportion of the population in the South than they did in the North, and all were closely related to or dependent on wealthy planters. They might vote Whig because they supported government promotion of banking, transportation, and manufacturing, but defending slavery almost always had a higher priority. New ideas were also slow to penetrate the South. Southern cities were small and the sparse rural population was widely scattered. The vehicles of new ideas—schools, lecturers, magazines, newspapers—so common in the North, reached few southerners. This cultural isolation heightened the planters' great influence over all aspects of life.

Slave Life

The material lives of slaves reflected the prosperity of the plantation system. Most slaves were somewhat better clothed and housed than the poorest whites of both the South and North. The slaves' food—particularly when supplemented by greens from their own garden plots and by game and fish that they caught—was probably better than that of unskilled workers in the North. On many large plantations, children, the sick, and the elderly received better care than northern society provided for these groups. But the slaves realized that planters gave them material favors primarily for the self-serving motive of protecting a valuable investment. Regardless of their standard of living, the blacks knew that they remained chattel—property—and could be disciplined at will and bought and sold as though they were horses or land. As Thomas

SLAVE LIFE
This is one of the few existing photographs of American slaves. It was taken on a Virginia plantation shortly after the arrival of Union troops in 1862. The disproportionate number of women and children may indicate that the men had joined the Union war effort. (Library of Congress)

Ruffin, a justice of the North Carolina Supreme Court, said in 1829, "The power of the master must be absolute to render the submission of the slave perfect."

The working conditions of slaves varied widely. On small farms, slaves might work alongside their masters. And on every plantation some slaves were household servants, "drivers" who helped white overseers in the fields, or skilled workers such as blacksmiths and carpenters. However, most slaves lived on farms or plantations that had more than twenty blacks and worked in the fields under the gang system.

The expansion of slavery into the Southwest made the practice even more oppressive during the 1840s and 1850s. The weather in Alabama, Mississippi, Louisiana, Arkansas, and Texas was hotter, the work routines more demanding, and the planters more brutal than farther east. The slave population in those states increased from about 500,000 in 1840 to more than 1.5 million in 1860. These slaves accounted for about a fifth of the South's 2.4 million slaves in 1840 and more than a third of the 4 million in 1860.

Many blacks came to the southwestern plantations through the growing domestic slave trade, which disrupted their lives by breaking up families and communities. Masters in the coastal and border states sold slaves "down the river" both to increase their profits and to punish those whom they regarded as difficult to handle.

In response to intensified work loads and disrupted lives, slaves increased their resistance to bondage, using the same tactics of evasion and sabotage that they had employed for generations. Most important, slaves continued to nurture family relationships for protection and support and to foster personal identities independent from those of their masters. By mid-century slave families had become unusually resilient, despite the lack of legal protection. Because slaves could not make contracts, marriages between them could not be legally binding. The North Carolina Supreme Court ruled in 1853:

> Our law requires no solemnity or form in regard to the marriage of slaves, and whether they "take up" with each other by express permission of their owners, or from a mere impulse of nature, in obedience to the command "multiply and replenish the earth" cannot, in the contemplation of the law, make any sort of difference.

Nevertheless, many slaves married outside the law and lived together throughout their lives. If not broken up by sale, couples usually maintained close nuclear families. Fathers helped their sons be as independent as possible from the discipline of the master. Mothers not only worked alongside men, but also cooked, kept gardens, and raised children, often nursing babies in the field.

During this period, slaves also developed particularly elaborate kinship networks. These networks included distant relations and even individuals who had no blood or marital ties but who shared in the life of the family. Elderly slaves, for example, often played a special role as community patriarchs, conducting religious services and disciplining difficult children. Young slaves learned to address their elders by kin titles, such as "Aunt" or "Uncle," preparing them for the day when they might be separated from their parents. Even when parted by sale, members of both nuclear and extended families kept track of one another. Many runaway slaves returned to their home plantations and, after emancipation during the Civil War, thousands sought to reunite their families. If distances were too great to maintain marriages, many slaves started new families in their new location. When the Union army registered black marriages in Mississippi at the end of the Civil War, it was found that the slave trade had separated about a fourth of the men over forty years old from their previous wives.

In their quarters, slaves built a community life rich with mutual obligations. They shared insights regarding the world of their masters and news from the outside world. Religion was central to their culture. The Christianity of the slaves focused on the endurance of the Israelites in Egypt and on the caring of Christ for the oppressed. They sometimes had to conduct their services and prayers at night or in the woods, in "bush meetings" to keep them secret from the masters. Religion offered a message of eventual liberation from life's sorrows, which helped most slaves endure their bondage. Organized prayer enabled them to express love for one another and to share burdens with others. Confident of their special relationship with God, the slaves prepared themselves spiritually for emancipation, which they regarded as deliverance to the Promised Land.

Resistance and Rebellion

Slave resistance sometimes took form in overt action. Thousands of slaves sought freedom in flight. However, their chances of escaping to the North or to Canada were slim, except for those who lived near a free state and received help. Such aid often came from the "underground railroad," an informal network of white and black abolitionists. Many escaped slaves, including Harriet Tubman, who returned to the South nineteen times to free hundreds of blacks, risked reenslavement by working with the "railroad." Fugitives from the deep South faced the hazards of white patrols with bloodhounds looking for runaway slaves. On public roads or paths, all blacks were presumed to be runaways unless they carried passes to prove otherwise.

A discontented slave might also be deliberately careless wih his master's property, losing or breaking tools or setting fire to houses or barns. He could make himself useless by cutting off his fingers or even committing suicide. Or he might turn on the master and kill him.

The planters used the fear of violent slave rebellion to build support for slavery among poor whites. The fear of massacre became a binding, cohesive force among the whites, who recognized that their power over slaves depended heavily on terror—and that slaves might want to repay the terror. Planters cited many slave rebellions to support their argument. In the Caribbean, slaves had ravaged Spanish regimes and in 1791 had begun a particularly bloody revolution on the island of Santo Domingo. That revolt overthrew French planters, repelled French, British and Spanish invasions, and culminated in the creation of the black republic of Haiti in 1803. Nat Turner's rebellion of 1831 provided a dramatic, firsthand example of the capacity of enslaved blacks to fight back. Local, small-scale disturbances and abortive revolts, such as that of Denmark Vesey in Charleston, South Carolina, in 1822, were common. As many as two hundred of these small uprisings may have occurred during the first half of the nineteenth century.

Slaves generally recognized, however, particularly after Nat Turner's defeat, how heavily the odds were stacked against successful rebellion. The ratio of blacks to whites in the South was lower than in any other slave society in the Western Hemisphere. The South was not an island that could be captured and cut off from the outside world. Southern whites were well armed, unified, and militant; and the South lacked jungles, mountains, and swamps where large numbers of black guerrillas could hide. Some of the reported revolts undoubtedly took place more in the minds of slaveowners than in the actions of their slaves. But even imagined revolts showed the whites' strong fear of black quests for freedom. Few planters were entirely certain about their security in the event of a rebellion. In 1856, William Proctor Gould of Green County, Alabama, warned his slaves not to become involved in an alleged conspiracy. Although they pledged their loyalty, Gould was still uneasy enough to note, "What they might have done if there had been an actual outbreak must forever remain unknown to us."

The antislavery movement reinforced whites' fear of revolts. Southerners feared that abolitionists would mobilize the slave community. The southerners linked Turner's insurrection to the

HARRIET TUBMAN
In 1849, Harriet Tubman (1823–1913) escaped from a Maryland plantation. During the next ten years she was a leader of the Underground Railroad and became a popular abolitionist speaker. During the Civil War she served as a spy for the Union Army and then set up schools for ex-slaves in North Carolina. In 1896 she played an active role in the founding of the National Association of Colored Women. (Library of Congress)

FREDERICK DOUGLASS ON SLAVE SONGS

The fiddling, dancing, and "jubilee beating" was carried on in all directions. The latter performance was strictly southern. It supplied the place of violin, or of other musical instruments, and was played so easily that almost every farm had its "Juba" beater. The performer improvised as he beat the instrument, marking the words as he sang so as to have them fall pat with the movement of his hands. Among a mass of nonsense and wild frolic, once in a while a sharp hit was given to the meanness of slaveholders. Take the following for example:

We raise de wheat,
Dey gib us de corn;
We bake de bread,
Dey gib us de crust;
We sif de meal,
Dey gib us de huss;
We peel de meat,
Dey gib us de skin;
And dat's de way
Dey take us in;
We skim de pot,
Dey give us de liquor,
And say dat's good enough
for nigger.
Walk over! walk over!
Your butter and de fat;
Poor nigger you cant get over dat. . . .

This is not a bad summary of the palpable injustice and fraud of slavery, giving, as it does, to the lazy and idle the comforts which God designed should be given solely to the honest laborer.

I did not, when a slave, understand the deep meaning of those rude and apparently incoherent sounds [of the slaves' songs]. I was myself within the circle; so that I neither saw nor heard as those without might see and hear. They told a tale of woe which was then altogether beyond my feeble comprehension; they were tones loud, long, and deep; they breathed the prayer and complaint of souls boiling over with the bitterest anguish. Every tone was a testimony against slavery, and a prayer to God for deliverance from chains.

The hearing of those wild notes always depressed my spirit, and filled me with ineffable sadness. I have frequently found myself in tears while hearing them. The mere recurrence to those songs, even now, afflicts me; and while I am writing these lines, an expression of feeling has already found its way down my cheek. To those songs I trace my first glimmering conception of the dehumanizing character of slavery. I can never get rid of that conception. Those songs still follow me, to deepen my hatred of slavery, and quicken my sympathies for my brethren in bonds. . . .

I have often been utterly astonished, since I came to the north, to find persons who could speak of the singing, among slaves, as evidence of their contentment and happiness. It is impossible to conceive of a greater mistake. Slaves sing most when they are most unhappy. The songs of the slave represent the sorrows of the heart; and he is relieved by them, only as an aching heart by its tears. . . .

---

first publication of William Lloyd Garrison's *The Liberator*. They also recognized the moral and the intellectual leadership that free blacks contributed to the antislavery movement. Southerners feared that pressures for emancipation would release a wave of violent rebellion. They knew those pressures would mount if the South became encircled by free-soil areas that could serve as bases for abolitionist raids on plantations and provide havens for runaway slaves. The free-soil concept, the planters believed, would inevitably bring insurrection and destruction of the white southern way of life.

Southern Imperialism

During the 1840s, the South aggressively used the federal government to protect its "peculiar institution," as slavery was sometimes called, in the West. Some planters wanted to make sure they did not run out of fertile land. Southern politicians also realized that every new free state in the West increased the threat of abolition by shifting power in Congress toward the North. Moreover, if the government did not protect slavery in the West, it would sanction what white southerners believed to be a denial of their rights as free Americans. They feared that if Congress failed to protect southern rights in the territories, it might not respect those rights in the South itself.

The anxieties of white southerners became more intense during the 1840s. Earlier, southerners had pressed for the acquisition of Louisiana and Florida in order to gain new lands where slavery could expand. American planters also cited the Monroe Doctrine to warn the British not to interfere with slavery anywhere in the Western Hemisphere. When Britain abolished slavery in the West Indies in 1831, southern planters became especially agitated. They feared that the British would use abolition in the West Indies to undermine the plantation economy of the United States—and thus make the British colonies more competitive in international markets. Southern planters also thought the British had a grand scheme to block American westward expansion by establishing an antislavery barrier from the West Indies through Mexican territory sweeping from Texas all the way to California. To prevent the formation of any such barrier, southern politicians launched a program of establishing and protecting slavery on their southern boundary. This policy led the United States toward a war of conquest against Mexico.

Accelerating Industrialization in the North

Industrialization accelerated during the 1840s and 1850s, binding the Northeast and the Northwest even more tightly together. By 1860, production in the industrial sectors of the North was surpassed only by that of Great Britain and France. Northern industrial production already was more than two-thirds that of either of those two countries, and it was increasing at a more rapid rate.

The quickening pace of industrialization expanded the material resources of the northern middle class. To the members of this class, their new levels of property ownership and consumption affirmed both the success of the economic system and their own commitment to the values

of an industrial society. Swift industrialization, however, continued to disrupt many lives. It also attracted immigrants who did not accumulate property and who rejected the evangelical Protestantism of the business class. Class distinctions, in both material and cultural terms, hardened.

Factories Triumphant

In the North, during the 1840s and 1850s, hundreds of manufacturers built factories that relied on modern technology and large numbers of workers. Factory owners extended the use of power-driven machines and assembly lines from the processing of agricultural produce to the manufacture of guns, watches, sewing machines, and agricultural machinery.

In the 1850s, some large industrialists, such as reaper manufacturer Cyrus McCormick of Chicago, developed power-driven conveyor belts to assemble their finished products. During that same decade, Samuel Colt built a factory in Hartford, Connecticut, that utilized all the machine tools needed to produce the six-shooter, which he had invented. By the late 1850s, the factory responded to the enormous demand of Americans for small arms by turning out sixty thousand weapons annually. Machine production also gained importance in industries where handicrafts had retained some significance during the 1820s and 1830s. In the 1850s, for exam-

COLT'S REPEATING PISTOL
This advertisement from the 1850s illustrated two features of Colt's revolvers: their inimitable design, displayed here to help customers recognize the genuine article; and parts which could be easily disassembled for cleaning, repair, or replacement. (Connecticut State Library Archives)

M'CORMICK'S ATENT VIRGINIA REAPER.

R.N. WHITE—ENGLISH PRAIRIE

THE MCCORMICK REAPER, 1851
The McCormick reaper was a complex piece of machinery, but it was designed to be operated and repaired by average farmers. This company advertisement indicates that the various parts of the reaper were "numbered and marked with paint, showing the connection of the parts one with another that they can readily be put together by the farmer." (State Historical Society of Wisconsin)

ple, sewing machines operated by young women in shoemaking shops began to replace the women and men who had stitched and bound shoes in an outwork system.

The most important machines included the stationary steam engine, used to power other machines and assembly lines. By 1840, manufacturers had exhausted available water-power sites and were forced to use more expensive steam power. However, the steam engine offered one advantage over water power; it enabled the most modern manufacturers to operate in the nation's largest cities—the great Atlantic seaports and the booming ports on the Great Lakes—rather than the smaller cities where falling water could be harnessed. During the 1840s modern manufacturers for the first time took advantage of all the benefits offered by a big-city location—easy access to the cheapest immigrant labor, highly developed markets for capital, sophisticated trading services, and urban consumers. Manufacturers in the seaports and the largest western cities, particularly Chicago, broke the near-monopoly that smaller inland cities had held on the most modern industries.

The manufacturers' growing demand for machinery stimulated the machine-tool industry, which became even more critical to the advance of industrialization. In the 1850s, the same machines that made parts for firearms were used to make parts for sewing machines. By the late 1850s, five Connecticut clockmakers used modern machine tools to make intricate works for half a million clocks a year. Some of these products remained well known for generations—Colt revolvers, Remington rifles, Singer sewing machines, Waltham watches, Yale locks, and McCormick reapers.

In 1851, at the Crystal Palace Exhibition in London, the first world's fair of the industrial era, Cyrus McCormick and Samuel Colt displayed their machine-tooled products. The amazement of British manufacturers quickly turned to anxiety when McCormick and Colt swiftly established factories in England and introduced American machinery and production techniques there. The British government dispatched two teams of technicians to the United States to investigate U.S. factories. They reported that many different industries were organized "in large factories, with machinery applied to almost every process, the extreme subdivision of labor, and all reduced to an almost perfect system of manufacture."

The increasing scale and complexity of production, however, made it difficult for manufacturers to estimate the demand for their products. During the 1850s, periods of overproduction

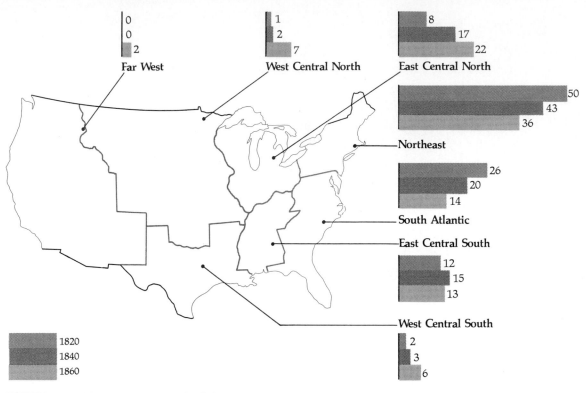

FIGURE 14.2 POPULATION BY REGION, 1820–1860

followed by the layoff and dismissal of workers became more common. One such episode coincided with the Panic of 1857—a crisis produced by an overexpansion of railroad investment—and a long depression followed. Unemployment remained at about 10 percent until the outbreak of the Civil War in 1861.

The Buoyant Northwest

By 1860, the United States possessed all the territory that later formed the contiguous forty-eight states. The westward movement had taken about half the nation's 31.4 million people west of the Appalachian Mountains. Most of them lived in the states of the old Northwest, around the Great Lakes, and in the Ohio and Mississippi valleys. Most settlers new to the West during the 1840s and 1850s migrated from New England and the Middle Atlantic states to Ohio, Indiana, Illinois, and Wisconsin—to wheat farms, to towns that serviced those farms, and to other, increasingly industrial towns. As people moved

westward, agriculture and industry developed in close conjunction, and the economies of the Northeast and Northwest became inextricably linked.

Federal land policy accelerated the pace of westward expansion. Most important was the Preemption Act, passed by Congress in 1841. Preemption recognized that people commonly settled on public land before purchasing it from the government; it also gave an advantage to actual settlers over land speculators. The act gave most American citizens and immigrants the right to buy 160 acres of land, provided they built a house on the land and made "improvements," such as clearing the land for crops. In 1854, the government further liberalized land policy in the Graduation Act, which allowed lands that had long been on the market to be sold below the official $1.25 per acre minimum.

The increasing availability of low cost, labor-saving machinery also quickened settlement, particularly on the fertile, grain-producing prairies bordering the Great Lakes. John Deere's steel plow, superior in strength to the cast iron plow, won widespread acceptance during the 1850s. In 1837, as a blacksmith in Grand Detour, Illinois, Deere had made his first steel plow from old saws; ten years later, in Moline, he opened a factory that used mass-production techniques. In addition, various companies—McCormick, Hussey, Atkins, and Manny—made reapers which grain farmers found invaluable. Previously, one worker with a cradle scythe cut two to three acres a day. In the 1850s, with a self-raking reaper, that farmer cut twelve acres daily. Largely because northwestern farmers had begun to use the products of modern factories in their fields, their productivity and incomes increased more than 20 percent during the 1850s.

Another product of industrial technology, the railroad, hastened the advance of farmers into the Northwest. As late as 1852, canals still carried twice as much tonnage as the railroads. During the next five or six years, railroad companies increased track mileage dramatically, built trunk lines across New York and Pennsylvania to provide through traffic to Chicago, and reduced their rates. By 1859, they carried more freight than did the canals. Railroads also lowered the costs of transporting farm goods and thus made western farming more profitable. In addition, they enabled farmers to settle in remote areas that canal or river transport did not serve and to produce crops for export to eastern markets.

Railroads also created new urban opportunities in the West. By stimulating an increased flow of goods, the railroads promoted commerce, particularly where trunk lines converged

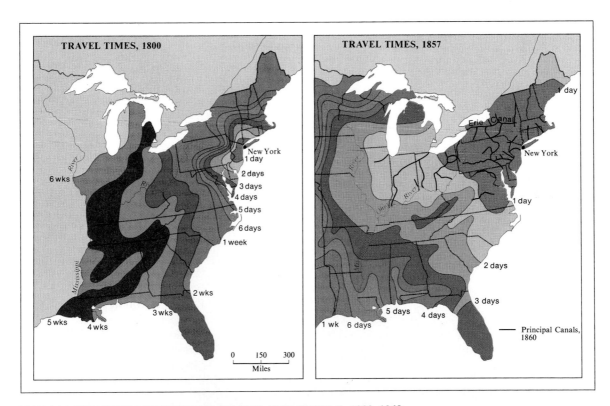

MAP 14.2 THE NEW MOBILITY OF GOODS AND PEOPLE, 1800–1860
This map shows how much the transportation revolution had dramatically decreased travel times for people and goods by 1860, as shown in the changing patterns on this map. In 1800, a traveller from New York required an entire day to reach Philadelphia and a full week to reach Pittsburgh or western New York state. In 1860, a day's travel on the railroad could take a New York traveller as far west as Cleveland. In a week the traveller could reach the Kansas Territory or the uppermost reaches of the Mississippi River.

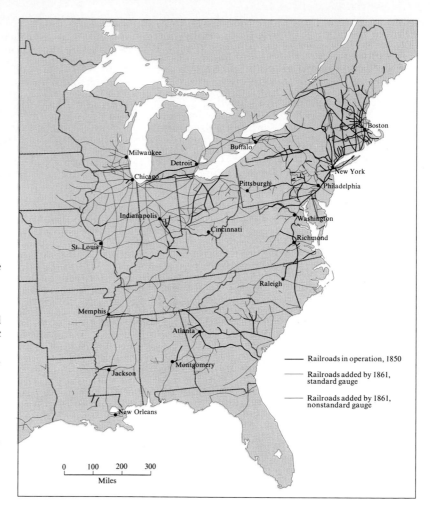

MAP 14.3 RAILROADS OF THE NORTH AND SOUTH, 1850–1860
The decade before the Civil War witnessed explosive growth in the nation's railroad network, but it was geographically uneven. The Northeast and Middle West acquired extensive, dense railroad linkages that stimulated economic development. The South built a much simpler system. Numerous, highly competitive companies built railroad lines, often using different track gauges that hindered the efficient flow of traffic and often made the transshipment of goods slow and expensive. Such problems were frustrating to the military, and proved especially severe in the South during the Civil War.

or rail routes met water transport. Springing up at these points were grain storehouses, warehouses, docks, flour mills, packing plants, and farm machinery factories, as well as mercantile and financial firms. In 1846, Cyrus McCormick moved from western Virginia to Chicago so he could manufacture his reapers closer to his grain-producing customers. Saint Louis and Chicago became boom towns largely because of the railroads. As early as 1860, they surpassed Boston and Baltimore in size and became the nation's third and fourth largest cities, respectively, behind New York and Philadelphia. Railroads undermined the economic base of other western cities, however. The trunk-line railroads reduced the importance of such cities as Cincinnati, Pittsburgh, Buffalo, and Rochester, which

had been key regional centers along water routes. Thousands of dockworkers, teamsters, and warehouse workers in those cities lost their jobs when the railroads provided efficient through traffic. During the depression of the late 1850s, many of these workers joined other unskilled laborers who roamed the country in search of casual employment or charity.

Because rails required high-quality iron, the western demand for railroads forced the American iron industry to modernize. By 1860, the railmills, located primarily in and around Philadelphia, were the largest and most technically advanced iron mills in the country. The engineering requirements for train engines had a similar effect on steam engine production. Moreover, to service complex locomotives, the railroads built a large network of machine shops that extended into the Northwest. These shops disseminated industrial skills and promoted the growth of a skilled labor force.

The spread of wheat production in the nation's interior also stimulated industry by lowering the cost of food for working people. Without a rapidly growing food supply to augment their diet, workers could not have physically endured the long hours of work that factories required. And without a cheap and rapidly increasing food supply, the working population would not have grown as rapidly. By 1850, Americans consumed an average of more than four thousand calories daily, compared with only two thousand or twenty-five hundred in 1700. The health of infants and nursing mothers

was probably better than in any other country, which helped make the death rate about half that of western Europe. By mid-century, the American diet was so ample that people born in the United States and raised on American diets had achieved heights and weights comparable to those of mid-twentieth-century Americans. The "breadbasket" of the Northwest had become vital to the health and productivity of the American people.

Business-Class Consumption

The income of Americans increased at unprecedented rates during the 1840s and 1850s. By the mid-1850s, the annual increase in per capita income approached 2.5 percent, a remarkable rate that the United States has never since matched. People with property or skills reaped the lion's share of this income bonanza and bought consumer goods that served as the badge of their economic success, and of their membership in the business class. The availability of inexpensive mass-produced goods, many of them new during the 1840s and 1850s, made the trappings of status even more accessible.

Homes became increasingly distinctive and affordable. They featured larger, more numerous bedrooms to enhance the privacy of each member of the family. The leading architectural philosopher of the era, Andrew Jackson Downing, lauded such designs in his most famous book, *The Architecture of Country Houses* (1850). Reinforcing Catharine Beecher's idealization of domesticity, Downing argued that his new houses would promote a "refinement of manners" and strengthen the life of the family, which was "the best social form." Within the single-family home, Downing proclaimed, "truthfulness, beauty, and order have the largest dominion." Ample homes would provide a medium for the success of republican ideas. By enabling average people to purchase homes, the Industrial Revolution was thought to advance the virtue of the citizenry.

Prosperous urban families furnished their new homes with an array of new comforts, decorations, and devices. Furnaces heated both interiors and water. Europeans marveled at them and at the American desire for warmth. One

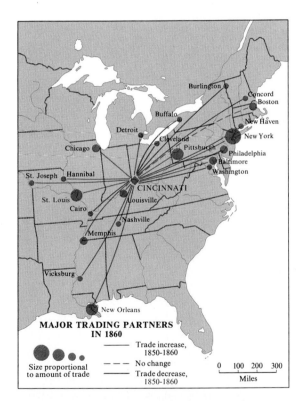

MAP 14.4 INCREASING INTERIOR TRADE
The growth of railroads greatly stimulated the development of cities within the interior. This map shows how the far-flung, growing trade of Cincinnati was distributed. During the 1850s, Cincinnati consolidated its trade with large eastern cities, including New York—its most important trading partner—while vigorously building linkages with cities to the west and south.

ADVERTISEMENT FOR STOVES, 1856
This broadside advertisement was an early effort to use mass-produced media to sell expensive household goods. Westchester Stove Works gave romantic names to the various stove models to appeal to prosperous urban families. The manufacturer also offered terms "the same as govern the general trade in both credits and discounts." (The New-York Historical Society. Bella C. Landauer Collection)

visitor complained that it was impossible to escape hot air: "It meets you the moment the street-door is opened to let you in, rushes after you when you emerge again, half-stewed and parboiled, into the wholesome air." In most homes, beds with springs of woven rope or iron wire replaced beds with wooden slats. Homemade featherbeds, mattresses, and down pillows spread rapidly after mass-produced ticking and sheeting became available in stores. Households acquired goods that made traditional chores more efficient. Beginning in the 1850s, some women purchased treadle-operated sewing machines. Most prosperous urban households now had stoves with ovens, including broilers and movable grates, instead of open hearths. Women used a wide variety of pots, pans, and kettles; some mechanical equipment, such as grinders and presses; and washboards. And these households had iceboxes that ice-company wagons filled daily. As early as 1825, for example, the Underwood Company of Boston marketed well-preserved Atlantic salmon in glass

jars. With the introduction of the Mason jar in 1858, households vastly increased their ability to preserve other perishable foods.

Even families with very modest incomes added decorative touches to their homes—sheet glass (rather than blown glass) in large windows that brought full sunlight into the interior; tin and glassware that caught the light; colorful curtains; ruffles and flounces for chairs; tablecloths; floor coverings; and wall prints. Many of these prints were advertised by Currier and Ives, the leading lithography firm of the nineteenth century, as "prints for the people." Others were simply the clipped pages of illustrated magazines. The proliferation of low-cost textiles, furniture, lamps, glass, and ceramics enabled almost every home to have a unique appearance. Mass-circulation newspapers in big cities advertised manufacturers and retailers of these goods, and large stores paved the way in promoting a consumer culture. In New York City, Broadway had many of the most modern stores, led by Alexander T. Stewart's. By the 1850s,

Stewart's was a six-story, white marble building with large plate glass windows and four hundred clerks.

The new household furnishings also included clocks. Before 1820, townspeople and villagers relied on public clocks or bells; country folk told time by the sun. By the 1840s, inexpensive clocks and watches had become the main methods of keeping time. One traveler in the West found them everywhere in the early 1840s: "In Kentucky, in Indiana, in Illinois, in Missouri, and here in every dell in Arkansas, and in cabins where there was not a chair to sit on, there was sure to be a Connecticut clock." Clocks had revolutionary effects. People could organize themselves to meet the more intense pace of daily life produced by the Industrial Revolution.

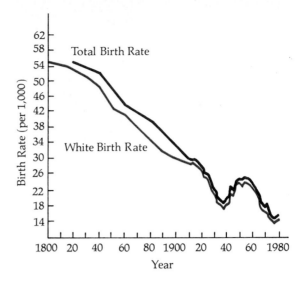

FIGURE 14.3 BIRTHRATE BY RACE

Family Planning

Another tangible hallmark of the emerging business class was its growing investment in young people. Parents aspiring to higher status and income for their children tried to provide them with a healthier environment, better food, basic academic skills, and the personal and social qualities appropriate to urban life. They began to spend more money on educating their children, kept them in school longer, and devoted more attention to their upbringing.

Partly because of the costs of education, some parents began to limit the size of their families. Acquainted with primitive but moderately effective means of birth control—abstinence, coitus interruptus, condoms fashioned from animal skins and intestines, and abortions induced by potent herbs—urban families from the business elite and the middle class led the movement to restrict family size. They, more than families that owned little property, recognized the value of urban-based skills. More important, they did not feel a pressing need for their children to bring home wages or to support them in old age. Rather, they felt more pressure to buy new goods and, in order to purchase more goods, to restrict the number of children they had.

Some rural parents in older agricultural areas also began to limit the size of their families. An important worry for these families was the rising price of land, which limited their ability to buy land for their children. Farmers, like urban middle-class parents, were also aware of the high return of skilled urban employment. Consequently, some farm families, especially in the East, began to practice birth control. The fertility rates in frontier areas declined more slowly. There, only the most highly mobile, disrupted families restricted family size. On the frontier, where the price of land remained low, the labor of children retained greater relative value.

Between 1800 and 1860, the average family size declined from 5.8 to 5.3 members, including adults. The birth rate, however, continued high—from forty-five to fifty live births per thousand people per year—compared with thirty per thousand in Europe. Most American parents remained confident of their ability to bear a large number of children and yet make sure that the children would lead useful, productive lives; they continued to have large families. As a consequence of the high birth rate and increasing immigration, the number of Americans rose from seventeen million in 1840 to thirty-one million in 1860. By 1860, Americans exceeded the British in number and were about to overtake both the Germans and French.

Immigration

In 1860, immigrants accounted for more than a fourth of the free white adult males in the United States and more than a third of those in the North. Between 1820 and 1860, about 2 million Irish immigrants settled in the United States along with 1.5 million Germans and 750,000 Britishers. Some of these immigrants were skilled workers but more than two-thirds were peasants, unskilled laborers, and farmers, dislocated by industrial and agricultural revolutions in Europe. Most of the newcomers took low-skilled jobs in factories, construction projects, docks, warehouses, and private homes. No federal legislation restricted immigration, and state immigration laws setting minimum health standards and excluding paupers were ineffective.

During the 1840s, manufacturers found it in-

THE STATUS OF IMMIGRANTS, 1855
The painter Charles F. Blauvelt was one of the rare artists of the period to make immigrants his subject, and to treat them with a degree of realism and sympathy. And perhaps he meant to highlight the generosity of blacks by suggesting that they would help lost immigrants even though the new immigrants, simply by virtue of the color of their skin, enjoyed higher status. (Charles Blauvelt. *A German Immigrant Inquiring His Way.* The North Carolina Museum of Art, Raleigh)

creasingly difficult to recruit and control unskilled American-born workers. When the manufacturers began to speed up production by taking advantage of new machines and steam power, many of their workers organized to resist. For example, in 1845, a group of workers in Lowell, Massachusetts, under the leadership of Sarah G. Bagley, a weaver, formed the Lowell Female Labor Reform Asociation to protest such a speedup. As working conditions became more grueling—and as their interests changed—most of the young women who had poured into factory work retired to the New England countryside and raised families.

Manufacturers in older industrial centers and in seaports thus turned to immigrants, both men and women, from Canada, Ireland, and the German states. Lacking the economic opportunities available to Americans, the immigrants were willing to work for longer periods of time, at lower wages, and with greater intensity. As a result, immigrants began to fill the unskilled labor force in the 1840s.

The poorest and most numerous of the immigrants were the Irish. They arrived in increasing numbers during the 1830s but began to come in force only in 1847, after a devastating potato famine drove them out of Ireland. They found new homes throughout much of the Northeast, especially in the cities of New England. By 1850, the Irish accounted for more than a third of the workers in Boston. Their labor enabled Boston industrialists to compete for the first time with manufacturers in the smaller mill towns of Massachusetts and Rhode Island. By 1860, each of the largest factories producing women's clothing in Boston employed about a hundred young Irishwomen. During the late 1840s and early 1850s, the Irish made only a modest contribution to the farm population. Most of them had been farmers in Ireland, but they were too poor to buy land in the United States.

Living conditions for many Irish immigrants, as for other unskilled immigrants and native-born day laborers, were only marginally better than the grinding poverty and rampant disease that had filled their lives in the Old World. Per capita consumption of all categories of food increased during the Industrial Revolution, and most immigrants were much better nourished than they had been in Europe. Even so, many

ADVICE TO PROSPECTIVE WELSH IMMIGRANTS, 1840

Benjamin W. Chidlaw, the first missionary of the American Sunday School Union in Ohio and Indiana, wrote a booklet of "Instructions for Inquirers" to encourage emigration from his native Wales and prepare settlers for the journey. It was translated from the Welsh by a relative in 1976.

Leaving our native land, our home and friends, travelling thousands of miles over sea and land, and becoming strangers in a foreign land is an important and sad experience. Before making such a long and unfamiliar journey in ignorance, people should seek the Lord's advice and give the matter very serious consideration. Many of the inhabitants of Wales have benefitted themselves and their offspring by going to America, exchanging poverty for plenty of those blessings that make life pleasant, but not without overcoming many difficulties and after untiring endeavors were they able to enjoy them. Others have worsened their situation by changing one country for another, all their pleasant expectations having resulted in disappointment and heart-break. . . .

Men with families, who are living comfortably and whose children after them have similar prospects, need not depart from their native land since they cannot expect to find anything better in any other country. . . . I advise those who are unaccustomed to work and who have no desire for it not to cross the great deep. . . . Although high wages are paid there, it is not a good place for living on the toil of others without doing anything yourself. Every freeholder there, if he is healthy and able to cultivate the land, cares for and works on his holding. The children are taught to work and thus, with the efforts of the children coupled with those of their parents, wealth increases. . . . It would not befit anyone who is "addicted to wine, clamouring in their cups," to go to America, they might as well suffer the indignity, shame, livelihood and grave of a drunkard here than there. Everyone who thinks of spending his time drinking in idleness should not expect much comfort in a land where intoxicating drinks are so plentiful and cheap. . . .

For young people who have worked hard and possess money America presents an opportunity to obtain good interest on their capital, or to purchase land in these new countries, and by leaving it for a few years they will find that it will have increased considerably in price and become very valuable. The Welsh tend to remain unfortunately in the old settlements, choosing high and rugged land; but having left their homes as well as the religious facilities they once possessed, they might as well endeavor to secure a good place and productive land, since the district is certain to flourish and religious amenities will follow. . . .

When going to America many difficulties have to be faced, leaving one country, travelling over sea and land, learning a new language and acquiring new customs and starting life anew—in a word, going to America is a revolution in a man's life.

---

unskilled laborers could not afford to buy the food they needed to keep up the intense pace of factory work. In addition, the stress and insecurity of work drove many unskilled workers to spend increasing portions of their income on the entertainment and alcoholic relief found in taverns. Malnutrition increased in the largest cities, resulting in higher rates of miscarriage and of death from infectious diseases.

Urban crowding, especially in the old commercial cities of the Northeast, threatened public health. Sanitation systems were primitive. Poorly sealed privies drained into drinking wells and open sewers ran through streets. Infectious diseases ravaged the weakened, malnourished poor. Epidemics of cholera, yellow fever, typhoid fever, smallpox, diphtheria, and tuberculosis struck the major cities. In the summer of 1849, major cholera epidemics hit New York, Saint Louis, and Cincinnati. More than five thousand people, most of them immigrants, died in New York. Many entire families succumbed.

Wealthy families moved out of the cities during the epidemics, while, as one observer wrote, the immigrants remained crowded "into a few wretched hovels, amidst filth and bad air, suffering from personal neglect and poisoned by eating garbage [at] which a well-bred hog on a western farm would turn up his snout." In 1860, mortality rates in New York, Philadelphia, and Boston reached a level of more than thirty-four deaths per thousand population annually, compared with only about fifteen per thousand in rural areas.

Irish Identity and Anti-Catholicism

In the United States, the French-Canadians, many Germans, and particularly the Irish relied on the Catholic church not only to sustain their spiritual lives but also to reinforce their sense of class and ethnic identity. The church's expansion closely paralleled the growth of Irish immigration, increasing from sixteen dioceses and seven hundred churches in the 1840s to forty-five dioceses and three thousand churches by the 1860s. Throughout the areas settled by Irish immigrants, traveling priests were replaced by resident ones. The Irish purchased many church buildings from Protestant congregations that had moved to more elegant quarters. In towns and cities, using the church as a foundation, the Irish also built a network of charitable societies, orphanages, militia companies, parochial schools, newspapers, social clubs, and political organizations. These community institutions supported the Irish immigrants in their search for housing, jobs, education, and security.

The new institutions had no equivalent in Ireland. They developed independently in the United States during the 1840s and 1850s in response to the desire of Irish immigrants to maintain their native culture, a culture to which existing American institutions were hostile or, at best, indifferent. The church network was important to immigrants who labored in large cities and especially to those who worked in big-city factories. It provided community services and a sense of group identity, much as a labor union might have done. The institutions that the Irish created had a great impact on later groups of Catholic immigrants. Because the Irish arrived early and because many spoke English, they built the church structure and the urban political machinery through which most European Catholic immigrants initially established a place for themselves in American life.

The relative autonomy of Catholic communities disturbed American Protestants, who comprised the dominant majority in most of the United States. During the 1830s, when Irish immigration started to increase, lurid anti-Catholic propaganda began to circulate. Its authors raised the specter of a sinister, highly organized menace that paralleled the free-soilers' description of the "Slave Power" conspiracy. According to the propaganda, the pope, acting through Catholics over whom he exerted total authority, plotted to subvert republican institutions.

In 1834, Samuel F. B. Morse, who invented the telegraph code, anonymously began to publish his *Foreign Conspiracy Against the Liberties of the United States*. This book came out under Morse's own name in 1835, and Protestant ministers of many denominations endorsed it. Morse declared that the "past history" of Roman Catholics and "the fact that they everywhere act together, as if guided by one mind, admonish us to be jealous of their influence, and to watch with unremitted care all their movements in relation to our free institutions." He warned in particular of the political facility of Irish Catholics. They "in an especial manner clanned together, and kept alive their foreign feelings, associations, habits and manners." Morse advocated the formation of an "Anti-Popery Union" to resist the perceived Catholic threat on all fronts.

Millions of young Americans read *Foreign Conspiracy* in Protestant Sunday schools and in public libraries and schools. It became a textbook for anti-Catholic crusaders. In 1838, the citizens of Sutton and Millbury, Massachusetts, asked Congress to investigate "whether there are not now those amongst us, who, by their oath of allegiance to a foreign despotic Prince or Power, are solemnly bound to support his interests and accelerate his designs."

The anti-Catholic movement became exceptionally intense because of the dislocations associated with industrialization. It appealed especially to artisans who had lost their jobs, or feared that they might lose them, as a consequence of the factory system. By attacking Catholics, they could blame cheap immigrant labor for their economic situation and, at the same time, persuade themselves that they at least had a superior culture and religion. These workers organized Native American Clubs, societies that called for an extension of the waiting period before naturalization from five to twenty-one years, a restriction of public offices to native-born Americans, and exclusive use of the (Protestant) Authorized Version of the Bible in public schools.

Workers who felt secure in their jobs—skilled factory workers, skilled laborers in the building trades, and white-collar employees—faced no direct threat from the immigrants. However, they feared that their children would face competition from immigrants, and they worried that Catholic preferences for parochial schools would weaken the public schools. This was fanned by proposals from Catholic clergy and Democratic legislators in many northeastern states to reserve Catholics' taxes for parochial schools. Evangelical ministers sometimes gave the temperance movement an anti-Catholic edge by emphasizing the abuse of alcohol—and consequent departures from good work habits—among Irish immigrants. Such appeals won recruits to the growing business class among native-born Protestant workers, and it impeded the development of a labor movement across ethnic and religious lines. Many Protestant laborers became convinced that they had more in common with their employers and other members of the business class than with Catholic workers.

In almost every city with a large Catholic immigrant population, the anti-Catholic movement became violent. In 1834, in Charlestown, Massachusetts, a quarrel between Catholic laborers in an Ursuline convent and Protestant workers in a neighboring brickyard turned into a full-scale riot. The anti-Catholic mob, persuaded that a young Protestant woman was being held against her will, drove out the residents of the convent and burned it to the ground. Larger urban riots erupted during the late 1830s and the 1840s as the Irish began to acquire significant political power in eastern cities. In Philadelphia, the violence peaked in 1844 after the Catholic bishop persuaded public school officials to use both Protestant and Catholic versions of the Bible. Anti-Irish rioting, provoked by the city's Native American Clubs, lasted for two months and escalated into open warfare between the Protestants and the Pennsylvania militia, causing many casualties.

In 1850, the secret anti-Catholic societies banded together in the Order of the Star Spangled Banner, and in 1854 they led in forming a new national political party, the American party. The members sometimes answer outsiders' questions by saying, "I know nothing." This gave the party the name that stuck, "Know-Nothing." The program of the Know-Nothings, however, was not mysterious. They supported the program of the Native American Clubs and advocated literacy tests for voters, which they thought would disenfranchise most recent immigrants. In the 1854 elections the Know-Nothings attempted to unite northern and southern voters behind a program of nativist opposition to Catholics and the "alien menace." They won a number of seats in Congress and gained control of the state governments of Massachusetts and Pennsylvania.

Decline of Whig Economics

The accelerating industrialization had a marked impact on politics. It strengthened the commitment of the urban middle class and prosperous farmers of the North to the values of the business elite, to the Whig party, and to the party's promotion of high tariffs, a national bank, and internal improvements. With the presidential election victory of William Henry Harrison, the Whig candidate in 1840, prospects for this program seemed highly promising.

The Whigs lost their opportunity, however, when Harrison died of pneumonia in 1841, one month after his inauguration. His successor was Vice-President John Tyler, a Virginian who was a far from typical southern Whig. Tyler opposed the urban commercial interests in his own state and had become a Whig because of his enthusiasm for states' rights. He had shared Andrew

Jackson's hostility to the Second Bank, but his disgust with Jackson's nationalism was too great for him to become a Democrat.

As president, Tyler's prime objective was to block the nationalizing economic program of his own party. He succeeded, vetoing two bills sponsored by Henry Clay to reestablish the national bank. He also blocked major protective tariffs. Tyler limited Whig successes to the repeal of the independent Treasury in 1841 and a modest increase in tariffs in 1842. The only major economic program enacted during his administration was one on which Democrats and Whigs could agree, the Preemption Act of 1841. Consequently, Clay broke with Tyler. Then all of Tyler's cabinet, except Secretary of State Daniel Webster, resigned. Tyler appointed Democrats to replace them but kept Webster in the cabinet in order to maintain a tie with New England and to claim that he had bipartisan support.

Remaining in office enabled Webster to achieve a Whig foreign policy objective—preventing war with Great Britain—that had major economic implications. Beginning in the late 1830s, a series of incidents had brought the two nations close to a third war. These incidents included the destruction in 1837 of an American ship, the *Caroline*, that was aiding Canadians rebelling against British rule; the "Aroostook War" in 1838–1839 between American and Canadian lumberjacks along the disputed border between Maine and Canada; and the British seizure in 1841 of an American brig, the *Creole*, sailing from Virginia to New Orleans with a cargo of about a hundred slaves. Supported by the business leaders of the Atlantic seaports, who feared that war with Britain would disrupt trade and interrupt recovery from the Panic of 1837, Webster negotiated the Webster-Ashburton Treaty, which the Senate ratified in August 1842. This treaty firmly established the Canadian-American boundary from the Atlantic Ocean to the Rocky Mountains and provided for a division of labor between the United States and Britain in policing the international slave trade. American naval squadrons assumed responsibility for capturing slave ships flying the American flag. Webster secretly funded newspaper editorials favoring his treaty, and talk of war subsided.

Tyler's defeat of Clay's American System gave the Democrats time to consolidate their opposition to the Whig economic proposals. The Democratic party mobilized workers, poor farmers in the North, and planters and small farmers in the South. Immigrant workers strongly opposed any economic programs that seemed to offer benefits to the wealthy. Also, Catholic immigrants hated the insistent Protestantism of the Whigs and appreciated the Democrats' greater acceptance of religious and economic diversity. These immigrants provided a new base of support for the Democratic party. In New York City during the 1840s, about 95 percent of the Irish Catholic electorate usually supported Democratic candidates.

In 1844, James K. Polk, a Jacksonian Democrat from Tennessee, defeated the Whig candidate, Henry Clay, in the presidential election. Clay's defeat was the final blow to the Whig program. In 1846, a Democratic Congress restored the independent Treasury and wiped out the 1842 tariff increase by passing the Walker Tariff. This law retained protection only in principle and seemed to herald the adoption of free trade by the United States. Further Whig defeats in 1846 diminished politicians' enthusiasm for campaigning on their traditional economic program. But congressional Whigs continued to advance their economic policies when they could, even if it meant cooperating with Democrats. In 1850, for example, they supported Senator Stephen A. Douglas of Illinois, a Democrat, in his successful effort to grant federal lands for the Illinois Central Railroad.

Northern Whigs also had to cope with southern efforts to gain control of the trans-Mississippi West, which, they believed, would block the expansion of free agriculture, assure control of the government for the Democratic representatives of slavery and immigrant labor, and permanently deny the Whigs their economic goals. Whig abolitionists were particularly fervent and attempted to commit their party to free-soil ideas. The stage was set for the replacement of Clay's American System by free-soil as the central economic program of the business class. During the 1840s, as northern Whigs inched toward that position, they drove a wedge between themselves and the southern Whigs, undermining their party's national base.

Party and Sectional Conflict over the West

During the 1840s, conflict over the legal status of slavery resulted when both northerners and southerners moved into western areas that were to be organized as territories in preparation for statehood. To southern planters, the chance that Americans could seize northern Mexico and secure it for slavery seemed a possible solution to their anxiety over the British and abolitionist threats to slavery. The South's ambitions produced a major fracture in the Whig party, and a lesser break in the Democratic party, between southerners loyal to slavery and northerners who supported free-soil. The issue of how to govern the territory taken from Mexico widened these splits, particularly among the Whigs. However, the threat to party unity, and to the Union itself, became so great that in 1850 leaders of both parties joined in framing a major sectional compromise.

The Texas Rebellion

The shift of national politics to a focus on slavery in the West began with a rebellion of Americans who had settled in Mexican territory north of the Rio Grande River. These people had migrated there after Mexico, which won independence from Spain in 1821, began to encourage immigration to its Texas district. During the 1820s, empresarios from the lower Mississippi Valley, led by Stephen F. Austin received grants for the best land in Texas. By 1830, about thirty thousand Americans lived in Texas, far outnumbering the four thousand Mexicans there. The American Texans, looking forward to planting cotton, had imported slaves by finding loopholes in Mexico's restrictions against slavery and the slave trade.

The Mexican government worried about the strength of the American immigrant community in Texas and about the possibility that American settlement would revive slavery in the country. In 1830, Mexico restricted American immigration and prohibited the importation of slaves. These actions, and the news that abolitionists planned to establish a refuge for free blacks in Texas, led the Americans to begin violent protests in 1832.

They launched a full-scale uprising in 1834, when the new Mexican president, Antonio Lopez de Santa Anna, arrested Austin.

The rebellious Texans found that they had powerful support in the United States. In March 1836, the news that Santa Anna had wiped out a Texas garrison defending the Alamo, in San Antonio, captured the attention of New Orleans and New York newspapers. Their correspondents at the scene romanticized the heroism of the Texans. Using some of the strongest anti-Catholic rhetoric of the day, the newspapers described the Mexicans as tyrannical butchers in the service of the pope. Thousands of adventurers, learning of Texan offers of land bounties, sailed to Texas from New York, the Gulf states, and the Mississippi Valley. Reinforced by many of these new arrivals and led by Sam Houston, the Texas rebels routed the Mexicans in the Battle of San Jacinto in April 1836. Texas then proclaimed its independence and adopted a constitution legalizing slavery. Mexico refused to recognize the new republic, but it abandoned any effort to reconquer it.

The Texans immediately voted by plebiscite for annexation by the United States. But President Andrew Jackson and his successor, Martin Van Buren, took no position regarding this issue, fearing it would lead to war with Mexico and divide the Democratic party. Privately, however, Jackson supported annexation and even encouraged the Texans to seize Mexican territory all the way to the Pacific Ocean.

The Annexation of Texas and "Oregon Fever"

Prospects for the annexation of Texas improved suddenly in 1843. That year, President John Tyler, whom congressional Whigs had read out of their party in 1841, decided to rally southern Democratic support for annexation so that he might win the Democratic nomination for president in 1844. He abandoned his remaining ties with northern Whigs and replaced Secretary of State Webster with a Virginian, Abel P. Upshur, who defended slavery as the foundation of "democracy" in the South. Together with John C. Calhoun, who had rejoined the Democratic party because he feared the economic program and abolitionist tendencies of the Whigs, Tyler and Upshur hatched a plot to annex Texas.

Tyler, Upshur, and Calhoun planned to obtain a new request from Texas for annexation and then to undertake a propaganda campaign to weaken northern opposition to annexation. They argued that annexation was necessary to prevent British domination of Texas and the West. In 1844, after Upshur died in an accident, Tyler appointed Calhoun as secretary of state, and the two leaders put their plan into effect. In April, Tyler submitted an annexation treaty to the Senate.

Calhoun encountered opposition from two leaders with presidential ambitions—Democrat Martin Van Buren, hoping to return to the White House, and Whig Henry Clay, a perennial candidate. Each feared he would alienate too many northern supporters by supporting annexation. Therefore, Clay and Van Buren joined in opposing ratification of the annexation treaty until Mexico approved it. They successfully united northern votes across party lines and defeated the treaty in Congress. Neither Van Buren nor

THE HAGER FAMILY
Most women joined their husbands' quest to Oregon with great misgiving and heartache. The hard journey uprooted many women in their childbearing years, and many died in childbirth along the trail. For those who survived, like the hauntingly beautiful young mother here with her child asleep in a packing crate, settlement meant continued hardship and uncertainty. (University of Oregon Library)

Clay foresaw, however, that during the presidential election of 1844, northern voters would link annexation of Texas with their own expansionist dreams for Oregon.

"Oregon fever" had gripped pioneers from the Ohio Valley since the late 1830s. By 1844, nearly five thousand people, attracted by glowing descriptions of the soil and climate of the Pacific Northwest, had followed the Oregon Trail and established farms in the fertile Willamette Valley. These settlers demanded that the federal government establish control over all of Oregon—to its northern boundary of 54° 40'. The British, who dominated the Oregon fur trade, had accepted the American claim only to the area south of the Columbia River; American diplomats pressed for title to at least the lands south of the forty-ninth parallel. Tyler and Calhoun argued that the British were determined to block the expansion of the republic into Oregon as well as Mexico.

Many Americans who might otherwise have opposed the extension of slavery accepted Tyler and Calhoun's linkage of the Texas and Oregon issues. Some may even have been persuaded by such popular propagandists as Robert J. Walker, a Mississippi planter and senator. In 1844, millions of copies of Walker's *Letter Relative to the Annexation of Texas* were distributed in the North. Addressing northern Democrats, he argued that Texas and, in turn, Mexico and Central America, would provide a safety valve to draw off slavery, slaves, and the race problem at the same time that southern soil wore out. Without a safety valve, Walker claimed, emancipated slaves ultimately would flood the northern economy or, if they remained in the South, cause a cataclysmic race war.

Economic issues had dominated the presidential campaign of 1840, but Texas and Oregon predominated in 1844. The Democrats had greater success than the Whigs in unifying their party on Texas. They passed over both Tyler, whose Whig background was too recent for many Democrats, and Van Buren, whom southern Democrats despised for failing to support their position on Texas. Instead, they selected James K. Polk of Tennessee, a slaveowner and advocate of national expansion. The Democrats called for annexation of Texas and taking all of Oregon. Polk's supporters chanted "Fifty-four forty or fight!" The Whigs nominated Henry

HEADING FOR THE GOLD FIELDS, 1849

Catherine Haun describes the trip she and her lawyer husband took to California from Iowa. Their relative prosperity enabled them to make unusually thorough preparations.

[We], being financially involved in our business interests near Clinton, Iowa, longed to go to the new El Dorado and "pick up" gold enough with which to return and pay off our debts. . . . Full of the energy and enthusiasm of youth, the prospects of so hazardous an undertaking had no terror for us, indeed, as we had been married but a few months, it appealed to us as a romantic wedding tour. . . .

At that time the "gold fever" was contagious and few, old or young, escaped the malady. On the streets, in the fields, in the workshops and by the fireside, golden California was the chief topic of conversation. Who were going? How was best to "fix up" the "outfit"? What to take as food and clothing? Who would stay at home to care for the farm and womenfolks? Who would take wives and children along? . . .

Some half dozen families of our neighborhood joined us and probably about twenty-five persons constituted our little band. . . . Flour ground at our own grist mill and bacon of home-curing filled the large, four-ox wagon while another was loaded with barrels of alcohol. The third wagon contained our household effects and provisions. . . . All meats were either dried or salted, and vegetables and fruit were dried. . . . For luxuries we carried a gallon each of wild plum and crabapple preserves and blackberry jam. Our groceries were wrapped in India rubber covers and we did not lose any of them—in fact still had some when we reached Sacramento.

The two-horse spring wagon was our bed-room and was driven by the Major—on good stretches of road by myself. A hair mattress, topped off with one of feathers and layed on the floor of the wagon with plenty of bedding made a very comfortable bed after a hard day's travel.

In this wagon we had our trunk of wearing apparel, which consisted of underclothing, a couple of blue check gingham dresses, several large stout aprons for general wear, one light colored for Sundays, a pink calico sunbonnet and a white one intended for "dress up" days. My feminine vanity had also prompted to include, in the quasi wedding trouseau, a white cotton dress, a black silk manteaux trimmed very fetchingly with velvet bands and fringe, also a lace scuttle-shaped bonnet having a face wreath of tiny pink rose-buds, and on the side of the crown nestled a cluster of the same flowers. . . . Should our dreams of great wealth, acquired over night come true it might be embarrassing not to be prepared with a suitable wardrobe for the wife of a very rich man!

In the trunk were also a few treasures; a bible, medicines, such as quinine, bluemass [a quinine derivative], opium, whiskey and hartshorn for snake bites and citric acid—an antidote for scurvey. . . . Our matches, in a large-mouthed bottle were carefully guarded in this trunk.

The pockets of the canvas walls of the wagon held every day needs and toilet articles, as well as small fire arms. The red shotgun was suspended from the hickory bows of the wagon camp. . . . It was more than three months before we were thoroughly equipped and on April 24th, 1849, we left our comparatively comfortable homes—and the uncomfortable creditors—for the uncertain and dangerous trip, beyond which loomed up, in our mind's eye, castles of shining gold. . . .

Source: Lillian Schlissel, *Women's Diaries of the Westward Journey.* New York: Schocken Books, 1982. 166–185.

Clay, who once again emphasized his American System. Throughout the campaign, however, Clay was defensive about his opposition to annexation of Texas. He finally suggested, but only hesitantly, that he might support annexation under certain circumstances.

The outcome of the election pointed to the popularity of Texas annexation, especially when linked with Oregon, and to the difficulty of even a skilled compromiser like Henry Clay in maintaining the Whigs as a national party. The desertion of both proslavery and abolitionist Whigs cost Clay the election. Many southern Whigs were willing to sacrifice the party's economic program in return for the annexation of Texas. Thousands of northern Whigs, disappointed

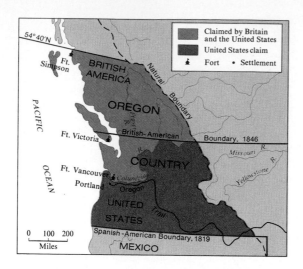

MAP 14.5 TERRITORIAL CONFLICT IN OREGON
The American and British governments disputed whether the Oregon Territory should be divided along the Columbia River, to include Ft. Vancouver, or the more northerly boundary that eventually divided the two countries. An agreement granting the citizens of each country equal access to Oregon enabled thousands of Americans to pour into the area.

with Clay's waffling on Texas and more interested in free-soil than in the American System, supported the new Liberty party and the first major abolitionist candidate, James G. Birney of Kentucky. Birney took away enough popular votes from Clay to deprive Clay of the electoral votes of New York and Michigan, with which he would have won. Polk became president, proclaiming that he had a mandate to create an American empire to the Pacific.

Recognizing the popularity of Texas annexation, northern Democrats now followed Polk rather than Van Buren. In February 1845, even before Polk's inauguration, northern Democrats in Congress closed ranks and led the approval of annexation. Texas entered the Union as a slave state in December 1845. Mexico denied the legality of American annexation of Texas and immediately broke diplomatic relations with the United States. Texas statehood, together with the admission of Florida that same year, gave slavery a temporary edge of fifteen slave states against thirteen free states. However, the admission of Iowa in 1846 and Wisconsin in 1848 reestablished the balance between free and slave states in the Senate.

The Mexican War

Polk entered the presidency determined to hold Texas, annex Oregon, and acquire New Mexico, Upper California, and perhaps even more territory. Americans had already discovered and exploited the economic opportunities of northwestern Mexico. From Santa Fe, a few Americans conducted a small but lucrative trade in gold, silver, furs, and mules. Since the 1820s, New England merchants who traded with China had stopped off in Upper California for sea-otter pelts and the products of the Franciscan missions. In the Sierra Nevada, Americans traded for furs. Pioneers who had turned southward on the way to Oregon became farmers in the Sacramento Valley. By 1845, about a thousand Americans lived in California, most of them in the interior. Their number grew swiftly, while the Mexican population of seven thousand, concentrated on the coast, remained stable. Meanwhile, Americans everywhere began to use the term "Manifest Destiny," coined in 1845 by a newspaper editor, to express their conviction that the United States had a divinely inspired mission to extend its civilization to the shores of the Pacific.

In December 1845, Polk delivered a bellicose message to Congress. He claimed that British intentions in the Pacific Northwest violated the policy, proclaimed by President Monroe in 1823, that the United States would not permit a European power to create a colony in North America. Polk intended to deny British claims to Oregon and to discourage them from taking California, which the British wanted as compensation for debts owed them by Mexico.

Polk's secretary of state, James Buchanan, had already advised his secret agent in the coastal town of Monterey that the United States would welcome a declaration of independence and a petition for annexation by American settlers in California. Meanwhile, secret orders went to the commander of the U.S. naval squadron in the Pacific. He was to seize San Francisco and other California ports if Mexico declared war on the United States. In December, shortly after Polk's message, Captain John C. Frémont, led an "exploring" party of heavily armed soldiers to California and established a base near Sacramento, despite orders from Mexican authorities to leave. In June 1846, the Americans in the interior staged a revolt, proclaimed the Bear Flag Re-

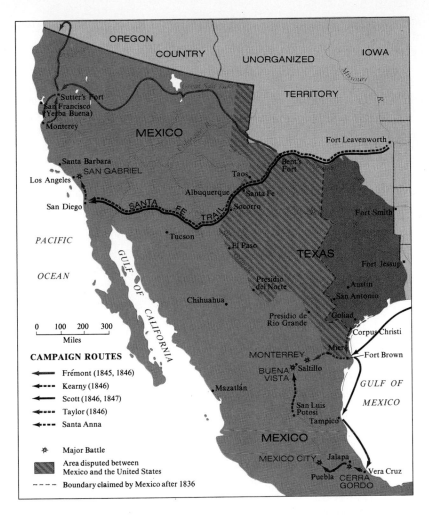

MAP 14.6 THE MEXICAN WAR
This map shows the major military expeditions which took the northern frontier of Mexico and then occupied Mexico City. In the last phase of the war, as Winfield Scott assembled his invasion army off the coast of Mexico, General Santa Anna tried to take advantage of the division of American forces by marching north and attacking the army of Zachary Taylor. The turning point of this phase of the war came at Buena Vista (February 1847), when Taylor's smaller forces repulsed Santa Anna, who had to return to defend Mexico City. Scott's most significant victory in his march on Mexico City came in the mountains, at Cerro Gordo.

public, and captured the Mexican town of Sonoma, all with the support of Frémont's forces.

President Polk then sent a secret emissary, John Slidell, to Mexico City. Polk instructed Slidell not to negotiate over the right of the United States to annex Texas. Slidell was further authorized to buy New Mexico and California for as much as $30 million. The Mexican government—perhaps hoping to embroil the United States in a war with Britain—rejected the legality of America's annexing Texas and refused to see Slidell. It also insisted on the Nueces River as the southern boundary of the Texas Republic.

Polk responded by creating an incident to provoke the Mexicans and thereby to justify taking California. In January 1846, he sent General Zachary Taylor to establish a fort south of the Nueces River. As Ulysses S. Grant, a young officer serving with Taylor, said much later, "We were sent to provoke a fight, but it was essential that Mexico should commence it." News of skirmishing between Mexican and American patrols reached Polk in early May. On May 9, he delivered the war message he had written long before. The president asserted that Mexico "has passed the boundary of the United States, has invaded our territory, and shed American blood on American soil." Congress declared war four days later.

As Polk had foreseen, American forces easily won control of New Mexico and California. A small army captured Santa Fe without opposition, occupied New Mexico, and marched to California. By the autumn of 1846, that force, joined by the navy and Frémont's army, took the fortified California towns of San Francisco, Monterey, Santa Barbara, Los Angeles, and San Diego. Meanwhile, Taylor's army won significant victories, crossing the Rio Grande and gaining control of northeastern Mexico.

While winning these easy victories, Polk worked to avoid a simultaneous war with Britain. He recommended that the Senate adopt the British proposal to divide Oregon at the forty-ninth parallel. The Senate agreed in June, ratifying the Oregon treaty.

At this point, Polk expected the Mexicans, having lost large territories and a potential ally, to sue for peace. He had underrated their national pride and strength. They would not agree to a peace, let alone a cession of territory. With the help of Winfield Scott, the commanding general of the army, Polk devised a plan to strike deep into the heart of Mexico and capture Mexico City itself. Late in 1846, Scott launched a seaborne campaign, storming the port of Vera Cruz and advancing 260 miles inland to Mexico City. With more than fourteen thousand troops and a talented group of West Point officers, most of them southerners, Scott persistently outflanked the enemy over difficult terrain. He never suffered a defeat. He occupied Mexico City in September 1847, and a new Mexican government was willing to make peace.

News of Scott's victory reached a Washington that was badly divided over its war aims. Such antislavery Whigs as Charles Francis Adams of Massachusetts and Joshua Giddings of Ohio— "Conscience Whigs," as they became known— had vehemently opposed the war as part of a proslavery conspiracy. Increasing numbers of northern Whigs had joined them, taking encouragement from the elections of 1846, which gave them control of Congress. These Whigs watched the casualties mount during the bloody and expensive march to Mexico City. They also took careful note that the Massachusetts legislature, in April 1847, declared the war unconstitutional. Even Daniel Webster and wealthy business leaders like Nathan Appleton—called "Cotton Whigs" because they were more conservative on slavery—opposed the war privately.

The Democrats also split over war aims. The most fervent expansionists decided that the rising cost of the war justified enlarging their ambitions. The party leaders—President Polk, Secretary of State Buchanan, and senators Stephen A. Douglas of Illinois and Jefferson Davis of Mississippi—all hoped that the United States could take at least a part of Mexico south of the

Rio Grande. But a vocal minority of northeastern Democrats, including key supporters of Martin Van Buren, opposed the extension of slavery into the territories and began to entertain free-soil ideas. They, along with many northwestern Democrats were also disappointed that Polk had failed to acquire more of Oregon. A few southern Democratic leaders worried that the Mexican people would oppose slavery and that the United States could not absorb the Mexicans, whom they regarded as an "inferior" people. This group included John C. Calhoun, who supported taking only Upper California and New Mexico, the most sparsely populated areas of Mexico.

Polk promoted party unity by steering a moderate course. He backed away from "All Mexico" and threw his support to Calhoun's policy. Polk endorsed the Treaty of Guadalupe Hidalgo, which promised that the United States would pay Mexico $15 million in return for Texas north of the Rio Grande and for New Mexico and Upper California. The treaty also provided that the United States would assume all the damage claims of its citizens, totaling $3.2 million, against the Mexican government. The Senate, agreeing with Polk that no more was possible, ratified the treaty in March 1848. The United States had taken northern Mexico, but it had yet to determine what the future of slavery would be there.

The Wilmot Proviso

In August 1846, during a House debate over a military appropriation bill, a free-soil Democrat, David Wilmot of Pennsylvania, proposed a strikingly simple amendment: The government would prohibit slavery in any area acquired from Mexico. This provision, known as the Wilmot Proviso, quickly became the rallying point for abolitionist opponents to the Mexican War.

During Scott's invasion of Mexico, the Wilmot Proviso gained bipartisan support. In the House, most Whigs and a minority of Democrats joined forces to pass it on several occasions, but the more heavily southern, more proslavery Senate killed the proviso each time. The state legislatures of fourteen northern states passed resolutions urging their senators to vote for it.

In the 1848 presidential election, the Democrats dumped Polk to appease the northern wing of the party. Their nominee was dull, elderly Senator Lewis Cass of Michigan. Cass was an expansionist who had advocated the purchase of Cuba and the annexation of Mexico's Yucatan Peninsula, but he had placed equal weight on acquiring all of Oregon. In an effort to hold both southerners and northerners in the party, the Democrats left their platform deliberately vague on the expansion of slavery.

In 1848, however, the Democrats faced a new challenge in trying to satisfy their northern constituencies. The Free Soil party, established on the foundation of the Liberty party, shrewdly nominated Martin Van Buren for president and the son of John Quincy Adams, Charles Francis Adams, for vice-president. Van Buren, though still a Democrat, had converted to free-soil beliefs. He remembered the role of southerners in denying him the Democratic nomination in 1844 and enthusiastically accepted the nomination. Adams inherited many of the Conscience Whig supporters of his father, who died in 1848 after distinguished service as an antislavery congressman from Massachusetts.

Even though northern Whig leaders generally supported the Wilmot Proviso, they avoided adopting any specific platform in favor of simply supporting an ideal presidential candidate—one who would appeal to both North and South, and who could be trusted not to veto the Wilmot Proviso. This candidate was the most popular military leader of the Mexican War, General Zachary Taylor. The fact that he came from Louisiana and owned a hundred slaves was less important to northern Whigs than the combination of his deep loyalty to the party, his popularity in the South, and his private opposition to the extension of slavery.

Taylor won 51 percent of the popular vote in the South and accumulated a massive electoral vote there. In the North, the Free Soil party hurt the Democrats more than it did the Whigs. Van Buren received 10 percent of the popular vote, pulling enough votes from Cass in New York to cost the Democrats the state and the election.

The victorious Whigs had not taken an official position on the critical issue of slavery in the territories. They had relied instead on Taylor's personality to satisfy their southern wing. In the future, neither southern Whigs nor southern Democrats would tolerate such ambiguity. The swift growth of the Free Soil party had left them all stunned and fearful. In response to the Free Soil party and the Wilmot Proviso, slaveowners became even more aggressive supporters of the expansion of slavery and demanded more from the two major parties.

Slavery in the Territories

All southern politicians now realized that they could not win national support for their territorial ambitions. After the election they played down their aspirations for Cuba and Mexico and concentrated instead on meeting the challenge of the Wilmot Proviso by firmly establishing slavery in the territories taken from Mexico. They developed three policies to achieve that objective.

John C. Calhoun advocated the most extreme expansionist position. He held that Congress had no constitutional authority to regulate slavery in the territories. It could not, therefore, exclude slavery from a territory even prior to admission to statehood. In Calhoun's view, the citizens of any state had the same rights as the citizens of any other state to take their property, including slaves, into territories owned commonly by the states. This argument won support from many Whigs in the deep South. But it repelled too many northerners of both parties to gain much support in Congress.

Most southern leaders of both parties advocated a more moderate position than Calhoun's—a simple extension of the Missouri Compromise line through the Mexican cession (the territory purchased from Mexico) to the Pacific coast. Their proposal would guarantee slaveowners access to at least some western territory, particularly southern California. It would remove the abolitionist threat from the South's western boundary. It would also almost certainly add some slave states to the Union. This approach appealed to some Democrats, including Polk, Buchanan, and Douglas. They hoped the offer of prohibiting slavery in northern territories would prevent free-soil Democrats from bolting the party. Free-soil advocates, however, uniformly denounced the extension of the Missouri Compromise line as a measure that would give the South too much. House passage of the Wilmot Proviso and the Free Soil party's gains in the election of 1848 gave free-soilers confidence that they could reject not only Calhoun's approach but also extension of the Missouri Compromise.

During the election campaign of 1848, the Democratic leaders began to turn to a third alternative—popular sovereignty. Supported first by the Democratic presidential candidate, Lewis Cass, popular sovereignty would leave slavery to the territorial governments. This doctrine had the attractive political features of seeming to be democratic and of shifting responsibility from Congress to the territorial legislatures.

However, the concept of popular sovereignty was vague on key issues. It did not specify at what point in a territory's development slavery could be legalized or prohibited; nor did it delineate the extent of the constitutional authority of the territorial governments over slavery. If Calhoun's doctrine were correct, territorial governments could consider the question of slavery only at the end of the territorial process, when they framed a constitution to apply for statehood. Until then, the federal Constitution, under Calhoun's theory, would protect slavery. Southern Democrats preferred this interpretation of popular sovereignty, believing that it gave slavery a good chance to become established in the territories. Free-soil advocates, on the other hand, believed that territorial legislatures, like Congress, had the power to exclude slavery. Therefore, territories could prohibit slavery as soon as they had been organized.

As long as each side left this ambiguity unexplored and simply followed whatever interpretation best served its interests, popular sovereignty held the greatest possibility for maintaining national unity on the slavery issue. The doctrine was tested far sooner than anyone expected.

MAP 14.7 THE CALIFORNIA GOLD RUSH
Hundreds of thousands of fortune seekers converged on the California gold fields beginning in 1849. Miners travelling by sea landed at San Francisco, which became California's instant metropolis. They outfitted their journey inland at Sacramento and Stockton, which were commercial outposts of San Francisco. The vast population influx placed great pressure on existing ranches for food and stimulated new farming enterprise in Sacramento, America, and San Joaquin river valleys, much of which survived the outmigration which ensued as the rich pickings from the mines were exhausted.

TIME LINE
SOCIAL TENSION AND SECTIONAL CRISIS

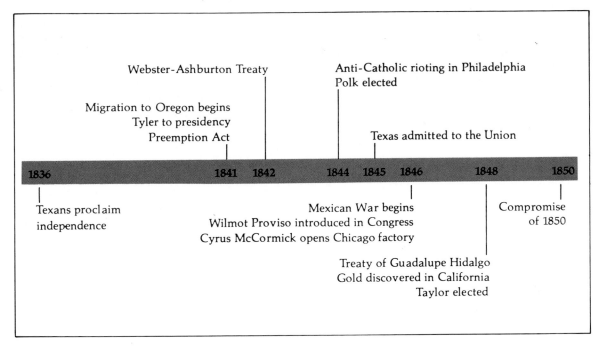

Webster-Ashburton Treaty

Anti-Catholic rioting in Philadelphia
Polk elected

Migration to Oregon begins
Tyler to presidency
Preemption Act

Texas admitted to the Union

| 1836 | 1841 | 1842 | 1844 | 1845 | 1846 | 1848 | 1850 |

Texans proclaim
independence

Mexican War begins
Wilmot Proviso introduced in Congress
Cyrus McCormick opens Chicago factory

Compromise
of 1850

Treaty of Guadalupe Hidalgo
Gold discovered in California
Taylor elected

California and the Compromise of 1850

In 1848, settlers in the Sacramento Valley discovered gold. A massive rush of new settlers to San Francisco and the gold fields of the Sierra Nevada foothills ensued. In 1849 alone, more than eighty thousand migrants arrived. Living in crowded, chaotic towns and mining camps, the "forty-niners" urgently needed effective government. Responding to their demands, President Zachary Taylor advised the Californians to apply for statehood immediately. Taylor's objectives were simple—to satisfy the forty-niners' demands, to avoid wrestling with the ambiguities of popular sovereignty, and to provide dramatic evidence that the Whigs could promote westward expansion without intensifying the slavery issue.

Taylor made this proposal in March 1849, when he took office. By October, California had ratified a constitution and applied for statehood. In the contest over the California constitution, slavery advocates fared poorly. Few of the many southerners who flocked to the gold fields owned slaves or wanted to own them. Only ranchers in sparsely populated southern California had a strong interest in promoting slavery. Consequently, the California constitutional convention, copying much of the new Iowa state constitution, prohibited slavery. When Congress convened, in December 1849, Taylor urged the admission of California and New Mexico as free states.

Southern defenders of slavery were startled and alarmed by the swift victory of the antislavery forces in California. They now questioned whether popular sovereignty would protect slavery in light of the vast numbers of northerners potentially interested in settling the new territories. The prospect of adding another free state to the Union also disturbed the southerners. California's admission would disrupt the exact balance of free and slave votes in the Senate. Moreover, the new state would create a base for abolitionists within the territory acquired from Mexico.

Southerners in Congress resisted Taylor's plan, touching off another major sectional confrontation. In passionate debates that lasted for eight months, Congress examined all the issues surrounding the present and future status of slavery. Southern leaders were willing to accept California's admission as a free state only if the federal government adequately guaranteed the future of slavery. They insisted on more than popular sovereignty in the Mexican cession. The most extreme position was taken by Calhoun, who doubted that the North and South could arrive at a lasting compromise. In what would be his farewell address, read to Congress on his behalf shortly before he died, Calhoun said the nation could prevent the South's secession and eventual civil war only by guaranteeing slavery in all the territories and by adopting a Constitutional amendment to establish a permanent balance of sectional power.

Antislavery advocates in both parties lent credence to Calhoun's prediction of civil war. Senators Salmon P. Chase, an Ohio Democrat, and William H. Seward, a New York Whig, urged the government to contain slavery within its existing limits. Their goal was its ultimate extinction. Seward declared that the government had a responsibility to "a higher law than the Constitution, which regulates our authority over the domain . . . the common heritage of mankind."

The issues were finally being clearly drawn, as were the risks to the future of the Union. Frightened by a clash that tore both parties along sectional lines—and stirred the fear that the Union might dissolve—senior Whigs and Democrats did their best to reach a compromise. Through a long, complex legislative process, Whigs Henry Clay and Daniel Webster and Democrat Stephen A. Douglas organized a package that, when implemented, consisted of five distinct laws. These laws were known collectively as the Compromise of 1850. The compromise attempted to mollify the South by removing the free states as havens for runaway slaves. It tried to satisfy the North by establishing the principle of popular sovereignty in the Mexican cession. The compromise (1) admitted California as a free state; (2) organized New Mexico as a territory on the basis of popular sovereignty; (3) organized Utah as a territory, also under popular sovereignty; (4) abolished the slave trade, but not slavery itself, in the District of Columbia; and (5) enacted a fugitive slave law that established severe federal punishment for obstructing the efforts of slaveholders to recover their slaves in any state.

The Compromise of 1850 only barely averted a secession crisis, and it failed to satisfy most southern Democrats and most northern Whigs. The former resisted admitting California under any terms. The latter opposed both the fugitive slave law and popular sovereignty. They held their ground even after Taylor died in July 1850 and was succeeded by Vice-President Millard Fillmore of New York, who supported popular sovereignty. In the end, northern Democrats and southern Whigs accounted for most of the votes for the compromise. Most congressional representatives of both the Whig northern business class and the Democratic southern planters were willing to risk the Union in order to control the West.

During the 1840s and 1850s, southern society became increasingly dependent on slavery. Planters used slavery more aggressively as a source of profits and developed an elaborate defense of it in order to control slaves, defeat abolitionism, and guarantee the loyalty of nonslaveholding whites. In response to the growing intensification of work and the disruption of their lives, slaves built elaborate networks of family and community support.

As northern industrialization accelerated, it bound together the Northeast and the Northwest and reinforced the power of the emerging business class. Class distinctions hardened, however, particularly because industrialization attracted immigrants, especially from Ireland, who were poor and Catholic. An anti-Catholic movement grew within the business class and gained support from artisans threatened by industrialization.

Their commitments to different labor systems forced the South and the North into direct conflict over the West. During the 1840s, the South sought to use the federal government to protect slavery in the West and to establish slavery in northern Mexico. Northern Whigs, however, feared that southern control of the West would block the expansion of free agriculture, assure control of the federal government for the Democratic representatives of planters and immigrants, and prevent the adoption of Henry Clay's American System.

This conflict severely strained the political system during the 1840s. In persuading the nation to undertake the Mexican War, the South provoked a major fracture in the Whig party. A lesser rift in the Democratic party formed between southerners loyal to slavery and northerners who embraced free-soil. The controversy over the status of slavery in the territories taken from Mexico became so great that the leaders of the two major parties adopted the Compromise of 1850 to try to preserve the Union. The compromise temporarily preserved the Second Party System, although most southern Democrats and northern Whigs did not support the compromise. They stood ready to risk the Union if they could dominate the West.

Suggestions for Further Reading

A Distinctive Society

Scholars have heatedly debated the issues of slavery's profitability and the productivity and welfare of slave labor. Most controversial is Robert W. Fogel and Stanley L. Engerman, *Time on the Cross: The Economics of American Negro Slavery* (1974), which should be read together with Paul A. David *et al.*, *Reckoning with Slavery* (1976).

The culture of the planter class and non-slaveholding whites can be explored in Catherine Clinton, *The Plantation Mistress* (1983); Clement Eaton, *The Freedom of Thought Struggle in the Old South* (1964); John Hope Franklin, *The Militant South 1800–1861* (1956); George M. Frederickson, *White Supremacy, A Comparative Study in American and South African History* (1981). John McCardell, *The Idea of a Southern Nation, Southern Nationalists and Southern Nationalism, 1830–1860* (1979); Frank L. Owsley, *Plain Folk of the Old South* (1949); William R. Taylor, *Cavalier and Yankee: The Old South and American National Character* (1961); and J. Mills Thornton III, *Politics and Power in a Slave Society, Alabama, 1800–1860* (1978).

The first study to describe slavery as repressive to blacks was Kenneth Stampp, *The Peculiar Institution* (1956). The first to emphasize the psychological costs of slavery was Stanley Elkins, *Slavery: A Problem in American Institutional and Intellectual Life* (Third Edition, 1976). Presenting more complete images of the lives of slaves are John W. Blassingame, *The Slave Community: Plantation Life in the Antebellum South* (1979); Eugene D. Genovese, *Roll, Jordan, Roll: The World the Slaves Made* (1974); Herbert D. Gutman, *The Black Family in Slavery and Freedom 1750–1925*; and Lawrence W. Levine, *Black Culture and Black Consciousness* (1977). On slave revolts, see Herbert Aptheker, *American Negro Slave Revolts* (1943); Stephen B. Oates, *The Fires of Jubilee: Nat Turner's Fierce Rebellion* (1975); and Eugene D. Genovese, *From Rebellion to Revolution: Afro-American Slave Revolts in the Making of the Modern World* (1979). On the ambiguous position of free blacks in slave society, see Ira Berlin, *Slaves Without Masters: The Free Negro in the Antebellum South* (1974).

Accelerating Industrialization in the North

The economic changes in the North during the 1840s and 1850s can be studied through many of the economic history sources listed for Chapter 11. In addition, on railroads see Albert Fishlow, *American Railroads and the Transformation of the Ante-Bellum Economy* (1965); Peter Temin, *Iron and Steel in Nineteenth-Century America* (1964); Allan G. Bogue, *From Prairie to Corn Belt: Farming on the Illinois and Iowa Frontier* (1968); Lee Soltow, *Men and Wealth in the United States, 1850–1870* (1975); and Colin Forster and G. S. L. Tucker, *Economic Opportunity and White American Fertility Ratios 1800–1860* (1972).

On the sources and character of European immigration, consult Maldwyn Allen Jones, *American Immigration* (1960); and Philip Taylor, *The Distant Magnet, European Emigration to the U.S.A.* (1971). The most useful introduction to the nature of immigrant communities during the 1840s and 1850s is Oscar Handlin, *Boston's Immigrants, A Study in Acculturation* (1959). See also Jay P. Dolan, *The Immigrant Church: New York's Irish and German Catholics 1815–1865* (1975) and Kathleen Neils Conzen, *Immigrant Milwaukee: 1836–1860* (1976). For the nativist reaction, consult Michael Feldberg, *The Philadelphia Riots of 1844: A Study of Ethnic Conflict* (1975); and Robert F. Hueston, *The Catholic Press and Nativism 1840–1860* (1976).

Party and Sectional Conflict

Study of 1840s expansionism should begin with Frederick Merk, *The Monroe Doctrine and American Expansion 1843–1849* (1972). On the coming of the Mexican War, consult David Pletcher, *The Diplomacy of Annexation: Texas, Oregon, and the Mexican War* (1973) and Charles G. Sellers, *James K. Polk, Continentalist 1843–1846* (1966). On Congressional politics during the 1840s, see Chaplain Morrison, *Democratic Politics and Sectionalism: The Wilmot Proviso Controversy* (1967) and Joel H. Silbey, *The Shrine of Party: Congressional Voting Behavior 1841–1852* (1967). On the Compromise of 1850 see Holman Hamilton, *Prologue to Conflict: The Crisis and Compromise of 1850* (1964).

15

TWO SOCIETIES AT WAR

he fateful decade of the 1850s began with the first armed struggles over slavery. It ended with a bloody war between the North and the South looming on the horizon. The first battles over slavery were fought not by soldiers, but between abolitionists and southerners who came into free states to recapture their escaped slaves. The violence escalated dramatically in 1854 in what became known as "Bleeding Kansas," where opponents and supporters of slavery fought a bitter guerrilla war for the future of the West. More fighting occurred in 1859, when John Brown, a veteran of the Kansas struggle, captured a federal arsenal in Virginia and tried to start a private war against slavery. By 1861 the political leaders of the South decided that they had to choose between slavery and the Union. They chose slavery—some quickly and jubilantly, others slowly and reluctantly. The North's Republican party, which had won the presidency for the first time, then had to make its own choice between war or a divided Union. It chose war, and the result was a conflict much more terrible, more total, and more deadly than any the American people had ever witnessed or could have imagined possible. When the Civil War ended, slavery, the Confederacy, and six hundred thousand soldiers were dead.

The Disruption of Union

Slavery shattered the Second Party System. By 1852, the Whig party was hopelessly fragmented by internal disputes, particularly over an 1850 law that made the federal government responsible for recapturing and returning runaway slaves who had managed to escape to free territory. The task of maintaining the political unity of the nation fell to the Democrats. This party had some strengths. On the question of slavery in new states, most Democratic leaders took the broadly appealing stance of supporting "popular sovereignty"—letting the people of the territories decide for themselves whether they would permit slavery. The Democrats also had a diverse base of voters. They had won the solid support of a large and growing number of immigrant voters in northern cities. They were supported by the many settlers of southern ancestry in the Ohio Valley. They also appealed to the many voters in all sections of the country who thought the Union was more important than the question of slavery or freedom for blacks.

But the Democrats had problems, too. Many southerners were not happy with the idea of popular sovereignty and instead wanted slaves to be recognized and protected as property everywhere in the Union. The Democrats also failed to satisfy voters who wanted to abolish slavery, and the party gradually lost a larger number of those who wanted to prohibit slavery in the western territories. There were also many northern voters who feared or resented immigrants, particularly the Catholics who formed a crucial part of the Democrats' urban base. Lastly, the Democrats had a theory of limited government that made it impossible for them to satisfy the growing number of northerners who wanted vigorous federal programs to promote economic development. In 1860, these disgruntled voters gathered behind the new Republican party. This party's social vision was essentially that of the northern business class. Armed with this vision, the party made profound and fundamental changes that affected all segments of American society.

The Fugitive Slave Act

The Compromise of 1850 was a political arrangement intended to prevent slavery from disrupting politics and government. As it turned out, however, the compromise brought slavery to center stage.

The most controversial element of the compromise was the Fugitive Slave Act. This act put the federal government at the disposal of slaveowners who were chasing runaway slaves. Federal judges or special commissioners determined the status of blacks who denied they were runaways. The accused blacks were denied jury trials or the right to testify. Federal marshals were instructed to support slave catchers, and could impose heavy penalties on anyone who helped a slave escape. Even slaves who had long ago fled to freedom could be subject to recapture. And blacks born free in the North ran the risk of kidnapping. To the South's political leaders, the Fugitive Slave Act was important not only because it might lead to the return of runaway slaves, but also because it acknowledged that the government recognized and protected their "property" everywhere.

Abolitionists immediately organized vigilante groups to block enforcement of the Fugitive Slave Act. In October 1850, Theodore Parker and other Boston abolitionists helped two slaves escape to freedom, driving a Georgia slavecatcher out of town. Four months later, a Boston mob snatched a fugitive slave from a federal marshal and spirited him to Canada. In October 1851, two thousand rioters in Syracuse, New York, broke into a courthouse and freed a fugitive slave. The plight of runaways and the appearance of slave catchers in northern communities dramatically personalized the message of abolitionism, and popular hostility to the Fugitive Slave Act grew. In fact, northern legislators and judges began overtly to resist federal authority. Several state legislatures passed "personal liberty" laws to protect accused fugitive slaves from federal officers. In 1857, the Supreme Court of Wisconsin, in the case of *Ableman v. Booth*, held that a state court had the power to declare an act of Congress unconstitutional. The Fugitive Slave Act, the court ruled, violated the Constitution and could not be enforced in Wisconsin.

Many people were outraged by the act. Harriet Beecher Stowe, an abolitionist who had lived in Cincinnati, poured her anger and her compassion into a remarkable novel, *Uncle Tom's Cabin*. Published first as a magazine serial in 1851–1852, the novel tells of a compassionate but weak master in Kentucky who is forced by debts to sell two slaves, Tom and a five-year-old boy, to a slave trader. Beautiful Eliza Harris, the boy's mother, refuses to be separated from her son. With the child in her arms, she crosses the Ohio River on cakes of ice just ahead of the vicious slave trader. Eliza escapes to freedom and reaches the house of an Ohio politician who has voted for a fugitive slave law, having set aside his "private feeling." His wife persuades him to trust his heart, rather than his head, and to help Eliza and her child on their way to Canada. Meanwhile, Tom is eventually sold to Simon Legree, a brutal master on a southern plantation. Legree beats Tom to death but never conquers the slave's Christian soul.

Uncle Tom's Cabin fueled the growing hostility to the Fugitive Slave Act in the North. In 1852, when the novel first appeared in book form, more than three hundred thousand Americans bought copies. Countless others saw the stage version, produced by theater companies throughout the North. For most of these people, Stowe's novel connected the abstract moral principles of abolitionism with heart-rending personal situations that they could respond to with anger or grief.

Fierce northern resistance to the Fugitive

Slave Act prompted special conventions in South Carolina, Georgia, Mississippi, and Alabama in 1850 and 1851. These conventions considered secession from the Union, but moderates persuaded them to support the Compromise of 1850 and not break with the Union yet. In turn, the moderates agreed to support secession if Congress modified the Fugitive Slave Act, abolished slavery anywhere, or refused to admit a state into the Union because it permitted slavery.

The Disintegration of the Whigs

The Whig party split over the Fugitive Slave Act. The dominant northern Whigs rejected the incumbent president, Millard Fillmore, who had tried to enforce the law, in favor of a military hero, General Winfield Scott. Their 1852 platform only softly endorsed the Compromise of 1850. Still, virtually no southern Whigs supported their party, and many went so far as to vote for the Democratic ticket.

Some southern Democrats wanted to nominate a candidate who supported Calhoun's position that the federal government should protect slavery in all the territories. Most realized, however, that this would ensure defeat for the party in the North. On the forty-ninth ballot, the Democratic convention passed over all the advocates of popular sovereignty, including Lewis Cass, Stephen Douglas, and James Buchanan, and chose Franklin Pierce of New Hampshire. The public knew Pierce only as a handsome and congenial New Englander with no identifiable enemies, but southern leaders had learned from Pierce's supporters that he would be sympathetic to the South's interests.

Pierce and the Democrats crushed the Whigs in the 1852 election. The Democratic consensus not only attracted southern Whigs but also won back many northern Democrats who had voted for the Free Soil party in 1848. These free-soilers were satisfied that the popular sovereignty provisions of the Compromise of 1850 would effectively prevent an expansion of slavery. Even Martin Van Buren, the former Free Soil candidate, supported Pierce. The Free Soil party got only about half the votes it had won four years earlier. General Scott carried only four of thirty-one states for the Whigs. They never again waged a national campaign.

Latin American Ambitions

The problem facing the Pierce administration was to quiet disputes about fugitive slaves and generate an atmosphere of national unity. Pierce and his advisers attempted a familiar Democratic strategy—a vigorous and expansionist foreign policy. President Fillmore had already sent Commodore Matthew C. Perry to "open" Japan to American merchants, and Pierce supported additional efforts to develop new trade. Furthermore, Americans of all parties believed the United States should support the liberal and nationalist revolutions that had flared throughout Europe in 1848. For example, the old Whig Daniel Webster, who served as secretary of state from 1850 until his death in 1852, had supported Hungary in its efforts to gain independence from Austria. Some Democrats organized the "Young America" movement to support the revolutions and to promote expansion into areas of Latin America still controlled by European monarchies.

The Pierce administration paid close attention to Latin America. Southern Democrats had blocked initiatives to annex Canada and acquire Hawaii. Instead, they forced Pierce to focus on Cuba. Earlier, Polk had tried unsuccessfully to purchase Cuba from Spain. From 1849 to 1851, southern expansionists tried to stir up a revolution in Cuba—in order to add it to the Union as a slave state—by funding three expeditions to the island by a Cuban exile, General Narciso Lopez. Pierce privately supported another expedition to Cuba, which was to be led by John A. Quitman, a former governor of Mississippi. Pierce instructed Pierre Soule, U.S. minister to Spain, to attempt "to detach that island from the Spanish dominion." After failing to purchase Cuba, Soule sent Pierce what became known as the Ostend Manifesto. In it, Soule declared that the United States would be justified "by every law, human and Divine," in "wresting" Cuba from Spain "if we possess the power." By November 1854, when the document arrived in Washington, Pierce realized that northern politicians would refuse to go to war for the purpose of adding a new slave state. Not wanting to lose support among northern Democrats, he persuaded Quitman to abandon his expedition. In 1855, the manifesto was leaked to the public and

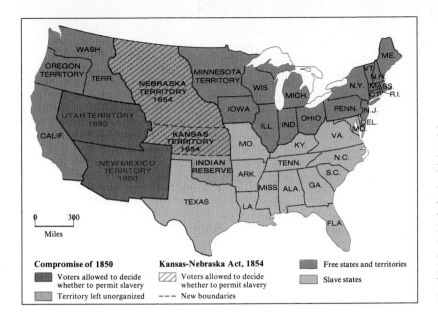

MAP 15.1 COMPROMISE OF 1850 AND THE KANSAS-NEBRASKA ACT
Vast territories were at stake in the contest over the westward extension of slavery. The Compromise of 1850 and the Kansas-Nebraska Act decided that the future of slavery in most of the West—in the Kansas, Nebraska, Utah, and New Mexico Territories—would be decided by popular sovereignty.

triggered a new wave of northern resentment against the South.

In 1854, another southern adventurer, William Walker led an invasion of Nicaragua. By 1855, he succeeded in making himself dictator of that country. He had a grand scheme to create and lead a new nation that included Central America and Cuba. Most of Walker's followers had the simpler mission of bringing Nicaragua into the Union as a slave state. In 1856, Walker announced the reestablishment of slavery in Nicaragua. His government was recognized by the Pierce administration and won an endorsement from the Democratic party in its platform. But Walker alienated his Central American neighbors, was driven out of power in 1857, and died before a Honduran firing squad in 1860. Foreign policy, it seemed, would not be the Democrats' key to national cohesion.

Kansas-Nebraska and the Republicans

The Democrats' hopes for generating a national consensus now depended primarily on the success of popular sovereignty. The doctrine was put to its first real test in a portion of the Louisiana Purchase where the federal government, under the Missouri Compromise, had prohibited the introduction of slavery.

Southerners had blocked the political organization of this land, except for the admission of Iowa to the Union in 1846 and the formation of the Minnesota Territory. Meanwhile, westerners had grown impatient. They wanted the government to organize this vast area into territories to open it for settlement. The leading Democratic spokesman for these westerners was a senator from Illinois, Stephen A. Douglas. He not only championed development of the West, but also wanted Chicago to become the eastern terminus for a transcontinental railroad. In addition, Douglas yearned to be president. He introduced a bill in 1854 to organize a large territory, to be called Nebraska.

Southerners, however, wanted to guarantee slavery in the territories and hoped that New Orleans, Memphis, or Saint Louis would be the eastern terminus for the transcontinental railroad. To win southern support for his bill, Douglas made two majors concessions. First, he agreed that the popular sovereignty provision of the Compromise of 1850 voided the Missouri Compromise's prohibition of slavery in the northern part of the Louisiana Purchase. Second, he advocated the formation of two new territories, Nebraska and Kansas, rather than one, giving slaveholders a chance to dominate the settlement of Kansas. These concessions attracted the support of almost all southerners in

Congress and the bill passed, despite the opposition of northern Whigs and half of Douglas's own northern Democrats.

Throughout the North, abolitionists and free-soilers expressed anger over the Kansas-Nebraska Act. Douglas had severely misread northern opinion. Now in need of new allies, northern Whigs began to cooperate with "Anti-Nebraska" Democrats. The two groups then joined with members of the Free Soil party, and in 1854 they organized a new party, reviving the Jeffersonian term "Republican" for themselves. The Republicans emphasized absolute opposition to the expansion of slavery into the territories—generalizing the principle of the Wilmot Proviso—and ran their first candidates in the congressional elections of that year. In these elections, they cooperated with the Know-Nothings, most of whom regarded the free-soil policy as advancing their program of excluding everyone but white Protestants from America. Together, the Republicans and Know-Nothings won a majority of seats in the House of Representatives in 1854. Suddenly there was a clear alternative to popular sovereignty and the Democrats.

Republican Ideology Versus the Defense of Slavery

Like most American political parties, the Republican party was a coalition. Its platform contained proposals designed to appeal to each of the groups that made up this alliance. But the party's ideas and political language were not just the sum of these proposals. Republican ideology was strongly shaped by a vision of the different kinds of human personalities that could develop in slave and free societies.

The Republican attack on slavery declared that slavery could produce only two classes of people, masters and slaves. The master class was shaped by a power that knew no limits. Limitless power could produce only people who knew no restraint on their passions and their wills, people accustomed to gratifying their every desire. In their dealings with slaves—and with their poorer white neighbors—such individuals would inevitably claim limitless privilege and inflict limitless injustice. This could only produce habits of submission and subservience, and ignorance and sloth, among both slaves and poor whites.

In the Republicans' description of free society, no person had unlimited power over another. The ancient divisions of society into permanent classes were eradicated by freedom and mobility. Abraham Lincoln, a Whig who became a Republican after the passage of the Kansas-Nebraska Act, said the basic fact about northern society was that "there is no permanent class of hired laborers among us." Every man had a chance to become an owner and an employer. And "if any continue through life in the condition of the hired laborers, it is not the fault of the system, but because of either a dependent nature which prefers it, or improvidence, folly, or singular misfortune." In the faith of Lincoln and his fellow Republicans, the typical men and women of such a society would not be submissive and subservient but proudly independent; not ignorant and lazy but creative, ambitious, and energetic. Such people would be disciplined not by authority but by their own free determination to meet their responsibilities to their families, their churches, and their communities.

Southern defenders of slavery developed their own theory in response to the Republicans'. Some of their defense of slavery rested where it had for decades, on simple racism—the conviction that black people lacked any capacity for freedom. These southerners also continued to defend slavery on sentimental grounds, insisting that masters were kindly and slaves grateful and affectionate. In the 1850s, a new defense of slavery began to take shape. In response to northern attacks on slavery and celebrations of free labor, southern writers and politicians began to attack free society and the kinds of personalities it produced.

This new defense of slavery argued that in a free labor system, labor becomes a mere commodity whose price is determined by the ruthless laws of the market. In the market, greed is the only morality, supply and demand the only law, and money the only goal. Every member of such a society, rich or poor, becomes grasping and selfish, concerned only with financial gain. Anyone who is too old, too weak, or too young to sell labor in the market is "free" only to be hungry and homeless. In such a world, neither the rich nor the poor has a sense of community, civic values, or responsibility for others.

Slavery, some argued, does resemble free labor because it forces some people to work to enrich others. But it produces a master class that differs from the ruling class of a capitalist society. Masters assume responsibility for their slaves—the old and the sick as well as the strong. The slaveowner, unlike the capitalist employer, is committed to community and civic responsibility. The master class in a slave society—whether in ancient Greece or Rome or the American South—cultivates the graces and virtues that can thrive only in a frankly aristocratic culture.

And so, in each section, ideologies were being shaped that defined the differences between North and South in ways that utterly precluded the possibility of political compromise. Each ideology suited the interests and the world view of the dominant group in the section that held it, the planters in the South and the business class

in the North. Northerners and southerners alike argued that slavery and free labor were not simply different labor systems but expressed different social orders that produced irreconcilably different kinds of men and women. Every passing year made it more likely that a majority of the voters in each section would be ready to decide that societies as different as the North and South could no longer be joined in a constitutional union that was, in Lincoln's ominous words, "a house divided."

"Bleeding Kansas"

Meanwhile, events in Kansas set the stage for the 1856 presidential election. In 1854, thousands of settlers began a rush for land in Kansas. Many of these settlers believed they had a mission to defend the fundamental principles of their society, whether northern or southern. On the side of slavery, Senator David R. Atchison of Missouri organized residents of his state to cross into Kansas and intervene in crucial elections.

FERRYING MISSOURI VOTERS TO THE KANSAS SHORE
At the time of the 1855 election of a territorial legislature in Kansas, there were probably no more than three thousand eligible voters among the Kansas settlers. Yet more than six thousand people voted in that first election. Missourians, taking advantage of a loosely drawn election law, poured across the border to vote for slavery. (Kansas Historical Society)

Opposing him were the agents of the New England Emigrant Aid Company, organized by abolitionists to colonize Kansas with free-soilers.

Violence peaked in 1856. A proslavery gang, seven hundred strong, sacked the free-soil town of Lawrence, destroying two newspaper offices, burning down buildings, and looting stores. In retaliation, a New York abolitionist named John Brown, together with his four sons and two helpers, murdered five proslavery settlers. The "Pottawatomie massacre," as the killings became known, provoked further retaliation and initiated a guerrilla war that cost about two hundred lives. Meanwhile, the Pierce administration recognized a territorial legislature that had been elected largely by Missourians who crossed the border simply to cast ballots. The legislature declared that questioning the legitimacy of slavery was a felony and that aiding a fugitive slave was a capital offense.

The violence focused the election of 1856 on Kansas. The Democrats, with their party's center of gravity now resting in the South, had to endorse the Kansas-Nebraska Act. But because of Pierce's close association with "Bleeding Kansas," the Democrats nominated James Buchanan of Pennsylvania, a party veteran who had no record on that volatile issue.

The Republicans counted on a sharp northern backlash against Democrats over "Bleeding Kansas." Their platform denounced the Kansas-Nebraska Act and insisted that the Wilmot Proviso, prohibiting slavery in the territories, be invoked. It also called for federal subsidies to railroads linking the Northeast with the Northwest, thus reviving the one element of the Whig economic program that was most popular among northern Democrats. The Republicans nominated John C. Frémont. Frémont, an army explorer, had a meager political record, but he was a genuine free-soiler and nationally famous for his role in the conquest of California.

Republicans focused their arguments on the expansion of slavery. They took the offensive, charging that the South, through the Democratic party, sought to extend slavery throughout the nation. Their solution for stopping the "Slave Power" was the Wilmot Proviso. They projected a messianic sense of destiny that even won over poet Walt Whitman, a former Democrat who campaigned for Republicans in 1856. "No man knows what will happen next," Whitman wrote, "but all know some such things are to happen as mark the greatest moral convulsions of the earth."

Many southern Democrats declared they would advocate secession if Frémont won the election. Fearful of such a cataclysm, and still believing in popular sovereignty, enough northern Democrats remained loyal to their party to give the 1856 election to Buchanan. He drew 1.8 million votes to 1.3 million for Frémont. But the Republican party had done very well in the free states. Frémont, attracting both former Whigs and free-soil Democrats, carried eleven states and Buchanan only five. Frémont would have won the electoral vote and the presidency with only a small shift of popular votes in Illinois and Pennsylvania. A dramatic and sudden restructuring of parties had taken place, and the crisis seemed only postponed. The Democratic party had bridged sectional conflicts by the slenderest of margins.

The Dred Scott Decision

The legal meaning of popular sovereignty was tested when the case of Dred Scott, a slave suing for his freedom, reached the Supreme Court in 1856. Scott had lived for a time with his master, an army surgeon, in Illinois and the Wisconsin Territory, where the Missouri Compromise had prohibited slavery. In his suit, which began in 1846, Scott claimed that his residence in free territory had made him a free man.

In March 1857, only two days after the inauguration of Buchanan, the Court reached a decision, in *Dred Scott v. Sanford*. The five southern Democrats on the Court, including Chief Justice Roger B. Taney of Maryland, and Buchanan—who privately twisted the arm of Justice Robert C. Grier, a fellow Pennsylvanian—had a specific political purpose in mind when they arranged this decision. They hoped to resolve the issue that threatened to disrupt the Union. Every justice wrote a separate opinion, but Taney's summarized the majority's position. He ruled that blacks, whether free or slave, could not be citizens of the United States. Scott, therefore, had no right to sue in a federal court.

DRED SCOTT
Dred Scott's odyssey began in Saint Louis in 1834, when he was sold to John Emerson and taken to Illinois, then to Fort Snelling in Wisconsin Territory, and finally back to Missouri. After Emerson died, Scott sued Emerson's wife for his freedom. Two months after the Supreme Court decision, the former Mrs. Emerson, who had married an antislavery politician from Massachusetts, freed Scott. (Missouri Historical Society)

Taney could have stopped there. Instead, he went on to make two broad points. First, he ruled that the Fifth Amendment prohibition against taking property without due process of law meant that Congress could not pass a law depriving persons of their slave "property" in the territories. So the Missouri Compromise had always been unconstitutional. Therefore, Scott's residence in the Wisconsin Territory could not have freed him. Second, Taney ruled that Congress could not extend to territorial governments any powers that Congress itself did not possess. Therefore, if Congress had no power to prohibit slavery in a territory, neither did the government of that territory. Thus, a majority of the Supreme Court endorsed the view set down by Calhoun that the people of a territory could prohibit slavery *only* at the moment of admission to statehood, not before.

Buchanan and the Supreme Court hoped that Republicans, out of respect for the Court, would accept this decision. But, in a stroke, the Democratic Supreme Court had declared the antislavery platform of the Republicans unconstitutional. It was a decision the Republicans could not tolerate. Led by Senator William H. Seward of New York, Republicans accused the Supreme Court and President Buchanan of participating in the "Slave Power" conspiracy. Respect for Chief Justice Taney fell so low that for the next nine years Congress refused to place his bust in the Supreme Court chambers with those of former chief justices.

The decision also undercut northern Democrats, including Stephen Douglas, who sought to protect their party's strength in the North with the popular sovereignty doctrine. The Court's decision in effect made it impossible for the people of a territory to prohibit slavery legally while settlers were moving in.

President Buchanan drove an even deeper wedge between himself and Douglas. Buchanan supported proslavery forces in Kansas, and in early 1858 he recommended the admission of Kansas as a slave state under the so-called Lecompton constitution, which the antislavery majority in Kansas had rejected in a referendum. Convinced that this was a parody of popular sovereignty, Douglas broke with Buchanan and southern Democrats by mobilizing western Democrats and Republicans in Congress to defeat approval of the Lecompton constitution. Kansas finally entered the Union as a free state in 1861, after secession was well under way.

Lincoln Versus Douglas

The highlight of the 1858 elections was Abraham Lincoln's eloquent challenge to Douglas's bid for reelection as a senator from Illinois. Lincoln's campaign attracted intense national interest because of Douglas's prominence, his break with the Buchanan administration, and the fact that he was struggling for political survival. Adding to the excitement was Lincoln's own reputation throughout the Old Northwest as a formidable attorney, politician, and stump speaker. He had been the best-known Whig in Illinois and was now the state's most powerful Republican. To increase his national exposure, Lincoln challenged Douglas to a series of seven debates.

During the debates, Lincoln attacked slavery as an institution that subverted equality of opportunity. He did express doubts about the innate abilities of blacks, and he explicitly rejected formulas that would give them social and political equality. But he declared that blacks were entitled to "all the natural rights enumerated in the Declaration of Independence." This meant, Lincoln explained, that "in the right to eat the bread, without leave of anybody else, which his own hand earns," the black was "the equal of every living man."

Lincoln thought he could see a master plan at work promoting slavery along several fronts. The scheme, he said, called for extending slavery throughout the territories and was evident in the Kansas-Nebraska Act (which Douglas had introduced), the *Dred Scott* decision, and Buchanan's cynical endorsement of the fraudulent Lecompton constitution for Kansas. The only solution, according to Lincoln, was to return to the Missouri Compromise and the principles of the Wilmot Proviso. For if the South could extend slavery into the West, it would eventually insist that slavery be legalized throughout the United States. Lincoln then pressed Douglas to explain how he could accept the *Dred Scott* decision and at the same time advocate popular sovereignty.

In a debate in Freeport, Illinois, Douglas responded by elaborating on a new formulation of popular sovereignty. In what became known as the Freeport doctrine, he asserted that settlers could exclude slavery from a territory in practice, if not legally, simply by not adopting local legislation to protect it. Douglas won reelection to the Senate by a narrow margin, on the appeal of the Freeport doctrine to those Illinois voters still grasping for a basis for harmony between the sections.

The Election of 1860

Southern Democrats were becoming increasingly nervous. They knew that the Republicans, who gained control of the House in 1858, might win a dramatic victory in 1860. Consequently, they insisted that the Democratic party and the fed-

JOHN BROWN
During his trial, John Brown (1800–1859), who had been cut and beaten during his capture, lay on a cot before the jury. Before sentencing he roused himself and declared: "Now, if it is deemed necessary that I should forfeit my life for the furtherance of the ends of justice, and mingle my blood with the blood of millions in this slave country whose rights are disregarded by wicked, cruel, and unjust enactments, I say let it be done." (Library of Congress)

eral government make specific commitments to protect slavery. They even demanded that Douglas and his followers reopen the international slave trade. The leaders of these Democrats included Senator Jefferson Davis, a Mississippi planter and Mexican War hero. Responding to Davis and the other southerners, Douglas, well aware that he would sacrifice his home base if he agreed to their terms, made it plain that if the Democratic party platform included such proposals in 1860, he would not support it.

A shocking event deepened the anxiety of southern Democrats even further. One night in October 1859, John Brown, leader of the Pottawatomie massacre, seized the federal arsenal at

Harpers Ferry, Virginia, with the assistance of eighteen heavily armed followers, both black and white. His explicit purpose was to arm a slave rebellion and create a black state within the South. Local militia and U.S. Marines, under the command of Colonel Robert E. Lee, quickly reclaimed the arsenal. They captured Brown and killed ten of his party. A Virginia court sentenced him to death.

Brown's hanging made him a martyr. Although Republican leaders dismissed him as a criminal, abolitionists depicted him almost as a saint. At a church meeting in Concord, Massachusetts, Henry David Thoreau described Brown as "an angel of light." It was necessary, Thoreau said, "that the bravest and humanest man in all the country should be hung." Such glorification of Brown horrified slaveholders, who assumed

that the abolitionists revealed the true sentiments and intentions of the entire North. They were convinced, more than ever, that a Republican victory at the polls would lead to the destruction of slavery.

When the Democratic party convened in April 1860, the southern wing was determined to force the party to defend slavery by embracing the program of Jefferson Davis and his followers. Northern Democrats, however, refused and insisted on nominating Douglas for the presidency. The southern delegates bolted, convened separately, and nominated Buchanan's vice-president, John C. Breckinridge of Kentucky. The Democratic party had finally broken apart.

The Republicans sensed victory. They made a cautious choice of a moderate presidential

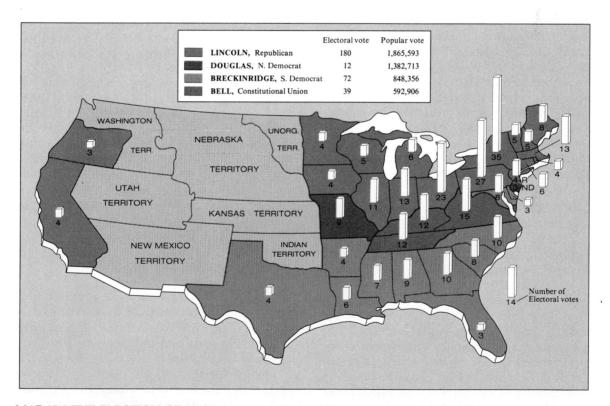

MAP 15.2 THE ELECTION OF 1860
Four presidential candidates vied for election in 1860. Douglas's few electoral votes are most striking in comparison with his strong showing in the popular vote. In most states, Douglas ran second to one of the two more extreme candidates—Lincoln and Breckinridge—who took all of the electoral votes of the states they won.

candidate, Abraham Lincoln, and passed over the best-known Republican, William H. Seward of New York, who had a reputation for being more radical than Lincoln on slavery. Lincoln also conveyed a compelling equalitarian image that could appeal to small farmers and workers.

The Republican platform attempted to strike a moderate tone. It adhered to free-soil doctrine but ruled out direct interference with slavery in the South. It denied the right of secession and appealed to Unionist sentiment there. It also endorsed the programs of economic development that had lain at the heart of Whig politics and had gained increasing support among Democrats in the Northwest, especially since the onset of depression conditions in 1857 and Buchanan's vetoes of internal improvement bills and homestead legislation.

Douglas was resigned to losing the North to Lincoln. He concentrated his efforts in the South. Underscoring the seriousness of the sectional crisis, he shattered tradition by campaigning personally. He warned southerners that the North would not allow them to destroy the Union and argued that *his* Democratic party provided the only feasible instrument for compromise. Competing with Douglas and also offering a Unionist message was John Bell, a former Tennessee senator who became the nominee of the Constitutional Union party, a residue of southern Whiggery.

In November, Lincoln won a plurality of the popular vote and a majority of the electoral vote. His victory in the North was overwhelming; he won every state there except New Jersey. In ten of the slave states, though, he failed to win a single electoral vote. Breckinridge won every state in the lower South and also carried Delaware, Maryland, and North Carolina. Bell carried the upper southern states where the Whigs had been strongest—Kentucky, Tennessee, and Virginia. Douglas's southern strategy failed completely. He carried only one state, Missouri, despite winning nearly a third of the popular vote. Even if Douglas had received the votes that went to Breckinridge and Bell, Lincoln would have been the victor because his votes were concentrated in the most populous states with the most electoral votes.

Secession and Civil War

Southern political leaders had pondered the implications of a possible Republican victory for years. A political party with support in only one section of the country had come to power. The Republicans had overcome differences between the Northeast and the West. They had been able to absorb abolitionism and still unify enough businessmen, workers, and farmers to achieve their victory. Worst of all—unlike any preceding president—Lincoln would take office owing not a single electoral vote to the South. To many southerners, it now seemed time to think carefully about the meaning of Lincoln's 1858 words:

> A house divided against itself cannot stand. I believe this government cannot endure, permanently half *slave* and half *free*. I do not expect the Union to be *dissolved*—I do not expect the house to *fall*—but I *do* expect it will cease to be divided. It will become *all* one thing, or *all* the other.

Many white southerners concluded that they could protect slavery only by leaving the Union and establishing their own nation. They believed in Calhoun's theory that the Constitution justified secession, and they were convinced that they were as true in their Americanism, and as stalwart in their defense of the republic, as were the Republicans in the North. The scale of secession, coupled with the profundity of the issues at stake, meant that the Republicans could unify the nation only at enormous cost.

The Secession Crisis

For most whites in the lower South, Lincoln's election called for immediate secession. Since the shock of John Brown's raid on Harpers Ferry, waves of hysteria over slave rebellion had swept through the region. The panic intensified during the presidential campaign. Fires of unknown origin and the deaths of whites under peculiar circumstances initiated reports of arson and poisoning. Southern whites knew that Lincoln considered slavery morally wrong. They believed he would appoint abolitionists or free blacks to federal jobs in the South and reopen

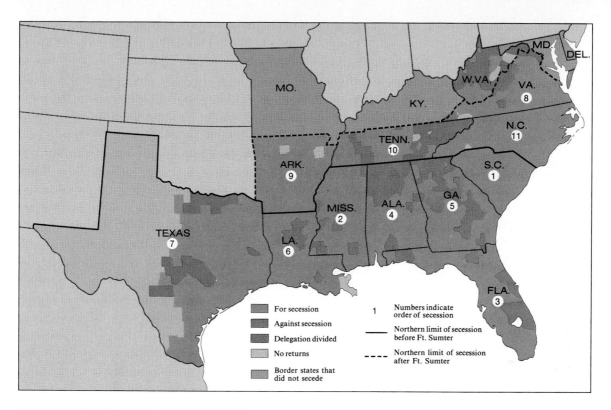

MAP 15.3 THE PROCESS OF SECESSION
The timing of the secession of the upper South pivoted upon the Union firing on Ft. Sumter. The map also shows the distribution of opinion among delegates to constitutional conventions or special sessions of legislatures that voted on secession. Comparing the order of secession with distribution of slaves on map 14.1 (page 411), it is clear that states with the highest concentration of slaves led the movement to secede.

the flow of abolitionist literature to southern blacks. By the time of Lincoln's election in November, whites in the lower South were united in a fear of cataclysm—a fear they believed no decent Christian or loyal American should have to endure.

On December 20, twenty-three days after Lincoln's election, South Carolina seceded. Six other cotton states called conventions or special sessions of legislatures to do the same. Vigilante groups formed, and military companies organized. Clergymen exhorted congregations to support secession. The "fire eaters"—dedicated, well-organized secessionist leaders such as Robert Barnwell Rhett of South Carolina, Robert Toombs of Georgia, and William Lowndes Yancey of Alabama, most of whom had advo-

cated secession since at least 1850—held control. Forty-two days after South Carolina's secession, Mississippi, Florida, Alabama, Georgia, Louisiana, and Texas left the Union. The secessionists formed the Confederate States of America, adopted a provisional constitution, and named Jefferson Davis as their provisional president. They moved so swiftly that all this had been done before James Buchanan left the White House.

The states that seceded first were those with the highest concentrations of slaves. Elsewhere in the South, the panic was less severe. Nonetheless, the political leaders of Delaware, Kentucky, Maryland, North Carolina, Tennessee, and Viriginia defended the right of any state to secede. In January 1861, the Virginia and

Tennessee legislatures pledged to resist any federal invasion of the seceded states. Leaders in the upper South wanted to make certain, however, that they had exhausted every reasonable option before they seceded. They proposed to seek concessions from the federal government that would relieve the anxieties of the seceding states and bring them back into the Union.

President Buchanan avoided any confrontation with the seceding states, fearing he might further accelerate the secession drive. In a message to Congress in December 1860, he denied the right of a state to secede but added that he believed the federal government lacked the power to force a state back into the Union. South Carolina quickly claimed that Buchanan's message implied recognition of the Confederacy and demanded that he should surrender Fort Sumter, in Charleston harbor. In January 1861, Buchanan tested the resolve of the secessionists by reinforcing the federal garrison at Fort Sumter. The South Carolinians, eager to provoke an attack, fired on an unarmed merchant ship as it entered the harbor. Buchanan backed off, declining to send the navy to reinforce the ship.

Buchanan worked instead with border-state congressmen to find concessions that would pacify the seceding states. The most important proposals came from Senator John J. Crittenden of Kentucky, an aging follower of Henry Clay. Crittenden proposed redrawing the Missouri Compromise line across the territories so that in all territories south of the line, the federal government would recognize and protect slavery.

Congressional Republicans, after consulting Lincoln, rejected Crittenden's plan. Lincoln worried that the compromise would encourage the South to embark on imperialist expansion in Latin America. He also was firm in his resolve not to repudiate free soil, the chief plank in the Republican platform.

In Lincoln's inaugural address on March 4, 1861, he left open the possibility of reconciliation. He promised to welcome the seceded states back into the Union after time had allowed their passion to cool. But he offered no concessions and was determined to persuade the secessionists that he fully intended to protect the Union.

He clearly stated that secession was illegal and that acts of violence in support of secession constituted revolution. He said, equally clearly, that he intended to enforce federal law throughout the Union and, specifically, to hold federal property in the seceded states. If force were necessary to preserve the Union, he promised to use it. The choice would be the South's—return to the Union or face war. Lincoln dispatched a relief expedition to Fort Sumter and informed South Carolina of his intentions.

On April 8, Jefferson Davis and his government received word of Lincoln's plans. The next day, they resolved to take the fort before Union reinforcements arrived. The Confederates did not seriously consider rejoining the Union and, in fact, welcomed Lincoln's coercion. They believed it would set the wavering southern states against the North and win foreign support for the Confederate cause.

The Confederates demanded Fort Sumter's surrender. The Union garrison refused, and the Confederates opened fire. On April 14, after two days of bombardment, the fort surrendered. The next day, Lincoln called seventy-five thousand state militiamen into federal service for ninety days to put down an insurrection "too powerful to be suppressed by the ordinary course of judicial proceedings." War had come.

The Confederate attack on Fort Sumter steeled northern resolve. The fort became a symbol of national unity and power, and its commander, Major Robert Anderson, became a national hero. Buoyed by public opinion, Lincoln strengthened the army and called on the states to provide troops to restore the Union. The pull of Unionism, supported by Lincoln's shrewd appeals to Unionist politicians and the use of military force, kept four border slave states—Maryland, Delaware, Kentucky, and Missouri—in the Union. The mountain counties of Virginia also stayed in the Union and were admitted in 1863 as the state of West Virginia. These crucial political victories prevented Washington, D.C., from being surrounded by enemy territory, assured Union transport down the Ohio River, and denied the Confederacy significant economic resources.

Lincoln's call to arms pushed the four states

of the upper South—Virginia, Arkansas, Tennessee, and North Carolina—into the Confederacy, however. The Confederacy thus doubled its population, gained the factories of Virginia, and won the symbolic victory of acquiring the homeland of Washington and Jefferson. The Confederacy had more than nine million people in its eleven states, about a third of the American population.

Military Stalemate, 1861–1863

For the North, the objective of the war was to force southerners to accept the legitimacy of the Union government—an enormously difficult task. The Confederacy stood willing and able to wage an extended and extremely damaging war. It was self-sufficient in food production. It had the advantage of fighting on familiar terrain. It could move troops and supplies quickly from one point to another along a defensive perimeter extending from Virginia to Louisiana. It had a long, irregular coastline that made blockade difficult. It had a strong military tradition and a near-monopoly of experienced military leaders. Above all, its white population had a passion for independence. To achieve independence, the Confedacy had to make the cost of the war high enough to induce the North to abandon the fight.

Gradually, the Union learned that it had to do more than win battles and occupy contested ground. It had to defeat southern society—to smash its armies, but also to break the ability and willingness of the southern people to supply new armies. A total war was required.

In 1861, the Union made immediate advances in the West. A small Union force stationed in Saint Louis defeated Confederates commanded by the governor of Missouri, Claiborne Jackson, who wanted his state to secede from the Union. In Ohio, General George B. McClellan assembled a Union force and occupied the mountain counties of western Virginia.

In the East, however, the Union suffered a major defeat. The Battle of Bull Run in 1861 revealed how unprepared the North was for a major war. In mid-July General Irvin McDowell, with an army of more than thirty thousand, advanced to attack P. G. T. Beauregard's Confeder-

ate force of over twenty thousand based at Manassas, thirty miles southwest of Washington. McDowell naively hoped to end the war in one battle. Since northern newspapers and southern spies had advertised the advance of McDowell's army, Beauregard had plenty of time to establish his army south of Bull Run, a small stream north of Manassas. McDowell attacked strongly on July 21, but panic swept through his inexperienced troops during Confederate counterattack. McDowell fell back to Washington, scrambling in retreat along with the many civilians who had come down from the capital with their Sunday picnic baskets to watch the battle. The Confederates lacked wagons and supplies to pursue and destroy McDowell's army. Lincoln replaced McDowell with McClellan, who had been so successful in the West, and increased the size of the Union army. It was clear now that the war would not be quick or easy.

In 1862, Confederate and Union commanders jockeyed for position around Washington and Richmond and their respective objectives. These commanders used virtually identical tactics, since almost all had been taught by the same instructors at West Point. After training 150,000 men during the winter of 1861–1862, McClellan, commander of the Army of the Potomac, began his Peninsula campaign against Richmond. He transported his troops by boat down the Potomac and Chesapeake Bay and then up the peninsula formed by the York and James rivers, toward the Confederate capital. But McClellan faced major problems. A Confederate army under Thomas J. ("Stonewall") Jackson marched rapidly north up the Shenandoah Valley, threatening Washington. To head off Jackson, Lincoln diverted thirty thousand troops from McClellen's army. But Jackson proved an able general; he defeated three Union armies in four battles. Then General Robert E. Lee, a new commander of the Army of Northern Virginia, with a force of eighty-five thousand, threatened to cut off McClellan from his base of supply on the York River. Although only twenty-five miles from Richmond, McClellan delayed his attack until Lincoln, exasperated with his cautious maneuvering, recalled the Army of the Potomac to the capital.

ANTIETAM'S AFTERMATH
This was the scene after Antietam in "Bloody Lane," a sunken road where two Union regiments had trapped Confederates in a barrage of rifle fire. This photograph and others from Antietam, taken by Mathew Brady, the most famous Civil War photographer, were the first photos Americans had ever seen of wartime carnage. (Library of Congress)

Lee, meanwhile, went on the offensive, moving overland toward Washington. In the Second Battle of Bull Run, on August 29–30, 1862, Lee routed a small Union army. He then struck north through western Maryland. He almost met with disaster after dividing his forces—sending Stonewall Jackson to capture Harpers Ferry—when a copy of his orders to Jackson fell into McClellan's hands. Once again, however, McClellan hesitated, and Lee had time to occupy a strong defensive position behind Antietam Creek, near Sharpsburg, Maryland. Although outnumbered eighty-seven thousand to fifty thousand, Lee repelled McClellan's attacks until Jackson's troops arrived. McClellan might have defeated Lee with another major effort, but the casualties appalled him. He let Lee fall back to Virginia while he buried the dead and set up field hospitals to nurse the wounded. September 17, 1862, proved to be the bloodiest single day in American military history. The dead numbered 4,800 and the wounded 18,500, of whom 3,000

soon died. (In contrast, only 6,000 Americans were killed or wounded on D-Day in World War II.)

Lincoln declared Antietam a major victory but believed that McClellan should have fought Lee to the finish. He replaced McClellan with Ambrose E. Burnside, who proved to be more daring but tactically incompetent. After losing large parts of the Army of the Potomac in futile attacks against the strongest part of the Confederate defenses of Richmond—at Fredericksburg, on December 13—Burnside relieved himself of command. Lincoln replaced him with Joseph ("Fighting Joe") Hooker.

In the West, Union and Confederate troops fought in 1862 for control of the great valleys of the Ohio, Tennessee, and Mississippi rivers. In April, Admiral David G. Farragut led a Union squadron of ironclad vessels up the Mississippi from the Gulf of Mexico and took New Orleans by surprise. In that one offensive, the Union captured the South's financial center and largest city, acquired a major base for future operations, and denied the Confederacy an important port.

In an even more brilliant tactical maneuver, a relatively unknown Union commander, Ulysses S. Grant, struck into Tennessee from Cairo, Illinois, and, using ironclad river boats, took Fort Henry, on the Tennessee River, and Fort Donelson, on the Cumberland. Grant then moved south to control critical railroad lines. Confederates under Albert Sidney Johnston and P. G. T. Beauregard caught Grant by surprise in the Battle of Shiloh, on April 6–7, 1862, but Grant relentlessly threw troops into the battle and forced a Confederate withdrawal. He then took Corinth, Mississippi, a major Confederate railroad junction, and by June controlled the Mississippi as far south as Memphis.

In 1863, strategy and tactics remained relatively unchanged on both sides, but the scale and intensity of fighting increased. In the West the Union continued to make major gains, and Grant remained the major figure. After hammering persistently at Confederate defenses around

Vicksburg, Mississippi, from the north, he swung his troops around the city. He besieged Vicksburg for six weeks, and it fell on July 4. Met almost immediately by Union forces advancing from New Orleans, Grant now controlled the whole length of the Mississippi. He had split the Confederacy, isolating its trans-Mississippi region.

Later in 1863, the Union also took complete control of the Tennessee River. Union forces under William S. Rosecrans occupied Chattanooga, Tennessee, on September 9 but, in the face of unusually strong Confederate forces, they failed to advance. Rosecrans was defeated by Braxton Bragg in the Battle of Chickamauga on September 19–20, and the Union troops retreated to Chattanooga, where they faced another siege by Bragg. Grant finally charged to the rescue and, in the Battle of Chattanooga on November 23–25, drove the Confederates into Georgia. The Union was now in position to divide the Confederacy again, this time in the East.

Facing great Union pressure in the west,

MAP 15.4 THE WESTERN CAMPAIGNS, 1861–1862
The great valleys of the Ohio, Tennessee, and Mississippi rivers were at stake during the early part of the Civil War. By the end of 1862, Union armies had kept Missouri in the Union and driven the Confederate armies out of Kentucky and half of Tennessee. They also controlled New Orleans and almost all of the Mississippi River, and at Shiloh they had proven that they could not be driven out of the lower South. Costing thirteen thousand Union and ten thousand Confederate dead, Shiloh also showed how bloody the war would become.

Confederate leaders wanted to send reinforcements. Lee persuaded them to invade the North instead. He argued that this would relieve the pressure on Vicksburg by drawing Union armies east, that it would enable his army to resupply itself from the rich northern countryside, and perhaps accomplish the capture of Washington or some other large Union city, thereby destroying the Union's will to fight. Lee began to move north, and in May defeated Hooker's Army of the Potomac at the Battle of Chancellorsville, in Virginia. Lee pressed on, determined to win a great victory on northern soil. He maneuvered his army west to the Shenandoah Valley and north through Maryland into Pennsylvania. The Union Army, now led by Hooker's replacement, General George C. Meade, pursued Lee, staying

between the Confederate forces and Washington. The two great armies finally encountered one another at Gettysburg, Pennsylvania, although neither commander chose the location for the momentous confrontation. Lee concluded that unless he engaged Meade's forces, he risked loss of his supply lines to Virginia. Meade could not let Lee control Gettysburg, where a junction of roads fanned out in a dozen directions.

On the first day of battle, July 1, Lee was able to bring more troops into action and drove Meade's advance guard to the south and west of town. Meade moved cautiously, waiting for the reinforcements that would give him numerical superiority. He placed his troops in well-defended positions on the hills outside town. Reinforcements for both sides arrived all day and

MAP 15.5 THE BATTLE OF GETTYSBURG
Lee's invasion of the North, following Confederate victories at Fredericksburg and Chancellorsville, was designed to threaten northern cities, to persuade Europeans that the Confederacy would win the war, and to strengthen the hand of the Peace Democrats, who argued that the South could not be defeated. Lee's strategy might have ended the war if he had won at Gettysburg.

ABRAHAM LINCOLN'S GETTYSBURG ADDRESS

On November 19, 1863, about four months after the Battle of Gettysburg, Lincoln delivered this address as he dedicated part of the battlefield as a national cemetery. Along with the words of "The Battle Hymn of the Republic," written by Julia Ward Howe, Lincoln's address became the most widely quoted statement of why the Union fought.

Four score and seven years ago our fathers brought forth on this continent, a new nation, conceived in Liberty, and dedicated to the proposition that all men are created equal.

Now we are engaged in a great civil war, testing whether that nation, or any nation so conceived and so dedicated, can long endure. We are met on a great battle-field of that war. We have come here to dedicate a portion of that field, as a final resting place for those who here gave their lives that this nation might live. It is altogether fitting and proper that we should do this.

But, in a larger sense, we can not dedicate—we can not consecrate—we can not hallow—this ground. The brave men, living and dead, who struggled here, have consecrated it, far above our poor power to add or detract. The world will little note, nor long remember what we say here, but it can never forget what they did here. It is for us the living, rather, to be dedicated here to the unfinished work which they who fought here have thus far so nobly advanced. It is rather for us to be here dedicated to the great task remaining before us—that from these honored dead we take increased devotion to that cause for which they gave the last full measure of devotion—that we here highly resolve that these dead shall not have died in vain—that this nation, under God, shall have a new birth of freedom—and that government of the people, by the people, for the people, shall not perish from the earth.

---

throughout the night. By the morning of the second day, Meade outnumbered Lee ninety thousand to seventy-five thousand. Although aware that he was outnumbered, Lee was confident in his troops and was bent on victory. He attacked Meade's army on both flanks. The flanking efforts failed. General George Ewell, assigned to attack the Union right, was unwilling to risk his men in an all-out assault against the well-entrenched forces on Cemetery Hill. General George P. Longstreet, assigned the Union left, was unable to attack swiftly enough to prevent Meade's forces from strengthening their hold on Little Round Top and Round Top.

Despite the failures of the previous two days, Lee decided to proceed with a final frontal assault on the center of the Union lines. He mistakenly believed that he faced demoralized Union troops stretched out in a thin defensive line. He also believed that an attack was the only alternative to a retreat into the South, with the loss, perhaps forever, of an opportunity to inflict a crushing psychological defeat on the North. On the third day, after the heaviest artillery exchange of the war, Lee ordered thirteen thousand men, commanded by General George E. Pickett, to take Cemetery Hill. Meade had reinforced the center of his line with artillery and his best troops. Lee's army charged across a mile of open terrain under massive, withering enemy fire. Ten thousand of Pickett's men were killed, wounded, or captured in the disastrous assault. The few Confederate soldiers who breached the Union fortifications were shot or forced to surrender. All told, Lee lost twenty-eight thousand men in these days of battle—one third of his army. Meade lost twenty-three thousand, but he held his position and emerged from Gettysburg with greater relative superiority over the Confederate forces.

Lee's Army of Northern Virginia was so weakened by the Battle of Gettysburg that he

THE RIFLE-MUSKET

In 1855, U.S. Secretary of War Jefferson Davis ordered an end to the production of the smooth-bore musket and began equipping American soldiers with rifle-muskets. Most Union infantrymen used the Springfield rifle, a rifle-musket manufactured by the U.S. armory at Springfield, Massachusetts or by private manufacturers copying Springfield designs. Confederate soldiers often used the Enfield rifle, a similar weapon manufactured in England. These new weapons accounted for most of the casualties of the war. They also revolutionized warfare and military strategy.

Hunting rifles dating back to the eighteenth century had tapered barrels that were rifled, or lined with spiral grooves. This kind of barrel gave the bullet greater speed and accuracy. Unlike the smooth barrels of muskets, however, the rifle grooves quickly accumulated gunpowder and so required frequent clean-

ing, an inconvenient and dangerous delay in combat.

In the early 1850s, an American mechanic named James S. Burton, working at the Harper's Ferry Armory, developed a new form of bullet based on the innovations of Captain Claude E. Minie of the French army. Burton's cylindro-conoidal bullet, radically different from the round bullets of the day, was cast with a cavity at its base. When the rifle hammer exploded powder at the base of the barrel, hot gas expanded this cavity and forced the bullet to engage the grooves of the rifling as it sped through the barrel. The bullet thus cleaned the grooves with each shot.

Infantrymen for the first time could be efficient, effective riflemen. Rifle-muskets built to fire the new bullets could hit targets half a mile away, whereas the maximum range of a musket was barely 250 yards. A veteran with a rifle-musket killed reliably at 300 yards; with a musket, his aim was

assured only at 100 yards or less.

The new gun was called a rifle-musket because it retained certain musket characteristics, which had limited the musket to use mainly as a defensive weapon. It fired a single shot, was loaded through the muzzle, and had a long barrel, usually forty inches. Like the musket, the rifle-musket was cumbersome and often fatal to load. Before aiming and firing, a soldier had to take out a paper-wrapped cartridge of gunpowder, rip open the cartridge with his teeth, pour the powder down the barrel, insert the bullet into the barrel, jam the bullet and powder down with a ramrod, half-cock the hammer, insert a percussion cap, and, finally, cock the hammer. Some soldiers could do all this while lying on their backs, but most, in order to fire two or three times a minute, had to load from a kneeling or standing position, often exposing themselves to enemy fire. Clearly, soldiers could

---

could never again invade the North. That the Confederate army survived at all was due largely to Meade, who was so pleased with his victory that he allowed the remaining Confederate soldiers to escape. Lincoln wrote Meade in fury that Lee "was within your easy grasp, and to have closed upon him would, in connection with our other late successes, have ended the war. As it is, the war will be prolonged indefinitely."

With better tactics, either side could have won the war in 1863. As events turned, the stalemate worked to the benefit of the North. The Confederacy had lost its best chance to weaken Union resolve, while the North gained time to build a war machine with the full strength of the industrial North behind it.

Lincoln Finds His General

President Lincoln slowly came to realize that Ulysses S. Grant had innovative approaches to warfare that produced results. Grant, bored by West Point orthodoxy since his cadet days, believed that conventional tactics would not win the war. In his decisive victories at Vicksburg and Chattanooga, he demonstrated his skill at rapidly deploying and supporting great armies by relying on railroads, the telegraph, and even ironclad ships. This mobility allowed Grant's troops to seize superior positions and exploit a new weapon, the rifle-musket, which northern factories mass-produced. This rifle could fire two shots a minute and was deadly accurate up to four hundred yards. Well-entrenched riflemen not reload and fire on the run.

The rifle-musket was not a modern rifle; it was not breech-loading and it did not fire multiple rounds. Modern rifles were refined during the war and adopted in limited quantities. But both sides preferred to stay with the rifle-musket because it had already proven to be much better than the muskets with which earlier wars had been fought. Most important, the increased range and accuracy and relatively quick reloading of the rifle-musket enormously strengthened defensive forces. Defenders could fire on attackers almost continually and, if the defenders were ensconced in well-protected positions with a broad field of vision—like the Union forces on Cemetery Hill—they could usually keep the attackers from getting close enough for hand-to-hand combat. (Bayonets accounted for less than 1 percent of all wounds in the Civil War.) If attacking forces broke through

defensive lines, they usually were so weakened that they had to retreat or surrender in the face of counterattacks. Elaborate entrenchments strengthened defensive positions even more. Used by both sides in almost every battle by 1863, these trenches, together with the rifle-musket, enabled infantrymen to turn back assaults by forces three to four times their size.

Infantry commanders, however, were slow to change the tactics of assault they had inherited from the days of the musket and bayonet. They used flanking maneuvers where possible; relied more heavily on "skirmishers," whose traditional role had been to explore the enemy's position; and experimented with deceptive rushing tactics. But for genuine effectiveness, these tactics required more than the voice and visual communication to which the Civil War armies were limited. Consequently, commanders still attacked in dense formations,

consisting of thousands of infantrymen, that assaulted enemy positions in successive waves. Officers tried to keep their men perfectly parallel to concentrate their fire and to hit the enemy line with maximum shock.

In battle after battle, charging infantrymen went down like harvested wheat. Many units in both armies suffered losses of 40 to 80 percent in a single engagement. By 1863, the extraordinary number of casualties had become psychologically and politically intolerable. The terrible losses at Gettysburg, in particular, finally forced a crisis in military tactics. Commanders on both sides began to try to avoid situations that required frontal assaults and to force or induce enemy troops to leave defensive positions. The trench warfare that developed around Petersburg, Virginia in the last weeks of the Civil War presaged the trenches of World War I, where another breed of weapons became necessary.

---

could repulse cavalry for the first time. The rifle was also cruelly effective against assaults of infantry in close-order formations, which Civil War commanders persisted in using, despite enormous casualties, because they could not control troops beyond voice or vision.

Not only did Grant excel in taking advantage of modern technology, but he also became convinced that heavy casualties would be necessary to end the war swiftly. Other Union commanders, more influenced by traditional, genteel military training, were reluctant to accept this view. Grant's tactics earned him a reputation as a butcher. He enhanced that reputation by destroying defeated armies and terrorizing civilians. Grant was certain that the southern people's will to resist had to be crushed, and he recognized a

stalemate would mean Confederate independence.

Frustrated by the military stalemate, and worried about re-election in 1864, Lincoln adopted Grant's approach to modern war. In March 1864, he placed Grant in charge of all the Union armies; until then, Lincoln himself had functioned as a general-in-chief. He also created a command structure more appropriate to the large, complex organization that the Union army had become. The president decided general strategy, and Grant inspired the military strategy. Instead of launching campaigns to take specific places, cities, and territory, the Union planned a simultaneous crushing advance of all its armies, supporting them with the maximum manpower and resources that could be mustered.

The Northern War Machine and Republican Policies

To wage a total war, the North had to develop the instruments of a modern state, especially a strong central government and a powerful presidency. The Lincoln administration introduced conscription, used force to suppress those in the largest cities and the border states who resisted the war effort, and taxed the people of the North at unprecedented levels. But developing a successful war machine required far more than coercion. It called for winning and holding the enthusiastic support of those who voted, paid taxes, and fought. Consequently, the Republicans worked hard both to implement their eco-nomic program and to gain public support. The direct result was mobilization on a scale the country had never experienced before. The indirect result was a rapid consolidation of the power of the business class.

Mobilization

As commander-in-chief, Lincoln assumed responsibility for directing mobilization, and he established the primacy of the presidency in the conduct of modern warfare. Secretary of War Edwin M. Stanton, appointed in 1862, reorganized the War Department and produced a dependable flow of supplies to the Union army. Stanton and Lincoln turned the nation's railroad system into the key logistical element of the war effort. They promoted the expansion of the rail-

LINCOLN WITH THE ARMY OF THE POTOMAC
This formal photograph records Lincoln's visit to McClellan's headquarters near the Antietam battlefield on October 3, 1862. On this visit, Lincoln vigorously urged McClellan to advance on Richmond. McClellan (facing the president) did not respond and Lincoln removed him from command a month later. (Library of Congress)

DRAFT RIOTS IN
NEW YORK CITY
The rioters went so far as to burn
down a black orphanage, the
Colored Orphan Asylum, on Fifth
Avenue. The riots—perhaps the
worst in all of U.S. history—
demonstrated that powerful issues of
class and race were not far from the
surface of American politics. (But
business-class denunciation of the
riots and of Peace Democrats
strengthened Lincoln's hand.) (From
Harper's Weekly. The Newberry
Library, Chicago)

roads, adding five thousand miles of track by the
end of the war and converting all lines to a standard rail gauge (see map 14.3 on railroad lines,
page 422).

The most difficult mobilization problem for
Lincoln was recruiting enough troops. The
dreadful carnage of 1862 discouraged men from
volunteering, and Lincoln and Stanton therefore
initiated conscription. Using the Militia Act of
1862, they imposed the draft on states that failed
to meet their quotas of volunteers. The threat of
the draft stimulated enough volunteers until
1863. Then, as the scale and intensity of the war
rose, Congress passed the Enrollment Act of
1863, which subjected to the draft all able-bodied
males, aged twenty to forty-five, who were either citizens or aliens who had applied for naturalization. The War Department, in draft calls
that extended through 1864, assigned each congressional district a quota based on its population. The district could meet the quota with
either conscripts or volunteers, to whom the federal government offered cash bounties. The act
allowed a draftee to provide a substitute or pay
a commutation fee of three hundred dollars that

exempted him from the draft. The Enrollment
Act produced only 46,000 draftees and 118,000
substitutes—about 10 percent of the Union soldiers—but, through the bounties, it stimulated
the voluntary enlistment or reenlistment of almost a million men.

Conscription and the high commutation fee—
at least half of a worker's annual income—provoked fierce resistance. The commutation fee
generated resentment among men who were un-
enthusiastic about the war, or even opposed it,
but could not buy their way out of the army.
The draft became a focal point for preexisting
hostility to Republicans, blacks, and the war effort. The resistance was greatest in districts that
were heavily urban, immigrant, Catholic, and
Democratic. In July 1863, after draftees' names
were announced, New York City became the
scene of ferocious antidraft rioting by immigrant
Irish workers worried about an influx of freed
slaves. After youths burned the draft office,
sacked the homes of some important Republicans, assaulted police, and lynched at least a
dozen blacks, Lincoln rushed in troops from
Gettysburg. Police and soldiers of the Army of

A UNION FIELD HOSPITAL
Under the pressure of heavy casualties and shifting battle sites, conditions at field hospitals were usually makeshift and chaotic. This one, at Savage Station, Virginia, served twenty-five hundred wounded in June 1862. It fell into Confederate hands as McClellan retreated during his Peninsula campaign. (Library of Congress.)

the Potomac, who had faced the Confederates two weeks earlier, killed more than a hundred rioters and suppressed the urban insurrection.

Lincoln's quashing of the antidraft riots was only one of the measures he used to suppress hostility to the war. In September 1862, he placed under martial law any person who discouraged enlistment, resisted the draft, or was guilty of any disloyal practice. He did this in order to subject them to trial by court-martial, rather than by a local jury. Suspending normal constitutional guarantees, such as habeas corpus, the Lincoln administration arrested and imprisoned nearly fifteen thousand individuals, mostly in the border states.

Mobilization for total war also required expansion and professionalization of the army's medical services. In 1862, Congress reorganized the Union Army Medical Bureau and Lincoln appointed an innovative surgeon general, William A. Hammond. Hammond and the bureau increased the number of surgeons, built more hospitals, organized a trained ambulance corps, and

integrated the services of the United States Sanitary Commission into the war effort. Organized early in the war by civilians, the Sanitary Commission provided vital health services. Through its seven thousand local auxiliaries, the commission gathered supplies; distributed clothing, food, and medicine to the army; raised the sanitary standards of camp life; and recruited nurses and doctors for the battlefield.

The results of all this organized effort were not readily visible. Disease—primarily dysentery, typhoid, and malaria—killed twice as many Union soldiers (about 250,000) as did combat. Surgeons took more lives by spreading infection than they saved by treating wounds and amputating limbs. However, the incidence of mortality from disease and wounds was substantially less than in other major nineteenth-century wars, partly because of the attention given to sanitation and the quality of food.

Most of the thousands of Sanitary Commission nurses and workers were women. Organized by Dorothea Dix, the first woman to receive a major federal appointment—as superintendent of female nurses—the nurses overcame prejudice against women treating the bodies of men and opened a new occupation to women. Nurse Clara Barton, who later founded the American Red Cross, recalled that "At the war's end, woman was at least fifty years in advance of the normal position which continued peace would have assigned her." Barton was overoptimistic. But the war effort did provide middle-class women with a great range of new civic involvement, unprecedented experience in large and complex bureaucracies such as the Sanitary Commission, and new jobs as clerks in government offices. Moreover, with the men away, women dramatically increased their responsibilities in schools, in their own households, and on their farms.

Total mobilization of northern society required a monumental financial effort. Wartime expenditures drove federal expenditures from less than 2 percent of the gross national product to an average of 15 percent, close to the level of about 20 percent in the 1980s. To finance these expenditures, the Republicans by 1863 had gone

far beyond their 1860 economic platform; they had built a revenue system appropriate to a modern state.

The Union government paid for the war by running deficits and borrowing money, raised through the sale of U.S. Treasury bonds. These policies financed two-thirds of the cost of Union mobilization. This enormous borrowing program succeeded for several reasons. The Treasury made the interest on the bonds payable in gold. Rising confidence, on both sides of the Atlantic, in a Union victory created a buoyant bond market. Also, the Treasury, which began to use the services of financier Jay Cooke in the summer of 1862, pioneered in techniques of bond marketing in both Great Britain and America. Bankers and wealthy people bought most of the bonds. But Cooke's newspaper advertisements and his twenty-five hundred subagents persuaded nearly a million Northerners—a fourth of all families—to buy them, too.

Another reason for the success of the borrowing program was the establishment of a national banking system, under the National Banking Acts of 1863 and 1865, as a deliberate effort to

UNION NURSES
More than three thousand women served on both sides as nurses during the Civil War. The Union nurses were more organized than the Confederate but only a minority served, for pay, under Dorothea Dix. The rest were unpaid volunteers and all nurses spent most of their time cooking and cleaning for their patients. (American Red Cross)

THE HOME FRONT, 1865

These excerpts from the diary of Sarah Beaulieu, a nineteen-year-old Wisconsin farm woman, indicate the new hardships and responsibilities women faced when all the men in the family went to war.

January 14

Cleaned as usual. Ma went to the P.O. to get a letter from Brother Bony [Napolean Bonaparte Beaulieu] which was very welcome, he being in the army, and we being very anxious about him.

February 13

Arose very early. About ten A.M. Bony took his departure, left Emma [Bony's wife] and I very lonely. He having to join his regt. at Cairo, Ill. having been home on a thirty day furlough.

March 27

Did our usual work. In the afternoon yoked up the oxen and drawed logs for firewood then went to sugar bush with Mother and brought down some sap on the little sleigh and had a queer time driving oxen.

March 28

Did the washing and in the afternoon had a sugaring off. Ate all the warm sugar I wanted for once this year.

March 30

Ironed the clothes and gathered sap in the evening. . . .

March 31

Moved about twenty bushels of potatoes with Ma's help and put them in the cellar. . . .

April 3

Emma and myself carried in fifty bushels of turnips out of the pit. We did not think it was so hard a job until after we got at it. . . .

April 5

Passed this day in the bush boiling sap. Did not do anything of importance. In the afternoon I went home and felt very bad. Went to bed early. . . .

April 13

Prepared to go to the Bay and pass examinations. If there is anything I dislike it is to have a man ask questions and be obliged to answer them in order to get that little paper licensing one to teach school.

April 14

Feel very tired having walked fourteen miles and at last arrived my place of destination [Green Bay]. . . .

April 16

Went to the Methodist Church in the forenoon. Every article was draped in mourning. . . . The assassination of our president has cast a gloom over every one.

April 25

Had only eight scholars. Passed the day in teaching those little minds in the right direction of their books.

April 26

Taught school one half day, cleaned the school house. . . . Went down to Mrs. Wagner's in the evening. Stayed all night, dressed that sick girl's hand which was so badly burned trying to save her mother.

April 29

Taught school, went home in the evening very lonesome and weary. I think I am getting very much like the old maid that sat down on Monday morning and cried because Saturday did not come twice a week. . . .

Source: W. Elliot Brownlee and Mary M. Brownlee, *Women in the American Economy, A Documentary History, 1675 to 1929.* New Haven: Yale University Press, 1976. 127–130.

---

induce bankers to purchase bonds. The acts placed a crippling tax on the notes issued by state-chartered banks and offered those banks national charters. The acts also required banks joining the national system to invest a third of their capital in United States bonds.

Taxes, almost all of them new, financed about 20 percent of the Union's mobilization. These taxes included the first income tax ever levied by the U.S. government (a graduated tax reaching a maximum rate of 10 percent), excise taxes on virtually all consumer goods, license taxes on a wide variety of activities (including every profession except the ministry), special taxes on corporations, stamp taxes on legal documents, and inheritance taxes. Each wartime Congress raised tariffs against foreign competition, doubling the average tariff rate by the end of the war.

The least important element of wartime finance was the issuing of money backed only by faith in the government. In February 1862, Congress passed the Legal Tender Act, authorizing the issue of $150 million of Treasury notes, which became known as "greenbacks." Congress required the public to accept greenbacks as legal tender, receivable for most debts public or private. Only tariff duties and interest on the national debt had to be paid in gold or silver coins, previously the only legal tender. This paper money, amounting to $500 million by the end of the war, financed 13 percent of the war's cost.

In developing programs of wartime mobilization, the Republicans built the financial foundations of a modern industrial nation-state. Borrowing, imposing taxes, and creating money mobilized huge sums for the Union cause and tied millions of Americans, especially members of the business class, to the welfare of the modern state.

The Republicans also used wartime mobilization to put through their own economic policies. By 1863, they had enacted virtually all the economic program they had inherited from Henry Clay and the Whigs.

Most enthusiastic about this program were Republicans who had begun their political careers as Whigs and had been waiting—some for more than twenty years—for this opportunity. They now received support from many farmers and workers who had been persuaded that this economic program would help prevent a return to the depression conditions of the late 1850s. Many former Democrats, drawn to the Republican party by their free-soil ideas, relaxed their resistance to national banking and protective tariffs. In addition, the war eliminated from Congress almost all southern Democrats who had opposed the Whig program. Most fundamentally, the Republicans muted social criticism that might have been directed at their style of economics. By celebrating economic opportunity in the North and by focusing on the threat that slavery posed to opportunity, they diverted attention from the failures and limitations of American industrialization. The southern challenge to northern society convinced many northern farmers and workers to support the nationalizing economic program of the Republican party and the business class.

Each element of the Republican economic program won a substantial following. The tariff received support from manufacturers and from laborers and farmers who feared cheap foreign labor. Capitalists, large and small, applauded the national banking system. In 1862, Congress passed the Homestead Act, giving heads of families or individuals twenty-one or older the right to 160 acres of public land after five years of residence and improvement. The act contained many loopholes, allowing many speculators to put together large accumulations of land, but numerous small farmers also acquired land, and almost all farmers regarded the legislation enthusiastically. In 1862, Lincoln followed through on the Republican promise to build transcontinental railroads. Congress chartered the Union Pacific and Central Pacific railways and subsidized them lavishly. It gave them twenty sections (twenty square miles) of federal land in alternate plots for every mile of track the railroads put down. Congress provided a similar charter and subsidy to the Northern Pacific in 1864.

Emancipation

Lincoln and his generals gradually redefined the war as a struggle not only against Confederate armies, but also against southern society. He and his party began to regard it as not just a war for the Union but against slavery.

A few abolitionist leaders had hoped in 1861 that the South would be allowed to secede, so as to rid the Union of the stain of slavery. But others shrewdly worked to get the Republican party to commit itself to making abolition a goal of the war. They argued on grounds not just of morality but of "military necessity." After all, they noted, the labor of the slaves enabled the Confederacy to feed and supply its armies. Frederick Douglass wrote that "the very stomach of this rebellion is the Negro in the form of a slave. Arrest that hoe in the hands of the Negro, and you smite the rebellion in the very seat of its life."

Union commanders in the field were the first to free any slaves. In May 1861, General Benjamin Butler, who had taken military control of Annapolis and Baltimore, refused to return three slaves who had escaped to his lines. He labeled them "contraband of war." His term stuck, and for the rest of the war, slaves found within the Union lines were known as "contrabands." By August 1861, a thousand contrabands camped with Butler's army. That same month, Lincoln

LETTER FROM A BLACK SOLDIER TO THE OWNER OF HIS DAUGHTER

Spotswood Rice, a former slave, writes to Kittey Diggs, 1864:

I received a letter from Cariline telling me that you say I tried to steal to plunder my child away from you now I want you to understand that mary is my Child and she is a God given rite of my own and you may hold on to hear as long as you can but I want you to remembor this one thing that the longor you keep my Child from me the longor you will have to burn in hell and the quicer youll get their for we are now makeing up a bout one thoughsand blacke troops to Come up tharough and wont to come through Glasgow and when we come wo be to Copperhood rabbels and to the Slaveholding rebbels for we dont expect to leave there root neor branch but we thinke how ever that we that have Children in the hands of you devels we will trie your the day that we enter Glasgow I want you to understand kittey diggs that where ever you and I meets we are enmays to each orthere I offered once to pay you forty dollars for my own Child but I am glad now that you did not accept it Just hold on now as long as you can and the worse it will be for you you never in you life befor I came down hear did you give Children any thing not eny thing whatever not even a dollars worth of expencs now you call my childrend your property not so with me my Children is my own and I expect to get them and when I get redy to come after mary I will have bout a powrer and autherity to bring hear away and to exacute vengencens on them that holds my Child you will then know how to talke to me I will asure that and you will know how to talk rite too I want you now to just hold to hear if you want to iff your conchosence tells thats the road go that road and what it will brig you to kittey diggs I have no fears about getting mary out of your hands this whole Government gives chear to me and you cannot help your self

Source: Ira Berlin, ed., *Freedom, A Documentary History of Emancipation, 1861–1867.* Cambridge: Cambridge University, 1982. 690.

---

signed into law a measure authorizing the seizure of all property—defined to include slaves—used to support the rebellion. This law applied only to slaves within reach of Union armies, and it did not actually emancipate them. But it did begin a process that ended in abolition.

Republicans opposed slavery and were ready for some kind of emancipation. But they divided into three groups over the timing and method. The conservatives, the smallest of the three groups, looked forward to slavery's ultimate end but believed that the federal government should only block the extension of slavery into the territories; emancipation in existing states, they believed, should be left to state governments. More numerous were the radicals, who wanted the government to abolish slavery everywhere immediately. The moderates, most numerous of all, wanted emancipation to proceed more rapidly than did the conservatives but feared that immediate abolition would cause a loss of Union support in the border states.

As battlefield casualties mounted, so did popular support for making slaveowners pay for the war with the loss of their slaves. So did moral enthusiasm for freeing the slaves, and so did the power of the radical Republicans, whose leaders included key congressional committee chairmen who could, and did, pressure the moderates. Charles Sumner, chairman of the Senate Committee on Foreign Affairs, and Thaddeus Stevens, chairman of the House Ways and Means Committee, were especially effective in influencing the leader of the moderates, Abraham Lincoln. Handsome and eloquent, Sumner had helped found the Free Soil party and had been elected to the Senate from Massachusetts by a coalition of Free Soilers and Democrats in 1850. In 1856, he had denounced both slavery and a South Carolina congressman, Preston Brooks, so passionately that Brooks attacked him with a cane and beat him senseless on the Senate floor. Thaddeus Stevens was at least as stern and uncompromising on slavery as Sumner, but more masterful in manipulating Congress, where he served as a representative from Pennsylvania from 1849 to 1853 and from 1859 until his death in 1868. Of all the Republicans in Congress, Stevens was probably the most completely committed to racial equality.

Together, Lincoln and congressional Republicans moved rapidly toward abolition, just ahead of the wave of public sentiment. Their measures were moderate, shaped by the practical objectives of winning the war. Thus, when Congress took its first step toward abolition in April 1862—abolishing slavery in the District of Columbia—it promised compensation to the former slaveowners in order to maintain their loyalty to the Union. Its second step, abolishing slavery in the national territories in June 1862, affected few slaves, but it represented the enactment of the Wilmot Proviso and the fulfillment of the free-soil platform.

Lincoln waited for a favorable turn on the battlefield before he extended emancipation significantly. After Antietam, he decided that the time had come. On September 23, 1862, the president issued the Emancipation Proclamation. He declared that on January 1, 1863, the slaves in all states still in rebellion would be free. He gave the rebellious states a hundred days to return to the Union and keep slavery intact. None chose to do so.

Lincoln was politically astute. He left slavery intact in the border states because he wanted to *keep* their loyalty. He left slavery untouched in areas occupied by Union armies—Tennessee, western Virginia, and southern Louisiana, including New Orleans—because he wanted to *win* their allegiance. The Emancipation Proclamation had no instant, practical effect on the life of a single slave. But as the Union armies advanced, it provided for the liberation of hundreds of thousands of slaves and clearly changed the meaning of the war.

After Lincoln issued the proclamation, emancipation accelerated. Before the war ended, two border states (Maryland and Missouri) freed their slaves, and three occupied Confederate states (Tennessee, Arkansas, and Louisiana) followed suit. On January 31, 1865, Congress began the final step toward full legal emancipation when it approved the Thirteenth Amendment, which prohibited slavery altogether. By the end of the year, the necessary number of states had ratified this amendment.

In the final, decisive phase of the war, emancipation had an unforeseen effect. It made many former slaves available to the Union war effort. By the end of the war, nearly two hundred thousand former slaves served as soldiers, sailors, and laborers. They contributed to the Union victory in a number of battles. The worst fears of the secessionists had come true; in a sense, the great slave rebellion had materialized.

BLACK SOLDIERS IN THE UNION ARMY
These were the proud soldiers of a guard detail of the 107th U.S. Colored Infantry at Fort Corcoran, near Washington, D.C. In January 1865, their regiment participated in the daring capture of Fort Fisher, which protected Wilmington, North Carolina, the last of the Confederate ports open to blockade runners. Their chaplain declared that in nine battles the regiment "never faltered, gave way, or retreated, unless ordered by the General commanding." (Library of Congress)

The Election of 1864

The 1864 presidential election tested support for Lincoln's policy of total war and support for emancipation. The Republican platform endorsed all his war measures, demanded unconditional surrender of the Confederacy, and called for a constitutional amendment to abolish slavery. To emphasize the need for restoration of the Union, the party temporarily renamed itself the National Union party and nominated for vice-president Andrew Johnson, a Tennessee Democrat who had remained loyal and stayed in the Senate.

Northern Democrats declared their opposition to emancipation but, beyond that, could not propose a clear alternative to Lincoln's program. Half the party, the War Democrats, wished to continue the war, while the other half, the Peace Democrats, wanted to grant an armistice and seek reunion on any available terms. This internal division nearly paralyzed the party. The Democratic presidential candidate, General George B. McClellan, wanted to continue the war, while his party's platform advocated an immediate armistice. The Republicans charged, with some accuracy, that groups of Peace Democrats—or "Copperheads" (poisonous snakes), as the Republican press called them—hatched treasonous plots in the border states and in the southern part of the Old Northwest.

Lincoln's victory was clear-cut but not a landslide. He increased his percentage of the popular vote from the 48 percent he had received in 1860 to 55 percent. His opposition was concentrated in border districts and the immigrant wards of large cities. Republicans also won 145 of the 185 seats in the House of Representatives and increased their Senate majority to 42 of 52 seats. The biggest shift of votes came from Union soldiers. The soldiers cast absentee ballots (or returned home, briefly furloughed by Lincoln, to cast ballots) in states such as Illinois and Indiana, where the Democrats had blocked absentee balloting. More than three-fourths of the Union troops voted for Lincoln. They wanted the war to continue until the Confederacy met Union demands, including emancipation. Grant wrote a friend that "the overwhelming majority received

by Mr. Lincoln and the quiet with which the election went off . . . will be worth more than a victory in the field both in its effect on the Rebels and in its influence abroad."

Lincoln's Foreign Policy

Throughout the war, the Lincoln administration worried that its mobilization of resources might be offset if the European powers provided economic or military aid to the Confederacy. Fears focused on Great Britain. It had great power; it imported four-fifths of its raw cotton from the South; and its intervention would free France's Napoleon III, who was bound by an entente to defer to the British in American affairs, to support the Confederacy and pursue his dream of creating an empire in Mexico. British and French aid might extend a military stalemate long enough to produce a Confederate victory.

Great Britain upset Lincoln by proclaiming its neutrality shortly after hostilities began. The administration protested that it was fighting a domestic insurrection and not a war, and that Britain's declaration of neutrality might be taken to imply recognition of the Confederacy. Lincoln feared that the British might next help break the naval blockade of the Southern coast that he had established in April 1861, at the outset of the war. The conflict came to a head over two issues: The Union seized a British steamer, the *Trent*, which was carrying Confederate commissioners to Britain and France; and the British built six cruisers for the Confederacy, including the *Alabama*, which sunk or captured more than one hundred Union merchant ships and the "Laird rams," two ironclads designed to break the blockade. Meanwhile the blockade tightened as Union troops captured ports and coastline, and cotton exports to Britain fell.

Lincoln, his secretary of state, William H. Seward, and the minister to Great Britain, Charles Francis Adams, handled these issues adroitly. They avoided provoking Britain into breaking its neutrality and they persuaded the British not to ship the Laird rams to the Confederacy. To his relief, Lincoln discovered that the diplomatic appeal of "King Cotton" was less powerful than he had feared. Before the war,

British textile manufacturers had built up their inventories, and they enjoyed the extremely high profits that these goods brought after the blockade started. Later in the war, raw cotton from Egypt and India began to replace American cotton. The British manufacturers and merchants who sold munitions and other supplies to both North and South, and the British shipowners who profited from the South's attacks on the North's merchant marine, had no interest in choosing sides and thus hastening an end to the war. British consumers hesitated to disrupt the northern grain trade that contributed to lower food prices. In addition, British workers and reformers proved to be enthusiastic champions of abolition. Perhaps most important, the Union victories at Antietam and Gettysburg, followed by the election of 1864, convinced the British of the military might and willpower of the Union.

The British had no desire to risk Canada or the British merchant marine by provoking the United States. Consequently, the British never recognized the Confederacy and remained neutral throughout the war.

Defeat of the Confederacy

By 1864, the stage was set for the last act in the drama of the Civil War. The Lincoln administration had put together a complex war machine and a powerful structure of command and production. Northern government, industry, and finance capital had been integrated. The transportation and communication network had been expanded. The well-funded production of weapons and supplies flowed efficiently and rapidly. Despite some resistance, the mechanism of

THE RUINS OF FREDERICKSBURG
Many southern towns suffered terrible damage to property, business activity, and people's way of life during the Civil War. In December 1863, Union artillery levelled the town of Fredericksburg, Virginia. Then Union soldiers fought house by house, street by street to clean out Confederate sharpshooters. The method of combat, and the totality of the destruction it produced, presaged World Wars I and II. (Brown Brothers)

TIME LINE
TWO SOCIETIES AT WAR

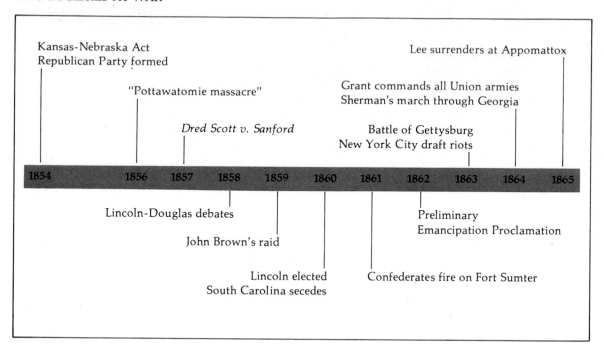

conscient, substitution, and enlistments worked well. Even the casualty lists only seemed to feed people's hatred of slavery and the rebellious planters. All the North's powerful advantages of population and resources stood ready to be used on the battlefield.

The South, on the other hand, had strained its resources, its constitution, and its people to the limit. In a struggle between armies, the South had a reasonable chance of forcing a stalemate and a decision by the North to end the fighting. But in a struggle between societies, a total war, the South could survive only as long as its people's will to resist held firm. For a year and a half, that will did hold. But continued resistance required ordinary southerners to believe two things: that the war could be won, and that it was a just war whose burdens fell alike on plain people and wealthy slaveholders. Both those beliefs were about to be destroyed by the superior power of the Union armies—and by the inherent economic and social weaknesses of the Confederacy.

Confederate Resources

The resources of the Confederacy could not match those of the Union in an endurance contest. The industrial base of the South was small, only about a tenth of the North's. Its share of the production of the ships, iron, textiles, locomotives, and firearms necessary for war was even smaller. Only in 1863, after capturing a hundred thousand Union rifles on battlefields and spending large sums to import British Enfield rifles, could the Confederacy provide each of its infantrymen with a modern weapon. It never developed adequate mobilization of food or clothing. Its health care and hospital system remained disorganized, although great numbers of southern women volunteered as nurses. Thousands of Confederate soldiers suffered from scurvy, and they died from camp diseases at higher rates than Union soldiers did.

The South also had far fewer people available for production and warfare. The slaves, who grew the crops that fed and clothed the Confederate armies, compensated for this disadvantage to some extent. However, many slaves refused to work as intensely as before covertly supported the Union armies, or even ran away to join the Union forces. While eight-hundred thousand men fought for the Confederacy, more than two million served the Union. The only way the Confederate armies could remain in the field was by requiring volunteers to reenlist. Far more Confederate than Union soldiers fought for the duration of the war.

The agricultural South also lacked the capital to sustain a massive, expensive war. After Gettysburg, investment in the Confederate cause became very risky, and even southern planters were cautious. Despite government pleas, most planters refused to pledge part of their cotton revenues to buy Confederate bonds. Moreover, they resisted higher taxes. Loans financed only about 35 percent of the Confederate war effort, whereas taxes covered less than 5 percent. Paper money which lacked backing in specie financed 60 percent of Confederate expenses. Consequently, after Vicksburg and Gettysburg, inflation in the Confederacy soared. By the spring of 1864, prices were forty-six times as high as they had been four years earlier. A year later, they had risen to ninety-two times their 1861 level.

Confederate Leadership

The Confederate leaders wanted to avoid creating a federal government as centralized and powerful as the one they had left. In their constitution, they implemented strong states' rights ideas by vesting sovereignty in the states. Governors could even thwart the will of President Davis by sabotaging the enforcement of conscription. Also, Davis never tried to build a political party comparable to the Republican party in the North—one that could promote national unity. While Lincoln centralized power and solidified his hold on the government, Davis's opponents nearly gained control of the Confederate Congress in November 1863. Consequently, the Confederate government found it impossible to adopt firm measures of finance, conscription, and martial law.

The Confederate leadership relied heavily on appeals to racial solidarity to maintain loyalty and support. Davis told whites that they were fighting to be able to expand westward into new territories and thereby protect their freedom. Without expansion, he said, "an overgrown black population" would "crowd upon our soil . . . until there will not be room in the country for whites and blacks to subsist in." Containment would destroy slavery "and reduce the whites to the degraded position of the African race." Alexander Stephens of Georgia made a similar appeal in a speech shortly after his election as vice-president of the Confederacy in 1861. He declared that the Confederacy's "cornerstone rests upon the great truth that the Negro is not equal to the white man, that slavery—subordination to the superior race—is his natural or normal condition." He argued that the alternative to slavery for blacks was serfdom for poor whites.

The Confederate military and economic setbacks of 1863 cracked the solid white South and exposed rising class resentment on the part of poor whites. Food riots broke out in southern cities. Orderly supply of armies became impossible. Farmers refused to accept Confederate money, and supply officers had to confiscate what they needed, leaving behind worthless IOUs. Nonslaveholding farmers refused to pay taxes, especially when the Confederate armies were far away. Everywhere, counterfeiters passed copies of the poorly designed and badly printed Confederate notes. Impoverished farm boys, describing the war as "a rich man's war and a poor man's fight," resisted conscription. Soldiers deserted on an increasing scale. To add to the South's troubles, secret societies of Unionists operated openly in the Appalachian Mountains, in the hill country of Alabama, in the Ozarks of Arkansas, in parts of Texas, and in all other areas where slavery barely existed. These Unionists aided northern troops and sometimes even enlisted in the Union army when it marched nearby.

In March 1865, the Confederacy exposed the depth of its manpower shortage in a revolutionary way. It decided to arm its own slaves. Earlier, Jefferson Davis had denounced the

ULYSSES S. GRANT
Grant put on his uniform for this picture, taken in July 1864 near Petersburg, but ordinarily he tried to identify with his men by wearing an old, white wool "slouch" hat and a well-worn, blue fatigue coat with little insignia of rank. Camp guards sometimes stopped Grant and asked him to identify himself. (Library of Congress)

Union's use of slaves as "the most execrable measure recorded in the history of guilty man," and Howell Cobb, a powerful Georgia politician, pointed out that "if slaves will make good soldiers our whole theory of slavery is wrong." Nonetheless, urged on by General Robert E. Lee, the Confederate Congress voted to enlist black soldiers. Davis added an executive order granting freedom to all blacks who served in the Confederate army. The war ended too soon, however, to reveal whether any slaves would seek freedom by joining their masters in defense of the Confederacy.

Closing Moves

The North's resources enabled Ulysses S. Grant to mount two great offensives in 1864. The South resisted bitterly, but the equally stubborn determination of the Union armies, combined with their superior strength, made both offensives successful.

In the East, Grant led the Army of the Potomac into Virginia. He waged a relentless cam-

MAP 15.6 THE CLOSING VIRGINIA CAMPAIGNS
During the last year of the war, the armies of Grant and Lee were locked in a deadly dance across the Virginia countryside. By challenging Lee's lines of communication with the rest of the Confederacy, Grant attempted to force Lee into open battles. Until April 1865, Lee successfully resisted, taking strong defensive positions that forced Grant to accept protracted sieges and steady casualties which threatened to undermine Northern support for the war.

GRANT PLANNING AN ATTACK
On June 2, 1864, the day this photograph was taken, Grant moved his headquarters to Bethesda Church, carried the pews out under the shade of surrounding trees, and planned the costly attack he would make at Cold Harbor the next day. While Grant leaned over the pew, gesturing at a map, other officers read reports of the war in newspapers that had just arrived from New York City. (Library of Congress)

paign to force Lee's surrender by destroying his army, regardless of the cost in Union lives. In the West, he sent General William Tecumseh Sherman from Tennessee into Georgia to take Atlanta and then advance to the sea, splitting the Confederacy once more and demoralizing its people. Grant aimed to inflict casualties on Lee's army until it could no longer fight. Sherman's mission was not so much to defeat armies as to bring the war home to the people of Georgia and the Carolinas until they stopped supporting it.

In Virginia, Grant accompanied the Army of the Potomac and directed it from the field, although General Meade remained technically the commander. Grant, with 115,000 men, advanced toward Richmond, hoping to force Lee's 75,000 troops to engage in battle and then wear him down with superior manpower. Lee, remembering Gettysburg, was careful not to attack unless he held a superior position. He attacked twice, in the Battle of the Wilderness on May 5–7 and the Battle of Spotsylvania Court House on May 8–12, but neither encounter was decisive. Grant then attacked Lee about ten miles from Richmond, near Cold Harbor, on June 1–3 but had to break off after losing 7,000 men in a frontal assault. During this month-long Wilderness campaign, Grant eroded Lee's forces, which suffered 31,000 casualties, but paid with 55,000 of his own. In Virginia, the war had become one of attrition.

In a surprise maneuver, Grant pulled away from Lee and Richmond, now heavily fortified, and swung south toward Petersburg, a major railroad center necessary for the supply of Richmond. By occupying it, he hoped to force Lee into a final battle. Lee, however, dug in at Petersburg first and denied Grant the advantage of position. In June 1864, Grant laid siege to Petersburg. Bloody, protracted trench warfare, which foreshadowed that of World War I, lasted until April 1865. The armies extended the trenches for almost fifty miles around Richmond and Petersburg, as Grant inched toward control of Richmond's railroads. One officer described the continual artillery firing and sniping as "endurance without relief; sleeplessness without excitement; inactivity without rest."

In Georgia, Sherman had a much easier time. His army outnumbered that of General Joseph E. Johnston, ninety thousand to sixty thousand. Johnston, unwilling to risk his smaller army, engaged Sherman in a set battle only once, at Kennesaw Mountain on June 27. On September 2, now opposed by General John B. Hood, who had replaced Johnston, Sherman took Atlanta. Hood then tried to lure Sherman northward, but Sherman remained in Atlanta, dispatching only enough cavalry to pursue and smash the weakened defending armies in Tennessee. He then set out across Georgia with his main force, on his "march to the sea." Sherman presented Savannah, Georgia, to Lincoln as a Christmas gift and then swept through the Carolinas, planning to join Grant at Petersburg.

As he marched, Sherman implemented

MAP 15.7 SHERMAN'S MARCH THROUGH THE CONFEDERACY
The Union victory at Chattanooga in November 1863 was almost as critical as those at Gettysburg and Vicksburg. Having already split the Confederacy along the Mississippi, the Union was now in position to split the Confederacy again with a line running from Kentucky through Tennessee and Georgia to the sea. Sherman took Atlanta and then, largely ignoring John B. Hood's failed invasion of Tennessee, swept to the Atlantic.

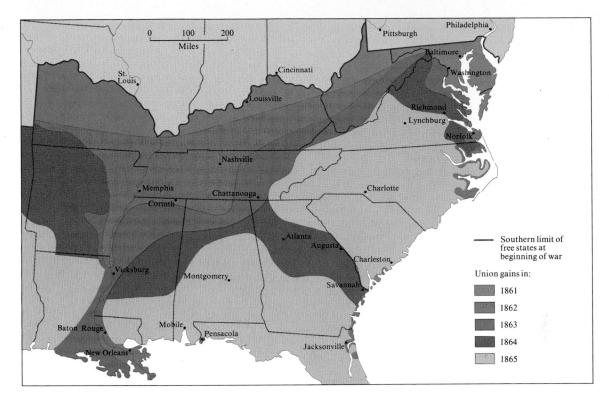

MAP 15.8 THE CONQUEST OF THE SOUTH, 1861–1865
This map reveals how slowly the Union took control of Confederate territory. Nearly half of the territory of the Confederacy held fast until the last year of the war. The Union victory depended far less on the ability of its armies to control territory than on their ability to control strategic lines of communication and to destroy the armies of the Confederacy.

Grant's concept of total war—destruction of the enemy's economic and psychological resources. He destroyed railroads, property, and supplies that the Confederates might use, and he terrorized the civilian population. A Union veteran wrote that "[we] destroyed all we could not eat, stole their niggers, burned their cotton & gins, spilled their sorghum, burned & twisted their R.Roads and raised Hell generally." By moving ruthlessly and freely through the heart of the Confederacy, Sherman demonstrated to southerners that the Confederacy could not resist the Union's organized forces. When Confederate families wrote to soldiers on the front about the terror, many of the men deserted and went home, demoralized, to support their loved ones.

In April 1865, Grant finally forced Lee into a showdown. He gained control of a crucial railroad junction and cut off Lee's supplies. Lee abandoned Richmond and turned west, hoping to meet Johnston in North Carolina. Grant pursued Lee, whose forces had been reduced to twenty-five thousand by casualties and desertions, and swiftly cut off his escape route. On April 9, at Appomattox Courthouse, Virginia, Lee surrendered. Almost exactly four years had passed since the Confederacy attacked Fort Sumter. Nine days later, Johnston surrendered to Sherman near Durham, North Carolina. The other Confederate generals surrendered by the end of May. There was no formal conclusion to the hostilities. The Confederate army and

GENERAL GRANT DESCRIBES
SHERMAN'S MARCH THROUGH GEORGIA

In his personal memoirs (1886), written on his deathbed, Grant described the organized way in which the Union Army conducted total war.

Sherman's army . . . numbered about sixty thousand effective men. All weak men had been left to hold the rear, and those remaining were not only well men, but strong and hardy, so that he had sixty thousand as good soldiers as ever trod the earth; better than any European soldiers, because they not only worked like a machine but the machine thought. European armies know very little what they are fighting for, and care less. . . .

The troops, both of the right and left wings, made most of their advance along the line of railroads, which they destroyed. The method adopted to perform this work, was to burn and destroy all the bridges and culverts, and for a long distance, at places, to tear up the track and bend the rails. Soldiers to do this rapidly would form a line along one side of the road with crowbars and poles, place these under the rails and, hoisting all at once, turn over many rods of road at one time. The ties would then be placed in piles, and the rails, as they were loosened, would be carried and put across these log heaps. When a sufficient number of rails were placed upon a pile of ties it would be set on fire. This would heat the rails very much more in the middle, that being over the main part of the fire, than at the ends, so that they would naturally bend of their own weight; but the soldiers, to increase the damage, would take tongs and, one or two men at each end of the rail, carry it with force against the nearest tree and twist it around, thus leaving rails forming bands to ornament the forest trees of Georgia. All this work was going on at the same time, there being a sufficient number of men detailed for that purpose. Some piled the logs and built the fire; some put the rails upon the fire; while others would bend those that were sufficiently heated; so that, by the time the last bit of road was torn up, that it was designed to destroy at a given place, the rails previously taken up were already destroyed.

---

government simply dissolved. After fleeing from Richmond, hoping that the South would continue to resist, Jefferson Davis was captured by Union cavalry in Georgia.

The armies of the Union had destroyed the Confederacy. During four years of war, they had also destroyed much of the South's productive capacity. Its factories, warehouses, and railroads lay in ruins, as did many of its farms and cities. Two hundred and sixty thousand Confederate soldiers—nearly one in three—had paid for secession with their lives. Most significant of all, the Union armies had not only ended slavery but destroyed the economic and social system which slavery had built..

The victory had not been easy for the Union, either. From Sumter to Appomattox, three hundred and sixty thousand Union soldiers had lost their lives. Hundreds of thousands of others had been maimed and crippled by Confederate fire. But the hard and bitter war was ended. Americans from the North and South, both blacks and whites, had to turn to the tasks of peace. Lincoln had spoken at Gettysburg of "finishing the work." But when the battles were finally over, it was time to decide exactly what that "work" was. Freed slaves faced the new and daunting questions of what freedom really would bring. Their former masters began to try to salvage what they could from defeat. People in all parts of the North pondered the meaning of a victory so costly and so complete. They wondered whether the "terrible, swift sword" of "The Battle Hymn of the Republic" should be put away in reconciliation or loosed again in a hard and bitter peace.

LEE'S SURRENDER
Lee arrived in full-dress uniform to surrender his army at the village of Appomattox Courthouse. Mathew Brady photographed Lee with his son, left, and an aide. Lee's solemn expression suggests the terrible burden of his memories. (Culver)

The Compromise of 1850 did not preserve the peace or the Second Party System for long. White abolitionists and slaveowners clashed in 1850, when the southerners recaptured slaves in northern communities under authority provided by the Fugitive Slave Act. When northern Whigs continued to oppose the Fugitive Slave Act, southern Whigs deserted their party.

The ability of the U.S. political system to hold the Union together came to rest on the national appeal of the Democratic party and its doctrine of popular sovereignty. Implementing the doctrine, however, meant voiding the Missouri Compromise's prohibition of slavery in the northern part of the Louisiana Purchase territory. This brought antislavery and proslavery forces into violent confrontation over "Bleeding Kansas" and split the Democratic party. Northern Whigs and abolitionists joined with "Anti-Nebraska" Democrats and anti-Catholic Know-Nothings to establish the Republican party and to call for free soil, which replaced Henry Clay's American System as the central economic program of the emerging business class.

In the 1860 elections, the Democrats divided along sectional lines because southerners sought more protection for slavery than northern Democrats would provide. When the Republicans took control of the federal government, the South concluded that it could no longer both preserve slavery and remain in the Union. The South seceded and used force to discourage the North from trying to maintain the Union.

The conflict became a total war, one of

unsurpassed cost in American lives and resources, because of the great strength of the
two regions and because of their conflict over
fundamental political and social values. The
Confederacy missed opportunities for a victory
in 1861–1863, while the Union learned that to
win the war it had to smash souther society. By

1864, the North had acquired the necessary military leadership and resources. During the process of waging total war, the Republicans called
for emancipation, enacted their economic program, and consolidated the power of the business class.

Suggestions for Further Reading

The Disruption of Union

General studies of the conflict between the North and
South that led to the Civil War include Avery O. Craven, *The Growth of Southern Nationalism, 1848–1861*
(1953); Roy F. Nichols, *The Disruption of American Democracy* (1948); and David M. Potter, *The Impending Crisis 1848–1861* (1976). On the Fugitive Slave Act, consult
Stanley W. Campbell, *The Slave Catchers* (1970); on
southern expansionism, see Robert E. May, *The Southern Dream of a Caribbean Empire 1854–1861* (1973); on
Kansas-Nebraska and "Bleeding Kansas," see James
A. Rawley, *Race and Politics: "Bleeding Kansas" and the
Coming of the Civil War* (1969) and Gerald W. Wolff, *The
Kansas-Nebraska Bill: Party, Section, and the Coming of the
Civil War* (1977). On Republicans and Know-Nothings,
see Eric Foner, *Free Soil, Free Labor, Free Men: The Ideol-
ogy of the Republican Party before the Civil War* (1970) and
Michael F. Holt, *The Political Crisis of the 1850s* (1978).
On Dred Scott, see Don E. Fehrenbacher, *The Dred
Scott Case: Its Significance in American Law and Politics*
(1978). On the rise of Abraham Lincoln, see Don E.
Fehrenbacher, *Prelude to Greatness: Lincoln in the 1850s*
(1962). And on the secession crisis, see Richard N.
Current, *Lincoln and the First Shot* (1963); J. Mills Thorn-
ton, *Politics and Power in a Slave Society, Alabama 1800–
1861* (1978); and Kenneth M. Stampp, *And the War
Came: The North and the Secession Crisis 1860–61* (1950).

Secession and Civil War

The most up-to-date, comprehensive one-volume survey of the Civil War is James M. McPherson, *Ordeal by
Fire, The Civil War and Reconstruction* (1982). The most
useful introduction to the military aspects of the war is
T. Harry Williams, *The History of American Wars* (1981).
Biographies crucial to understanding the Civil War include Richard N. Current, *Old Thad Stevens* (1942); Da-

vid Donald, *Charles Sumner and the Rights of Man* (1970);
William McFeely, *Grant, A Biography* (1981); Stephen B.
Oates, *With Malice Toward None: The Life of Abraham
Lincoln* (1977); Benjamin F. Thomas, *Abraham Lincoln*
(1952); and James G. Randall, *Mr. Lincoln* (1957). To
study northern society and politics during the war,
consult Adrian Cook, *The Armies of the Streets: The New
York City Draft Riots of 1863* (1974); Emerson D. Fite,
*Social and Economic Conditions in the North During the
Civil War* (1910); George M. Frederickson, *The Inner
Civil War: Northern Intellectuals and the Crisis of Union*
(1965); David Gilchrist and W. David Lewis (eds.), *Eco-
nomic Change in the Civil War Era* (1965); Frank I. Kle-
ment, *The Copperheads in the Middle West* (1960); Mary
E. Massey, *Bonnet Brigades: American Women and the
Civil War* (1966); Joel Silbey, *A Respectable Minority: The
Democratic Party in the Civil War Era* (1977); and Hans
Trefousse, *The Radical Republicans* (1969). On the Con-
federacy, see Clement Eaton, *A History of the Southern
Confederacy* (1954); Charles W. Ramsdell, *Behind the
Lines in the Southern Confederacy* (1944); Charles P. Ro-
land, *The Confederacy* (1960); and Emory M. Thomas,
The Confederate Nation: 1861–1865 (1979).

The Northern War Machine and Republican
Policies

Studies of slaves and emancipation during wartime in-
clude Herman Belz, *Reconstructing the Union: Theory
and Policy During the Civil War* (1969); Ira Berlin (ed.),
*Freedom: A Documentary History of Emancipation, The
Black Military Experience* (1982); John Hope Franklin,
The Emancipation Proclamation (1963); William B. Hessel-
tine, *Lincoln's Plan of Reconstruction* (1960); James M.
McPherson, *The Struggle for Equality: Abolitionists and
the Negro in the Civil War and Reconstruction* (1964); and
Benjamin Quarles, *The Negro in the Civil War* (1953).

16

THE UNION
RECONSTRUCTED

*W*hen the armies of the Confederacy surrendered in 1865, the United States still remained deeply divided. A flourishing, triumphant North confronted a beaten, shattered
South. While the people in the North had managed to maintain a high degree of unity during
the war, the South was now divided between
bitter, fearful whites and exultant, hopeful former slaves.

Abraham Lincoln had spoken in his second
inaugural address of the need to "bind up the
nation's wounds." The necessity of rebuilding
the Union was clear, but many questions remained unanswered. Who would control the rebuilding? How long should the rebuilding last?
How far should it go?

Three basic viewpoints emerged in answer to
these questions. Some people defined the task of
rebuilding as *restoration*. They wanted to restore
the southern states to what Lincoln called "their
proper practical relation with the Union." This
would mean getting loyal, pro-Union state governments into place, restoring southern states'
representatives in Congress, and freely exercising federal power in the South.

Other people felt that some degree of *reconstruction* of the South was necessary and that the
Union should be very different from what it had
been before 1860. For those who held this view,
the end of slavery should be followed by steps
to ensure a measure of political and even eco-

nomic equality for the ex-slaves. Steps should
also be taken to make the Republican party as
strong a political force in the South as it was in
the North.

Finally, many white southerners and some
northern sympathizers maintained that the problem was one of *redemption*. The Union's total victory had temporarily deprived the dominant
majority in the South of control over its own
economic, social, and political systems. The
Union would be rebuilt only when southerners
had regained the same degree of power over
their own affairs that the citizens of Indiana or
Massachusetts had.

The era of Reconstruction—which historians
conventionally date as the years from 1865 to
1877—was shaped by continual, often confused
struggles among the men and women who held
one version or another of these views. In these
struggles, every kind of tactic was brought to
bear—the assassination of one president and the
impeachment of another; three amendments to
the Constitution and a welter of new legislation;
nighttime terrorism by robed whites in the
South; patient work and resistance by southern
blacks; and compromise, maneuvering, and
deals by politicians on all sides.

The outcome was as mixed and as unclear as
the struggles themselves; no single position
emerged triumphant. By 1877, political leaders
on all sides were ready to say that what Lincoln

had called "the work" was complete. But for many Americans, especially the freed slaves, the work clearly had not been completed, but merely abandoned and left to the slow, frustrating, and imperfect processes of history. It became apparent to many Republicans that they had been much less successful in reconstructing the South than they had been at quickening and consolidating the successes of industrial capitalism in the nation as a whole.

Presidential Restoration

At first, the initiative for rebuilding the Union rested with the president. Lincoln and his successor, Andrew Johnson, both believed that the southern states had never legally left the Union, that Reconstruction was simply a process of restoring governments loyal to the Union, and that this process could take place quickly, largely under presidential direction.

Lincoln saw much evidence that a swift reconciliation between North and South could be achieved. Former Confederate soldiers accepted defeat. After Lee's surrender, his Virginia troops heeded his advice to "go home . . . and help build up the shattered fortunes of our old state." Most ex-slaves also hoped to live in peace with whites. They pleaded to acquire the land they tilled, but they did not plot violence against their former masters. Northerners had accomplished their original war aims—the defeat of southern resistance and the crushing of the "Slave Power"—and had even made slavery unconstitutional. Some northerners insisted on making the South pay for the 360,000 Union deaths. But the typical Union soldier viewed the conflict more compassionately, believing that 260,000 Confederate dead, plus surrender, were payment enough. After Lee surrendered at Appomattox, Grant's soldiers willingly shared their ample rations with hungry Confederates.

Lincoln underestimated Republican demands for a thorough Reconstruction of the South. Had he survived, Lincoln might have demanded more of the ex-Confederates. But Andrew Johnson agreed with the racial attitudes and policies of the defeated Confederacy and did not want to advance the fortunes of the Republican party. He refused to adjust his policies to take account

SMOLDERING RESISTANCE IN THE SOUTH
This engraving, subtitled "Verdict, 'Hang the D——
Yankee and Nigger,' " appeared in *Harper's Weekly* in March 1867. It may have led readers to recall the killing of the Republicans who attended the black suffrage convention in New Orleans the previous summer. We have no reliable estimates of the total number of Republicans, white and black, killed in retaliation by ex-Confederates during Reconstruction. (Library of Congress)

of the opinions of Republican leaders in Congress, and his Reconstruction policy was distinctly sympathetic to the ex-Confederates.

Restoration Under Lincoln

Reconstruction actually began during the war. Lincoln sought to subvert the southern war effort by employing a policy of moderation and reconciliation in the large portions of the South occupied by federal troops. He ignored the imprecise constitutional status of the southern states and relied on his military powers as commander-in-chief to justify his actions.

In December 1863, Lincoln offered a general amnesty to all Confederates except the high-ranking officials of the Confederacy. His simple plan called for Confederates to take an oath (1) pledging their future loyalty to the Union and (2) accepting the Union's wartime acts and proclamations concerning slavery. When just 10 percent of the people who had voted in 1860 had taken the loyalty oath, they could reconstitute their state's government.

Lincoln aimed this plan at former southern Whigs, many of whom he knew well. He hoped they would step forward, declare allegiance to the Union, and take charge of southern state governments. Lincoln's constitutional assumption was simple; states could not legally secede and were therefore still in the Union. (In 1869, in *Texas v. White*, the Supreme Court accepted Lincoln's interpretation, ruling that secession was impossible under the Constitution.)

Lincoln's plan was opposed by members of his own party in Congress, including even his fellow moderates. The most strenuous criticism came from a group of radical Republicans, most of whom had abolitionist backgrounds. Led by Senator Charles Sumner of Massachusetts and Congressman Thaddeus Stevens of Pennsylvania, these radical Republicans wanted the federal government to go beyond abolishing slavery and, in Stevens's words, to "revolutionize Southern institutions, habits, and manners." Stevens declared that "The foundations of their institutions . . . must be broken up and relaid, or all our blood and treasure will have been spent in vain." In particular, the radical Republicans wanted the federal government to ensure that blacks would participate in southern society with full equality.

All radicals agreed full equality required a federal guarantee of voting rights for ex-slaves. Without the vote, blacks could not be genuinely independent from their former masters. Some radicals, however, believed that the vote alone was not enough. Thaddeus Stevens, for example, believed that the redistribution of land to the ex-slaves was the solution.

The radicals assumed that the ex-slaves had the capacity to become full citizens if only they were given political participation and economic independence. Most Republicans had a more pessimistic view of what could be accomplished for or by the freed blacks. They believed that blacks were simply not competent to exercise the franchise, much less to take their place as economically independent farmers. The moderates

also worried that any effort to make drastic changes in the economic and social relationships between the races would only provoke resistance and violence from southern whites.

Yet the moderates agreed with the radicals that Lincoln's program of restoration was too lenient. In its place, moderates and radicals joined in advancing three propositions. First, the leaders of the Confederacy should not be allowed to return to power in the South. Second, the abolition of slavery should be guaranteed by an amendment to the Constitution, and the former Confederate states should be forced to accept this amendment before they could return to the Union. Third, steps should be taken to establish the Republican party as a major, even dominant, force in southern political life. The moderates and radicals rejected the new governments that Lincoln had established in Louisiana, Arkansas, and Tennessee.

Republicans in Congress set to work on their own theory of Reconstruction. Legally, they argued, the seceded states *had* left the Union and were now the equivalent of conquered provinces. As territories, they were constitutionally subject to congressional rule rather than administration by the executive branch. To translate their theory into practice, Congress passed the Wade-Davis bill in July 1864. This bill prescribed the conditions necessary for former Confederate states to regain membership in the Union. A majority of the state's adult white males would have to swear an oath of allegiance to the Union. Each southern state would have to write a new constitution. These constitutions would have to abolish slavery, disenfranchise Confederate civil and military leaders, and repudiate all state war debts. Finally, to make sure that the new constitutions would be made by the friends of the Union, the Wade-Davis bill required that the constitutions had to be written by men who could swear an oath that they had never carried arms against the Union or aided the Confederacy in any way—a statement that became known as the "ironclad oath."

The Wade-Davis bill went much further than Lincoln's plan, but it did not satisfy most radicals. Like Lincoln's plan, the bill did not propose to establish any federal control over race relations in the South, and it did not guarantee the political participation of blacks in new southern governments. Nevertheless, the basis for a compromise between Lincoln and the congressional Republicans clearly existed. Skillfully, Lincoln kept his options open. He did not openly challenge Congress by vetoing the bill. Instead, he executed a "pocket" veto by not signing it before Congress adjourned. At the same time, he began informal talks with members of Congress clearly aimed at producing a compromise solution when the war finally ended.

Whether Lincoln and his party could have found a unified approach to Reconstruction became one of the great unanswered questions of American history. On April 14, 1865—Good Friday—Lincoln was shot in the head at Ford's Theater in Washington, by a half-crazed actor named John Wilkes Booth. Ironically, Lincoln might have been spared if the war had dragged on longer, for Booth and his associates had originally plotted to kidnap the president to force a negotiated settlement. After Lee's surrender, Booth became desperate for revenge. In the middle of the play, he leapt to Lincoln's box, shot him at close range, stabbed a member of the president's party, and fled the theater. Booth was hunted down and killed by Union troops. Eight people were eventually convicted as accomplices by military courts and four of them were hanged. Abraham Lincoln never regained consciousness. He died on April 15. The Union—and hundreds of thousands of ex-slaves for whom his name had become synonymous with freedom—went into profound mourning. Even Lincoln's critics suddenly conceded his greatness. Millions of Americans waited in silence to watch the train bearing his body back to Illinois for burial.

The presidency now belonged to Andrew Johnson. Even before the last Confederate armies had surrendered in Alabama, a dramatic change in the prospects for Reconstruction had taken place. At one stroke, John Wilkes Booth had accomplished two important things. He sent Lincoln to martyrdom and convinced many northerners that harsher measures against the South were necessary. He also gave the presidency to a Tennesseean, a former Democrat, whose plan of restoration was even milder than Lincoln's. Now there would be no compromise between an elected president and his party in Congress. There would be only a deepening contest in the North for control of Reconstruction and an equally deep struggle in the South for control of the economic, social, and political life of the old Confederacy.

Johnson's Plan for Restoration

Andrew Johnson's middle name was Jackson, in honor of the president who had shaped the Democratic party in the 1830s. Johnson had much in common with Andrew Jackson. He had been born poor but had become a man of wealth—including slaves—in Jackson's Tennessee. His political career had led from the Tennessee legislature to the United States Senate. He shared Jackson's commitment to the preservation of the Union. In fact, the Republicans had handed him the vice-presidency in an effort to promote wartime political unity.

Johnson also had some other political attitudes that were closer to Jackson's than to Lincoln's. He opposed the Republican policy of promoting economic development through tariffs or federal subsidies to railroads. He hated what he called the "bloated, corrupt aristocracy" of the Northeast and charged that the Republican economic program reinforced the power of this elite. Johnson also despised blacks. He accepted their legal freedom, but he wanted to maintain white supremacy through the systematic denial of rights to blacks. Johnson's interest in Reconstruction extended no further than punishing the ex-slaveholding elite—another class that he resented. But he did not require revenge on the scale that most Republicans demanded. For Johnson, simply establishing his personal power over the planters was satisfaction enough. Because he opposed the Republican economic and racial plans, Johnson did not want to see the Republican party prevail in either the North or the South.

Despite their differences, Johnson and the Republican Congress could have avoided a deadlock. Northern Democrats and some moderate Republicans were close in their racial attitudes and policies. Most Republicans in Congress favored the moderate approach to Reconstruction outlined by the Wade-Davis bill. Most ex-Confederates, accepting their defeat in total war, were prepared to submit to a somewhat punitive Reconstruction.

But Johnson risked confrontation with Congress when he announced his own lenient plan and proceeded to execute it during the summer of 1865, when Congress was not in session. Johnson was so thoroughly convinced that Reconstruction should be an exclusively executive function that he believed consultation with Congress was unnecessary. In his view, the southern states had retained all their constitutional rights. He insisted on only three conditions— that they revoke ordinances of secession, abolish slavery, and repudiate the debts they had acquired during the rebellion. Johnson's plan offered amnesty and a return of all property, except slaves, to almost all southerners if they took an oath of future allegiance to the Union. He excluded several categories of southerners from his amnesty—high-ranking Confederate officers and civil officials and, revealing his distaste for planter aristocrats, persons with taxable property of more than twenty thousand dollars. (These individuals were invited to petition Johnson personally. He intended to humble them, but then grant most of them pardons.) By December, all of the former Confederate states had functioning governments and were ready to rejoin the Union under Johnson's plan.

Congressional Reconstruction

Most Republicans supported Johnson's program at first, despite his failure to consult with Congress. They hoped to amend his program so that it would achieve the objectives of the Wade-Davis bill. They also hoped that southern governments would respond positively to Johnson's conciliatory attitude and offer the vote to at least those blacks who were literate and owned property—probably no more than 10 percent of adult black men. In fact, Johnson unofficially advised the southern states to undertake limited enfranchisement of blacks.

But the president soon made more political mistakes. He continued to insult Congress and refused to spearhead a Reconstruction policy that would satisfy moderate Republicans. Provoked by Johnson, Congress took control of Reconstruction and in 1866–1867 imposed a more radical program than Republicans had proposed in the Wade-Davis bill.

As a result, Reconstruction was highly erratic. While Johnson's policy of restoration had encouraged the ex-Confederates, congressional Reconstruction punished them. This alternating policy intensified southern resistance to federal power. The peace that seemed so close at hand in 1865 turned out to be long in coming.

Congress Versus Johnson

Johnson's first mistake was a serious blunder in his relations with Congress. In an August 1865 telegram, Johnson told the provisional governor of Mississippi that if he gave the vote to literate blacks, "the radicals, who are wild upon negro franchise, will be completely foiled." When the telegram became public, it not only enraged radical Republicans but embarrassed moderates. To compound Johnson's problem, provisional governments in the South made no effort to enfranchise blacks. Moderate Republicans began to doubt Johnson's leadership on the suffrage issue. More important, they became increasingly sympathetic to the plight of southern blacks.

During the fall of 1865, news reports from the South further undermined the president's leadership. Northerners read of frequent attacks on ex-slaves and Union supporters and of control of southern governments by ex-Confederates. Moreover, southern voters sent to Congress nine prominent individuals who had served in the Confederate Congress, seven officials from Confederate state governments, four generals and four colonels from the Confederate army, and even Alexander Stephens, the vice-president of the Confederacy. Radical Republicans such as Sumner and Stevens began to attack Johnson for his failure to reconstruct the South properly.

Meanwhile, Johnson increasingly viewed himself as the savior of the Democratic party. He believed he could build a coalition of southerners, northern Democrats, and conservative Republicans under the Democratic banner. Democrats in both the North and the South praised Johnson as the leader they needed to restore their party on a national basis. Northern Democrats, who had strong antiblack feelings, wholeheartedly endorsed Johnson's racial policy.

Moderate Republicans watched Johnson with

ANDREW JOHNSON
The president was not an easy man. This photograph of
Andrew Johnson (1808–1875) conveys some of the
personal qualities that contributed so centrally to his
failure to reach agreement with Republicans on a program
of moderate Reconstruction. (Library of Congress)

increasing dismay and agitation. As the president warmed to Democratic applause, he granted more and more pardons to wealthy southerners—to an average of one hundred pardons a day in September. By December, when Congress convened, Republicans had become convinced that they had to do more to protect the rights of the ex-slaves and to establish the Republican party in the South.

The moderate Republicans controlled Congress when it convened in December 1865. They rejected the newly elected southern representatives—some of whom were ex-Confederate officials—until Johnson would agree with Congress on a Reconstruction program. To develop that program, moderates formed a joint House-Senate committee charged to cooperate with the president. When the Joint Committee on Reconstruction conducted hearings on conditions in the former Confederacy, it heard alarming reports from army officers, federal officials, and white and black southerners. The level of violence was rising, and southern legislatures were enacting Black Codes—laws designed to keep

blacks in a condition close to slavery. These laws, passed by every state of the former Confederacy, were written to ensure that blacks remained on the land as agricultural laborers, and that they worked there under terms highly favorable to white landowners.

Moderate Republicans drafted two bills to meet these complaints. The first extended the life of the Bureau of Refugees, Freedmen, and Abandoned Lands. Known commonly as the Freedmen's Bureau, this agency had been created in March 1865 to feed and clothe refugees of both races, to rent confiscated land to "loyal refugees and freedmen," and to draft and enforce labor contracts between ex-slaves and planters. The bureau also cooperated with voluntary associations, such as the Freedmen's Aid Societies, which sent missionaries and teachers to the South to establish schools for ex-slaves. The new bill empowered the bureau to establish courts to protect the rights of ex-slaves until the southern states had been restored to the Union. The bill also sought to extend the occupation by ex-slaves of land confiscated from planters by the Union on the Sea Islands, off the coast of South Carolina and Georgia.

Republicans almost unanimously approved the Freedmen's Bureau bill but, in February 1866, Johnson vetoed it. He argued that the bill was unconstitutional because the Constitution did not authorize a "system for the support of indigent persons" and because "there was no Senator or Representatives in Congress from the eleven States which are to be mainly affected by its provisions." The veto enraged moderates. They could not accept Johnson's implication that *any* Reconstruction legislation they passed without southern representation was necessarily unconstitutional. Moderates tried to override the veto but failed, just barely, to collect the two-thirds majority they needed.

Democrats applauded Johnson's firmness. To celebrate, a group of them went to the White House to serenade him. The president emerged to deliver a speech that suggested to many that he was drunk. Johnson went so far as to accuse the radical Republicans of being traitors who were plotting to assassinate him.

Johnson's veto and his unwise address to the Democrats pushed the moderate Republicans close to a complete break with the president. But they still expected his cooperation on their second major piece of legislation, a civil rights bill. This bill defined the citizenship rights of the ex-slaves—such as the rights to own and rent property, to make contracts, and to have access to the courts—and guaranteed that anyone appealing a case involving these rights could take the case to a federal court. Republicans passed it in March 1866, declaring that blacks had the right to enjoy "full and equal benefit of all laws and proceedings for the security of person and property as it is enjoyed by white citizens." Republicans intended the bill to wipe out the Black Codes and thus ensure the eradication of slavery. They did not mean to guarantee that blacks could vote.

Again, however, Johnson vetoed the bill against the advice of his cabinet. He called it unconstitutional and, with the votes of Democratic wards in the large cities in mind, argued that it discriminated against whites by providing citizenship for newly freed slaves while immigrants had to wait five years for the privilege.

Johnson's veto persuaded almost all moderate Republicans that they must take charge of Reconstruction and adopt a completely independent plan. In April, they overrode Johnson's veto and passed the Civil Rights Act of 1866. In July—after amending the Freedmen's Bureau bill to require ex-slaves to buy the confiscated land on the Sea Islands which they occupied—they passed the bill over a second Johnson veto.

The Fourteenth Amendment

At the same time, the Joint Committee on Reconstruction drafted and submitted to Congress its proposal for the Fourteenth Amendment to the Constitution. This amendment went beyond the Civil Rights Act of 1866 by providing blacks a constitutional guarantee of citizenship and encouraging, although not guaranteeing, black suffrage. The resistance of ex-Confederates and President Johnson had persuaded moderates to adopt a more radical position.

Section 1 of the amendment declared that all native-born or naturalized persons—including blacks—were citizens. No state could abridge "the privileges or immunities of citizens of the United States," or deprive "any person of life, liberty, or property, without due process of law," or deny anyone "the equal protection of the laws." The writers of the amendment in-

tended these phrases to be vague. While they did not foresee that "equal protection," for example, might eventually prohibit racial segregation in schools and other public facilities (as the Supreme Court ruled in 1954), they hoped that the scope and force of this amendment would grow over time.

The amendment's key political provision was Section 2, which penalized any state that denied suffrage to a portion of its adult male citizens. The amendment would reduce the state's representation in Congress by the percentage of adult male citizens denied the vote. Republicans hoped this provision would induce southern states to extend the vote to blacks. But the amendment did not force enfranchisement. Radicals criticized this point, arguing that Congress should take steps to guarantee the vote for blacks. Radicals also complained that the amendment would have little effect on northern states that refused to give blacks the vote.

Johnson attacked the Fourteenth Amendment, despite its moderation. Disregarding precedent, he campaigned personally in the 1866 congressional elections to promote candidates who supported his own views on the matter. In August and September, he made a railroad tour from Washington to Chicago and Saint Louis and back, charging that Congress had acted illegally by approving the Fourteenth Amendment without the participation of all the southern states. He declared that southerners were loyal, while the real traitors were the radical Republicans who were stalling restoration of the Union.

Under Johnson's assault, moderate Republicans escalated their attacks on Democrats. They reminded northern voters of vicious race riots over suffrage that had occurred in Memphis and New Orleans during the late spring and early summer of 1866. In New Orleans, a white mob had attacked the delegates to a black suffrage convention and killed forty people, including thirty-seven blacks. In what became known as "waving the bloody shirt," Republicans went so far as to blame the Democrats for the Civil War. Governor Oliver Morton of Indiana described the Democratic party as "a common sewer and loathsome receptacle, into which is emptied every element of treason North and South, every element of inhumanity and barbarism which has dishonored the age."

The 1866 congressional elections brought a

humiliating defeat for the president. The Republicans won a three-to-one majority in Congress and gained control of every northern state, as well as West Virginia, Missouri, and Tennessee. The moderates interpreted the elections as a clear call for Reconstruction, rather than mere restoration, of the South. They finally accepted the radical proposition that the federal government must guarantee black suffrage.

Radical Reconstruction and the Impeachment of Johnson

In the months following the elections of 1866, moderates and radicals together hammered out a more rigorous plan of Reconstruction. By March, Congress had passed, over Johnson's persistent vetoes, the Reconstruction Acts of 1867. These acts divided the South into five military districts and placed each district under a military commander, who had the responsibility for registering voters. The acts ordered the commanders to register all adult black males but allowed them considerable discretion in registering former Confederates. After registering voters, the commander would call on them to elect a convention to write a state constitution that had to include guarantees for black suffrage. Congress would readmit the state to the Union only if its voters ratified the new constitution, if the new constitution proved acceptable to Congress, if the new state legislature approved the Fourteenth Amendment, and if enough states had already ratified the Fourteenth Amendment to make it part of the Constitution.

Some radicals did not believe that even these measures went far enough to guarantee equality for blacks. They advocated distribution of land to ex-slaves, federal support for black schools, and continued disenfranchisement of ex-Confederates. One radical, George W. Julian, a congressman from Indiana, warned that without such measures, "the power of the great landed aristocracy in these regions, if unrestrained by power from without, would inevitably assert itself." Nonetheless, the radicals accepted the new Reconstruction policies as all they could get in 1867.

Republicans also took action to ensure that President Johnson did not thwart Reconstruction by exercising his executive authority. Congress passed the Tenure of Office Act, which required congressional consent for the removal of any government officer whose appointment required congressional approval. Republicans chiefly wanted to protect Secretary of War Stanton, a Lincoln appointee and the only member of Johnson's cabinet to support congressional Reconstruction. As commander of the armed forces in the South, Stanton could do much to prevent Johnson from frustrating congressional Reconstruction. Congress also required the president to issue orders to the army through its general, Ulysses S. Grant, who also supported a more radical Reconstruction. In effect, Congress attempted to reconstruct the presidency as well as the South. A crisis was clearly at hand.

In August 1867, after Congress adjourned, Johnson made his move. He fired Stanton and replaced him with Grant on a temporary basis, hoping Grant would be more cooperative. He next replaced four Republican generals who commanded southern districts, including Philip H. Sheridan, Grant's favorite cavalry general.

Johnson had misjudged Grant. Grant wrote a letter protesting the president's thwarting of Congress and deliberately leaked it to the press. After Congress overruled Stanton's suspension, Grant resigned, allowing Stanton to resume his office. Johnson's public protests against Grant's resignation led Grant to emerge openly as an enemy of the president.

Johnson decided to test, unequivocally, the constitutionality of the power granted to Congress by the Tenure of Office Act. In February 1868, he again dismissed Stanton. Stanton barricaded the door of his office, refusing to admit the replacement whom Johnson had appointed. Republicans in Congress responded by charging the president with criminal misconduct in office. The Constitution gave the House the power to impeach—to charge formally—federal officials for "Treason, Bribery, or other high Crimes and Misdemeanors," and the Senate the power to convict them, with a two-thirds majority needed in each house. But impeachment and conviction were drastic steps; Congress had removed federal judges from office, but never before had it seriously considered removing a president. After a year of political struggle, on February 24, 1868, radicals and moderates in the House joined to impeach the president. A radical-dominated committee was appointed to bring to the Senate charges of "high crimes and misdemeanors" against Johnson; it concentrated on alleged violations of the Tenure of Office Act.

The Senate, acting as a court, failed to convict Johnson. On May 26, after deliberating for eleven weeks, thirty-five senators voted for conviction—one vote short of the two-thirds required. Seven moderate Republicans had broken ranks, voting with twelve Democrats in support of Johnson. These Republicans reached their decision partly because they feared Benjamin Wade, the radical Republican who, as president pro tempore of the Senate, was next in the line of succession. Primarily, they worried about the precedent of Congress deposing a president over an issue of policy. They believed that the Civil War had demonstrated the need for a strong federal government administered by a powerful executive. Without a strong presidency, the moderate Republicans doubted whether the nation could preserve internal unity, advance the Republican economic program, and defend itself against foreign enemies. The Radical Republicans had failed to convict Johnson, but they had defeated him. For the remainder of his term, Johnson let Reconstruction proceed under congressional direction.

In November 1868, the Republicans won a major electoral victory. The impeachment controversy had led Grant, already the North's most popular war hero, to the Republican presidential nomination. He had supported congressional Reconstruction, "waved the bloody shirt," and yet urged peace between the sections. Grant's opponent was Horatio Seymour, a former governor of New York, who almost declined the nomination, certain that Grant would win. In the face of rising violence in the South, Seymour and the Democrats received little support for their claim that the government should let southern state governments reorganize on their own. Grant won about the same share of the northern vote (55 percent) as Lincoln had in 1864, collected a majority of the national popular vote, and received 214 of 294 electoral votes, including those of six of the eight reconstructed states. The Republicans kept majorities of at least two-thirds in both houses of Congress.

With this strong mandate, Republicans added the last major piece of Reconstruction legislation. They drafted the Fifteenth Amendment, which forbade states to deny their citizens the right to vote on the grounds of race, color, or previous condition of servitude. Once again, some radicals would have preferred more. They had wanted the amendment to go farther and to prevent state governments from using property or literacy qualifications that state governments might use to disenfranchise blacks. But moderates had wished to keep these tactics available to northern and western states that wanted to deny immigrants the vote and therefore opposed a more rigorous proposal. Still, the Fifteenth Amendment was much tougher in protecting black suffrage than the Fourteenth. Passing the amendment in February 1869, Congress required the unreconstructed states of Virginia, Mississippi, Texas, and Georgia to ratify it before they could be readmitted to the Union.

The Issue of Women's Suffrage

The constitutional amendments enacted during Reconstruction could have dramatically changed the legal status of women. The Fourteenth Amendment, however, was even more conservative on suffrage for women than on suffrage for blacks. In referring to "adult male citizens," the amendment wrote the term "male" into the Constitution for the first time and, in effect, sanctioned the denial of the vote to women. Abolitionists such as Elizabeth Cady Stanton and Susan B. Anthony were deeply disappointed. They had led the drive to collect almost four hundred thousand signatures in support of the Thirteenth Amendment, which abolished slavery, and had hoped that abolitionists would unite behind universal suffrage. Many male abolitionists supported women's suffrage, but they did not think the public was ready for the idea. As Wendell Phillips told feminists, "One question at a time. This hour belongs to the Negro." Feminists did not oppose the ratification of the Fourteenth Amendment, but, through the American Equal Rights Association—which they formed in 1866, at their first women's rights convention since the Civil War—they sought to win support for their position among male abolitionists and launched a universal suffrage campaign at the state level.

The Fifteenth Amendment, like the Fourteenth, disappointed those who sought the vote for women; it made no reference to sex and thus allowed states to deny suffrage to women. Stanton and Anthony had already concluded that feminists should develop a political position independent of any political party. The two women broke with Republican abolitionists and refused to support the amendment unless it was accompanied by a sixteenth amendment enfranchising women. Stanton argued that ratification of the Fifteenth Amendment alone would create an "aristocracy of sex." She declared, "All manhood will vote not because of intelligence, patriotism, property or white skin, but because it is male, not female." In promoting a sixteenth amendment, she made a special appeal to women of the business class:

> American women of wealth, education, virtue and refinement, if you do not wish the lower orders of Chinese, Africans, Germans and Irish, with the low ideas of womanhood to make laws for you and your daughters . . . to dictate not only the civil, but moral codes by which you shall be governed, awake to the danger of your present position and demand that woman, too, shall be represented in the government!

Not all advocates of women's suffrage agreed with the tactics of Stanton and Anthony. Lucy Stone, Frederick Douglass, and other former abolitionists formed the New England Woman Suffrage Association in 1868 to maintain an alliance with Republicans and to support the Fifteenth Amendment. They believed that this was the best way to enlist the support of the Republican party for women's suffrage after Reconstruction issues had been settled.

These two different strategies came to characterize long-standing differences within the women's rights movement. In 1869, the American Equal Rights Association split into two organizations as a result of the debate over the Fifteenth Amendment. One group was the National Woman Suffrage Association, which elected Stanton as its first president. It relied on local suffrage societies that Stanton and Anthony's efforts had triggered in communities around the country. In response, the women of the New England Woman Suffrage Association, including Lucy Stone, formed the American Woman Suffrage Association. They elected Henry Ward Beecher, a prominent Brooklyn minister, as president and cultivated strong ties with Republicans and male abolitionists. For twenty-one years, these two national organizations competed for the leadership of the women's movement. The American Association tended to focus on suffrage, while the National Association developed a more comprehensive

A CYNIC'S VIEW OF
WOMEN'S SUFFRAGE
This antifeminist Currier and Ives lithograph appeared in 1868 and was called "The Age of iron, or Man as He Expects to Be"—after his wife's emancipation. As the quote above by Elizabeth Cady Stanton indicates, the feminists were willing to invoke traditional morality in response to their opponents. (Museum of the City of New York. Harry T. Peters Collection)

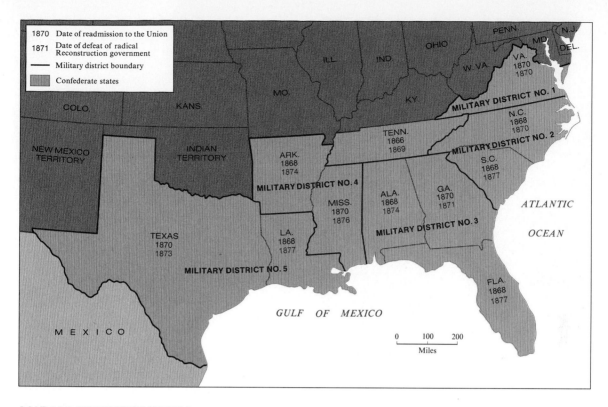

MAP 16.1 RECONSTRUCTION
The federal government grouped states of the ex-Confederacy into military districts during radical Reconstruction. The two dates in each state indicate when the state was re-admitted to the Union, and when radical Republicans lost control of the state government. All the ex-Confederate states rejoined the Union during the period 1868–1870, but the periods of radical rule varied widely. Radicals lasted only a few months in Virginia; they held until the end of Reconstruction in Louisiana, Florida, and South Carolina.

feminist position. The contest over the Fifteenth Amendment had finally disconnected the women's rights movement from abolitionism, and women now began to develop political strategies independent of other reform movements.

The South During Reconstruction

Between 1868 and 1871, all the southern states met the stipulations of Congress and rejoined the Union. Reconstruction governments under Republican control remained in power for periods ranging from a few months for Virginia to nine years for South Carolina, Louisiana, and Florida. In each government, the Republican party drew its support from a coalition of blacks, whites who had not owned slaves, and white settlers from the North.

Southern Republicans, black and white, did their best to reconstruct southern society. But during the 1870s, the ex-Confederates resisted effectively and exhausted the northern Republicans, who abandoned their southern allies. Even if the southern Republicans had prevailed, they would not have produced an economic revolution in the South. Most Republicans, North and South, remained too steadfastly loyal to established property rights to redistribute wealth on behalf of ex-slaves or poor whites.

Reconstruction Governments

Blacks played an important role in Reconstruction governments, although they did not dominate in any state. In Alabama, Florida, South Carolina, Mississippi, and Louisiana, where blacks constituted a majority of all registered voters, they contributed heavily to Republican

HIRAM R. REVELS

In 1870 Hiram R. Revels was elected to the U.S. Senate from Mississippi to fill Jefferson Davis's former seat. Revels was a free black from North Carolina who had migrated North and attended Knox College in Illinois. He recruited blacks for the Union army and, as an ordained Methodist minister, served as chaplain of a black regiment in Mississippi, where he settled after the war. (Library of Congress)

victories. In South Carolina, blacks briefly held a majority in one house of the legislature. In other states, they held positions of importance, but never in proportion to their numbers.

Black political leaders came largely from an elite that had been freed before the Civil War. Most of them had been artisans, shopkeepers, teachers, and ministers in southern towns and cities. However, a significant minority had been slaves. An ex-slave named Blanche K. Bruce was one of two black U.S. senators from Mississippi. He had received tutoring on the Virginia plantation of his white father and then escaped during the Civil War to Hannibal, Missouri, where he established a school for blacks. He moved to Mississippi in 1869 and entered politics; he was elected to the Senate in 1874—the only black elected to a full term in the Senate until 1966. All

the black leaders of the Reconstruction South emphasized the need for blacks to vote, and they supported state programs to improve schools and roads.

The Republicans who dominated the reconstructed state governments were satirized and stereotyped by resentful southern whites. Nonslaveholding whites were labeled "scalawags"—worthless, runty animals—by their Democratic opponents. Settlers from the North were called "carpetbaggers"—transient exploiters who carried all their property in cheap suitcases called carpetbags. Carpetbaggers held more than half the Republican governorships in the South and almost half of the South's seats in Congress. Black Republicans were mocked and scorned as ignorant field hands who could only play at politics like children.

Actually, few southern Republicans conformed to these stereotypes. Many carpetbaggers sought personal profit, but they also brought capital and skills to invest in the region's future. Most had been Union army officers who fell in love with the South—its climate, people, and economic opportunities. Many were college graduates and professionals—lawyers, engineers, and teachers. Some scalawags were wealthy ex-Whigs; others were not rich but did often own their own farms. They wished to see a South free of a slaveowning aristocracy and usually had fought against, or at least refused to support, the Confederacy.

The Republican governments in the South were often accused of corruption and incompetence. But corruption and incompetence were common in the northern states and in the federal government during Reconstruction. Southern Republicans modernized state constitutions, extended the right to vote, and made more offices elective than had been traditional in the South. They built roads in areas where roads had never existed. They supervised the rebuilding of the region's blasted railroad network and subsidized investment in manufacturing and transportation. They undertook major public works programs. And they did all this without major federal financing.

Perhaps the main accomplishment of the southern Republicans came in the area of education. They built public schools that served more people, black and white, than free education had ever reached in the prewar South. Blacks of all ages rushed to attend newly established schools, even where they had to pay tuition. An elderly black man in Mississippi explained his desire to go to school: "Ole missus used to read the good book to us . . . on Sunday evenin's, but she mostly read dem places where it says, 'Servants obey your masters.' . . . Now we is free, there's heaps of tings in that old book we is just suffering to learn." By 1877, hundreds of thousands of black children went to school. A child in Augusta, Georgia, explained his presence there in simple terms: "I'm going to school now to try to learn something I hope will enable me to be of some use to my race."

Like politicians everywhere, southern Republicans usually focused on immediate tasks and problems. But beneath their day-to-day efforts—and their mistakes—lay a reasonably coherent idea. The South, they believed, needed to be fundamentally reconstructed. Their goals were to end southern dependence on a cotton agriculture that rested on the unskilled labor of blacks and to create a growing economy based on manufacturing, capital investment, and skilled labor. Southern Republicans fell far short of making this vision a reality. But they accomplished much more of it than their critics, northern or southern, gave them credit for.

The Planters' Reaction

Most ex-slaveowners opposed the Republican program, especially the effort to expand political and economic opportunities for blacks, because it threatened their vested interest in traditional agriculture and their power and status in southern society. A few planters supported subsidized manufacturing, but most wished only to rebuild the transportation system. In any case, the former slaveowners set aside political differences among themselves and united to defeat the Republicans. Their appeals for racial solidarity and southern patriotism focused mass hostility against the Republicans on black suffrage and social status rather than economic issues.

The planters concentrated on recapturing exclusive political control of southern state governments. They used any means, both legitimate and illegitimate, at their disposal. In the eight states where whites formed a majority of the population—all except Louisiana, Mississippi, and South Carolina—planters sought to return ex-Confederates to the rolls of registered voters and unite them under the Democratic banner. Calling themselves the "redeemers," planters and their supporters organized secret societies to frighten blacks and Republican whites from

A FREEDMEN'S SCHOOL
This 1866 sketch from *Harper's Weekly* of a Vicksburg, Mississippi school run by the Freedmen's Bureau illustrates the desire for education by ex-slaves of all ages. Because most southern blacks were farmers, schools commonly offered night classes that left students free for field work during the day. (From *Harper's Weekly*. The Newberry Library, Chicago)

CARPETBAGGER DESCRIBES THE KU KLUX KLAN

Albion W. Tourgée (1838–1905) was a carpetbagger in North Carolina. He described his continual harassment by the Ku Klux Klan in The Invisible Empire *(1880).*

Another thing which shows that . . . [to say the Klan] was merely the work of rough spirits of the lower classes is a libel on the common people of the South, is the fact that the best classes never prosecuted nor denounced these acts, but were always their apologists and defenders. Besides that, they kept the secrets of the Klan better than the Masons have ever kept the mysteries of their craft. It was an open secret in families and neighborhoods. Ladies met together in sewing-circles to make the disguises. Churches were used as places of assembly. Children were intrusted with secrets which will make them shudder in old age. . . . It was a holy trust which the Southern cause had cast upon them, and they would have died rather than betray it.

The fact has been overlooked, too, that whenever positive information has been obtained as to the membership of the Klan, it has been shown to have had its full proportion of the best classes. Two judges, two sheriffs, one State solicitor, one leading editor, four members of the legislature, one Congressman, and numerous lawyers and planters and professional men, are shown by the testimony in *one* State alone, to have been among its members. The confessions of members showed the officers and leading men of the Klans always to have been men of standing and influence in their communities.

There is no sort of doubt that it originated with the best classes of the South, was managed and controlled by them, and was at all times under their direction. It was their creature and their agent to work out their purposes and ends. It was just as much their movement as was the war of rebellion, and animated by similar motives.

---

voting or taking other political action. These societies coerced whites into joining the Democratic party and used intimidation and terror to prevent blacks from supporting the Republicans. The most widespread of these groups, the Ku Klux Klan, was organized in Tennessee in 1865 and quickly spread throughout the South.

The Klan's first leader was Nathan Bedford Forrest, a celebrated Confederate cavalry officer, and its initial organization was based on Confederate army units. Forrest had led the Confederate cavalry that took Fort Pillow in Tennessee in 1864. He had captured the black Union soldiers who held the fort and killed them. In 1868, during an interview in Memphis, Forrest warned Republicans that they would suffer the same fate if they tried to suppress the Klan. "I intend to kill the radicals," Forrest said. He was watching their houses, he added, and "when the fight comes not one of them would ever get out of this town alive."

As Reconstruction advanced, terrorism became more blatant and more elaborate. Paramilitary groups, with names such as Rifle Clubs and Red Shirts, operated openly. They became most visible in Mississippi, where their procedures became known as the Mississippi Plan. In essence, they mobilized and armed whites in virtually every community in order to determine the outcome of elections by force.

The first step in the Mississippi Plan was to compel the state's white Republicans to become Democrats. Overt violence was often used against whites, as it was against blacks, but the tactics also included social ostracism. A white Republican who succumbed explained that the Democrats made it "too damned hot for us to stay out. . . . No white man can live in the South in the future and act with any other than the Democratic party unless he is willing and prepared to live a life of social isolation and remain in political oblivion."

The second step was the relentless intimidation of black voters. In Mississippi's 1875 elec-

INTIMIDATION OF BLACK VOTERS

The following testimony was given by Harriet Hernandes, a black resident of Spartanburg, South Carolina, July 10, 1871, to the Joint Congressional Select Committee investigating conditions in the South.

Question: How old are you?

Answer: Going on thirty-four years. . . .

Q: Are you married or single?

A: Married.

Q: Did the Ku-Klux come to your house at any time?

A: Yes, sir; twice. . . .

Q: Go on to the second time. . . .

A: They came in; I was lying in bed. Says he, "Come out here, sir; come out here, sir!" They took me out of bed; they would not let me get out, but they took me up in their arms and toted me out—me and my daughter Lucy. He struck me on the forehead with a pistol, and here is the scar above my eye now. Says he, "Damn you, fall." I fell. Says he, "Damn you, get up." I got up. Says he, "Damn you, get over this fence!" and he kicked me over when I went to get over; and then he went on to a brush pile, and they laid us right down there, both together. They laid us down twenty yards apart, I reckon. They had dragged and beat us along. They struck me right on the top of my head, and I thought they had killed me; and I said, "Lord o' mercy, don't, don't kill my child!" He gave me a lick on the head, and it liked to have killed me; I saw stars. He threw my arm over my head so I could not do anything with it for three weeks, and there are great knots on my wrist now.

Q: What did they say this was for?

A: They said, "You can tell your husband that when we see him we are going to kill him. . . ."

Q: Did they say why they wanted to kill him?

A: They said, "He voted the radical ticket, didn't he?" I said, "Yes," that very way. . . .

Q: When did [your husband] get back home after this whipping? He was not at home, was he?

A: He was lying out; he couldn't stay at home, bless your soul! . . .

Q: Has he been afraid for any length of time?

A: He has been afraid ever since last October. He has been lying out. He has not laid in the house ten nights since October.

Q: Is that the situation of the colored people down there to any extent?

A: That is the way they all have to do—men and women both.

Q: What are they afraid of?

A: Of being killed or whipped to death.

Q: What has made them afraid?

A: Because men that voted radical tickets they took the spite out on the women when they could get at them.

Q: How many colored people have been whipped in that neighborhood?

A: It is all of them, mighty near. . . .

---

tions, in which the Republican party went down to defeat, local Democratic clubs paraded as full militia companies. They identified black leaders in assassination lists called "dead-books"; broke up Republican meetings; provoked rioting that left hundreds of blacks dead; and threatened voters, who still lacked the protection of the secret ballot. The Republican governor of the state, Adelbert Ames, a Congressional Medal of Honor winner from Maine, appealed for federal troops, but President Grant refused, fearing damage to Republicans in northern elections. Ames con-templated organizing a state militia to resist, but he decided against it, believing that only blacks would join. Rather than escalate the scale of the racial war, he conceded victory to the terrorists.

To defeat the paramilitary forces, southern Republicans needed federal military aid. The Grant administration and moderate Republicans in Congress were unwilling to enlarge what had already become a costly, bloody guerrilla war. In 1870–1871, however, Congress passed the Force Acts, which authorized the president to use military force and martial law to suppress felonies and conspiracies fomented by the Ku Klux Klan. Under these acts, federal agents penetrated the Klan and gathered evidence that provided the basis for thousands of arrests. Federal grand juries indicted more than three thousand Klansmen. The Justice Department, however, lacked the resources necessary to prosecute effectively, especially when Justice Department attorneys faced all-white juries. Only about six hundred offenders received convictions, and only a handful of these served significant prison sentences.

Meanwhile, northern Republicans began to lose heart. They continued to "wave the bloody shirt" but found that it had less effect with each election. Northerners had grown weary over the bloodshed and money needed to support Reconstruction. Most northern Republicans, including even some radicals, concluded that ex-slaves should be able to enjoy their freedom without additional federal assistance. Republicans moved toward a consensus that the federal government had accomplished its Civil War objectives and should end Reconstruction.

Because of the lack of federal help, Republican governments in the South found themselves gradually overwhelmed by ex-Confederate politicians in daylight and by terrorists at night. In 1870, the Democrats, supported by a vigorous Klan, recovered power in Virginia, Georgia, and North Carolina. They overthrew Republicans in Texas in 1873, in Alabama and Arkansas in 1874, and in Mississippi in 1875. By 1877, Republican governments and token U.S. military units remained in only three states—Louisiana, South Carolina, and Florida.

The Plight of the Ex-Slaves

Even at its most effective stage, Reconstruction was as much a scheme to promote the Republican party as to assist the ex-slaves. After receiving their political rights, the blacks were expected to fend for themselves. This meant that the actual outcome of the legal abolition of slavery depended largely on thousands of contests between ex-slaves, acting individually and collectively, and an increasingly unified white South, led by the planter class. Despite the odds against them, the ex-slaves won some modest economic gains. But these gains came only

within the restrictions of a form of debt peonage that replaced slavery. Blacks and many whites remained mired in a poverty that both racism and economic forces reinforced powerfully.

Land Reform Fails

To former slaves, freedom had a specific, positive meaning—control over their own lives. But they knew that to have genuine freedom in an agricultural economy, they had to own land.

Emancipation and the advancing Union armies raised black expectations of land ownership. Union officers often left slaves in control of plantations. General Sherman promoted land ownership for blacks by reserving coastal land in Georgia and South Carolina—the Sea Islands and abandoned plantations within thirty miles of the coast—for black refugees and by giving them "possessory titles" to forty-acre tracts. By the end of the war, the Freedmen's Bureau had placed about ten thousand families on half a million acres of this land. Reports of such actions inspired hope among blacks throughout the South. Many continued to work on their old plantations in the hope that they would own some of the land after the war. For example, when planter Thomas Pinckney returned to his South Carolina plantation, his slaves told him, "We ain't going nowhere. We are going to work right here on the land where we were born and what belongs to us." An ex-slave on a Georgia plantation offered to sell to his former master the share of the plantation he expected to receive after the federal redistribution.

Then, in May 1865, Andrew Johnson's amnesty ended all land redistribution. It allowed pardoned Confederates to recover their land if Union troops had confiscated or occupied it. In October, Johnson ordered General Oliver O. Howard, head of the Freedmen's Bureau, to tell blacks on the Sea Islands that they did not hold legal title to the land, and to advise them to come to terms with the legal, white landowners. Howard reluctantly obeyed. The dispossessed blacks replied, "Why do you take away our lands? You take them from us who have always been true, always true to the Government! You give them to our all-time enemies! That is not right!" When some of the Sea Island blacks refused to deal with the restored white owners,

Union soldiers forced them to leave or to work for their old masters. The Freedmen's Bureau did help more than two thousand black families buy their own land in the Sea Islands. But by the end of 1866, the bureau had returned the rest of the land to its white owners.

The only other Reconstruction land-redistribution measure was the Southern Homestead Act of 1866, which designated more than forty million acres of public land in Alabama, Arkansas, Florida, Louisiana, and Mississippi for grants of eighty acres to settlers who cultivated the land for five years. Congress prohibited anyone who had supported the Confederacy from filing a claim until 1867. Yet few ex-slaves or poor white Unionists could exploit this advantage. The cost of equipping new farms was too great. Fewer than seven thousand ex-slaves claimed land and only about a thousand eventually qualified for ownership.

Congressional Republicans never seriously considered a massive redistribution of land in the South. Given their commitment to property rights, such a policy seemed too radical. Most Republicans believed it was unconstitutional as well, for it would deprive landowners of their property without due process of law. Massive redistribution would also endanger, Republicans believed, southern economic recovery. Only Thaddeus Stevens insisted that Reconstruction meant little unless the federal government redistributed land.

The former slaves, however, realized how important land was to freedom. Where they had occupied lands, they resisted removal. Often led by black veterans of the Union army, the ex-slaves fought pitched battles with plantation owners and bands of ex-Confederate soldiers. Whenever possible, the owners attempted to disarm and intimidate the returning black veterans. A black veteran from Maryland wrote, "The returned colard Solgers are in Many cases beten, and their guns taken from them, we darcent walk out of an evening . . . they beat us badly and Sumtime Shoot us."

In this warfare, federal troops often backed the local whites. The necessities of fighting a total war had briefly carried land reform further than even most radical Republicans had wanted to go. Subsequently, the government ensured that land ownership in the South would remain concentrated in the hands of the planters.

Planters Versus Ex-Slaves

Planters now tried to establish a labor system that was as close to slavery as they could make it. High cotton prices provided a powerful inducement for planters to restore the status quo in labor relations. Moreover, on paper, emancipation had cost the slaveowners about $3 billion—the value of their capital investment in former slaves—a sum that equaled nearly three-fourths of the nation's economic production in 1860. In reality, however, their losses depended on the extent to which they lost control over their former slaves. Planters therefore attempted to control the freed blacks and to substitute low wages for the food, clothing, and shelter that the blacks had received as slaves.

WAGE LABOR OF EX-SLAVES
This photograph, taken shortly after the Civil War, shows former slaves being led from the cotton fields. Although they now worked for wages, they were probably organized into a gang not far removed from the earlier slave gangs. Their plug-hatted crew leader is dressed much as his slave-driving predecessor would have been. (The New-York Historical Society)

MAP 16.2 THE BARROW PLANTATION
Comparing the maps of this central Georgia plantation
reveals the changing patterns of black residence and
farming after the Civil War. In 1860, the slave quarters
clustered near the planter's house, which sat above them
on a small hilltop. The free sharecroppers of 1881 built
their cabins along the spurs or ridges of land between the
streams, scattering their community over the plantation.
A black church and school were built by this date. A
typical sharecropper on the plantation earned most of his
income from growing cotton.

The ex-slaves resisted, however. During the
growing seasons of 1865 and 1866, thousands of
former slaves abandoned their old plantations
and farms. Many sought better lives in the
towns and cities of the South. Others remained

in the countryside but either refused to work in
the cotton fields or reduced their hours there.
They worked instead on their own garden plots,
guaranteeing themselves a subsistence level of
rations during the postwar disruptions.

Meanwhile, they fortified the institutions that
had sustained their spirit during the days of
slavery. Black families moved away from the
slave quarters, usually building homes scattered
around or near their old plantations and farms.
Sometimes they established all-black villages.
Families strengthened the ties they had long
nurtured. Husbands, wives, and children often
reunited, sometimes after journeys of hundreds
of miles. Couples stepped forward to record
their marriages. When they could, mothers res-
cued their children from the control of planters
and overseers. One mother pleaded for the return of her daughter so the girl could go to
school and church. She explained that her
daughter "never was in a church in her life, and
don't know the Lord's prayer." Another mother
fought to free her daughter from the ex-master
to whom she had become apprenticed after the
war. "Our condition is bettered but little," she
said, because parents and children were separated. "Give us our children, and don't let them
be raised in the ignorance we have."

Blacks moved their religion completely into
the open, building their own churches and
founding independent organizations within the
Baptist and Methodist churches. Many women
refused to work in the fields. They insisted on
staying at home, where they tended elaborate
gardens, managed households, and brought education and religion to their children.

In the fields, ex-slaves refused to submit to
the grueling gang labor that had been the major
tool for their economic exploitation. Now they
wanted a pace of work and independence that reflected their new status. What was freedom all
about if not to have a bit more leisure time, to
work less intensely than they had as slaves, and
to work for themselves and their families?

This modest ambition ran counter to deeply
entrenched attitudes among planters and poor
whites. Emancipation had not destroyed the
racist assumptions and fears that the planters
had fostered in order to maintain and defend
slavery. One Freedmen's Bureau commissioner

in Mississippi wrote that wherever he went, he heard "the people talk in such a way as to indicate that they are yet unable to conceive of the negro as possessing any rights at all." He explained:

> The whites esteem their property by natural right, and however much they may admit that the individual relations of masters and slaves have been destroyed by the war and by the President's emancipation proclamation, they still have an ingrained feeling that the blacks at large belong to the whites at large, and whenever opportunity serves they treat the colored people just as their profit, caprice or passion may dictate.

Thus, former slaveowners and the poorer whites who looked to them for leadership continued to maintain the South's caste system, which rested on racist attitudes that united whites across class lines.

In 1865–1866, planters led the movement to enact the Black Codes, an extract of which appears on page 500. The codes varied from state to state, but almost all of them required the arrest of an ex-slave for vagrancy if he or she were found without employment. In most cases, the vagrant could not pay the fine required to be released from jail, and the county court hired him or her out to an employer. Several courts established specific hours of labor, spelled out the duties expected of laborers, and declared that any laborer who did not meet these standards was a vagrant. The codes usually restricted employment opportunities outside agriculture by establishing licensing procedures for blacks who wished to pursue skills or "irregular job work."

With the sanction of state law, local governments narrowly circumscribed the lives of blacks. They set curfews, required employer-issued passes for black agricultural workers, insisted that blacks who wished to live in town obtain white sponsors, and sharply regulated meetings of blacks, both inside and outside churches. Fines and forced labor were the penalties for violators.

The Black Codes, or similar laws, remained on the books throughout the South even during radical Reconstruction. If challenged by the federal government, state legislatures usually relaxed only marginal provisions. In any case, congressional intervention did not reach the local level. Then, when the "redeemers" came to power, southern states usually established new, even more stringent regulations.

The planters often received support from a source that surprised most of them—the agents of the federal government. Most army officers and federal marshals accepted the basic assumption behind the Black Codes—that ex-slaves were suited only for agricultural labor. In fact, even during the war, Union army officers tended to sympathize with the planters. Officers usually left planters who expressed their loyalty to the Union in control of their plantations and their former slaves.

After Appomattox, representatives of the federal government quickly came to support the economic interests of the planters. As one Louisiana ex-slave described the process, "Whenever a new Provost Marshall comes he gives us justice for a fortnight or so; then he becomes acquainted with planters, takes dinners with them, receives presents; and then we no longer have any rights, or very little." In disputes between employers and laborers, federal marshals generally sided with the planters and sustained their authority. Army commanders complied with the requests of planters for help in forcing blacks to work. The officers expelled former plantation workers from towns and cities and punished blacks for disobedience, theft, vagrancy, and erratic labor.

Even most agents of the Freedmen's Bureau supported the planters. They interpreted their instructions to promote a transition to free labor to mean that they should teach ex-slaves to be reliable agricultural workers. They preached the gospel of work to the blacks. To discourage labor violence, they warned that it was better "to suffer wrong than to do wrong." They urged former slaves to vindicate the cause of abolition by staying at home and working even harder than they had under slavery. One bureau official told ex-slaves that their former master "is not able to do without you, and you will . . . find him as kind, honest, and liberal as other men" and "you can be as free and as happy in your old home, for the present, as anywhere else in the world."

. . . All freedmen, free negroes and mulattoes in this State, over the age of eighteen years, found on the second Monday in January, 1866, or thereafter, with no lawful employment of business, or found unlawfully assembling themselves together, either in the day or night time, and all white persons so assembling themselves with freedmen, free negroes or mulattoes, or usually associating with freedmen, free negroes or mulattoes, on terms of equality, or living in adultery or fornication with a freed woman, free negro or mulatto, shall be deemed vagrants, and on conviction thereof shall be fined in a sum not exceeding, in the case of a freedman, free negro, or mulatto, fifty dollars, and a white man two hundred dollars, and imprisoned at the discretion of the court, the free negro not exceeding ten days, and the white man not exceeding six months. . . .

[I]n case any freeman, free negro or mulatto shall fail for five days after the imposition of any fine or forfeiture upon him or her for violation of any of the provisions of this act to pay the same, . . . it shall be, and is hereby, made the duty of the sheriff of the proper county to hire out said freedman, free negro or mulatto, to any person who will, for the shortest period of serve, pay said fine and forfeiture and all costs: *Provided*, A preference shall be given to the employer, if there be one, in which case the employer shall be entitled to deduct and retain the amount so paid from the wages of such freedman, free negro or mulatto, then due or to become due; and in case said freedman, free negro, or mulatto cannot be hired out, he or she may be dealt with as a pauper.

. . . Every freedman, free negro, and mulatto shall, on the second Monday of January, one thousand eight hundred and sixty-six and annually thereafter, have a lawful home or employment, and shall have written evidence thereof as follows, to-wit: if living in any incorporated city, town, or village, a license from the mayor thereof; and if living outside of an incorporated city, town, or village, from the member of the board of police of his beat, authorizing him or her to do irregular and job work; or a written contract, as provided in section six in this act, which licenses may be revoked for cause at any time by the authority granting the same.

All contracts for labor made with freedmen, free negroes, and mulattoes for a longer period than one month shall be in writing, and in duplicate, attested and read to said freedman, free negro, or mulatto by a beat, city or county officer, or two disinterested white persons of the county in which the labor is to be performed, of which each party shall have one; and said contracts shall be taken and held as entire contracts, and if the laborer shall quit the service of the employer before the expiration of his term of service, without good cause, he shall forfeit his wages for that year up to the time of quitting.

. . . If any person shall persuade or attempt to persuade, entice, or cause any freedman, free negro, or mulatto to desert from the legal employment of any person before the expiration of his or her term of service, or shall knowingly employ any such deserting freedman, free negro, or mulatto, or shall knowingly give or sell to any such deserting freedman, free negro, or mulatto, any food, raiment, or other thing, he or she shall be guilty of a misdemeanor, and, upon conviction, shall be fined not less than twenty-five dollars and not more than two hundred dollars and the costs; and if said fine and costs shall not be immediately paid, the court shall sentence said convict to not exceeding two months' imprisonment in the county jail, and he or she shall moreover be liable to the party injured in damages.

The minority of Freedmen's Bureau agents who did side with the blacks were stymied by northern racism, lack of funds, understaffing, lack of coordination within the bureau, and uncooperative military authorities. Overall, the Freedmen's Bureau helped the planters reestablish control over their labor force. It also gave legitimacy in the north to the policies of the planter elite.

Sharecropping and Debt Peonage

The Freedmen's Bureau did, however, change the way planters controlled the labor of their ex-slaves. It established a contract labor system by encouraging, even compelling, planters and ex-slaves to agree on written contracts through a formal bargaining process. The labor contract system was a poor substitute for land ownership. But it helped the freedmen attain something else they badly wanted—the elimination of gang labor.

As early as 1865, the written contracts between ex-slaves and planters provided that the ex-slaves would work for wages. However, the contracts also provided for less supervision, a slower pace, and more free time than under slavery, as well as the elimination of drivers and overseers from the plantations. By 1866, however, bargaining between planters and ex-slaves had become more difficult, partly because a shrinking money supply in the South reduced the cash available to pay wages. To resolve the growing number of conflicts, Freedmen's Bureau agents introduced a form of compensation that was common, though not typical, in northern agriculture. This was the payment of agricultural workers in shares of the crop, rather than in wages.

At first, ex-slaves were enthusiastic about sharecropping, and it swept through the South. Former slaves found that sharecropping in-

creased their control over working conditions. It also allowed them to improve their standard of living. Under typical sharecropping contracts, sharecroppers turned over between half and two-thirds of their harvested crops to their landlords. The owner's share was not necessarily excessive, because the landlord commonly provided land, seed, fertilizer, tools, and assistance in marketing. The sharecropping system bound together laborers and owners of land and capital in a common sharing of risks and returns.

Sharecropping did not lead to land ownership for many slaves. Some ex-slaves managed to save enough through sharecropping to rent land. As tenant farmers, they could sell their own crops directly to market. Some of these renters were finally able to purchase their own land; by 1910, black farmers owned nearly a third of all the land they cultivated. But black farm owners usually occupied marginal land—in the coastal swamps of Georgia and South Carolina, for example—and the land often cost more than its productivity warranted. Blacks had to

SHARECROPPING
This sharecropping family seems proud of their new cabin and their crop of cotton, which they planted in every available bit of ground. But the presence of their white landlord in the background suggests the forces that led families like this one into debt peonage. (Brown Brothers)

pay high prices for land throughout the South, especially in the most fertile areas, because they were willing to pay a premium for the badge of freedom and because white planters restricted their access to land ownership. Some planters made agreements among themselves not to sell land to blacks or intimidated blacks who tried to buy land. Others devised a system of debt peonage that tied ex-slaves to the land and enabled planters to depress their earnings.

The financial condition of blacks was extremely difficult. Sharecropping and renting of land enabled ex-slaves to increase their incomes but also broadened their financial needs. They wanted more food and better clothing than they had had under slavery; sharecroppers often needed more supplies than their landlords were willing to provide; and renters had to purchase all their seed, fertilizer, and equipment. The purchase of major farm supplies almost always required borrowing. Southern banks, however, were reluctant to lend money to black farmers, whom they saw as bad risks, and cash was generally in short supply.

The owners of country stores stepped in. Eager to lend money to sharecroppers, they furnished everything the black farmers needed and extended credit for the purchases. The country merchants took advantage of the weak bargaining power of the ex-slaves by charging unusually high prices and interest rates. In effect, they were rural loan sharks.

Once the black sharecroppers fell into debt to the country merchants, high interest rates made it difficult for them to settle their accounts. At best, after paying their debts, the sharecroppers broke even. Most sharecroppers fell deeper and deeper into debt. Most southern states gave this system legal force by allowing a merchant to take a lien on crops. This gave merchants a legal right to take the crops to settle the sharecropper's debts, and to seek criminal prosecution of a sharecropper who could not pay the full amount of interest owed. Indebted black farmers faced imprisonment and forced labor unless they toiled on the land according to the instructions of the merchant-creditor. Increasingly, merchants and landlords cooperated to maintain this lucrative system and many landlords themselves became merchants. The ex-slaves had been trapped in the vicious circle of debt peonage.

The North During Reconstruction

The Republicans failed to break the hold of the planter elite on the South, but they did succeed in completing economic reconstruction of the North. They enacted nearly all their nationalizing economic program—a system of national banking, tariff protection, and subsidies for internal improvements—despite resistance from Democrats. The adoption of the Republican program accompanied and promoted unprecedented economic growth and industrial and territorial expansion.

A Dynamic Economy

The destruction and waste of the Civil War disrupted the nation's economic life, but economic growth—gains in productivity—resumed quickly after the fighting ended. By the 1870s, Americans became more productive and their economy expanded faster than ever before. Northeastern industry led the way, particularly iron and steel and railroad construction. The production of iron more than doubled between the end of the Civil War and 1870; it more than doubled again by 1880. Steel production grew even more rapidly—fivefold between 1865 and 1870 and then nearly twenty times by 1880. The era began the "age of capital," a period that lasted until World War I and that was marked by great increases in investment in factories and railroads. It also began the era of big business, characterized by the rise of giant corporations.

As impressive as America's industrial expansion was its territorial growth. During the 1860s, the United States began to seize its potential as a great continental power, integrating its vast western territory into its economy. Northern capitalists built transcontinental railroads. Settlers poured into the Great Plains region. Beginning in 1859, with the discovery of gold near Pike's Peak, miners rushed to Colorado and then to Nevada and the Black Hills of South Dakota. During the late 1860s, Texas cattlemen started their great drives to northern railheads, beginning the creation of the Cattle Kingdom. And the United States launched its wars against western Indians. By 1870, territorial governments had

EXPANSION IN THE MOUNTAIN STATES
The growth of towns like Virginia City, Nevada, pictured here in 1866, helped transform the United States into a wealthy, transcontinental nation. Virginia City's residents built their town, including five newspapers and a stock exchange, around the gold mines that had been discovered in the surrounding Comstock Lode just before the Civil War began. (Library of Congress)

been formed throughout the West. Nevada became a state in 1864, with Nebraska following in 1867 and Colorado in 1876.

During the Civil War, Republicans implemented the economic program that they had inherited from the Whigs. After the war, northern acceptance of the Republican economic programs grew. Economic expansion seemed to validate the promises of renewed prosperity that Republicans had made in 1860. Also, the North's military victory seemed to prove that its society was stronger than the South's and to justify Republican programs as contributing to that strength. In addition, the successful experience of wartime mobilization encouraged Americans

to relax their traditional hostility to concentration of social power.

Many young soldiers—and women who had served in the Sanitary Commission—now accepted the state as a large, centralized entity. Wartime service had been their first direct experience of participation in a complex organization. For the first time, they had lived and worked within an explicit hierarchy that imposed a high degree of job specialization and rigorous discipline. Their service also had taken them, most for the first time, far from their homes and placed them in intimate contact with people who came from distant places and yet served in the same cause. This collective and disciplined national service predisposed many northerners to accept the Republican party and the federal government as agencies of national economic reorganization and, increasingly, to accept large corporations as instruments necessary for prosperity.

Republicans expanded their economic programs, rather than shrinking the federal government back to its prewar scale. They strengthened government regulation of the banking system, winning praise from investors who appreciated a more predictable economic environment. Republican Congresses continued to promote the development of a national transportation system by expanding railroad subsidies and establishing the Atlantic and Pacific Railroad in 1866 and the Texas Pacific in 1871. Republicans expanded the national postal system, funded major river and harbor development, and established a permanent army and navy. They also provided the cavalry forces required to clear the Indians from the Great Plains; military spending accounted for 60 percent of the federal budget by 1880. The Homestead Act subsidized the settling of the Great Plains. To some extent, all these programs stimulated the growth of a national economy and in turn lubricated the Republican political machine.

Even more central to the popularity of the Republican party was an elaborate system of pensions for Union veterans and their dependents. The Civil War pension program, which the government continually extended and broadened, had a distinct welfare component that became especially important during the severe depressions of the 1870s and 1890s. But the prime purpose of the pensions was to solidify the political loyalty of the families of the men who had served in the Union army.

The government financed its bountiful programs with the revenues raised from the tax system introduced during the Civil War. Postwar Congresses kept in force the high tariffs that had proved surprisingly lucrative. Congress also retained taxes on alcohol and tobacco that the Republican party at first had justified as emergency measures. These taxes not only financed the new Republican programs but also provided the funds for repayment of the Union's wartime debts. Wealthy Americans owned most of the war bonds issued by the government. The government repaid these investors out of the proceeds from the tariffs and sales taxes. Because the taxes increased the cost of everyday items, the mass of the American people were actually paying far more on the war debt in proportion to their income than were wealthy people. Republicans praised this redistribution of wealth, for it transferred significant amounts of money from poorer people to richer people, who were more able and likely to save and invest, and thereby increased the supply of capital, raised the rate of capital formation, and accelerated the rate of economic growth—all changes that benefitted the Republican-dominated business class.

Republican Foreign Policy

Americans were heavily preoccupied during the 1860s and 1870s with the development of their own territory. Nonetheless, some Republican leaders were alert to new possibilities for expansion abroad. Perhaps the most important advocate of expansion was William H. Seward, who had been Lincoln's secretary of state and continued in that post under Johnson. Believing in the importance of foreign commerce to the long-term health of the republic, Seward promoted the acquisition of colonies that could be used as trading bases in the Caribbean and the Pacific.

Johnson and Seward inherited their major foreign policy issues from the Civil War. The most pressing one was Mexico. The French emperor, Napoleon III, had intervened in a civil war there and created a puppet government under Archduke Maximilian, the brother of the emperor of Austria. Johnson and Seward decided not to tolerate this assertion of European power so close to the United States. In 1866, Johnson sent fifty thousand battle-hardened veterans to the Mexican border, while Seward negotiated the withdrawal of French troops. The French troops withdrew in 1867, leaving Maximilian to a Mexican firing squad.

The American government was also annoyed over Great Britain's allowing the *Alabama* and other Confederate cruisers to sail from British shipyards to raid Union commerce. Seward claimed that Britain had violated international laws of neutrality and owed compensation for damages. Britain, fearing that Americans might build ships for British enemies in some future war, accepted Seward's legal point and agreed to submit the "Alabama Claims" to arbitration. However, Charles Sumner, chairman of the Senate Foreign Relations Committee, insisted that the compensation cover "indirect" damages. He included lost shipping revenue and the costs of Britain's prolonging the war. Estimating these costs at more than $2 billion, he hoped to acquire Canada as part of a settlement. Sumner's demands blocked a solution during Johnson's presidency.

Meanwhile, Seward's expansionist ambitions met with only mixed success. Supporting naval demands for a base in the Caribbean, Seward negotiated a treaty with Denmark to purchase the Virgin Islands, but Congress rejected the $7.5 million price tag. Congress also turned down his proposal to annex Santo Domingo (now the Dominican Republic), which had won independence from Spain in 1865. Seward did persuade Congress to purchase the small Midway Islands west of Hawaii, after his effort to acquire the Hawaiian Islands had failed. Most important, Seward convinced the Senate, in 1867, to ratify a treaty to buy Alaska from Russia and to appropriate the $7.2 million for the purchase. Critics referred to Alaska as "Johnson's Polar Bear Garden" and "Seward's Folly," but its acquisition promised to obstruct any further British ambitions in North America. Also, the price was reasonable when weighed against even the low estimates that Congress made of Alaska's fish, fur, lumber, and mineral resources.

When Ulysses S. Grant became president in 1869, he promoted expansion in the Caribbean. He was influenced by American investors and adventurers in Santo Domingo, including Orville E. Babcock, a former military aide of Grant's who had become his personal secretary in the White House. Grant proposed a treaty to annex the country as a colony for American blacks dissatisfied with Reconstruction. The Senate defeated Grant's imperial ambition in 1870. Leading the attack was Charles Sumner, who feared that annexation would threaten the indepen-

dence of the neighboring black republic of Haiti. "These islands by climate, occupation, and destiny . . . belong to the colored people," he declared.

Grant's secretary of state was genteel Hamilton Fish, a former Whig who had been governor of New York and a U.S. senator. Fish had less interest than Seward in acquiring new territory and concentrated on settling differences with Britain. Part of his goal was to strengthen the ties of capital and commerce between the two nations. Interest in annexing Canada still remained high, but Fish finally persuaded Grant in 1870 that Parliament's passage of the British North America Act of 1867, uniting Canada in a federation (the Dominion of Canada), had removed any serious Canadian interest in annexation. Fish then quickly negotiated the Treaty of Washington, which both the Senate and Parliament ratified in 1871. This treaty submitted for arbitration all the outstanding issues between the two countries, including the "Alabama Claims." In 1873, the British government obeyed the ruling of an international tribunal established under the treaty and presented a $15.5 million check to the United States government. A period of unprecedented good will between America and Britain followed.

The Politics of Corruption

The Republican economic program became the primary target of the Democratic party, which tried to reestablish its national base of power. This was not an easy task, because the key elements of Republican policy had wide support. The Democrats tried to avoid attacking specific Republican programs on narrow economic grounds. Instead, they renewed their traditional assault on "special privilege."

Democrats warned that Republican programs created islands of privilege, enabling wealthy individuals to buy favors from the federal government and the Republicans to buy support from the people whom their programs served. The result, Democrats charged, was an increasing concentration of wealth and power and a corruption of the republic. In stressing corruption, the Democrats aimed to attract members of the business class to their party. They appealed to Americans who valued honesty in their economic and political lives and who believed in the ideal of a society composed of independent and virtuous farmers, artisans, and small entrepreneurs. The Democrats wished to restore a competitive economy, one that they argued had been lost during the Industrial Revolution and the Civil War.

During Grant's first term, some Republicans also criticized the management of Reconstruction and the northern economy. These dissidents included some radicals, such as Charles Sumner, who regarded Grant's Reconstruction policies as too conservative. The most important among them, however, included long-time Republicans like Charles Francis Adams, who were wealthy, well-educated members of established northeastern families. They resented and disapproved of the professional politicians who had become crucial to the party.

The dissident Republicans, like the Democrats, specifically attacked Grant for turning the Republican party into a self-serving bureaucracy. They criticized him for relying too heavily on professional politicians in executive positions, especially cabinet posts. These Republicans faulted their party for requiring government workers to pay a portion of their salaries into the party's treasury. They coined the term "Grantism" to describe this new spoils system of party patronage.

The dissident Republicans developed a unified program and a political strategy. They hoped to convince their party to endorse a program of civil service reform, beginning with a merit system to replace the system of rewarding party workers with public offices. They proposed a civil service commission to administer competitive examinations as the basis for appointments. Having mobilized fellow Republicans around this program, they planned to replace Grant as the party's nominee in 1872.

When the dissidents failed to win control of the Republican party, they set up their own party. They called themselves Liberal Republicans to indicate their commitment to liberty, competition, and limited government. They emphasized civil service reform and—to attract Democratic support—advocated amnesty for all former Confederates and removal of troops from

THE GRANT SCANDALS
This cartoon pointed to Grant's inability or unwillingness to deal with corruption among his friends—like General William W. Belknap, who received a bribe of nearly $25,000 for an appointment he made at an army post (Fort Sills). In 1876 the House impeached Belknap, but Grant allowed him to escape conviction by accepting his resignation before the Senate could put him on trial. (The Bettmann Archive)

the South. For president, the Liberal Republicans nominated Horace Greeley, the influential editor and publisher of the *New York Tribune.*

The Democrats attempted to steal the Liberal's thunder by also nominating Greeley. However, they made their endorsement with no great enthusiasm. Greeley supported reconciliation with ex-Confederates, but he had earlier favored radical Reconstruction, and his support for high tariffs conflicted with those of the Democrats.

In the election of 1872, Grant won an even larger percentage of the popular vote—56 percent—than he had in 1868. He received a higher percentage of the popular vote than any candidate since Andrew Jackson in 1828. Grant carried every northern state. And, because Democrats had not yet established control over presidential voting in the South, he lost only Georgia and Texas in the states of the former Confederacy.

The issue of corruption in the Republican party erupted in 1873 as a series of government scandals came to light. A congressional committee confirmed newspaper reports, first published during the 1872 campaign, of a complicated deal in which high-ranking Republicans appeared to have cheated the taxpayers. The scandal centered on Crédit Mobilier, a construction company that contracted for work on the Union Pacific Railroad. It turned out that key Union Pacific stockholders also controlled Crédit Mobilier and had arranged for enormous purchases, sometimes for services never delivered, paid for in Union Pacific stock and federal subsidies, from Crédit Mobilier. To prevent a congressional investigation, the corporate insiders had sold Crédit Mobilier stock at a discount to several members of Congress. The Republican Congress, however, censured only Oakes Ames, a Massachusetts congressman who had been the agent for Crédit Mobilier.

An even more dramatic scandal involved the "Whiskey Ring," a network of large whiskey distillers and Treasury agents who defrauded the Treasury of excise taxes on liquor. The ring was organized by a mediocre Union general, John A. McDonald, whom Grant had appointed supervisor of internal revenue. It was centered in the major distilling centers of Saint Louis, Milwaukee, Chicago, and Indianapolis. Between 1868 and 1873, it diverted as much as $4 million from the Treasury. The conspirators divided the spoils among the distillers, the McDonald organization, and the campaign chests of the Republican party in the Midwest. The ring reached into the White House, where Grant's private secretary, Orville Babcock, kept a protective eye on McDonald's activities.

Secretary of the Treasury Benjamin Bristow destroyed the ring. Appointed in 1874, after his predecessor had resigned under charges of corruption, Bristow launched an extensive investigation. In 1875, he brought indictments against more than 350 distillers and government officials. More than 100 men went to prison, although the courts acquitted Babcock.

The Whiskey Ring scandal crushed whatever prospects Grant might have had for a third term. Grant was known to be a crony of Babcock's and to have gone to extraordinary lengths to protect him, despite his command to Bristow, "Let no guilty man escape." The scandals stung the public all the more for coming in the midst of a pro-

longed depression from 1873–1877. Nearly 15 percent of the labor force was unemployed by 1876, and thousands of farmers went bankrupt. Precipitating the depression was the Panic of 1873, which involved the bankruptcy of the Northern Pacific Railroad and its major investor, Jay Cooke. Cooke's favored role as a financier of the Civil War, and the extensive Republican subsidies to railroads, suggested to many Americans that Republican financial manipulations had caused the depression.

The ongoing depression, and the apparent unresponsiveness of the Grant administration to the widespread economic distress, further wounded Republicans. Especially damaging was the money issue. Rapidly decreasing prices prompted small farmers and other people heavily in debt to call for an inflated money supply that they hoped would stabilize prices. Republicans aggravated such people's distress by insisting that Civil War bondholders be paid back fully in gold, even though they had bought their bonds with devalued greenbacks and had received only the guarantee that the interest on the bonds would be paid in gold. In early 1874, the Democrats responded by pushing through Congress a bill that would have increased the number of greenbacks in circulation and eased the money pinch. But Grant vetoed it, fueling Democratic charges that Republicans served only the special interests of capitalists.

In the election of 1874, the Democrats gained in both houses of Congress and won a majority of the seats in the House of Representatives. For the first time since the war, they would control a branch of the federal government. Before the new Congress met in 1875, however, the lame-duck Republicans passed the Resumption Act of 1875. This act provided that the federal government would exchange gold for greenbacks. The new law not only made federal paper money as "good as gold," but it also added to the deflation.

The Political Crisis of 1877

Republican leaders entered the 1876 campaign in a spirit of foreboding. If they were to stem the Democratic momentum, they had to shake themselves free of the atmosphere of scandal that had grown up around Grant. They turned to a little-known Ohioan, Rutherford B. Hayes. Hayes had been governor of Ohio for three scandal-free terms. He had a good Civil War record, a reputation for honesty, and a record of support for civil service reform. He also was a moderate on Reconstruction and a former Whig whose strategy called for appealing to southern conservatives—especially former southern Whigs—to join the Republican cause.

For their part, the Democrats were determined to make the most of the Grant scandals. They nominated Governor Samuel J. Tilden of New York, who had built a political career on his reputation as a fighter of corruption. Tilden had helped break the control of an infamous Democratic machine, the Tweed Ring, over New York City politics. The party wrote a platform that emphasized reform, especially of the civil ser-

vice. They promised to save the nation from "a corrupt centralism which has honeycombed the offices of the Federal government itself with incapacity, waste, and fraud."

On election night, the outcome seemed clear. Headlines announced that Tilden had won. Democrats celebrated, and the Republican party plunged into gloom. In Ohio, Hayes simply went to bed, convinced he had been defeated. A majority of the voters, 52 percent, had supported Tilden. The Democrats had made deep inroads in the North, carrying New York, New Jersey, Connecticut, and Indiana. They apparently had swept every southern state.

But before dawn, at Republican campaign headquarters in New York City, two or three sleepless politicians put together a daring strategy. In three southern states—Louisiana, South

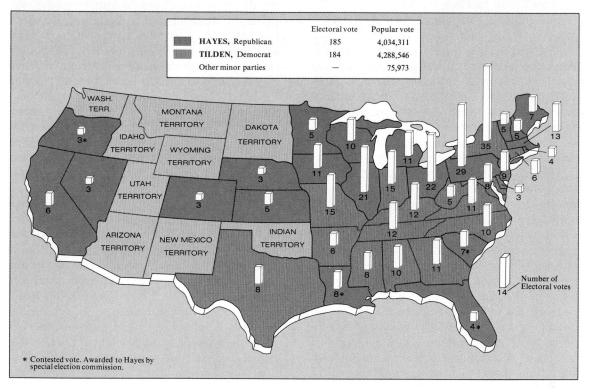

	Electoral vote	Popular vote
HAYES, Republican	185	4,034,311
TILDEN, Democrat	184	4,288,546
Other minor parties	—	75,973

* Contested vote. Awarded to Hayes by special election commission.

MAP 16.3 THE ELECTION OF 1876
The Democratic candidate, Tilden, made such inroads in Northern states that Hayes, the Republican candidate, could not win the electoral college without the contested votes of three states in the deep South, despite the fact that he carried most northern and western states.

ANTI-REPUBLICAN SENTIMENT, 1876
This Democratic cartoon portrays Union soldiers, with bayonets fixed, coercing blacks to vote
Republican. The carpet bag in the foreground identifies the politics of the civilian at the voting table.
To the far left, the individual casting a watchful eye on the proceedings is probably an ex-planter,
supposedly powerless in the new politics of the South. (Culver)

TIME LINE
THE UNION RECONSTRUCTED

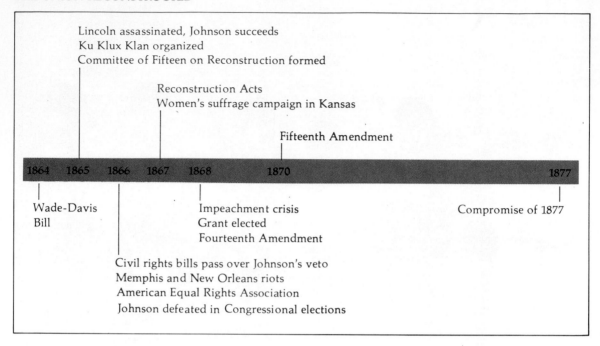

Carolina, and Florida—Republicans still controlled election procedures. If they could argue that Democratic fraud and intimidation had affected the election result in those states, they could certify Republican victories and report Republican electoral votes. Of course, newly elected Democratic officials in the three states would send in electoral votes for Tilden. As a result, there would be two sets of electoral votes from those states when Congress met to count the electoral votes early in 1877. If Congress accepted all the Republican votes, Hayes would have a one-vote electoral majority. The audacious announcement came: Hayes had carried the three southern states and won the election.

The months between the election in November and the inauguration the following March were filled with rumors: There might be a violent coup by Democrats if the Republicans tried to steal the election; President Grant might use the military to prevent Tilden from taking office; there might be a new election, or even be a new civil war. While the rumors flew, various inter-

ests tried to gain some advantage from the situation. Railroad promoters jockeyed for new federal subsidies, promising to deliver blocs of support in Congress to the party that made the best promises. Politicians on all sides flirted with the opposition, hoping for rewards.

In the end, political compromise and accident won out. Congress decided to appoint an Electoral Commission to settle the question. The commission would include seven Republicans and seven Democrats. The fifteenth and deciding vote would go to Justice David Davis of the Supreme Court, a man with a reputation for being free of party loyalty. But Davis resigned from the Court at the crucial moment, and the deciding vote fell to a lifelong Republican. When the commission completed its careful investigation of the election results in Florida, Louisiana, and South Carolina, the decision on each state was made by a straight party vote of eight to seven.

It next remained to be seen whether Congress would accept the result. The Senate was Republican, the House Democratic. Southern Democrats held the balance of power and Hayes's representatives sought their support. Some of these southerners were convinced that Hayes made promises to the "negotiators"—to confine federal troops to their barracks throughout the South, to appoint Democrats to major offices, and to support construction of a railroad across Texas to the West Coast. In any case, enough southerners in the House supported accepting the commission's findings to make Hayes president.

This sequence of events is often referred to as the Compromise of 1877, but historians remain uncertain whether any kind of deal was really struck. Hayes had promised in his campaign to end the military occupation of the South. He had also planned to appoint a few Democrats to his cabinet. And his faction of the Republican party did not support the Texas railroad scheme. The alleged compromise may have been a fiction created by southern Democrats to justify their votes for Hayes.

The only certainty was that Reconstruction had ended. Those who had wanted *restoration* could be satisfied that the southern states had returned to their "proper practical relation with the Union." Those who had sought *reconstruction* could boast of three amendments to the Constitution, the end of slavery, public schools for black children, and some access to the land for ex-slaves, even if it was mostly as debt-ridden sharecroppers and tenant farmers. Those who had favored *redemption* could point to the fact that all the southern states were now firmly in the control of southern politicians and voters.

---

*A*fter the Civil War ended in 1865, the Thirteenth Amendment made slavery unconstitutional. However, President Abraham Lincoln's plan for quickly restoring the Union encountered opposition from radical Republicans in Congress, who believed that ex-slaves must vote, and moderate Republicans, who wished to punish the South and establish their party in southern states. Lincoln was assassinated before he could negotiate a unified Republican position.

Possibilities for a swift sectional reconciliation continued into the administration of Andrew Johnson, but he could not satisfy both moderate Republicans and the defeated Confederacy. His difficulties in working with Congress resulted in an erratic policy that intensified the South's resistance to federal power.

Congressional Reconstruction extended the civil rights of ex-slaves through the Fourteenth Amendment, protected black suffrage through the Fifteenth Amendment, and encouraged the formation of southern state governments controlled by supporters of the Union. Northern Republicans, however, failed to equip these governments to defeat the old planter elite, which through appeals to racial solidarity, and by terror and intimidation, overturned all the Reconstruction state governments by 1877. Ex-slaves won some modest economic gains during Reconstruction, but without access to land ownership they became ensnared in a system of debt peonage and once again found themselves dependent on the planters.

In the North, Republicans enacted their entire economic program. Democrats attacked the program with a Jacksonian critique of "special privilege," but most northerners came out of the Civil War more receptive to concentrations of power. Many believed that the Republican program was necessary for sustained prosperity. Scandals during the Grant administration inflamed opposition to the Republicans but Republicans took the election of 1876 by capitalizing on the South's hunger for an end to Reconstruction and for greater influence in national politics. What is sometimes called the Compromise of 1877 kept the Republicans in control of the federal government by cementing an alliance with southern economic elites.

Suggestions for Further Reading

Presidential Restoration, Congressional Reconstruction

The most central studies of Reconstruction politics include Michael Les Benedict, *A Compromise of Principle: Congressional Republicans and Reconstruction* (1974); David Donald, *The Politics of Reconstruction 1863–1867* (1965); W. E. B. Du Bois, *Black Reconstruction* (1935); John Hope Franklin, *Reconstruction* (1965); Eric L. McKitrick, *Andrew Johnson and Reconstruction* (1966); Kenneth M. Stampp, *The Era of Reconstruction* (1965); and Hans L. Trefousse, *Impeachment of a President: Andrew Johnson, the Blacks, and Reconstruction* (1975).

The South During Reconstruction and the Plight of the Ex-Slaves

On conditions in the South during Reconstruction, including the experience of blacks, consult Robert Cruden, *The Negro in Reconstruction* (1969); Richard N. Current, *Three Carpetbag Governors* (1967); Robert Higgs, *Competition and Coercion: Blacks in the American Economy 1865–1914* (1977); Peter Kolchin, *First Freedom: The Responses of Alabama's Blacks to Emancipation and Reconstruction* (1972); Leon F. Litwack, *Been in the Storm So*

Long, *The Aftermath of Slavery* (1979); James M. McPherson, *The Abolitionist Legacy: From Reconstruction to the NAACP* (1975); Howard N. Rabinowitz, *Race Relations in the Urban South 1865–1890* (1977); Roger L. Ransom and Richard Sutch, *One Kind of Freedom, The Economic Consequences of Emancipation* (1977); Willie Lee Rose, *Rehearsal for Reconstruction, The Port Royal Experiment* (1964); Allen W. Trelease, *White Terror: The Ku Klux Klan Conspiracy and Southern Reconstruction* (1972); and Joel Williamson, *After Slavery: The Negro in South Carolina During Reconstruction 1861–1877* (1965).

The North During Reconstruction

On national politics after the Civil War, including the retreat from Reconstruction, see Paul H. Buck, *The Road to Reunion 1865–1900* (1937); Morton Keller, *Affairs of State: Public Life in Late Nineteenth Century America* (1977); Robert Kelley, *The Transatlantic Persuasion, The Liberal–Democratic Mind in the Age of Gladstone* (1968); William S. McFeely, *Grant: A Biography* (1981); K. I. Polakoff, *The Politics of Inertia: The Election of 1876 and the End of Reconstruction* (1973); John G. Sproat, *"The Best Men": Liberal Reformers in the Gilded Age* (1968); and C. Vann Woodward, *Reunion and Reaction* (1956).

17

THE NEW INDUSTRIAL ORDER

During the last three decades of the nineteenth century, the productive capacity of the United States reached phenomenal levels. The gross national product—that is, the value of goods and services produced—increased six-fold between 1869 and 1899. This productive growth was linked above all to the industrializing sector of the economy. Manufacturing, which had accounted for roughly a third of total commodity output in 1869, accounted for more than half in 1899. By this time, the signs of industrialization could be seen almost everywhere—an industrial labor force of about nine million persons, a landscape of factories and mines, and two hundred thousand miles of railroad tracks.

Fundamentally, however, no break had occurred from the nation's industrial past. The essential characteristic of modern economic development is its capacity for sustained gains in economic efficiency—in obtaining a continually increasing output from a given input of labor and capital. Rising productivity is the basic difference between modern and preindustrial economies. A nation with a preindustrial economy might have a high standard of living, if it has abundant natural resources or a favorable population-to-land ratio. But such societies lack the means to become more efficient. The American colonies, for example, were prosperous at an early point. Only late in the colonial period, however, did the first signs of rising productivity appear. Sustained productivity gains began more than three decades before the Civil War. In the late nineteenth century, the United States maintained and gradually increased the momentum for higher productivity set in motion during the earlier stages of its industrial revolution.

The cumulative impact of industrialization made late nineteenth-century Americans keenly aware that they lived in a new age. What had been partial and limited became general and widespread. America turned into a land of factories, machines, and railroads.

New patterns of business organization were devised. For the first time, enterprise was conducted on a large scale. This, in turn, necessitated new ways of thinking about how to run a business. Methods of modern management emerged.

Working people deeply felt the effects of industrialization. Craft traditions came into sharp conflict with the mechanized factory. The demand for workers stimulated a mass migration of rural people, mainly from European villages, into American industry. After much trial and error, the modern trade-union movement began. Industrialism had become America's way of life.

A Maturing Industrial Economy

Before the Civil War, industrialism in America was overshadowed by a larger agricultural economy. The United States had a national transportation network, but it was based on rivers and canals, not railroads. There was a factory system, but it was limited to producing light consumer goods, such as boots, textiles, and clocks. There also was keen entrepreneurship, but no systematic management or large-scale enterprise. America's industrial revolution had started. It was completed in the late nineteenth century.

The Railroads

The maturing industrial economy required, above all, a transportation system capable of welding the nation into a vast, unified market. Until around 1850, transportation on canals and rivers had kept pace with the interior development of the country. But these waterways did not extend much beyond the Mississippi River. And, while suitable for bulky raw materials, canal barges and riverboats could not provide the year-round, on-time service demanded by the growing industrial and commercial sectors of the economy. Railroads performed this task far better. They had started in the 1830s as feeders for the river and canal traffic but quickly grew into

a system rivaling water transportation. By the 1860s, the dominance of the railroads was assured for both goods and passengers.

Railroad construction burst ahead during the postwar era. In 1870, the nation had about fifty-three thousand miles of track. Most of it lay east of the Mississippi, but it included the first transcontinental railroad linking the Pacific Coast to the rest of the nation. Between 1870 and 1882, the rail network doubled in size, mainly as a result of construction west of the Mississippi and across the continent into southern California and the Pacific Northwest. A final surge of building, which doubled the amount of track again by 1902, filled in the gaps in the South and elsewhere. In 1914, the U.S. railroad network covered over 250,000 miles, more than the rest of the world combined. Virtually every populated area in the country had come within reach of railroad service.

Railroad transportation became highly efficient. The early system, built by competing local companies, had been a jumble of discontinuous segments. Gauges of track varied widely and physical connections were lacking at terminal points between railroads. Many rivers had no railroad bridge. Also, each railroad company reserved the use of its track exclusively for its own equipment. As late as 1880, a shipment of heavy textile machinery had to go through eight transfers en route from Massachusetts to South Carolina.

CENTRAL PACIFIC'S CRACK ENGINE NO. 149
The railroads created a new notion of time. How fast could a person cross the continent? In 1876, a troupe of actors, scheduled to present Shakespeare's *Henry V* in San Francisco, made the trip from New York City in eighty-four hours, a new record. The Central Pacific's engine No. 149 carried them at top speed on the last leg from Ogden, Utah. (Southern Pacific Transportation Company)

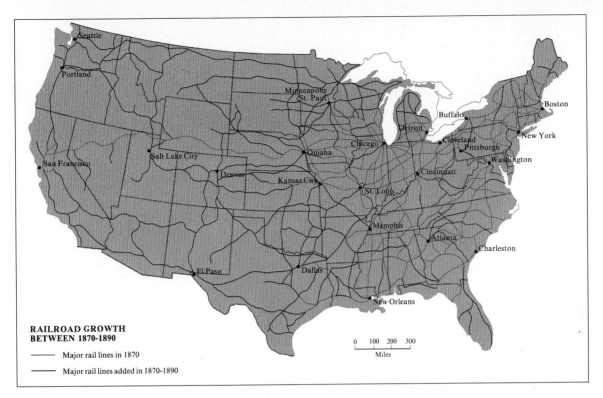

MAP 17.1 EXPANSION OF THE RAILROAD SYSTEM, 1870–1900
In 1870, the nation had 53,000 miles of rail track; in 1890, 167,000 miles. That burst of construction essentially completed the nation's rail network. Statistics confirm what a visual inspection of the map tells us. The main areas of expansion were in the South and west of the Mississippi. The Great Plains and intermountain sectors accounted for over 40 percent of all construction from 1870 onward. By 1890, the West was well served, both in the Pacific northwest and the southwest.

Beginning with the Civil War years, however, pressures increased for integration of the railroad. Track was hastily laid through Philadelphia, Richmond, and other cities in both the North and South to transport huge shipments of troops and equipment. The postwar economy, as it grew more complex and interdependent, demanded a better-organized rail system. Much railroad integration took place through the expansion of the great trunk lines connecting different regions of the country. The Pennsylvania and New York Central railroads pushed west from the East Coast to the Midwest, and the Illinois Central and the Burlington thrust south and west from Chicago. By the end of the 1880s, a standard rail gauge had been adopted across the country. Through the use of fast-freight firms and elaborate accounting procedures among railroads, the network served shippers as if it were a single unit. Breaks in transit, freight transfers between cars, and other causes of delayed rail service became as obsolete by 1900 as handwoven cloth might have seemed back in 1850.

At the same time, railroad technology was advancing. Heavier locomotives with four sets of driving wheels nearly tripled the pulling power of freight trains between 1866 and the turn of the century. To control the great mass and length of the freight trains, George Westinghouse invented the automatic coupler, the air brake, and friction gear for starting and stopping a long line of cars. Beginning in the 1870s, iron rails gave way to steel rails capable of withstanding the tremendous stress and heavy use of the latest freight traffic.

Integrated service and advancing technology increased the efficiency of the railroads. Productivity gains for the carriers advanced more rapidly than for the economy as a whole, averaging 2 percent a year between 1870 and 1910. These increases resulted in a sharp drop in freight rates from 1.12 cents per ton-mile in 1870 to 0.75 cents in 1910.

Considered as a transportation system, the railroads brilliantly met the needs of the maturing industrial economy. However, the dynamism that underlay this achievement did not stem from any orderly plan or design, but from the competitive energy of a free-wheeling market economy. The federal, state, and city governments provided assistance, especially before the 1870s, through extensive land grants and a variety of financial aids. But the actual enterprise of building railroads remained, with a few early exceptions, entirely in private hands.

Railroad construction differed from other kinds of nineteenth-century enterprise because it required, more than anything else, enormous amounts of capital. That was why—long before other businesses did so—the railroads organized themselves as corporations capable of raising funds from the public through the sale of stocks and bonds. Finance became the central arena of entrepreneurial activity in railroading.

The key figures were those with access to capital—their own and/or that of others. For example, John Murray Forbes, a Bostonian who had made his fortune in the China trade, went on to develop the Chicago, Burlington and Quincy Railroad into the preeminent midwestern system by the 1870s. A more aggressive figure was Cornelius Vanderbilt, who left the steamboat business in 1863 to invest his fortune in the New York Central. Vanderbilt and his son William built the Central into an east-west trunk line rivaled only by the Pennsylvania Railroad. They did so primarily through the acquisition of connecting lines and an intensive construction program. Forbes and the Vanderbilts aimed at creating well-constructed, well-financed railroad systems.

Jay Gould, a very different kind of rail entrepreneur, started out as a stock-market speculator. Gould earned early notoriety by his amazing manipulation of Erie Railroad stock in the 1860s and his nearly successful corner of the gold market in 1869. Many people at the time—and historians long after—considered Gould a "robber baron," one who loots commerce and gives nothing in return. But Gould did give something

in return. His great talent lay in gaining control over weak properties—the Erie, the Union Pacific, the Wabash, and the Southwest lines during the 1880s—and making them turn a profit. Some of this success came from stock manipulation, but Gould also earned his money by the kind of management he gave his railroads. He cared little for improving his properties, but he was a fierce competitor—for good reason. Gould's railroads generally had heavy bonded indebtedness, and only a high volume of traffic enabled them to meet the interest charges. His wealthier rivals, such as Forbes and the Vanderbilts, bitterly resented his ruthless rate-cutting tactics, but shippers and consumers benefited from the lower transportation costs that resulted. Gould's stock speculations also had the effect of attracting fresh capital into the railroad industry, money that might not otherwise have gone there. In the free-market economy in which American railroads grew, even a buccaneer like Jay Gould made a positive contribution.

Railroad development in the United States was often sordid, fiercely competitive, and subject to boom and bust. When the panic of 1893 hit, fully a third of the industry (by track mileage) went into receivership. Yet vast sums of capital were raised—$15 billion by 1914—and an integrated, highly advanced transportation system emerged.

Basic Industry

The nation's first manufacturing industries—textiles, boots and shoes, paper, and furniture—had been very much a part of the larger agricultural economy. They processed farm and forest materials and relied on the traditional sources of hand and water power. These industries made primarily consumer goods that substituted for homemade or artisan-made products. In the early industrial economy before 1850, there was not much call for heavy industry. It took increasing demands from such fields as railroad building, urban construction, and metal fabrication to develop a substructure of the mining and metal-processing industry.

Central to this development was iron making, which had become extensive well before the Civil War. The early iron makers engaged in small-batch production of wrought iron, a malleable metal ideal for use on farms and in small shops. In 1856, the English inventor Sir Henry Bessemer perfected a new process for refining iron. Unlike the puddling furnaces that made wrought iron, Bessemer converters produced steel, a harder, more durable metal, and did so in large amounts with little labor. Others took up this invention earlier, but Andrew Carnegie demonstrated its revolutionary importance.

Carnegie, an all-American success story, had arrived from Scotland in 1848 at the age of

TABLE 17.1 INCREASING OUTPUT OF HEAVY INDUSTRY, 1870–1910

	Bituminous Coal (Thousands of tons)	Rolled iron and steel (Thousands of tons)	Copper (tons)	Industrial machinery (in millions of dollars)
1870	20,471	850*	14,112	110.4**
1880	50,757	3,301	30,240	98.6***
1890	111,302	6,746	129,882	185.6
1900	212,318	10,626	303,059	347.6
1910	417,111	24,216	544,119	512.4

*Approximate total.
**Data for 1869.
***Data for 1874.

twelve with his poverty-stricken family. He became a telegraph operator and then went to work for the Pennsylvania Railroad, where he rapidly climbed the managerial ladder. Carnegie resigned in 1865, wealthy from a series of successful speculations, to manufacture iron bridges for the railroads. Keenly aware of the possibilities of the Bessemer converter, Carnegie embarked in 1872 on a project aimed at the fullest exploitation of the new refining process. He built a massive steel-rail mill outside of Pittsburgh that had the most advanced equipment of the day. Equally important, the mill integrated all the stages of production—smelting, refining, and rolling—into a single operation that began with iron ore and ended with finished steel rails. Carnegie's mill, called the Edgar Thompson Works, fully repaid its investment in a few years, and came to be a model for the modern steel industry. Large, integrated steel plants swiftly replaced the older blast furnaces and puddling mills, and steel became a product essential for the further industrial growth of the nation.

The production of copper and other noniron metals went through a similar development. Copper output grew phenomenally, from eight thousand tons in 1860 to eight hundred thousand tons in 1914. Simultaneously, a change occurred in the use of copper. It had been used mainly for household products until the Civil War. Now it became a key ingredient in oil refining, the production of electrical generators and such other new fields as telephone communication.

The growth of the metal industries depended on the intensive exploitation of the country's mineral resources. Major discoveries of rich iron ore deposits occurred from the 1850s onward,

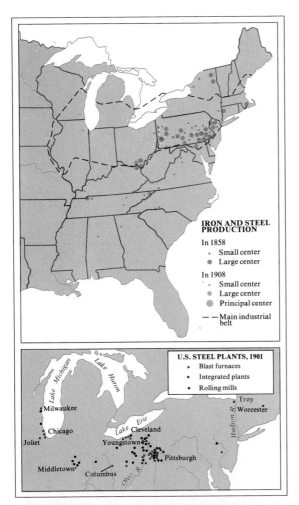

MAP 17.2 CHANGING PATTERN OF IRON AND STEEL PRODUCTION

Before the Civil War, the iron industry was concentrated in eastern Pennsylvania and northern New Jersey. During the late nineteenth century, the rapid development of the railroads and manufacturing spurred growth in steel production. The industry shifted westward, with a new trend toward integrated mills exemplified by the network of U.S. Steel Corporation plants around Pittsburgh.

IRON AND STEEL

Iron was not a product new to the nineteenth century in the sense that plastic was new to the twentieth century. Early Europeans made iron tools and weapons at least a thousand years before Christ. Nor did the underlying processes change, for they are dictated by the nature of iron metallurgy. Iron ore must be smelted into metal; the raw metal must be refined to acquire desired properties such as malleability or hardness; and the refined iron must be shaped into useable forms. What did begin to change, slowly at first, were the techniques for carrying out these processes. Only as iron became available in large quantities and at low cost could the Industrial Revolution proceed.

Metallurgical innovation took place in two great waves. The first began in smelting late in the Middle Ages, when blast furnaces appeared in Belgium around 1340. Ore was melted in a charcoal-burning furnace to which limestone had been added. A blast of air then set off a combustion process that combined carbon from the charcoal with the molten iron while its impurities combined with the limestone to form a slag. The slag was drawn off from the top of the furnace while the molten iron was tapped from the bottom into

sand forms resembling piglets feeding from a sow—hence the term "pig iron."

By the eighteenth century, the shortage of wood for charcoal had become acute in England. The substitution of coke, made by superheating coal, broke this bottleneck in iron production. An improved refining furnace, with separate chambers for the fuel and iron, was also developing. In 1784, Henry Cort invented the puddling furnace. Molten iron collected in the hollowed-out bottom, where it was worked with a long bar or paddle by hand from the outside. The resulting product was a malleable iron called *wrought iron*. Cort also made a crucial advance in the finishing stage at this time. For the laborious hammering process, he substituted the rolling mill, which shaped iron as it passed through grooved rolls.

This iron technology—blast furnace, puddling furnace, and rolling mill—formed the metallurgical basis for England's industrial revolution in the first half of the nineteenth century. Endowed with ample forests, the United States was slow to adopt the coke-using technology, but by 1860 it had caught up fairly well with England technologically and was producing nearly a million tons of iron annually. The

iron industry, as it had developed to this point, met America's needs very well. Wrought iron was admirably suited for farm use because it was malleable and easily worked, and was also suitable for the localized machine- and engine-building characteristic of early industrialism. But wrought iron was too soft for the increasingly heavy service it received as railroad track. The search for a harder, more durable metal resulted in the invention in 1856 of an entirely different refining process by Henry Bessemer, an Englishman.

The Bessemer converter was a pear-shaped, tilting vessel open at the top, with a bottom perforated by many holes. Molten pig iron flowed into the top while the converter was tilted on its side. Air was blasted at great force through the perforated bottom, and the converter then swung back to its upright position. The resulting combustion set off a spectacular display of flame and smoke. Within fifteen minutes, the impurities in the molten iron had burned off and the flames died down. The converter was again tilted on its side and, after manganese and other chemicals had been added, the purified iron was emptied into ingot molds.

The refined metal, called *steel*,

first in upper Michigan and then in the huge Mesabi Range of Minnesota. These ores were readily shipped down the Great Lakes to the great steel-making centers in Illinois, Ohio, and Pennsylvania. Michigan was also the site of the first major copper finds before the Civil War, followed by discoveries in Arizona in the 1870s, and in the more extensive Montana fields during

the 1880s. With the invention of the flotation refining process, it became possible to utilize the lower-grade copper ores of these western fields. Coal mining, a minor enterprise before 1850, grew rapidly thereafter, first in the anthracite region of eastern Pennsylvania, and then in the soft-coal Appalachian fields from West Virginia through western Pennsylvania and into Ohio.

had a hardness somewhere between that of wrought iron and the expensive crucible steel that had long been used for fine tools and weapons. The Bessemer process had one significant drawback; it operated successfully only with expensive, low-phosphorous iron. The open-hearth method, developed shortly after the Bessemer process, could handle low-quality iron and was more economical and flexible. By World War I, the open-hearth method was rapidly becoming the dominant refining process. But the Bessemer converter had given life to the modern steel industry.

The device that Bessemer had invented to produce a better metal also proved vastly more efficient than the hand-operated puddling furnace. The Bessemer converter turned out great quantities of steel with virtually no labor. This forced changes up and down the line. To feed the converters' appetite for pig iron, blast furnaces grew ever larger and, with the introduction of the hot blast, much more efficient. To handle the flow of steel from the converters, rolling mills became increasingly mechanized and automatic, so that the steel could move continuously through progressively narrower rolls set in tandem. By means of

a variety of metal-handling devices, the stages of production became integrated, enabling the iron to proceed "with perfect regularity" from the blast furnace to the Bessemer converter to its emergence from the rolling mill as a finished rail or girder. The integrated steel plant of 1900, capable of producing twenty-five hundred tons or more a day, was vastly more efficient than the small blast furnaces and iron mills of 1860.

The revolution in steelmaking changed the face of American industrialism. The geographic concentration of industrial activity intensified. The places best located in relation to raw materials, transportation, and markets—Pittsburgh, the steel towns along the Great Lakes, and Birmingham, Alabama—became the great centers of steel production.

A second result involved the scale of business enterprise. The principal steel companies evolved into vertically integrated firms that controlled their own raw materials, some of their transport facilities, and the marketing of their products. For the workers, the effects were no less sweeping. The skills of the puddler, heater, and hand roller became obsolete; gang labor was largely replaced by ore- and metal-handling equipment; and face-to-

face relationships with employers disappeared. The typical steelworker of 1900 was a machine-tender in an impersonal, bureaucratic business organization.

Steel made possible dramatic changes in transportation and construction. With steel rails capable of withstanding heavy traffic, and steel locomotives capable of ever greater pulling power, the railroads became the primary carriers of the nation's enormous volume of goods. The efficiency of the railroads rose nearly 70 percent between 1870 and 1900, and freight charges per ton-mile fell by almost the same amount—thanks largely to the use of steel for rails and equipment. In the growth of America's cities, steel played a key role in the construction of skyscrapers, trolley lines, and subways, and the vast underground complexes of pipe that supplied the urban millions with water and gas and carried away their sewage. Steel battleships asserted the nation's new role as a world power. Without steel, the emerging automobile industry would not have grown, nor a host of other American industries. It is no wonder that historians have called the last decades of the nineteenth century America's Age of Steel.

Coal production, scarcely half a million tons in 1860, reached 270 million tons in 1900.

Coal, in turn, was the key to the intensive use of energy in industrial production. The steam engine, limited initially to service as a power source for ships and locomotives, came into increasing use as a driver of machinery during the second half of the century. Steam was as impor-

tant as water power for industrial purposes by 1870, and six times as important twenty years later. At the Philadelphia Centennial Exhibition of 1876, visitors gazed in wonder at the enormous Corliss reciprocating engine, shown on page 520, with a fly wheel thirty feet in diameter and the capacity to drive all the other exhibits in Machinery Hall.

Steam power became increasingly efficient, first through refinements in the reciprocating engine, then by means of the steam turbine in the 1880s, and finally by coupling the steam turbine to the electric generator in the 1890s. The transformation of coal energy into electric power greatly increased the flexibility of industry. Once electricity could be drawn from distant generating plants, the power needs of factories no longer dictated where they would be located. And, as small electric motors became the power source for machines, factory design no longer was determined by the transmission of power by belts and shafts from the plant's steam engines. These advantages led to the rapid adoption of electric power by manufacturers after 1900.

Following the Civil War, the modern metal-producing industries were established, the nation's mineral resources came under intensive exploitation, and energy was harnessed to the manufacturing system. Production of steel, coal, and horsepower grew after 1870 at rates far exceeding that of manufacturing production. The industrial substructure came into its own during this period, enabling the manufacturing economy to forge ahead rapidly.

Mass Markets and Large-Scale Enterprise

Meanwhile, business organization underwent fundamental change. Until well into the industrial age, economic activity had characteristically been carried on in small units. Now, for the first time, American enterprise became big business.

Early manufacturers had typically produced in limited quantities, mainly for nearby markets. No firm tried to control the flow of its product very far through the industrial process. As distribution widened, producers relied on wholesale merchants and commission agents to market their goods. From the making of raw materials at one end, goods normally passed through numerous hands on their way to the final sale to the customer. Both industry and commerce were carried on by many small, independent entrepreneurs. Shops and factories had an average of about eight employees in 1870.

Then the scale of economic activity began to change markedly. "Combinations of capital on a scale hitherto wholly unprecedented constitute one of the remarkable features of modern business methods," the economist David A. Wells

THE CORLISS ENGINE
The symbol of the Philadelphia Centennial in 1876 was the great Corliss engine, which towered over Machinery Hall and powered all the equipment on exhibit there. Yet, the Corliss engine also signified the incomplete nature of American industrialism at that time; it soon became obsolete. Westinghouse turbines generating electricity would power the nation's next great world's fair, held in Chicago in 1893. (Culver)

wrote in 1889. He already could see "no other way in which the work of production and distribution can be prosecuted." The increasing scale of enterprise seemed "in a certain and large sense, not voluntary on the part of the possessors and controllers of capital, but necessary or even compulsory."

What was there in the nation's economic activity that led to Wells's sense of inevitability? The dynamic features of American growth—availability of capital, receptivity to technology, and the emergence of a heavy industrial base—certainly played a part. They enabled large-scale enterprise to occur. But the key lay in the American market. Immigration and a very high birthrate swelled the population. People flocked into the cities, and the railroads brought these dense consuming markets within the reach of distant producers. The telegraph, which came into widespread use by the Civil War, eliminated communications barriers. Unlike Europe, America was not carved up into many national markets; no political frontiers impeded the flow of goods within the country. Nowhere else did manufacturers have an internal market so vast and accessible for their products.

The impact of the expanding markets on the scale of enterprise can best be seen in the fresh-meat trade. Until the Civil War, this business had hardly changed since the preindustrial era. In every city, butchers purchased livestock directly from nearby farmers and butchered the animals in local slaughterhouses. The diet of city dwellers, especially the poor, depended mostly on salt pork and smoked pork.

With the coming of the railroads, a partial revolution occurred in the fresh-meat business. Cattle raising shifted to the grazing ranges of the Great Plains and to feed lots in the Corn Belt of the prairie states. Chicago, the rail terminal for the upper Midwest, established itself as the hub of the American meat trade. The Union Stock Yards, which opened in Chicago in 1865, immediately became the world's greatest livestock market. Cattle were shipped by railroad from Chicago to eastern cities, where, as before, they were slaughtered in local "butchertowns." By means of regional specialization and an efficient rail network, the meat trade serviced an exploding urban population and, without further development, might have done so indefinitely.

Gustavus F. Swift, a shrewd Massachusetts cattle dealer who settled in Chicago in 1875, saw the future differently. The system of marketing fresh meat seemed inefficient to him. Livestock deteriorated enroute to the East, and local slaughterhouses wasted by-products and labor. Production might be concentrated in Chicago, as it already was for preserved pork products, if dressed beef could be kept fresh in transit. The Chicago pork-packing plants had converted to year-round operation in the 1860s through the development of primitive refrigeration. After Swift's engineers solved the problem of air circulation, he built a fleet of refrigerator cars and established a central beef-packing house at the Chicago stockyards.

This was only the beginning of Swift's activities. No refrigerated warehouses were available in the cities to which he shipped chilled beef, so Swift had to build his own network of branch houses. Then he established a fleet of wagons to distribute his products to retail butcher shops. Swift constructed additional facilities to handle the fertilizer, chemicals, and other usable by-products from his slaughtering operations, and he took on other perishable commodities, including dairy products, to fully utilize his refrigerated cars and branch houses. As the demand grew, he built more packing houses in other stockyards centers, such as Kansas City, Fort Worth, and Omaha.

Step by step, Swift created a new kind of enterprise, the vertically integrated firm—that is, a national company capable of handling within its own structure all the functions of an entire industry. In effect, Swift and Company replaced a large number of small firms that had operated locally. Four other meat packers, which, like Armour and Company, had originated as pork packers, followed Swift's lead. By the end of the 1890s, these firms, all of them nationally organized and vertically integrated, produced nearly 90 percent of all the meat shipped in interstate commerce.

The development of the refrigerator car had made all this possible in the fresh-meat trade. In most other fields, no such single event was so decisive. But other manufacturers did share Swift's perception that the essential step was to identify a mass market. They, like Swift, moved quickly to set up national distribution systems to reach that market. The Singer Sewing Machine Company formed its own sales organization, using both retail stores and door-to-door salesmen. The McCormick Harvesting Machine Company set up a franchise network of dealers. Through such distribution systems, manufacturers provided technical information, credit, and repair facilities for their products. These companies, as did the meat packers, became vertically integrated firms that served a national market.

To gain the benefits of mass distribution, retail business went through a comparable change. Montgomery Ward and Company and Sears, Roebuck and Company developed into national mail-order houses for rural consumers. From Vermont to California, farm families selected identical goods from mail-order catalogues, and became part of the nationwide consumer market. In the cities, mass distribution followed different strategies. Department stores, pioneered by John Wanamaker in Philadelphia, spread to every substantial city in the country. Sometimes this growth occurred through the efforts of a wholesale merchant, but more often—as with R. H. Macy of New York—it came through the addition of departments to a dry goods store. An alternative route to urban distribution was the establishment of extensive chain store systems, in which the Great Atlantic and Pacific Tea Company and the F. W. Woolworth Company were the leaders. Woolworth used the slogan "Large purchases for cash direct from manufacturers explain the high values we offer."

American society prepared citizens to be consumers of standardized goods. The high rate of geographic movement broke down loyalties to local custom and regional distinctiveness that were so strong in Europe. Social class in America, though by no means absent, was blurred at the edges. Equally important, it did not involve special symbols of appearance. Foreign visitors often noted that ready-made clothing made it difficult to tell shop girls from debutantes on the city streets.

The receptivity to standardized goods should not be exaggerated. For example, Gustavus Swift encountered great resistance to his Chicago beef. How could it be wholesome weeks later in Boston or Philadelphia? Cheap prices helped, but advertising perhaps had a greater influence. Modern advertising was born during the late nineteenth century, bringing brand names and

QUAKER OATS
Like crackers, sugar, and other nonperishable foods, oatmeal had traditionally been marketed to consumers in bulk from barrels. In 1882, the grain merchant Henry P. Cowell completed the first continuous-process mill for oatmeal, cutting production costs and greatly increasing output. He also struck on the idea of selling oatmeal in boxes of standard size and weight to a national market. Broadsides showing the Quaker Oats man soon appeared in every American town, advertising a product of reliable quality and uniform price. (Collection of Business Americana, Smithsonian Institution, Courtesy of Quaker Oats Company)

an urban landscape increasingly cluttered by billboards and signs. By 1900, advertisers spent more than $90 million annually for space in newspapers and magazines. Advertisements urged readers to bathe with Pears' soap, to munch Uneeda biscuits, to sew on a Singer machine, and to snap pictures with a Kodak camera. The shaping of these tastes became a major function of American business. An increasing amount of entrepreneurial effort went into the active molding of demand for brand names.

In heavy industry, on the other hand, markets required neither the active shaping, nor the extensive distribution systems called for in selling consumer goods. Steel companies, which sold mostly to such large users as railroads and bridge builders, did not develop extensive marketing organizations. But they did need reliable supplies of raw materials. Andrew Carnegie saw this most clearly. By 1900, he had made his steel company fully self-contained. He had acquired his own coal and iron mines, and built a fleet of ore boats and connecting railroads to carry the raw materials to his western Pennsylvania mills. Other basic steel producers followed this pattern as best they could, and so did the big firms in oil, copper, explosives, and other fields dependent on mined materials. The motive of all these companies was primarily defensive. In a world of limited resources, the big user did well to corner his share before others grabbed it.

Heavy industry thus followed a different pattern of vertical integration—back toward raw materials rather than forward toward the consumer. But in either case, the result was the vertically integrated firm.

Mass Production

Mass marketing, which caused a revolution in American business organization, had an equally decisive effect on production methods. Once products became standardized and production became high-volume, changes in manufacturing processes followed almost inevitably. After the Civil War, as mass marketing expanded, mass production systems came into their own.

For example, great advances accompanied the creation of a national market for dressed beef. The huge packing houses that sprang up in Chicago quickly improved the traditional methods of killing and processing cattle. At the Armour plant in 1907, the work was divided into seventy-eight distinct jobs. Workers performed all these tasks extremely efficiently and at high speed as the carcasses moved along hooked to overhead conveyors. In a ten-hour day, a gang of 157 workers handled 1,050 cattle, many more per employee than if one skilled butcher did everything. Machinery did not replace workers; rather savings resulted from a minute division of labor.

The concept of mass production could be applied even outside factories. The women's clothing industry discovered that the division of tasks might be organized efficiently through a system of subcontracting. Cloth, after being cut in the central shop, was sent out to be sewn and finished in small shops. It often went through further distribution as homework to be done in the shabby tenements of immigrant ghettos in large cities. This was called a "sweated" trade because the low piece rates paid for the work forced people to work extremely long hours and usually involved the labor of wives and children. The production of women's clothing, though performed largely outside of factories, was a genuine mass production industry. It manufactured large volumes of standardized goods at low cost.

The main thrust, however, was toward the large factory, and the central method was mechanization. After work had been subdivided into simple, repetitive tasks, machines generally could be designed to replace hand labor. The main opportunity to do so came with products that could be assembled from standardized, interchangeable parts. These items included agricultural implements, sewing machines, typewriters, and bicycles. The advantages of mass production for such products had been evident to such early inventor-entrepreneurs as Eli Whitney and Simeon North in the manufacture of guns and clocks. But it had taken many years to devise metal-cutting machines—the machine tools—that were speedy, automatic, and, above all, precise. It was essential to eliminate the need for "fitting"—that is, the costly hand-filing of parts before they could be assembled. A separate industry had emerged by the Civil War that specialized in machine tools for new industries making products assembled from interchangeable parts. The machine-tool industry did most of the innovative work, culminating in the turret lathe. This machine made a complex series of cuts automatically and with great speed and accuracy.

The brilliant inventive process that resulted in the turret lathe was directed at the manufacture of high-volume standardized goods. This connection between technology and markets could be seen vividly in the automobile industry. The "horseless carriage," a curiosity when it first appeared in the 1890s, quickly became serious business. By 1900, about eight thousand cars were chugging along the nation's roads. Most of the early buyers were wealthy, but the future of the automobile lay with the development of a mass market.

Of the pioneer car makers, Henry Ford saw this fact most clearly. Ford was the classic tinkerer turned manufacturer. Born on a Michigan farm in 1863, he had moved to Detroit and worked as a machinist at the Edison Illuminating Company. Like many others, Ford became fascinated by automobiles, especially racing cars.

ℋENRY FORD: MASS PRODUCING THE MODEL T

During the season 1908–1909 we continued to make Models "R" and "S," four-cylinder runabouts and roadsters, the models that had previously been so successful. . . . But "Model T" swept them right out. We sold 10,607 cars—a larger number than any manufacturer had ever sold. The price for the touring car was $850. . . . This season demonstrated conclusively to me that it was time to put the new policy in force. . . . Therefore in 1909 I announced one morning, without any previous warning, that in the future we were going to build only one model, that the model was going to be "Model T," and that the chassis would be exactly the same for all cars, and I remarked:

"Any customer can have a car painted any color that he wants so long as it is black."

I cannot say that any one agreed with me. The selling people could not of course see the advantages that a single model would bring about in production. . . . They thought that our production was good enough as it was and there was a very decided opinion that lowering the sales price would hurt sales . . . The impression was that a good car could not be built at a low price, and that, anyhow, there was no use in building a low-priced car because only wealthy people were in the market for cars. . . .

We were, almost overnight it seems, in great production. How did all this come about?

Simply through the application of an inevitable principle. By the application of intelligently directed power and machinery. In a little dark shop on a side street an old man had labored for years making axe handles. Out of seasoned hickory he fashioned them, with the help of a draw shave, a chisel, and a supply of sandpaper. Carefully was each handle weighed and balanced. No two of them were alike. . . . His average product was eight handles a week. . . . And often some of these were unsaleable—because the balance was not true.

Today you can buy a better axe handle, made by machinery, for a few cents. And you need not worry about the balance. They are all alike—and every one is perfect. Modern methods applied in a big way have not only brought the cost of axe handles down to a fraction of their former cost—but they have immensely improved the product.

It was the application of these same methods to the making of the Ford car that at the very start lowered the price and heightened the quality. . . .

A Ford car contains about five thousand parts—that is counting screws, nuts, and all. Some of the parts are fairly bulky and others are almost the size of watch parts. In our first assembling we simply started to put a car together at a spot on the floor and workmen brought to it the parts as they were needed in exactly the same way that one builds a house. . . .

The first step forward in assembly came when we began taking the work to the men instead of the men to the work. We now have two general principles . . . a man shall never have to take more than one step . . . [and] no man need ever stoop over.

Along about April 1, 1913, we first tried the experiment of an assembly line. We tried it on assembling the fly-wheel magneto. We try everything in a little way first—we will rip out anything once we discover a better way, but we have to know absolutely that the new way is going to be better than the old before we do anything drastic.

I believe that this was the first moving line ever installed. The idea came in a general way from the overhead trolley that the Chicago packers use in dressing beef. We had previously assembled the fly-wheel magneto in the usual method. With one workman doing a complete job he could turn out from thirty-five to forty pieces in a nine-hour day, or about twenty minutes to an assembly. What he did alone was then spread into twenty-nine operations; that cut down the assembly time to thirteen minutes, ten seconds. Then we raised the height of the line eight inches—this was in 1914—and cut the time to seven minutes. Further experimenting with the speed that the work should move at cut the time down to five minutes. In short, the result is this: by the aid of scientific study one man is now able to do somewhat more than four did only a comparatively few years ago.

MODEL T'S
Henry Ford introduced his Model T in 1908. He became a pioneer in the use of assembly line techniques, and the Ford Motor Company sold more than fifteen million Model T's during the next nineteen years. Ford mass-produced his cars by making them all alike, ". . . just like one pin is like another pin . . ." Here, workers complete final assembly. (The Bettmann Archive)

His interest quickly shifted after he launched his own company in 1903 with the aid of wealthy backers. "I will build a motor car for the multitude," Ford declared. This car was the Model T, which Ford introduced in 1908. It was designed specifically to match his conception of mass production of automobiles:

> The way to make automobiles is to make one automobile just like another automobile, to make them all alike, to make them come through the factory alike—just like one pin is like another pin when it comes from the pin factory.

If the pin was the simplest mass-produced item, the automobile was the most complex. But volume and standardization made it subject to the same principles of production.

Assembly was the bottleneck. Even after the parts of a car had been mass-produced, the vehicle was still assembled individually by skilled craftsmen. In a stroke of genius, Ford proposed that the assembly of automobiles also be broken down into simple, repetitive tasks. This could be accomplished by moving the unfinished vehicle past a series of work stations on a continuous motor-driven chain conveyor. The moving assembly line was limited at first to engines, transmissions, and frames. It began to turn out finished Model T's at Ford's new plant in Highland Park, Michigan, in 1914. The mass market that Ford created with his Model T had given rise to the modern assembly line plant and the first giant automobile company.

The Merger Movement

For a Swift, a Carnegie, or a Ford, growing larger meant becoming more efficient. These men saw vertical integration as a form of innovation that, like technology, meant lower operating costs. For many others, however, big business provided an answer to entirely different concerns. Economic concentration offered an escape from the fearsome competition of an uncontrolled marketplace.

After the Civil War, the business cycle became subject to violent fluctuations. From 1873 to 1878 and again from 1893 to 1897, severe depressions gripped the United States. Lesser panics struck in 1884, 1888, 1903, and 1907. Part of the problem came from the nation's weak financial structure. The banking system was apt to

FIGURE 17.1 PERFORMANCE OF THE ECONOMY

collapse under stress, and the money supply was too inflexible for the needs of the growing economy. These weaknesses were compounded by the boom-and-bust character of American investment—feverishly overbuilding capacity in good times and then sharply curtailing activity when demand began to slacken.

Businessmen, even if they could not understand the underlying causes of the volatile economy, knew the consequences—lost earnings for stronger firms and bankruptcy for weaker ones. During the depression of the 1870s, wholesale prices fell about 30 percent. The rate of business failures doubled as forty-seven thousand firms went under. In hard times, the marketplace turned into a jungle.

Despite their lip service to free enterprise, unrestrained competition held few charms for American businessmen. Even before the Civil War, they had sought the shelter of pools—that is, agreements to share the market and to avoid price cutting. Such pacts violated the common-law principle against conspiracies in restraint of trade, however, and therefore, could not legally be enforced. Depressed markets, moreover, almost invariably tempted stronger firms to break away and grab a larger share of the available business. This occurred especially in industries with high fixed costs, such as the railroads and, increasingly, manufacturing as well. Firms were often better off operating at lower prices, or even at a loss, than not operating at all. For a strong competitor like Andrew Carnegie, who could make a profit even on rock-bottom prices, there was "nothing like meeting the market, taking the business and running full." Carnegie said

this when he pulled out of the steel-rail pool in 1894.

If voluntary pools did not work, the only solution was a business strategy that would bring competing firms under a single head. John D. Rockefeller was the pioneering figure in this activity. Rockefeller had been a rising young commission merchant in nearby Cleveland at the time that Colonel E. L. Drake drilled the world's first oil well in western Pennsylvania in 1859. Within a few years, Rockefeller moved into the refining end of the new petroleum industry. His product was kerosene, for which great demand quickly developed for use as an illuminating fuel. Production grew even more rapidly, however. The petroleum industry became intensely competitive and subject to severe booms and busts. Rockefeller's response was two-pronged. He built the Standard Oil Company into a highly efficient and often ruthless competitor. But he also did what he could to reduce the competitive intensity of the oil business, among other ways by buying into rival firms.

Rockefeller's empire building hit a legal snag, however, because his Ohio corporation charter prohibited him from acquiring holdings outside the state. After trying a variety of subterfuges, Rockefeller in 1882 conceived of the *trust* as the answer to his problem. Under this arrangement, participating firms assigned their stock to a board of trustees and in return received certificates entitling them to dividends on the earnings of the trust. The board took full control of all the properties, managing and disposing of them as it saw fit. In this way, Rockefeller hoped to avoid the limitations imposed by his Ohio incorporation and bring his rivals under the control of Standard Oil. Although firms in other industries followed Rockefeller's lead, however, the trust encountered increasing legal problems during the 1880s.

Then a better legal instrument emerged for bringing competing firms under a common management. This was the holding company, a corporation with the power to purchase stock in other corporations. If just one state granted such privileges, the corporation could operate throughout the country. In 1889, the New Jersey legislature provided holding-company privileges in the state's general incorporation law. The promoter of this legislation was James B. Dill, a corporate lawyer. New Jersey was willing because it wanted the revenues expected from the fees and taxes paid by the new corporations. Delaware, West Virginia, and other states soon joined New Jersey in issuing charters to holding companies.

Although a legal, efficient device was now available, a national merger movement did not begin until after the terrible depression of the 1890s. Chastened by the cutthroat competition of that depression, firms rushed to sell out. Bringing them under the control of a holding company was a formidable task. First, a syndicate had to be set up to provide risk capital. Then negotiations were conducted for the purchase—usually through an exchange of stock—of the firms slated to be part of the new combine. Finally, a large volume of holding-company stock had to be marketed in an orderly way. This procedure was primarily a venture in finance, and no one could handle it better than an investment banker.

Investment bankers were financial middlemen who raised capital for American business. After the Civil War, a handful of large investment-banking firms had risen to eminence—J. P. Morgan and Company and the Kuhn, Loeb Company in New York; Lee, Higginson and Company in Boston; and the Drexel Company in Philadelphia. They operated largely to serve the financial needs of the railroads. These firms underwrote—that is, sold at their own risk—issues of railroad stock. They channelled the new securities into allied banks and insurance companies and to large investors in both America and Europe. When a railroad went into receivership, in-

vestment bankers handled the reorganization, a task similar to that of organizing an industrial holding company. The investment bankers, because of their railroad experience and their strategic place in the financial system, played the key role in the merger movement that began in the late 1890s.

When the merger movement began, in 1897, others tried to play the promotional role. The barbed-wire manufacturer John W. ("Bet-A-Million") Gates organized the American Steel and Wire Company, and other promoters launched mergers in tin plate, biscuits, and other fields. But as the financial stakes rose, the professionals

J. PIERPONT MORGAN
J. P. Morgan was the giant among American financiers. He had served an apprenticeship in investment banking under his father, a leading Anglo-American banker in London. A gruff man of few words, Morgan had a genius for instilling trust, and the strength of will to persuade others to follow his lead and do his bidding—qualities the great photographer Edward Steichen captured in this portrait. (The Museum of Modern Art, New York. Gift of A. Conger Goodyear)

entered the picture. In 1898, J. P. Morgan organized the Federal Steel Company, and thereafter investment bankers largely preempted the field. Such new giants as the International Harvester Company, the American Car and Foundry Company, the American Can Company, and United States Steel were the handiwork of Wall Street.

Morgan and his Wall Street compatriots left no doubt about the main purposes of these giant mergers. Their objective, as earlier with the railroads, was to bring order to industries "demoralized" by cutthroat competition. The investment bankers claimed to be marketplace reformers and advocates of "fair" competition, as opposed to "bitter, relentless, overbearing, tyrannical conduct, calculated to drive out the weak." They were interested in changing marketplace behavior, rather than achieving savings and efficiency through mergers.

Once in operation, however, the new combines commonly moved to take advantage of their great size. As the National Biscuit Company reported in 1901, four years after its creation for the admitted purpose of monopolizing the industry:

> We turned our attention and bent our energies to improving the internal management of our own business, to getting the full benefit for purchasing our raw materials in large quantities, to economizing the expense of manufacture, to systematizing and rendering more effective our selling department.

The company shifted from bulk sales for grocery cracker barrels to packaged goods under the brand name Uneeda Biscuit. It embarked on a major advertising campaign, built up global purchasing and marketing systems, and concentrated production in a few giant plants. National Biscuit originally intended "to control competition. We soon satisfied ourselves that within the company itself we must look for success."

Not all mergers ended this way, but those that did not generally failed. The profitable ones rationalized their operations, exploited their advantage of size, and moved in the direction of vertical integration. They thus joined the mainstream of large-scale American enterprise. Whether the starting point had been to benefit from the efficiencies of size, as with Swift, or to control competition, as with National Biscuit, the result was essentially the same. The vertically integrated corporation had come of age.

The Managerial Revolution

At one time, observed the railroad expert Marshall M. Kirkman in 1896, it had been thought "practically impossible to manage a great railway effectively." On the early roads, "management had been personal and autocratic; the superintendent, a man gifted with energy and clearness of perception, moulded the property to his own will. But as the properties grew, he found himself unable to give his personal attention to everything. Undaunted, he sought to do everything and do it well. He ended by doing nothing."

It is not hard to understand the mistake of the early railroad superintendent. How could he know that methods which had worked brilliantly in the past would not work in the future? And where, in a world of small businesses, was there a model for running an enterprise other than by personal and direct control over its activities? How else could a business be run? No problem was harder to see clearly, or, once discovered, more taxing on the business imagination. Nor was any industrial success, once achieved, fated to have more enduring consequences than the mastery of the techniques of modern management.

As trunk lines thrust westward from Baltimore, Philadelphia, and New York before the Civil War, they came up against a managerial crisis that had not troubled shorter roads. In 1856, in a classic statement of the problem, the Erie Railroad official Daniel C. McCallum compared a fifty-mile road and a five hundred-mile road. On the short road, the superintendent could personally attend to every detail, "and any system, however imperfect, may prove comparatively successful." But not on long roads: "I am fully convinced that in the want of a system lies the true secret of their failure." McCallum had crucial insight in realizing the need for a system—a formal administrative structure—in the operation of large-scale, complex enterprises. He knew he was working in the dark: "We have no precedent or experience upon which we can fully rely."

The railroads were the most complex form of nineteenth-century enterprise. They had to raise huge amounts of capital, and their properties stretched over ever greater distances. They employed armies of workers—nearly fifty thousand on the Pennsylvania system by 1890. And, unlike the leisurely traffic on the canals, trains had to be precisely scheduled and closely coordinated. Even after the telegraph became an indispensable operating tool in the 1840s, train accidents took a heavy toll.

Step by step, always under the prod of necessity, the early trunk lines pioneered in the main elements of modern business administration. They separated overall management from day-to-day operations and departmentalized operational activities along functional lines—maintenance of way, rolling stock, and traffic. The Erie Railroad was the first to divide its system into manageable geographic units. Then came the careful definition of the lines of communication upward to the central office. When Albert Fink perfected his cost-accounting system for the Louisville and Nashville Railroad after the Civil War, managers at last had precise data on which to assess the performance of their roads. By the end of the 1870s, the managerial crisis on the railroads had been resolved.

As industrial enterprises became comparably complex, they confronted the same kind of managerial problems. However, industry drew on the experience of the railroads. Sometimes there were direct linkages, as with Andrew Carnegie, who had been a Pennsylvania Railroad executive before going into steel. Starting in 1879, J. P. Morgan attended the monthly directors' meetings of the New York Central and applied what he learned to the manufacturing mergers he later promoted. Whether by trial and error or through the railroad influence, large companies everywhere moved toward a modern management structure. Successful firms, such as Armour and Company, the Singer Sewing Machine Company, and the McCormick Harvesting Machine Company, solved the problems of administering far-flung business empires.

By the beginning of the twentieth century, the main lines of managerial strategy had taken hold throughout large-scale American industry. With few exceptions, vertically integrated firms followed a centralized, functionally departmentalized plan (see Figure 17.2 on page 530). The central office housed a number of departments, each charged with the overall responsibility for a specific area of activity—purchasing, auditing, production, transportation, or sales. These functionally defined departments provided "middle management," and they represented the heart of the managerial revolution in American industry.

Although managers of operating units in the field functioned much like earlier factory owners, middle managers undertook entirely new tasks. They grappled with the complex problems of directing the flow of goods through the integrated enterprise from the purchase of raw materials to the final sale. They were key innovators, equivalent in matters of business practice to engineers in improving technology.

Their superiors, the top executives, could not claim such a complete achievement. The firms that developed through internal growth had been built by individual entrepreneurs. The founding families—the Swifts, Armours, and McCormicks—still largely maintained control into the twentieth century. They were generally reluctant to surrender the tight supervision with which they or their fathers had developed the companies. In 1907, J. Ogden Armour spent his days reading operational reports and issuing orders to his buying, processing, and selling departments. All middle managers reported directly to him. Priding himself on his knowledge of the company and absorbed in the details of its operation, Armour had neither the time, the staff, nor the inclination to engage in long-term, strategic planning or systematic evaluation of his firm's performance. Armour typified an entire generation of owner-managers. Brilliant in creating the subordinate administrative structure, they normally were slow to apply managerial principles to their own tasks.

The large-scale firms formed by mergers had an advantage here. Their top executives were more likely to be salaried officials. They also were inclined to introduce a systematic approach into the central office as well as to the reorganization of the various units of the merged company. Even here, however, absorption in day-to-day activity gave top management little opportunity for long-term planning. It would take further experimentation, prompted by the emergence of the multi-industry firm in the 1920s, for top management to begin to be liberated from the actual direction of industrial activity.

In twenty-five years, the face of American industry had been transformed. By the turn of the century, the hundred largest companies controlled roughly a third of the nation's total productive capacity. The day of the small manufacturer had not passed. He still flourished, or at least survived, in many fields. But he was no longer the dominant figure in American enterprise, and his sphere of activity narrowed every year. The future lay with big business.

The World of Work

In a free-enterprise system, profit drives the entrepreneur. But the industrial order is not populated only by profit makers. It includes—in vastly larger numbers—wage earners. What is done for profit always acts directly and powerfully on those working for wages. Never did those actions have more profound consequences than in the late nineteenth century. During that period, the modern factory system transformed the lives of American workers.

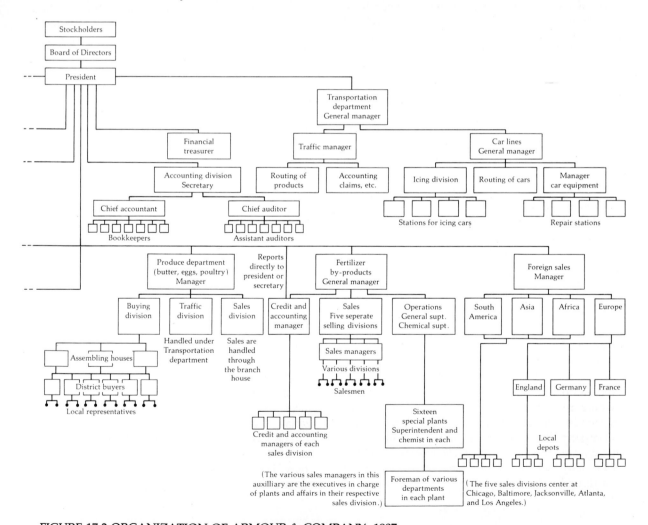

FIGURE 17.2 ORGANIZATION OF ARMOUR & COMPANY, 1907

Autonomous Labor

No one supervised the pick miner. He was a tonnage worker, paid for the amount of coal he produced. He provided his own pick and other tools, worked at his own pace, and knocked off early when he chose. He also used his own judgment in his "room" in the coal mine. Such autonomous craftworkers, almost all of whom were men, flourished in many branches of nineteenth-century industry. They were mule spinners in cotton mills; puddlers and rollers in iron works; molders in stovemaking; and machinists, glass blowers, and many other types of skilled workers.

Within the shop, they abided by the *stint*, a limit placed by the workers themselves on the amount that they should produce each day. This informal system of limitation on output infuriated efficiency-minded engineers. But to the craftworker it signified personal dignity; "unselfish brotherhood" with his fellow employees; and protection against rate cutting, irregular work, and even drunken debauchery. The craftworker took pride in a "manly" bearing, both toward his fellows and toward the boss. One day, a shop in Lowell, Massachusetts, posted regulations requiring all employees to be at their posts in work clothes at the opening bell and remain, with the shop door locked, until the dismissal bell. A machinist promptly packed his tools and quit, declaring that he had not "been brought up under such a system of slavery."

Underlying this ethical code was a keen sense of the craft group, each of which had its own history and customs. Among hat finishers, masters of the art of applying fur felting to hats, an employed man always "asked for" a jobless friend. It would have been unthinkable for the friend himself to request work from a foreman. The hatters had a language of their own. When a hatter was hired, he was "shopped"; if fired, he was "bagged"; when he quit work, he "cried off"; and when he took an apprentice, the boy was "under teach." The hatters, most of whom worked in Danbury, Connecticut, or Orange, New Jersey, formed a distinctive, self-contained community.

The craftworker's skills were crucial to nineteenth-century production. He also was valued for the responsibilities he assumed. He hired his own helpers, supervised their work, and paid them out of his earnings. In an era when the scale of production was expanding, autonomous craftworkers relieved their employers of the mounting burdens of shop-floor management. Many factory managers tried to shift responsibility to employees. A system of inside contracting developed in metal-fabricating firms that did precise machining and complex assemblying. Contracter-employees hired and paid their own men and supervised them completely. They received a contracted rate for the output of their units, plus regular wages as employees. In the New England machine tool industry, which often produced on a to-order basis, inside contractors bid for custom jobs instead of serving as virtual department heads. If a man lost a bid, he sometimes went to work for the winning contractor.

The skilled worker was one central figure of nineteenth-century industry; the common laborer was the other. Great numbers of these laborers had been needed to dig canals, lay railroad tracks, and build cities. They were equally important in heavy industry. Until the last years of the century, virtually all hauling of materials was done by hand. In the steel mills, a third or more of the workers shoveled coal and iron ore from freight cars and wheeled barrows to furnaces. They also handled the tons of metal that passed through the mill daily at every stage of steel production. The steel companies regarded a strong back as the only requirement for all this work. They kept no personnel records on day laborers, considering them to be a floating labor force. The men worked in gangs, and the foreman or gang boss had complete responsibility for them. He hired them, told them what to do, and disciplined and fired them. He was their actual employer.

Dispersal of authority was thus characteristic of nineteenth-century industry. The aristocracy of workers—the craftsmen, the inside contractors, and the foremen—had a high degree of autonomy. However, their subordinates often paid dearly for that independence. The opportunities for abuse were endless. Any worker who paid his helpers from his own pocket might be tempted to exploit them. In the Pittsburgh area, foremen were known as "pushers," notorious for driving their gangs mercilessly. Many foremen also practiced favoritism. For example, they might promote only the sons of craftsmen from the position of helper. On the other hand, industrial labor in the nineteenth century was on a human scale. The crucial relationships were face-to-face, and cohesive ties could develop within a work force. Striking craftworkers commonly received the support of helpers and laborers, and labor gangs sometimes walked out on behalf of a popular foreman.

Systems of Control

As technology advanced and modern management emerged, so did controls over the work process. Workers might have preferred the older system of autonomous work, but they had no choice. They increasingly lost the proud independence that characterized nineteenth-century work.

When undercutting machines appeared in coal mines in the 1880s, they deprived the miner of the pick work that was his most prized skill. "Anyone with a weak head and a strong back can load machine coal," grumbled one Kentucky miner. "But a man has to think and study every day like you was studying a book if he is going to get the best of the coal when he uses only a pick." Similar complaints came throughout the industrialization era from craftworkers whose skills fell victim to machinery—from hand-loom weavers early in the nineteenth century to glassblowers a hundred years later.

The division of labor had the same effect on other skilled workers. "A man never learns the machinist's trade now," a craftworker complained in 1883. In the manufacture of sewing machines, "the trade is so subdivided that a man is not considered a machinist at all. One man may make just a particular part of a machine and may not know anything whatever about another part of the same machine." Such a worker, noted an observer, "cannot be master of a craft, but only master of a fragment."

Although many skilled workers drifted downward into the semiskilled ranks, skilled work itself did not disappear. But its relationship to the production process changed. If weavers, puddlers, and glassblowers became machine tenders, the machines themselves demanded skilled installers and repairers. In the early automobile industry, skilled assemblers soon found themselves replaced by the repetitious, specialized work of the assembly line. But this development led to a new aristocracy of autoworkers, the tool-and-die men and mechanics who prepared and maintained the production lines. It was not so much that mass production eliminated skilled jobs—which actually increased proportionately after 1910—as that it separated them from the production process.

Technology took hold of the pace of operations. The machine, not the worker, determined how fast production would go. In continuous-flow operations, as on an assembly line or in a mechanized rolling mill, the individual worker got caught up in an entire system of externally paced activity. "If you need to turn out a little more," boasted a superintendent at Swift and Company, "you speed up the conveyor a little and the men speed up to keep pace." Complaints about speedups were a sure sign of workers' loss of control over their jobs.

The impact of machinery on workers was essentially unintentional. It amounted to a by-product of decisions made for technological reasons. Employers doubtless recognized that mechanization would better enable them to discipline their workers. But this was only an incidental benefit in addition to the efficiencies that came from the machinery itself. Only slowly, and rarely before 1900, did employers realize that the management of labor might yield the kind of returns that they had gained from technology.

Reform of factory administration began in the 1880s. It aimed at giving managers the means, previously lacking, to control the operations of large industrial plants. As orderly procedures extended down from the central office, workers found themselves subject to general rules and to standard terms of work. Hiring and firing increasingly became the responsibility of the personnel office rather than the foreman. Even so, the actual handling of workers yielded only slowly to central direction. Authority on the shop floor, where the foreman still remained boss, was most resistant of all.

The foreman's traditional rough-and-ready ways always stood as a rebuke to the systematic approach of managerial reformers. Why was it not possible, asked the industrialist Henry R. Towne, to devise "some better method of bringing out of the men the best that is in them in doing their work?" This question applied especially to workers not subject to the discipline of machines or assembly lines.

Among the early management reformers, Frederick W. Taylor took work itself as his special province. Others had experimented with incentive and profit-sharing programs. Taylor, beginning with his landmark essay "A Piece Rate System" (1895), proposed a method for getting the maximum work from the individual worker. He proposed two basic reforms. The first would eliminate the brain work involved in what workers did and give it entirely to managers. The managers would assume "the burden of gathering together all of the traditional knowledge which in the past has been possessed by the workmen and then of classifying, tabulating, and reducing this knowledge to rules, laws, and formulae." The second reform, a logical consequence of the first, would deprive workers of the authority they had normally exercised on the shop floor. Workers would "do what they are told promptly and without asking questions or making suggestions. . . . The duty of enforcing . . . rests with the *management* alone."

Once they had the knowledge and power, according to Taylor, managers would put labor on a "scientific" basis. This meant subjecting each task to a "time-and-motion" study, in which an engineer with a stopwatch tried to measure precisely the steps in each task. A personnel office would hire and train the right person for each job. The worker would be paid at a differential rate—that is, a certain amount if he met the stopwatch standard. He would earn at a higher rate for any greater output. Taylor claimed that his techniques would guarantee the optimum level of worker efficiency.

Taylor called his method "scientific management." It was not, in practice, a roaring success. His reforms called for a total restructure of factory administration. No company ever adopted Taylor's entire system, and the few that tried to do so paid dearly for the effort. The differential-rate method, which was widely used, met stubborn resistance. "It looks to me like slavery to have a man stand over you with a stopwatch," complained one iron molder. A union leader insisted that "this system is wrong, because we want our heads left on us." Workers deliberately slowed up to fool the time-and-mo-

tion man, and they often prevented the incentive rate from pushing up production.

Yet Taylor, a brilliant publicist, achieved something of fundamental importance. He and his disciples spread his scientific-management teachings throughout American industry. Taylor's successors devised more sophisticated techniques than his simple economic psychology, which assumed an automatic response to the reward of more money. A threshold had been crossed into the modern era of labor management.

So the circle closed in on American workers. With each advance, the quest for efficiency cut deeper into their cherished autonomy. Mechanization, systematic administration, and the growing scale of industrial activity diminished workers and cut them down to fit the productive system. The process occurred unevenly. For textile workers, the loss had come early. Miners and iron workers felt it much more slowly. Others, such as workers in the building trades, escaped the process almost entirely. But increasing numbers of workers found themselves in an environment that crushed any sense of mastery or even understanding.

Industrial Recruits

Wherever industrialism took hold, it set people in motion. Artisans moved into factories. Farm folk migrated to manufacturing centers. An industrial labor force emerged. These events took place in all industrializing nations. But the United States built its work force in a distinctive way. Unlike European countries, it could not rely primarily on its own population.

For one thing, the demand for labor was enormous. American industry required five times as many workers in 1910 as in 1870. No less important, people born in the United States after the 1850s could no longer be attracted into factories. It was not that rural people, who still made up about 75 percent of the population in 1870, refused to leave their farms. Large numbers of them migrated from agricultural areas after 1870. Many went westward and remained farmers. About half did move to cities, but they tended to avoid factory work. The desirable jobs—those of puddlers, rollers, molders, and machinists—required advanced industrial skills not held by rural Americans. They did have a basic education. They could read and calculate, and they understood American institutions and ways of doing things. City-bound white Americans were better qualified for the multiplying white-collar jobs in offices and retail stores than for manual jobs in factories.

As for rural blacks, even the lowest factory job probably seemed better than the debt peonage of southern cotton agriculture. Racial barriers kept them out of factories. In the South, industrial jobs were generally reserved for whites. A trickle of blacks began to migrate northward and westward, roughly eighty thousand between 1870 and 1890, and another two hundred thousand from 1890 to 1910. Most of them settled in cities, but few found factory work. The

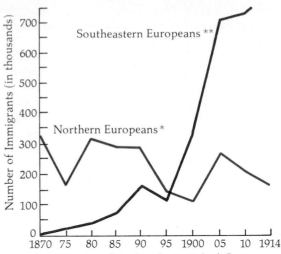

* Includes immigrants from Great Britain, Ireland, Germany, and the Scandinavian countries.
** Includes immigrants from Poland, Russia, Italy, and other Baltic and Eastern European countries.

FIGURE 17.3 AMERICAN IMMIGRATION, 1870–1914

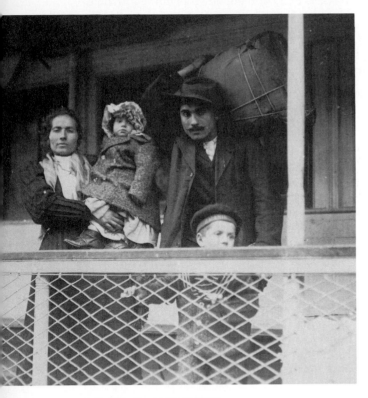

IMMIGRANT WORKERS
Many native-born Americans resented the influx of peasant immigrants from eastern and southern Europe that began in the 1880s. In fact, however, the newcomers, more than any other group, manned the machines, laid the railroad tracks, and did the heavy construction labor in the nation's cities. They were, in truth, Europe's gift— its most vigorous and energetic people. (Lewis Hine. International Museum of Photography at George Eastman House)

great majority of the men ended up as casual laborers and janitors, the women as maids and laundresses. Only 7 percent of all black American males worked in industry in 1890. Industrial employers excluded blacks because of an apparently limitless supply of foreign workers on which they could draw.

The exodus from the Old World had started in the 1840s when the potato famine sent more than a million Irish peasants fleeing to America. During the following years, other traditional rural economies were disrupted by the commercialization of agriculture and an increasing imbalance between population and land. The erosion of peasant agriculture struck first in Germany and Scandinavia. Then it spread east into Austria-Hungary and Russia and south into Italy and the Balkans. In industrial districts of Europe, the force of economic change also cut loose many workers in the declining artisan trades. A total of about 25 million immigrants arrived in America between 1870 and 1914.

Ethnic origin largely determined the kind of work that the immigrants found in their new country. Many western Europeans were seasoned artisans and industrial workers. They generally sought the same types of jobs they had held in the Old World. The nineteenth-century occupational structure took on an ethnic character—the Welsh as tin-plate workers, Germans as machinists and traditional artisans, Belgians as glass workers, and Scandinavians as seamen on Great Lakes boats. For common labor, employers had long counted on the brawn of rural immigrants to dig canals, lay railroad tracks, and provide unskilled labor in factory and construction gangs. These workers included primarily the Irish but also other western European peasants, as well as French Canadians in New England, Mexicans in the Southwest, and Chinese in California.

As industrialization advanced, the demand for unskilled workers increased and the nation's dependence on European craft skills moderated. These developments helped trigger the remarkable shift of immigration away from northern Europe that started in the 1880s. More than nine million people migrated to America from eastern and southern Europe between 1900 and 1914. Italian and Slavic immigrants, almost wholly lacking in industrial skills, flooded into the lowest rungs of American industry. Heavy, low-paid factory labor became essentially the domain of the recent immigrants. Blast-furnace jobs, a

job-seeking investigator heard, was "Hunky work," not suitable for him or any other American.

Other factors beside skill levels determined where immigrants ended up in American industry. Most of the newcomers arrived alone, but they moved within well-defined networks. The immigrants followed relatives or fellow villagers already in America, joined their households as family members or boarders, and relied on them to find a job. A high degree of ethnic clustering resulted, even within one factory. At the Jones and Laughlin steel works in Pittsburgh, the carpentry shop was German, the hammer shop Polish, and the blooming mill Serbian. Sometimes this clustering process led to unlikely ethnic concentrations. Bulgarians made up the unskilled labor force of Granite City, Illinois. Numerous Greeks became coal miners in central Colorado, although few worked in mines elsewhere.

Distinctive ethnic characteristics also determined the jobs that immigrants found. For example, men from Italy sought construction and road work because their village society made them amenable to a gang form of organization

FIGURE 17.4 CHANGES IN THE LABOR FORCE, 1870–1910

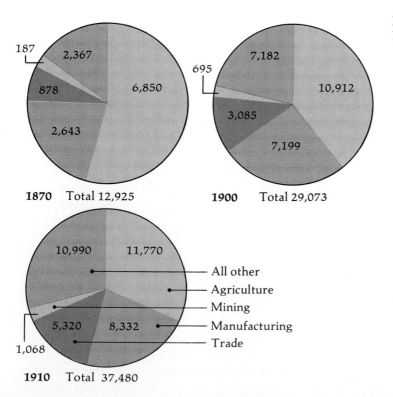

187

2,367

878

6,850

2,643

1870   Total 12,925

695

7,182

10,912

3,085

7,199

1900   Total 29,073

10,990   11,770

5,320   8,332

1,068

1910   Total 37,480

—— All other
—— Agriculture
—— Mining
—— Manufacturing
—— Trade

under a *padrone* (boss). Eastern European Jews flocked into the needle trades because many had tailoring skills. The industry also suited, or could be adopted to, their family and religious needs. The sweating system, which involved the subcontracting of sewing jobs from a central shop, enabled Orthodox Jews to stay in their own neighborhoods. They could observe the Saturday Sabbath, put their wives and daughters to work in the safety of the tenement, and make an easy jump from worker to entrepreneur.

The immigrants entered a modern industrial order, but they saw their surroundings through peasant eyes. With the disruption of the traditional rural economies of eastern and southern Europe, many peasants had begun to lose their land. This meant an intolerable decline into the class of dependent, propertyless servants. Peasants could avoid such a bitter fate only if they had money to buy property. In Europe, job-seeking peasants commonly tried seasonal agricultural labor, or temporary work in nearby cities. America represented merely a larger leap, made possible by the cheap and speedy steamship transportation across the Atlantic. The peasant immigrants, most of them young and male, came with the purpose of earning enough money, and then returning to their native villages.

As long as the work lasted, the peasant worker rarely was inclined to protest against low wages, harsh conditions, or the hardships of his life. When work ran out, as it almost always did, there was a safety valve. In the depression year of 1908, more Italians and Austro-Hungarians returned to Europe than arrived. As many as half of the new immigrants returned to their homelands. No one knows how many saved enough money to fulfill their peasant goals and how many left for lack of work. Clearly, however, the peasants' reasons for coming, and their tendency to leave in bad times, made them an ideal labor supply for the new industrial order.

A few fields, such as railroading, had mostly native-born workers. Southern industry also relied on workers native to the region. Overall, however, immigrants manned American industry. They comprised 60 percent of the labor force of the nation's principal manufacturing and mining industries in 1910.

Working Women

The late nineteenth-century economy also relied on women's labor. Their participation in the work force increased steadily. The female population grew by nearly half between 1870 and 1900, but the number of woman workers jumped by almost two-thirds. They made up more than a fourth of the nonfarm labor force in 1900. Women, like immigrants, entered the industrial economy from another world. The role they found as wage earners was shaped by the fact that they were women. Contemporary beliefs about womanhood largely determined which women entered the work force and how they were treated once they became wage earners.

Wives were not supposed to hold jobs. In 1890, less than 5 percent of all married women worked outside their homes. Employment was acceptable before marriage, at least for young women not in the respectable middle class. For women in America, wage work was typically an adolescent experience that ended when they got married. The majority of all employed women in 1890 were from sixteen to twenty-four years old. When older women worked, remarked one observer, it "was usually a sign that something had gone wrong"—their husbands were missing, jobless, or incapacitated.

Since women were considered inherently different from men, it followed that they should not be permitted to do "men's work." And, regardless of the value of their labor, they could not be paid at men's rates. At the turn of the century, woman workers fell into three roughly equal categories. A third worked as maids or other types of domestic servants. Another third held white-collar jobs also identified as "female" in teaching, nursing, and sales. Sex-typing affected the third of the women in industrial occupations as well. Few worked in the crafts, as supervisors, or as day laborers. Most female industrial workers were classified as "operatives"—machine tenders and hand workers. Women were heavily concentrated in the garment trades and textile mills, but could be found throughout industry in "light" occupations—as packers, inspectors, assemblers, or as sausage stuffers in packing houses.

Sex-typing of work was legitimatized by the

sentimental view of women as the weaker sex. But powerful interests also played a role. Craftworkers protected their male domain, and employers profited from cut-rate work. Wherever they worked, women earned wages below those of the lowest male occupations. In 1914, female industrial workers averaged $7.75 a week, $3 less than unskilled males and $5 less than the average for all industrial employees.

The objection to working wives, also expressed in sentimental and moral terms, was likewise based on solid necessity. From the standpoint of the industrial economy, the basic economic unit consisted of the individual em-

ployee. For the worker, however, the family was the real economic unit. In this family economy, the wife contributed crucially. Her household services were not considered as income-producing, nor given a monetary value. But her husband knew that his household could not function without her labor. Therefore, the wife's place was in the home.

Working-class families, especially those below the skilled ranks, required more than one income. Hardly half of these families, one expert estimated in 1912, got along on the husband's earnings alone. Additional funds came mainly from sons and daughters, children as well as

THE MODERN OFFICE

Office work provides a prime example of the process of sex-typing in American employment. During the nineteenth century, most clerks and secretaries were men, and their jobs were regarded as stepping stones to partnerships or senior business positions. As paperwork multiplied in bureaucratic firms, secretarial duties were redefined as women's work, at lower pay relative to men's jobs and with no prospect for advancement. The chap in this office will surely find another line of work . . . or replace the male supervisor standing on the left. (Culver) adults. In 1890, about 20 percent of the children between the ages of ten and fifteen held jobs.

The immigrants arriving after 1890 relied heavily on the family economy. The high proportion of unmarried males among southern and eastern Europeans put a premium on household labor. As a result, the wife was indispensable in an immigrant family that boarded single workers. Moreover, in an era when people began to value education more highly, many immigrants persisted in treating children as contributors to the family economy. People who placed a high value on education, such as Jewish immigrants, saw their children rise more rapidly into the middle class than did those who preferred the income of their offspring. Finally, some immigrant groups, especially the Italians, objected strongly to the employment of wives outside the home. If the wife was to contribute to the family income, she could do so only within the household, either by doing work at home or keeping boarders.

Despite the immigrant influence, the family economy was changing. Obstacles to child labor appeared. By the 1890s, all the northern industrial states had laws prohibiting the employment of young children and regulating the work hours of teenagers. Most of those states also required children from eight to fourteen years old to go to school for a certain number of weeks each year. At the same time, jobs designated as female were increasing rapidly in teaching, office work, and shops, though not significantly in manufacturing. Finally, the pressure for higher family incomes increased in the twentieth century with the advent of automobiles, appliances, and other durables.

Working-class families continued to rely on second incomes, but this money was more likely to come from the wife than the children. By 1920, the proportion of working married women had doubled from what it had been in 1890. For working-class women, entry into the labor market went forward even more rapidly. About a fifth of the wives of unskilled and semiskilled men in Chicago had jobs in 1920. Wage-earning women, including many wives, were on their way to becoming a primary part of America's labor force.

The Labor Movement

Wherever industrialism has taken hold, workers have responded collectively. However, the method they have used to organize themselves has varied from one industrial society to another. In the United States, workers were especially uncertain about the path to take. Only after the 1880s did the American labor movement settle into a fixed course.

Unionists and Reformers

By the late nineteenth century, craftworkers regarded trade unionism as an old story. Unions had long since become central to their working lives. Apprenticeship rules regulated entry into a trade, and the closed shop excluded nonunion and incompetent workers. In the carpenters' unions, the walking delegates—that is, the local union officials—served as employment agents for building contractors and the journeymen workers. Union rules specified the terms of work, sometimes in minute detail. Above all, trade unionism defended the craftworker's traditional skills and rights.

The union also symbolized the social identity of a craft. Hatters took pride in their drinking prowess, an on-the-job privilege jealously guarded, and their unions sometimes resembled drinking clubs. More often, however, the craft union had an uplifting character. A Birmingham iron puddler claimed that his union's "main object was to educate mechanics up to a standard of morality and temperance, and good workmanship." The International Association of Machinists boasted of an elaborate ritual, an expression of fraternalism common to most craft unions. The railroad brotherhoods especially stressed insurance and mutual aid because operating trains was a highly risky occupation. On the job and off, the union played a big part in the lives of craftworkers.

Labor organizations, sometimes sparked by fraternal spirit but more often by the need to defend wage rates, can be traced back to the eighteenth century. The first unions were local groups of workers in the same trade. These organizations grew into national unions. The first to survive, the International Typographical Union, was formed in 1852. By the 1870s, molders, iron and steelworkers, bricklayers, and members of about thirty other trades had formed national unions. Almost invariably, the first order of business was to create a national "traveling card" for wandering journeymen. If work was available in a community, the local union admitted a traveling member and expected him to observe union standards. If he did not do so, the local gave him a meal and a bed and then sent him on his way, traveling card in hand. By thus creating a kind of national citizenship, the national union asserted control over the labor market of its trade. As national product markets emerged, a second motivation developed for building national unions. Because goods flowed from different points into a common market, a union had to coordinate bargaining and organize nonunion areas. The union served workers' crucial interests in this effort to standardize labor costs among competing producers.

The protection of job interests was not the only source of collective activity by working people. Distress over the impact of industrialization on their lives had an equally strong effect.

In 1883, a New York wagon driver named Thomas B. McGuire testified before a Senate committee. He had saved three hundred dollars from his wages, "thinking that I might become something of a capitalist eventually." But he soon failed. "A man in the express business today owning one or two horses and a wagon cannot even eke out an existence from the business," McGuire complained. "The competition is too great from the Adams Express Company and all those other monopolies." McGuire's prospects seemed no better in the hack, or taxi business:

Corporations usually take that business themselves. They can manage to get men, at starvation wages, and put them on a hack, and put a livery on them with a gold band and brass buttons, to show that they are slaves—I beg pardon; I did not intend to use the word slaves; there are no slaves in this country now—to show that they are merely servants.

Slave or liveried servant, the symbolic meaning was the same to McGuire. He was speaking of the crushed aspirations of the independent American workingman.

What would satisfy the Thomas McGuires of the nineteenth century? Only the restoration of a world in which "monopoly" and special privilege did not deprive workers of the chance to rise. In such a world, no distinction would exist between capital and labor. All would be "producers" in what was commonly called the "cooperative commonwealth." This ideal inspired wave after wave of labor-reform movements. They took the form of workingmen's parties in the 1830s, land-reform groups in the 1840s, the National Labor Union after the Civil War, and finally, the Noble Order of the Knights of Labor.

The Knights of Labor started in 1869 as a secret society of Philadelphia garment cutters. The organization gradually spread to other cities and emerged in 1878 as a national movement. Led by Grand Master Workman Terence V. Powderly, the Knights purged themselves of the secrecy and religious verbiage objectionable to the Catholic church. They retained the elaborate ritual and ceremony that appealed so strongly to the fraternal spirit of the nineteenth-century worker. The Knights of Labor typified the American labor-reform tradition. Their goal was to "give voice to that grand undercurrent of mighty thought, which is today [1880] crystallizing in the hearts of men, and urging them on to perfect organization through which to gain the power to make labor emancipation possible."

But how was "emancipation" to be achieved? The Knights tried a number of solutions, including cooperation. Funds would be raised and cooperative enterprises set up, and as these flourished and spread, American society would be transformed into a cooperative commonwealth. But little was actually done. In reality, the Knights concentrated mainly on "education." Powderly regarded the organization as a vast labor lyceum that almost anyone could join. The cooperative commonwealth would arrive in some mysterious way as more and more "producers" became members and learned the group's message in lectures, discussions, and publications. Social evil would not end in a day, but "must await the gradual development of educational enlightenment."

Labor reform might have seemed a far cry from hard-headed, job-conscious unionism. But both were in reality embedded in a single workers' culture. Workers saw no conflict between the two loyalties. Many carried membership cards in both the Knights of Labor and a trade union. The careers of many labor leaders, including Powderly, likewise embraced both kinds of activity. For many years, even the functional lines were indistinct. At the local level, little separated a trade assembly of the Knights from a local trade union; both engaged in fraternal and bargaining activities.

After 1884, the Knights began to act increasingly like a trade union. Boycott campaigns defeated "unfair" employers across the country. With the economy on the upswing, the Knights began to win strikes, including one against Jay Gould's Southwestern railway system in 1885. Workers flocked into the organization, and its membership jumped from a hundred thousand to perhaps seven hundred thousand in less than a year. For a brief time, the Knights stood poised as a potential industrial-union movement capable of bringing all workers within their fold. Craft unions barred women, but the Knights welcomed them and, to a lesser degree, blacks. The Knights could boast that their "great work has been to organize labor which was previously unorganized."

The rapid growth of the Knights of Labor frightened the national craft unions. The unions tried to keep their locals away from the Knights, but without success. The craft unions then began to insist on a clear separation of roles. In May 1886, they offered the Knights a "treaty" that excluded trade-union groups from the organization, leaving to it only its reform functions. When the Knights rejected the treaty, the craft unions formed the American Federation of Labor (AFL) in December.

The AFL embodied the belief of the national unions that they constituted a distinctive movement. The federation, in effect, locked into place the trade-union structure as it had evolved by the 1880s. Underlying this structure was the conviction that workers henceforth had to take the world as it was, not as they dreamed it might be. Their collective strength had to be carefully conserved to improve their lives in the present time. American trade unionism had determined to follow a course of tough-minded realism.

The architect of the AFL, and its president for nearly forty years, was Samuel Gompers. Gompers, a cigar maker from New York City, hammered out the philosophical position that would define American "pure and simple" unionism. First, there would be a steady focus on concrete, short-term gains. Second, unions would rely on economic power rather than politics. Third, they would limit their membership to workers, organized on strictly occupational lines. Finally, the union strongly rejected the theories and grand schemes that had excited the labor reformers. The steady growth of the trade unions after the formation of the AFL seemed to justify Gompers' confidence that he had hit on the correct formula for the American labor movement.

The Knights of Labor faded away. The organization had not been able to sustain its swift growth of 1885–1886 and, after a series of disastrous strikes, had retreated from the trade-union field. Grand Master Workman Powderly turned back to the rhetoric of labor reform. But the appeal to wage earners had disappeared. In its declining years, the Knights survived mainly in small-town America, no longer a workers' movement.

Industrial Battleground

The Noble Order of the Knights of Labor was the last of the nineteenth-century labor reform movements. The difference between the real world of industrial struggle and the idealism of labor reform had become too great. There was no unifying population of "producers," but only employers and workers deeply divided by conflicting interests. Nor was either side responsive to uplifting "education." Labor and management settled their differences by means of strikes, lockouts, boycotts, court-ordered injunctions and even pitched battles. As industrialism advanced in the late nineteenth century, so did the intensity of industrial warfare.

It was not that workers received no share of the returns of industrialism. Real wage rates—that is, the purchasing power of earnings—had advanced at a rate of roughly 1.5 percent a year from the beginning of industrialism. In 1870,

MAP 17.3 THE GEOGRAPHY OF AMERICAN LABOR STRIKES
Labor unrest flared up in the 1880s in patterns that revealed trigger points for strikes and a "ricochet" effect speading them to neighboring localities. Early strikes blanketed areas of heavy industry, particularly in southern New England, Pennsylvania, and Illinois. By 1894, few parts of the Northeast had remained unaffected. In the Middle West, farming districts inhibited the spread of strikes. In the South, which was thinly industrial and plainly hostile to unions, strikes were rare.

workers earned 50 percent more in real terms than in 1840; the same was true in 1910 compared with 1870. However, the labor system contained a high degree of instability. Employers quickly cut wages when business slackened. Why should they do otherwise? asked a vice-president of the Burlington Railroad. "The labor question is one of supply and demand," he said. "When work is scarce and labor plenty . . . laborers . . . must take what they can get or remain idle." Continual uncertainty about their jobs troubled workers the most. In Massachusetts, they could expect to be unemployed an average of several months a year even during normal periods. The much longer sieges of joblessness that came in hard times caused catastrophe in the lives of workers and their families.

In July 1877, a great wave of strikes hit the nation's railroads. Wage cuts triggered the strikes, but the scope and violence of the conflict stemmed from more deep-seated causes. The United States had been in a·severe depression since 1873. Unemployment may have run as high as 25 percent, and suffering was widespread. When the Baltimore and Ohio railroaders walked out on July 16, many idle men and boys joined them. Crowds cheered in railway towns along the B&O tracks as the strikers attacked railroad property and prevented trains from running. The strike spread rapidly across the rail network. In Pittsburgh, the Pennsylvania Railroad roundhouse went up in flames on July 21, followed by the Union Depot the next day. Rioters and looters roamed freely. For nearly a week, riotous strikes swept other cities, including San Francisco, Saint Louis, Omaha, and

Chicago. President Rutherford B. Hayes called up the National Guard, which gradually restored order, and the strikes collapsed. But for a while, the nation had seemed on the edge of revolution.

In 1886, another series of strikes hit the nation. This time the primary issue was the length of the work week, not wages or jobs. The work week had actually been falling, from sixty-six hours in 1860 to sixty hours in 1886, but not fast enough for American workers. As the intensity of work increased, and the value placed on leisure time rose, so did the demand for a shorter work day. "Eight hours for work, eight hours for rest, eight hours for what we will." With this slogan, the national trade unions called for an eight-hour day, effective May 1, 1886. Large numbers of organized and unorganized workers heeded the call, and strikes broke out in cities throughout the country.

The strongest fight for the eight-hour day took place in Chicago. On May 3, a battle erupted between McCormick strikers and strikebreakers. To protest the deaths of four strikers, Chicago anarchists called a meeting for the next evening at Haymarket Square. They used a pro-

vocative appeal: "Workingmen, arm yourselves and appear in full force." The meeting went off peacefully, but when police moved in at the end to break it up, someone threw a bomb and several policemen were killed. The anarchist organizers were arrested and, with no evidence against them, found guilty. Four were executed, one committed suicide, and the others received long prison sentences. They were victims of one of the great miscarriages of American justice. And in the wake of nationwide hysteria against the anarchists and strikers, employers largely defeated the campaign for an eight-hour day.

Employers strongly opposed collective dealings with workers. They commonly compiled blacklists of union members. Industrial spies kept tabs on shop sentiment and disrupted unions. Employers required workers to sign yellow-dog contracts, which were guarantees that, as a condition of employment, they would not join a union or engage in a strike. When a union did form, employers fought to deny it recognition and to maintain an open shop. Industrial warfare resulted at least as much from the militancy of antiunion employers as from the determination of workers to improve their lot in life.

LABOR STRIFE, 1912
The grievances voiced by textile workers in Lawrence, Massachusetts, resulted in one of the most dramatic strikes in American history. The companies tried to frighten the strikers into submission. Troops were brought in, picketing was prohibited, and strikers were arrested and, in some cases, given a year or longer in jail. But the men held out through the bitter cold of January and February, and won their demands. It was a rare instance in which immigrant workers, striking spontaneously, prevailed against the power of corporate industry. (Library of Congress)

STRIKING AGAINST THE AMERICAN WOOLEN COMPANY

Samuel Lipson gave the following testimony before the U.S. Committee on Rules in 1912.

Mr. Berger: Why did you go on strike?

Mr. Lipson: I went on strike because I was unable to make a living for my family.

Mr. B: How much wages were you receiving?

Mr. L: My average wage . . . is from $9 to $10 a week.

Mr. B: What kind of work do you do?

Mr. L: I am a weaver.

Mr. B: You are a skilled workman?

Mr. L: Yes, sir; for years. . . .

Mr. B: You are a member of the strike committee, are you not?

Mr. L: Yes, sir.

Mr. B: Tell us the immediate cause of the strike.

Mr. L: The workers in the American Wool Co.'s mills had meetings and discussed the question of what we can do to make a living. . . . They tried to speed up the machinery in order to make us do 56 hours work in 54 hours time, and tried to cut off the pay at the same time. . . . It was unbearable. . . .

Mr. B: You were required to do 56 hours work in 54 hours time, because a law has recently passed in Massachusetts cutting down the hours of labor to 54 per week?

Mr. L: Yes, sir. . . .

Mr. B: How many nationalities are there represented among the workers at Lawrence?

Mr. L: Sixteen nationalities.

Mr. B: Mention some of them.

Mr. L: There are Germans, Polish, English, Italians, Armenians, Turks, Syrians, Greeks, Belgians, some from France, Jewish, Lithuanians. . . .

Mr. B: How many of the workers of Lawrence are women and children? How many are men?

Mr. L: I cannot tell you about how many, but I can tell you that the majority of them are women and children, and as we are speeding up, these children are doing more work. . . . If they do not speed up, they are fired out.

Mr. B: If the children do not speed up, they lose their places in the mills?

Mr. L: Yes, sir; and the women who are used in the same place are pushed out sometimes and the children take their places.

Mr. B: Do they have any accidents in the factory?

Mr. L: Yes, sir.

Mr. B: Give a few instances of accidents.

Mr. L: There is a girl over there, Camella Teoli, and everyone present can see her. She is an Italian girl, but also speaks English. She started to work in the spinning department, on a machine that is a long one, with three or four different sides. The machine was speeded up and was running with such speed that her hair was caught and her scalp was cut by the machine. Her scalp was torn down, as you see. . . .

Mr. B: She has not sued the company?

Mr. L: No, sir. That happened two years ago, and she is working to keep up the family. They are poor and she and the father are working to keep up the family. The youngest is a little older than a year.

Mr. B: She would not stand much chance on a lawsuit against the American Woolen Co. The American Woolen Co. is a powerful concern.

Mr. L: Yes, sir; that is true.

Mr. B: What are the demands of the strikers now?

Mr. L: The demands are 15 per cent increase in wages, based on 54 hours work per week, and double pay for overtime. The reason I wish to call your attention to the demand for 15 per cent increase is this: These people work sometimes only two or three days in a week. Her father works only three days in a week, and has $2.88 per week for the family, and they absolutely live on bread and water. If you would look at the other children, you would see that they look like skeletons. . . .

Mr. B: What reception did the strikers get from the mill owners? . . .

Mr. L: They said if we did not like it to get out.

In the steel industry, the decisive attack on trade unionism came with the Homestead lockout of 1892. The Carnegie Steel Company's plant at Homestead, Pennsylvania, had a history of friendly dealings with the Amalgamated Association of Iron and Steel Workers. But by 1892, technological advances had reached the point where the company no longer regarded skilled union men as indispensable. In addition, the accompanying productivity gains created continuing difficulties with the union over the renegotiation of wage rates. The men went on strike on June 29 following a wage cut. Andrew Carnegie and Henry Clay Frick, his second-in-command, had decided to get rid of the union. Frick locked the men out of the plant on July 1, and the strikers decided to prevent strikebreakers from entering. On July 6, when Frick tried to bring in three hundred guards by barge under cover of darkness, the armed strikers were waiting on the shore of the Monongahela River. The strikers won the bloody gun battle that followed, but the Pennsylvania militia arrived a few days later and restored law and order. The company, having broken the strike, reopened the plant.

On the railroads, the battle over trade unionism was renewed on a larger scale two years later. Pullman, Illinois, was a model factory town, built and wholly owned by the sleeping-car magnate George N. Pullman. When the Panic of 1893 hit, Pullman cut wages but kept rents at their high predepression levels. The workers protested in May 1894. The Pullman Company fired their leaders, and the men struck. They belonged to the American Railway Union (ARU), which had recently been formed by the labor leader Eugene V. Debs to represent all railroad workers. In response to the strikers' plea, the ARU directed its members not to handle Pullman sleeping cars, which were attached to trains but were owned and serviced by the Pullman Company. The railroads, although they dealt with the brotherhoods of conductors, locomotive engineers, and firemen, strongly opposed the unionization of their other employees. The Pullman boycott by the ARU gave the railroads their chance to break that union. The General Managers' Association, which represented the railroads serving Chicago, insisted on running the Pullman cars, and a farflung rail strike began.

At this point, the federal government intervened. Attorney General Richard Olney, a former railroad lawyer, had close connections with the General Managers' Association. He sent troops to keep the trains running on the grounds that they carried U.S. mail. When this tactic did not work, Olney got court injunctions prohibiting the ARU leaders from conducting the strike. Debs and the other leaders refused to obey and were held in contempt of court and jailed. The great rail boycott of 1894 had been crushed by this naked use of government power on behalf of the railroad companies.

The American labor movement could make only limited headway against such concentrated resistance. Following the return of prosperity in 1897, unions expanded in some areas, especially in the building trades, transportation, and coal mining. AFL membership climbed from about half a million in 1897 to more than two million in 1904, roughly 10 percent of the nonagricultural work force. Although the number of union members continued to grow slowly, the proportion of organized workers no longer increased. The struggle for recognition went especially badly against unions in such mass-production industries as meat packing, steel, and metal-fabricating. Organized labor settled for the areas of traditional craft strength and gave up on the broad industrial sector characterized by large-scale organization and modern technology. By the second decade of the twentieth century, the AFL had become an arrested movement.

Radicals

Conservatism was the hallmark of Samuel Gompers and his brand of trade unionism. The AFL accepted the economic status quo and sought only to increase labor's share of the economic benefits. It had not been easy for the labor movement to accept such a limited objective. Only after much struggle had pure and simple unionism prevailed against nineteenth-century labor reform. If the Knights of Labor was dead, however, a tougher-minded kind of radicalism—Marxian socialism—took its place in the fight for the loyalty of American workers in the early 1900s.

German refugees had brought the ideas of Karl Marx, a German philosopher and revolu-

THE "RED SPECIAL"
Eugene V. Debs ran for president on the Socialist ticket three times before World War I—in 1904, 1908, and 1912—crisscrossing the country in whistle-stop campaigns in the "Red Special." He had no use for a train in his fourth try, in 1920, because his opposition to the war had landed him in prison. Debs never had a chance of winning, but the campaigns enabled him to spread the gospel of Socialism. (Brown Brothers)

tionary, to America after the revolutions of 1848 in Europe. Marx offered a powerful economic critique of capitalism. His prescription for revolution through class struggle produced the most durable of radical movements throughout the industrial world. Although little noticed in most parts of American society, Marxian socialism struck deep roots in the growing German-American communities of Chicago and New York. There, spilling over from European debates, a bitter dispute flared during the 1870s over a central question of organizational strategy. Should the emphasis be on political action or on the economic organization of workers? The political wing won, and in 1877 it formed the Socialist Labor party.

The overriding problem of the Socialists was how to broaden the popular base of their political movement. This meant, in part, breaking down ethnic barriers and attracting American-born voters. Equally important was gaining the support of the trade unions. These issues came

to a head during the 1890s when Daniel DeLeon began to dominate the Socialist Labor party. A brilliant theorist and inflexible leader, DeLeon preferred a pure party to a popular one. He had little interest in appealing to the American voter, and even less in dealing with what he called the "labor fakers" of the AFL. DeLeon's rigid beliefs prompted a revolt that resulted in the formation of the Socialist Party of America.

The Socialist party dedicated itself to building a broad-based radical movement. The key figure was Eugene Debs. Born in 1855 in Terre Haute, Indiana, Debs served for thirteen years as national secretary and treasurer of the Brotherhood of Locomotive Firemen. Finally repelled by the craft-union exclusiveness he saw on the railroads, Debs began to support industrial unionism. He formed the American Railway Union in 1893 and, in the Pullman boycott the next year, felt the full force of the opponents of organized labor. The union was crushed and Debs was jailed. He came out a radical and, shortly, an

TIME LINE
THE NEW INDUSTRIAL ORDER

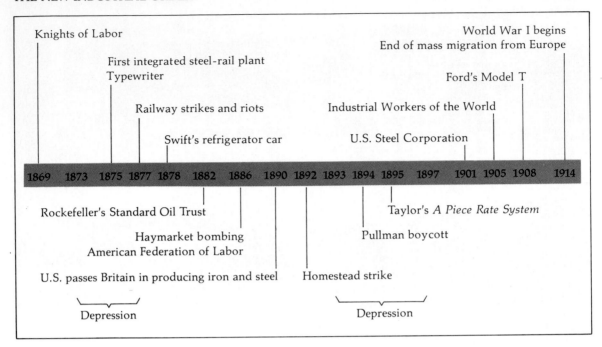

avowed Socialist. Debs, a spellbinding campaigner, was a superb spokesman for the Socialist party. He had the common touch and talked socialism in an American idiom.

The Socialist party grew steadily under Debs. By 1910, it had a national network of branches and state organizations, and numerous elected officials in American cities. The Socialists broke through the ethnic barriers of the past. They won a considerable middle-class following and were highly successful at attracting women activists. Conciliatory toward the AFL, the Socialists developed a large following in the trade unions. They represented as much as 40 percent of the vote at AFL conventions.

Failure to advance beyond that point put a fatal limitation on the prospects of the Socialist party. Without the trade-union base on which European parties relied, American socialism could not hope to prevail. In the West, radical unionism had sprung up among the metal miners. For a decade, beginning with the Cripple Creek strike in Colorado in 1894, they fought a bitter industrial war in western mining areas. As in the Pullman strike, government power sup-

ported the employers. Experience radicalized the metal miners. Their union, the Western Federation of Miners, served as the nucleus for a rival to the AFL. The new labor organization, the Industrial Workers of the World (IWW), was formed in 1905. Its objective was a labor movement suited to the needs of socialism—industrially organized, militant toward employers, and fully supportive of Socialist policies.

The IWW swiftly settled on its own radical course. It turned strongly antipolitical and severed its ties with political socialism. The Wobblies, as IWW members were called, fervently supported the Marxian class struggle, but strictly in the industrial field. By action at the point of production and by an unending struggle against employers—ultimately by a general strike—the workers themselves would bring about a revolution. A workers' society would emerge, run directly by them through their industrial unions. The term *syndicalism* describes this workers' radicalism.

In the East, the Wobblies acted as a shock force, leading strikes of industrial workers, most of them immigrants, but leaving behind no permanent organization. The IWW played this role in a series of strikes at McKees Rocks, Pennsylvania, in 1909; Lawrence, Massachusetts, in 1912; Paterson, New Jersey, in 1913; and Akron, Ohio, in 1913. But its true calling came in the West, where the IWW organized lumberjacks, construction men, miners, and itinerant farm workers following the harvest. To reach these rootless workers the Wobblies engaged in a series of free-speech fights in hostile western towns. In the field, the IWW relied on on-the-job organizers, and pressure tactics against bad bunkhouse conditions. In the West, the IWW became, in effect, a kind of trade union for the dispossessed.

American radicalism flourished during the years after 1900, but only on a limited basis. Socialists and Wobblies lived, in a sense, on the tolerance of society. They later would be crushed without ceremony. Nevertheless, they had served a larger purpose. American radicalism, by its sheer vitality, bore undying witness to what was exploitative and unjust in the new industrial order.

---

*A*merican industrialism took its modern shape during the last decades of the nineteenth century. First an efficient railroad system provided access to national markets. Then a heavy industrial base developed to supply materials, equipment, and energy for manufacturers. The scale of enterprise grew very large, and the vertically integrated firm became the predominant form of business organization. Mass production, the high-volume output of standardized goods, became the prevailing system of manufacturing.

Workers felt these developments most strongly in the loss of control over the labor process. The enormous demand for labor also led to a great influx of immigrants into the industrial economy, making ethnic diversity a distinctive feature of the American working class. After a lengthy period of uncertainty, the labor movement committed itself to pure and simple unionism. The long struggle for organization against the determined opposition of employers had begun.

Suggestions for Further Reading

A Maturing Industrial Economy

The most useful introduction to the economic history of this period is Edward C. Kirkland, *Industry Comes of Age, 1860–1897* (1961). A more sophisticated analysis, but still comprehensible to the attentive student, can be found in W. Elliott Brownlee, *Dynamics of Ascent* (rev. ed., 1979). For up-to-date essays on many of the topics covered by this chapter, the student is advised to consult Glenn Porter, ed., *Encyclopedia of American Economic History* (3 vols: 1980).

On railroads, a convenient introduction is John F. Stover, *American Railroads* (1970). The growth of the railroads as an integrated system has been treated in George R. Taylor and Irene D. Neu, *The American Railway Network, 1861–1890* (1956). Thomas Cochran, *Railroad Leaders, 1845–1890* (1953) is a pioneering study of the industry's entrepreneurs. Julius Grodinsky, *Jay Gould: His Business Career, 1867–1892* (1957) is a complex study demonstrating the contributions this railroad buccaneer made to the transportation system. Books like Cochran's and Grodinsky's have gone a long way to resurrecting Gilded Age businessmen from the debunking tradition first set forth with great power in Matthew Josephson, *Robber Barons: Great American Fortunes* (1934). Peter Temin, *Iron and Steel in the 19th Century* (1964) is the best treatment of that industry. Joseph F. Wall, *Andrew Carnegie* (1970) is the definitive biography of the great steelmaster. Equally definitive on the oil king is Allan Nevins, *A Study in Power: John D. Rockefeller* (2 vols: 1953). Harold C. Passer, *The Electrical Manufacturers, 1875–1900* (1953) treats both the entrepreneurial and technological aspects of this emergent industry. John B. Rae, *American Automobiles* is an excellent introductory account, and James J. Flink, *America Adopts the Automobile, 1895–1910* (1970) is a lively account of the start of the great American love affair. On the presiding genius, the major biography is Allan Nevin and Frank E. Hill, *Ford* (3 vols: 1954–62). A less deferential, but very shrewd, account is Keith T. Sward, *The Legend of Henry Ford* (1948).

On the emergence of modern management, the magisterial work is Aldred D. Chandler, *The Visible Hand: The Managerial Revolution in American Business* (1977), not an easy book, but one that will amply repay the labors of the interested student. Also worth reading is Chandler's earlier *Strategy and Structure: Chapters in the History of Industrial Enterprise* (1962). The standard treatment of industrial combination is Ralph L. Nelson, *Merger Movements in American Industry* (1959), as is Vincent P. Carosso, *Investment Banking in America* (1970) on the related subject of high finance. The kingpin of investment banking received somewhat irreverent treatment in Frederick Lewis Allen, *The Great Pierpont Morgan* (1949). On the money question, the definitive book is Milton Friedman and Anna J. Schwartz, *Monetary History of the United States, 1867–1960* (1963).

The World of Work

To understand the impact of industrialism on American workers, three collections of essays make the best starting points: Herbert G. Gutman, *Work, Culture and Society in Industrializing America* (1976); David Montgomery, *Workers' Control in America* (1979); and Michael S. Frisch and Daniel J. Walkowitz, eds, *Working-Class America: Essays on Labor, Community and American Society* (1983). On the introduction of Taylorism, the most useful book is Daniel Nelson, *Managers and Workers: Origins of the New Factory System* (1975). For a sweeping analysis of long-term change in American labor relations, see David M. Gordon *et al.*, *Segmented Work, Divided Workers: The Historical Transformation of Labor in the U.S.* (1982). There are two valuable recent collections of essays on immigrant workers: Richard Ehrlich, ed., *Immigrants in Industrial America* (1977), and Dirk Hoerder, ed., *American Labor and Immigration History, 1877–1920: Recent European Research* (1983). David Brody, *Steelworkers in America: The Nonunion Era* (1960)

is a study of workers in a single industry. John Bodnar, *Immigration and Industrialization: Ethnicity in an American Mill Town* (1977) is an important case study of a single community. On women workers, the best introduction is Alice Kestler-Harris, *Out To Work* (1982). Leslie Woodcock Tentler, *Wage-Earning Women: Industrial Work and Family Life, 1900–1930* (1979) is a thoughtful treatment of the impact of industrial work on female identity. On black workers, the best introduction is William H. Harris, *The Harder We Run: Black Workers since the Civil War* (1982).

The Labor Movement

The pioneering work of the American labor movement is John R. Commons *et al.*, *History of Labor in the U.S.* (4 vols, 1918–1935), of which vols II and IV cover the period of this chapter. The standard book on the struggle between labor reform and trade unionism is Gerald N. Grob, *Workers and Utopia, 1865–1900* (1961). It should be supplemented by Leon Fink, *Workingmen's Democracy: The Knights of Labor and American Politics* (1983), which captures cultural dimensions of labor reform not seen by earlier historians. The founder of the AFL is the subject of a lively, brief biography by Harold Livesay, *Samuel Gompers and Organized Labor in America* (1978). Among the many books on individual unions, Robert Christie, *Empire in Wood* (1956) best reveals the way pure-and-simple unionism worked out in practice. On industrial conflict, the most vivid book is Robert V. Bruce, *1877: Year of Violence* (1959). Almont Lindsay, *The Pullman Strike* (1943) is definitive on that battle. The best book on the IWW is Melvyn Dubofsky, *We Shall Be All* (1969). On socialism, David Shannon, *The Socialist Party of America* (1955) remains the standard account. There is, however, a fine new biography of that party's leader that supercedes previous studies, Nick Salvatore, *Eugene V. Debs: Citizen and Socialist* (1982). A dimension of American radicalism long neglected has recently received sensitive attention in Mari Jo Buhle, *Women and American Socialism, 1870–1920* (1982).

18

THE CITY

For the first two hundred years of its history, America remained a land of farmers. In 1820, barely 5 percent of the people lived in cities with a population of ten thousand or more. But after that, decade by decade, the urban population swelled, turning into a flood after midcentury. The greatest growth took place in the great metropolitan centers. In 1900, nearly a tenth of the nation—6.5 million persons—lived in cities of over a million. Another tenth made their homes in urban centers of between a hundred thousand and a million. The late nineteenth century, an economist remarked in 1899, was "not only the age of cities, but the age of great cities."

The growth of the cities had enormous implications for American society. The city was the arena of the nation's vibrant economic life. Here the factories went up, and here the multitudes of working people settled. Here, too, lived the millionaires and the new and growing urban middle class of white-collar workers and businessmen. For all these people, the city was more than a place to make a living. It provided the setting for an urban culture unlike anything seen before in the United States. City people, though vastly different among themselves, became distinctively and recognizably urban.

Urbanization

The march to the cities seemed inevitable to nineteenth-century Americans. "The greater part of our population must live in cities—cities much greater than the world has yet known," declared the Congregational minister and social critic Josiah Strong in 1898. "In due time we shall be a nation of cities." There was "no resisting the trend," said another writer. Urbanization became inevitable because of its link to another inevitability that gripped America—industrialization.

Sources of City Growth

During the earlier stages of industrialism, manufacturing had been scattered in the countryside. Mills and factories needed waterpower from the falls of streams, close access to sources of fuel and raw materials, and workers drawn from the surplus farm population. Cities, on the other hand, had engaged primarily in commerce. Located strategically along transportation routes, they were the places where merchants bought and sold goods, distributed them to the interior, or shipped them into the world market. Before

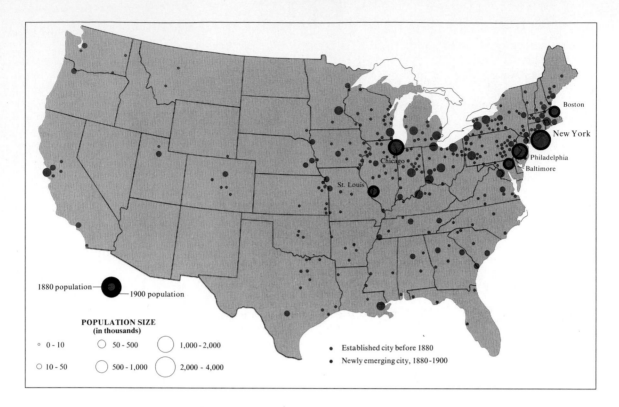

MAP 18.1 THE GROWTH OF AMERICA'S CITIES, 1880–1900
The number of Americans living in urban places more than doubled between 1880 and 1900. The most
dramatic increases occurred in the largest metropolitan centers. New York went from 1.2 million to
3.4 million, Chicago from 0.5 million to 1.7 million. Many small towns also grew rapidly, including
Seattle, Duluth, Sioux City, and Birmingham, which all grew to fifty thousand by 1900.

the Civil War, urban growth resulted primarily
from commerce, not industry. Of the fifteen
largest cities in 1860, only five had as many as 10
percent of the labor force in manufacturing activity.

After midcentury, industrialism began to
abandon the countryside. With the arrival of
steampower, mill operators no longer had to lo-
cate along streams. In the iron industry, coal
replaced charcoal as the primary fuel, so iron
makers did not have to be near forests. Improved transportation, especially on the railroads, gave entrepreneurs a greater choice in selecting the best sites in relation to supplies and
markets. Geographic concentration of industry
resulted. Ironmasters gravitated to Pittsburgh
because of its access not only to coal and iron-
ore sources but also to markets for iron and steel

products. Chicago, ideally located between livestock suppliers and consuming markets, became
a great meat-packing center in the 1870s.

Many smaller industrial cities depended on a
high degree of economic specialization. Youngs-
town, Ohio, and Johnstown, Pennsylvania,
specialized in iron and steel; Brockton and Ha-
verhill, Massachusetts, in boots and shoes; Troy,
New York, in collars and cuffs; and East Liverpool, Ohio, in pottery. Other cities processed the
raw materials of their regions. Sacramento
canned fruits and vegetables, Richmond made
cigarettes, Minneapolis milled grain, and Memphis handled lumber and produced cottonseed
oil.

Geographic concentration was one industrial
source of urban growth in the late nineteenth
century. Another was the increasing scale of

production that became characteristic of modern industry. A factory that employed thousands of workers created a small city in its vicinity. If the plant went up in an outlying area, a company town resulted. For example, Aliquippa, Pennsylvania, became body and soul the property of the Jones and Laughlin Steel Company. More often, firms built near a large city so they could draw on its labor supply and transportation facilities. George Pullman located his sleeping-car works and model town southwest of Chicago, and George Westinghouse put up his electrical plant in East Liberty near Pittsburgh. Sometimes the nearby metropolis spread and absorbed the smaller city, as happened with Pullman, Illinois. Elsewhere, as in northern New Jersey or south of Chicago and across the state line into Indiana, smaller communities merged and formed an extended urban-industrial area.

The established commercial cities also contributed to urban growth. They benefited from the tendency of a maturing industrial economy to create complex marketing and administrative structures. The greatest centers—New York and Chicago—became headquarters for corporations operating across the country. Finance, publishing, distribution, advertising, and fashion were concentrated in the metropolitan centers. Commercial cities attracted certain kinds of industry as well. They had warehouse districts readily convertible to small-scale manufacturing, and they offered ample transportation and service facilities. They also had abundant supplies of cheap labor because they served as gateways for immigrants. Boston, Philadelphia, Baltimore, and San Francisco became hives of small-scale, labor-intensive industrial activity. New York's enormous pool of immigrant workers made it a magnet for men's and women's clothing, cigar making, and diversified light industry. Preeminent as a city of trade and finance, New York also ranked as the nation's largest manufacturing center.

The 1900 census made clear the urban-industrial link. The nation's 209 principal cities, with about a third of the total population, accounted for two-thirds of the nation's industrial activity. The connection also could be seen in the country's regional development. By 1870, a core industrial area had formed from New England down through the Middle Atlantic states to Maryland. This region, with thirty of the fifty-two U.S. cities of more than twenty-five thousand people, had an urban population ratio twice the national average in 1870. Forty years later, the original industrial core was nearly three-quarters urbanized. It had thrust westward to include the Great Lakes states, which became the heartland of America's heavy industry. The centers of this new industrial activity—Pittsburgh, Cleveland, and Detroit—each grew from roughly a hundred thousand to half a million people between 1870 and 1910.

City Building

Cities grew larger under the impact of industrialism. But in so doing, they encountered staggering obstacles. How would so many people move around, communicate, and meet their physical needs? The city demanded innovation no less than did industry itself and, in the end, compiled an equally impressive record of technological achievement.

The preindustrial city had been a compact place, densely settled on a harbor. As late as 1860, Philadelphia covered only six square miles. A person could walk anywhere in the city within forty-five minutes from the foot of Chestnut Street on the Delaware River. Residential and working places remained almost as near each other as they had been in the colonial period. A Philadelphian, whether worker or businessman, normally had only a short distance to go in his everyday affairs.

As cities grew through the years, the need increased for an efficient means of urban transportation. The first step, dating back to the 1820s, was the omnibus, an elongated version of the horse-drawn coach. Once placed on iron tracks, these vehicles could be built to carry up to forty passengers. They were also able to move more rapidly through congested city streets.

Horsecars, as the first streetcars were called, provided the primary means of urban transit from the 1850s to the 1890s. The horse was not an ideal source of locomotion. It moved slowly, had limited pulling power, and left piles of manure behind. Among various early improvements on horsecars, cable cars seemed the most promising. The first ones ran in San Francisco in 1873, and more than twenty other cities used

TRAFFIC JAM IN DOWNTOWN CHICAGO, 1905
The purpose of urban transit systems—streetcars, elevated lines, and subways—was to move masses
of people rapidly and efficiently through the city. Sometimes the results compounded problems that
the transportation networks had been designed to solve. By attracting more people and business
activity, better transportation brought more congestion as well, like this scene of temporary gridlock
at Randolph and Dearborn streets in Chicago. (The Bettmann Archive)

them during the 1880s. Pulled by an endless underground cable, a cable car could run only at a
slow, unvarying speed; systemwide breakdowns
occurred frequently. The electric trolley quickly
replaced it except in hilly San Francisco. This
type of railway was the work primarily of Frank
J. Sprague, an electrical engineer who had
worked with the famous inventor Thomas A.
Edison. In 1887, Sprague designed an electric-
trolley system, utilizing an overhead power line,
for Richmond, Virginia. After Sprague's success,
electric railway construction spread across the
country. The horsecar, which had accounted for
about 70 percent of the surface transit in 1890,
virtually disappeared by 1900.

Meanwhile, congestion led to efforts to move
public transit off the streets. In 1879, the first elevated lines went into operation on Sixth and
Ninth avenues in New York City. Powered at
first by steam engines, the "els" converted to
electricity following Sprague's invention. Chicago developed elevated transit most fully. New
York, because of its crowded downtown area,
next turned to the subway. Although Boston
opened a short underground line in 1897, the
completion in 1904 of a subway running the
length of Manhattan demonstrated the full potential of underground rapid transit. The new subway system, (the *New York Times* predicted), "will
open up a region now thinly settled," in which

"a population of ten millions can be, and we believe will be, housed comfortably, healthfully and relatively cheaply." The subway would especially delight "all who travel with the sole purpose of 'getting there' in the least time possible."

Construction techniques also forged ahead. The key breakthroughs occurred in new building materials that made it possible to construct commercial buildings of greater height, interior space, and fire resistance. With the availability by the 1880s of construction steel and mass-produced durable plate glass, a wholly new way of construction opened up. A steel skeleton would support the building, and the walls, hitherto weight-bearing, would serve as curtains enclosing the structure.

In 1885, the architect William Le Baron Jenney designed the ten-story Home Insurance Building in Chicago on this principle. The steel-girdered structure liberated aesthetic perceptions. A Chicago school of architecture sprung up, dedicated to the design of buildings whose form expressed, rather than masked, their structure and function. The masterpiece of the Chicago school was Louis Sullivan's Carson, Pirie, Scott and Company department store (1908). Chicago pioneered in skyscraper construction, but New York, with its unrelenting need for prime downtown space, took the lead after the mid-1890s. The climax of New York's construction surge came with the completion in 1913 of the fifty-five story Woolworth Building. The colossal "Cathedral of Commerce" towered over its neighbors and marked the beginning of the modern Manhattan skyline.

The railroads, which played a vital role in the development of the industrial city, gave rise to the other distinctive forms of urban construction. Rivers, the earlier lifelines of trade, now became barriers that interrupted rail traffic and hindered city expansion. The second half of the nineteenth century became the great age of bridge construction. Hundreds of iron and steel bridges went up during this period. Some, such as the Eads Bridge (1873) spanning the Mississippi River at Saint Louis and the Brooklyn Bridge (1883) over New York's East River, are still in use. The Brooklyn Bridge, a giant suspension structure linking Brooklyn and Manhattan (pictured on page 554), took fifteen years to build. The architectural critic Lewis Mumford called

this engineering marvel "the first product of the age of coal and iron to achieve completeness of expression."

On the other hand, the magnificent rail terminals that graced the great cities tried to mask that modernity. Reflecting the architectural forms of ages past, the terminals were marvels of structural design in their soaring interiors and use of steel, glass, and stone. New York's Grand Central Station (1913), built in the French baroque style, was completely electrified. It made superb use of underground space and had a loop system that enabled trains to turn around without reversing course. New York's other

MANHATTAN'S FIRST SKYSCRAPER
The Tower Building at 50 Broadway was completed in 1889. To the modern eye, the first New York skyscraper seems modest and old fashioned. Compared with its squat neighbors, however, it was a revolutionary building based on new principles of construction and expressing a new form of slender, soaring architecture. (Museum of the City of New York)

THE BROOKLYN BRIDGE
This engraving celebrated the opening of the Brooklyn Bridge, an event of great importance in the city's history. Metropolitan growth in the 1870s made rivers as much barriers to urban development as they were lifelines in the city's economy. Structures like the Brooklyn Bridge were the crucial links in forming unified metropolitan areas. Brooklyn Bridge joined Manhattan and Brooklyn, providing quick transport for land shipment, streetcars, pedestrians, and, later, automobiles. (*Bird's Eye View of the Great New York and Brooklyn Bridge, 1883*. The New-York Historical Society)

great terminal, Pennsylvania Station (1910), was modeled after a Roman bath.

If the railroad was the economic lifeline of the industrial city, electricity was the source of its quickening tempo. The telephone, patented by Alexander Graham Bell in 1876, sped up communication beyond anything imagined previously. By 1900, 1.5 million telephones linked urban decision makers into a network of instant communication. Electricity also lit up the city and extended its activity into the night beyond what had been possible in the gaslight era. Charles F. Brush's electric arc lamps, first installed in the windows of the Wanamaker department store in Philadelphia in 1878, soon illuminated stores, hotel lobbies, and city streets throughout the country. Meanwhile, Thomas Edison experimented with filaments for his vacuum bulb, which, beginning in 1880, brought electric lighting into homes. Before electricity had any significant effect on industry, it lifted and lowered elevators, powered streetcars and subway trains, and lit up cities. No other invention so transformed America's urban life.

The Private City

City building was very much an exercise in private enterprise. The great innovations—the telephone, the trolley car, electric lighting, the skyscraper, and the elevator—had been spurred by the lure of profit. The investment opportunities looked so tempting that new cities sprang up almost overnight from the ruins of the Chicago fire of 1871 and the San Francisco earthquake of 1906. Likewise, real estate interests, anxious to develop subdivisions, often played an instrumental part in pushing horsecar lines out from the central districts of cities.

When urban transit began to mature, it followed the same consolidation route as in the industrial sector. In the early 1880s, Peter A. B. Widener and William L. Elkins teamed up to unite much of Philadelphia's streetcar system within the Philadelphia Traction Company. They did the same with Charles T. Yerkes in Chicago and with William C. Whitney and Thomas Fortune Ryan in New York. By 1900, their syndicate controlled streetcar systems in more than a hundred cities and had expanded to include gas works and electric lighting as well. The city, like industry, became an arena for enterprise and profit.

There was a difference, however. The city served as a dwelling place for multitudes of people, and what might improve their lives did not necessarily spell profit for entrepreneurs. Moreover, the burden of rights lay on the side of the community. There could be no "complete definition of 'a city purpose,' " the New York state courts ruled in an 1897 case authorizing New York City to build a municipally owned subway. A city had to determine its needs and then carry out those responsibilities as it saw fit. If a city chose to have services provided by others, it did so by, in effect, turning a private corporation into a municipal instrumentality. Even the use of privately owned land was subject to whatever regulations the city might choose to require.

But if municipal powers were thus broadly interpreted by law, cities generally hesitated to use them. America produced what the urban historian Sam Bass Warner has called the "private city," one shaped primarily by the actions of many private individuals. All these persons pursued their own goals and tried to maximize their own profit. Almost everyone believed that the sum of such private activity would far exceed what the community could accomplish through public effort. This meant that the city itself handled only functions, such as police protection, street construction, and sewage disposal, that could not be undertaken efficiently or profitably by private enterprise. The division of responsi-

bility, although varying greatly from city to city, almost always deferred to what favored the interests of private capital. And the functions remaining with the city were to be handled in a way that would encourage private enterprise within its precincts. This system unleashed tremendous energies for city building. But the nation paid an enormous price for such unrestricted development. A century later, we are still adding up the costs in the quality of American urban life.

Some of those costs could be seen right away. No one could deny the blight that spread along streets on which elevated trains operated. An English visitor observed in 1879:

> The nineteen hours and more of incessant rumbling day and night from the passing trains; the blocking out of a sufficiency of light; the full, close view passengers on the cars can have into rooms on the second and third floors.

Skyscrapers shut out the light and added to downtown congestion. People regarded such conditions as sad but inevitable costs of progress.

Other consequences were more clearly the result of deliberate choice. Priority went to projects considered vital to a city's economic development. Thus, bridge construction flourished. Grand public buildings, which stood as symbols of a city's eminence, enjoyed great popularity. Philadelphia's City Hall, said one critic, had been "projected on a scale of magnificence better suited for the capitol of an empire than the municipal building of a debt-burdened city." On the other hand, the condition of the streets, mainly a matter of convenience for the people, often remained scandalously bad. "Three or four days of warm spring weather," declared a New York journalist in 1893, would turn Manhattan's garbage-strewn, snow-clogged streets into "veritable mud rivers."

The farther from marketplace concerns, the less likely a project was to arouse the interest of city fathers. In 1877, Philadelphia still had about eighty-two thousand privies and cesspools. They gave way only slowly to centralized sewage systems. It took still longer for underground sewage pipes to replace the stinking gutters that connected individual houses to sewer mains.

THE LOWER EAST SIDE, NEW YORK CITY
As cities grew, land values in core areas skyrocketed. For the immigrant poor, with nowhere else to go, the result was incredible crowding in the confined spaces of tenement houses. Life necessarily spilled out into the streets. Much of the neighborhood business was transacted from pushcarts and with peddlers. The streets also offered a bit of fresh air, a chance to socialize with the neighbors, and a playing area for children. Street life was, all things considered, one of the pluses of downtown congestion. (Library of Congress)

Untreated sewage emptied into nearby bodies of water, sometimes poisoning a city's own water supply, as happened with typhoid-ridden Pittsburgh. Or the sewage might pollute the water of users downstream. Coastal cities disposed of garbage in an equally heedless way. They simply towed it out to sea in scows and dumped it in the outgoing tide.

Industrial wastes, accumulated in huge slag heaps, poured into the streams and rivers, and belched from factory stacks. A visitor to Pittsburgh noted "the heavy pall of smoke which constantly overhangs her . . . until the very sun looks coppery through the sooty haze." As for the lovely hills rising from the rivers, "they have been leveled down, cut into, sliced off, and ruthlessly marred and mutilated, until not a trace of their original outlines remain." Pittsburgh presented "all that is unsightly and forbidding in

appearance, the original beauties of nature having been ruthlessly sacrificed to utility."

These failures of the industrial city resulted not only from the low value placed on the quality of urban life. The city's dynamism confounded efforts to provide adequate services. New York's Croton aqueduct, when completed in 1842, was hailed as "more akin in magnificence to the ancient and Roman aqueducts [than anything] achieved in our times." Yet, less than a decade later, the growing city's water requirements had outstripped the capacity of the aqueduct. In 1885, New York started to build a second and larger aqueduct. That one also failed to meet the city's needs, and so New York built still another aqueduct a hundred miles away in the Catskill Mountains. Each new facility and innovation seemed to fall short, not merely outstripped by the rising demand, but also contributing to that demand. This occurred with urban transportation, high-rise building, and modern sanitation systems. They attracted more users, created new necessities, and caused additional crowding and shortages.

Dynamic urban growth had the most disastrous impact on the living conditions of the poor. In the preindustrial city, these people had lived on a makeshift basis. They occupied small wooden structures in the alleys and back streets and, increasingly, in the subdivided homes of wealthy families who had fled to other neighborhoods. When rising land values after the Civil War made this practice uneconomical, speculators began to build houses specifically for low-income people. In New York, the dreadful result was the "dumbbell" tenement, so shaped as to be able to utilize nearly all the standard twenty-five by hundred foot lot. A five-story building of this type could house twenty families in cramped, airless apartments. In New York's eleventh ward, an average of 986 persons occupied each acre, a density matched only in Bombay, India. In other cities, the pressure for space was not quite as severe. Chicago, Boston, and Saint Louis housed their poor in two- and three-story buildings, and Philadelphia and Baltimore had dingy row-houses. But people everywhere considered these districts to be blights on the city. A Hull House investigator described Chicago's Halsted Street in 1896:

. . . The filthy and rotten tenements, the dingy courts and tumble-down sheds, the foul stables and dilapidated outhouses, the broken sewer pipes, the piles of garbage fairly alive with diseased odors, and . . . children filling every nook, working and playing in every room, eating and sleeping in every windowsill, pouring in and out of every door, and seeming literally to pave every scrap of "yard."

People recognized the problem but seemed unable to solve it. Reformers favored model tenements financed by public-spirited citizens willing to accept limited dividends on their investments. When such private philanthropy failed, cities tried to impose basic housing codes, a movement that resulted in New York's Tenement Reform Law of 1901. However, it was much easier to set standards than to enforce them. Commercial development had pushed up land values in downtown areas. Only high-density, cheaply built housing could earn a sufficient profit for the landlords of the poor. This basic economic fact defied nineteenth-century solutions. Since housing was not considered a "natural monopoly," it was unthinkable for public money to be spent "competing with private enterprise in housing the masses." It was even less permissible to interfere with the free labor market so that the poor might earn enough to afford better housing.

FIGURE 18.1 FLOOR PLAN OF A DUMBBELL TENEMENT

HOW THE OTHER HALF LIVES IN NEW YORK CITY (1890)

The reading public was shocked by the revelations in Jacob Riis's photographs and newspaper articles for the New York Tribune. *He later published his collected observations as* How the Other Half Lives, *from which this passage is excerpted.*

Down below Chatham Square, in the old Fourth Ward, where the cradle of the tenement stood, we shall find New York's Other Half at home, receiving such as care to call and are not afraid. . . .

Leaving the Elevated Railroad where it dives under the Brooklyn Bridge at Franklin Square, scarce a dozen steps will take us where we wish to go. With its rush and roar echoing yet in our ears, we have turned the corner from prosperity to poverty. We stand upon the domain of the tenement.

Suppose we look into one? No—Cherry Street. Be a little careful, please! The hall is dark and you might stumble over the children pitching pennies back there. Not that it would hurt them; kicks and cuffs are their daily diet. They have little else. Here where the hall turns and dives into utter darkness is a step, and another, another. A flight of stairs. You can feel your way, if you cannot see it. Close? Yes! What would you have? All the fresh air that ever enters these stairs comes from the hall door that is forever slamming, and from the windows of dark bedrooms that in turn receive from the stairs their sole supply of the elements God meant to be free, but man deals out with such niggardly hand. That was a woman filling her pail by the hydrant you just bumped against. The sinks are in the hallway, that all the tenants may have access—and all be poisoned alike by their summer stenches. Hear the pump squeak! It is the lullaby of tenement-house babes. In summer, when a thousand thirsty throats pant for a cooling drink in this block, it is worked in vain. But the saloon, whose open door you passed in the hall, is always there. The smell of it has followed you up. Here is a door. Listen! That short hacking cough, that tiny, helpless wail—what do they mean? They mean that the soiled bow of white you saw on the door downstairs will have another story to tell—Oh! a sadly familiar story—before the day is at an end. The child is dying with measles. With half a chance it might have lived; but it had none. That dark bedroom killed it.

"It was took all of a suddint," says the mother, smoothing the throbbing little body with trembling hands. There is no unkindness in the rough voice of the man in the jumper, who sits by the window grimly smoking a clay pipe, with the little life ebbing out in his sight, bitter as his words sound: "Hush, Mary! If we cannot keep the baby, need we complain—such as we?"

Such as we! . . . What sort of an answer, think you, would come from these tenements to the question "Is life worth living?"

One case that came to my notice some months ago in the Seventh Ward tenement was typical enough . . . There were nine in the family: husband, wife, an aged grandmother, and six children; honest, hard-working Germans, scrupulously neat, but poor. All nine lived in two rooms, one about ten feet square that served as parlor, bedroom, and eating room, the other a small hall room made into a kitchen. The rent was seven dollars and a half a month, more than a week's wages for the husband and father, who was the only breadwinner in the family. That day the mother had thrown herself out of the window, and was carried up from the street dead. She was "discouraged," said some of the other women from the tenement, who had come in to look after the children while a messenger carried the news to the father at the shop.

By relying on entrepreneurial development, the city invoked powerful self-seeking forces within its public life. Americans generally believed that municipal services could be provided most efficiently by private enterprise. Unfortunately, the profit motive operated entirely differently in the public sector than in the marketplace. Transit and utility companies considered it only smart business to keep pliable the city officials who granted them franchises and regulated their operations. "Private ownership of natural monopolies in cities is the chief source of corruption in city government," Mayor Hazen Pingree of Detroit stated in 1891. In city after city for the next twenty years, reform leaders battled the private utilities. The reformers faced a problem that cities had brought upon themselves—the price of making city building a function of entrepreneurial development.

The private city went counter to the creation of a rationally planned environment. America did not lack an urban vision. On the contrary, an abiding rural ideal had exerted a powerful influence on cities for many years. Frederick Law Olmsted, who designed New York's Central Park before the Civil War and many other city parks in later years, wanted cities that exposed people to the beauties of nature. One of Olmsted's projects, the Chicago World's Fair of 1893, gave rise to the influential "City Beautiful" movement. The results included larger park systems, broad boulevards and parkways, zoning laws after the turn of the century, and even planned suburbs.

Cities usually heeded urban planners too little and far too late. "Fifteen or twenty years ago a plan might have been adopted that would have made this one of the most beautiful cities in the world," the Kansas City Park Commissioners reported in 1893. At that time, "such a policy could not be fully appreciated." Nor, even if Kansas City had foreseen its future, would it have shouldered the "heavy burden" of trying to shape its development. The American city had placed its faith in the dynamics of the marketplace, not the restraints of a planned future.

The city symbolized energy and enterprise, with its vaulting skyscrapers, rushing subways and street traffic, and hum of business activity. A British visitor called New York City "colossal, great in height, in spirit, in emotion . . . its great buildings, its spreading luxury, its lights, its air of skeptical pleasure, its moral anaesthesia, its cool ferocity . . . the microcosm of the new civilization of America." But the city also had slums, congestion, suffering, and ugliness. No city reflected the industrial age more than Chicago, a village of four thousand in 1840 and a metropolis of a million in 1890. The famous English author Rudyard Kipling described Chicago in 1899:

> Streets . . . long and flat and without end . . . interminable vistas flanked with nine, ten, and fifteen storied houses . . . no colour in the streets and no beauty—only a maze of wire ropes overhead and dirty stone flagging underfoot. A cab driver . . . said that Chicago was a

MAP 18.2 THE EXPANSION OF CHICAGO
Chicagoans in 1865 depended on slow horse-car transport to get around town. By 1900 the city limits had expanded enormously, accompanied by equally dramatic extension of streetcar service, by then all electrified. Elevated trains also now helped ease congestion in the urban core. New streetcar lines, some beyond the city limits, were important to suburban development in coming years.

live town, and that all the creatures hurrying by were engaged in business.

Kipling passed judgment on Chicago: "This place is the first American city I have encountered. . . . Having seen it, I urgently desire never to see it again."

Upper Class/Middle Class

Wealth, more than anything else, has determined social class in the United States. By that measure, American society was highly stratified during the nineteenth century. The top 1 percent of Americans held about a fourth of all wealth, and the upper 5 percent owned fully one half. The middle class, made up of the next 30 percent, owned the other half of the nation's wealth. The bottom two-thirds of the population shared what remained. This sharply unequal division of wealth occurred early in America's industrial revolution and continued well into the twentieth century with little change. Late nineteenth-century industrialism apparently did not have much impact on the distribution of wealth in America. However, it did alter greatly the ways in which the resulting distinctions of social class expressed themselves. Such expression was mainly a function of urbanism, because the city became the arena in which social differentiation took place in the industrial age.

In the compact commercial city, the marks of class had depended neither on where people lived nor with whom they rubbed elbows. Class distinctions had been expressed by the way men and women dressed, how they behaved, and the deference they demanded from or granted to others. As the industrial city grew, these interpersonal marks of class began to lose their force. In the anonymity of a large city, recognition and deference no longer served very well as mechanisms for conferring status. Instead, people began to rely on external signs. These included conspicuous consumption of material goods, exclusive associations in clubs and similar social organizations, and, above all, choice of neighborhood.

Residential segregation was hastened by the changing physical layout of the industrial city. A city's economic activities, as they grew more complex, invariably became separated along distinct territorial lines. A downtown area emerged, usually in what had been the original commercial city. Downtown, in turn, broke up into shopping, financial, warehousing, light-manufacturing, hotel and entertainment, and red-light districts. Although somewhat fluid at their edges, all these districts were well-defined areas of specialized activity. Moving out from the center, industrial development tended to follow the arteries of transportation—railroads, canals, and rivers—and, at the city's outskirts, to spread out into complexes of heavy industry. This process acted strongly against the traditional urban living patterns of the commercial city. People wanted to flee at night as far as they could from the places of their employment. Advances in urban transportation gave them a much greater degree of physical mobility.

A person's place of residence had previously depended primarily on the location of his work. Now it became much more a reflection of his personal means and social preference.

The Urban Elite

As early as the 1840s, Boston merchants took advantage of the new railway service to move out of the congested central city. Fine rural estates appeared in Milton, West Roxbury, Newton, and other outlying towns. In 1848, roughly 20 percent of Boston's businessmen made the long trip from countryside to downtown office. They traveled on 118 trains that served stations within fifteen miles of the center of Boston. Ferries that plied between Manhattan and Brooklyn or New Jersey served much the same purpose for New Yorkers. As urban development engulfed downtown residential areas and as transportation services improved, the exodus from cities by the well-to-do spread across America. Wealthy families in Cincinnati settled on the scenic hills rimming the crowded, humid tableland that ran down to the Ohio River. On those hillsides, a traveler noted in 1883, "the homes of Cincinnati's merchant princes and millionaires are found ... elegant cottages, tasteful villas, and substantial mansions, surrounded by a paradise of grass, gardens, lawns, and tree-shaded roads." Residents of the area, called Hilltop, founded five country clubs, the Cincinnati Riding Club, the New England Society, five downtown gentlemen's clubs, and many other institutions that assured an exclusive social life for Cincinnati's elite.

Despite the temptations of suburban life, many of the very richest people preferred the heart of the city. Chicago had its Gold Coast; San Francisco, Nob Hill; Denver, Quality Hill; and Manhattan, Fifth Avenue. The New York novelist Edith Wharton recalled how the comfortable midcentury brownstones—"all so much

THROWING A GREAT PARTY DURING HARD TIMES

Frederick Townsend Martin describes the lavish affair his brother and sister-in-law put on for the crème de la crème of New York society in 1897 during a severe national depression.

Every year my brother Bradley and his wife spent their winters in New York, when they entertained largely. One morning at breakfast my brother remarked—

"I think it would be a good thing if we got up something; there seems to be a great deal of depression in trade; suppose we send out invitations for a concert."

"And pray, what good will that do?" asked my sister-in-law, "the money will only benefit foreigners. No, I've a far better idea; let us give a costume ball at so short notice that our guests won't have time to get their dresses from Paris. That will give an impetus to trade that nothing else will."

Directly Mrs. Martin's plan became known, there was a regular storm of comment. . . .

We were besieged by reporters, but my brother and his wife invariably refused to discuss the matter. Threatening letters arrived by every post, debating societies discussed our extrava-gance, and last, but not least, we were burlesqued unmercifully on the stage.

I think every one anticipated a disturbance, but nothing of the kind took place, and the evening passed without any untoward incident.

The best way I can describe what is always known as the "Bradley Martin Ball," is to say that it reproduced the splendour of Versailles in New York, and I doubt if even the Roi Soleil himself ever witnessed a more dazzling sight. The interior of the Waldorf-Astoria Hotel was transformed into a replica of Versailles, and rare tapestries, beautiful flowers and countless lights made an effective background for the wonderful gowns and their wearers. I do not think there has ever been a greater display of jewels before or since; in many cases the diamond buttons worn by the men represented thousands of dollars, and the value of the historic gems worn by the ladies baffles description.

My sister-in-law personated Mary Stuart, and her gold embroidered gown was trimmed with pearls and precious stones. Bradley, as Louis XV, wore a Court suit of brocade, and I rep-resented a gentlemen of the period. The whole thing appealed most strongly to my imagination. . . .

The power of wealth with its refinement and vulgarity was everywhere. It gleamed from countless jewels, and it was proclaimed by the thousands of orchids and roses, whose fragrance that night was like incense burnt on the altar of the Golden Calf.

I cannot conceive why this entertainment should have been condemned. We Americans are so accustomed to display that I should have thought the ball would not have been regarded as anything very unusual. Every one said it was the most brilliant function of the kind ever seen in America, and it certainly was the most talked about.

After the ball the authorities promptly raised my brother's taxes quite out of proportion to those paid by any one else, and the matter was only settled after a very acrimonious dispute. Bradley and his wife resented intensely the annoyance to which they had been subjected, and they decided to sell their house in New York and buy a residence in London.

---

alike that one could understand how easy it would be for a dinner guest to go to the wrong house"—gave way to the " 'new' millionaire houses," which then spread northward beyond Fifty-ninth Street and up Fifth Avenue along Central Park. On the other side of the park, along Central Park West at Seventy-second Street, stood the monumental Dakota Apartment House, completed in 1884. It was furnished so luxuriously, one admiring journalist wrote, as to "guarantee to the tenants comforts which would require unlimited wealth to procure in a private residence." However, most millionaires preferred private homes that reflected wealth. Great mansions, reminiscent of European aristocratic houses and filled with Old World artifacts, lined Fifth Avenue at the turn of the century.

The creation of fashionable areas in the heart of a city showed the ability of the rich to assert their will over the larger society. But great fortunes did not automatically mean high social standing. An established elite stood astride the

THE BREAKERS
The favorite summering place of the New York elite was the historic colonial port of Newport, Rhode Island. The opulent mansions there were known as "cottages." Among the grandest was The Breakers, built in 1892 at a cost of $5 million. Richard Morris Hunt, a favorite architect of the Newport set, designed it for Cornelius Vanderbilt II in the style of an Italian palace. The Breakers had seventy rooms, thirty-three of them to house the small army of servants. The ornate dining room is shown in this photograph. (The Preservation Society of Newport County, R.I.)

social heights even in such relatively raw cities as San Francisco and Denver. It had only taken a generation—and sometimes less—for money made in commerce or real estate to shed its tarnish and become "old" and genteel. In more venerable cities, such as Boston, wealth passed intact through several generations. A high degree of intermarriage occurred there among the Brahmin families. By withdrawing from trade, and by asserting a high cultural and moral code, the proper Bostonians kept moneyed newcomers at bay. Elsewhere, urban elites tended to be more open, but only to the socially ambitious who were prepared to make visible and energetic use of their money.

New York's Metropolitan Opera was one of the products of this ongoing struggle among the wealthy. The Academy of Music, home to the city's opera since 1854, was controlled by the Livingstons, the Bayards, the Beekmans, and other old New York families. Frustrated in their efforts to purchase boxes at the academy, the Vanderbilts and their allies determined to sponsor a rival opera house. In 1883, with its

glittering opening to the strains of *Faust*, the Metropolitan asserted its ascendancy over the field and, in due course, won the patronage of even the Beekmans and Bayards. During this battle of the opera houses, the Vanderbilt circle achieved social recognition.

New York became the home of a national elite. The most successful people gravitated from everywhere to this preeminent center of American economic and cultural life. Manhattan's extraordinary vitality, in turn, kept the city's high society fluid and relatively open. The tycoon Frank Cowperwood, in Theodore Dreiser's novel *The Titan* (1914), reassured his unhappy wife that if Chicago society would not accept them, "there are other cities. Money will arrange matters in New York—that I know. We can build a real place there, and go in on equal terms, if we have money enough." New York thus came to be a magnet for millionaires. The city attracted them not only by its importance as a financial center, but also by the opportunities it offered for display and social recognition.

From Manhattan radiated out an extravagant

life of leisure in such resort centers as Saratoga Springs, New York; Palm Beach, Florida; and Newport, Rhode Island. Newport featured a grand array of summer "cottages," crowned by the Vanderbilts' Marble House and The Breakers. To these resorts, and elsewhere, the affluent traveled in great comfort by private railway car. A style of living emerged that was incredible for its lavish excess, ranging from yachting and horseracing to huge feasts at such luxurious restaurants as Sherry's and Delmonico's. "Our forefathers would have been staggered at the cost of hospitality these days," remarked one New Yorker.

This infusion of wealth shattered the older elite society of New York. Seeking to be assimilated into the upper class, the flood of moneyed newcomers simply overwhelmed it. Then followed a curious process of reconstruction, a deliberate effort to define the rules of conduct and identify those who properly belonged in New York society. In 1888, the first *Social Register* appeared. It announced that it would serve as a "record of society, comprising an accurate and careful list of its members, with their addresses, many of the maiden names of the married women, the club addresses of the men, officers of the leading clubs and social organizations, opera box holders, and other social information."

The career of Ward McAllister as arbiter to New York society was even more significant. He instructed the socially ambitious on how to select guests, set a proper table, arrange a ball, and launch a young lady into society. McAllister fostered an ordered social round of assemblies, balls, and dinners that defined the boundaries of an elite society. The key lay in the creation of sponsored associations by social leaders, "organized social powers, capable of giving a passport of society to all worthy of it." McAllister himself played a part in this selective process. He had the idea of the "Four Hundred," the true cream of New York society. His list corresponded to those invited to Mrs. William Astor's great ball of February 1, 1892.

Social registers, junior leagues, and lesser versions of Ward McAllister soon popped up in cities throughout the country. They represented the price paid for the fluidity at the height of the social order.

Americans were adept at making money, noted the journalist E. L. Godkin in 1896, but they lacked the European traditions for spending it. "Great wealth has not yet entered our manners," Godkin remarked. "No rules have yet been drawn to guide wealthy Americans in their manner of life." In their struggle to find the rules and establish the manners, the moneyed elite made an indelible mark on urban life. If there was magnificence in the American city, it was mainly their handiwork. And if there was conspicuous waste and vulgarity, it was likewise their doing. In a democratic society, wealth finds no easier outlet than through public display.

The Middle Class

The middle class left a much smaller imprint on the city. Its members, unlike the rich, preferred privacy and retreated into the domesticity of suburban comfort and family life.

The emerging corporate economy spawned a new salaried middle class. Bureaucratic organizations required managers, accountants, and clerks. Advancing technologies needed engineers, chemists, and designers. The distribution system sought salesmen, advertising men, and buyers. These salaried ranks increased sevenfold between 1870 and 1910, much faster than any other occupational group. The traditional middle class—independent businessmen and professionals—also grew but only at a third of the rate of salaried personnel. Nearly nine million people held white-collar jobs in 1910, more than a fourth of all employed Americans.

The middle class, particularly its salaried portions, was an urban population. Some lived within the city, in the rowhouses of Baltimore or Boston, or in the comfortable apartment houses of New York or other metropolitan centers. But far more preferred to escape from the clamor and congestion of the city. They were attracted by a persisting "rural ideal." They agreed with the landscape architect Andrew Jackson Downing, who thought that "nature and domestic life are better than society and manners of town." With the extension of rapid transit service from the city center, middle-class Americans followed the wealthy into the countryside. All sought what a Chicago developer promised of his North Shore subdivision in 1875—"qualities of which the city is in a large degree bereft, namely its pure air, peacefulness, quietude, and natural scenery."

MIDDLE-CLASS DOMESTICITY

For middle-class Americans of the late nineteenth century, the home was a place of nurture, a refuge from the world of competitive commerce. Perhaps that explained why their residences were so heavily draped and cluttered with bric-a-brac, every space filled with overstuffed furniture. All of it emphasized privacy—and the pride of possession. The young woman shown playing the piano symbolizes another theme of American domesticity—wives and daughters as ornaments, and as bearers of culture and refinement. (Museum of the City of New York)

No major American city escaped rapid suburbanization during the last third of the nineteenth century. City limits everywhere expanded rapidly. By 1900, more than half of Boston's people lived in "streetcar suburbs" outside the original city. When the United States Bureau of the Census began to designate "metropolitan districts" in 1910, it found that about 25 percent of the urban population lived outside the city limits.

The suburbs were middle-class territory. But the middle class was not monolithic. It ranged from prosperous businessmen and lawyers to clerks and traveling salesmen who earned no more than foremen and craftworkers. There was no better map of class standing than the geography of the suburbs, because where a family lived told where it ranked. The farther the distance from the center of the city, the finer the houses and the larger the lots. This arrangement reflected the ability to pay, and the work situations that went with varying income levels. The well-to-do had the leisure and flexible schedules to travel the long distance into town. People closer in wanted a direct transit line convenient to home and office. Lower-income suburbanites were likely to have more than one wage earner in the family, less security of employment, and to hold jobs requiring movement around the city. They needed easy access to crosstown transit lines, which ran close to the city center.

Divisions within suburbs, although always a precise measure of economic ranking, never became rigidly fixed. People in the center who wanted to better their lives moved to the cheapest suburbs. Fleeing from these newcomers, those already settled pushed the next higher group farther out in search of space and greenery.

Suburbanization was the sum of countless individual decisions. Each move represented an advance in living standards—not only more light, air, and quiet, but also better housing than the city afforded. The housing had more space and better design, as well as indoor toilets, hot water, central heating, and, by the turn of the century, electricity. Even the inner suburbs came to regard these amenities as standard comforts. The suburbs also restored a basic opportunity that had seemed sacrificed by rural Americans who had moved to the city. In the suburbs, home ownership again became a norm. "A man is not really a true man until he owns his home," propounded the Reverend Russell H. Conwell in his sermon, "Acres of Diamonds."

The small town of the rural past had fostered community life. Not so the suburbs. The grid street pattern, while efficient for laying out lots and providing utilities, offered no natural focus for group life. Nor did stores and services that lay scattered along the trolley-car streets. Not even schools and churches were located to make them the centers of community life. Suburban development conformed to the economics of real estate and transportation, and so did the thinking of middle-class home seekers entering the suburbs. They wanted a house that gave them good value and convenience to the trolley line.

The need for community had lost some of its meaning for middle-class Americans. Two other attachments assumed greater importance. One was work, the other, family.

Families

The family had been the primary productive unit in the preindustrial economy. Farmers, merchants, and artisans had carried on their work within a family setting. The value of family members could be reckoned by their economic contribution. The family circle included not only blood relatives, but all others living and working within the household. With the onset of industrialism, the family gradually lost its function as a productive unit. Throughout the city, members of the household left the home to help earn the family's living. Families also stopped producing for their own consumption. Almost all men's clothing was ready-made by 1900, and so was a growing share of food that came in the form of packaged and canned goods. Urban families reduced the number of their children and excluded all but nuclear members. The typical middle-class family of 1900 consisted of husband, wife, and three children.

Within this small circle, relationships between family members became intense and affectionate. "Home was the most expressive experience in life," recalled the literary critic Henry Seidel Canby of his growing up in the 1890s. "Though the family might quarrel and nag, the home held them all, protecting them against the outside world." In a sense, the family served as a refuge against the competitive, impersonal business world into which its employed members plunged daily. The suburbs provided a fit setting for middle-class families. The quiet, tree-lined streets created a domestic world insulated from the hurly-burly of commerce and enterprise. The symbol of middle-class suburbia was the house, standing on its own lot as an expression of family sanctity.

The burdens of this domesticity fell heavily on the wife. It was nearly unheard of for her to seek an outside career; that was her husband's role. She had the job of managing the household. "The woman who could not make a home, like the man who could not support one, was condemned," Canby remembered. But with better household technology, greater reliance on purchased goods, and fewer children, the wife's workload declined in these years. Moreover, servants still played an important part in middle-class households. The 1910 census reported about two million domestic servants, the largest job category for women.

The easing of household work put greater stress on the need for higher quality homemaking. This was the theme of Catharine Beecher's bestselling book *The American Woman's Home* (1869) and of such magazines as the *Ladies' Home Journal* and *Good Housekeeping*, which first appeared during the 1880s. The wife did more than make sure that food was on the table, that clothes were washed and mended, and that the house was kept clean. She had the higher calling of bringing sensibility, beauty, and love to the household. She made the home a refuge for her husband and a place of nurture for their children.

The wife's role, difficult under the best of circumstances, was made even harder by deep-rooted problems. Foremost was the denial of any sexual basis to the affectionate relationship at the heart of the family. "The majority of women (happily for society) are not very much troubled with sexual feeling of any kind," a popular medical text assured its readers. "What men are habitually women are only exceptionally. . . . Love of home, of children, and of domestic duties are the only passion they feel." Toward their husbands, another manual stated, wives should hold only "motherly tenderness. . . . The higher a woman rises in moral and intellectual culture, the more is the sensual refined away from her nature, and the more pure and perfect and predominating becomes her motherhood." In the face of the male's natural sexual appetites, brides should "struggle as resolutely to secure extreme temperance after marriage as they do to maintain complete abstinence before the ceremony."

Womanly virtue, even if a happy marriage depended on it, by no means put the wife on equal terms with her husband. The law established her subordinate role. It denied political rights to women—in 1890, only four states gave them the right to vote—and subjected them to discriminatory treatment. For example, the husband, but not the wife, could sue for divorce on grounds of adultery. More important, custom dictated the wife's submission to her husband. She relied on his ability as the family breadwinner and, despite her superior virtues and graces, ranked his inferior in vigor and intellect. Her mind could be employed "but little and in trivial matters," wrote one prominent physician, and her proper place was as "the companion or ornamental appendage to man."

Bright, independent-minded women understandably rebelled against marriage. The marriage rate in the United States fell to its lowest point during the last forty years of the nineteenth century. More than 10 percent of the women of marriage age remained single, and the rate was much higher among college graduates and professionals. Only half of the Mount Holyoke College class of 1902 married. When Frances Perkins, a member of the class, married in 1913, she upset her New York social-work colleagues. They thought they had lost her, but her husband's illness forced Perkins to resume her career. She eventually became the first woman cabinet member, serving as secretary of labor under President Franklin D. Roosevelt.

For middle-class women who did marry, the price was often high. A substantial number of families broke apart, but most of these domestic mishaps remained unrecorded because of the stigma attached to divorce. In a Chicago suburb in the 1880s, at a time when divorce was virtually unknown there, about 10 percent of the households had an absent spouse. The national divorce rate increased from 1.2 per thousand marriages in 1860 to 7.7 in 1900. It was more difficult to document the other ways women responded to marriages that denied their autonomy or sexual desires. Middle-class women became the principal victims of neurasthenia, a disorder whose symptoms included depression and general disability. Some unhappy housewives found "silent friends" in opium and alcohol, both often dispensed in well-laced patent medicines.

A happier release came through the companionship of other women. In an age that defined separate men's and women's spheres, close ties commonly formed between schoolmates, cousins, and mothers and daughters. The intimacy and intensity of such attachments can be sensed in surviving letters of separated friends. Such enduring female ties yielded emotional gratification not often found in marriage. Husbands, absorbed in business, frequently played a secondary and remote role in the lives of their wives. The women's own sphere often filled that emotional vacuum.

The middle-class family had long faced a difficult dilemma. Many couples wished to limit the number of their children, but birth control was not an easy matter. Antipornography laws, pushed through by the social-purity campaigner Anthony Comstock during the 1870s, banned distribution of birth control information through the mail. Many states classified such material as obscene literature and prohibited its sale. Abortion became illegal except to save the mother's life. Although the practice of abortion was probably widespread, it was expensive, dangerous, and considered shameful. Family limitation could be best achieved by delaying marriage and then by practicing abstinence. The repressive sexuality within the family resulted from practical necessities. A fulfilling sexual relationship could not be squared with the desire to limit and space childbearing.

Somewhere around 1890, change set in. Although the birth rate continued to decline, more young people got married and at an earlier age. These developments reflected a sexual revolution within the American middle-class family. With the growing acceptability of contraception, the Comstock laws notwithstanding, people no longer tightly linked sex and procreation. This crucial change initiated the sexual emancipation of women. In succeeding editions of his book *Plain Home Talk on Love, Marriage, and Parentage*, for example, the physician Edward Bliss Foote began to favor a healthy sexuality that gave pleasure to both female and male. During the 1890s, the artist Charles Dana Gibson created the image of the "new woman" in his drawings for *Life* magazine. The Gibson girl was tall, spirited, athletic, and chastely sexual. Such clothing constrictions as bustles, hoop skirts, and hourglass corsets gave way to shirtwaists and other natural styles that did not hide or disguise the female form.

The children of the middle class went through their own revolution. In the past, American children everywhere had been regarded chiefly as economic assets—added hands for the family farm, shop, or counting house. That no longer held true for the urban middle class. Parents stopped treating their children as working members of the family. In the old days, remarked the author Ralph Waldo Emerson in 1880, "children had been repressed and kept in the background; now they were considered, cosseted, and pampered." There was such a thing as "the juvenile mind," lectured Jacob Abbott in his book *Gentle Measures in the Management and Training of the Young* (1871). The family had the responsibility of providing the nurturing environment in which the young personality could grow and mature. Preparation for adulthood became increasingly linked to formal education. School enrollment went up one and a half times between 1870 and 1900. High school attendance, while still covering only a small percentage of teenagers, increased at the fastest rate. The years between childhood and adulthood began to stretch out, and a new stage of life—adolescence—emerged. Rooted in an extended period of family dependency, adolescence at the same time shifted much of the socializing role from parents to peer group. A youth culture started to take shape. It became one of the hallmarks of American life in the twentieth century.

City People

When the budding writer Hamlin Garland and his brother arrived in Chicago from rural Iowa in 1881, they knew immediately that they had entered a new world: "Everything interested us. . . . Nothing was commonplace, nothing was ugly to us." In one way or another, every city-bound migrant, whether from the American countryside or a foreign land, experienced something of this exhilaration and wonder. But with the freedom, opportunity, and boundless variety, there also came profound disorder and uncertainty. The urban world would be utterly unlike the rural communities that the newcomers had left. In the countryside, every person had been known to his or her neighbors. In the city, people were not only strangers but strangers from many lands who spoke many languages. Rural roles and obligations had been well understood, but the only predictable relationships in the city were those dictated by the marketplace.

The newcomers could never recreate in the city the worlds they had left behind. But new ways developed to meet the social needs of urban dwellers—to give them a sense of their place in the community; to teach them how to function in an impersonal, heterogeneous environment; and to make the complex, dynamic city understandable. An urban culture emerged, and through it a new breed of American entirely at home in the modern city.

Immigrants

For immigrants, ethnic identity played the crucial role in forming an urban community. Beginning in the 1880s, observers invariably reported that only foreign-born people lived in the poorer downtown areas. "One may find for the asking an Italian, a German, a French, African, Spanish, Bohemian, Russian, Scandinavian, Jewish, and Chinese colony," remarked the Danish-American journalist Jacob Riis in his study of lower New York in 1890. "The one thing you shall vainly ask for in the chief city of America is a distinctively American community." This foreign-born concentration stemmed partly from

JEWISH ETHNIC CONCENTRATIONS

Hungarian   Galician   Russian

Romanian   Mixed Levantine and Romanian

NEIGHBORHOOD INSTITUTIONS

1. Newspaper Row
2. Chatham Square Library
3. Beth Israel Hospital
4. Israel Elchanan Yeshiva
5. Educational Alliance
6. Henry Street Settlement
7. Machzike Talmud Torah
8. Hebrew Sheltering House
9. Hebrew Technical School for Girls
10. Home for the Aged
11. Jewish Maternity Hospital
12. Beth Hamedrash Hagadol
13. Yiddish Rialto
14. Thalia Theater
15. People's Bath
16. Police Headquarters
17. Public School 63
18. Music School Settlement
19. Asch Building
20. Astor Library
21. Hebrew Technical School for Boys
22. Labor Temple

MAP 18.3 THE JEWISH LOWER EAST SIDE, NEW YORK CITY

Jews from Eastern Europe, disembarking in New York City, concentrated in Manhattan's Lower East Side and, within that area, settled among others from their home regions. The same feeling of group identity led to a remarkable flowering of ethnic institutions built by Jewish immigrants to meet their own educational, cultural, and social needs.

economic necessity—the need to live near jobs and the inability to afford better housing. Of all urbanites, immigrant working people had the least freedom to choose where they lived. Their poverty dictated that they be concentrated in the industrial districts and the congested downtown area.

The immigrants did not settle randomly in the tenement districts, however. Even where this seemed to happen, as in Philadelphia, closer study revealed ethnic groups clustering in individual houses and portions of blocks. More commonly, as Riis discovered, an ethnic group took over an entire neighborhood. In New York, Italians crowded into the Irish neighborhoods west of Broadway, and Russian and Polish Jews pushed the Germans out of the lower East Side. A dense colony of Hungarians lived around Houston Street, and Bohemians occupied the upper East Side between Fiftieth and Seventy-sixth streets.

One could also spot a clustering within ethnic groups of people from the same province or even village. Among New York Italians, for example, Neapolitans and Calabrians populated the Mulberry Bend district, and Genoese lived on Baxter Street. Other northern Italians occupied the eighth and fifteenth wards west of Broadway, and southern Italians moved into "Little Italy" far up in Harlem. In 1903, along a short stretch of Elizabeth Street, lived several hundred families from Sciacca, a Sicilian fishing town.

From the feeling of companionship that drew ethnic groups together, a variety of institutions sprung up to meet their needs. Wherever substantial numbers of immigrants lived, newspapers appeared. In 1911, the twenty thousand Poles in Buffalo, New York, supported two daily papers. Immigrants throughout the country avidly read *Il Progresso Italo-Americano* and the Yiddish language *Jewish Daily Forward*, both published in New York City. Conviviality could always be found on street corners, in barbershops and club rooms, and in saloons. A 1905 survey showed that Chicago had as many saloons as grocery stores, meat markets, and dry-goods stores together. Italians marched in saint-day parades, Bohemians gathered in singing socie-

TABLE 18.1 FOREIGN-BORN POPULATION OF PHILADELPHIA, 1870 AND 1910

	1870	1910
Irish	96,698	83,196
German	50,746	61,480
Austrian	519	19,860
Italian	516	45,308
Russian	94	90,697
Hungarian	52	12,495
Foreign-born population	183,624	384,707
Total population	674,022	1,549,008

SOURCE: Allen F. Davis and Mark Haller, *The Peoples of Philadelphia* (Philadelphia: Temple University Press, 1973).P.

ties, and New York Jews patronized a vibrant Yiddish theater. To provide help in times of sickness and death, the immigrants organized mutual-aid societies. The Italians of Chicago had sixty-six of these organizations in 1903, composed mainly of people from particular provinces and towns. Immigrants built a rich and functional institutional life in urban America to an extent unimagined in their native villages.

Most urban blacks, like the immigrants, were newcomers to the cities. Settled black populations in northern cities began to be outnumbered in the late 1800s by migrants from the South. By 1910, New York ranked as the nation's second largest black urban center, after Washington, D.C. New York's ninety-one thousand blacks represented scarcely 3 percent of its 1910 population, but they had a rich community life. They created a flourishing press, fraternal orders, and a middle class that catered to their needs. Newcomers found the black churches particularly important in their lives. Manhattan's Union Baptist Church, housed like many others in a storefront, attracted the "very recent residents of this new, disturbing city" and made Christianity come "alive Sunday mornings."

Religion had an equally important part in the lives of the immigrants. They found greater difficulty, however, establishing churches as they had known them in the old country. These people stubbornly opposed any change from familiar church practice. Also, the ground had been preempted to some degree by others who had already planted their religions in America.

(After K. Conzen)

0   ½   1
Mile

Mississippi River

Laborers

"Good class"

"Good class"

Mechanics and laborers   Menominee

Artisans and laborers

Artisans
and
laborers

Laborers

Lake
Michigan

River

	1850	1890
Native	→	
German	→	
Irish	→	
Polish		
Scandinavian		
Black		
Mixed (both dates)		

Central business district (1890)

Industrial zone (1890)

MAP 18.4 THE URBAN ETHNIC MOSAIC:
MILWAUKEE, 1850–1890
Neighborhoods in American cities developed strong class
and ethnic identities in the second half of the nineteenth
century. Core areas near downtown Milwaukee
expanded outward as immigrant populations increased
and new residents arrive. Artisans and laborers tended to
settle near their places of work in and near the industrial
zone. The "good class" (upper and middle classes) and
German residents have remained dominant in certain
areas throughout Milwaukee's history.

By the time the eastern European Jews began
their mass migration in the 1880s, about 250,000
Jews lived in America, mostly of German origin.
The German Jews, well established and increasingly properous, had long since begun to embrace Reform Judaism. Reform Jews abandoned
religious practices "not adapted to the views and
habits of modern civilization." They thus practiced a form of Judaism very remote from the pious orthodoxy of the Yiddish-speaking Jews.
The eastern Europeans founded their own Orthodox synagogues, often in vacant stores and
ramshackle buildings. The number of synagogues in the United States jumped from 270 in
1880 to 1,901 in 1916.

Many Jews found it difficult to adhere to the
traditional form of their religion. In the insulated
villages of eastern Europe, Judaism comprised
not only worship and belief, but an entire way
of life. Not even the closely confined urban
American ghetto could recreate the communal
environment for strict religious observance. "The
very clothes I wore and the very food I ate had
a fatal effect on my religious habits," confessed
the hero of Abraham Cahan's novel *The Rise of
David Levinsky* (1917). "If you ... attempt to bend
your religion to the spirit of your surroundings,
it breaks. It falls to pieces." Levinsky shaved off
his beard and plunged into the Manhattan clothing business. If Orthodox Judaism survived this
shattering of faith, it did so only by sharply reducing its claims on the lives of the faithful.

The Catholic church faced much the same
problem. The issue, explicitly defined within the
church as "Americanism," turned on how far
Catholicism should respond to American society. Catholics fought out the question on many
fronts, including parochial schooling, education
for the clergy, and relations with non-Catholics.
What was the church's place in a pluralistic society that denied religion any state support or automatic claim to people's allegiance? Bishop John
Ireland of Saint Paul, Minnesota, felt that "the
principles of the Church are in harmony with
the interests of the Republic." But traditionalists,
led by Archbishop Michael A. Corrigan of New
York, denied the possibility of such harmony.
They argued, in effect, for insulating the church
from a hostile environment.

In 1895, Pope Leo XIII announced his support
of the traditionalists. He denied "that in America
is to be sought the type of the most desirable
status of the Church." The pope regretted the
absence of the benefits that came from public
support and urged Catholics "to prefer to asso-
ciate with Catholics, a course which will be very
conducive to the safeguarding of their faith."
Catholicism, because of its hierarchical structure,
had a better chance than Judaism to resist American influences.

The church's traditional wing had the support
of immigrant Catholics, who wanted to preserve
their religion as they had known it in Europe.
But the needs of the immigrants extended beyond purely religious matters. The church also
had to express their ethnic identities. These
Catholics wanted their own parishes, where

they could celebrate their own customs and holidays, speak their own languages, and educate their children in their own parochial schools. When they became numerous enough, they also demanded their own bishops. German Catholics had pressed these ethnic claims for years, and so did the southern and eastern Europeans who flocked to America from the 1890s on.

The church had difficulty responding. Ironically, the institutional strength that preserved Catholicism against "Americanism" made it resistant to the demands of its immigrant congregations. Their claims seemed to challenge the Irish-Catholic hierarchy and, more importantly, the integrity of the church itself. The desire for ethnic parishes did more than divide Catholics; it also led to demands for local control of church property. In addition, to appoint bishops with jurisdiction over specific ethnic groups meant cutting across the diocesan structure of the church.

The severity of the conflict depended partly on the religious traditions of each ethnic group. Italians, for example, had a strong anticlerical feeling, much strengthened by the papacy's opposition to the unification of Italy. Italian men also had a tradition of religious apathy. On the other hand, the church played such an important part in the lives of Polish immigrants that they sometimes tolerated no interference from the Catholic hierarchy. In 1907, fifty parishes formed the Polish National Catholic Church of America, which adhered to Catholic ritual without recognizing the pope's authority.

On the whole, however, the church reconciled its authority with the ethnic needs of the immigrant faithful. It met the demand for representation in the hierarchy by appointing Polish and other immigrant priests as auxiliary bishops within existing dioceses. Before World War I, American Catholics worshiped in more than two thousand foreign-language churches and in many others that were bilingual. The Catholic church became a central institution for the expression of ethnic identity in urban America.

Protestantism and the City

Protestant churches, the products of rural, middle-class America, in some ways encountered even greater challenges in the cities than Judaism or Catholicism. Beginning with the Irish migrations of the 1840s, urban populations fell increasingly outside the Protestant faith. At the same time, Protestant congregations abandoned the older residential neighborhoods. Many formerly prosperous churches found themselves stranded in bleak working-class districts. Seventeen Protestant churches moved out of lower Manhattan during the twenty years after 1868 when the area below Fourteenth Street filled up with immigrants.

Nearly every major city retained great downtown churches where wealthy Protestants worshiped. Some of these churches, richly endowed, took pride in nationally prominent pastors, including Henry Ward Beecher of Plymouth Congregational Church in Brooklyn and

URBAN REVIVALISM
In rural America, the church was as familiar to the community as the schoolhouse, and churchgoing was a normal part of the routine of life. In anonymous city life, faith found fewer established outlets. The revivalist Dwight L. Moody discovered an enormous, pent-up need when he began to preach in American cities in 1875. This crowd of five thousand in Brooklyn at Moody's maiden service prompted the trolley company to lay additional track to accommodate the faithful. (From *Harper's Weekly*. The Newberry Library, Chicago)

Phillips Brooks of Trinity Episcopal Church in Boston. The eminence of these churches, with their fashionable congregations and imposing edifices, emphasized the growing remoteness of Protestantism from mainstream urban life. "Where is the city in which the Sabbath day is not losing ground?" lamented a minister in 1887. The families of businessmen, lawyers, and doctors could be seen in any church on Sunday morning, he noted, "but the workingmen and their families are not there."

To counter this decline, the Protestant churches responded in two ways. They evangelized among the unchurched and indifferent, for example, through the Sunday-school movement that blossomed in these years. Protestants also made their churches instruments of social uplift. Starting in the 1880s, many city churches provided such facilities as reading rooms, day nurseries, clubhouses, and vocational classes. Sometimes the churches linked evangelism and social uplift. The Salvation Army, which arrived from England in 1879, spread the gospel of repentance among the urban poor. A decade later, it added an assistance program that ranged from soup kitchens to homes for fallen women. When all else failed, the down-and-outers of American cities knew they could count on the Salvation Army.

The Young Men's and Women's Christian Associations attracted large numbers of the young single people who flocked into the cities. No other organizations better met the needs of young adults for physical recreation, education, or companionship. Nor did other groups so effectively combine these services with an evangelizing appeal in the form of Bible classes, nondenominational worship, and a strong religious atmosphere.

The need of many people to unite religion with social uplift could be seen in the enormous popularity of a book called *In His Steps* (1896). The author, the Reverend Charles M. Sheldon, told the story of a congregation that resolved to live by Christ's precepts for one year. "If the church members were all doing as Jesus would do," Sheldon asked, "could it remain true that armies of men would walk the streets for jobs, and hundreds of them curse the church, and thousands of them find in the saloon their best friend?"

Yet the most potent form of urban evangelism said little about social uplift. From its beginnings in the eighteenth century, revivalism had steadfastly focused on the individual. It stressed sinfulness and the need for redemption. The solution of earthly problems would follow the conversion of the people to Christ. Beginning in the mid-1870s, revival meetings swept through the cities. The pioneering figure was Dwight L. Moody, a former Chicago shoe salesman and YMCA official. After preaching two years in England, Moody returned to America in 1875. With his talented chorister and hymnwriter, Ira D. Sankey, Moody staged revival meetings that drew thousands of people. He preached an optimistic, uncomplicated, nondenominational message. Eternal life could be had for the asking, Moody shouted as he held up his Bible. His listeners needed only "to come forward and take, TAKE!" Many other preachers followed in Moody's path. The most notable was Billy Sunday, a hard-drinking outfielder for the Chicago White Stockings who mended his ways and found religion. Like Moody and other city revivalists, Sunday was a farm boy. His rip-snorting cries against "Charlotte-russe Christians" and the "booze traffic" carried the ring of rustic America. By realizing that many people remained villagers at heart, revivalists had found the key for bringing city dwellers back into the church fold.

Leisure

City people divided life's activities into separate units, setting workplace apart from home, and working time apart from free time. Leisure became a defined function, marked by the clock and enjoyed in distinctive ways and at designated places. Urban dwellers, in the impersonal, anonymous world they inhabited, increasingly found themselves the paying customers of commercial entertainment.

Amusement parks, such as Elitch's Gardens, which opened in Denver in 1890, went up at the end of trolley lines in cities across the country. Coney Island became immensely popular among New Yorkers. Theatrical entertainment likewise attracted huge audiences. Chicago had six vaudeville houses in 1896, and twenty-two in 1910. Evolving from cheap variety and minstrel

THE SEASHORE
Earlier generations of Americans would have shaken their heads at the sight of swarms of city dwellers heading for the beach on a hot Sunday. Didn't they know about the physical risks of "exposing one's complexion to the harmful rays of the sun" or the moral dangers of mixed bathing in various stages of undress? By 1900, the beach had become one of the great urban institutions of weekend play. (New Haven Colony Historical Society)

shows, vaudeville moved from boisterous beer halls into grand theaters. It cleaned up its routines, making them suitable for the entire family, and turned into thoroughly professional entertainment handled by national booking agencies. With its standard program of nine acts of singing, dancing, and comedy, vaudeville attained the popularity that the movies later achieved.

Of all forms of diversion, none was more specific to the city, nor so spectacularly successful, as professional baseball. The game's promoters decreed that baseball had been created in 1839 by Abner Doubleday in the village of Cooperstown, New York. Actually, baseball was neither of American origin—it developed from the English game of rounders—nor a product of rural life. Organized play began in the early 1840s in New York City, where a group of gentlemen enthusiasts competed among themselves on an empty lot. They wrote the first modern rules in 1845. The next year, as the New York Knickerbockers, they lost to the New York Nine, 23 to 1, in the first game between two organized baseball teams. During the next twenty years, the aristocratic tone of baseball disappeared. Clubs sprang up across the country and intercity competition developed on a scheduled basis. In 1868, baseball became openly professional, following the example of the Cincinnati Red Stockings in sign-

ing players to contracts at a negotiated salary for the season.

Big-time commercial baseball came into its own with the launching of the National League in 1876. The team owners were profit-minded businessmen who ran the sport and carefully shaped it to please the fans. Wooden grandstands gave way to the concrete and steel stadiums of the early twentieth century, such as Fenway Park in Boston, Forbes Field in Pittsburgh, and Shibe Park in Philadelphia.

For the urban multitudes, baseball grew into something more than an occasional afternoon at the ball park. Fans, by rooting for the home team, found a basis for identifying themselves with the city they lived in. Amid the diversity and anonymity of urban life, the common experience and language of baseball acted as a bridge among city people. Students of the game have suggested that baseball was peculiarly attuned to city life. It followed strict, precise rules, which suggested an underlying order to the chaotic city. Far from respecting the rules, however, the players tried to get away with whatever they could in order to win. Did this not match the competitive scramble of urban life? The blue-coated umpires, the symbols of authority, were scorned by players and derided by fans. What better substitutes for the resentment against the

THE NATIONAL PASTIME
This color lithograph commemorates the opening game of the 1889 season, with the Boston Base-Ball Club taking on the New York Base-Ball Club. The National League was then scarcely twelve years old. The fielders played barehanded, but otherwise the game remains today much as the artist pictured it a century ago, even down to the umpire's characteristic stance. What was there about baseball that almost overnight made it the national game and has kept it there virtually unchanged for a century? (Historical Pictures Service)

powers-that-be who ruled the lives of city people? Baseball, like many other emerging urban institutions, served as a mechanism for inducting people into the life of the modern city.

The press undertook this task in a clear-eyed, calculated way. Until Benjamin H. Day founded the *New York Sun* in 1833, American newspapers had limited themselves to a diet of mercantile news and political advocacy. The *Sun* promised "all the news of the day," cost only a penny—hence the term "penny press"—and aimed for a broad audience. When James Gordon Bennett founded the *New York Herald* in 1835, he said he wanted "to record the facts . . . for the great masses of the community." Journalism defined the news to be whatever interested city readers. The *Herald* covered crime, scandal, and sensational events. After the Civil War, *Sun* editor Charles A. Dana added the human-interest story which made news of ordinary, insignificant happenings. Newspapers also targeted specific audiences. A women's page offered recipes and fashion news, separate sections covered sports and high society, and the Sunday supplement helped fill the spare weekend hours.

Newspaper wars erupted periodically, as when Joseph Pulitzer, the owner of the *St. Louis Post-Dispatch* invaded New York in 1883 by buying *The World*. In 1895, William Randolph Hearst, who owned the *San Francisco Examiner*, bought the *New York Journal* and challenged *The World*. Hearst developed a sensational style of newspaper reporting and writing called *yellow journalism*. In his combative zeal, he often abandoned the journalistic canon of telling the truth. The *Journal*'s sensational reporting of the civil war in Cuba enabled Hearst's paper to win its circulation battle with *The World*—and helped bring on the Spanish-American War of 1898.

"He who is without a newspaper," said the great showman P. T. Barnum, "is cut off from his species." Barnum was speaking of city people and their hunger for information. By meeting this need, newspapers revealed their sensitivity to the public they served.

The Higher Culture

The great cities implanted the institutions of higher culture into American society. A hunger for the cultivated life did not, of course, originate in cities. Before the Civil War, the lyceum movement had sent lecturers to the remotest of towns bearing messages of culture and learning. The Chautauqua movement, founded in upstate New York in 1874, carried on this work of cultural dissemination in the last decades of the nineteenth century. However, large cultural institutions, such as museums, public libraries, opera companies, and symphony orchestras, could flourish only in metropolitan centers.

The first outstanding art museum, the Corcoran Gallery of Art, opened in Washington, D.C., in 1869. New York's Metropolitan Museum of Art started in rented quarters two years later. In 1880, the museum moved to its permanent site in Central Park and launched an ambitious program of art acquisition. J. P. Morgan became chairman of the board in 1905, thus assuring the Metropolitan's preeminence. The Boston Museum of Fine Arts was founded in 1876, and Chicago's Art Institute in 1879. By 1914, virtually every major city, and about three-fifths of all cities with more than a hundred thousand people, had an art museum.

Top-flight orchestras also appeared, first in New York under the conductors Theodore Thomas and Leopold Damrosch in the 1870s. Symphonies started in Boston and Chicago during the next decade. National tours by these leading orchestras planted the seeds for orchestral societies in many other cities. Public libraries grew from modest collections (in 1870 only seven had as many as fifty thousand books) into major urban institutions. The greatest library benefactor was Andrew Carnegie, who announced in 1881 that he would build a library in any city prepared to maintain it. By 1907, Carnegie had spent more than $32.7 million to establish about a thousand libraries throughout the country.

If the late nineteenth century was the great age of money making, it was also the great age of money giving. Surplus private wealth flowed in many directions, particularly to universities. These schools included Vanderbilt, Tulane, and Stanford universities, all named for their chief benefactors, and the University of Chicago, founded by John D. Rockefeller. Urban cultural institutions also received their share, partly as a matter of civic pride. To some extent, patronage of the arts also served the need of the newly rich to establish themselves in society, as in the founding of the Metropolitan Opera in New York. But the higher culture, beyond being merely a commodity of civic pride and social display, received support out of a sense of cultural deprivation.

"In America there is no culture," pronounced the English critic G. Lowes Dickinson in 1909. Science and the practical arts, yes, "every possible application of life to purposes and ends," but "no life for life's sake." Such condescending remarks received a respectful hearing in the United States because of a deep sense of cultural inferiority to the Old World. In 1873, Mark Twain and Charles Dudley Warner had written a novel, *The Gilded Age*, satirizing America as a land of money grubbers and speculators. This enormously popular book touched a nerve in the American psyche. Its title took root in historical literature as a characterization of late nineteenth-century America, denoting especially the nation's materialism and cultural shallowness. Some members of the upper class, including the novelist Henry James, despaired of the country and moved elsewhere. Others spent their lives in the kind of perpetual alienation that Henry Adams described in his caustic memoir *The Education of Henry Adams* (1907).

The more common response was to try to raise the nation's cultural level. The newly rich had a hard time doing this. They did not have much opportunity to cultivate a taste for art, and a great deal of what they collected was mediocre and garish. On the other hand, George W. Vanderbilt, grandson of the roughhewn Cornelius Vanderbilt, became a patron of the Art Students League in New York and an early champion of French Impressionism. The enthusiasm of moneyed Americans—not always well-directed—largely fueled the great cultural institutions that arose in many cities during the Gilded Age.

A deeply conservative idea of culture sustained this generous patronage. The aim was to embellish urban life, not to probe or reveal its meaning. "Art," says the hero of the Reverend Henry Ward Beecher's sentimental novel *Norwood* (1867), "attempts to work out its end solely by the use of the beautiful, and the artist is to select out only such things as are beautiful."

Culture had also become firmly linked to femininity. In America, remarked one observer, culture was "left entirely to women. . . . It is they, as a general rule, who have opinions about music, or drama, or literature, or philosophy. . . . Husbands or sons rarely share in those interests." Men represented the "force principle," said the clergyman Horace Bushnell, and women symbolized the "beauty principle."

The treatment of life, said one highly successful editor, "must be tinged with sufficient idealism to make it all of a truly uplifting character. . . . We cannot admit stories which deal with false or immoral relations. . . . The finer side of things—the idealistic—is the answer for us." The "genteel tradition," as this literary school came to be called, dominated American cultural agencies, such as universities and publishing companies, from the 1860s on.

Rebellion against the genteel tradition sparked the main creative impulses of late nineteenth century American literature. Realism became the rallying cry of a new generation of writers. Their champion, William Dean Howells, resigned in 1881 as editor of the *Atlantic Monthly* magazine, stronghold of the genteel tradition. He became editor of *Harper's Monthly* magazine and began to call for literature that "wishes to know and to tell the truth" and seeks "to picture the daily life in the most exact terms possible." In a series of realistic novels—*A Modern Instance* (1882), *The Rise of Silas Lapham* (1885), and *A Hazard of New Fortunes* (1890)—Howells captured the world of the urban middle class.

Henry James, a far greater writer, also treated the novel as "a direct impression of life" and aimed above all at achieving "an air of reality." He wrote about the world of leisured Americans, and his central concern was the study of moral decay and regeneration. This concern, often set in motion by the confrontation of American innocence with European corruption, appears in *The American* (1877), *Portrait of a Lady* (1882), and *The Golden Bowl* (1904).

The nostalgia of urbanized Americans helped sustain a vigorous literature of local color and regionalism. These writings included the mining camp stories of Bret Harte, the Uncle Remus tales of Joel Chandler Harris, the Indiana poetry of James Whitcomb Riley, and the New England fiction of Sarah Orne Jewett. Such literature fit comfortably within the genteel tradition, for it was generally sentimental, reassuring, and morally uplifting.

Mark Twain was an entirely different kind of regional writer. Starting as a western journalist and humorist, Twain avoided the influence of the Eastern literary establishment. His greatest novel, *The Adventures of Huckleberry Finn* (1884), violated the custom of keeping "low" characters in their proper place for the amused inspection of the culturally superior reader. Huck, an outcaste boy, seizes control of the story. The words are his, and so is the innocence with which he questions right and wrong in America. No other novel so fully engaged the themes of racism, in-

MARK TWAIN
On steamboats navigating treacherous stretches of the Mississippi River, the leadsman would peer over the bow and call out "mark twain," signifying a depth of two fathoms (twelve feet). Samuel L. Clemens (1835–1910), once a Mississippi pilot, took "Mark Twain" as a pen name when he worked for the Virginia City *Enterprise*. It signified Twain's deep roots in Mississippi country. His best writing, including *Huckleberry Finn*, united the world of the Mississippi with a sharp, perspicacious view of the human condition. (Mark Twain Memorial, Hartford, Ct.)

TIME LINE
THE CITY

Chicago Fire

Twain and Dudley's *The Gilded Age*

Moody launches urban revivalist movement

Telephone
National Baseball League

Electric arc-light system in Philadelphia

Woolworth Building, New York City

San Francisco earthquake

New York Tenement Reform Law

| 1871 | 1873 | 1875 | 1876 | 1878 | 1879 | 1883 | 1885 | 1888 | 1893 | 1895 | 1897 | 1900 | 1901 | 1906 | 1913 |

Edison's incandescent light bulb

New York City's Metropolitan Opera
Joseph Pulitzer buys the
New York *World*
Brooklyn Bridge opens

Jenney's steel-girded skyscraper, Chicago

Chicago World's Fair

Electric trolley line in Richmond, Virginia

First comic strip, "The Yellow Kid"

Boston's subway

Dreiser's *Sister Carrie*

---

justice, and brutality in nineteenth-century America.

No comparable writing about city life appeared during these years. Realistic novels stopped short of the immigrant slums and working-class neighborhoods or ventured into them hesitantly and without much comprehension. Howells, for example, insisted that the United States was not like Europe: "The sum of cold and hunger is certainly very small, and wrong from class to class is also inappreciable. We invite our novelists, therefore, to concern themselves with the more smiling aspects of life, which are the more American."

Nevertheless, the hard realities of city life crept irresistibly into American fiction. Stephen Crane's *Maggie: A Girl of the Streets* (1893), privately printed because no publisher would touch it, told unflinchingly of the destruction of a slum girl. In another urban novel, Henry Blake Fuller's *The Cliff-Dwellers* (1893), the city itself occupied the center of the author's imagination. This story traces the fortunes of the occupants— "cliff-dwellers"—of a Chicago skyscraper. In *McTeague* (1899), Frank Norris captured the

sights, sounds, and, most acutely, the smells of the city. One reviewer called the story "a study in stinks." Although set in San Francisco, Norris insisted that it "could have happened in any big city, anywhere."

These novels stressed the insignificance of the individual, and his or her helplessness in the face of urban life. This approach, called "naturalism," was inspired by the French novelist Emile Zola, by the contemporary zeal for scientific objectivity, and by the theory of evolution proposed by the British naturalist Charles R. Darwin. Thus, Frank Norris's character McTeague, more animal than man, is the creature of his instincts and his environment, and he cannot escape coming to a bad end. In Norris's *The Octopus* (1901), the implacable force is the Southern Pacific Railroad; in *The Pit* (1903) it is the Chicago grain market. The city itself, however, most powerfully influenced the naturalistic writers.

The best of these authors, Theodore Dreiser, surmounted the crude determinism of Frank Norris. But the city people in his great novels— *Sister Carrie* (1900), *Jenny Gerhardt* (1911), *The Financier* (1912), and *The Titan* (1914)—are no less hostage to an urban world they cannot under-stand. Dreiser sought to capture this world in all its detail, "to talk about life as it is, the facts as they exist, the game as it is played." Visiting his fiancee's Missouri farm home in 1894, Dreiser had been struck by "the spirit of rural America, its idealism, its dreams." But this was an "American tradition in which I, alas!, could not share."

Said Dreiser, "I had seen Pittsburgh. I had seen Lithuanians and Hungarians in their 'courts' and hovels. I had seen the girls of the city—walking the streets at night." The city had entered the American imagination. By the early 1900s, it had become a main theme of American art and literature.

---

*A*merica, an agrarian society since its birth, became increasingly urbanized after the Civil War. In 1900, about 20 percent of the population lived in cities of a hundred thousand or more. City growth stemmed primarily from industrialization—the concentration of industry at key points, the increasingly large scale of production, and the need for commercial and administrative services best located in urban centers. A burst of innovation, including the telephone, electric lighting, rapid transit systems, and steel frame buildings, solved the problems arising from the concentration of an extremely large population in a confined area.

Within the city, geography defined the social order of the population. The poor were found in the centers and the factory districts, the middle class spread out into the suburbs, and the rich lived insulated either in exclusive central sections or beyond the suburbs. A distinctive urban culture emerged that enabled city dwellers to accommodate themselves to the world of the city.

The great cities of the United States became the sites of a higher culture, including art museums, opera and symphony companies, and libraries. From the late nineteenth century on, American life would increasingly be defined by what happened in the nation's cities.

Suggestions for Further Reading

Urbanization

A useful introduction to urban history is Charles N. Glaab and A. Theodore Brown, *History of Urban America* (1967). The pioneer study for the late nineteenth century is Arthur M. Schlesinger, *The Rise of the City* (1936). Blake McKelvey, *The Urbanization of America, 1860-1915* (1963) provides an account of events that took place within the context of the city. A sampling of innovative scholarship in the field can be found in Stephan Thernstrom and Richard Sennett, eds., *19th Century Cities: Essays in the New Urban History* (1969).

Allan Pred, *Spatial Dynamics of U.S. Urban Growth, 1800-1914* (1971) traces the patterns by which cities utilized the space in which they grew. The impact of trolley-line building is revealed in the pioneering book by Sam B. Warner, *Streetcar Suburbs* (1962). In a subsequent work, *The Private City: Philadelphia in Three Periods* (1968), Warner broadened his analysis to show how private decision-making shaped the character of the American city. Urban construction is treated in Carl Condit, *American Building Art: Nineteenth Century* (1969), and the emergence of a distinctively American style in his *Chicago School of Architecture* (1964). Another aspect of city building is subtly analyzed in Alan Trachtenberg, *Brooklyn Bridge* (1965). The problems of meeting basic needs can be conveniently studied in Stanley K. Schultz and Clay McShane, "To Engineer the Metropolis: Sewers, Sanitation, and City Planning in Late-Nineteenth-Century America," *Journal of American History* 65 (September 1978): 389-411. Eric H. Monkonnen, *Police in Urban America, 1860-1920* (1981) and David B. Tyack, *The One Best System: A History of American Urban Education* (1974) give accounts of two of the key services demanded by city people. The struggle to reshape the chaotic nineteenth-century city can be explored in Laura Wood Roper, *FLO: A biography of Frederick Law Olmstead* (1973) and William H. Wilson, *The City Beautiful Movement in Kansas City* (1964).

Upper Class/Middle Class

The study of urban classes can properly begin with Stephan Thernstrom's social-mobility analysis, *The Other Bostonians: Poverty and Progress in an American City, 1880-1970* (1973), which contains also a useful summary of mobility research on other cities. Frederic C. Jaher, *The Urban Establishment: Upper Strata in Boston, New York, Charleston, Chicago, and Los Angeles* (1982) is a major comparative study of the elites in America's cities. Dixon Wecter, *The Saga of American Society* (1937) is a lively account of the development of American high society. The flavor of this process can best be captured in Ward McAllister, *Society as I Have Found It* (1890). The tensions of middle-class life in the industrial cities are revealed in Richard Sennett, *Families Against the City: Middle Class Homes of Industrial Chicago, 1872-1890* (1970). Kathryn Kish Sklar, *Catharine Beecher: A Study of American Domesticity* (1973) details the life and influence of the key exponent of the cult of domesticity that ruled middle-class home life in the late nineteenth century. Other aspects of this development emerge from Gwendolyn Wright, *Moralism and the Model Home: Domestic Architecture and Cultural Conflict in Chicago, 1873-1913* (1980), Susan Strasser, *Never Done: A History of American Housework* (1983), and David M. Katzman, *Seven Days A Week: Women and Domestic Service in Industrializing America* (1978). A useful collection on family history is Michael Gordon, ed., *The American Family in Social-Historical Perspective* (1973). Carl N. Degler, *At Odds: Women and the Family in America* (1980) is the leading interpretive survey of the subject. Contemporary notions of male and female are skillfully captured in John S. and Robin M. Haller, *The Physician and Sexuality in Victorian America* (1974).

City People

There is a rich literature on immigrants and the city. Among the leading books are: Moses Rischin, *The Promised City: New York's Jews, 1870-1914* (1962); Joseph Barton, *Peasants and Strangers: Italians, Rumanians and Slovaks in an American City, 1890-1950* (1975); Humbert S. Nelli, *The Italians in Chicago, 1860-1920* (1970). On blacks in the city, see Gilbert Osofsky, *Harlem: The Making of a Ghetto, 1890-1930* (1966) and Allan H. Spear, *Black Chicago, 1860-1920* (1966). The problems that Protestantism encountered in the city are treated in Henry F. May, *Protestant Churches and Urban America* (1949) and Aaron I. Abell, *The Urban Impact on American Protestantism* (1943). The starting point on urban revivalism is William G. McLoughlin, *Modern Revivalism* (1959). For the Catholic church, see Robert D. Cross, *The Emergence of Liberal Catholicism in America* (1958) and, ed., *Church and City, 1865-1910* (1967). In *City People: The Rise of Modern City Culture in 19th Century America* (1982), Gunther Barth shows how the department store, baseball, and newspapers helped to shape a distinctive city culture. There is an imaginative accounting of another urban institution in John F. Kasson, *Amusing the Million: Coney Island at the Turn of the Century* (198). On the fostering of high culture in the American city, see Daniel M. Fox, *Engines of Culture: Philanthropy and Art Museums* (1963). The best introduction to intellectual currents within the emerging urban society is Alan Trachtenberg, *The Incorporation of America: Culture and Society, 1865-1893* (1983). An important case study of working-class leisure is Roy Rosenzweig, *Eight Hours for What We Will: Workers & Leisure in An Industrial City, 1870-1920* (1983).

$\mathscr{S}$EPARATE SPHERES

"The most enlightened of both sexes," a speaker told the graduating class of Mount Holyoke College in 1876, believe "there is a difference of kind in their natural endowments and that there is for each an appropriate field of development and action." The women of Mount Holyoke did not hoot the speaker off the platform, for he was voicing one of the accepted truths of nineteenth-century, middle-class America. Men and women "are different, widely different from each other," asserted the prominent Boston physician Edward Clarke. What was more, "we should cultivate the difference of the sexes, not try to hide it or abolish it."

This was a notion certified by the mightiest scientific authority of the age. In *The Descent of Man* (1871), Charles Darwin proposed that sexual divergence was a consequence of evolution. Motherhood had rendered women dependent on men and thus to some degree removed them from the struggle for survival by which the species evolved. Darwin postulated a hierarchy of mental attributes—climbing from instinct to emotions, intuition, imagination, and, finally, reason. The male brain, as it had evolved, operated best at the higher range, the female brain at the lower range. There was no question, admitted the physiologist Frances Emily White after reading Darwin's book, that men's ancient role as hunters and warriors had resulted in "more robust intellects," while women's family role had produced qualities of "tenderness and love . . . and devotional sentiment."

Physically, too, women were the weaker sex. Medical opinion at the time conceived of the human body as endowed with a finite, nonreplenishable amount of energy. In women's bodies, this energy went primarily to the reproductive organs. It was, said one doctor reverentially, "as if the Almighty, in creating the female sex, had taken the uterus and built a woman around it." Too much mental activity would lead to the atrophy of the female organs and/or to physical breakdown. To conserve their body energy, Dr. Clarke advised women students at Vassar against any studies during menstruation, and a maximum of a third less than male college students at other times. A booming patent medicine industry grew rich catering to, in the words of a Lydia Pinkham advertisement (plate 1), "the peculiar weaknesses of women."

PLATE 1
(Schlesinger Library, Radcliffe College)

Given their profound differences, men and women had to live entirely different kinds of lives. The ideal man had "indomitable energy"; he enjoyed "a *robust health*—full of vigor." He had the will to win, to exert his "force and authority as a man." His field of battle was preeminently the competitive marketplace; "the whirl and contact with the world . . . is the inheritance of our sex." Money-making was strictly a masculine affair, whether it involved the risk-taking of the entrepreneur, the prudence of the banker, the easy fellowship of the salesman, or the brawn of the ironworker (plate 2). So, too, with politics. Politicians dealt in the currency of power, entirely a masculine concern, and party activity was rich with the ritual and camaraderie in which the American male took delight (plate 3, on page 582). No wonder the suffragist demand for the right to vote met ridicule

PLATE 2
(Thomas P. Anshutz. *Ironworkers–Noontime*. The Fine Arts Museums of San Francisco. Gift of Mr. & Mrs. John D. Rockefeller 3rd)

PLATE 3
The Levi P. Morton Association, the local Republican party, Newport, Rhode Island. (Newport County Historical Society)

PLATE 4
(Kansas Collection, University of Kansas Libraries. Joseph J. Pennell Collection)

and disbelief. Equally sacred were such male precincts as the fraternal order, the volunteer fire department, the saloon, and, everywhere, the barbershop. Rudy Sohn's barbershop (plate 4) was surely a mecca for the menfolk of Junction City, Kansas. The regulars deposited their shaving mugs on Rudy's wall racks and came in weekly for a shave and trim, hot towels, and some easy male talk amid the aroma of hazel water and stale cigar smoke.

"There is something enervating in feminine companionship," acknowledged *Cosmopolitan* magazine. "The genuine man feels that he must go off alone or with other men, out in the open air, roughing it among the rough as a mental tonic." A rich young man like Theodore Roosevelt might try his luck in the Wild West or Africa; those of lesser means took their shotguns and fishing gear to woods closer at hand (plate 5). The first college football game took place between Rutgers and Princeton in 1869. In the organized mayhem of football (plate

PLATE 6
The Yale Game, about 1900. (New Haven Colony Historical Society. The T. S. Bronson Collection)

PLATE 7
Mrs. Glessner's reading group met weekly to discuss fine literature. The ladies in attendance represented many of the "best" families in Chicago. (Chicago Historical Society)

PLATE 8
(Martin W. Sandler Collection)

6), the young American male could show the stuff he was made of.

Woman's place, on the other hand, was in the home. "Real womanhood" consisted above all of the nurturing qualities that made for a good wife and mother. "We owe to women the charm and beauty of life," said one educator. "For purity of thought and heart, for patient courage, for recklessly unselfish devotion, for the love that rests, strengthens and inspires, we look to women." Theirs was the nurturing function in life. Within the family, gender roles were sharply differentiated. In an 1895 portrait of a family in Portland, Oregon, the husband sits in dignity, his eye on some serious piece of business, while his wife plays lovingly on the floor with the children (plate 8). In such families, husbands remained in some ways strangers to their wives. The women's emotional world, recaptured from surviving correspondence, revolved much more around other women—sis-ters and cousins, and old school chums who became lifelong, intimate friends. A special feminine sphere—as closed to men as the barbershop world was closed to women—grew from such attachments. Leisure time, a precious commodity to nineteenth-century homemakers, found only a limited compass of social and cultural activity among other women, as in the Methodist–Episcopal church picnic in Junction City, Kansas in 1896 (plate 9).

Women's sphere, though deeply enshrined in American life, did not remain unchanged. Some degree of liberation from the endless drudgery of housework came in the late nineteenth century with the advent of central heating, inside plumbing and hot water, electricity, kitchen appliances, store-bought bread, and mass-produced clothing. In the city, women's sphere began to take on a more public character. Of the new urban institutions catering to women, the most important was the department store, which became a temple for their emerging role as consumers. Similarly, seeking to attract the trade of women, the New Amsterdam National Bank of New York set aside a special section decorated to suit the tastes of their new customers (plate 10, on page 586).

For the daughters of the middle class, higher education became available through limited access to state universities, as well as through the new women's colleges, led by Vassar in 1865. In most of these institutions, academic excellence distinctly took a back seat. Women's colleges, said Dean Briggs of Smith, "exist not for the competition of women with men, but for the ennobling of women as women. They do not, or should not exist primarily for higher learning." Ironically, anxiety about women's frailty led to a strong emphasis on physical fitness in the women's colleges (plate 11, on page 586).

The process of modified liberation went steadily forward.

PLATE 9
(Kansas Collection, University of Kansas Libraries. Joseph J. Pennell Collection)

During the 1890s, there was much talk of the "new woman" (plate 12). As she became better educated, more robustly active, and an increasingly public presence in reform movements and at the workplace, the rigidities of separate sphere began to break down. In the twentieth century, more and more of life's activities came to be shared by men and women.

Today, the vast majority of people rejects, both in law and by belief, the notion of female inferiority—which is why nineteenth-century views on sexual divergence sound so quaint. But stereotyping by sex still lives. Consider the masculine appeal of a 1915 tobacco ad (plate 13), with its "live-wire" men enjoying their whiskey and the ladies tucked away in the music room. The modern reader may smile at "Bull" Durham's blatant sexism, but is the message of Virginia Slims—"You've Come a Long Way, Baby"—any less rooted in sex stereotyping? The more things change. . . .

PLATE 10
(Museum of the City of New York. The Byron Collection)

PLATE 11
Gymnasium, Wellesley College, 1893. (Photo by Seaver. Wellesley College Archives)

The "Clubby" Smoke—"Bull" Durham

You start something lively when you produce "Bull" Durham in a crowd of live-wires and start "rolling your own". That fresh mellow-sweet fragrance of "Bull" Durham makes everyone reach for "the makings." A hand-rolled "Bull" Durham cigarette brims over with zest and snap and the sparkle of sprightly spirits.

GENUINE

"BULL" DURHAM
SMOKING TOBACCO

Made of rich, ripe Virginia-North Carolina leaf, "Bull" Durham is the mildest, most enjoyable tobacco in the world. Its unique aroma and pleasing flavor give you wholesome, lasting satisfaction.

No other cigarette can be so full of life and youthful vigor as a fresh-rolled cigarette of "Bull" Durham. "Roll your own" with "Bull" Durham and you'll discover a new joy in smoking.

THE AMERICAN TOBACCO COMPANY

Ask for FREE package of "papers" with each 5c sack

PLATE 13
(The Newberry Library, Chicago)

PLATE 12
John Singer Sargent's painting, *Mr. and Mrs. Isaac Newton Phelps Stokes* (1897), captures on canvas the essence of the "new woman" of the 1890s. Nothing about Mrs. Stokes, neither in how she is dressed nor in how she presents herself, suggests physical weakness or demure passivity. She confidently occupies center stage, a fit partner for her husband, who, indeed, is relegated to the shadows of the picture. (The Metropolitan Museum of Art. Bequest of Edith Minturn Stokes)

587

19

RURAL AMERICA

*D*uring the last third of the nineteenth century, American society seemed to be at odds with itself. From one angle, the nation looked like an advanced industrial society, with great factories and mills and enormous, crowded cities. But from another angle, America looked like a nation still absorbed in conquering a continent, with settlers streaming toward lonely farms and ranches in the open spaces of the West, and Americans repeating the old dramas of "settlement" they had been performing over and over since 1607. Not until 1890 did the Census Bureau declare that the frontier no longer existed: the country's "unsettled area has been so broken into . . . that there can hardly be said to be a frontier line."

That same year, 1890, the country surpassed Great Britain in the production of iron and steel. Newspapers told about Indian wars and labor strikes in the same edition. The army's massacre of Indians at Wounded Knee, South Dakota, the final tragedy in the suppression of the Plains tribes, occurred only eighteen months before the great Homestead strike of July 1892.

This conjunction of events, unrelated though they might seem, did not occur entirely by accident. The final surge of westward development across the Great Plains was powered primarily by the dynamism of American industrialism. Much the same could be said for the history of rural America in those years. The South rebuilt its plantation agriculture on the basis of a sharecropping tenant system after the Civil War. But though the South remained rooted in its historic cotton culture, it also entered the industrial age.

Its future, for better or worse, was locked into the industrial revolution going on in the North. The nation's farmers, too, had one foot in the Jeffersonian past and the other in the industrial age. The distress they experienced during this period resulted basically from their imperfect integration into the world of the corporation and the international market. Rural America could no longer be understood on its own terms. Its history had become linked ever more tightly to the larger industrial society.

The Great West

Before the Civil War, the vast lands west of the Mississippi Valley—people called it the Great West—had seemed of little importance. Until the 1840s, Americans assumed the Great West would always remain beyond the frontier of white settlement. Accustomed to woodlands and ample rainfall, farmers hung back from the dry country that began several hundred miles west of the Mississippi River.

The Great West consisted of two parts. At roughly the ninety-eighth meridian, running from what are now North and South Dakota down through central Texas, the tall grass of the prairies gave way to the short buffalo grass of semiarid country. This region, the Great Plains, extended to the Rocky Mountains. Beyond the mountains lay a high, arid plateau that spread to the Sierra and Cascade ranges. Schoolbooks referred to the Great Plains as the Great American Desert. Major Stephen H. Long, after exploring the region west of the ninety-eighth meridian in

1820, declared it "almost wholly unfit for cultivation, and of course uninhabitable by a people depending upon agriculture for their subsistence."

Whites generally considered the Great Plains best left to the native American inhabitants—the Apache and Comanche in the Southwest; Arapaho and Pawnee on the central plains; and Crow, Cheyenne, and Sioux to the north. During the eighteenth century, as horses spread northward after being brought to Mexico by Spanish explorers, the Plains Indians had become horsemen. Superb hunters and fierce warriors, they created an essentially new culture that centered on the horse, the buffalo, and the open land. To their hunting grounds now came the woodland Indians as well. After the War of 1812, the nation pursued a relentless policy of removing the eastern tribes beyond the Mississippi to the prairie lands bordering the Great Plains.

In 1834, Congress formally created a permanent Indian country in the Great West. The army built border forts from Lake Superior to the Red

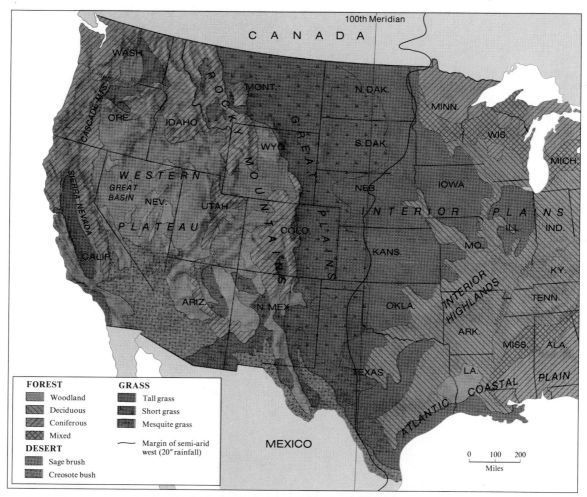

MAP 19.1 NATURAL ENVIRONMENT OF THE WEST
As settlers crossed the Mississippi River, and especially as they pushed into the Great Plains beyond the line of semi-aridity, they sensed the overwhelming power of the environment to determine their fate. In a landscape without trees for fences and barns, without adequate rainfall, farmers had to relearn their business. The West lacked the navigable rivers that had earlier eased pioneer travel, and placed nearly impenetrable barriers of mountains and desert between settlers and the beckoning West Coast. Nowhere did environment so impress itself on settlers—and on the historians who wrote about them—than in the West.

River to keep the Indians in and the whites out. In 1838, the commanding general of the area, Edmund Gaines, recommended that the forts be constructed of stone because they would be there forever. The creation of an Indian country supported the contemporary belief that the Great American Desert could serve only as home, in the words of the explorer Zebulon M. Pike, "to the wandering and uncivilized aborigines of the country."

First Intruders; Wagon Trains, Railroaders, Miners

Solemnly committed to the Indians, the Great West was put to new, more profitable uses almost immediately. The first break came with the acquisition and settlement of the Oregon and California regions during the 1840s. Instead of serving as a buffer against the British and the Mexicans, the Indian country became a bridge to the Pacific. The first wagon train headed west from Missouri for Oregon in 1842. Thousands then traveled the Oregon Trail to the Willamette Valley or, cutting south beyond Fort Hall, down into California. These migrants had no interest in the land they crossed; they considered it barren ground. But their journey marked the intrusion of the modernizing world on the Indian's last remaining habitat.

The rapid white settlement of the Pacific region raised a demand almost at once for a transportation system across the continent. As early as 1853, the federal government began surveying railway routes to the Pacific. A sectional stalemate over the proposed transcontinental route delayed railroad construction for a decade. Wagon freight lines, stagecoaches, and the horseback riders of the Pony Express furnished the first regular links westward. A telegraph line reached San Francisco in 1861. The tracks of the Union Pacific and Central Pacific railroads finally converged at Promontory, Utah, in 1869, uniting the continent by rail. An orgy of western railway building followed, stimulated partly by the availability until 1871 of generous government subsidies. By 1883, after being interrupted by the Panic of 1873, three more continental routes had

been completed—the Southern Pacific line to New Orleans; the Santa Fe to Kansas City; and the Northern Pacific from Portland, Oregon, to Saint Paul, Minnesota.

On the heels of this traffic across the plains and mountains, and generally in advance of the railroads, came the exploitation of the mineral wealth of the Great West. The rush to California had been triggered in 1848 by the discovery of gold in the foothills of the Sierras. By the mid-1850s, disappointed forty-niners, as the prospectors were called, had spread throughout the West in hope of striking it rich elsewhere.

Beginning in 1858, gold was discovered on the Nevada side of the Sierras, in the Colorado Rockies, and along the Fraser River in British Columbia. New strikes occurred in Montana and Wyoming during the 1860s, in the Black Hills of South Dakota in the 1870s, in the Coeur d'Alene region of Idaho during the 1880s, and in the Yukon area of Alaska in 1896.

As the news spread of each gold strike, a wild, remote area turned almost overnight into a mob scene of prospectors, traders, gamblers, prostitutes, and saloonkeepers. At least a hundred thousand fortune seekers flocked to the Pikes Peak area of Colorado in the spring of 1859. Always trespassers on government or Indian land, the prospectors made their own law. The mining codes, devised at community meetings, limited the size of claims to what a man could reasonably work. This kind of popular lawmaking also became an instrument for excluding or discriminating against the Mexicans, Chinese, and blacks in the gold fields. And it turned into hangman's justice for the many lawless men who infested the mining camps.

The heyday of the prospector was always very brief. He was equipped only to skim gold from the surface of the earth and from streambeds. To extract the metal locked in the underground lodes required mine shafts and crushing mills, and these took capital, technology, and business organization. The original claim holders quickly sold out after taking the surface gold or when a generous bidder came along. At every gold-rush site, the prospector soon gave way to entrepreneurial development and large-scale mining.

MAP 19.2 DEVELOPMENT OF THE WEST, 1860–1890
Development in the West followed an uneven pattern. The first organized settlements—Mormon
around Salt Lake, miners and farmers in California and Oregon—were far from other populated areas.
Mining sprang up in isolated spots on the broad terrain of wilderness. The transportation routes of
wagon trains, cattle trails, and railroads crossed wide expanses of unpopulated land. The land itself
was valued so little that the federal government granted over 180 million acres free to railroads as an
inducement to build across unsettled territory.

Orderly law and government followed at this stage. The mining country was organized into territories and then into states of the Union. Rough mining camps turned into cities. Nevada's Virginia City, once a baudy, ramshackle mining camp, boasted a stock exchange and five newspapers a few years after the Comstock lode opened in 1859. By 1875, Virginia City's population had reached twenty thousand. The great

fortunes of the mining kings brought restaurants, hotels, opera, Shakespearean theater, and similar amenities to communities that had been wilderness a decade earlier.

In its final stage, the mining frontier passed into the industrial world. At some sites, gold and silver proved less important than the commoner metals with which they had been intermixed. Beginning in the mid-1870s, copper

HYDRAULIC MINING IN THE BOISE BASIN, IDAHO
Hydraulic mining, invented in the California gold fields in 1853, was a highly efficient method that yielded profits even with low-grade concentrations of gold. The technology was simple—it used high-pressure water under gravity feed to wash away hillsides of gold-bearing soil. Although building the necessary reservoirs, piping systems, and sluices required heavy investment, the profits from hydraulic mining helped transform western mining into big business. But, as Mary Brown's painting from 1875 suggests, hydraulic mining destroyed the natural landscape. (Idaho State Historical Museum)

mining thrived in the Butte district of Montana, especially after the opening of the fabulous Anaconda mine, and also flourished in the Globe and Copper Queen fields of Arizona. In the 1890s, the Coeur d'Alene silver district, following earlier finds at Leadville, Colorado, became the nation's main source of lead and zinc.

In short order, industrialism established itself at these remote places in the Great West. Entrepreneurs raised capital, built rail connections, devised advanced technology to treat the lower-grade copper deposits, constructed smelting facilities, and recruited a labor force. As elsewhere on the industrial scene, trade-union organization appeared among the miners. And, as elsewhere, the western metal industries joined enthusiastically in the merger movement that took place at the end of the century. The Anaconda Copper Mining Company and other Montana mining firms came under the control of the Amalgamated Copper Company in 1899. That same year, the American Smelting and Refining Com-

pany brought together the bulk of the nation's lead-mining and copper-refining properties. Still Blackfeet and Crow country in the 1860s, the Butte copper district was a center of industrial capitalism barely thirty years later.

The Cattle Frontier

As with copper and lead mining in the mountain country, market demand pushed the relentless exploitation of the Great Plains. This vast grass region supported enormous herds of buffalo. Some trade in buffalo hides had gone on for years between the Indians and the white trading posts that first began to dot the Great Plains in the 1820s. In the early 1870s, eastern tanneries conducted successful experiments in curing buffalo hides, and a ready market developed among shoe and harness manufacturers. Parties of professional hunters, armed with high-powered rifles, swept across the plains and began a systematic slaughter of the buffalo. The great herds almost vanished within ten years. Many people spoke out against this mass killing, but no method existed here, any more than in gold-rush country, to curb men bent on making a quick dollar. Besides, as General Philip H. Sheridan assured the Texas legislature, the extermination of the buffalo brought benefits. The Indians would be starved into submission, he noted, and feeding grounds would open up for a more valuable commodity, the Texas longhorn.

Since the eighteenth century, these tough Spanish cattle had spread westward across Texas from the grasslands between the Rio Grande and the Nueces River. About five million longhorns roamed the region in 1865, largely untended and unclaimed, and hardly worth bothering about because they could not be marketed. That year, however, the Missouri and Pacific Railroad reached Sedalia, Missouri. At that terminal, connecting as it did to hungry eastern markets, the three-dollar longhorn might command forty dollars. This realization set off the famous Long Drive. Cowboys herded Texas cattle a thousand miles or more north to the railroads as the lines pushed west into Kansas.

At Abilene, Ellsworth, and, beginning in 1875, Dodge City, stockmen sold the cattle and the trail-weary cowboys went on a binge. The wide-open cow towns, like the mining camps, captured the nation's imagination as symbols of the Wild West. But the Long Drive, colorful though it seemed, was actually a makeshift method of bridging a gap in the developing transportation system. As soon as railroads reached the Texas range country in the 1870s, stockmen abandoned the hazardous and wasteful Long Drive for a more settled kind of ranching.

Meanwhile, longhorns had been introduced to the upper Great Plains and demonstrated their ability to survive the harsh winter climate. In hardly a decade, starting in the late 1860s, the Great Plains changed into ranching country. The land itself was treated as a free commodity, available to anyone who seized it and put it to use. A hopeful rancher would spot a likely area along a creek, and claim 160 acres under the Preemption Act of 1841. By a common usage that quickly began among cattlemen, the rancher had a "range right" to all the adjacent land rising up to the "divide," where the land sloped down to the next creek. As herds multiplied, and as they improved through crossbreeding with Hereford and Angus cattle, the stockman quickly became a substantial rancher. But he remained very much a pioneer in relying on himself and, through stockmen's associations, on his fellow ranchers to protect his rights.

A boom during the early 1880s hastened the end of open-range ranching. Eastern and British investors rushed in to capitalize on the high profits. Overgrazing depleted the grasslands. Cattle prices slumped at the Chicago stockyards beginning in 1882, and collapsed as stockmen

THE COWBOY AT WORK
Open-range ranching, where cattle from different ranches grazed together, gave rise to distinctive traditions. At the roundup, cowboys separated the cattle by owner and branded the calves. The cowboy, traditionally a colorful figure, was really a kind of farmhand on horseback, with the skills to work on the range. He earned twenty-five dollars a month, plus his food and a bed in the bunkhouse, for long hours of grueling, lonesome work.
(Culver)

dumped stricken cattle during the cold weather and drought of 1885–86. The winter that followed, the most terrible in memory, wiped out vast herds. Open-range ranching came to an end. Cattlemen built fences around their land and laid in hay crops for winter feed. No longer would cattle be left to fend for themselves on the open range. The Great Plains turned into ordinary ranch country. Sheep raising, previously scorned as unmanly work and resisted as a threat to the grass, now became respectable. Some cattlemen even sold out to the despised "nesters," who wanted to try farming the Great Plains.

The Farmers' Frontier

Powerful forces had been pushing against the mental barrier of a Great American Desert ever since the Civil War. As the midwestern states filled up, farmers began to look hungrily farther west. Farmers in Europe, especially in Scandinavia, also were eager to find a place in America. Land speculators, steamship lines, and the western states and territories all encouraged settlement of the Great Plains. Railroads, anxious to sell their huge land holdings and develop traffic for their routes, became especially active sponsors of settlement programs.

Federal land policy also offered a strong attraction. The Homestead Act of 1862 enabled settlers to obtain up to 160 acres of public land free, except for a filing fee, if they lived on it for five years. This law included aliens who had filed their first naturalization papers. Beginning in 1873, settlers could claim an additional 160 acres if they planted trees on at least a fourth of the land.

None of these forces, however, could have pushed the agricultural frontier far out on to the plains without the intervention of a highly inventive society. The notion of a Great American Desert, illusion though it was, did point to a plain truth: the grasslands could not be worked by the known methods of American farmers.

Consider the absence of woodland. Determined pioneers could manage the problem of shelter by cutting dugouts in the side of a hill. Then they built sod houses, using strips of turf cut from the ground. These crude homes served—often for years—until the settler had

earned enough money to buy the lumber for a proper house and barn. But what about fencing to protect the crops? A furious patent race developed to meet this crucial need. In 1874 Joseph F. Glidden, an Illinois farmer, invented barbed wire, which provided a cheap, effective barrier against roaming cattle.

The arid climate presented a tougher problem. The eastern, high-grass prairie received enough rain for grain crops. But the annual rainfall averaged below twenty inches west of ninety-eighth meridian. The Mormons who lived in the area near Great Salt Lake had demonstrated how irrigation could turn a wasteland into a garden. But the Great Plains lacked the surface water needed for irrigation. The answer lay in dry-farming methods, which involved

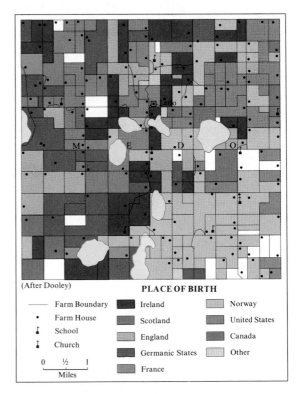

MAP 19.3 THE RURAL ETHNIC MOSAIC: BLUE EARTH COUNTY, MINNESOTA, 1880
What could have been more natural for emigrants like Ida Lindgren, especially given the isolation and hardship she describes (see document at right), than to settle next to others sharing common ties to a homeland? This map of Medo township reveals that in rural America, no less than in the cities, ethnicity determined spatial patterns of living.

SWEDISH EMIGRANT IN FRONTIER KANSAS

Like many emigrants, Ida Lindgren did not find it easy to adjust to the harsh new life on the frontier. Her diary entries and letters home show that the adjustment for the first generation was never complete.

Diary entry: 15 May 1870, Lake Sibley, Nebraska

What shall I say? Why has the Lord brought us here? Oh, I feel so oppressed, so unhappy! Two whole days it took us to get here and they were not the least trying part of our travels. We sat on boards in the work-wagon packed in so tightly that we could not move a foot, and we drove across endless, endless prairies, on narrow roads; no, not roads, tracks like those in the fields at home when they harvested grain. No forest but only a few trees which grow along the rivers and creeks. And then here and there you see a homestead and pass a little settlement. The Indians are not so far away from here, I can understand, and all the men you see coming by, riding or driving wagons, are armed with revolvers and long carbines, and look like highway robbers.

Diary entry: No date. Probably written in July 1870.

Claus and his wife lost their youngest child at Lake Sibley and it was very sad in many ways. There was no real cemetery but out on the prairie stood a large, solitary tree, and around it they bury their dead, without tolling of bells, without a pastor, and sometimes without any coffin. A coffin was made here for their child, it was not painted black, but we lined it with flowers and one of the men read the funeral service, and then there was a hymn, and that was all.

Manhattan, Kansas, 25 August 1874

Beloved Mamma,

It has been a long time since I have written, hasn't it? . . . when one never has anything fun to write about, it is no fun to write. . . . We have not had rain since the beginning of June, and then with this heat and often strong winds as well, you can imagine how everything has dried out. There has also been a general lamentation and fear for the coming year. We are glad we have the oats (for many don't have any and must feed wheat to

the stock) and had hoped to have the corn leaves to add to the fodder. But then one fine day there came millions, trillions of grasshoppers in great clouds, hiding the sun, and coming down onto the fields, eating up *everything* that was still there, the leaves on the trees, peaches, grapes, cucumbers, onions, cabbage, everything, everything. Only the peach stones still hung on the trees, showing what had once been there.

Manhattan, Kansas, 1 July 1877

. . . It seems so strange to me when I think that more than seven years have passed since I have seen you all . . . I can see so clearly that last glimpse I had of Mamma, standing alone amid all the tracks of Eslöv station. Oliva I last saw sitting on her sofa in her red and black dress, holding little Brita, one month old, on her lap. And Wilhelm I last saw in Lund at the station, as he rolled away with the train, waving his last farewell to me. . . .

Source: H. Arnold Barton, ed. *Letters from the Promised Land.* Minneapolis: University of Minnesota Press, 1975. 143–145, 150–156.

---

deep planting to stimulate the capillary action of ground moisture to roots and quick harrowing after rainfalls to turn over a dry mulch that slowed evaporation.

Dry farming produced a low yield per acre. To be economical, a semiarid farm had to operate on a scale much larger than an eastern farm. Therefore, it had to rely much more on machinery. The epitome of western mechanized farming took place on the corporate farms that

covered up to a hundred thousand acres in the Red River Valley in the Dakota Territory. But family farms, which remained the norm elsewhere, could not operate with less than three hundred acres of cereal crops and so required machinery for plowing, planting, and harvesting. Such basic inventions as the McCormick reaper came before the Civil War, but the swift growth of the farm-equipment industry occurred later in response to the western demand.

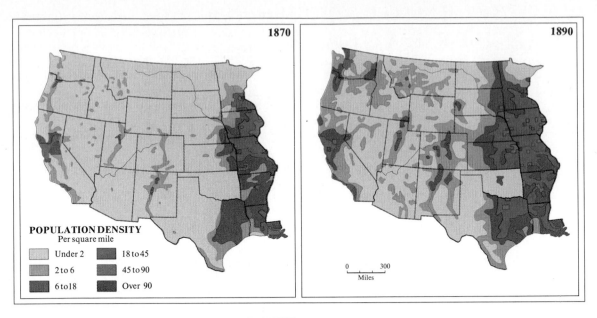

MAP 19.4 GROWING POPULATION IN THE WEST
Western population more than tripled between 1870 and 1890, from 1 million to 3.2 million. In 1890, the superintendent of the Census reported that for the first time in the country's history "there can hardly be said to be a frontier line"; that is, an unbroken line beyond which lay land with fewer than two people per square mile. However, the western population was still scattered amidst vacant land rather than spread in the continuous settlement to be found farther east. Except for a few urban centers, it remained sparsely populated by the standard of the rest of the country.

The push into semiarid lands, despite barbed wire, dry-farming methods, and harvesting machines, involved a great deal of wish fulfillment. The Great Plains happened to experience a wet cycle between 1878 and 1886. "As the plains are settled up we hear less and less of drouth, hot winds, alkali and other bugbears that used to hold back the adventurous," remarked one Nebraska man. Some settlers attributed the increased rainfall to soil cultivation and tree plantings, which somehow generated air moisture and caused more rain. Others credited God. As one settler on the southern plains remarked, "The Lord just knowed we needed more land an' He's gone and changed the climate." No matter how they explained it—and no matter how much scientists warned otherwise—settlers moved westward convinced that the land would receive permanently increased rainfall.

The last frontier thrust across the continental United States was on. More land came under cultivation between 1870 and 1900 than in the previous 250 years. More than a million people went west from the settled Midwest during the 1880s. Northern Europe contributed its share, too. At the peak of the "American fever" in 1882, over 105,000 Scandinavians emigrated to the United States. Swedish and Norwegian became the primary languages of entire areas of Minnesota and Dakota. By 1880, Kansas had 850,000 people. Dakota, which had been very thinly settled when it became a territory in 1861, had twenty thousand inhabitants in 1873. Its population jumped to 135,000 in 1880 and all the way to 550,000 in 1885. The dry years that followed pushed Dakota's population back to 500,000 by 1890, and a comparable departure of drought-stricken farmers occurred up and down the Great Plains. But that vast region, where buffalo herds had thrived a few decades earlier, had been conquered. About half the nation's cattle and sheep, a third of its cereal crops, and nearly three-fifths of its wheat came from the newly settled lands in 1900.

The Indians

And what of the Indians who had inhabited the Great West? Basically, their fate has been told in the foregoing account of western settlement. "The white children have surrounded me and have left me nothing but an island," lamented the great Sioux chief Red Cloud in 1870, the year after the completion of the transcontinental railroad. "When we first had all this land we were strong; now we are all melting like snow on a hillside, while you are grown like spring grass." Every advance of the whites—the Oregon-bound wagon train, the railroad, the buffalo hunter, the miner, the cattleman, the farmer—intruded on the Indians' world. The whites took away the tribes' sustenance, decimated their ranks, and shoved the remnants into remote and barren corners of their former domain. No historical equation could have been more precise or implacable: The progress of the white settlers meant the death of the Indian.

The provision for a permanent Indian country, written into federal law and into treaties with various tribes, was swept away in the westward march of the settler. As early as 1854, upon creating the Kansas and Nebraska territories, the United States formally canceled the Indian policy of 1834. By 1860, all the resettled eastern tribes, treaties notwithstanding, had been forced to cede their lands in Kansas and Nebraska and move farther west. The Plains Indians presented a more formidable barrier. As miners and other pioneers thrust into Indian lands from the late 1850s on, war broke out all along the frontier from the Apache in the Southwest, the Cheyenne and Arapaho in Colorado, to Sioux in the Dakota Territory.

The fierce resistance led to the formulation in 1867 of a new policy for dealing with the Plains Indians. The necessity of moving them out of the path of western development caused hardly any discussion. Neither did the idea that the Indians should be placed on reservations. Efforts to do this had already helped stir up the tribes' anger. What was new was a planned approach to wean the Indians from their nomadic way of life. Under the guidance of the Indian Office, they would be wards of the government until they learned "to walk on the white man's road."

The government set aside two extensive areas for the Indians. It designated the southern quarter of the Dakota Territory—two-thirds of present-day South Dakota—for the northern Plains Indians. The government assigned what is now Oklahoma to the southern Plains Indians, as well as to the five Civilized Tribes—the Choctaw, Cherokee, Chickasaw, Creek, and Seminole—and other eastern Indians already there. Scattered reservations went to the Navaho and Apache in the Southwest and the mountain Indians in the Rockies and beyond. As in the past, the transfer of land went through the legal process of treatymaking. And, as in the past, the whites bribed and tricked the Indian chiefs and in the end forced them to accept what they could not prevent. The Indians had now been provided with homes off "the great road" of the white man. "All who cling to their old hunting-grounds are hostile and will remain so till killed off," stated the western commanding general of the army in 1868.

The Plains Indians inevitably tried to hold on to their way of life. Their subjection was equally inevitable. The native Americans had long been weakened by the white man's whiskey and his diseases. Smallpox had first struck the Indians in the Southwest as early as 1801. It took its heaviest toll in the late 1830s, when a terrible epidemic ravaged the tribes from the upper Missouri River to northern Texas. The Indians never recovered from these losses. They suffered equally from the erosion of their means of subsistence. As the buffalo disappeared, so did the Indian's ability to fight. Hunger and exposure defeated him just as often as did the federal troops.

The wars went on for nearly a decade—in Kansas in 1868–69, in the Texas Red River Valley in 1874, and finally in the climactic Sioux War of 1875–76. Indians occasionally won a victory. In 1876, they wiped out the troops under the immediate command of General George A. Custer on the Little Bighorn River in the Montana Territory. However, the day of reckoning was merely postponed. The Indians had no chance against the overwhelming strength of the soldiers and the relentless white settlement of the land.

Homesick bands of southern Cheyenne learned this bitter truth in 1878 when they

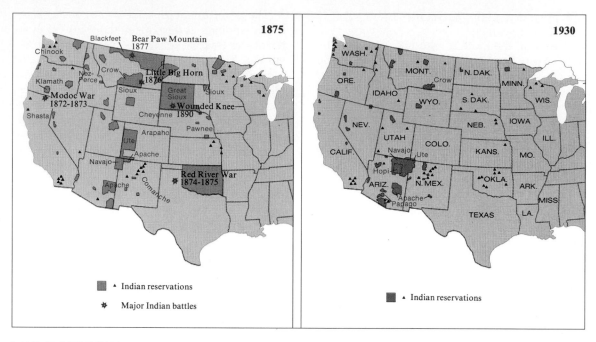

MAP 19.5 THE WESTERN INDIANS
The Plains Indians, who considered the lands they hunted as rightfully theirs, resisted in a series of sporadic wars the federal government's plan of 1867 to confine them to reservations. Even so, the reservations provided extensive land and enabled the Indians to live as tribal peoples. But from 1875 on, as whites discovered the reservations' mineral wealth and fertile lands, the Indians lost the land granted to them in 1867. By 1930, little but barren and arid lands remained in their hands.

escaped from their reservation in the Indian Territory of Oklahoma. Along the route to the Indians' hunting grounds in the Wyoming Territory, lay three railroads, numerous telegraph lines, and ranchers and homesteaders eager to report the Cheyennes' movements. The Indians made their way through Kansas and Nebraska, but the army eventually brought them to bay. The government permitted the surviving remnants, who preferred death to returning to the reservation, to stay on their native land.

Not the Indian, but the white man wrecked the reservation policies of 1867. Prospectors discovered gold in 1874 in the Black Hills, part of the Sioux reservation in Dakota. Unable to hold back the prospectors or to buy out the Indians, the government opened up the Black Hills to gold seekers at their own risk. The Sioux War, touched off chiefly by this influx, gave the government the excuse to force the cession of the western third of the Sioux reservation.

The Indian Territory of Oklahoma met the same fate. Two million acres in the heart of the territory had not been assigned to any tribe. White homesteaders coveted the fertile land of this area. The "Boomer" movement, stirred up initially by railroads running across the Indian Territory during the 1880s, agitated ceaselessly to open this so-called Oklahoma District to whites. In 1889, the government gave in and opened the Oklahoma District to the Homestead Law. On April 22, 1889, a horde of homesteaders rushed in and staked out the entire district within a few hours. Two tent cities—Guthrie with fifteen thousand people and Oklahoma City with ten thousand—were in full swing by nightfall.

The completion of the land-grabbing process came, ironically, at the hands of the Indians' avowed friends. The native Americans never lacked sympathizers, especially in the East. Their mistreatment after the Civil War resulted in a reform movement led by the Indian Rights Association. The movement got a big push from the writer Helen Hunt Jackson, whose powerful book *A Century of Dishonor* (1881) told the story of the unjust treatment of the Indians. The reformers, unfortunately, had little sympathy for the tribal way of life. They could think of no better solution to the Indian problem than assimilation into white society.

From 1871, when Congress had prohibited any more Indian treaties, the government moved consistently to undermine tribal authority. An education program began in 1879. The Indians would be trained for farming and manual work, as well as for citizenship, at boarding schools and at day schools on the reservations. The goal was *severalty*, the individual, rather than tribal ownership of land. However, the Indians found this idea alien and repugnant. It had failed dismally in earlier experiments with land allotments distributed to about 1,750 Chippewa in 1871.

The reformers remained unshaken in their conviction that land ownership would transform the Indians into prudent, hard-working members of white society. With their blessing, the Dawes Severalty Act of 1887 authorized the president to divide tribal lands, giving 160 acres to each family head and smaller plots to other individuals. The land would be held in trust by the

THE CHEROKEE STRIP
This photograph captures the wild race into the Cherokee Strip in the northern part of the Oklahoma Territory on September 16, 1893, the second such "run" that opened the region to white settlement. The winners staked out their claims under the Homestead Act, and looked forward to a prosperous future on the richest farmland in America. Those who lost out hoped for better luck as other parts of the territory opened up. The Indians who had owned the land had nothing to hope for, because this process spelled the end of their way of life. (Oklahoma Historical Society)

BLACK ELK: A HOLY MAN'S MEMORY OF WOUNDED KNEE

We heard that Big Foot was coming down from the Badlands with nearly four hundred people. Some of these were from Sitting Bull's band. They had run away when Sitting Bull was killed, and joined Big Foot on Good River. There were only about a hundred warriors in this band, and all the others were women and children and some old men. They were all starving and freezing, and Big Foot was so sick that they had to bring him along in a pony drag. They had all run away to hide in the Badlands, and they were coming in now because they were starving and freezing. . . .

It was in the evening when we heard that the Big Foots were camped over there with the soldiers, . . . In the morning [December 29, 1890] I went out after my horses, and while I was out I heard shooting off toward the east, and I knew from the sound that it must be wagon guns [cannon] going off. The sounds went right through my body, and I felt that something terrible would happen. . . .

A little way ahead of us, just below the head of the dry gulch, there were some women and children who were huddled under a clay bank, and some cavalrymen were there pointing guns at them. . . .

I had no gun, and when we were charging, I just held the sacred bow out in front of me with my right hand. The bullets did not hit us at all.

When we drove the soldiers back, they dug themselves in, and we were not enough people to drive them out from there. In the evening they marched off up Wounded Knee Creek and then we saw all that they had done there.

Men and women and children were heaped and scattered all over the flat at the bottom of the little hill where the soldiers had their wagon-guns, and westward up the dry gulch all the way to the high ridge, the dead women and children and babies were scattered. . . .

After the soldiers marched away, I heard from my friend, Dog Chief, how the trouble started, and he was right there by Yellow Bird when it happened. This is the way it was:

In the morning the soldiers began to take all the guns away from the Big Foots, who were camped in the flat below the little hill where the monument and burying ground are now. The people had stacked most of their guns, and even their knives, by the tepee where Big Foot was lying sick. Soldiers were on the little hill and all around, and there were soldiers across the dry gulch to the south and over east along Wounded Knee Creek too. The people were nearly surrounded, and the wagon-guns were pointing at them.

Some had not yet given up their guns, and so the soldiers were searching all the tepees, throwing things around and poking into everything. There was a man called Yellow Bird, and he and another man were standing in front of the tepee where Big Foot was lying sick. They had white sheets around and over them, with eyeholes to look through, and they had guns under these. An officer came to search them. He took the other man's gun, and then started to take Yellow Bird's. But Yellow Bird would not let go. He wrestled with the officer, and while they were wrestling, the gun went off and killed the officer. As soon as the gun went off, Dog Chief told me, an officer shot and killed Big Foot who was lying sick inside the tepee.

Then suddenly nobody knew what was happening, except that the soldiers were all shooting and the wagon-guns began going off right in among the people.

Many were shot down right there. The women and children ran into the gulch and up west, dropping all the time, for the soldiers shot them as they ran. There were only about a hundred warriors and there were nearly five hundred soldiers. The warriors rushed to where they had piled their guns and knives. They fought soldiers with only their hands until they got their guns.

Dog Chief saw Yellow Bird run into a tepee with his gun, and from there he killed soldiers until the tepee caught fire. Then he died full of bullets.

It was a good winter day when all this happened. The sun was shining. But after the soldiers marched away from their dirty work, a heavy snow began to fall. The wind came up in the night. There was a big blizzard, and it grew very cold. The snow drifted deep in the crooked gulch, and it was one long grave of butchered women and children and babies, who had never done any harm and were only trying to run away.

Source: *Black Elk Speaks: Being the Life Story of a Holy Man of the Ogalala Sioux*, John G. Niehardt, ed. New York: William Morrow, 1932. 257–268.

WOUNDED KNEE
In December 1890, U.S. soldiers massacred about two hundred Sioux men, women, and children in the Battle of Wounded Knee in South Dakota. It was the last big fight on the northern plains between the Indians and the whites. Black Elk, a Sioux chief, related that ". . . After the soldiers marched away from their dirty work, a heavy snow began to fall . . . and it grew very cold." The body of Yellow Bird lay frozen where the medicine man had fallen. (Smithsonian Institution, National Anthropological Archives)

government for twenty-five years, and the recipients would be made citizens. Remaining reservation lands would be sold off, the proceeds to be placed in an Indian education fund.

Disaster for the Indians followed. As the law was applied in stages in the coveted Indian Territory, white settlers moved into reservation after reservation. When Oklahoma became a state in 1907, Indians made up a scattered minority among half a million whites. They received little profit from their own land holdings. Their vulnerability spawned an industry of fraud and a flood of leasing scams, and then seizure once the land could be sold. The government invoked severalty even against tribes that resisted strongly. Only land too barren to evoke white greed was spared.

Of the 138 million acres of land owned by Indians in 1887, less than two-fifths, mainly desert, remained theirs in 1934. That year, the government moved to repair the damage caused by the misguided assimilation policy of nineteenth-century reformers. But what had been taken from the Indians could not be restored. "Sympathy and sentiment never stand in the way of the onward march of empire," an Oklahoma editor commented in 1907, the year that his state, Indian land twenty years earlier, joined the Union.

The South

"The South is the Bonanza of the future," the railway magnate Chauncey Depew declared in 1890. He added that "great and sudden opportunities for wealth" no longer existed in the West. So his message was: "Go South, Young Man." Northern investors and promoters did indeed find rich pickings in Louisiana timberlands and Alabama iron fields. But as a region, the South was not the West. The onrush of the western movement had simply swept away the Indian and Mexican civilizations. The social order of the Old South, changed but not crushed by the Civil War and Reconstruction, acted as a brake on the forces transforming the rest of the United States.

The Southern Economy

Long after the Civil War, the South lagged behind. In 1912, southerners had half the per capita wealth and less than two-thirds the per capita income of other Americans. Despite some growth of cities and industries, they remained a rural people. From 1850 into the twentieth century, two out of three southerners east of the Mississippi made a living from the land.

Farming and poverty are not, of course,

necessarily linked. But in the South, they were. Plantation agriculture ended after the Civil War, but not large land-holding. The freed slaves resisted the gang labor their former owners would have preferred and became tenant farmers instead. They worked on a crop-sharing basis, exchanging their labor for the use of land, house, implements, and sometimes seed and fertilizer. Lack of capital prevented them from renting on a cash basis and thrust them into debt to carry their families through the season. The local storekeeper "furnished" the sharecropper and took as collateral a lien on his growing crop. A crop lien, in effect, transferred the crop to the storekeeper, leaving the sharecropper only the proceeds that remained—if any—after his debts had been paid. Nor, once he had established credit with one store, was the sharecropper free to shop around. As a result, merchants imposed terribly high prices on farmers seeking credit. The price of corn in Georgia during the 1880s ran 35 percent higher on credit than for cash. The sharecropper who could not pay at the end of the season fell into permanent debt to the merchant. Their bargaining relationship, already unequal, now became wholly one-sided. And if the storekeeper was also the landowner, or was conspiring with the landowner, the debt became a pretext for forced labor. Many indebted sharecroppers found themselves in virtual peonage.

It would be hard to imagine a less progressive system of commercial agriculture. Sharecropping committed the South inflexibly to cotton, despite soil depletion and unprofitable prices. Crop diversification declined after the Civil War, and sharecroppers raised less grain and fewer animals than had the earlier plantations. With leases on a year-to-year basis, neither tenant nor owner had any incentive to invest in long-term improvements. The results included ramshackle buildings; implements in disrepair; and scrawny, untended livestock. At a time of rapid advances in agriculture and farm mechanization, cotton growing remained tied to the mule, the plow, and the hoe. The crop-lien system lined merchants' pockets with earnings—economists estimate the expropriation rate at 13.5 percent—that might otherwise have helped improve agricultural production.

An appalling waste of human resources also held back the South. A freed slave, previously deprived of managerial experience and basic ed-

ucation, had neither the opportunity nor much incentive for self-improvement as a sharecropper. In 1880, more than 75 percent of the black sharecroppers remained illiterate.

All these impediments combined to produce a stagnant agricultural system. Cotton production per capita recovered very slowly from the wreckage of the Civil War. In 1900, it stood at only 75 percent of the level of 1860.

Despite its lagging agriculture, the South had high hopes of a new start after Reconstruction. A highly influential group of young publicists, including Henry W. Grady, editor of the *Atlanta Constitution*, put forth the credo of a "New South." Henry Watterson, editor of the *Louisville Courier-Journal*, declared that "the ambition of the South is to out-Yankee the Yankee." Throughout this New South, imbued with the spirit of industrial capitalism, people shared Watterson's conviction that "the easygoing days . . . have passed away . . . never to return. . . . The South has learned that 'time is money.' "

The small industrial sector of the South, unlike agriculture, recovered rapidly from the devastation of the Civil War. By 1870, the railway system had been rebuilt and manufacturing output exceeded prewar levels. In 1879, with both Reconstruction and the economic depression ended, a railroad boom developed. Track mileage doubled in the next decade. The timber industry expanded greatly in the Gulf states, along with an even more dramatic surge of coal and iron production in Alabama. Northern and English capital played the key role in all these advances. Only the southern textile industry did not depend on outside investors. In the towns of the Piedmont region of North Carolina and Georgia intense public spirit generated enough local capital to build about four hundred cotton mills by 1900.

In other respects, however, the Piedmont mills typified the southern approach to industrial development. Their competitive edge over the older New England mills stemmed partly from more modern machinery but far more from cheap labor. Recruiting exclusively from among poor whites in the surrounding hill country, the industry featured paternalism, long hours, and low wages. An 1897 report estimated the cost of cotton labor as 40 percent lower in the South than in New England. Southern chambers of

A Model Mill.

THE INDUSTRIAL SOUTH
No development so buoyed the hopes of New South proponents as the success of the region's textile industry. After 1877, new mills sprung up in South Carolina, North Carolina, and Georgia. Investors received a high return—average profits ran at 22 percent in 1882. Cotton mill employment, boasted the Charleston *News & Courier*, creates new jobs for "the necessitous masses of poor whites" and exposes them "to elevated influences, encourages them to seek education, and improves them in every conceivable respect." This 1887 engraving conveys the South's sense of pride in its new industrial prowess. (The Newberry Library, Chicago)

commerce pushed this kind of advantage to the limit. As one publicist wrote in 1897, "We must induce capital for manufacture to come here by offering cheaper money, cheaper taxation, cheaper labor, cheaper coal, and cheaper power, and much more public spirit."

The burst of industrial development did not liberate the South from its long-resented status as a colonial economy controlled by the North. The southern economy, always reliant on outside financing and distribution, fell even further under northern domination as a result of the merger movement that occurred in the 1890s. The region's railroads were reorganized and consolidated into a few large, cooperating systems, including J. P. Morgan's Southern Railway, controlled by investment bankers on Wall Street. The United States Steel Corporation acquired much of the southern iron industry. By monopolizing pipelines and refining facilities, Standard Oil and its allies exerted a stranglehold on the booming Texas oil fields that went into production starting in 1901.

Southerners headed many regional operations, but basic policy flowed from the controlling interests in the North. These interests aimed at maintaining the interregional status quo. Freight rate differentials encouraged the flow of raw materials but severely handicapped southern manufactured goods in competitive markets. In iron and steel, U.S. Steel created a price structure that protected its capital investment in Pittsburgh. Purchasers of Alabama steel had to pay Pittsburgh prices—despite the lower southern production costs—plus freight charges from Pittsburgh, even though the shipment originated in Birmingham. Southern users of steel were thus severely penalized, the Alabama steel industry lagged in spite of its natural advantages, and Pittsburgh retained its dominant position.

Contrary to the hopes of proponents of the New South, industrialism did not lift the region out of its rural poverty. Industrial output increased, but not enough to have much effect on the dominance of the agricultural sector. The industry that did develop was characteristically extractive, such as forestry and mining. In 1910, nearly two-thirds of the South's labor force worked in the production of raw materials, compared with hardly an eighth in the Middle Atlantic and New England states. Processing rarely went beyond coarse, semifinished goods, even in the textile industry. Relying on cheap, low-skill labor, southern industry fed on the region's poverty and backwardness. Long after Reconstruction, the South remained a tributary economy, a supplier on unequal terms to the advanced industrial heartland of the North.

Race, Class, and Politics

The commercial ambitions of the New South made a deep mark on southern politics. The dominant group was a business elite of new entrepreneurs and older plantation owners committed to southern economic development. Their method of exerting power, however, was strongly influenced by the political inheritance of Reconstruction. With the Republicans wholly discredited, the South became a one-party region. Whoever controlled the Democratic party controlled southern politics.

Because the Reconstruction struggle had been about home rule, the Democrats could portray themselves as the party of southern patriotism. In seizing control of the Democratic party, the economic elite thus had enormous advantages. Not only was there no effective opposition party. Members of the economic elite could cloak themselves in the mantle of the lost cause of the Civil War, and as the champions of southern *redemption* from black Republican rule. The conservative Democrats indeed called themselves the Redeemers.

The test of the Redeemers was their ability to exclude competing interests from the public arena. Class antagonism played a part in southern society. There had been long-smoldering differences between upland farmers and the planters. Fresh sources of conflict now arose in the tenant-farmer system—which increasingly included whites as well as blacks—and in an emerging industrial working class. Under the Redeemers, the South adopted highly conservative state policies. These included less public spending, the defense of property rights, and all possible encouragement of enterprise and investment.

Among the resulting disagreements, the most explosive was the question of heavy state debts incurred during Reconstruction. Failing to pay these obligations in full, conservatives argued, would undermine the public credit and frighten away outside capital. But the cost of such financial integrity would be borne by the people. In states such as Virginia, the burden of Reconstruction debt meant the virtual termination of all social services, including education. Where

creditor interests refused to compromise, Readjuster movements sprang up in the poorer farming areas, committed to a reduction of Reconstruction debts.

The Readjusters won some victories. Under the leadership of General William H. Mahone, they controlled Virginia from 1879 to 1883. But the Readjusters could not capture the Democratic machinery. When they allied themselves with the Republicans or appealed to black voters, they became vulnerable to Democratic charges of treason. The Democrats did not hesitate to resort to the rough tactics of Reconstruction days. In Mississippi, South Carolina, and Virginia, the Readjuster movements were defeated in an outbreak of bloodshed and stuffed ballot boxes. These ruthless actions reflected the confidence of a ruling class exercising its claim to political dominance.

The foundation of that claim lay in the white-supremacist order that rose from the ashes of slavery. "The white laboring classes here," wrote an Alabamian in 1886,

> are separated from the Negroes, working all day side by side with them, by an innate consciousness of race superiority. This . . . excites a sentiment of sympathy and equality on their part with the classes above them, and in this way becomes a healthy social leaven.

White workers expressed this "innate consciousness of race superiority" by claiming privileged rights above the blacks. Blacks were systematically driven from the many skilled jobs they had held since the Civil War. Blacks also found themselves entirely excluded, except as janitors, from textile work and tobacco processing.

The social marks of inferiority—segregation and deference—had equally great psychological importance because they asserted that "the lowest white man counts for more than the highest Negro." The pressure for a rigid system of social segregation came primarily from poor whites. "The best people of the South do not demand this separate [railroad] car business," wrote a North Carolina black man. By accepting segregation, he declared, they were "pandering to the lower instincts of the worst class of whites in the South."

In times of economic distress, the logic of class solidarity strongly challenged the doctrine of white supremacy. Blacks and whites worked together in many places, such as coal mines and timber camps and on the waterfronts of southern seaports. There, they sometimes organized together into trade unions and even went on strike side by side. During the mid-1880s, the Knights of Labor preached the message of interracial unionism with considerable effect.

In this predominantly agricultural region, it meant more that distressed white farmers showed some willingness to work with black farmers to achieve their common goals. "They are in the ditch just like we are," asserted a white Texan. Beginning in 1886, white dirt farmers began to agitate for agrarian reform through the Southern Farmers' Alliance. Black farmers formed a separate organization, the Colored Farmers' Alliance, but the two bodies worked together. Once the farmers' movement entered politics in 1890, this formal racial division began to be overcome.

Unable to capture the Democratic party, the Southern Farmers' Alliance formed independent parties in a number of states. It joined with western movements to form the People's party, commonly called the Populist party, in 1891. The southern Populists needed the black vote. "The accident of color can make no difference in the interest of farmers, croppers, and laborers," stated the Populist leader Thomas E. Watson of Georgia. "You are kept apart that you may be separately fleeced of your earnings." By organizing interracially as a third party representing southern dirt farmers, the Populists endangered the structure of conservative southern politics.

The one-party system survived, but at a terrible cost to racial justice in the South. In the contest for the black vote, the conservative Democrats had the advantages of money, power, and paternalistic ties. They also attacked the Populists at their most vulnerable point—that they were courting "Negro domination." When all this did not suffice, fraud at the polls enabled the Democrats to defeat the opposition in Alabama, Georgia, and elsewhere. The race issue, instrumental in bringing down the Populists, also reconciled them to defeat. The embittered poor whites, deeply ambivalent all along about interracial cooperation, turned their fury on the blacks. Southern conservatives, chastened by the Populist show of strength, encouraged this anger.

The Populist struggle tragically produced a brand of white supremacy more virulent and impenetrable than anything the blacks had faced since emancipation. The color line, hitherto incomplete, became rigid and comprehensive. Starting in Florida in 1887, state after state in the South passed laws requiring segregated seating in trains. Such racial legislation, known as Jim Crow laws, soon spread to every type of public facility, even cemeteries. Southern schools had been segregated since the Civil War and social custom had dictated considerable racial separation. But in the 1890s, the South became for the first time a fully segregated society by law as well as fact. The Supreme Court of the United States soon ratified the South's decision. In the case of *Plessy v. Ferguson* (1896), the Court ruled that segregation was not discriminatory—that is, it did not violate black civil rights under the Fourteenth Amendment—if blacks had accommodations equal to those of whites. The "separate but equal" doctrine held for nearly half a century.

The pressure for Jim Crow laws came from poor whites, but Southern conservatives generally took the lead in depriving blacks of their right to vote. Black disfranchisement came through the constitutional adoption, beginning with Mississippi in 1890, of literacy tests, property requirements, and poll taxes. The conservatives called such actions "reforms" because without black voters, they argued, there would be no reason for electoral corruption.

The poor whites favored disfranchisement as another expression of militant white supremacy. Their own voting rights were only partially protected from the literacy tests by special exemptions and lenient enforcement, and not at all from the property and poll-tax requirements. They might have objected more had they not been given a voice within the Democratic party. From the 1890s on, a new brand of Southern politician spoke for the poor whites. He no longer appealed to their class interests, but to their racial prejudices. Tom Watson, the fiery Georgia Populist, rebuilt his political career as a brilliant practitioner of race baiting. Starting in the early 1900s, he and other racial demagogues thrived throughout the Deep South.

Race hatred became an accepted part of southern life, manifested in a wave of lynchings and race riots and in the public vilification of blacks. For example, Benjamin R. Tillman, a leading South Carolina Democrat, described them as "an ignorant and debased and debauched race." This ugliness came from several sources, including intensified competition between white and black workers during the depression of the 1890s and the reaction against a less submissive black generation born after slavery. The nationwide spread of a pseudoscientific theory of racist inferiority also played a part, as did American imperialism and its subjugation of Filipinos, Hawaiians, and Hispanics.

But what had triggered the anti-black offensive was the crisis over Populism. Thereafter, white supremacy propped up the one-party system that had emerged from Reconstruction. If political power had to be shared, it would be on terms agreeable to the southern elite—the exclusion from the political process of any challenge to the economic status quo.

The Black Response

Where did this leave the blacks? In 1890, blacks comprised more than half the population of Grimes County, a cotton-growing area of east Texas. They had managed to keep the local Republican organization going after Reconstruction and regularly sent black representatives to the Texas legislature during the 1870s and 1880s. Also remarkably, the local Populist party that appeared in 1892 among white farmers proved immune to the Democrats' charges of "black rule." A Populist-Republican coalition swept the county elections in 1896 and 1898, surviving well after the collapse of the national Populist movement.

In 1899, defeated Democratic office seekers and prominent citizens of Grimes County organized the secret White Man's Union. Armed men prevented blacks from voting in town elections that year. The two most important black county leaders were shot down in cold blood. Night riders terrorized both white Populists and black Republicans. When the Populist sheriff proved incapable of enforcing the law, the game was up. The White Man's Union, now out in the open, became the county Democratic party in a new guise. The Democrats won Grimes County by an overwhelming vote in the 1900 election. The day after the election, members of the

Union laid siege to the Populist sheriff's office. They killed his brother and a friend and drove the sheriff, badly wounded, out of the county forever.

The White Man's Union ruled Grimes County for the next fifty years. The whole episode was the handiwork of the county's "best citizens," suggesting how respectable the naked use of force had become in the service of white supremacy. The Union intended, as one of its leaders said, to "force the African to keep his place." After 1900, blacks could survive in Grimes County only if they tended to their own business and stayed out of trouble with whites.

Booker T. Washington, the top black leader of

BOOKER T. WASHINGTON
In an age of severe racial oppression, Booker T. Washington (1856–1915) emerged as the acknowledged leader of black people in the United States. He was remarkable both for his ability as a spokesman to white Americans and his deep understanding of the aspirations of black Americans. Born a slave, Washington suffered the oppression common to all blacks after emancipation. But, having been befriended by several whites as he grew to manhood, he also understood what it took to gain white support in the black struggle for equality. (Library of Congress)

his day, responded to that grim reality in a famous speech in Atlanta in 1895. Washington marked out a line of retreat from the defiant stand of older black abolitionists. (Frederick Douglass, the greatest of that group, died the same year that the Atlanta speech launched Washington into national prominence.) Washington was conciliatory toward the South, calling it a society that blacks understood and loved. He considered "the agitation of the question of social equality (as) the extremest folly." Washington accepted segregation, provided that blacks had equal facilities. He accepted educational and property qualifications for the vote, providing that they applied equally to blacks and whites.

Washington's doctrine came to be known as the Atlanta Compromise. His approach was "accommodationist" in the sense that it avoided any direct assault on white supremacy. Despite the humble face he put on before white audiences, Washington did not concede the struggle, any more than did the Grimes County blacks, who, many decades later, still talked about the battles they had fought and lost during the Populist years. Behind the scenes, Washington fought skillfully against Jim Crow laws and disfranchisement. More important, his Atlanta Compromise, while abandoning the field of political protest, opened up a second front of economic struggle.

Washington sought to capitalize on a southern dilemma about the economic role of the black population. Racist dogma dictated that blacks be kept down and that they conform to their image as lazy, shiftless workers. But for the South to prosper, it needed an efficient labor force. Washington made this need the target of his efforts. Founder of Tuskegee Institute in Alabama in 1881, Washington advocated industrial education—that is, manual and agricultural training. He preached the virtues of thrift, hard work, and property ownership. His industrial-education program won generous support from northern philanthropists and businessmen and, following his Atlanta speech, applause from progressive supporters of the New South.

Washington assumed that black economic progress would be the key to winning black political and civil rights. He regarded members of the white southern elite as his crucial allies because ultimately only they had the power to act.

More importantly, they could "see the close connection between labor, industry, education, and political institutions." When it was in their economic interest, and when they had grown dependent on black labor and black enterprise, white men of business and property would recognize the justice of black rights. As Washington put it, "There is little race prejudice in the American dollar."

For twenty years after his Atlanta address, Washington dominated organized black life in America. He was the authentic voice of black opinion in an age of severe racial oppression. No black dealt more skillfully with the leaders of white America. Washington wielded more political influence than any other black of his generation. The black community knew him as a hard taskmaster. Intensely jealous of his authority, he did not regard opposition kindly. Black politicians, educators, and editors stood up to him at their peril.

Even so, a rift began after 1900, especially among younger, educated blacks. They thought Washington was conceding too much. He instilled black pride, but of a narrowly middle-class and utilitarian kind. What about the special genius of blacks that W. E. B. DuBois celebrated in his collection of essays called *The Souls of Black Folk* (1903)? And what of the "talented tenth" of the black population whose promise could only be stifled by industrial education? At the same time, blacks became increasingly impatient with Washington's silence over segregation and lynchings. The key critic was DuBois, a Harvard-educated sociologist and educator. In 1905, demanding "aggressive action," DuBois helped found the Niagara Movement. The reform atmosphere of the Progressive era also brought a new, though small, group of white allies on the scene. The National Association for the Advancement of Colored People (NAACP), organized by blacks and whites in 1909, absorbed the Niagara Movement and became a biracial vehicle in the fight for black rights. By the time of Washington's death in 1915, his approach had been superseded by a strategy that relied on the courts and political leverage, not on black self-help and accommodation.

History has proved Washington's Atlanta Compromise wrong in contending that only economic strength would give civil rights to blacks.

These rights have been gained without prior achievement of economic equality. But in taking the route of legal protest, the NAACP largely overlooked the bedrock plight of the mass of black people. Washington wisely emphasized the attack on black poverty and ignorance, each of which feeds the other. He also realized shrewdly that the evil race relations of the post-Reconstruction South was rooted in its backward economic order. As long as share-cropping cotton agriculture prevailed, and as long as the southern economy remained subservient to the industrial North, the South would not abandon the oppressive racial system that had been forged out of slavery.

Before Washington died, two events produced changes that would have far-reaching consequences for the economic future of poor blacks. In 1892, the boll weevil moved from Mexico into Texas. During the next thirty years, this small beetle spread throughout the South, attacking the cotton fields and forcing farmers to grow other crops. The second event, World War I, created a sudden demand for black labor and set off a massive, long-term migration to the North. The blacks who left the South found opportunity in northern industry, while those who remained had a stronger bargaining position.

Progress came slowly for the regional economy as a whole. It took much longer than nineteenth-century optimists had expected for the New South to come fully into its own. Now that the South has reached that goal, Booker T. Washington's expectations seem at least partly fulfilled. In the enterprising atmosphere of the modern South, the heart seems to have gone out of racial oppression.

The Agricultural Interest

In the South, the typical farmer was a sharecropper. Elsewhere in the country, he was an independent freeholder. The freeholder tradition was deeply rooted in the Jeffersonian ideal of a nation of virtuous yeoman farmers and was enshrined in the policy of free land for the settler. Family farms predominated throughout rural America in the late nineteenth century. The average farm comprised about 150 acres and employed an average of fewer than one hired hand. Farm ownership also was widespread. In 1880, owners occupied 75 percent of Iowa's farms. In an age of trusts and corporations, the farmer succeeded as did no other group in retaining the *forms* of economic individualism. But his *functions* took him far from the self-sufficient yeoman farmers of Jeffersonian America. He had been fully inducted into the modern economic order.

The Farming Business

American farmers of 1880 stood at the center of a vast and complex system of trade. They depended on the railroads to carry their crops to market. A highly sophisticated network of commodity exchanges determined prices and found buyers throughout the country and beyond. Great processing industries turned wheat into flour, livestock into dressed meat, and fruit and vegetables into canned goods. Only through this modern commercial system could farmers gain access to the expanding urban markets in the United States and overseas. About 20 percent of American agricultural production went abroad during the late nineteenth century.

TABLE 19.1 FREIGHT RATES FOR TRANSPORTING CROPS

Grand Island to Omaha (150 miles)				Grand Island to Chicago (650 miles)			
Date effective	Corn	Wheat	Oats	Date effective	Corn	Wheat	Oats
	(In cents per hundredweight)				(In cents per hundredweight)		
January 1, 1883	18	19½	18	January 7, 1880	32	45	32
April 16, 1883	15	16½	15	September 15, 1882	38	43	38
January 10, 1884	18	19½	18	April 5, 1887	34	39	34
March 1, 1884	17	19½	17	November 1, 1887	25	30	25
August 25, 1884	20	20	20	March 21, 1890	22½	30	25
April 5, 1887	10	16	10	October 22,1890	22	26	22
November 1, 1887	10	12	10	January 15, 1891	23	28	25

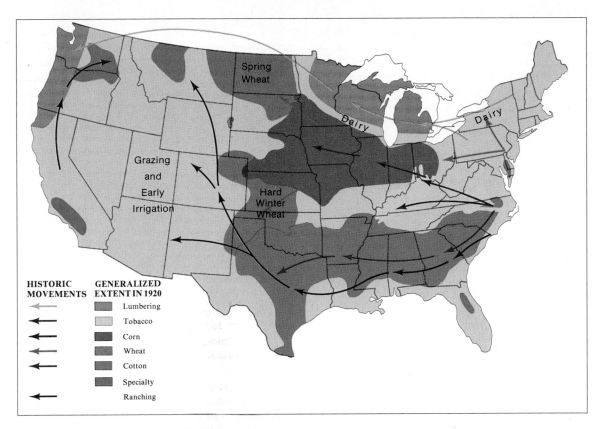

MAP 19.6 AGRICULTURAL REGIONS, 1900
The development of agricultural regions reflected the commercial bent of American agriculture—that is, growing crops for market rather than home consumption. Regional specialization matched climate and soil to the most suitable crops. Many crops moved west along with settlers. For some commodities, such as dairy products, the crop region simply expanded. Wheat, which was usually replaced by other crops after early years of settlement, concentrated finally on the Great Plains and the northwest. Agricultural regions continue to shift somewhat, as in the recent decline of cotton in the South and its growth in California.

American farmers were likewise well supplied with modern goods and services. They met their credit needs through mortgage companies that drew on eastern and European capital. The McCormick Reaper Company, John Deere and Company, and other manufacturers sold them labor-saving farm machinery. Other industries supplied an increasing share of household and farming needs. "The old rule that a farmer should produce all he required is part of the past," noted a farm journal. "Agriculture, like all other business, is better for its subdivisions, each one growing that which is best suited for his soil, skill, climate and market, and with its proceeds purchasing his other needs."

Farmers eagerly followed this advice. Subsistence farming persisted in infertile, hilly areas, and general farming, in which no crop represented as much as 40 percent of a farm's total production, went on throughout rural America. But farmers everywhere tended to concentrate on a cash crop, though not, as in the cotton South, to the exclusion of some gardening and small-stock raising. As a result, a high degree of regional specialization developed by the end of the century.

Distinct crop regions emerged. The wheat belt lay on the western edge of the Midwest from North Dakota down to Kansas and into northern Texas. Wheat had long been a virgin crop, the first to be planted when new land opened up. As the frontier moved on, wheat growing moved steadily westward. Wheat settled on the Great Plains, partly because of the suitability of the land and partly because of the arrival of hardy Russian varieties. Russian wheat prospered in the harsh plains climate and produced a bread flour superior to the soft wheat of milder regions. From Iowa eastward ran the corn belt, which devoted most of its product directly to livestock raising. The dairy belt, north of the corn belt, stretched from Minnesota as far east as New York and New England. It produced the nation's milk, butter, and cheese. In California, wheat raising gave way to orange groves and a wide variety of fruits and vegetables.

This agricultural specialization served as the best indicator of the commercial path taken by American farmers. But there were many other signs as well, such as the attitude toward land. Americans had little of the passionate identification with the soil that held European peasants to their inherited plots. In 1910, more than half the farmers lived on different land than they had inhabited five years earlier. The farmer saw his acreage as a commodity to be bought and sold, and to be valued for the price it could bring on the market. Most farmers believed they could earn as much profit, if not more, from the appreciation of the land's value as from the crops it produced. This attitude fostered the willingness to operate on borrowed capital. In boom times, farmers rushed into debt to extend their land holdings.

The commercial spirit also made farmers enthusiastic about the innovations of the industrial age. Farm machinery cut production costs for the leading crops by about half between 1850 and 1900. The railroad, especially the prospect of local rail service, delighted the western pioneers. They happily supported whatever inducements might be necessary, such as the public purchase of railway bonds, to lure the line to their towns.

Agrarian Distress

Farmers participated eagerly in the new industrial order. They embraced its entrepreneurial spirit, yet found themselves more victims than beneficiaries of the modern economy. The late nineteenth century was a time of deep agricul-

A WISCONSIN FARM FAMILY
On the frontier, pioneers struggled to tame the land and bring in the first cash crop. But as the frontier receded, as it had in Wisconsin by the late nineteenth century, farming settled down into a seasonal routine of plowing, planting, and harvesting. In this portrait, the young farmers proudly display their corn (the cash crop), ample produce, good health, and, in the woman's starched apron and the infant's white smock, their respectability. (State Historical Society of Wisconsin)

tural discontent. For thirty years, protest movements swept across the farm belt.

Part of the farmers' anger stemmed from the harshness of rural life. No one labored longer or harder. The farmer worked an average of sixty-eight hours a week in 1900, twelve hours longer than industrial workers; he had worked only six hours longer in 1850. Mechanization had not actually reduced work loads on farms as it had in factories. Crop acreage tended to increase with the availability of planting and harvesting machinery. Most other chores remained on the farmer's shoulders.

For the farm wife, the burdens increased. Larger harvests meant more field hands for whom to cook and clean up. At the same time, her own work in the kitchen remained almost unaffected by the conveniences and appliances that were becoming common in many urban homes. She and the children, as soon as they were old enough, also pitched in with the farm chores and field work. "Many a time a shudder has passed through the mother heart of me," said a Missouri woman in 1909, "at the sight of some little fellow struggling with the handles of a plow, jerking and stumbling over cloddy ground from daylight till dark. Boys 'making a full hand,' 'helping Pa.' " Farm children in 1900 attended school only two-thirds as many days as did city children, and they left school at an earlier age.

The farmer may have accepted how hard he labored, and how he wore out his wife and sacrificed his children, for the living he wrested from the soil. He found it harder to swallow the widening discrepancy in the quality of life between farm and city. In an age of rapidly advancing urban education, his children still attended gloomy, ungraded one-room schools—hardly the little red schoolhouses of popular mythology. Electricity, indoor plumbing, and paved roads had not yet come to the farm. The rural diet consisted of salt pork, bread, and potatoes for much of the year. A nationwide survey in 1918 by the U. S. Public Health Service showed that farm sanitation remained primitive. On two-thirds of all farms the water supply was threatened by "potentially dangerous contamination from privy contents."

Hardest of all was the sense of isolation from the variety and pleasures that farm people associated with urban life. Isolation was worst on the Great Plains, with its cruel winters and the long, empty distances. But farm life everywhere tended to be lonely and circumscribed. Rural neighborhoods, even in long-settled areas, amounted to three or four square miles where perhaps a dozen families lived. As one writer remarked, "the end of the neighborhood was almost the end of the world." Hamlin Garland and other authors of the late nineteenth century wrote powerfully about the dreariness of the countryside and the lure of the city. "I hate farm life," grumbled one of Garland's heroines. "It's nothing but fret, fret and work the whole time, never going any place, never seeing anybody but a lot of neighbors just as big fools as you are. I spend my time fighting flies and washing dishes and churning. I'm sick of it all."

Understandably, when farmers formed organizations, they provided for social activity first of all. The Patrons of Husbandry, familiarly known as the Grange because its branches were called granges, became a rural social center through its dances, picnics, and lectures. It encouraged women as well as men to join. Oliver H. Kelley, the government clerk who founded the Grange in 1867, hoped that participation by "the young folks of both sexes . . . will have a tendency to instill in their minds a fondness of rural life, and prevent in great measure so many of them flocking to the cities."

The hunger for social activity cemented organizational ties, but the dynamism of farmers' movements came from economic grievances. The farmers' basic problem was their imperfect participation in the economic transformation of the late nineteenth century. They embraced the era's commercialism, welcomed its technology and products, and sent their crops into a network of national and international markets. In one way, however, farmers did not change. They remained individual operators in a world of business consolidation and large-scale enterprise. In certain ways, they were acutely aware of their predicament.

One solution for farmers might have been to create their own versions of large-scale enterprise. Cooperative activity, especially through stores and creameries, had started before the Civil War. The Grange took up the cooperative idea in a big way by organizing bulk purchasing

A PIONEER COUPLE TWENTY YEARS LATER
Life on the frontier was harsh, but things improved through the years. The first photograph shows Mr. and Mrs. Ephraim Finch in front of their log-and-mud hut in Nebraska during the 1880s. This bleakness, common on the frontier, fed the agrarian discontent of those years. Twenty years later, the Finches posed again to record their prosperity. Their hut has given way to a handsome frame house, and the trees they may have planted as a wind break have grown into tall shade trees. (Nebraska State Historical Society)

from manufacturers, along with scattered cooperative banks, insurance companies, grain elevators, and processing plants. In Iowa, the state Grange started to manufacture farm implements in 1873. The Southern Farmers' Alliance, which became active in the middle 1880s, likewise strongly encouraged cooperation, especially for marketing cotton and operating cotton gins. The ambitious Texas Exchange began as a statewide cotton marketer in 1887. In an attempt to break the oppressive crop-lien system, it quickly evolved into a comprehensive marketing and purchasing exchange. However, banks and suppliers refused to do business with it, and the organization collapsed, as did most cooperative ventures of this era. The opposition by private business was too unrelenting, cooperative managers too unskilled, and the farmers themselves too individualistic.

Residual benefits did remain, among them an efficient mail-order business that emerged from farmers' hostility to middlemen. In 1872, Montgomery Ward and Company was founded specifically to "meet the wants" of the Grange. The early cooperative activity also led to more permanent institutions after the turn of the century, especially for dairy farmers and fruit growers.

Cooperative stores, grain elevators, and telephone exchanges became familiar parts of the countryside throughout rural America. As a solution to the organizational weakness of the late nineteenth-century farmer, however, cooperative movements had to be accounted a failure.

Another alternative for the farmers would have been to enlist the power of government against economic monopoly. Western farmers, generally served by only one grain elevator or railroad, felt continually cheated on storage charges and wheat grading. They also complained about paying freight rates higher than those farther east. The Grange, itself strictly a social-education organization, gave rise to independent political parties during the early 1870s that captured a number of state legislatures on antimonopoly platforms. The resulting Granger laws regulated grain elevators, fixed maximum railroad rates, and prohibited discriminatory practices against small and short-haul shippers. In *Munn v. Illinois* (1876), the Supreme Court upheld these laws on the ground that such enterprises involved the public interest. Reversing that decision in *Wabash v. Illinois* (1886), a more conservative Court ruled that the states lacked the power to regulate interstate commerce. By then, however, a movement had started for federal regulation of the railroads. The passage of the Interstate Commerce Act (1887), partly as a result of the Wabash case, made railroad regulation a permanent part of American public policy.

Farmers turned to cooperatives and government regulation out of a deep sense of economic disadvantage. But their difficulties did not actually stem from the monopoly power of the suppliers of goods and services. Manufacturers, railroads, and banks lacked the degree of market control ascribed to them by angry farmers. From 1865 to 1890, manufacturers could not establish a relative price advantage over agriculture. In fact, the wholesale price of all commodities fell at a slightly faster rate than did farm product prices during those years. Nor did the heavy transportation costs for grain shipments result primarily from the monopoly power of the railroads. More important factors were the increasing distance from farms to Chicago, the principal grain market; the thin settlement on the Great Plains; and the seasonality of grain shipments.

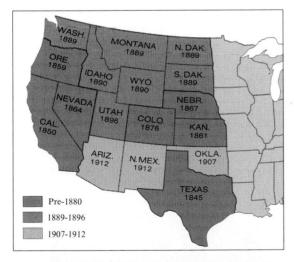

MAP 19.7 STATEHOOD FOR WESTERN STATES
In the Northwest Ordinance of 1787, the United States made a crucial political decision: the western territories, when sufficiently populated, would be admitted to the union as states "on an equal footing with the original states in all respects whatsoever." The entry of the western states had considerable political consequences. They were the seat of the Populist protest of the 1890s. And because each new state gained two votes in the Senate, the 4.4 million western citizens (scarcely 6 percent of the nation's total) had a disproportionate voice in national policy.

After the 1870s, as railroad technology improved and the volume of western traffic increased, freight rates fell steadily and east-west differentials narrowed. Even the much-maligned mortgage companies could not rig credit markets in the western states. Their interest rates matched those in the rest of the country. Farmers sometimes fell victim to suppliers, railroads, and moneylenders. But the impact of such abuses was not great enough to account for unprofitable farming.

Agrarian discontent centered on the Great Plains. This was the grain belt of the 1880s. Ten years earlier, when the grain belt lay farther east, Iowa, Illinois, and Wisconsin had been the scene of the Granger agitation. The special militancy of grain growers resulted partly from the nature of their market, which was international, highly volatile, and unpredictable. Grain prices, depressed in the late 1870s, surged in 1880. Chicago prices for a bushel of No. 2 corn went from 37.7 cents to 67.5 cents in 1882, and No. 2 wheat rose from $1.05 to $1.16.

Such price increases triggered a second weakness. A speculative climate tended to prevail in freshly settled areas. With grain prices on the rise, the price of land was rapidly bid up. In Harrison Township, Nebraska, first settled in 1872, land that sold for eight dollars an acre in 1880 sold for twenty-five dollars and up a few years later. At that price, the purchaser in effect gambled that grain prices—and land prices—would continue to rise. But grain prices collapsed in 1883–84. Anyone who had taken out a mortgage and bought land at twenty-five dollars an acre in Harrison Township could not hope to meet his payments, at 6 percent interest, at the prevailing price for wheat. "One is almost tempted to draw the moral that the would-be purchaser . . . had almost better throw his money away than invest it in farming operations in Nebraska," an investigator concluded in 1892.

Such advice came too late—and, in any case, it would not likely have been taken by the western farmer. His predicament seemed fundamental to him and to stem not from individual errors of judgment but from deep-rooted inequities in the economic system. As grain prices sank after 1884 and foreclosures swept across the grain belt, the western farmer turned to the one course of action that seemed able to rescue him—politics.

Populism and After

A second cycle of agrarian organization began in the 1870s. In the South, the leading groups were the Southern Farmers' Alliance and the Colored Farmers' Alliance; in the western states, most important was the National Farmers' Alliance of the North West. Originally intended as social and mutual-aid societies, these organizations increasingly began to take up the economic grievances of sharecroppers and grain farmers. In both the South and West, they tried to gain a hearing from the major political parties. When this did not succeed, the farmers turned to independent politics. In 1890, they won control of the Nebraska and Kansas legislatures, and captured several governorships as well as eight state legislatures in the South. Two years later, the southern and western organizations joined together in Saint Louis to form the Populist party. In the 1892 elections, the Populists, with James B. Weaver, an Iowa congressman, as their presidential candidate, won a million votes—9 percent of the total—and carried four states. For the first time, agrarian protest showed potential as a national political movement.

Populism contained a strong radical bent. Severe economic distress, Populists felt, could stem only from some basic evil. They identified this evil as the control of the "money power" over the levers of the economic system. "There are but two sides," proclaimed a Populist manifesto. "On the one side are the allied hosts of monopolies, the money power, great trusts and railroad corporations. . . . On the other are the farmers, laborers, merchants and all the people who produce wealth. . . . Between these two there is no middle ground." This reasoning allied agriculture with labor and identified farmers and workers as a single producer class. In 1887, the Southern Farmers' Alliance changed its name to the Farmers' and Laborers' Union of America, and the Populists sought to ally themselves with the labor movement.

The Populist platform of 1892 revealed the scope of the party's program. It called for nationalization of the railroads; protection of the land, including natural resources, from monopoly and alien ownership; a graduated income tax; and postal savings banks. The Populist platform also included the Southern Alliance's sub-treasury plan, by which farmers could borrow money at a nominal 2 percent interest with their crops serving as collateral. In addition, the Populists adopted resolutions supporting organized labor, veterans' pensions, and such political reforms as the secret ballot and direct election of senators. Finally, the Populists called for the unlimited coinage of silver. From a comprehensive program, this currency question became the overriding issue of the Populist party.

Until 1873, the nation had operated on the bimetallic standard, by which silver and gold had served as legal tender at a ratio of sixteen to one. At a given unit of monetary value, sixteen parts of silver equaled one part of gold. Because of the scarce supply of silver, its market price rose above its official value. Hence, silver disappeared from currency circulation and in 1873 was officially dropped as a medium of exchange, putting the nation on a gold standard. Soon thereafter, great silver discoveries occurred in Nevada, Arizona, and elsewhere in the West. With this new supply, silver prices dropped swiftly in relation to gold. If the government returned to the bimetallic standard, at the ratio of

MARY ELIZABETH LEASE
As members of a political movement, the Populists were short on cash and organization, but long on rank-and-file zeal and tub-thumping oratory. No one was more rousing on the stump than Mary Elizabeth Lease, who came from a Kansas homestead and pulled no punches. "What you farmers need to do," she urged in her speeches, "is to raise less corn and more *Hell!*" (Brown Brothers)

sixteen to one silver would flow into the Treasury and greatly expand the volume of currency. Although the Sherman Silver Purchase Act of 1890 permitted limited Treasury purchases, the Populists began to demand free silver.

The reasons were in part narrowly economic. Farmers would benefit from free silver because it was inflationary. A larger money supply would raise farm prices and reduce the burden of farm debt; farmers would be paying back cheaper dollars than they had borrowed. But free silver was also defended in radical terms, based on a conspiracy theory about eastern bankers and "goldbugs." Their stranglehold on the money supply, according to this theory, was the central evil of the capitalist system and the primary means of exploiting the producing classes. *Coin's Financial School* (1894), a powerful pamphlet by William H. Harvey, trumpeted this message at the height of the free-silver agitation.

However, the Chicago Socialist Henry Demarest Lloyd, Georgia's Tom Watson, and other left-wing Populists clearly saw the conservative logic behind free silver. It meant money in the pockets of western farmers and hefty party contributions from silver-mining interests. These mine operators, scornful though they might be of the Populist program, yearned for the day when the government would buy all the silver they could produce—at a premium price.

On the other hand, free silver had no appeal for city workers. Any chance of a farmer-labor alliance that might transform Populism into an American version of a social-democratic party would be doomed. As Lloyd complained, free silver was "the cowbird of reform," stealing in and taking over the nest that others had built.

Events soon proved the truth of Lloyd's jibe. When the Democratic party came out for free silver in the 1896 presidential election, the Populists could not prevent themselves from being absorbed into the Democratic campaign and from losing their independent identity. With the victory of William McKinley, a Republican, Populism died.

Populism did not disappear because farmers had changed their minds about the need for a larger money supply. They had made the right economic analysis, only it was not free silver that came to their rescue. During the 1890s, gold was discovered in South Africa, Colorado, and Alaska. New refining techniques, especially the cyanide method, greatly increased ore yields. The gold discoveries did for the embattled farmers just what they had hoped to accomplish through free silver. Prices rose nearly 50 percent between 1897 and 1914, and their debt burdens eased.

Moreover, the growing urban population increased the demand for farm products. As domestic markets began to absorb the farm surplus, farm exports dropped sharply after 1900. Wheat went from 72 cents a bushel in 1896 to 98 cents in 1909, corn from 27 cents to 57 cents, and cotton from 6 cents to 14 cents a pound. Farm prices rose faster than those of other products, and, as a result, so did the real income of farmers. A new spirit of prosperity and optimism took hold in the "golden age" of American agriculture before World War I.

Farmers abandoned Populism because rising prices eased their economic distress shortly after the 1896 election. More deep-seated changes, already underway, would ensure that, even in the harshest times, they would not express their discontent through a twentieth-century version of Populism. The farmers' sense of deprivation and inferiority—that they were "rubes" and "hicks," and that life was inherently better in the city—began to subside after 1900. The new prosperity helped bring about this significant change in their feelings. More farmers could afford to expand and modernize their houses. They purchased labor-saving home appliances and farm machinery to lighten field work.

New inventions helped ease the isolation and monotony of rural life. The telephone became commonplace, not so much because of the spread of commercial service, but through the determined efforts of farmers themselves. Telephone cooperatives became the most numerous type of farm cooperatives in the early twentieth century. The automobile, especially after the Ford Model T came on the market in 1908, spread across rural America. President Theodore Roosevelt's Country Life Commission, formed in 1908, took a sunny view of farm society: "There has never been a time when the American farmer was as well off as he is today, when we consider not only his earning power, but the comforts and advantages he may secure."

The farmer's self-conception also underwent an irreversible transformation. As long as farmers remained in the majority, they naturally

TIME LINE
RURAL AMERICA

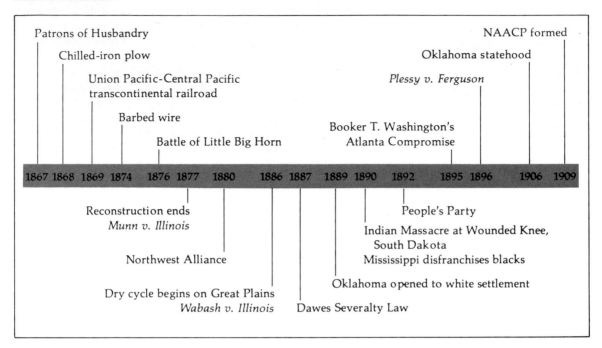

Patrons of Husbandry

Chilled-iron plow

Union Pacific-Central Pacific
transcontinental railroad

Barbed wire

Battle of Little Big Horn

Booker T. Washington's
Atlanta Compromise

Plessy v. Ferguson

Oklahoma statehood

NAACP formed

1867 1868 1869 1874 1876 1877 1880 1886 1887 1889 1890 1892 1895 1896 1906 1909

Reconstruction ends
Munn v. Illinois

Northwest Alliance

Dry cycle begins on Great Plains

Wabash v. Illinois

Dawes Severalty Law

Oklahoma opened to white settlement

Mississippi disfranchises blacks

Indian Massacre at Wounded Knee,
South Dakota

People's Party

considered themselves as representative of the American norm. They could readily regard their own economic distress as a general disorder of the entire nation. Pushed far enough, they might seek to mobilize their fellow producers—farmers and workers—to seize political power. In short, they could become Populists. But by the opening of the twentieth century, farmers no longer composed the majority of the population. In 1910, only about a third of the labor force earned a living from the soil. The farmers' realization that their number could only decrease with each census persuaded them to abandon the Jeffersonian illusion of a rural yeomanry.

"Now the object of farming is not primarily to make a living, but it is to make money," stated an agricultural writer in 1904. "To this end it is to be conducted on the same business basis as any other producing industry." This commercial spirit expressed itself in a fresh interest in improved farming methods and marketing techniques and, above all, in the recognition of

supply and demand as the farmers' central concern. Federal assistance, which went back to the Morrill College Land Grant Act of 1862, expanded to provide many new marketing and educational services for farmers. The budget of the Department of Agriculture increased thirty-fold between 1890 and 1920. New farm organizations sprang up, such as the Farmers' Educational and Cooperative Union, the American Society of Equity, and, strongest of all, the American Farm Bureau Federation. These groups cultivated a strong service orientation and concerned themselves chiefly with the profitable marketing of agricultural commodities. They avoided politics except to advance farmers' practical needs, and they acted in these cases as interest groups, not as a political movement.

All these developments reflected the new reality facing the farmer. Agriculture had been at the heart of American life. In the twentieth century, it was but one more economic interest—an important one, but now subordinate in the larger scheme of the modern industrial order.

In the late nineteenth century, rural America was drawn increasingly into the orbit of the new industrial way of life. The surge across the Great Plains and the Rockies, the final phase of the westward movement, was strongly linked with the nation's economic development. Industry needed mineral resources; the cities demanded agricultural products; and the railroad, barbed wire, and other symbols of an industrial age made the conquest of the West relatively easy. Doomed by the swift penetration of their lands, the western Indians were largely the victims of events that occurred far off in the nation's industries and cities.

The South, emerging from the ravages of the Civil War and Reconstruction, tried to follow the example of the industrial North, but with only mixed success. Southern politics were strongly influenced by entrepreneurial values, and southerners made strenuous efforts to encourage industrial development. However, the South remained locked into its deep-rooted heritage of staple-crop agriculture and racial division. As the nation's underdeveloped region, it remained subordinate to the more advanced economy of the North.

Western farmers also stood in an uncomfortable relationship to the industrial sector. Operating as family farmers in an age of increasing organization and complexity, they found farming persistently unprofitable. The causes of their difficulty baffled them, which led to the rise of Populism, a protest movement that briefly challenged the two party system during the 1890s. After 1897, farm prices rose and a new age of prosperity began for farmers. The flow of the new products of industrialism—telephones, household appliances, and automobiles—began to relieve the isolation and hardship of farm life.

Suggestions for Further Reading

The Great West

The liveliest and most sensitive introduction to western history is Robert V. Hine, *The American West* (2nd ed. 1984). The seminal statement on the significance of the frontier is in Frederick Jackson Turner, *The Frontier in American History* (1950). Another highly influential work is Walter P. Webb, *The Great Plains* (1931), which stresses man's adaptation to the western climate and environment. A good regional survey is Robert G. Athearn, *High Country Empire: High Plains and Rockies* (1960). The best book on western mining is Rodman Paul, *Mining Frontiers of the Far West: 1848–1880s* (1963). For the farming pioneers, see Everett Dick, *Sod-House Frontier* (1954), and on the cattlemen, Lewis Atherton, *The Cattle Kings* (1961) and Robert R. Dykstra, *Cattle Towns* (1968). Cowboys receive full treatment in Joe B. Frantz and Julian E. Choate, *American Cowboy: Myth and Reality* (1955).

Native Americans

A useful introduction to Native American history is William T. Hagan, *American Indians* (1961). Two valuable collections by deans of the subject are Wilfred E. Washburn, ed., *Indian and White Man* (1964) and Francis Paul Prucha, *Indian Policy in the United States: Historical Essays* (1981). Ralph K. Andrist, *Long Death: Last Days of the Plains Indians* (1964) tells that tragic story eloquently. The most recent study of white attitudes is Richard Drinnon, *Facing West: The Metaphysics of Indian-Hating and Empire-Building* (1980).

The South

On the South, the seminal book for the post-Reconstruction period is C. Vann Woodward, *Origins of the New South, 1877–1913* (1951), which still defines the terms of discussion among historians. Two recent books stress the continuities between the Old South planters and the post Civil War economic development: Dwight B. Billings, *Planters and the Making of "New South": North Carolina, 1865–1900* (1979) and Jonathan M. Wiener, *Social Origins of the New South: Alabama, 1860–1885* (1978). The standard book on New South thought is Paul M. Gaston, *The New South Creed: A Study of Southern Myth-making* (1973). Gaston's book can profitably be read in conjunction with a much older study, Paul M. Buck, *The Road to Reunion, 1865–1900* (1937).

The economic aftermath of slavery and the plantation system is treated with great insight by two economists, Roger Ransom and Richard Sutch, *One Kind of Freedom* (1977). Pete Daniel, *Shadow of Slavery* (1972) gives a vivid account of peonage. The classic book on segregation is C. Vann Woodward, *The Strange Career of Jim Crow* (2nd rev. ed. 1968), but it should be supplemented by Howard N. Rabinowitz, *Race Relations in the Urban South, 1865–1890* (1978). Disfranchisement is treated with great analytic sophistication in

J. Morgan Kousser, *The Shaping of Southern Politics: Suffrage Restriction and the Establishment of the One-Party South, 1880–1910*, and as an aspect of progressivism in Jack Temple Kirby, *Darkness at the Dawning: Race and Reform in the Progressive South* (1972). Rayford W. Logan, *The Betrayal of the Negro* (new ed. 1965) is the standard history of blacks after Reconstruction. August Meier, *Negro Thought in America, 1880–1915* (1963) is a key analysis of black accommodation and protest. The pre-eminent exponent of accommodation has been the subject of a superb two-volume biography by Louis B. Harlan, *Booker T. Washington: The Making of a Black Leader* (1973) and *Wizard of Tuskegee* (1983).

The Agricultural Interest

On agriculture, the standard works are Fred A. Shannon, *The Farmer's Last Frontier, 1860–1897* (1945) and Gilbert C. Fite, *The Farmer's Frontier, 1865–1900* (1966). Women's role on the frontier is now beginning to receive its due. See especially Julie Roy Jeffrey, *Frontier Women: The Trans-Mississippi West* (1979). The flavor of farm life can best be captured in fiction: Hamlin Garland, *Main-Travelled Roads* (1891), Willa Cather, *My Antonia* (1918), and O. E. Rolvag, *Giants in the Earth* (1927).

Populism

The standard work on Populism is John D. Hicks, *The Populist Revolt* (1931). Richard D. Hofstadter, *Age of Reform* (1955) advanced an interpretation that stressed the darker side of Populism, in which intolerance and paranoia figured heavily. Hofstadter's thesis, which dominated debate among historians for some years, has now given way to a much more positive assessment of Populism. The key book here is Lawrence Goodwyn, *Democratic Promise: The Populist Movement in America* (1976), which argues that it was the last broadly-based, radical response to industrial capitalism. Goodwyn stresses the Southern roots of Populism, and has consequently stimulated other work studying this aspect of subject—for example, Steven Hahn, *The Roots of Southern Populism: Yeoman Farmers and the Transformation of the Georgia Upcountry, 1850–1890* (1983). The carry-over of southern Populism into twentieth-century agrarian socialism has received detailed study in James R. Green, *Grass-Roots Socialism: Radical Movements in the Southwest* (1978). A highly stimulating book that traces the evolution of other strands of Populism into twentieth-century agrarian conservatism is Grant McConnell, *The Decline of Agrarian Democracy* (1953).

20

THE PUBLIC WORLD OF LATE NINETEENTH-CENTURY AMERICA

*I*n times of national ferment, as a rule, public life becomes magnified. Leaders emerge. Electoral campaigns debate great issues. The powers of government expand. That had certainly been true of the Civil War era. The crises of Union and Reconstruction had tested to the utmost the nation's public institutions and resources. The transforming economic changes that followed Reconstruction did not bring a comparably large political response. As the sectional crisis lost its force during the 1870s, so did the nation's commitment to activist government. Political life went on, but was drained of its earlier potency. In the 1880s there were no Lincolns, no great national debates, and little exercise of state power. Public life was vigorous in other ways—highly organized and rife with cultural conflict—but not through the formal, governmental processes by which a nation confronts its central concerns.

The rule enunciated above—that great events call forth great politics—applied to the new industrial age, but with a lag in the political response. Eventually, enough social pressure built up to require government action. Equally important, industrialism made the United States—whether or not the nation desired it—a world power. That change in itself was a political event. Both truths came home to the country during the 1890s. By the end of that decade, public life had taken on new meaning in America.

Domestic Politics

Late nineteenth-century America was richly endowed with brilliant political observers—James Bryce of Great Britain, Moisei Ostrogorski of Russia, and a young American political scientist named Woodrow Wilson. Unanimously, they deplored the politics they saw in post-Reconstruction America. "The conditions of public life in this country," wrote Wilson in his *Congressional Government* (1885), "are not what they were in the early years of the federal government; they are not what they were even twenty years ago. . . . Since [the Civil War] we . . . are perplexed at finding ourselves denied a new order of statesmanship to suit the altered conditions."

National Politics

The presidents of the period from 1877 to 1897 were estimable men. Rutherford B. Hayes (1877–1881), James A Garfield (1881), and Benjamin Harrison (1889–1893) all had distinguished war records. Hayes had served well as governor of Ohio for three terms, and Garfield as a congressional leader for many years. Chester A. Arthur (1881–1885), despite his cloudy reputation as a machine politician, had demonstrated fine administrative skills in heading the New York Custom House. Grover Cleveland (1885–1889 and 1893–1897), the only Democratic president of these years, had made his mark as reform mayor of Buffalo and governor of New York. None of these men was a strong or charismatic leader. Cleveland, the most aggressive and high principled, asserted himself in a largely negative way; he vetoed a record number of bills. But circumstances, more than their personal qualities, explain why these presidents did not make a larger mark on history.

The executive functions of the presidency did not amount to much in those days. As late as 1901, the White House staff consisted of three secretaries and half a dozen clerks, doorkeepers, and messengers. During the 1880s, the government departments were sleepy places carrying on largely routine duties. The civil service had mostly low-quality employees, and the diplomatic service received little attention. The army and navy handled mainly frontier duty and coastal patrol. The government was not responsible for social welfare, education, or economic regulation. So modest were its functions, in fact, that the government continually wound up with a financial surplus in the 1880s. The problem of how to reduce federal revenues ranked as one of the most troublesome issues of the decade.

The presidents spent much time dispensing political patronage through the spoils system, which gave public offices as rewards for party services. Civil service reform became a national issue after Charles Guiteau, a disappointed office seeker, assassinated President Garfield in 1881. The Pendleton Act of 1883 created a civil service list of jobs to be filled through examination by the new Civil Service Commission. The list origi-

nally included only 10 percent of all federal jobs. Each president added to it, generally at the close of his term in order to safeguard some of his appointees. But patronage remained a preoccupation in the White House. Cleveland groaned over the "damned, everlasting clatter for office." Benjamin Harrison spent four to six hours a day dealing with office seekers during the first eighteen months of his term.

The presidents took a back seat to Congress on national policy making. But they consistently defended the integrity of the presidency against congressional encroachment. This matter primarily involved appointments, over which Congress had asserted broad jurisdiction in the Tenure of Office Act of 1867 during the battle with President Johnson over Reconstruction policy. From

GROVER CLEVELAND
In the years after Reconstruction, Americans did not look for charismatic personalities or dramatic leadership in their presidents. They preferred men who accepted the limits of executive power, men of "sound conservatism." Grover Cleveland fitted this bill to perfection. For political reformers, Cleveland had the additional virtues of independence and personal integrity. Cleveland best represented the late nineteenth-century ideal of the American president. (Culver)

Rutherford B. Hayes on, each president of this era stubbornly held on to his appointive powers. Many fierce scraps developed with such congressional leaders as Senator Roscoe Conkling of New York until the Tenure Act was repealed in 1887. Nevertheless, the presidents had no thought of leading Congress on policy matters. The presidency, insisted Cleveland, was "essentially executive in nature." A good president ought to give efficient, honest service and veto measures that he considered ill advised or extravagant, as Cleveland regularly did with veterans' pension bills. Otherwise, policy making should be left to Congress. Scarcely any important legislation originated in the White House during these years.

American government, complained Professor Woodrow Wilson of Princeton University in 1885, was congressional government. But Congress was not well set up to do its work. In the House of Representatives, the rules had grown so complicated and numerous that they frequently brought business to a standstill. In neither the House nor the Senate could the party leadership exert discipline over the members. Nor did either party ever stay in power long enough to design or push through a legislative program. From 1877 to 1893, neither Democrats nor Republicans controlled both houses for more than a single congressional term. Most of the time, the Democrats controlled the House, the Republicans the Senate. Consequently, the ability of Congress to take forceful action was extremely limited.

The major parties, for their part, had little stomach for strong programmatic positions. Historically, they represented somewhat different traditions—the Democrats favoring states' rights and limited government, the Republicans supporting government encouragement of economic development. But after Reconstruction, neither party was eager to translate these differences into well-defined positions. On most leading national issues of the day—civil service reform, the currency, and regulation of the railroads and trusts—the divisions occurred within the parties, not between them. The laws that resulted could not be clearly identified as either Democratic or Republican legislation.

The tariff was something of an exception. After the Republicans came to power in 1861, they had increased tariffs, and the protective walls remained high for the next half century. It was an article of Republican faith, as President Harrison said in 1892, that "the protective system . . . has been a mighty instrument for the development of the national wealth and for protecting the home of the workingman from the invasion of want." The Democrats, free traders by tradition, regularly attacked Republican protectionism.

Actually, however, the parties disagreed only about the degree of protection. More important, congressmen voted their own local interests on tariffs, regardless of party rhetoric. All tariff bills consisted of patchworks of many bargains among special interests. In 1887, President Cleveland made a mighty effort to sharpen the battle. He devoted his entire annual message to Congress to tariff reform. Then he made tariffs the issue of his 1888 campaign for reelection. His narrow defeat seemed to confirm the political wisdom of evading the issue. "They told me it would hurt the party," he later wrote. "Perhaps I made a mistake from the party standpoint; but damn it, it was right. I had at least that satisfaction."

The major parties treated issues gingerly partly because they feared each other. The Democrats, in retreat immediately after the Civil War, quickly regrouped and, by the end of Reconstruction, stood on virtually equal terms with the Republicans. Every presidential election from 1876 to 1892 was decided by a thin margin, and neither party gained commanding control over Congress. Political caution seemed wise; any false move on national issues might tip the balance to the other side.

James Bryce, accustomed to philosophical divisions between English Tories and Liberals, grumbled about the indistinctness of American politics. "Neither party has any principles, any distinctive tenets," he wrote in his classic *American Commonwealth* (1888). Perhaps Lord Bryce exaggerated when he added, "All has been lost, except office or the hope of it." But electoral success had unquestionably taken precedence over party principle. This was evident particularly in the way the Republican party treated its Civil

War legacy. The major unfinished business was black rights in the South. Republicans gave lip service to the Blair Education Bill, appropriating federal funds to combat illiteracy, and the Lodge Election Bill, providing federal supervision for southern congressional elections, but let both pro-black measures die in 1890. The Republican administrations, more interested in building white support in the South, backpedaled on the race issue and gradually abandoned the blacks to their fate.

The Republicans were not so willing to abandon their identification with the Civil War itself. In every election campaign until the 1890s, Republican orators "waved the bloody shirt" against the "treasonous" Democrats. People considered service in the Union army to be the best claim for public office. One third of the Republican congressmen of the 1880s had a war record, and veterans' benefits always stood high on the Republican agenda. The Democrats played the same game in the South as the defenders of the Lost Cause. Bryce criticized American politicians for "clinging too long to outworn issues and . . . neglecting . . . the problems which now perplex the country."

The campaigns were not, in fact, intended to address those problems. The main thing was to avoid making too clear a statement on any issue of real controversy. After speaking in the 1880 campaign, James Garfield often confided in his diary, "I think no harm has been done." The personal reputations of the candidates overshadowed everything else in the hard-fought election of 1884. Was it more important that Grover Cleveland, a man of impeccable public honor, had years earlier fathered an illegitimate child? Or that James G. Blaine, perhaps the most gifted Republican of his generation, had taken favors from the railroads? In the midst of all the mudslinging, the issues got lost.

The issues did not, on the whole, absorb the politicians of the 1880s. The Republicans fought bitterly among themselves after President Grant left the White House in 1877. For the next six years, the party was divided into two clashing factions—the Stalwarts, who followed Senator Roscoe Conkling of New York, and the Halfbreeds, led by Representative Blaine of Maine. The split resulted from a personal feud between Conkling and Blaine, and it lasted because of a furious struggle over patronage. The Halfbreeds represented a newer Republican generation, more inclined to give lip service to political reform and less committed to the old Civil War issues. But principle actually had litle to do with the war between Stalwarts and Halfbreeds.

Although standards of conduct rose after the Grant years, a backroom atmosphere continued to pervade Gilded-Age politics. Congressmen

THE REPUBLICAN CONVENTION IN UPROAR
At the 1880 Republican convention in Chicago, the Stalwarts blocked Blaine, the Halfbreeds blocked Grant, and Garfield carried off the nomination. To placate the Stalwarts, one of their own—Chester A. Arthur of New York—was nominated as vice president. Garfield won the election but was shot on July 2, 1881 by a demented office-seeker, Charles Guiteau, who shouted: "I am a Stalwart and Arthur is President!" Guiteau was a madman, but he was prompted by the same emotions that had excited the convention—not over policy, but over control of the party, and the spoils that came with it. (From *Harper's Weekly*. The Newberry Library, Chicago)

still openly accepted railroad passes, took gifts and favors from the lobbyists swarming around Capitol Hill, and engaged routinely in private business activities that conflicted with their legislative responsibilities. "A remarkable nonchalance underlies the sound and fury of partisan politics," observed Henry Jones Ford the journalist.

The characteristics of public life in the 1880s—the inactivity of the federal government, the evasiveness of both political parties, and the absorption in politics for its own sake—came from the conviction that little was at stake in public affairs. Both parties shared a deep suspicion of activist government. In 1887, President Cleveland vetoed a small appropriation for drought-stricken Texas farmers with the remark that "though the people support the Government, the Government should not support the people." Government activity was in itself considered a bad thing. All that the state can do, said Senator Conkling, "is to clear the way of impediments and dangers, and leave every class and every individual free and safe in the exertions and pursuits of life. . . . Wealth can never be conjured out of the crucible of politics." Conkling was expressing the doctrine of laissez faire, which reigned supreme in late nineetenth-century America.

The Ideology of Individualism

In 1885, the cotton manufacturer Edward Atkinson gave a talk to the restless textile workers of Providence, Rhode Island. They had, he told them, no cause for discontent. "There is always plenty of room on the front seats in every profession, every trade, every art, every industry," Atkinson declared. "There are men in this audience who will fill some of those seats, but they won't be boosted into them from behind." Every man, he added, gets what he deserves. For example, Cornelius Vanderbilt had amassed a fortune of $200 million by building the New York Central Railroad. Atkinson went through some rapid calculations. Every person in the audience consumed about a barrel of flour a year. In 1865, it had cost $3.45 to ship that barrel from Chicago to Providence. In 1885, the New York Central carried it for 68 cents, taking 14 cents as profit,

while the workingman saved nearly $3. "Wasn't Vanderbilt a cheap man for you to employ as a teamster?" Atkinson asked. "Do you grudge him the fourteen cents?"

Atkinson's homely talk went to the roots of conservative American thought—that any man, however humble, could rise as far as his talents would carry him; that everyone received his just reward, great or small; and that the success of the individual contributed to the progress of the whole. This message appeared in a wide variety of writings, from the rags-to-riches tales of Horatio Alger to the stream of success manuals with such titles as *Thoughts for the Young Men of America, or a Few Practical Words of Advice to those Born in Poverty and Destined to be Reared in Orphanages* (1871). It was a lesson celebrated in the lives of such self-made men as Andrew Carnegie, whose book *Triumphant Democracy* (1886) paid homage to a nation in which a penniless Scottish child could rise from bobbin boy to steel magnate.

From the pulpit came the assurances of Bishop William Lawrence of Massachusetts that "Godliness is in league with riches." American Protestantism closely linked one's earthly calling and eternal salvation. This link enabled a conservative ministry to make morally reassuring the furious acquisitiveness of industrial America. "To secure wealth is an honorable ambition," intoned the Baptist minister Russell H. Conwell in his lecture "Acres of Diamonds," which became phenomenally popular. "Money is power. Every good man and woman ought to strive for power, to do good with it when obtained." Carnegie elevated this notion of stewardship into a formal doctrine that he called "the gospel of wealth," the responsibility of the rich to put their wealth to good social use. This should be done not by coddling the less privileged, Carnegie noted, but by providing the libraries, education, and cultural and scientific institutions by which they might prepare themselves for life's challenges.

The intellectual base of American individualism had long rested on classical economics. This economic theory, launched by the British economist Adam Smith in *The Wealth of Nations* (1776), postulated a self-regulating, competitive economy. Classical economics was fading as an intellectual formulation though it was still preached in classrooms, on editorial pages, and from lecture platforms. Relying on unproven principles, it seemed increasingly sterile and more a dogma than a theory that invited research.

The defense of individualism fell increasingly to a sociological theory more in keeping with the scientific spirit of the age. In his great book *The Origin of Species* (1859), the English naturalist Charles R. Darwin presented a theory to explain the evolution of plants and animals. In nature, Darwin wrote, all living things struggle and compete. Individual members of a species are born with certain characteristics that better enable them to survive. Future generations inherit these characteristics, and the species evolves.

This process, which Darwin called natural selection, created a revolution in biological science. It also had profound social implications. The British philosopher Herbert Spencer proposed the theory of Social Darwinism. He developed an elaborate analysis of how society evolves through constant competition among its members. In America, William Graham Sumner, a Yale sociology professor, became the leading exponent of Social Darwinism. Competition, said Sumner, is a law of nature that "can no more be done away with than gravitation." Furthermore, "if we do not like the survival of the fittest, we have only one possible alternative, and that is the survival of the unfittest. The former is the law of civilization; the latter is the law of anti-civilization." Who are the fittest? "The millionaires. . . . They may fairly be regarded as the naturally selected agents of society. They get high wages and live in luxury, but the bargain is a good one for society."

The political meaning of Social Darwinism was clear and convincing. As Sumner put it, "Minimize to the utmost the relations of the state and industry." Social Darwinism also inculcated deep belief in social determinism. "The great stream of time and earthly things will sweep on just the same in spite of us," Sumner wrote in his famous essay "The Absurd Attempt to Make the World Over" (1894). "That is why it is the greatest folly of which a man can be capable to sit down with a slate and pencil to plan out a new social world." As for the government, it had "at bottom . . . two chief things . . . with which to deal. They are the property of men and the honor of women. These it has to defend against crime."

This antigovernment appeal not only paralyzed political initiative. It also shifted the governmental balance away from the executive and legislative branches. "The task of constitutional government," declared Sumner, "is to devise institutions which shall come into play at critical periods to prevent the abusive control of the powers of a state by the controlling classes in it." Sumner meant the judiciary. From the 1870s on, the courts increasingly took the role that he assigned to them. During this period, judicial attack was directed mainly against legislative activism by the states. The number of decisions striking down state social welfare and regulatory laws rose markedly in the 1880s and after. The Supreme Court's crucial weapon in this campaign was the Fourteenth Amendment (1868), which prohibited the states from depriving "any person of life, liberty, or property, without due process of law." This due-process clause, intended to protect the civil rights of the freed slaves, gradually became a tight restraint against state interference with economic and business activity. The Supreme Court erected similar barriers against the federal government through narrow interpretations of the Constitution. It ruled in 1895 that the power to regulate interstate commerce did not cover manufacturing and that the power to tax did not extend to personal incomes.

Judicial supremacy went far beyond these negative functions. At a time when electoral politics were hesitant and disreputable, the legal system filled the void in effective governance. When Congress took up the issue of economic regulation in the 1880s, it passed laws designed to let the courts define their precise meaning as well as enforce them. The Interstate Commerce Act of 1887 and the Sherman Antitrust Act of 1890 were little more than the shells of effective legislation. With increasing aggressiveness, the courts took over the shaping of public policy on economic affairs.

Power conferred status. The legal profession and the courts, not politics, attracted the ablest men and held the public's esteem. A Wisconsin judge boasted: "The bench symbolizes on earth the throne of divine justice. . . . Law in its highest sense is the will of God." Judicial supremacy reflected the low esteem to which American politics sank after Reconstruction.

Cultural Politics

Yet, for all its formal weakness, politics figured centrally in the nation's life. Proportionately more voters turned out in presidential elections from 1876 to 1896 than at any other time in American history. Party loyalty ran high, and voting swings rarely occurred from one election to the next. This loyalty extended to party membership. In 1880, a fourth of the Republican voters in New York City were dues-paying party members. National conventions attracted huge crowds. "The excitement, the mental and physical strains," remarked an Indiana Republican after the 1888 convention, "are surpassed only by prolonged battle in actual warfare, as I have been told by officers of the Civil War who later engaged in convention struggles." The convention he described had nominated the colorless Benjamin Harrison on a routine platform. What was all the excitement about? Why did politics mean so much to late nineteenth-century Americans?

For one thing, politics had a vibrant part in the nation's culture. American journalist George M. Towle told an English audience that America "is a land of conventions and assemblies, where it is the most natural thing in the world for people to get together in meetings, where almost every event is the occasion for speechmaking." Such orators as Robert G. Ingersoll, who delivered the soaring Republican nominating speech of 1876 in which James G. Blaine became the "Plumed Knight," drew enormous crowds at campaign meetings. During the election season, party paraphernalia flooded the country—handkerchiefs, mugs, posters, and buttons emblazoned with the Democratic donkey or the Republican elephant, symbols that had been adopted in the 1870s. In 1888, pictures of the twenty-five presidential hopefuls appeared on cards, like baseball players, packed into Honest Long Cut tobacco. The campaigns had the suspense of baseball pennant races, plus the excitement of the circus coming to town. In an age before movies and radio, politics ranked as one of the great American forms of mass entertainment.

Party loyalty was a deadly serious matter, however. The emotions of the Civil War lasted a long time in both North and South. The Ohio Republican party, recalled the urban reformer Brand Whitlock of his youth, was "a synonym for patriotism, another name for the nation. . . . It was inconceivable that any self-respecting person should be a Democrat." The two parties did, in fact, represent different sorts of people. Republicans prided themselves on being the respectable elements of northern society. Senator George F. Hoar of Massachusetts described Republicans as "the men who do the work of piety and charity in our churches . . . administer the school systems, own and till their own farms . . . perform the skilled labor in the shops." Class played a role, too. The more money a man had, the more likely he would vote Republican.

More important, however, were religion and ethnic background. The two parties drew on different ethnocultural sections of northern society. Statistically, Democrats tended to be foreign born and Catholic, Republicans native-born and Protestant. Among Protestants, the more pietistic the theology—that is, the more personal and direct the person's relationship to God—the more likely the Republican identification. In political terms, this translated into a party policy favorable to using the powers of the state to legislate public morality and regulate individual behavior. On the other hand, the Democrats favored "the largest individual liberty consistent with public order," as the state platform in Ohio put it.

During the 1880s, ethnocultural tensions began to build up in many cities. Education became an arena of bitter conflict. One issue concerned the place of foreign languages in schools. Immigrant groups, especially the Germans, wanted their children taught in their own language. However, native-born Americans pushed through laws making English the language of instruction. In Saint Louis, a heavily German city, a fight developed over whether the teaching of German should continue to be compulsory for all students.

Religion was an even more divisive school issue. Reading from the Protestant Bible in school angered Catholics. They also fought a losing battle over public aid for parochial schools. By 1900, such aid had been prohibited by twenty-three states. In Boston, a furious controversy broke out in 1888 over the use of an anti-Catholic history text. After the school board withdrew the offending book, angry Protestants mounted a

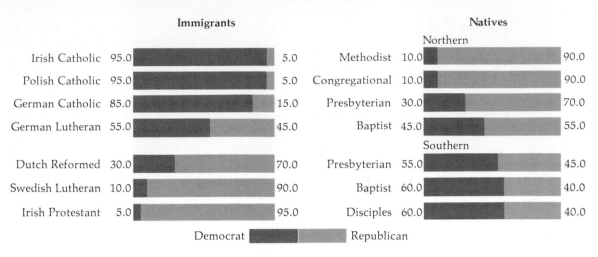

Immigrants

		Democrat		Republican	
Irish Catholic	95.0				5.0
Polish Catholic	95.0				5.0
German Catholic	85.0				15.0
German Lutheran	55.0				45.0
Dutch Reformed	30.0				70.0
Swedish Lutheran	10.0				90.0
Irish Protestant	5.0				95.0

Natives

Northern

Methodist	10.0			90.0
Congregational	10.0			90.0
Presbyterian	30.0			70.0
Baptist	45.0			55.0

Southern

Presbyterian	55.0			45.0
Baptist	60.0			40.0
Disciples	60.0			40.0

Democrat ▮▮ ▮▮ Republican

FIGURE 20.1 ETHNOCULTURAL VOTING PATTERNS, 1870–1892

drive, threw the moderates off the board, and put the text back into the curriculum.

Similar tensions developed over the regulation of public morals. Evangelical Protestants renewed their efforts to enact and enforce Sunday blue laws. The Nebraska Supreme Court approved a ban on Sunday baseball as a blow struck in "the contest between Christianity and wrong." But German and Irish Catholics, who saw nothing evil in a glass of beer and a ball game on Sunday considered the ruling a blow against their personal freedom. The same kind of ethnocultural conflict flared in the liquor question. Upon introducing the first national prohibition amendment in 1876, Senator Henry W. Blair of New Hampshire declared: "Upon discussion of this issue Irishman and German will in due time demonstrate that they are Americans." Although the Blair amendment languished, the antiliquor movement intensified. The Women's Christian Temperance Union, formed in 1874, became a powerful force throughout the country. Many states adopted strict licensing and local option laws governing the sale and consumption of alcoholic beverages. Indiana permitted drinking, but only joylessly in rooms containing "no devices for amusement or music . . . of any kind."

All these issues—education, temperance, and observance of the Sabbath—were contested along ethnic and religious lines. Because they were also party issues—more so than tariffs,

CARRY NATION UNDER ARREST
Opponents of alcohol had traditionally advocated temperance; that is, self restraint. The Women's Christian Temperance Union took a more coercive approach. It demanded legal prohibition of alcohol. Some prohibitionists turned to direct action. Carry Nation became famous for her ax-wielding attacks on saloons. She meant to draw attention to the struggle, and so gladly went to jail—where she is headed in this photograph, taken in Enterprise, Kansas in 1901. (Kansas State Historical Society)

currency, or civil service reform—they gave deep significance to party affiliation. Crusading Methodists thought of Republicans as the party of morality. For embattled Irish or German Catholics, the Democratic party was the defender of their freedom. Fought out mostly at the state and local levels, such ethnocultural issues as public education and the liquor question gave an importance to party politics that would have been scarcely apparent to anyone focusing exclusively on national elections.

Organizational Politics

Political life also was important because of the remarkable organizational activity that it generated. By this time each of the major parties had evolved a formal, well-articulated structure. At the base lay the precinct or ward, whose meetings could be attended by all party members. County, state, and national committees ran the ongoing business of the parties. Nominating conventions, corresponding to the electoral units of the state and federal systems, determined party rules, adopted platforms, and selected the party's candidates for public office.

At election time, the party functioned mainly to get out the vote. In the South, where a Democratic nomination was equivalent to election, little organized effort went into election day. As a result, fewer people voted than anywhere else in the country. In states or communities with hard-fought elections, however, the parties put on intensive efforts organized down to the individual voter. In Indiana, for example, the Republicans appointed ten thousand "district men" in 1884, each responsible for turning out a designated group of voters. The Pennsylvania Republican party maintained a list of eight hundred thousand voters, each classified according to his degree of voting reliability.

Only professionals could manage such a highly organized political system. The German sociologist Max Weber remarked that Americans regarded "politics as a vocation." This factor, above all else, gave American politics its special character. The distinguishing trait of American politicians, James Bryce observed, was "that their whole time is more frequently given to political work, that most of them draw an income from politics . . . that they . . . are proficient in

the arts of popular oratory, of electioneering, and of party management." The party system required professionals, and professionalism created careers. Politics, like professional sports and trade unionism, served as an avenue of upward mobility for many who, because of ethnic or class background, had been barred from the more conventional opportunities of industrial America.

Party administration was, on the face of it, highly democratic. Representation emanated either directly, as in county committees and district conventions, or indirectly, as at the state and national levels, from the membership in wards and precincts. In practice, however, the professionals ran the parties. They did this through unofficial, internal organizations called machines, which consisted of insiders willing to accept discipline and do work in exchange for the rewards of patronage and/or graft. The machines tended toward one-man rule, though more of a consensual than of a dictatorial nature. Each state party had a "boss," such as, in New York during the 1890s, the Republican Thomas C. Platt and the Democrat David B. Hill. Sometimes the state leader held public office—the U.S. Senate was preferred because senators were selected by the state legislature. Therefore, the office lay directly in the hands of the parties. But public office was not necessary for the boss to do his job.

The organizational development of political parties had started in the 1830s with the first mass parties and had grown more refined through the years. Now the machine began to play a central role in city politics. It did so primarily in response to a crisis in city governance at a time of explosive urban growth. City governments, which had taken shape in a simpler age, consisted of an accumulation of unplanned, overlapping, highly decentralized jurisdictions. In some cities, each ward had its own school board and ran its own schools. Administration was a largely unknown art. At the same time, enormous responsibilities for services and construction passed to the cities. In an age of laissez faire, the city stood as a great exception; the importance of the public sector in the urban economy could not be denied. Also, the older governing elites—the merchants in most cases—lost their capacity to run things. Rapid urban growth multiplied the number and complexity of interest groups, ranging from businessmen to labor unions to a variety of ethnic and reform movements. These groups often found it impossible to agree on matters of urgent city business.

Into the breach stepped the party machines. They alone seemed capable of getting things done. In Cincinnati, George B. Cox's Republican machine was widely greeted as an answer to the problems of an increasingly ungovernable city. In New York City, the Tammany Hall machine came to life after many years of weakness following the Tweed Ring scandals of 1871. A party machine had two great strengths, its highly developed organization and its strategic location between the public and private sectors.

For immigrants and tenement dwellers, the machine acted as a rough-and-ready social service agency. It provided work for the jobless, a helping hand for a bereaved family, and intercession against an unfeeling city bureaucracy. As a Boston ward boss remarked, "There's got to be in every ward somebody that any bloke can come to—no matter what he's done—and get help. *Help, you understand; none of your law and justice, but help.*" The machine also served a similar function for a different clientele. Entrepreneurs of many kinds wanted something from the city. Contractors sought city business; gas companies and traction firms wanted licenses and privileges; manufacturers needed services and not-too-nosy inspectors; and the liquor trade and numbers racket relied on a tolerant police force. All of them went to the machine boss and his lieutenants. In addition to these daily functions, the machine continually mediated among conflicting interests and oiled the wheels of city government. It became an integral part of the urban order.

Of course, all these services of the machine exacted a price. The tenement dweller gave his vote. The businessman wrote a check. Those who became the machine's beneficiaries enabled it to function. There were additional costs as well, including corruption. The Tammany ward boss George Washington Plunkitt often insisted that he had no need for kickbacks and bribes. He favored what he called "honest graft," the easy profits that came to political insiders from sure-fire investments—for example, the purchase of a vacant lot soon to be needed for a city

project—and easy-term partnerships. One way or another, legal or otherwise, most machine politicians died fairly well off.

The machine's operations also affected the tone of party politics. Absorbed in the tasks of power brokerage, the machine boss tended to see issues as somewhat irrelevant. The influence of the machine system had a lot to do with the absence of strong programs in electoral politics.

And yet, the record was by no means wholly negative. For one thing, the machine system contained some means for its own reform. From an organizational perspective, corruption amounted to a form of inefficiency. As fund-raising operations became better regulated, the diversion of funds into private pockets largely ceased. Charles F. Murphy, the dour Tammany leader of the early twentieth century, was a far cry from Boss William M. Tweed, who ended his days in jail. The machine influence also raised the standards of government in certain ways. As seasoned machine politicians rose to higher office, their professionalism and party discipline measurably improved the performance of state legislatures and Congress. Above all, the party machines filled a void in the nation's public life. They did informally much of what the governmental system left undone. "Nowhere else in the world," observed Henry Jones Ford, "has party organization had to cope with such enormous tasks, . . . and its efficiency in dealing with them is the true glory of our political system."

For all its effectiveness, machine politics never managed to win public legitimacy. The social elite of the cities—professionals, intellectuals, well-to-do businessmen, and old-line families—deeply resented politics that left little room for public service by the "best men." There was, too, a genuine clash of values. For political reformers the operative terms were "disinterestedness" and "independence"—the opposite of the self-serving careerism and the party regularity fostered by the machine system.

In 1884, this public-spirited elite split from the Republican party because they could not stomach its presidential candidate, James G. Blaine, whom they associated with corrupt party politics. Spurred by their efforts for Grover Cleveland, the Mugwumps, as they became known, grew into something of a national movement,

A REFORMER'S VIEW OF WARD POLITICS IN BOSTON

There are usually in the tenement-house sections several distinctly political clubs. Standing at the head of these clubs is the "machine club." It is now quite the custom of those in control of the party, and known as the "machine," to have such an organization. All the men in the ward having good political jobs are members. It is a question of bread and butter with them. In addition to City employees the various machine workers are enrolled. The room of the club is ordinarily very pleasant. There are, of course, in these clubs the usual social attractions, among other things poker and drinking. At the head of the club stands the boss of the ward.

One of the bosses whom the writer knows is fairly typical. He is considered the "prince of jolliers," on account of his alluring ways. He has for many years been in public office of one kind or another. His early opportunities were small. His native abilities, however, enable him to fulfill his official duties with real effectiveness—when political business does not interfere. The politician must provide something with which to feed his hungry followers. The jobs that he tries to get for his followers, however, are not secured as the private employer seeks men—for efficiency. The motive of the boss in seeking favors from the City government is to satisfy claims against him and to maintain himself.

On the whole, partly for the love of position and power, and partly from a good heart, the boss enjoys doing good turns for men. Stories are told by his admirers of his generous deeds. For instance, he has been known to pay the funeral expenses of poor people who have no insurance. At Christmas time and Thanksgiving he gives turkeys to certain needy families. This all sounds very generous; but the chief admirers of the boss cannot deny that when the supremacy in the ward is at all endangered, he makes capital of all his good deeds. In other words, every man to whom he has granted a favor is made to feel that the boss expects a vote.

Votes are his business—they mean money, power. The boss can never be a disinterested member of society. He is forced to make men act and vote with him,—the weaker their wills, the fewer their convictions, the better for him. He gives another drink to the drunkard: he has a vote. The only morality he seeks in men is loyalty to him. The merit system he regards always with a horror and indignation which would be amusing if it were not so serious. . . .

There are certain lesser figures characteristic of ward politics known as "heelers." They do the dirty work. As a rule, they prefer to serve the well-established boss, as he can best protect them if they are found out and prosecuted in the execution of their villainy. As a rule, a "heeler" is a broken-down "bum," afraid of work, fond of his cups, in touch with loafers and the semi-criminal class, more of a fox than they, energetic enough in a campaign, possessed of a strong dramatic sense, loving the excitement of ward politics with its dark plots and wire pulling, glad to be lifted into temporary importance by having money to spend on the "boys."

In analyzing ward politics, it is necessary to understand something of the morale of the various groups of voters. As to race complexion, in the local wards the Irish voters prevail. Next in number are the Jews. There is a good sprinkling of "Yankees," a term which for political purposes includes the British element. Foreigners other than those mentioned do not cut much of a figure in politics. It goes without saying that the greatest degree of political activity is found among the Irish. The Jews, however, are commencing to take considerable interest in politics. There seems to be a special antipathy ordinarily on the part of the Irish for the Jews. Not so with the Irish politician. He solves the race problem in short order. He fraternizes with the Jew, eats with the Jew, drinks with the Jew, and dickers with him in politics. . . .

In noting the various classes of voters in these wards, it is also necessary to keep steadily in mind the large number of unemployed men. The few secure a job; the many get promises. Those who get jobs are the slaves of the boss. According to the ethics of the district, a man who receives a job is under the most sacred obligations to the politician who bestowed it. The lack of employment, therefore, is one of the most important factors working in the interest of the boss and boss rule.

spawning good-government campaigns across the country. Although they scored some municipal victories, the Mugwumps achieved greater importance as the nation's opinion molders. They controlled the respectable newspapers and journals and occupied a strategic place in the urban world.

Most of all, the Mugwumps defined the terms of political debate. They stressed not the usefulness of the machine system, but its violation of American political values. The potency of their attack helped win their campaign for the Australian secret ballot in 1888. This reform, adopted throughout the United States in the early 1890s, eliminated the means by which the parties kept tabs on voters. Instead of submitting a party-supplied ticket at the polling place, citizens now chose candidates on an official ballot in the privacy of a voting booth.

The Mugwumps injected an elitist bias into respectable political thinking. Mark Twain was not alone in proclaiming "an honest and saving loathing for universal suffrage." Corrupt politics, remarked another writer in 1897, seemed to arise from "the ignorance and corruption of the people, and therefore . . . a growing class in America desires to restrict the suffrage, to have less frequent elections to take power from the people." In the South, such reform thinking rationalized the disfranchisement of blacks. Elsewhere, antidemocratic sentiment had a less decisive though widely felt impact. The expansion of suffrage, which had been going on for half a century, went into reverse after the 1870s as northern states began to impose literacy tests and restrict alien voting rights.

The Republican Ascendancy

The Mugwump bible was *The American Commonwealth*. In that book, Lord Bryce deplored the absence of serious debate in American national life. A basic political fact that inhibited debate between the parties was their evenly balanced strength. In the late 1880s, that stalemate began to break down, at first in favor of the Democrats. Their support within the immigrant populations of key northern states strengthened as ethnocultural tensions intensified, especially over the liquor question. This issue also drew Republican votes into the Prohibition party and forced the

Republicans to compete by taking a harder line on liquor and other ethnocultural issues.

In the 1890 elections, the number of Democrats in the House of Representatives jumped from 159 to 235. Democrats also won state offices in Pennsylvania, Massachusetts, and other normally Republican states. Two years later, Grover Cleveland, who had lost his bid for reelection in 1888, regained the presidency.

But then the Panic of 1893 hit, and the pendulum swung toward the Republicans. The party in power usually gets blamed if the economy falters, but Cleveland compounded the costs to the Democratic party. Although farmers were suffering terribly from deflated prices, Cleveland adhered to his defense of the gold standard. The Republicans had passed the highly protectionist McKinley tariff in 1890. But Cleveland could not deliver on his campaign promise of tariff reduction. The Wilson-Gorman Tariff of 1894, which he let go into law without his signature, caved in to special interests and cut average tariff rates only slightly.

The president had no answer for the jobless except a call for law and order. His response to the unemployed who came to Washington pleading for federal relief under the leadership of Jacob S. Coxey was to arrest Coxey and to disperse his followers. In July, when the Pullman strike turned into a national railway walkout, Cleveland called out federal troops to crush the strikers. His record did little to reassure a nation in the throes of a terrible depression.

The result was a Democratic disaster in the 1894 elections. The party lost nearly a third of its congressional seats and suffered severe setbacks in the states. A sweeping political realignment was in the making.

The catalyst was the money question, by far the most explosive economic issue of the late nineteenth century. The economy had suffered from deflationary pressures ever since the Civil War. The wholesale price index went steadily downward. It was 30 percent lower in 1880 than in 1870, nearly 20 percent lower in 1890 than in 1880. The favored solution by those who felt injured by this persistent deflation of prices—especially debtors, users of imported goods, those generally lacking in market power—was to increase the money supply. But many Americans considered it unwise, even immoral, to tamper

COXEY'S ARMY
During the winter of 1893–1894, with unemployment at more than 18 percent, desperate workers began to demand public relief. An Ohio labor reformer, Jacob S. Coxey, called them to march on Washington to present their grievances to Congress. When "Coxey's Army" reached Washington in April 1894, police dispersed the few hundred demonstrators and arrested Coxey for trespassing on the Capitol lawn. (The Bettmann Archive)

with the currency. The stability of the economic order, they thought, depended on "sound" money.

The battle was fought first, in the decade after the Civil War, over the greenback issue. The Lincoln administration had helped finance the war by printing paper notes, or greenbacks. After the war, sound money men, dominant in both parties, moved to retire some of the greenbacks and back the rest with specie, that is, to make the paper money exchangeable for gold from the U.S. Treasury. Despite strong opposition, this policy prevailed, and went fully into effect in 1879. The money fight then shifted to the free coinage of silver. If the United States would return to the bimetallic standard (which it had abandoned in 1873), and if the Treasury would accept all silver offered at the old ratio of sixteen to one with gold, the volume of currency would balloon overnight, and the nation's deflation would be reversed.

Until the 1890s, the battle between inflationists and sound money men had cut across party lines. Under the pressure of the economic depression, the money question became a more clear-cut partisan issue.

Within the Democratic party, the silver wing gained strength. President Cleveland, though a determined sound-money advocate, had difficulty maintaining the gold standard in the face of mounting pressures on U.S. gold reserves. In 1893, at Cleveland's urgent behest, Congress repealed the Sherman Silver Purchase Act of 1890. This action canceled a hard-won concession to the silver interests for monthly public purchases of a limited amount of silver at prevailing market rates. In 1895, as his administration's difficulties deepened, Cleveland turned to a syndicate of private bankers led by J. P. Morgan to finance gold purchases needed to replenish the Treasury's depleted gold reserves. The administration's secret negotiations with Wall Street, once discovered, raised a furor among Democrats.

Free silver also attracted the Democrats because of the challenge posed by the Populist party. Normally, third parties serve to define issues, not to contend seriously for political power. But as the 1896 elections approached, the Populists appeared to be making a real challenge. They had taken up the free-silver issue in hope of broadening their appeal beyond the limited areas of their strength among the distressed farmers of the South and West. With the growing popular support for free silver, they had a chance; but the silver Democrats intended to beat them to the punch.

In 1896, at their national convention in Chicago, the Democrats repudiated Cleveland and the gold standard. The leader of the triumphant silver Democrats was William Jennings Bryan, a

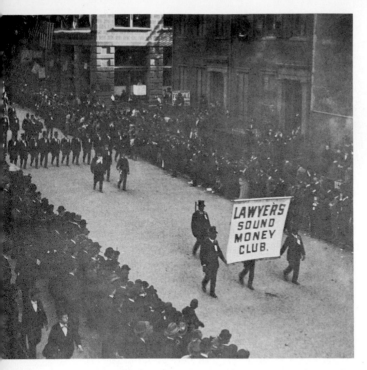

LAWYERS MARCH FOR THE GOLD STANDARD
Presidential campaigns of the late nineteenth century
were always hard-fought. In 1896, big issues were at
stake. Would the country stay on the gold standard, or
dramatically increase the money supply through the free
coinage of silver? Lawyers paraded in the streets of New
York City to demonstrate their conviction that the
nation's fate hung on "sound money" and on the election
of the Republican William McKinley. (The New-York
Historical Society)

Nebraska congressman. Only thirty-six years old
and not yet a national figure, Bryan was already
a consummate politician. He had quietly been
building up delegate support while keeping a
distance between himself and convention poli-
ticking. Bryan probably had the presidential
nomination locked up even before he electrified
the convention with his stirring attack on the
gold standard: "You shall not press down upon
the brow of labor this crown of thorns, you shall
not crucify mankind upon a cross of gold."
Bryan's nomination meant that the Democrats
had identified themselves as the party of free silver; his "cross of gold" speech meant he would
turn the money question into a national crusade.

The Republicans took up the challenge. Their
key party figure was Mark Hanna, a wealthy

Cleveland ironmaker, a brilliant political manager, and an exponent of the new industrial capitalism. Hanna's candidate, Ohio congressman
William McKinley, personified the virtues of Republicanism, standing solidly for prosperity,
protection, and honest money. While Bryan
broke with tradition and criss-crossed the country in a furious whistle-stop campaign, the dignified McKinley received delegations at his home
in Canton, Ohio. As Bryan orated with passionate moral fervor, McKinley talked of industrial
progress and a full dinner pail.

The Republicans, beating a strategic retreat
from the politics of morality, aimed to escape the
ethnocultural issues that had hurt their popularity just before the depression. McKinley himself
represented a mixed district in northeastern
Ohio. In appealing to his immigrant and working-class constituents, he had learned the art of
easy tolerance, as expressed in his phrase, "live
and let live." Of the two candidates, the prairie
orator Bryan, with his Christian rhetoric and
moral righteousness, presented a more alien image to traditional Democratic voters in the big
cities.

No election since Reconstruction had evoked

WILLIAM JENNINGS BRYAN
Already a polished campaigner at 36, William Jennings
Bryan (1860–1925) took his free silver crusade across the
country, speaking at every whistlestop to crowds of
voters. Bryan's campaign style was exuberant and
forceful. Here he strides, beaming confidently, to the
speaker's platform at a Democratic rally in California.
(American Heritage)

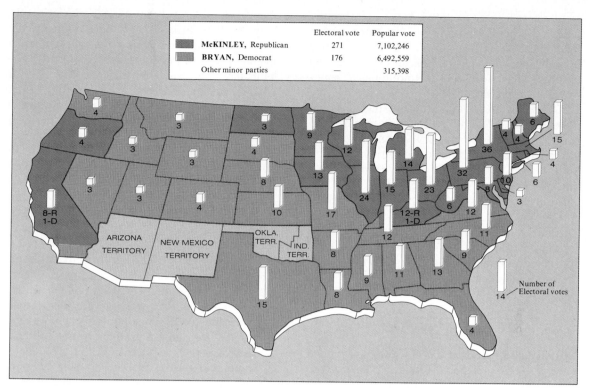

MAP 20.1 ELECTION OF 1896

The 1896 election was one of the decisive elections in American political history. Not only did the Republican party win by its largest popular margin since 1872, but it also established a firm grip on the key midwestern and middle Atlantic states—especially New York, Indiana, Ohio and Illinois—the decisive states for all the elections since Reconstruction. The 1896 election broke a party stalemate of twenty years duration, and began a period of Republican dominance that lasted until 1932.

such a sharp division over issues. The gold Democrats bolted to a splinter Democratic ticket or supported McKinley; silver Republicans went over to the Democrats. The Populists, meeting after the Democratic convention, accepted Bryan as their candidate. The free-silver issue had become so vital that they could not do otherwise. For all practical purposes, despite their best efforts, the Populists found themselves absorbed into the Democratic silver crusade.

Not since 1860 did the United States have such a hard-fought election, and over stakes that loomed so high. The nation's currency had exceptional social significance in American life. For the middle class, sound money meant the soundness of the social order. Now, with workers tramping the streets and farmers up in arms, Bryan's fervent assault on the gold standard struck fear in many hearts. Republicans de-

nounced the Democratic platform as "revolutionary and anarchistic." They called Bryan's supporters "social misfits who have almost nothing in common but opposition to the existing order and institutions." The formidable party machinery was pumped up to the limit. Contributions flowed from businessmen in record amounts. Hanna's network kept close tabs on the race in every state; and about fourteen hundred Republican orators went out on the hustings. The political debate reached a level of intensity and significance unequaled since the days of the Lincoln-Douglas debates.

McKinley won handily with 271 electoral votes to 176 for Bryan. He kept the Republican ground that had been won in 1894 and also pushed into Democratic strongholds, especially in the cities. Boston, New York, Chicago, and Minneapolis, all taken by Cleveland in 1892, went for McKinley in 1896. Bryan ran strongly only in the South, in silver-mining states, and in the Populist West. The gains his evangelical style brought him in some Republican rural areas fell far short of what he lost in traditionally Democratic urban districts.

The paralyzing equilibrium of American politics ended in 1896, and the Republicans emerged as the majority party. They accomplished the victory by exploiting both the economic and cultural aspects of party allegiance. The Republicans persuaded the nation that they were the party of prosperity and they reduced their burden of being the party of morality. In 1896, too, electoral politics regained its place as an arena for national debate. The silver question quickly subsided; other issues such as social reform and the trusts lay ahead.

An Emerging World Power

"A policy of isolation did well enough when we were an embryo nation," remarked Senator Orville Platt of Connecticut at the beginning of the 1890s. "But today things are different. . . . We are 65 million people, the most advanced and powerful on earth, and regard to our future welfare demands an abandonment of the doctrines of isolation." Platt had his facts right. The United States had become the equal, by any population or economic measure, of the greatest world powers of the late nineteenth century. He also concluded correctly that the nation would move into the world arena. Equally significant, however, was the senator's need to make the case for a more vigorous international role. Americans were slow to shed their identity as an "embryo nation." Not many of them agreed with Platt's call for "an abandonment of the doctrines of isolation."

The Roots of Expansionism

For almost a century after George Washington's farewell address, the United States followed his advice against involvement in permanent alliances with foreign powers. The westward push of Americans across the continent had brought the nation into periodic conflict with other powers, and so did the Civil War. But to a remarkable degree, the development of the United States went ahead in isolation. Geography helped. Wide oceans kept the world at a distance. Relying on British naval supremacy to maintain freedom of the seas, the United States let its navy rot away after the Civil War. Nor did any European conflicts entangle the United States as had happened during the Napoleonic era. The balance of power, erected at the Congress of Vienna in 1815, held firm for almost a hundred years.

The European powers of the nineteenth century expressed their national prowess primarily through empire building. This activity did not tempt the United States. Even so ardent an American nationalist as the young Theodore Roosevelt saw the folly of overseas expansion. "We want no unwilling citizens to enter our Union," he wrote in 1886. "European nations war for the possession of thickly settled districts which, if conquered, will for centuries remain alien and hostile to the conquerers; we, wiser in our generation, have seized the waste solitudes that lay near us."

Some Americans, few in number but well placed, took the opposite view. William H. Seward, secretary of state under Presidents Lincoln and Johnson, dreamed of an American empire, perhaps with a capital in Mexico, that extended into South America and across the Pacific to Asia. President Grant had been an eager, if less grandiose, expansionist. His successors lacked Grant's enthusiasm, but some kind of scheming was always afoot, especially in the State Department, for overseas projects.

Little came of it, however. Seward's only notable success was the purchase from Russia of Alaska in 1867. Grant's strongest efforts could not persuade the Senate to purchase Santo Domingo in 1870, and later moves to acquire bases in Haiti, Cuba, and Venezuela were also blocked. So were repeated efforts to gain approval for construction of a canal across Central America to link the Atlantic and Pacific oceans. However, the United States strongly opposed any foreign undertaking of such a project; no canal would be tolerated unless under American control. The Monroe Doctrine, which declared the Western Hemisphere off limits to European expansionism, played a big role in the thinking of James G. Blaine, secretary of state briefly in 1881 and later under President Benjamin Harrison from 1889 to 1892. Blaine was an avid Pan-

Americanist, a believer in closer ties among the nations of the Western Hemisphere. The Washington Conference of 1889, held at his instigation, called for economic cooperation and reciprocal trade and set up an agency that became the Pan-American Union.

In the Pacific, American interest centered on Hawaii. American missionaries had long been active among the natives on the islands. With a climate ideal for raising sugar cane, Hawaii also attracted many American planters and investors. Nominally an independent nation, Hawaii fell increasingly within the American orbit. In 1875, a treaty of commercial reciprocity declared that no Hawaiian territory could be ceded to a third power. A second treaty in 1887 added U.S. naval rights at Pearl Harbor.

Having encouraged the sugar economy in Hawaii, the United States withdrew Hawaii's trading advantages in the McKinley Tariff of 1890. All foreign sugar could now enter the United States duty free, while domestic producers received a special subsidy to compensate for the drop in sugar prices. Anxious to gain that benefit, American planters in Hawaii began to plot for annexation to the United States. Aided by the U.S. minister to Hawaii, they revolted in January 1893 against Queen Liliuokalani, who had begun to reassert native control over the islands. Before annexation could be approved by the Senate, Grover Cleveland returned to the presidency. Following an investigation of the Hawaiian episode, he withdrew the treaty. To annex Hawaii, he declared, would violate both America's "honor and morality" and its "unbroken tradition" against acquiring territory far from the nation's shores.

By the 1890s, however, the anticolonial tradition encountered powerful crosscurrents. One source of expansionist thinking was Social Darwinism. If animals and plants evolved through the survival of the fittest, so did nations. "Nothing under the sun is stationary," warned the American historian Brooks Adams in *The Law of Civilization and Decay* (1895). "Not to advance is to recede." By this criterion, the United States had no choice; if it wanted to survive, it had to expand.

Linked to Social Darwinism was a spreading belief in racial inequality. On both sides of the Atlantic, Anglo-Saxonism had come into great vogue, proclaiming the English-speaking "race" inherently superior. John Fiske, an American philosopher and historian, popularized Social Darwinism and Anglo-Saxonism by lecturing the nation on its future responsibilities. "The work which the English race began when it colonized North America," Fiske declared, "is destined to go on until every land on the earth's surface that is not already the seat of an old civilization shall become English in its language, in its religion, in its political habits, and to a predominant extent in the blood of its people."

Fiske entitled his famous lecture "Manifest Destiny." He revived the notion that had justified the nation's thrust across the continent half a century earlier. Now, in the 1890s, with the frontier officially declared at an end, Manifest Destiny turned outward. The young historian Frederick Jackson Turner suggested as much in his landmark essay "The Significance of the Frontier in American History" (1893). "He would be a rash prophet who should assert that the expansive character of American life has now entirely ceased," Turner wrote. "Movement has been its dominant fact, and, unless this training has no effect upon a people, the American energy will continually demand a wider field for its exercise." A strong current of ideas, deep-rooted in American experience and ideology, had set the nation on a course of overseas expansion.

Economic forces did the same thing. The gross national product quadrupled between 1870 and 1900, and industrial output quintupled. As the economy burst ahead, so did American exports. In 1876, for the first time, the United States became a net exporter, initially because of the agricultural trade, but increasingly in manufacturing as well. Industrial exports exceeded industrial imports by 70 percent in 1900. Only about 7 percent of the national output left the country. Even so, the development of foreign markets loomed large in business thinking and became urgent once the panic of 1893 struck. Unlike farmers, who blamed the scarce money supply, industry attributed the depression to overproduction. Foreign markets seemed the only likely outlets for the American surplus.

In Europe, however, protectionist sentiment was rising. Even worse, markets elsewhere in the world were being closed off. European imperialism, which had slackened in the middle of the century, suddenly revived after 1880. The European powers carved up Africa and, along

FIGURE 20.2 BALANCE OF U.S. IMPORTS AND EXPORTS, 1870–1914

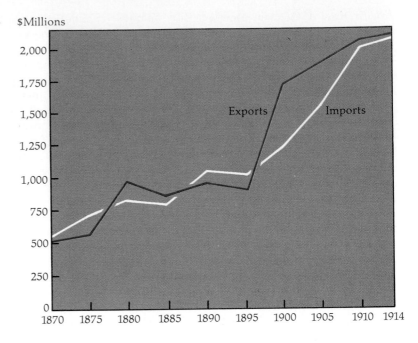

with Russia and Japan, pressed into China during the 1890s. As their navies grew, they posed a challenge to U.S. interests even in Latin America. These underdeveloped parts of the world seemed crucially important because they, not Europe, constituted the future consumers of American goods. The China market, above all, exerted a powerful hold on the American mercantile imagination. Many felt that the China trade, although actually negligible, would one day be the key to American prosperity. Therefore, the underdeveloped world must not be closed to the United States—and this, in turn, spelled overseas expansion.

"Whether they will or not, Americans must now begin to look outward. The growing production of the country requires it." So wrote Captain Alfred T. Mahan, America's leading naval strategist, in his book *The Influence of Seapower upon History* (1890). The United States should no longer regard the oceans as barriers, but as "a great highway . . . over which men pass in all directions." To traverse that highway required a merchant marine, which had fallen on hard times since its heyday in the 1850s, and a powerful navy to protect American commerce. "When a question arises of control over distant regions . . . it must ultimately be decided by naval power," Mahan advised. To sustain that navy and commerce, the United States needed strate-

gic overseas bases. Here technology played a part because, having converted to steam, navies required coaling stations distant from home. Otherwise, Mahan warned, warships were "like land birds, unable to fly far from their own shores."

Mahan called first of all for a canal across Central America to connect the Atlantic and Pacific oceans. Such a canal would enable the eastern United States to "compete with Europe, on equal terms as to distance, for the markets of East Asia." Guarding its approaches would require bases in the Caribbean Sea. It also would be necessary to annex Hawaii in order to extend American power into the Pacific, a step that Mahan called "natural, necessary, irrepressible." Mahan discriminated carefully between colonies as potential markets, and colonies as strategic bases necessary to gain access to markets. His interest lay strictly in the second kind, as did that of nearly all the economic expansionists of the 1890s. They sought strategic territory by which American power could be asserted where Americans wanted to trade rather than extensive colonies of the European type.

Mahan's thinking struck a resonant chord among other great-power exponents. They included navy men, diplomats, publishers like Whitelaw Reid of the *New York Tribune*, and such young politicians as Governor Theodore Roosevelt of New York and Senator Henry Cabot Lodge of Massachusetts. The influence of these men, few in number but strategically placed, increased during the 1890s. They pushed steadily for what Lodge called a "large policy." One result was the rebuilding of the U.S. Navy. Begun in the mid-1880s, the naval program shifted after 1890 from shore defense to an offensive strategy, which meant the construction of a battleship fleet. This "large policy," warned Carl Schurz, the antiexpansionist editor of the *New York Evening Post,* aimed at acquiring "such territory, far and near, as may be useful in enlarging our commercial advantages, and in securing to our navy facilities desirable for the operations of a great naval power."

A growing nationalism attended the great-power sentiment. It infected even the antiexpansionist Cleveland administration. For years, a border dispute had simmered between Venezuela and British Guiana. On July 20, 1895, Secretary of State Richard Olney sent a bristling note to London; Cleveland called it Olney's "twenty-inch gun." Invoking the Monroe Doctrine, Olney accused Britain of aggressive actions against Venezuela. He warned that the United States could not tolerate any European attempt to overthrow an American state. "Today the United States is practically sovereign upon this continent, and its fiat is law upon the subjects to which it confines its interposition," Olney asserted. In support of that bombastic claim, the United States said it was prepared to take on all comers. The British agreed in 1896 to the American demand for arbitration, and the crisis passed.

No series of events better caught the American mood—the nation's growing sense of power and nationalism. People called it "jingoism." The United States, eager to step onto the world stage, needed only the right occasion.

The Spanish-American War

In February 1895, Cuba rebelled against Spanish rule. A bloody standoff developed; the Spaniards controlled the towns, the insurgents the countryside. During the fall of 1897, the brutal Spanish commander, General Valeriano Weyler, adopted a policy of "reconcentration." The Spaniards forced the entire population into armed camps and treated any Cuban on the outside as a rebel. The strategy, while militarily effective, took a dreadful toll among the Cubans. Thousands died of starvation, exposure, and dysentery.

Cuban rebellions had occurred since the 1820s and were always troublesome to the United States. The last uprising, which lasted from 1868 to 1878, had raised serious tensions with Spain. These tensions now became intolerable.

A wave of sympathy for the Cuban rebels swept across the United States. As in the past, Cuban exiles skillfully played on public opinion. But now they got help from a yellow press eager to capitalize on the situation. Locked in a circulation war, William Randolph Hearst's *New York Journal* and Joseph Pulitzer's *New York World* elevated the atrocities and skirmishes into front-page news. However, more than sentiment brought the United States into conflict with Spain. The Cuban troubles involved American interests, especially large investments in Cuban sugar. As in past rebellions, the Spaniards arrested American citizens and destroyed American property. The United States considered its new strategic plans even more important. If a canal across Central America were to be built and Caribbean bases acquired, the United States could not tolerate a chronically unstable Cuba.

On September 18, 1897, the American minister asked the government in Madrid "whether the time has not arrived when Spain . . . will put a stop to this destructive war." If Spain could not give assurances of an "early and certain peace," he warned, the United States would take whatever steps it "should deem necessary to procure this result."

At first, the Spanish response sparked some hope. The conservative regime fell, and a liberal government, upon taking office in October 1897, moderated the Cuban policy. Spain recalled Weyler, eased reconcentration, and adopted an autonomy plan. But Madrid's incapacity soon became clear. In January 1898, Spanish loyalists in Havana rioted against the grant of autonomy. The Cuban rebels, encouraged by the prospect of American intervention, then demanded full independence.

Relations between the United States and Spain worsened. On February 9, the *New York Journal* published a private letter of Dupuy de Lôme, the Spanish minister to the United States. He insulted President McKinley and suggested

"REMEMBER THE MAINE!"
The U.S.S. *Maine* enters Havana harbor on a courtesy call in late January 1898, en route to disaster. On the evening of February 15, a mysterious blast sent the battleship to the bottom. Although no evidence ever linked the Spanish authorities to the explosion, the event fed the emotional fires preparing the nation for war with Spain. (National Archives)

that the American government was not acting in good faith. A week later, the U.S. battleship *Maine* blew up and sank in Havana harbor, with the loss of 260 men. The findings of a naval board of inquiry, issued on March 21, proved highly damaging to the Spanish position. The explosion, the board reported, had been caused by a mine, not, as experts had widely suspected, by an internal malfunction, on the *Maine*. No evidence linked the Spaniards to the explosion, but they had failed to meet their responsibility of protecting the American vessel from such an attack.

Spanish sovereignty had broken down. This was the theme of a memorable speech by Senator Redfield Proctor of Vermont after a visit to Cuba. His account of the conditions there led to the conclusion that Spain had lost its claim to rule Cuba.

President McKinley did not seek war. He had no stomach for the martial spirit sweeping the country. His supporters in the business world likewise preferred peace. With the economy finally coming out of depression, they strongly wanted to avoid any disturbances. But, in the end, McKinley had no choice. Whipped up by the lurid journalism of the Hearst newspapers, angered by the awful spectacle of the sunken Maine, the American people were calling for blood.

In late March, Spain made a series of desperate concessions, climaxed by an offer on April 5 to suspend hostilities in Cuba for six months. However, not even this proposal guaranteed the restoration of order as demanded by Washington. In any case, the public pressure on McKinley could no longer be resisted. The president's message to Congress on April 11 was remarkably restrained. McKinley did not ask for war, but for authorization to intervene at his discretion. He identified the United States as an "impartial neutral" between Spain and Cuba, withheld recognition of the rebels, and remained silent on Cuban independence.

McKinley did not come close to satisfying the war hawks in the Senate. They pushed through a joint congressional resolution that asserted Cuban independence, required Spanish evacuation of the island, and directed the president to use force to achieve those goals. McKinley signed the resolution. Spain broke off diplomatic relations with the United States, and Congress declared war on April 25, 1898.

The United States did not go to war with the intention of seizing Spanish territory. The most avid interventionists in the Senate were western Democrats and Populists. They were eager for an independent, republican Cuba as a matter of principle, but they were also strongly antiexpansionist. As part of the war resolution following McKinley's message of April 11, they sponsored the Teller amendment in which the United States disclaimed any intention of taking Cuba. The amendment also pledged "to leave the government and control of the island to its people." Nor did conventional expansionist projects make much headway at that time. During the spring of 1898, neither a canal bill nor a Hawaiian annexation measure got through the Senate. Yet the Spanish-American War, once it started, quickly set the United States on an imperial course.

The crucial event occurred not in Cuba but far off in another Spanish colony, the Philippines. Acting on standing orders in the event of war, Commodore George Dewey's small fleet set sail immediately from Hong Kong. The Americans cornered the Spanish fleet in Manila harbor on May 1 and destroyed it. The victory produced euphoria in the United States. Immediately, part of the army being trained on the Gulf of Mexico for the Cuban campaign was diverted to the Philippines. Manila, the Philippine capital, fell on August 13, 1898.

Dewey's victory meant that Manila Bay, the western Pacific base long coveted by naval strategists, would not be returned to Spain. At this time, too, the great powers were carving up China. If American commerce wanted a place in that glittering market, the power of the United States would have to be projected into Asia.

American businessmen, foot draggers in the race to war, now rushed to the flag. "With a strong foothold in the Philippine Islands, we can and will take a large slice of the commerce of Asia," asserted Mark Hanna, now an Ohio senator. "That is what we want . . . and it is better to strike while the iron is hot." The logjam on Hawaii also broke, and annexation won approval in July 1898. The decision on Manila had enhanced the strategic importance of Hawaii as a half-way station in the mid-Pacific. Overnight, expansionism had been legitimized.

The campaign in Cuba, the main theater of operations, was something of an anticlimax. The

FIGHTING THE FILIPINOS
The United States went to war against Spain in 1898 partly out of sympathy with the Cuban struggle for independence. Yet the United States found it necessary to use very much the same brutal tactics to put down the Filipino struggle for independence as the Spaniards had used against the Cubans. Here the Twentieth Kansas Volunteers march through the burning village of Caloocan. The regiment's commander, Colonel Frederick Funston, vowed to "rawhide these bullet-headed Asians until they yell for mercy." (From *Harper's Weekly*. The Newberry Library, Chicago)

U.S. forces made short work of the demoralized, outgunned Spaniards. Their fleet was bottled up in Santiago harbor. The ill-prepared U.S. army, greatly augmented by volunteers, landed east of Santiago late in June. On July 1, American troops assaulted San Juan Hill; Colonel Theodore Roosevelt's dismounted Rough Riders led the attack on nearby Kettle Hill. Despite heavy casualties, the Americans took the heights commanding Santiago and its harbor. They sank the Spanish fleet on July 3 when it made a suicidal daylight attempt to run the American blockade.

Three weeks later, Spain sued for peace. The two nations signed an armistice in which Spain agreed to give up Cuba and cede Puerto Rico and Guam, one of the Mariana Islands in the Pacific, to the United States. American forces would occupy Manila pending a peace treaty that would decide the fate of the Philippines.

The Imperial Experiment

"Without any original thought of complete or even partial acquisition," admitted President McKinley, "the presence and success of our arms at Manila imposes upon us obligations which we cannot disregard." Thus the imperial entanglements began. McKinley's few advisers who knew anything about the Philippines assured him that Manila could not be held without taking the entire archipelago of over 7,000 islands. The defeat of Spain had created a power vacuum. Germany and Japan were on the prowl and were interested in the Philippines. The Americans considered the Filipinos incapable of immediate self-rule. By taking the Philippines, the United States would assume "the white man's burden" and bring the blessings of western civilization to "our little brown brothers."

MAP 20.2 SPANISH-AMERICAN WAR
The swift American victory in the Spanish-American War derived from overwhelming U.S. naval superiority. Dewey's destruction of the Spanish fleet in Manila harbor doomed the Spaniards in the Philippines. In Cuba, American ground forces won a hard victory on San Juan Hill, but they were ill-equipped and poorly supplied. With the United States in control of the seas, however, the Spaniards saw no choice but to give up the battle for Cuba. Had they chosen to fight on, it would not have seemed the "splendid little war" of which McKinley's next secretary of state, John Hay, boasted.

THE IDEALS AND REALITIES OF SUBDUING THE FILIPINOS

Major General Arthur MacArthur, Commanding General, U.S. Forces in the Philippines, to the Senate Committee on the Philippines, 1902.

From the beginning of civilization man has tried to mitigate and escape as far as possible from the consequences of his own barbarous environment. In pursuance of these laudable efforts, the human race, from time immemorial, has been propagating its higher ideals by a succession of intellectual waves, one of which is now passing through our mediumship, beyond the Pacific, and carrying therewith everything that is implied by the beautiful flag which is a symbol of our nationality.

At the time I returned to Manila [May 1900] to assume the supreme command it seemed to me that we had been committed to a position by process of spontaneous evolution. . . . [O]ur permanent occupation of the islands was simply one of the necessary consequences in logical sequence of our great prosperity, and to doubt the wisdom of [occupation] was simply to doubt the stability of our own institutions and in effect to declare that a self-governing nation was incapable of successfully resisting strains arising naturally from its own productive energy. . . . [O]ur conception of right, justice, freedom, and personal liberty was the precious fruit of centuries of strife; that we had inherited much in these respects from our ancestors, and in our own behalf have added much to the happiness of the world, and as beneficiaries of the past and as the instruments of future progressive social development we must regard ourselves simply as the custodians of imperishable ideas held in trust for the general benefit of mankind. In other words, I felt that we had attained a moral and intellectual height from which we were bound to proclaim to all as the occasion arose the true message of humanity as embodied in the principles of our own institutions.

All other governments that have gone to the East have simply planted trading establishments; they have not materially affected the conditions of the people. They have perfected organizations which have systematized living conditions, but have not planted an idea that would be self-sustaining. There is not a single establishment, in my judgment, in Asia to-day that would survive five years if the original power which planted it was withdrawn therefrom.

The contrasting idea with our occupation is this: In planting our ideas we plant something that can not be destroyed. To my mind the archipelago is a fertile soil upon which to plant republicanism. . . . We are planting the best traditions, the best characteristics of Americanism in such a way that they never can be removed from that soil. That in itself seems to me a most inspiring thought. It encouraged me during all my efforts in those islands, even when conditions seemed most disappointing, when the people themselves, not appreciating precisely what the remote consequences of our efforts were going to be, mistrusted us; but that fact was always before me—that going down deep into that fertile soil were the imperishable ideas of Americanism.

F. A. Blake, Red Cross worker, quoted in the San Francisco Call, *March 30, 1899.*

I never saw such execution in my life and hope never to see such sights as met on all sides as our little corps passed over the field, dressing wounded legs and arms nearly demolished, total decapitation, horrible wounds in chest and abdomen, showing the determination of our soldiers to kill every native in sight.

Richard T. O'Brien, M Company, 26th Infantry Volunteers, U.S. Army, to the Senate Committee on the Philippines, 1902.

[H]ow the order started and who gave it I don't know, but the town was fired on. I saw an old fellow come to the door, and he looked out: he got a shot in the abdomen and fell to his knees and turned around and died. . . .

After that two old men came out, hand in hand. I should think they were over 50 years old, probably between 50 and 70 years old. They had a white flag. They were shot down. At the other end of the town we heard screams, and there was a woman there; she was burned up, and in her arms was a baby, and on the floor was another child. The baby was at her breast, the one in her arms, and this child on the floor was, I should judge, about 3 years of age. They were burned. Whether she was demoralized or driven insane I don't know. She stayed in the house.

The Spaniards had little choice. They ceded the Philippines to the United States and received a payment of $20 million in return. The Treaty of Paris, signed in December 1898, encountered harder going at home. Events in the Philippines reawakened traditional antiexpansionism. An organized movement formed in many cities, starting with Boston, and grew into the formidable Anti-Imperialist League in October 1899. The Philippine issue delayed the treaty in the Senate for weeks. Senator George Hoar of Massachusetts protested that annexation violated the Constitution. "The power to conquer alien people and hold them in subjugation is nowhere expressly granted [and] nowhere implied," he protested. With only a vote to spare, the Senate approved the treaty on February 6, 1899.

Two days earlier, on February 4, fighting had broken out between American and Filipino patrols on the edge of Manila. Shortly after the destruction of the Spanish fleet, the United States Navy had brought the Filipino leader Emilio Aguinaldo back from exile to help organize local resistance to the Spaniards. Aguinaldo quickly asserted his nation's independence and, confronted by American annexation, turned his guns on the U.S. forces.

The ensuing conflict far exceeded the ferocity of the war just concluded with Spain. Fighting tenacious guerrillas, the United States Army resorted to the same tactics used by the Spaniards in Cuba, moving the people into the towns, carrying out indiscriminate attacks beyond the perimeters, and burning crops and villages.

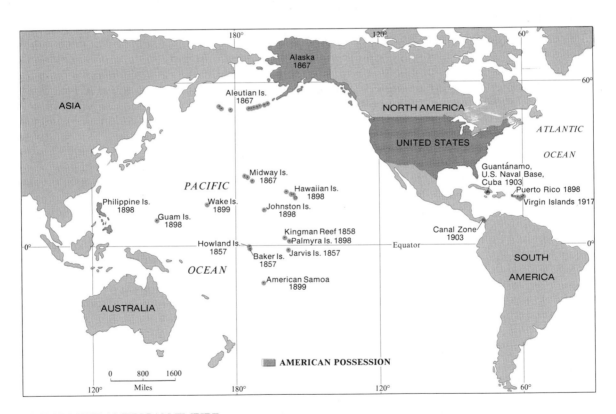

MAP 20.3 THE AMERICAN EMPIRE
In 1890, the great strategist Captain Alfred T. Mahan wrote that the United States should regard oceans no longer as protective barriers but rather as "a great highway" across which America would carry on world trade and exert its naval power. That was precisely what resulted from the empire the United States acquired in the wake of the Spanish-American War. The Caribbean possessions, the Panama Canal, and strategically located holdings that spanned the Pacific gave the United States commercial and naval access to a new, wider world.

TIME LINE
THE PUBLIC WORLD OF LATE NINETEENTH-CENTURY AMERICA

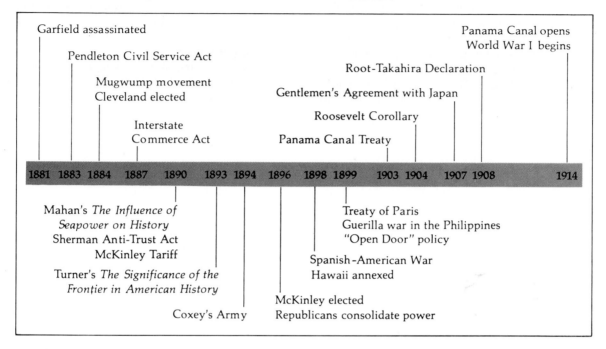

Atrocities became commonplace. The U.S. forces specialized in the "water cure"—forcing water into a person's stomach and then pounding it out—to force captured guerillas to talk. In more than three years of warfare, forty-two hundred Americans and thousands of Filipinos died. The fighting ended in 1902, and Judge William Howard Taft, appointed governor by President McKinley, set up a civilian government. He intended to make the Philippines a model of American road building and sanitary engineering.

In a few years, the United States had acquired a modest overseas empire—Hawaii, Puerto Rico, Guam, and the Philippines. In 1900, this overseas expansion concluded with the acquisition in the South Pacific of several islands of Samoa, over which the United States, Germany, and Great Britain had established a joint protectorate in 1889.

In the 1900 election, the Democrats nominated William Jennings Bryan for a second try against McKinley. An avid antiexpansionist, Bryan declared imperialism the "paramount is-

sue" in the campaign. But, sensing his opposition to imperialism to be a losing cause, he backed away from it by election day. McKinley's convincing victory nevertheless suggested popular satisfaction with America's overseas adventure.

Yet a strong sense of misgiving also was evident. Americans had not anticipated the brutal methods needed to subdue the Filipino guerillas. In addition, there were disturbing political issues to be resolved. Did the Constitution extend to the acquired territories? Did their inhabitants automatically become citizens? In 1901, the Supreme Court ruled negatively on both questions; these were matters for Congress to decide. In its report on administration for the Philippines, the special commission appointed by McKinley recommended ultimate independence after an indefinite period of U.S. rule, during which the Filipinos would prepare for self-government.

The colonial adventure had clearly ended. But this did not mean any renunciation of America's pursuit of global power. The United States had stepped permanently onto the world stage.

*A*fter Reconstruction ended in 1877, national politics became less issue-oriented and, as a formal process, less important in American life. This situation resulted from weaknesses in governmental institutions, from the prevailing philosophy of laissez faire, and from the paralysis of evenly matched political parties. Yet the politics of the period from 1877 to 1893 had great vigor. For one thing, politics provided the arena in which the nation's ethnocultural conflicts could be fought out. Equally important, the party machines performed crucial functions that properly belonged to, but were still beyond the capacity of, government institutions.

During the 1890s, national politics again became an important arena. Threatened by the rise of Populism, the Democratic party committed itself to free silver and made the 1896 election a contest over issues of great significance. The Republicans won decisively, ending the paralyzing party stalemate that had lasted twenty years and assuring themselves of political dominance for the next thirty years.

At the same time, the nation's growing population and industrial strength gave the United States the potential to be a world power. After a century of self-absorption and relative isolation, Americans began to push into the international arena after 1890. In 1898, the United States won the Spanish-American War and, as a result of the victory, acquired an overseas empire. The nation clearly had joined the great powers of the world.

Suggestions for Further Reading

Domestic Politics

The best introduction to the politics of the late nineteenth century is John A. Garraty, *The New Commonwealth, 1877–1890* (1968). Much more detailed is Morton Keller, *Affairs of State: Public Life in late 19th Century America* (1977). Among other books that deal with aspects of national politics are: Ari Hoogenboom, *Outlawing the Spoils: The Civil Service Reform Movement, 1865–1883* (1961); Robert D. Marcus, *Grand Old Party: Political Structure in the Gilded Age* (1971); H. Wayne Morgan, *From Hayes to McKinley: National Party Politics, 1877–1896* (1969); and David J. Rothman, *Politics and Power: The Senate, 1869–1901* (1966). On the development of public administration, see Leonard D. White, *The Republican Era, 1869–1901* (1958) and Stephen Skowronek, *Building a New American State: The Expansion of National Administrative Capacities* (1982).

The ideological basis for conservative national politics is fully treated in Robert L. Bannister, *Social Darwinism: Science and Myth* (1979); Sidney Fine, *Laissez Faire and the General Welfare State, 1865–1901* (1956); Richard Hofstadter, *Social Darwinism in American Thought* (rev. ed., 1955); and Robert G. McCloskey *American Conservatism in the Age of Enterprise* (1951).

The ethnocultural dimensions of party politics have been studied in Paul Kleppner, *The Cross of Culture: A Social Analysis of Midwestern Politics* (1970) and in Richard Jensen, *The Winning of the Midwest, 1888–1896* (1971). A sophisticated reinterpretation of urban machine politics is to be found in David C. Hammack, *Power and Society: Greater New York at the Turn of the Century* (1982). See also John M. Allswang, *Bosses, Machines and Urban Voters: An American Symbiosis* (1977), and Zane Miller, *Boss Cox's Cincinnati* (1968). Among the many books on the liberal reformers, the most useful are Geoffrey T. Blodgett, *Gentle Reformers: Massachusetts Democrats in the Cleveland Era* (1966) and John G. Sproat, *The Best Men: Liberal Reformers in the Gilded Age* (1965).

The money question is elucidated in Walter Nugent, *Money and American Society, 1865–1880* (1968) and Allan Weinstein, *Prelude to Populism: Origins of the Silver Issue* (1970). On the crisis of the 1890s, see especially Peter H. Argersinger, *Populism and Politics: William Alfred Peffer and the People's Party* (1974); Robert F. Durden, *Climax of Populism: The Election of 1896* (1965); and Paul W. Glad, *McKinley, Bryan and the People* (1964).

An Emerging World Power

Good introductions to the diplomatic history of this period are Foster R. Dulles, *Prelude to World Power, 1865–1900* (1965) and Robert L. Beisner, *From the Old Diplomacy to the New, 1865–1900* (1975). A highly influential interpretation of American expansionism is Walter LaFeber, *The New Empire, 1860–1898* (1963). Other important books dealing with aspects of American expansionism are David Healy, *U.S. Expansionism: Imperialist Urge in the 1890s* (1970); Thomas McCormick, *China Market* (1967); Robert Seager, *Alfred T. Mahan* (1977); William C. Widenor, *Henry Cabot Lodge and the Search for an American Foreign Policy* (1980). Frank Freidel, *Splendid Little War* (1958), but David F. Trask's, *The War With Spain* (1981) provides a fuller account of the conflict. Robert L. Beisner, *Twelve Against Empire* (1968) treats the anti-imperialist response in the United States. On the occupation of the Philippines, see Leon Wolff, *Little Brown Brother* (1961), and for the subsequent history, Peter Stanley, *A Nation in the Making: The Philippines and the U.S., 1899–1921* (1974).

21

THE PROGRESSIVE ERA

*O*n the face of it, the political ferment of the 1890s ended after the 1896 election. The bitter struggle over free silver left the victorious Republicans no stomach for political crusades. The McKinley administration devoted itself to maintaining business confidence: sound money and high tariffs were the order of the day. The main thing, as party chief Mark Hanna said, was to "stand pat and continue Republican prosperity." Insofar as the Republicans felt a need to express crusading zeal, they channeled it into the public's absorption with overseas expansion.

Yet surface appearances were deceiving. The depression of the 1890s had unveiled harsh truths not acknowledged in better days. One such discovery was the power of vested economic interests. In Wisconsin, for example, utility and transit companies had raised fares, reduced services, and demanded and received special tax relief—all at the expense of the public. This discovery of corporate arrogance launched movements in Wisconsin for tax reform, municipal ownership of utilities, and progressive politics. The labor unrest of the 1890s produced a similar response. When the American Railway Union went on strike in 1894, the Cleveland administration plotted with the railroad operators, issued injunctions against the strikers, and sent in troops to restore railroad service. The architect of this policy, Attorney General Richard Olney, took little satisfaction from his success. He asked himself what might

be done in the future to avoid the need for such one-sided intervention. Olney began to advocate labor legislation, first expressed in the Erdman Mediation Act of 1898, that would regulate labor relations on the railroads and prevent crippling rail strikes. In such ways did the crisis of the 1890s turn the nation's thinking toward reform.

The problems themselves, however, went back much further in U.S. history. For more than half a century, Americans had been absorbed in the furious development of their country. Now, at the beginning of the twentieth century, they paused, looked around, and began to add up the costs. Industrialization had led to a frightening concentration of economic power in corporate hands, and an equally troubling growth of a large and restless working class. The great cities spawned widespread misery and corrupt machine politics. The heritage of an earlier America seemed to be succumbing to the demands of the new industrial order.

These problems had concerned reformers in the past, and many of the progressive generation had become active long before 1900. Nor were most reform prescriptions freshly minted. What made the progressive years distinctive was primarily a matter of emphasis. Reform, earlier a marginal activity, became a central and absorbing concern. It was as if social awareness had reached a critical mass around 1900 that set reform activity going as a major, self-sustaining phenomenon of early twentieth-century America.

Reform Impulses

Historians have sometimes spoken of a progressive "movement." But, except as this term refers to Theodore Roosevelt's Progressive party of 1912, progressivism was not a movement in any meaningful sense. There was no single progressive constituency, no agreed-upon agenda, and no unifying organization or leadership. At different times and places, different social groups became active. The arena might be private, as with settlement-house work, or on any of several public levels. People who were reformers on one issue might be conservative on another. The term *progressivism* refers not to a single movement but to a widespread, many-sided effort after 1900 to build a better society in the United States. Progressive reformers shared only this objective, plus an intellectual style that can be called "progressive."

The Progressive Mind

Intellectual climates change. It is usually hard to explain *why* they change but not so difficult to tell *when* new ideas take hold. Such a change of ideas clearly seemed to be in the wind as the twentieth century began.

The new age stressed realism. Americans wanted the facts; they wanted to confront reality. John Sloan, George Luks, William Glackens, and other young artists, many of them trained as newspaper illustrators, began to paint city streets and factory life. The art of this "Ashcan School" portrayed the ugly, commonplace world of the tenement, the rush hour, and the prize fight. The social counterpart of realistic painting was the scientific investigation. The federal government launched massive statistical studies of immigration, of women's and children's labor, and of working conditions in many industries. Vice commissions studied the morals of a number of cities. Among private investigative efforts, the classic was the multivolume *Pittsburgh Survey* (1911–1914). Financed by Margaret Olivia Sage and other New York City philanthropists, it described living and working conditions of the steel district in great detail.

The facts were important because they formed the basis for corrective action. When the young journalist Walter Lippmann wrote *Drift and Mastery* (1914), he asserted the Progressive's confidence in people's ability to act purposefully and constructively. This sense of mastery expressed itself in many ways. For example, people had great faith in the capacity of experts. When Robert M. La Follette became governor of Wisconsin in 1900, he relied heavily on the University of Wisconsin for advice and personnel. "The close intimacy of the university with public affairs explains the democracy, the thoroughness, and the scientific accuracy of the state in its legislation," boasted one La Follette supporter in 1912. "It, as much as any other influence, kept Wisconsin true to the progressive movement during these years."

One of the most admired experts was Frederick W. Taylor, who had devised scientific management as a technique for cutting labor costs in factories. Scientific management also seemed to offer solutions to waste and inefficiency in municipal government, in schools and hospitals, and even in homes and churches. "The fundamental principles of scientific management are applicable to all kinds of human activities," Taylor stressed, and could solve all the social ills that arise "through such of our acts as are blundering, ill-directed, or inefficient." Nothing, Taylor suggested, lay beyond the human capacity to improve through "scientific," purposeful action.

The essential thing was to resist intellectual formulations that denied people this sense of mastery. Such had been the effect of Herbert Spencer's Social Darwinism, with its elaborate laws for the automatic development of society. Spencer now came under severe attack from scholars who, while accepting social evolution, denied that it could not be made subject to human direction. Man could "shape environmental forces to his own advantage," argued the sociologist Lester F. Ward. Society could advance through "rational planning" and "social engineering."

A comparable struggle went on in many academic disciplines. This involved an attack on what has been termed nineteenth-century "formalism," in which abstract theory, not empirical inquiry, formed the heart of the scientific method. In economics, for example, the market

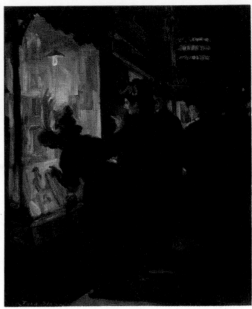

REALISM OF THE ASHCAN SCHOOL

Newspapers still relied on drawings to illustrate the news before the turn of the century. John Sloan, for example, came of age as an artist doing on-the-spot drawings of tenement fires, mine explosions, and political campaigns for the Philadelphia *Press*. The apprenticeship shaped the way he, and others of the "ashcan" school, saw the urban world. His *Wake of the Ferry* (left) captured the somber mood, *Shop Window* (right) something of the joys of city life. (Left, The Phillips Collection, Washington; Right, The Newark Museum. Gift of Mrs. Felix Fuld)

was presumed to be perfectly competitive, and hence always subject to the laws of supply and demand. Such a perfect system had no room for reform, which would only disrupt what could not be improved.

Critics of classical economics—they called themselves "institutional economists"—denied that the market ever operated this perfectly. They conducted field research to determine how institutions and power relationships actually controlled the operation of the marketplace. In his *The Theory of the Leisure Class* (1899) and *The Instinct of Workmanship* (1914), the economist Thorstein Veblen lampooned the classical economists' abstract image of the economic man. In the real world, he noted, people acted not out of pure economic calculation, but from complex human motives ranging from vanity to pride in their work.

No field was more a victim of nineteenth-century formalism than the law. After Recon-

struction, the courts had elevated the Fourteenth Amendment into a set of eternal principles in defense of the rights of property. The key clause denied to the states the power to "deprive any person of life, liberty, or property, without due process of law." Intended to protect the civil rights of the freed slaves, the due-process clause gradually became a bar against state regulation of the economy. Any such interference violated the property rights of persons—who were defined to include corporations—under the due-process clause. The Supreme Court, in *Lochner v. New York* (1905), invalidated a maximum-hours law for bakers in New York on the grounds that it violated the contractual rights of both employers and workers. Dissenting, Justice Oliver Wendell Holmes saw this interpretation as a fictional equality outside the real world of labor-management relations. Holmes had earlier asserted the essence of progressive jurisprudence in *The Common Law* (1881): "The life of the law has not been logic; it has been experience. The felt necessities of the time, even the prejudices which judges share with their fellow-men, have had a good deal more to do than the syllogism in de-termin-ing the rules by which men shall be governed."

The lawyer Louis D. Brandeis acted successfully on Holmes's dictum in *Muller v. Oregon* (1908), a case that involved a ten-hour law for women working in Oregon laundries. Brandeis set aside the usual legal arguments about constitutional meaning. Instead, he drew upon social research that showed how long hours damaged women's health. "Sociological jurisprudence," as Dean Roscoe Pound of the Harvard Law School termed it, called for "the adjustment of principles and doctrines to the human conditions they are to govern rather than assumed first principles." Only as the courts came to accept this legal view—as they did in *Muller v. Oregon*—could progressive legislation move forward.

The philosopher William James took up the task of attacking the core ideas of formalism. James denied the existence of absolute truths. His philosophy of "pragmatism" judged ideas by their consequences and used ideas as guides to action that produced desired results. Philosophy should concern itself with solving problems, said James, not with contemplating ultimate ends. James's most important disciple was John Dewey. Like James, Dewey had a great interest in psychology, and even more in applying psychological insights to education. In his Laboratory School at the University of Chicago, Dewey broke from the rigid curriculum of traditional education and instead stressed problem solving and practical activity as the keys to children's educational growth. Nowhere could the intellectual bent of progressivism in action be seen better than in Dewey's experiments. Fittingly, they came to be known as progressive education.

Progressive reformers prided themselves on being tough minded. They wanted to confront and know social reality. The had confidence in people's capacity to take purposeful action. But there was another side to the progressive mind. It was deeply infused with idealism. Progressives framed their intentions in terms of high principle. The progressive cause, pronounced Theodore Roosevelt, "is based on the eternal principles of righteousness."

Much progressive idealism came from the past, from a refurbishing and sharpening of American values. Abraham Lincoln loomed large in the minds of Progressives. For many, the Great Emancipator had been a guide from childhood, and they identified their own efforts with the early Republican party and with the abolitionist struggle. Past values found clearest expression in the battle for political reform. "Go back to the first principles of democracy; go back to the people," Robert La Follette told his audience when he first launched his attack on Wisconsin machine politics in 1897. Political reformers typically described theirs as a work of political restoration. They frequently said they had converted to reform after discovering how far the actual practice of party politics had drifted from their inherited ideals of representative government.

Progressive idealism also derived from American radical traditions. Many Progressives traced their conversion to reform to Henry George's *Progress and Poverty* (1879), with its plea for the *single tax* to crush the evils of land monopoly. George, a social reformer, believed that the government should get all its funds from a tax on land. Other Progressives found inspiration in the journalist Edward Bellamy's *Looking Backward* (1888), with its utopian vision of an ordered, affluent American socialism; or in the writer Henry Demarest Lloyd's *Wealth Against Commonwealth* (1894), with its powerful indictment of a predatory Standard Oil Company. In later years, this radical tradition came to be transmitted mainly through the Socialist party. It was no coincidence that socialism and progressivism flourished during the same period. Both drew, to some degree, on the same sources of discontent. Walter Lippmann and many other young reformers passed through socialism on their way to progressivism.

The boundaries between progressivism and socialism were often clouded, especially at the municipal level. In about 350 cities where Socialists won public office between 1910 and 1919, they could hardly be distinguished from other reform administrators. On the other hand, strong tensions arose between socialism and progressivism. The more militant Socialists, such as Eugene V. Debs, had little but contempt for moderate reform; they called for Marxian class struggle and revolution. Nevertheless, they had a stimulating effect on progressivism. In the business sector, corporate reformers acted partly out of fear of the socialist appeal among workers. And, despite the discomfort it caused, socialism asserted ideals that served as a beacon for more moderate reformers.

The most important source of progressive idealism, especially among social reformers, was religion. Within the Protestant churches, confrontation with cities had given rise to the new doctrine of the Social Gospel. For the Reverend Walter Rauschenbusch, the shaping experience was his ministry at a German Baptist congregation near the squalid Hell's Kitchen area of New York City. Shocked by the conditions he found there, Rauschenbusch fought for more playgrounds and better housing in slum neighborhoods. The churches had to reassert the "social aims of Jesus," Rauschenbusch argued. The "Kingdom of God on Earth" would be achieved, he said, not by striving only for personal salvation, but by struggling for social justice. Many clergymen agreed with Rauschenbusch that unrestrained American capitalism was only "semi-Christian." The Social Gospel, increasingly heard from urban Protestant pulpits after the turn of the century, led to the formation of the Federal Council of Churches in 1908. The council aimed at "promoting the application of the law of Christ in every relation to human life."

The Social Gospel addressed the concerns of the Protestant ministry, but the underlying religious sentiment extended far beyond formal church boundaries. Progressive leaders characteristically grew up in families imbued with evangelical piety. Many went through a religious crisis, having sought and failed to experience a conversion, and ultimately settled on a career in social work, education, journalism, or politics. There they could translate inherited religious belief into modern secular action. Jane Addams, for example, had taken up settlement-house work with this intent. By uplifiting the poor in tenement districts, settlement workers would themselves be uplifted. They would experience "the joy of finding the Christ which lieth in man, but which no man can unfold save in fellowship."

As a result, progressive thought contained a pervading Christian undercurrent. The phil-

osopher John Dewey thus called democracy "a spiritual fact" and the "means by which the revelation of truth is carried on." Only in democracy, "through community of action, did the incarnation of God in man (man, that is to say, as organ of universal truth) become a living present thing." Theodore Roosevelt launched his Progressive party with the battle cry, "We stand at Armageddon and we battle for the Lord." His supporters at the party's national convention of 1912 marched around the hall singing "Onward Christian Soldiers."

The progressive mode of thought—idealistic in intent and tough minded in approach—nurtured a new kind of reform journalism. A growing urban audience had already given rise to a rash of popular magazines, including *Munsey's, McClure's,* and *Collier's.* Unlike the highbrow *Atlantic Monthly* or *Harper's,* these journals sold for only ten cents and catered to a broad audience. They attracted people, publisher Frank A. Munsey remarked, by low prices, attractive formats, and "good cheer and human interest throughout." After the magazines discovered a popular appetite for the exposure of evil, investigative journalism became their hallmark. Lincoln Steffens wrote about the corrupt ties between business and political machines in the cities. Ida M. Tarbell (pictured on page 650) attacked Standard Oil, and David Graham Phillips told how money controlled the Senate. William Hard exposed industrial accidents in "Making Steel and Killing Men" (1907) and child labor in "De Kid Wot Works at Night" (1908). Others described prostitution, Wall Street abuses, and adulterated food. Hardly a sordid corner of American life escaped the scrutiny of these brilliant and tireless reporters. They were moralists as well. They made their writing powerful not only by uncovering facts, but also by telling the facts with great indignation.

President Roosevelt, among many others, thought they went too far. In a 1906 speech, he compared them to the man with the muckrake in *The Pilgrim's Progress,* by the seventeenth-century English preacher John Bunyan. The man was too absorbed with raking the filth on the floor to look up and accept a celestial crown. Thus, the term "muckrakers" became attached to journalists who exposed the underside of American life. Their efforts were, in fact, health-

IDA TARBELL TAKES ON ROCKEFELLER
A popular biographer of Napoleon and Lincoln in the 1890s, Ida Tarbell turned her formidable journalistic talents to muckraking. Her first installment of "History of the Standard Oil Company" appeared in *McClure's Magazine* in November 1902. John D. Rockefeller, she wrote, "was willing to strain every nerve to obtain for himself special and illegal privileges from the railroads which were bound to ruin every man in the oil business not sharing them with him." As Tarbell built her case, a crescendo of criticism rained down on Rockefeller. A more sympathetic cartoon in the magazine *Judge* pleads with Rockefeller's critics: "Boys, don't you think you have bothered the old man just about enough?" (Ida M. Tarbell Collection, Allegheny College; Culver)

giving. More than any other group, the muck-rakers called the people to arms.

Political Reformers

Progressives wanted to know and confront social reality. They infused their efforts with a deep sense of ideals. They were confident of the human capacity to take purposeful action. This much Progressives had in common. But, once in action, they revealed more complicated characteristics. Different groups took up different reforms, and, to a greater or lesser degree, they did so for reasons of self-interest. Nowhere were these cross-currents stronger than among political reformers.

In many cities, the demand for better government came from local businessmen. They complained that the economic burdens of old-fashioned party rule had become too heavy. Taxes went up while services fell short of the businessmen's growing needs. There had to be a stop, as one manufacturer said, to "the inefficiency, the sloth, the carelessness, the injustice and the graft of city administrations." The solution, argued John Patterson of the National Cash Register Company as early as 1896, lay in putting "municipal affairs on a strict business basis." Cities should be run "not by partisans, either Republican or Democratic, but by men who are skilled in business management and social service."

In 1900, a hurricane devastated Galveston, Texas. Local businessmen took over and, during the course of rebuilding the city, replaced the mayor and board of aldermen with a five-man commission. The Galveston plan, although widely copied, had a serious flaw. It gave too much power to the individual commissioners. Dayton, Ohio, resolved this problem in 1912 by giving the legislative duties to a nonpartisan commission and the administrative functions to an appointed city manager. The commission-manager system soon became the preferred way to run an American city "in exactly the same way as a private business corporation." Municipal political reform was preeminently the work of the business community, and overtly a matter of the balance sheet. Efficient government amounted to good business.

It was also a species of power-grab. Municipal reformers favored city-wide elections, nonpartisanship, and professional city administration. All these reforms attacked means by which ethnic and working-class groups gained access to political power and influence. As a result, municipal control moved into the hands of the urban middle class. In fact, municipal reform contained a decidedly antidemocratic bias. "Ignorance should be excluded from control," said former Mayor Abram Hewitt of New York in 1901. "City business should be carried on by trained experts selected upon some other principle than popular suffrage."

A different kind of political progressivism opposed such elitist reform. Mayor Brand Whitlock of Toledo, Ohio, believed "that the cure for the ills of democracy was not less democracy, as so many people were always preaching, but more democracy." Shoe manufacturer Hazen S. Pingree, an early example of this breed of urban politician, led the Republicans to victory against the Democratic machine in Detroit in 1889. Although drafted by a business coalition, Pingree skillfully appealed for support from trade unions and ethnic groups. His administration not only attacked municipal corruption and inefficiency, but also concerned itself with the needs of Detroit's working people. They swept him back into office by a large majority in 1893. A number of other cities likewise came under the leadership of such progressive mayors, including Samuel M. "Golden Rule" Jones in Toledo, Tom Johnson in Cleveland, and Mark Fagan in Jersey City. By combining popular programs and campaign magic, they won over the urban masses and challenged the rule of the entrenched machines.

The democratic Progressives found their major battleground at the state level. Robert La Follette in Wisconsin, Harold U'Ren in Oregon, Hiram Johnson in California, and Woodrow Wilson in New Jersey profoundly altered state government in America. They did so, like business reformers in cities, by means of structural reforms. However, the state Progressives did not aim at restricting popular representation. They worked to expand it. The most important reform was the direct primary election, by which candidates were nominated by popular vote rather than by party conventions and caucuses. The direct election of senators, enacted into law in 1913 by the Seventeenth Amendment, deprived the party-dominated state legislatures of that power. Other democratizing reforms included the initiative, the referendum, and the recall.

In city halls and state houses, political Progressives pictured themselves as democratic idealists. They wanted to return to "the people" what had been stolen by corrupt bosses and the vested interests. La Follette vowed "never to abandon the fight until we have made government truly representative of the people." This rhetoric was sincere but it did not tell the whole

ROBERT M. LAFOLLETTE
LaFollette was transformed into a political reformer when a Wisconsin Republican boss attempted to bribe him in 1891 to influence a judge in a railway case. As he described it in his *Autobiography*, "Out of this awful ordeal came understanding; and out of understanding came resolution. I determined that the power of this corrupt influence . . . should be broken." As Wisconsin governor in 1901, he rooted out the old machine politics and made Wisconsin a "laboratory for democracy." (State Historical Society of Wisconsin)

story. For political reform aimed as much at winning office as it did at purifying politics.

The progressive generation of political reformers did not consist of refurbished Mugwumps of the 1880s. Many Progressives were seasoned politicians. La Follette, for example, had followed a conventional party career—lawyer, district attorney, and then a congressman for three terms—before breaking with the Wisconsin Republican machine after 1890 and turning to reform politics. If they were newcomers—as was Woodrow Wilson, the president of Princeton University, when he won election as governor of New Jersey on the Democratic ticket—they showed a quick aptitude for politics and gained a solid mastery of the trade.

The Progressives had little sympathy for the disinterested amateurism of the Mugwumps. They accepted the party system but operated within it entirely differently than did the party regulars. George Washington Plunkitt of Tammany Hall had scorned the value of rhetoric and speechmaking in politics. But not the Progressives. They used the skills of the political campaigner to dramatize issues and generate grass-roots support, often as a way of seizing control from machine politicians.

The welling up of reform sentiment gave such politicians their chance, and they seized it. "I was merely expressing a common and widespread, though largely unconscious, spirit of revolt among the people," La Follette said of his fight with the Wisconsin Republican machine. After three defeats, he finally gained the Republican nomination for governor in 1900 by his skillful, persistent appeal to rank-and-file voters. Once in office, he immediately pushed through a direct primary law. This democratic reform expressed his political ideals; it also suited his particular political talents perfectly. The direct primary gave La Follette the means to maintain his control over the Republican party in Wisconsin. Through good times and bad, he kept it until his death twenty-five years later.

What was true of La Follette was more or less true of all successful progressive politicians. They supported democratic ideals and made skillful use of the reforms that expressed those ideals. Once in office, they asserted control over their parties. From Golden Rule Jones and Tom Johnson in city halls, to Hiram Johnson in the California governorship, to Roosevelt and Wil-

son in the White House, the progressive politicians beat the party bosses at their own game. They practiced a new kind of politics. In a reform age, it could be a more effective way to power than the backroom techniques of the old-fashioned machine politicians.

Social Feminism

Among the groups activated by the reform ferment, none played a more crucial role than American women. For half a century after the Seneca Falls convention of 1848, the women's rights movement had concentrated mainly on gaining the vote. By 1900, this effort had fully succeeded in only four states—Wyoming, Colorado, Idaho, and Utah. The rival campaign for a women suffrage amendment to the Constitution, once promising, also failed. The formation of the National American Women Suffrage Association in 1890 restored unity to the movement, but the old momentum had been lost. The pioneering generation of Elizabeth Cady Stanton, Lucy Stone, and Susan B. Anthony was passing from the scene, to be replaced by less visionary and skillful leaders. The women's rights movement went through the "doldrums," as suffragists called it, from the mid-1890s to 1910.

During those years, reform energies drifted from the voting issue. Women turned instead toward social uplift—protecting working women and children, improving the lives of immigrants and slum dwellers, and assisting destitute families. These social-reform causes, although taken up by men as well, came to be identified especially with woman progressives.

Middle-class women had long borne much of the burden for humanitarian work in American cities. During the Civil War, ladies' aid societies sprang up almost everywhere to assist soldiers and their families. Afterward, vocational schools, orphan asylums, and "homes for the friendless" assisted war widows and orphans. As their number multiplied in the cities, working women became the principal concern of organized charity, especially through social clubs and job exchanges.

After the depression of the 1870s, the need to coordinate various relief agencies led to the creation of charity-organization societies. Voluntary investigators visited needy families, assessed their problems, and certified them to the appropriate agencies. Women did most of this work, in keeping with the traditional concept of the woman as a nurturer. She appropriately filled this role for society as well as within her own family and continued to do so as the nation entered the progressive era.

Social uplift, the special province of American women, now showed a new brand of aggressiveness. After many years of dedicated charity work, Mrs. Josephine Shaw Lowell of New York City concluded that it was not enough to give assistance to the poor. "If the working people had all they ought to have, we should not have the paupers and criminals," she declared. "It is better to save them before they go under, than to spend your life fishing them out afterward." Mrs. Lowell founded the New York Consumers League in 1890. Her goal was to improve the wages and working conditions of the female clerks in the city's stores. To help bring pressure on reluctant merchants, the league issued a "White List"—a very short one at first—of shops that met its standards. The league then expanded its interest beyond retail stores and spread to other cities. The National Consumers League was founded in 1899. Under the crusading leadership of Florence Kelley, formerly a chief factory inspector in Illinois, it became a

powerful lobby for protective legislation for women and children.

Among its achievements, none was more important than the *Muller v. Oregon* decision (1908), which validated the Oregon Ten-Hour Law for woman laundry workers. The Consumers League had pushed that law through the state legislature and successfully defended it before the Supreme Court. The Muller case opened the way for protective legislation throughout the country. Women's organizations became a mighty force in state legislatures and Congress on behalf of women and children. Their victories included the first law providing public assistance for mothers with dependent children, in Illinois in 1911; the first minimum wage law for women and children, in Massachusetts in 1912; and the creation of the children's and women's bureaus in the U.S. Labor Department, in 1912 and 1920, respectively. In 1916, Congress passed a national child labor law banning the products of child labor from interstate commerce. Two years later, however, the Supreme Court declared this law unconstitutional.

A second thrust of social feminism, equally as strong as public advocacy, aimed at direct engagement with the underprivileged of industrial America. The settlement-house movement

SAVING THE CHILDREN
In the early years at Hull House, toddlers sometimes arrived for kindergarten tipsy from breakfasts of bread soaked in wine. To settlement-house workers, education in childcare seemed the obvious answer to such ignorance, and so began the program to send visiting nurses into immigrant homes. They taught mothers the proper methods of caring for children—including, as this photograph shows, the daily infant bath, in a dishpan if necessary. (Chicago Historical Society)

THE MAKING OF A SOCIAL FEMINIST

Jane Addams's autobiography Twenty Years at Hull House *(1910) is as good an account as we have of the motives that led to social feminism.*

The winter after I left school was spent in the Woman's Medical College of Philadelphia, but the development of the spinal difficulty which had shadowed me from childhood . . . inevitably put aside the immediate prosecution of a medical course, and although I had passed my examinations . . . I was very glad to have a physician's sanction for giving up clinics and dissecting rooms and to follow his prescription for spending the next two years in Europe. . . .

The long illness left me in a state of nervous exhaustion with which I struggled for years, traces of it remaining long after Hull-House was opened in 1889. At the best it allowed me but a limited amount of energy, so that doubtless there was much nervous depression at the foundation of the spiritual struggles which this chapter is forced to record. . . .

One of the most poignant of these experiences, which occurred during the first few months after our landing upon the other side of the Atlantic, was on a Saturday night, when I received an ineradicable impression of the wretchedness of East London, and also saw for the first time the overcrowded quarters of a great city at midnight. A small party of tourists were taken to the East End by a city missionary to witness the Saturday night sale of decaying vegetables and fruit. . . . On Mile End Road, from the top of an omnibus which paused at the end of a dingy street lighted by only occasional flares of gas, we saw two huge masses of ill-clad people clamoring around two hucksters' carts. . . . They were huddled into ill-fitting, cast-off clothing, the ragged finery which one sees only in East London. . . . Yet the final impression was not of ragged, tawdry clothing nor of pinched and sallow faces, but of myriads of hands, empty, pathetic, nerveless and work-worn, showing white in the uncertain light of the street, and clutching forward for food which was already unfit to eat. . . .

For two years in the midst of my distress over the poverty . . . thus suddenly driven into my consciousness . . . there was mingled a sense of futility, of misdirected energy, the belief that the pursuit of cultivation would not in the end bring either solace or relief. I gradually reached a conviction that the first generation of college women had taken their learning too quickly, had departed too suddenly from the active, emotional life led by their grandmothers and great-grandmothers. . . .

This, then, was the difficulty, the assumption that the sheltered, educated girl has nothing to do with the bitter poverty and the social maladjustment which is all about her, and which, after all, cannot be concealed, for it breaks through poetry and literature in a burning tide which overwhelms her; it peers at her in the form of heavy-laden market women and underpaid street laborers, gibing her with a sense of her uselessness. . . .

It is hard to tell just when the very simple plan which afterward developed into the Settlement began to form itself in my mind. It may have been even before I went to Europe for the second time, but I gradually became convinced that it would be a good thing to rent a house in a part of the city where many primitive and actual needs are found, in which young women who had been given over too exclusively to study, might restore a balance of activity along traditional lines and learn of life from life itself. . . .

In those early days we were often asked why we had come to live on Halsted Street when we could afford to live somewhere else. . . . In time it came to seem natural to all of us that the Settlement should be there. If it is natural to feed the hungry and care for the sick, it is certainly natural to give pleasure to the young, comfort to the aged, and to minister to the deep-seated craving for social intercourse that all men feel.

In addition to the neighbors who responded to the receptions and classes, we found those who were too battered and oppressed to care for them. To these, however, was left that susceptibility to the bare offices of humanity which raises such offices into a bond of fellowship.

From the first it seemed understood that we were ready to perform the humblest neighborhood services. We were asked to wash the new-born babies, and to prepare the dead for burial, to nurse the sick, and to "mind the children."

Perhaps even in those first days we made a beginning toward that object which was afterwards stated in our charter: "To provide a center for a higher civic and social life; to institute and maintain educational and philanthropic enterprises, and to investigate and improve the conditions in the industrial districts of Chicago."

began in London in 1884, when Oxford University students founded Toynbee Hall. Inspired by that example, two young women, Jane Addams and Ellen Gates Starr established Hull House on Chicago's West Side in 1889. During the next fifteen years, scores of settlement houses sprang up in the slum neighborhoods of the nation's cities. The houses served as community centers run by middle-class settlement residents. Hull House had meeting rooms, an art gallery, clubs for children and adults, and a kindergarten. Jane Addams herself led battles for garbage removal, playgrounds, better street lighting, and police protection. At the Henry Street Settlement in New York, Lillian D. Wald made visiting nursing a major service. Mary McDowell, head of the University of Chicago Settlement, installed a bathhouse, a children's playground, and a citizenship school for immigrants.

Beyond the modest good they did in slum neighborhoods, settlement houses served as a breeding ground for social feminism. The residents were expected to work full-time, and so the settlement house helped break the convention of social uplift as a female avocation. At least half the female residents went on to lifelong careers in some branch of social service. The settlement houses thus contributed strongly to the emerging profession of social work. To a remarkable degree, too, the leaders of social reform—both men and women—served settlement-house apprenticeships. The settlement houses became "spearheads of reform," as one historian called them.

On the surface, social feminism seemed to divert energy from the struggle for women's suffrage. But it was a diversion richly repaid. In a famous essay, Jane Addams spoke of the "subjective necessity" of the settlement house. She meant that it was as much a response to the middle-class women eager to serve as it was to the needs of city slum dwellers. Addams herself was a case in point. She had grown up in a comfortable Illinois family and graduated from Rockford College. Then she faced an empty future—an ornamental wife if she married, a sheltered spinster if she did not. Hull House became her salvation. It gave her contact with what she thought was the real world plus a useful career and a sense of purpose and personal worth.

Hundreds of other college-educated women who found their calling in social reform shared

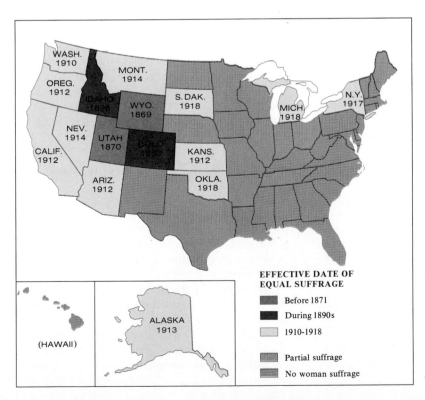

MAP 21.1 WOMAN SUFFRAGE BEFORE 1920
As a reform movement, the fight for woman suffrage was remarkable for the persistent resistance it encountered. By 1910, after more than sixty years of agitation, only four lightly populated western states had granted women full voting rights. A number of other states granted partial suffrage, limited mostly to voting for school boards and such issues as taxes. After 1910, as the effort shifted to a national struggle for a constitutional amendment, ten states were added to the short list of full suffrage. The most stubborn resistance was in the South.

Addams's experience. Almost inevitably, they became suffragists. Why should a woman capable of running a settlement house or lobbying a bill be denied the right to vote? Suffrage, moreover, became linked to social feminism. If women had the right to vote, they and their male supporters argued, more enlightened legislation and better government would certainly result. Social feminism thus broadened the base of the suffrage movement. Some social reformers, believing that working women should be enabled to help themselves, founded the National Women's Trade Union League in 1903. Financed and led by wealthy supporters, the league organized women workers, played a considerable role in their strikes, and, perhaps most importantly, developed working-class leaders. Rose Schneiderman, for example, became a union organizer among the garment workers in New York City; Agnes Nestor led the woman glove workers in Illinois; and both were lobbyists for women's protective legislation. Such trade-union women identified their cause with the broader struggle for women's rights.

A genuine sense of sisterhood developed that cut across class lines. Well-to-do women rallied to the side of immigrant girls in the great shirt-waist-makers' strike of 1909 in New York City. Socialites and sweatshop girls marched side by side in the city's suffrage parades. When the state of New York held referenda on women's suffrage in 1915 and 1917, strong support came from the Jewish and Italian precincts inhabited by unionized garment workers. The women's rights movement thus expanded beyond its original base in the middle class.

Meanwhile, suffrage activity was reviving nationwide. Women won the right to vote in the state of Washington in 1910, in California in 1911, and in four more western states during the next three years. Women also started to shift their tactics. Beginning in 1903, suffragists in England had picketed, assaulted politicians, and gone on hunger strikes in jail. The effectiveness of this disruptive strategy impressed suffragists in the United States.

The most important of the new militants was Alice Paul, a young Quaker. Rejecting the slower route of enfranchisement by the states, Paul took aim at a constitutional amendment that would give women across the country the

SUFFRAGISTS ON PARADE, 1913
After 1910, the suffrage movement went into high gear. Suffragist leaders decided to demand a constitutional amendment rather than battle for the vote state by state, and to adopt the direct-action methods pioneered by English suffragists. The great parade of women—and near riot—in Washington, D.C. at Woodrow Wilson's inauguration served notice on the new president that the suffragists meant business. (The Bettmann Archive)

right to vote. In 1914, Paul organized the militant National Women's party. The National American Woman Suffrage Association (NAWSA), from which Paul had split off, was also rejuvenated. Carrie Chapman Catt, a skilled political organizer from the New York movement, took over as national leader in 1915. Under her guidance, the NAWSA brought a broad-based organization to the campaign for a federal amendment.

Urban Liberalism

At first, progressivism was a product of middle-class America. In almost every case, the initiative for reform came from the educated, the native born, and the economically comfortable. But progressivism changed over time, and its constituency shifted.

When Hiram Johnson ran for governor of California in 1910, he was the candidate of the middle class and the countryside. Johnson had first attracted attention as the successful prosecutor of the San Francisco political boss Abe Ruef. In his platform, Johnson pledged to purify California politics and to curb the Southern Pacific Railroad, the dominating power in the state's economic and political life. By his second term, Johnson was championing social and labor legislation. His original base of support had strongly eroded and had been replaced by the immigrant, working-class vote that kept him in power for years.

These events illustrated the most enduring achievement of progressivism—the activation of America's working people as a force in reform politics. The cities served as the main arena for this development. Historians have called the result *urban liberalism*—that is, a reform movement by city people for social protection attained by state intervention.

Thirty minutes before quitting time on Saturday afternoon, March 25, 1911, fire broke out at the Triangle Shirtwaist Company in downtown New York. The flames trapped the workers, mostly young immigrant girls. Forty-seven leaped to their deaths; another hundred never made it to the windows. The tragedy caused a national furor and led, two months later, to the creation of the New York State Factory Commission. During four years of work, the commission developed a remarkable program of labor reform, totalling fifty-six laws that dealt with such matters as fire hazards, unsafe machines, home work, and wages and hours for women and children. The chairman of the commission was Robert F. Wagner; the vice-chairman, Alfred E. Smith. Both were Tammany Hall politicians and Democratic party leaders in the state legislature. Wagner and Smith sponsored the resolution establishing the commission, participated fully in its work and, most important, marshalled the party regulars to pass the proposals into law. All this the two men did with the approval of the Tammany machine. The labor code that resulted was the most advanced in the United States.

Tammany's reform role reflected a trend in American cities. Urban political machines increasingly saw their limits as social agencies in the modern industrial age. Only the state could prevent future Triangle fires or cope with the evils of factory work and city life. Also, a new generation had entered machine politics. Al Smith and Robert Wagner, men of social vision, absorbed the lessons of the Triangle investigation. They formed durable ties with such middle-class progressives as the social worker

THE TRIANGLE SHIRTWAIST FIRE

The doors were the problem. Most were locked (to keep the working girls from leaving early); the few that were open became jammed by bodies trying to escape the flames. When the fire trucks finally came, the ladders were too short. Compared to those caught inside, the girls who leaped to their deaths were the lucky ones. "As I looked up I saw a love affair in the midst of all the horror," a reporter wrote. A young man was helping girls leap from a window. The fourth "put her arms about him and kiss[ed] him. Then he held her out into space and dropped her." He immediately followed. "Thud—dead, Thud—dead . . . I saw his face before they covered it. . . . he was a real man. He had done his best." (Brown Brothers)

Frances Perkins, who came to the commission as representative of the New York Consumers League.

For all their organizational strength, moreover, the urban machines could not ignore the voters' sentiments. In the successes of such middle-class reform politicians as Toledo's Sam Jones and Cleveland's Tom Johnson, the urban machines saw the appeal of progressive programs in working-class wards. The political universe of the machines had changed. In the age of the direct primary, more attention had to be paid to opinion in the precincts.

Political reform was, of course, hailed as an assault on the machine system, and some measures did threaten the machine. City-wide elections diluted the vote of the working-class wards, nonpartisan ballots undercut party loyalty, and commission government threatened the spoils system. The machines strongly resisted these reforms. The commission-manager system was confined largely to middle-sized cities where machine politics had not been so well entrenched.

Reforms aimed at broadening popular participation in politics were far less threatening. Democratization actually put a premium on the organizational resources of the urban machines. This was clearly the case, for example, with the direct primary. The machines, while forced to work harder, generally succeeded as well at bringing out the vote in party primaries as at manipulating conventions and caucuses. Moreover, democratizing reforms had a highly favorable effect on the urban-rural balance in state politics. Cities in industrial states had invariably been underrepresented in the state legislatures. In Connecticut, an extreme case, rural towns of a few hundred people had as much representation as did Hartford and New Haven. Any shift to a popular vote, such as primary elections and the direct election of senators, benefited the populous cities, and hence the urban machines.

Always highly pragmatic in their operations, the city machines adopted urban liberalism without much ideological struggle. The same could not be said of the trade unions, the other important institution that represented American workers. During its early years, the American Federation of Labor (AFL) had strongly opposed state interference in labor's affairs. Samuel Gom-

pers preached that workers should not seek "at the hands of government what they could accomplish by their own initiative and activities." Economic power and self-help, not the state, would be the workingman's salvation. Voluntarism, as trade unionists called this antistate doctrine, did not die out, but it weakened substantially during the progressive years.

Organized labor enlisted, although reluctantly, in the cause of urban liberalism—partly for defensive reasons. In the early twentieth century, the labor movement came under severe attack by open-shop employers, who had powerful legal weapons. For one thing, they could sue unions under the Sherman Antitrust Act. In the Danbury Hatters (*Loewe v. Lawler*) case (1908), the Supreme Court found a union boycott to be a conspiracy in restraint of trade. The Court awarded triple damages to the company. More injurious was the routine use of injunctions against unions during labor disputes. Upon an employer's plea of irreparable damages, a sympathetic judge would, without evidence or testimony, prohibit the union from carrying on a strike or boycott.

Only a political response might blunt this assault on labor's crucial economic weapons. In its Bill of Grievances of 1906, the AFL demanded immunity from court attack. The labor organization then campaigned to "reward our friends and punish our enemies" in congressional elections. Getting a cold reception from the Republicans, organized labor moved into closer alliance with the Democratic party, notwithstanding an official AFL policy of nonpartisanship.

Having breached the political barriers for defensive reasons, the labor movement had difficulty denying the case for social legislation. The AFL, after all, claimed to speak for the entire working class. When muckrakers exposed exploitation, and middle-class Progressives came forward with solutions, how could the labor movement fail to respond? Gompers served on the Triangle factory commission, and if—according to Frances Perkins—he was a less eager student than the Tammanyite members, learn he did. In state after state, organized labor joined the battle for progressive legislation and increasingly became its strongest advocate. Conservative labor leaders found some consolation by making a careful distinction: protective laws were for women and children, who lacked the ability to defend themselves.

But the lure of beneficial legislation proved too strong. Accident rates took an appallingly high toll in American mills and mines. Liability laws were archaic and heavily favored the employer. Under the common law, which still governed in this field, an injured worker could sue for damages, but he or she had little hope of succeeding. Nothing cried out more for reform than the plight of maimed workers and penniless widows. In Germany and England, accident-insurance systems guaranteed compensation regardless of fault. Efforts to adopt similar insurance laws in America quickly received the support of the trade unions. Between 1910 and 1917, workmen's compensation for industrial accidents and illnesses went into effect in all the industrial states.

If for factory illness and injury, why not state-mandated insurance for unemployment, old age, and the other hazards of industrial life? Conservative unionists argued that workmen's compensation should be considered a special case. They insisted that labor was better off gaining protection through collective bargaining, rather than through the enactment of laws. But the logic of social insurance could not be resisted for long. Because the needs of working people for security could be met only through state action, the labor movement eventually supported social insurance.

Not only social-welfare goals shaped urban liberal politics. It was also influenced by the sharpening attack on the ethnocultural claims of city voters. Old-stock, evangelical Protestants had long agitated for the political imposition on society of their moral and cultural norms. During the progressive period, these activities took a new lease on life. The Anti-Saloon League, which called itself "the Protestant church in action," became a formidable force in many states. Prohibition linked up with other reform concerns: the saloon made for dirty politics, poverty, and bad labor conditions. Old battles heated up again over the social purposes of education. The schools ought not to perpetuate foreigners' ways, but "to civilize, to Christianize, and to Americanize them."

The moral-reform agenda expanded to include a new objective, immigration restriction.

Large numbers of southern and eastern Europeans had entered the United States since the 1890s. Many Americans, including respected social scientists, believed these new immigrants threatened American society. Its Anglo-Saxon population would be "mongrelized" and its Puritan heritage swamped by "inferior" Mediterranean and Slavic cultures. This ethnic argument, though misconceived, appealed strongly to a wide spectrum of middle-class, native-born Americans. The Immigration Restriction League spearheaded a movement to end America's historic open-door policy.

These moral-cultural issues, expressed in reform terms, were as much a part of the progressive spirit as were the social-reform concerns of the settlement houses and the National Consumers' League. But urban liberals bitterly resented the demands for prohibition and immigration restriction. They considered such "reforms" to be attacks on the personal liberty and worthiness of urban immigrants. Prohibition, protested a Catholic economist, was "despotic and hypocritical domination." The Tammany politician Martin McCue accused the Protestant ministry of "seeking to substitute the policeman's nightstick for the Bible."

A hard-fought but unequal battle resulted. The first federal immigration-restriction law, setting up a literacy test, went into effect in 1917. In 1921, the Dillingham Act imposed a quota system that discriminated flagrantly against southern and eastern Europeans. In 1920, the Eighteenth Amendment made prohibition the law of the land.

By fighting these measures, urban liberalism gained an ethnocultural identity. Urban-liberal leaders championed both the economic needs of city dwellers and their right to follow their religious and cultural preferences. In many ways, certainly until the Great Depression of the 1930s, ethnocultural issues provided a stronger basis for urban-liberal politics. And because the Democrats were the party identified with tolerance and diversity, they became the beneficiaries of the rise of urban liberalism. The growing size of the city vote destined the Democrats to become the majority party. The shift from Republican domination, although not completed until the New Deal came to power in the 1930s, began during the progressive era.

Progressivism and National Politics

The gathering forces of progressivism reached the national scene only slowly. Reformers had been activated· by immediate concerns, by problems that affected them directly, and by evils visible and tangible to them. Washington seemed remote from the battles they were waging in their cities and states. But progressivism was bound to come to the capital. In 1906, Robert La Follette went from the governor's office in Wisconsin to the United States Senate. Other seasoned Progressives, also ambitious for a wider stage, made the same move. By 1910, a highly vocal progressive bloc was making itself heard in both houses of Congress.

Problems of a nationwide character had begun to emerge, most of them stemming from the country's economic growth. As the economy had become more industrialized, it had also become more national in scope. At the same time, the economy began to function in ways that made Americans increasingly uneasy. At the national level, progressivism concerned itself mainly with reform of the economic system—the railroads, consumer protection, exploitation of natural resources, finance, and, above all, corporate power. Such reform demanded a great expansion of government power, which had resided mostly at the state and local levels in the nineteenth century.

During the progressive era, the center of power shifted decisively to Washington. There it remained, continually becoming stronger, during the twentieth century. The modern American state had its origins in national progressivism.

The Square Deal

Theodore Roosevelt brought progressivism into national politics. Sheer accident set him on that course. Roosevelt had not wanted the Republican nomination for vice-president under William McKinley in 1900. Then, soon after the inauguration, an anarchist named Leon F. Czolgosz assassinated President McKinley. By this twist of fate, Roosevelt became president on September 14, 1901.

Roosevelt was cut from much the same cloth as other progressive politicians, except for his rather aristocratic background. He came from a wealthy, old-line New York family, attended Harvard, and might well have chosen the life of a leisured, literary gentleman. Instead, scarcely out of college, he plunged into Republican politics and in 1882 entered the New York state legislature. His reasons matched the high-minded motives of other budding Progressives. Like most of them, Roosevelt had received a moralistic, Christian upbringing. A political career would enable him to act constructively on those beliefs. Roosevelt always identified himself— loudly—with the side of righteousness. On the other hand, he did not scorn power and its uses. He showed contempt for the amateurism of the Mugwumps, whom he called "those political and literary hermaphrodites," and much preferred the professionalism of party politics. Roosevelt rose in the New York party because he skillfully translated his moral fervor into broad popular support and thus forced himself on reluctant state Republican bosses. Other emerging progressive politicians followed the same route of party advancement.

After returning from the Spanish-American War as the hero of San Juan Hill, Roosevelt won the New York governorship in 1898. During his single term, he clearly indicated his inclinations toward reform. Roosevelt pushed through civil-service reform and a tax on corporate franchises. He discharged the corrupt superintendent of insurance over the Republican party's objections and asserted his confidence in the government's capacity to improve the life of the people. Ironically, in an attempt to neutralize him, the party bosses promoted Roosevelt to what normally would have been a dead-end job as vice-president. Mark Hanna, hearing of McKinley's assassination, knew "that damn cowboy" would make trouble in the White House.

Roosevelt moved cautiously at the outset. In his first official statement, he reassured the nation that he would "continue absolutely unbroken" McKinley's policies. The conservative Republican bloc in Congress greatly limited his freedom of action. He treated the Senate leader, Nelson W. Aldrich of Rhode Island, with kid gloves. Roosevelt spent much of his energy, through the skillful use of the patronage powers of his office, gaining control of the Republican

JOHN MUIR AND PRESIDENT ROOSEVELT IN YOSEMITE

John Muir, one of America's great naturalists, considered the defense of the nation's forests against commercial exploitation a battle "between landscape righteousness and the devil." Yosemite became a national park in 1890, largely through Muir's crusading efforts. He accompanied Roosevelt on a camping trip through the park in 1903, when this photograph was taken, and helped persuade the president to create sixteen national monuments and double the number of national parks. (Library of Congress)

party. He had fully accomplished this task by the time Senator Hanna died in 1904. But Roosevelt was also restrained by uncertainty about what reform role the federal government ought to play. At first, the new president might have been described as a Progressive without a cause.

Even so, Roosevelt gave early evidence of his activist bent. He devoted part of his first annual message to conservation. Roosevelt, an ardent outdoorsman, loved the West and had invested—unprofitably—in Dakota cattle ranching in the 1880s. A national movement began in the late nineteenth century to conserve the country's natural resources and scenic wonders against reckless exploitation. Yellowstone National Park, the first national park, had been established in 1872, and the withdrawal of timberlands from development had begun under the Forest Re-serve Act of 1891. Roosevelt added more than 125 million acres to the national forest reserve and brought mineral lands and waterpower sites into the reserve system. In 1902, he backed the Newlands Reclamation Act, which designated the proceeds from public land sales for irrigation development in arid regions. His administration strongly upgraded the management of public lands and, to the chagrin of some Republicans, energetically prosecuted violators of federal land laws. In the cause of conservation, Roosevelt demonstrated his enthusiasm for exercising executive authority and his disdain for those who sought profit "by betraying the public service."

The same inclinations influenced Roosevelt's handling of the national anthracite coal strike of 1902. Hard coal was the main fuel for home heating. As cold weather approached with no settlement in sight, the government faced a national emergency. The United Mine Workers, led by John Mitchell, were willing to submit to arbitration, but the coal operators adamantly opposed any recognition of the union. Roosevelt's advisers told him there was no legal basis for federal intervention. Nevertheless, the president took the unprecedented step of calling both sides to a conference at the White House on October 1, 1902. When the conference failed, Roosevelt threatened the operators with a government take-over of the mines. He also persuaded the financier J. P. Morgan to use his considerable influence with them. At this point, the coal operators caved in. The strike ended with the appointment by Roosevelt of an arbitration commission to rule on the issues, another unprecedented step. Roosevelt did not especially support organized labor, but he became infuriated by what he labeled the "arrogant stupidity" of the mine employers.

"Of all the forms of tyranny the least attractive and the most vulgar is the tyranny of mere wealth," Roosevelt wrote in his autobiography. He was prepared to deploy all his presidential authority against the "tyranny" of irresponsible business.

The growing concentration of corporate power brought the issue to a head. For more than thirty years, the structure of business enterprise had been evolving into the modern form of the large-scale, vertically integrated corporation. Following the depression of the 1890s, this process of business concentration suddenly accelerated. Earlier, companies had grown mainly through internal expansion, but now corporate growth occurred through an astonishing scramble to merge rival firms. The resulting trusts greatly increased the degree of concentration in the economy. The term *trust,* which had applied to a specific legal form of business control introduced by Standard Oil in the 1880s, was used more broadly after 1900 to describe all business combinations. Of the seventy-three largest industrial companies in 1900, fifty-three had not existed three years earlier. By 1910, 1 percent of the nation's manufacturers accounted for 44 percent of the total industrial output.

The sheer power of the new combines was not the only disturbing factor. Most of them were heavily "watered"—that is, capitalized in excess of their real value. Financiers had taken huge fees for their underwriting services and, even worse, had not relinquished control over the trusts they had fathered. Almost overnight, a "money power" seemed to have gained a stranglehold on the American economy. Roosevelt's sense of the nation's uneasiness became evident as early as his first annual message, in which he referred to the "real and grave evils" of economic concentration. But what weapons could the president use?

Economic concentration threatened the free competition of the marketplace. Under the common law, which America had inherited from England, any person could sue for damages against injury caused by conspiring competitors or by a monopolistic firm. These common-law rights had been enacted into statute law in many states during the 1880s, and then, because the magnitude of the problem exceeded state jurisdictions, were incorporated into the Sherman Antitrust Act of 1890. Free competition was more vigorously defended in two ways under this federal law. First, the law considered an action in restraint of trade as a crime and hence subject to more severe punishment than liability for damages to an injured party. Second, the law enabled the government, as well as injured parties, to bring suit in the federal courts against violators.

Neither the Cleveland nor the McKinley administrations had been much inclined to enforce the Sherman Act, except against organized labor. Of the eighteen suits brought before 1901, half were against trade unions. Court rulings were equally negative. In *United States v. E. C. Knight* (1895), the Supreme Court ruled that manufacturing was not covered by the Constitution's commerce clause and hence lay beyond the reach of federal regulation. This ruling crippled the Sherman Act but did not kill it. The potential of the act rested, above all, in the fact that it incorporated common-law principles of unimpeachable validity. In the right hands, the Sherman Act could be a strong weapon against the abuse of economic power.

Roosevelt made his opening move when he strengthened the government's capacity to enforce the law. In 1903, despite considerable opposition, Congress established the Bureau of Corporations within the newly created Department of Commerce and Labor. Empowered to investigate business practices, the bureau provided the factual record on which the Justice Department could mount antitrust suits. The first suit had already been filed in 1902 against the Northern Securities Company, a combination of the railroad systems of the Northwest. In 1904, the Supreme Court ordered Northern Securities dissolved, the first such action against a holding company. The next year, in an antitrust case against the major meat packers, the Court reversed the Knight doctrine excluding manufacturing from federal antitrust law.

In 1904, Roosevelt handily defeated a weak Democratic candidate, Judge Alton B. Parker, for a second term. President in his own right, Roosevelt stepped up the attack on the trusts. He took on forty-five of the nation's giant firms, including Standard Oil, American Tobacco, and DuPont. The president accompanied these actions with a rising crescendo of rhetoric. He became the nation's trustbuster, a crusader against "predatory wealth."

Actually, Roosevelt's bark was worse than his bite. He was not antibusiness, and he regarded large-scale enterprise as a natural result of modern industrialism. Only firms that abused their power deserved punishment. But how would those companies be identified? Under the common law, and under the Sherman Act as originally intended, it had been up to the courts to decide whether a given restraint of trade was "unreasonable." The Supreme Court unexpectedly rejected this "rule of reason" in *United States v. Trans-Missouri* (1897). The very fact of conspiracy or monopoly, irrespective of the impact on the market, was sufficient under the Sherman Act. So, if the rule of reason were to survive, it would have to be exercised by those who initiated prosecutions. Roosevelt welcomed the responsibility of making his own distinctions between "good" and "bad" trusts.

In November 1904, shortly after the Bureau of Corporations began to investigate the United States Steel Corporation, the company chairman, Elbert H. Gary, met with Roosevelt. Gary proposed an arrangement: cooperation in exchange for preferential treatment. The company would open its books to the Bureau of Corporations. If the bureau found evidence of wrongdoing, the company would be advised privately and given a chance to set matters right. Roosevelt accepted this "gentlemen's agreement," which was followed by one with International Harvester the next year. J. P. Morgan controlled both firms. From the financier's standpoint, the arrangement seemed entirely sensible. Two great powers, one political and the other economic, met as equals and settled matters between them. For Roosevelt, the gentlemen's agreements eased a serious dilemma. He could accommodate the realities of the modern industrial order while maintaining his public image as the champion against the trusts.

Roosevelt turned his attention to the railroads as well. The main lines of national policy, as with the trusts, had already been laid down. Under the Interstate Commerce Act of 1887, the government established the nation's first regulatory agency, the Interstate Commerce Commission (ICC), to oversee the railroads. But, as with the Sherman Act, railroad regulation remained pretty much a dead letter in its early years. Stymied by a hostile Supreme Court, the ICC lapsed into a mere collector of statistics. Roosevelt was determined to put teeth into the law. The Elkins Act of 1903 empowered the ICC to act against discriminatory rebates—that is, reductions on published rates for preferred or powerful customers. Then, with the 1904 election behind him, Roosevelt pushed for firmer regulation of the railroads.

The central issue was the setting of rates. This power had been denied the ICC, but Roosevelt considered it essential. Senator Nelson Aldrich

and his conservative bloc opposed it just as firmly. In 1906, after nearly two years of wrangling, Congress passed the Hepburn Railway Act. This law gave the ICC the power to set and put into effect maximum rates upon complaint of a shipper, and also the authority to examine railroad books and prescribe uniform bookkeeping. But Roosevelt gave up his demand for limited court review of ICC rate decisions. He also failed to get physical valuation—that is, an inventory of railroad property and equipment—as the basis for fixing fair rates.

The Hepburn Act stood as a testament to Roosevelt's skills as a political operator. He had maneuvered brilliantly against determined opposition and come away with the essentials of what he wanted. Despite grumbling by Senate progressives, Roosevelt was satisfied. He had achieved a landmark expansion of the government's regulatory powers over business.

These powers then began to extend to consumer protection, an area where the muckrakers

CAMPAIGNING FOR THE SQUARE DEAL
When William McKinley ran for president in 1896, he sat on his front porch in Canton, Ohio, and received delegations of voters. That was not Theodore Roosevelt's way. He considered the presidency a "bully pulpit," and he used the office brilliantly to mobilize public opinion and to assert his leadership. The pre-eminence of the presidency in American public life begins with Roosevelt's administration. Here, at the height of his crusading powers, he stumps for the Square Deal in the 1904 election. (Library of Congress)

FILTH AND CHICANERY IN CHICAGO MEAT-PACKING, 1906

Novelist Upton Sinclair is best remembered for his virulent attack on the meat-packing industry, The Jungle. *This brief excerpt indicates why his novel prompted a wave of investigations and regulatory legislation.*

When Jurgis had first inspected the packing plants with Szedvilas, he had marveled while he listened to the tale of all the things that were made out of the carcasses of animals, and of all the lesser industries that were maintained there; now he found that each one of these lesser industries was a separate little inferno, in its way as horrible as the killing-beds, the source and fountain of them all. The workers in each of them had their own peculiar diseases. . . .

There were the "hoisters," as they were called, whose task it was to press the lever which lifted the dead cattle off the floor. They ran along upon a rafter, peering down through the damp and the steam, and as old Durham's architects had not built the killing room for the convenience of the hoisters, at every few feet they would have to stoop under a beam, say four feet above the one they ran on, which got them into the habit of stooping, so that in a few years they would be walking like chimpanzees. Worst of any, however, were the fertilizer men, and those who served in the cooking rooms. These people could not be shown to the visitor—for the odor of a fertilizer man would scare any ordinary visitor at a hundred yards, and as for the other men, who worked in tank rooms full of steam, and in some of which there were open vats near the level of the floor, their peculiar trouble was that they fell into the vats; and when they were fished out, there was never enough of them left to be worth exhibiting—sometimes they would be overlooked for days, till all but the bones of them had gone out of the world as Durham's Pure Leaf Lard! . . .

There was never the least attention paid to what was cut up for sausage; there would come all the way back from Europe old sausage that had been rejected, and that was mouldy and white—it would be dosed with borax and glycerine, and dumped into the hoppers, and made over again for home consumption. There would be meat that had tumbled out on the floor, in the dirt and sawdust, where the workers had tramped and spit uncounted billions of consumption germs. There would be meat stored in great piles in rooms; and the water from leaky roofs would drip over it, and thousands of rats would race about on it. It was too dark in these storage places to see well, but a man could run his hand over these piles of meat and sweep off handfuls of the dried dung of rats. These rats were nuisances, and the packers would put poisoned bread out for them, they would die, and then rats, bread, and meat would go into the hoppers together. . . . All of their sausage came out of the same bowl, but when they came to wrap it they would stamp some of it "special," and for this they would charge two cents more a pound.

---

truly made their mark. In 1905, Samuel Hopkins Adams published a series of articles on the patent-medicine business in *Collier's Weekly*. The first paragraph opened with these riveting words:

> Gullible America will spend this year some seventy-five millions of dollars in the purchase of patent medicines. In consideration of this sum it will swallow huge quantities of alcohol, an appalling amount of opiates and narcotics, a wide assortment of varied drugs ranging from powerful and dangerous heart depressants to insidious liver stimulants; and, far in excess of all other ingredients, undiluted fraud. For fraud, exploited by the skillfullest of advertising bunco men, is the basis of the trade.

In the Agriculture Department, the chemist Harvey W. Wiley had long been analyzing the chemical adulteration of food products. He began to test the additives on twelve healthy, young male volunteers who had agreed to serve as guinea pigs in the public interest. Wiley's

"Poison Squad" captured national attention. Numerous pure food and drug bills, introduced in Congress in 1905, had been stymied by industry lobbies. Then, in 1906, Upton Sinclair's novel *The Jungle* appeared. Sinclair had aimed at exposing labor exploitation in the Chicago meat-packing houses, but his graphic descriptions of rotten meat and filthy conditions excited—and sickened—the nation. President Roosevelt, hitherto not greatly concerned about consumer issues, now threw his weight into the legislative battle. Congress passed the Pure Food and Drug and Meat Inspection acts within months.

During the 1904 presidential campaign, Roosevelt had taken to calling his program the "Square Deal." This kind of labeling was new to American politics. It introduced a political style that dramatized issues, mobilized public opinion, and asserted leadership. But the Square Deal meant something of substance as well. After many years of passivity and weakness, the federal government had reclaimed the large role it had abandoned after the Civil War. Now, however, the target became the new economic order. When companies misused corporate power, the government had the responsibility of correcting matters and assuring Americans of a "square deal." Under Roosevelt's leadership, progressivism had come to national politics.

The Aftermath of Colonial Expansion

Theodore Roosevelt left a similar imprint of vigorous action—laced with prudence—on the conduct of the nation's foreign affairs. He had been thrust into the presidency in 1901 just as the United States was concluding its brief burst of overseas expansion by subduing the Filipino independence movement. The next step was to exploit the resulting strategic opportunities in the Caribbean and the Pacific. This was Roosevelt's main foreign policy task, and he welcomed it.

In the 1890s, Roosevelt had been an exuberant expansionist and an admirer of the geopolitics of Captain Alfred T. Mahan. "All the great masterful races have been fighting races," Roosevelt declared. Nothing would be worse for the United States, already too commercial for his aristocratic taste, than "slothful and ignoble peace." But a nation's power had to be used only for good ends and, in particular, to keep the world from sliding into anarchy. Roosevelt stated his foreign policy in a colorful phrase, "Speak softly and carry a big stick." The international forces for disorder were such, he maintained, as to "render it incumbent on all civilized and orderly powers to insist on the proper policing of the world." This view licensed the United States to exert power as needed in regions that, because of the country's overseas expansion, had fallen under its direct influence.

A canal across Central America headed Roosevelt's agenda. After persuading Britain in 1901 to give up its treaty right to a joint canal enterprise, Roosevelt proceeded to more troublesome matters. During the 1880s, a company headed by Ferdinand M. de Lesseps, a French engineer, had started to build a canal across the isthmus of Panama, a province of Colombia. De Lesseps had previously directed the construction of the Suez Canal. The United States agreed to pay $40 million for the company that owned the de Lesseps assets. The Roosevelt administration then entered into negotiations with Colombia to lease the strip of land through which the canal would run. The Colombian legislature voted down the proposed treaty, partly because the company's rights would soon expire and the sale to the United States could then be renegotiated to Colombia's benefit. Furious over what seemed to him a breach of faith, Roosevelt contemplated outright seizure of Panama but settled on a more devious solution.

The key intermediary in the sale of the de Lesseps assets, an engineer named Philippe Bunau-Varilla, let Roosevelt know that an independence movement was brewing in Panama. The United States in turn informed Bunau-Varilla that American naval ships were steaming toward Panama. When the U.S.S. *Nashville* dropped anchor at Colon on November 3, 1903, the revolution against Colombian rule went off on schedule. The United States recognized Panama the next day. Less than two weeks later, with Bunau-Varilla serving as representative of the new republic, Panama signed a treaty with the United States. The agreement granted the United States a perpetually renewable lease on a canal zone. The Panama Canal, completed in 1914, gave the United States a commanding

THE PANAMA CANAL

The Canal Zone was acquired through devious means in which Americans could take no pride (and which led in 1978 to the Senate's decision to restore the property to Panama). But the building of the Panama Canal itself was a triumph of American ingenuity and drive. Dr. William C. Gorgas cleaned out the malarial mosquitoes that had earlier stymied the French. Under Col. George W. Goethals, the U.S. army overcame formidable obstacles of terrain and construction in a mighty feat of engineering. This photograph shows the lower main gates of the Miroflores Locks on July 5, 1913 as the canal nears completion. (Historical Pictures Service)

commercial and strategic position in the Western hemisphere.

Next came the task of making the Caribbean Basin secure. The countries there, said Secretary of State Elihu Root, had been placed "in the front yard of the United States" by the Panama Canal. Therefore, as Roosevelt put it, they had to "behave themselves." In the case of Cuba, this was readily managed in the settlement following the Spanish-American War. Before the United States withdrew from Cuba in 1902, it reorganized Cuban finances and concluded a sanitation program that eliminated yellow fever from the island. This disease had ravaged Cuba for many years. As a condition for gaining independence, Cuba was required to include in its constitution a proviso called the Platt Amendment. The amendment gave the United States the right to intervene if Cuban independence were threatened or if Cuba failed to maintain internal order. Cuba also granted the United States a permanent lease on Guantanamo Bay, where the U.S. Navy built a large base.

Roosevelt believed that instability in the Caribbean invited the intervention of European powers. For example, Britain and Germany blockaded Venezuela in 1902–1903 for failing to meet its debt payments. In 1904, Roosevelt announced that the United States would act as

"policeman" of the region, stepping in "however reluctantly, in flagrant cases . . . of wrongdoing or impotence." This policy became known as the Roosevelt Corollary to the Monroe Doctrine. Under its cloak, the United States intervened regularly in the internal affairs of Caribbean states. In 1905, the United States took over the custom and debt management of the Dominican Republic. When similar financial intervention by the United States touched off a rebellion in Nicaragua in 1912, American marines landed and occupied the country.

Roosevelt's thinking was primarily strategic; his successor, William Howard Taft, took a more commercial view. American investments in the Caribbean region grew dramatically during the Taft administration, from 1909 to 1913. The United Fruit Company owned about 160,000 acres in Central American countries by 1913, and U.S. investments in Cuban sugar plantations quadrupled in fifteen years. Taft quickly intervened when disorder threatened American property. But he also regarded business investment as a force for stability in underdeveloped areas. Taft spoke for "dollar diplomacy," the aggressive coupling of American diplomatic and economic interests abroad.

In the Far East, commercial interests had always stood at the forefront. In 1899, with China carved up into spheres of influence, Secretary of State John Hay sent an "Open Door" note to the occupying powers seeking assurances of equal trading opportunities for all nations. The replies were noncommittal or ambiguous, but Hay chose to interpret them as accepting the American position. When a secret society of Chinese nationalists launched the Boxer Rebellion in 1900, the United States joined the campaign to raise the siege of the foreign legations in Peking. America took the opportunity to assert a second principle to the Open Door, the preservation of China as a "territorial and administrative entity." As long as the legal fiction of an independent China survived, so would American claims to equal access to the China market.

In the wake of the Spanish-American War, the United States had quickly consolidated its strategic position in the Pacific. The partition of the Samoan Islands in 1900 with Germany secured America's South Pacific anchor and completed the network of U.S. island bases. The naval strength of the United States could now be projected across the Pacific, where the nation faced strong rivals in Asia. The European powers had acceded to American claims to preeminence in the Caribbean, including the Roosevelt Corollary. But Britain, Germany, France, and Russia were strongly entrenched in the Far East, with no inclination to defer to American interests. The United States also confronted a strategically placed Asian nation—Japan—that had vital interests at stake.

Japan was a rising world power. It had unveiled its military strength in the Sino-Japanese War of 1894–1895, which began the dismemberment of China. The Anglo-Japanese Alliance of 1902 removed the English naval challenge to Japan in the Far East. In 1904, provoked by Russian assaults on Manchuria, Japan suddenly attacked the czar's fleet at Port Arthur, Russia's leased port in China. In a series of brilliant victories, the Japanese demolished the Russian military forces in Asia. Roosevelt, anxious to restore some semblance of a power balance, mediated a settlement of the Russo-Japanese War at Portsmouth, New Hampshire, in 1905. Japan emerged as the predominant power in North Asia.

Despite his bombastic rhetoric, Roosevelt took an accommodating stance toward Japanese expansionism. However, a surge of anti-Oriental feeling in California complicated his efforts. In 1906, the San Francisco school board placed all Asian students in a segregated school, infuriating Japan. The "gentlemen's agreement" of 1907, in which Japan agreed to restrict immigration to the United States, smoothed matters, but the periodic resurgence of racism in California led to continuing tensions with the proud Japanese. Roosevelt meanwhile moved to balance Japan's military power by increasing American naval strength in the Pacific. American battleships visited Japan in 1908 and then made a global tour in an impressive display of sea power. Late that year, near the end of his administration, Roosevelt achieved his accommodation with Japan. The Root-Takahira Agreement between the two nations confirmed the status quo in the Pacific, as well as the principles of free oceanic commerce and equal trade opportunity in China.

However, William Howard Taft entered the White House in 1909 convinced that the United States had been shortchanged. Throughout his administration, Taft pressed for a larger role in the Far East for American bankers and investors, especially in the railroad construction going on in China. Taft hoped that American capital could serve as a counterbalance against Japanese power and as a lever for increased commercial opportunities. When the Chinese Revolution of 1911 toppled the ruling Manchu dynasty, Taft supported the Chinese Nationalists as a new counterforce to the Japanese. The United States thus entered a long-term conflict with Japan that ended in war thirty years later.

The triumphant thrust across the Pacific lost its luster. The United States had become embroiled in a distant struggle that promised many future liabilities but little of the fabulous profits that had lured Americans to Asia. It was a chastening experience for an emerging world power.

The New Nationalism

During his two terms as president, Theodore Roosevelt struggled to bring a modern corporate economy under control. He was well aware that his Square Deal had built on nineteenth-century foundations. In his final presidential speeches, Roosevelt dwelt on the need for a reform agenda for the twentieth century. When he left office in

1909, he thought he had arranged matters so there would be steady movement in that direction. He was mistaken. By the time Roosevelt returned in 1910 from a year-long safari in Africa, turmoil reigned in Washington. Modern progressive reform would come, not from thoughtful debate or careful planning, but in political battle.

The agencies of historical change sometimes take strange forms. A person out of tune with the times can, by the sheer friction he or she generates, serve as the catalyst for great events. Such became the fate of William Howard Taft, Roosevelt's handpicked successor. Taft was an estimable man in many ways. He had been an able jurist and a superb administrator. He had served Roosevelt loyally and well as governor general of the Philippines and as secretary of war. But he was not by nature a progressive politician. Taft was incapable of dramatizing issues or of stirring the people. He disliked the give-and-take of politics, he distrusted power, and he generally deferred to Congress. Moreover, Taft was, in different ways than Roosevelt, deeply conservative. He sanctified property rights, he revered the processes of the law, and, unlike Roosevelt, he found it hard to trim his means to fit his ends.

By 1909, the reform ferment had unsettled the Republican party. On the right, the conservatives were girding themselves against further losses. Under Senator Aldrich, they still dominated on Capitol Hill and had strong influence in the party. On the other hand, progressive Republicans were rebellious. They had broad popular support, especially in the Midwest, and, in Robert La Follette, a fiery leader. And they were not about to be pawned off. The resourceful Roosevelt had somehow stymied them. No more compromise for them. To reconcile these conflicting forces within the Republican party would have been a daunting task for the most accomplished politician. For Taft, it spelled disaster.

First there was the tariff. Taft had campaigned for "a sizable reduction." Senator Aldrich won him over during the lengthy drafting process and he came out for the protectionist Payne-Aldrich Tariff Act of 1909, which especially favored eastern industry. Then Taft infuriated his former tariff-cutting allies by touring the country and touting the new tariff legislation as the "best" ever passed.

Next came the battle over "Uncle Joe" Cannon, the Speaker of the House of Representatives. Joseph G. Cannon of Illinois, a died-in-the-wool conservative, virtually controlled the flow of legislation in the House. Progressives were determined to depose him. Taft abandoned them in exchange for Cannon's help on administration legislation. A House revolt broke the Speaker's power in 1910. Cannon's defeat was regarded as a defeat for the president as well.

Most damaging to Taft was the Pinchot-Ballinger affair. U.S. Chief Forester Gifford Pinchot, an ardent conservationist and chum of Roosevelt's, accused Taft's Secretary of the Interior, Richard A. Ballinger, of involvement in a scheme to transfer public coal lands in Alaska to a private syndicate. When Pinchot went public with the charges in January 1910, Taft fired him for insubordination. A true conservationist, Taft compiled a stronger record of protecting the wilderness than had Roosevelt. Somehow it did not matter. In the eyes of the Progressives, the Pinchot-Ballinger affair marked Taft for life as a friend of the "interests."

Solemnly pledged to carrying on in Roosevelt's tradition, Taft managed to work his way into the conservative Republican camp in less than two years. While doing so, he helped transform the reformers into a distinct faction of the party. By 1910, they were calling themselves "Progressives" or, in more belligerent moments, "insurgents." Taft responded by trying to purge them in the Republican primaries that year. This vendetta climaxed Taft's record of disastrous leadership.

The Progressives emerged much stronger and angrier than before. They formed the National Progressive Republican League in January 1911 and began a drive to take control of the Republican party. La Follette was the Progressives' leader and their designated presidential candidate, but they knew their best hope would be Theodore Roosevelt.

Roosevelt, home from Africa, yearned to re-enter the political fray. He was not easily reconciled to the absence of power and would have been troublesome for Taft under any circumstances. As it was, the president's handling of the Progressives fed Roosevelt's mounting sense of outrage. But Roosevelt was too loyal a party man to defy the Republican establishment, and too astute a politician not to recognize that a party split would benefit the Democrats. He could be spurred into rebellion only by the discovery of a true clash of philosophies.

Taft again proved obliging. He attacked the problem of economic concentration—the overriding issue of the day—in a way that crystallized Roosevelt's thinking and led him to formulate a policy called the New Nationalism.

From the first, Roosevelt had been troubled by the Sherman Antitrust Act. To enforce competition seemed to him to fly in the face of the inevitable modern tendency toward economic concentration. By distinguishing betwen good and bad trusts, Roosevelt had managed to reconcile public policy and economic reality. But this was a makeshift solution, depending as it did on a president inclined to stretch his powers to the limit. Taft had no such inclination. His legalistic mind rebelled at the discretionary use of presidential authority. The Sherman Act was on the books. "We are going to enforce that law or die in the attempt," Taft promised grimly. Attorney General George W. Wickersham stepped up the pace of antitrust actions, taking no notice of the "gentlemen's agreements."

Giant business firms found themselves caught in a legal dilemma. If they competed freely, they would drive out weaker companies and be guilty of monopoly. But if they tried to share the market with these companies, they would be guilty of conspiracy in restraint of trade. Taft's blindness to this dilemma forced some big-business leaders, especially those active in the National Civic Federation, to advocate a basic shift of public policy away from the Sherman Act.

This conclusion was driven home to Roosevelt in a peculiarly painful way. A government suit against the United States Steel Corporation in 1911 charged that the firm had violated the antimonopoly clause of the Sherman Act by acquiring the Tennessee Coal and Iron Company in 1907. That acquisition had been personally approved by Roosevelt as a necessary step—so U.S. Steel representatives explained it to him—to prevent a financial collapse on Wall Street. The suit thus amounted to a humiliating attack on Roosevelt. Either he had conspired to circum-vent the Sherman Act or he had been tricked by U.S. Steel. Nothing was better calculated to propel Roosevelt into action than an issue that was both an affair of personal honor and a question of broad principle.

The country did not have to choose between breaking up big business and submitting to corporate rule, Roosevelt argued. There was a third way. The federal government could be empowered to oversee big business to make sure it acted in the public interest. In a speech in Osawatomie, Kansas, in August 1910, Roosevelt discussed what he termed the New Nationalism. The central issue, he said, was human welfare versus property rights. In modern society, property had to be controlled "to whatever degree the public welfare may require it." The government would become "the steward of the public welfare."

This formulation removed the restraints from Roosevelt's thinking. Ultimately, he did not stop short of advocating government price fixing for corporate industry. He took up the cause of social justice, adding to his program a federal child labor law, federal workmen's compensation, regulation of labor relations, and a minimum wage for women. Then, recognizing the courts as a bastion of conservatism, Roosevelt took them on by proposing sharp curbs on their powers and even popular recall of court decisions.

Beyond these specifics, the New Nationalism presented a new political philosophy. As propounded in Herbert Croly's *The Promise of American Life* (1909), the New Nationalism called for uniting rival strains in the American political tradition. From Hamilton's federalism, it took reliance on strong national government; from Jefferson's republicanism, regard for the interests of the common man. The New Nationalism marked a genuine break from America's political past.

Early in 1912, Roosevelt announced his candidacy for the presidency and immediately swept the progressive Republicans into his camp. A bitter and divisive battle ensued. Taft proved a tenacious opponent. Roosevelt virtually swept the field in states that held primary elections. But Taft controlled the party organizations elsewhere. The party regulars dominated the national convention, and they threw the nomination to Taft.

Roosevelt, considering himself cheated out of the nomination, led his followers into a new Progressive party. In a crusading campaign, he offered New Nationalism to the people.

The New Freedom

A rival reform philosophy was emerging within the Democratic party. Demoralized since the free-silver campaign of 1896, the Democrats had come to life in the 1910 elections. They won a number of traditionally Republican governorships and gained a solid majority in the House of Representatives for the first time since 1892. William Jennings Bryan, after fourteen years as party leader and three tries at the presidency, reluctantly made way for a new generation of leaders who had been swept into office by the reform wave.

The ablest, by all odds, was Woodrow Wilson of New Jersey. A noted political scientist, he had served for eight years as president of Princeton University. Then, defeated in a controversy over graduate-school education at Princeton, he resigned to accept the Democratic nomination for governor of New Jersey in 1910. Wilson compiled a brilliant record as governor and won the Democratic presidential nomination in 1912. He could identify himself as a reformer by his achievements in New Jersey—defeat of the boss system and passage of a direct primary law, workmen's compensation, and regulation of railroads and utilities.

Wilson had, to a fault, the qualities of moral certainty that characterized the progressive politician. A brilliant speaker, he almost instinctively assumed the mantle of righteousness—and, by the same token, had little tolerance for the views of his critics. At the time of his presidential nomination, Wilson had no national reform program. Only during the election campaign did he hammer out a coherent program to oppose Roosevelt's New Nationalism.

The New Freedom, as Wilson called his program, had its roots in old-fashioned Jeffersonian ideas. Born and bred in Virginia, Wilson was by tradition a states-rights Democrat. He supported low tariffs and disliked big government and special privilege. He believed in an independent, self-reliant citizenry. Wilson fashioned these traditional notions into a modern reform agenda.

July 13 1912   THE NEW RIDER   Price 10 Cents

ON TO THE WHITE HOUSE
At the Democratic convention, Woodrow Wilson only narrowly defeated the front-runner, Champ Clark of Missouri. *Harper's Weekly* triumphantly depicted Wilson immediately after his nomination—the scholar-turned politician riding off on the Democratic donkey, his running mate, Thomas R. Marshall, hanging on behind. *Harper's* editor, George Harvey, had identified Wilson as of presidential timber as early as 1906, long before the Princeton president had thought of politics, and worked on his behalf ever since. (The Newberry Library, Chicago)

Louis D. Brandeis, known as the "people's lawyer," gave Wilson a sophisticated critique of economic concentration. Bigness did not mean efficiency, Brandeis argued. On the contrary, the trusts were inherently wasteful compared to firms vigorously competing in a free market. Nor would the public interest be served by governmental oversight of big business. The more likely result would be a comfortable alliance between regulators and regulated. The country needed not a powerful trade commission, Brandeis concluded, but a better Sherman Antitrust

Act that would "so restrict the wrong use of competition that the right use of competition will destroy monopoly."

As he warmed to the debate, Wilson drew the issue in the fundamental terms of slavery and freedom. "This is a struggle for emancipation," he proclaimed in October 1912. "If America is not to have free enterprise, then she can have freedom of no sort whatever." Wilson also scorned Roosevelt's social-welfare program. It might be benevolent, he declared, but it also would be paternalistic and contrary to the traditions of a free people. The New Nationalism represented a future of collectivism, Wilson warned, whereas the New Freedom would conserve the political and economic liberties of the individual.

Wilson won the 1912 election. But did Americans prefer the New Freedom to the New Nationalism? One cannot judge by the outcome of the election. The Republican vote was divided.

Taft ran a poor third, but he kept Roosevelt from winning. Wilson received 42 percent of the popular vote—fewer votes than Bryan got against Taft in 1908—but won by a landslide in electoral votes. One sign of the reform-minded nature of the 1912 electorate was a record nine hundred thousand votes for the Socialist candidate, Eugene V. Debs. But because of the party splits, the 1912 election could not be considered a national referendum between the New Nationalism and the New Freedom.

Likewise on the matter of implementation. Would a victorious Roosevelt have put the New Nationalism into effect? This question also remains unanswerable. Roosevelt would certainly have had a hard time of it. Since the Progressive party had fielded only a presidential ticket, with no congressional candidates, Congress probably would have posed tremendous obstacles. Not only did Wilson win the presidency, but his

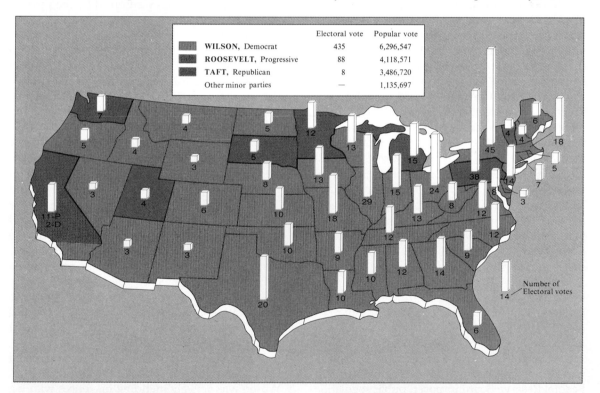

	Electoral vote	Popular vote
WILSON, Democrat	435	6,296,547
ROOSEVELT, Progressive	88	4,118,571
TAFT, Republican	8	3,486,720
Other minor parties	—	1,135,697

MAP 21.2 ELECTION OF 1912
The 1912 election reveals why the two-party system is so strongly rooted in American politics. The Democrats, although a minority party, won an electoral landslide because the Republicans became, in effect, two parties for the election. The disastrous result indicated the enormous incentive for major parties against splintering. The Socialists, despite a record vote of 900,000, got no electoral votes at all, suggesting the fatal weakness of third parties in the American political system. To vote Socialist in 1912 meant, in effect, to throw away one's vote.

party, for the first time since the 1850s, gained control of both houses of Congress. Yet the Democratic program eventually enacted was a far cry from Wilson's campaign pronouncement of the New Freedom.

Upon entering the White House, Wilson chose a flank attack on the problem of economic power. So long out of office, the Democrats were hungry for tariff reform. From the prevailing average of 40 percent, the Underwood Tariff Act of 1913 pared rates down to an average of 25 percent and applied the sharpest cuts to the trust-dominated industries. Democrats confidently expected the Underwood Tariff to spur competition and reduce prices in American markets.

The administration then turned to the nation's banking system, whose key weakness was the absence of a central reserve bank. In practice, this role had been assumed by the major New York banks, which accepted the deposits of lesser banks and assisted them if they came under pressure. However, if the New York institutions themselves weakened, the entire system could totter and even collapse. This had nearly happened during the Panic of 1907. The need for a reserve system became widely accepted, but the form it should take was hotly debated. Wall Street wanted a centralized system, controlled by the bankers. Rural Democrats and their spokesman, Senator Carter Glass of Virginia, preferred a decentralized network of reserve banks. Progressives of both parties agreed that the essential factor should be public control over the reserve system. The bankers, who had come under severe criticism from a congressional investigation of the "money trust" early in 1913, were on the defensive in this contest.

President Wilson, no expert to begin with, learned quickly and reconciled the reformers and bankers. The monumental Federal Reserve Act of 1913 gave the nation a banking system resistant to financial panic. The act delegated reserve functions to twelve district reserve banks, which would be controlled by the member banks. The Federal Reserve Board imposed public regulation on this regional structure. In one stroke, the act strengthened the banking system considerably and placed a measure of restraint on the "money trust."

Having dealt with tariff and banking reform, Wilson turned at last to the central issue of the New Freedom. The issue of economic concentration had seemed straightforward enough during the 1912 campaign. Roosevelt wanted to abandon the antitrust approach, while Wilson wished to make the existing Sherman Act airtight. Wilson's thinking had been crystallized by the recent Supreme Court decision in *Standard Oil v. United States* (1911), which ordered the dissolution of the oil trust. In this case the Court reasserted the "rule of reason"—that is, judicial discretion over what constituted illegal restraints of trade. At another time, this restoration to the Sherman Act of an ancient rule of the common law might have caused little controversy. But in 1911, the Standard Oil ruling seemed intended to weaken the antitrust act. In response, Wilson proposed revisions to the Sherman Act so tightly drawn as to nullify the rule of reason, including explicitly prohibiting such practices as price discrimination and interlocking directorates. Precise prohibitions, vigorously enforced by the government, made up the New Freedom approach to the problem of monopoly.

In midcourse, Wilson changed his mind. In its final version, the Clayton Antitrust Act of 1914 added the following phrase to the prohibited business practices: "where the effect may be to substantially lessen competition or tend to create a monopoly in any line of commerce." These words, in effect, amounted to a return to the rule of reason. The motive for Wilson's retreat was partly practical. He had lost confidence in the effectiveness of rigid legal prohibitions, and his adviser, Louis Brandeis, now advocated a regulatory approach. The idea of a powerful trade commission came from Roosevelt, but he had intended it to replace the antitrust law. Brandeis proposed that the trade commission enforce competition. The Federal Trade Commission Act of 1914 gave the FTC broad powers to investigate companies and to issue "cease and desist" orders against unfair trade practices that violated antitrust law.

However, the Clayton and FTC acts involved more than a tactical shift. By the spring of 1914, Wilson was actively mending his fences with big business. "The antagonism between business and Government is over," he proclaimed. To the chagrin of Brandeis, Wilson's appointees to the FTC were probusiness and disinclined to act as watchdogs over industrial activity. Cooperation, not prosecution, became the commission's watchword. Wilson himself showed little enthusiasm for trust busting—far less, certainly, than had Taft.

In the end, Wilson came close to the position Roosevelt had held under the Square Deal. Wilson welcomed business leaders, including J. P. Morgan, to the White House. In addition, the Justice Department announced its willingness to advise corporations about how to avoid antitrust actions. The Wilson administration thus raised the "gentlemen's agreements" pioneered by Roosevelt to the status of official national policy.

On social policy, too, Wilson drifted from the principles of the New Freedom. During the campaign, he had denounced the social program of the New Nationalism as paternalistic. Compared to his dealings with big business, Wilson proved resistant to "class" legislation for labor and agriculture. He accepted cosmetic language in the Clayton Act stating that labor and farm organizations were not illegal combinations. But he rejected the exemptions they wanted for immunity from antitrust prosecution.

The labor vote had grown increasingly important to the Democratic party, however. As the prospect of a second presidential campaign loomed larger, Wilson lost some of his scruples about prolabor legislation and championed a host of landmark bills beneficial to American workers. These included the Seamen's Act of 1915 and a model federal workmen's compensation law, a federal child labor law, and the Adamson eight-hour law for railroad workers, all in 1916. Likewise, after stubbornly resisting earlier farm-credit measures, Wilson approved in 1916 the Federal Farm Loan Act, providing the low-interest rural-credit system long demanded by farmers.

Four years in the White House carried Woodrow Wilson far from his Jeffersonian principles. In the end, he presided over a major intrusion of the federal government into people's lives. Wilson encountered the same kind of dilemmas that confronted all successful Progressives—the claims of moral principle versus the unyielding realities of political and economic life. Progressives were high minded but not radical. They saw evils in the system, but they did not consider the system itself evil. They also prided themselves on being realists as well as moralists. So it stood to reason that Wilson, like other Progressives who achieved power, would drift to the center.

Progressivism and the Mexican Intervention

Foreign affairs offered a better chance for holding to the moral ground of progressive idealism. So it seemed, at any rate, to Woodrow Wilson. For one thing, foreign matters did not involve the exasperating complexity of domestic America—those stubborn interests and demands that required constant trimming of Wilson's high-minded policy. The world stage seemed a simpler place for progressive reform, because the objective was to bring other nations into conformity with American ideals. Moreover, the power equation appeared more favorable beyond the nation's borders. The United States was a great power, overwhelmingly so in relation to its neighbors to the south. Mexico seemed less formidable in world affairs than, for example, the House of Morgan in domestic politics.

To think in this vein, of course, betrayed Wilson's inexperience in world politics. He had far less knowledge about international affairs than had Theodore Roosevelt a decade earlier. Wilson's choice for secretary of state, William Jennings Bryan, knew more about diplomacy. But he, like Wilson, had a strong missionary and moralistic approach. Both of them deplored William Howard Taft's "dollar diplomacy" as the extension abroad of the business influence they were trying to curb at home. It seemed to Wilson "a very perilous thing to determine the foreign policy of a nation in terms of material interest."

Wilson aimed to foster the "development of constitutional liberty in the world" and, above all, to extend it to the nation's neighbors in Latin America. In a major policy speech in October 1913, he vowed to them that the United States would "never again seek one additional foot of territory by conquest." The president said he would strive to advance "human rights, national integrity, and opportunity" in Latin America. To do otherwise would make "ourselves untrue to our own traditions." Guided by such a moral policy, future generations would arrive at "those great heights where there shines unobstructed the light of the justice of God."

Mexico became the first object of Wilson's ministrations. A cycle of revolutions had begun there in 1911. The long dictatorship of Porfirio Diaz was overthrown by Francisco Madero, who

TIME LINE
THE PROGRESSIVE ERA

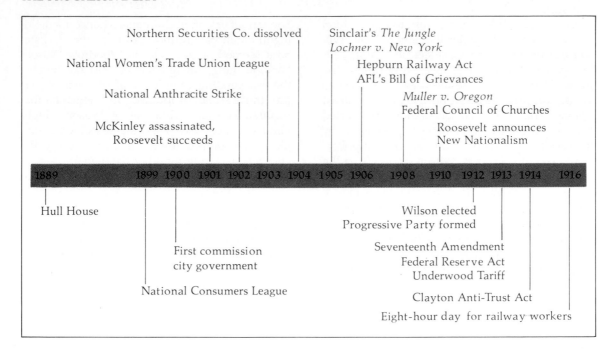

Northern Securities Co. dissolved

National Women's Trade Union League

National Anthracite Strike

McKinley assassinated,
Roosevelt succeeds

Sinclair's *The Jungle*
Lochner v. New York
Hepburn Railway Act
AFL's Bill of Grievances
Muller v. Oregon
Federal Council of Churches
Roosevelt announces
New Nationalism

1889   1899 1900 1901 1902 1903 1904 1905 1906   1908   1910 1912 1913 1914   1916

Hull House

First commission
city government

National Consumers League

Wilson elected
Progressive Party formed

Seventeenth Amendment
Federal Reserve Act
Underwood Tariff

Clayton Anti-Trust Act

Eight-hour day for railway workers

spoke much as Wilson did about liberty and constitutionalism. But before Madero could get very far with his reforms, he was deposed and murdered in February 1913 by his chief lieutenant, Victoriano Huerta. Other powers quickly recognized Huerta's provisional government, but the United States had not yet acted when Wilson entered the White House the next month.

Wilson abhorred Huerta and called his coup a "usurpation" and Huerta himself a murderer. Wilson pledged "to force him out." The United States denied recognition to Huerta's government, although this policy opposed America's long-standing tradition of recognizing new governments. Wilson also subjected Mexico to other pressures, including the threatened use of force. By intervening in this way, Wilson insisted, "we act in the interest of Mexico alone. ... We are seeking to counsel Mexico for its own good." Wilson meant he intended to put the Mexican revolution back on the constitutional path started by Madero.

Wilson's determination was strengthened by the emergence of armed opposition to Huerta in northern Mexico under Venustiano Carranza.

This constitutionalist movement, as it became known, gave Wilson some grounds for denying recognition to Huerta—his government did not fully control the country. More important, it signified to Wilson the vitality of the reformist politics that he wanted to foster in Mexico.

The Constitutionalists were ardent nationalists. They had no desire for American intervention in Mexican affairs. Moreover, they wanted a complete revolution. Carranza angrily rebuffed Wilson's efforts to bring about elections through a compromise between the rebels and the Mexican government. He also vowed to resist by force any intrusion of U.S. troops in his country. All he wanted from Wilson, Carranza asserted, was recognition of the Constitutionalists' belligerent status so they could purchase arms in the United States. In exchange for vague promises to respect property rights and "fair" foreign concessions, Carranza finally got his way in 1914. American weapons began to flow to his troops.

The American contribution to the Constitutionalists' cause went much further than selling them arms. For one thing, Wilson isolated Huerta diplomatically. Huerta's crucial support came from the British, who wanted to ensure a steady flow of Mexican oil for their fleet. Under intense pressure from Washington, the British withdrew recognition from Huerta in late 1913—in return for making the United States the guarantor of British property interests in Mexico. When it became clear that neither the loss of British support nor the supplying of Carranza would turn the trick against Huerta, the United States threw its own forces into the game.

Using the pretext of a minor insult to the U.S. Navy at Tampico, Wilson ordered the occupation of the major port of Vera Cruz on April 21, 1914. This action cost 19 American and 126 Mexican lives. With Wilson preparing for a thrust at Mexico City, the Huerta regime began to crumble. Carranza nevertheless condemned the United States for intervening, and his own forces came close to engaging the Americans. When he entered Mexico City in triumph in August 1914, Carranza had some cause to thank the United States. But if any sense of gratitude existed, it was overshadowed by the anti-Americanism inspired by Wilson's insensitivity to Mexican pride and revolutionary zeal.

The later phases of the Mexican revolution dragged the United States ever more deeply into the unprofitable morass of interventionism. No sooner had the Constitutionalists triumphed than Carranza was challenged by his northern general, Pancho Villa. This illiterate but shrewd former bandit had carefully cultivated American representatives in Mexico and won their support in his bid for power against Carranza. But Carranza defeated Villa and drove him northward.

Meanwhile, World War I had broken out, and the United States became entangled with Germany over submarine attacks on civilian ships. The stakes of continued friction with Mexico began to rise. The Wilson administration granted *de facto* recognition to the Carranza government on October 9, 1915.

Pancho Villa was not finished, however. Reduced to the status of a bandit leader, he began to attack U.S. citizens. He killed sixteen Americans after taking them from a train in Chihuahua in January 1916, and then crossed the border and razed the town of Columbus, New Mexico, in March. If Villa wanted to stir up trouble between Washington and Mexico City, he succeeded thoroughly. Wilson sent troops led by General John J. Pershing into Mexico after the elusive Villa. Carranza accepted this action at first, but he grew alarmed as the Americans penetrated deeply into his country. Pershing's force continually increased in size so that it resembled an army of occupation more than a punitive expedition. Mexican public opinion demanded that

IN PURSUIT OF
PANCHO VILLA
Pancho Villa's attacks on American citizens were an early example of the terrorism that bedevils American foreign policy in the 1980s. Similarly, Pershing's punitive expedition into Mexico in response was an early demonstration of the difficulties great powers encounter in trying to seize terrorists able to melt away into a larger civilian society. The invading U.S. troops captured some of Pancho Villa's followers, but the wily Villa (center) and his main force got away. (The Bettmann Archive)

Pershing withdraw immediately. But Americans insisted that the threat to U.S. security be stamped out first. Armed clashes with Mexican troops began.

At the brink of war, the two governments backed off. Tempers cooled during a period of inconclusive negotiation, and the U.S. troops began to withdraw early in 1917. With its new constitution ratified and elections completed, the Carranza government received official recogni-

tion from Washington on March 13, 1917, less than a month before the United States entered World War I.

This sad chapter in Mexican-American relations might have been worthwhile if it had taught Woodrow Wilson a lesson, but it did not. The same mixture of high principle, bullying methods, and masked national interest played itself out on a grander stage at Versailles in 1919—with far more tragic results.

A new chapter in American reform began at the start of the twentieth century. For decades, the problems resulting from industrialization and city growth had been mounting. Now, after 1900, a broad progressive movement sprang up that dominated the nation's public life until World War I intervened. The unifying element in the reform activity was a common intellectual outlook, highly principled and idealistic as to goals, and confident of the human capacity to find the means.

Beyond this shared outlook, progressivism broke up into diverse, often conflicting, groups. Political reformers, for example, included business groups concerned chiefly with improving the efficiency of city government. There also were state reformers, such as Robert La Follette, who opposed privilege and wanted to democratize the political process. Both groups worked—in different ways—to enhance their power against entrenched party machines.

Progressivism also drew new groups into reform activity. Social welfare became very much

the province of American women, and the social feminism that resulted had a strong influence on the struggle for women's rights. In the cities, working people and immigrants also became reform minded and thereby set in motion a new political force, urban liberalism.

At the national level, attention focused primarily on controlling the economic power that had become concentrated in corporate business. This overriding problem led to Theodore Roosevelt's Square Deal, then his New Nationalism, and finally to Woodrow Wilson's New Freedom. During the course of these developments, a troubling weakness of progressivism became apparent: righteous idealism could not be easily accommodated to the need for compromise in the real world of power and diversity. Wilson managed well enough on the domestic front, but not when he encountered the outside world. This problem became apparent in the American involvement in the Mexican revolution. The stakes grew vastly higher after the United States entered World War I.

Suggestions for Further Reading

Reform Impulses

The best narrative treatments of the Progressive era are two volumes in the New American Nation Series: George E. Mowry, *The Era of Theodore Roosevelt: 1900–1912* (1958) and Arthur S. Link, *Woodrow Wilson and the Progressive Era: 1900–1917* (1954). Harold U. Faulkner, *The Quest for Social Justice, 1898–1914* (1931) is a useful portrait of the social setting within which progressivism developed. The most influential interpretation of

progressive reform, although its arguments have been effectively disputed, is Richard Hofstadter's *Age of Reform* (1955). A radical critique that stresses the reforming role of big business is James Weinstein, *The Corporate Ideal in the Liberal State, 1900–1918* (1968). Robert H. Wiebe, *The Search for Order, 1877–1920* (1967) places progressive reform in a broader context of organizational development.

The progressive mind has been studied from many different angles. The religious underpinnings are stressed in Robert M. Crunden, *Ministers of Reform: The Progressives' Achievement in American Civilization, 1889–1920* (1982). In *The New Radicalism in America, 1889–1963* (1965), Christopher Lasch sees progressivism as a form of cultural revolt. Samuel Haber traces the influence of Frederick W. Taylor in *Efficiency and Uplift: Scientific Management in the Progressive Era* (1964). On the intellectual basis for progressivism, the key book is Morton White, *Social Thought in America: The Revolt Against Formalism* (1975). For leading figures in this anti-formalist tradition, see Samuel Konefsky, *The Legacy of Holmes and Brandeis* (1956) and David Riesman, *Thorstein Veblen* (1963). On political thinkers, the most useful book is Charles Forcey, *The Crossroads of Liberalism: Croly, Weyl, Lippmann and the Progressive Era* (1961). Clarke A. Chambers, *Paul U. Kellog and the Survey* (1971) treats one of the key social investigators. For the muckrakers, see Louis Filler, *Crusaders for American Liberalism* (1938); Harold S. Wilson, *McClure's Magazine and the Muckrakers* (1970); and, for documents, Arthur and Lila Weinberg, eds., *The Muckrakers* (1961). To savor fully this brand of journalism, the reader should turn to Lincoln Steffens, *The Shame of the Cities* (1904) and, for one career, *The Autobiography of Lincoln Steffens* (1931).

Political Reform

Political reform has been the subject of a voluminous literature. Wisconsin progressivism can be studied in David P. Thelen, *The New Citizenship: Origins of Progressivism in Wisconsin, 1885–1900* (1972); Thelen, *Robert LaFollette and the Insurgent Spirit* (1976); and Robert S. Maxwell, *LaFollette and the Rise of Progressivism in Wisconsin* (1956). Other important state progressives are treated in Spencer C. Olin, *California's Prodigal Son: Hiram Johnson and the Progressive Movement* (1968); Robert F. Wesser, *Charles Evans Hughes: Politics and Reform in New York State, 1905–1910* (1967); and Richard Lowitt, *George W. Norris: The Making of a Progressive* (1963). On city reform, see Bradley R. Rice, *Progressive Cities: The Commission Government Movement* (1972); Jack Tager, *The Intellectual as Urban Reformer: Brand Whitlock and the Progressive Movement* (1968); and Melvin G. Holli, *Reform in Detroit: Hazen S. Pingree and Urban Politics* (1969).

Social Reform

On social feminism, the reader should begin with Allen F. Davis, *American Heroine: Jane Addams* (1973) and George Martin, *Madame Secretary: Frances Perkins* (1976). The connection to working women is effectively treated in Nancy S. Dye, *As Equals and Sisters, Feminism, the Labor Movement, and the Women's Trade Union League of New York* (1980). On the ideology of women's suffrage, see Aileen Kraditor, *Ideas of the Women's Suffrage Movement, 1890–1920* (1965). The best treatment of the settlement-house movement is Allen F. Davis, *Spearheads of Reform* (1967). The struggle for tenement-house reform is ably covered in Roy Lubove, *The Progressives and the Slums, 1890–1917* (1962). The seminal essay on urban liberalism is J. Joseph Huthmacher, "Urban Liberalism and the Age of Reform," *Mississippi Valley Historical Review* 44 (September 1962): 231–241. Huthmacher's ideas have been fully developed in John D. Buenker, *Urban Liberalism and Progressive Reform* (1973). The relationship to organized labor can be followed in Irwin Yellowitz, *Labor and the Progressive Movement in New York City* (1965). The rise of American nativism has received authoritative treatment in John Higham, *Strangers in the Land* (1955). James H. Timberlake, *Prohibition and the Progressive Crusade* (1963) covers another important aspect of progressive moralism.

Progressivism and National Politics

National progressivism is best approached through its leading figures. Good biographies include: William Harbaugh, *Power and Responsibility: The Life and Times of Theodore Roosevelt* (1961); G. Wallace Chessman, *Theodore Roosevelt and the Politics of Power* (1969); John Morton Blum, *The Republican Roosevelt* (1954); Donald E. Anderson, *William Howard Taft* (1973); Arthur S. Link, *Woodrow Wilson* (5 vols., 1947–65); John Morton Blum, *Woodrow Wilson and the Politics of Morality* (1956). Aspects of national progressive politics can be followed in James Penick, *Progressive Politics and Conservation: The Ballinger-Pinchot Affair* (1968); Robert Wiebe, *Businessmen and Reform* (1962); Gabriel Kolko, *The Triumph of Conservatism* (1963); James Holt, *Congressional Insurgents and the Party System* (1969). On the South, a comprehensive treatment is provided by Jack Temple Kirby, *Darkness at the Dawning: Race and Reform in the Progressive South* (1972).

On progressive diplomacy, the starting point remains Howard K. Beale, *Theodore Roosevelt and the Rise of America to World Power* (1956). On the thrust into the Caribbean, see Walter LaFeber, *The Panama Canal* (1979); Dana G. Munroe, *Intervention and Dollar Diplomacy in the Caribbean, 1900–1921* (1964); and David Healy, *The United States in Cuba, 1898–1902* (1963). Akira Iriye, *Pacific Estrangement: Japanese and American Expansion, 1897–1911* (1972) covers the Pacific theatre effectively. The Mexican involvement is treated in P. Edward Haley, *Revolution and Intervention: The Diplomacy of Taft and Wilson with Mexico, 1910–1917* (1917). There is a lively and critical analysis of Wilson's misguided policies in Robert E. Quirk, *An Affair of Honor: Woodrow Wilson and the Occupation of Vera Cruz* (1962). The revolution as experienced by the Mexicans is brilliantly depicted in John Womack, *Zapata and the Mexican Revolution* (1968).

22

PROGRESSIVISM GOES TO WAR

The course of American participation in World War I was fundamentally shaped by the progressive period that preceded it. The connections between progressivism and the war may not be immediately obvious. What greater contrast could there be to agitating for domestic reform than fighting a foreign war?

In fact, many Americans saw close links between the two experiences. Reformers eagerly embraced wartime America as an opportunity to put progressive ideals into practice. Educator and philosopher John Dewey argued that wars represented a "plastic juncture" when societies became more open to reason and new ideas. Business could be rationalized, class unity promoted, and scientific efficiency strengthened. In the collective effort of fighting and winning a war, society could be improved. Dewey's optimistic view matched the spirit of the times. Unfortunately, a dissenting observation by Randolph Bourne, an outspoken pacifist and intellectual who had once been a pupil of Dewey's, came closer to reality. "If the war is too strong for you to prevent," Bourne asked, "how is it going to be weak enough for you to control and mold to your liberal purposes?"

Progressivism also influenced the wartime roles of business and government. Mobilization encouraged large-scale industrial organization and set in motion an unparalleled expansion of the national administrative structure. The war experience completed the process of industrial development begun during the nineteenth century and accelerated the centralizing tendencies prominent in economic and political life since the late nineteenth century. As a result of World War I, the United States moved closer to the model of a corporate bureaucratic state that would prevail in the modern era, where the lines between the public and private sectors became increasingly blurred. However, older patterns of informal, localized power coexisted with the new bureaucratic order well into the twentieth century.

Foreign policy showed the link between progressivism and World War I most clearly. The crusading spirit of progressivism spilled over into world affairs, as it had during the Mexican crisis. President Woodrow Wilson declared that American participation would "make the world safe for democracy," "end all wars," and "bring peace and safety to all nations." Imperialism and power politics would give way to morality and good deeds. By pegging American involvement to such lofty goals, Wilson virtually guaranteed disappointment. Even if America won the war, his ideals for world reformation were too far-reaching for practical attainment.

Fighting the War

"It would be the irony of fate if my administration had to deal chiefly with foreign affairs," Woodrow Wilson confided to a friend early in his first term. His remark proved prophetic when Archduke Francis Ferdinand of Austria was assassinated in the Bosnian town of Sarajevo on June 28, 1914. The Great War—few anticipated a second world war just a generation later—erupted in August. Initially it pitted the Allies (Great Britain, France, Japan, Russia, and, in 1915, Italy) against the Central Powers (Germany, Austria-Hungary, Bulgaria, Romania, and Turkey). Early in the war, most Americans saw no reason to get involved in a war among Europe's imperialistic powers. So firmly did they support nonintervention that Wilson won reelection in 1916 with the slogan "He kept us out of war." But several months later, in April 1917, the president stood before Congress and asked for a declaration of war.

The Perils of Neutrality

The entry of the United States into World War I has often been portrayed as a sharp break from the nation's traditional isolation from world affairs. This view is only partly correct. The war did represent America's first sustained participation in European political affairs; after the conflict ended, the United States attained what seems a permanent place as a great world power. Yet the country had hardly been uninvolved in world affairs before 1917. America's dramatic industrial growth and increasing agricultural production during the nineteenth century had led to a search for new and wider markets. The United States found them not only in Europe or Africa, where Great Britain and Germany dominated, but also in Mexico, Canada, South America, and the Far East.

To accompany this economic expansion, American leaders developed a philosophy that provided the ideological basis for U.S. diplomacy.

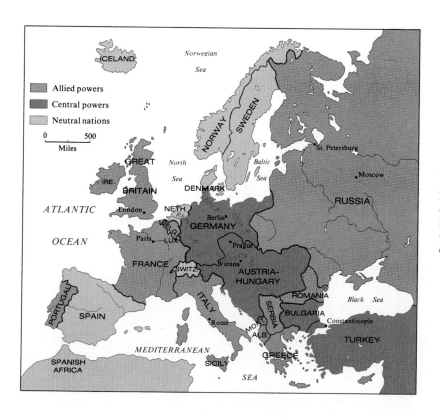

MAP 22.1 EUROPE AT THE START OF WORLD WAR I By early August 1914, a complex set of interlocking alliances had drawn the major European powers into war. At first, the United States held aloof from the conflict. The *Plain Dealer*, a Wabash, Indiana, newspaper, captured the prevailing isolationist sentiment when it noted, "We never appreciated so keenly as now the foresight of our fathers in emigrating from Europe." Not until April 1917 did the United States enter the war on the Allied side.

LOVE AND CRISIS IN THE PRESIDENT'S LIFE

The White House
13 September 1915

Monday morning, 9:50

My precious Darling,

The weight of public matters rests rather grievously upon me this morning and I have been obliged to fill the morning with many important engagements, beginning with the Secretary of State in half an hour, but there is one resource for me always: I can turn to you (what would it not be worth to me if I could *go* to you) and all the burden will fall away with the realization of your love and vital, comprehending sympathy.

The Secretary and I will be obliged this morning, I fear, to make some decisions that *may* affect the history of the country more than any decisions a President and Secretary of State ever made before and it gives me such a steadiness and added *balance* in my thinking that you have come to my side and put your hand in mine and given your splendid life to sustain mine. . . .

Your own
Woodrow

Source: Edwin Tribble, *A President in Love: The Courtship Letters of Woodrow Wilson and Edith Bolling Galt.* Boston: Houghton Mifflin, 1981. 178.

Expansion depended on a peaceful world order based on principles of international law and harmony. Specifically, capitalism flourished in an atmosphere of low national trade barriers, freedom of the seas, and strong support for neutrality rights. The Open Door policy in China, stressing free trade rather than spheres of influence, represented a commitment to such liberal capitalist expansion. The United States has followed this path throughout the world ever since.

Of course, commitments to free trade and peaceful economic expansion in the world marketplace served America's own national interests. For example, a strong belief in neutrality rights—the freedom to trade with nations on both sides of a conflict—suited the country's expansive trade policies. Similarly, persistent calls for national self-determination and the dismantling of European colonial empires opened new areas to American trade.

The economic expansion of the United States in the late nineteenth and early twentieth centuries raised the nation's stature as a world power. A combination of provincialism and arrogance made it feel superior to the great European powers. America had remained free of large standing armies, entangling alliances, and, excepting the Caribbean and Pacific acquisitions in the wake of the Spanish-American War, overseas imperial expansion. The prevailing American belief that the United States was different and better than the rest of the world played an important role in the national identity. It eventually compelled Woodrow Wilson to commit the United States to war.

Before the outbreak of war in 1914, Europe had enjoyed more than four decades of peace following the Franco-Prussian War of 1870. This peace was at best fragile. Chancellor Otto von Bismarck's unification of the German empire in 1871, coupled with Germany's dramatic industrial development, introduced a new force into world affairs, both diplomatically and economically. The rush of imperialism in the late nineteenth century represented another potentially divisive factor. Between 1880 and 1895, the major European powers acquired extensive colonial empires throughout the world. Africa, carved up among Britain, France, Germany, Italy, Belgium, and Portugal, became the main target for European imperialism, but domination extended to the Far East as well.

With the heyday of imperialist expansion in the late nineteenth century came increasing friction and rivalry among the great powers. In

1879, Bismarck proposed a military alliance that linked Germany with Austria-Hungary; the inclusion of Italy in 1882 completed the Triple Alliance. In response, France initiated the Franco-Russian alliance in 1894. Britain, with the oldest and most extensive colonial empire, initially stayed free of such entangling alliances. Then, in 1904, the British and French became allies through the *Entente Cordiale* (cordial understanding). In 1907, an alliance called the Triple Entente linked Britain, France, and Russia.

Skillful diplomacy and an unwillingness to resort to war kept minor disturbances from escalating into major conflicts throughout most of the late nineteenth and early twentieth centuries. The complex alliance system, however, had the potential for bringing a host of countries into war over a comparatively minor incident. Following the assassination of Archduke Francis Ferdinand in 1914, Austria declared war on Serbia. The assassin was a Bosnian student who lived in Serbia, and Austria-Hungary suspected that Serbia had been involved in the murder of the heir to the Austrian throne. The alliance system that had kept Europe out of war since 1870 now quickly pulled all the major powers into the conflict.

President Wilson called on the United States to remain neutral in thought and action. Two factors—economic and political ties with the Al-lies, and a commitment to neutrality rights and freedom of the seas—eventually undermined the nation's determination to steer clear of the European war. The United States enjoyed strong cultural and historic bonds with England and France, and its economic ties across the Atlantic were even stronger. Supplying the needs of the Allies had started an economic boom in the United States, and Wilson did not want to deflate the prosperity. American trade with England and France grew from $825 million in 1914 to $3.2 billion in 1916. By the time America officially entered the war in 1917, U.S. bankers had loaned the Allies $2.5 billion. In contrast, American trade with and loans to Germany in that year totaled only $29 million and $27 million, respectively.

Despite these American ties to the Allied cause, many British policies strained relations with the United States. Most troublesome was disagreement over neutrality rights. British naval policy conflicted with America's long-standing commitment to freedom of the seas. The British based their strategy against Germany on a blockade of continental Europe. They aimed to cripple the enemy's war effort by cutting off military supplies and starving the German people into submission. Such a blockade violated international law, which differentiated between "contraband," mainly munitions, and "non-contraband,"

THE PRESIDENT AND MRS. EDITH GALT
For Woodrow Wilson, love and war were interwoven. Wilson's first wife, Ellen, died in August 1914, just as war was breaking out in Europe. The next year the president carried on an intense courtship of Washington widow Edith Galt at the height of the submarine crisis. Here they attend a World Series game in Philadelphia shortly after their engagement. They were married in December 1915. (Library of Congress)

items such as foodstuffs or raw cotton. Although Germany legally was supposed to be able to import non-contraband items during wartime, Britain's blockade honored no such distinction. Neutral nations such as the United States were effectively prevented from trading at all with Germany and its allies. The United States chafed at the British infringement of the trading rights of neutral nations, but could do little else because of Britain's domination of the seas.

Meanwhile, Germany developed its own response to the British blockade. The Germans could not match the British in sea power, so they turned to a devastating weapon, a submarine called the U-boat, short for *Unterseeboot* (undersea boat). In 1915, Germany announced that its submarines would attack enemy ships caught transporting military supplies in the war zone between the European continent and the British Isles. Traditional rules of naval warfare required that the crew and passengers be allowed to leave their ship before an attacking vessel sank it. If a submarine surfaced to carry out this requirement, however, it lost its greatest advantage—surprise—and left itself vulnerable to attack. The Germans began sinking enemy ships without warning.

What if a U-boat attacked a neutral trading vessel or an unarmed passenger ship by mistake? This situation occurred when the Germans sank a British passenger liner, the *Lusitania*, off the Irish coast on May 7, 1915. Almost 1,200 people died when the *Lusitania* went down, including 128 Americans. The fact that the passenger ship carried military contraband came to light only later.

Woodrow Wilson sent a strong letter to Germany protesting this assault on the freedom of nonbelligerents to travel on the high seas. However, the president would not ban Americans from traveling on the ships of Germany's enemies to avoid such incidents in the future. The *Lusitania* episode divided Wilson's government into pro- and anti-British factions. Secretary of State William Jennings Bryan resigned in protest. Bryan could not support Wilson's harsh criticism of Germany's violation of neutrality rights, which he also feared might risk war, while at the same time the president remained silent about Britain violating American rights with its blockade.

Throughout 1915 and 1916, Wilson had tried at several points to mediate an end to the European conflict through his aide Colonel Edward House. However, House concluded that neither side was interested in serious peace negotiations. In the meantime, Wilson tried to remain flexible yet firm in his response to the German submarine attacks. His policy paid off, at least temporarily, when Germany agreed in May 1916 to end the unrestricted assaults. For the Germans, the danger of drawing the United States into the war over neutrality rights and freedom of the seas far offset the benefits of attacking British ships. A temporary lull set into the naval war. On land, the Allies and the Central Powers continued to grind each other down in the bloody stalemate of trench warfare that characterized the fighting during World War I. Between February and June 1916, for example, 350,000 French soldiers and 330,000 Germans died as Germany tried to break through the French lines at Verdun. The front did not move.

After the sinking of the *Lusitania,* Wilson had confided to a cabinet member, "I wish with all my heart I saw a way to carry out the double wish of our people, to maintain a firm front in respect of what we demand of Germany and yet do nothing that might by any possibility involve us in war." The events of early 1917 diminished whatever hope Wilson had of staying out of the conflict. On January 31, Germany announced the resumption of unrestricted submarine attacks, a decision dictated by the impasse of the ground war. Germany planned boldly to sever the trade links between America and the Allies. Even if submarine attacks brought the United States into the war, the Germans hoped to destroy Allied shipping and defeat the Allied armies before the Americans could join the fighting. In response, Wilson broke off diplomatic relations with Germany on February 3.

In March, U-boats started to attack American ships without warning, sinking three U.S. ships on March 18 alone. While these attacks continued to push the United States toward war, another event jolted American public opinion. The State Department released evidence of German interference in Mexican affairs—the so-called Zimmerman telegram, a communication from Germany's state secretary for foreign affairs to the German minister in Mexico City. In a direct snub to the Monroe Doctrine's warning to European powers not to interfere with nations of the Western Hemisphere, Germany urged Mexico, which American policymakers still considered a revolutionary trouble spot, to enter the war against the United States. In return, Germany promised to help Mexico recover its "lost provinces" of Texas, New Mexico, and Arizona. This threat to the territorial integrity of the United States brought the war even closer to home.

On April 2, 1917, President Wilson went before a special session of Congress and asked for a declaration of war. He had concluded that in order to influence the shape of the postwar peace, America would have to enter the fighting. The United States declared war on April 6, but six senators and fifty members of the House voted against the action. They included Representative Jeannette Rankin of Montana, the first woman elected to Congress. "I want to stand by my country," she declared, "but I cannot vote for war."

Setting War Aims

Woodrow Wilson linked American participation in the war with lofty ideals. "It is a fearful thing to lead this great peaceful people into war, into the most terrible and disastrous of all wars, civilization itself seeming to be in the balance," he stated when calling for a declaration of war.

> But the right is more precious than peace, and we shall fight for the things which we have always carried nearest our hearts—for democracy, for the right of those who submit to authority to have a voice in their own Government, for the rights and liberties of small nations, for a universal dominion of right by such a concert of free peoples as shall bring peace and safety to all nations and make the world itself at last free.

Several factors led Wilson to justify the war in ideologically charged terms. In the first place, as reflected by the lack of unanimity in Congress, the nation remained deeply divided about the war. From 1886 to 1916, almost twenty million immigrants had come to the United States. The 1910 census estimated that a third of the population was foreign born, or had at least one parent born abroad. While the sympathies of these new

Americans gravitated towards the Allies, such loyalty was potentially unstable. Irish-Americans felt anger at the harsh British suppression of Ireland's Easter Rebellion in 1916. Many recent immigrants traced their heritage to one of the Central Powers. German-Americans made up the largest, best-established ethnic group in the United States. Many aspects of German culture, including music and Germany's university system, were widely admired. Such factors limited support for American involvement on the Allied side.

A strong antiwar movement also limited the support for American participation in the war. Pacifist sentiment was broad but diffuse. Progressive Republican senators, such as Robert La Follette of Wisconsin and George Norris of Nebraska, opposed Wilson's call for armaments. Practically the entire political left, led principally by Eugene Debs and the Socialist party, spoke out forcefully against the war. Strong pacifist groups, among them the American Union Against Militarism and the Women's Peace party, also mobilized popular opposition. Feminists Jane Addams and Crystal Eastman were especially outspoken against war as an instrument of national policy. So were the prominent industrialists Andrew Carnegie and Henry Ford, who bankrolled antiwar activities. Ford spent half a million dollars in December 1915 to send more than a hundred men and women on a "peace ship" to Europe in the hope of hastening a negotiated end to the war.

Ironically, the 1916 election had not served as an American referendum on European affairs. The Republicans passed over Theodore Roosevelt and his prowar belligerence in favor of Justice Charles Evans Hughes of the Supreme Court, a former reform governor of New York. The Democrats renominated Wilson. Many observers saw little difference between the foreign policies of the two candidates, although the Democrats picked up votes with their widely circulated campaign slogan about keeping the United States out of war. They won a narrow victory over a Republican party reunited after its 1912 split. Despite polling three million more votes than he had received in 1912, Wilson defeated Hughes by only about six hundred thousand popular votes and a twenty-three-vote majority in the electoral college. This slender

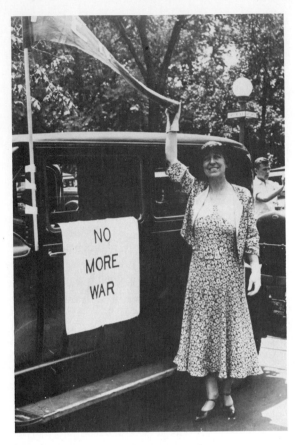

JEANNETTE RANKIN
Jeannette Rankin, a former suffrage organizer, was the
first woman elected to Congress, in 1916. She actively
supported protective legislation, prohibition, and
"preparedness that will make for peace." Her vote against
U.S. entry into World War I in 1917 cost her the chance
for election to the Senate in 1918. In 1940, Rankin once
again won election to Congress from Montana. True to
her lifelong commitment to pacifism, she cast the only
vote against U.S. entry into World War II. (The Bettmann
Archive)

margin limited Wilson's options both in mobilizing the nation for war and planning the postwar
peace.

The president's personality also played a
prominent role in his decision to justify the war
in sweeping terms. Wilson, the child of a Presbyterian minister, approached foreign affairs
with missionary zeal. He never doubted the superiority of the Christian values he had learned
as a boy. In his mind, private morality and public policy were two sides of the same coin. Such

an orientation had guided his response to the
Mexican situation several years earlier.

Throughout his terms as president, Woodrow
Wilson eloquently articulated a vision of a new
international order based on American ideals. In
January 1917, he proposed a "peace without victory," reminding his audience that only "a peace
among equals" would last. At other times, he
called for security against aggression; an end to
secret diplomacy; and the right of nations, large
and small, to choose their own sovereignty. He
envisioned a permanent international tribunal to
settle disputes and uphold national rights of self-
determination and freedom. His goal, Wilson
stated, was "not a balance of power, but a community of power; not organized rivalries, but an
organized common peace."

Wilson declared his highest ideals in January
1918, when he announced his Fourteen Points in
a speech to Congress. Although the outcome of
the war was still in doubt in early 1918, the Fourteen Points represented Wilson's blueprint for
the peace to follow. The president called for
open diplomacy, "absolute freedom of navigation upon the seas," removal of economic barriers to trade, an international commitment to
territorial integrity, and arms reduction.

More specifically, the fifth point reaffirmed
Wilson's long-standing commitment to national self-determination and an end to colonial
empires. He proposed redrawing national
boundaries following the breakup of the
Austrian-Hungarian, Russian, and German empires, including the creation of an independent
Polish state. The highlight of Wilson's vision
was the last point, the creation of a multinational
organization "for the purpose of affording
mutual guarantees of political independence and
territorial integrity to great and small States
alike." This League of Nations became Wilson's
obsession.

The Fourteen Points matched the spirit of
progressivism. Widely distributed as propaganda during the final months of the war, they
proposed to extend the benefits of the American
way of life—democracy, freedom, and peaceful
economic expansion—to the rest of the world.
The League of Nations would serve as a kind of
Federal Trade Commission for the world.

Unfortunately, Wilson's lofty pronouncements did not sit well with America's allies.

Britain, for example, had much to lose from open diplomacy and freedom of the seas. Wilson's call for self-determination of colonial peoples clashed with Allied plans for the acquisition of Germany's colonies at the end of the war. Furthermore, his humanitarian vision of a world made safe for democracy and peaceful economic expansion struck many European leaders as a self-centered view. They thought Wilson had conveniently defined the interests of the world as synonymous with those of the United States. The Fourteen Points produced the first of many misunderstandings that doomed both the Treaty of Versailles and the League of Nations.

Over There

After the declaration of war, many Americans were surprised to learn that their country planned to send troops to Europe. They had naively assumed that the nation's participation could be limited to military and economic aid. The United States had always avoided having a large standing army in peacetime; it had only 175,000 soldiers, mostly life-time volunteers, on active duty in 1915. The government turned to conscription to field a substantial fighting force.

On June 5, 1917, more than 9.5 million young men registered for military service. By the end of the war, almost 4 million men, plus a few thousand female navy clerks and army nurses, were in uniform. Nearly 3 million men were inducted by a draft lottery; the rest volunteered. Over 300,000 men evaded the draft, and another 4,000 were classified as conscientious objectors. During the eighteen months that the United States fought in the war, 50,000 American servicemen were killed in action. Another 60,000 died from other causes, mainly the influenza epidemic that swept the world in 1918–1919. The nation suffered minimal casualties compared with the 8 million soldiers lost by the Allies and the Central Powers. The French lost far more soldiers in the siege of Verdun than the United States did in the entire war.

American troops were eager to serve. As the novelist John Dos Passos recalled, "We had spent our boyhood in the afterglow of the peaceful nineteenth century. . . . What was war like? We wanted to see with our own eyes." Yet the Americans were slow to have an impact on the

European fighting. By June 1917, only 15,000 American troops had landed in France; the number reached 87,000 by the fall. Allied commanders pleaded for American reinforcements to be assigned to their units to replace men lost in battle, but American leaders were unwilling to put their soldiers under the command of the British and the French. Instead, the United States created an independent fighting unit, the American Expeditionary Force (AEF). General John J. Pershing, who had recently returned from pursuing Pancho Villa and his bandits in Mexico, led the AEF.

At first, the United States contributed more at sea than on land. German submarines were sinking Allied ships at the alarming rate of about nine hundred thousand tons a month when the

THE CALL TO ARMS
To build popular support for the war effort, the government called on the services of such artists as Howard Chandler Christy, Charles Dana Gibson, and James Montgomery Flagg. This 1917 recruiting poster by Flagg was adapted from a June, 1916 cover of *Leslie's Illustrated Weekly Newspaper*. The model was the artist. Four million copies of this poster were printed during World War I. (Library of Congress)

THE FLYING ACES
Although airplanes were not yet the decisive factor they would become in World War II, the exploits of American flyers captivated the popular imagination. Tales of such daredevil pilots fighting it out in the skies like medieval knights in combat provided more thrills than reports of monotonous trench warfare. One of America's best known aces was former professional race car driver Eddie Rickenbacker (right), who was credited with twenty-six "victories" over enemy aircraft. (The Bettmann Archive)

ness of the government headed by Czar Nicholas II, and a revolution overthrew his repressive regime in March 1917. The new government headed by Alexander Kerensky pledged to press for victory against Germany. Russian peasants, however, were sick of suffering deprivation and heavy casualties because of a war that seemed distant and unrelated to their lives. A new leader, Vladimir Ilych Lenin, rapidly gained power by promising "peace, land, and bread" for all Russians. Lenin, who had been living in exile in Switzerland when the March revolution took place, followed the teachings of German revolutionary theorist Karl Marx, especially Marx's emphasis on the inevitability of class struggle between the ruling class and the workers. The Germans arranged Lenin's safe passage home, hoping to promote internal strife in Russia. Lenin and a group of Bolshevik revolutionaries arrived in Petrograd (now Leningrad) in

United States entered the war in mid-April. The U-boats had seriously crippled the attempt to send supplies and munitions to the Allies and threatened the transport of American troops to the European front. Adopting a plan that aimed for safety in numbers, the government immediately began sending armed convoys across the ocean. The plan worked. No American soldiers were killed on their way to Europe. A stepped-up American naval campaign cut the Allied shipping losses to four hundred thousand tons a month by late 1917 and two hundred thousand tons by April 1918.

Meanwhile, revolutionary changes in Russia were affecting the course of the war. The strain of fighting the Germans had exposed the weak-

THE MEUSE-ARGONNE CAMPAIGN
The Meuse-Argonne produced its share of heroes. Corporal Alvin York, a conscientious objector from Tennessee, singlehandedly killed twenty-eight Germans and took one hundred twenty-three prisoners during this offensive. The popular fascination with York suggested a deep-seated need to anoint individual heroes in what was becoming an increasingly depersonalized and mechanized war. (The Bettmann Archive)

MAP 22.2 U.S. PARTICIPATION ON THE WESTERN FRONT, 1918 When American troops finally reached the European front in significant numbers in 1918, the Allied and Central powers had been grinding each other down in a war of attrition for almost four years. New, long-range artillery and the concentrated fire of machine guns gave a tremendous advantage to defensive positions. Huge massed armies faced each other across a front that contained more than 25,000 miles of trenches. The influx of American troops and supplies broke the stalemate. Successful offensive maneuvers by the American Expeditionary Force included Belleau Wood, Château Thierry, and the Meuse-Argonne campaign.

April. In November, Lenin led the Bolshevik seizure of power, completing the Russian Revolution.

The new Bolshevik government quickly sued for peace with the Germans to end the unpopular war and consolidate its position at home. Peace talks opened at Brest-Litovsk in December 1917, and the Bolsheviks signed a treaty with Germany in March 1918 in which they surrendered to German control the territory of Poland, the Baltic provinces, and the Ukraine. With Russia knocked out of the war, Germany could turn its full force to the stalemate on the western front. On March 21, 1918, the Germans launched a major offensive that advanced within fifty miles of Paris. Allied leaders intensified their calls for fresh American troops. About seventy thousand American soldiers helped the French repel the Germans in the battles of Château-Thierry and Belleau Wood. The German offensive ground to a halt after a summer of fighting.

American reinforcements now began to arrive in force. Fresh troops flooded the ports of Liverpool in England and Brest and Saint Nazaire in France—245,000 in May, 278,000 in June, and 306,000 in July. In September 1918, General Pershing launched a major assault that pitted a million American soldiers against vastly outnumbered and exhausted German troops. The successful forty-seven-day Meuse-Argonne campaign near Verdun pushed the enemy back across the Somme River and broke the German defenses.

World War I ended on November 11, 1918, with the signing of an armistice. The flood of American troops and supplies during the last six months of fighting provided the Allied margin of victory.

"You're In the Army Now"

About two million American soldiers were in France when the war ended. Two-thirds of them had seen at least brief action on the western front. However, most American doughboys escaped the horrors of sustained trench warfare that had sapped the morale of Allied and German troops. The war in France became a great adventure for many young Americans because they experienced the war more as tourists than as soldiers. Large numbers of recruits had barely traveled beyond their hometowns before joining the army, and the journey across the ocean to Europe was a monumental event in their lives. In France, the young men were struck by how old everything seemed, compared to an America just one generation removed from the closing of the frontier.

High progressive ideals set the tone for military service. One reform instituted by the army was the Stanford-Binet intelligence test. Army psychologists, who administered the test to all recruits, expressed shock at the level of illiteracy among draftees—as high as 25 percent. Racial and ethnic variations also turned up in the test scores. But these lower scores stemmed from the cultural biases of the tests rather than innate differences in intelligence among ethnic groups. How many recent immigrants or rural blacks could be expected to know who wrote "The Raven"; the city in which the Overland car was manufactured; or the importance of the painter Rosa Bonheur? The army dropped the test in 1919, but revised versions of intelligence tests soon became a standard part of the American educational system.

The military forces also adopted progressive solutions to the vices of alcohol and sex. Reflecting the anti-liquor fever taking hold in America, the army banned drinking by soldiers in uniform and declared army bases and the surrounding localities officially dry. This experiment in imposed temperance added momentum to the adoption of national prohibition in 1920.

The army mounted an ambitious program of sex education. In an era when people rarely discussed sex in public, the army program represented an attempt to bring the subject into the open. Concerned that venereal disease might sap the strength of the fighting men (antibiotics had not yet been developed), the army launched an anti-VD campaign. As soldiers ate dinner in their mess halls, they looked up at posters that proclaimed "A German Bullet is Cleaner than a Whore" or "How could you look the flag in the face if you were dirty with gonorrhea?" In France, the army continued its campaign against venereal disease, although it never totally stopped American soldiers from patronizing French prostitutes. Army-issue condoms and safety razors (a novelty that changed the shaving habits of an entire generation of men) were two of the souvenirs that American soldiers brought home from France.

Reformers had expressed high hopes for the democratization and educational potential of military service. Theodore Roosevelt, whose offer to raise an independent regiment was politely but firmly refused by President Wilson, hoped that army duty would foster class unity. "The military tent where they all sleep side by side will rank next to the public school among the great agents of democratization," Roosevelt predicted. Yet the army reflected the same problems that afflicted American society at large. About a fifth of the American soldiers had been born in another country, leading some people to call the

A BLACK VETERAN RETURNS HOME
Black soldiers received segregated and unequal treatment at every stage of their military service. When the war ended, black veterans faced hostility from many whites alarmed that blacks no longer "knew their place." (Amistad Research Center)

AEF the American Foreign Legion. At a camp in Georgia, the army assigned Italians and Slavs to ethnically segregated units. These men were commanded by officers who spoke their language, and the troops were even serviced by cooks trained in the respective culinary traditions.

Black soldiers received the worst treatment, a reflection of their subordinate position in American society. White Southerners became especially alarmed at training blacks to bear arms, and few whites from any part of the country would have consented to serve under a black officer. As a result of such prejudice, blacks were organized into rigidly segregated units, in all but a few cases under the control of white officers. In addition, blacks were always assigned to the most menial tasks. Despite the official policy of segregation designed to minimize contact between black and white recruits, racial violence erupted at several camps. The worst incident occurred in Houston, where black members of the Twenty-fourth Infantry's Third Battalion killed seventeen white soldiers who had goaded them. The army immediately tried more than a hundred black soldiers in military courts. Thirteen were executed within days, and six more were later hanged.

Despite such incidents, over four hundred thousand black men volunteered or were drafted for military service. Blacks made up 13 percent of the armed forces. In France, black soldiers found the French far more willing to socialize with them on an equal basis than were many white American soldiers. Despite documented cases of extreme heroism, no black received the Congressional Medal of Honor, the nation's highest military award. As with President Wilson's lofty ideals and the actual course of the war, the black experience in World War I reflected the persistent gap between progressive rhetoric and reality.

Mobilizing the Home Front

Fighting World War I required extraordinary economic mobilization on the home front. Business, the work force, and the public all cooperated to win the war. At the height of mobilization, a fourth of the gross national product went for war production. Business and government proved especially congenial partners. Their cooperation put into action the New Nationalism urged by Theodore Roosevelt during the 1912 presidential campaign.

Financial and Economic Mobilization

The war forced government and business to organize and perform on an unprecedented scale. This process had begun even before the formal declaration of war, as the United States geared up as the arsenal for Allied supplies and financing. Almost overnight, America reversed its historic debtor position to that of creditor toward other nations as the Allies bought more U.S. exports and paid for them in gold. In addition, U.S. financial institutions increasingly provided capital for foreign investment on the world market now that the British pound sterling was diverted to the Allied war effort. This American export capital guaranteed the nation a major role in international financial affairs from then on.

The monetary cost of World War I reached $32 billion, a huge sum for a government unaccustomed to large expenditures. The United States raised about a third of this amount from taxes; the rest came from loans, especially the popular Liberty Loans that encouraged public support for the war effort. The government also helped pay for the war by using the Federal Reserve System to expand the money supply, which made it easier to borrow money. Even so, the federal debt increased from $1 billion in 1915 to $20 billion in 1920. Federal expenditures never again dropped to their prewar levels.

The debt obligations and money expansion fueled inflation, and the consumer price index doubled during the war. Inflation, however, proved a more politically acceptable way of paying for the war than increasing income taxes or imposing a federal sales tax. The Sixteenth Amendment to the Constitution, which allowed a federal income tax, had been in effect only since 1913. Few Americans except those in the top income brackets had to file federal returns. Because inflation raised incomes and thus brought more households into the tax system, the war emergency accustomed a broader cross section of the population to paying higher taxes to support the expanded functions of the government.

In addition to raising money, mobilization required coordination of economic production. The government never seriously considered exercising total control over the economy. But the war hastened the creation of a national administrative structure to match the consolidated power of the business and banking communities. For the most part, the government turned to those who knew the capacities of the economy best—the nation's business leaders. These executives flocked to Washington, regarding war work as both a duty and an opportunity for professional advancement.

Economic mobilization operated within a series of boards and agencies that tried to rationalize and coordinate the national economic structure. A network of industrial committees linked war agencies to organizations in private industry. Government leaders utilized a combination of public and private power to enforce their decisions.

The Fuel Administration, directed by President Harry Garfield of Williams College, allocated coal resources. Its task became more difficult during the especially severe winter of 1917–1918, when coal shortages occurred in major northeastern cities and industries. At one point, Garfield ordered all factories east of the Mississippi River to shut down for four days. By raising the price of coal to artificially high levels, the Fuel Administration eventually stimulated production of coal from previously unprofitable mines to meet the nation's energy needs.

The Railroad War Board, under Secretary of the Treasury William G. McAdoo, brought order to the nation's sprawling transportation system by nationalizing the railroads in December 1917. The government guaranteed railroad owners a "standard return" equal to average earnings between 1915 and 1917. It also promised that the carriers would be returned to private control no later than twenty-one months after the war. Railroad workers received wage hikes totaling $300 million, which were financed by rate increases passed on directly to shippers and the public. The government quickly returned the railroads to private ownership after the armistice.

Perhaps the most successful government agency was the Food Administration, led by Herbert Hoover, a Stanford-trained engineer.

Using the slogan "Food will win the war," Hoover expanded domestic production of wheat and other grains from forty-five million acres in 1917 to seventy-five million in 1919. This increased production not only fed the large domestic market, but also allowed a threefold rise in food exports to war-torn Europe. At no time did the government contemplate domestic food rationing. Much of Hoover's success resulted from the voluntary cooperation of consumers who patriotically followed government reminders to "Serve Just Enough" and "Use All Left-Overs." Wheatless Mondays, Meatless Tuesdays, and Porkless Thursdays and Saturdays enabled substantial conservation of food resources. Hoover emerged from the war as one of the nation's most admired public figures.

The central agency for wartime mobilization was the War Industries Board (WIB), established in July 1917. After a fumbling start, the Wilson administration reorganized the board under the direction of Bernard Baruch, a Wall Street financier, in March 1918. Baruch's financial experience and his ability to cajole American business to cooperate with the government contributed significantly to the success of the WIB.

The WIB reflected the ambiguities that characterized business–government cooperation during the early twentieth century. While it emphasized cooperation over competition, it left patterns of private power undisturbed. Baruch organized the WIB around specific commodities and industries, whose administrators then negotiated such issues as market allocation with their equivalents in private industry. This frequent consultation blurred the lines between the needs of business and government.

Bernard Baruch was no economic dictator, but the WIB produced an unparalleled expansion of the federal government. The board allocated scarce resources, gathered economic data and statistics, controlled the flow of raw materials, ordered conversion of factories to war production, set prices, imposed efficiency and standardization procedures, and coordinated purchasing. The board had the authority to compel compliance, but Baruch preferred to win voluntary acceptance from business. He saw himself as a partner of business, not its enemy. To a large degree, business supported this government expansion because federal growth coincided with its interests so well.

The fundamental reason for America's successful economic mobilization lay less in administrative theory than in hard cash. Corporate profits soared, aided by the suspension of antitrust laws and competitive bidding during wartime. Profits on war work were further guaranteed through "cost-plus" contracts—that is, industries' profits came on top of their actual production costs. War profits created about forty-two thousand new millionaires, and produced an economic boom that continued uninterrupted until 1920.

With the signing of the armistice in November 1918, the United States scrambled to dismantle its wartime apparatus. The government had no comprehensive plans to guide the economy through postwar reconversion. Concentrated power in the hands of business and government could be tolerated by business executives and the general public in an emergency, but not yet as a permanent feature of the American economy.

Although U.S. participation in the war lasted only eighteen months, it left an important legacy for the modern bureaucratic state. Entire industries had been organized as never before, linked to a maze of government agencies, congressional committees, and executive departments. These changes had been under way before 1917, but the war accelerated them. The partnership between business and government had been mutually beneficial, a lesson that both partners would put to use well in the modern era.

Manpower and Womanpower

Wars cannot be won just by a nation's armed forces and its business and government executives. Such crises demand the participation and cooperation not only of the work force but of the entire civilian population. However, World War I produced fewer rewards for the workers who produced the war products than for their managers in Washington.

Labor's position improved during the war, although it remained a junior partner to business and government. Samuel Gompers, leader of the American Federation of Labor (AFL), traded labor's support of the war for a voice in government policy. This bargain proved acceptable to government and business leaders concerned with averting strikes that could cripple war production. Gompers represented labor's interests on both the National Defense Advisory Commission and the National War Labor Board (NWLB). In addition, the War Labor Policies Board, headed by Felix Frankfurter, a Harvard law professor, coordinated labor and welfare programs in government and industry. This board established the United States Employment Service, which placed four million workers in war jobs.

Far more important to workers themselves were the actions of the National War Labor Board. The NWLB functioned more as a judicial than an administrative body; labor leaders often called it "labor's Supreme Court." Comprised of representatives of labor, management, and the public, the NWLB was co-chaired by former President William Howard Taft, representing management, and Frank P. Walsh, a labor lawyer. During the eighteen months of the NWLB's existence, it arbitrated about 1,250 cases. The board's decisions favored labor more often than management, giving important federal support to the goals of the labor movement.

The board stipulated that workers not disrupt war production through strikes or other disturbances. In return, it supported the right of workers to organize unions and required employers to deal with shop committees. The board established an eight-hour day for war workers, with time-and-a-half pay for overtime; it also endorsed equal pay for woman workers. The NWLB had ample power to enforce its decisions and intervene in unresolved disputes. For example, NWLB examiners supervised elections for shop committees in the steel industry. When the Smith and Wesson arms plant in Springfield, Massachusetts, flouted NWLB rules by discriminating against union employees, the federal government took over the firm.

Following years of hostility toward labor by management and the federal government, such actions by the National War Labor Board improved labor's status and power. From 1916 to 1919, AFL membership grew by almost a million workers, reaching nearly three million by the end of the war. Few of these wartime gains lasted, however. Wartime inflation ate up most of the wage hikes, and a virulent postwar anti-union movement drove union membership into a rapid decline that lasted until the 1930s. The labor movement did not yet have enough power to bargain on an equal basis with business and government.

Small gains also occurred for certain groups of workers. When men go to war, the resulting labor shortage usually makes jobs available to workers normally excluded from them. Blacks, for example, found jobs in northern defense industries that never would have accepted them in peacetime. The magnet of industrial jobs and an escape from the southern agricultural system lured between 400,000 and 450,000 blacks to northern and western cities during the war. Henry Ford sent agents to the South to recruit black workers for his automobile plants and even provided special trains to bring them north. In Detroit, blacks shared in the unprecedented five-dollar daily wage that Ford had instituted in 1914. This migration of blacks from the South represented one of the most fundamental population shifts of the twentieth century.

Mexican-Americans in California, Texas, New Mexico, and Arizona also found their lives improved by wartime labor needs. Many left their segregated *barrios* (neighborhoods) for industrial opportunities in northern cities. Some Mexican-Americans, however, fearing they would be drafted into the army, had returned to Mexico. The exodus of all these workers increased the labor shortage in agriculture. The government quickly exempted agricultural workers from the draft, whereupon the migration resumed. At least a hundred thousand Mexican-Americans entered the United States between 1917 and 1920.

Women made up the largest group that took advantage of new opportunities in wartime. White women and, to a lesser degree, black women, like black and Mexican-American men, found jobs open to them in factories and war industries as never before. About four hundred thousand women joined the labor force for the first time. In addition, many of the nation's eight million women who already held jobs switched from low-paying fields, such as domestic service, to higher-paying industrial work. Americans soon got used to the novel sight of woman

WARTIME OPPORTUNITIES
Women took on new jobs during the wartime emergency, working as mail carriers, police officers, drill-press operators, and farm laborers attached to the Women's Land Army. These three women clearly enjoyed the camaraderie of working in a railroad yard in 1918. When the war ended, women usually lost such employment. (National Archives)

streetcar conductors, train engineers, and defense workers. But everyone—including the women themselves—believed that these jobs would return to men after the war.

World War I proved even more liberating for middle-class women outside the work force. Women's clubs and groups had grown steadily since the nineteenth century, and they turned much of their organizational energy to the war effort. Suffragist leaders such as Carrie Chapman Catt and Anna Howard Shaw mobilized women's support for the war through the Women's Committee of the Council of National Defense. Housewives played a crucial role in the success of Herbert Hoover's Food Administration. Other groups, including the American Red Cross and the Young Women's Christian Association (YWCA), sent volunteers to the front lines in France.

Professional women also found opportunities in government service. Mary Van Kleeck, an industrial sociologist and expert on the problems of woman wage earners, joined the Army Ordnance Department and the Department of Labor to lobby for equal pay and better working conditions for woman workers. Pauline Goldmark, a social reformer from the National Consumers' League, acted as a women's rights advocate at the Railroad Administration. Mary Anderson, a trade unionist who had been Van Kleeck's assistant, became the first director of the Women's Bureau, established by the Labor Department in 1920. Women's groups failed, however, to get a woman named to the National War Labor Board.

The war had an important impact on the battle for woman suffrage as well. A small minority of radical feminists, led by Alice Paul and her Congressional Union, opposed the war. But the main suffrage organization, the National American Woman Suffrage Association (NAWSA), threw the support of its two million members solidly behind the Wilson administration. Carrie Chapman Catt, president of the organization, realized that women had to prove their patriotism in order not to jeopardize the suffrage movement.

Women's wartime contributions helped push their campaign for suffrage to its successful conclusion. Especially effective was a simple moral question. How could the United States fight to make the world safe for democracy while denying half its citizens their democratic right to vote? Woodrow Wilson, who had converted to woman suffrage in 1916 but preferred to leave the matter to the states, withdrew his opposition to a federal woman suffrage amendment in January 1918. The constitutional amendment quickly passed the House but took eighteen months to get through the Senate. Then came another year of hard work for ratification by the states. Finally, on August 26, 1920, Tennessee gave the Nineteenth Amendment the last vote it needed. The goal that had first been declared at the Seneca Falls convention in 1848 won approval seventy-two years later, partly because of women's contributions to the war effort.

Promoting National Unity

Whereas the successful climax of woman suffrage confirmed John Dewey's prediction that social progress could occur in a war context, the excesses committed in the name of building national unity corroborated Randolph Bourne's warnings about the passions that could get out of control during wartime. Widespread support for the war was never a foregone conclusion. Many citizens felt far removed from the conflict. Why should they sacrifice their sons and their taxes in a European imperialist conflict far across

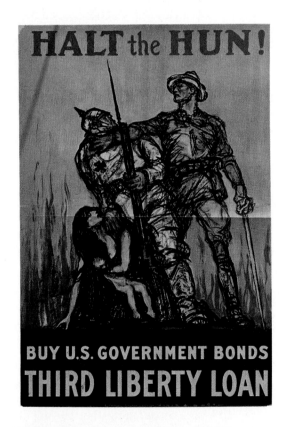

DRUMMING UP PATRIOTIC DOLLARS
This poster made it clear who the enemy was, and what was the proper patriotic American response. Treasury Secretary William McAdoo reinforced the point when he said in 1917, "Every person who refuses to subscribe or who takes the attitude of let the other fellow do it, is a friend of Germany and I would like nothing better than to tell it to him to his face. A man who can't lend his government $1.25 per week at the rate of 4 percent interest is not entitled to be an American citizen." (Historical Pictures Service)

the Atlantic Ocean? Support for the war remained tentative from immigrants who had ties to the Central Powers. Pacifist sentiment continued strong even after the United States declared war. Because of such domestic opposition, the Wilson administration recognized the need to manufacture support for the war. "It is not an army we must shape and train for war, it is a nation," the president said.

Wilson chose the Committee on Public Information (CPI) to promote public backing for the war. This government propaganda agency, headed by the reform journalist George Creel, acted as a magnet for reformers and muckraking journalists, such as Ida Tarbell and Ray Stannard Baker. The CPI professed high goals, such as educating citizens about democracy, promoting national unity, Americanizing immigrant groups, and breaking down the isolation of rural life. Indirectly, it acted as a nationalizing force by promoting the development of a common national ideology.

The CPI touched the lives of practically every American during World War I. In these days before radio and television, the CPI depended heavily on the printed word. It distributed seventy-five million pieces of literature during the war. At local movie theaters before the feature presentation (which might be a CPI-supported film, such as *The Prussian Cur* or *The Kaiser, Beast of Berlin*), a volunteer called a "four-minute man" made a short speech supporting the war. About seventy-five thousand volunteers delivered more than 755,000 speeches during the war. They reached an audience estimated at more than three hundred million, three times the population of the United States at the time. Yet the tactics of the CPI often went too far, overriding the right of individual expression in favor of national conformity in wartime. By early 1918, for example, the CPI was encouraging the four-minute men to use inflammatory stories of alleged German atrocities in their speeches to build support for the war effort.

As a spirit of total conformity pervaded the home front, many Americans found themselves the targets of suspicion. Local businesses donated ads to newspapers and magazines which asked citizens to report to the Justice Department "the man who spreads pessimistic stories, cries for peace, or belittles our efforts to win the war." Posters encouraged Americans to join the army or be on the lookout for German spies. One of the most popular posters, called "Spies and Lies," began by warning that "German agents are everywhere." An unintended byproduct of this wartime propaganda was the stimulation of the advertising industry, which became a major force in shaping patterns of consumption in the 1920s. More aggressive were quasi-vigilante groups, such as the American Protective League. This organization mobilized about 250,000 self-appointed "agents" to spy on their neighbors, fellow workers, and innocent bystanders. The American Protective League (whose members were furnished with badges issued by the Justice Department) and groups including the Sedition Slammers and the Boy Spies of America staged violent raids against draft evaders and other war opponents in 1918.

German-Americans bore the brunt of the Americanization campaign. The CPI urged ethnic groups to give up their old-world customs and become "Unhyphenated Americans." In an orgy of hatred generated by propaganda about German militarism and war atrocities, everything German became suspect. German music, especially opera, was banished from the concert repertoire. Publishers removed pro-German references from textbooks, and many communities banned the teaching of the German language. Sauerkraut became "liberty cabbage," and hamburgers were called "liberty sandwiches" or Salisbury steaks. Even the German measles got a new name, "liberty measles."

In this campaign for total conformity, the government tolerated little criticism of American values and institutions. Militant suffragists became early targets of repression. When women chained themselves to the White House fence and burned copies of President Wilson's speeches on democracy to protest female disenfranchisement, the government swiftly retaliated. The suffragists, charged with obstructing traffic and blocking sidewalks, were sentenced to seven months in jail. To protest these stiff sentences as well as the terrible conditions in prison, the women prisoners went on hunger strikes and were forcibly fed. Public shock at their treatment made them martyrs and ultimately aided the suffrage cause. But the suffragists' status as white middle-class women

$\mathcal{L}$ETTERS FROM PRISON

Suffragist Rose Winslow smuggled out descriptions of the treatment she and militant feminist Alice Paul, founder of the National Woman's Party, endured in Occoquan prison.

The women are all so magnificent, so beautiful. Alice Paul is as thin as ever, pale and large-eyed. We have been in solitary for five weeks. There is nothing to tell but that the days go by somehow. I have felt quite feeble the last few days—faint, so that I could hardly get my hair brushed, my arms ached so. But to-day I am well again. Alice Paul and I talk back and forth though we are at opposite ends of the building and a hall door also shuts us apart. But occasionally—thrills—we escape from behind our iron-barred doors and visit. Great laughter and rejoicing!

Alice Paul is in the psychopathic ward. She dreaded forcible feeding frightfully, and I hate to think how she must be feeling. I had a nervous time of it, gasping a long time afterward, and my stomach rejecting during the process. I spent a bad, restless night, but otherwise I am all right. The poor soul who fed me got liberally besprinkled during the process. I heard myself making the most hideous sounds. . . . One feels so forsaken when one lies prone and people shove a pipe down one's stomach.

We still get no mail; we are "insubordinate." It's strange, isn't it; if you ask for food fit to eat, as we did, you are "insubor-dinate"; and if you refuse food you are "insubordinate." Amusing. I am really all right. If this continues very long I perhaps won't be. I am interested to see how long our so-called "splendid American men" will stand for this form of discipline.

All news cheers one marvelously because it is hard to feel anything but a bit desolate and forgotten here in this place.

All the officers here know we are making this hunger strike that women fighting for liberty may be considered political prisoners; we have told them. God knows we don't want other women ever to have to do this over again.

Source: Doris Stevens, *Jailed for Freedom.* New York: Schocken Books, 1976; originally published 1920. 188–191.

---

protected them from some of the harsher reprisals meted out to others who dared to criticize the government during wartime.

The main legal tools for curbing dissent were the Espionage Act of 1917 and the Sedition Act of 1918. The espionage law set stiff penalties for antimilitary actions and empowered the federal government to ban treasonous material from the mails. The definition of treason was left to the discretion of the postmaster general. The sedition law went further, punishing anyone who might "utter, print, write or publish any disloyal, profane, scurrilous, or abusive language about the form of government in the United States, or the uniform of the Army or the Navy." More than a thousand persons were convicted under these broad restrictions on freedom of speech in wartime.

One tempting target for repression was the Industrial Workers of the World, the labor organization whose members were known as Wobblies. IWW organizers spoke out against militarism and threatened to disrupt war production in the western lumber and copper industries. In September 1917, the Justice Department arrested 113 top IWW leaders for interfering with the war effort. Vigilante groups contributed their own reprisals. A mob in Butte, Montana, dragged IWW organizer Frank Little through the streets and hanged him from a railroad trestle. By the end of the war, the Wobblies were decimated.

Socialists, who also criticized the war and the draft, encountered similar attacks. The postmaster general banned their publications from the mails. Party leader Eugene Debs drew ten years in jail for stating that the master classes caused wars while the subject classes fought them. Victor Berger, a Milwaukee socialist, was twice prevented from taking his seat in the United States House of Representatives. Berger had served in the House from 1911 to 1913. He was reelected in 1918 and 1919, but the House refused to seat him because he had been jailed under the Espionage Act for his antiwar views. The Supreme Court reversed Berger's sentence in 1921, and he served in the House again from 1923 to 1929.

Rarely did the Supreme Court overturn the wartime excesses. In *Schenck v. United States* (1919), Justice Oliver Wendell Holmes ruled in a unanimous decision that if an act of speech constituted a "clear and present danger to the safety of the country," Congress could constitutionally restrict it. The defendant, an official of the Socialist party, had been convicted for mailing pamphlets that urged army recruits to resist induction. In *Abrams v. United States* (1919), the Court upheld the conviction of Jacob Abrams, an immigrant printer who had distributed pamphlets denouncing American military intervention in Russia to destroy the Bolshevik regime. Holmes dissented in this case, seeing no clear threat to the conduct of the war. He and Justice Louis Brandeis made up the minority in the 7 to 2 decision. During a national war emergency, limits on freedom of speech were tolerated that would not have been acceptable in peacetime.

An Unsettled Peace

The mobilization of the home front and the defeat of Germany were major accomplishments, but they came at a price. Following the armistice, dormant problems rose to the surface. Woodrow Wilson confronted the task of making the Allies live up to the high ideals he had put forward as the basis for peace. He then faced a Senate hostile to the treaty he brought home. At the same time, ethnocultural and racial tensions that had smoldered during the war erupted in violence and strife. And fears of domestic radicalism boiled over in the Red Scare.

Versailles and the League of Nations

President Wilson scored an early victory when the Allies accepted his Fourteen Points as the basis for the peace negotiations that began in January 1919. But other factors limited Wilson's ability to enforce his views of a just peace. Despite the president's plea to make the November 1918 elections a referendum on the peace settlement, American voters returned a Republican majority

to Congress. Nevertheless, Wilson failed to appoint even one Republican senator to the United States delegation to the peace conference. His shortsightedness later helped doom the treaty's chances for approval in the Senate.

The peace delegation sailed for Europe in December 1918. Wilson toured the major European capitals and received a tumultuous welcome. To Europeans, the American president represented the hope for national self-determination that had become a major justification for the war. In Paris, two million people lined the Champs-Elysees to pay tribute to "Wilson the Just." This lofty reception encouraged Wilson to press ahead with his plans to dominate the peace conference.

Twenty-seven countries sent representatives to the peace conference in Versailles, near Paris. The victorious Allies did not invite either Germany or Russia. Wilson firmly opposed the

TRIUMPHANT WOODROW WILSON
After the armistice, Woodrow Wilson toured Europe to popular acclaim. His heady reception from millions of adoring Europeans, who saw him as the embodiment of the long-sought goal of national self-determination, contrasted sharply with the cool reception he received from leaders of the European powers. When the Versailles treaty was in trouble with the U.S. Senate, Wilson pursued the same tactic of taking his case directly to the people, this time with disastrous results. (Library of Congress)

WILSON'S DIPLOMACY AT PARIS

Journalist Walter Lippmann reflects on the Peace Conference at Paris, 1919.

Five great powers sent plenipotentiaries to Paris and with them came delegates from a host of small nations, provisional governments, and classes. Together they constituted the representatives of a coalition that had won at terrible cost a complete mastery of the organized military and economic power of the world. The process of victory had entailed the destruction of established authority in four of the great empires, and out of their ruin had issued angry, frightened, resentful, and wildly hopeful masses of men. It was by flashes black night and golden morning, the new day and the end of the world.

At Paris men looked out upon two continents in revolt, upon conflicts and aspirations more intricate and more obscure than any they had ever been called to resolve. . . . Through it all the primary problem of the conference was to find men who had sufficient authority to negotiate a peace. Soon there was discovered a truth, which political science seemed to have ignored: that you cannot wage war with or dictate peace to an unorganized people. . . .

For an understanding of what has happened at Paris these last six or seven months, it is necessary to study the peculiar technique of the Wilson diplomacy as it operated in contact with these imponderables. . . . The facts are, I believe, about as follows. Throughout the war he was increasingly convinced that the masses in Europe were passionately determined upon the kind of peace which he himself desired. When he "clarified" this common thought he found himself the acknowledged spokesman of the populations of Europe, and gradually he came to believe that no power on earth could successfully resist this democratic insistence. "Statesmen must follow the common clarified thought or be broken." Therefore, why become involved in the complications of governmental diplomacy when all that will be swept aside by popular demand? Why commit the governments (who, by the way, could have been committed to anything while they needed American military assistance) when the people accept the President's leadership? All the rest can be ignored so long as the heart of the people is expressed. . . .

Source: Walter Lippmann, *The Peace Conference. The Yale Review,* July 1919. 710–711, 716, 719.

Bolshevik regime. The outcome of the Russian Revolution troubled him so greatly that he approved the landing of American troops in Siberia in 1918, supposedly to aid thousands of trapped Czechoslovakian soldiers. Actually, Wilson wanted to topple the new Soviet state. He continued to be deeply disturbed by Lenin's calls for a proletarian revolution to liberate the world from capitalism and imperialism. Even though Lenin did not attend the peace conference, leaders of many nations began to see that the new Soviet state was changing the complexion of power in Eastern Europe—and the world.

The Big Four—Wilson, Prime Minister David Lloyd George of Great Britain, Premier Georges Clemenceau of France, and Prime Minister Vittorio Orlando of Italy—did most of the negotiating at Versailles. The three European leaders sought a peace that differed radically from Wilson's plan. They put a high priority on punishing Germany through heavy reparations. They also planned to treat themselves to the spoils of war. In fact, secret treaties among Britain, France, and Italy had already divided up territory of the defeated German empire. Issues of self-interest separated the three nations, but they agreed that they did not want Wilson to write the peace settlement unilaterally.

It is a tribute to Woodrow Wilson that he managed to influence the peace agreement as much as he did. His presence at Versailles softened some of the harshest demands for reprisals against Germany. National self-determination, a fundamental American principle enunciated in Wilson's Fourteen Points, found fulfillment in the creation of the independent states of Austria, Hungary, Poland, Yugoslavia, and Czechoslovakia from the defeated empires of the Central

Powers. The establishment of a *cordon sanitaire* (sanitary zone) of the new nations of Finland, Estonia, Lithuania, and Latvia further served Wilson's determination to isolate the new Bolshevik state from the rest of Europe.

The president also won limited concessions regarding the colonial empires of the defeated powers. Wilson had favored complete independence for the colonies involved; the Allies did not favor such a challenge to the system of prewar imperialism which they hoped to maintain. The resulting compromise put the colonies under a mandate system of protectorates. France and England received parts of the old Turkish and German empires in the Middle East and Africa, and Japan assumed responsibility for the former German colonies in the Far East.

However, Wilson had to back down from his goals on many other issues in the Fourteen Points. Certain topics, such as freedom of the seas and free trade, never even made the agenda because of Allied resistance. Wilson's call for "open covenants of peace openly arrived at" was mocked by the secret negotiating sessions held by the Big Four at Versailles. Wilson yielded to French and British demands for a guilt clause, which provided the justification for the heavy restitution demanded from Germany. Wilson agreed to reparations of $33 billion, even though he realized that this staggering amount could cripple the Germans' ability to rebuild their devastated economy.

In the face of his many disappointments, Wilson consoled himself with the peace conference's commitment to his proposed League of Nations. He acknowledged that the treaty had defects. But he expressed confidence that they could be resolved by a permanent international organization that brought nations together for the peaceful resolution of disputes.

German leaders reacted with dismay at the severity of the treaty, but they had no choice but to accept it. On June 28, 1919, representatives of the participating nations gathered in the Hall of Mirrors in the Palace of Versailles to sign the treaty. Wilson sailed home immediately after the ceremony and presented the treaty to the Senate on July 10. To reject it, he piously declared, "would break the heart of the world." The treaty was already in trouble, however, with support in the Senate far short of the two-thirds vote

necessary for ratification. Would Wilson compromise? "I shall consent to nothing," he told the French ambassador. "The Senate must take its medicine."

Opposition to the Versailles treaty came from several sources. One group, called the "irreconcilables," consisted of such Western progressives as William E. Borah of Idaho, Hiram W. Johnson of California, and Robert M. La Follette of Wisconsin. They disagreed fundamentally with the premise of permanent U.S. participation in European affairs. Moreover, they were horrified at the severity of the treaty's sanctions against Germany.

Less dogmatic, but more influential, were a group of Republicans led by Senator Henry Cabot Lodge of Massachusetts. By raising objections to the peace settlement Wilson had negotiated, Republicans sought to capitalize politically on the controversy with an eye toward the 1920 election. They expressed strong reservations about the break with American isolationism represented by membership in the League of Nations. Lodge's Republicans proposed a list of amendments that, scholars now agree, would not have seriously weakened the peace treaty. Most of these changes centered around Article X, the section of the League of Nations covenant calling for collective security measures if a member nation were attacked. Lodge correctly argued that this provision restricted Congress's constitutional authority to declare war. More importantly, Lodge and many other senators felt that the treaty imposed unacceptable restrictions on the freedom of the United States to pursue a unilateral foreign policy.

Wilson still refused to budge, especially to placate Lodge, his hated political rival. Sensing widespread popular support for the treaty, the president launched an extensive speaking tour to take his case to the American people. He brought large audiences to tears with his impassioned defense of the treaty. But the strain proved too much for the ailing sixty-three-year-old president, and he collapsed in Pueblo, Colorado, in late September. Two weeks later in Washington, Wilson suffered a severe stroke that left him paralyzed on one side of his body.

While his wife, Edith Galt Wilson, and his physician oversaw the routine business of government, Wilson slowly recovered. But he was never the same again. He had delusions of making the 1920 election campaign "a great and solemn referendum" on the League of Nations, and even hoped to run for a third term as president. Neither dream ever became a serious possibility. Woodrow Wilson died in 1924, "as much a victim of the war," David Lloyd George noted, "as any soldier who died in the trenches."

We will never know whether a healthy Wilson could have mobilized public support for the League of Nations and gained Senate ratification. If he had allowed the Democrats to compromise, the treaty might have been saved. From his sickbed, however, Wilson ordered the Democratic senators to vote against all Republican amendments. The treaty came up for a vote in November 1919 and failed to be ratified. Another attempt several months later fell seven votes short of approval, and the issue was dead.

The United States never signed the Versailles treaty nor joined the League of Nations. Many wartime issues remained only partially resolved, notably the future of Germany, the fate of colonial empires, and rising nationalist demands for self-determination. These unsolved problems played a major role in the coming of World War II and its aftermath.

Racial Strife and Labor Unrest

Woodrow Wilson spent only ten days in the United States between December 1918 and June 1919. This remarkable fact illustrates his total preoccupation with the peacemaking process at Versailles. For more than six months, Wilson was practically an absentee president. Unfortunately, many urgent domestic problems demanded his attention.

The immediate postwar period brought a severe decline in race relations throughout the country. In the South, the number of lynchings rose from forty-eight in 1917 to seventy-eight in 1919. Southern whites lynched several blacks who were still wearing their military uniforms. Northern blacks also faced hostility. Serious racial violence broke out in more than twenty-five northern cities, and the resulting death toll for the summer of 1919 reached 120.

The riots in northern cities resulted from the northward migration set in motion by World War I. Superficially at least, northern cities promised new freedoms. But southern blacks faced a difficult readjustment to the diverse urban environment from life in the rural South, with its traditional patterns of deference to whites. In turn, white northerners had never seen so many blacks before; ethnic groups such as Italians and Poles were especially hostile. Violence between blacks and whites erupted as early as 1917 in East Saint Louis, Illinois. Nine whites and more than forty blacks died in a riot sparked by competition over jobs at a defense plant.

One of the worst race riots took place in Chicago in July 1919. It began at a Lake Michigan beach when a black teenager named Eugene Williams swam into the area of water customarily reserved for whites. Someone threw a rock that hit him on the head, and he drowned. The incident touched off five days of rioting in which twenty-three blacks and fifteen whites died. Extensive property damage also occurred.

Chicago on the eve of the riot was a tinderbox waiting to ignite. The arrival of fifty thousand black newcomers during the war years had strained the city's social fabric. In politics, black male voters often provided the balance of power in close elections. Blacks and whites competed for jobs, and the more heavily unionized white population deeply resented blacks who became strikebreakers. White stockyard workers considered the words "Negro" and "scab" synonymous. Blacks and whites competed for scarce housing as well. Blacks soon overflowed the racially segregated South Side into Chicago's intensely ethnic neighborhoods. Even before that sultry July afternoon at the beach, tensions had erupted in bombings of black homes and other forms of harrassment.

Chicago blacks did not sit meekly by as whites destroyed their neighborhoods. They fought back, both in self-defense and for their rights as citizens. World War I had an indirect effect on their actions. Many blacks had served in the armed forces. The rhetoric about democracy and self-determination raised their expectations, too.

Workers had similar hopes as a result of the war. The war years had provided important breakthroughs for many industrial emloyees, including higher pay, shorter hours, and better working conditions. Relations between labor and

RACIAL VIOLENCE IN CHICAGO

Much of the violence perpetrated against blacks during the 1919 Chicago race riot was perpetrated by white teenagers and young men, many of Irish descent, who belonged to gangs such as the "Dirty Dozen" and "Our Flag." A city commission later concluded that without the gang activities, "it is doubtful if the riot would have gone beyond the first clash." (Chicago Historical Society) management had also improved. Soon after the armistice, however, many employers returned to older patterns of hostility toward union activity. Many consumers blamed workers for the rising cost of living, and some people continued to identify unions with radicalism and foreigners. Nevertheless, workers hoped to expand their wartime gains. The worst problem was rapidly rising inflation, which threatened to wipe out their wage increases.

More than four million workers went on strike in 1919. The year began with a walkout by shipyard workers in Seattle. Their action spread into a general strike that crippled the city. In the fall, the Boston police force struck. The idea of public employees trying to unionize shocked many Americans. Governor Calvin Coolidge of Massachusetts propelled himself into the political spotlight by declaring, "There is no right to strike against the public safety by anybody, anywhere, any time." Harvard undergraduates acted as strikebreakers after university president A. Lawrence Lowell promised that their grades would not suffer. The strike failed, and the entire police force was fired. The public supported this harsh reprisal, and Coolidge received the Republican vice-presidential nomination in 1920 largely because of his stand against the striking police officers.

The most extensive labor disruption in 1919 was the great steel strike. More than 350,000 steelworkers walked off the job in late September. The main issue was union recognition, but strikers were also protesting such conditions as twelve-hour shifts and seven-day weeks. Elbert H. Gary, chairman of the United States Steel Corporation, refused to meet with representatives of the steelworkers' union to discuss their demands. The company hired Mexican and black strikebreakers and maintained steel production at about 60 percent of the normal level.

The continued high production rate doomed the strike. Striker solidarity began to slacken as winter approached; by January, the strike had collapsed. The union charged that U.S. Steel's "arbitrary and ruthless misuse of power" had crushed the strike. Just as important to the union's defeat was the lack of public support for the goals of organized labor. Unions had made important gains during the war, but they were unable to hold on to them.

The Red Scare

In addition to postwar racial violence and labor unrest, another cause for concern soon arose— fear of radicalism. Wartime hatred of the German Hun was quickly replaced by postwar hostility toward the Bolshevik Red. The Russian Revolution of 1917 set these fears in motion. The call of the Communist International, an organization established in the Soviet Union in 1919 to export revolution globally, threatened the American vision of a world order based on democracy, capitalism, and international harmony. Americans suddenly began seeing radicals everywhere.

Ironically, as the public became increasingly concerned about domestic Bolshevism, American radicalism rapidly lost members and political power. No more than seventy thousand Americans belonged to the fledgling U.S. Communist party or the Communist Labor party in 1919. The IWW and the Socialist party had been broken by wartime repression and internal dissension. Yet the public and the press continued to blame almost any disturbance on radicals. "REDS DIRECTING SEATTLE STRIKE—TO TEST CHANCE FOR REVOLUTION," warned a typical newspaper headline in January 1919.

Then a series of bombings shocked the nation in early spring. "The word 'radical' in 1919," one historian observed, "automatically carried with it the implication of dynamite." Thirty-six mail bombs addressed to prominent government officials were discovered by an alert postal worker before they exploded. Many people immediately suspected that the intended bombings had been timed to coincide with the communist celebration of International Labor Day on May 1. In June, a bomb exploded outside the Washington townhouse of the recently appointed attorney general, A. Mitchell Palmer. His family escaped unharmed, but the bomber was blown to bits. One of Palmer's neighbors, Assistant Secretary of the Navy Franklin D. Roosevelt, called the police. Despite intensive efforts, law enforcement agencies never traced the origin of a single bomb.

As hysteria mounted in the fall, the federal government became involved. President Wilson's debilitating stroke prevented him from providing decisive leadership. Attorney General

Palmer, a former Democratic member of Congress from Pennsylvania who had been a strong supporter of Woodrow Wilson's in 1912, assumed leadership. Angling for the presidential nomination, Palmer rode the crest of public hysteria about domestic radicalism into 1920.

Palmer set up an antiradicalism division in the Justice Department and appointed a young government attorney named J. Edgar Hoover to direct it. Hoover's division shortly became the Federal Bureau of Intelligence. In November 1919, on the second anniversary of the Russian Revolution, the attorney general staged the first of what became known as "Palmer raids." These attacks on the headquarters of radical organizations captured such supposedly revolutionary booty as a set of drawings that turned out to be blueprints for an improved phonograph, not sketches for a bomb. The dragnet netted thousands of aliens who had committed no

crime, but were suspect for their anarchist or revolutionary beliefs or merely their immigrant backgrounds. Lacking the protection of U.S. citizenship, they faced deportation without formal trial or indictment. In December 1919, the *U.S.S. Buford*, nicknamed the "Soviet Ark," embarked for Finland and the Soviet state with a cargo of 294 deported radicals. Its passengers included two famous anarchists, Emma Goldman and Alexander Berkman.

The peak of Palmer's power came with his New Year's raids in January 1920. In one night, with the greatest possible newspaper publicity, Palmer rounded up six thousand radicals. Agents invaded private homes, union headquarters, and meeting halls. The government held both citizens and aliens without specific charges and denied them legal counsel, a violation of their civil liberties. Some prisoners were even forced to march through the streets handcuffed

THE OUTBREAK OF INFLUENZA
The influenza epidemic of 1918–1919 strained the resources of a public health system already fully mobilized for the war effort. Novelist Mary McCarthy recalled in *Memories of a Catholic Girlhood* how "no hospital beds were to be had and people went about with masks or stayed shut up in their houses, and the awful fear of contagion paralyzed all services and made each man an enemy to his neighbor." McCarthy lost both her parents to influenza that terrible winter. (Chicago Historical Society)

TIME LINE
PROGRESSIVISM GOES TO WAR

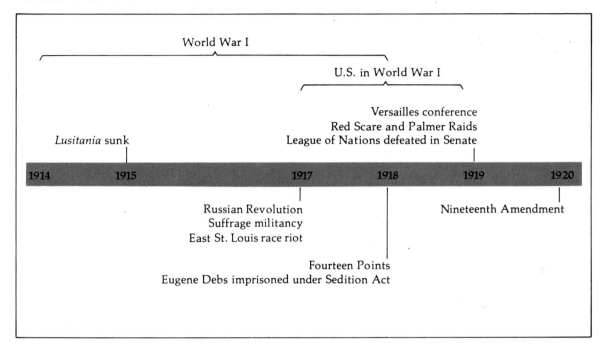

and chained to one another. One of the few moments of comic relief came when "patriotic" prisoners in a Chicago jail rioted when they were ordered to share cells with arrested radicals. "There are some things at which even a Chicago crook draws the line," a local newspaper reported.

Palmer was riding high, and his ambitions for the presidency swelled. But then he overstepped himself. Palmer predicted that May Day 1920 would bring a major plot to overthrow the United States government. Buildings were put under protection, state militia called up, and police put on twenty-four-hour alert to defend the nation against revolutionary violence. Not a single incident occurred. The hysteria of the Red Scare began to abate as the summer of 1920 passed without major labor strikes or renewed bombings.

One dramatic episode kept the wartime legacy of antiradicalism alive well into the next decade. In May 1920, at the height of the Red Scare, Nicola Sacco, a shoemaker, and Bartolomeo Vanzetti, a fish peddler, were arrested for the robbery and murder of a shoe company paymaster in South Braintree, Massachusetts. Sacco and Vanzetti were self-proclaimed anarchists and Italian aliens who had evaded the draft; both were armed at the time of their arrest. Regardless of their guilt or innocence, serious doubts still remain about whether they received a fair trial from the American judicial system.

Sacco and Vanzetti were convicted in 1921 and sat on death row for six years. Shortly before his death in the electric chair on August 23, 1927, Vanzetti claimed triumph.

> If it had not been for these thing, I might have live out my life among scorning men. I might have die, unmarked, unknown, a failure. Now we are not a failure. This is our career and our triumph. Never in our full life can we hope to do such work for tolerance, for justice, for man's understanding of man, as now we do by an accident.

World War I had caught the United States at a crossroads. The triumphs and tragedies between 1917 and 1920 were as much a response to the forces of industrialization, immigration, and urbanization as they were to the demands of a people at war. Over the past half century, the country had completed a fundamental transformation from a predominantly agricultural economy to an industrial one. Its population, which had been swelled by millions of immigrants from Europe and Russia, had become increasingly concentrated in urban areas. At the same time, the United States had broken from its former isolationist stance to take on a more active role in world affairs. By 1920,. the United States stood on the threshold of the modern era.

---

*D*uring World War I, the United States confronted international challenges caused by the outbreak of hostilities in 1914 and domestic tensions related to the nation's emergence as a modern industrial society. America entered the war in 1917 because of violations of its neutrality rights at sea, but, more broadly, because the country's foreign policy reflected the same moral concerns that animated the domestic reform movement. After the war ended in 1918, the Versailles treaty only partially reflected the hopes of President Woodrow Wilson for such international goals as freedom of the seas, peaceful economic expansion, and national self-determination. His postwar plans suffered a worse blow when the Senate refused to ratify the treaty, which included U.S. participation in the League of Nations.

On the home front, the conduct of the war was also shaped by the progressive period which preceeded it. The war called for a mobilization of economic resources that accelerated the concentration of power in the federal government and large corporations. The government tried to mobilize the minds of the American people as well but succeeded mainly in inflaming passions. Certain groups, such as woman suffragists, found new opportunities during the war. But others became targets of repression, including blacks who migrated to northern cities, labor activists who called widespread strikes, and Socialists and other radicals who criticized the government. Domestic tensions erupted in race riots in many northern cities, and in the Red Scare of 1919–1920.

Suggestions for Further Reading

David M. Kennedy, *Over Here: The First World War and American Society* (1980), provides a comprehensive overview. For the links between the progressive era and the war, see Robert M. Crunden, *Ministers of Reform: The Progressives' Achievement in American Civilization, 1889–1920* (1982). Ellis W. Hawley, *The Great War and the Search for a Modern Order, 1917–1933* (1979), stresses the continuities between the war years and the 1920s.

Fighting the War

On American entry into World War I, see Ernest May, *The World War and American Isolationism* (1959); Ross Gregory, *The Origins of American Intervention in the First World War* (1971); and Daniel Smith, *The Great Departure: The United States and World War I, 1914–1920*

(1965). There is a large body of material on the policies and personality of Woodrow Wilson, beginning with Arthur Link's five-volume biography (1947–1965), as well as his *Wilson the Diplomatist* (1957). See also Alexander L. George and Juliette L. George, *Woodrow Wilson and Colonel House: A Personality Study* (1956), and John M. Blum, *Woodrow Wilson and the Politics of Morality* (1956). Later studies of Wilson include Edwin Weinstein, *Woodrow Wilson: A Medical and Psychological Biography* (1981), and John Milton Cooper, Jr., *The Warrior and the Priest: Woodrow Wilson and Theodore Roosevelt* (1983).

For American military participation in the war, Russell Weigley, *The American Way of War* (1973); Edward M. Coffman, *The War to End All Wars* (1968); and Harvey deWeerd, *President Wilson Fights His War* (1968), provide useful introductions. They can be supplemented by Laurence Stallings, *The Doughboys: the Story of the AEF, 1917–1918* (1963), and A. E. Barbeau and Florette Henri, *The Unknown Soldiers: Black Troops in World War I* (1974).

Over Here: Mobilizing the Home Front

Robert D. Cuff, *The War Industries Board: Business-Government Relations During World War I* (1973), provides an excellent case study of war mobilization. See also Stephen Skowronek, *Building a New American State: The Expansion of National Administrative Capacities, 1877–1920* (1982); Charles Gilbert, *American Financing of World War I* (1970); David F. Noble, *America by Design* (1977); and Paul A. C. Koistinen, "The 'Industrial-Military Complex' in Historical Perspective: World War I," *Business History Review*, 41 (1967), 378–403. Valerie Jean Conner, *The National War Labor Board* (1983), covers federal policies toward labor.

Maurine Greenwald, *Women, War, and Work* (1980), provides a good overview of women's wartime experiences. Anne F. Scott and Andrew Scott, *One Half the People* (1975), and Eleanor Flexner, *Century of Struggle* (1959), cover the final stages of the woman suffrage campaign. For the experiences of Mexican-Americans, see Rodolfo Acuna, *Occupied America* (1980), and Wayne Cornelius, *Building the Cactus Curtain: Mexican Migration and U.S. Responses from Wilson to Carter* (1980). Efforts to promote national unity are covered in Stephen Vaughn, *Holding Fast the Inner Lines: Democracy, Nationalism, and the CPI* (1980); Paul L. Murphy, *World War I and the Origin of Civil Liberties* (1979); George Blakey, *Historians on the Homefront* (1970); and Frederick Luebke, *Bonds of Loyalty: German-Americans and World War I* (1974).

An Unsettled Peace

N. Gordon Levin, Jr., *Woodrow Wilson and World Politics* (1968), offers a stimulating interpretation of Wilson's diplomacy. For more on Versailles and the League of Nations, see Thomas Bailey, *Woodrow Wilson and the Great Betrayal* (1945); Ralph A. Stone, *The Irreconcilables: The Fight Against the League of Nations* (1970); John A. Garraty, *Henry Cabot Lodge* (1953); and Arno J. Mayer, *Politics and Diplomacy of Peacemaking: Containment and Counter Revolution at Versailles* (1967). On American intervention in Russia, see George F. Kennan, *The Decision to Intervene* (1958); John L. Gaddis, *Russia, the Soviet Union, and the United States* (1978); and Peter Filene, *Americans and the Soviet Experiment, 1917–1933* (1967). Ronald Steel's fine biography *Walter Lippmann and the American Century* (1980) offers another view of the Versailles conference.

Robert K. Murray, *The Red Scare* (1955), summarizes the antiradicalism of the immediate postwar period. See also James Weinstein, *The Decline of Socialism in America, 1912–1923* (1967); John Higham, *Strangers in the Land* (1955); and Burl Noggle, *Into the Twenties* (1974). David Brody, *Labor in Crisis* (1965), describes the steel strike of 1919, while William M. Tuttle, Jr., covers racial strife in *Race Riot: Chicago in the Red Summer of 1919* (1970). For an introduction to the complicated Sacco and Vanzetti case, see Louis Joughin and Edmund Morgan, *The Legacy of Sacco and Vanzetti* (1948), and Roberta Strauss Feuerlicht, *Justice Crucified* (1977).

PART THREE

STATE AND

1920 TO

THE PRESENT

Just as no single turning point indicates the onset of industrialization in early nineteenth century America, no event or date marks the emergence of the United States as a mature industrial society. By the early twentieth century, however, a different mode of organization shaped American economic, political, and social life than had prevailed in industrializing America. Many of the outlines of modern America were firmly in place by the 1920s. The period following World War II produced a noticeable quickening in the pace of change.

One of the most dramatic changes of the twentieth century has been the growth of a postindustrial state with a significant impact on all aspects of soci-

S O C I E T Y

ety, especially economic life. Two world wars greatly increased the concentration of political and economic power in the federal government and the presidency, as did the Great Depression. By the 1960s, the United States had erected an extensive federal apparatus that accepted responsibility for the basic social well-being of its citizens. It also intervened in the economy when private initiatives could not maintain steady economic growth.

The United States also assumed a dramatically different stance in foreign affairs than the position it had held through most of the nineteenth century. The critical turning point occurred after 1945, when the United States emerged from World War II committed to a foreign policy that included a wide-ranging involvement in international affairs. The most consistent thrust of American foreign policy ever since has been the tendency to interpret international events in terms of a deep-rooted conflict between Communism and the Free World. The Korean and Vietnam wars were a direct outgrowth of this Cold War mentality.

A third theme characterizing present-day America is that its citizens are increasingly drawn into a web of interlocking national experience, fostered by the development of a mass culture based on technological innovations such as radio, movies, and television as well as the widespread dissemination of the values of consumerism. In addition, the growth of metropolitan areas has given the nation an increasingly urban tone while geographic mobility has broken down old regional differences.

A fourth theme of twentieth-century life has been its growing social and political diversity. The political domination by elite white males has been undercut by the broader participation in public life of labor, women, and blacks, and other ethnic and racial minorities. During the period after World War II, and especially in the 1960s, many groups challenged American society to make good on its promise of liberty and equality for all. The resulting hard-won reforms dramatically expanded the democratic system, although the promise of full equality remains unfulfilled. The saga of civil rights and the fight against discrimination, like so many other stories in modern America, does not yet have an ending.

The final section of this book continues our attempt to relate the contours of ordinary lives and individual decisions to broader historical forces and patterns. Yet the focus shifts somewhat as we enter the twentieth century. To a remarkable extent, outside events now impinge directly on individual lives. The actions of an expanding federal bureaucracy, the tensions of international relations, the complexity of sprawling metropolitan areas, and the economic impact of giant multinational corporations have broken down older patterns of local autonomy and isolation. Because state and society have become inextricably entwined in the modern era, the structures of a complex bureaucratic society increasingly circumscribe and control the conditions under which Americans live.

Despite the nationalizing trends so evident in twentieth-century economic, political, and cultural life, however, the collective American experience continues to be defined as much by diversity as by uniformity or consensus. There is not one American story, but many. How we live is still fundamentally shaped by age, gender, religion, ethnic or racial background, and socioeconomic class. Describing the ongoing diversity of American social history, while at the same time connecting it to the centralizing tendencies in a mass bureaucratic society, offers clues to the complexity of American history from the 1920s to the present.

23

THE 1920s:
TOWARD A CORPORATE
ECONOMY
AND MASS CULTURE

*M*odern America began in the 1920s. In economic organization, political outlook, and cultural values, the 1920s have more in common with the United States of the 1980s than with the industrializing America of the late nineteenth century. Although this transformation did not occur overnight, by the 1920s there was little doubt that the United States had entered a new age.

By the 1920s, the process of industrialization was complete and the foundations of the modern corporate economy were firmly in place. Large-scale bureaucracies run by sophisticated tools of modern management, planning, and production strategies dominated the economy. The business–government partnership accelerated by World War I expanded on an informal basis throughout the "New Era" of the 1920s, and the successful performance of the economy seemed to confirm the efficacy of these capitalist choices. Even though the prosperity of the 1920s could not be sustained on a permanent basis, the economic reverses of the Great Depression in the

1930s did not wipe out the corporate organizational structure of the previous decade. This bureaucratic order reached its height in the postwar prosperity of the 1940s and 1950s.

The 1920s also represented an important watershed in the development of a mass national culture. The invention of the radio, the growing popularity of movies, and the spread of mass circulation magazines fostered a sense of shared national experience that broke down older patterns of isolation and provincialism. Advertising glorified new values of consumption and spending, although only the more prosperous members of the middle class could afford this expensive lifestyle. Meanwhile, the automobile had a revolutionary impact on both the nation's values and its landscape, signaling, among other things, a new emphasis on leisure and amusement that has come to characterize the modern era.

Such changes were troubling to many Americans. The 1920s were marked by deep controversy over the extent to which modern secular

ONE SIDE OF THE TWENTIES
Rarely has a decade been defined so predominantly in cultural clichés as the 1920s—flappers, bathtub gin, speakeasies, the Charleston, and gangsters shooting it out on the streets of Chicago. John Held, Jr.'s cover for *McClure's* magazine suggests why one historian satirized the decade as "one long party" where "everyone had a hangover (known as the depression) in the morning." This version of the 1920s tells only part of the story. Most Americans were too concerned with earning a living and raising a family to learn the latest dance craze. (Culver)

Corporatism, the Mesh of Public and Private Power

The booming economic prosperity of the 1920s provided the backdrop for the business and government initiatives during that decade. After a brief but sharp downturn in 1921 and 1922, the economy took off. Between 1922 and 1929, the gross national product, which is the total value of the nation's output of goods and services, grew by 40 percent, from $74.1 billion to $103.1 billion. Per capita income rose from $641 in 1921 to $847 in 1929. After 1922, unemployment hovered around 3 or 4 percent and inflation was negligible. Behind this economic growth lay new management and production techniques, especially the wide-spread introduction of electricity into factories and a strong increase in worker productivity. The automobile industry became the symbol of mass production and mass consumption. The world admired the extraordinary economic accomplishments of the United States.

Corporate Capitalism

The 1920s brought the triumph of the managerial revolution that had been reshaping the structure of the American economy since the late nineteenth century. Large-scale corporate organizations with bureaucratic structures of authority replaced older, family-run businesses. Ownership was divorced from control, and the visible hand of management replaced what the eighteenth-century economist Adam Smith had called the invisible hand of market forces.

A wave of mergers took place, surpassed in intensity only by the heyday of combinations in the 1880s and 1890s. There were 368 mergers in 1924 and 1,245 in 1929. The largest numbers of mergers occurred in rapidly growing industries such as chemicals (led by Du Pont), electric power (Westinghouse and General Electric), and automobiles (General Motors). By 1930, the two hundred largest corporations controlled just under half the nonbanking corporate wealth in the United States and received 43 percent of the corporate income. This concentration of economic power did not produce monopolies; rarely did

values should prevail. Cultural and political conflict broke out over such issues as immigration restriction, prohibition, and race relations. Rural Americans, now a minority, felt threatened by the country's increasingly urban tone. Despite such ambivalence about the transformations under way in American culture, the 1920s stand as a major turning point in the shift from older values characterized by self-denial and the Protestant work ethic to a fascination with consumption, leisure, and self-realization that is the essence of modern times.

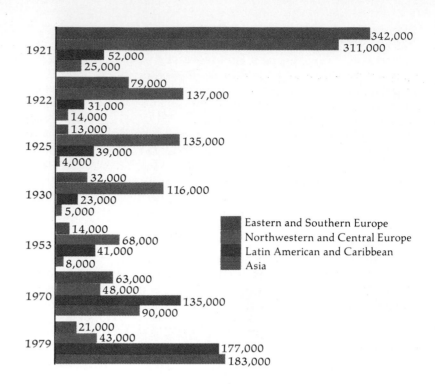

FIGURE 23.1 AMERICAN
IMMIGRATION SINCE
WORLD WAR I

any corporation control an entire industry. Rather, oligopolies, in which a few large producers controlled the market of an industry, became the norm.

By 1920, techniques of modern business enterprise dominated many industries, especially in manufacturing. The multi-unit enterprise coordinated production and distribution through divisions organized by functions, such as sales, operations, and investment. Alfred P. Sloan, Jr., an engineer and mid-level manager at General Motors in the 1920s, further refined the structure when he devised a bureaucratic strategy that relieved top management of all day-to-day control of production. The managers in the central office concentrated solely on long-range planning, while a series of autonomous, integrated divisions met short-range production goals. General Motors' innovative structure set the pattern for large companies in the 1920s and 1930s.

Perhaps the most important management change of the 1920s came with a greatly increased commitment to research and development within the corporate framework. This decision involved using current earnings to finance future profits. The increase in resources generated by the merger movement provided an

important source of capital for this purpose. By 1927, more than a thousand corporations had set up independent research programs to improve products or services, reduce production costs, or develop new products. The formal incorporation in 1925 of Bell Laboratories, the research arm of the American Telephone and Telegraph Company, reflected this trend.

Running these huge modern corporate structures called for a new breed of men. (Women found few opportunities in the corporate hierarchy until the 1960s and 1970s.) Professionalization of management became the watchword, especially emphasis on knowledge of management theory and techniques. Professionalization entailed a growing reliance on graduate training at business schools, such as Wharton and Harvard; the organization of professional societies and journals; and the growth of management consultants. Many of these new managers had engineering training. The chief executives in the 1920s at General Motors, General Electric, Singer, Du Pont, and Goodyear had been engineering classmates at the Massachusetts Institute of Technology.

The expansion and consolidation of the nation's financial resources paralleled its corporate growth. Total bank assets rose from almost $48 billion in 1919 to $72 billion in 1929. Rising deposits in savings accounts and business and loan associations, along with life insurance accounts and policies, accounted for much of the gain. Mergers between Wall Street banking establishments enhanced New York's role as the financial center of the United States. About 250 banks, 1 percent of the nation's total, controlled almost half its banking resources in 1929.

Business leaders enjoyed enormous popularity and respect in the 1920s. Their reputations often surpassed those of the rather lackluster politicians of the day. Styling themselves as trustees of the public interest, they promoted service and social responsibility through business. Many drew parallels between religious activity and business leadership. As President Calvin Coolidge solemnly declared, "The man who

HENRY FORD AND THOMAS EDISON
Henry Ford (1863–1947) and Thomas Alva Edison (1847–1931), two of the decade's most widely respected (and richest) business leaders, were also good friends. Edison (right), inventor of the phonograph, electric lighting, and motion pictures, was a founder of the company that eventually became General Electric. Henry Ford (left) revolutionized the auto industry with the introduction of the Model T in 1908 and was one of the most influential industrialists of the twentieth century. (Library of Congress)

builds a factory builds a temple. The man who works there worships there." The secularization of religion, and the glorification of business, reached its height in *The Man Nobody Knows* (1925), a book by advertising executive Bruce Barton. The man was Jesus Christ, whom Barton portrayed as the founder of modern business. Christ, he wrote, "picked up twelve men from the bottom ranks of business and forged them into an organization that conquered the world." Americans made Barton's parable an instant bestseller.

Henry Ford ranked as the most respected business leader of the decade, and a genuine folk hero as well. His background as a poor farm boy who made good symbolized the values of rural society and American individualism in a rapidly changing world. Ford was widely revered as a pioneer in labor relations for introducing the five-dollar-a-day wage in 1914. His factories, especially the Rouge plant in suburban Detroit, represented the triumph of mass production. Ironically, this American capitalist hero achieved great popularity in the Soviet Union, where he won respect as an economic innovator. At a time when the United States and the Soviet Union did not have formal diplomatic relations, Ford sold the Russians twenty-five thousand tractors between 1920 and 1926.

Although labor lagged behind business in reaping the benefits of technological advance, workers shared in the prosperity of the 1920s. Business supported higher wages as a deliberate strategy to increase consumer buying power. Shorter work weeks, down to five and a half days, including a half day on Saturday, gave workers more leisure time.

The 1920s also were the heyday of a system of labor relations that stressed management's obligation for the well-being of employees. Corporations provided their own programs—called "welfare capitalism"—as a calculated substitute for unions. Paternalism tinged such systems, but they provided benefits to workers at a time when federally guaranteed unemployment compensation and old age pensions did not exist. The corporate programs were not, however, primarily concerned with workers' security. Management's long-term goals included control over the workplace; the open, or nonunion, shop; and worker loyalty.

Welfare capitalism took several forms. For example, workers could increase their stake in a company's success by purchasing the firm's stock below the stock market price. By 1927, about eight hundred thousand workers had invested more than $1 billion in 315 companies. Some firms subsidized mortgages or contributed to employee savings funds; others set up insurance and pension plans. Many voluntarily adopted programs for consultation between management and the elected representatives of the workers. These employee representation plans, actually a device to avert unionization, were called the American Plan so as to establish the idea that unions were un-American.

Welfare capitalism represented a form of labor relations squarely in keeping with the values of the 1920s. It provided freedom from government interference to both workers and managers, placing the responsibility for economic welfare on the private rather than the public sector. The system had serious gaps, however. It offered no protection against unemployment. Only a minority of companies provided pension plans and stock-purchase programs. Most welfare capitalism programs appeared in the largest, most prosperous firms, such as General Electric and U.S. Steel. Furthermore, corporate profits dictated the nature of the programs. The Proctor & Gamble Company guaranteed its soap-manufacturing workers forty-eight weeks of employment a year because of the steady public demand for soap. The firm did not extend a similar pledge to workers who processed vegetable oils, which were subject to severe sales fluctuations.

In general, welfare capitalism satisfied management's main objective: it reversed the advance of unionization. Union membership dropped from 5.1 million in 1920 to 3.6 million in 1929. At the same time, the number of strikes fell dramatically from the 1919 level. Welfare capitalism seemed to represent the wave of the future in industrial relations.

The Economy

America's transition from a wartime to peacetime economy hardly foreshadowed the strong economic record of the 1920s. Runaway inflation was the worst problem during the immediate postwar period. Prices jumped by a third in 1919 and tripled their 1914 level by 1920. Feverish economic activity accompanied the inflation. However, the postwar boom was more a reflection of

consumers' desire to buy goods before prices rose even higher than of solid economic growth.

The inflationary bubble burst in 1920 when the Wilson administration sharply reduced federal expenditures in an attempt to balance the budget. The national deficit had risen to the unprecedented level of $13 billion. In contrast, the largest deficit during the period between the Civil War and World War I was about $89 million, recorded in 1899 and 1909. The Federal Reserve System also tightened credit in 1920 because its previous expansive money polices had encouraged people to borrow and spend, thereby pushing prices even higher. The resulting recession demonstrated that the government still had much to learn about protecting the stability of economic life.

The recession of 1920–1921 was the sharpest short-term downturn the United States had ever faced. Production fell, unemployment reached 10 percent, and the demand for goods and services slackened. Nearly five million Americans were out of work. Foreign trade dropped by almost half, from $13.5 billion in 1920 to less than $7 billion in 1921. Prices fell so dramatically— more than 20 percent—that the contraction wiped out much of the inflation of World War I. Fortunately, the recession lasted only a short time. Recovery started by 1922 and continued until 1929, broken only by brief, mild downturns.

One sector of the economy, agriculture, never fully recovered from the 1920 recession. During the inflationary period from 1914 to 1920, farmers had piled up large debts for mortgages and farm equipment as they expanded production in response to government incentives, increased demand, and rising prices. When the war ended, a glut of agricultural products hit the world market. Furthermore, the government withdrew price supports for wheat on May 31, 1920. Farm income plunged as the price of wheat dropped 40 percent, corn 32 percent, and hogs 50 percent. Total net farm income, which peaked at more than $10 billion in 1919, barely reached $4.1 billion in 1921.

Each year brought larger agricultural surpluses, which depressed farm prices even further. Farmers turned to the political system for help. The McNary-Haugen bill, a far-reaching attempt to create federal price supports for agricultural products, used the idea of a "fair exchange

SIGNS OF PROSPERITY
The success of the automobile industry provided a major component of the prosperity of the 1920s. With the introduction of the moving assembly line in 1914, the time it took Ford workers to assemble an auto dropped from fourteen hours to ninety-three minutes. By 1929, there were more than twenty-three million cars on the road, many of them caught up in traffic jams like the one pictured above. Billboards advertising brand-name products were another manifestation of the growth of a mass national culture. (Museum of Science & Industry, Chicago)

value" to guarantee that farmers earn at least their production costs, no matter what price prevailed on the world market. A 1924 bill applying this principle only to grain failed in Congress. When cotton, rice, and tobacco were added to win southern farm support, the measure twice passed, only to draw presidential vetoes in 1927 and 1928. Coolidge opposed the measure as an unhealthy government intrusion into the economy, a view seconded by the eastern business interests that controlled the Republican party. By the end of the decade, farmers had seen their share of the national income plunge from 16 percent in 1919 to 8.8 percent just ten years later.

Most other sectors of the economy fared considerably better during the 1920s. The value of total new construction increased from $6 billion in 1921 to $12 billion in 1927. Manufacturing output expanded 64 percent during the decade, fueled by a 40 percent increase in worker productivity. New industries turning out automobiles, chemicals, electric power, radios, aircraft, and movies stimulated economic growth. The demand for goods and services kept unemploy-

ment low throughout the 1920s, but the expanded demand was not so strong that it produced inflation.

This record of low unemployment and low inflation represented a significant accomplishment, but the economy contained several soft spots. In addition to agriculture, certain "sick industries," including coal and textiles, did not share in the prosperity of the 1920s. Unemployment remained far higher than the national average for workers in those industries. Moreover, seasonal or part-time work often cut workers' income, a fact not adequately reflected in the rather primitive economic statistics of that time. This underside of economic life foreshadowed the Great Depression of the 1930s.

As the economy expanded, its international dimensions enlarged correspondingly. America's emergence as the world's largest creditor nation, a reversal of its pre–World War I debtor status, represented a dramatic shift of power in the world capital markets. During the 1920s, the United States had the world's most productive economy, with great capacity to compete in markets abroad. The most visible aspect of this outward thrust was the dramatic extension of private investment, which more than doubled between 1919 and 1930. By the end of the 1920s, foreign investment stood at $15.2 billion.

Manufacturers led the way in foreign investment. Automobile companies found it cheaper to ship car parts to assembly plants outside the country and build the vehicles there than to export the finished products. Ford had major facilities in England, Canada, and throughout the British Empire; General Motors took control of such established firms as Vauxhall in England and Opel in Germany. Electric companies, including General Electric, built new plants in Latin America, China, Japan, and Australia. The International Telephone and Telegraph Corporation, founded in 1920, owned twenty-four factories in Europe by 1929. It employed ninety-five thousand workers outside the country, more than any other U.S. company. Underlying this increase of multinational economic activity was a growing foreign demand for the fruits of American mass production, such as radios, telephones, automobiles, and sewing machines.

Other U.S. companies invested internationally during the 1920s not so much to increase their foreign markets as to obtain supplies or take advantage of lower production costs. They concentrated their investments mainly in Latin America and Canada. The three major American meat packers—Swift, Armour, and Wilson—built packing plants in Argentina to capitalize on lower livestock prices. Fruit growers such as the United Fruit Company, searching for tropical products unavailable in the United States, developed vast tracts of land in Costa Rica, Honduras, and Guatemala. American capital dominated sugar plantations in Cuba and rubber plantations in the Phillipines, Sumatra, and Malaya.

American companies also made massive investments in mining and oil, concentrating on South American and Canadian sources. Chile attracted the greatest U.S. investment in mining; the Anaconda Copper Corporation owned Chile's largest copper mine. Led by Standard Oil of New Jersey, American oil companies put new emphasis on acquiring foreign oil. These firms retained extensive investments in Mexico but, discouraged by the tough bargaining of the Mexican government, turned to Venezuela as well.

By 1929, Venezuela ranked second only to the United States in oil production. American companies did not begin to pump oil from the Persian Gulf area of the Middle East until the 1930s.

American banks supported U.S. enterprises abroad. The banks not only facilitated direct corporate investments, but also made extensive loans of their own. Lending by American banks, particularly to foreign governments, became especially active after 1925.

The strong European demand for American private capital resulted primarily from the need to finance economic recovery after World War I, especially in Germany. The Allies' need for dollars to pay off wartime loans also contributed to the demand. As late as 1930, the Allies still owed the United States $4.3 billion. American political leaders, responding to the disenchantment with the nation's costly participation in the war, rigidly demanded payment. "They hired the money, didn't they?" scoffed President Calvin Coolidge.

The United States made repayment more difficult because of its high protective tariffs. The Fordney-McCumber Tariff of 1922 raised protectionism to an all-time high. Such tariffs, desired by American manufacturers who feared that foreign competition would reduce their high profits, limited the volume of European imports allowed into the United States. In turn, the difficulty in selling goods in the United States made it more difficult for European nations to use dollars to pay off their debts.

American business was concerned about debt repayment. The American banking community, and many U.S. corporations with European investments, opposed excessively high tariffs and urged modification of the debt structure. They recognized that a rapidly recovering Europe and a free-trade environment would help American business. Conversely, banks feared that a weak European economy might undermine their long-term loans and investments.

In 1924, the United States, France, Great Britain, and Germany, at the prodding of the United States, jointly agreed to a plan to promote European financial stability. The Dawes plan, named for Charles G. Dawes, a Chicago banker who negotiated the agreement, involved substantial American loans to Germany and a reduction in the amount of reparations owed the Allies. But the Dawes plan hardly provided a permanent solution. The international economic system was inherently unstable. It depended on the flow of American capital to Germany, reparations payments from Germany to the Allies, and the repayment of debts to the United States. If the outward flow of capital from the United States slowed or stopped, the whole international financial structure could collapse. This economic instability helped turn the recession that began in 1929 into a depression of worldwide proportions by the 1930s.

The Republican Ascendancy

The 1920 election returned the Republicans to power. Their domination of national politics in the 1920s stemmed from a reorientation in the national party system during the 1890s. Between 1894 and 1896, the Republican party broke the stalemate that had characterized national politics since the 1870s. William McKinley's presidential victory in 1896 marked the beginning of Republican control of the national government that lasted, with the exception of Woodrow Wilson's two terms, until 1932.

The Republicans built their party around various blocs of voters, drawn chiefly from the native-born Protestant middle class. This group included owners of small businesses, white collar workers, and farmers. To this solid base the Republicans added skilled workers who approved the party's promises of protection of home industries through high tariffs. They also relied on the black vote, traditionally Republican since Lincoln had freed the slaves and the Democratic party had fallen under the domination of southern politicians. In addition, wealthy industrialists supported Republican policies that encouraged business and economic development. These corporate leaders supplied the substantial cash resources that formed the party's stable financial base. Geographically, Republican strength was concentrated in the Northeast and West.

Throughout the first third of the twentieth century, the Democratic party had difficulty competing with its more popular and better-financed rival. Democrats had two main bases of support, the Solid South, consisting of the former Confederate states, and northern urban political machines, such as Tammany Hall in New

WARREN HARDING AND CALVIN COOLIDGE
The political careers of New Era political leaders Warren G. Harding (1865–1923) and Calvin Coolidge (1872–1933) present a study in contrasts. Harding (left), a small-town politician from Marion, Ohio, was prone to cronyism and mediocrity. Calvin Coolidge (right), of Vermont, was cut from a different cloth: taciturn, upright, stern, and capable. In the wake of the Harding scandals, Coolidge reassured citizens' faith in Republican government by his unimpeachable ethics. (Culver)

York. Until they could broaden their support and build an effective national organization to rival the Republican party, the Democrats would remain a minority party.

Woodrow Wilson had temporarily overcome the Democrats' weakness by exploiting the split in the Republican party in 1912 and by capturing electoral support from reform-minded progressives and western farmers. By 1918, Wilson's progressive coalition was floundering. In 1920, the Democrats passed over the ailing Wilson in favor of Governor James M. Cox of Ohio. Assistant Secretary of the Navy Franklin D. Roosevelt received the vice-presidential nomination. The Democratic platform urged ratification of U.S. participation in the League of Nations and a continuation of Wilsonian progressivism. Cox and Roosevelt lost in a landslide to Warren G. Harding and Calvin Coolidge.

President Harding was hardly a towering national figure. He had built an uninspiring record in Ohio state politics before winning election to the United States Senate in 1914. With a

Republican victory almost a certainty in 1920, party leaders wanted a presidential candidate they could dominate after he had taken office. Genial, loyal, and mediocre, "Uncle Warren" fit the bill.

Harding realized his limitations and assembled a strong cabinet to help him guide the government. Charles Evans Hughes, former presidential candidate and Supreme Court justice, headed the State Department. Secretary of Agriculture Henry C. Wallace set up conferences that brought farmers together with government agencies such as the Bureau of Agricultural Economics. Financier Andrew W. Mellon ran the Treasury Department, where he engineered a massive tax cut to reduce the federal surplus. Most of the benefits went to the wealthy, fulfilling Mellon's goal of releasing money for private investment.

By far the most active member of the Harding administration was Secretary of Commerce Herbert Hoover. Hoover made Commerce the most important cabinet position in both the Harding and Coolidge administrations. Cynics grumbled that he not only ran his own department, but also acted as undersecretary for all the others.

Hoover embodied the business–government cooperation that dominated the 1920s. Unlike Secretary of the Treasury Mellon, who sought the least amount of federal activity possible, Hoover supported expansion of the federal government in what he called the spirit of "associationalism." He developed his ideas to meet the needs of highly competitive, disorganized industries such as agriculture, construction, and mining. Hoover sought to eliminate waste, stabilize prices, and assure general economic stability in these volatile sectors of the economy through voluntary cooperation in the public interest. He used persuasion, educational conferences, and fact-finding commissions to accomplish his broad goals.

The key to Hoover's vision of "associated individualism" was his promotion of trade associations. These groups, which numbered about two thousand by 1929, represented almost every major industry and commodity. Serving as instruments of voluntary cooperation, they proved especially important in industries where excessive competition hampered productivity. Trade associations attempted to bring stability to modern economic life through conferences, conventions, publicity, lobbying, and trade practice controls. Statistics gathered by the Commerce Department and private groups, such as the National Bureau of Economic Research, aided corporate planning and the allocation of investments and markets. The Commerce Department's trade conferences provided a supportive climate for this exchange of information. The Republican-dominated Federal Trade Commission, conveniently ignoring antitrust laws that forbade such arrangements in restraint of trade, then approved the resulting agreements.

Unfortunately, many of Harding's lesser appointments fell far short of Hoover. The president was personally an honest man, but several of his appointees, often his cronies from his days in Ohio politics, lacked ethical standards. "My God, this is a hell of a job," Harding told journalist William Allen White in 1923. "I have no trouble with my enemies. . . . But my damned friends, my God-damn friends, White, they're the ones that keep me walking the floor nights!" Alice Roosevelt Longworth, Theodore Roosevelt's sharp-tongued and witty daughter, described Harding as a "slob" and characterized the mood at the White House as "a general atmosphere of waistcoat unbuttoned, feet on desk, and spittoons alongside."

Harding died unexpectedly in San Francisco in August 1923 after making the first presidential trip to Canada and Alaska. Evidence of widespread fraud and corruption in his administration had just started coming to light. The worst scandal concerned the government's leasing of oil reserves in Teapot Dome, Wyoming, and Elk Hills, California, to private companies. Secretary of the Interior Albert Fall eventually was convicted of taking almost half a million dollars in bribes. He became the first cabinet officer in American history to serve a prison sentence.

Harding's death catapulted Vice-President Calvin Coolidge into the White House. In contrast to Harding's political cronyism, Coolidge represented Vermont rectitude. He believed in limited government and performed all his presidential duties in four hours a day. As vice-president, "Silent Cal" often sat through entire dinner parties without uttering a word. His dinner partner once challenged him by saying, "Mr. Coolidge, I've made a rather sizable bet with my friends that I can get you to speak three words this evening." Replied Coolidge, "You lose." Alice Longworth quipped that Coolidge had been weaned on a pickle, but his unimpeachable morality reassured voters in the wake of the Harding scandals. Coolidge soon announced he would run for president in 1924.

The 1924 campaign featured a third-party challenge by Senator Robert M. La Follette of Wisconsin, who ran on the Progressive ticket. His candidacy mobilized progressive reformers and labor leaders, as well as farmers discontented over plunging farm prices. The Progressive party platform called for nationalization of the railroads, public ownership of utilities, and the right of Congress to overrule Supreme Court decisions. The platform also favored election of the president directly by the voters, rather than by the electoral college.

The Democrats were even more divided than usual when they gathered in the sweltering July heat of New York City to nominate a candidate for president in 1924. Their convention, the first to be broadcast live on national radio, lasted seventeen days, prompting humorist Will Rogers to joke, "This thing has got to come to an end. New York invited you people here as guests, not to live." The convention became hopelessly deadlocked between Governor Alfred E. Smith of New York, who had the support of northern urban politicians, and William G. McAdoo of California, Wilson's secretary of the treasury (and son-in-law), the western and southern choice. McAdoo also had the backing of a large faction of the Ku Klux Klan. The delegates needed 103 ballots to agree on compromise candidate John W. Davis, a Wall Street lawyer who had served as a West Virginia congressman and ambassador to Great Britain. To attract rural voters, Democrats chose Governor Charles W. Bryan of Nebraska, brother of William Jennings Bryan, for vice-president.

The Republicans won impressively. Coolidge received 15.7 million popular votes to 8.4 million for Davis and scored a decisive victory in the electoral college. Despite La Follette's vigorous campaign, he could not draw many midwestern farm leaders away from the Republican party; his labor support also proved soft. La Follette got almost 5 million popular votes but won only the support of Wisconsin in the electoral college.

Perhaps the most significant fact about the 1924 election was voter apathy. Only 52 percent of the electorate bothered to take part. Although voter participation had been declining since its nineteenth-century high, the turnout in 1924 was low partly because so few of the nation's newly enfranchised women voted. In 1920, the first presidential election since passage of the Nineteenth Amendment, barely a third of the women eligible to vote did so. Most people still considered politics a male preserve. Putting polling places in schools and churches, rather than their former location in saloons, helped women feel more comfortable with their new political role. By the end of the decade, women's voting turnout was on the rise, encouraged by the extensive education campaigns undertaken by the recently founded League of Women Voters.

Rather than forming their own party, women sought integration into the traditional political system. The two major parties only grudgingly granted women token positions. In 1920, Harriet Taylor Upton of Ohio, a former officer of the National American Woman Suffrage Association, became a vice-chairman of the Republican National Committee. In 1924, Emily Newell Blair, a former Missouri suffragist, took over the same position for the Democrats. In most cases, however, political officeholding for women remained a "widow's game." Both Miriam ("Ma") Ferguson of Texas and Nellie Tayloe Ross of Wyoming won election as their states' governors in 1924, but only after their husbands, because of impeachment or death, respectively, could not run. About two-thirds of the women in Congress were named to fill their late husbands' unexpired terms.

Women played more influential roles as lobbyists. The Women's Joint Congressional Committee, a Washington coalition of ten major women's organizations, lobbied for reform legislation of interest to women. Its major accomplishment was winning the passage in 1921 of the Sheppard-Towner Federal Maternity and Infancy Act, one of the nation's first federally funded health care programs. In an attempt to reduce the high rates of maternal and infant mortality, Congress appropriated $1.25 million for medical clinics, educational programs, and visiting-nurse projects. The Sheppard-Towner law passed because politicians feared that women would vote them out of office otherwise.

As one supporter noted, "If the members could have voted in the cloak room, it would have been killed." Once politicians realized that women did not vote as a bloc, they cut off appropriations for the program after 1929.

A New National Culture

In millions of homes during the 1920s, Americans sat down to a breakfast of Kellogg's corn flakes and toast prepared in a General Electric toaster. After breakfast, they got into their Ford Model T to go about the day's business, perhaps shopping at one of the new chain stores that had spread across the country. In the evening, the family gathered to listen to favorite radio programs such as "Great Moments in History" and "True Story." Or they read the latest issue of the *Saturday Evening Post* or *American Mercury*. On Friday or Saturday night, the family might hop into the car to see the latest Charlie Chaplin film at the local movie theater. Similar scenes took place throughout the United States. Millions of Americans shared the same daily experiences, signaling the development of a national culture.

Not every family participated in this new way of life, however. Urban blacks, rural farmers, and recent immigrants could rarely afford it. Other Americans found that the new values conflicted with religious and cultural mandates to work hard and live frugal lives. But, the patterns of consumption and leisure that appeared during the prosperous 1920s quickly became entrenched in American culture.

Toward a Mass National Culture

Nineteenth-century America was dominated by small towns and rural settlements where people felt in control of their own destinies and had little contact with outside forces. Even in the nineteenth century, however, community self-reliance and isolation were breaking down rapidly. The railroads, symbols of the new industrial order, threatened the older settled ways. Railroads brought in outside goods and ideas, and they took away products and people. By the 1920s, the isolation of most rural communities had been permanently shattered by forces even more powerful than the railroads. Automobiles, paved roads, parcel post service, movies, radios,

THE MAGIC OF THE MOVIES
Moving picture theaters were primarily located in working-class neighborhoods around the turn of the century. In order to lure the more prosperous middle class to this new form of mass entertainment, movie theaters in the 1920s featured lavish interiors decorated to mimic European palaces. The recently restored Chicago Theatre shows the architectural grandeur of the vintage picture palaces of the era. (© Don DuBroff and Russell B. Phillips)

THE GREAT HEART-THROB, RUDOLPH VALENTINO

In *The Shiek* (1921), Rudolph Valentino portrayed a British aristocrat disguised as an Arab chieftain who seduces a liberated Englishwoman, played by Agnes Ayres. When Valentino suddenly died in 1926 at the age of thirty-one, the lines of loyal fans at his funeral stretched for eleven blocks. (MOMA/Film Stills Archive)

telephones, mass circulation magazines, brand names, and chain stores—all lessened geographical isolation. Americans became linked by an ever-expanding web of national experience.

The movie industry probably did more than anything else to promote the diffusion of common values and attitudes throughout the United States. Its growth coincided with America's transformation into a predominantly urban, industrial society. Movies were the most popular, and probably the most influential, element of the new urban-based mass media. By the end of the 1920s, the nation had almost twenty-three thousand movie theaters. In Muncie, Indiana, a city of thirty-five thousand people, nine theaters operated seven days a week, with a rotating schedule of films. Muncie became famous as the typical American city, "Middletown," of Robert and Helen Lynd's 1929 sociological study.

National weekly movie attendance grew dramatically from 40 million in 1922 to 95 million in 1929, and reached 115 million in 1930. The introduction in 1927 of "talkies," movies with sound,

contributed to this growth. *The Jazz Singer* (1927), starring Al Jolson, was the first feature-length talking picture. Silent films soon became obsolete.

Movies began in working-class nickleodeons around the turn of the century, but by the 1920s they had reached into middle-class neighborhoods. The major film studios built elaborate movie palaces in most large cities. A doorman in a frock coat opened the car door at the curb and directed moviegoers to the ticket booth. Then a white-gloved usher showed the patrons to their seats. People joked that they would pay their way into these lavish theaters just to see the rest rooms. "Mama, does God live here?" asked a small moviegoing child in a *New Yorker* cartoon of the period.

Movies became big business, one of the main growth industries of the decade. During the first years of the twentieth century, most films had been made in New York City or in Fort Lee, New Jersey. After 1910, moviemakers started flocking to southern California, which had cheap land, plentiful sunshine, and mountains, deserts, cities, and the Pacific Ocean within easy access for use as scenery. Los Angeles was also a notoriously anti-union town, another attraction. Also flocking to California were the new movie stars. Actors such as Buster Keaton, Charlie Chaplin, Harold Lloyd, Mary Pickford, Douglas Fairbanks, and Clara Bow (the "It" girl), became national idols. Foreign distribution of films made Lloyd, Chaplin, and other stars familiar to European audiences as well. It also stimulated the market for the American material culture so lavishly documented on movie screens.

Movies fed the materialistic desires of a mass consumption economy. They stimulated fantasy and encouraged new patterns of leisure and recreation. They established national trends in clothing and hairstyles. Movies also served as a form of sex education. Though not salacious, they thrived on themes of romance and desire. Rudolph Valentino, best known as the hero of *The Sheik* (1921), symbolized passion on the screen. The message was not wasted on the nation's youth. "It was directly through the movies that I learned to kiss a girl on her ears, neck, and cheeks, as well as on the mouth," confessed one boy. Many girls noticed that actresses kissed with their eyes closed, and so they did, too. A sociologist concluded that movies made young people more "sex-wise, sex-excited, and sex-absorbed" than any previous generation. The links between movies and changing patterns of morality and sexuality have remained strong ever since.

Other instruments of mass culture also helped establish national standards of taste and behavior. In 1922, ten magazines claimed a circulation of at least 2.5 million; twelve others sold a million copies of each issue. The *Saturday Evening Post*, the *Ladies' Home Journal*, *American Mercury*, *Collier's Weekly*, and *Good Housekeeping* could be found in homes throughout the country. *Reader's Digest*, *Time*, and *The New Yorker* all began publication in the 1920s, with *The New Yorker* snidely boasting that it was "not for the old lady in Dubuque." People in all parts of the United States read the same articles, thanks to syndicated columns and features in newspapers. They also read the same best-selling books, partly as the result of the founding of the Book of the Month Club in 1926.

The newest instrument of mass culture truly was a child of the 1920s. Professional radio broadcasting began on November 2, 1920, when station KDKA in Pittsburgh carried the presidential election returns. By 1929, about 40 percent of the nation's households had a radio. (Map 25.2 on page 782 shows how far radio had spread by 1938.) More than eight hundred stations were broadcasting, most of them loosely grouped in two major networks, the Columbia Broadcasting Service and the National Broadcasting Company. American radio stations, unlike those in Europe, operated for profit, not as government monopolies. The U.S. government licensed the stations, however.

Americans loved radio. They listened avidly to the World Series and other sports events, as well as to variety entertainment shows featuring the Cliquot Club Eskimos, the Lucky Strike Orchestra, and the A & P Gypsies, all sponsored by advertisers of major brand name products. One of the most popular radio shows of all time, "Amos 'n' Andy," premiered on the NBC network in 1929. This comedy series featured black characters played by white actors. Soon fractured phrases from "Amos n' Andy" like "I'se regusted" and "Check and double check" became part of everyday speech. So many people

"tuned in" (another new phrase in the 1920s) that the country almost seemed to come to a halt at the time of favorite programs.

New Patterns of Leisure

The 1920s sometimes seem to have consisted of one fad after another—crossword puzzles, miniature golf, contract bridge, flagpole sitting, and Mah-Jongg (a Chinese game played with small tiles). Crazes reflected the diffusion of popular culture by the media and the increased leisure time Americans enjoyed. One of the most significant developments in modern life has been the growing freedom of many workers from constant physical toil on the job. The work week shrank an average of four hours per decade from 1900 to 1950, and some workers even won the right to paid vacations. As a result, Americans had more time to spend in leisure activities.

Public recreation flourished during the 1920s. Urban communities opened baseball diamonds, tennis courts, swimming pools, and golf courses, many built by state or municipal governments. In the New York metropolitan area, city planner Robert Moses masterminded the creation of a vast system of parks, playgrounds, and picnic areas. His greatest achievement was Jones Beach on Long Island. Moses created not only the beach; he also built limited-access highways from Manhattan to the Long Island shore. Any New Yorker with a car (an important limit on the democratic impulse of consumption) could escape to a free public beach in less than forty minutes.

As recreational facilities grew, so did professional sports, reflecting a trend toward the commercialization of leisure. People could watch a sports event in a comfortable stadium or listen to it on the radio. Millions followed boxing. The rematch between Jack Dempsey and Gene Tunney in 1927 featured the famous "long count" that enabled Tunney to recover from a knockdown and win the bout. This fight was one of the most talked about events of the year, probably surpassed only by Charles A. Lindbergh's solo flight across the Atlantic Ocean.

Baseball drew between nine and ten million fans each year. The sport was tarnished by the "Black Sox" scandal of 1919, when some Chicago White Sox players accepted gamblers'

CHARLES A. LINDBERGH

In 1928, *Time* magazine chose Charles A. Lindbergh (1902-1974) as its first Man of the Year. Lindbergh had successfully made the first solo nonstop flight between New York and Paris the year before in *The Spirit of St. Louis*. For the 3,610 mile, 33½-hour flight, Lindbergh took only five sandwiches and one day's worth of tinned rations. "If I get to Paris," he later explained, "I won't need any more, and if I don't get to Paris, I won't need any more either." Lindbergh captivated America because he personified the mastery of new technology (the airplane) in combination with the traditional American virtues of individualism, self-reliance, and hard work. His charm and boyish good looks didn't hurt, either. At the time of his record-breaking flight, he was twenty-five years old. (Missouri Historical Society)

bribes to throw the World Series. But baseball bounced back into popular favor with the rise of new heroes, most notably Babe Ruth of the New York Yankees. Nicknamed the "Sultan of Swat," Ruth electrified crowds by hitting more home runs—and hitting them farther—than any other player up to that time. Ruth's record of 714 career homers stood until Henry Aaron of the Atlanta Braves surpassed it in 1974. Yankee Stadium became known as the "house that Ruth built."

Newspapers heightened popular interest in sports. Their coverage of games and fights proved especially well suited to the tabloid, a small-sized newspaper featuring sensational stories and photojournalism. One of the chief beneficiaries of the heightened journalistic enthusiasm for sports was college football. The annual Harvard-Yale and Rose Bowl games received national coverage. Football fans could not read enough about the Four Horsemen of Notre Dame, the most famous backfield in college football history. In 1924, Red Grange of the University of Illinois became known throughout the country for scoring five touchdowns the first five times he carried the ball against the University of Michigan.

Other sports also gave the public numerous heroes to follow and admire. Bobby Jones ranked as the decade's best golfer. Bill Tilden dominated men's tennis, while Helen Wills and Suzanne Lenglen reigned in the women's game. The decade's best-known swimmer, male or female, was Gertrude Ederle, who shattered all records in 1927 by swimming the English Channel in just over fourteen hours. The muscle-bound bodybuilder Charles Atlas made his weight-lifting program nationally famous with the testimonial "I was a 97-pound weakling." Thanks to the attention of the media, the popularity of sports figures rivalled the fame of movie stars.

A musical innovation called jazz provided a different kind of entertainment. Jazz originated in the South but achieved nationwide prominence after black musicians brought its new rhythms to Chicago, New York, and other northern cities. Phonograph records spread the appeal of jazz by capturing its spontaneous improvisational excitement. All the early jazz musicians were black, including Ferdinand ("Jelly Roll") Morton and Louis Armstrong, who got his start with Joseph ("King") Oliver's Creole Jazz Band. White musicians such as Benny Goodman and Bix Beiderbecke later took up jazz, which became so popular that the 1920s are often called "the Jazz Age."

Consumption and Advertising

The 1920s were a critical decade in the development of the American consumer society. Consumption became a dominant cultural ideal among the middle class, often providing the criterion for self-worth that character, religious affiliation, and social standing formerly supplied. Americans were encouraged to believe that they could not live without the abundance of products and styles that appeared during the decade. Spending money became a form of self-fulfillment and gratification of personal needs.

The unequal distribution of income, however, limited the adoption of these new patterns of consumption to the more prosperous members of the middle class. About 65 percent of America's families had an income of less than $2,000 a year at the height of prosperity in the 1920s. The average family income for the bottom 40 percent of the population was $725. With that amount, a family would spend an average of about $290 a year for food, $190 for housing, and $110 for clothing. These expenditures left only $135 for everything else.

A dramatic increase in installment buying partially overcame this problem. With easier credit and buying on time, families could spend on the basis of future, as well as current, income. It is difficult to realize how revolutionary the philosophy of "buy now, pay later" was to consumers. Before World War I, most urban families paid cash for everything except the major purchase of a home. Then, during the 1920s, the automobile overcame people's fears of buying on time. Probably two-thirds of the cars in the United States in the 1920s were bought on the installment plan. Once consumers saw how easily they could finance the purchase of a car, they moved on to radios, refrigerators, and sewing machines. "A dollar down and a dollar forever," a cynic remarked. By 1929, the provision of consumer credit by banks, finance companies, credit unions, and other institutions exceeded $7 billion a year. It had become the tenth largest business in the United States.

Many of the new products were electric appliances, for which consumers spent about $667 million in 1927. By 1930, 85 percent of the nation's nonfarm households had the electricity necessary to run such gadgets. The most popular appliances were irons and vacuum cleaners, followed by phonographs, sewing machines, and washing machines. Radios, whose production increased twenty-five-fold in the 1920s, sold for around $75. One of the most expensive items was a refrigerator, which at the beginning of the

Proud that it is a Frigidaire

DELCO-LIGHT COMPANY, Dept. V-45, DAYTON, OHIO
Subsidiary of General Motors Corporation
The World's Largest Builder of Electric Refrigerators

Frigidaire
ELECTRIC REFRIGERATION

ADVERTISING ON A NATIONAL SCALE
Refrigerators did not save as much time or labor as other appliances such as irons and vacuum cleaners, but they did have advantages. For example, food stayed fresh longer, which reduced the need to shop every day. In the 1920s, refrigerator manufacturers launched major advertising campaigns to promote the advantages of their product over the old-fashioned icebox. Their advertising budgets peaked at $20 million in 1931, approximately $7 for every refrigerator sold. (The Newberry Library, Chicago)

decade cost $900. Technology quickly brought the price down, but even a $180 refrigerator remained beyond the reach of many families, who continued to use iceboxes.

This new technology, much of it concentrated in the home, had dramatic implications for women. The appliances promised liberation from the drudgery of domestic chores. An electric iron was easier to use than an iron heated on the stove, and a vacuum cleaner worked quicker and more efficiently than a broom. A washing machine saved hours of toil over a washboard, and clothes came out much cleaner. Paradoxically, however, the time that women spent on housework did not decline. Since fewer poor women were entering domestic service, more middle-class women began to do their own housework; electric servants replaced human ones. Technology often raised standards of cleanliness as well. A man could wear a clean shirt every day, not just on Sunday, and a house could be vacuumed daily rather than weekly. All this made more work for women.

Advertising became big business in the 1920s. By 1929, advertisers spent an average of $15 annually for every man, woman, and child in the United States, a total of $3.4 billion. That year, advertising comprised 3 percent of the gross national product, comparable to its share in the post–World War II period. Many major advertising firms were founded, some with direct or indirect links to the expanding field of psychology. The advertising pioneer Edward Bernays was the nephew of the controversial Austrian psychoanalyst Sigmund Freud. The prominent psychologist John B. Watson left Johns Hopkins University in 1922 to become vice-president of the J. Walter Thompson advertising agency.

Psychology played an important role in advertising. Since few of the new products could be considered basic necessities, ads had to create a desire to buy. Advertisers often used the implied approval of science, represented by the white-coated doctor who appeared in many advertisements, to sell their products. Ad writers also sold products by calling attention to people's insecurities. They came up with a variety of socially unacceptable diseases, including "sneaker smell," "paralyzed pores," "vacation knees," "ashtray breath," and the dreaded "B.O." (body odor). After the term *halitosis* was discovered in an obscure British medical journal, the ugly-sounding word made many consumers buy Listerine mouth wash to prevent bad breath.

Advertising claims soared higher and higher. Not only would a toothpaste prevent "pink toothbrush" (bleeding gums), it would also assure a dazzling smile and improve the buyer's love life. Zelda Fitzgerald, the wife of novelist F. Scott Fitzgerald and herself a novelist, reflected this faith in advertising when she confessed, "I still believe that one can learn to play the piano by mail and that mud will give you a perfect complexion." Yet American consumers were not passive victims of evil "captains of consciousness" who manipulated their every whim and desire. America gloried in its role as the world's first mass consumption economy.

The Automobile Culture

The automobile, the predominant symbol of the 1920s, typified the new consumer-based economy. "Why on earth do you need to study what's changing this country?" a Middletown (Muncie, Indiana) resident challenged the sociologists. "I can tell you what's happening in just four letters: A-U-T-O!" Showpiece of modern capitalism and the ultimate consumer toy, the automobile revolutionized patterns of leisure and consumption. Cars changed the nation's vernacular with such phrases as "filling station," first recorded in 1921. They even affected patterns of crime, providing gangsters with a "getaway car" and the option of "taking someone for a ride." Cars touched so many aspects of American life that the word *automobility* was coined to describe their revolutionary impact on production methods, the nation's landscape, and even American values.

The automobile stimulated the prosperity of the 1920s. Car sales climbed from 1.5 million in 1921 to 5 million in 1929, when Americans spent $2.58 billion on new and used autos. By the late 1920s, a new Ford Model T cost only $295. Decreasing cost, combined with installment buying, increased yearly car registrations from 8 million in 1920 to 23 million in 1929. By the end of the decade, Americans owned about 80 percent of the world's automobiles, with an average of one car for every five people.

The growth of the auto industry had a multiplier effect on the American economy. In 1929, 3.7 million workers directly or indirectly owed their jobs to the automobile. Auto production stimulated basic industries, such as steel, petroleum, chemicals, rubber, and glass. The advertising industry also grew hand in hand with the automobile, which was one of the most heavily marketed products of the decade. Highway construction became a billion-dollar-a-year activity, financed by federal subsidies and state gasoline taxes. Because everyone wanted more roads, gas taxes were probably the most popular taxes ever proposed. Car ownership also spurred the suburban boom and contributed to real estate speculation. It spawned the first shopping center, Country Club Plaza, in Kansas City in 1922. Not even the twenty-five thousand people killed each year in traffic accidents, 70 percent of them pedestrians, could diminish America's love affair with the automobile.

Nowhere was this infatuation more evident than in the changing patterns of leisure. Americans took to the roads and became a nation of tourists. The American Automobile Association reported that about forty-five million people took vacations by automobile in 1929. Of the $10 billion spent on recreation in 1930, two-thirds went for cars and related expenses. People regarded automobiles as instruments of personal freedom far preferable to trains, with their predetermined tracks and timetables. Only twelve motorists had driven across the United States in 1912, but twenty thousand made the trip in 1921. With improved roads, motorists could average more

than forty-five miles per hour. By the 1930s, they drove three hundred to four hundred miles a day. Autocamps and tourist cabins, the forerunners of motels, began to offer services for traveling motorists.

People did not have to travel such long distances to experience the impact of the automobile. Will Kennicott, the main character of Sinclair Lewis's popular novel *Main Street* (1920), confessed to four loves, in no particular order—his wife, his automobile, his medical practice, and hunting. City dwellers could escape from urban crowding for a day in a rural area, in the mountains, or at the seashore. Cars broke down the isolation of rural and farm life.

Young people loved cars because they made possible a social life independent of parental supervision. Contrary to many parents' views, sex was not invented in the back seat of a Ford. But a Model T offered more privacy and comfort than the family living room or front porch. City elders in Muncie, Indiana, overreacted by calling automobiles "prostitution on wheels." Cars, like

THE AUTOMOBILE VACATION

This contented couple was autocamping in Yellowstone Park in 1923. Autocamping was portrayed as a great liberation from seedy hotels and rigid railroad timetables. When farmers complained about auto tourists' tendency to camp right in their fields, towns instituted auto camps. When auto camps became associated with transients and hobos in the depression, tourist cabins (with a spot to park your car next to the cabin) became the vogue. By the 1940s, it was just a short step to the modern motel chain. (Library of Congress)

MIDDLETOWN RESIDENTS TALK ABOUT THEIR AUTOMOBILES

In 1929, Robert and Helen Lynd conducted a pioneering sociological study of community life in Muncie, Indiana. In their book on the findings, they named the location "Middletown."

"We'd rather do without clothes than give up the car. We used to go to his sister's to visit, but by the time we'd get the children shoed and dressed there wasn't any money left for carfare. Now no matter how they look, we just poke 'em in the car and take 'em along."

"We don't spend anything on recreation except for the car. We save every place we can and put the money into the car. It keeps the family together."

"No, sir, we've *not* got a car. *That's* why we've got a home."

"The Ford car has done an awful lot of harm to the unions here and everywhere else. As long as men have enough money to buy a second-hand Ford and tires and gasoline, they'll be out on the road and paying no attention to union meetings."

"We don't have no fancy clothes when we have the car to pay for. The car is the only pleasure we have."

"He don't like to go to church Sunday night. We've been away from church this summer more'n ever since we got our car."

"I'll go without food before I'll see us give up the car."

"An automobile is a luxury, and no one has a right to one if he can't afford it. I haven't the slightest sympathy for any one who is out of work if he owns a car."

Source: Robert S. Lynd and Helen Merrell Lynd, *Middletown: A Study in Modern American Culture.* New York: Harcourt, Brace, 1929. 254–257, 362.

---

movies, changed the ways that American youth discovered sex.

The Model T was the most popular car of the decade. The Ford Motor Company manufactured fifteen million Model Ts between 1908 and 1927. Charles Lindbergh drove one when he was not flying, and Buffalo Bill Cody used one to promote his traveling Wild West show. Even the Mexican bandit chief Pancho Villa retreated to the mountains in a Model T. The "Tin Lizzies," as the dependable Model T's were affectionately nicknamed, came in one color. "Any customer can have a car painted any color he wants so long as it is black," said Henry Ford, keeping a close eye on costs. A Model T required a mechanically inclined driver. The motorist had to hand-crank the car to start it and then keep one hand on the accelerator and the other on the wheel while driving. The only way to check how much gas remained was to remove the front seat and peer into the tank. As late as 1919, only about 10 percent of the nation's cars had a roof.

People eventually became discontented with the plain Model T's. Ford faced stiff competition from General Motors, whose five automobile divisions produced products for specialized markets. The luxury Cadillac featured the highest prices and lowest volume of sales; the Chevrolet boasted the cheapest price tag and highest sales; Oldsmobile, Pontiac, and Buick were geared to incomes in between. GM cars also offered such conveniences as self-starters and foot accelerators. Henry Ford finally bowed to consumer demands for yearly style changes, optional colors, and greater comfort when he introduced the Model A in 1927. Consumers trusted Ford so completely that four hundred thousand of them made a down payment on the Model A before even seeing its design or knowing its cost. (The price ranged from $495 to $570.) More than a million New Yorkers visited the Ford showroom during the five days after the new model was unveiled. The Model A lived up to consumers' high expectations, and helped make the automobile a permanent part of American culture.

Another Part of the Twenties

Not all Americans accepted the secular values that characterized the mass consumption society of the 1920s. In addition to the families who could not afford such a life-style, others opposed the new values as an affront to a more traditional way of life rooted in small towns and farming communities. In Dearborn, Michigan, a suburb of Detroit, Henry Ford created Greenfield Village, a nostalgic memorial to the world of his youth, just as his automobiles were transforming the rural countryside. Many Americans shared Ford's ambivalence about the dramatic changes in society. Their conservative outlook represented another part of the Twenties.

Urban Majority/Rural Minority

One of the most conspicuous features of modern America has been the rapid growth of cities. In 1920, 52 percent of the population lived in urban areas, compared with 28 percent in 1870, only fifty years earlier. When the 1920 census revealed that city people outnumbered rural dwellers for the first time, Americans realized that a dramatic transition had taken place. It produced feelings as intense as those that had greeted the 1890 announcement of the end of the frontier.

Actually, the 1920 report did not represent as great a turning point as it seemed. The census bureau had distinguished between urban and rural populations for the first time in 1870, setting the dividing line at a population of 8,000. In 1900, it lowered the number to 2,500, which would hardly fill more than a village. If urban areas had been defined as population centers of more than 10,000, a more realistic standard, as late as 1930 only 47.6 percent of the population would have been classified as urban.

Yet there was no mistaking the trend. Americans were moving to the cities in ever-increasing numbers. By 1929, ninety-three cities had a population of over 100,000. In the 1920s, New York City exceeded 7 million and the population of Los Angeles doubled to more than 1.2 million. The growth outside the major cities was even more impressive. Extended metropolitan areas and suburbs sprang up, encouraged by cheap land and better highway transportation. This trend started long before the post-World War II suburban boom.

As rural dwellers felt mounting threats to their cultural and economic superiority, they often lashed out at the most convenient symbol, the city. The essential rootlessness of urban life offended traditional community standards, and the frantic emphasis on consumption mocked values of thrift and character. Automobiles, radios, and mass circulation magazines brought these unwelcome facts of life into previously isolated rural areas.

The conflict between cultures that had been building since the late nineteenth century took on special force in the 1920s. Farmers continued to struggle after the recession of 1920–1921, and rural communities lost people to urban areas at an alarming rate. During the 1920s, about six million Americans left the farms for the cities, including many blacks who abandoned the South altogether for the greater freedom of northern society. The boundaries of political districts did not reflect this population shift, however, and rural areas still controlled most state legislatures. Battles over the equitable use of tax dollars, especially for city services, intensified the rural–urban political conflict.

Yet it would be wrong to describe this conflict as just a futile last-ditch effort on the part of rural America to hold onto political and cultural dominance. The lives of many rural people had changed in response to the same forces that influenced urban life. The old ideal of the self-reliant yeoman farmer was giving way to a new model of the farmer as entrepreneur. Much of the new technology enhanced rural life, especially electricity and automobiles. Rural people were tempted by the new values trumpeted by radio programs, magazines, and movies. Even though they tried to resist, many Americans found more to attract than to repel them in the new ways. The cultural conflict in the 1920s may have been so heated because both rural and urban dwellers realized how far they had already strayed from older values.

Dissenters to the New Values

The 1920s brought an upsurge in political mobilization centering around cultural issues. This political action included a willingness to use coercion or legislation to enforce a specific point of view. Americans troubled by the growing number of immigrants turned to national legis-

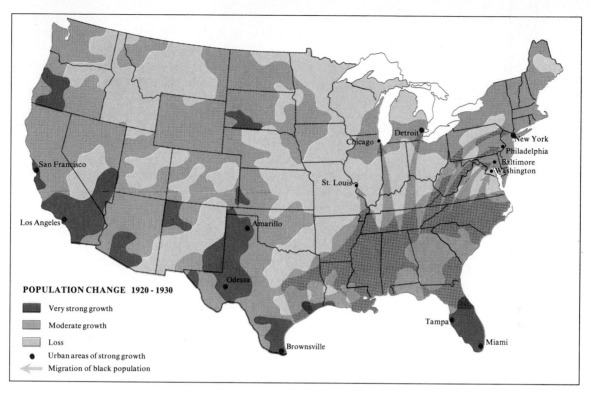

MAP 23.1 THE SHIFT FROM RURAL TO URBAN POPULATION, 1920–1930
Despite the increasingly urban tone of modern America after 1920, regional patterns of population growth and decline were far from uniform. Cities in the South and West grew most dramatically, as southern farmers moved to more promising areas in familiar climates. One important component of the growth of northern cities, such as New York and Chicago, was the migration of southern blacks set in motion by World War I.

lation to restrict the flow. The Ku Klux Klan rose again to defend white Anglo-Saxon Protestantism against the intrusion of blacks, Catholics, Jews, and immigrants. Fundamentalist religious leaders fought what they considered the inroads of science in the nation's classrooms. And prohibition imposed the views of the nondrinking majority on a vocal and thirsty minority.

Tension between city and country played a part in all these conflicts, but it was not the sole cause. Resistance to change and a desire to stop the clock of progress, feelings that transcended the urban–rural polarity, probably had a greater influence. Many city dwellers had been born and raised in rural areas or small towns, and memories of the nineteenth century still had a strong hold on their lives. In many ways, these cultural conflicts resembled those of the 1970s, when conservative groups proposed constitutional amendments on abortion, school prayer,

and school busing in an effort to legislate social values.

The successful drive against immigration in the 1920s tapped deep feelings of nativism in the United States. Native-born white Americans doubted the nation's ability to absorb the growing number of newcomers who brought different values and customs with them. Many of the new immigrants were Catholics or Jews, whose religion clashed with the country's dominant Protestant tone. Large numbers came from peasant backgrounds, which gave them little preparation for participation in democratic forms of government. Senator William Bruce of Maryland called such immigrants "indigestible lumps" in the "national stomach."

Prejudice against Orientals had already closed off immigration from Japan and China. In 1917 the United States established a literacy test for all immigrants. This requirement proved to be only a slight deterrent, however. If immigrants were determined to find a new life in America, they also were prepared to learn enough reading and writing skills to pass a simple test. Demands for stricter limits intensified.

In 1921, Congress passed a bill limiting the number of immigrants to 3 percent of each national group, based on the 1910 census. President Wilson refused to sign the bill, but it was reintroduced after Warren Harding took office in 1921. The new law produced results that same year. During the fiscal year ending in June 1921, 805,228 immigrants entered the United States; the number dropped to 309,556 in fiscal 1922.

For many citizens, a quota system that admitted 300,000 immigrants a year was a sieve with too many holes. As a result, the National Origins Act of 1924 limited immigration to 2 percent of each nationality as reflected in the 1890 census. Congressional leaders chose the 1890 cutoff because at that time, few immigrants had arrived from the "undesirable" areas of southeastern Europe and Russia. The 1924 quotas cut the total annual immigration to 164,000 persons, with national origins heavily favoring Great Britain, Ireland, and Germany. The law admitted only 4,000 Italians. It excluded Japanese and Chinese immigrants entirely.

An even more restrictive system took force in 1929. A ceiling of 150,000 persons annually was placed on incoming immigration, to be apportioned on the basis of the national origins revealed in the 1920 census. President Herbert Hoover lowered the quota even further in 1931. The next year, during the depth of the Great Depression, more foreigners left the United States

RESURGENCE OF THE KKK
The Ku Klux Klan was not limited to the South. Here a group of Klansmen conduct an initiation rite outside of Milwaukee, Wisconsin. Note the juxtaposition of the symbols of the Ku Klux Klan—white robes and burning crosses—with the traditional symbol of patriotism, the American flag. (FPG)

THE KLAN COMES TO KOKOMO, INDIANA

The Konklave was an important day in my life. I was nine years old, with a small boy's interest in masquerades and brass bands. But I was also a Catholic, the son of a Catholic who taught in the public schools and who consequently was the object of a good deal of Klan agitation. If anything worse was to come, the Konklave probably would bring it. Every week or so the papers had been reporting Klan atrocities in other parts of the country—whippings, lynchings, tar-and-feather parties—and my father and my family were logical game in our locality. . . .

As we sat on our front porch after watching the parade, we could see the Klansmen of our neighborhood trickling home. Some still wore their regalia, too tired to bother with taking it off before they came into sight. Others carried little bundles of white: they were the ones who still made some pretense of secrecy about being members. One of the last to come down the street was old Mrs. Crousore, who lived a few doors away. Her white robe clung damply, and

her hood was pushed back. As she climbed her steps and sank solidly into a rocking chair on her porch, we could hear her groan, "Oh, my God, my feet hurt!"

Mrs. Crousore spoke with such feeling that her words seemed to summarize the whole day. My parents adopted her comment as a family joke. July 4, 1923, became for us the day when Mrs. Crousore's feet hurt. But it was clear to me when I grew a little older that my parents needed that joke as much as Mrs. Crousore needed her rocking chair. There were wild rumors in the town in the months that followed: Father Pratt, the pastor at St. Patrick's Church, was on the list for tar-and-feathering; the church was going to be burned; the Klan was going to "call" on the Jewish merchants; it was going to "get" my father and Miss Kinney, another Catholic who taught in the public schools. Considering all the violent acts committed by the Klan elsewhere in the country, it seemed quite possible that any or all of these notions might mature into action.

As it turned out none of them

did. . . . Perhaps the answer lay in the dead level typicalness of the town: a population overwhelmingly white Protestant, with small, well-assimilated numbers of Catholics, Jews, foreigners, and Negroes, and an economy nicely balanced between farming and industry. There were few genuine tensions in Kokomo in 1923, and hence little occasion for misdirected hate to flame into personal violence.

It may be asked why, then, did the town take so wholeheartedly to the Klan, which made a program of misdirected hate? And the answer to that may be, paradoxically enough, that the Klan supplied artificial tensions. Though artificial, and perhaps never quite really believed in, they were satisfying. They filled a need—a need for Kokomo and all the big and little towns that resembled it during the early 1920s.

Source: Robert Coughlan, "Konklave in Kokomo," in Isabel Leighton, ed., *The Aspirin Age, 1919–1941.* New York: Simon & Schuster, 1949, 1976. 107, 110–111.

---

than entered. In contrast, 1,285,000 immigrants had entered the country in 1907, the peak year of immigration.

America had always been a nation of immigrants. Whoever could afford the passage to the United States was free to seek a new life there. But now the gates were closing tight. The sole loophole, which grew in significance through the years, permitted unrestricted immigration from countries in the Western Hemisphere. Central and Latin Americans crossed the border in increasing numbers, filling the places vacated by the cutoff of immigration from Europe and the Far East.

The National Origins Act was just one example of the rise of nativism during the 1920s. Colleges instituted quotas to limit the enrollment of Jewish students, and many law firms refused to hire Jewish lawyers at all. Henry Ford spoke for many Americans when he warned of the menace of the "International Jew." Ford became so closely identified with anti-Semitism that decades passed before some Jewish families could bring themselves to buy one of his cars.

The most striking example of nativism in the 1920s was the revival of the Ku Klux Klan. Confirming the power of the media, the Klan found encouragement in D. W. Griffith's epic film *Birth of a Nation* (1915), a glorification of white southerners fighting to overturn the social and political changes introduced by the Civil War and Reconstruction. Racism pervaded the movie, and its plot pandered to fears of sexual relations between whites and blacks. White audiences everywhere cheered the famous scene in which the Klan rode to the rescue of endangered white southern womanhood.

Unlike its earlier version in the post-Civil War era, the Ku Klux Klan did not limit its activities to harassment of blacks. Its targets were just as likely to be immigrants, especially Catholics and Jews. Nor did the Klan have only rural supporters. The modern Klan was organized in Atlanta and appealed to both city and rural people. It had long outgrown its southern base, finding significant support in the far West, Southwest, and Midwest, especially in Indiana. At the height of its power in 1925, the Klan had almost four million members.

The Ku Klux Klan appealed to Americans who believed in its slogan, "native, white, Protestant supremacy." Hiram Wesley Evans, an "Imperial Wizard" or boss of the Klan, claimed the Klan spoke for "the great mass of Americans of the old pioneer stock" who were deeply distressed by the moral breakdown in society:

> One by one all our traditional moral standards went by the boards, or were so disregarded that they ceased to be binding. The sacredness of our Sabbath, of our homes, of chastity, and finally even of our right to teach our own children in our own schools fundamental facts and truths were torn away from us. . . . We found our great cities and the control of much of our industry and commerce taken over by strangers, who stacked the cards of success and prosperity against us. . . . So the Nordic American today is a stranger in large parts of the land his fathers gave him.

Members of the Klan, who wore white hoods and robes at Klan gatherings, developed an elaborate hierarchy of leaders and passwords that filled the emotional needs of its members. But the Klan did not merely practice harmless rituals. Its standard activities included nightriding, arson, tarring and feathering, and other forms of physical intimidation.

After 1925, the Klan declined rapidly, the victim of internal scandals and a changing national climate. Especially damaging was the revelation that Grand Dragon David Stephenson, the Klan's national leader, had kidnapped and sexually assaulted his former secretary, driving her to suicide. The passage of the 1924 immigration act also contributed to the Klan's eclipse.

The religious debate between modernists and fundamentalists represented another example of the cultural conflict that raged in the 1920s. Modernists, or liberal Protestants, attempted to bring religion more in line with modern secular values, especially to reconcile the often contradictory views of religion and science. Fundamentalists believed in a literal interpretation of the Bible. Popular speakers, among them Billy Sunday and Aimee Semple McPherson, promoted their versions of fundamentalist evangelicalism throughout the 1920s.

The modernist-fundamentalist controversy soon entered the political arena, especially in legislation designed to prevent the teaching of evolution in schools. The scientific theories in Charles Darwin's *On the Origin of the Species* (1859) conflicted with the Biblical account of creation in the book of Genesis, which claimed that God created the world in six days. In 1925, Tennessee passed a law providing that "it shall be unlawful . . . to teach any theory that denies the story of the Divine creation of man as taught in the Bible, and to teach instead that man has descended from a lower order of animals."

The newly formed American Civil Liberties Union (ACLU) decided to challenge the constitutionality of the Tennessee law. Its test case involved a teacher named John T. Scopes, who had taught evolution in his high school biology class in Dayton, Tennessee. The famous criminal lawyer Clarence Darrow defended Scopes. The prosecuting attorney was William Jennings Bryan, three-time presidential candidate, spellbinding orator, and a fundamentalist.

The Scopes trial in July 1925 became known as the "monkey trial." That nickname had a double meaning, referring both to Darwin's theory that human beings descended from other primates, and the circus atmosphere that surrounded the trial. Darrow ridiculed Bryan's "fool religion," and Bryan called Darrow "the greatest atheist and agnostic in the United States." More than a hundred journalists crowded into the sweltering Dayton courthouse, and Chicago radio station WGN broadcast the trial live.

Scopes, who readily admitted that he had broken the Tennessee law, played only a minor role as the trial quickly turned to volatile questions of faith and scientific theory. The judge rebuffed defense efforts to call expert scientific witnesses on evolution. He considered such testimony as hearsay because the experts had not been present when lower forms of life evolved. Darrow countered by calling Bryan to the stand as an expert on the Bible. Under oath, Bryan asserted his belief that Jonah had been swallowed by a "big fish," Eve created from Adam's rib, and the world created by God in six days. He hedged, however, about whether the days were literally twenty-four hours long, an inconsistency which Darrow ruthlessly exploited.

Even so, the jury took only eight minutes to find Scopes guilty. The Tennessee Supreme Court upheld the controversial law on appeal, and the statute remained technically in force until the state legislature repealed it more than thirty years later. However, the Tennessee Supreme Court overturned Scopes's sentence on the technicality that his hundred-dollar fine had been incorrectly set by the trial judge rather than the jury. The reversal of Scopes's conviction prevented further appeal of the case. As the 1920s ended, science and religion faced each other in an uneasy standoff.

The longest-running cultural debate of the 1920s involved prohibition. The Eighteenth Amendment to the Constitution prohibited the manufacture, transport, or sale of intoxicating liquors in the United States after January 16, 1920. The law did not forbid people to drink liquor, however.

Prohibition is often described as a repressive denial of individual freedom. Yet it was viewed by many people at the time as a progressive reform. The twentieth-century crusade for prohibition had roots in Protestant urban areas, where it drew support from reformers concerned about good government and public morality. It also picked up substantial backing in rural communities. Liquor was equated with all the sins of the city, including prostitution, crime, machine politics, and public disorder. In addition, religious groups such as the Methodists and Baptists who counted their greatest strength in rural areas, condemned drinking.

On the other hand, alcoholic beverages, especially beer and whiskey, played an important role in certain ethnic cultures, especially those of German and Irish immigrants. Most saloons were in working-class neighborhoods and

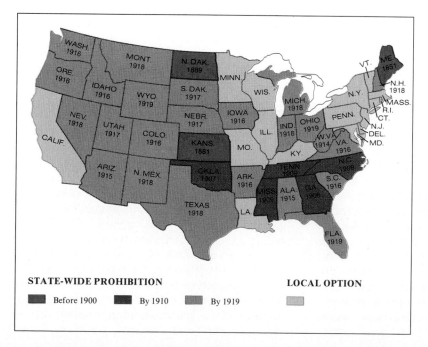

STATE-WIDE PROHIBITION

- Before 1900
- By 1910
- By 1919

LOCAL OPTION

MAP 23.2 PROHIBITION ON THE EVE OF THE EIGHTEENTH AMENDMENT
Prohibition had already made strong headway in the states before the adoption of the Eighteenth Amendment in 1919. States such as Maine, North Dakota, and Kansas had been dry since the nineteenth century; by 1919, two-thirds of the states had already passed laws banning liquor. Most states that resisted the trend were industrial centers or had large immigrant populations. In the intense anti-German hysteria of World War I, the fact that many major U.S. breweries—such as Pabst and Busch—had German names made beer drinking unpatriotic in many people's minds.

THE ADVENTURES OF IZZY AND MOE, PROHIBITION AGENTS

Government agents Isadore (Izzy) Einstein and Moe Smith carried out many raids on illegal liquor stills and speakeasies. Their exploits gained the air of legend as the Prohibition dragged on.

What the newspapers enjoyed most about Izzy and Moe was their ingenuity. Once they went after a speakeasy where half a dozen dry agents had tried without success to buy a drink. The bartender positively wouldn't sell to anyone he didn't know. So on a cold winter night Izzy stood in front of the gin-mill, in his shirt sleeves, until he was red and shivering and his teeth were chattering. Then Moe half-carried him into the speakeasy, shouting excitedly:

"Give this man a drink! He's just been bitten by a frost!"

The kindhearted bartender, startled by Moe's excitement and upset by Izzy's miserable appearance, rushed forward with a bottle of whiskey. Moe promptly snatched the bottle and put him under arrest.

On one of his swings around the so-called enforcement circuit, Izzy made up a sort of schedule showing the length of time it took him to get a drink in various cities. New Orleans won first prize, a four-star hiss from the Anti-Saloon League. When Izzy arrived in the Crescent City he climbed into an ancient taxicab, and as the machine got under way he asked the driver where he could get a drink.

"Right here, suh," said the driver, and pulled out a bottle. "Fo' bits."

Time—thirty-five seconds.

Source: Herbert Asbury, "The Noble Experiment of Izzie and Moe," in Isabel Leighton, *The Aspirin Age, 1919–1941*. New York: Simon & Schuster, 1949, 1976. 40–41, 47.

---

served as gathering places for workers at the end of the day. Members of political machines conducted much of their business in bars. Urban dwellers who regarded liquor and saloons as an important part of their heritage therefore opposed prohibition.

Prohibition caused a temporary decline in drinking in the early 1920s, but several factors undermined its long-term success. America's coastlines and borders enabled liquor smugglers to operate with ease, and organized crime, already a factor in major cities, supplied a ready-made distribution network for bootleg liquor. Government appropriations for enforcement of prohibition were woefully inadequate. In addition, many people abused its exemptions. For example, doctors could prescribe alcohol for medicinal reasons, and churches could use wine for sacramental purposes. Sacramental consumption soon rose to a hefty eight hundred thousand gallons a year. People even learned to make alcoholic beverages at home, hence the term "bathtub gin." However, beer proved more difficult to manufacture and distribute illegally than hard liquor, and beer consumption dropped considerably after 1920. Working-class people had to turn to hard liquor if they wanted to drink.

Once people showed their willingness to flout the law, prohibition had little chance of success. In a typical incident off Coney Island, people on the beach cheered a rum runner who eluded a Coast Guard boat. Illegal saloons called speakeasies flourished openly in all major cities; New York had more than thirty thousand of them. Attorney General William D. Mitchell conceded in 1929 that liquor could be bought "at almost any hour of the day or night, either in rural districts, the smaller towns, or the cities." More than any other issue, prohibition gave the decade its reputation as the Roaring Twenties.

Just before prohibition took effect in 1920, the Yale Club of New York bought a fourteen-year supply of wine and hard liquor. That hoard lasted comfortably throughout the prohibition era. By the middle of the decade, prohibition was clearly failing. The "wets" (those who supported repeal) gained over the "drys." Organizations such as the Women's Organization for National Prohibition Repeal, headed by Pauline Sabin, a wealthy New York Republican, mobilized extensive support among national leaders and organizations. Even a committee appointed by President Hoover in 1931 to study prohibition could not agree on a final report endorsing the law.

The onset of the Great Depression hastened repeal. People argued that liquor production would pump up the faltering economy and provide jobs. On December 5, 1933, the Eighteenth Amendment was repealed. Ironically, drinking had become more socially accepted than it had been before the prohibition experiment began its rocky course.

The 1928 Election

Emotionally charged issues such as prohibition eventually spilled over into national politics. The Democratic party, which drew on Protestant rural supporters in the South and West as well as voters from northern city political machines, was especially susceptible to the urban–rural cultural conflicts of the 1920s. The 1924 Democratic national convention had already revealed intense polarization between the party's urban forces and its rural wing.

The Democrats approached the 1928 campaign in somewhat stronger shape. Senator Robert La Follette had died in 1925, ending the threat of another challenge by the Progressive party. William Jennings Bryan's collapse and death just a week after his impassioned defense of fundamentalism in the Scopes trial removed another potential spoiler. Former contender William McAdoo, well into his sixties, was considered too old for the nomination. As a result, Al Smith, just elected to his fourth term as governor of New York, stood in a commanding position to win the Democratic nomination. In 1924, the Democrats had needed more than a hundred ballots to select a candidate. In 1928, they nominated Smith on the first try.

Alfred E. Smith brought strengths and weaknesses to the Democratic ticket. He was the first national presidential candidate to reflect the aspirations of city dwellers, especially the urban working classes. The grandson of Irish immigrants, Smith had worked his way up in politics from Tammany Hall to the governor's chair in Albany. He was proud of his urban background and adopted "The Sidewalks of New York" as his campaign song. Democrats hoped Smith would attract recent immigrants and working people who traditionally voted Republican. The

prominent role of Belle Moskowitz, a New York social worker who served as Smith's political adviser, enhanced his attraction to woman voters and liberal urban Jews.

But Smith had several liabilities that offset his appeal to urban voters. He did not speak well on the radio, and sprinkled his speeches with "ain't" and "he don't" in a heavy New York accent. At times, he seemed to flaunt his eastern manners. Joking with reporters who inquired about the needs of states west of the Mississippi River, Smith asked in reply, "What states *are* west of the Mississippi?" His early career in Tammany Hall troubled many voters, suggesting, unfairly, that he was little more than a typical machine politician. Smith's stand on prohibition presented an even bigger problem. Although committed to enforcing prohibition if elected president, he made no secret of his opposition to the law. Smith drank openly during the 1920s. And he chose John J. Raskob, a wealthy business entrepreneur and one of the nation's most ardent "wets," as head of the Democratic National Committee.

Smith's Catholicism proved by far the most damaging handicap to his campaign. In 1928, Protestant Americans were not ready to elect a Roman Catholic president. Although Smith staunchly insisted that his religion would not interfere with his performance as president, his Catholic faith cost him support from Democrats and Republicans alike. Members of the Protestant clergy, who already opposed Smith because he had flouted prohibition, led the drive against him. "No Governor can kiss the papal ring and get within gunshot of the White House," declared a Methodist bishop from Buffalo. A Baptist minister warned, "If you vote for Al Smith, you're voting against Christ and you'll all be damned."

Smith marked a new kind of presidential candidate for the Democrats, and so did the Republican nominee, Herbert Hoover. In 1927, President Coolidge issued a ten-word announcement: "I do not choose to run for President in 1928." His unexpected declaration opened the field. Hoover led from the start. His popularity and power as secretary of commerce under Harding and Coolidge left no room for contenders such as Vice-President Charles G. Dawes and former Governor Frank O. Lowden of Illinois.

As a professional administrator and engineer, Hoover symbolized the new managerial and technological elite that was restructuring the modern economic order. He had never been elected to any political office. During his campaign, in which he gave only seven speeches, Hoover promised that his vision of individualism and cooperative endeavor would banish poverty from the United States. Many people considered Hoover more progressive than Smith.

Hoover won a stunning victory. He received 58 percent of the popular vote to Smith's 41 percent, and 444 electoral votes to 87 for Smith. For the first time since Reconstruction, a Republican candidate carried Virginia, Texas, and North Carolina, largely because many Democratic voters refused to vote for a Catholic. The participation of eligible voters in the election rose from 52 percent in 1924 to 56.9 percent in 1928, with women accounting for a large share of the increase. Many Catholic and immigrant women cast their ballots for Smith, but native-born Republican women supported Herbert Hoover in even greater numbers.

The 1928 election reflected important underlying political changes. The Democratic turnout, despite the party's overwhelming loss, increased substantially in the big cities. Smith won the heavily industrialized states of Massachusetts and Rhode Island. The Democrats were on their way to a new identity as the party of the urban masses and ethnic voters, a reorientation completed by the New Deal.

In 1928, no Democratic candidate, let alone a Catholic, could have won the presidency. With a prosperous economy, a stable international situation, strong support from the business commu-

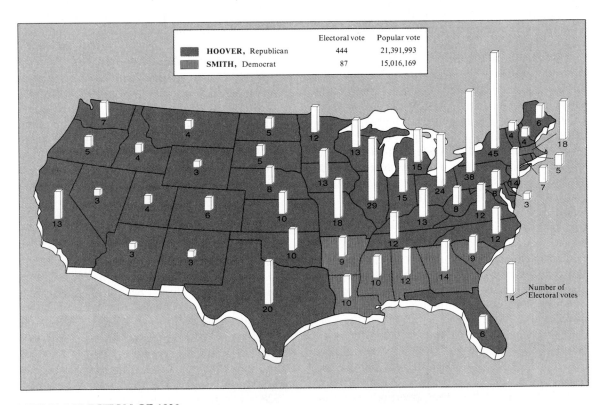

	Electoral vote	Popular vote
HOOVER, Republican	444	21,391,993
SMITH, Democrat	87	15,016,169

MAP 23.3 ELECTION OF 1928
Historians still debate the extent to which 1928 was a critical election—that is, one that produced a significant realignment in voting behavior. Although Republican candidate Herbert Hoover swept the electoral college, Democrats were heartened that Alfred E. Smith won the heavily industrialized states of Rhode Island and Massachusetts. For the first time, the Democratic ticket carried the nation's twelve largest cities, indicating strong support from immigrants and urban dwellers.

TIME LINE
THE 1920s: TOWARD A CORPORATE ECONOMY AND MASS CULTURE

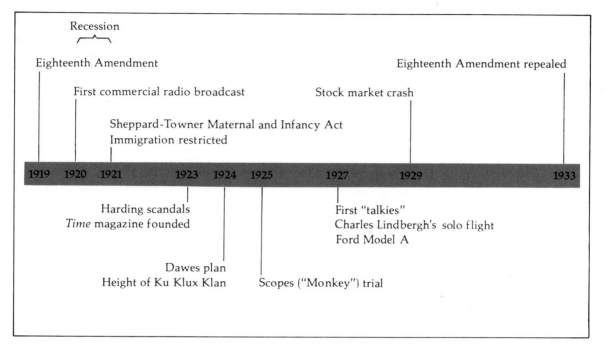

nity, and their status as the majority party, the Republicans were unbeatable. Ironically, Herbert Hoover's victory gave him the unenviable task of leading the United States when the Great Depression struck in 1929. Having claimed credit for the prosperity of the 1920s, the Republicans found it difficult to disassociate themselves from blame for the depression. Twenty-four years passed before a Republican won the presidency again.

The 1920s cemented the partnership between business and government that had been accelerated by World War I. The Republican party controlled the national government and, with the exception of the 1920–1921 recession, the economy performed well. The automobile industry symbolized the new mass production techniques that dominated economic life in the United States.

During the 1920s, a national culture began to develop. It was characterized by the wide diffusion of ideas and values through movies, radio, and other mass media; new patterns of leisure and amusement; and a heightened emphasis on consumption and advertising. These new lifestyles captured the popular imagination, but they were limited to a minority of the population. Only families with at least a middle-class income had enough money to afford cars, radios, vacuum cleaners, and toasters. Credit and installment buying stretched family incomes.

Not everyone welcomed the new secular values of the 1920s. Conflicts arose over prohibition, fundamentalist religion, the Ku Klux Klan, and immigration restriction. These cultural disputes spilled over into politics, especially affecting the already fractured Democratic party. The 1928 election showed that the nation could not yet accept a Catholic presidential candidate. The Republican ascendancy continued under Herbert Hoover, who looked forward to a term filled with even greater prosperity and progress.

Suggestions for Further Reading

General overviews of the 1920s are provided by Ellis Hawley, *The Great War and the Search for a Modern Order, 1917–1933* (1979); William Leuchtenberg, *The Perils of Prosperity* (1958); George Soule, *Prosperity Decade* (1947); Frederick Lewis Allen, *Only Yesterday* (1931); and Geoffrey Perrett, *America in the Twenties* (1982). Robert S. Lynd and Helen Merrell Lynd, *Middletown: A Study in Modern American Culture* (1929), remains a superb sociological study of American life and values in the 1920s. John Braeman, Robert H. Bremner, and David Brody, eds., *Change and Continuity in 20th Century America: The Twenties* (1968), offers interpretations of the decade's major trends.

Business and Politics in the 1920s

Alfred Chandler provides a stimulating introduction to business life in *Strategy and Structure* (1962) and *The Visible Hand* (1977). Further discussion of corporate developments can be found in Louis Galambos, *Competition and Cooperation* (1966); Robert Himmelberg, *The Origins of the National Recovery Administration: Business, Government, and the Trade Association Ideal, 1921–1933* (1976); James Gilbert, *Designing the Industrial State* (1972), and J. W. Prothro, *The Dollar Decade: Business Ideas in the 1920s* (1954). Irving Bernstein, *The Lean Years* (1960), and David Brody, *Steelworkers in America* (1960) and *Workers in Industrial America* (1980), cover labor developments.

The domestic and international aspects of the economy are treated in Jim Potter, *The American Economy Between the World Wars* (1974), and Joan Hoff Wilson, *American Business and Foreign Policy, 1920–1933* (1968) and *Ideology and Economics: U.S. Relations with the Soviet Union, 1918–1933* (1974). L. Ethan Ellis, *Republican Foreign Policy, 1921–1933* (1968), and William Appleman Williams, *The Tragedy of American Diplomacy* (1962), offer interpretations of foreign policy.

General introductions to politics in the 1920s are found in John D. Hicks, *Republican Ascendancy* (1960); Arthur M. Schlesinger, Jr., *The Crisis of the Old Order* (1957); and Robert Murray, *The Politics of Normalcy* (1973). Biographies of the decade's major political figures include Donald McCoy, *Calvin Coolidge* (1967); David Burner, *Herbert Hoover* (1979); and Joan Hoff Wilson, *Herbert Hoover: Forgotten Progressive* (1975). On women in politics in the 1920s, see J. Stanley Lemons, *The Woman Citizen* (1973); William H. Chafe, *The American Woman* (1972); and Clarke A. Chambers, *Seedtime of Reform* (1963).

Towards a National Culture

Daniel Boorstin, *The Americans: The Democratic Experience* (1973), provides an excellent introduction to the emerging mass culture. On movies, see Robert Sklar, *Movie Made America* (1975), and Lary May, *Screening Out the Past* (1980). Erik Barnouw, *A Tower in Babel: A History of American Broadcasting in the United States to 1933* (1966), discusses radio. Stewart Ewen, *Captains of Consciousness* (1976), and Daniel Pope, *The Making of Modern Advertising* (1983), cover the new patterns of consumption and advertising, while Paula Fass, *The Damned and the Beautiful* (1977), treats American youth in the 1920s. The impact of the automobile on modern American life is amply documented by James Flink, *The Car Culture* (1975); John Rae, *The American Automobile* (1965); Ed Cray, *Chrome Colossus: General Motors and Its Times* (1980); Bernard A. Weisberger, *The Dream Maker* (1979); and Reynold Wik, *Henry Ford and Grass Roots America* (1972). Good sources for Charles Lindbergh are his two accounts, *"We"* (1927) and *The Spirit of St. Louis* (1953). See also Leonard Mosley, *Lindbergh: A Biography* (1976), and Walter S. Ross, *The Last Hero: Charles A. Lindbergh* (1968).

Cultural Conflicts

Paul Carter, *Another Part of the Twenties* (1977), outlines the decade's deeply felt cultural controversies. Background on rural and urban life is provided by Don Kirschner, *City and Country: Rural Responses to Urbanization in the 1920s* (1970); Zane Miller, *The Urbanization of America* (1973); and William Wilson, *Coming of Age: Urban America, 1915–1945* (1974). John Higham, *Strangers in the Land* (1955), and Maldwyn A. Jones, *American Immigration* (1960), describe immigration restriction. Kenneth Jackson, *The Ku Klux Klan in the City, 1915–1930* (1965), and David Chalmers, *Hooded Americanism* (1965), cover the KKK's rise and fall. Ray Ginger, *Six Days or Forever?* (1958), and Norman F. Furniss, *The Fundamentalist Controversy, 1918–1933* (1954), cover religion. On prohibition, see Andrew Sinclair, *Prohibition: The Era of Excess* (1962); Joseph R. Gusfield, *Symbolic Crusade* (1963); and Norman Clark, *Deliver Us from Evil* (1976). The treatment of the 1928 election found in David Burner, *The Politics of Provincialism* (1967), and Oscar Handlin, *Al Smith and His America* (1958), should be supplemented by Allan J. Lichtman's quantitative study, *Prejudice and the Old Politics* (1979).

24

THE NEW DEAL: TOWARD THE MODERN WELFARE STATE

For most Americans, the year 1929 means only one thing—the stock market crash that touched off the Great Depression. By 1932, more than a fourth of the nation's workers were unemployed, and industrial production had fallen to barely half the 1929 level. President Herbert Hoover, once the symbol of business prosperity, had become the scapegoat for the depression.

Against this backdrop, the nation turned to Franklin Delano Roosevelt, whose New Deal administration restored confidence in the capitalist economic system. The New Deal also set into motion far-reaching changes in the role of the federal government, notably the emergence of a modern state of significant size. In addition to accepting responsibility for managing the economy, the government now guaranteed a wide range of social and economic benefits for ordinary Americans. During the 1930s, more than a third of the population received direct government assistance from such new federal programs as Social Security, farm loans, relief, and mortgage guarantees. Roosevelt became one of the most popular presidents in United States history and won election an unprecedented four times.

The New Deal represented an important period of political and economic reform, but its programs were hardly revolutionary. Even before the deepening depression, President Hoover had taken the first steps toward involving the federal government more actively in economic life. The New Deal also built on the organizational and bureaucratic structure that had been developed in World War I and refined during the 1920s.

The New Deal's welfare state—that is, the federal government's acceptance of primary responsibility for the individual and collective welfare of the people—was limited in many respects. Many social welfare programs of the New Deal represented contradictory responses to the emergency of the depression. Benefits were small and programs operated haphazardly. The government expanded during the 1930s, but World War II, not the New Deal, gave the United States a massive federal bureaucracy and large budget deficits. And not until the Great Society programs of President Lyndon Johnson in the 1960s did the welfare system reach significant numbers of America's poor. Many of the achievements—and problems—commonly ascribed to the New Deal belong to a later era.

WALL STREET, OCTOBER 1929
When the stock market collapsed, Julius Rosenwald, the chairman of Sears, Roebuck and Company, offered to guarantee the accounts of Sears employees who had bought stocks on margin. Comedian Eddie Cantor jokingly asked for a job as a Sears office boy. (UPI)

Herbert Hoover and the Great Depression

In 1932, the journalist William Allen White wrote an article about the outgoing president entitled "Herbert Hoover—The Last of the Old Presidents, or the First of the New?" Like historians ever since, White concluded that Hoover had been a little of both. Hoover's early efforts to fight the depression are now credited with foreshadowing many New Deal programs, and his reputation among historians has risen steadily through the years. Hoover, who lived until 1964, offered a simple explanation for the improvement in his historical stature. He told Chief Justice Earl Warren of the Supreme Court that he had simply managed "to outlive the bastards."

The Causes of the Depression

The Great Depression began slowly and without much notice. Consumer spending declined after 1927, and housing construction slowed. In 1928 and 1929, inventories piled up and manufacturers began to cut back production and lay off workers. The reduced incomes and buying power reinforced the downturn. By the summer of 1929, the economy was clearly in a recession, although at that point not as severe as the downturn that had begun in 1920.

The economy had tolerated minor recessions before without suffering long periods of excessive unemployment and slack industrial production. But this time was different. By 1933, the United States had sunk into the worst economic collapse in its history, which seemed particularly bitter coming on the heels of the high-income, high-employment boom of the 1920s.

Among the causes of the Great Depression, a flawed stock market played an important, but not dominant, role. By 1929, the market had become the symbol of the nation's prosperity and an icon in American middle-class culture. Financier John J. Raskob captured the "get rich" mentality in a *Ladies Home Journal* article called "Everyone Ought to Be Rich." Invest fifteen dollars a month on sound common stocks, Raskob advised, and the investment will grow to eighty thousand dollars in twenty years. Such inflated expectations drove stock prices up and up in

1928 and 1929. Contrary to popular wisdom, however, not everyone played the stock market. About four million Americans owned stock in 1929; with their families, they represented about 10 percent of the nation's households. A mere 1.5 million had a portfolio large enough to require the services of a stock broker.

As the frenzied stock market speculation continued, investors assumed, incorrectly, that stock prices could rise indefinitely, more rapidly than any concrete measure of industrial progress. A noted economist proclaimed in mid-October 1929 that "Stock prices have reached what looks like a permanently high plateau." Neither the government nor the Federal Reserve System did anything to dampen the speculative fever.

"Black Tuesday"—October 29, 1929—went down in history as the day the bubble burst, but actually the stock market had been sliding since early September. The 1929 recession had already cast doubt on the likelihood that stock prices would continue to rise indefinitely. When small, inexperienced investors suddenly found themselves heavily in debt and began to sell their stocks, others followed suit to protect their investments. Waves of panic selling developed quickly. By November, stock values had fallen from a peak of $87 billion (at least on paper) to $56 billion. The market eventually bottomed out at $18 billion in 1933. The precipitous decline of stock prices became known as the Great Crash.

The stock market crash intensified the course of the Great Depression in several ways. It wiped out the savings of many thousands of Americans and damaged commercial banks that had invested in corporate stocks. Less tangibly, it smashed the optimism of people who had seen the stock market as the crowning symbol of America's limitless economic prosperity. This crisis of confidence prolonged the depression.

However, the stock market crash does not adequately explain either the severity or the length of the Great Depression, especially the deep plunge between 1931 and 1933. Other factors that contributed to the prolonged decline included the legacy of "sick" industries from the 1920s, the growing inequality of wealth, an unstable international financial situation, and the monetary policies of the Federal Reserve System.

Important segments of the economy had not shared equally in the prosperity of the 1920s. Agriculture was in the worst shape; farmers had never recovered from the sharp depression that followed World War I. Farmers faced high fixed costs for equipment and mortgages incurred during the inflationary war years. At the same time, overproduction and surpluses drove prices even lower, causing farmers to default on mortgage payments and risk foreclosure of their farms. In 1929, farmers' yearly income averaged only $223, compared to $870 for other occupations. Because about a fourth of the nation's gainfully employed workers in 1929 were engaged in farming, the difficulties in agriculture weakened the general economic structure.

The economic troubles of certain basic industries also marred the otherwise prosperous 1920s. Many of these problems dated back to World War I or the depression of 1920–1921. The textile industry, for example, had moved steadily into decline after the war. Textile firms abandoned New England for the cheaper labor markets of the South but continued to be hurt by decreasing demand and excess capacity. The railroad industry likewise declined, hit by shrinking passenger revenues, stagnant freight levels, and inefficient management. The railroads also faced stiff new competition from truck transportation on publicly subsidized highways.

Mining and lumbering, which had expanded in response to wartime demands, found themselves with a productive capacity too great for peacetime. Coal mining was especially troubled, battered by overexpansion, technological obsolescence, and a legacy of bitter labor struggles. As with the railroads, coal faced competition from new sources, including hydroelectric power, fuel oil, and natural gas. Herbert Hoover, while secretary of commerce, had plans to help these ailing industries, but the trade associations that he promoted did little to stabilize or revitalize them.

The country's unequal distribution of wealth also contributed to the deepening depression. During the 1920s, the share of national income going to families in the upper- and middle-income brackets increased. The tax policies of Secretary of the Treasury Andrew Mellon contributed to this concentration of wealth by easing personal tax rates, eliminating excess-profits taxation, and expanding deductions that favored

BOULDER DAM
In 1928, Congress passed the Boulder Canyon Project Act, which provided for the construction of a dam on the Colorado River at the Arizona-Nevada border for flood control purposes. The $175 million cost of the dam, now called Hoover Dam, was to be repaid through the sale of electricity from the project's power plant. Under a compromise agreement, the government sold hydroelectric power only at wholesale to specified private and municipal distributors, not to the public. (Historical Pictures Service)

wealthy individuals and corporations. The lowest 40 percent of the population received only 12.5 percent of the aggregate family personal income in 1929, while the top 5 percent got 30 percent. With this unequal base of purchasing power, not enough people could afford the levels of consumer spending necessary to revive the economy after the depression began.

As the Great Depression ground on relentlessly after 1929, it became self-feeding. The longer the economy contracted, the more expectations of continued depression built up, which further inhibited the consumption and investment necessary to stimulate economic recovery. Business investment plummeted 88 percent from 1929 to 1933. Consumers were afraid to spend—even if they had any money. Jobless workers struggled to keep their families from destitution. The economy showed some signs of recovery in the summer of 1931 as many inventories were eliminated and low prices encouraged renewed consumption, but the upturn did not last. The economy plunged again in late fall.

At this point, the chronically depressed agricultural sector exerted pressure on the commercial banking system, further deepening the economic contraction. The nation's banks had already been weakened by the stock market crash. When agricultural prices and incomes fell even more steeply in 1930, farmers went over the

edge into bankruptcy. Bank failures, particularly in the cotton belt, came one after another after the harvest of 1930. By November and December, the defaulting of rural banks on their obligations touched off failures of urban banks. The wave of bank failures drove fearful depositors to withdraw their savings, further worsening the banking crisis.

A change in the nation's monetary policy in 1931 added to the banking problems. During the first phase of the depression, the Federal Reserve System had reacted cautiously. In October 1931, the system took a gravely incorrect step. The New York Reserve Bank significantly increased the discount rate—that is, the interest rate it charged to loan money to member banks. It also sharply curtailed the amount of money it placed in circulation through the purchase of government securities. Through these actions, the Federal Reserve severely limited the ability of the banking system to meet domestic demands for currency and credit. By March 1933, when the economy reached its lowest point, the money supply had fallen by about a third of its August 1929 level.

The main effects of an inadequate money supply were to force prices down and deprive business of investment funds. In the face of such a substantial contraction of the money supply, the American people could have pulled the country out of the depression only by spending more rapidly. But because of falling prices, rising unemployment, and a banking system in crisis, they preferred to save their dollars. And many Americans believed that savings were safer under a mattress than in a bank, which further limited the amount of money in circulation.

The economic problems of the United States soon had an impact on the rest of the world. The international economic system had been out of kilter since World War I. It could function only as long as American banks exported enough capital for European countries to repay their debts and continue to buy American manufactured goods and agricultural products. As the depression worsened, American financiers reduced foreign investments and consumers cut purchases of European goods, making debt repayment even more difficult. European demand for American exports fell drastically. The critical reduction of American capital exports turned the depression into an international event. No other major trading nation, however, was as severely affected as the United States.

A further blow to the international economic system occurred in 1931 when Great Britain abandoned the gold standard. This action deprived the world market of a system for the orderly adjustment of values of international currencies. Forty-one countries had followed Britain's example by 1932. Fear spread in Europe that the United States also would abandon the

gold standard. Consequently, holders of dollars abroad began to demand gold, and gold flowed out of the United States. In an attempt to reverse this flow, the Federal Reserve drove up short-term interest rates in October 1931. This policy successfully attracted gold holders to U.S. investments, thereby saving the gold standard, but at a high cost. Because of the Federal Reserve's contraction of the money supply, the banking system could not meet internal demands for currency.

Herbert Hoover later blamed the international economic situation for the severity of the depression in the United States. He had a point, although domestic factors far outweighed international ones in causing America's protracted collapse. When the depression hit, no single country stepped forward to provide leadership and stability for the world market, as Britain had done prior to World War I. Nations raised tariff barriers and imposed exchange controls to hoard precious gold, dollars, and pounds sterling. Such economic nationalism, by the United States and many other countries, prolonged the depression. The world economy finally showed signs of recovery by 1933, although progress remained uneven.

The Republican Response

President Hoover's reaction to the Great Depression was shaped by the commitment to associationalism that he had exhibited as secretary of commerce. He turned to the business community for help in pulling the nation out of the depression. Hoover asked business to maintain wages voluntarily, keep up production, and work with the government to build confidence in the soundness of the system. Greeting a business delegation in June 1930, the president announced, "Gentlemen, you have come sixty days too late. The Depression is over."

Hoover also used public budgets to encourage recovery. Soon after the stock market crash, he cut taxes and called on the state and local governments to increase capital outlays. In 1930 and the first half of 1931, he increased the federal public works budget. In addition, Hoover eased the international crisis by bringing about, early in the summer of 1931, a moratorium on the payment of Allied debts and reparations. The federal government's efforts to encourage

TABLE 24.1 AMERICAN BANKS AND BANK FAILURES, 1920–1980

Year	Total Number of Banks	Total Assets	Bank Failures
1920	30,909	$53.1 billion	168
1929	25,568	72.3	659
1931	22,242	70.1	2,294
1933	14,771	51.4	4,004
1934	15,913	55.9	61
1940	15,076	79.7	48
1950	14,676	179.2	5
1960	14,019	282.9	2
1970	14,187	611.3	7
1980	14,870	1543.5	10
1985	—	—	—

SOURCE: *Historical Statistics of the United States: Colonial Times to 1970*, pp. 1019, 1038–1039; *Statistical Abstract of the United States, 1981* (Washington, D.C.: U.S. Government Printing Office, 1981), pp. 510–511.

THE "1932ND PSALM"

Hoover is my Shepherd, I am in want,
He maketh me to lie down on park benches,
He leadeth me by still factories,
He restoreth my doubt in the
Republican Party.
He guided me in the path of the
Unemployed for his party's sake,
Yea, though I walk through the alley of soup
  kitchens,
I am hungry.
I do not fear evil, for thou art against me;
Thy Cabinet and thy Senate, they do discomfort
  me;
Thou didst prepare a reduction in my wages;
In the presence of my creditors thou annointed my
  income with taxes,
So my expense overruneth my income.
Surely poverty and hard times will follow me
All the days of the Republican administration.
And I shall dwell in a rented house forever.
Amen.

Source: E. J. Sullivan, "The 1932nd Psalm." *Seaman's Journal* 46 (October 1932): 259. Quoted in Robert S. McElvaine, *Down & Out in the Great Depression.* Chapel Hill: University of North Carolina Press, 1983. 34.

---

recovery were moderately effective, but the depression continued.

By 1931, more drastic action became necessary. Hoover, however, faced a cruel dilemma that had been set in motion by the Federal Reserve's contraction of the money supply. He could continue budget deficits and thereby encourage recovery through increased government spending. But this course pitted the borrowing needs of the federal government against those of private investors, which would drive up interest rates. Fearing that significantly higher interest rates would choke recovery, Hoover asked Congress in December 1931 for tax increases to raise revenues by a third and balance the budget. The resulting Revenue Act of 1932 represented the largest peacetime tax increase in the nation's history. But higher taxes seriously impeded both consumption and investment. Along with monetary restriction, they contributed to the unique severity of the Great Depression.

The Hoover administration took additional steps to fight the deepening depression. It spent $700 million, an unprecedented sum for the time, on public works. Hoover supported the Glass-Steagall Banking Act of 1932, which made government securities available to back Federal Reserve notes in order to counter credit contractions from gold withdrawals. This step temporarily propped up the ailing banking system.

Hoover remained adamant in his refusal to consider any plan for direct federal relief for unemployed Americans. Throughout his career, he had advocated that private organized charity meet social welfare needs. During World War I, Hoover headed the Commission for Relief of Belgium, a private group that distributed five million tons of food to relieve the suffering of Europe's civilian populations. In 1927, Hoover coordinated the massive rescue and cleanup operation after a devastating Mississippi River flood left 16.5 million acres of land under water in seven states. This effort involved both private charities, including the Red Cross and the Rockefeller Foundation, as well as such government agencies as the U.S. Public Health Service and the National Guard. The success of these and other predominantly private responses to public emergencies confirmed Hoover's belief that private charity, not federal aid, was the "American way." Meanwhile, charities and state and local relief agencies struggled to meet the growing needs of the unemployed.

The centerpiece of Hoover's new initiative to combat the depression was the Reconstruction Finance Corporation (RFC). Modeled on the War Finance Corporation of World War I, and developed in collaboration with the business and banking communities, the RFC represented the first federal institution set up to intervene directly into the economy during peacetime. The RFC provided federal loans to railroads, financial institutions, banks, and insurance companies in an attempt to get the economy moving again. This financial strategy has sometimes been called "pump priming." Money loaned at the top of the economic structure stimulates production, which in turn creates new jobs and increases consumer spending. Benefits thus "trickle down" to the rest of the economy.

The RFC received $500 million, but the agency's cautiousness in lending money limited its impact. In July 1932, Congress doubled this amount and authorized loans to the states totaling $300 million for relief and public works. Once again acting far too cautiously, the RFC lent only $30 million by the end of 1932. Furthermore, it allocated and spent only 20 percent of the $1.5 billion appropriated for public works projects.

The Reconstruction Finance Corporation stands as a watershed in American political history. When voluntary cooperation failed, the president turned to federal action to stimulate the economy. Yet Hoover's break with the past had clear limits. In many ways, his support of the RFC amounted to simply another example of the philosophy of encouraging business confidence. Compared with previous presidents, Hoover responded on an unprecedented scale. Compared to the nation's needs during the Great Depression, his programs were too little and too late.

The 1932 Election

As the depression deepened, hatred of Herbert Hoover became widespread. His declarations that nobody was starving and that hoboes were better fed than ever before seemed cruel and insensitive. His apparent willingness to bail out businesses and banks, but not to feed starving Americans, added to his cold-hearted image. New terms entered the vocabulary, including "Hoovervilles" (shanty towns where people lived in packing crates and other makeshift homes), waving "Hoover flags" (empty pockets turned inside out), and sleeping under "Hoover blankets" (newspapers). Newspaper columnist Russell Baker remembered his aunt's exaggerated recital of Hoover's faults:

> People were starving because of Herbert Hoover. My mother was out of work because of Herbert Hoover. Men were killing themselves because of Herbert Hoover, and their fatherless children were being packed away to orphanages . . . because of Herbert Hoover.

The final straw came in the summer of 1932 with Hoover's handling of the "Bonus Army." A ragtag group of about fifteen thousand unemployed World War I veterans had hitchhiked to Washington to demand that their bonuses, originally scheduled for distribution in 1945, be paid immediately. While they unsuccessfully lobbied

Congress, members of the "Bonus Expeditionary Force" (parodying the wartime American Expeditionary Force) camped out in the capital, a visible reminder of the despair of the unemployed. "We were heroes in 1917, but we're bums now," one veteran remarked bitterly. When the marchers refused to leave their camp, Hoover called out riot troops led by General Douglas MacArthur, assisted by Majors Dwight D. Eisenhower and George S. Patton, to clear the area. More than a hundred bonus marchers were injured in the fight that followed. Most Americans found the spectacle of the U.S. Army firing on U.S. citizens deeply disturbing.

The Bonus Army was not the only sign of unrest in the summer of 1932. Midwestern farmers had watched the price of wheat fall from three dollars a bushel in 1920 to barely thirty cents in 1932. Now they joined together in the Farm Holiday Association under the charismatic leadership of Milo Reno, the sixty-four-year-old former president of the Iowa Farmers' Union. Reno failed in an attempt to organize a farm strike to

HOOVERVILLES
By 1930, shantytowns had sprung up in most of the nation's cities. In New York City, squatters camped out along the Hudson River railroad tracks, built makeshift homes in Central Park, or lived in the city dump. Such shantytowns were called "Hoovervilles," a pointed reference to the increasingly unpopular president. (Brown Brothers)

keep products out of markets until prices rose. At the same time, groups of unemployed citizens in many cities battled local authorities over inadequate relief. Rent riots and hunger marches occurred frequently. Mayor Anton J. Cermak of Chicago challenged a congressional committee to send either relief or troops.

Despite the unrest among city dwellers and farmers, the nation was not in a revolutionary mood as it approached the 1932 election. Despair and apathy, more than anger, characterized the feelings of most Americans. The Republicans, who could find no credible way to dump an incumbent president, unenthusiastically renominated Herbert Hoover. The Democrats turned to Governor Franklin Delano Roosevelt of New York, who capitalized on that state's record of innovative responses to relief and unemployment to win the nomination.

Franklin Roosevelt's route to the governor-

ROOSEVELT IN WARM SPRINGS
President Franklin D. Roosevelt, shown here in Warm Springs, Georgia, in 1933, was a consummate politician who loved the adulation of a crowd. He began to spend several months a year at Warm Springs in 1924 to rehabilitate his polio-stricken legs. Later, he often went there to escape the pressures of Washington. (UPI)

ship, and from there to the White House, began on a Hudson River estate north of New York City. Born into a wealthy family in 1882, Franklin attended the Groton School, Harvard, and Columbia Law School. Roosevelt gave up his law career in 1910 for a seat in the New York legislature. He served as assistant secretary of the navy in the Wilson administration, which earned him the vice-presidential nomination on the losing Democratic ticket in 1920. He consciously modeled his career on that of his distant cousin, Theodore Roosevelt, whose niece Eleanor he married in 1905.

Franklin Roosevelt's strategy of following his cousin's path to the White House was sidetracked by an attack of polio in 1921, which left him paralyzed from the waist down for the rest of his life. Roosevelt battled back from his infirmity, emerging from the ordeal a stronger, maturer personality. "If you had spent two years in bed trying to wiggle your toe," he later commented, "after that anything would seem easy." Eleanor Roosevelt strongly supported her husband's return to public life, serving as his stand-in during the 1920s. She and Louis Howe, Roosevelt's devoted political aide, masterminded his reentry into Democratic politics. Roosevelt won the New York governorship in 1928 and the Democratic presidential nomination in 1932.

The 1932 campaign foreshadowed little of the New Deal. Roosevelt hinted at new approaches to the depression but stated his goals in vague, unspecific terms. "The country needs and, unless I mistake its temper, the country demands bold, persistent experimentation," he said. Roosevelt won easily, receiving 22.8 million votes to Hoover's 15.7 million. Despite the economic collapse, Americans remained firmly committed to the two-party system. The Socialist party candidate, Norman Thomas, got fewer than a million votes. The Communist party, which had successfully organized hunger marches in major cities, drew only 100,000 votes for its candidate, party leader William Z. Foster.

The 1932 election reflected the American people's desire for a change in leadership. But it also represented a major step toward the forging of the New Deal coalition that would dominate political life for the next four decades. In 1932, Roosevelt won with the support of the Solid South, which returned to the Democratic fold after de-

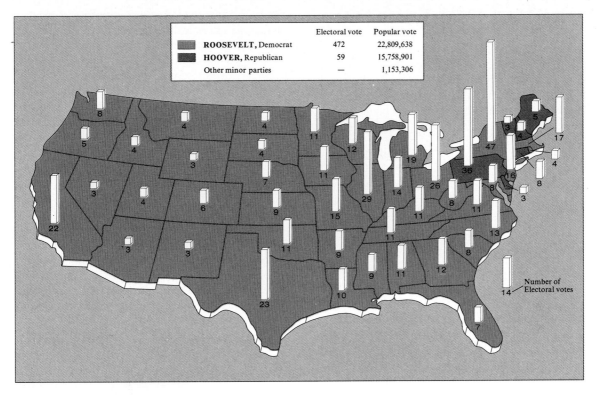

		Electoral vote	Popular vote
	ROOSEVELT, Democrat	472	22,809,638
	HOOVER, Republican	59	15,758,901
	Other minor parties	—	1,153,306

Number of Electoral votes

MAP 24.1 THE ELECTION OF 1932

Franklin Roosevelt's convincing election victory over Herbert Hoover in 1932 resulted from realignments in the Democratic party and dissatisfaction with the incumbent president, who had become the scapegoat for the Great Depression. The candidates of the Communist and Socialist parties could not rally voters even during the gravest economic crisis that the American capitalist system had ever faced. Together they received fewer than a million votes of almost 40 million cast.

fections in 1928 because of Al Smith's religion and views on prohibition. Roosevelt also drew substantial support in the West. An increasingly large urban vote continued the trend first noticed in the 1928 election, when the Democrats successfully appealed to recent immigrants and ethnic groups in the nation's cities. However, the voters hardly gave Roosevelt an unlimited mandate to reshape American political and economic institutions. Many people voted against Hoover as much as for Roosevelt.

Having spoken, the voters had to wait until March before Roosevelt could put his new ideas into action. (The long interval between the presidential election and inauguration never occurred again. The passage of the Twentieth Amendment in 1933 moved the inauguration permanently to January.) In the worst winter of the depression, Americans could do little but hope

things would get better. According to the most conservative estimates, from 20 to 25 percent of the work force was unemployed. The percentage stood as high as 50 percent in Cleveland, 60 percent in Akron, and 80 percent in Toledo.

By the winter of 1932–1933, the depression had totally overwhelmed public welfare institutions. Private charity and local public relief, whose expenditures had risen dramatically over earlier levels, still reached only a fraction of the needy. Hunger haunted cities and rural areas alike. When a teacher tried to send a coal miner's daughter home from school because she was weak from hunger, the girl replied, "It won't do any good . . . because this is sister's day to eat." In New York City, hospitals reported ninety-five deaths from starvation. This was the America that Roosevelt inherited when he took the oath of office on March 4, 1933.

The New Deal Takes Over

Franklin Roosevelt's promise of a New Deal for the American people reassured them that hard times could be overcome. "So, first of all, let me assert my firm belief that the only thing we have to fear is fear itself," he boldly proclaimed in his inaugural address. The restoration of hope and confidence was perhaps Roosevelt's greatest contribution during the depression decade of the 1930s. The specific means for ending the depression remained less clear. The New Deal was not a carefully formulated plan. Its ideology contained many contradictions. But it provided a measure of economic security against the worst depression in United States history.

The Hundred Days

Franklin Roosevelt first used the term *New Deal* in his acceptance speech at the Democratic National Convention of 1932, but he hardly realized that he had named his era. Plucked from deep in the speech by the newspaper cartoonist Rollin Kirby, the term came to stand for the Roosevelt administration's response to the depression. The federal government dominated political and economic life so thoroughly during the 1930s that the term *New Deal* is often used as a synonym for the decade itself.

The New Deal represented many things to many people, but one unifying factor was the personality of its master architect, Franklin Roosevelt. As one historian aptly noted, the New Deal was "a very personal enterprise." Roosevelt, a superb politician, crafted his administration's program in response to shifting political and economic conditions, rather than by following a set ideology or plan. He experimented with one idea, and if it did not work, he tried another. Roosevelt used people in the same way. Senator Huey Long of Louisiana complained, "When I talk to him, he says 'Fine! Fine! Fine!' But Joe Robinson [the Senate majority leader] goes to see him the next day and again he says 'Fine! Fine! Fine!' Maybe he says 'Fine!' to everybody." Roosevelt remained unperturbed by criticism that his administration did not follow a consistent ideological course. "I have no expectation of making a hit every time I come to bat," he disarmingly told critics. "What I seek is

the highest possible batting average." Roosevelt parlayed this experimental tone into a highly effective political and governmental style.

The first problem that Roosevelt confronted was the banking crisis. On the eve of his inauguration, thirty-eight states had closed their banks and banks operated on a restricted basis in the rest. By 1933, about nine million depositors had lost their savings, a total of $2.5 billion. Senator "Cotton Ed" Smith of South Carolina began carrying his cash in a money belt on the Senate floor rather than entrust it to a bank. On March 6, two days after Roosevelt's inauguration, the president declared a national "bank holiday," a euphemism for closing all the banks. Three days later, Congress passed Roosevelt's proposed banking bill, which permitted banks to reopen beginning on March 13, but only if a Treasury Department inspection showed they had sufficient cash reserves to operate on a sound basis.

THE CCC
The Civilian Conservation Corps (CCC) was one of the most popular New Deal programs. Over ten years, it enrolled 2.75 million young Americans who worked for a dollar a day on such projects as soil conservation, disaster relief, reforestation, and flood control. Because the CCC was limited to men only, critics asked, "Where is the she-she-she?" (Wide World)

MAP 24.2 THE TENNESSEE VALLEY AUTHORITY
The need for dams to control flooding and erosion in the Tennessee River Basin, a seven-state area
with some of the country's heaviest rainfall, had long been recognized. Early in the New Deal, the
Tennessee Valley Authority won approval to develop the region's resources under public control.
From 1933 to 1952, the TVA built twenty dams and improved five others. The cheap hydroelectric
power generated by the dams brought electricity to more local residents than ever before.

The House approved the plan after only thirty-eight minutes of debate.

The Banking Act, developed in consultation with banking leaders, was a conservative document. Herbert Hoover could have proposed it. The difference was the public's reaction. On the Sunday evening before the banks reopened, Roosevelt made his first "fireside chat" to a radio audience estimated at sixty million. In simple terms, he reassured the people that the banks were now safe—and they believed him. When the banks reopened on Monday morning, deposits exceeded withdrawals. "Capitalism was saved in eight days," observed Raymond Moley, a Columbia University professor who had served as Roosevelt's speechwriter in the 1932 campaign. The banking bill did its job. More than four thousand banks failed in 1933, but only sixty-one closed their doors in 1934.

The Banking Act was the first of fifteen pieces of major legislation enacted by Congress during the opening months of the Roosevelt administration. This legislative session, which came to be called the "Hundred Days," remains one of the most productive ever. Congress created the Home Owners Loan Corporation to refinance home mortgages, and 20 percent of the nation's homeowners took advantage of this opportunity to make their home ownership more secure. The Federal Deposit Insurance Corporation (FDIC) insured bank deposits up to $2,500. The Civilian Conservation Corps (CCC) sent 250,000 young men to live in camps where they performed reforestation and conservation work. The Tennessee Valley Authority (TVA) received legislative approval for its imaginative plan of government-sponsored regional development and public power. The price of electricity in the seven-state Tennessee valley area soon dropped from ten cents a kilowatt hour to three cents. And in a move that lifted public spirits immeasurably, Roosevelt legalized beer in April. Full repeal of prohibition came eight months later, in December 1933.

The Roosevelt administration targeted three areas for immediate attention—curbing agricultural overproduction, stimulating business recovery, and providing for the unemployed. Agriculture received top priority. The Agricultural Adjustment Act (AAA) was developed by Secretary of Agriculture Henry A. Wallace and Assistant Secretary Rexford Tugwell, a Columbia University economist and agricultural expert, in close collaboration with leaders of major farm organizations. A domestic allotment system for seven major commodities (wheat, cotton, corn, hogs, rice, tobacco, and dairy products) gave cash subsidies to farmers in return for cutting production; these benefits were financed by a tax on processing. New Deal planners hoped prices would rise in response to the federally subsidized scarcity.

The AAA stabilized the farm situation, but its benefits were distributed unevenly. The subsi-

dies for reducing production went primarily to large and medium-sized farm owners, who in turn often cut the acreage of their renters and sharecroppers while continuing to farm their own more profitable land. In the South, this inequality of New Deal benefits had a racial component, because many sharecroppers were black and the land owners and government administrators were white.

The New Deal attacked the problem of economic recovery with the National Industrial Recovery Act, which created the National Recovery Administration (NRA). This agency drew on the World War I experience of Bernard Baruch's War Industries Board and extended the trade association thrust of the Coolidge and Hoover administrations. The NRA set up a system of industrial self-government to handle the problems of overproduction, cutthroat competition, and price instability. This objective would be achieved through codes of fair competition, tailored to prevent the specific practices within each industry that had forced prices downward. In effect, these legally enforceable agreements suspended

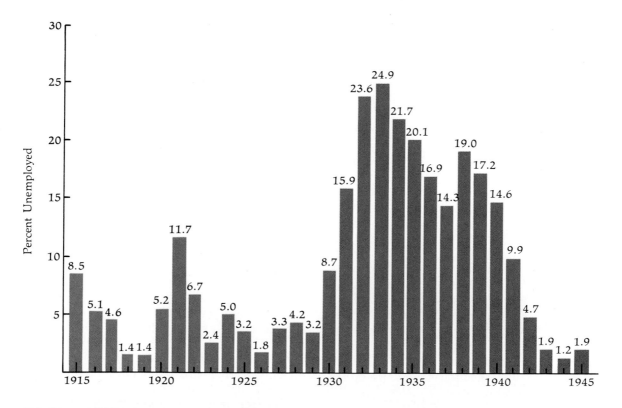

FIGURE 24.1 UNEMPLOYMENT, 1919–1945

the antitrust laws. Each code also contained provisions covering working conditions. For example, the codes established minimum wages and maximum hours and outlawed child labor completely. Under Section 7(a), workers received the right to organize and bargain collectively "through representatives of their own choosing."

General Hugh Johnson, a colorful if somewhat erratic administrator, headed the NRA. He oversaw negotiations for more than six hundred NRA codes, ranging from large industries, such as coal, cotton, and steel, to dog food, costume jewelry, and even burlesque theaters. The code process theoretically included equal input from management, labor, and consumers, but business trade associations basically set the terms. Because large companies dominated the trade associations, the code-drafting process further solidified the power of large businesses at the expense of smaller enterprises. Labor had little input, consumer interests almost none.

The early New Deal also addressed the critical problem of unemployment. The total exhaustion of private and local sources of charity made some form of federal relief essential in this fourth year of the depression. Roosevelt moved reluctantly toward federal responsibility for relief. The Federal Emergency Relief Administration (FERA), set up in May 1933 under the direction of Harry Hopkins, a New York social worker, was a matching federal-state program designed to keep people from starving until other recovery measures had a chance to take hold. Hopkins spent $5 million in his first two hours in office. When told that some of the projects he had just authorized might not be sound in the long run, Hopkins replied, "People don't eat in the long run—they eat every day." During its two-year existence, the FERA spent $1 billion.

Roosevelt always maintained a strong distaste for the dole. Wherever possible, his administration promoted work relief, no matter how makeshift, over cash subsidies. The Public Works Administration (PWA), under Secretary of the Interior Harold L. Ickes, received a $3.3 billion appropriation in 1933 for a major public works program. However, Ickes's cautiousness in initiating projects limited the PWA's effectiveness in spurring recovery or providing jobs. In November 1933, Roosevelt assigned $400 million in PWA funds to a new agency, the Civil Works

Administration (CWA), headed by Harry Hopkins. Within thirty days, the CWA put four million men and women to work repairing bridges, building highways, constructing public buildings, and setting up community projects. CWA workers received fifteen dollars a week. The CWA, regarded as a stopgap measure to get the country through the winter of 1933–1934, lapsed the next spring after spending all its funds.

When an exhausted Congress recessed in June 1933, much had been accomplished. Rarely had a president so dominated a legislative session. A mass of "alphabet agencies," as the New Deal programs came to be known, flowed from Washington. They gave the impression of action, but they had not turned the economy around. A slight economic boom occurred that summer, but the depression stubbornly persisted.

Nevertheless, Americans saw a ray of hope. In April 1933, at the height of the excitement of the Hundred Days, Walt Disney released a cartoon film called *Three Little Pigs*. Echoing FDR's assertion that they had nothing to fear but fear itself, many people hummed the cartoon's theme song, "Who's Afraid of the Big Bad Wolf?" as they started down the road toward renewed confidence.

Consolidating the New Deal

If the measures taken during Franklin Roosevelt's first hundred days had cured the Great Depression, the rest of the New Deal probably would not have occurred. Legislative action now turned to structural reform rather than the emergency recovery measures of 1933. Roosevelt still hoped for a balanced budget; he still abhorred the idea of direct federal relief. However, as a politician aiming to create a coalition capable of winning reelection in 1936, Roosevelt responded to popular demands to do more. He also recognized the need to try additional wide-ranging solutions to the depression.

During Roosevelt's first term, the nation's basic economic institutions got some much-needed reform. In 1934, the stock market came under federal regulation through the establishment of the Securities and Exchange Commission (SEC). The commission had the power to regulate buying stocks on credit, which was called margin buying, and to restrict speculation by people with inside information on corporate plans. The Holding Company Act of 1935 similarly reformed the structures of utility companies.

The banking system came under scrutiny as well. The Banking Act of 1935 represented a significant consolidation of federal control over the nation's banks. The law authorized the president to appoint a new Board of Governors of the Federal Reserve System. This reorganization squarely placed control of interest rates and other money market policies at the federal level rather than with regional banks. By requiring all large state banks to join the Federal Reserve System by 1942 in order to use the federal deposit insurance system, the law further encouraged the centralization of the nation's banking system.

Roosevelt had no special hostility toward the business community. He heartily accepted the capitalist system but realized that modern industrial life required certain structural changes in order to bring the system under more explicit federal control. "To preserve we had to reform," Roosevelt commented succinctly. Even though he styled himself as the savior of capitalism, he provoked strong hostility from many well-to-do Americans. To the wealthy, Roosevelt became simply "That Man," a traitor to his class. Business leaders and conservative Democrats formed the Liberty League in 1934 to organize public opposition to the New Deal.

The New Deal also faced mounting criticism from those who claimed that it had not gone far enough. The chief challenges came from three individuals, each of whom presented an alternative vision of social change. Perhaps the most benign was Francis Townsend, a Long Beach, California, doctor who spoke for the nation's elderly. Americans greatly feared the poverty of old age because so few of them had pension plans. In 1934, Townsend proposed an Old Age Revolving Pension Plan, which would give two hundred dollars a month to citizens above the age of sixty. To receive payment, people would have to retire from their jobs, thereby easing unemployment by opening the positions to others, and spend the money within the month. Townsend clubs soon sprang up throughout the country.

More overtly political challenges to Roosevelt's leadership came from Father Charles

"THE KINGFISH"
Huey Long, the Lousiana governor and senator, still ranks as one of the most controversial figures in American political history. Long inspired one of the most powerful political novels of all time, Robert Penn Warren's *All The King's Men*, which won a Pulitzer Prize in 1946. (UPI)

Coughlin and Senator Huey Long of Louisiana, both of whom attracted large followings. Coughlin, a parish priest in the Detroit suburb of Royal Oak, had turned to the radio in the mid-1920s to enlarge his pastorate. By 1933, about forty million Americans listened to the "Radio Priest." In many Roman Catholic neighborhoods during the summer, Coughlin's sermon could be heard blaring from open windows. He supported the New Deal at first but soon broke with Roosevelt over the president's refusal to support economic measures such as nationalization of the banking system and expansion of the money supply. Coughlin organized the National Union for Social Justice in 1935 to promote his views as an alternative to "Franklin Double-Crossing Roosevelt." As a Catholic priest, and because he had been born in Canada, Coughlin could not run for president, but his rapidly growing constituency became a factor in the 1936 election.

Huey Long represented the most direct political threat to Roosevelt. Flamboyant and outrageous, yet politically shrewd and enormously popular, Long built roads, public works, and schools for his backward state after his election as governor in 1928. He maintained virtual dictatorial control over Louisiana's political machine, even after being elected to the United States Senate in 1930. Long supported Roosevelt in 1932 but made no secret of his own ambitions. In 1934, he published a book called *My First Days in the White House.*

By 1934, Long had broken with the New Deal, arguing that its programs did not go far enough. Like Coughlin, he soon headed his own national movement, which had about four million followers in 1935. His Share-Our-Wealth Society attacked the unequal distribution of wealth in the United States. Long proposed taxing all incomes over $1 million and all inheritances over $5 million, and distributing the money to the rest of the population. Every family would be guaranteed about $2,000 annually, he predicted. Meanwhile, the "Kingfish" (Long's nickname, from a character in the popular radio show "Amos 'n' Andy") criticized what he considered the New Deal's inadequate social welfare programs. His rapid rise in popularity suggested a potentially large volume of public dissatisfaction with the Roosevelt administration. The president's strategists feared that Long might form a third party by combining his forces with those of Coughlin and Townsend, enabling the Republicans to win the 1936 election.

By 1935, Roosevelt had abandoned his hope of building a classless coalition of rich and poor, workers and farmers, and rural and urban dwellers. Pushed from the Left to do more, and bitterly criticized by the Right for what he had already done, the president had no choice but to abandon the middle ground. For both political and ideological reasons, and with an eye fixed firmly on the 1936 election, Roosevelt moved dramatically to the left, thwarting such opponents as Long and Townsend.

Historians use the term *Second New Deal* to describe the outpouring of legislation that followed. Roosevelt's change of direction benefited organized labor first. The rising number of strikes in 1934, about eighteen hundred involving a total of 1.5 million workers, reflected a growth of rank-and-file militancy. Labor demanded permanent legislation that would protect labor's rights to organize and bargain col-

lectively. That year, Senator Robert F. Wagner of New York, one of labor's staunchest supporters in Congress, introduced legislation to replace the ineffective Section 7(a) of the NRA. Only when Congress was on the verge of passing Wagner's bill did Roosevelt reluctantly support the legislation. He signed the National Labor Relations Act, also known as the Wagner Act, on June 5, 1935. The new law, proudly called "labor's Magna Carta," spurred unionization in all sectors of the economy.

The Wagner Act placed the weight of the federal government on labor's side in the struggle to organize. It upheld the right of workers to join unions by outlawing many unfair labor practices, such as engaging in industrial espionage, firing or blacklisting workers because of union activities, and supporting company unions. The act established the nonpartisan National Labor Relations Board (NLRB) to protect workers from employer coercion, and to supervise representation elections and enforce the guarantee of collective bargaining. If a union won a majority of the votes in a secret election, usually conducted by the NLRB, it was entitled to recognition as the sole bargaining agent for all the employees in a factory or other appropriate bargaining unit. The NLRB had the authority to issue cease and desist orders to force employers to comply.

The Social Security Act, signed by President Roosevelt on August 14, 1935, was the second major piece of legislation enacted in this period. The law was a partial response to the political mobilization of the nation's elderly through the Townsend and Long movements. It also represented the prodding of social reformers such as Grace Abbott, head of the Children's Bureau, and Secretary of Labor Frances Perkins, the first woman cabinet member. The Social Security Act provided for old-age assistance through a federal-state pension fund to which both employers and employees contributed. The use of payroll deductions, rather than financing the plan with general tax revenues, was designed to insulate the Social Security program from political attack. The act also provided for a joint federal-state system of unemployment compensation, funded by an unemployment tax on employers.

Having addressed the problems of labor and the elderly, Roosevelt now confronted the needs

ROOSEVELT AND CIVIL RIGHTS
President Roosevelt moved cautiously on civil rights.
When blacks voted overwhelmingly Democratic in 1936,
however, Roosevelt increasingly took note of their
importance to the New Deal coalition. Here he meets
with scientist George Washington Carver at the Tuskegee
Institute in 1939. (Franklin D. Roosevelt Library)

of the millions of Americans still out of work in
the sixth year of the depression. Harry Hopkins,
who had run the Federal Emergency Relief Administration from 1933 to 1935, took command of
the Works Progress Administration (WPA), the
main federal relief agency for the rest of the depression. Whereas the FERA had supplied
grants to the states for relief programs, the WPA
put relief workers on the federal payroll. Between 1935 and 1943, the WPA employed 8.5
million Americans and spent $10.5 billion. The
agency constructed 651,087 miles of roads,
125,110 public buildings, 8,192 parks, 853 air-
ports, and built or repaired 124,087 bridges.

The WPA, though an extravagant operation
by the standards of the 1930s (it gave rise to a
new word, "boondoggling," and such nick-
names as "We putter around" and "We poke
along"), never reached more than a third of
the nation's unemployed. Its average wage of
$55 a month, although well below the govern-
ment-defined subsistence level of $1,200 a year,
enabled workers to eke out a bare living.

Furthermore, the money they spent offered a
stimulus to renewed economic production. The
government cut back the program severely in
1941 and ended it in 1943. The WPA was no
longer needed in the full-employment economy
resulting from World War II.

One final measure of the Second New Deal
showed Roosevelt's willingness to push reforms
considered too controversial earlier in his presidency. Much of the business community had
already turned violently against Roosevelt in
protest of such federal measures as the NRA,
the Social Security Act, and the Wagner Act.
In 1935, he antagonized the wealthy further by
proposing a tax reform bill that called for federal
inheritance and gift taxes, higher personal income tax rates in the top brackets, and increased
corporate taxes. Conservatives quickly labeled
this legislation an attempt to "soak the rich."
Roosevelt was more interested in the political advantage of such a bill, especially defusing some
of the popularity of Huey Long's Share-Our-
Wealth plan, than in its actual results. The final
version of the bill increased tax revenues by only
$250 million a year.

As the 1936 election approached, the broad
range of New Deal programs brought many new
voters into the Democratic coalition. Some had
been personally helped by federal programs;
others benefited because their interests had
found new support in the expanded functions of
the government. Roosevelt could now count on
a potent urban-based coalition of workers, organized labor, blacks, ethnic groups, Catholics,
Jews, liberals, intellectuals, progressive Republicans, and middle-class families concerned about
old-age dependence and unemployment. At the
same time, the Democrats held on, though
somewhat uneasily, to their traditional sources
of strength among white southerners.

To run against Roosevelt, the Republicans
chose Governor Alfred M. Landon of Kansas,
who accepted the general precepts of the New
Deal but criticized the inefficiency and expense
of many of its programs. The Republicans could
not compete with Roosevelt's popularity and
his potent New Deal coalition. The expected
third-party challenge from the combined Long-
Coughlin forces fizzled in the aftermath of
Long's assassination by a Baton Rouge doctor in
September 1935.

Roosevelt won the 1936 election in one of the biggest landslides in United States history. He received 60.8 percent of the popular vote and carried every state except Maine and Vermont. Landon fought such an uphill battle that columnist Dorothy Thompson quipped, "If Landon had given one more speech, Roosevelt would have carried Canada." The New Deal was at high tide.

Stalemate

"I see one-third of a nation ill-housed, ill-clad, ill-nourished," the president declared in his second inaugural address in January 1937. Roosevelt's frank appraisal suggested that he was considering the further expansion of the welfare state that had begun to form late in his first term. However, retrenchment, controversy, and stalemate, not further reform, marked the second term.

Only two weeks after his inauguration, Roosevelt stunned Congress and the nation by asking for fundamental changes in the structure of the Supreme Court. He believed a grave constitutional crisis called for this drastic judicial reorganization. Simply put, the Supreme Court seemed on the verge of invalidating the entire New Deal. On "Black Monday," May 27, 1935, the Court struck down a farm mortgage act on the grounds that it deprived creditors of property without due process of law. That same day, in the case of *Schecter v. United States*, the Supreme Court unanimously ruled the National Industrial Recovery Act an unconstitutional delegation of legislative power. (The so-called "sick-chicken" case concerned a Brooklyn, New York firm convicted of violating NRA codes by selling diseased poultry.) Roosevelt publicly claimed that the Court's narrow interpretation returned the Constitution to "horse-and-buggy days." In 1936, the Court struck down the Agricultural Adjustment Act, the Guffey-Snyder Coal Conservation Act, and New York's minimum wage law. With the Wagner Act, the TVA, and Social Security coming up on appeal, the whole future of New Deal reform legislation appeared in doubt.

In response to this threat, Roosevelt proposed adding one new justice to the Court for each one over the age of seventy. This scheme, which would have increased the number of justices from nine to fifteen, smacked of political expediency. Roosevelt's opponents accused him of trying to "pack" the Court with justices favorable to the New Deal. The president's proposal was also regarded as an assault on the institution of the Supreme Court and on the principle of separation of powers. The issue became moot when the Supreme Court, in what journalists called "a switch in time that saved nine," upheld several key pieces of New Deal legislation, including Washington state's minimum wage law and the Wagner Act.

Charitably one could say that Roosevelt had lost a skirmish but won the war. Within four years, he reshaped the Supreme Court to suit his liberal philosophy with seven new appointments, including those of Hugo Black, Felix Frankfurter, and William O. Douglas. Yet his handling of the Court issue was a costly blunder at a time when he was vulnerable to the lame-duck syndrome that often afflicts second-term administrations. (No one yet suspected that FDR would break tradition and become the first president to seek a third term.) Throughout his second term, a conservative coalition in Congress, composed mainly of southern Democrats and Republicans from rural areas, blocked or impeded further social legislation. One of the few pieces of reform legislation to win passage was the 1938 Fair Labor Standards Act. This law made permanent the minimum wage and maximum hours provisions and the abolition of child labor first tried in the NRA codes.

The "Roosevelt recession" of 1937–1938 probably dealt the most devastating blow to the president's political standing during his second term. It showed that policymakers still did not understand the impact of their fiscal instruments on the national economy. Until that point, the economy had been making steady progress. The gross national product had grown at a yearly rate of about 10 percent from 1933 to 1937. Industrial output finally reached 1929 levels in 1937, as did real income. Unemployment declined from 25 percent to 14 percent, which meant that almost half the people without a job in 1933 had found one by 1937. Many Americans agreed with Senator James F. Byrnes of South Carolina that "the emergency has passed."

The steady improvement cheered Roosevelt. Reflecting his basic fiscal conservatism, he had never overcome his dislike of large deficits and huge federal expenditures for relief. Accordingly, he slashed the federal budget in 1937. Congress cut the WPA's funding in half between January and August, laying off about 1.5 million WPA workers. Adding to the nation's economic woes, the withholding of $2 billion from workers' paychecks to fund the new Social Security system reduced purchasing power. On another front, the Federal Reserve, fearing inflation, tightened credit. The stock market promptly collapsed, and unemployment soared to 19 percent, leaving more than ten million workers without a job. Roosevelt found himself in the same situation that had confounded Hoover. Having taken credit for the recovery between 1933 and 1937, he now had to take the blame for the recession.

Roosevelt spent his way out of the downturn. Large WPA appropriations and a resumption of public works poured enough money into the economy to snap it out of the recession by early 1938. Roosevelt and his economic advisers were groping toward the general theories being advanced by John Maynard Keynes, a British economist. Keynes proposed that governments use deficit spending to stimulate the economy when private spending proved insufficient. The increase in federal defense spending for World War II, which finally ended the Great Depression, provided the most striking confirmation of Keynesian theory.

By 1938, the New Deal had basically run out of steam. It had no climax; it simply withered away. For six years, Franklin Roosevelt had inspired public confidence that hard times could be overcome. He had pragmatically sought solutions to the depression and found them in Keynesian economics. Roosevelt showed himself to be a superb politician, successfully balancing demands for more government programs with his own assessment of what was politically feasible. His political skill and enormous personal popularity cemented the formation of the Democratic coalition that had started to develop in the 1920s.

Throughout the New Deal, however, Roosevelt always demonstrated clear limits on how far he was willing to go. His instincts were basically conservative, not revolutionary; he saved the capitalist economic system by reforming it. He created new public instruments to make economic life more predictable, initiatives that rein-forced the ongoing private efforts to ensure stability in a modern industrial economy. The New Deal has been credited with a major expansion of the governmental role, but mainly the emergency of the depression pushed Roosevelt in that direction. Under normal circumstances, he would have served out his second term and a new president would have been elected in 1940. Roosevelt won election to a third term—and eventually a fourth—only because events in Europe became so serious that a change in leadership seemed dangerous.

The New Deal's Impact on Society

The New Deal was, as one historian put it, "somehow more than the sum of its parts." To understand its impact on society, we must look beyond the new federal programs coming out of Washington and consider broader changes in American political and social life. The New Deal set in motion a major expansion of presidential power and engendered a dramatic growth in the federal bureaucracy. The Roosevelt administration opened unprecedented opportunities for groups such as women, blacks, and labor to play larger roles in public life. It also laid the groundwork for the modern welfare system that shapes American life today.

The Growth of the Presidency and the Federal Bureaucracy

Every president since the 1930s has lived in the shadow of Franklin Roosevelt. Few of his successors have matched his raw political talent or had the opportunities offered by the twin crises of depression and war in which to act "presidentially." By concentrating public attention so dramatically on the presidency and the national state, Roosevelt raised expectations that the federal government could solve major problems in social and economic life. These promises have proven difficult to deliver.

President Roosevelt established unusually close rapport with the American people. Many credited him with the positive changes in their lives, saying "He gave me a job" or "He saved my home." Ordinary citizens felt he was their

ROOSEVELT'S RELATIONS WITH THE PRESS

T.R.B. (Richard Lee Strout), columnist for The New Republic, *recalls Roosevelt's press conferences.*

Roosevelt started off having two press conferences a week. He continued that until the war came; then he had one press conference a week. Altogether, I think he had a thousand press conferences. I was present at practically all of them. One press conference was held in the morning for the afternoon papers, one in the afternoon for the morning papers the next day. We'd gather outside and there'd be anywhere from fifty or more reporters. At big times, 200 reporters might be there. We'd go in and stand around his desk. It was covered with dolls, totems, and knick-knacks. It was like a meeting of a club.

Television has destroyed the press conference as we knew it, destroyed the old freedom, the intimacy, the lack of inhibition, and that jocular familiarity between two antagonists that we had then. We were antagonists, but we liked each other and we laughed and we had a perfect understanding of what each was trying to do and there was a certain degree of affection.

The publishers of papers were generally hostile, but the reporters were won by his personality. We might not have agreed with his politics, but we had a symbiotic relationship. He got everything he could from us and we got everything we could from him. We nearly always got a good story. . . .

People often ask me why Roosevelt's being crippled was concealed from the public: "Why didn't you say so when you wrote a story about him? Why didn't you say he was in a wheelchair? Why didn't you say he was heaved up or heaved down?" We just took it for granted. Everybody knew it. It was common knowledge. . . . That had nothing to do with politics.

Source: Reprinted by permission of the publishers from *The Making of the New Deal: The Insiders Speak* ed. by Katie Louchheim, Cambridge, Mass.: Harvard University Press, © 1983 by the President and Fellows of Harvard College. 13–14.

---

friend. "Mr. Roosevelt is the only man we ever had in the White House who would understand that my boss is a son of a bitch," remarked one worker. Roosevelt's masterful use of the new medium of radio fostered this personal identification. During an early fireside chat (he broadcast sixteen during his first two terms), Roosevelt interrupted his text to ask for a glass of water. After swallowing audibly, he told his listeners, "My friends, it's very hot here in Washington tonight." An average of five thousand to eight thousand letters a week poured into the White House throughout the 1930s. One person had handled public correspondence during the Hoover administration, but it took a staff of fifty under Roosevelt. Further reflecting the new importance of communicating with the public, Roosevelt became the first president to engage a press secretary.

Much of the mail was addressed to Eleanor Roosevelt. While her husband's expansion of the personalized presidency had roots in the administrations of Theodore Roosevelt and Woodrow Wilson, the nation had never seen a First Lady like Eleanor Roosevelt. Franklin and Eleanor's marriage represented one of the most successful political partnerships of all time. He was a pragmatic politician, always aware of what could or could not be done. She was an idealist, a gadfly, always pushing him—and the New Deal—to do more. Eleanor Roosevelt observed in her autobiography,

He might have been happier with a wife who was completely uncritical. That I was never able to be, and he had to find it in other people. Nevertheless, I think I sometimes acted as a spur, even though the spurring was not always wanted or welcome. I was one of those who served his purposes.

Eleanor Roosevelt underestimated her influence. She served as the conscience of the New Deal.

The First Lady kept up her own career during her husband's four terms. She held press

"For gosh sakes, here comes Mrs. Roosevelt!"

A FIRST LADY WITHOUT PRECEDENT

Eleanor Roosevelt's globe-trotting travels provoked comment from both her family and the press. The famous *New Yorker* cartoon shown above reflected the First Lady's tendency to turn up in odd places. She did indeed soon go down in a coal mine to visit the miners. (Drawing by Robert Day; © 1933, 1961 The New Yorker Magazine, Inc.)

conferences for woman journalists, wrote a popular syndicated news column called "My Day," and traveled extensively throughout the country. Some people wondered why the First Lady could not be content to stay home at the White House like a good wife. But most admired her determination to support the causes she believed in. A Gallup poll in January 1939 showed that 67 percent approved of Eleanor Roosevelt's conduct, a higher approval rate than the president's at that time. In 1938, *Life* magazine hailed her as the greatest American woman alive.

During the Roosevelt years, basic institutional changes occurred in the office of the presidency. From the beginning, Roosevelt centralized decision making in the White House and dramatically expanded the role of the executive branch in initiating policy. In drafting legislation and setting policy, he still relied on the advice of his talented cabinet. But he was just as likely to turn to advisers and administrators scattered throughout the New Deal bureaucracy. His closest advisers, such aides as Raymond Moley, Rexford Tugwell, and Adolph Berle, became known as the "Brain Trust."

Roosevelt's attempts to reorganize the executive branch proved more controversial. In 1937 and 1938, Congress refused to consider a Roosevelt plan that would have consolidated all independent agencies into cabinet-rank departments, extended the civil service system, and created the new position of auditor general. The conservative coalition in Congress blocked the reorganization plan, effectively playing on lawmakers' fears that the president's bid for centralized executive management would dramatically reduce congressional power. Opponents also linked Roosevelt's attempt to reorganize the executive branch with popular fears about fascism and dictatorship. He had to settle for a weak bill in 1939, allowing him to create the Executive Office of the President and name six administrative assistants to the White House staff. The White House also took control of the budget process by moving the Bureau of the Budget to the Executive Office from its old home in the Treasury Department.

The growth of the office of the presidency was part of the general expansion of the federal bureaucracy set in motion by the New Deal's programs. The number of civilian government employees, which had reached 579,000 in 1929 under Herbert Hoover, exceeded a million in 1940. This expansion represented an 80 percent increase in just a decade. The number of federal employees who worked in Washington grew at an even faster rate, doubling between 1929 and 1940. Power became centered increasingly in the nation's capital, not in the states.

Eager young people flocked to Washington to join the New Deal. Lawyers in their mid-20s fresh out of Harvard found themselves drafting major legislation or being called to the White House for strategy sessions with the president. Paul Freund, a Harvard Law School professor who worked in the Reconstruction Finance Corporation and the Department of Justice, remembered, "It was a glorious time for obscure people." Many young New Dealers went on to distinguished careers in government or public service but recalled that nothing ever matched the excitement of the early New Deal.

Along with the growth in the federal bureaucracy came greatly expanded federal budgets. In 1930, the Hoover administration spent $3.1 billion and had a surplus of almost $1 billion. With the increase in federal programs to fight the depression, federal expenditures grew steadily—$4.8 billion in 1932, $6.5 billion in 1934, and $7.6 billion in 1936. In 1939, the last year before war mobilization affected the federal budget, expenditures hit $9.4 billion. Government spending outstripped receipts throughout this period, producing yearly deficits of about $3 billion. Roosevelt came close to balancing the budget in 1938, but only at the cost of a major recession. The deficit climbed toward $3 billion again as soon as he spent his way out of the so-called Roosevelt recession.

The New Deal has often been associated with the beginnings of big government and bureaucracy. It did spend money and run up deficits at a rate unprecedented for the time. But the real step toward big government spending came during World War II, not the depression. Federal outlays in the 1930s never topped $9.4 billion a year. They routinely surpassed $95 billion in the 1940s. Deficits grew from $4 billion annually during the depression to $50 billion during the war. Although the deficit declined in the postwar era, government expenditures never returned to their pre–World War II levels.

Minorities and the New Deal

The growth of the federal government in the 1930s increased the potential impact that its decisions (and its spending) had on various constituencies. The New Deal considered a broader cast of characters worthy of inclusion in the political process, especially if they were organized into pressure groups. Politicians realized the importance of satisfying the concerns of certain blocs of voters in order to cement their allegiance to the Democratic party. Sympathetic government administrators promoted the interests of groups previously overlooked. As a result, native Americans, women, blacks, and labor received more attention from the federal government and had a higher visibility in public life than ever before.

Native Americans made up one of the nation's most disadvantaged and powerless minorities. Their annual average income in 1934 totaled only forty-eight dollars, and their unemployment rate was three times the national average. Concerned New Deal administrators,

such as Secretary of the Interior Harold Ickes and Commissioner John Collier of the Bureau of Indian Affairs, tried to correct some of these inequalities. The Indian Reorganization Act of 1934 reversed the Dawes Severalty Act of 1887 by promoting more extensive self-government through tribal councils and constitutions. The government also changed the former emphasis on integration into American society by now pledging to pay greater attention to preserving Indian languages, arts, traditions, and other tribal heritages. The economic problems of native Americans were so severe, however, that no practical change in federal policy could have produced dramatic results.

Women as a group also received government attention during the 1930s. In the experimental climate of the New Deal, unprecedented numbers of women accepted positions in the Roosevelt administration. The New Deal included the first woman cabinet member, director of the mint, assistant secretary of the treasury, head of a major WPA division, and judge of the circuit court of appeals. Many of these women were close friends as well as professional colleagues, and they cooperated in an informal network to advance both feminist and reform causes.

Eleanor Roosevelt exemplified the growing prominence of women in public life. Close behind her in importance came Secretary of Labor Frances Perkins and Mary (Molly) Dewson, a social reformer-turned-politician who headed the Women's Division of the Democratic National Committee. By 1936, the Women's Division had organized eighty thousand women at the grassroots level. Dewson pushed an issue-oriented program that educated women about what the New Deal had done for their communities.

Without the vocal support of prominent women such as Eleanor Roosevelt, Molly Dewson, and the rest of the female political network, women's needs during the depression might have been totally overlooked. Grave flaws still marred the treatment of women in New Deal programs. For example, although NRA codes raised wages and improved working conditions for four million workers, a fourth of the codes adopted a lower minimum wage for women than for men performing the same jobs. Women received little help from such New Deal agencies as the Civil Works Administration or Public

ELEANOR ROOSEVELT AND CIVIL RIGHTS
One of Eleanor Roosevelt's greatest contributions was her commitment to civil rights. She developed an especially fruitful working relationship with Mary McLeod Bethune of the National Youth Administration. This photograph shows Bethune and the First Lady at a conference on black youth in 1939. (Franklin D. Roosevelt Library)

Works Administration, whose construction projects were considered unsuitable employment for female workers. Only 7 percent of the CWA workers were women. The Civilian Conservation Corps, which benefited 2.5 million young men, excluded women entirely. The Fair Labor Standards Act and the Social Security Act did not cover major areas of female employment, such as domestic service.

Women fared somewhat better under the Works Progress Administration. At the WPA's peak, 405,000 women were on its rolls. Still, at a time when women accounted for about 23 percent of the labor force, they comprised only between 14 percent and 19 percent of the WPA workers. The Women's and Professional Projects Division of the WPA, headed by Ellen Sullivan Woodward, a Mississippi social worker, created hundreds of programs to put women to work. For the most part, however, progress for women did not come from specific attempts to single

them out as a group. It occurred as part of the broader effort to improve the economic security of all Americans.

Black Americans had a similar experience. They benefited more from the general social and economic programs of the New Deal than from any concerted commitment to promote civil rights. There were striking parallels between the situation of blacks and women. (For black women, who belonged to both groups, race proved more important than gender in determining treatment from the New Deal.) Mary McLeod Bethune, an educator who became head of the Office of Minority Affairs of the National Youth Administration, headed the "black cabinet." This informal network worked for fairer treatment of blacks by New Deal agencies in the way that the women's network advocated feminist causes. Both groups benefited greatly from the support of Eleanor Roosevelt. The First Lady's promotion of equal treatment for blacks in the New Deal ranks as one of her greatest legacies.

The vast majority of the American people did not regard civil rights as a legitimate objective for federal intervention in the 1930s. The New Deal provided little specific aid for blacks, for whom hard times were a permanent feature, not just a product, of the 1930s. Franklin Roosevelt repeatedly refused to support a federal antilynching bill, claiming it would antagonize southern members of Congress whose support he needed for passage of New Deal measures. Many New Deal programs reflected prevailing racist attitudes. CCC camps segregated blacks, and many NRA codes did not protect black workers.

At the same time, blacks received enormous benefits from New Deal relief programs directed toward poor Americans regardless of race or ethnic background. Public works projects channeled funds into black communities. Blacks made up about 18 percent of the WPA's recipients, although only 10 percent of the population. Such agencies as the Resettlement Administration fought for the rights of black tenant farmers in the South. Many blacks reasoned that the tangible aid coming from Washington outweighed the discrimination that marred many New Deal programs.

Help from the WPA and other economic programs, and a belief that the White House—at least Eleanor Roosevelt—realized their plight, caused a dramatic change in blacks' voting behavior. Since the Civil War, blacks had voted Republican, a loyalty resulting from Abraham Lincoln's freeing of the slaves. As late as 1932, black voters in northern cities overwhelmingly supported Republican candidates. Then, in fewer than four years, blacks turned Lincoln's portrait to the wall and substituted that of Franklin Roosevelt. They gave him 71 percent of their votes in 1936. Black voters have remained overwhelmingly Democratic ever since.

The Rise of Organized Labor

During the 1930s, labor became a legitimate arena for federal action and intervention. At the same time, organized labor claimed a place in the national political life of the United States. Its dramatic growth in the 1930s represented one of the most important social and economic changes of the decade.

LABOR STRIFE
Despite the guarantees of the 1935 National Labor Relations Act, the drive for union recognition often provoked confrontations, and even violence, between workers and management. In this photograph, workers battle guards during the General Motors strike in Flint, Michigan in 1937. (Wide World)

THE SIT-DOWN STRIKE
The sit-down tactic pioneered by the United Auto Workers was soon used by other members of the work force, including the sales clerks at Woolworth's shown above. Sit-down strikes, however, were unpopular with many nonunion members, who saw them as assaults on property rights. The Supreme Court outlawed the practice in 1939. (The Archives of Labor and Urban Affairs, Wayne State University)

Several factors produced the breakthrough for labor. They included the inadequacy of welfare capitalism in the face of the depression, New Deal legislation such as the Wagner Act, the rise of the Congress of Industrial Organizations (CIO), and the growing militancy of rank-and-file workers. By the end of the decade, the number of unionized workers had tripled to almost nine million, covering 23 percent of the nonfarm work force. Union strength grew rapidly in manufacturing, transportation, and mining. Organized labor won not only the battle for union recognition, but also higher wages, seniority systems, and grievance procedures. Labor also greatly expanded its political involvement.

The CIO served as the cutting edge of the union movement. It did so by promoting industrial unionism—that is, it organized all the workers in an industry, both skilled and unskilled, into one union. John L. Lewis, leader of the United Mine Workers and a founder of the CIO, was the leading exponent of industrial unionism. His philosophy put him at odds with

RANK AND FILE MEMBER REMEMBERS EARLY DAYS OF THE CIO

I got in the mills in 1936, and I [was] fortunate to be caught up in a great movement of the people in this country. And that doesn't happen very often in one's lifetime, but it's an experience that I think is important to anyone who has been able to participate in a movement of this kind. . . . It's indeed a very important event in his or her life. Because a movement of the kind that we had in the Steelworkers Union and in the CIO was a movement that moved millions of people, literally, and changed not only the course of the working man in this country, but also the nature of the relationship between the working man and the government and between the working man and the boss, for all time in this country. . . .

I was hired at the Inland Steel Company in 1936. And I remember I was hired at 47 cents an hour, which was the going rate, and at a time when there were no such things as vacations, holidays, overtime, insurance, or any of the so-called fringe benefits everybody talks about today. But the worst thing—the thing that made you most disgusted—was the fact that if you came to work and the boss didn't like the way you looked, you went home; and if he did like the way you looked, you got a promotion. Anything and everything that happened to you was at the whim and will of the fellow who was your boss and your supervisor. . . . When the CIO came in, the people were ready to accept a change. And because they were ready to accept a change, it was not a difficult task to organize the people in the steel mills. Thousands upon thousands of them, in a spontaneous movement, joined the steelworkers' organization at that time. And they did it because conditions in the mill were terrible, and because they had become disgusted with the political set-up in this country and the old tales told by the Republican Party about the free enterprise system in this country in which any man was his own boss, and there was no sense in having an organization, and organizations and unions were anti-American, and so on. All this fell off the backs of the people at that time. They realized that there was going to be a change—both a political and an economic change—in this country, and there was.

Source: John Sargent, interviewed in Alice and Staughton Lynd, eds., *Rank and File: Personal Histories by Working-Class Organizers.* Princeton, N.J.: Princeton University Press, 1973. 105–106.

---

the American Federation of Labor, which favored organizing workers on a craft-by-craft basis. Lewis began to detach himself from the AFL in 1935, and the break became complete by 1938. Although the CIO generated much of the excitement on the labor front during the 1930s, the AFL gained more than a million new workers between 1935 and 1940. The two organizations reunited in 1955.

The CIO scored its first major victory in the automobile industry. On December 31, 1936, General Motors workers in Flint, Michigan, staged a sit-down strike. They vowed to stay at their machines until management agreed to bargain collectively with them. The workers lived in the factories and machine shops for forty-four days before General Motors recognized the United Automobile Workers (UAW). The CIO soon won a second major victory, this time at the United States Steel Corporation. Despite a long history of bitter opposition to unionization (as demonstrated in the 1919 steel strike), "Big Steel" capitulated without a fight and recognized the Steel Workers Organizing Committee (SWOC) on March 2, 1937.

The victory in the steel industry was not complete, however. A group of companies known as "Little Steel" chose not to follow the lead of U.S. Steel in making peace with the CIO. Steelworkers struck the Republic Steel Corporation plant in South Chicago. On the afternoon of May 31, 1937, strikers and their families gathered for a holiday picnic and rally outside the plant gates. Tension mounted, rocks were thrown, and the police fired on the crowd, killing ten protesters. All were shot in the back. A newsreel photographer recorded the scene, but Paramount Pictures suppressed the film of the "Memorial Day Massacre," considering it too inflammatory. The road to recognition for labor, even with New Deal protections, was often still violent.

The 1930s were one of the most active periods of labor solidarity in American history. The sit-down tactic spread rapidly. In March 1937, 167,210 workers staged 170 sit-down strikes. Labor unions called nearly five thousand strikes that year and won favorable terms in 80 percent of them. Rank-and-file militancy, not union leadership, fueled many of labor's breakthroughs.

The CIO attracted new groups to the union movement. Blacks, for example, found the CIO's commitment to racial justice a strong contrast to the AFL's long-established patterns of exclusion and segregation. Woman workers, about eight hundred thousand strong, also found a limited welcome in the CIO. Women participated in major CIO strikes and served as union organizers, especially in textile organizing drives in the South. Blacks and women held few union leadership positions, however.

Women found other ways beside joining a union to participate in the labor movement. The Women's Emergency Brigade, a group of wives, sisters, and girlfriends of striking workers, supplied food and first aid in the Flint sit-down strike against General Motors in 1937. Wearing distinctive red berets and armbands, they picketed, demonstrated, and occasionally resorted to such tactics as breaking windows to counter the tear gas used against the strikers. After the strike, however, UAW leaders politely but firmly told the women to go back home where they belonged.

Labor's new vitality spilled over into political activity. The AFL had always stood aloof from partisan politics, but the CIO quickly allied itself with the Democratic party. Through Labor's Nonpartisan League, the CIO gave $770,000 to Democratic campaigns in 1936. Labor also provided one of the few solid lobbies behind President Roosevelt's plan to reorganize the Supreme Court. In the 1940s, the CIO's Political Action Committee became a permanent and sophisticated contributor to the Democratic war chest.

Despite these breakthroughs, the labor movement never developed into as dominant a force in American life as had seemed possible in the heyday of the late 1930s. Roosevelt never made the growth of the labor movement a high priority. Many workers remained indifferent or even hostile to calls for unionization. Large numbers of middle-class Americans felt alienated by sit-down strikes, which they considered attacks on private property.

The Wagner Act, the New Deal's greatest contribution to labor, guaranteed unions a permanent place in American industrial relations. The effect of New Deal legislation in changing actual working conditions was not revolutionary, however. Collective bargaining, while an important gain, did not redistribute power in American industry; it merely granted labor a measure of legitimacy. Management even found that unions could be useful as a buffer against rank-and-file militancy. In addition, New Deal programs diffused some of the radical spirit prevalent before 1937 by channeling significant social welfare benefits to workers. The labor movement, which had seemed on the verge of even greater breakthroughs when the 1930s ended, entered a period of stalemate and consolidation over the next several decades.

The New Deal Legacy

The New Deal stands as a creative, exciting period of American history. The national government, no longer a distant or insignificant force, now occupied the center of the nation's political and economic activity. For the first time, people experienced the federal government as a concrete part of everyday life through mortgage guarantees, farm subsidies, NRA codes, social insurance, and work relief. The rapidly growing level of federal expenditures had emerged as a central factor in modern economic life. In 1939, a British observer summed up this new orientation: "Just as in 1929 the whole country was 'Wall Street conscious,' now it is 'Washington conscious.'"

While the New Deal took the federal government in new directions, it did so in a pragmatic, nonrevolutionary manner. Neither Franklin Roosevelt nor the American people wanted a fundamental restructuring of American economic or social life. The New Deal basically preserved the existing system of corporate capitalism by

TIME LINE
THE NEW DEAL: TOWARD THE MODERN WELFARE STATE

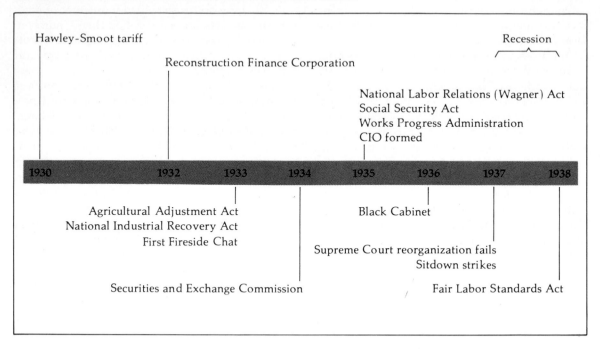

grafting a limited welfare state onto a capitalist foundation. It neither sought nor accomplished a radical redistribution of income. During the 1930s, the poorest 40 percent of the nation's families increased their share of the national income only marginally, from 12.5 percent in 1929 to 13.5 percent in 1941. The share of the top 5 percent of families dropped from 30 percent to 24 percent. Most of the redistributed income went to the middle class, whose share of income rose from 33 percent to 39 percent during the 1930s. These limited changes were as much the result of economic factors as of direct government action.

Despite the conservative thrust of the New Deal, the political and economic history of the 1930s had a wide-reaching impact on the decades that followed. The Roosevelt administration set precedents and made decisions that have shaped American institutions ever since. The New Deal represented the politicization and bureaucratization of modern American life. It brought three major changes—a new federal role in the management of the economy, the founda-

tions of the nation's welfare state, and the solidification of the New Deal coalition.

During the 1930s, the government made a concrete commitment to intervene in the economy when private instruments of power proved insufficient to guarantee economic stability. New legislation regulated the stock market more tightly and reformed the Federal Reserve system by placing more power in the hands of Washington policy makers. It also brought many practices of modern corporate life under federal regulation. The New Deal basically continued the pattern begun during the progressive era of using federal regulation of economic practices to bring order and regularity to modern industrial life.

The modern welfare system began to take shape about 1935 with the passage of the Social Security Act. One of Social Security's most important components was categorical assistance, such as aid to the blind, deaf, and disabled, and to dependent children. These were the so-called "deserving poor," people who could not support themselves through no fault of their own. The categorical assistance programs have grown dramatically since the 1930s. Aid to Dependent Children, which covered only 700,000 youngsters in 1939, by 1974 had become Aid to Families of Dependent Children with 10.8 million Americans on the welfare rolls. Programs that had formed merely a small part of the New Deal gradually grew through the years until they made up most of the American welfare system.

The other component of the emerging welfare system, old age pensions and unemployment compensation, did not amount to welfare at all. These benefits were funded by contributions from employers and employees, not by general revenues. Their greatest drawback was their failure to reach a significant minority of American workers. For example, the Social Security program excluded domestic servants and farm workers entirely for many years. Another problem, especially with unemployment compensation, stemmed from the fact that state governments administered these programs. Benefits varied widely from state to state, with the South consistently providing the lowest amounts. Payments were so low that people could barely get by on Social Security or unemployment compensation without additional resources. The social insurance system also failed to protect the chronically unemployed. After exhausting their unemployment insurance, they were at the mercy of inadequate state and local general relief.

In assessing the foundations of America's welfare state, it is hard to escape the limited nature of the New Deal commitment. The New Deal offered more benefits than American citizens had ever had before, but its safety net had many holes. Franklin Roosevelt never willingly embraced large expenditures for social welfare programs. He stated forcefully in January 1935 that the government "must and shall quit this business of relief." The government operated under the assumption that once the depression had been overcome, full employment and an active economy would take care of welfare needs. Policymakers hoped, although unrealistically, that poverty would simply wither away. It did not do so. When later administrations con-

fronted the persistence of inequality and unemployment in modern industrial society, they grafted welfare programs to the modest jerry-built system left over from the New Deal.

To its credit, the New Deal recognized that poverty was a structural economic problem, not a matter of personal failure. After hard times ended, the federal commitment to economic security for citizens remained. In fact, it grew steadily during the period after World War II. Yet the American welfare system would always be marked by its birth during the crisis atmosphere of the Great Depression. The pressing emergency needs to restore jobs, incomes, and morale precluded the development of a coherent blueprint for the modern welfare state.

Even if the early welfare system set some ill-advised, or perhaps fatal, economic and social precedents, it was brilliant politics. The frenzied activity of the New Deal gave Americans hope and confidence that the nation would pull through the depression. The Democratic party courted the allegiance of citizens who benefited from New Deal programs. Organized labor aligned itself with the administration that had promoted it as a legitimate force in modern industrial life. Blacks voted Democratic in direct relation to the economic benefits that poured into their communities. The unemployed also looked kindly on the Roosevelt administration. According to one of the earliest Gallup polls, 84 percent of those on relief voted the Democratic ticket in 1936.

The Democratic party did not attract only the down and out. Roosevelt's magnetic personality and the dispersal of New Deal benefits to families throughout the social structure brought middle-class voters, many of them first- or second-generation immigrants, into the Democratic fold. The New Deal thus completed the transformation begun in the 1920s toward a party reflecting the interests of ethnic groups, city dwellers, organized labor, blacks, and a broad cross section of the middle class. All these people benefited from and supported the expansion of federal initiatives represented by the New Deal. These voters provided the backbone of the Democratic coalition for decades to come.

*T*he economic prosperity of the 1920s rested on shaky grounds. After the stock market crash of 1929, the economy entered a downward spiral that did not bottom out until 1932–1933. The Hoover administration authorized the first direct federal intervention into the economy during peacetime in an attempt to win business and public confidence. However, such measures did not end the Great Depression, and the nation turned to Franklin D. Roosevelt and the Democrats in 1932.

Roosevelt's New Deal did not cure the depression, but it restored confidence that hard times could be overcome. Through a variety of legislation that touched the economy, agriculture, labor, and unemployment, the New Deal

got the country moving again. Yet it could hardly be called revolutionary. The commitment toward meeting Americans' welfare needs remained limited.

The New Deal led to a dramatic expansion of the federal government. Washington suddenly became a force that touched individual lives. The New Deal also set in motion other changes, including the growth of the presidency and a larger role in public life for blacks, women, and labor. It cemented the reorientation of the Democratic coalition begun in the 1920s. By 1938, however, the New Deal had run out of steam and hard times were far from over. World War II finally broke the depression's grasp.

Suggestions for Further Reading

William E. Leuchtenberg, *Franklin D. Roosevelt and the New Deal* (1963), remains the best concise introduction to the New Deal. Other useful surveys include Robert S. McElvaine, *The Great Depression* (1984); Albert Romasco, *The Politics of Recovery* (1983); and Paul Conkin, *The New Deal* (1967). Arthur M. Schlesinger, Jr., *The Age of Roosevelt* (three volumes, 1957–1960), and Frank Freidel's multivolume biography, *Franklin D. Roosevelt* (four volumes, 1952–1973), examine the era and its leading protagonist in detail.

Hoover and the Great Depression

Historians and economists continue to debate the causes of the Great Depression. See John Kenneth Galbraith, *The Great Crash* (1954); Milton Friedman and Anna Schwartz, *The Great Contraction, 1929–1933* (1965); and Peter Temin, *Did Monetary Forces Cause the Great Depression?* (1976). For general overviews of economic developments, see Charles Kindelberger, *The World in Depression* (1973), and Jim Potter, *The American Economy Between the Wars* (1974). Irving Bernstein, *The Lean Years* (1960), offers a compelling portrait of hard times during the Hoover years.

Hoover's response to the depression is chronicled in Alfred Romasco, *The Poverty of Abundance* (1965), and Jordan Schwartz, *The Interregnum of Despair* (1970). See also David Burner, *Herbert Hoover* (1978), and Joan Hoff Wilson, *Herbert Hoover: Forgotten Progressive* (1975). Eliot Rosen, *Hoover, Roosevelt, and the Brain Trust* (1977), treats the transition between the two administrations, as does Frank Freidel, *Launching the New Deal* (1973). For the 1932 election and the beginnings of the New Deal coalition, see David Burner, *The Politics of Provincialism* (1967); Samuel Lubell, *The Future of American Politics* (1952); and John Allswang, *The New Deal in American Politics* (1978).

The New Deal Response

The New Deal has inspired a voluminous bibliography. Frank Freidel, *Launching the New Deal* (1973) covers the first hundred days in detail. Monographic studies include Bernard Bellush, *The Failure of the NRA* (1975); Thomas K. McCraw, *TVA and the Power Fight* (1970); John Salmond, *The Civilian Conservation Corps* (1967); Susan Kennedy, *The Banking Crisis of 1933* (1973); and Michael Parrish, *Securities Regulation and the New Deal* (1970). Ellis Hawley, *The New Deal and the Problem of Monopoly* (1966), provides a stimulating account of economic policy. Agricultural developments are covered in Van L. Perkins, *Crisis in Agriculture* (1969); Richard S. Kirkendall, *Social Scientists and Farm Politics in the Age of Roosevelt* (1966); David Conrad, *The Forgotten Farmers* (1965); Paul Mertz, *The New Deal and Southern Rural Poverty* (1978); and Sidney Baldwin, *Poverty and Politics: The Rise and Decline of the Farm Security Administration* (1968). Alan Brinkley, *Voices of Protest* (1982), describes the Coughlin and Long movements; see also T. Harry Williams, *Huey Long* (1969). Roy Lubove, *The Struggle for Social Security* (1968), and J. Joseph Huthmacher, *Senator Robert Wagner and the Rise of Urban Liberalism* (1968), cover major initiatives from the Second New Deal.

The second term has drawn far less attention than the 1933–1936 period. James McGregor Burns, *Roosevelt: The Lion and the Fox* (1956), provides an overview. For the Supreme Court fight; see Joseph Alsop and Turner Catledge, *168 Days* (1938), and Leonard Baker, *Back to Back* (1967). The growing opposition to the New Deal is treated in James T. Patterson, *Congressional Conservatism and the New Deal* (1967), and Frank Freidel, *FDR and the South* (1965). See also Richard Polenberg, *Reorganizing Roosevelt's Government* (1966), and Barry Karl, *Executive Reorganization and Reform in the*

New Deal (1963). James T. Patterson, *The New Deal and the States* (1969), examines changing patterns of federalism, while Charles Trout, *Boston: The Great Depression and the New Deal* (1977), examines the impact of the New Deal on one city.

The New Deal's Impact on Society

For minorities and the New Deal, see Harvard Sitkoff, *A New Deal for Blacks* (1978); Raymond Wolters, *Negroes and the Great Depression* (1970); and Nancy J. Weiss, *Farewell to the Party of Lincoln* (1983). Donald Parman, *Navajoes and the New Deal* (1976), summarizes Indian policy. On women and the New Deal, see Susan Ware, *Beyond Suffrage* (1981). Joseph Lash, *Eleanor and Franklin* (1971), provides a comprehensive account of Eleanor Roosevelt's activities, which can be supplemented by her autobiographies, *This Is My Story* (1937) and *This I Remember* (1949). George Martin, *Madam Secretary* (1976), covers the career of Frances Perkins. Also of interest is Perkins's memoir, *The Roosevelt I Knew* (1946).

Irving Bernstein, *The Turbulent Years* (1970), chronicles the story of the labor movement in compelling detail through 1941. Additional studies include Peter Friedlander, *The Emergence of a UAW Local* (1975); Melvin Dubofsky and Warren Van Tine, *John L. Lewis* (1977); Sidney Fine, *Sit-Down: The General Motors Strike of 1936–1937* (1969); and David Brody, *Workers in Industrial America* (1980).

The creation of the New Deal's welfare system is treated in James T. Patterson, *America's Struggle Against Poverty* (1981), which carries the story through 1980. See also John Garraty, *Unemployment in History* (1978), and Otis Graham, *Towards a Planned Society: From Roosevelt to Nixon* (1976). Katie Louchheim, ed., *The Making of the New Deal: The Insiders Speak* (1983), provides an engaging introduction to some of the men and women who shaped the New Deal.

25

THE SOCIAL FABRIC
OF DEPRESSION
AMERICA

*T*he 1930s represent a distinct historical unit in the history of the United States. The decade symbolically began with the stock market crash of October 29, 1929, and ended with the bombing of Pearl Harbor by the Japanese on December 7, 1941. More than any other factor, the Great Depression provides the unifying theme for the decade.

Yet not every event of the 1930s can or should be interpreted through a depression-focused lens. For many people, times had always been hard. They did not experience a radical change for the worse during the depression. One historian who studied oral histories collected during the 1930s by the Works Progress Administration (WPA) expressed surprise at how rarely people actually mentioned the depression by name. "The Depression was not the singular event it appears in retrospect," she concluded. "It was one more hardship."

On the other hand, the depression loomed larger in the interviews conducted by the writer Studs Terkel during the 1960s. As the years went by between the hard times and the present, people's recollections of the depression's impact grew. More and more, survivors of the decade told uncomprehending children and grandchildren, "If you only understood how we struggled during the depression."

By interpreting the 1930s solely in terms of the depression, we also run the risk of ignoring important elements of continuity that shaped American institutions in the twentieth century. Family values and gender definitions remained stable. The popular culture of the 1920s survived, and even expanded, during the depression. For example, movies, radio, and mass-circulation magazines played important roles in keeping spirits up while Americans waited for good times to return.

Almost all our impressions of the 1930s are in terms of black and white. Widely distributed photographs taken at the time by government photographers have etched this stark visual image of depression America. Yet conditions were not uniformly grim. The depression was not on everyone's mind twenty-four hours a day. People continued their daily routine of work, family, and leisure. Literature and the arts flourished. The novelist Josephine Herbst noticed "an almost universal liveliness that countervailed universal suffering."

Hard Times

"Mass unemployment is both a statistic and an empty feeling in the stomach," observed a perceptive historian. "To fully comprehend it, you have to both see the figures and feel the emptiness." As the legions of unemployed exceeded a fourth of the nation's work force, many Americans began to lose faith in the Horatio Alger ethic of upward mobility through hard work. Many of the down-and-out blamed themselves for their misfortune.

The Invisible Scar

Some people actually got rich in the Great Depression. Joseph P. Kennedy, the father of the future president, increased his family fortune substantially during the 1930s by buying real estate and stocks that few others could afford. Chicago millionaire W. Clement Stone claimed that any ambitious young person could start at the bottom as he himself had and work to the top by taking advantage of depression-induced opportunities. All the person had to have, said Stone, was what he called PMA (Positive Mental Attitude). Such success stories merely reinforced the intense sense of personal failure among Americans who felt confused and unneeded as they lost jobs, homes, and self-respect.

"You could feel the depression deepen," recalled the writer Caroline Bird, "but you could not look out the window and see it." Many people never saw a bread line or a man selling apples on the street corner. The depression caused a private kind of despair that often simmered behind closed doors. "I've lived in cities for many months broke, without help, too timid to get in bread lines," the writer Meridel LeSueur remembered. "I've known many women to live like this until they simply faint on the street from privations, without saying a word to anyone. A woman will shut herself up in a room until it is taken away from her, and eat a cracker a day and be as quiet as a mouse. . . ."

The victims of the depression were a varied group. The depression did not create poverty; it merely publicized the conditions of the poor. People who had always been poor were joined

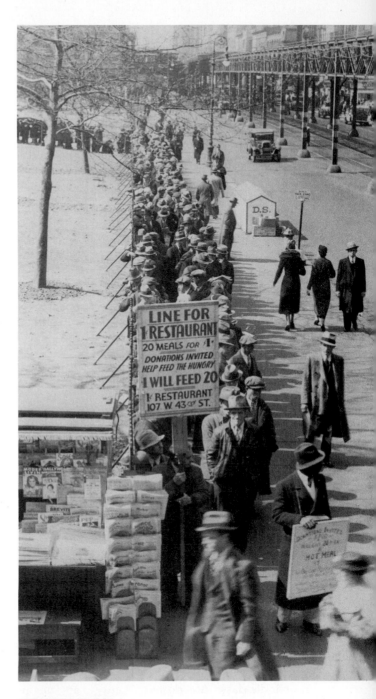

THE BREADLINE
Some of the most vivid images from the depression were breadlines and men selling apples on street corners. Women rarely appeared in breadlines, perhaps due to the different standards of "respectability" for men and women. (Franklin D. Roosevelt Library)

by the newly poor. These formerly solid working-class and middle-class families strongly believed in the work ethic and the American dream but suddenly found themselves floundering in a society that no longer had a place for them. They were proud people who felt humiliated by their plight. "What is going to become of us?" asked an Arizona man. "I've lost twelve and a half pounds this last month, just thinking. You can't sleep, you know. You wake up at 2 A.M. and you lie and think."

Hard times were especially distressing for old people, who had struggled all their lives and now faced total destitution in their final years. The loss of savings in bank failures contributed to their plight. In a cartoon from the 1930s, a squirrel asks an old man on a park bench why he had not saved for a rainy day when times were good. "I did," the man replies listlessly. No wonder older Americans responded enthusiastically to Francis Townsend's plan for old-age pensions and cheered the passage of the Social Security Act in 1935. But many still felt bitter. A man from Lincoln, Nebraska wrote to Eleanor Roosevelt in 1934. "Now as we are Old and down and out of no reason of our own," he asked, "would it be asking too much of our Government and the young generation to do by us as we have tried our best to do by them even without complaint."

Children, on the other hand, often escaped the sense of bitterness and failure that gripped their elders. Some youngsters thought it was fun to stand in a soup line. They did not feel ashamed. Yet the experience of hard times matured children quickly. A ten-year-old girl was thinking more about family survival than childhood playthings when she wrote President Roosevelt in 1935. "We have no one to give us a Christmas present," she said, "and if you want to buy a Christmas present please buy us a stove to do our cooking and to make good bread."

Downward mobility was especially hard for middle-class Americans. "Lady," an unemployed Pittsburgh man told FERA investigator Lorena Hickok, "you just can't know what it's like to have to move your family out of the nice house you had in the suburbs, part paid for, down into an apartment, down into another apartment, smaller and in a worse neighborhood, down, down, down, until finally you end

up in the slums." Before a laid-off chauffeur started his relief construction job, he spent the day watching how the other men handled their picks and shovels so he could "get the hang of it and not feel so awkward." A wife broke into tears when her husband, formerly a white-collar worker, put on his first pair of overalls to go to work.

The key to surviving the depression was maintaining self-respect. One man spent two years painting his father's house; in fact, he painted it twice. Keeping up appearances, keeping life as close to normal as possible, was an essential strategy. Camaraderie and cooperation helped many families and communities survive because other people found themselves in the same boat. When a truck driver "accidentally" dumped a load of oranges or coal off the back of his truck, he probably was contributing to the welfare of the neighborhood. Hoboes developed an elaborate system of sidewalk chalk marks to tell one another at which back doors they could get a meal, an old coat, or some spare change.

When hard times struck, families coped as best they could. Many appealed directly to Franklin or Eleanor Roosevelt. More than 450,000 letters poured into the White House in the week following the president's inauguration. People believed that the Roosevelts sincerely cared about their lives. "Never before have we had leaders in the White House to whom we felt we could go with our problems," an Alabama woman wrote Eleanor Roosevelt, "for never before have our leaders seemed conscious of the masses. The knowledge that my President is trying to uplift 'the forgotten man' has made me bold to write to you." Sometimes citizens approached the White House with specific requests, such as a loan to pay the electric bill, or one of the First Lady's cast-off coats. More often, they wrote poignant descriptions of situations that had no easy solution.

After savings and credit had been exhausted, many families faced the humiliation of going on relief. Seeking aid from the government offended people's values of self-help or the traditional pattern of reliance on relatives, neighbors, and institutions such as churches in times of need. A young caseworker tearfully remembered her embarrassment when investigating the homes of these proud people:

The father was a railroad man who had lost his job. I was told by my supervisor that I really had to *see* the poverty. If the family needed clothing, I was to investigate how much clothing they had at hand. So I looked into this man's closet . . . he was a tall, gray-haired man, though not terribly old. He let me look into the closet—he was so insulted. . . . He said, "Why are you doing this?" I remember his feeling of humiliation . . . this terrible humiliation. He said, "I really haven't anything to hide, but if you really must look into it. . . ." I could see he was very proud. He was so deeply humiliated. And I was, too. . . .

Despair, apathy, and cynicism were common reactions to such experiences. Here is how some Americans described their plight: "We're about down and out and the only good thing about it that I see is that there's not much farther down we can go." "A man over forty might as well go out and shoot himself." "It's funny. A lot of times I get offered a drink. It seems like people don't want to drink alone. But no one ever offers me a meal. Most of the time when I take a drink it makes me sick. My stomach's too empty." "No work, no hope; just live from one day to the next. Maybe better times are coming. Personally I doubt it." "New Deal? They forgot to cut the deck. That's what we say around here."

Such hardships left deep wounds. Author Caroline Bird called them the "invisible scar." An elderly civil servant told Studs Terkel that she had bought a plot of land outside Washington so that if the depression ever recurred, she would have something to live off. Labor organizer Larry Van Dusen described another common reaction: "The depression left a legacy of fear, but also a desire for acquisition—property, security. I now have twenty times more shirts than I need, because all during that time, shirts were something I never had." Some people concluded that the system was rotten and had to be changed, but most drew a different lesson. Virginia Durr, a white civil rights activist from Alabama, observed, "The great majority reacted by thinking money is the most important thing in the world. Get yours. And get it for your children. Nothing else matters. Not having that stark terror come at you again." For many Americans, "that stark terror" of losing control over their lives summed up the Great Depression.

Blacks and the Depression

Black Americans viewed the despair of the depression differently than most whites did. One black man told Studs Terkel the reaction of a typical black male: "It didn't mean too much to him, the Great American Depression, as you call it. There was no such thing. The best he could be is a janitor or a porter or shoeshine boy. It only became official when it hit the white man." The novelist and poet Maya Angelou recalled the same sentiments from her childhood in Stamps, Arkansas. "The country had been in the throes of the Depression for two years before the Negroes in Stamps knew it," she said. "I think that everyone thought the depression, like everything else, was for the white folks." Writer Langston Hughes expressed it most forcefully: "The depression brought everybody down a peg or two. And the Negroes had but few pegs to fall."

Black Americans felt little of the shame and personal guilt experienced by many whites during the depression. Discrimination and limited opportunities had always been such a large part of their lives that they had no reason to blame themselves for their misfortune. That attitude hardly helped them overcome the staggering obstacles they faced in the 1930s, however.

As late as 1940, more than 75 percent of the nation's black population lived in the South, including nearly all of the black farmers. Only 20 percent of these farmers owned their own land. The rest toiled on the bottom rung of the exploitative southern agricultural system, working as tenant farmers, farm hands, and sharecroppers. They rarely earned more than an average of $200 a year. The yearly earnings of black women cotton pickers in one Louisiana parish averaged only $41.67.

Throughout the 1920s, southern agriculture had suffered from falling prices and overproduction. The depression made an already desperate situation even worse. Such New Deal programs as the Agricultural Adjustment Administration displaced as many as two hundred thousand black tenant farmers from their land. When white owners cut back on production to get their government subsidy checks, they simply let the blacks go and continued to farm their own land. The Resettlement Administration was one of the few New Deal agencies that supported the rights

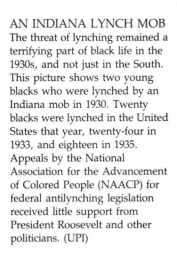

AN INDIANA LYNCH MOB
The threat of lynching remained a terrifying part of black life in the 1930s, and not just in the South. This picture shows two young blacks who were lynched by an Indiana mob in 1930. Twenty blacks were lynched in the United States that year, twenty-four in 1933, and eighteen in 1935. Appeals by the National Association for the Advancement of Colored People (NAACP) for federal antilynching legislation received little support from President Roosevelt and other politicians. (UPI)

of black sharecroppers, but angry southerners in Congress soon cut its appropriations drastically.

Some black farmers fought back by joining the Southern Tenant Farmers Union (STFU), one of the few southern groups that welcomed both blacks and whites. "It won't do no good for us to divide because there's where the trouble had been all the time," an elderly black farmer reminded the organizing committee. "The same chain that holds you holds my people, too. If we're chained together on the outside we ought to stay chained together in the union."

The STFU, founded in 1934, encountered repression and violent harassment from landowners who had a stake in keeping black and white sharecroppers divided and unorganized. The Southern Tenant Farmers Union could do little to reform an agricultural system so dependent on one crop, cotton. It won only slight improvements in the treatment of tenant farmers by New Deal programs.

The Scottsboro case reflected the harsh social and political discrimination that almost all blacks faced in the South during the 1930s. On March 25, 1931, a freight train pulled into Scottsboro,

Alabama carrying a number of hoboes and transients who had caught a free ride on the rails. Acting on a tip from the conductor, sheriff's deputies arrested nine black men for fighting with some white hoboes.

Suddenly, two white women wearing men's clothing stepped off the boxcar and claimed they had been raped by the nine blacks. The officers accepted without question the accusations of the women, Victoria Price and Ruby Bates, and barely kept an angry white crowd from lynching the men. Within two weeks, juries composed entirely of white males found the nine defendants guilty of rape and sentenced eight of them to death. One defendant, a minor, escaped the death penalty. The U.S. Supreme Court overturned the sentences in 1933 and ordered new trials on the grounds that the defendants had been denied adequate legal counsel.

The youth of the Scottsboro defendants, their rapid trials, and especially their harsh sentences stirred public protest. The case aroused emotions centering on the issues of class, race, gender, and sectional suspicion. The International Labor Defense (ILD), a labor organization loosely affiliated with the Communist party, took over the defense of the so-called "Scottsboro boys." White southerners resented not only the presence of these radical lawyers, but also that all were northerners and Jews. Southerners felt they should be left alone to deal with the episode, as local custom demanded. Some believed they should be congratulated because the accused men had been brought to trial rather than lynched on the spot.

The southern myth of the inviolate honor and chastity of white womanhood also complicated the case. No evidence confirmed that the two women had had sexual intercourse on the train, and their stories contained many inconsistencies and unsupportable claims. Ruby Bates eventually recanted her story and agreed that the Scottsboro boys had been framed by racism. In the South, however, when a white woman claimed to have been raped by a black man, her word was always accepted over that of the accused rapist. As one court observer remarked, Victoria Price "might be a fallen woman, but by God she is a white woman."

The case dragged on through the courts for the next decade. Five of the defendants were convicted and sentenced to long prison terms in trials held in 1936 and 1937. The charges against the other four were dropped in 1937. Four of the convicted men were paroled in 1944. The fifth escaped to Michigan, whose governor refused to return him to Alabama.

The Scottsboro case received wide coverage in black communities of both the North and the South. Coupled with an increase in lynching in the early 1930s, it provided a strong inducement for black Americans to head for northern cities. The lure of the North was offset, however, by the lack of economic opportunities caused by the depression. Consequently, the black exodus of the 1930s totaled only about half of that in the 1920s. About four hundred thousand black men and women left the South during the 1930s. By 1935, eleven northern cities had a black population of more than a hundred thousand. Two of the most popular destinations were Harlem in New York City and the South Side of Chicago.

Harlem presents a case study of what awaited blacks when they journeyed north. Harlem had been New York's first suburb, a neighborhood of wealthy city families in the late nineteenth century. As late as 1900, blacks made up only a small minority of the Harlem population. Then came the great migration from the South set in motion by the social and geographic mobility of World War I. At the same time that blacks moved into Harlem, second-generation Italians and Jews began to move out.

Harlem reached the height of its fame in the 1920s, when it became a mecca for both whites and blacks. Adventurous New Yorkers associated Harlem with the Cotton Club and other glittering jazz palaces catering to white audiences. Meanwhile, black intellectuals founded the literary movement called the Harlem Renaissance, which celebrated racial pride and cultural identity in the midst of white society. Such authors as Alain Locke, Claude McKay, Langston Hughes, Jean Toomer, Jessie Fauset, and Zora Neale Hurston represented the "New Negro" in fiction. These cultural developments had little impact on the masses of black Americans, however.

During the 1920s, the black population of New York City increased by about 115 percent, putting a drastic strain on Harlem's resources. This once prosperous middle-class community was on its way to becoming a slum. The depression made a bad situation worse. Residential segregation kept blacks from moving elsewhere. They paid excessive rents while unscrupulous realtors allowed housing to deteriorate rapidly. Crowded living conditions caused disease and death rates to rise severely; tuberculosis became one of Harlem's leading causes of death. Unemployment there climbed to 50 percent, as whites now clamored for jobs traditionally held by blacks—domestic servants, elevator operators, garbage collectors, and waiters.

In March 1935, Harlem exploded in the nation's only major race riot of the decade. Its residents were angry about the lack of jobs, a slowdown in relief, and pervasive economic exploitation of the black community; the white-owned stores, although dependent entirely on black trade, would not employ blacks. The arrest of a teenage black shoplifter, followed by rumors that he had been severely beaten by white police officers, triggered the riot. False reports of his death increased the panic, and the city mobilized five hundred police officers. Four blacks were killed, and property damage totaled $2 million.

Reflecting the harsh conditions experienced by black Americans in northern cities, black religious and colonization movements gained support during the 1920s and 1930s. In the 1920s, the Universal Negro Improvement Association (UNIA) promoted racial pride and black separatism under the leadership of Jamaican-born Marcus Garvey. Based in Harlem, the UNIA was the first mass movement among the nation's black working class. At its height, it claimed four million followers. Garvey urged blacks to return to Africa because, he said, they would never be treated justly in countries ruled by whites. Amy Jacques Garvey attracted black women by combining her husband's black nationalism with a feminist outlook emphasizing women's contributions to cultural and political life.

The Universal Negro Improvement Association grew rapidly in the early 1920s. It published a newspaper called *Negro World* and opened "liberty halls" for its followers in major northern cities. The UNIA also undertook extensive business ventures as part of its support for black capitalism. The most ambitious project was the Black Star Line, a steamship company to ferry cargo between the West Indies and the United States, and to provide passage to Africa for American blacks. This venture caused the downfall of the UNIA. Financial irregularities in raising money led to mail fraud indictments against Garvey and several of his associates. Garvey was convicted in 1925 and sentenced to five years in prison. President Calvin Coolidge paroled him in 1927, and Garvey was deported to Jamaica. His movement collapsed without his charismatic leadership.

During the 1930s, a black religious leader named Father Divine rose to fame in Harlem. Divine promised his loyal followers a kingdom in heaven that recognized no distinctions of sex, race, color, or economic status. He became noted for establishing shelters and soup kitchens staffed by the Divine Peace Mission. At the height of the Great Depression, Divine provided three thousand free meals a day for Harlem's destitute. Unlike Marcus Garvey, Divine did not bar whites from his movement.

Although the "Divine Deal" competed with the New Deal for the loyalty of many Harlem residents, Father Divine's cult had little impact on political development. In politics, Harlem be-

came overwhelmingly Democratic by 1936, a striking confirmation of the shift in black allegiance to the New Deal. In 1920, only 3 percent of Harlem's blacks voted for the Democratic ticket of James M. Cox and Franklin D. Roosevelt. By 1928, 28 percent of them supported Al Smith. The percentage rose to 50.8 percent for Roosevelt in 1932.

The impact of the New Deal programs on economic conditions in Harlem, especially the increased expenditures in the wake of the 1935 riot, raised Roosevelt's support to 81.3 percent in the 1936 election. The president maintained that level of popularity in the black community in 1940. The number of black voters in Harlem rose 78 percent during the 1930s, far outstripping the population increase from migration. Despite the harshness of the depression—or, more likely, because of it—national politics assumed a new relevance for black Americans in northern cities.

Dust Bowl Migrations

Like black Americans, farmers had long experienced depressed economic conditions. That situation merely continued in the 1930s. For farmers on the Great Plains, however, things got worse—much worse. In Oklahoma, Arkansas, and Texas, the decade became known as the "Dirty Thirties" because of the dust storms that blighted the land. A drought that began in 1930 and lasted until 1941 was the worst in the history of the country. Throughout the decade, the three words most often repeated by farmers were "if it rains."

Dust became a part of everyday life. When the clouds of dust rolled in, street lights blinked on in what seemed like nighttime darkness. Dust seeped into houses and, one historian wrote, "blackened the pillow around one's head, the dinner plates on the table, the bread dough on the back of the stove." The dust storms were not confined to the Plains. In May 1934, the wind took dust clouds to Chicago, where the grime fell like dirty snow, dumping the equivalent of four pounds of debris for every person in the city. Several days later, the same clouds blackened the skies and dirtied the streets of Buffalo, Boston, New York and Washington.

Farmers who moved onto the semiarid Great Plains after the 1870s had always risked the rav-

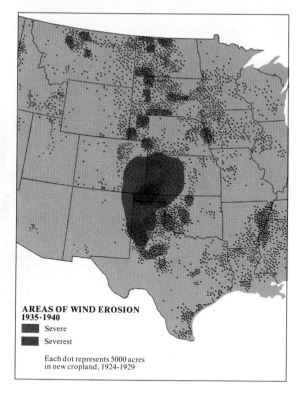

AREAS OF WIND EROSION
1935-1940

■ Severe

■ Severest

Each dot represents 5000 acres
in new cropland, 1924-1929

MAP 25.1 THE DUST BOWL
A U.S. Weather Bureau scientist called the drought of the
1930s "the worst in the climatological history of the
country." Conditions were especially severe in the
southern plains, where the dramatic increases in farming
on marginal land had already strained production before
the drought struck. Winds whipped the loosened topsoil
into devastating dust storms. One dust-storm blackout in
Amarillo, Texas lasted eleven hours.

ages of drought. Even in wet years, the average
rainfall of twenty inches or less was barely
enough to raise grain crops. But low rainfall
alone did not cause the Dust Bowl, an area of
the Great Plains that included parts of Oklahoma, Texas, New Mexico, Colorado, and Kansas. The aggressive expansion of the farming
frontier beyond its natural limits destroyed the
delicate ecological balance of the plains. After
marginal land had been stripped of its natural
vegetation, nothing remained to hold the soil
when the rains dried up and the winds came.

This ecological disaster caused an exodus
from the land. The term "Okies" (for Oklaho-
mans) came into use to describe the members of
farm families who loaded all their belongings

into a beat-up Ford and headed west along
Route 66 to the promised land of California.
John Steinbeck's classic novel *The Grapes of Wrath*
(1939) immortalized this saga. Its central character, Ma Joad, symbolized the family's attempt to
keep its spirit unbroken in the face of economic
and social disaster.

Families like the Joads abandoned their land
not only because of drought, but also as a result
of economic forces that had changed American
agriculture. Large-scale commercialized farming
was spreading to the plains. The Joads had
farmed with animals. After the bank foreclosed
their mortgage, a gasoline-engine tractor, the
symbol of mechanized farming, plowed under
their crops and pushed down their house.

California had already undergone massive
changes that created a type of agriculture vastly
different from the traditional farming the Joads
left behind. Farming in California was large
scale, intensive, and diversified. In the late nineteenth century, the Imperial Valley had been
arid wasteland; only the introduction of irrigation made farming possible. Growers at first cultivated wheat, but soon switched to fruits and
vegetables. The steady supply of cheap labor
provided by Chinese, Mexicans, Okies, and,
briefly, even Hindustani made such farming economically feasible. Carey McWilliams, whose
Factories in the Field (1939) rivaled *The Grapes of
Wrath* in focusing national attention on migrant
workers, noted that California agriculture was
basically industrial in nature.

> Ownership is represented not by physical
> possession of the land, but by ownership of cor-
> porate stock; farm labor, no longer pastoral in
> character, punches a time clock, works at piece
> or hourly wage rates, and lives in a shack or
> company barracks, and lacks all contact with the
> real owners of the farm factory on which it is
> employed.

Encouraged by handbills promising good jobs
in California, at least 350,000 Okies headed west
during the 1930s. White, native-born Americans
had made up about 20 percent of the migratory
farm labor force before the depression, but their
proportion increased to more than 85 percent by
the late 1930s. Since growers needed only
175,000 workers at the peak of the picking season, many more people wanted a job than could

MIGRANT LABOR IN CALIFORNIA

By the 1930s, about thirty-five thousand Filipinos were working as migrant laborers in California, including these lettuce workers in Salinas. At first, Filipinos were highly desired as migratory workers because they worked long hours for low wages. But they soon began to demand higher wages. In 1934, three thousand Filipino lettuce workers went on strike near Salinas. The strike was brutally broken, and many of the workers were driven from the community. (Library of Congress)

find one. This surplus of labor assured the growers a cheap and usually docile wage force willing to work at any price. That price was incredibly low in the 1930s. The average yearly family income for farm workers in California ranged from $350 to $450, less than a third of the subsistence level.

Thousands of Mexican-American workers in the Southwest also found grim conditions. The 1930 census reported 617,000 Mexican-Americans, but the number had dropped to 377,000 by 1940. A formal deportation policy instituted by the U.S. government caused part of the decline, although many more Mexicans left voluntarily when work ran out or because they feared deportation. The deportation of Mexican-Americans was not simply a response to the arrival of migrants from the Dust Bowl. The largest number of Mexican-American deportations occurred under the Hoover administration, well before the Dust Bowl exodus reached its peak. Many southwestern communities realized that it was cheaper to send the migrant workers back to Mexico than to support them on relief during the winter, when there were no crops to pick. A one-way train ticket cost the equivalent of a week's relief allotment in 1932.

The experience of Mexican-Americans in the 1930s reflected ongoing ambivalence in the United States about whether to encourage or discourage migration across the border. The first *bracero* (day-laborer) program promoting Mexican immigration had been established during World War I to meet the labor shortages caused by mobilization. The importation of cheap Mexican labor continued throughout the 1920s. After the forced exodus in the depression, the tide changed again. Mexican workers found themselves coaxed back when World War II caused another labor shortage. A second bracero program, started in 1942, remained in effect on an informal basis until 1964.

Except for short periods following the two world wars and during the Great Depression, Mexican migration to the United States—both legal and illegal—has increased steadily throughout the twentieth century. The influx of Spanish-speaking migrants with their own distinct culture helped shape the patterns of life in the Southwest.

The experiences of a young Mexican-American in the 1930s named Cesar Chavez influenced him to become a farm union organizer. Chavez was a child of ten when his father lost his farm near Yuma, Arizona, in 1934. The Chavez family became migrant workers in California, joining the army that followed the crops. They experienced continual discrimination, including rejection by many restaurants whose signs proclaimed "White Trade Only." The family never stayed long in one place because Cesar's father became involved in several bitter labor strikes that hit the Imperial Valley in the mid-1930s. All these strikes failed, but they gave young Chavez a heritage of labor organizing that he used in founding a national farm workers' union in 1962.

Family Values

"We didn't go hungry, but we lived lean." That poignant memory sums up the experiences of many American families during the Great Depression. The vast majority were neither very rich nor very poor. For most, the depression did not mean losing millions of dollars in the stock market or leaving an expensive boarding school because their parents could no longer pay the bills. Nor did it mean living in cardboard "Hoovervilles" or going on relief. The husband in a typical family in the 1930s had a job, and his wife was a homemaker. Life was not easy, but it consisted of "making do" rather than stark deprivation.

MEXICAN-AMERICAN POVERTY IN TEXAS
In 1937, Antonia and Pablo Martinez lived in a one-room house in San Antonio, Texas, with his parents and older brother. If either Pablo or Antonia worked in 1937, it was probably in San Antonio's pecan-shelling industry, which depended heavily on the cheap labor of Mexican-Americans. (The San Antonio Light Collection, U. T. Institute of Texan Cultures)

The Family Faces the Great Depression

Sociologists who studied family life during the 1930s found that the depression usually intensified existing trends of behavior. For example, if a family had been stable and cohesive before the depression, it now pulled together to surmount the new obstacles. If, however, a family had shown signs of disintegration, the dislocations of the depression made the situation worse. On the whole, the researchers thought far more families hung together than broke apart.

The depression encouraged a return to traditional values. Church attendance rose slightly. The family unit again became the center of leisure activities, replacing the expensive commercial amusements of the 1920s. Spending the evening at home listening to the radio became a popular pastime, as did reading books borrowed from the public library. People enjoyed such bestsellers as Pearl Buck's *The Good Earth* (1931), Hervey Allen's *Anthony Adverse* (1933), Dale Carnegie's *How to Win Friends and Influence People* (1936), and Margaret Mitchell's *Gone With the Wind* (1936). Columnist Russell Baker recalled another activity that everyone could afford: "Talking was the Great Depression pastime. Unlike the movies, talk was free. . . . "

The depression directly affected demographic trends in the 1930s. The marriage rate fell from 10.14 per thousand persons in 1929 to 7.87 in 1932. Temporary postponements of marriage became permanent in many cases. Elsa Ponselle, a Chicago schoolteacher who later became the principal of one of the city's largest elementary schools, recalled her experience:

> Do you realize how many people in my generation are not married? . . . It wasn't that we didn't have a chance. I was going with someone when the Depression hit. We probably would have gotten married. He was a commercial artist and had been doing very well. . . . Suddenly he was laid off. It hit him like a ton of bricks. And he just disappeared.

The marriage rate rebounded after 1933, but the number of women aged twenty-five to thirty in 1930 who never married was 30 percent higher than in 1925. Since people could not afford the legal expense necessary to dissolve an unhappy marriage, the divorce rate dropped as well. The birthrate was the demographic factor most sensitive to the depression. It had fallen steadily since 1800, but it dropped from 21.3 live births per thousand population in 1930 to 18.4 three years later, a 13 percent decrease. The 1933 level, if maintained, would have led to a population decline.

Economic factors played a dominant role in the falling birthrate. Many people regarded pregnancy as a misfortune because they worried about bringing a child into a world with such limited opportunities. The birthrate rose slightly after 1934 but had reached only 18.8 by the end of the decade. In contrast, the birthrate increased to 25 per thousand population at the height of the baby boom following World War II.

The extensive limitation of births during the Great Depression required access to effective contraception. The production of diaphragms and condoms was one of the few businesses that thrived in the 1930s. Abortion remained illegal, but hard times increased the number of women who visited an abortionist to end an unwanted pregnancy. Such abortions were risky because many abortionists operated under unsanitary conditions that caused illness or death. Between

eight thousand and ten thousand women died each year from botched abortions.

The 1930s marked a significant stage in the long history of the birth control movement in America. A 1936 federal court decision in the case of *United States v. One Package of Japanese Pessaries* struck down all federal bans on the dissemination of contraceptive information. Doctors now had wide discretion in prescribing birth control for married women, which became legal in all the states except Massachusetts and Connecticut. Public support of birth control also increased. A 1936 Gallup poll found that 63 percent of those interviewed favored the teaching and practice of contraception.

Margaret Sanger played a major part in encouraging popular acceptance of birth control in America. She had started her career as a public health nurse in the slums of New York in the 1910s. Anxious immigrant women continually asked Sanger to tell them the "secret" of how to avoid having more babies. When a patient who had been referred to her died from the effects of an illegal abortion, Sanger dedicated her life to birth control. At first, she linked forces with socialist movements aimed at the working class. But by the 1920s, she appealed for support almost entirely to the middle class, which she identified as the key to the movement's success. Sanger also courted the medical profession, pioneering in the establishment of birth control clinics staffed by doctors. In the process, birth control became less a feminist demand and more a medical issue.

Birth control had long been a private decision between individuals. Its public acceptance increased greatly during the 1930s because of the widespread desire to limit family size for economic reasons. In 1942, the American Birth Control League, an organization Sanger had founded in 1921, became Planned Parenthood, an organization that remains very active today.

MARGARET SANGER AND BIRTH CONTROL
Margaret Sanger was probably the twentieth century's most influential birth control reformer. In 1923, she opened the first doctor-staffed birth control clinic in the United States. By 1938, more than three hundred such clinics operated nationwide. Here she testifies before a Senate subcommittee in 1931 in support of a bill to legalize the distribution of birth control information. (UPI)

Women and the Depression

Men and women experienced the Great Depression differently. In many ways, the depression disrupted women's lives less than men's. Millions of men lost their jobs, but few of the nation's twenty-eight million homemakers lost theirs. In fact, women's roles in the home took on greater importance.

ONE WOMAN'S STRUGGLE FOR AN EDUCATION DURING THE DEPRESSION

Frances Ridgway's story of life in rural Michigan speaks for the experiences of many depression-era women.

The Depression caused my family to change their way of living. There were six of us kids and in order to feed us all, my parents traded their town home for an eighty-acre farm. There was no electricity there, no running water, and no flush toilet. And the house was back off the road a half a mile.

But my father thought at least we could eat, living on a farm. And we did, even if it was only beans. My mother would put up 600 or 700 quarts of beans every year.

When I reached twelve years old, I wanted to go to high school; but back in northern Michigan they didn't encourage farm girls to get much of an education. Now, I really insisted that my parents let me go live with this family who paid me two dollars a week to take care of the house and kids.

I did that kind of work for the better part of four years. Sometimes I stayed at home, but when I did I'd have to walk almost four miles to get to the place where the school bus stopped.

I'll tell you, I washed and I cleaned and did all the dirty work, you know. Anyway, when I started that first year of high school, I had six dollars saved, and that was enough to buy all my supplies until Christmas. I supplemented my income in another way, by writing all the book reports for the boys on the football team at a nickel apiece. And you know for a nickel you could get a big, thick pad of paper.

During my senior year I got an NRA grant of six dollars a month for helping the teachers correct papers. I thought that was wonderful.

But on the whole, it was hard. I was so very poor. I had one skirt I made out of an old coat in home economics class. And I wore NRA pants. You know, my family got food supplements, and they'd come in sacks that had NRA stamped on them. My mother'd dye them a dark seal brown, but the NRA was still there. My brothers used to always call my NRA pants, "Nuts Running America." I forget . . . I think it meant National Recovery Act.

Anyway, I had no clothes and no money but I finished at the top of my class and I competed for a scholarship and won. It was to Wellesley, a big Eastern college for women. Well, of course, that was out of the question. I didn't even have the money to get there, let alone all the extras I'd need.

But I had a goal for myself. Ever since I was twelve years old there was one major goal in my life . . . one thing . . . and that was to never be poor again. I wasn't especially attractive, and I was poor. I couldn't do anything about the one, but I made up my mind I wasn't always going to be poor.

Source: Frances Ridgway, quoted in Jeane Westin, *Making Do: How Women Survived the '30s.* Chicago: Follett, 1976. 152–153.

The difference in the depression's impact resulted from the traditional gender roles that governed male and female behavior in the 1930s. Men had been trained from childhood to be breadwinners for their families. If they no longer could fulfill this expectation, they considered themselves failures. Women, on the other hand, saw their self-importance increase as they struggled to keep their families afloat. The sociologist Robert Lynd noticed this phenomenon in the follow-up study of Middletown (Muncie, Indiana) published in 1937:

The men, cut adrift from their usual routine, lost much of their sense of time and dawdled helplessly and dully about the streets; while in the homes the women's world remained largely intact and the round of cooking, housecleaning, and mending became if anything more absorbing.

A woman recalled her own experience:

I did what I had to do. I seemed to always find a way to make things work. I think hard times is harder on a man, 'cause a woman will

RURAL ELECTRIFICATION

In 1935, less than one tenth of the nation's 6.8 million farms had electricity. For millions of farm families, this stark fact meant a life of unremitting toil made even harsher by the lack of mechanical aids. Farm families used an average of two hundred gallons of water a day. Any household or barnyard chore that involved water—and most did—meant pumping the water from a distant well and carrying it to the house or barn in a pair of buckets weighing as much as sixty pounds full. If hot water were needed, it had to be heated on a wood stove that required constant tending. Meeting a family's yearly water needs took sixty-three eight-hour days and involved carrying the water a total of 1,750 miles.

The lack of electricity affected farm wives especially hard. A Farm Belt senator recalled "hundreds of thousands of women . . . growing old prematurely; dying before their time." Canning, a necessity because families had no way to store food by refrigeration, kept women over boiling cauldrons of peaches, berries, or vegetables, often in the worst summer heat before the freshly harvested produce spoiled. Washday, traditionally Monday, involved three large zinc washtubs for washing, rinsing, and bleaching. One week's wash consisted of at least four to eight loads, each requiring three washtubs of clean water hauled from the well. Few farm households could afford commercial soap, and so they used lye, which roughened women's hands and did not get ground-in dirt out of soiled clothes too well. If farm women dreaded washday on Monday, they hated ironing on Tuesday even more. Ironing was another all-day job. The iron, a six- or seven-pound wedge of metal, had to be heated on the stove. Because the metal did not retain heat for more than a few minutes, it usually took several irons to do a single shirt. The women in Texas's Hill Country called them "sad irons."

After a day that began in pitch darkness and continued with backbreaking work for twelve hours, evenings brought few comforts. Reading strained the eyes because the only available light came from cumbersome kerosene lamps that provided the equivalent of 25 watts of light at best. Children's eyes might be strong enough to read in the semidarkness, but few older folks could read without squinting. In addition, the absence of electricity meant no radios to provide a bit of amusement or some contact with the world beyond the boundaries of the darkened farmhouse.

Electricity brought relief from

do something. Women just seem to know where they can save or where they can help, more than a man. It's just a worry for him, and he feels so terrible when he can't take care of his family.

Women made many contributions to family survival during the depression years. With the national median annual income at $1,160, a typical woman had $20 to $25 a week to feed, clothe, and provide shelter for her family. Deflation had lowered the cost of living so that milk sold for 10 cents a quart, bread 7 cents a loaf, and butter 23 cents a pound. Yet housewives still had to watch every penny. Two friends who often bought hamburger split the two pounds that sold for 25 cents and took turns keeping the extra penny. Eleanor Roosevelt described these women's lives: "It means endless little economies and constant anxiety for fear of some catastrophe such as accident or illness which may completely swamp the family budget." The line between making do and doing without was often thin.

Despite the hard times, Americans managed to maintain a fairly high level of consumption. Continuing the pattern of the 1920s, much of this buying was done by households in the middle-income range, the 50.2 percent of American families with an income of $500 to $1,500 in 1935. Several factors enabled these families to approximate their former standard of living despite the pay cuts or unemployment common in the depression. Deflation lowered the cost of living almost 20 percent between 1929 and 1935. Families also made different choices of how to spend their lower incomes. For example, telephone use and clothing purchases dropped sharply during the depression. People had a harder time giving up cigarettes, movies, radios, and newspapers, once considered luxuries but now regarded as necessities. An automobile proved to be one of the most depression-proof items in the family budget. Sales of new cars the drudgery and isolation of farm life. A host of farm machines and appliances powered by electricity became available by the 1930s. An electric milking machine saved hours of manual labor, most of it previously done in pitch darkness or by the faint glow of a kerosene lamp before dawn so farmers could conserve the daylight hours for outdoor chores. An electrically powered water pump lightened many farm chores, especially hauling water for family use or the stock. Electric irons, vacuum cleaners, and washing machines lightened women's work in the home. Studies had shown that farmers found so many uses for electricity that they would be good customers. But power companies claimed the cost of running lines to individual farms would be so high that the idea was economically unfeasible. The main reason rural electrification moved so slowly, however, was that power companies made plenty of money in urban areas and had no incentive to expand into the rural countryside.

In 1935, the New Deal made a federal commitment to bring power to rural America. The Rural Electrification Administration, an independent agency, promoted the formation of nonprofit farm cooperatives to bring electricity to their localities. Local farmers, for a five-dollar down payment each, could form an association to apply for low-interest federal loans to cover the cost of installing power lines for their area. Each household was committed to a monthly minimum usage, usually about three dollars, but the rates came down as usage increased. By 1940, 40 percent of the nation's farms had electricity. The rate reached 90 percent by 1950.

The human impact of rural electrification was especially poignant. A small child later told his mother, "I didn't realize how dark our house was until we got electric lights." One farm woman remembered, "I just turned on the light and kept looking at Paw. It was the first time I'd ever really seen him after dark." Another family, caught unawares by the timing of the hookup, saw their house from a distance and thought it must be on fire. A rural cooperative held a mock funeral for their kerosene lamps, and schoolteachers noticed that children did better at school when they could do their homework by light. Along with the automobile, electricity probably did more than any other technological innovation to break down the barriers between urban and rural life in twentieth-century America.

"BLUE MONDAY"
Laundry was one of women's hardest household chores. Although this woman did not have to haul water from an outdoor well, she still had to pump it by hand in order to do the wash because her home lacked electricity. She also had to wring out the wet clothes manually, another arduous task. (The Bettmann Archive)

dropped, but gasoline sales stayed stable, suggesting that people turned to used cars or kept their old models longer.

To maintain family lifestyle, housewives often substituted their own labor to provide goods and services they had formerly purchased. These economies financed such budget items as cars and movies, which could not be manufactured at home. Women sewed their own clothes and canned fruits and vegetables. They practiced small economies such as buying day-old bread and heating several dishes in the oven at once to save fuel. Women who previously employed servants began to do all their own housework. In countless ways around the home, women took up the slack, making a contribution whose dollar value would be impossible to calculate. Women generally accepted this new work stoically. "We had no choice," remembered one housewife. "We just did what had to be done one day at a time."

Some families maintained their lifestyle in the 1930s through "deficit living"—that is, using installment payments and credit to stretch their income. This strategy added about 10 percent to a family income under $500, and 2 to 5 percent for a family in the $500 to $1,500 range. By 1936, consumer credit in the United States had increased 20 percent over 1929 levels. A Middletown resident reflected the growing dependence on installment buying as a tactic for family survival. "Most of the families I know are after the same things today that they were after before the Depression," she said, "and they'll get them in the same way—on credit."

Other families kept up their standard of living by sending an additional member of the household into the work force. At the turn of the century, this additional family worker probably would have been a child or young adult. In the 1930s, it was increasingly a married woman. The depression, instead of expelling women from the work force, solidified their place in it. The 1940 census reported almost eleven million women in the work force, a small increase over 1930. By the end of the depression, women made up about a fourth of the labor force, again a small rise from the start of the decade.

Important changes in the backgrounds of working women had occurred by the 1930s. At the turn of the century, the typical woman with a job was young, single, and poor, in most cases a recent immigrant. By the 1930s, more native-born, middle-class, and older women had entered the labor market. Most dramatic was the 50 percent increase in this decade of married women employed outside the home.

Working women, especially married ones, did not have an easy time during the depression. Even if their husband had no job, working wives still had almost total responsibility for housework and child care. They also faced harsh and widespread accusations that they had stolen jobs from men. A 1936 Gallup poll asked whether wives should work when their husbands had a job, and a resounding 82 percent of the people interviewed said no. Many states adopted laws that prohibited the employment of married women; such laws were especially widespread in the field of education. Ironically, the proportion of married female school teachers rose from 17.9 percent in 1930 to 24.6 percent in 1940. From 1932 to 1937, even the federal government would not allow a husband and wife to hold government jobs at the same time.

Norman Cousins, editor of the *Saturday Review of Literature*, offered a quick solution that reflected the resentment women faced when they entered the work force. After calculating that the number of employed women roughly equaled the 1939 unemployment total, he suggested this tongue-in-check remedy: "Simply fire the women, who shouldn't be working anyway, and hire the men. Presto! No unemployment. No relief rolls. No depression."

The attempt to make women scapegoats for the depression rested on shaky grounds, both morally and economically. Most women worked because of economic necessity. A sizable minority were the sole support of their families; their husbands had either left home or could not find work. Furthermore, women rarely took jobs away from men, and men had difficulty moving into women's jobs. "Few of the people who oppose married women's employment," observed one feminist in 1940, "seem to realize that a coal miner or steel worker cannot very well fill the jobs of nursemaids, cleaning women, or the factory and clerical jobs now filled by women." Norman Cousins failed to understand that the economy had always been roughly divided between "men's" and "women's" jobs. Custom, rather than law or economics, dictated this practice and made crossovers fairly uncommon.

The division of the work force by gender gave women a small edge during the depression. Many fields with large numbers of female employees, including clerical and sales work, and service and trade occupations, suffered less from economic contraction than did such male areas as steel, mining, and manufacturing. A woman could sometimes find a job even if her husband could not, because women cost less to hire. Women earned from sixty to sixty-three cents for every dollar earned by men. As a result, female unemployment rates, although extremely high, were somewhat lower than men's. This small bonus came at a heavy price, however. The jobs held by women reinforced the traditional stereotypes of female work. Women found themselves even more concentrated in low-paying, no-advancement jobs when the depression ended than when it began.

During the Great Depression, there were few feminist demands for reallocation of power to women either at home or on the job. On an individual basis, women's self-esteem probably rose because of their importance to family survival. Both men and women, however, continued to believe that the two sexes should have fundamentally different roles and responsibilities. The substantial contributions by women in the 1930s actually reinforced their overall identification with the home. The foundation had been laid for the so-called feminine mystique of the 1950s.

Hard Times for Youth

The depression hit the nation's twenty-one million young people especially hard. Unlike children who only dimly glimpsed the sacrifices of life in the 1930s, adolescents knew that "making do" usually meant "doing without." Writer Maxine Davis, who traveled ten thousand miles in 1936 interviewing the nation's youth, described them as "runners, delayed at the gun." She added, "The depression years have left us with a generation robbed of time and opportunity just as the Great War left the world its heritage of a lost generation."

Studies of social mobility confirm that the young men who entered their twenties during the depression era had less successful careers than those before or since. Thoughts of marriage also had to be shelved until at least the prospect of a job came into sight. Lowered expectations became so demoralizing that about 250,000

young people simply took to the road as hoboes and "sisters of the road," the term for female tramps.

Young people who stayed home spent increasing time in school because job prospects appeared so dim. Public schools did not charge tuition, and they provided warmth from the elements, an important consideration in winter. For the first time, most young Americans from fourteen to eighteen went to high school. Less than half the nation's youth attended high school in 1930, but three-fourths of them did in 1940. Changing expectations for boys, who had traditionally dropped out of school at an earlier age than girls in order to work, contributed to this expansion of the high school population.

Although a majority of American teenagers went to high school, college remained the privilege of a distinct minority. With times so rough, the "college of hard knocks" was all most depression-era youths could expect. Yet about 1.2 million young people, or 7.5 percent of the population between eighteen and twenty-four, attended college in the 1930s. Women made up 40 percent of these undergraduates. After 1935, college became a little easier to afford because of the National Youth Administration (NYA), which gave part-time employment to more than 2 million college and high school students. This New Deal agency also provided work for 2.6 million out-of-school youths.

College students were a studious group in the 1930s; financial sacrifices encouraged their seriousness of purpose. The schools never lost their share of men who happily accepted a "gentleman's C" as a grade in a course, or of women who were hunting for a husband. On the other hand, the influence of fraternities and sororities on campus life declined during the depression. Large numbers of students became involved in various political movements. Fueled by disillusionment with World War I, thousands of them took the "Oxford Pledge" never to support a war in which the United States might be involved. In 1936, the Student Strike Against War drew support from several hundred thousand students who cut classes to demonstrate on campuses throughout the country.

Despite the economic sacrifices demanded by the depression, adolescence became increasingly institutionalized in the 1930s. Through high school and college attendance, organized athletics, and extracurricular activities, young people developed their own values and patterns of behavior. Peer culture, rather than parents, influenced their values and tastes. Teenagers throughout the country read the same comics, wore the same style clothes, flocked to the same movies, hung out at corner drugstores, and borrowed the family Ford. The expansion of education at both the secondary and collegiate levels provided one environment for the growth of these new customs.

The rise of the youth culture in twentieth century America had a close link to changes in the family. As the family unit lost many of its economic functions during industrialization, it became an emotional unit; affection and nurture replaced production as its central function. Power in the family became more democratically distributed. Families grew increasingly child conscious; the declining birth rate reflected parents' desire to have fewer children in order to better provide for them. Young people's fashions, fads, and values, closely tied to an ethos of consumption, were increasingly disseminated by such mass media as magazines and movies. Youth culture took its place as another example of the modern secular way of life.

Popular Culture

Popular culture played an important role in pulling the United States through the trauma of the Great Depression. Such diversions as movies and radio programs provided a welcome outlet from the quiet desperation of daily life. The mass culture first recognized in the 1920s flourished in the following decade.

Movies were the most popular entertainment during the 1930s. More than 60 percent of the American people saw at least one movie every week. The films of the depression decade transported moviegoers to a world where hard times appeared only infrequently. Yet these motion pictures offered more than escapism. "Hollywood," observed one film historian about the decade, "directed its enormous powers of persuasion to preserving the basic moral, social and economic tenets of traditional American culture."

Films from the 1930s reflected the values of popular culture at the time. Gangster films were especially popular in the grim early years of the depression. Two of the most successful ones were *Little Caesar* (1930), starring Edward G. Robinson, and *The Public Enemy* (1931), in which

DANCING CHEEK TO CHEEK
During the Great Depression, Americans turned to such cheap recreational activities as listening to the radio and going to the movies. Hollywood film companies produced a number of gala musicals, and one of the most popular attractions of the 1930s was the dance team of Fred Astaire and Ginger Rogers. Astaire and Rogers starred together in ten movies. (The Bettmann Archive)

James Cagney shoved a grapefruit in Mae Clark's face. The extravagant Busby Berkeley musicals that replaced gangster movies in popularity suggest an upswing in the public mood around the time of Franklin Roosevelt's election and inauguration. Three blockbusters, *42nd Street*, *Golddiggers of 1933*, and *Footlight Parade*, appeared in 1933. The 1930s also featured the "screwball comedy"—sophisticated, fast-paced romantic comedies with top stars such as Clark Gable and Claudette Colbert in *It Happened One Night* (1934), John Barrymore and Carole Lombard in *Twentieth Century* (1934), Katharine Hepburn and Cary Grant in *Bringing Up Baby* (1938), and Irene Dunne and Grant in *The Awful Truth* (1938). The Marx brothers kept people laughing with such irreverent classics as *Animal Crackers* (1930) and *Duck Soup* (1933). The bawdy Mae West titillated audiences with such lines as "Why don't you come up and see me some time?" and "I used to be Snow White, but I drifted." Walt Disney produced 198 cartoons during the depression in addition to such feature-length classics as *Snow White and the Seven Dwarfs* (1937) and *Fantasia* (1940).

Movies influenced the consumer culture, even at the height of the depression. One of the decade's top box-office stars was a curly-headed little girl named Shirley Temple, who made twenty-one films by 1941. Soon Shirley Temple dolls, books, and clothes flooded the market. Similarly, sales of peroxide hair rinse skyrocketed in the 1930s because of the popularity of such blond stars as Jean Harlow, Carole Lombard, and Mae West. Undershirt sales fell drastically after Clark Gable, a leading sex symbol of his day, took off his shirt in *It Happened One Night* and revealed his bare chest.

Although movies had the greatest influence on popular values, they competed with newspapers' ability to provide quick coverage of news events. The kidnapping of the twenty-month-old son of Charles and Anne Morrow Lindbergh in 1932 instantly became a major national news story. Seventy-five days later, searchers found the child's body in the woods near the Lindbergh home in New Jersey. "BABY DEAD" ran the headlines, and everyone knew what the two words meant. Other leading news events of the depression years included the birth of the Dionne quintuplets in Canada in 1934; the gunning down of John Dillinger, Public Enemy Number One, by the FBI in 1934; the abdication in 1936 of King Edward VIII of Great Britain so he could marry "the woman I love," an American divorcee named Wallis Warfield Simpson; aviator Amelia Earhart's disappearance on a round-the-world flight in 1937; and the fiery crash of the *Hindenburg*, a German dirigible, at Lakehurst, New Jersey in 1937.

Radio took over an increasingly large place in popular culture during the 1930s. About 13 million households had a radio set in 1930, and 27.5 million owned one in 1939. Listeners tuned in to daytime serials such as "Ma Perkins" and "John's Other Wife." "The Betty Crocker Hour" offered useful household hints. Ventriloquist Edgar Bergen and his impudent dummy, Charlie McCarthy, delighted Sunday night audiences with their comedy routines. Twenty million listeners followed the adventures of the Lone Ranger three times a week.

One of the most famous radio programs in history took place on a Sunday night in October 1938. Actor Orson Welles's "Mercury Theater of the Air" broadcast a modern rendition of *The War of the Worlds* (1898) by the English writer H. G. Wells. Orson Welles used fictional news bulletins interspersed with simulated on-the-spot reports to describe the landing of an imaginary meteor near Princeton, New Jersey which supposedly unleashed death-ray wielding Martian invaders on the unsuspecting countryside. Even though the broadcast included four announcements that the attack was just a dramatization, mass hysteria broke out. The event seemed so realistic that many people fled from their homes. No one doubted the power of radio anymore.

There may have been a deeper reason that people so readily accepted Orson Welles's dramatic production as an actual event. During September 1938, radio programs had been interrupted repeatedly by ominous news bulletins about a possible European war between England and Germany. Even the news on September 30 of the Munich Agreement, which prevented war for another year, did not erase public fears of im-

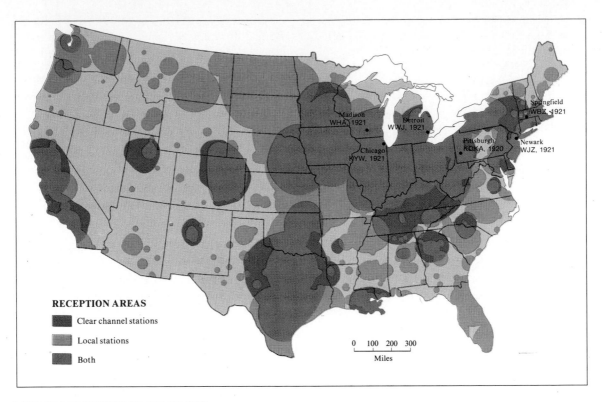

RECEPTION AREAS

▮ Clear channel stations

▮ Local stations

▮ Both

0   100   200   300
Miles

MAP 25.2 THE SPREAD OF RADIO
In 1938, more than twenty-six million American households, or about three-quarters of the population, had a radio. Four national networks dominated the field, broadcasting news and entertainment across the country. Powerful clear-channel stations reached listeners hundreds of miles distant. Independent local stations opened in large and small cities. By the period covered in this map, only a few sparsely populated areas were beyond radio's reach.

minent catastrophe. When Welles staged his monumental hoax a month later, he convinced large numbers of people that the United States had been invaded. Popular culture increasingly reflected America's involvement in the complexities of international political and economic life. Three years later when radios announced that the Japanese had attacked Pearl Harbor, Americans realized this news flash was not a joke.

Culture and Commitment

The depression had a tremendous impact on creative expression in the United States. Few decades have had a greater contrast in their literary themes than the 1920s and 1930s. During the prosperous Twenties, many artists felt so alienated by what they saw as the anti-intellectual and complacent tone of American life that they

settled in Europe, especially in France. Ernest Hemingway's *A Farewell to Arms* (1929), which portrayed the disillusionment with World War I, and F. Scott Fitzgerald's *The Great Gatsby* (1925), which questioned the mindless pursuit of material wealth and riches, reflected many writers' disenchantment with American values.

A different tone animated most cultural expression in the depression-plagued Thirties. A collective sense of cooperation and community replaced alienation. As a result of the depression, American artists redefined their relationship to society. Social and economic questions could no longer be ignored, action toward common goals became necessary to surmount the crisis, and world events overshadowed domestic literary concerns. Not all the creative leaders of the 1930s fitted neatly into the pattern of socially relevant art. Yet the critic Malcolm Cowley expressed the spirit of the times when he said in 1939 that never had there been a decade "when literary events followed so closely on the flying coat-tails of social events."

New Deal Culture

Federal One, a WPA project which put unemployed artists, actors, and writers to work, was a unique example of federal patronage of the arts. The depression had dried up traditional sources of private patronage. Like most Americans, creative artists had nowhere to turn except Washington. Such WPA projects never lost sight of their initial purpose—to provide subsistence for needy artists. But their spirit and goals extended far beyond mere relief. New Deal administrators sought to redefine the relationship between artists and the community, so that art no longer would be consumed only by the elite who could afford to pay. "Art for the millions" became a popular New Deal slogan.

The New Deal's call for a fusion of democracy with art drew a talented group of administrators to Washington in the 1930s. Nicholas Sokoloff, conductor of the Cleveland Symphony Orchestra from 1918 to 1933, headed the Federal Music Project, which employed fifteen thousand musi-

cians. Government-sponsored orchestras toured the country, presenting free concerts of classical and popular music. The Music Project, like many other New Deal programs, emphasized American themes as part of the nation's introspective and nationalistic mood during the depression. Composer Aaron Copland wrote his *Billy the Kid* and *Rodeo* suites for the WPA, compositions which specifically incorporated western folk melodies. Musicologist Charles Seeger, and his wife, composer Ruth Crawford Seeger, undertook the extensive project of collecting and cataloguing examples of the American folk tradition.

The Federal Art Project (FAP) employed many of the twentieth century's leading painters, muralists, and sculptors. They received government assistance at a point in their careers when the lack of private patronage would have prevented them from continuing their work. Jackson Pollack, Alice Neel, Willem de Kooning, and Louise Nevelson all received support from the FAP. Under the direction of Holger Cahill, an expert on American folk art, the FAP was best known for sponsoring the murals that decorated public buildings and post offices throughout the country. The FAP commissioned Victor Arnautoff to paint the *City Life* mural for San

RELIEF BLUES
Between 1934 and 1939, an Italian immigrant named O. Louis Guglielmi found work on the Federal Art Project of the WPA, to which he submitted this painting in 1937. Entitled *"Relief Blues,"* it represents the social concern and urban realism prominent in American painting of the 1930s. The starkness of the room and its occupants is intensified by the bright red slippers, the pink rose on the floor, and the red lipstick and nail polish of the woman on the left. (National Museum of American Art, Smithsonian Institution. Transfer from The Museum of Modern Art)

CONSTRUCTION OF A DAM

Social realist painter William Gropper, a cartoonist for *New Masses,* portrayed the contributions of labor in modern industry. His mural of dam construction was commissioned for the Department of the Interior Building in Washington, D.C. The heroic, dynamic style was typical of public art during the depression. (William Gropper. *Construction of a Dam,* Study for the Mural. National Museum of American Art, Smithsonian Institution. Transfer from U.S. Department of Interior, National Park Service)

Francisco's Coit Tower. Huge WPA murals covered the walls and ceilings of terminals at the newly constructed La Guardia airport in New York; later, as artistic tastes changed, the murals were painted over. FAP art tended towards socially relevant themes, such as work scenes, family life, and pioneers struggling to tame the land. No one claimed that all the results were great art. As Franklin Roosevelt diplomatically remarked, "Some of it good, some of it not so good, but all of it native, human, eager and alive."

Former journalist Henry Alsberg headed the Federal Writers' Project (FWP), which employed about five thousand writers at its height. Young FWP writers who later achieved fame included Saul Bellow, Ralph Ellison, Arna Bontemps, Margaret Walker, Jack Conroy, Conrad Aiken, Tillie Olsen, and John Cheever. The black folklorist and novelist Zora Neale Hurston finished three novels while on the Florida FWP, among them *Their Eyes Were Watching God* (1937). This story's central character, Janie Crawford, typifies the proud, determined, and beautiful black women who appear in Hurston's fiction. Richard Wright won the 1938 *Story* magazine prize for the best tale by a WPA writer. He used his spare time on the project to complete *Native Son* (1940), the bitter novel about Bigger Thomas, a black man who finds expression in a white-dominated world only through hatred and violence.

The Federal Writers' Project produced more than a thousand publications. It collected oral histories of Americans in many walks of life, including a set of two thousand narratives of former slaves. The 150-volume *Life in America* series included *Baseball in Old Chicago* and *These Are Our Lives,* a set of oral histories from people in North Carolina, Tennessee, and Georgia. Part of the series consisted of ethnic studies, such as *The Italians of New York, The Armenians of Massachusetts,* and *The Hopi.*

The most ambitious FWP project was a set of state guidebooks to the United States. Fifty-one state and territorial guides, thirty city guides, and twenty regional guides, including *U.S. One, Maine to Florida,* and *The Oregon Trail,* were published, mostly by commercial presses. These guides combined tourism, folklore, and history, and they reflected the resurgence of interest in everything American. The guides became widely popular, but the choice of subjects occasionally annoyed politicians and state boosters. For example, the 675-page Massachusetts guide gave only fourteen lines to the Boston Tea Party and five to the Boston Massacre, while alloting thirty-one to the Sacco-Vanzetti case.

Anzia Yezierska, a novelist who had won

fame with her 1925 novel *Bread Givers* but then had fallen on hard times, joked about her new job on the Writers' Project: "The Savior of Art! At the bargain price of $23.86 per artist." An unexpected by-product was the camaraderie that creative artists found by working together. Yezierska reveled in this new spirit:

> A new world was being born. A world where artists were no longer outcasts, hangers-on of the rich, but backed by the government, encouraged to produce their best work. . . . Each morning I walked to the Project as light-hearted as if I were going to a party. The huge barracks-like Writers' Hall roared with the laughter and greetings of hundreds of voices. . . .

Of all the federal creative programs, the Federal Theatre Project (FTP) was the most ambitious. American drama thrived in the 1930s, the only time that the United States has had a federally supported national theater. Under the gifted direction of Hallie Flanagan, former head of Vassar College's Experimental Theater, the Theatre Project reached an audience of twenty-five to thirty million in the four years of its existence. Talented directors, playwrights, and actors, including Orson Welles, John Huston, Arthur

Miller, E. G. Marshall, and John Houseman, offered their services.

The Theatre Project's most successful productions included T. S. Eliot's *Murder in the Cathedral*, Mark Blitzstein's *The Cradle Will Rock*, William Shakespeare's *Macbeth* with an all-black cast in a Haitian voodoo setting, and the *Swing Mikado*, a jazz rendition of the Gilbert and Sullivan operetta. Sinclair Lewis's *It Can't Happen Here* opened simultaneously in eighteen cities across the country, including productions in Spanish and Yiddish. Also popular were mini-plays called "living newspapers," among them *Triple A Plowed Under*, about farm problems, and *Power*, concerning public ownership of utilities.

The theater was one of the most politically committed fields of American creative life in the 1930s. However, Congress proved unwilling to appropriate federal funds for its often controversial productions, and the Federal Theatre Project was terminated in 1939. Federal One limped on under federal-state sponsorship until 1943, when wartime priorities dealt it a final blow.

Public support for permanent government patronage of the arts never developed during the 1930s. The arts programs remained tied too closely to their original relief-oriented purpose of

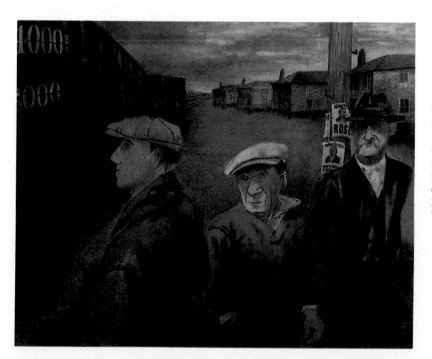

SCOTT'S RUN, WEST VIRGINIA
Ben Shahn was a multi-talented social realism artist—a painter, lithographer, muralist, and photographer. His art always had a point of view. Some of his best-known work was a series of twenty-three paintings in defense of Sacco and Vanzetti. This 1937 tempera painting depicts a railroad depot shut down by a coal miners' strike. (Whitney Museum of American Art, New York)

feeding hungry artists. But while federal support lasted, it fostered an enormous outburst of creativity that made a substantial and lasting contribution to American artistic expression.

The Documentary Impulse

The WPA arts projects were influenced by a broad artistic trend called the "documentary impulse." It attempted to combine social relevance with distinctively American themes, an approach that characterized artistic expression in the 1930s. The documentary impulse, probably the decade's most distinctive genre, influenced practically every aspect of American culture—literature, art, music, film, dance, theater, and radio.

The documentary impulse was the communication of real life, the presentation of actual facts and events in a way that aroused the interest and emotions of its audience. It emphasized observation and narration, but without relying on overembellished prose for impact. A photograph or some other visual image often supplied the emotional force that words could not convey. This technique exalted the ordinary, finding beauty and emotion in subjects not usually considered the province of art. It tried to make you, the audience, experience the subject as though you were actually on the scene.

The documentary impulse influenced every facet of American creative expression in the 1930s. It can be seen in John Steinbeck's fiction, especially *In Dubious Battle* (1935) and *The Grapes of Wrath* (1939), and in Erskine Caldwell's *Tobacco Road* (1932). John Dos Passos's *U.S.A.* trilogy used actual newspaper clippings, dispatches, and headlines throughout its fictional story. The *March of Time* newsreels, which movie audiences saw before the feature film, presented visual images of the world in a pre-television age. The standard opening of radio news broadcasts, "We now take you to . . .", did the same thing. Filmmaker Pare Lorentz commissioned the composer Virgil Thompson to create music that set the mood for such documentary movies as *The Plow that Broke the Plains* (1936) and *The River* (1936). The new photojournalism magazines, including *Life* and *Look*, founded in 1936 and 1937, respectively, reflected this documentary approach. So

did many creative works of the New Deal, from the living newspapers of the Federal Theatre Project to the American Guide series and oral history interviews prepared by the Federal Writers' Project. The New Deal actually institutionalized the documentary impulse. It frequently sent investigators, such as Lorena Hickok and Martha Gellhorn, into the field to report on conditions of people on relief.

The camera was the prime instrument of the documentary impulse. The use of cameras to document social conditions and awaken social consciousness dated back to the probing photography of Jacob Riis and Lewis Hines at the turn of the century. When the nation entered another period of intense social and economic questioning in the 1930s, photographers revived and updated this technique. Such great photographers as Dorothea Lange, Walker Evans, and Margaret

THE POWER OF PHOTOGRAPHY
"Migrant Mother" by Dorothea Lange is perhaps the most famous documentary photograph of the 1930s. Lange spent only ten minutes in the pea picker's camp in California where she captured this image, and did not even get the name of the woman whose despair and resignation she so powerfully recorded. (Library of Congress)

Bourke-White permanently shaped the image of the Great Depression.

Documentary photography became widely popular in *Life, Look,* and in other magazines and books that combined photography with narration. *You Have Seen Their Faces* (1937), by Margaret Bourke-White and Erskine Caldwell, studied southern agriculture, emphasizing the physical and emotional devastation of sharecropper poverty. Dorothea Lange collaborated with the social economist Paul Taylor on several projects about migrant labor conditions. Lange and Taylor produced *An American Exodus: A Record of Human Erosion* (1939), a study of the effects of drought and mechanization on farmers in the Dust Bowl and the South.

The ultimate documentary collaboration between a photographer and a writer remains *Let Us Now Praise Famous Men* (1941), by James Agee and Walker Evans. Agee's rich prose describing the lives of three white tenant farm families in the South—he devoted fifty thousand words simply to an inventory of tenant homes—was framed by Evans's stark photographs of rural life. Through the years, this book has come to epitomize life in the 1930s. Ironically, only about six hundred copies were sold in 1941, the year it was published.

The federal government played a leading part in compiling the photographic record of the 1930s. In 1935, Roy Stryker, a Columbia economics instructor who had been a teaching assistant under brain trust member Rexford Tugwell, took charge of the Historical Section of the Resettlement Administration. He had a mandate to document and photograph the American scene for the government. Stryker gathered a talented group of photographers for this massive task, including Walker Evans, Dorothea Lange, Ben Shahn, Arthur Rothstein, Marion Post Wolcott, and Russell Lee. The government hired these photographers solely for their professional skills. Unlike the Federal Art and Federal Writers' Projects, the Historical Section, which later became part of the Farm Security Administration (FSA), was not established to provide relief for struggling photographers. The collection of FSA photographs ranks as the best visual introduction to life in the United States during the depression decade.

The Popular Front

By the mid-1930s, ominous developments on the international scene resulted in new forms of political action by writers and other intellectuals. Many literary figures participated in the "popular front," a broad leftist movement dedicated to stopping the spread of fascism throughout the world. In this leftward shift, the Communist party played a leading role.

The mid-1930s marked the Communist party's greatest appeal in American society. No longer a small sectarian group, the party had about a hundred thousand members at its peak in 1939. For many recruits, the depression was the main influence that led them to join. Marxism, having predicted the collapse of capitalism, provided an alternative vision of social and economic organization. Communists could be found scattered throughout all walks of life in the 1930s—working-class activists, intellectuals, housewives, union organizers, farmers, blacks, and even a few New Deal administrators. Yet one fact distinguished Communists from other activist groups in political life during the 1930s. American Communists could debate for hours the latest directive from Moscow, but they could never change it. Moscow demanded total loyalty for the party line developed in the Soviet Union.

From 1929 to 1935, the Communist party of the United States conducted activities on several fronts. Communists organized marches of the unemployed, led unionizing drives, and reached out to oppressed groups, such as industrial workers and blacks. The party's support of the defendants in the Scottsboro case represented an attempt to win over blacks in the South as part of its worldwide fight against racism. These recruiting attempts produced little success. Fewer than a thousand blacks joined the Communist party in the early 1930s. "It's bad enough being black, why be red?" was a common reaction. After five years of the gravest depression ever faced by capitalism, the party had fewer than thirty thousand members.

The Communist party had a powerful impact on the collective consciousness of American writers in the 1930s. As a literary historian has observed, however, "It was the times, not the party, that made them radicals." In 1932, fifty-two writers, including Sherwood Anderson, Erskine Caldwell, Malcolm Cowley, John Dos Passos, Theodore Dreiser, Granville Hicks, and Edmund Wilson, pledged their support to William Z. Foster, the party's presidential candidate. While some writers actually joined the Communist party, many others considered themselves only "fellow travelers." They sympathized with the party's objectives, wrote for the *Daily Worker* and other party newspapers, or associated with organizations sponsored by the party. Author Mary McCarthy recalled the fascination that the party held for her and other intellectuals: "For me, the Communist Party was *the* party, and even though I did not join it, I prided myself on knowing that it was the pinnacle."

During the 1930s, many writers wrote so-called proletarian novels, which glorified Marxist themes. The books of such committed communist writers as Michael Gold and Joseph Freeman represented this literary genre at its best, although much of this radical writing was wooden and formalistic. In many novels with proletarian themes, the plot built to a stirring climax where the main character, always a member of the working class, suddenly proclaimed the need for revolutionary change. Many proletarian novels centered on real events. The textile strike in Gastonia, South Carolina, in 1929 inspired six fictional works.

The American Writers' Congress, sponsored by the Communist party in 1935, typified the rapport between the party and major writers and intellectuals. Theodore Dreiser, Josephine Herbst, Langston Hughes, Meridel LeSueur, Nathanael West, Genevieve Taggard, and Richard Wright signed the call for the conference. The participants explored the relationship between revolutionary activism and creative work and discussed the tensions between ideology and art.

The courting of intellectuals was part of an important shift in Communist party tactics in response to the rise of fascism. Adolf Hitler had

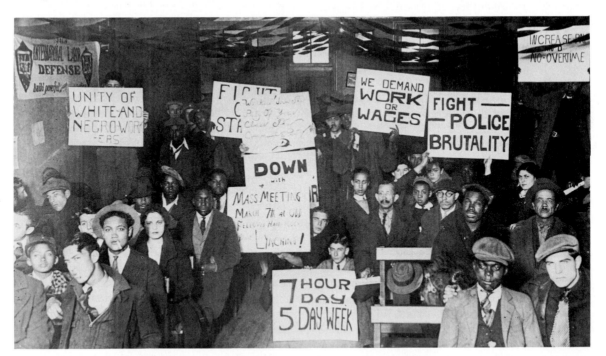

AMERICAN COMMUNISTS
The Communist party played an active role in the social and political ferment of the 1930s.
Communists organized demonstrations by the unemployed and homeless, participated in strikes and
labor-organizing drives, and mobilized public opposition to fascism with the so-called popular front.
This 1930 photograph shows that the party took seriously, both ideologically and in social relations,
its commitment to ending racism. (Library of Congress)

THE MASSES VERSUS THE MILITIA

Marching! Marching!, *excerpted here, won the 1935 New Masses contest for a novel on an American proletarian theme.*

It's day. For hours we've been coming together, eager to start. . . . We're coming from all directions. Some of us carry banners and slogans. Hey, what's the delay? If we're all here, let's start. . . .

As we near a street corner, a worker bursts into view, running toward us, waving his arms. "MILITIA!" he yells. "They've called out the militia!" . . . The ugly news leaps from mouth to mouth. "Christ's sake!" says a scared voice, "they're going to shoot us. They wont shoot." A woman shrills, "We aint afraid!" just as Matt raises both hands for our attention and yells, "Are we going to let them stop us?" "NO!" we roar. "Let's go!" "Fall in, everybody!" The line reforms, straightens, and we're marching again. We come to the corner and round it. We march steadily to the next corner, turn it, and swing into Broadway. "There they are!" The street seems jammed with them, guns held ready—a dung-colored mass drawn up against us. Bayonets! They've got bayonets! The sun glints on their helmets and flashes steel-bright from the points of their bayonets. "Jesus Christ!" whispers someone. "They're just young kids—strangers! They'll shoot! They dont know what they're doing . . ." thinking *Our boys wouldnt gas and shoot their own fathers and mothers and brothers and sisters . . .* A few of us gasp, flinching the way horses do from the menace of snakes, but we dont stop or slow. We keep marching, but we tighten, looking ahead . . . some of us thinking *Jeez! Bayonets! Machine guns! They got gas masks in those bags around their necks on their chests—gas!* and others *For God's sake, you guys, dont shoot us! Come over to our side. Why should you kill us? We are your brothers.*

For a few seconds we hear only the sound of our own feet, the steady pound of ourselves marching forward. Then suddenly Annie turns and waves a signal to our marshals. Each lifts a hand for a moment while a word is spoken from rank to rank. The signalling hands go down in unison and we're all singing:

"Hold the fort for we are coming;
Workingmen be strong! . . ."

Source: Clara Weatherwax, *Marching! Marching!* New York: John Day, 1935. 253–256.

---

seized absolute power in Germany the day after Franklin Roosevelt was inaugurated in 1933. Hitler's Nazi regime concentrated all economic and political power in a centralized state. Benito Mussolini had introduced fascism in Italy when he took control of that country in 1922. When Italy invaded Ethiopia in 1935, the League of Nations could not stop the aggression. Hitler began to rearm Germany and prepared to seize the Rhineland, in violation of the Versailles treaty. Fears grew of a world war caused by the advance of fascism.

Fearful of fascist aggression, the Soviet Union attempted to mobilize support in democratic countries. Both in Europe and the United States, communist parties called for a "popular front." The party now welcomed cooperation with any group concerned about the threat of fascism to such areas as civil rights, organized labor, and world peace. Communists sought to ally themselves with liberal political movements throughout the country, adopting the slogan, "Communism is 20th Century Americanism." Despite earlier scorn of the New Deal as reactionary and insincere, the party now supported President Roosevelt and worked for his reelection in 1936. Eleanor Roosevelt, once depicted as a slave of the ruling class, received praise for her humanitarianism. This effort at joining forces with American liberal groups in the mid-1930s represented the height of the party's impact on the United States.

The popular-front strategy became even more urgent with the outbreak of the Spanish Civil War in 1936. Army forces led by Generalissimo Francisco Franco led a rebellion against the elected coalition government. Franco received strong support from the fascist regimes in Germany and Italy. Only the Soviet Union and Mexico backed the Spanish government forces,

TIME LINE
THE SOCIAL FABRIC OF DEPRESSION AMERICA

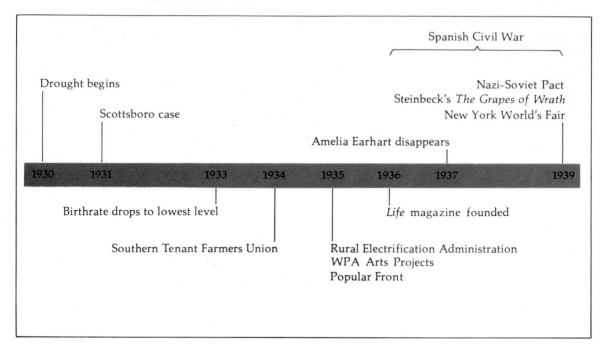

called the Loyalists. The governments of the United States, Great Britain, and France sympathized with the Loyalists but stayed neutral. In the United States, strict neutrality legislation in 1935, 1936, and 1937 forbade arms shipments to either side. Since Franco was receiving substantial military aid from Germany and Italy, the neutrality policy doomed the Loyalists.

Most American activists and intellectuals expressed shock at the policy of nonintervention. The Spanish Civil War became the most vital issue of their generation. "People of my sort," observed writer Malcolm Cowley, "were more deeply stirred by the Spanish Civil War than by any other international event since the World War and the Russian Revolution." Ernest Hemingway immortalized the Spanish conflict in his famous novel *For Whom the Bell Tolls* (1940).

Approximately thirty-two hundred American men and women volunteered to fight on the Loyalist side. Calling themselves the Abraham Lincoln Brigade, they formed part of an international force of soldiers, ambulance drivers, and military personnel who aided the Loyalist cause. Years later, survivors recalled the struggle as the

"good fight." Outnumbered and inadequately supplied, more than half the American volunteers died in the carnage of Spain. By 1939, the Spanish Republic had fallen to Franco's forces.

Although American intellectuals applauded the Soviet Union's active support of the Spanish Loyalists, many literary figures began to feel uncomfortable in leftist circles. The Communists remained suspicious of intellectuals, many of whom were too independent to submit to party discipline. A number of writers found it increasingly difficult to satisfy both their artistic urges and the party's demand for fiction that reflected working-class concerns. Rumors of political repression by the Soviet leader Joseph Stalin also distressed them.

The final blow came in August 1939, when the Soviet Union, eager to avoid war, signed a nonaggression pact with Nazi Germany. Germany thus had a free hand to invade Poland, while the Soviet Union in return shared in the division of that unfortunate country. This harsh act and Stalin's willingness to deal with Hitler came as a bitter blow to many supporters of the popular front. Die-hard communist members loyally accepted the policy change, but others left the party in disgust. The heyday of American Communism ended abruptly.

With the signing of the Nazi-Soviet pact, the world again stood on the brink of war. Now that Germany no longer feared fighting a war on two fronts, the Nazis moved closer to their goal of European—and ultimately world—conquest. Although many Americans considered themselves isolationists—they hoped the United States could remain aloof from European conflicts— they began to realize that the nation faced an even greater enemy than the economic problems that had gripped it for the past decade. Barely twenty years after the war to end all wars, the United States prepared once again to enter another worldwide struggle for the survival of democracy.

$\mathcal{T}$he Great Depression left an "invisible scar" on people who lived through the 1930s. Those who wanted to work blamed themselves if they could not find a job. The depression did not make as much difference to black Americans, for whom times had always been hard. But things did get worse for farmers in the Midwest, who also had experienced hard times in the 1920s. A drought created the Dust Bowl, forcing many farmers off their land.

Despite the devastating impact of the depression, many aspects of American life and culture continued to conform to traditional patterns. Families pulled together, although women took on expanded roles, and often new jobs, to help support their households. Young people adapted by staying in school longer. Families turned to forms of popular culture, especially movies and radio programs, to take their minds off their troubles.

The collapse of the economy encouraged a reassertion of American values in literature and other forms of culture. This artistic flowering was partly supported by a unique experiment in government patronage of the arts through the WPA. Another feature of cultural expression in the 1930s involved documenting the American experience. Many writers blended artistic concerns with intense political commitment. This activism culminated in the popular front, where liberals and Communists joined together to oppose the spread of fascism, especially in the Spanish Civil War. The brief alliance ended when the Soviet Union signed an agreement with Nazi Germany, bringing the world to the brink of war again.

Suggestions for Further Reading

Hard Times

A wealth of material brings the voices of the 1930s to life. The Federal Writers' Project, *These Are Our Lives* (1939); Tom Terrill and Jerrold Hirsch, eds., *Such as Us: Southern Voices of the Thirties* (1978); and Ann Banks, ed., *First-Person America* (1980), all draw on oral histories collected by the Works Progress Administration during the 1930s. See also Richard Lowitt and Maurine Beasley, eds., *One Third of a Nation: Lorena Hickok Reports the Great Depression* (1981), and Robert S. McElvaine, ed., *Down & Out in the Great Depression* (1983), for first-hand accounts. Evocative secondary sources are Studs Terkel, *Hard Times: An Oral History of the Great Depression* (1970), and Caroline Bird, *The Invisible Scar* (1966).

Developments in the black community during the 1920s and 1930s are covered in Gilbert Osofsky, *Harlem: The Making of a Ghetto* (1966); Nathan Huggins, *Harlem Renaissance* (1971); and Gunnar Myrdal, *An American Dilemma* (1944). David Cronin, *Black Moses* (1962), and Theodore Vincent, *Black Power and the Garvey Movement* (1970), describe Marcus Garvey, and they can be supplemented by Robert Weisbrot, *Father Divine and the Struggle for Racial Equality* (1983). Dan T. Carter, *Scottsboro* (1969), remains the classic depiction of this case. Donald Grubbs, *Cry from Cotton* (1971), tells the story of the Southern Tenant Farmers Union.

Donald Worster, *Dust Bowl* (1979), evokes the plains during the "dirty thirties." The first volume of Robert Caro's biography of Lyndon Johnson, *The Path to Power* (1982), contains a moving portrait of the harshness of farm life before electricity. For more on rural electrification, see D. Clayton Brown, *Electricity for Rural America* (1980), and Marquis Childs, *The Farmer Takes a Hand* (1952). The experiences of Mexican-Americans during the 1930s are treated in Rodolfo Acuna, *Occupied America* (1981); Wayne Cornelius, *Building the Cactus Curtain* (1980); and Mark Reisler, *By the Sweat of Their Brow* (1976).

Family Values

Descriptions of family life in the 1930s include Robert and Helen Lynd, *Middletown in Transition* (1937); Mirra Komarovsky, *The Unemployed Man and His Family* (1940); and Rogert Angell, *The Family Encounters the Depression* (1936). Russell Baker's autobiography, *Growing Up* (1982), provides an often humorous description of family life in the 1930s. For more on youth, see Maxine Davis, *The Lost Generation* (1936), and Eileen Eagen, *Class, Culture and the Classroom* (1981). Frederick Lewis Allen, *Since Yesterday* (1939), provides an overview of the popular culture of the 1930s. Specific studies of movies include Robert Sklar, *Movie Made America* (1975); Andrew Bergman, *We're in the Money* (1971); and Molly Haskell, *From Reverence to Rape: The Treatment of Women in the Movies* (1974).

Material on women in the 1930s is found in Susan Ware, *Holding Their Own* (1982); Winifred Wandersee, *Women's Work and Family Values, 1920–1940* (1981); Lois Scharf, *To Work and To Wed* (1980); and Alice Kessler-Harris, *Out to Work* (1982). For the special dimensions of rural women's lives, see Margaret Hagood, *Mothers of the South* (1939). Jeane Westin, *Making Do: How Women Survived the '30s* (1976), is a lively account

drawn from interviews. The birth control movement is surveyed in Linda Gordon, *Woman's Body, Woman's Right* (1976), and James Reed, *From Private Vice to Public Virtue* (1978). See also *Margaret Sanger: An Autobiography* (1938).

Culture and Commitment

The various New Deal programs have found their historians in Jerry Mangione, *The Dream and the Deal: The Federal Writers' Project, 1935–1943* (1972); Monty Penkower, *The Federal Writers' Project* (1977); Richard McKinzie, *The New Deal for Artists* (1973); and Jane DeHart Mathews, *The Federal Theater, 1935–1939* (1967). General studies of cultural expression include William Stott, *Documentary Expression and Thirties America* (1973); Richard Pells, *Radical Visions and American Dreams* (1973); and R. Alan Lawson, *The Failure of Independent Liberalism, 1933–1941* (1971). See also Karen Becker Ohrn, *Dorothy Lange and the Documentary Tradition* (1980).

Daniel Aaron, *Writers on the Left* (1961), provides the best overview of literary currents in the decade. For selections from the 1930s, see Harvey Swados, ed., *The American Writer and the Great Depression* (1966). Material on the relationship between intellectuals and the Communist party is in Harvey Klehr, *The Heyday of American Communism* (1984), and Irving Howe and Lewis Coser, *The American Communist Party* (1957). Warren Susman, "The Thirties," in Stanley Coben and Lorman Ratner, eds., *The Development of an American Culture* (1970), contains a provocative analysis of culture and commitment in the 1930s.

THE NEW YORK WORLD'S FAIR OF 1939–1940

On April 30, 1939, two hundred thousand people clogged the turnstiles on opening day of the New York World's Fair. At a cost of $160 million, a marshy dump in Queens called Flushing Meadows, which writer F. Scott Fitzgerald once described as "a valley of ashes," had been transformed into a sparkling 1,216-acre showplace with the theme "Building the World of Tomorrow." Sixty countries, thirty-three states, and major industries and business companies contributed exhibits and pavilions. The fair's backers optimistically predicted it not only would stimulate the local depression-ravaged economy, but also would demonstrate that hard times could be overcome, that democracy could survive the threats of fascism and communism, and that the alienated individual could be reintegrated into modern society. The 1939 World's Fair thus was a cultural document of American values and aspirations at a crucial crossroads between the Great Depression and World War II.

"This is *your* Fair, built for *you*, and dedicated to *you*," the fair's organizers proclaimed. "Here are the materials, ideas and forces at work in our world. ... You are the builders; we have done our best to persuade you that these tools will result in a better World of Tomorrow; yours is the choice." After grimly struggling for a decade to overcome the hard times brought on by the Great Depression, many Americans were more than ready to embrace this rosy vision of a future of social harmony,

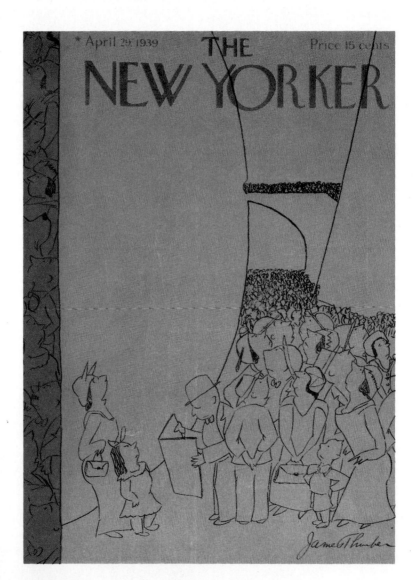

PLATE 1
Cartoonist James Thurber drew this cover for the April 29, 1939 issue of *The New Yorker* magazine to celebrate the official opening of the World's Fair. The fair had so many exhibits that few visitors could see everything in one day. In fact, the average visitor came to the fair 2.3 times. (The Newberry Library, Chicago)

interdependence, and material prosperity.

The principal symbols of the 1939 Worlds Fair were two huge structures called the Trylon and the Perisphere. The Trylon, a tall, thin pyramid, and the Perisphere, a globe, dominated the landscape, "a dazzling white reminder of a world that somehow science and technology might achieve" (plate 2). The fair's theme was further carried out by exhibits covering seven major facets of modern life—production and distribution, transportation, communications and business systems, food, medicine and public health, science and education, and community interests. The concepts of social harmony and interdependence were reinforced by the fair's physical layout, which radiated like the spokes of a wheel from the Trylon and the Perisphere. (plate 3).

Not only did the two structures serve as focal points of the fair, but the Perisphere also housed one of the most popular theme exhibits, Democracity, a diorama of a planned community in the year 2039. As created by industrial designer Henry Dreyfuss, Democracity consisted of Centerton (the business and cultural hub), Pleasantvilles (residential suburbs), and Millvilles (light industrial areas) (plate 5, on page 798). Greenbelt tracts provided land for recreation and agriculture, and a system of highways linked the various sections. Visitors took a six-minute trip into the future via two rotating balconies. The tour featured a narration by popular newscaster H. V. Kaltenborn synchronized to music by black composer William Grant Still.

The theme exhibits prepared by the fair's organizers were complemented, indeed often overshadowed, by the plazas and pavilions erected by American business. The fair unabashedly dedicated itself to the promotion and celebration of the world's first mass-consumer-based society. Visitors were viewed as po-

PLATE 2
Joseph Binder's prize-winning poster was widely distributed for publicity and advertising. Its prominent featuring of the Trylon and Perisphere was typical of the World's Fair promotional material, as was its crisply stylized lettering and composition. (The Queens Museum. Gift of Carla Binder)

PLATE 3
This stylized map appeared in *The New Yorker*. It helped visitors find exhibits within the fair's seven thematic zones, such as Government, which included the Court of Peace and Lagoon of Nations (upper left); and Transportation (lower left), which housed the General Motors and Ford exhibits. The amusement section (right) was deliberately separated from the rest of the fair by a wide boulevard. (The Newberry Library, Chicago)

tential customers for the goods and services lavishly displayed by American businesses eager to acquaint consumers with their products. The D. E. Leathers family of Clarendon, Texas, chosen as a "typical American family," received a Ford Super Deluxe Fordor sedan from the Ford Motor Company, and many visitors sported a Heinz pickle pin, one of the souvenirs handed out by the exhibitors. With its emphasis on consumption spread democratically throughout society by a beneficial capitalist system, historian Warren Susman noted, "the Fair became a rather generalized advertisement for something the 1930s had begun to call the American way of life."

The World's Fair offered a stimulating visual experience, especially at night, when light, fire, color, water, and sound created dazzling multi-media displays (plate 7, on page 799). Most of the buildings featured large, blank walls enlivened by colorful murals, sculpture (plate 8, on page 800), and landscaping. Other architectural innovations included "streamlining" (industrial design characterized by rounded contours and smooth surfaces), extensive use of clear plastics such as Lucite and Plexiglas, and fluorescent interior lighting. A final novelty was air conditioning.

The most popular exhibit was the General Motors Futurama, a glimpse of motorized America in 1960. Long lines formed at the entrance of the Futurama, which handled as many as twenty-eight thousand visitors a day. The exhibit simulated a cross-country trip by carrying visitors in moving chairs with individually synchronized commentary throughout the one-third mile tour. The most striking aspect of the scale model was the extensive arterial highway system, where seven-lane superhighways enabled mo-

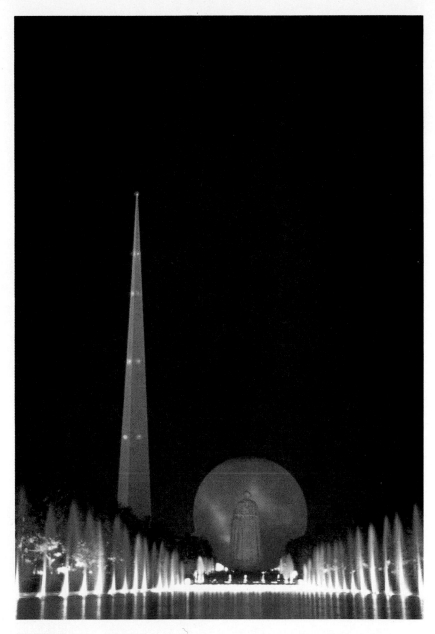

PLATE 4

The World's Fair featured spectacular "sound and light" shows every night. This view, which looks from the Court of Peace to the Theme Center, shows the vibrancy of the night illumination in a way that resembles the photographs of earth sent by the Apollo spacecraft three decades later. The statue is of George Washington, the 150th anniversary of whose inauguration the fair was also dedicated to commemorate. (Alex Siodmak)

PLATE 5
The Democracity diorama was contained in the Perisphere at the fair's Theme Center. To enter, visitors stepped on an escalator that took them up to one of two balconies revolving in opposite directions. Once the six-minute rotation was complete, visitors exited by way of the Helicline, a 950-foot spiral ramp that encircled the Trylon and Perisphere. (Richard Wurts. Museum of the City of New York)

PLATE 6
The focal point of the Ford exhibit was "The Road of Tomorrow," a spiral, three-tiered ramp on which new model cars circled for more than half a mile over the building and through its Garden Court. The Ford Motor Company frequently used pictures of its World's Fair pavilion in its national advertising (this one ran in *The New Yorker*) as a way of stimulating consumer interest in Ford products. (The Newberry Library, Chicago)

torists to drive at speeds up to a hundred miles an hour through city and countryside alike. This glorification of the private automobile was hardly surprising in an exhibit funded by a major car company. At the end of the tour, visitors exited into an intersection that was an exact replica of the Futurama's final stop. No wonder consumers began to believe that the future was now.

Another popular exhibit was the Westinghouse time capsule (plate 9, on page 801), a container more than seven feet long. Officials of the fair filled it with such items as a Mickey Mouse cup, newsreel footage of Jesse Owens's victory in the hundred-yard dash at the 1936 Olympics in Berlin, a copy of Margaret Mitchell's epic novel *Gone With the Wind*, and the 1938 Sears, Roebuck catalog.

Fair visitors sampled a wide range of exhibits promoting the latest in technological innovations for the home and workplace. The Westinghouse exhibit featured a seven-foot robot named Elektro, and General Electric offered a kitchen with talking appliances. The Consolidated Edison exhibit showed a totally electrified diorama of metropolitan New York, complete with streetlights, moving subways, and busy factories (plate 10). RCA showcased live television transmissions from the fair, the first demonstration of TV's potential for mass communication and entertainment. Every day, American Telephone and Telegraph let 150 persons make a free long-distance phone call (then still something of a novelty) to anywhere in the country while the rest of the crowd listened in.

The amusement zone of the fair offered more traditional entertainment, such as the 250-foot-high parachute jump sponsored by Life Savers. Another popular attraction was Billy Rose's Aqua-

PLATE 7
Gallup pollsters found that the USSR Pavilion was the best liked of the foreign exhibits. With its 79-foot stainless steel figure of a worker with a red star (irreverently nicknamed "Big Joe" or "the Bronx Express Straphanger"), the Soviet Pavilion was the second tallest structure at the fair after the Trylon. (Peter M. Warner)

cade, which featured Buster Crabbe, (who played Flash Gordon in the movies), Olympic gold medalists Johnny Weissmuller and Eleanor Holm, and other Hollywood stars performing in a ten-thousand-seat aquatic amphitheater.

Twenty-six million Americans visited the New York World's Fair in 1939, but attendance fell far short of its backers' projections. Many people stayed away because of the seventy-five-cent general admission fee (twenty-five cents for children under fourteen), which was a lot of money at a time when a subway ride in New York cost only a nickel. The Futurama and many of the other most popular exhibits charged an additional admission fee. A family could expect to spend about fourteen dollars for admissions, food, and souvenirs on a day-long trip to the fair. Such entertainment was simply too extravagant for many Americans still struggling to recover from hard times.

In an attempt to recoup its financial losses, the World's Fair was extended for the 1940 season. Reflecting the worsening international situation, the 1940 fair took a more sober theme: "For Peace and Freedom." Attendance rose after the admission fee was dropped to fifty cents (see plate 11, on page 802), but the 1939–1940 fair ended with a $19-million deficit. The fair's temporary structures were razed, and the Trylon and Perisphere were melted down for scrap metal as part of the country's defense mobilization for World War II. The Flushing Meadows site languished until it hosted the 1964–1965 New York World's Fair. By then, the technological progress and material prosperity of postwar America had made even the most futuristic predictions of the 1939 World's Fair looked tame indeed.

PLATE 8
Augusta Savage's sculpture "The Harp" depicts a choir supported by the arm of God. The figure in front holds the opening bars of James Weldon Johnson's "Lift Every Voice and Sing," often referred to as the black national anthem. Savage was the only black artist to receive a commission from the fair's organizers. (Richard Wurts. Museum of the City of New York)

PLATE 9

The Westinghouse Corporation buried this sleek, futuristic, streamlined time capsule at the Flushing Meadows site with instructions not to open it for five thousand years. The capsule included newsreel footage of such events as veterans at the 75th anniversary of Gettysburg and Howard Hughes's record-breaking round-the-world flight in 1938, along with detailed instructions on how to build a movie projector. (Westinghouse Historical Collection)

PLATE 10

Commonwealth Edison's "City of Light" diorama filled an entire city block. In just twelve minutes, an entire city day passed before the spectators, including a spectacular thunderstorm that caused the lights in the city to flick on in response to the darkened skies. Some of the diorama's model structures, such as the Empire State Building pictured above, were as tall as three stories. (Walter Dorwin Teague Associates)

PLATE 11
The National Cash Register building
totalled daily attendance at the fair.
Deeming it too blatant in its
commercialism, fair organizers
banished the cash register to the
Amusement Zone, where it stood
next to the parachute jump ride.
(Alex Siodmak)

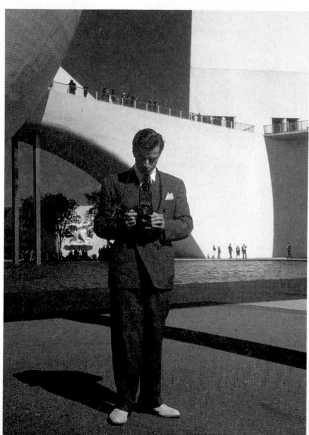

PLATE 12
Professional photographer Alex Siodmak poses with
his camera in front of the Helicline. Who knows
how many family scrapbooks are filled with aging
Kodak snapshots of the 1939 World's Fair, legacies
of amateur photographers who attempted to record
what the fair meant to them. (Alex Siodmak)

26

THE WORLD
AT WAR

World War II ranks with the New Deal as a crucial period of political and economic change. Mobilization pumped money and confidence into the economy, ending the Great Depression. Most Americans at last had money in their pockets. Due to wartime shortages, however, they had little to spend it on. The result was a pent-up demand for a variety of goods and services that extended the wartime prosperity into the postwar period. Despite widespread fears, the depression did not return.

The task of fighting a global war accelerated the growing influence of the federal government on all aspects of American life, one of the themes that has defined the modern era. World War II hastened the concentration of power in the presidency and extended federal intervention in the regulation and management of economic life. Mobilization of the country's vast industrial resources demanded cooperation between top-level business executives and political leaders in Washington. Their joint action solidified the partnership that had been growing since World War I.

Fighting a world war also caused dramatic social changes on the home front. The labor move-ment, fresh from its victories in the late 1930s, strengthened its position. Geographic mobility increased as families followed loved ones entering the armed services or took jobs in defense industries. The war opened new opportunities for women, the "Rosie the Riveters" who filled men's jobs in war plants and other factories. Blacks used the war against Nazi racism as a weapon to challenge notions of white supremacy and discrimination in the United States. They sowed the seeds of the civil rights movement of the 1950s and 1960s.

Perhaps the most far-reaching effect of World War II was America's break with its traditional isolation from international affairs. After the war, the United States accepted a leading role in world diplomacy and a permanent peacetime military establishment. Henry Luce, the publisher of *Life* magazine, confidently predicted the beginning of the "American century" when the war was over. In 1945, the United States stood alone as the only major power to come out of the war physically unscathed and in possession of the secret of the atomic bomb. Those two factors gave force to the predictions of world supremacy.

WARTIME PROSPERITY
War mobilization brought prosperity to many American households. This photograph, taken in 1942, shows the Hall family of Sheffield, Alabama, at ease in their home, part of a defense housing project connected with the TVA. Although the picture's cheerfulness may have been posed, it reflects the new levels of comfort prosperity brought. (Library of Congress)

Internationalism Replaces Isolationism

International developments during the 1930s threatened the fragile world peace that had prevailed since the end of World War I. Fascism took control in Germany and strengthened its hold in Italy, while Japanese militarism grew in the Far East. The League of Nations, set up by the Versailles treaty to resolve potential disputes, proved too weak to deal with those threats to peace. The United States, which had never ratified the treaty or joined the League, followed its own isolationist course. By 1939, however, President Franklin D. Roosevelt was leading the nation toward war.

Depression Diplomacy

Fighting the Great Depression took top priority during Roosevelt's first term, but the president remained deeply interested in foreign affairs. Franklin Roosevelt was an internationalist. He wanted the United States to play a prominent role in a system of worldwide economic and po-

litical interdependence that would foster the long-term prosperity necessary for a lasting peace. Conditions in the early 1930s did not encourage such a policy. Only when the United States regained a stable economy at home could it be an effective leader abroad.

In dealing with the international economy, Roosevelt put national interests first. At an economic conference in London in 1933, his message that the United States would not participate in world plans to stabilize currency killed any hope of common action. The president was announcing to the world that he wanted to promote domestic recovery—in this case, keeping control over the value of the dollar—even at the expense of international cooperation.

Political involvement in international affairs remained limited in the early New Deal. One of Roosevelt's few initiatives was formal recognition of the Soviet Union. Mutual distrust had prevailed since the Bolshevik Revolution of 1917 and the U.S. intervention in 1918 and 1919, and the two countries had never formalized diplomatic relations. The lure of trade with the Soviets led to recognition in November 1933.

In general, Roosevelt steered clear of Europe

and Asia during the 1930s and worked to consolidate American influence in the Western Hemisphere. His diplomatic strategy, which combined both political and economic goals, became known as the Good Neighbor Policy. Under the Reciprocal Trade Agreements Act of 1934, the president was empowered to raise or lower tariffs, without congressional approval, in return for reciprocal concessions from other nations. Secretary of State Cordell Hull negotiated a series of agreements, mainly with European and Latin-American countries where the United States already played the leading role in trade. The volume of trade with nations of the Western Hemisphere rose 100 percent in the 1930s.

As a corollary to economic expansion, the United States also voluntarily renounced the use of military force and armed intervention in the Western Hemisphere. At the Pan-American Conference in Montevideo, Uruguay, in December 1933, Hull proclaimed that "No state has the right to intervene in the internal or external affairs of another." The U.S. Congress agreed in 1934 to repeal the Platt Amendment, a relic of the Spanish-American war that had asserted the right of the United States to intervene in Cuba's internal affairs.

During the first two years of the Roosevelt administration, relatively few citizens were concerned about foreign affairs despite the significant international events taking place. In 1933, Adolf Hitler became chancellor of Germany, and the *Reichstag* (legislature) soon gave him dictatorial powers. Hitler took the title of *Fuhrer* (leader) and outlawed all political parties except his own National Socialists, also called Nazis. They were fiercely anti-semitic. The 1935 Nuremberg laws deprived Jews of all citizenship rights and forbade intermarriage between Jews and Gentiles. Hitler announced that he planned to rearm Germany, a violation of the Versailles treaty, and he withdrew German membership in the League of Nations. A Nazi slogan declared ominously, "Today Germany, tomorrow the world."

In the United States, Hitler's rise to power produced no widespread call for collective security or joint international action. On the contrary, it encouraged a dramatic rise in the isolationist sentiment. Reflecting a long-standing determination to stay clear of dangerous foreign entanglements, most American political leaders sought to strengthen democracy at home rather than commit U.S. resources abroad.

In 1934 and 1935, Senator Gerald P. Nye, a North Dakota Republican, conducted a congressional investigation that revived disillusionment with American participation in World War I. Nye initially looked into the profits of munitions makers during World War I. He widened the investigation to examine the influence of economic interests on America's decision to join the war effort in 1917. Nye's committee concluded that profiteers, whom they called "merchants of death," had maneuvered the United States into the war to save their investments.

Most of the Nye committee's charges were dubious, but they added momentum to the growing isolationist movement. In late 1934, President Roosevelt revived a proposal supported by the Republican administrations of Calvin Coolidge and Herbert Hoover for the United States to join the World Court. This proposal amounted to a mild internationalist gesture that had greater symbolic than actual importance. In January 1935, reflecting the rising isolationist sentiment, Congress rejected participation in the World Court.

The Neutrality Act of 1935 had a greater impact. This law was explicitly designed to prevent a recurrence of the events that had pulled the United States into World War I by, in effect, abandoning the country's rights as a neutral nation under international law. The Neutrality Act imposed an embargo on arms trade with countries at war, and declared that American citizens could travel on belligerent ships only at their own risk. Congress expanded the Neutrality Act in 1936 to include loans to belligerents and, in 1937, made it even stricter by adopting a "cash and carry" provision. If a country at war wanted to purchase nonmilitary goods from the United States, it had to pay cash and pick up the supplies in its own ships. Congress intended this restriction to prevent American trading ships from being the targets of attack. Roosevelt did not like the legislation, which gave him no discretion to decide whether some belligerents, such as the Spanish Loyalists, deserved American military support. Because of the rising tide of isolationism, however, he had no choice but to accept the verdict of Congress.

The Storm Clouds Gather

In 1936, Hitler and Mussolini joined forces in the Rome-Berlin Axis, a political and military alliance. That same year, German troops occupied the Rhineland, again violating the Versailles treaty. The Nazis also increased their persecution of Jews. In 1938, Hitler sent his troops into Austria and proclaimed an *Anschluss* (union) between Germany and Austria.

France and Great Britain, as they had been doing since Hitler started on his road of conquest, hoped he would go no further. But the German dictator was already aiming to seize part of Czechoslovakia, the strategic keystone of Europe. War seemed imminent because Czechoslovakia had a firm alliance with France. At the Munich Conference in September 1938, Prime Minister Neville Chamberlain of Britain and Prime Minister Edward Daladier of France capitulated to Hitler. They agreed to let Germany annex the Sudetenland, the German-speaking section of Czechoslovakia, in return for Hitler's pledge that he would seek no more territory.

Despite Chamberlain's announcement that the Munich agreement guaranteed "peace in our time," Hitler overran the rest of Czechoslovakia within six months and threatened to march into Poland. Britain and France realized the folly of their policy of appeasement and prepared to take a stand over Poland. Hitler, meanwhile, had signed his nonaggression pact with the Soviet Union, protecting Germany from having to wage war on two fronts. He attacked Poland on September 1, 1939, and Britain and France declared war on Germany two days later. World War II had begun.

For more than two years after war broke out in Europe, the United States debated its course of action. Most Americans held two contradictory positions. The overwhelming majority supported the Allies. A 1939 poll showed 84 percent wanted an Allied victory, 2 percent supported the Nazis, and 14 percent had no opinion. On the other hand, most Americans also did not want to be drawn into another European war. This strong isolationist sentiment severely limited President Roosevelt's options.

As early as 1936, Roosevelt had foreseen the possibility of U.S. participation in another European war, but he had determined to stay in line with public opinion. During the 1936 campaign, the president made a stirring antiwar statement: "I have seen war . . . I have seen blood running from the wounded. I have seen men coughing out their gassed lungs . . . . I have seen children starving. I have seen the agony of mothers and wives. I hate war." In October 1937, Roosevelt seemed to take a small step away from isolationism. He spoke against "the present reign of terror and international lawlessness" and called on peace-loving nations to oppose such aggression through a "quarantine."

Roosevelt's 1937 statement reflected rhetorical opposition to militarism more than a specific call for collective security. Domestic affairs, including the prevailing isolationism, made it impossible for him to risk a foreign policy confrontation at the beginning of his second term. A Gallup poll at this time showed that two-thirds of the American people believed the United States had made a mistake in entering World War I.

By 1939, Roosevelt had embarked on what *Time* magazine later called his "thousand-step road to war." After hostilities broke out, he made no secret of his sympathies. "This nation will remain a neutral nation," he stated, "but I cannot ask that every American remain neutral in thought as well." The president wanted to supply the Allies with military supplies, an action forbidden by the Neutrality Act's embargo on the sale of arms to warring nations. After a bitter battle in Congress, he won a slight modification of the neutrality laws. The Allies now could buy weapons from the United States, but only on a "cash and carry" basis.

A false calm settled over Europe after the German conquest of Poland in September 1939. This "phony war" lulled many Americans into thinking that their arms supply policy would be enough to defeat Germany in a war of attrition. Hitler soon shattered that complacency. On April 9, 1940, Nazi *Panzer* forces (armored troops) overran Denmark in a few hours. Norway fell to the Nazi *blitzkrieg* (lightning war) soon after, followed by Holland and Belgium. Next, the Germans stormed into France, bypassing the fixed defenses of the Maginot line and quickly defeating the massed English and French troops. By June 1940, only England stood between the United States and Hitler's plans for world domination.

Toward War

In the midst of the Nazi blitzkrieg, the United States prepared for the 1940 election. Would Roosevelt seek an unprecedented third term? He had not designated a successor as head of the Democratic party, and the situation in Europe in the spring of 1940 convinced him to run again. He submitted to a "draft" at the Democratic National Convention. Although the delegates acclaimed Roosevelt's renomination, they balked at his choice of Secretary of Agriculture Henry A. Wallace for vice-president to replace John Nance Garner of Texas, a conservative who had long since broken with the New Deal. The nomination of the liberal Wallace went through only after Eleanor Roosevelt flew to the convention in Chicago and asked the delegates to put politics aside in a national crisis.

The Republicans nominated a political newcomer, Wendell Willkie of Indiana, president of the Commonwealth and Southern Electric Utilities Company. Willkie, a former Democrat, supported many of the New Deal's domestic and international policies and tried to portray himself as a man of the people. This strategy led crusty Secretary of the Interior Harold Ickes to call him "a simple barefoot Wall Street lawyer." The platforms of the two parties differed only slightly. Both pledged aid to the Allies but stopped short of calling for American participation in the war.

Roosevelt may have clinched his election victory when he declared on October 30, 1940, "I have said this before, but I shall say it again and again and again: Your boys are not going to be sent into any foreign wars." Willkie's spirited campaign resulted in an election closer than the ones in 1932 or 1936. But Roosevelt still received 55 percent of the popular vote and won a lopsided victory in the electoral college.

The debate about America's stance toward the European war continued. Journalist William Allen White and the influential Committee to Defend America by Aiding the Allies led the interventionist side. In 1940, such isolationists as Charles Lindbergh, Senator Gerald Nye, and former NRA administrator Hugh Johnson formed the America First Committee, which agitated to keep the nation out of the war. The *Chicago Tribune*, the Hearst newspapers, and other conservative publications gave full support to the isolationist cause, especially in the Midwest.

Despite the efforts of the America First Committee, the United States moved closer to involvement in 1940 and 1941. The number of Americans who believed that a German victory would threaten national security increased from 43 percent in March 1940 to 69 percent after the fall of France. In June 1940, Roosevelt brought two prominent Republicans, Henry Stimson and Frank Knox, into his cabinet as secretary of war and of the navy, respectively, to give a bipartisan character to the war preparations.

During the summer of 1940, the president traded fifty old destroyers to Great Britain for the right to build military bases on British possessions in the Atlantic. This trade circumvented the 1939 neutrality legislation. Roosevelt also began putting the American economy and government on a defense footing by creating the National Defense Advisory Commission and the Council of National Defense in May 1940. In October of that year, Congress instituted the first peacetime draft registration and conscription in American history. When the draft law came up for extension in 1941, it passed by a single vote.

The United States virtually entered the war when Congress passed the Lend-Lease Act in March 1941. This legislation enabled the nation to serve, in Roosevelt's words, as the "arsenal of democracy." Great Britain, already at war for eighteen months and under nightly bombing attacks from the German air force, could no longer afford to pay cash for supplies. Roosevelt decided to "get away from the dollar sign." In a fireside chat to build support for Lend-Lease, Roosevelt used the analogy of lending a neighbor a garden hose to put out a fire: "I don't say to him, . . . 'Neighbor, my garden hose cost me fifteen dollars; you have to pay me fifteen dollars for it.' . . . I don't want fifteen dollars—I want my garden hose back after the fire is over." Under the Lend-Lease Act, the president was empowered to "lease, lend, or otherwise dispose of" arms and other equipment to any country whose defense was vital to the security of the United States.

As in World War I, supplying the Allies brought German attacks on American and Allied ships. By September 1941, Nazi submarines and American vessels were fighting an undeclared naval war in the Atlantic. In October, Congress

PEARL HARBOR
The USS *Shaw* roils in flames and smoke after receiving a direct hit during the Japanese attack on
Pearl Harbor on December 7, 1941. It was early Sunday morning in Hawaii and many American
servicemen were still asleep. More than twenty-four hundred Americans were killed. The Japanese
suffered only light losses. (FPG)

authorized the arming of merchant vessels. Roosevelt still hesitated to ask for a declaration of war against Germany without an actual enemy attack.

The final provocation came from Japan, not Germany. Conflict between Japan and the United States had been building throughout the 1930s. Japanese military advances, including the conquest of Manchuria in 1931 and the occupation of northern China in 1937, upset the balance of political and economic power in the Far East. The United States had long enjoyed the economic benefits of the Open Door trade policy, but Japan now controlled the region's rich raw materials and large markets. Nevertheless, the U.S. government avoided taking a strong stand, even when provoked. The Japanese sank an American gunboat, the *Panay*, in the Yangtze River near Nanking in 1937. The United States allowed Japan to apologize for the incident and pay more than $2 million in damages, and it was quickly forgotten.

Japanese intentions soon became more expansive. In 1940, Japan signed a diplomatic pact with Germany and Italy. In response, Roosevelt imposed an embargo on shipments of scrap metal to Japan. By the fall of 1941, after Japanese troops occupied French Indochina, the United States had effectively cut off trade with Japan, including vital oil shipments. Before its supplies ran down, Japan would either have to decide for war or accept American demands that it cease its expansionist activities in east Asia.

In September 1941, the government of Prime Minister Hideki Tojo began secret preparations for war. By November, American military intelligence had learned that Japan was planning an attack, but the United States did not know where it would come. Military strategists assumed that the Japanese would attack British Malaya, the American-controlled Philippines, or Thailand. In fact, Japan had selected the United States naval base at Pearl Harbor in Hawaii as the target. Early on Sunday morning, December 7, 1941, Japanese bombers attacked Pearl Harbor, killing more than twenty-four hundred Americans. Eight battleships, three cruisers, and three destroyers—practically the entire Pacific fleet—and almost two hundred airplanes were destroyed or heavily damaged.

President Roosevelt went before Congress the next day and, calling December 7 "a date that will live in infamy," asked for a declaration of war against Japan. The Senate unanimously voted for war, and the House concurred by a vote of 388 to 1. The lone dissenter was Jeannette Rankin of Montana, who had also opposed American entry into World War I. Three days later, Germany and Italy declared war on the United States, and the United States in turn declared war on them.

Mobilizing for Victory

Pearl Harbor Day is etched in the memories of several generations of Americans who remember precisely what they were doing when they heard about the Japanese attack. Many felt relief that the period of indecision and waiting had finally ended.

Coordinating the massive shift from civilian to war production, and assembling the necessary work force, taxed the powers of the government agencies set up to do the job. As in World War I, the nation confronted a number of fundamental questions. For example, how much power should the federal government wield over the economy? What benefits should go to workers as opposed to industrialists? What role should politics play in the conduct of the war?

Defense Mobilization

Defense mobilization not only ended the Great Depression, but it caused the economy to more than double during World War II. In 1940, the gross national product stood at $99.7 billion; it reached $211 billion by 1945. After-tax profits of American business companies rose from $6.4 billion in 1940 to $10.8 billion in 1944. In addition, agricultural output increased by one third.

During the war, the federal government spent $186 billion on war production, sometimes as much as $250 million a day. The peak of mobilization occurred in late 1943, when two-thirds of the economy was directly involved in the war effort, as opposed to only one quarter in World War I. The aircraft industry, whose 46,638 workers had produced 5,865 planes in 1939, peaked in 1944 with more than 2.1 million employed and 96,369 planes produced. By 1945, a total of 86,000 tanks, 296,000 airplanes, 15 million rifles and machine guns, 40 billion bullets, 4 million tons of artillery shells, 64,000 landing craft, and 6,500 naval ships had been produced. Mobilization on this gigantic scale energized the economy after years of depression.

The federal bureaucracy also expanded dramatically, growing far more than it had during the eight years of the New Deal. The number of government civilian employees increased from a million to 3.8 million. At the height of wartime hiring, the government gave the civil service exam two or three times daily. The federal budget rose from $9.4 billion in 1939 to $95.2 billion in 1945. The national debt grew sixfold, topping out at $258.6 billion in 1945.

Taxes paid about half the cost of the war, compared with 30 percent in World War I. The Revenue Act of 1942, which President Roosevelt called the "greatest tax bill in American history," set the foundation for the modern tax structure. This law increased corporate income taxes to a maximum of 40 percent and set a flat rate of 90 percent on excess profits. It also expanded the number of people who had to file a return from thirteen million in 1941 to fifty million in 1942. The system of payroll deductions and tax withholding started in 1943. Bond drives and war loans, in which people put their savings at the disposal of the government through the purchase of long-term Treasury bonds, financed the remaining cost of the war. In addition to encouraging patriotism, war bonds withdrew money from circulation and thus helped hold down inflation.

As Woodrow Wilson had done during World War I, Roosevelt turned to business leaders to run the war economy. Defense preparations had been underway since 1940; before Pearl Harbor, 25 percent of the economy was already devoted to war production. In January 1941, Roosevelt established the Office of Production Management under William Knudsen, the president of General Motors. After Pearl Harbor, Roosevelt disbanded that agency and replaced it with the more powerful and comprehensive War Production Board (WPB). Donald Nelson, a former executive of Sears, Roebuck and Company, headed the WPB.

The War Production Board awarded defense contracts, evaluated military and civilian requests for scarce resources, and oversaw the conversion of industries to military production. Many business leaders, with the depression still on their minds, hesitated to invest heavily in plant expansion or new production. Therefore, the government granted generous tax write-offs for plant construction, approved contracts with cost-plus provisions that guaranteed profits, and promised that industries could keep the plants after the war. As Secretary of War Henry Stimson said, "If you . . . go to war . . . in a capitalist country, you have to let business make money out of the process or business won't work."

In the interest of efficiency and production, the WPB found it easier to deal with major corporations than with small businesses. The fifty-six largest corporations received about three-fourths of the war contracts, and the top ten obtained a third. This allocation system, along with the suspension of antitrust prosecution during the war, hastened the concentration of business in large corporate structures. In 1940, the largest hundred companies manufactured 30 percent of the nation's industrial output. Their share grew to 70 percent by the end of the war.

However, Roosevelt remained unsatisfied with the overall mobilization performance. Nelson and the WPB had allowed the armed forces too much control over priorities. There were too many government agencies, often with overlapping jurisdictions and mandates. In late 1942, Roosevelt persuaded Justice James F. Byrnes to resign from the Supreme Court and head the Office of Economic Stabilization and, after 1943, the Office of War Mobilization. Byrnes soon became the second most important person in the administration and finally brought order to production goals for civilian and military needs.

The results were remarkable. Shipbuilding showed the strength of American productive capacity. By 1941, the German navy had sunk about 12 million tons of Allied, mainly United States, shipping in the North Atlantic, crippling transatlantic transport. The speedy production of new transport vessels called Liberty ships became a high priority. An experienced sailor, Roosevelt called these easy-to-build but hardly graceful ships "ugly ducklings." Ugly or not, the United States produced 19 million tons of merchant shipping by 1943, up from a million tons just two years earlier.

The achievements of Henry J. Kaiser, a West Coast shipbuilder, typified the shipyard produc-

tion miracles. In less than a year, by using the mass production techniques of the automobile industry, Kaiser cut the time needed to build a transport ship from three hundred days to seventeen. He motivated workers through high pay and attractive fringe benefits, including one of the country's first prepaid medical programs.

Kaiser's name became synonymous with getting things done fast. Although not all industries could boast such relative freedom from snafus (an acronym coined during the war from the expression *situation normal, all fouled up*), business and government compiled an impressive record. As in World War I, American industrial might contributed significantly to the military victory.

Labor and the War Effort

A huge hole opened in the American work force when more than thirteen million men entered military service. The backlog of depression-era unemployment quickly disappeared, and the United States faced the reverse problem, a critical labor shortage. About seven million new workers took jobs in the nation's defense industries. They included great numbers of women and blacks who found employment opportunities for the first time. Many of these wartime gains did not last, however. The upward occupational mobility of women and blacks in defense industries evaporated when the veterans came home. And organized labor faced increasing public hostility to its demands for a larger role in industrial life.

Government planners "discovered" the nation's women while casting about for workers to fill the jobs vacated by departing servicemen. The recruiting campaign stressed patriotism. One poster urged, "Longing won't bring him back sooner . . . GET A WAR JOB!" Another showed a woman announcing, "I'm proud . . . my husband *wants* me to do my part." To supplement the emotional appeal of getting loved ones back sooner, government recruiters stressed how easy war work would be for women: "Millions of women find war work pleasant and as easy as running a sewing machine, or using a vacuum cleaner." Women would take to riveting machines and drill presses "as easily as to electric cake-mixers and vacuum

"ROSIE THE RIVETER"
War mobilization created an ideological climate supporting larger roles for women in the workplace. Between 1940 and 1945, the female labor force grew by more than 50 percent. Yet many female defense workers, probably including the riveter shown here, lost their jobs when the war ended. (Library of Congress)

cleaners." The artist Norman Rockwell created a popular image of these patriotic women with his "Rosie the Riveter" cover for the *Saturday Evening Post.*

The government directed its propaganda campaign at housewives, and about six million women responded by taking jobs for the first time. In addition, women who already had employment gladly abandoned low-paying "women's" jobs, such as domestic service and clerical work, for higher-paying work in defense factories. Female riveters, welders, blast furnace cleaners, and drill press operators suddenly filled the nation's factories. Women made up 36 percent of the labor force in 1945, compared with 24 percent at the beginning of the war. An overwhelming majority said they wanted to keep their jobs when the war ended.

However, government planners regarded women's war work as temporary; women were just filling in while the men were away. For this reason, employers offered such benefits as day care for children and flexible hours on a limited basis only. Because women maintained responsibility for home care as well as their defense jobs, they had a higher absentee rate than men did.

Often, the only way to get shopping done or take a child to the doctor was to skip work. Women war workers also faced discrimination on the job. In shipyards, women with the most seniority and responsibility earned $6.95 a day, while the top men made as much as $22.

When the servicemen came home and the war plants returned to peacetime operations, men soon displaced the Rosie the Riveters. Many women, however, refused to put on aprons and go back home. Women's participation in the labor force dropped temporarily following the war, but then it rebounded steadily for the rest of the 1940s. After being fired from defense plants, women simply took a cut in pay and returned to the jobs they had traditionally held in restaurants, telephone exchanges, laundries, offices, and domestic service. By 1950, 29.1 percent of the nation's adult women belonged to the labor force, far higher than prewar levels.

Organized labor also seized wartime opportunities made available by the need for skilled workers in the mobilization effort. No dramatic labor changes occurred, but the war confirmed that the industrial breakthroughs of the 1930s had become permanent. By the end of the war, almost fifteen million workers, a third of the nonagricultural labor force, belonged to unions.

Organized labor began the war with a rush of patriotic unity. On December 23, 1941, representatives of major unions made a "no strike" pledge for the duration of the war. This pledge was not binding, however. To maintain industrial peace, in January 1942 President Roosevelt set up the National War Labor Board (NWLB), composed of representatives of labor, management, and the public. The board established wages, hours, and working conditions and had the authority to order government seizure of plants that did not comply. The government took control of forty plants during the war.

The NWLB handled 17,650 disputes affecting twelve million workers. It faced two controversial issues, union membership and wage increases. Union organizers favored either the union shop or the closed shop, but management preferred the open shop. (In a union shop, the employees must belong to a certain union or join it within a specified period. In a closed shop, the employer may hire only members of a union. An open shop employs both union and nonunion workers.) As a compromise, the NWLB imposed

THE SHIPYARD DIARY OF A WOMAN WELDER

Back to work and more welding. I "dis-improved" as rapidly after lunch as I had improved during the morning. One girl stopped to ask, "How you doin'?" and watched me critically. "Here, let me show you, you're holding it too far away." So she took over, but she couldn't maintain the arc at all. She got up disgusted, said, "I can't do it—my hand shakes so since I been sick," and I took over again. But she was right. I held it closer and welded on and on and on. . . .

We were called to another safety lecture—good sound advice on Eye Safety. . . . Only Chile has a higher accident rate than the United States. Last year the shipyard had fairly heavy absenteeism, but this year they hope to build an extra ship on the decrease in absenteeism. He cautioned us about creating hazards by wearing the wrong kind of clothing, and told us not to wear watches or rings. After it was over, Missouri was bothered about her wedding ring. It hadn't been off in fourteen years. She was willing to take it off, but only if necessary.

The lecturer brought up the rumor that arc welding causes sterility among women. He said that this was untrue, and quoted an authoritative source to prove its falsity. . . . Actually, welders had *more* children than other people. "No, thanks," said the first girl; "I don't like that either!" . . .

I, who hate heights, climbed stair after stair after stair till I thought I must be close to the sun. I stopped on the top deck. I, who hate confined spaces, went through narrow corridors, stumbling my way over rubber-coated leads—dozens of them, scores of them, even hundreds of them. I went into a room about four feet by ten where two shipfitters, a shipfitter's helper, a chipper, and I all worked. I welded in the poop deck lying on the floor while another welder spattered sparks from the ceiling and chippers like giant woodpeckers shattered our eardrums. I, who've taken welding, and have sat at a bench welding flat and vertical plates, was told to weld braces along a baseboard below a door opening. On these a heavy steel door was braced while it was hung to a fine degree of accuracy. I welded more braces along the side, and along the top. I did overhead welding, horizontal, flat, vertical. I welded around curved hinges which were placed so close to the side wall that I had to bend my rod in a curve to get it in. I made some good welds and some frightful ones. But now a door in the poop deck of an oil tanker is hanging, four feet by six of solid steel, by *my* welds. Pretty exciting!

Source: Augusta Clawson, *Shipyard Diary of a Woman Welder*. New York: Penguin, 1944, quoted in Rosalyn Baxandall, Linda Gordon, and Susan Reverby, eds., *America's Working Women: A Documentary History, 1600 to the Present*. New York: Random House, 1976. 288–289.

---

the principle of maintenance of membership. Workers did not have to join a union, but those already in a union had to maintain their membership during the life of the contract.

Pressure for wage increases caused a more serious disagreement. In contrast to the deflation that characterized the depression, inflation pushed prices up throughout the war. Because management wanted to keep production (and profits) running smoothly, it expressed willingness to pay the higher wages demanded by workers. Such raises, however, would have conflicted with the public policy of keeping inflation as low as possible. In 1942, the NWLB established the "Little Steel Formula," which granted a 15 percent wage increase to match a similar increase in the cost of living since January 1, 1941. Although the NWLB froze hourly wages in principle, it allowed them to rise another 24 percent by 1945. Actually, incomes rose as much as 70 percent because workers earned overtime pay, which was not covered by wage ceilings. The tremendous increase in worker output during World War II resulted largely from working overtime.

Despite higher wages than anyone had dreamed possible during the depression, many union members felt cheated as they watched corporate profits soar while their wages remained frozen. The high point of dissatisfaction came in 1943. A nationwide railroad strike was narrowly averted. But then John L. Lewis led more than half a million United Mine Workers out on strike to demand higher wages than the Little Steel Formula allowed. Lewis won concessions, but he alienated Congress and became one of the most disliked public figures of the 1940s for defying the government.

Congress countered Lewis's activism by passing the Smith-Connally Labor Act of 1943, which required a thirty-day cooling-off period before a strike and prohibited strikes in defense industries entirely. Nevertheless, about fifteen thousand strikes occurred during the war. This number represented less than a tenth of 1 percent of working hours, but the public perceived the disruptions as far larger. Unionized labor won acceptance during the war years but also faced increasing hostility from other social groups.

Politics in Wartime

At a press conference late in 1943, President Roosevelt playfully announced that "Dr. Win the War" had replaced "Dr. New Deal." The reform agenda of the New Deal had been dormant since 1938. During the 1940s, Roosevelt rarely pressed for further social and economic change, thus placating conservative members of Congress whose support he needed to conduct the war in a bi-partisan spirit. With little argument, he agreed to drop several popular New Deal programs. In 1943, the National Youth Administration, the Works Progress Administration, and the Civilian Conservation Corps were dismantled. Severe budget cuts crippled the Farm Security Administration, which had represented the interests of poor farmers. The rapidity with which the government terminated these agencies suggests that they had been a response to the crisis of the depression rather than a commitment to expanding federal programs to promote the general welfare. Such programs as Social Security remained untouched, however.

The war years brought a significant decline in the reform spirit that had flourished in Washington during the 1930s. Unlike World War I, few public figures talked about using the war to bring about social change. Business leaders replaced the reformers and social activists who had staffed New Deal relief agencies in the 1930s. These business executives became known as "dollar-a-year men" because they volunteered for government service while remaining on their corporate payrolls.

Roosevelt had hoped politics could be shelved for the duration of the war, but that proved to be an unreasonable expectation. In the 1942 election, the Republicans picked up seats in both houses of Congress and increased their share of state governorships. These gains reflected the general tendency of the party out of power to improve its position in off-year elections. The Republicans also benefited from a low voter turnout. The decline resulted from dislocations caused by servicemen's going into the armed forces and the difficulty of many voters in meeting residency requirements after moving to new localities.

Roosevelt himself had hardly given up politics for the duration. After concluding that continuation of the war made a fourth term necessary, he went on a mild offensive to attract Democratic voters. In his state of the union address in 1944, the president called for a second Bill of Rights. As the basis of postwar prosperity, he pledged such rights as a job, adequate food and clothing, a decent home, proper medical care, and an education.

The president's sweeping commitment remained largely rhetorical. Congressional support did not exist in 1944 for this vast extension of the welfare state. It was possible, however, to win some of these pledges for a special group of American citizens, the returning veterans. The GI Bill of Rights, passed in 1944, provided education, job training, medical care, pensions, and mortgage loans for men and women who had served in the armed forces during the war.

"I am an old campaigner and I love a good fight," Franklin Roosevelt had said during the 1940 election. He approached the 1944 campaign with the same verve, but the years of the presidency had taken their toll. When Republicans tried to raise the issue of his health, the sixty-two-year-old Roosevelt replied by making several strenuous campaign appearances, including a four-hour, fifty-mile drive in pouring rain through New York City. Concern about presidential succession prompted the Democrats to drop Vice-President Henry Wallace, whose outspoken support for labor, civil rights, and further domestic reform was too extreme for many party leaders. In Wallace's place, they chose Senator Harry S. Truman of Missouri. Truman had become known for heading a Senate investigation of government waste and inefficiency in defense contracts during the war.

The Republicans nominated New York Governor Thomas E. Dewey. Dewey, only forty-two years old, had won fame for his fight against organized crime while serving as a U.S. attorney. He accepted the broad outlines of the welfare state and belonged to the internationalist wing of the Republican party. The 1944 election was the closest since 1916. Roosevelt received 53.4 percent of the popular vote. The Democrats lost ground among farmers, but most ethnic groups remained solidly Democratic. Roosevelt got his customary support from the South, augmented by the overwhelming allegiance of servicemen and women, who voted by absentee ballot. His margin of victory came from the cities. In urban areas with more than a hundred thousand people, the president drew 60 percent of the vote.

Roosevelt also received strong support from organized labor. Under the prodding of CIO leaders Sidney Hillman and Philip Murray, labor contributed more than $1.5 million, or about 30 percent of the Democratic party's election funds. The CIO's Political Action Committee conducted door-to-door canvassing drives and voter registration campaigns. This venture into electoral politics reflected a change in labor's priorities to include political action as well as union organizing drives. Organized labor continued to play a significant role in the Democratic party after the war.

The Home Front

In contrast to World War I, there was almost no domestic opposition to the nation's role in World War II. Americans fought for their way of life and for the preservation of democracy against the forces of Nazi and Japanese totalitarianism. People on the home front had a job to do just like the soldiers in uniform. A national mood characterized by unity, determination, and commitment made World War II perhaps America's last truly patriotic war.

At the same time, many Americans remember the war years as much for the return of prosperity as anything else. Not only did unemployment disappear, but per capita income rose from $691 in 1939 to $1,515 in 1945. Despite geographical dislocations and shortages of various items, about 70 percent of the people on the home front admitted midway in the war that they had personally experienced "no real sacrifices."

"For the Duration"

Although the United States did not suffer the physical devastation that ravaged much of Europe and the Far East, the war affected the lives of those who stayed behind. Families with a loved one anywhere near the front lines wondered every time they saw the Western Union boy on his bicycle whether they might receive the dreaded telegram from the War Department telling them that their son or husband or father would not be coming home. Other Americans put up with far less traumatic experiences. "Don't you know there's a war on?" became the standard reply to almost any request that could not be fulfilled. People calmly accepted the fact that their lives would be different "for the duration."

Many Americans on the home front contributed enthusiastically to the war effort. They took defense jobs, worked on civilian defense committees, performed volunteer work, collected old newspapers and scrap material, donated blood, and served on local rationing or draft boards. All seven war loan drives were over-subscribed. Advertising campaigns displaying the popular "V for Victory" slogan stressed patriotic unity. About twenty million home "victory gardens" produced 40 percent of the vegetables grown in the United States.

Movie attendance soared during the 1940s. Workers on the home front had few other places to spend their first steady income in years. Theaters operated around the clock to accommodate war workers on the swing and night shifts. Many movies featured patriotic themes. In *Since You Went Away* (1943), Claudette Colbert held her family together when her husband went off to war; near the end of the film, she took a job as a welder in a shipyard. In *Casablanca* (1943), Humphrey Bogart and Ingrid Bergman renewed an old love affair against the backdrop of freedom fighters escaping from Nazi persecution in North Africa. At the end, the previously cynical Bogart character joined the fight against fascism.

The war caused much geographical mobility. When men volunteered or were drafted into the

HOME-FRONT PATRIOTISM
The sale of defense bonds and stamps by the government raised money for the war effort and encouraged patriotism. These housewives from the Parent–Teacher Association of Turlock, California, did their part for the U.S. Treasury Department in a booth set up in a local store in 1942. (Library of Congress)

armed services, their families often followed them to their training bases or points of debarkation. The lure of high-paying defense jobs also resulted in migration. About fifteen million Americans changed their residences during the war years, and half of them moved into another state. This movement was not simply an exodus from rural to urban areas, although the pace of urbanization increased. About 5.4 million people left farms, but 2.5 million moved onto them. A million southerners, black and white, went north, but 600,000 migrants moved south. The greatest number of people went west. California, the center of much defense production, gained 1.4 million newcomers.

Migration often strained family cohesion. Harriet Arnow's novel *The Dollmaker* (1954) described a family's wartime uprooting. Gertie Nevels, her husband Clovis, and their children leave eastern Kentucky for Detroit. The family settles in a miserably inadequate housing project filled with other migrants from the rural South.

Clovis gets a job in a defense plant, but his wages barely keep up with the inflated expenses of urban life in wartime. One son flees back home to Kentucky. A daughter, deeply disturbed by the move, distractedly falls beneath the wheels of a train and is killed. Gertie Nevels finds her only solace in woodcarving. But in a final act of desperation, she cuts up the Christ figure she has been whittling so she can make trinkets to sell for money to feed her family.

For most Americans, the dramas of everyday life occurred on a less dramatic scale. The Office of Price Administration and Civilian Supply (OPA) oversaw the home front consumer economy, allocating domestic resources and trying to keep inflation down. By February 1942, retail prices were rising at the rapid rate of 2 percent a month. In April, the OPA froze most prices and rents at their March 1942 level. When loopholes, especially concerning food prices, undermined the effort, Congress passed the Anti-inflation Act, which stabilized wages, prices, and salaries. The Consumer Price Index rose 28.3 percent between 1940 and 1945, but most of the inflation occurred before 1943.

During the war, almost anything that Americans ate, wore, or used was subject to rationing or regulation. Rubber became the first scarce item. The Japanese conquest of Malaya and the Netherlands East Indies cut off 97 percent of America's imports of natural rubber, a serious threat to war production. By late 1944, an entirely new industry devoted to the production of synthetic rubber supplied 762,000 tons a year, most of it for the war effort.

Meanwhile, the government ordered the rationing of tires to conserve rubber, a hard sacrifice for the nation's thirty million drivers. Rubber campaigns recycled such items as old boots, heating bottles, doormats, and tires. Many people put their cars up on blocks for the duration. Bicycle tires were also in short supply. If people walked instead, they risked wearing out their shoes. By 1944, the annual allotment was two pairs per person, barely half the average number purchased before the war.

Gasoline and fuel oil became the next items to be rationed. German attacks on oil tankers crossing the Atlantic from the Middle East had disrupted supplies. Shortages of fuel oil forced schools and restaurants to shorten their hours, and home thermostats to be lowered to 65 degrees. Gasoline rationing, introduced in December 1942, was both a response to depleted gasoline supplies and an attempt to save wear on precious rubber tires. Rationing categories ranged from "nonessential" to "unlimited." An "A" (nonessential) card entitled a motorist to buy four gallons of gasoline a week, the equivalent of about sixty miles of driving. That ration was later cut in half. To discourage additional fuel consumption, Congress imposed a nationwide speed limit of thirty-five miles per hour. Highway death rates dropped dramatically.

People found it harder to cut back on eating than on driving. Many food commodities were in short supply during the war. Sugar quickly disappeared from grocery shelves, and the government soon rationed it at the rate of eight to twelve ounces per person a week. However, the manufacturers of such products as Coca-Cola and Wrigley's chewing gum received unlimited sugar quotas by convincing the government that these items helped the morale of the men and women in the armed forces.

By the midpoint of the war, a complicated system of rationing points and coupons regulated how much meat, butter, and other food Americans could buy. The government limited butter to one pound per person monthly, barely a fourth of the prewar consumption level. The food restrictions resulted in a black market, especially in meat. Most people cooperated with the restrictions, but almost a fourth thought that buying items on the black market was occasionally justified.

Shortages of consumer durables also hit the home front. Following the Great Depression, people finally had enough money to buy refrigerators, cars, and radios. But they found that rubber, copper, steel, and other necessary components had been earmarked for war production. The last Ford rolled off the assembly line in 1942 as automobile plants converted to bomber production. To dampen consumer demands, many companies ran advertisements encouraging delayed gratification. After the war, they told the public, you can buy that new house and fill it with all the appliances that were temporarily unavailable.

But some purchases just could not wait. One of the most highly desired items on the black market was women's stockings. In the 1930s, women had worn silk stockings, but they switched to nylons when the war with Japan cut off imports of silk. Unfortunately, nylon was essential to war production. Thirty-six pairs of nylons equalled one parachute. A besieged hosiery executive jested, "We could figure a way to knit them of grass one day and the next day there would be a priority on grass." Many women began wearing slacks in public, a dramatic fashion change of the 1940s. The strict rationing of food and other items eased in the summer of 1944, when victory appeared on the horizon.

Seeds of Change for Black Americans

"A wind is rising throughout the world of free men everywhere," Eleanor Roosevelt wrote during the war, "and they will not be kept in bondage." This rising wind characterized the experience of black Americans. The war disrupted a number of traditional patterns, both of society in general and of race relations in particular, and many barriers to racial equality tottered or broke down.

The first evidence that the war might encourage greater black activism came in 1941. A. Philip Randolph, head of the Brotherhood of Sleeping Car Porters, a black union, announced a "March on Washington" to protest the exclusion of black workers from defense plants. Of the nation's 100,000 aircraft workers in 1940, only 240 were black, and most of them were janitors. Black leaders demanded that the government require defense contractors to integrate their work forces. Randolph predicted that a hundred thousand black Americans would march in the demonstration at the capital. Roosevelt, though not a strong supporter of civil rights, feared the public embarrassment of such a massive protest. Even more, he feared a disruption of war preparations. The president agreed to meet many of Randolph's demands, and the union leader cancelled the march.

The compromise between Randolph and Roosevelt involved the issuance of an executive order. The government declared it to be the policy of the United States "that there shall be no discrimination in the employment of workers in defense industries or government because of race, creed, color, or national origin." The president established the Fair Employment Practices Committee (FEPC) in the Office of Production Management to enforce that policy.

This federal commitment to guaranteeing black employment rights was unprecedented but still limited in scope. It did not, for example, affect segregation in the armed forces. Moreover, the FEPC, which could not require compliance with its orders, often found that the needs of defense production took precedence over fair employment.

The FEPC received more than eight thousand complaints, of which it resolved about a third. By 1944, blacks made up 8 percent of the defense workers, probably more as a result of the labor shortage than of the FEPC prodding. Nevertheless, they got great satisfaction from the symbolic federal action against discrimination in the work force.

Spurred by the new economic opportunities in defense and factory work, black migration from the South increased dramatically after the temporary lull during the depression. More than a million blacks moved to defense centers in California, Illinois, Ohio, and Pennsylvania. Their need for jobs and housing led to racial conflict in a number of northern cities.

Detroit, the new home of a large number of southern migrants, both black and white, experienced some of the worst racial violence. Many incidents occurred because of competition over scarce housing. Early in 1942, black families encountered resistance and intimidation when they tried to move into the Sojourner Truth housing project in Hamtramck, a Polish community of Detroit. Similar tensions erupted into major violence in 1943, when a race riot in Detroit left thirty-four people dead, twenty-five of them blacks. Racial conflicts broke out in forty-seven cities throughout the country.

Tensions in the cities extended beyond hostility between whites and blacks. The activities of Hispanic youths in Los Angeles polarized that city. These young people organized *pachuco* (youth) gangs that dressed in a distinctive style including broad felt hats, pegged trousers, pocket knives on gold chains, and long greased hair. They became known as "zoot suiters." White hostility toward the Hispanic gangs had been smoldering for some time. In July 1943, rumors that a gang had beaten a sailor set off a four-day riot, during which white servicemen entered Hispanic neighborhoods and attacked zoot suiters. The sailors took special pleasure in slashing the pegged pants of their Hispanic targets. The attacks occurred within full view of white police officers who did nothing to stop the violence.

On the other hand, a new mood of militancy among the nation's minorities appeared during the war years. Black leaders effectively suggested parallels between Germany's treatment of Jews and racial discrimination against blacks in America. Although the full horror of Hitler's extermination of six million Jews in concentration camps did not become widely known until after the war, black leaders capitalized on the revulsion felt by many Americans at Hitler's anti-semitism. Civil rights leaders pledged themselves to a "Double V" campaign—victory over Nazism abroad and victory over racism and inequality at home.

Encouraged by the ideological climate of the war years, black organizations reported a large

A ZOOT SUITER
Zoot suit fashions gained wide popularity among young Americans during the war. In 1943, this well-dressed teenager greased his hair in a ducktail and wore a loosely cut coat with padded shoulders (called "fingertips") that reached mid-thigh, baggy pleated pants cut tight ("pegged") around the ankles, and a long gold watch chain. The easy fit of a zoot suit accommodated the current dance craze, the jitterbug. (UPI)

increase in membership. The National Association for the Advancement of Colored People (NAACP) grew ninefold to 450,000. In 1942, A. Philip Randolph helped found the Congress of Racial Equality (CORE). Unlike the NAACP, which favored lobbying and legal strategies, CORE used more aggressive tactics, including mass demonstrations and sit-ins. In 1944, CORE forced several restaurants in Washington, D.C., to serve blacks. Pickets carried signs that read "Are You for Hitler's Way, or the American Way? Make Up Your Mind."

A heightened awareness of civil rights surfaced in other ways as well. The Swedish sociologist Gunnar Myrdal wrote a monumental study of race relations, *An American Dilemma: The Negro Problem and Modern Democracy* (1944). Other books that focused national attention on black issues included such novels as Richard Wright's *Black Boy* (1945) and Lillian Smith's *Strange Fruit* (1944). In 1944, in the case of *Smith v. Allwright*, the Supreme Court ruled that Texas's all-white primary election, a common device used to disfranchise blacks in southern states, was unconstitutional. Following the Court's decision, Congressman Wright Patman of Texas vowed that blacks would vote in his district "over my dead body." Soon, however, Patman began courting black voters at church picnics and other social events in his successful re-election campaigns. These wartime developments laid the groundwork for the civil rights explosion of the 1950s and 1960s.

Japanese Relocation

Events such as the Detroit race riot of 1943 recalled the widespread racial tensions during World War I. But in most other ways, the home fronts of the two wars differed greatly. In the 1940s, German culture and German-Americans did not come under suspicion; nor did Italian-Americans suffer persecution. Leftists and Communists faced little domestic repression, mainly because the Soviet Union became an ally of the United States after the Pearl Harbor attack. The lack of war hysteria largely reflected the strong patriotic consensus in support of the nation's war aims.

One glaring exception marred the wartime record of tolerance and patriotism: the internment of Japanese-Americans on the West coast. The racial prejudice and hysteria directed at them serve as a reminder of how fragile civil liberties can be in wartime.

At first, the West Coast remained calm after Pearl Harbor. But then, partly reflecting the region's vulnerability to attack, coastal residents began to demand protection against the threat of supposed Japanese spies. The Japanese-Americans, who lived clustered in highly visible communities, were a small, politically impotent minority. California's long history of racial antagonism against both Japanese and Chinese immigrants helps explain why the Japanese, rather than German- or Italian-Americans, were singled out. "A Jap's a Jap," an army general

MAP 26.1 WRA
RELOCATION CAMPS
In 1942, the government ordered 112,000 Japanese-Americans living on the West Coast into internment camps in the nation's interior because of their supposed threat to public safety during wartime. The freedom of 150,000 Japanese-Americans in the multi-racial, multi-ethnic society of the U.S. territory of Hawaii was not restricted. In California and other states, they were a highly visible and vulnerable minority.

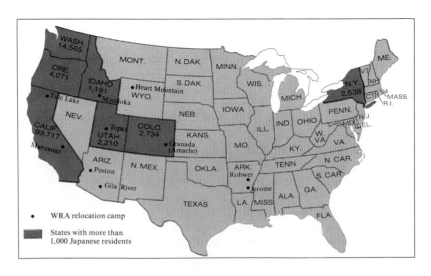

THE INSULT AND INJURY OF INTERNMENT

Peter Ota remembers his family's internment in an American prisoner of war camp during World War II.

It was just my sister and myself. I was fifteen, she was twelve. In April, 1942, we were evacuated to Santa Anita. At the time we didn't know where we were going, how long we'd be gone. We didn't know what to take. A toothbrush, toilet supplies, some clothes. Only what you could carry. We left with a caravan.

Santa Anita is a race track. The horse stables were converted into living quarters. My sister and I were fortunate enough to stay in a barracks. The people in the stables had to live with the stench. Everything was communal. We had absolutely no privacy. When you went to the toilet, it was communal. It was very embarrassing for women especially. . . .

We had orders to leave Santa Anita in September of 1942. We had no idea where we were going. Just before we left, my father joined us. . . . I can still picture it to this day: to come in like cattle or sheep being herded in the back of a pickup truck bed. We were near the gate and saw him come in. He saw us. It was a sad, happy moment, because we'd been separated for a year.

He never really expressed what his true inner feelings were. It just amazes me. He was never vindictive about it, never showed any anger. I can't understand that. A man who had worked so hard for what he had and lost it overnight. There is a very strong word in Japanese, *gaman*. It means to persevere. Old people instilled this into the second generation: you persevere. Take what's coming, don't react.

He had been a very outgoing person. Enthusiastic. I was very, very impressed with how he ran things and worked with people. When I saw him at Santa Anita, he was a different person.

We were put on a train, three of us and many trains of others. It was crowded. The shades were drawn. During the ride we were wondering, what are they going to do to us? We Niseis [first-generation Japanese Americans] had enough confidence in our government that it wouldn't do anything drastic. My father had put all his faith in this country. This was his land.

Oh, it took days. We arrived in Amache, Colorado. That was an experience in itself. We were right near the Kansas border. It's a desolate, flat, barren area. The barracks was all there was. There were no trees, no kind of landscaping. It was like a prison camp. Coming from our environment, it was just devastating. . . .

When I think back to my mother and father, what they went through quietly, it's hard to explain. [Cries.] I think of my father without ever coming up with an angry word. After all those years, having worked his whole life to build a dream—an American dream, mind you—having it all taken away, and not one vindictive word. His business was worth more than a hundred thousand. He sold it for five. When he came out of camp, with what little money he had he put a down payment on an apartment building. It was right in the middle of skid row, an old rooming house. . . . He died a very broken man.

Source: Peter Ota, interviewed in Studs Terkel, *"The Good War."* New York: Pantheon, 1984. 29–30, 32–33.

---

stated. "It makes no difference whether he is an American citizen or not."

Mounting fears on the West Coast in early 1942 brought a far-reaching decision from Washington. President Roosevelt approved a War Department plan to intern Japanese-Americans in relocation camps for the duration of the war. In March, Milton Eisenhower, a career civil servant and brother of General Dwight D. Eisenhower, took over the War Relocation Authority, a civilian agency created to carry out the policy. Few public leaders opposed the plan. The Supreme Court upheld its constitutionality as a legitimate exercise of power during wartime in *Hirabayashi v. United States* (1944), ruling that "residents having ethnic affiliations with an invading enemy may be a greater source of danger than those of different ancestry."

The relocation announcement shocked Japanese-Americans, of whom more than two-thirds were native-born American citizens of Japanese ancestry. They comprised the *Nisei* generation, the children of the foreign-born *Issei* generation. The government gave families barely a few days to dispose of their belongings and prepare for relocation. They could take with them only what they could carry. Eager speculators snatched up Japanese real estate for a fraction of its value. Businesses that had been developed over a lifetime had to be liquidated overnight. A Japanese-American piano teacher got only $30 for her treasured piano. Another woman broke every piece of her family's heirloom porcelain rather than accept $17.50 from a secondhand dealer. The government later estimated the total financial loss at $400 million, but Congress appropriated only $38 million to compensate Japanese-Americans after the war.

Relocation took place in two stages. First the government sent the Japanese-Americans to temporary assembly centers, such as the Santa Anita racetrack in Los Angeles, where they lived in stables that horses had occupied a few days earlier. Then they were moved to ten permanent camps away from the coast. These camps, located in California, Arizona, Utah, Colorado, Wyoming, Idaho, and Arkansas, "were in places where nobody had lived before and no one has lived since," one historian commented. Milton Eisenhower had hoped to pattern the relocation camps on the CCC youth camps of the New Deal, but the barbed wire and enforced communal living mocked his hopes. The relocation centers, although sometimes compared to Nazi concentration camps, most closely resembled Indian reservations.

All ten camps were located in hot, dusty climates, and their primitive conditions made family life nearly impossible. Communal bathroom and dining facilities undermined morale even more. The lack of privacy was hardest to bear; only flimsy partitions separated the hastily built rooms. When one baby cried, babies cried up and down the barracks. Eight people often lived in a room that measured only twenty-five by twenty feet. Small families might have strangers assigned to their room. Generational differences between the Issei, who had an average age of fifty-five, and the Nisei, who averaged seventeen years old, added to the tensions. Everyone found boredom a major problem.

Almost every Japanese-American in California, Oregon, and Washington was involuntarily detained for some period during World War II,

a total of approximately 112,000 people. The 15,000 Japanese-Americans who lived outside the West Coast war zone were not affected. Cracks soon appeared in the relocation policy. Japanese-Americans had played important roles in agriculture, and the labor shortage in farming led the government to furlough seasonal agricultural workers as early as 1942. In addition, about forty-three hundred young people who had been in college when the relocation order came were allowed to return to their studies—if they transferred out of the West Coast military zone.

Some young men took advantage of another route out of the camps. Their government, despite imprisoning them, allowed Japanese-Americans to volunteer for military service in Europe. The 442nd Infantry Combat Team, composed entirely of Nisei volunteers, became the most decorated unit in all the armed forces. Its battle and casualty record provided convincing proof of the loyalty of Japanese-Americans.

Most Japanese-Americans accepted relocation. They hoped that by proving their loyalty, they would be accepted again after the war. Many Japanese-Americans of the third generation, called the *Sansei*, some of whom were born in the internment camps, and the fourth generation, the *Yonsei*, do not understand why their elders did not protest more strongly. With each generation, the memory of the wartime deprivation grows dimmer, but nothing can erase this shameful episode from the national conscience.

Victory

The United States gave top priority to fighting Germany, but the battle against the Japanese on the islands of the Pacific was just as difficult. Coordinating the massive military effort strained the Grand Alliance of the United States, Great Britain, and the Soviet Union. In wartime diplomacy lay the seeds of the Cold War that followed victory.

Fighting on Two Fronts

The overall strategy for winning the war resulted from give-and-take discussions among the dominant personalities of the Grand Alliance: Franklin Roosevelt, Prime Minister Winston Churchill of Great Britain, and Joseph Stalin, premier of the Soviet Union. Roosevelt's strong commitment to Britain's survival provided the basis for a strong, if not always smooth, relationship with Churchill. The two men first met at a secret conference aboard a cruiser off the Newfoundland coast in 1941. Stalin, on the other hand, was something of a mystery. He and Roosevelt did not meet until the Teheran Conference in November 1943. Although the United States and Great Britain disagreed on such issues as the postwar fate of colonial empires, the potential for conflict with the Soviet Union was far greater because of the profound differences between their economic and political systems and their opposed visions of the world order of the future. This uncertainty affected both the conduct of the war and the plans for the postwar peace.

The Atlantic Charter, drafted by Roosevelt and Churchill in the summer of 1941, provided the ideological foundation of the Allied cause. It bore similarities to the Fourteen Points proclaimed by Woodrow Wilson in 1918. The Atlantic Charter affirmed the sovereign rights of nations and the freedom of each nation to choose its form of government. The charter called for postwar economic collaboration and guarantees of political stability to ensure freedom from want, fear, and aggression. It condemned territorial gains achieved as the spoils of victory.

The Allied commitment to national self-determination represented the most striking element of continuity with Wilson's Fourteen Points. It became the thorniest problem to confront the three leaders. Roosevelt's hope for self-determination in Eastern Europe conflicted with Stalin's demand for a band of satellite states under Soviet control for protection against invasion from the west. To a lesser degree, the issue caused Roosevelt's disagreement with Churchill over the fate of the British colonial empire after the war. Despite such conflicts, Roosevelt hoped that the Allies could maintain friendly relationships that would survive the war and provide the basis of a constructive postwar system. At the heart of this postwar cooperation would be an international organization, the United Nations, that would serve as a forum to resolve tensions and prevent further aggression.

These long-term goals interacted with the military necessities of fighting a global war. Defeating Germany always occupied top military priority, with Japan relegated to a secondary position. One way to wear down the Germans lay in opening a second front on the European continent, preferably in France, as soon as possible. The Russians strongly argued for this strategy, because a second front would draw German troops away from the fighting on Russian soil. Roosevelt assured Stalin informally that such a front would be opened in 1942.

The two-year delay in opening a second front proved to be one of the most damaging blows to the harmony among the three main Allies. The issue came up so many times that Soviet Foreign Minister Vyacheslav Molotov was said to know only four English words, "yes," "no," and "second front." The delay resulted from a combination of military priorities and British opposition. In 1942, the Allies did not have the necessary equipment, especially landing craft, to mount a successful invasion across the English Channel

"Wisht I could stand up an' git some sleep."

WILLIE AND JOE
World War II contributed its share of humor as well as horror. Cartoonist Bill Mauldin won a Pulitzer Prize in 1945 for his drawings, which featured realistic portrayals of the war through the eyes of Willie and Joe, two common soldiers. Here, as grimy, exhausted infantrymen, they huddle on the beachhead at Anzio following the Allied invasion of Italy. (By permission of Bill Mauldin and Wil-Jo Associates, Inc.)

MAP 26.2 EUROPE, 1942–1945
The height of German control came in 1942. The Allies countered first in North Africa in 1942–1943, and then moved onto the European mainland via the Italian peninsula in 1943–1944. In the meantime, the Soviets had begun to push the Germans back from Russian territory. In 1944–1945, Allied activity concentrated in Northern Europe with the successful D-Day invasion in France and the push toward Berlin that ended the war in May 1945.

against the heavily defended French coast. Churchill adamantly opposed launching the invasion, fearing that the Allies would be trapped in a destructive ground war in France as had happened during World War I.

The repeated delays in opening the second front meant that for most of the war, the Soviet Union bore the brunt of the land battle against Germany. The Soviets lost as many as 20 million military and civilian dead during the war, about 8 percent of their people. In contrast, 292,000 Americans were killed and 671,000 wounded in the fighting. These casualties represented less than half of 1 percent of the population. Roosevelt and Churchill's unfulfilled pledges angered Soviet leaders, who were already suspicious about American and British intentions. This mistrust and bitterness carried over into the postwar world.

At first, the military news was so bad that it

threatened to swamp the alliance completely. During the first six months of 1942, the Allies suffered severe defeats everywhere. German armies pushed deeper into Soviet territory and started an offensive in North Africa that menaced the Suez Canal. At sea, German submarines were crippling the transatlantic convoying of American supplies to Europe.

The news from the Pacific was even grimmer. In the wake of Pearl Harbor, Japan had scored quickly with seaborne invasions of Hong Kong, Wake Island, and Guam. Japanese forces conquered much of Burma, Malaya, and the Philippines, as well as the Solomon Islands. Japan achieved this huge expansion of territory in only three months.

A major turning point of the war occurred in the winter of 1942–1943, when the Soviets halted the German advance in the Battle of Stalingrad. Now came the task of pushing the Germans back through eastern Europe. By October 1943, Soviet armies stood on the east bank of the Dnieper River, ready to drive through the Ukraine into Romania. At the same time, the Allies launched a major offensive in North Africa, Churchill's substitute for a second front in France. Between November 1942 and May 1943, Allied troops defeated Germany's crack Afrika Korps led by General Erwin Rommel. From Africa the Allied command planned an invasion of Sicily and the Italian mainland, following Churchill's strategy of attacking Europe through what he called its "soft underbelly." By mid-1943, the fascist regime of Benito Mussolini had fallen. The Allies invaded Italy in the fall of 1943 but encountered such heavy resistance that they did not enter Rome until June 1944.

The long-awaited invasion of France came on D-Day—June 6, 1944. That morning, after an agonizing delay because of bad weather, an armada of Allied troops and equipment moved across the English Channel. The beaches of Normandy where the Allies landed—Utah, Omaha, Juno, Gold, and Sword—soon became household words in the United States. Under the command of General Dwight D. Eisenhower, more than 1.5 million soldiers landed on the beaches during the next few days. Allied troops liberated Paris in August and drove the Germans out of most of France and Belgium by September.

By the autumn of 1944, the German military situation looked hopeless. All that year, long-range Allied bombers had made daring daylight raids that damaged Nazi military and industrial installations. The massive air campaign killed about 305,000 people and wounded 780,000, showing that civilians no longer remained free from attack.

Despite the Allied assault, the Germans were not ready to give up. In December 1944, German forces in Belgium mounted an attack that started the Battle of the Bulge, named for the dent it made in the Allied defenses. After weeks of heavy fighting in what turned out to be the final

HITTING THE BEACH AT NORMANDY
These American reinforcements landed on the Normandy beach two weeks after D-Day, June 6, 1944. More than a million Allied troops came ashore during the next month. The Allies liberated Paris by August and pushed the retreating Nazi forces back behind the German border by September. (UPI)

German attack of the war, the Allies regained their momentum. Their goal was Berlin. American and British troops led the drive from the west, and Soviet troops advanced on the German capital from the east through Poland. On April 30, in what remained of Berlin, Hitler committed suicide. Germany surrendered on May 8, 1945, which became known as V-E (Victory in Europe) Day.

The United States still faced the task of defeating Japan. Throughout the war, policymakers had balanced their commitment to defeat Germany with the need to fight Japan. Unlike the combat in Europe, which was shared by U.S., British, French, and Russian troops, American forces did almost all the fighting in the

A NEW TYPE OF NAVAL WARFARE
The battles of Coral Sea and Midway in 1942 marked a revolution in naval warfare. For the first time, major sea battles were waged—and decided—primarily by planes launched from aircraft carriers. American planes such as these dive bombers sank four carriers during the Battle of Midway. (Frank Scherschel, *Life* Magazine © 1942 Time, Inc.)

Pacific. By early 1945, victory over Japan was in sight.

The tide had begun to turn on April 18, 1942, when Colonel James H. Doolittle led sixteen American bombers on the first air raid on Tokyo. On May 7–8, in the decisive Battle of the Coral Sea near southern New Guinea, American naval forces halted the Japanese offensive that had threatened to engulf Australia. Then, at the island of Midway in June, the Americans inflicted extensive damage on the Japanese fleet. Dive bombers and fighters, launched from the aircraft carriers *Enterprise*, *Hornet*, and *Yorktown*, provided the margin of victory in both battles.

From that point on, the American military command under General Douglas MacArthur and Admiral Chester W. Nimitz took the offensive in the Pacific. For the next eighteen months, American forces advanced arduously from one island to the next, winning major victories at Tulagi and Guadalcanal in the Solomon Islands and at Tarawa and Makin in the Gilberts. They reached the Marshall Islands in early 1944. In October 1944, MacArthur began the reconquest of the Philippines by winning the Battle of Leyte Gulf, a massive naval encounter. The Japanese lost practically their entire remaining fleet, while the Americans suffered only minimal losses.

The island-hopping campaign in the Pacific moved slowly toward an invasion of Japan. For a successful assault on the Japanese mainland, the Americans needed the islands of Iwo Jima and Okinawa. Airstrips there would put U.S. planes within striking distance of Tokyo. American Marines won the battles for Iwo Jima (February 14–March 20, 1945) and Okinawa (April 1–June 10) in some of the fiercest fighting of the war. At Iwo Jima, the Marines sustained more than twenty thousand casualties, including six thousand dead; at Okinawa, the toll reached thirteen thousand dead and nearly forty thousand wounded.

By mid-1945, Japan's land troops, naval ships, and air force had suffered devastating losses. American bombing of the mainland had killed about 330,000 civilians and crippled the Japanese economy. In a last-ditch effort to stem the tide, Japanese pilots began *kamikaze* (suicide) missions, crashing their planes into American ships. This desperate action suggested that Japan would not soon surrender despite its overwhelming losses.

MAP 26.3 WAR IN THE PACIFIC: THE EXTENT OF JAPANESE CONTROL, 1942–1943

After the attack on Pearl Harbor in December 1941, the Japanese rapidly extended their domination in the Pacific, both on land and at sea. The Japanese flag soon flew as far east as the Marshall and Gilbert Islands and as far south as the Solomon Islands and parts of New Guinea. Japan also controlled the Philippines, much of Southeast Asia, and parts of China, including Hong Kong. This great territorial expansion occurred in just three months.

MAP 26.4 WAR IN THE PACIFIC: THE ALLIED RESPONSE, 1944–1945

The American counterattack began in mid-1942, when the Battle of the Coral Sea stopped further Japanese expansion to the south. Allied forces retook the islands in the Central Pacific in 1943 and 1944, and the Philippines in early 1945. The capture of Iwo Jima and Okinawa put U.S. bombers in position to attack the Japanese mainland. Instead of a land invasion, with the tremendous potential loss of American lives, the United States chose to end the war quickly by dropping atomic bombs on Hiroshima and Nagasaki in August 1945.

The American Fighting Force

During World War II, the armed forces of the United States numbered more than 15 million men and women. The army enlisted the most—about 10.5 million—but almost 4 million served in the Navy, 600,000 in the Marines, and 240,000 in the Coast Guard. Although stationed in deserts, jungles, and tropical rain forests, American service personnel faced no more risk from disease than they would have at home. Medical advances cut the death rate in battle in half from the World War I level, thanks to new drugs such as penicillin and sulfa.

Draft boards registered about 31 million men between the ages of eighteen and forty-four. The draft age was lowered from twenty to eighteen in 1942. The government gave physical examinations to about a sixth of the male population prior to induction for military service. More than half the men failed to meet the minimum physical standards, which required a height of 5 feet; weight of 105 pounds; correctable vision; at least half the number of natural teeth; and no flat feet, hernia, or venereal disease. Defective teeth and eyes, traceable largely to inadequate dental and medical care, caused the greatest number of rejections.

War correspondents, including Ernie Pyle and John Hersey, reported on the GIs (short for "government issue") for readers back in the United States. "The American soldier," wrote Pyle, "is a born housewife. . . . I'll bet there's not another army in the world that makes itself a 'home away from home' as quickly as ours does." (Pyle was killed in a foxhole by a Japanese bullet during the battle for Iwo Jima.) Cartoonist Bill Mauldin created two scruffy infantrymen named Willie and Joe for the armed services newspaper *Stars and Stripes*. "Do retreatin' blisters hurt as much as advancin' blisters?" Willie asked Joe during the Italian campaign. "Joe," said Willie in another drawing, "yesterday ya saved my life an' I swore I'd pay ya back. Here's my last pair of clean socks." Such books as *A Bell for Adano* (1944) by John Hersey, *Mister Roberts* (1946) by Thomas Heggen, and *The Naked and the Dead* (1948) by Norman Mailer immortalized the war in fiction. James Jones's *From Here to Eternity* (1951) described army life in Hawaii just before the Japanese attacked Pearl Harbor.

War reporters often portrayed the GIs as ordinary boys doing their patriotic duty. John Hersey described a bunch of Marines in Guadalcanal:

> When you looked into the eyes of those boys, you did not feel sorry for the Japs: you felt sorry for the boys. The uniforms, the bravado . . . were just camouflage. . . . They were just American boys. They did not want that valley or any part of its jungle. They were ex-grocery boys, ex-highway laborers, ex-bank clerks, ex-schoolboys, boys with a clean record . . . not killers.

But, of course, soldiers were trained to kill. Another Marine who had fought at Guadalcanal painted a different picture of war than John Hersey, calling it a matter of simple survival: "The only way you could get it over with was to kill them off before they killed you. The war I knew was totally savage."

Another popular theme was the ethnic and racial diversity of the American forces. A film critic noted that almost every war movie featured "one Negro, one Jew, a Southern boy, and a sprinkling of second-generation Italians, Irish, Scandinavians and Poles." *Time* reported that the men who liberated France sounded like "the roster of an All-American eleven." Soldiers with names such as Czeklauski, Pucilowski, Hakenstod, Gemmill, Christensen, and Dreiscus fought side by side with old-stock Americans named Thacker, Walsh, Eaton, and Tyler.

Most reporters ignored the class distinctions and racial discrimination prevalent in the armed forces, much of it directed against the approximately seven hundred thousand blacks in uniform. Blacks served in all branches of the armed forces, but they were assigned the most menial duties; a great number served as messmen on navy ships, for example. The army segregated black and white blood banks, a practice without genetic or scientific merit. Race riots broke out on several military bases. The NAACP and other civil rights groups chided the government with such reminders as, "A Jim Crow army cannot fight for a free world," but the military remained rigidly segregated.

About 350,000 American women, both black and white, enlisted in the armed services and achieved permanent status in the military establishment. There were about 140,000 WACS (Women's Army Corps), 100,000 WAVES

WOMEN AVIATORS
WASPs like this flyer piloted every type of military aircraft, from the huge B-29 bombers to sleeker fighter craft. Barred from combat duty, women pilots mainly ferried planes and supplies for the Army Air Force throughout the United States and Canada. The treatment of WASPs reflected the sexism and racism of the armed forces: women's monthly pay was $70 less than comparable men's pay, and the program remained all white. Because women pilots never achieved full military status, they were ineligible for military and veterans' benefits when the war ended. (U.S. Air Force)

(Women Appointed for Volunteer Emergency Service in the Navy), 23,000 members of the Marine Corps Women's Reserve, and 13,000 SPARS in the Coast Guard. (The word SPAR comes from *Semper Paratus*, the Coast Guard motto, and *Always Ready*, the English translation.) In addition, about 1,000 WASPs (Women's Airforce Service Pilots) flew sixty million miles ferrying planes and supplies in noncombat areas. A third of the nation's registered nurses volunteered for military duty. About 60,000 served in the army, and 14,000 in the navy.

As with blacks, the armed forces limited the type of duty allowed for women. They barred women from combat, although nurses and medical personnel often served in battle, sometimes risking capture. Many jobs assigned to women in military service reflected stereotypes of women's roles in civilian life—office work, communications, and health care. The pin-up pictures widely distributed to the troops—Betty Grable in a bathing suit, Rita Hayworth in a flimsy nightgown, and, for the black soldiers, the tempestuous singer Lena Horne—were probably closer to the average GI's view of women than was a WAC in uniform.

By the spring of 1944, about a million soldiers had finished their military duty, which averaged

sixteen months, and were returning home. The war had been a dirty, bloody job, not an idealistic fight. Visions of marriage, a house in the suburbs, and a new car sustained many soldiers through its horror and tedium. By 1947, veterans and their families made up a fourth of the American population.

Wartime Diplomacy and the Onset of the Atomic Age

Throughout the war, the three leaders of the Grand Alliance met to discuss the progress of the fighting and to plan the postwar peace. In January 1943, Roosevelt and Churchill met in Casablanca, Morocco; Stalin declined to attend because the Soviet Union's battle against the Germans had reached a crucial point. In November 1943, Roosevelt finally met Stalin for the first time at a conference in Teheran, Iran. Roosevelt expressed confidence that the personal rapport he developed with Stalin would aid postwar harmony among the superpowers.

At Teheran, Roosevelt and Churchill agreed to Stalin's demand for a second front within six months. In return, Stalin promised to join the fight against Japan after the war in Europe ended. Churchill and Roosevelt also agreed to Stalin's demand to redraw Poland's borders to give the Soviet Union more territory. The three men disagreed sharply, however, about the governments that should control the rest of Poland and the neighboring eastern European states. Their failure to resolve these territorial questions in 1943 affected the postwar peace significantly. By the time of the next Big Three conference early in 1945, Soviet troops occupied most of Eastern Europe.

The three leaders held their last, and by far most controversial, wartime conference in February 1945 at Yalta, a Black Sea resort. Victory in Europe was in sight, but no agreement had been reached on the shape of the peace to come. Roosevelt was concerned about maintaining Allied unity after the war. Stalin had become increasingly inflexible on the issue of Eastern Europe, arguing that he needed friendly governments there to provide a buffer for Soviet national security. Roosevelt acknowledged the legitimacy of this demand, but he also hoped for democratically elected regimes in Poland and the neighboring countries.

The compromise reached at Yalta was open to multiple interpretations. Admiral William D. Leahy, Roosevelt's chief military aide, described the agreement as "so elastic that the Russians can stretch it all the way from Yalta to Washington without technically breaking it." As early as 1943, Roosevelt had implied that Stalin could have a free hand in Eastern Europe, but he had neglected to inform the American public of his promises. At Yalta, Roosevelt and Churchill agreed in principle to the idea of a Soviet sphere of influence in Eastern Europe, but they left its actual dimensions deliberately vague. In return, Stalin pledged to hold "free and unfettered elections" at an unspecified time. These elections never took place.

The Yalta conference also proceeded with plans to divide Germany into four zones, to be controlled by the United States, Great Britain, France, and the Soviet Union. Berlin, which lay in the middle of the Soviet zone, would also be partitioned among the four powers. The issue of German reparations remained unsettled.

The Big Three did agree on an international organization to prevent future wars and aggression. Roosevelt, determined to avoid Woodrow Wilson's mistakes, had already cultivated congressional support for American participation in a postwar organization. Realizing that such an

THE LIVING DEAD
When Allied troops advanced into Germany in the spring of 1945, they came face to face with what had long been rumored—concentration camps, Adolf Hitler's "final solution of the Jewish question." The Nazis liquidated six million Jews, plus about as many Poles, Gypsies, and Magyars, in death camps such as Buchenwald, shown here; Dachau; Bergen-Bilsen; and the extermination center at Auschwitz, Poland. (Margaret Bourke-White, *Life* Magazine © 1945 Time, Inc.)

TIME LINE
THE WORLD AT WAR

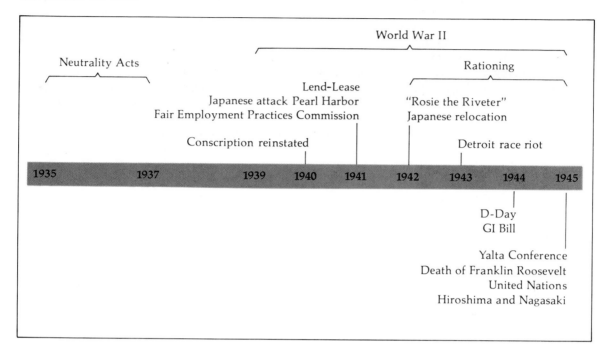

organization would be impotent without Soviet participation, he also courted Soviet support for it.

British, American, and Soviet representatives had met at Dumbarton Oaks, an estate in Washington, D.C., in September 1944 to begin planning the structure of the organization. At Yalta, the Big Three agreed that the Security Council of the United Nations should consist of five major powers—the United States, Britain, France, China, and the Soviet Union—plus six elected nations on a rotating basis. They also decided that the permanent members of the Security Council should have veto power over decisions of the United Nations General Assembly, in which all nations would be represented. Roosevelt, Churchill, and Stalin announced that the United Nations would convene in San Francisco on April 25, 1945.

Roosevelt returned to the United States in February, visibly exhausted from his fourteen-thousand-mile trip. When he reported to Congress on the Yalta agreements, he made an unusual acknowledgment of his physical infirmity. Referring to the heavy steel leg braces he always wore, he asked Congress to excuse him

if he gave his speech sitting down. Roosevelt by now was a very sick man, suffering from heart failure and hypertension. On April 12, 1945, during a short visit to his vacation home in Warm Springs, Georgia, the president suffered a cerebral hemorrhage and died. He was only sixty-three years old. Many Americans could not imagine any leader other than Franklin Roosevelt in the White House. Those who reached adulthood in the 1930s and 1940s had never known another president.

V-E Day came less than a month after Roosevelt's death and Harry Truman's ascent to the presidency. The war in the Pacific ended after the United States dropped an atomic bomb on two Japanese cities, Hiroshima on August 6, and Nagasaki on August 9. The awesome new weapons killed a hundred thousand people at Hiroshima and sixty thousand at Nagasaki. Tens of thousands more Japanese died slowly of radiation poisoning. Japan surrendered on September 2, 1945, which President Truman designated as V-J (Victory over Japan) Day. World War II had ended, but the atomic age of insecurity had just begun.

The development of the atomic bomb was

closely linked to wartime military strategy. In December 1938, German scientists had discovered that the nuclei of atoms could be split into even smaller parts, a process called fission. With materials prepared from uranium, a chain reaction of nuclear fission would release tremendous amounts of energy. American scientists, many of them refugees from Nazi Germany and fascist Italy, produced the first controlled chain reaction on December 2, 1942, at the University of Chicago.

Scientists soon began working frantically to harness such nuclear reactions for military purposes. Their goal was the development of an atomic bomb for use against Germany or, later, Japan. The secret research, called the Manhattan Project, cost $2 billion, involved the construction of thirty-seven installations in nineteen states, and employed 120,000 people, including most of the country's top physicists.

President Roosevelt followed the bomb's progress closely. He and his planners had a dual purpose for rushing the project. They wanted to use the bomb to end the war without the dreadful number of American casualties that had been predicted for an invasion of Japan. At the same time, policymakers hoped that the sole possession of such a powerful weapon by the United States would make the Soviet Union more flexible in international affairs after the war ended. Ironically, instead of lessening tensions, the atomic bomb propelled the United States and the Soviet Union into a deadly arms race conducted in an atmosphere of fear and mistrust.

Until the last moment, the scientists did not know if the atomic bomb would work. On July 16, 1945, near Alamogordo, New Mexico, they watched in wonder as the test bomb exploded into a huge mushroom cloud. President Truman received news of the successful detonation in Potsdam, near Berlin, where he was about to meet with Churchill and Stalin. Truman, who had not even known about the bomb before he became president, was ecstatic about the potential of the new weapon. He ordered the use of atomic weapons against Japanese cities and, following the destruction of Hiroshima, exclaimed to aides, "This is the greatest thing in history."

Others were not so sure. J. Robert Oppenheimer, one of the leading scientists in the Manhattan Project, watched the test on that early July morning in the New Mexico desert. Overwhelmed by its frightening power, he recalled the words from the *Bhagavad Gita*, the Hindu bible: "I am become Death, Destroyer of Worlds."

The international situation deteriorated rapidly throughout the 1930s, and the world was again at war by 1939. Although strong isolationist sentiment opposed American participation, President Roosevelt began mobilizing public opinion for U.S. intervention. The Japanese attack on Pearl Harbor on December 7, 1941, brought the nation into World War II.

Defense mobilization ended the Great Depression. As had happened during World War I, mobilization led to a dramatic expansion of the federal bureaucracy. On the home front, the war resulted in rationing and shortages of many items. Geographical mobility increased as labor shortages opened job opportunities for women, blacks, and Mexican-Americans. The ideological climate of fighting Nazism aided the cause of civil rights. However, Japanese-Americans on the West Coast suffered a devastating denial of civil liberties when the government moved them into internment camps in the nation's interior.

World War II was a global war, consisting of massive military campaigns in both Europe and the Pacific. The war news was bleak at first, but by 1943 the Allies had started to move toward victory. At the same time, Roosevelt attempted to maintain harmony among the United States, Great Britain, and the Soviet Union. Many of the problems that plagued the postwar world resulted from disagreements in wartime diplomacy.

Of all the major powers that fought in World War II, only the United States emerged physically unharmed. And at the end of the war, only the United States had the powerful new weapon, the atomic bomb.

Suggestions for Further Reading

John Morton Blum, *V Was For Victory* (1976), offers a good introduction to American politics and culture during the war years. Also useful are Richard Polenberg, *War and Society* (1972); Geoffrey Perrett, *Days of Sadness, Years of Triumph* (1973); and Richard Lingeman, *Don't You Know There's A War On?* (1970).

Internationalism Replaces Isolationism

Depression and wartime diplomacy are effectively covered in Robert Dallek, *Franklin D. Roosevelt and American Foreign Policy, 1932–1945* (1979). For more on American policy between the wars, see Lloyd Gardner, *Economic Aspects of New Deal Diplomacy* (1964), and Selig Adler, *The Uncertain Giant* (1966). William L. Langer and S. Everett Gleason provide a detailed chronology of American entry in *The Challenge to Isolation, 1937–1940* (1952) and *The Undeclared War, 1940–1941* (1953); see also Robert Divine, *The Reluctant Belligerent* (1965). Selig Adler, *The Isolationist Impulse* (1957); Manfred Jonas, *Isolationism in America* (1966); and Wayne S. Cole, *Charles A. Lindbergh and the Battle Against American Intervention in World War II* (1974), discuss American public opinion. Warren T. Kimball, *The Most Unsordid Act* (1969), describes the Lend-Lease controversy of 1939–1941. Roberta Wohlstetter, *Pearl Harbor* (1962), and Herbert Feis, *The Road to Pearl Harbor* (1950), describe the final chain of events that led to American entry.

Mobilizing for Victory

George Flynn, *The Mess in Washington* (1979); Bruce Catton, *War Lords of Washington* (1946); Donald Nelson, *Arsenal of Democracy* (1946); and Gerald T. White, *Billions for Defense* (1980), discuss America's economic mobilization. Alan Winkler, *The Politics of Propaganda* (1978), covers the Office of War Information. On labor's role during war, see Joel Seidman, *American Labor From Defense to Reconversion* (1953); Nelson Lichtenstein, *Labor's War at Home: The CIO in World War II* (1982); Howell Harris, *The Right to Manage* (1982); and Paul Koistinen, *The Hammer and the Sword: Labor, the Military, and Industrial Mobilization, 1920–1945* (1979). James C. Foster, *The Union Politic* (1975), details the CIO's political involvement. For more on politics in wartime, see James McGregor Burns, *Roosevelt: The Soldier of Freedom* (1970).

Women's roles in wartime are covered by Susan Hartmann, *The Home Front and Beyond* (1982); Karen Anderson, *Wartime Women* (1980); Leila J. Rupp, *Mobilizing Women for War* (1978); and William Chafe, *The American Woman* (1972).

The Home Front

Additional material on America's home-front experience can be gleaned from Richard Polenberg, ed., *The War at Home* (1968), and Lester Chandler, *Inflation in the United States, 1940–1948* (1951). Alan Clive, *State of War* (1979), provides a case study of Michigan during World War II. The experience of black Americans is treated by A. Russell Buchanan, *Black Americans in World War II* (1977); Neil Wynn, *The Afro-American and the Second World War* (1975); and Louis Ruchames, *Race, Jobs, and Politics* (1953). August Meier and Elliott Rudwick, *CORE* (1973), describes the founding of this important civil rights organization. Richard Dalfiume, *Desegregation of the U.S. Armed Forces* (1969), covers black soldiers in the military. Two compelling accounts of Japanese relocation are Audre Girdner and Anne Loftus, *The Great Betrayal* (1969), and Roger Daniels, *Concentration Camps, USA* (1972).

Victory

Extensive material chronicles the American military experience during World War II. Albert R. Buchanan, *The United States and World War II* (two volumes, 1962), and Russell F. Weigley, *The American Way of War* (1973), provide overviews. Cornelius Ryan, *The Last Battle* (1966), and John Toland, *The Last Hundred Days* (1966), describe the end of the fighting in Europe. For the Far East, see John Toland, *Rising Sun: The Decline and Fall of the Japanese Empire* (1970); William Manchester, *American Caesar* (1979) on General Douglas MacArthur; and Barbara Tuchman, *Stilwell and the American Experience in China* (1971).

American diplomacy and the strategy of the Grand Alliance are surveyed in Dallek, *Franklin D. Roosevelt and American Foreign Policy;* William McNeill, *America, Britain, and Russia, 1941–1946* (1953); and Gaddis Smith, *American Diplomacy during the Second World War* (1965). The relationship between the wartime conferences and the onset of the Cold War are treated by Walter LaFeber, *America, Russia, and the Cold War* (1976); John L. Gaddis, *The United States and the Origins of the Cold War* (1972); and Herbert Feis, *Between War and Peace* (1960). Martin Sherwin, *A World Destroyed* (1975), provides a compelling account of the development of the atomic bomb; it can be supplemented by Gar Alperovitz, *Atomic Diplomacy* (1965), and Gregg Herken, *The Winning Weapon* (1980).

27

AFFLUENCE AND ITS CONTRADICTIONS

By 1945, four years of war-induced prosperity had made the American people the richest in the world. Over the next two decades, the gross national product more than tripled, and Americans became even more affluent. Industrial workers in the largest smokestack industries found their unions accepted at last, and their wages rose and fringe benefits expanded. Employees of the successful large corporations— New York accountants, Georgia factory managers, Chicago engineers, San Francisco advertising executives, Dallas office managers—saw their incomes increase as well. Soon they were able to move their families into new houses in the suburbs, where they joined the doctors, lawyers, bankers, and brokers who serviced the growing metropolitan areas.

At the heart of this postwar prosperity lay the involvement of the federal government in national economic life; by the mid-1950s, federal expenditures accounted for a fifth of the gross national product. Another component of postwar prosperity was the "baby boom"—the dramatic rise in the nation's birthrate—which heightened demand for goods and services by the expanding middle class. Increased federal outlays for defense and domestic programs, combined with galloping consumer spending,

seemed to promise a continually rising standard of living.

Meanwhile, the nation's economy underwent sweeping structural and technological changes. Agriculture declined as an occupation, white-collar employment rose, and women entered the labor force in unprecedented numbers. Bureaucracies grew larger and corporations more diversified. Such changes often proved disruptive to individual American workers—the farmers who were forced off their land, the alienated assembly-line workers, the bored clerical workers who watched the clock from 9 to 5, and the middle-level managers who tried desperately to fit into impersonal corporate bureaucracies. The bountiful advantages of affluence were tempered by unsettling changes in the lives of ordinary Americans.

Postwar society was also characterized by the growing concentration of population in metropolitan areas. Urbanization, one of the most momentous changes of the nineteenth and early twentieth centuries, had slowed to a trickle during the Great Depression. After 1940, urban migration accelerated once again, with the new arrivals settling not just in cities but in their surrounding suburbs. Poor migrants from rural areas, Puerto Rico, and Mexico, lured by dreams of better jobs and housing, moved into the central cities. The more affluent migrants moved to suburban housing developments on the surrounding fringe. State and local governments struggled to cope with both kinds of growth.

Between 1945 and the mid-1960s, affluence and abundance permeated most—but not all—aspects of American society. In certain areas, those themes of the immediate postwar period continued to characterize American social and economic life through the 1970s. At the same time, underlying contradictions tempered the complacency that went with being the richest nation in the world. These lurking problems in the economic, social, and political spheres eventually surfaced, setting the tone for American life from the 1960s to the present.

Technology and Economic Change

After 1945, technological change transformed one sector of the American economy after another. In agriculture, large-scale agribusiness replaced the old family farm. Industry increasingly relied on automation, and the nation became a society of white-collar clerks rather than producers of goods. Meanwhile, business corporations diversified both domestically and internationally. Accompanying these structural changes was the steady performance of the American economy. The country's gross national product grew from $213 billion in 1945 to more than $500 billion in 1960; by 1970, the GNP approached $1 trillion. Much of this growth was fueled by increased federal spending, especially for defense.

The Economic Record

The impact of war mobilization laid the foundations for postwar economic developments. The United States enjoyed overwhelming political and economic advantages at the end of World War II. Unlike the Soviet Union, which had lost more than 20 million citizens, or Western Europe and Japan, whose landscapes and economies had been devastated by the fighting, the United States emerged physically unscathed from the war. In fact, the U.S. economy was in far stronger shape in 1945 than when the war began. Consumers had accumulated wartime

CONSUMER CULTURE
This 1962 painting by Tom Wesselman mocks the consumer culture that it so lavishly illustrates with a table well stocked with brand-name goods. Realistic painting in the 1960s took on an air of cynicism, especially as practiced by artists such as Andy Warhol. Wesselman's *Still Life* treats the most ordinary objects of American life as icons, hinting at the new power of consumerism in popular culture. (*Still Life No. 24.* The Nelson-Atkins Museum of Art, Kansas City, Mo. Gift of the Guild of the Friends of Art)

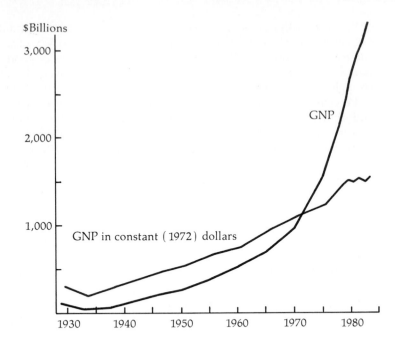

FIGURE 27.1 GROSS
NATIONAL PRODUCT,
1929–1983

savings of $140 billion, which created a strong market for the consumer goods that had been unavailable during the war. The federal government eased conversion to a peacetime economy by allowing businesses to buy factories built for the war effort at a fraction of their cost. In addition, business quickly applied the scientific and technological innovations developed for war production, such as plastics and synthetic fibers, to the production of consumer goods.

To working Americans, the steady growth of the gross national product meant a 25 percent rise in real income between 1946 and 1959. Most Americans rightly felt they had more money to spend than ever before. In 1940, 43 percent of American families owned their homes; by 1960, 62 percent did. But while the standard of living was rising, there was no redistribution of income. The percentage of income received by each segment of the population was substantially the same as it had been in 1939 and in 1910. Americans were living better, but the concentration of income remained unchanged—the top tenth still earned more than the bottom half.

One reason ordinary Americans felt better off was that inflation finally had been brought under control by the 1950s, a boon to both investors and individuals on fixed incomes. Inflation had skyrocketed during the immediate postwar

reconversion period; it averaged 7 percent per year in the 1940s. By contrast, inflation slowed to 2 to 3 percent annually during the 1950s. It stayed low until 1965, when the increased military spending for the Vietnam War set off an inflationary spiral that pushed inflation rates to the 7 to 10 percent range for the next fifteen years. The dramatic rise in world oil prices after 1973 further fueled inflation.

Despite high rates of economic growth, a rise in real income, and low inflation, there was an unevenness to the postwar economy that qualified the rosy picture of economic success and affluence. The economy was plagued by periodic recessions accompanied by high unemployment. At the height of the 1948–1949 recession, unemployment hit 8 percent, although it soon fell to 3 percent with the partial mobilization for the Korean War. Twice when the Eisenhower administration cut defense spending (at the end of the Korean War in 1953 and again in 1957–1958), recessions set in. In the severe 1957 recession, unemployment exceeded 8 percent. Even in nonrecessionary years, the unemployment rate ranged from 4.1 to 5.5 percent, meaning that between 2.7 and 3.7 million workers could not find work. The unemployment rate for nonwhite men averaged 10.6 percent between 1955 and 1959, more than double the rate for white males. During the early 1960s, the general unemployment rate ranged from 5 to 6 percent.

These persistent levels of high unemployment show that not all Americans shared in the general prosperity. The permanently unemployed, the aged, female-headed households, and non-whites all found themselves at a significant disadvantage. Economist John Kenneth Galbraith, whose book *The Affluent Society* (1958) surveyed the modern economic structure, admitted that the poor were only an "afterthought" in the minds of economists and politicians, who assumed that poverty was well on its way to extinction. Yet, as he noted, more than one family out of thirteen in the 1950s had a cash income of less than a thousand dollars. Not until the publication of Michael Harrington's forceful *The Other America* (1962) did most middle- and upper-class Americans begin to wake up to the fact that between 40 and 50 million Americans—a fourth of the population—were poor.

The Agricultural Revolution

In the major postwar transformations that the economic system underwent, no sector changed more dramatically than agriculture. The number of American farmers had grown until 1910, and even in 1935 nearly a third of all gainfully employed Americans were farmers or farm workers. As late as the end of World War II, a fourth of the American work force consisted of farmers. During the next twenty-five years, however, 25 million people left rural America; by 1969, only 5 percent of the population lived on farms. A federal task force on rural development called this shift "one of the largest migrations of people in recorded history," rivaling European immigration to the New World and America's westward expansion.

This farm-to-city migration was the result of two interrelated trends—a technological revolution in agriculture that reduced the need for labor, and the steady decline of the small, often subsistence, family farm. These agricultural developments in turn dovetailed with the growing metropolitanization of American life.

New technology brought an astonishing increase in agricultural productivity after 1945. Before the war, the typical American farm had been a small, modestly equipped family enter-

prise where horses and mules outnumbered tractors. In 1935, an hour of labor produced about 2½ pounds of cotton, 2 bushels of wheat, just over 1 bushel of corn, 33 pounds of milk, or 3 chickens. In the next two decades, the massive application of new technology—such as harvesting machines, better seed, and improved chemical fertilizers and pesticides—revolutionized farming. By 1978, a single hour's labor produced 50 pounds of cotton, 11 bushels of wheat, 25 bushels of corn, 250 pounds of milk, or 100 chickens. This improved output often had unforeseen consequences. While chemicals such as DDT were initially hailed as miracles of modern science, the publication of Rachel Carson's book *Silent Spring* in 1962 forced consumers and government officials to confront the hazards such pesticides posed to human life.

Mechanization also enabled a farmer to manage a larger farm. Between 1940 and 1980, the average size of an American farm grew two and a half times, from 180 acres to 450. Such

IMPROVED FARM MACHINERY
This machine could plant multiple rows of corn or soybeans while dispensing fertilizer and insecticide. The rising cost of farm machinery was one of the factors that threatened the survival of small family farms. In the late 1940s, a tractor cost a maximum of about $1,500. By the mid-1970s, it cost between $20,000 and $30,000, with some models approaching $100,000. (USDA, Soil Conservation Service)

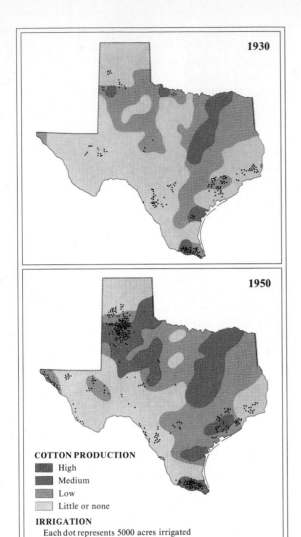

MAP 27.1 AGRICULTURAL ADVANCES IN TEXAS

In Texas, as elsewhere, the major changes in cotton production after 1930 included government price supports begun by the New Deal; greater reliance on chemicals and pesticides; and the growing use of machinery. Irrigation was largely responsible for increased production in arid regions of southeastern and northern Texas.

large-scale agriculture required major capital investments, beginning with investment in increasingly expensive land. Between 1940 and 1955, the cost of fuel and repairs for farm machines quadrupled, the cost of fertilizer quadrupled, and total operating costs tripled. Family farms often lacked the capital to compete with

the large, technologically advanced farm units. In 1948, the 10 percent of American farms with the most acreage produced 24 percent of the total farm output. By 1974, their share had more than doubled to 55 percent.

The technological revolution transformed the lives of many of those who remained on the land. American farmers had long sought to produce the crops that would bring the greatest return in the market, but they had often hedged their bets by producing a diversified array of crops for sale as well as for home consumption. As long as they had relied on horses and mules, farmers had also enjoyed considerable self-sufficiency in terms of energy and fertilizer.

All this now came to an end. Each farmer began to specialize in the one or two crops that yielded the highest return on investment. Land formerly devoted to oats and hay to feed farm animals was now planted for corn, soybeans, or other cash crops. The farmer relied on outside industrial sources for fertilizer, feed, seed, and pesticides and for the energy needed to run the expanding array of gasoline-powered equipment. Farm families increasingly purchased consumer goods from commercial sources, rather than producing them at home.

After 1940, American farmers lost their intimate connection with the land. They now managed specialized organizations—small factories that poured industrial materials into the land and extracted raw products for immediate sale. Farming had become a business enterprise,

TABLE 27.1 TRENDS IN AMERICAN FARMING, 1935–1980

	Number of farms (thousands)	Farm population (thousands)	Percent of total population
1935	6,814	32,161	25.3%
1940	6,350	30,547	23.1
1945	5,967	24,420	17.5
1950	5,648	23,048	15.2
1956*	4,514	18,712	11.1
1960	3,963	15,635	8.7
1965	3,356	12,363	6.4
1970	2,949	9,712	4.7
1975	2,521	8,864	4.2
1980	2,428	6,051	2.7

*Data unavailable for 1955.
Source: Gilbert Fite, American Farmers (Bloomington: Indiana University Press, 1981). 101.

closely tied to other business enterprises. These ties made farmers, like other businesspeople, increasingly dependent on national and international market conditions, on scientific and technological developments, and on federal economic and farm policies.

The fuller integration of farmers into the national economy, and the diminishing number of Americans who made farming their occupation, greatly reduced the differences between rural and urban life. Farmers, once a major force in political life, no longer wielded much clout in electoral politics except in the United States Senate, where a bloc of farm states still affected national policy. At the same time, the introduction of electricity and labor-saving machinery on the farm lessened the harshness of farm life. Measurable farm income, which ranged from only 40 to 60 percent of the national average between the 1930s and 1950s, rose above 80 percent—and briefly to 110 percent—in the 1970s. As farm income rose and farming came to resemble other occupations, those who remained on the farm increasingly shared the experiences, views, and aspirations of other Americans.

White-Collar World

A revolution in American industry paralleled the revolution in agriculture. Well into the 1940s, the United States had been a nation of goods producers. By 1956, however, a majority of Americans were white-collar workers. The sociologist C. Wright Mills captured the new white-collar world in this riveting image: "What must be grasped is the picture of society as a great salesroom, an enormous file, an incorporated brain, a new universe of management and manipulation." In many ways, this shift of American workers into commerce, government, services, and the professions was as significant a watershed as the closing of the frontier in 1890. Soon panelists on the popular TV quiz show "What's My Line?" learned to ask their mystery guests this question: "Do you deal in services?"

Numbers suggest the dimension of the shift. In 1940, two-thirds of all workers held blue-collar jobs that required them to use physical strength and skills to make products. From 1947 to 1957, the number of factory workers dropped 4 percent, while the ranks of clerical workers rose 23 percent and those of salaried middle-class work-

THE RISING WHITE-COLLAR WORK FORCE
These salespeople at Macy's department store in New York, photographed in 1956, represented the increase in service and retail jobs that characterized the postwar economy. Sales jobs, although not paying high salaries, were considered respectable for women, partly because the flexible hours allowed female workers to combine employment with their family roles. (Eliot Elisofon, *Life* Magazine © 1956 Time, Inc.)

ers jumped 61 percent. A new middle class was created by America's transformation from a society of producers to one of white-collar workers. The new middle class consisted of corporate managers, salaried professionals (such as teachers, professors, and researchers), salespeople, and office workers. They earned a salary, which distinguished them from self-employed entrepreneurs and from service and blue-collar workers who earned an hourly wage. These new members of the middle class had taken advantage of the great expansion of high school and college education after the 1920s, and the explosion of universities after 1945, to make themselves much better educated than their elders. Their new skills enabled them to advance more quickly, and at a younger age, than previous generations. Such advancement usually led them through the giant corporate structures—big business, government agencies, universities, and other bureaucratic organizations—that came to dominate the twentieth century.

The upper level of new middle class had little time to identify with any particular residential community. Atlas Van Lines estimated in the 1950s that corporate managers moved an average of fourteen times—once every two and a half years—during their careers. Perpetually mobile IBM managers joked that the company's initials stood for "I've Been Moved."

Switching jobs, or even careers, necessitated such personality traits as adaptability and the ability to get along in a variety of situations. Corporate managers worked hard, sometimes with the assistance of the resident corporate psychologist, to be "well adjusted." Their philosophy was "Evade, don't confront." Sociologist David Riesman contrasted the stern, formal, "inner-directed" small business and professional types of earlier years with the new managers of the postwar world. He concluded that members of the new middle class were "other-directed," more concerned about their relations with their immediate associates than about adherence to fundamental principles. Sociologist William Whyte painted a more somber picture of these "organization men" as "the ones of our middle class who have left home spiritually as well as physically to take the vows of organization life."

The new middle class accepted a strong role for the federal government in modern economic life. The managers of large corporations and their professional neighbors had shed the small entrepreneur's traditional opposition to government regulation. Many of the new middle class voted Democratic. They had seen their families hurt by the Great Depression and felt that the New Deal and wartime changes had given them opportunities far superior to those available to their parents. "As the poor and underprivileged prospered and climbed they remained loyal to the Democratic party," journalist Samuel Lubell concluded in 1952. "The new middle class . . . seems as Democratic by custom as the older middle class elements are instinctively Republican."

The Changing World of Work

The new hierarchy of work confused old patterns of status and class. In the late nineteenth century, an office job as a secretary was a prized

FIGURE 27.2 LABOR UNION STRENGTH, 1900–1984

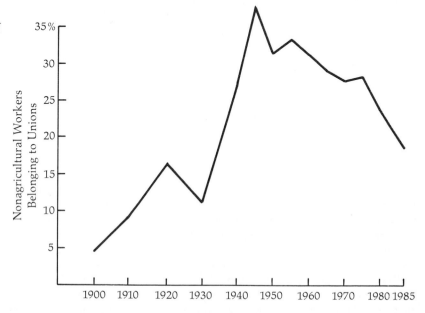

STEELWORKER IN LORDSTOWN, OHIO

They use time, stopwatches. They say, It takes so many seconds or hundreds of seconds to walk from here to there. We know it takes so many seconds to shoot a screw. We know the gun turns so fast, the screw's so long, the hole's so deep. Our argument has always been: That's mechanical; that's not human.

The workers said, We perspire, we sweat, we have hangovers, we have upset stomachs, we have feelings and emotions, and we're not about to be placed in a category of a machine. When you talk about that watch, you talk about it for a minute. We talk about a lifetime. We're gonna do what's normal and we're gonna tell you what's normal. We'll negotiate from there. We're not gonna start on a watch-time basis that has no feelings.

When they took the unimates on, we were building sixty [Vegas] an hour. When we came back to work, with the unimates, we were bulding a hundred cars an hour. A unimate is a welding robot. It looks just like a praying mantis. It goes from spot to spot to spot. It releases that thing and it jumps back into position, ready for the next car. They go by them about 110 an hour. They never tire, they never sweat, they never complain, they never miss work. Of course, they don't buy cars. I guess General Motors doesn't understand that argument.

Source: Gary Bryner, interviewed in Studs Terkel, *Working.* New York: Pantheon, 1974, 190–191.

---

position for a working woman, a badge of upward social mobility and respectability, as well as an opportunity for increased pay. By the 1950s, the jobs of office workers were not too different from those of factory operatives—narrow, repetitive, and lacking in control and autonomy. Confounding the old formula that work with your brain counted for more than work with your hands, many unionized factory operatives had higher incomes than those in service or professional occupations such as teaching and social work.

The changing structural composition of the work force and the shifting nature of work itself posed challenges for the labor movement in the postwar world. Labor unions reached the peak of their strength immediately after the war. By 1955, the schisms of the 1930s had healed enough that Walter P. Reuther of the United Automobile Workers could lead the CIO back into an alliance with the AFL. This merger created a single organization, the AFL-CIO, that represented more than 90 percent of the nation's 17.5 million union members. George Meany, a New York building-trade unionist, headed this organization from 1955 to 1979.

New priorities shaped labor-management relations after World War II. Postwar inflation and changing patterns of consumption produced demands for higher incomes. Wage increases brought many workers real incomes that were secure, predictable, and steadily rising. In exchange, union leaders promised labor peace and stability—that is, fewer strikes. In 1950, General Motors and the United Automobile Workers signed a contract containing two key provisions. An escalator clause provided that wages would be adjusted to reflect changes in the cost of living, and a productivity clause guaranteed that wages would rise as productivity in the industry increased. In 1955, autoworkers won a guaranteed annual wage.

These contracts shared a common tendency to emphasize union members' status as consumers rather than workers. George Meany accepted the thrust of government-subsidized business prosperity; his goal was to ensure that labor got its share. Workers paid for these improved wages not only by limiting the number and duration of strikes, but also by putting aside their traditional claims for control over the pace of work. In return for higher wages and fringe benefits, workers allowed technologically minded managers to exert increasing control over their lives on the job.

But labor still had to fight for legitimacy in postwar society. The most virulent antilabor attack came in 1947, when Congress passed the Taft-Hartley Act. This law outlawed the closed shop and restricted the political power of unions by prohibiting the use of union dues for political activity. It allowed the president to declare a

60-day cooling-off period in strikes with national impact. Unions especially disliked Section 14b of the act, which allowed states to pass "right to work" laws to prohibit the union shop. Taft-Hartley chipped away at some of the protections guaranteed by the 1935 National Labor Relations Act and showed that the New Deal labor reforms remained controversial a decade after their passage.

The displacement of American jobs by expansion abroad posed another problem for labor leaders and workers alike. Between 1957 and 1967, General Electric built sixty-one plants overseas. Its rationale was simple: why pay workers in its Ashland, Massachusetts plant $3.40 an hour when workers in Singapore would be glad to do the work at 30 cents an hour? By the 1960s and 1970s, plant closings and relocations had become rampant, costing the United States close to a million jobs between 1966 and 1971, according to an AFL-CIO estimate. General Instruments transferred TV-tuner production from New England to Portuguese and Taiwanese factories, and over three thousand jobs at home were lost. Zenith radio laid off more than seven thousand American workers when it relocated production to Taiwan.

Unions found it difficult to develop a consistent response to the foreign threat. Labor was at a distinct disadvantage because large industrial corporations had international mobility; they could take their operations anywhere. Union workers, though, could not follow jobs out of the country. Even moving to different parts of the United States to follow work, as when companies left the Northeast for the South or West, was difficult. Switching occupations entirely was harder still, especially for older workers. "People are not fungible," observed one study of the global corporation. "The man who assembles radios cannot easily become a computer programmer or a packaged-food salesman."

The labor movement also faced displacement of union workers by automation. Mechanization had long threatened skilled workers, but, by the 1950s, new technology affected the jobs of unskilled factory operatives as well. By 1977, four hundred thousand workers in the steel industry produced twice as much steel as six hundred thousand had in 1947. Similar patterns held in the automobile industry, which had pioneered the assembly line. In 1952, Ford Motor Company introduced automatic drilling machines at a Cleveland engine plant, enabling 41 workers to do a job that formerly employed 117. By the 1970s, automatic machines equipped with sensors not only determined whether engine blocks had been produced in accordance with specifications, but also corrected the defects.

When labor leader Walter Reuther inspected one of these automated engine plants, a Ford manager kidded him: "Well, you won't be able to collect dues from all these automated machines." "You know," Reuther replied, "that is not what is bothering me. What is bothering me is, how are you going to sell cars to all of these machines?" Reuther's reply was right on the mark. Without workers earning sufficient income to continue buying consumer goods, the American economy would falter.

These structural changes affected the labor movement in the postwar period. During the momentous 1930s and 1940s, unions had organized heavy industries such as mining, manufacturing, construction, and transportation, but these sectors were no longer growing. The labor movement had to look elsewhere for new recruits, such as the less skilled, often black or Hispanic, workers in the lower-paying service and agricultural sectors or the millions of secretaries and file clerks in the nation's offices. The union movement needed to expand its industrial midwestern base into southern and western states, areas of rapid economic growth that were traditionally antiunion. Organized labor also had to woo younger workers who now saw unions as part of management, rather than as advocates of the rank and file. Finally, it had to branch out to organize white-collar employees in such previously untapped professions as teaching, nursing, and municipal services.

Organized labor met some, but not all, of these new challenges. By the mid-1950s, the labor movement had stalled. The unionized percentage of the nonagricultural work force peaked at 35.5 percent in 1946 and held level until 1954. Then union membership began a steady decline—31.4 percent in 1960, 27.3 percent in 1970, 23 percent in 1980, and 18.8 percent in 1984. This erosion of the labor movement stood in stark contrast to labor's vitality at the end of the New Deal.

Corporations in an Unpredictable World

Successful corporate managers adopted four strategies to cope with risk and uncertainty in the postwar economic world. They tapped federal money for research and development, diversified their range of products, expanded their multinational operations, and sought to improve their ability to plan. In the struggle to survive and expand in the changing postwar economy, giant corporations had a distinct advantage. In 1968, the five hundred largest corporations controlled 64 percent of all industrial sales in the United States. By 1973, the annual sales of General Motors were greater than the gross national products of Switzerland, Pakistan, or South Africa.

The pattern of business-government partnership that had been accelerated by World War II continued to characterize modern corporate life in the postwar period. According to the National Science Foundation, federal money underwrote 90 percent of the cost of research on aviation and space, 65 percent on electricity and electronics, 42 percent on scientific instruments, 24 percent on automobiles, and 20 percent on chemicals. With the government footing part of the bill, corporations transformed new ideas into useful products faster than ever before. After the Pentagon backed IBM's investment of $5 billion in integrated circuits in the 1960s, the new devices, crucial to the computer revolution, were in commercial production within three years.

Diversification was the most important corporate strategy of the postwar era. The classic corporation of the early twentieth century had produced a single line of products. After World War II, the most successful managers developed new product lines and moved into new markets. Because the largest corporations could afford research laboratories, they diversified more easily. CBS, for example, hired the Hungarian inventor Peter Goldmark, who developed color television during the 1940s, long-playing records in the 1950s, and a video recording system in the 1960s. As head of CBS Laboratories, Goldmark patented more than a hundred new devices.

Postwar managers also diversified through mergers, acquiring other firms to make it easier to invest in expanding new markets. The nation's third great merger wave (the first two had taken place during the 1890s and the 1920s) climaxed during the 1960s. International Telephone and Telegraph became a diversified conglomerate corporation by acquiring Continental Baking, Sheraton Hotels, Avis Rent-a-Car, Levitt and Sons home builders, and Hartford Fire Insurance. Ling-Temco-Vought, another conglomerate, simultaneously produced steel, built ships, developed real estate, and brought cattle to market. In 1947, the largest two hundred corporations accounted for 30 percent of all value added by manufacturing. By 1972, the largest two hundred, now heavily diversified, accounted for 43 percent of this sum.

Expansion into foreign markets also helped managers build giant corporations. International strategies enabled American business to enter new areas when domestic markets became saturated or when American recessions cut into sales. By the 1970s, such corporations as Gillette, IBM, Mobil, and Coca-Cola earned more than half their profits abroad. ITT had a worldwide payroll of 425,000 workers in seventy countries.

In their effort to direct large organizations through the uncertainties of the postwar economy, managers placed increasing emphasis on a fourth master strategy, planning. Always anxious to know how much they could sell and when a competing product might take over their markets, corporate planners tried to take economic, technological, and social trends into account as they weighed and balanced corporate investments. Top executives were increasingly recruited for their business-school training, their ability to manage information, and their skill in corporate planning, marketing, and investment. As a result, corporate managers found themselves working more closely with their counterparts in other corporations, large banks, investment firms, economic research organizations, and the federal government.

The predominant thrust of modern corporate life after 1945 was consolidation of economic and financial resources in oligopolies, where a few large producers controlled the national and, increasingly, the world market. In 1970, the top four U.S. firms produced 91 percent of all motor vehicles; the top four in tires produced 72 percent, in cigarettes 84 percent, and in detergents

70 percent. In 1970, the four largest banks held 16 percent of the nation's banking assets; the top fifty banks held 48 percent.

A case study of the beer industry illustrates this growing concentration of economic power. Beer has always been a highly profitable, high-volume business. At the end of World War II, the United States had about 450 breweries. Each produced a distinctive-tasting brand of beer, due to variations in the local water and differences in brewing techniques. New York City alone had more than a dozen beers, many of which were brewed by family-run businesses.

In the early 1950s, this pattern of competing products and regional diversity changed dramatically. Large corporations went after the national market that had been created in part by advertising on network television. National companies such as Anheuser-Busch developed a beer that could be manufactured anywhere in the country, no matter what the local water was like. They then used modern marketing techniques to push this homogenized product.

Soon the national brands were driving out local competition. Whereas the seven leading beers in 1946 had accounted for barely 20 percent of national sales, by 1970 the ten largest breweries had captured 70 percent of the beer market. In 1960, the number of breweries had dropped to 170; by 1970, it was down to 70. American consumers could find the beer advertised on their favorite television programs at local supermarkets, but they were choosing among a much smaller selection of beers with much blander taste. In beer, as in many other consumer industries, oligopolistic concentration and a national consumer market cut the variety of products—and thus the diversity of American life.

Cities and Suburbs

In the postwar years, Americans lived predominantly in metropolitan areas, largely because available jobs and housing were concentrated there. Economic activity in the twenty-five largest metropolitan areas picked up considerably after 1945. This growth did not occur in the central cities, which lost 300,000 jobs, but in the surrounding suburban areas, which gained an astounding 4 million jobs. By the late 1960s, suburbs surpassed cities in the number of manufacturing jobs they offered. Only in white-collar office work did inner-city employment rise.

These patterns of employment and economic growth reinforced the growing gap between city dwellers and their suburban neighbors. Metropolitan areas developed a striking pattern of residential segregation that persists to this day. Poorer people, many of them nonwhites, clustered in the decaying inner cities, while the more prosperous middle class flocked to the suburbs.

Metropolitan Life

As early as 1880, demographers had noticed the appearance of sprawling metropolitan areas centered around one or more large cities and including scattered suburbs and satellite towns. That year, the U.S. Census identified twenty-five such regions, ranging in size from New York–Brooklyn–Newark, with 6,500,000 people, to Portland, Oregon, with 215,000. In 1920, the Census Bureau announced that urban population had surpassed rural for the first time, a major turning point in the modern era. By then, a dozen metropolitan areas—located on the Atlantic Coast, near the Great Lakes or the Ohio River, or in California—had at least a million people each. Pilots flying along the East Coast at night began to notice that they could no longer distinguish one city from the next; a continuous strand of light stretched from Newport News, Virginia, past New York, and up to Boston. After World War II, metropolitan regions became the dominant form of American settlement. They had two-thirds of the people in 1960, and three-fourths by 1980.

The growth of new metropolitan areas was most striking in the South and West, where large portions of the population had traditionally been rural and impoverished. Miami, strengthened by the capital and expertise of thousands of refugees from Fidel Castro's revolution in Cuba in 1959, developed into an important center for the management of trade with Latin America. Texas cities grew as the petrochemical industry expanded rapidly after 1945; the oil and gas industries, together with the banks and law firms that served them, concentrated in Hous-

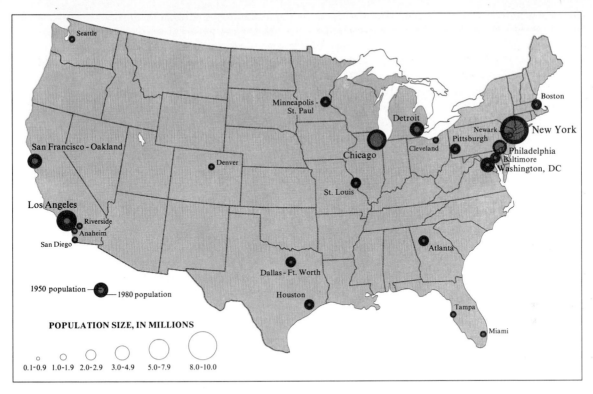

MAP 27.2 METROPOLITAN GROWTH, 1950–1980

A metropolitan area is generally defined as a central city which, in combination with its surrounding territory, forms an integrated economic and social unit. The U.S. Census Bureau introduced the "Standard Metropolitan Statistical Area" in 1950, but later changes in the definition of what comprises an SMSA makes it difficult to generalize from the 1950 figures. This map compares the population of central cities in 1950 with population figures for the more broadly defined metropolitan areas in 1980 to illustrate the extent and geographic distribution of metropolitan growth in the postwar period.

ton. Other expanding cities included Atlanta, Baton Rouge, Long Beach, Mobile, and Phoenix. By the 1970s, boosters were heralding the booming metropolitan economies of the "Sun Belt." Overall, the South and West grew twice as fast as the Northeast between 1940 and 1970.

California provided the most dramatic example of this new growth. Acting as a magnet that pulled people from all parts of the country, California absorbed 2.6 million people in the 1940s and added 3.1 million more in the 1950s. Much of this growth was spurred by expansion of defense industries, such as aircraft and electronics. By 1970, California had about a tenth of the entire U.S. population. Reflecting this growth, California was allotted twenty-five electoral votes in 1940 but forty-five in 1970; by contrast, New York's declined from forty-seven to forty-one in the same period. The only state that rivaled this

phenomenal growth was Florida, which added 3.5 million people, many of them older or retired Americans, between 1940 and 1970. State growth of another kind was represented by the admission of Alaska and Hawaii to the union in 1959.

During the postwar era, professional sports mirrored the new patterns of geographical and sectional growth, heralding a broader definition of a "big-league city." In 1958, baseball's Brooklyn Dodgers moved to Los Angeles and the New York Giants went to San Francisco. Teams in other professional sports also followed the sprawling metropolitan population. The New England Patriots played football in Foxboro, Massachusetts, halfway between Boston and Providence; the Detroit Lions moved to Pontiac, Michigan; and the Los Angeles Rams played in suburban Orange County.

While the older metropolitan areas in the

Northeast grew less rapidly than the new Sun-belt centers, they experienced fundamental changes in their economies. Boston and nearby Lowell, Lawrence, and Salem, Massachusetts, lost most of their textile and manufacturing jobs, but high-technology industries that produced Polaroid instant cameras and Digital and Wang computers gave new life to the New England economy. Several high-tech companies moved into rehabilitated mill buildings, with whirring disk drives replacing clanking textile looms. New York City lost many of its garment-making and printing jobs, but outlying areas profited from the relocation of corporate headquarters to sub-urbs such as White Plains, New York, and Stam-ford, Connecticut. Grumman and Northrup developed an important airplane and weapons-manufacturing industry on Long Island.

Their similar appearances and economies gave metropolitan regions less sharply defined social and economic profiles than had prevailed in the late nineteenth and early twentieth centu-ries. In 1940, the average person in the three wealthiest regions of the country—the Far West, the Middle Atlantic states, and New England—had 95 percent more income than the average American in the three poorest sections—the South Atlantic, the Southwest, and the South Central states. In 1960, incomes in the wealthiest sections were 50 percent higher than those in the poorest sections; in 1980, they were only 20 per-cent higher. The advent of metropolitan econo-mies and the dramatic decline in subsistence farming caused by the agricultural revolution en-abled people in the southern and mountain states to have incomes similar to those earned elsewhere in the nation. The migration of poor blacks and whites out of rural areas such as Ap-palachia into northern cities provided a further equalizer by relocating rural poverty to urban areas. Regional economic inequalities that had persisted since Reconstruction finally began to disappear.

Urban Neighborhoods, Urban Poverty

"The world's image of Los Angeles," wrote a British critic, "is of an endless plan endlessly gridded with endless streets, peppered endlessly with ticky-tacky houses clustered in indistin-guishable neighborhoods, slashed across by endless freeways that have destroyed any community spirit that may once have existed." This view, widely held, was somewhat unfair. It ignored the rich diversity of social life in Los An-geles—and every other metropolitan area. The differentiation of neighborhoods reflected cul-tural preferences and economic and racial pres-sures.

Migration from other parts of the country and from abroad added to the growth and ethnic di-versity of the nation's urban population. The War Brides Act of 1946 and the Displaced Per-

SUBURBAN SPRAWL
This new housing development, built in Los Angeles in 1965, symbolized the dramatic growth that characterized many Sun Belt cities during the postwar period. In 1940, Los Angeles was the nation's fifth largest city with a population of 1.5 million. By the early 1980s, 3 million people lived in Los Angeles, and 7.5 million in its metropolitan area. Los Angeles passed Chicago, which had been number two (hence its nickname, "the Second City"), since 1900. (© Bruce Davidson, Magnum)

sons Act of 1948 permitted large numbers of people from southern and eastern Europe and from Asia to enter the United States. The Immigration Act of 1965 abolished the national quota system imposed in 1924 and set a new annual limit of 290,000 immigrants—170,000 from the Eastern Hemisphere, 120,000 from the Western. Husbands, wives, and children of U.S. citizens were exempt from these quotas, as were specially identified groups of refugees from Cuba and Indochina. Altogether, about 350,000 immigrants entered the United States each year during the 1960s. More than 400,000 came yearly during the 1970s. Most of these new arrivals ended up in the nation's metropolitan areas.

Chicanos (Mexican-Americans) represented one of the largest waves of postwar migrants, swelling populations in southwestern cities. Whereas most Mexican-Americans had lived in rural areas before World War II, 80 percent lived in cities by 1960, making them more urbanized than the general population. Southwestern cities with a high proportion of Chicano citizens included Los Angeles, Long Beach, El Paso, and Phoenix. Large numbers of Mexican-Americans also settled in Chicago, Detroit, Kansas City, and Denver. By the 1970s, five million Mexican-Americans lived in the United States legally (along with perhaps two million illegal aliens), making them one of the nation's largest ethnic groups and a growing force in American political and cultural life.

Another major group of Hispanic migrants came from the American-controlled territory of Puerto Rico. Residents of this island had been American citizens since 1917, but before World War I fewer than two thousand had migrated to the mainland. Migration increased dramatically after World War II, as Puerto Ricans were lured by the promise of better economic opportunities and social services. The inauguration of cheap, direct air service between San Juan and New York City made Puerto Ricans this country's first group to immigrate by air, not boat.

Most of the Puerto Rican migrants went to New York, where they settled first in East ("Spanish") Harlem and then in other areas throughout the city's five boroughs. This massive influx, which grew from 70,000 in 1940 to 613,000 just twenty years later, transformed the ethnic composition of the city. More Puerto Ri-

cans now lived in New York City than in San Juan. They faced conditions common to all recent immigrants—crowded and deteriorating housing, segregation, unemployment or restriction to menial jobs, poor schools, and the problems of a bilingual existence.

Black Americans were the other major group of migrants to the postwar cities. Blacks had been leaving the South since Reconstruction, but 77 percent of the black population still lived there as late as 1940, predominantly in rural areas. By 1960, a majority of blacks lived in the North; by 1970, four-fifths of the northern blacks were urban dwellers. Black Americans thus incurred the double dislocation of moving from South to North, and from a rural to an urban environment, all within a generation or two. (These dislocations applied to Puerto Ricans and Mexican-Americans as well.) Like all other migrants, blacks responded to both "push" and "pull" factors. On the one hand, they were pushed out of the South when the agricultural revolution and mechanized farming ended the traditional southern dependence on sharecropping and tenant farming. On the other hand, they responded to the pull of a better life, economically and socially, in northern cities.

The nation's cities saw their nonwhite populations swell at the same time that whites flocked to the suburbs. From 1950 to 1960, the nation's twelve largest central cities lost 3.6 million whites while gaining 4.5 million nonwhites. During the 1950s, the nonwhite population of Washington, D.C., rose from 35 to 55 percent of the total, and Chicago's from 14 to 24 percent. The pattern continued in the 1960s as New York's black and Hispanic population grew from 14 to 21 percent of the total, Los Angeles's from 13.5 to 18 percent, and Detroit's from 29 to 44 percent.

By the time that blacks, Mexican-Americans, and Puerto Ricans moved into the inner cities in the 1940s and 1950s, urban America was in dire shape. Housing continued to be a crucial problem. One common response to the problem of deteriorating inner-city housing in the 1950s was urban renewal—that is, razing blighted urban neighborhoods and replacing them with modern, supposedly better buildings. Urban renewal often produced grim high-rise housing projects that destroyed feelings of neighborhood pride

CLAUDE BROWN TALKS ABOUT BLACK MIGRATION

I want to talk about the first Northern urban generation of Negroes. I want to talk about the experiences of a misplaced generation, of a misplaced people in an extremely complex, confused society. . . . The characters are sons and daughters of former Southern sharecroppers. These were the poorest people of the South, who poured into New York City during the decade following the Great Depression. These migrants were told that unlimited opportunities for prosperity existed in New York and that there was no "color problem" there. They were told that Negroes lived in houses with bathrooms, electricity, running water, and indoor toilets. To them, this was the "promised land" that Mammy had been singing about in the cotton fields for many years.

Going to New York was good-bye to the cotton fields, good-bye to "Massa Charlie," good-bye to the chain gang, and, most of all, good-bye to those sunup-to-sundown working hours. One no longer had to wait to get to heaven to lay his burden down; burdens could be laid down in New York.

So, they came, from all parts of the South, like all the black chillun o' God following the sound of Gabriel's horn on that long-overdue Judgment Day. The Georgians came as soon as they were able to pick train fare off the peach trees. They came from South Carolina where the cotton stalks were bare. The North Carolinians came with tobacco tar beneath their fingernails.

They felt as the Pilgrims must have felt when they were coming to America. But these descendants of Ham must have been twice as happy as the Pilgrims, because they had been catching twice the hell. Even while planning the trip, they sang spirituals such as "Jesus Take My Hand" and "I'm On My Way" and chanted, "Hallelujah, I'm on my way to the promised land!"

It seems that Cousin Willie, in his lying haste, had neglected to tell the folks down home about one of the most important aspects of the promised land: it was a slum ghetto. There was a tremendous difference in the way life was lived up North. There were too many people full of hate and bitterness crowded into a dirty, stinky, uncared-for closet-size section of a great city.

Before the soreness of the cotton fields had left Mama's back, her knees were getting sore from scrubbing "Goldberg's" floor. Nevertheless, she was better off; she had gone from the fire into the frying pan.

The children of these disillusioned colored pioneers inherited the total lot of their parents—the disappointments, the anger. To add to their misery, they had little hope of deliverance. For where does one run to when he's already in the promised land?

Source: Claude Brown, *Manchild in the Promised Land.* New York: Macmillan & Co., 1965. vii–viii.

---

and created a combat zone for street crime. Local residents were rarely consulted about whether they wanted their neighborhoods "renewed." Complained one resident of an East Harlem housing project:

> Nobody cared what we wanted when they built this place. They threw our houses down and pushed us there and pushed our friends somewhere else. We don't have a place around here to get a cup of coffee or a newspaper even, or borrow fifty cents. Nobody cared what we need. But the big men come and look at that grass and say, "Isn't it wonderful! Now the poor have everything!"

Between 1949 and 1961, urban renewal projects demolished almost 150,000 buildings and displaced 500,000 people. By 1967, the number of razed structures topped 400,000, and 1.4 million urban dwellers had been forced to relocate.

Urban renewal projects often benefited the wealthy at the expense of the poor. Many downtown "revitalization" projects supplanted established ethnic neighborhoods with expensive rental housing or shiny office buildings where suburban commuters worked. Boston's West End, a flourishing, if poor, Italian community, was razed by a private developer between 1958 and 1960 to build Charles River Park, an apartment complex whose rents were far too steep for the old-time residents. West Enders were forced into less desirable parts of the city, cut off from the vitality of their former neighborhood.

Despite such urban "gentrification," the cities were increasingly becoming a place of last resort for the nation's poor. Unlike earlier immigrants, for whom cities were gateways to social and economic betterment, inner-city residents in the postwar period faced diminishing hopes for improvement. Lured by the promise of plentiful jobs, migrants found that many of these supposed opportunities had relocated to the suburban fringe. Steady employment was thus out of reach for those who needed it most.

That the poor were increasingly trapped in the cities was due largely to racism. Migrants to the city, especially blacks, faced racial hostility and institutional barriers to mobility. Blacks were barred by explicit covenants and informal practices from moving into better neighborhoods. A 1968 federal commission, set up to investigate the race riots that rocked northern cities in the 1960s, concluded ominously that there were "two increasingly separate Americas"—a white society located in suburbs and peripheral areas, and an inner city made up of blacks, Mexican-Americans, and other disadvantaged groups. This widespread metropolitan segregation remains one of the most striking and disturbing aspects of modern urban life.

THE BLIGHT OF URBAN RENEWAL
The West End area of Boston is shown as it looked in 1960, after an urban renewal program had cleared the land. Of the thriving community where seven thousand people had lived just eighteen months earlier, only Saint Joseph's Catholic Church still stood (far right). Within two years, the site was covered with twenty-four hundred units of luxury housing, whose rents far exceeded what the former residents could afford. (Herbert Gans. Reprinted from *The Urban Villagers*, Updated and Expanded edition, Free Press 1982)

The Growth of Suburbia

As late as 1945, many cities had pastures and working farms on their outskirts. Just five or ten years later, these cities were surrounded by tract housing and shopping centers. Between 1950 and 1960, the population of fourteen of the nation's fifteen largest cities shrank, while the suburbs surrounding these cities grew dramatically. New York, despite the influx of Puerto Rican migrants, lost 2 percent of its population in the 1950s, but its suburbs grew by 58 percent. The population of Nassau County, on Long Island, grew from just over 400,000 people in 1940 to 1.3 million twenty years later. The population of Orange County, outside Los Angeles, doubled in the 1940s and then tripled from that level in the 1950s. Other areas that underwent rapid growth included San Mateo County, south of San Francisco; Cook and DuPage counties, north and west of Chicago; and Prince Georges County in Maryland, outside Washington, D.C. By 1960, more people lived in suburbs than in cities.

What spurred this dramatic suburban growth? Automobiles and highways played a crucial role. Suburbanites needed cars to get to work or to take children to school and piano lessons. About 90 percent of suburban families owned cars, and 20 percent had more than one. Whereas twenty-five million cars had been registered in 1945, the number rose to fifty-one million in 1955 and ninety million in 1970.

The car culture that first emerged in the 1920s expanded dramatically during the 1950s, with cars becoming personal metaphors for status and success. With gas cheap, no one cared about fuel efficiency, and cars became heavier and more stylized; the fins of a Chevrolet added two feet to the chassis. One of the most popular cars was the 1957 "Chevy," of which 1.5 million were manufactured. The Chevy came in sixteen solid and fifteen two-tone colors and cost between $1,885 and $2,757.

More cars required more highways, which were funded largely by the federal government. In 1947, the government authorized the construction of 37,000 miles of highway. In 1956, it increased its commitment by another 42,500 miles in the greatest civil engineering project of world history. The new roads would be at least four lanes wide and would link the entire country in an integrated interstate system. (The national highway network was also promoted to speed civilian evacuation in the event of nuclear attack.) Gas taxes and user fees for commercial vehicles provided the necessary funds. Federal expenditures for highway construction rose correspondingly from $429 million in 1950 to $4.6 billion in 1970.

The interstate system of the 1960s changed both the cities and the countryside. It rerouted traffic through rural areas, bypassing old main roads like Route 1 and Route 66 and creating new communities of gas stations, fast-food outlets, and motels at anonymous cloverleaf exchanges. In urban areas, new highways cut wide swaths through urban neighborhoods, forcing relocation and readjustment. Cities were soon plagued by the problems that cars brought to

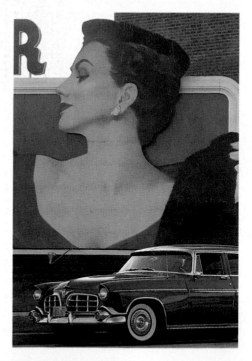

IMAGES OF AFFLUENCE
Two dominant and interrelated themes of postwar consumer culture were advertising and automobiles. By 1960, annual advertising expenditures topped $10 billion, mainly for consumer goods such as tobacco, legal drugs and alcohol, home furnishings, and automobiles. (© Elliott Erwitt, Magnum)

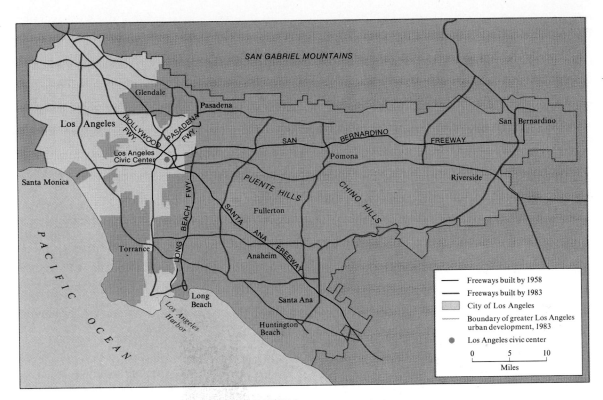

MAP 27.3 THE LOS ANGELES FREEWAY SYSTEM
Los Angeles epitomizes a metropolitan area dominated by the automobile. The city's famous freeway system consists of 650 miles of high-speed expressways (only the major arteries are shown on this map). In the 1920s and 1930s, Los Angeles had one of the nation's best public transportation systems. By the 1960s, however, automobiles accounted for 95 percent of the travel within the city.

modern life—air pollution from exhausts and traffic jams at rush hours. Critics now complained about "autosclerosis," a hardening of the urban arteries.

Highway construction had far-reaching effects on patterns of consumption and shopping. Instead of taking a train into the city to shop or walking to a corner grocery store, people now hopped into their cars and drove to suburban shopping malls and supermarkets. Although the first mall had appeared in the 1920s, there were only eight in 1945. The number mushroomed to almost four thousand by 1960. Contractors who built the shopping centers knew that suburbanites soon would arrive. "People have path-habits like ants," one builder noted.

The federally constructed highways threatened the demise of mass transit. Los Angeles, a city now largely dependent on freeways, had a viable mass transit system as late as the 1940s. On Long Island, master builder Robert Moses planned an extensive expressway system and deliberately omitted the option of adding a mass transit system along its right of way, thereby condemning Long Island to reliance on only cars and freeways. The Highway Trust Fund set up in 1956 specifically prohibited use of its collected fees to promote urban mass transit. By 1960, two-thirds of all Americans drove to work each day.

Another spur to suburban development was the availability of mortgage money from the Federal Housing Administration and the Veterans Administration. Before World War II, banks usually demanded a 50 percent down payment for homeowner's loans and granted no more than ten years to pay back the balance. After the war, the FHA required only a 5 to 10 percent down payment and gave homeowners up to thirty years to pay back mortgages at the modest rate of 2 to 3 percent. The Veterans' Administration was even more lenient, requiring only a token one-dollar down payment from those who had served their country during the war. By 1955, these two agencies wrote 41 percent of all non-farm mortgages.

In the end, people flocked to the suburbs because they followed the available housing. Very little new housing had been built during the depression or war years, and when World War II veterans wanted to establish households and families, they faced a critical housing shortage. The 1950s witnessed a dramatic surge in construction. By 1960, a fourth of all housing in the country had been built during the preceding decade.

The suburban housing market was revolutionized by a Long Island building contractor named Arthur Levitt and Sons, which cut costs and sped production by applying mass-production techniques to home construction. In 1947, Levitt's basic four-room house, complete with kitchen appliances and an attic that could be finished on weekends into two additional bed-

rooms, was priced at less than ten thousand dollars. Levitt did not need to advertise; word of mouth brought more customers than the firm could handle.

Levitt built planned communities in New York, New Jersey, and Pennsylvania. The developments contained few old people and even fewer unmarried adults. Even the trees were young. Owners had to agree to cut their lawns once a week between April and November and not to hang out the laundry on weekends. When residents complained that the streets and the houses were so similar that they could not find their way home, the developer added more variety in style and site placement. A sociologist who studied a Levittown community by living in it for two years concluded, "Whatever its imperfections, Levittown is a good place to live." Soon other developers were snapping up cheap farmland surrounding urban areas, further hastening the exodus from both the farm and the central city.

These suburban developments were almost exclusively for whites. Levittown homeowners had to sign a covenant with this restrictive clause, "No dwelling shall be used or occupied by members of other than the Caucasian Race," although "the employment and maintenance of

A NATION OF JOINERS
Suburban life was relentlessly organized. Although some suburban organizations, such as churches and PTAs, attracted both men and women, many were limited to one sex. In Fullerton, California, in 1959, men would have joined the male-only Kiwanis, Lions, or Elks, while women would have belonged to the Business and Professional Women or other women's clubs. (© Eve Arnold, Magnum)

other than Caucasian domestic servants" was permitted. Not until 1960 did Levitt sell houses directly to blacks. Even then, the company carefully screened black families and made sure that no two black families lived next door to each other.

While suburbia was often portrayed as a homogeneous, even bland, environment, there were strong cultural and class variations among the suburbs. Older, wealthy suburbs already occupied the most pleasant locations, including the hills of northwest Atlanta, the gracious lakes of Minneapolis, the spectacular hills north and west of Los Angeles, Chicago's North Shore, and the heights well to the east of Cleveland's industrial Cuyahoga Flats. When the less affluent firefighter, plasterer, machine-tool maker, or sales clerk moved to the suburbs, he or she was far more likely to move to a modest Levittown than to an upper-class suburb such as Winnetka, Illinois; Scarsdale, New York; or Shaker Heights, Ohio. Blacks shut out of white suburbs established their own communities, such as Lincoln Heights, outside Cincinnati; Robbins, on the edge of Chicago; and Kinloch, near St. Louis. In well-equipped living quarters at bargain prices, even working-class and black families could share in the ultimate postwar suburban dream "to give every kid an opportunity to grow up with grass stains on his pants."

State and Local Government

The task of governing cities and suburbs fell to state and local governments. The average citizen lived under multiple layers of government—local, county, state, and federal—but local governments often had the greatest impact on people's daily lives. They collected taxes, ran the schools, supplied fire and police protection, picked up the trash, and cleaned the streets. State governments licensed the services of workers ranging from beauticians to lawyers, enforced building and health codes, and protected workers through child-labor laws and workers' compensation.

Like the federal government, state and local governments experienced rapid growth in the postwar period. In fact, their expenditures and payrolls increased much faster than the nondefense activities of the federal government during

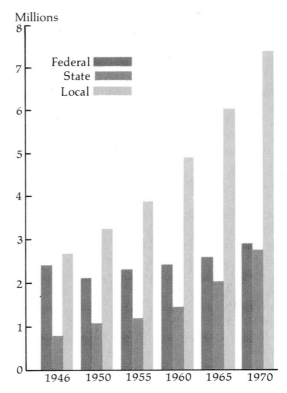

FIGURE 27.3 FEDERAL, STATE, AND LOCAL EMPLOYEES, 1946–1970

this time. State and local expenditures totaled $18 billion in 1949; by 1979, they had risen to more than $300 billion, accounting for two-thirds of total government spending on domestic programs. Employment by local governments grew from 3.2 million in 1950 to 7.4 million in 1970. (The number of federal government employees rose from 2.1 million to 2.8 million in the same period.) By the 1970s, roughly one of six Americans worked for some government bureaucracy.

State and local revenues came primarily from taxation. In 1954, state and local governments relied on property and sales taxes for almost half their revenues. In the following two decades, dependence on property and sales taxes declined somewhat, while state and city income taxes doubled. Federal aid, which supplied 8.5 percent of local and state budgets in 1954, accounted for 19.9 percent by 1976.

State and local governments spent more money on education than on any other item.

Expenditures for education in 1974–1975 took up 39.1 percent of states' budgets and 45 percent of local budgets. Funding covered not only primary and secondary schools; 80 percent of college students attended publicly supported institutions. Although education remains primarily a state and local affair, the federal government has increased its contribution to education since the 1960s through direct aid to educational institutions and programs such as guaranteed student loans and work-study. The rest of the state and local budget covers welfare and social services (the second largest category), highways, health and hospitals, and other services.

Central cities and their surrounding suburban areas often have grossly unequal resources to meet local needs. Since the property tax still provides a sizable part of local budgets, a wealthy community such as Grosse Pointe in suburban Detroit can far more easily provide funds for first-rate schools, clean streets, public recreational facilities, and police and fire protection than can Detroit, whose tax base shrank as businesses and wealthy citizens relocated in the suburbs. While many of the problems of urban life—sewage, traffic, pollution, and police and fire protection—are shared by the cities and their surrounding areas, existing forms of government do not readily allow for cooperation. Political fragmentation is the rule. There are more than a thousand governmental units in the Chicago area, and fourteen hundred in the New York City region. Suburban communities remain reluctant to surrender their fiscal independence, to say nothing of the tradition of local self-rule, to the huge cities with their myriad social and economic problems.

Many urban planners turned their gaze to federal funding to equalize the disparity between the inner cities and the surrounding suburban rim. A national urban policy, they argued, could supply the funding to deal with problems on a metropolitan-area-wide scale. Indeed, the general expansion of federal functions in the 1960s did produce greater attention to the cities—the creation of the Department of Housing and Urban Development (HUD), the Model Cities program, and such antipoverty programs as VISTA and Head Start. These programs, however, hardly dented the massive problems facing urban areas. The needs of the cities have remained a low priority on the national agenda.

The Affluent Society

In 1955, the United States, which accounted for only six percent of the world's population, produced and consumed more than a third of the planet's goods and services. The steady performance of the economy allowed a level of affluence for a wider segment of society than anyone would have dreamed possible during the dark days of the depression. Many members of the new middle class, as well as working-class people who could afford this lifestyle, settled in the sprawling suburban developments that proliferated in the postwar period. The suburbs offered an opportunity to live the child-centered existence that was the hallmark of family culture after World War II.

Consumer Culture

In some respects, the postwar consumer culture seemed like a return to the 1920s—an overabundance of new gadgets and appliances, the expansion of consumer credit and advertising, more leisure time, the growing importance of the automobile, and the development of new types of mass media. Yet there was a difference. The postwar economy was far better balanced than that of the 1920s; no depressed agricultural sector detracted from the prosperity and no Great Depression lurked on the horizon. Furthermore, by the 1950s the American economy was more geared toward the production of consumer goods than thirty years earlier. Consumption had become integral to middle-class culture. Due to rising incomes, even blue-collar families now had discretionary income to spend on consumer goods.

As in the 1920s, though, the postwar prosperity was helped along by a dramatic increase in consumer credit, which enabled families to stretch their incomes. Between 1946 and 1958, short-term consumer credit rose from $8.4 billion to almost $45 billion. A hefty portion of this increase involved financing for the purchase of automobiles on the installment plan. The Diners Club credit card, introduced in 1950 and followed by the American Express card and Bank Americard in 1959, was initially geared toward the business traveler. But by the 1960s and 1970s, the ubiquitous plastic credit cards had revolutionized personal and family finances.

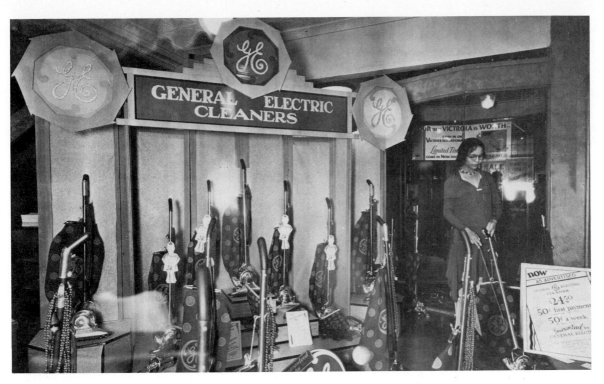

BUY NOW, PAY LATER
Most advertising was geared to American women, who were urged to find fulfillment in buying
things for their homes. Companies like General Electric made the process easier by offering credit
terms for the purchase of vacuum cleaners and other appliances. (FPG)

One symbolic casualty of the consumer credit phenomenon was the pawnshop, which no longer found much call for its services.

Along with expanded consumer credit came a spurt in advertising. In 1951, businesses spent more on advertising ($6.5 billion) than taxpayers did on primary and secondary education ($5 billion); by 1960, advertising expenditures topped $10 billion. To assure continued growth in sales of consumer commodities, advertising sought to "create the wants it seeks to satisfy," as John Kenneth Galbraith put it. Businesses also relied on the idea of planned obsolescence—that is, frequent style changes and minor improvements to make consumers trade in old products for newer, fancier models.

Advertising promoted a variety of new consumer appliances to fill the suburban home. Production of some of these appliances had been halted by wartime priorities; others were new to the postwar market. In 1946, automatic washing machines replaced the old machines that re-

quired wringing out clothes by hand. Electric dryers came on the market that same year. In 1955, 1.2 million dryers were sold, twice the 1953 total, and commercial laundries across the country went out of business as more American homemakers chose to do their own laundry. Another new item on the market was the home freezer, which enabled families to eat seasonal foods, such as fruits and vegetables, all year. The availability of home freezers in turn encouraged the frozen-food industry, which grew dramatically in the 1960s and 1970s, as people spent less time cooking for themselves.

While washing machines, freezers, and refrigerators lightened housekeeping chores, other gadgets offered more frivolous benefits. Blenders, first patented in 1922, originally came in two speeds, on and off. The 1950s brought high and low, and then intermediate speeds. "It was crazy," admitted one executive, "the more buttons, the better they sold. We got as high as sixteen, and the things still couldn't do much more than whip cream." Due in part to the purchases of electrical gadgets for the home, consumer use of electricity doubled during the 1950s.

Consumers had more time to spend money than ever before. In the 1920s, workers toiled six days a week, and few employers offered paid vacations. By the 1960s, the average worker put in a five-day week, with eight paid holidays each year (double the 1946 standard) plus a paid two-week vacation. In 1950, Americans devoted a seventh of the gross national product to spending on leisure and entertainment. One growth area in the 1950s was the travel industry. Americans traveled both domestically (encouraging the dramatic growth in motel chains, roadside restaurants, and fast-food eateries) and internationally, aided by the strong U.S. dollar abroad and the introduction of jet air travel in 1958.

One of the most widespread leisure activities was watching television. TV's leap to cultural prominence was swift and overpowering. In 1947, there were only ten broadcasting stations in the entire country, and a meager 7,000 sets were manufactured. Just three years later, Americans had purchased 7.3 million TV sets. By 1955, 66 percent of all American families had

at least one television set; by 1970, 96 percent. More Americans owned a TV set than a refrigerator.

Television transformed American life, fostering a mass national culture in a way similar to, but far more completely than, radio's effect in the 1920s. Television promoted homogeneity, encouraged consumption through its incessant commercials, and reduced regional and ethnic differences by its national network programming. By assuming such a central role in American popular culture, television supplanted radio, whose stars quickly made the transition to the "tube," and movies, which had enjoyed cultural predominance from the 1920s through the 1940s. Movie attendance plummeted throughout the postwar period.

Television also encouraged the consumerism and advertising that had characterized mass culture since the 1920s. New items entered the home. For example, 1954 brought the introduction of the frozen TV dinner of turkey, peas, and mashed potatoes. Now a family could eat a meal in front of the television without having to talk. *TV Guide* became the most successful new periodical of the 1950s. Television even affected city services. In 1954, the Toledo water commissioner

"FATHER KNOWS BEST"
The television program "Father Knows Best" made its debut in 1953. Its title reflected the patriarchal basis of family life at the time. One historian described the character of Robert Anderson, played by Robert Young, as having "no politics, no opinions, and no connections with the world about him"—in short, a perfect organization man of the 1950s. (Wide World)

wondered why water consumption rose dramatically during certain three-minute periods. The answer? All across Toledo, TV watchers flushed their toilets during commercials.

What Americans saw on television, besides the omnipresent commercials, was a world that reflected the complacent self-image of American society that prevailed until the political and social upheavals of the 1960s—a predominantly white, Anglo-Saxon world of nuclear families, suburban homes, and middle-class life. The popular show "Father Knows Best," starring Robert Young and Jane Wyatt, typified this norm. We never knew what Father actually did, except that he left home each morning wearing a suit and carrying a briefcase. Mother was a full-time housewife, parent to three children, and personification of all the negative stereotypes about women. For example, she drove badly and was hopelessly emotional. While the new medium did offer some serious programming, notably live theater and documentaries, Federal Communications Commissioner Newton Minow concluded in 1963 that television was "a vast wasteland."

Women—Back to the Home

"The suburban housewife was the dream image of the young American woman," feminist Betty Friedan has said of the 1950s. "She was healthy, beautiful, educated, concerned only about her husband, her children, and her home." Friedan herself gave up a psychology fellowship and a career as a journalist to marry, move to the suburbs, and raise three children. "Determined that I find the feminine fulfillment that eluded my mother . . . I lived the life of a suburban housewife that was everyone's dream at the time," she said.

The 1950s were characterized by a pervasive, indeed pernicious, insistence that women's proper place was in the home. There was nothing new about such emphasis on domesticity. What Betty Friedan tagged the "feminine mystique" of the 1950s—that "the highest value and the only commitment for women is the fulfillment of their own femininity"—bore remarkable similarities to the nineteenth-century's cult of true womanhood. But women's lives had changed dramatically since the nineteenth cen-

tury, due to increased access to education and jobs and the greater availability of consumer goods and services. It was much harder to convince women to stay in their homes in the 1950s than it had been in the 1850s.

The updated version of the cult of domesticity drew on new elements of twentieth-century science and culture, even Freudian psychology, to give it more force. It claimed that feminism was a neurosis and that women who sought careers were sexually maladjusted. And reflecting the consumer culture, the feminine mystique insisted that women's primary role was to buy appliances and other consumer goods for her home and family. The mass media, such as women's magazines and advertisements, pushed this message relentlessly. "Love is said in many ways," ran an ad for toilet paper. "It's giving and accepting. It's protecting and selecting . . . knowing what's safest for those you love. Their bathroom tissue is Scott Tissue always." Another ad played on the housewife's insecurity by asking, "Can a woman ever feel right cooking on a dirty range?"

The dislocations of the war years made both men and women yearn for a return to traditional family values. A popular 1945 song was "Gotta Make Up for Lost Time." The average age of marriage for women dropped to twenty, and a third of all young women in 1951 were married by the time they reached nineteen. This generation approached life with an optimism and confidence notably absent from the depression generation of the 1930s. The GI Bill and other federal programs aided their quest for unprecedented levels of material security.

The most dramatic result of this family- and consumer-oriented life-style was the postwar "baby boom." After a century and a half of declining family size, the birthrate suddenly shot up. In contrast to the Great Depression, when the birthrate had dropped to a low point of 18.4 per 1,000 population, the annual rate peaked at 25.3 per 1,000 by 1957. (The American rate approached that of the developing nation of India.) Families now had an average of almost four children. Caring for such large households further encouraged women to define themselves as full-time mothers.

Suburbia was child-centered. When asked why they had moved to the suburbs, most new

HOME LIFE IN THE 1950s: THE IDEAL
This photograph reflects an idealized picture of family life
in the 1950s. Taken in Long Island in 1958, it suggests the
theme of "togetherness," a word coined by *McCall's*
magazine in 1954. Many popular magazines promoted
the notion of an idyllic home life for women who made a
full-time career of home-making, regardless of family size.
(© Eve Arnold, Magnum)

homeowners gave the same answer: "We did it
for the children." Scarred by the depression,
parents eagerly sought the wider opportunities
that suburban living offered the next generation.
Children's lives were relentlessly organized.
Their mothers put them in play groups at the
age of three, the Little League or dancing lessons
at eight, and tennis lessons at twelve. Parents
flocked to the PTA, cheered the high school
football team, and applauded the school play.

For their child rearing, parents increasingly
relied on the advice of experts, notably Dr. Benjamin Spock, whose best-selling book *Baby and
Child Care* sold a million copies a year after its
publication in 1946. Dr. Spock urged mothers to
abandon the rigid feeding and baby-care schedules of an earlier generation. New mothers
found Spock's common-sense approach liberating, but it did not totally soothe their insecurities. If they wanted to work outside the home,
they felt guilty about neglecting their family. If
mothers were too protective of their children,

they might hamper their adjustment to a normal
adult life. Dr. Spock could only recommend that
mothers be constantly available to respond to
their children's needs.

In large part because of the baby boom, the
American population rose dramatically in the
postwar period: from 140 million in 1945 to 179
million in 1960, and 203 million in 1970. After the
baby boom produced between 20 and 30 million
more Americans than had been expected, demographers predicted that the population would
reach 300 million by the end of the century.
When the boom tapered off in the mid-1960s
and the birthrate entered a period of steady decline, demographers revised their predictions
and estimated a population of 250–260 million
for the year 2000.

In addition to the rising birthrate and immigration, the declining death rate contributed to
the population growth. Life expectancy at birth
had improved steadily over the first half of the
twentieth century, from forty-seven years in
1900 to sixty-three years in 1940. Continued improvements in diet, public health, and surgical
practices lengthened the life span. So did "miracle drugs," such as penicillin, introduced in 1943;
streptomycin in 1945; cortisone in 1946; and ter-
ramycin in 1949. When Dr. Jonas Salk perfected
a polio vaccine in 1954, he became a national
hero. Life expectancy at birth continued to increase—to seventy years by 1960 and seventy-
four years by 1980.

The baby boom had a broader impact on
American society than simply reinforcing
women's domestic roles and confounding demographers' predictions. The consumer needs of
all those babies fueled the economy as families
bought food, diapers, toys, and clothing for their
expanding broods. When the children got a little
older, manufacturers discovered a vital teenage
market for stereos, records, clothes, and cars.
Family spending on consumer goods joined federal expenditures on national security as the basis for the unparalleled prosperity and economic
growth that characterized American society
through the 1960s.

The baby boom also encouraged a major expansion of the nation's educational system. The
new middle class, America's first college-
educated generation, placed a high value on
education. To make schools into showplace

community centers, suburbanites approved 90 percent of the proposed school bond issues during the 1950s. By 1970, school expenditures accounted for 7.2 percent of the gross national product, double the 1950 level.

The effects of the baby boom are still felt. In the 1950s, children provided plenty of patients for doctors and dentists, students for teachers, and customers for tricycles and swings—and, later, stereos and cars. In the 1960s, the baby-boom generation participated in a broad expansion of higher education, especially at the college level. Not coincidentally, it also contributed to the ranks of student protesters in the late 1960s. By the 1970s, when the baby boom generation entered the workplace, it had to compete for a limited number of jobs in what had become a stagnant economy. In the 1980s, the delayed marriages and later childbearing of the career-oriented baby boomers temporarily caused the birthrate to rise again.

An awareness that the baby boomers were voting finally seeped into politics. At least one major Democratic presidential candidate of the 1980s, Senator Gary Hart of Colorado, specifically addressed his campaign of new ideas to the young people who were the products of the 1950s and 1960s. More successful was his Republican opponent, Ronald Reagan, who nostalgically promised to restore the social conditions of the 1950s and early 1960s, when the baby boomers were growing up. The decisions made by couples in the immediate postwar period to have large families will continue to ripple through American social and economic life for decades to come.

The Great Contradiction—Women at Work

Although women's domestic roles were glorified in the 1950s, a contradictory pattern also emerged—a dramatic rise in the number and kind of women who worked for pay outside the home. Economist Eli Ginzberg later called this trend "the single most outstanding phenomenon of our century."

When World War II ended, women war workers wanted to hold on to their high-paying, skilled jobs, but they stepped aside for returning veterans. Women felt betrayed, however, when,

HOME LIFE: ONE REALITY
This young mother in New Rochelle, a suburb of New York City, was photographed in 1955. Her frenzied situation hints at why twenty-four thousand American women responded to a 1960 *Redbook* magazine article entitled "Why Young Mothers Feel Trapped." (© Elliott Erwitt, Magnum)

after all the veterans had been placed in jobs, plants began to hire and train new young male workers, rather than call the experienced women back to their old positions. Their inability to keep or regain skilled jobs did not send these women back to the home, however. They simply returned to jobs that women traditionally had held. By 1960, there were twice as many women at work as in 1940.

The increase in the number of working women was paralleled by another change of equally significant proportions—the dramatic rise in the number of older, married, middle-class women who took jobs. At the turn of the century, the average female worker was a young recent immigrant who worked only until she married. By mid-century, the average woman worker was in her forties, was married, and had children in school. In 1940, only 15 percent of all wives worked. This percentage doubled by 1960, hit 40 percent by 1970, and passed 50 percent by 1980. Woman workers were not just part-time

TIME LINE
AFFLUENCE AND ITS CONTRADICTIONS

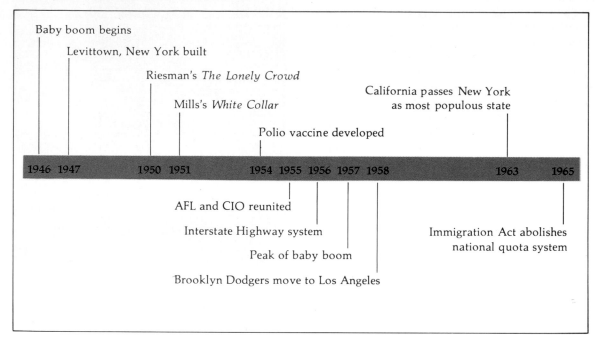

employees; 50 percent of them worked full-time in 1950, and the proportion rose to 70 percent by 1975.

Why did women enter the paid labor force? Many worked to supplement their family income. For many families, postwar inflation and changing consumption habits required two incomes. The wages that many men earned even in the prosperous 1950s and 1960s could not pay for all the necessities of new middle-class life— cars, houses, vacations, and college for the children. The structural needs of the economy were an equally significant factor; there was a demand for workers in fields traditionally filled by women. The shortage was especially acute in clerical work, a predominantly female field that expanded as rapidly as any other white-collar sector in the economy. Teachers to staff the nation's burgeoning school systems were also in demand. Lower-paying jobs went to women in growing sectors such as restaurant and hotel work, hospitals, and beauty care—jobs that critical observers accurately called the "pink-collar ghetto."

Occupational segmentation remained a fun-

damental characteristic of women's work in the postwar period. More than 80 percent of all working women held jobs in stereotypical "women's work," as salespersons, health-care technicians, waitresses, flight attendants, domestic servants, receptionists, telephone operators, and secretaries. In 1960, women represented only 3.5 percent of all lawyers and 6.1 percent of all physicians, but 97 percent of the nurses, 85 percent of the librarians, and 57 percent of the social workers. Along with women's jobs went women's pay, which averaged 63.9 percent of men's in 1955 and dropped to 60 percent in 1963. By the 1970s, a woman earned only 59 cents for every dollar earned by a man.

How could the society of the 1950s so steadfastly uphold the domestic ideal while an increasing number of wives and mothers took jobs? In many ways, the dramatic increase was kept invisible by the women themselves, who, fearing public disapproval of their decisions, usually interpreted their work in very individual terms: "I took a job to put Susie through college, but I still believe a woman's place is at home." The absence of an active feminist movement in the 1940s and 1950s meant that few public figures or organizations paid attention to this major demographic and social shift. Finally, when women took on jobs outside the home, they invariably maintained full responsibility for child care and household management, which allowed families and society to avoid the full implications of women's new roles. As one overburdened woman noted, she now had "two full-time jobs instead of just one—underpaid clerical worker and unpaid housekeeper."

While the American Dream became a reality after 1945 for more citizens than had ever seemed possible, not everyone shared equally in this postwar prosperity. Many people—dis-placed mill workers and coal miners, destitute old people, female-headed households, blacks and Hispanics—watched the affluent society from the outside and wondered why they were not permitted to share in its bounty. These contrasts between the lure of the city for the poor and minorities and the reality of its segregated existence, between affluence and "the other America," between a heightened emphasis on domesticity and widening opportunities for women, would spawn protest and change in the turbulent 1960s. Amid the booming prosperity of the late 1940s and 1950s, however, these fundamental social and economic contradictions were barely noticed.

---

*P*ostwar affluence rested on several foundations. The most important was federal intervention in the economy, especially in the form of defense spending to maintain permanent mobilization. Spending for consumer goods also fueled the prosperity, playing an especially important role in the reconversion to a peacetime economy. Technological change stimulated increased productivity, notably in agriculture and industry.

Much of the economic activity in the postwar period concentrated in the growing metropolitan areas, especially in their expanding suburbs. Metropolitan areas exhibited a striking dichotomy as poor migrants settled in the inner city while the more affluent took their families to the suburbs. For the new middle class, the postwar period brought a higher standard of living and access to an array of new consumer goods. Blacks, Puerto Ricans, and Chicanos rarely shared in this affluence, however.

The structural changes transforming the American economy had a strong impact on individual Americans. White-collar workers now outnumbered blue-collar employees, and more women joined the work force. The labor movement could not maintain its momentum from the 1930s. Many of the smoldering contradictions of the postwar period—an unequally shared affluence, institutionalized racism that limited opportunities for nonwhite Americans, and tensions in women's lives—soon surfaced in the social-protest movements of the 1960s.

Suggestions for Further Reading

Technology and Economic Change

W. Elliot Brownlee, *Dynamics of Ascent* (1979), covers the postwar period more extensively than most surveys of economic history. For an even more detailed picture, see Harold G. Vatter, *The U.S. Economy in the 1950s* (1963). Herman P. Miller, *Rich Man, Poor Man* (1971), and Gabriel Kolko, *Wealth and Power in America* (1962), discuss inequality in income distribution. Michael Harrington, *The Other America* (1962), documents the persistence of poverty. John Kenneth Galbraith's lively books, *American Capitalism* (1952), *The Affluent Society* (1958), and *The New Industrial State* (1967), shaped much of the public discussion of the economy in the period. Robert L. Heilbroner, *The Limits of American Capitalism* (1965), is equally readable and more critical.

John L. Shover, *First Majority-Last Minority* (1976), analyzes the transformation of rural life in America. It can be supplemented by Willard W. Cochrane and Mary E. Ryan, *American Farm Policy, 1948–1973* (1976), and Gilbert C. Fite, *American Farmers: The New Minority* (1981).

David Brody, *Workers in Industrial America* (1980); David Montgomery, *Workers' Control in America* (1979); and James R. Green, *The World of the Worker* (1980), provide stimulating overviews of labor in the twentieth century. On the impact of technology and automation, see Elting E. Morison, *From Know-How to Nowhere* (1974), and David F. Noble, *Forces of Production: A Social History of Industrial Automation* (1984). Harry Braverman, *Labor and Monopoly Capital* (1974), looks at the degradation of work from a Marxist perspective. Studs Terkel's superb oral history, *Working* (1974), lets people from all walks of life talk about what they do and how they feel about it.

The most influential study of the new middle class is still David Reisman, with Nathan Glazer and Ruel Denney, *The Lonely Crowd* (1950). William H. Whyte, *The Organization Man* (1956), provides a similar perspective. See also the work of C. Wright Mills, especially *White Collar* (1951) and *The Power Elite* (1956). Samuel Lubbell describes middle-class voting patterns in *The Future of American Politics* (1956) and *Revolt of the Moderates* (1956).

Alfred D. Chandler, *The Visible Hand* (1977), is the definitive history of American corporate structure and strategy. Myra Wilkin, *The Maturing of Multinational Enterprise* (1974), and Richard J. Barnet and Ronald E. Muller, *Global Reach* (1974), describe American business abroad. See also Robert Sobel, *The Age of Giant Corporations* (1972).

Cities and Suburbs

There is extensive literature on the growth of urban areas and their surrounding suburbs. Zane L. Miller, *The Urbanization of Modern America* (1973), and Blake McKelvey, *The Emergence of Metropolitan America, 1915–1966* (1968), provide comprehensive overviews; Sam Bass Warner, Jr., *The Urban Wilderness* (1972), is more interpretive. Herbert J. Gans, *The Urban Villagers* (1962), tells the story of an Italian community in Boston displaced by urban renewal. Jane Jacobs, *The Death and Life of Great American Cities* (1961), is an opinionated look at urban problems. Stephen Thernstrom, *The Other Bostonians* (1973), suggests why blacks in urban areas did not find upward social mobility. Robert A. Caro, *The Power Broker* (1974), provides a case study of the impact of highways on the landscape of metropolitan New York City through the career of Robert Moses.

Jon C. Teaford, *City and Suburb: The Political Fragmentation of Metropolitan America, 1850–1970* (1979), surveys the impact of suburban growth on American life. Standard texts on suburbia include Robert C. Wood, *Suburbia: Its People and their Politics* (1959), and William M. Dobriner, *Class in Suburbia* (1963). Michael N. Danielson, *The Politics of Exclusion* (1976), describes how blacks were kept out of suburbia. Zane Miller, *Suburb* (1981), is a case study of Forest Park, Ohio. Herbert Gans, *The Levittowners* (1967), describes the two years he spent as a participant-observer in that New Jersey community. Bennett M. Berger, *Working-Class Suburb* (1960), and Scott Donaldson, *The Suburban Myth* (1969), question the homogeneity of the suburban experience.

The Affluent Society

An excellent introduction to postwar society that stresses the consumer culture is William E. Leuchtenberg, *A Troubled Feast* (1979). Other useful overviews highlighting social and economic developments are Godfrey Hodgson, *America In Our Time* (1976); Carl Degler, *Affluence and Anxiety* (1968); Geoffrey Perrett, *A Dream of Greatness* (1979); James Gilbert, *Another Chance* second edition, 1986; and David Potter, *People of Plenty* (1954). See also Douglas T. Miller and Marion Nowak, *The Fifties: The Way We Really Were* (1977), and Jeffrey Hart, *When the Going was Good! American Life in the Fifties* (1982).

Eric Barnouw, *The Image Empire* (1970), chronicles the impact of television. Other treatments of the mass media include Marshall McLuhan, *Understanding Media* (1964); Frank Mankiewicz and Joel Swerdlow, *Remote Control: Television and the Manipulation of American Life* (1978); and Edward J. Epstein, *News from Nowhere* (1973). Robert Sklar, *Movie-Made America* (1975), shows how movies reacted to the threat from television. Vance Packard's influential *The Hidden Persuaders* (1957) unmasks the advertising industry.

Richard Easterlin, *American Baby Boom in Historical Perspective* (1962) and *Birth and Future: The Impact of Numbers on Personal Welfare* (1980), analyzes the demographic changes, as does Landon Y. Jones, *Great Expectations: America and the Baby Boom Generation* (1980). Developments in medicine are treated in James Bordley and A. McGehee Harvery, *Two Centuries of American Medicine* (1976).

Betty Friedan, *The Feminine Mystique* (1963), provides a witty perspective on the lives of educated suburban women, which should be contrasted with Mirra Komarovsky, *Blue Collar Marriage* (1962). William H. Chafe, *The American Woman* (1972), and Carl Degler, *At Odds* (1980), survey women's public and private roles; Alice Kessler-Harris, *Out to Work* (1982), concentrates on women at work. For an interpretive overview of women in the 1950s, see Eugenia Kaledin, *Mothers and More* (1984).

28

THE POLITICS OF POST-NEW DEAL AMERICA

*T*he New Deal and World War II made the federal government the single most important force in American life. In 1929, the government employed fewer than six hundred thousand people, spent $3.1 billion, and comprised about 3 percent of the total national economic activity. By 1953, the government spent $75 billion a year, employed more than 2.5 million people (4 percent of the civilian work force), and accounted for 17 percent of the gross national product. During the 1960s, federal budgets surpassed $150 billion, making up 20 to 25 percent of the GNP. Outlays for national defense caused most of this growth in the federal budget, but increased federal responsibilities for social welfare programs also played a role. These structural changes in the scope of federal activity underlay postwar political developments.

The major debate within the political system from 1945 to 1968 concerned the purposes that this vastly expanded federal power ought to serve. With the memory of the Great Depression still fresh, many citizens wanted the government to use its power to ensure economic stability and growth. At the same time, such groups as blacks and labor unions wanted the federal government to intervene actively to improve social and political conditions. Other citizens, however, opposed any extension of federal power, especially in sensitive areas such as civil rights.

Other unresolved questions animated postwar politics. Could the New Deal coalition of labor unions, black voters, urban dwellers, and ethnic groups survive and regroup after the death of its charismatic leader, Franklin D. Roosevelt? What new goals would it set? The postwar years saw a widening of the New Deal agenda to encompass topics not addressed in the 1930s, most notably civil rights. Little of this platform was translated into legislation in the 1940s and 1950s, but it came to fruition during the Democratic 1960s. The Democratic coalition was inherently unstable, however, torn among its diverse constituencies and their conflicting priorities for the exercise of federal power. The impact of the "new politics" on national elections after 1960, which focused attention on candidates rather than on traditional party structures, also weakened the New Deal coalition. After the 1960s, it struggled to maintain its predominance in the political system.

In the 1950s and 1960s, some of the most dramatic decisions affecting people's daily experiences came from the Supreme Court. Unlike the New Deal years, when the Supreme Court played an obstructionist role, during the postwar period the Supreme Court often acted as a catalyst for sweeping social change. The court decisions of this period arguably had as great an impact on American society as anything proposed by the president or Congress. So much of this judicial dynamism was linked to Earl Warren, the Chief Justice from 1953 to 1969, that the Supreme Court of these years is often referred to as the Warren Court.

These postwar political developments occurred against a backdrop of dramatic new responsibilities in foreign affairs. The United States and the Soviet Union were locked in an intense ideological confrontation, called the cold war, throughout most of the postwar period. The desire of American leaders to stop the worldwide spread of communism led to vastly increased defense spending, the forging of permanent diplomatic and military alliances with other nations, and the deployment of U.S. military forces in Korea and Vietnam. Insecurities about the nation's new role abroad fueled fears of communist infiltration and internal subversion at home, a reflection of the blurring of the lines between international and domestic events that characterized the postwar period.

As commander-in-chief of the world's most powerful military apparatus and manager of an ever-growing federal bureaucracy, the president became the most important policymaker in the political system. Franklin Roosevelt's enormously successful four terms in office had heightened expectations for presidential leadership. Increasingly, many citizens looked to Washington for solutions to national and local problems. The four presidents who followed Roosevelt—Harry S Truman, Dwight D. Eisenhower, John F. Kennedy, and Lyndon B. Johnson—all grappled with the responsibilities and challenges of this new presidential power.

Harry Truman and the Fair Deal

When Harry Truman was summoned to the White House on April 12, 1945, after learning of Roosevelt's death, he asked the president's widow, "Is there anything I can do for you?" Eleanor Roosevelt responded with another question, "Is there anything we can do for you? For you are the one in trouble now." Truman, not content to be a caretaker president for a Roosevelt fifth term, wanted to be a strong president in his own right. He kept the fractious New Deal coalition alive by proposing new federal programs to advance the interests of the varied groups that comprised it. His "Fair Deal" shaped the Democratic party's agenda for the next twenty years.

The Man from Missouri

Many observers asked, "Who the hell is Harry Truman?" when Franklin Roosevelt chose him as his running mate in the 1944 presidential campaign. Widely regarded as a political lightweight, Truman had been an unsuccessful small-town haberdasher in Missouri before rising through state and national politics, partly due to his connections with Tom Pendergast's Democratic machine in Kansas City. His Senate investigations into waste and inefficiency in the war mobilization effort won him a spot on the 1944 ticket.

Truman brought a complex character to the presidency. Alternately humble and cocky, thick-skinned and easily outraged, he had none of Roosevelt's patrician ease. Yet he handled affairs with an assurance and crisp dispatch that has endeared him to later generations. "If you can't stand the heat, stay out of the kitchen," he liked to say of presidential responsibility. Two mottoes graced his desk. One was "The buck stops here"; the other was a remark by fellow Missourian Mark Twain, "Always do right. This will gratify some people and astonish the rest."

When Harry Truman took over the presidency, Americans welcomed him with an initial approval rate of 87 percent, according to Gallup polls. Within a year, his popularity had dropped to 32 percent and new phrases such as "To err is Truman" had entered the political language. What had happened? New to the presidency, Truman had to oversee the complex conversion of a war economy to a peacetime one. At the same time, he had to grapple with deteriorating relations with the Soviet Union. When the economy suffered and the cold war worsened, Americans blamed their president.

The main problem was inflation. While consumers sought the end of wartime restrictions and price rationing, Truman feared economic chaos if all controls were lifted immediately. In the summer of 1945, he eased industrial controls but retained the wartime Office of Price Administration. When the OPA was disbanded in 1946, prices soared. That year saw an annual inflation rate of 18.2 percent. The persistence of shortages of food and products also irritated consumers.

The rapidly rising cost of living prompted demands for higher wages by the nation's workers. By 1945, the number of union members had swelled to more than 14 million—two-thirds of all workers in the mining, manufacturing, construction, and transportation industries. The labor movement had held the line on wages during the war but now was angered as corporate profits doubled while real wages declined due to inflation and the end of wartime overtime pay. Determined to make up for their war-induced sacrifices, workers mounted strikes in major sectors of the economy, crippling the automobile, steel, and coal industries. By the end of 1946, 5 million workers had idled factories and mines for a total of 107,476,000 work days.

HELEN GAHAGAN DOUGLAS
Representative Helen Gahagan Douglas of California, a former Broadway and film star, illustrated a 1947 speech supporting the reestablishment of price controls by bringing a market basket of food to a press conference. Douglas served in Congress from 1944 until 1950, when she was defeated in a bid for the Senate by Representative Richard M. Nixon. (Western History Collections, University of Oklahoma Library)

Truman never doubted his proper course of action. It was the president's job to ensure domestic tranquillity and economic stability, even if it meant alienating organized labor, an important component of the Democratic coalition. "If you think I'm going to sit here and let you tie up this whole country, you're crazy as hell," Truman told leaders of a nationwide railroad strike in the spring of 1946. Truman seized the nation's railroad system and asked Congress for power to draft striking workers into the army, a move that infuriated labor. The president also took a tough stand against labor leader John L. Lewis and the striking United Mine Workers by seizing control of the mines that spring. Such actions won Truman support from Americans fed up with labor disruptions, but he incurred the enmity of organized labor.

These domestic upheavals did not bode well for the Democrats at the polls. In the 1946 elections, Republicans capitalized on popular dissatisfaction with the myriad reconversion problems with the simple slogan "Had enough?" The Republicans gained control of both houses of Congress for the first time since 1928. Truman and the Democrats seemed thoroughly repudiated.

Unity had returned to the Democratic coalition by the time of the 1948 presidential election, however. The most dramatic reversal came from labor. The Republican Congress elected in 1946 was determined to undo the New Deal's social welfare measures, and it singled out labor legislation as a special target. In 1947, Congress passed the Taft-Hartley Act, a direct challenge to several provisions of the 1935 National Labor Relations Act. Truman issued a ringing veto of the Taft-Hartley bill in June 1947, calling it "bad for labor, bad for management, and bad for the country." Congress easily overrode Truman's veto, but his action brought labor back into the Democratic fold.

The 1948 Election

Most observers believed that Truman faced an impossible task in the presidential campaign of 1948. The Republicans were united and well led. They maintained the loyal support of most middle- and upper-income Protestants outside the South, and many farmers and skilled workers. Eager to attract votes from traditional Democratic

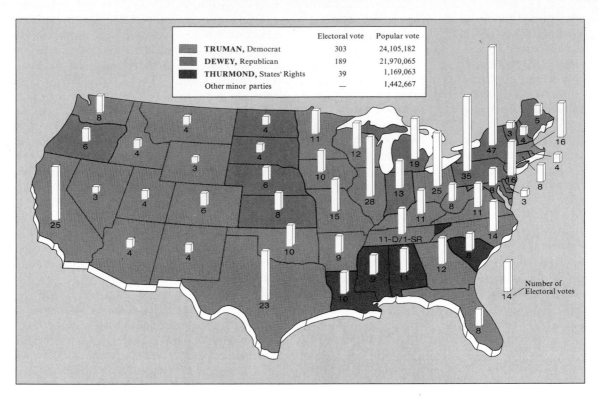

MAP 28.1 ELECTION OF 1948
Political adviser Clark Clifford planned Truman's successful electoral strategy in 1948, arguing that the president should concentrate his campaign in urban areas where the Democrats had their greatest strength. In an election marked by low turnout, Truman held onto enough support from the Roosevelt coalition of blacks, union members, and farmers to defeat Dewey by more than two million votes.

constituencies, they rejected their own conservative favorite, Senator Robert A. Taft of Ohio, in favor of a moderate, Governor Thomas E. Dewey of New York. A renowned prosecuting attorney, Dewey had demonstrated his attractiveness as a national candidate in his 1944 campaign against Roosevelt. To increase their appeal in the West, the Republicans nominated Earl Warren, governor of California, for vice-president. Their brief platform promised to continue most New Deal reforms. Dewey was so certain of victory that he acted, as one journalist observed, "like a man who has already been elected and is merely marking time, waiting to take office."

Truman, in contrast, led a party in severe disarray. Both the left and right wings of the Democratic party split off and nominated their own candidates. Henry A. Wallace, a former New Dealer whom Truman had fired as secretary of commerce in 1946 over disagreements on foreign policy, chose to run as the candidate of the new Progressive party. Wallace advocated increased government intervention in the economy and more power for labor unions. Most controversially, he called for greater cooperation with the Soviet Union, saying in 1946, "The tougher we get, the tougher the Russians will get."

Southern Democrats also bolted the party. At the Democratic national convention, leaders such as Mayor Hubert H. Humphrey of Minneapolis and gubernatorial candidate Adlai E. Stevenson of Illinois had pushed through a strongly prolabor, procivil rights platform, which called for the repeal of Taft-Hartley, the establishment of a permanent Fair Employment Practices Commission, and federal antilynching and antipoll tax legislation. The civil rights plank was too much for the southerners. They had grudgingly supported Roosevelt's and Truman's internationalist foreign policy and a greater role for the government in the economy, but they would not tolerate federal interference in race relations. Three days after the convention, southern Democrats met in Birmingham, Alabama to set up the States' Rights, or Dixiecrat, party. They nominated Governor J. Strom Thurmond of South Carolina for president.

In spite of the fractured Democratic coalition and confident Republican opposition, Truman fought back with one of the most effective presidential campaigns ever waged. He dramatically called Congress back into summer session to give the Republicans a chance to enact their platform into law. When, predictably, they failed to do so, he launched a strenuous cross-country speaking tour, hitting out at the "do-nothing Republican Congress." He also hammered away at the Republicans' support for the antilabor Taft-Hartley Act and their opposition to full-parity price supports for farmers. Truman struck just the right chord. At his rallies enthusiastic listeners took up the cry, "Give 'em hell, Harry!"

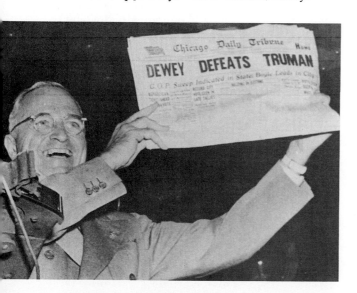

TRUMAN TRIUMPHANT
In one of the most famous photographs in American political history, Harry S Truman gloats over an inaccurate headline in the *Chicago Tribune*. Pollsters had predicted an overwhelming victory for Thomas E. Dewey. Their primitive polling techniques, however, did not reflect the dramatic shift in support for Truman during the last days of the campaign. (Saint Louis Globe Democrat)

Truman won a remarkable victory, receiving 49.6 percent of the vote to Dewey's 45.1 percent. Strom Thurmond and the Dixiecrats carried four southern states. Henry Wallace failed to carry a single state. Truman basically owed his election to the ongoing vitality of the Democratic coalition. As *The New Republic* observed, "Harry Truman won this election because Franklin Roosevelt had worked so well." Truman retained the support of organized labor and Jewish and Catholic voters in the big cities; the allegiance of northern black voters to the Democratic party offset the southern losses to the Dixiecrats. (The discovery that the Democrats could capture the presidency without the Solid South paved the way for later civil rights legislation.) Most important, Truman appealed effectively to people like himself who hailed from the farms, towns, and small cities in the nation's heartland. He had grasped something the pollsters had missed: "Everybody's against me but the people."

Truman's Fair Deal

On September 6, 1945, just four days after Japan surrendered to end World War II, Truman staked his claim to domestic leadership with a call for expanded federal responsibilities that he named the Fair Deal. Against a backdrop of abundance, rather than the austerity that had shaped the New Deal, Truman phrased his proposals in terms of the rights of individual citizens—the right to a "useful and remunerative" job, stable prices, protection from monopoly, good housing, "adequate medical care," "protection from the economic fears of old age," and a "good education." Soon Truman added support for civil rights as well.

Despite a generally hostile Congress, the Truman administration accomplished much of this agenda. The minimum wage was raised from forty cents an hour to seventy-five; the Social Security system was extended to cover ten million new workers and its benefits raised by 75 percent. The National Housing Act of 1949 declared as public policy "the goal of a decent home and a suitable living environment for every American family" and called for the construction of 810,000 units of low-income housing.

With the Employment Act of 1946, the federal government also began to develop tools to pursue a coherent economic policy. The legislation formally integrated Keynesian ideas into American economic policy, proposing federal fiscal planning on a permanent basis, not just in times of crisis such as the Great Depression. Beside supporting the use of government spending to spur economic growth, the Employment Act envisioned the use of tax policy as a tool for managing the economy—cut taxes to spur economic growth; raise taxes to slow inflation. Yet the act failed to establish clear economic priorities, such as the proper weight between the commitment to full employment and the need for a balanced budget. And the new three-member Council of Economic Advisers, appointed by the president and directly responsible to the White House, played only an advisory role. On balance, however, the Employment Act of 1946 marked an important turning point toward federal responsibility for the performance of the economy.

The Truman administration also made civil rights a national political issue for the first time. Several factors explained this shift. Black expectations had been raised by wartime opportunities. In addition, Truman realized that black voters played an increasingly large role in the Democratic party as they migrated from the South, where they were effectively disenfranchised, to northern cities. Finally, Truman was sensitive to the world's view of the American government's treatment of blacks, especially since the Soviet Union often compared segregation of southern blacks with the Nazis' treatment of the Jews.

Truman's civil rights proposals included a federal anti-lynching law, federal protection of voting rights (such as an end to poll taxes), and a permanent federal agency to guarantee equal employment opportunities. A filibuster by southern conservatives effectively blocked such legislation in Congress, but Truman found other means to advance the cause of civil rights. By executive order, he began the process of desegregating the armed forces. He ordered the Justice Department to prepare *amicus curiae* (friend of the court) briefs in Supreme Court cases such as *Shelley v. Kraemer* (1948), which struck down as unconstitutional restrictive covenants designed to enforce residential segregation. He appointed a National Civil Rights Commission, whose recommendations called for an expanded federal role in civil rights that foreshadowed much of the legislation of the 1960s.

Despite such accomplishments, the Democratic coalition in the 1940s was not strong enough to overcome the opposition of various interest groups on several key items on the Fair Deal agenda. The American Medical Association squashed the movement for national health insurance by denouncing it as the first step toward "socialized medicine." Catholics successfully opposed any aid-to-education proposal that omitted subsidies for parochial schools. Filibusters by southern senators prevented congressional action on civil rights. Farmers refused to join labor in supporting the outright repeal of Taft-Hartley. While the Fair Deal forestalled any wholesale attacks on the New Deal, with the exception of the revisions to the National Labor Relations Act contained in Taft-Hartley, the Truman administration could not mobilize popular and congressional support for enlarged federal responsibilities in the economic and social spheres.

Two further factors limited the Fair Deal's chances for legislative success. One was the outbreak of the Korean War in 1950. The United States sent troops to repel an attack on South Korea by North Korean Communists, draining both money and energy away from domestic reform. The other was the nation's growing fear of internal subversion. The anticommunist crusade was just one manifestation of the increasing preoccupation with the cold war that was seeping into all facets of American life. Truman's own administration played a major role in fueling these domestic tensions.

The Great Fear

The deterioration of relations with the Soviet Union after 1945 and the onset of the cold war underlay the domestic repression that gripped the country in the late 1940s and early 1950s. Americans often call this phenomenon "McCarthyism," after Senator Joseph R. McCarthy of Wisconsin, the decade's most vocal anticommunist. But this "great fear" was actually much broader than the work of just one man. The obsessive concern over internal subversion reflected a deep-seated American insecurity spawned by worsening cold war tensions. Few Communists were actually found in positions of power; far more Americans became innocent victims of the false accusations and innuendoes that flourished in the postwar climate of fear.

In the 1930s, liberals and Communists had cooperated in a "popular front" against fascism. By the mid-1940s, however, deteriorating relations with the Soviet Union made that totalitarian state seem as large a threat to the American way of life as fascism had been a decade earlier. Some postwar liberals, notably Henry Wallace and his followers in the Progressive party, continued to seek cooperation with the Soviet Union and were not disturbed by the presence of communist activists in their political movement. Yet many other liberals, best represented by the Americans for Democratic Action, founded in 1947, broke from the popular front by including a strident anticommunist plank in their political agenda.

Similarly, Communists had been active in the labor-organizing drives of the 1930s, and their contributions were welcomed, if not openly acknowledged. By the late 1940s, however, the labor movement reversed itself and suddenly purged Communists from its membership. CIO president Phillip Murray denounced communist sympathizers as "skulking cowards . . . apostles of hate." Unions that refused to oust their left-wing leaders, such as the United Electrical, Radio and Machine Workers of America, were expelled from the CIO.

The federal government also undertook its own antisubversion campaign. In 1947, President Truman outraged many supporters by ordering a comprehensive investigation into the loyalty of all federal employees. More than six million individuals were subjected to security checks, and fourteen thousand underwent intensive FBI investigation. Two thousand resigned, although not a single case of espionage was found.

The case of Dorothy Bailey, a forty-one-year-old graduate of Bryn Mawr College and the University of Minnesota, typified the abuses of the federal program. A fourteen-year veteran of the U.S. Employment Service, Bailey lost her job because an unidentified informer claimed she was a Communist and associated with known Communists. Brought before the District of Columbia regional loyalty board, she denied the charge. No evidence against her was introduced and no

witnesses testified to support the charges, but she lost her job anyway.

Soon many state and local governments, colleges and universities, and private institutions and businesses undertook their own antisubversion campaigns. All 11,000 faculty members at the University of California were required to take a loyalty oath; UCLA alone fired 157 who refused to do so. In Hollywood, ex-FBI agents circulated a blacklist of actors, directors, and writers whose names had been mentioned in congressional investigations or whose associations and friends had been described as dubious. Industry executives denied the existence of any such list, but for ten years, hundreds of people were shut out of work in the entertainment industry. The Weavers, a popular group of folk singers, were blacklisted after 1954, and politically active actors such as Zero Mostel and John Garfield had difficulty finding work. One day Jean Muir headlined the popular radio show "The Aldrich Family"; the next she was out of a job, fired, the network said, not because she was a Communist but because gossip about her had made her too "controversial."

The House Committee on Un-American Activities (HUAC) played an especially active role in fanning the anticommunist hysteria. HUAC had been ferreting out supposed Communists in government since its 1938 investigation into the New Deal's Federal Theatre Project. In 1947, HUAC intensified its crusade by holding widely publicized hearings on communist infiltration in the film industry. For example, HUAC members objected to the 1944 film *Song of Russia*—made while the United States was still allied with the Soviet Union—because the director had shown Communists smiling. Novelist Ayn Rand, called as an expert witness, explained, "It is one of the stock propaganda tricks of the Communists to show these people smiling." When asked if no one in the Soviet Union ever smiled, Rand replied, "If they do, it is privately and accidentally. Certainly, it is not social. They don't smile in approval of their system." A group of writers and directors, soon dubbed the "Hollywood Ten," went to jail for contempt of Congress when they cited the First Amendment rather than testify about their past associations.

HUAC next took up, with a vengeance, the case of Alger Hiss, a former New Deal State

PETE SEEGER TESTIFIES BEFORE THE HOUSE COMMITTEE ON UN-AMERICAN ACTIVITIES (1955)

Seeger, a folksinger, songwriter, and member of the Weavers, was one of many performers and artists called to testify before HUAC.

Mr. Tavenner: When and where were you born, Mr. Seeger?

Mr. Seeger: I was born in New York in 1919.

Mr. Tavenner: What is your profession or occupation?

Mr. Seeger: Well, I have worked at many things, and my main profession is a student of American folklore, and I make my living as a banjo picker—sort of damning, in some people's opinion. . . .

Mr. Tavenner: You said that you would tell us about the songs. Did you participate in a program at Wingdale Lodge in the State of New York, which is a summer camp for adults and children, on the weekend of July Fourth of this year? [Witness consulted with counsel.]

Mr. Seeger: Again, I say I will be glad to tell what songs I have ever sung, because singing is my business.

Mr. Tavenner: I am going to ask you.

Mr. Seeger: But I decline to say who has ever listened to them, who has written them, or other people who have sung them.

Mr. Tavenner: Did you sing this song, to which we have referred, "Now Is the Time," at Wingdale Lodge on the weekend of July Fourth?

Mr. Seeger: I don't know any song by that name, and I know a song with a similar name. It is called " Wasn't That a Time." Is that the song?

Chairman Walter: Did you sing that song?

Mr. Seeger: I can sing it. I don't know how well I can do it without my banjo.

Chairman Walter: I said, Did you sing it on that occasion?

Mr. Seeger: I have sung that song. I am not going to go into where I have sung it. I have sung it many places. . . .

Chairman Walter: I direct you to answer the question. Did you sing this particular song on the Fourth of July at Wingdale Lodge in New York?

Mr. Seeger: I have already given you my answer to that question, and all questions such as that. I feel that is improper to ask about my associations and opinions. I have said that I would be voluntarily glad to tell you any song, or what I have done in my life.

Chairman Walter: I think it is my duty to inform you that we don't accept this answer and the others, and I give you an opportunity now to answer these questions, particularly the last one.

Mr. Seeger: Sir, my answer is always the same.

Source: Eric Bentley, ed., *Thirty Years of Treason: Excerpts from Hearings before the House Committee on Un-American Activities, 1938–1968.* New York: Viking, 1971. 686, 690.

Department official who had accompanied Franklin Roosevelt to Yalta. The case against Hiss rested on the 1948 testimony of former Communist Whittaker Chambers, a senior editor at *Time.* Chambers claimed that Hiss had passed him classified documents in the 1930s as part of his duties as a member of a secret communist cell in the government. Congressman Richard M. Nixon of California orchestrated the HUAC investigation of Hiss, which culminated in the dramatic release of the so-called Pumpkin Papers, microfilm that Chambers had hidden in a pumpkin patch on his Maryland farm. (This supposedly incriminating cache, when declassified, contained only Navy Department documents on life rafts and fire extinguishers.) Since the statute of limitations on espionage had expired by 1949, Hiss was charged instead with perjury for denying Chambers's charges before HUAC. The first trial resulted in a hung jury; the second found Hiss guilty of perjury in early 1950.

The hysteria soon became worse. In 1946, Senator Joseph McCarthy, a Marine Corps veteran, had won election in the 1946 Republican landslide with the slogan "Wisconsin Needs a

Tail Gunner in the Senate." In late 1949, McCarthy discovered that an anticommunist attack on a liberal Madison, Wisconsin newspaper brought him favorable attention. In a February 1950 speech in Wheeling, West Virginia, he launched what one columnist later called his string of "multiple untruths" by declaring, "I have here in my hand a list of the names of 205 men that were known to the Secretary of State as being members of the Communist Party and who nevertheless are still working and shaping the policy of the State Department." McCarthy never revealed the names on his list, later changing the number to 81, then to 57.

McCarthy's political genius was his ability to make his name synonymous with the issue of subversives in government. Politicians who attacked him exposed themselves to charges of being soft on communism, the kiss of death in the postwar political climate. McCarthy's supporters at first were more visible than his detractors; such Democratic congressmen as John F. Kennedy of Massachusetts thought "McCarthy may have something." But President Truman called McCarthy's charges "slander, lies, character assassination," although he could do nothing to curb them. Even when Republican Dwight D.

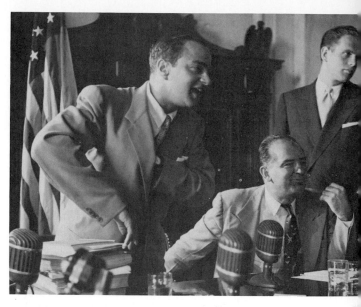

THE MCCARTHY ERA
Senator Joseph R. McCarthy of Wisconsin became famous in the early 1950s when he charged that Communists held many positions in the government. This photograph shows McCarthy and his two chief aides on the Senate Committee on Government Operations, Roy Cohn (left) and G. David Schine (right). (© Eve Arnold, Magnum)

Eisenhower was elected president in 1952, he did not publicly challenge his party's most outspoken senator.

The momentum of international events allowed McCarthy to retain credibility, despite his failure to identify a single Communist in government. Alger Hiss was convicted in 1950. The Korean War broke out soon after, embroiling the United States in a frustrating fight against communism in a faraway land. And in a sensational but isolated case, Julius and Ethel Rosenberg were accused in 1951 of passing atomic secrets to the Soviet Union. They were convicted, and were executed in 1953.

In 1954, McCarthy finally overreached himself by launching an investigation into possible subversion in the U.S. Army. The lengthy televised hearings brought McCarthy's smear tactics and leering innuendoes into the nation's living rooms, and support for him declined. Later that year, the Senate voted 67 to 22 to censure McCarthy. He died three years later at the age of forty-eight, his name forever attached to a period of political repression of which he was only the most flagrant manifestation.

NIXON AND THE HISS CASE
As a member of the House Un-American Activities Committee, Richard Nixon (far right) parlayed his aggressive questioning of Alger Hiss, a former State Department official, into a national political reputation. In his memoirs called *Six Crises* (1962), Nixon devoted the first chapter to the Hiss case. (UPI)

Modern Republicanism

The Republican party found it difficult to rival the New Deal coalition. The party's greatest strength lay in the largely Protestant and rural states of the Midwest. Since only a third of the nation's registered voters were Republicans, however, the party had to find a candidate who could attract Democrats and independents. Republican leaders quickly realized that General Dwight D. Eisenhower would be just such a candidate. His election in 1952 did not carry with it a stable Republican majority to replace the prevailing Democratic coalition, but it led the party back to national power and slowed the expansion of the federal government.

The Soldier Turned Politician

Dwight Eisenhower's status as a war hero was his greatest political asset. Born in 1890 and raised in Abilene, Kansas, he graduated from the United States Military Academy at West Point in 1915. General Douglas MacArthur chose him as his aide in the early 1930s, and Eisenhower rose dramatically through the ranks. After Pearl Harbor, he came to Washington under the sponsorship of a second mentor, General George C. Marshall. By 1944, Eisenhower was Supreme Commander of Allied Forces in Europe, where he directed the D-Day invasion of France. To hundreds of thousands of soldiers, and to the millions who followed the war on newsreels, he was simply "Ike," the best known and best liked of the nation's military leaders.

By 1952, Eisenhower had placed himself in a superb position for a presidential campaign. As a professional military man, he could insist that he stood "above politics." While in the army, in fact, he had never voted because he felt that such political activity would represent an intrusion of the military into civilian affairs. Many Democrats had hoped to make him their candidate for president in 1948, and again in 1952. Eisenhower did want the office, but as a Republican.

When conservative candidate Senator Robert A. Taft of Ohio did well in the early primaries, Eisenhower resigned his military position to campaign. He quickly proved an effective politician. He defeated Taft in primaries in New Hampshire, Pennsylvania, and New Jersey and took delegates away from Taft in a tough fight at the Republican National Convention. Eisenhower then asked Senator Richard M. Nixon of California to be his running mate. Young, tirelessly partisan, and with a strong anticommunist record from his crusade against Alger Hiss, Nixon brought an aggressive campaign style, as well as ideological and regional balance, to the ticket.

The Democrats never seriously considered renominating Harry Truman, who by 1952 was a thoroughly discredited leader. During the last two years of his presidency, his public approval rating had never risen above 32 percent and at one point had plunged to 23 percent. Lack of popular enthusiasm for the Korean War dealt the severest blow to Truman's support, but a series of widely publicized scandals involving federal officials in bribery, kickback, and influence-peddling schemes caused voters to complain about the "mess in Washington." With a certain relief, the Democrats turned to Governor Adlai E. Stevenson of Illinois, who enjoyed the support of respected liberals such as Eleanor Roosevelt and of organized labor. To appease southern voters, the Democratic convention nominated Senator John A. Sparkman of Alabama for vice-president.

Throughout the 1952 campaign, Stevenson advocated New Deal–Fair Deal policies with an almost literary wit and eloquence, but Eisenhower's artfully unpretentious speeches proved more effective with the voters. Eager to get maximum support from a broad electorate, Eisenhower played down specific questions of policy. Instead, he attacked the Democrats with the "K_1C_2" formula—"Korea, Communism, and Corruption." In a campaign pledge that clinched the election, he vowed to go to Korea to end the stalemated war if elected. Stevenson lamely quipped, "If elected, I shall go to the White House."

The only slip in the Republican campaign was the revelation that wealthy Californians had set up a secret "slush fund" for Richard Nixon. While Eisenhower contemplated dropping Nixon from the ticket, the vice-presidential candidate adroitly used television to appeal directly for voters' sympathy. He had not misused campaign funds, he asserted. Whereas Truman appointees had accepted mink coats from contractors—a reference to a widely reported case involving a loan examiner for the Reconstruction Finance Corporation—his wife wore only a "Republican cloth coat." Nixon did admit accepting one gift, a puppy his young daughters had named Checkers. That gift he would not give back, he declared earnestly. Nixon's televised pathos turned an embarrassing incident into an advantage. He effectively bypassed traditional Republican leaders by winning support from the general public to keep him on the ticket. The "Checkers speech" showed how the mass media—notably the new medium of television—were fundamentally changing the political process.

The Republican campaign paid off handsomely, with Eisenhower winning 55 percent of the popular vote. He carried all the northern and western states and won majorities in four southern states. Although Eisenhower won a great personal victory, Republican candidates for Congress ran far behind him. They won control of the House of Representatives by a slender margin of four seats; in 1954, Democrats regained control of both houses, an advantage they held for the rest of the Eisenhower years. When the enormously popular Eisenhower won an easy

reelection over Adlai Stevenson in 1956, he became the only president to win election while his party lost control of both houses of Congress.

The "Hidden-Hand" Presidency

Seeking a middle ground between liberalism and conservatism, Eisenhower offered "modern Republicanism" as an alternative to the Democrats' New Deal and Fair Deal. He did his best to set a quieter national mood, to slow down the pace of public life. As columnist Richard L. Strout observed in *The New Republic*, "The less he does the more they love him. Here is a man who doesn't rock the boat." Even Democratic challenger Adlai Stevenson agreed that "it is time for catching our breath." The nation's voters put it more simply in a popular slogan: "I Like Ike."

Yet Eisenhower was no stooge as president. Several historians have characterized his style of leadership as the "hidden-hand presidency." They point to Eisenhower's deft behind-the-scenes maneuvering while maintaining a public demeanor of a benign leader who did not concern himself with partisan questions. They also cite the president's skillful handling of the press. When his press secretary, James Hagerty, asked what he would say at a press conference about

PRESIDENT IKE
Arthur Krock of *The New York Times* characterized President Dwight D. Eisenhower's news conferences as events "in which numbers and genders collide, participles hang helplessly and syntax is lost forever." Eisenhower's vagueness and confusion in public contrasted with his more decisive and effective style behind the scenes. (UPI)

a tricky foreign policy issue, Eisenhower replied, "Don't worry, Jim. If that question comes up, I'll just confuse them." He proved just as adept in personnel situations. In a characteristic move, Eisenhower recognized the outspoken anticommunism of Clare Booth Luce, an author, playwright, and former Republican member of Congress from Connecticut, by making her the nation's second woman ambassador. At the same time, by sending Luce to Italy, he removed her strident opinions from the Washington scene.

Eisenhower's presidential style deliberately avoided confrontation. He refused to speak out publicly, for example, against Senator Joseph McCarthy. Likewise, he displayed little leadership in the emerging area of civil rights. Inadvertently, though, he contributed to the advance of the black cause. In September 1953, he named Governor Earl Warren of California as chief justice of the Supreme Court. Warren's quiet persuasion convinced the Court to rule unanimously in *Brown v. Board of Education of Topeka* (1954) that racial segregation in the public schools was unconstitutional. Eisenhower remained disturbed by the decision, asserting, "I don't believe you can change the hearts of men with laws or decisions." Nonetheless, in 1957 he sent federal troops to enforce the integration of Central High School in Little Rock, Arkansas. Congress also passed the Civil Rights Act of 1957, a weak bill most notable for being the first national civil rights legislation passed since Reconstruction.

Eisenhower presided over other cautious increases in federal activity. When the Soviet Union launched the first satellite (called *Sputnik*, or "earth traveler") into space in 1957, Eisenhower supported a U.S. space program to catch up with the Russians. Arguing that the cold war required more scientists and experts on foreign affairs, he persuaded Congress to appropriate additional money for college and university scholarships, as well as increased support for research and development in universities and industry. He also yielded to demands of interest groups for increased federal outlays on veterans' benefits, unemployment compensation, housing, and Social Security. The minimum wage was raised from seventy-five cents an hour to a dollar. The creation of the new Department of Health, Education, and Welfare (HEW) confirmed the federal commitment to welfare programs. When HEW head Oveta Culp Hobby, the second woman to hold a cabinet position, suggested that it would be "socialized medicine" for the government to offer free distribution of the new Salk polio vaccine, she was forced from office by the adverse public reaction.

Under the Eisenhower administration, the government undertook new commitments on a more massive scale. It sponsored the construction of the Saint Lawrence Seaway to link the Great Lakes with the Atlantic Ocean. In a move that drastically altered the American landscape and favored the trend toward privately owned automobiles rather than mass transit, the Federal Highway Act of 1956 authorized $26 billion over a ten-year period for the construction of a nationally integrated highway system. Projects such as the Saint Lawrence Seaway and interstate highways were the largest public works programs to date, surpassing anything the New Deal had undertaken.

Dwight Eisenhower realized that the vast federal budget, which reached almost 23 percent of the gross national product by the late 1950s, gave the government a major responsibility for the overall health of the nation's economy. The president made the fight against inflation, not full employment, his top economic priority. Eisenhower and his advisers believed their policies would encourage business confidence and lead to prosperity, but the economy grew only at the modest rate of 2.9 percent per year between 1953 and 1960—too slowly to absorb all those who sought work. Furthermore, Eisenhower's drive for a balanced budget and stable prices contributed to the recessions of 1953–1954, 1957–1958, and 1960–1961.

Modern Republicanism, it turned out, resisted the unchecked expansion of federal power but did not cut it back in any tangible fashion. The responsibilities now accepted by the federal government—which included social welfare programs inherited from the New Deal, a commitment to managing the economy, and increased defense expenditures necessitated by the United States' larger role abroad—negated any return to the limited Republican government that had prevailed in the 1920s. When Eisenhower retired from public life in 1961, the government had become an even greater presence in everyday life than when he took office.

The New Politics and the 1960 Campaign

The crucial question for the Republicans in 1960 was whether they could maintain their hold on the presidency without popular Dwight D. Eisenhower. The Twenty-Second Amendment now limited a president to two terms. A Republican-controlled Congress had passed the measure in 1951 to prevent another long-term presidency such as Franklin Roosevelt's. Ironically, it precluded another Eisenhower term.

The Republicans turned without opposition to Vice-President Richard M. Nixon, who like a good junior executive had patiently served Eisenhower, gaining experience and waiting for his turn at the top. Nixon campaigned for an updated version of Eisenhower's policies, carefully staking out a position between the Republican conservative wing, now led by Senator Barry M. Goldwater of Arizona, and the moderate wing represented by Governor Nelson A. Rockefeller of New York. Nixon was hampered, however, by the occasionally lukewarm support he received from Eisenhower. Asked whether Nixon had helped make any major policy decisions in his administration, Eisenhower replied, "If you give me a week I might think of one."

After two unsuccessful tries with Adlai Stevenson as their candidate, the Democrats turned to Senator John Fitzgerald Kennedy of Massachusetts, who beat out Hubert Humphrey and Lyndon Johnson for the nomination. An alumnus of Harvard and a World War II hero, Kennedy had inherited his love of politics from his grandfathers, both of whom had been colorful Boston politicians. His wealthy father, Joseph P. Kennedy, had headed the Securities and Exchange Commission and served as ambassador to Great Britain under Roosevelt. First elected to Congress in 1946, John Kennedy moved to the Senate in 1952. Ambitious, hard-driving, and deeply aware of style, he made full use of his many advantages to become, as novelist Norman Mailer put it, "our leading man." Besides his youth—he was only forty-three—Kennedy's greatest disadvantage was his Catholicism.

The 1960 campaign marked the introduction to the national scene of political practices called the "new politics." Originally developed in California in the late 1940s and early 1950s, this political style was well suited to a state that was growing so fast that it did not have entrenched political machines or active party organizations. California covered such a huge territory that candidates had to rely on billboard and newspaper advertising, radio spots, and television ads rather than personal contact with voters to win statewide office. The state also lacked the strong union tradition that influenced politics in other parts of the country.

Charisma, style, and personality, rather than issues and platforms, were the hallmarks of the new politics. The media were the key to the new approach, and politicians paid special attention to the ability of television to reach individual voters. (By 1960, 88 percent of the nation's households owned at least one TV set.) Professional media consultants now advised candidates on their proper image, and professional pollsters

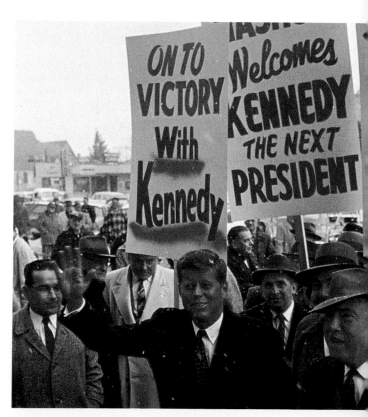

THE NEW POLITICS COMES TO NEW HAMPSHIRE
John Fitzgerald Kennedy, the first Catholic ever elected president, was also the first Democratic presidential nominee from New England in over one hundred years. Here the Massachusetts senator campaigns in neighboring New Hampshire, whose primary he won handily in February 1960. (Hank Williams. *Life* Magazine © 1960 Time, Inc.)

not only told candidates whether they were leading their opponents, but also what ideas to stress in order to get elected.

The spread of the new politics contributed to a decline in the role of traditional political party organizations at the national level. The new politics targeted its appeal to enthusiastic amateurs outside the traditional party organization, rather than to the ward bosses, state committee officials, and party machines that once delivered the votes on election day. By using the media, campaigns could bypass the party structures to touch, if only with a thirty-second commercial, the ordinary citizen.

Running such campaigns took money, however, and the required funds often far exceeded those available through the traditional party coffers. Once candidates began to seek campaign funds from other sources (wealthy donors, mass mailings, or, by the 1970s, from political action committees set up by corporations, labor unions, or special interest groups to channel contributions to candidates), the influence of political parties diminished even further. In addition, party loyalty declined as growing numbers of voters identified themselves as independents, a major shift from patterns of political behavior in the nineteenth and early twentieth centuries. The combination of these factors made it increasingly difficult to maintain the New Deal coalition.

John Kennedy was a perfect candidate to take the new politics to the national level in 1960, and his campaign altered the nature of American presidential contests. His family's wealth and the contributions he raised from sources outside traditional party donors paid for this expensive campaign. Thanks both to his media advisers

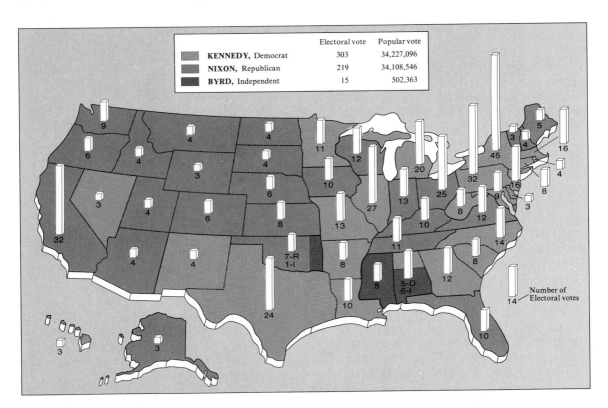

	Electoral vote	Popular vote
KENNEDY, Democrat	303	34,227,096
NIXON, Republican	219	34,108,546
BYRD, Independent	15	502,363

Number of Electoral votes

MAP 28.2 ELECTION OF 1960
The election of 1960 produced the closest popular vote since 1884. Kennedy won twelve states, including Illinois, by less than 2 percent of the two-party vote tally, and lost six others, including California, to Nixon by a similarly small margin. Kennedy won 303 electoral votes, the same number that President Truman had received in 1948, but his margin of victory was far slimmer, showing how the electoral college vote can be misleading as an indicator of popular support.

and to his personality, he projected a superb television image. His mastery of this method enabled him to appeal directly to the voters, rather than through the Democratic party.

Another innovation of the 1960 campaign was a series of four televised debates between the two major candidates. These debates further confirmed the new dominance of mass media in political life. Nixon, a far less photogenic personality than Kennedy and at an added disadvantage because he was recovering from a minor illness, looked sallow and unshaven under the intense studio lights. Kennedy, by contrast, looked vigorous, cool, and self-confident on the TV screen, and he dispelled voters' doubts that he was not as well prepared for the presidency as the former vice-president. Confirming that appearances swayed political perceptions, voters who listened to the first debate on the radio concluded that Nixon had won, whereas TV viewers judged in Kennedy's favor.

Despite the ground Kennedy picked up in the debates, he won only the narrowest of victories, receiving 49.7 percent of the popular vote to Nixon's 49.5 percent. Kennedy had successfully appealed to the diverse elements of the Democratic coalition, attracting large proportions of Catholic voters and blacks and strengthening his party's appeal to the middle class. Yet only 120,000 votes out of a total of 69 million cast separated the two candidates, and the shift of a few thousand votes in key states such as Illinois would have reversed the election results. Although Kennedy had campaigned on a promise to get America moving again, the electoral results hardly gave him a popular mandate for sweeping change.

The Politics of Expectation

During the 1960s, Americans placed new demands on the federal government. John F. Kennedy's brilliant articulation of the aspirations of many Americans, enhanced by his youth and self-confidence, enabled him to reconstitute the Democratic coalition. Kennedy's shocking assassination in November 1963, and the extraordinary energy of his successor, Lyndon Baines Johnson, then set in motion a remarkable expansion of federal power. In 1964, big-city Catholics,

the middle class, and many southern whites joined organized labor and blacks in one of the largest and most diverse political coalitions ever assembled in the United States.

For a brief period in 1965–1966, this coalition held together. Under Johnson's leadership, the Democrats enacted nearly all of the legislative program Harry Truman had outlined in 1946. By making the federal government far more powerful than ever before, the new legislation encouraged the constituents of the Democratic coalition to redouble their demands. By 1968, this dramatic expansion of federal power had raised unanticipated problems for the coalition.

Kennedy's Thousand Days

The administration of John Fitzgerald Kennedy began amid great promise. "Let the word go forth from this time and place," he orated in his inaugural address, "to friend and foe alike, that the torch has been passed to a new generation of Americans, tempered by war, disciplined by a hard and bitter peace, proud of our ancient heritage." Unlike his predecessor, Kennedy believed the federal government ought to be strong, visible, and active and that the president should set the tone for such leadership. In foreign policy, he remained a resolute cold warrior. At home, his "New Frontier" would be built on patriotism and service. "Ask not what your country can do for you," he insisted at his inauguration. "Ask what you can do for your country."

Kennedy's dramatic emphasis on the importance of the federal government attracted unusually bright and ambitious people to his administration. Robert S. McNamara, former president of the Ford Motor Company, introduced "systems analysis" techniques to the Department of Defense. Republican banker C. Douglas Dillon brought the corporate managers' desire for expanded markets and stable economic growth to the Department of the Treasury. The president's younger brother Robert took over the Department of Justice as attorney general, and his brother-in-law Sargent Shriver headed the popular Peace Corps. A host of "honorary Kennedys," trusted advisers and academics from leading universities, flocked to Washington to join the New Frontier.

Kennedy expected his appointees to move

quickly. "The deadline for everything is the day before yesterday," exclaimed one cabinet member. House Speaker Sam Rayburn was skeptical about this vigorous approach to government. Kennedy's people "might be every bit as intelligent as you say," he told his old friend Lyndon Johnson, "but I'd feel a whole lot better about them if just one of them had run for sheriff once."

The expansive vision of presidential leadership that Kennedy and his advisers brought to the White House stood in stark contrast to their rather meager legislative accomplishments. Kennedy was hampered by his lack of a popular mandate, which left him with a tiny Democratic majority of two in the Senate and twenty-two in the House. A conservative coalition of southern

THE AMERICAN SPACE PROGRAM
Marine Lieutenant Colonel John Glenn, shown preparing for his historic 1962 flight, became the first American to orbit the earth. The space program had cold war overtones as the United States tried to catch up and surpass early successes of the Soviet Union, including beating the Russians to the moon. (FPG)

Democrats and western and midwestern Republicans effectively stalled most liberal initiatives.

One domestic program that did win both popular and congressional support was increased funding for space exploration. In 1958, seven astronauts had been chosen for America's Mercury space program. On May 5, 1961, just three months after Kennedy took office, Alan Shepard became the first American launched into space; on February 2, 1962, John Glenn became the first American to orbit the earth. (Soviet cosmonaut Yuri Gagarin held the distinction of being the first person in space with his 108-hour flight in April 1961.) At the height of American fascination with space in 1961, Kennedy proposed that "this nation should commit itself to achieving the goal, before this decade is out, of landing a man on the moon and returning him safely to earth." To accomplish this mission, achieved in July 1969, he supported the creation of a massive new federal agency, the National Aeronautics and Space Administration (NASA).

The Peace Corps was the New Frontier program that most captured the public imagination. The idea, Kennedy explained on March 1, 1961, was to create "a pool of trained American men and women" to be sent "overseas by the United States government or through private organizations and institutions to help foreign countries meet their urgent needs for skilled manpower." Thousands of idealistic Americans, most of them recent college graduates, responded to the call, agreeing to devote two or more years to such tasks as teaching English to Philippine schoolchildren and helping African villagers obtain adequate supplies of water. As Kennedy aide Arthur M. Schlesinger, Jr., explained, the Peace Corps embodied Kennedy's desire "to replace protocol-minded, striped-pants officials by reform-minded missionaries of democracy who mixed with the people, spoke the native dialects, ate the food, and involved themselves in local struggles against ignorance and want."

Kennedy's most striking domestic achievement was his successful use of modern economics to shape fiscal policy. Initially Kennedy had shared the belief of many conservative business leaders that the federal government could best contribute to economic growth by reducing the national debt and maintaining a balanced budget. However, at the urging of Walter Heller, chairman of the Council of Economic Advisers, Kennedy decided on a different course to stimulate the economy. Rather than increase federal spending to accomplish this result, he proposed a dramatic cut in the taxes paid by businesses and the public. A tax cut, he argued, would leave more money in the hands of taxpayers, enabling them to increase their investments and purchases, and thus bring about economic growth by creating more wealth and jobs. For a time, federal expenditures would exceed federal income, but after a year or two, the expanding economy would raise taxpayers' incomes, leading in turn to higher tax revenues.

Congress predictably balked at this unorthodox proposal. But Lyndon Johnson pressed for it after Kennedy's assassination and signed it into law in February 1964. The Kennedy-Johnson tax cut of 1964 marked the first purposeful use of the federal budget—fiscal policy—to encourage steady economic growth. Although economic expansion started before the effects of the tax cut could be felt, Kennedy and his economic advisers got credit for it anyway. The gross national product grew at a rate of 5 percent during the 1960s, nearly twice the rate achieved during the Eisenhower administration. Much of this growth, however, was fueled by massive defense expenditures for the escalating Vietnam War.

Kennedy's interest in stimulating economic growth did not include a corresponding commitment to spending for domestic needs. John Kenneth Galbraith, his most liberal economic adviser, had argued that it would be better to stimulate the economy by expanding social programs than by cutting taxes: What is the advantage, Galbraith asked, "in having a few more dollars to spend if the air is too dirty to breathe, the water is too polluted to drink, the commuters are losing out in the struggle to get in and out of cities, the streets are filthy, and the schools are so bad that the young, perhaps wisely, stay away"? Kennedy rejected such advice, advocating increased spending only for weapons and space, and sent Galbraith off as ambassador to India.

The president did not entirely ignore the legislative agenda Franklin Roosevelt and Harry Truman had set for the Democratic party. He proposed federal aid to elementary and secondary schools, federal investment in mass transportation, medical insurance for the elderly funded through Social Security, and wilderness preservation. But he failed to define any of these proposals in terms satisfactory to a majority in Congress and all were defeated.

Dissension within the Democratic coalition was particularly evident in the case of aid to education. Most northern Democrats favored such aid, but they disagreed about important details. Blacks and civil rights advocates insisted that federal school aid go only to desegregated schools, while Catholics insisted that federal assistance be extended to parochial systems. After great effort, Kennedy persuaded black leaders to accept a school aid plan that ignored existing segregation, but he told southern whites that federal aid would not be guaranteed to segregated schools in the future. Because Kennedy was himself a Catholic, however, he feared angering Protestants if he proposed a bill that permitted aid to parochial schools. In the absence of a bill acceptable to all these groups, the education proposal died in committee.

Kennedy failed to provide decisive leadership in other domestic fields. He ignored women's issues and appointed fewer women to federal positions than Eisenhower or Truman had. Most tellingly, he never made civil rights a top priority. He believed he would need the votes of southern whites to win reelection in 1964, and he sought to hold them in the Democratic coalition by delaying the civil rights reforms he had promised during the 1960 campaign. He doubted such measures would pass in any case. "There is no sense in raising hell," he insisted, "and then in not being successful."

Some of the most controversial decisions of the early 1960s, however, came not from the Kennedy administration, but from the Supreme Court under the leadership of Chief Justice Earl Warren. This activist Supreme Court came to represent for many Americans an intrusive federal presence they had not sought and did not want. In *Gideon v. Wainright* (1963), *Escobedo v. Illinois* (1964), and *Miranda v. Arizona* (1966), the Supreme Court greatly expanded the rights of suspects accused of crimes. Tackling the issue of reapportionment in *Baker v. Carr* (1962) and *Reynolds v. Sims* (1964), the Court put forth the

THE WARREN COURT
This photograph of the Supreme
Court was taken in 1965, with Chief
Justice Earl Warren in the middle of
the front row. Until President Ronald
Reagan named Sandra Day
O'Connor to the Court in 1981, all
pictures of the nation's highest court
showed nine solemn robed men. (©
Fred Ward, Black Star)

doctrine of "one person, one vote," which substantially increased the representation of urban
areas, with their concentration of black and Hispanic residents, at the expense of rural regions.
Perhaps the most controversial decision of all
was *Engel v. Vitale* (1962), which outlawed prayer
in public schools as a violation of the First
Amendment's injunction that "Congress shall
make no law respecting an establishment of religion." President Kennedy, like President Eisenhower before him, could only pledge to uphold
the law of the land, even when he disagreed
with the scope of judicial activism.

By late 1963, Kennedy had realized little of his
promise. He had expanded the government
through his space and arms programs, his intervention in the economy, and his successful effort
to attract able people to federal service. While
partisans later claimed he planned to expand antipoverty, health, and education programs; commit federal resources to civil rights; withdraw
American troops from Vietnam; and reduce tensions with the Soviet Union, we will never know
what he might have accomplished.

On November 22, 1963, Kennedy went to
Texas, a state he needed to win in order to be
reelected in 1964. As he rode in an open car past
the Texas School Book Depository in Dallas, he
was shot and killed by an assassin's bullet. Before Air Force One left Dallas to take the presi-

dent's body back to Washington, a grim-faced
Vice-President Lyndon Johnson was sworn in as
president. Kennedy's stunned widow, Jacqueline, still wearing a bloodstained pink suit,
looked on.

By 1 P.M. Dallas time, just thirty minutes after
the shooting, 68 percent of the adults in the
United States, about seventy-five million people,
knew that Kennedy had been shot. By late afternoon, the proportion had risen to 99.8 percent,
showing how within a few hours, the mass media could connect practically every person in the
nation. As on Pearl Harbor Day in 1941, people
never forgot what they were doing when they
first heard Kennedy had been shot. The shock
that greeted the assassination reflected the personal identification that ordinary Americans felt
with the occupant of the White House, a situation quite different from the last assassination of
an American president, that of William McKinley in 1901.

Americans suspended normal activities for
four days as they sought reassurance in ceremonies of grief and continuity. All three major
television networks canceled their commercial
programs, and an estimated audience of 100 million Americans collectively mourned the slain
president. They saw 250,000 people pay their
last respects as Kennedy's body lay in state in
the Capitol rotunda; they watched as his coffin

was drawn up Pennsylvania Avenue on a horse-drawn caisson, led by a riderless horse with reversed boots in the stirrups; they admired the dignified bearing of Jacqueline Kennedy as she and her two young children walked behind the casket; and they joined the procession past a million mourners to the burial place in Arlington National Cemetery on a hill overlooking the city of Washington. These shared televison images bound the American people together at a time of national grief.

Kennedy's buoyant youth, the trauma of his assassination, and the collective sense that Americans had been robbed of a promising leader contributed to a powerful Kennedy mystique. This mythologizing process had begun even before his tragic death. In June 1963, about 59 percent of the people surveyed claimed to have voted for Kennedy, and after the assassination, this figure rose to 65 percent. British journalist Godfrey Hodgson called it "a posthumous landslide."

The Kennedy assassination also set off a national wave of self-examination. Americans debated whether the murder of the president had been an isolated act or the symbol of a deep tragic flaw in the democratic system. (The argument that there was something wrong with the nation gained credence two days after the assassination, when Kennedy's accused killer, Lee Harvey Oswald, a twenty-four-year-old loner who had spent three years in the Soviet Union, was himself gunned down by Jack Ruby, a Dallas nightclub owner, on live network television.) Chief Justice Earl Warren warned ominously about "forces of hatred and malevolence" that made such acts possible, and newspapers and magazines asked, "What sort of nation are we?" Later in the 1960s, many Americans overwhelmed by the social conflict of that decade looked back on November 22, 1963, as the day when things began to come apart.

Johnson and the Great Society

Without offering any radical or sweeping programs, John Kennedy fostered an atmosphere conducive to challenging the status quo, a climate that has been called the "politics of expectation." President Lyndon Johnson, through his astonishing energy and genius for compromise,

translated these unformed strivings for change into a concrete program.

Born in the central Texas hill country in 1908, Johnson had served in Washington since 1932 as congressional aide, New Deal administrator, congressman, senator, senate majority leader, and finally vice-president. He had far more legislative experience than any modern president, and he used his talent to great effect. A man of singular force, he often got his way by using what one journalist called the "Johnson treatment." Approaching unsuspecting colleagues, he moved "in close, his face a scant millimeter from his target, his eyes widening and narrowing, his eyebrows rising and falling. From his pockets poured clippings, memos, statistics. Mimicry, humor, and the genius of analogy made the Treatment an almost hypnotic experience." Johnson invariably left his targets overwhelmed and bruised—and willing to go along.

Johnson seized the initiative almost as soon as Kennedy's assassination thrust him into the presidency. He called for rapid passage of New

THE "JOHNSON TREATMENT"
Lyndon B. Johnson, a shrewd and adroit politician, learned many of his legislative skills while serving as Majority Leader of the Senate from 1953 to 1960. Here, in characteristic LBJ style, he zeroes in on Senator Theodore Francis Green of Rhode Island. After succeeding John Kennedy in the White House, Johnson remarked, "They say Jack Kennedy had style, but I'm the one who's got the bills passed." (George Tames, *The New York Times*)

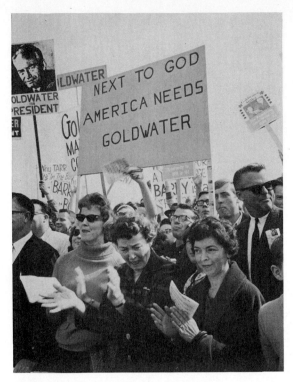

COMPAIGNING FOR GOLDWATER
Lyndon B. Johnson's election to the presidency in 1964 was made easier when the Republicans nominated Senator Barry Goldwater of Arizona as their candidate. Goldwater rallied conservatives behind the motto, "In your heart you know he's right." Democrats effectively played on fears that Goldwater might support the use of nuclear weapons by countering, "In your heart you know he might." (© Declan Haun)

Frontier proposals, especially the tax cut and civil rights legislation, as a memorial to the slain president. Dramatically reminding Congress that he himself, a Texan, had supported civil rights, he made it difficult for any southerner to oppose the issue. "I urge you again, as I did in 1957 and again in 1960," he told Congress, "to enact a civil rights law so that we can move forward to eliminate from this nation every trace of discrimination and oppression that is based upon race or color."

By June, black pressure and Johnson's sure-handed tactics had their impact. Breaking a southern filibuster, the Senate approved the most far-reaching civil rights legislation since Reconstruction. The 1964 Civil Rights Act guaranteed equal access to public accommodations and schools and prohibited discrimination by em-

ployers and unions. It granted new powers to the U.S. attorney general to enforce these guarantees and established the Equal Employment Opportunity Commission to prevent job discrimination by race, religion, national origin, or sex.

If 1964 was a year of liberal triumph in Congress, it was a year of conservative retrenchment within the Republican party. The Republican nominee for president in 1964 was Senator Barry Goldwater of Arizona. Goldwater, who was determined to offer "a choice, not an echo," campaigned against the expansion of federal power in such areas as the economy and civil rights. Goldwater's crisp speeches rejected efforts to build a moderate coalition. "Extremism in the defense of liberty is no vice," he stated. "Moderation in the pursuit of justice is no virtue."

President Johnson easily won his party's nomination. Reaffirming his commitment to the liberal Democratic agenda, but putting some distance between himself and the Kennedy administration, Johnson passed over Robert F. Kennedy for vice-president in favor of Senator Hubert H. Humphrey of Minnesota, who in 1948 had introduced the controversial civil rights plank that split the party. An attempt by an avowed segregationist, Governor George C. Wallace of Alabama, to exploit a white backlash against civil rights showed early momentum but then fizzled. The Johnson-Humphrey ticket won by one of the largest margins in history, receiving 61.1 percent of the popular vote. It even surpassed the 1936 landslide of that great coalition builder, Franklin D. Roosevelt, Johnson's political idol and mentor. Johnson's sweeping victory brought with it Democratic gains in Congress and state legislatures.

Lyndon Johnson held an expansive view of presidential leadership. Eager to make his own mark on American history and only too aware that the liberal majority in Congress was likely to be short-lived, Johnson pressed for prompt legislation to achieve his "Great Society." "Hurry boys, hurry," he urged his staff. "Get that legislation up to the Hill and out. Eighteen months from now ol' Landslide Lyndon will be Lame-Duck Lyndon." As he forcefully put it, "There are some administrations that do and some that don't. This one is gonna do."

The Eighty-ninth Congress enacted more social-reform measures than any session since Roosevelt's first term, offering something for every important element of the Democratic coalition. Responding to growing black demands, Johnson increased federal support for civil rights. The Voting Rights Act of 1965 authorized the attorney general to send federal examiners to the South to register voters. In 1963, only a fourth of all southern blacks were registered to vote; when Johnson left office in 1969, their ranks had swelled to two-thirds.

Johnson also found a way to break the congressional deadlock on aid to education. The Elementary and Secondary Education Act of 1965 authorized $1 billion in federal funds to benefit impoverished children attending Catholic schools, rather than aiding the schools themselves. With his flair for the dramatic, Johnson signed the education bill in the one-room Texas schoolhouse he had attended as a child.

The Eighty-ninth Congress also gave Johnson the votes to enact the federal health insurance legislation first proposed by President Truman. Realizing it could no longer block federal health insurance in its entirety, the American Medical Association proposed that federal funds be used to pay doctors as well as hospitals. The resulting compromise was an expansive new program that included both Medicare, a plan for the elderly funded from an increment to Social Security payroll taxes, and Medicaid, a health plan for welfare recipients paid for by general tax revenues. By 1975, the cost of Medicare reached $18 billion. Medicaid grew more slowly at first, but by the mid-1970s it covered twenty-four million people and cost $14 billion annually. Few policymakers had anticipated that Medicare and Medicaid costs would spiral so dramatically.

The middle class benefited from Democratic programs as much as the poor did. Federal urban renewal and home mortgage assistance aided those who could afford to live in single-family homes or in modern apartments. Medicare assistance went to every elderly person covered by Social Security, regardless of need. Much of the federal aid to education benefited the children of the middle class. Johnson successfully pressed for expansion of the national park system, for legislation to improve the quality of the air and water, for increased land-use planning, and, at the insistence of his wife, Lady Bird Johnson, for the Highway Beautification Act of 1965. That year also saw the creation of the National Endowment for the Arts to support the performing and creative arts, and the National Endowment for the Humanities, which encouraged efforts to understand and interpret the nation's cultural and historical heritage.

Although Johnson's programs offered something for every constituency in the Democratic coalition, he always insisted that the top priority of his Great Society was "an end to poverty in our time." The problem of poverty was very real. As political activist Michael Harrington had pointed out in his book *The Other America: Poverty in the United States* (1962), the poor were everywhere, but their poverty was curiously invisible in affluent America. Poor people made up about a fourth of the American population; three-fourths of the poor were white. The poor in the United States were isolated farmers and miners in Appalachia, country folk recently uprooted from the land, blacks mired in urban ghettos, Hispanics in migrant labor camps and urban barrios, native Americans on reservations, women trying against all odds to raise families on their own, and the abandoned and destitute elderly. Modern American technology had "made a longer, healthier, better life possible," Harrington observed, yet it left the poor "on the fringe, on the margin": "They watch the movies and read the magazines of affluent America, and these teach them that they are internal exiles."

New Deal social welfare programs had failed to reach these people. Since unemployment insurance ran out after a few months, it did nothing to protect against extended joblessness. Social Security and other social-insurance programs provided benefits to workers who paid for them through special taxes; such measures did not cover farm workers, hospital janitors and orderlies, laundry workers, or women who cared for their children at home or cleaned other people's houses. Social welfare programs such as Old Age Assistance, Aid to Dependent Children, and Aid to the Blind carried strict restrictions regarding eligibility.

The Office of Economic Opportunity (OEO), established by the omnibus Economic Opportunity Act of 1964, became the Great Society's showcase in the "War on Poverty." OEO programs were so numerous and diverse that they recalled the alphabet agencies of the New Deal. Sargent Shriver, who left the Peace Corps to head the new agency, admitted, "It's like we

MICHAEL HARRINGTON DESCRIBES "THE OTHER AMERICA" (1962)

There are perennial reasons that make the other America an invisible land.

Poverty is often off the beaten track. It always has been. The ordinary tourist never left the main highway, and today he rides interstate turnpikes. He does not go into the valleys of Pennsylvania where the towns look like movie sets of Wales in the thirties. He does not see the company houses in rows, the rutted roads (the poor always have bad roads whether they live in the city, in towns, or on farms), and everything is black and dirty. And even if he were to pass through such a place by accident, the tourist would not meet the unemployed men in the bar or the women coming home from a runaway sweatshop. . . .

These are the normal and obvious causes of the invisibility of the poor. They operated a generation ago; they will be functioning a generation hence. It is more important to understand that the very development of American society is creating a new kind of blindness about poverty. The poor are increasingly slipping out of the very experience and consciousness of the nation. . . .

Clothes make the poor invisible too: America has the best-dressed poverty the world has ever known. For a variety of reasons, the benefits of mass production have been spread much more evenly in this area than in many others. It is much easier in the United States to be decently dressed than it is to be decently housed, fed, or doctored. Even people with terribly depressed incomes can look prosperous. . . .

And finally, the poor are politically invisible. It is one of the cruelest ironies of social life in advanced countries that the dispossessed at the bottom of society are unable to speak for themselves. The people of the other America do not, by far and large, belong to unions, to fraternal organizations, or to political parties. They are without lobbies of their own; they put forward no legislative program. As a group, they are atomized. They have no face; they have no voice. . . .

These, then, are the strangest poor in the history of mankind.

They exist within the most powerful and richest society the world has ever known. Their misery has continued while the majority of the nation talked of itself as being "affluent" and worried about neuroses in the suburbs. In this way tens of millions of human beings became invisible. They dropped out of sight and out of mind; they were without their own political voice.

Yet this need not be. The means are at hand to fulfill the age-old dream: poverty can now be abolished. How long shall we ignore this underdeveloped nation in our midst? How long shall we look the other way while our fellow human beings suffer? How long?

Source: Michael Harrington, *The Other America: Poverty in the United States.* New York: Macmillan, 1962. 11–13, 170.

---

went down to Cape Kennedy [the NASA space center in Florida] and launched a half dozen rockets at once."

The War on Poverty produced some of the most significant and controversial measures of the Johnson administration. Head Start provided free nursery schools designed to prepare disadvantaged preschoolers for kindergarten. The Job Corps and the Neighborhood Youth Corps trained young people. Upward Bound gave low-income teenagers the skills and motivation to plan for college. The Appalachian Regional Development Act, the Metropolitan Area Redevelopment Act, and the Demonstration Cities Act were intended, like foreign aid, to spur development of impoverished areas. Volunteers in Service to America (VISTA), modeled on the Peace Corps, provided technical assistance to the rural poor. The Community Action Program encouraged the poor to organize to demand "maximum feasible participation" in the decisions that affected them. Community Action organizers worked closely with the two thousand lawyers employed by the Legal Services Program to provide the poor with free access to the legal system.

The OEO quickly drew criticism, however. VISTA and Community Action Program agents had encouraged poor people to mount militant demands for public services long withheld by unresponsive local governments controlled by middle- or upper-class politicians. Community organizers on the government payroll in Syracuse, New York, for example, formed tenants' rights groups to protest conditions in public housing, conducted voter registration drives to unseat unpopular elected representatives, and even used public funds to bail out activists arrested for protesting at local welfare offices. Legal Services lawyers challenged welfare and housing administrations in class-action suits. Needless to say, such activism upset entrenched political elites. Such mayors as Sam Yorty in Los Angeles and Richard J. Daley in Chicago vociferously resisted OEO guidelines for including poor people in program planning and administration.

The Great Society also tried to reduce poverty by expanding long-established social insurance and welfare programs. It broadened Social Security to include waitresses, cleaning people, farm workers, and hospital employees. Benefits for the elderly were raised, extended to include Medicare, and (in 1972) indexed to rise with inflation. Social welfare expenditures also increased rapidly, especially for Aid to Families with Dependent Children (AFDC). Housing programs provided $3 billion worth of public housing and rent subsidies annually by 1974. The Food Stamp program, begun in 1964 largely to stabilize farm prices, grew into a major program of assistance to low-income families.

In the end, however, the War on Poverty did little to reduce poverty or redistribute wealth. Using a definition of poverty as half the median family income, the poverty line in 1963 was set at three thousand dollars. That year, 20 percent of the population lived below the poverty line. In 1976, the median family income had risen to fifteen thousand dollars, but 20 percent of the nation still received less than half that amount. Technological change and economic growth had raised everyone's material standard of living so that the poor were better off in an absolute

sense. Relatively, however, they remained as far behind the middle class as ever. In effect, the War on Poverty and related welfare efforts simply provided the nation's poor with about the share of income they had always received.

The ambiguous accomplishments of the Great Society suggest the difficulties of promoting fundamental political and economic change through federal initiatives. Its record also reveals contradictions inherent in the New Deal coalition. These contradictions had been lurking in political life ever since Franklin Roosevelt and Harry Truman began to expand the impact of the

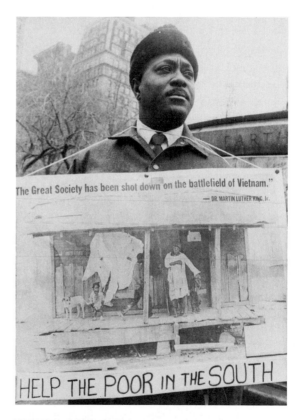

BUTTER, NOT GUNS
This placard graphically protested that the Vietnam War diverted money from government social and economic programs aimed at aiding the nation's poor. Many Americans shared this view, and antiwar demonstrations spread across the United States. The protesters included students on hundreds of college campuses. (© Michael Abramson, Gamma-Liaison)

TIME LINE
THE POLITICS OF POST-NEW DEAL AMERICA

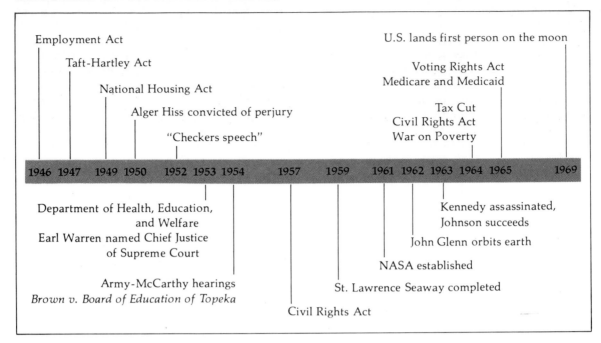

federal government on American society. John Kennedy and Lyndon Johnson had brought an extraordinarily diverse set of groups into the New Deal coalition—middle-class and poor; white, black, and Hispanic; Protestant and Catholic; urban and rural. As the functions and responsibilities of the government grew, so did demands for further action from this widening cast of politically organized constituencies. Yet the demands of certain groups—such as the cry of blacks for civil rights and of the urban poor for increased political power—conflicted with the interests of other Democratic supporters, such as white southerners and northern political bosses eager to maintain the status quo. In the end, the New Deal coalition, which had fostered a vast and powerful federal government, could not sustain a consensus over the purposes that such a government ought to serve.

The Great Society was not just a victim of the factionalism of the Democratic coalition. It was also, in the haunting phrase of civil rights leader Martin Luther King, Jr., "shot down on the battle-fields of Vietnam." In 1966, the government spent $22 billion on the Vietnam War and only $1.2 billion on the War on Poverty. Nearly two hundred thousand American soldiers were fighting in Vietnam by the end of 1965, four hundred thousand by the end of 1966, and half a million a year later. After 1966, as Lyndon Johnson turned his full attention to the escalating war, the domestic programs of the Great Society fell by the wayside.

Johnson never admitted to the American people the extent of the nation's growing involvement in Vietnam; nor did he confront the true cost of ending poverty through legislative activism. At a time of nearly full employment, his failure to press for a tax increase to cover the expanded budget commitments at home and abroad led to a growing deficit and accompanying high inflation. Johnson's attempt to carry out simultaneously, in historian Garry Wills's apt phrase, a "welfare" and "warfare" state provoked by 1968 a profound crisis from which the Democratic coalition has yet completely to recover.

The growth of the federal government dominated the postwar period. The major concern in postwar politics was the purposes that this expanded federal power should serve. The concentration of power in Washington also led to a corresponding growth in the responsibilities of the president, whom citizens now invested with rising expectations of leadership. John F. Kennedy especially stimulated this "politics of expectation."

The Democratic party set much of the legislative agenda for the postwar period, expanding the reforms first introduced by Franklin Roosevelt in the 1930s. Harry Truman's Fair Deal won only limited legislative victories but added civil rights to the national political agenda. The Republican administration of Dwight Eisenhower did not seek to roll back the New Deal and, in fact, presided over cautious increases in federal power. Lyndon Johnson, building on the wave of public emotion after Kennedy's assassination, significantly expanded the welfare state with his Great Society.

In political party organization, the two decades after 1945 were dominated by the Democratic coalition first assembled during the New Deal—labor, blacks, urban dwellers, ethnic groups, and a large section of the middle class who had benefited from New Deal programs. Between 1952 and 1960, despite the personal popularity of President Eisenhower, the Republicans were unable to establish a majority to overtake the vital New Deal coalition. By the late 1960s, however, the consensus of the Democratic party was threatened by controversy over social programs at home and the escalating Vietnam war abroad.

Suggestions for Further Reading

Three lively books provide excellent introductions to the politics of the postwar period: William Manchester, *The Glory and the Dream: A Narrative History of America, 1932–1972* (1973); Godfrey Hodgson, *America in Our Time* (1976); and William E. Leuchtenberg, *A Troubled Feast: American Society Since 1945* (1979).

Harry Truman and the Fair Deal

Harry S. Truman's *Memoirs* (1955–1962) tell his story in characteristically pointed language; see also Merle Miller's oral history, *Plain Speaking* (1980). Eric F. Goldman, *The Crucial Decade and After—America, 1945–1960* (1961), offers an account of the period. The best description of Truman's presidency is Alonzo L. Hamby, *Beyond the New Deal: Harry S. Truman and American Liberalism* (1973). See also Richard J. Donovan, *Conflict and Crisis* (1977). Critical perspectives are presented in Barton J. Bernstein, ed., *Politics and Policies of the Truman Administration* (1970). Arthur M. Schlesinger, Jr., states the case for Fair Deal liberalism in *The Vital Center* (1949).

The story of the Democratic coalition can be traced in Samuel Lubbell, *The Future of American Politics* (1965); V. O. Key, *Politics, Parties, and Pressure Groups* (1964); Angus Campbell, ed., *Elections in the Political Order* (1967); and Everett C. Ladd and Charles Hadley, *Transformations of the American Party System* (1978). The 1948 campaign is described in Irwin Ross, *The Loneliest Campaign* (1968), and Jules Abels, *Out of the Jaws of Victory* (1959). The best account of Henry Wallace's challenge to Truman is Norman D. Markowitz, *The Rise and Fall of the People's Century: Henry A. Wallace and American Liberalism* (1973). Joseph P. Lash, *Eleanor: The Years Alone* (1972), describes the former First Lady's continuing work for liberal causes. James T. Patterson, *Mr. Republican: A Biography of Robert A. Taft* (1972), is the best account of Truman's chief Republican critic.

Stephen K. Bailey's model *Congress Makes a Law* (1957) covers the battle over the Employment Act of 1946. Other aspects of the Truman administration are treated by Arthur F. McClure, *The Truman Administration and the Problems of Postwar Labor* (1969); Allen J. Matusow, *Farm Policies and Politics in the Truman Years* (1967); and Susan Hartmann, *Truman and the 80th Congress* (1971).

The literature on McCarthyism is voluminous and intense. David Caute, *The Great Fear* (1978), provides a vivid introduction, which can be supplemented by Victor Navasky, *Naming Names* (1980), and Athan G. Theodaris, *Spying on Americans* (1978). Two biographies are Thomas C. Reeves, *The Life and Times of Joe McCarthy* (1982), and David Oshinsky, *A Conspiracy So Immense* (1983); but Richard Rovere's *Senator Joseph McCarthy* (1959) still commands attention. Michael P. Rogin, *The Intellectuals and McCarthy* (1967), analyzes McCarthy's base of support, while Robert Griffith, *The Politics of Fear* (1970), and Richard Fried, *Men Against McCarthy* (1976), look at the politics involved.

Allen Weinstein, *Perjury: The Hiss-Chambers Case* (1978), covers the still-debated Alger Hiss case. Walter and Miriam Schneir, *Invitation to an Inquest* (1965), and Ronald Radosh and Joyce Milton, *The Rosenberg File*

(1983), cover the Rosenberg case. Lillian Hellman offers her biting memoir of the period in *Scoundrel Time* (1976). Eric Bentley, ed., *Thirty Years of Treason* (1971), collects excerpts from testimony before the House Committee on Un-American Activities.

Modern Republicanism

Two standard overviews of the Eisenhower administration, Herbert S. Parmet, *Eisenhower and the American Crusades* (1972), and Charles C. Alexander, *Holding The Line* (1975), can be supplemented by Fred I. Greenstein, *The Hidden-Hand Presidency* (1982), and Stephen Ambrose, *Eisenhower the President* (1984). Blanche Wiesen Cook, *The Declassified Eisenhower* (1984), contrasts the covert activities of the administration with its public image. For scientific developments, consult James R. Killian, Jr., *Sputnik, Scientists, and Eisenhower* (1976). Richard M. Nixon, *Six Crises* (1962), offers the perspective of the vice-president.

For the Supreme Court, useful surveys include Archibald Cox, *The Warren Court* (1968); Alexander Bickel, *The Supreme Court and the Idea of Progress* (1970); and Philip B. Kurland, *Politics, the Constitution, and the Warren Court* (1970). Anthony Lewis, *Gideon's Trumpet* (1964), narrates one of the era's most famous cases.

The Politics of Expectation

The best histories of politics in the 1960s are Allen J. Matusow, *The Unraveling of America: A History of Liberalism in the 1960s* (1984); Jim F. Heath, *Decade of Disillusion: The Kennedy-Johnson Years* (1975); and James L. Sundquist, *Politics and Policy: The Eisenhower, Kennedy, and Johnson Years* (1968).

The indispensible account of the 1960 presidential campaign is Theodore H. White, *The Making of the President—1960* (1961). Arthur M. Schlesinger, Jr., *A Thousand Days* (1965), and Theodore Sorenson, *Kennedy* (1965), offer uncritical, but highly readable accounts of the New Frontier. See also Roger Hilsman, another Kennedy aide, *To Move a Nation* (1967). Critical views appear in David Halberstam, *The Best and the Brightest* (1972); Henry Fairlie, *The Kennedy Promise: The Politics of Expectation* (1973); and Gary Wills, *The Ken-*

nedy Imprisonment (1980). The best account of President Kennedy's assassination is William Manchester's overwritten *The Death of the President* (1967); Anthony Summer's *Conspiracy* (1980) provides a careful review of the ongoing controversy.

Lyndon Johnson's own account of his presidency is *The Vantage Point* (1971). Doris Kearns, *Lyndon Johnson and the American Dream* (1976), and Merle Miller, *Lyndon: An Oral Biography* (1980), are based on extensive conversations with Johnson. Rowland Evans and Robert D. Novak offer a vigorous portrait in *Lyndon B. Johnson: The Exercise of Power* (1966), and Robert A. Caro provides a critical interpretation of Johnson's early career in *The Path to Power* (1982). Eric F. Goldman, *The Tragedy of Lyndon Johnson* (1969), and George E. Reedy, *The Twilight of the Presidency* (1975), are sympathetic but critical views from former aides. For the 1964 election, see Theodore H. White, *The Making of the President—1964* (1965). Barry M. Goldwater presented his ideas in *The Conscience of a Conservative* (1960), which can be supplemented by Phyllis Schlafly, *A Choice Not an Echo* (1964).

Michael Harrington called attention to poverty in *The Other America* (1962). Other accounts of poverty include Harry M. Caudill, *Night Comes to the Cumberlands* (1963); J. Wayne Flynt, *Dixie's Forgotten People* (1979); and Susan Estabrook Kennedy, *If All We Did Was to Weep at Home* (1979). Sar A. Levitan describes the war on poverty in *The Great Society's Poor Law* (1969) and, with Robert Taggart, argues that it was quite effective in *The Promise of Greatness* (1976). Charles R. Morris, *A Time of Passion* (1984), offers thoughtful reflections from a former antipoverty administrator. Daniel P. Moynihan criticizes the community action programs in *Maximum Feasible Understanding* (1969). Other critical discussions of antipoverty programs include John Donovan, *The Politics of Poverty* (1973); Peter Marris and Martin Rein, *Dilemmas of Social Reform* (1973); and Richard Cloward and Frances Fox Piven, *Poor People's Movements* (1978). Marvin E. Gettleman and David Mermelstein, eds., *The Great Society Reader* (1965), criticize the prevailing assumptions behind many Johnson initiatives.

29

PERMANENT
MOBILIZATION AND
THE COLD WAR

*W*orld War II brought about a revolution in American foreign policy, ending two centuries of isolation from world diplomatic affairs. Before the war, the United States had no formal alliances, no troops stationed on foreign soil, and only a small defense budget. After 1945, the United States willingly sought a lasting, indeed dominant, role in international affairs. A state of permanent mobilization has characterized American society ever since, whether or not the United States has been formally at war. By the late 1960s, the military budget exceeded $80 billion annually, more than 1.5 million military personnel were stationed in a hundred foreign countries, and the United States had entered into defense treaties with forty-eight other nations.

American postwar foreign policy combined both old and new concerns. In keeping with the ideals enunciated by Woodrow Wilson during World War I, the United States continued to promote the peaceful expansion of its capitalist economic system throughout the world. It also maintained support for political democracy, national self-determination, and the breakup of colonial empires. Yet new policy directions rivaled, and finally overshadowed, those economic and

political considerations. The most striking aspect of postwar American foreign policy was strident ideological confrontation with the Soviet Union, accompanied by military and diplomatic efforts to contain the spread of communism. The desire to maintain military parity with the Soviets, and the corresponding Soviet push to match American strength, set in motion the arms race that dominated the postwar period.

The dramatic shift in American foreign policy after 1945 had important domestic repercussions. Permanent mobilization required higher defense expenditures and a military draft. Every neighborhood seemed to have at least one son in military service. It fostered the creation of a powerful military establishment that linked the armed services with scientific and corporate communities in the cause of national security. Finally, permanent mobilization led to a revolution in American government, as the executive branch assumed an almost uncheckable authority over the conduct of foreign affairs. In keeping with the centralization of American life and culture throughout the twentieth century, decisions made in Washington, and in other capitals across the world, now had an impact on ordinary lives.

The Origins of the Cold War

The defeat of Germany and Japan did not bring stability to the world. Within a year of the end of World War II, the United States was engaged in a global ideological struggle with the Soviet Union that historians call the cold war. The U.S. government developed a cold war mentality, characterized by a fear of communist expansion and a tendency to interpret all revolutionary activity as part of a monolithic communist movement controlled by Moscow. The Soviet Union, in turn, viewed American economic and political initiatives throughout the world as a threat to its security. Cold war assumptions still fundamentally shape American and Soviet diplomatic and military priorities today.

Descent into Cold War

Franklin Roosevelt had hoped that the establishment of the United Nations would provide a forum to resolve postwar conflicts and promote freedom throughout a stable, peaceful world. Unlike the disagreements that had doomed American participation in the League of Nations after World War I, the Senate ratified the United Nations by a margin of 80 to 2 in July 1945. Roosevelt had died that April, and the United Nations became in part a memorial to his hopes for postwar peace and cooperation. One of the United Nations' most tireless supporters—and a member of the U.S. delegation from 1946 to 1953—was the president's widow, Eleanor Roosevelt.

The planning for the United Nations was done at the Dumbarton Oaks Conference in Washington in 1943–1944, the Yalta conference in early 1945, and in San Francisco later that spring. It reflected President Roosevelt's aspirations for international cooperation and collective security—that is, the maintenance of the security of all member nations by common action. Yet elements of the United Nations charter explicitly continued traditional patterns of international relations. While the General Assembly granted one vote to each member nation, the Security Council functioned strictly along the lines of traditional big-power diplomacy. The United States, Great Britain, France, the Soviet Union, and China each had veto power over any Security Council action. Because any superpower could veto Security Council sanctions leveled against its own aggression or that of its allies, the United Nations was fundamentally hampered in its quest for collective security. Yet since neither the Soviet Union nor the United

ELEANOR ROOSEVELT, U.N. REPRESENTATIVE
Eleanor Roosevelt won over her fellow members of the United Nations delegation by doing her homework and standing firm on her convictions. Republican John Foster Dulles admitted to her, "I feel I must tell you that when you were appointed I thought it terrible and now I think your work here has been fine!" Eleanor Roosevelt was proudest of her role in drafting the 1948 Universal Declaration of Human Rights. Here she entertains delegates from UNESCO at her home in Hyde Park, New York. (FPG)

States was willing to entrust its national security totally to an international organization, the veto was a necessary condition to induce all the superpowers to participate.

Although Roosevelt heartily supported the United Nations, he also believed it was essential for the United States to continue good relations with the only other power whose strength realistically rivaled that of the United States in 1945, the Soviet Union. Yet events in the immediate postwar period, especially the sensitive issue of Soviet domination of Eastern Europe, proved far too controversial to be settled amicably between the two great powers. Within twenty-four hours of taking over the presidency, Harry Truman questioned whether the United States could cooperate with its former wartime ally. "We must stand up to the Russians," he stated privately. America and Russia's descent into cold war had begun, and the United Nations could do nothing to stop it.

Why did the Grand Alliance fall into disarray so quickly in the immediate postwar period? Profound disagreements marred American and Russian priorities for the postwar world. The Soviet Union, embittered by the German invasion and the loss of twenty million Soviet civilians during the war, put its own security needs first. The United States wanted to continue Wilsonian policies of encouraging national self-determination throughout the world. The administration was also responsive to the political realities of the large Polish-American community in the United States, a voting block that was staunchly opposed to Soviet control of Eastern Europe. In addition to the disagreements about self-determination, American and Soviet leaders disagreed over whether the world market should operate under capitalist or state-controlled systems. Soviet control of Eastern European economies, and American fears that such domination would reach throughout the emerging Third World, threatened American plans for free-market principles and international trade in the postwar world.

Other deep-seated causes added to the climate of suspicion between the United States and the Soviet Union. Soviet leaders had not forgotten that President Wilson had dispatched American troops onto Russian soil in 1918 and 1919 to undermine the fledgling Bolshevik regime. They remembered their exclusion from the Versailles conference. The initiation of diplomatic relations in 1933 did little to break the ice. Wartime pressures only heightened the level of distrust, even though the two powers fought on the same side. Especially damaging was Roosevelt's and Churchill's repeated delay in implementing their promise to open a second front in Europe to relieve the Soviets of the brunt of fighting the Germans.

The immediate aftermath of the war did nothing to ease tensions. Soviet leaders were especially angered by Truman's reaction to events in Eastern Europe. As the Soviet army drove the Germans out of Russia and back through Romania, Bulgaria, and Hungary, Soviet-sponsored, procommunist provisional governments were established in those countries. At the Yalta conference, both American and British diplomats, including President Roosevelt, had in effect agreed to recognize this Soviet "sphere of influence" in the region along its borders, even though it conflicted with America's traditional commitment to national self-determination. But as soon as the war ended, Truman backed away from the Yalta pledges. The new president berated Soviet Foreign Minister V. M. Molotov for imposing a Soviet-controlled government on Poland. Molotov had never "been talked to like that in my life," he told Truman. "Then keep your agreements!" Truman retorted.

American officials feared that Stalin was not just establishing a buffer zone to protect the Soviet Union from invasion from the West, but was embarking on a plan for worldwide domination. Republican Senator Arthur Vandenberg of Michigan rose in the Senate to ask, "What is Russia up to now? We ask it in Manchuria. We ask it in Eastern Europe and the Dardanelles. We ask it in Italy. . . . We ask it in Iran. . . ." One of the few leaders to urge a more conciliatory approach was Secretary of Commerce Henry A. Wallace, who warned that Truman's pronouncements ignored the Soviet Union's "dire economic needs and disturbed sense of security." When Wallace continued to question Truman's emerging hard line toward the Soviets, the president removed him from office.

Far more in line with Truman's attitudes were those of Winston Churchill, whom Truman invited to Fulton, Missouri, in March 1946 for a major foreign policy address. The former British prime minister had always opposed Soviet ambitions in Europe. Now, out of power and eager to regain a forum for his views, he warned ominously about the "expansive tendencies" of the Soviet Union: "From Stettin in the Baltic to Trieste in the Adriatic, an iron curtain has descended across the Continent." If the West hoped to preserve peace and freedom in the face of the Soviet challenge, Churchill declared, it must remember that "there is nothing they admire so much as strength, and there is nothing for which they have less respect than for military weakness." Churchill's widely publicized "iron curtain speech" helped convince many Americans that the Soviet Union posed a dangerous threat to national security.

The Containment Policy

By 1946, these new perceptions of the Soviet Union led American diplomats to conclude that it was futile to bargain with the Russians. Instead, they turned to containment, a strategy designed to limit Soviet and communist expansion. In one version or another, containment has defined the foreign policy of every subsequent administration, both Democratic and Republican.

George F. Kennan, an intense, scholarly diplomat who had devoted his entire career to the study of Russia, provided the rationale for containment. From his post at the U.S. embassy in Moscow, Kennan sent his superiors in Washington an eight-thousand-word cable in February 1946. At the "bottom of the Kremlin's neurotic view of world affairs," Kennan asserted, was "the traditional and instinctive Russian sense of insecurity." The Soviet Union saw the world as irrevocably divided into socialist and capitalist camps, and the "basic Soviet instinct" held "that there can be no compromise with rival power and the constructive work can start only when Communist power is dominant." Kennan concluded, "Impervious to logic of reason, [the Soviet Union] is highly sensitive to logic of force. For this reason it can easily withdraw—and usually does—when strong resistance is encountered at any point."

Kennan's analysis impressed George C. Marshall, who was about to cap his distinguished military and diplomatic career by becoming secretary of state. Marshall brought Kennan to Washington, and, working closely with President Truman, they developed the containment policy. As Kennan argued in 1947, the Soviets moved "inexorably along the prescribed path, like a persistent toy automobile wound up and headed in a given direction, stopping only when it meets unanswerable force." It was necessary, therefore, to pursue a policy of "firm containment, designed to confront the Russians with unalterable counterforce at every point where they show signs of encroaching upon the interests of a peaceful and stable world." Such a policy left little room for such international organizations as the United Nations.

The first test of containment came in Greece in 1947. Local communist-inspired guerrillas, whom American advisers mistakenly believed were controlled by Moscow, had fought for control of Greece since the end of 1944. By 1946, they were engaged in a full-scale civil war against anticommunist forces aided by Great Britain. Early in 1947, the British informed Truman that they could no longer afford to assist the Greek anticommunists. "If Greece was lost," Truman feared, Stalin "would then direct the communist parties of Italy and France to grab for power" and thus threaten to bring the industrially developed regions of Western Europe into the Soviet sphere.

To counter this perceived menace, the president announced what became known as the Truman Doctrine. In order to win acceptance for an unprecedented change in the U.S. stance toward the rest of the world, the president followed the advice of Senator Vandenberg "to scare the hell out of the country." Not just Greece, but freedom itself, was at issue, Truman declared. He painted a picture of a world deeply polarized between two competing ways of life, one "based upon the will of the majority," the other based "upon the will of a minority forcibly imposed upon the majority." It was clear where American loyalties lay:

It must be the policy of the United States to support free peoples who are resisting attempted subjugation by armed minorities or outside pressures. . . . The free peoples of the world look to us for support in maintaining their

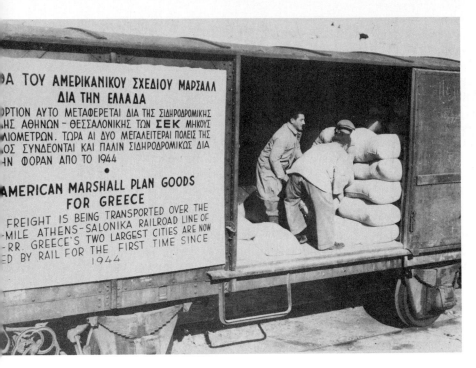

ΘΑ ΤΟΥ ΑΜΕΡΙΚΑΝΙΚΟΥ ΣΧΕΔΙΟΥ ΜΑΡΣΑΛΛ
ΔΙΑ ΤΗΝ ΕΛΛΑΔΑ
PTION ΑΥΤΟ ΜΕΤΑΦΕΡΕΤΑΙ ΔΙΑ ΤΗΣ ΣΙΔΗΡΟΔΡΟΜΙΚΗΣ
ΗΣ ΑΘΗΝΩΝ - ΘΕΣΣΑΛΟΝΙΚΗΣ ΤΩΝ ΣΕΚ ΜΗΚΟΥΣ
ΙΟΜΕΤΡΩΝ. ΤΩΡΑ ΑΙ ΔΥΟ ΜΕΓΑΛΕΙΤΕΡΑΙ ΠΟΛΕΙΣ ΤΗΣ
ΟΣ ΣΥΝΔΕΟΝΤΑΙ ΚΑΙ ΠΑΛΙΝ ΣΙΔΗΡΟΔΡΟΜΙΚΩΣ ΔΙΑ
ΗΝ ΦΟΡΑΝ ΑΠΟ ΤΟ 1944
•
AMERICAN MARSHALL PLAN GOODS
FOR GREECE
FREIGHT IS BEING TRANSPORTED OVER THE
-MILE ATHENS-SALONIKA RAILROAD LINE OF
-RR. GREECE'S TWO LARGEST CITIES ARE NOW
ED BY RAIL FOR THE FIRST TIME SINCE
1944

THE MARSHALL PLAN
Many people in European cities lived on subsistence diets after World War II. "The patient is sinking while the doctors deliberate," Secretary of State George C. Marshall declared after traveling to Europe and the Soviet Union to survey the war's devastation. In 1948, Congress established the Marshall Plan to help European nations cooperate in economic recovery. At first, humanitarian and military aid were equally important components of American assistance to war-torn Europe, but from the 1950s on, the United States tended to emphasize military assistance. (Wide World)

freedoms. If we falter in our leadership, we may endanger the peace of the world—and we shall surely endanger the welfare of our own Nation.

The Truman Doctrine represented an important step in the shift of foreign policy formulation from Congress to the executive branch. Despite the breadth and open-endedness of this military and political commitment, Congress quickly approved Truman's request for $400 million in aid to Greece and Turkey in a bipartisan show of support. This appropriation reversed the postwar policy of sharp cuts in foreign spending.

One of the few voices raised against the containment doctrine was that of Walter Lippmann, one of the nation's most respected journalists. In 1947, Lippmann criticized containment as a "strategic monstrosity" that threatened to require unlimited defense expenditures and involve the United States unnecessarily in disputes throughout the world. "The Eurasian continent is a big place," Lippmann noted drily, "and the military power of the United States has certain limitations." Containment could be implemented "only by recruiting, subsidizing, and supporting a heterogeneous array of satellites, clients, dependents, and puppets." American efforts to make "Jeffersonian Democrats" out of Asian peasants would prove futile and costly, he asserted. Although conflicts in China, Korea, and Vietnam later demonstrated the validity of Lippmann's critique, it had little impact on public opinion at the time.

A few weeks after Congress approved aid to Greece, Secretary of State Marshall proposed a plan to provide economic as well as military aid to Europe. In Truman's words, the Marshall Plan was "the other half of the walnut." By bolstering the free-world economy, Marshall and Truman believed, the United States could forestall the economic dislocation thought to give rise to communism. European economies had not recovered from the war, and the cold, hard winter of 1946–1947 brought even worse privation. Crowds of gaunt, haggard people had begun to heed communist-led attacks on the governments of Italy and France. Speaking at the Harvard University commencement in June 1947, Marshall urged the nations of Europe to work out a comprehensive recovery program and then ask the United States for aid. "Any government willing to assist in the task of reconstruction," he promised, "will find full cooperation on the part of the United States."

Congress overwhelmingly approved funds for the Marshall Plan. Over the next four years the United States contributed nearly $13 billion to a highly successful recovery effort. Western European industrial production increased 64 percent, and such revived economic activity opened new areas for American trade. U.S. policymakers saw this economic revitalization as creating a hospitable climate for democratic developments in the region, a further wedge against Soviet encroachment.

The Marshall Plan did not specifically exclude Eastern Europe or the Soviet Union, but it did require that all participating nations exchange economic information and work toward the mutual elimination of tariffs and other trade barriers. Soviet leaders denounced these conditions and forbade their new satellites to participate. In February 1948, a pro-Soviet coup prevented Czechoslovakia from participating in the Marshall Plan. Later that year, when Stalin's agents failed to unseat Yugoslavia's tough, resourceful leader, Marshal Tito, Stalin expelled Yugoslavia from the Soviet bloc.

Germany, which was jointly administered by the Soviet Union, the United States, France, and Great Britain, continued to be a bone of contention. Especially troublesome was the fate of Berlin, the capital, which lay deep within the Soviet zone of occupation. The Soviet Union had installed a communist regime in East Berlin and demanded control over the entire city, including the sectors of West Berlin governed by the Western allies. The allies refused, and when Western nations took steps to revive the Berlin economy in the spring of 1948, the Soviet Union imposed a blockade on all highway, rail, and river traffic to West Berlin. Truman replied with an airlift. For nearly a year, American and British pilots, who had been dropping bombs on Berlin only four years earlier, flew in 2.5 million tons of food and fuel, nearly a ton for each Berlin citizen. By late 1949, Stalin lifted the blockade, which by then had made West Berlin a symbol of resistance to communism.

The Berlin airlift and the crises in Czechoslovakia and Yugoslavia led to a dramatic turning

MAP 29.1 COLD WAR EUROPE
The core of the American alliance system with Western Europe was the North Atlantic Treaty Organization (NATO), established in 1949. Twelve nations signed the original pact, whose central article read: "The parties agree that an armed attack against one or more of them in Europe or North America shall be considered an attack against them all." The U.S. Senate ratified the treaty by a vote of eighty-two to thirteen.

point in U.S. diplomatic history. In 1949, for the first time since the American Revolution, the United States bound itself to Western Europe by a formal military alliance. Arguing that it was necessary to meet the Soviet threat with "an inclusive security system," Truman orchestrated the creation of the North Atlantic Treaty Organization (NATO). On April 4, 1949, the United States, Britain, France, Italy, Belgium, The Netherlands, Luxembourg, Denmark, Norway, Portugal, Iceland, and Canada agreed that "an armed attack against one or more of them in Europe or North America shall be considered an attack against them all." In May 1949, these nations also agreed to the creation of the German Federal Republic (West Germany). All assumed that it would join NATO, which it did in 1955.

Distressed by the aggressive American effort to promote a new economic and political order in Western Europe, the Soviet Union tightened its grip on Eastern Europe. It created a separate government for East Germany, which now became the German Democratic Republic. The Soviets also sponsored an economic association called COMECON (1949) and a military alliance for Eastern Europe, the Warsaw Pact (1955). The postwar division of Europe was nearly complete.

Containment Militarized

September 1949 brought another shock to U.S. policymakers. American military intelligence detected a sudden rise in radioactivity, proof that the Soviet Union had set off an atomic bomb. The United States' atomic monopoly, which some military and political advisers had argued would last for decades, had ended in less than four years. The nation had lost a major bargaining chip with which to confront the Russians. To many Americans, the world looked even more threatening now that the Soviets had the bomb.

The end of American atomic supremacy forced a major reassessment of the nation's foreign policy. To devise a new blueprint for diplomatic and military priorities, Truman turned to the National Security Council (NSC), an advisory body charged with assisting the president to set defense and military priorities. The NSC formed part of the unified military establishment set up by the National Security Act of 1947,

which created a single Department of Defense to replace the previous Departments of War and the Navy. The newly established Joint Chiefs of Staff coordinated army, navy, and air force policy. And a new Central Intelligence Agency (CIA) gathered and analyzed military intelligence. These bureaucratic structures were a concrete reminder of permanent mobilization.

In April 1950, the National Security Council delivered its report to President Truman. This document, known as NSC-68, reflected the bleak assumptions that American policymakers held about the Soviet Union. In their view, the Soviet Union aimed for world domination:

> The Kremlin is inescapably militant because it possesses and is possessed by a world-wide revolutionary movement, because it is the inheritor of Russian imperialism, and because it is a totalitarian dictatorship. . . . It is quite clear from Soviet theory and practice that the Kremlin seeks to bring the free world under its dominion by the methods of the cold war.

Since Moscow possessed tremendous military power that enabled the Soviet Union to "back up infiltration with intimidation," policymakers predicted an "indefinite period of tension and danger."

NSC-68 made several specific recommendations. It favored further development of the hydrogen bomb, an advanced weapon that was a thousand times more destructive than the atomic bombs that had destroyed Hiroshima and Nagasaki. (The United States exploded its first hydrogen bomb in late 1952, and the Soviet Union followed suit in 1953.) It supported increases in American conventional forces and a strong system of Western alliances. Most important, it called for an increase in taxes to finance "a bold and massive program of rebuilding the West's defensive potential to surpass that of the Soviet world." NSC-68 suggested that the administration mobilize an American consensus on the need for "sacrifice" and "unity" that would justify defense budgets totaling up to 20 percent of the gross national product, four times their level at the time.

The need for increased defense spending was directly linked to the end of atomic supremacy. The United States had been relying too heavily on atomic deterrence at the expense of its conventional military arsenal. Now that the nation's atomic monopoly had been broken, a general buildup of the American military arsenal was needed. The Korean War, which began just two months after NSC-68 was completed, provided the impetus necessary to put this new policy into practice. Before 1950, the military budget stood at $13.5 billion. In just six months, Truman more than tripled it to nearly $50 billion.

The Cold War in Asia

American cold war ideology was developed primarily to prevent Soviet expansion beyond its sphere of influence in Eastern Europe. As the mutual suspicion between the United States and the Soviet Union hardened, cold war containment doctrines formed the basis of the American stance toward Asia as well. American policymakers soon found, however, that it was much more difficult to apply the containment doctrine to Asia than to Europe, where China, rather than the Soviet Union, was the dominant force.

The "Fall" of China

A civil war had been raging in China since the 1930s. Communist forces led by Mao Zedong (Mao Tse-tung) and Zhou Enlai (Chou En-lai) contended for power with conservative nationalist forces under Jiang Jieshi (Chiang Kai-shek). Jiang had strong connections with the Chinese business community and with the western world. His wealthy wife had been educated at Wellesley College in Massachusetts. In contrast, Mao was the son of struggling peasants. He was a tough, uncompromising leader, indifferent to personal comfort and absolutely dedicated to revolution. Mao inspired loyalty in his associates and won the devotion of China's overtaxed, land-hungry peasants. By the mid-1940s, Mao's forces were gaining the upper hand.

The Truman administration, somewhat reluctantly, stuck with its nationalist allies until the bitter end. Betwen 1945 and 1949, the United States provided more than $2 billion to Jiang's forces, to no avail. In 1947, General Albert Wedemeyer, who had tried to work with Jiang, reported to President Truman that "until drastic political and economic reforms" were undertaken by the "corrupt, reactionary, and ineffi-

cient Chinese National government, United States aid cannot accomplish its purpose." By 1949, nearly half the nationalist troops had defected, and Jiang's regime had been forced off the Chinese mainland and onto the island of Formosa (Taiwan). Wedemeyer attributed Jiang's defeat to "lack of spirit," not lack of equipment. "In my judgment," he said, "they could have defended the Yangtze with broomsticks if they had had the will to do it." Assistant Secretary of State Dean Acheson agreed, declaring that "China lost itself."

Many Americans, however, viewed Mao's success as a defeat for the United States. A pronationalist "China lobby," supported by such Republicans as Senators Karl Mundt of South Dakota and William S. Knowland of California, protested that the State Department was responsible for the "loss of China." Publisher Henry R. Luce, born in China to missionary parents, spread these accusations through his magazines, including *Time* and *Life*. Bowing to pressure from the China lobby, most of the State Department's experts on the Far East were forced to resign during the McCarthy period for supposedly having been too sympathetic to the Chinese Communists. The United States refused to recognize the new communist state, instead giving recognition to the nationalists ensconced on Taiwan. For almost twenty years afterward, American administrations acted as if mainland China, the world's most populous country, did not exist.

The Korean War

Although Truman acknowledged that communist success in China raised urgent questions for American foreign policy, he recognized the limits of American power in Asia. In December 1949, his new secretary of state, Dean Acheson, clarified American policy. The United States, he said, would help Asian nations realize their own aspirations but would consider itself bound to protect only a "defensive perimeter" that ran from the Aleutian Islands in Alaska to Japan, the Ryukyus (a chain of small islands that stretch from Japan to Taiwan), and the Philippines. If an attack occurred outside this perimeter—on Korea, Taiwan, or Southeast Asia, for example—"the initial reliance must be on the people attacked to resolve it and then upon . . . the United Nations."

A test of this new policy came quickly, but events unfolded quite contrary to Acheson's pronouncement. On June 25, 1950, North Korean troops launched a surprise attack across the thirty-eighth parallel, the line at which the United States and the Soviet Union had partitioned Korea in 1945. North Korean leader Kim Il Sung may have expected Truman to ignore this armed challenge to the U.S.–supported government of Syngman Rhee in South Korea. If so, he was badly mistaken. The president immediately ordered General Douglas MacArthur in Japan to send American troops to help Rhee, and asked the U.N. Security Council to authorize a "police action" against the invaders. Since the Soviet Union was temporarily boycotting the Security Council to protest the exclusion of the People's Republic of China from the U.N., it could not veto Truman's request, and the United Nations voted to send a peacekeeping force.

The outbreak of the Korean War further tipped the balance of foreign policy formulation from Congress to the president. When Republican Senator Robert A. Taft of Ohio objected that the president should have obtained congressional approval before committing American troops to Korea, Truman boldly insisted that he already had all the power he needed as commander-in-chief of the armed forces and as executor of the treaty binding the United States to the United Nations.

The rapidly assembled United Nations army in Korea remained overwhelmingly American. On September 15, 1950, U.N. commander Douglas MacArthur launched a brilliant amphibious attack at Inchon, far behind the lines of the North Korean invasion, which had cut deeply into the south. Within two weeks, the U.N. forces controlled Seoul, the South Korean capital, and almost all the territory up to the thirty-eighth parallel.

Stimulated by this success, General MacArthur sought authority to lead his forces across the thirty-eighth parallel into North Korea itself. Truman's initial plan had been to restore the 1945 border; now he agreed to the broader goal of creating "a unified, independent and democratic Korea." The Chinese government in Beijing (Peking) warned repeatedly that such a move would provoke its retaliation. American officials failed to take these warnings seriously. In late 1950, MacArthur drove rapidly northward, confident that he would reach the Chinese border at the Yalu River by Christmas. Just after Thanksgiving, however, a massive Chinese counterattack forced a retreat. By January 1951, communist troops had reoccupied Seoul. "They really fooled us when it comes right down to it, didn't they?" a senator later asked Secretary of State Acheson. "Yes, sir," he replied. Two months later, the American forces and their allies counterattacked, regained Seoul, and pushed back to the thirty-eighth parallel. Then a stalemate set in.

Truman and his advisers in Washington decided to work for a negotiated peace. They did not wish to tie down large numbers of U.S. troops in a remote corner of Asia, far from what they considered more strategically important

MAP 29.2 THE KOREAN WAR

The first months of the Korean War featured dramatic shifts in control up and down the six-hundred-mile peninsula. By September 1950, North Korean troops had overrun most of the territory below the thirty-eighth parallel. Then General Douglas MacArthur's amphibious landing at Inchon routed the North Koreans and enabled United Nations forces to push north almost to the Chinese border. The UN troops were forced to retreat to the thirty-eighth parallel, however, and the war became a stalemate for the next three years.

trouble spots in Europe and the Middle East. The Soviet Union, not China, remained the focus of their cold war strategy. If the Korean War became a general war with China, insisted General Omar N. Bradley, chairman of the Joint Chiefs of Staff, it would be "the wrong war, in the wrong place, with the wrong enemy."

MacArthur disagreed. Headstrong, arrogant, and brilliant, he fervently believed the nation's future opportunities lay in Asia, not in Europe. Disregarding Truman's instructions, MacArthur traveled to Taiwan and urged the nationalists to join in an attack on communist China. He pleaded for American use of the atomic bomb against targets in China. In an inflammatory letter to the House Minority Leader, Republican Joseph J. Martin of Massachusetts, he denounced the Korean stalemate. "We must win," MacArthur declared. "There is no substitute for victory."

Martin released MacArthur's letter on April 6,

MacARTHUR'S RETURN FROM KOREA
General Douglas MacArthur received a tumultuous welcome in San Francisco in 1951, the first time the popular general had set foot on the American mainland in fourteen years. The public outcry over President Harry Truman's dismissal of MacArthur for insubordination reflected frustration with the stalemated Korean War. (© Wayne Miller, Magnum)

1951, as part of a concerted Republican campaign to challenge President Truman's conduct of the war. The strategy backfired. On April 11, Truman relieved MacArthur of his command in Korea and Japan, accusing him of insubordination. "MacArthur left me no choice," Truman later insisted. "Even the Joint Chiefs of Staff came to the conclusion that civilian control of the military was at stake. . . . I didn't let it stay at stake very long."

Truman's decision was highly unpopular. According to a Gallup poll, 69 percent of the American people supported MacArthur rather than Truman. The general returned to tumultuous receptions in San Francisco, Chicago, and New York. In Washington, he delivered an impassioned address to a joint Congressional session that ended with a line from an old West Point ballad, "Old soldiers never die, they just fade away." But when the shouting died down, Truman had the last word. Failing to get the Republican presidential nomination in 1952, MacArthur did indeed fade away from public view.

The war dragged on for more than two years after MacArthur's dismissal. The armistice ultimately negotiated in July 1953 left Korea divided very near the thirty-eighth parallel. North Korea remained firmly allied with the Soviet Union; South Korea signed a mutual defense treaty with the United States in 1954, tying itself to the American sphere of influence in the Pacific. During the next thirty years, American and Japanese investments helped South Korea rapidly expand its economy.

The Korean War had only a limited domestic impact on the United States. The government did not control the economy to the extent it had during World War II. Limited mobilization stimulated the economy and reduced unemployment, contributing to the general prosperity that characterized the 1950s.

Few soldiers felt the patriotic fervor that had characterized service during World War II. Struggling against subzero cold and snow, the men grew to hate the endless fighting and "those damned hills of Korea." One griped, "You march up them but there's always the sinking feeling you are going to have to march right back down." A corporal from Chicago asserted, "I'll fight for my country, but I'm damned if I see why I'm fighting for this hellhole." When an Oregon newspaper prominently

THE KOREAN WAR
The American GI's who fought in Korea were often younger brothers of the men who had served in
World War II. Fighting in Korea was grim duty; it lacked the patriotic fervor that had characterized
service in the 1940s. The most popular expression of weary GI's in Korea was the fatalistic, "Well,
that's the way the ball bounces." (UPI)

ran the same news dispatch from Korea two
days in a row, not a single reader called the repetition to its attention.

Conditions did improve for black soldiers
during the Korean War. Although President Truman had signed an executive order desegregating the armed forces in 1948, little progress had
been made before the war began. During the
rapid mobilization, demands for efficiency (such
as processing draftees) outweighed customary
mores (such as keeping black and white draftees
separate), thus speeding up the integration process. The generally successful experience of an
integrated armed services during the Korean
War hastened the emergence of the civil rights
movement later in the 1950s.

The Korean War cost the United States 34,000
dead, 103,000 wounded, and $54 billion in mili-
tary expenditures. It showed the nation's willingness to take concrete steps to stop communist
aggression, no matter how remote from its
shores, and it reminded Americans that containment required a heavy, ongoing commitment. In
contrast to the triumphs on World War II battlefields, however, the protracted stalemate
proved frustrating. "If we are so powerful,"
many asked, "why can't we win?" When an ar-

mistice was finally signed in 1953, few public
celebrations took place. Similar frustration surrounding a limited war to stop the spread of
communism in Asia surfaced little more than a
decade later over American intervention in
Vietnam.

Extending Containment

Although Dwight D. Eisenhower promised to
take a new look at American defense policy
when elected president in 1952, his two terms
continued the nation's commitment to containment. His secretary of state, John Foster Dulles,
accused the Russians of looking "upon anybody
who is not for them as against them," but the
same could have been said of the United States.
Despite the Eisenhower administration's attempt
to hold down the defense budget, the 1950s saw
the growth of what Eisenhower himself labelled
the "military-industrial complex." At the same
time, the new Republican leaders faced a challenge that had also plagued previous Democratic
administrations—to develop a consistent policy
toward the new nations created by the breakup
of imperialism in the wake of World War II.

Alliances and Arms

Dwight Eisenhower had earned a reputation for excellent judgment in military and diplomatic affairs while serving as the commander of NATO military forces in Europe in 1951–1952. As president, he worked closely with Secretary of State Dulles to define the administration's foreign policy. Dulles, an experienced international lawyer and diplomat, was an outspoken critic of "atheistic communism." Rather than just limiting further Soviet expansion, he argued, the United States ought to promote the "liberation" of the "captive nations" of Eastern Europe.

At the beginning of the Eisenhower administration, the Soviet Union briefly appeared more interested in better relations with the West. Joseph Stalin died in March 1953, and his duties were assumed by Georgi Malenkov, who adopted a more conciliatory tone toward the West. After an intraparty struggle that lasted until 1956, Nikita S. Khrushchev solidified his position as Stalin's successor. He soon startled communists thoughout the world by denouncing Stalin as "a distrustful man, sickly and suspicious," and detailing publicly for the first time Stalin's "crimes" and "tortures" of the 1930s and 1940s. Khrushchev likewise surprised Westerners by calling for "peaceful coexistence" between communist and capitalist societies. He also seemed more willing to tolerate different approaches to communism, such as that developed by Yugoslavia's previously ostracized leader Marshal Tito. When Polish leader Wladislaw Gomulka, who had once been jailed in a Stalinist purge, insisted that his nation's communists be allowed to work out Poland's problems in their own way, Khrushchev agreed.

On the other hand, Khrushchev made certain that Russia's Eastern European satellites did not deviate too far from the Soviet path. When a nationalist revolt erupted in Hungary in 1956, Soviet tanks rapidly moved into Budapest. Demonstrating their willingness to use massive force to retain control in Eastern Europe, the Soviets crushed the revolt and installed a puppet regime. Despite Dulles's rhetoric, the United States responded only by loosening immigration quotas for Hungarian refugees.

The Soviet repression of the Hungarian revolt confirmed that American policymakers had few, if any, options to "roll back" Soviet power in Eastern Europe short of going to war with the USSR. An alternative strategy, already in force, sought to limit communist expansion through a permanent alliance structure. Truman, Marshall, and Acheson had established key military alliances in Europe and Asia. Dulles added new agreements with nations that bordered on the Soviet Union and China—the Baghdad Pact (1953), with Great Britain and nations on the Soviet Union's Middle Eastern flank (Turkey, Iran, Iraq, and Pakistan); bilateral defense treaties with South Korea and the nationalist Chinese regime on Taiwan (1954); and the creation of the Southeast Asia Treaty Organization (SEATO) in 1954. The secretary of state regarded the establishment of these overtly anticommunist alliances as an imperative. "Neutrality," Dulles maintained, was not only "obsolete" but "immoral."

Firm in the righteousness of his cause, Dulles did not shrink from covert interventions against governments that were, in his opinion, too closely aligned with communism. For such tasks, he used the Central Intelligence Agency, which was headed by his brother, Allen Dulles. During the Eisenhower administration, the CIA moved beyond its original mandate of intelligence gathering to active—if secret—involvement in the internal affairs of countries where such covert action suited American objectives.

In the 1950s, the CIA successfully directed the overthrow of several foreign governments. When Iran's nationalist premier, Mohammed Mossadegh, seized British oil properties in 1953, CIA agents helped the young shah, Mohammed Reza Pahlevi, depose him. Using both economic leverage and a repressive secret police, the shah soon solidified his power within Iran. In 1954, the CIA supported a coup in Guatemala against popularly elected Jacobo Arbenz Guzman, who had expropriated 250,000 acres held by the American-owned United Fruit Company and accepted arms from the communist government of East Germany. The CIA also tried, unsuccessfully, to overthrow Achmed Sukarno of Indonesia in 1958 and Fidel Castro of Cuba in 1961. Eisenhower specifically approved these efforts. "Our traditional ideas of international sportsmanship," he wrote privately in 1955, "are scarcely applicable in the morass in which the world now flounders."

Although Eisenhower strongly opposed communism, he hoped to keep the cost of containment at a manageable level. To encourage the nation's allies to bear some of the responsibility for maintaining large armed forces, his administration increased the flow of American military aid. Truman had emphasized foreign economic assistance; the United States sent more than $22 billion abroad between 1946 and 1952, more than twice the amount spent on military aid. Eisenhower reversed the priorities. He reduced economic aid to $18 billion between 1953 and 1961, while increasing military aid to more than $19 billion.

Eisenhower and Dulles also devised the policy of "massive retaliation" or "brinksmanship."

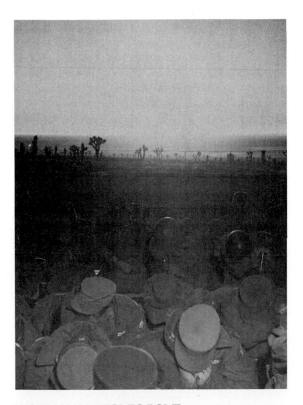

TESTING AN ATOMIC BOMB
Throughout the 1950s, the Atomic Energy Commission conducted above-ground atomic tests, including this one at Camp Desert Rock in Nevada in 1957. Thousands of soldiers were exposed to fallout during the tests. The AEC, ignoring or suppressing medical evidence to the contrary, mounted an extensive public relations campaign to convince local residents that the tests did not endanger their health. (U.S. Army)

They believed the United States could economize by developing an effective nuclear deterrent rather than relying solely on expensive conventional armed forces. Nuclear weapons delivered "more bang for the buck." If the nation's major foreign enemy were a worldwide communist movement led by Moscow, they reasoned, the United States did not need to keep a large number of soldiers under arms, because atomic weapons could threaten the Soviet Union directly and force it to back down. To this end, the Eisenhower administration expanded its commitment to develop the hydrogen bomb, which the United States tested in the atmosphere between 1954 and 1958. The administration also supported research to develop the long-range bombing capabilities of the Strategic Air Command. To improve U.S. defenses against an air attack from the Soviet Union, the administration installed the Distant Early Warning (DEW) line of radar stations in Alaska and Canada in 1958.

These efforts did little to improve the nation's security, as the Soviets matched the United States weapon for weapon in an escalating arms race. The Soviet Union carried out its own atmospheric tests of hydrogen bombs between 1953 and 1958 and developed a fleet of long-range bombers. It won the race to build an intercontinental ballistic missile (ICBM) and beat the United States into space with the *Sputnik* space probe of October 1957. The United States successfully launched its own ICBM in 1958 and by 1960 had deployed Polaris nuclear submarines carrying atomic-tipped missiles within striking distance of Soviet targets. Soviet leaders raced to produce equivalent weapons.

While the Soviet Union viewed the Eisenhower-Dulles policies of anticommunist alliances and massive deterrence as inherently hostile, Eisenhower continued to work toward a negotiated arms limitation agreement. Although preliminary discussions with Soviet leaders between 1955 and 1957 had not yielded the "open skies" mutual arms inspection treaty he had wanted, they did produce plans for a summit meeting with Khrushchev in May 1960. Then, on May 5, an American spy plane was shot down over Soviet territory. Rejecting the opportunity to deny personal knowledge of the flight, Eisenhower replied that he had authorized this and many

other secret flights by high-flying U-2 recon-
naisance aircraft over the Soviet Union. Eisenhower's last chance to negotiate an arms
agreement evaporated.

The Emerging Third World

Though preoccupied with the Soviet Union
throughout the postwar period, American policymakers faced another challenge: developing a
coherent policy toward the new nations that
were rapidly emerging from the disintegrating
European empires in Africa and Asia. At the
outset of World War II, there had been five geo-
political blocs—the Western Hemisphere, in
which the United States was preeminent; the European continent, split between Britain and Germany; the center of the Eurasian land mass,
dominated by the Soviet Union; the Pacific Basin
and Southeast Asia, controlled by Japan, China,
or Western imperialist powers; and Africa and
the Middle East, also under Western European
influence. When the war ended, the latter two
areas came up for grabs.

Nationalism, socialism, and religious fanata-
cism had already inspired powerful anticolonial
movements before World War II; such forces intensified and spread, especially in the Middle
East, Africa, and the Far East, during the 1940s
and 1950s. The end to colonial empires fulfilled
a goal the United States had sought in vain after
World War I, and the nation in general welcomed the independence of the new states. At
the same time, both the Truman and Eisenhower administrations were so caught up in cold
war polarities that they often failed to recognize
that indigenous nationalist or socialist movements in these emerging nations had their own
goals and were not always under the strict control either of local communists or the Soviet
Union. This failure to appreciate the complexity
of local conditions limited the effectiveness of
American policy toward the emerging Third
World.

The Middle East presented the most serious
challenges in the 1950s. Egypt had gained independence from Britain in 1952. When Gamal
Abdel Nasser came to power in 1954, he pledged
to lead not just Egypt but the entire Middle East
out of its dependent, colonial relationship
through a form of pan-Arab socialism. Nasser

obtained arms and promises of economic assistance from the Soviet Union in return for Egyptian cotton. When the Soviets offered to finance
a dam on the Nile River at Aswan, Secretary of
State Dulles countered with an offer of American
assistance. Nasser refused to distance himself
from the Russians, however, and in July 1956,
Dulles abruptly withdrew the U.S. offer.

Retaliating against the withdrawal of American financial aid, Nasser nationalized the Suez
Canal, over which Britain had retained administrative authority. Nasser said he would use the
tolls from the canal to build the dam himself. After several months of fruitless negotiation, Britain and France, in alliance with Israel (which had
become an independent state in 1948), responded by retaking the canal by force. When
Eisenhower and the United Nations condemned
this action, they reluctantly pulled back. Egypt
was left more angry and defensive than ever—
but it controlled the canal. In the end, these
events increased, rather than decreased, Soviet
influence in the Third World and produced dissension among the leading members of the
Western European alliance.

In early 1957, still preoccupied with East-West
conflict, the president persuaded Congress to
approve the "Eisenhower Doctrine." This policy
stated that American forces would assist any
Middle Eastern nation "requiring such aid,
against overt armed aggression from any nation
controlled by International Communism." Invoking the doctrine, Eisenhower sent the U.S.
Sixth Fleet to the Mediterranean Sea to aid King
Hussein of Jordan in 1957. A year later, Eisenhower landed eight thousand troops to back up
a pro-United States government in Lebanon.

The attention that the Eisenhower administration paid to developments in the Middle East
in the 1950s confirmed that American policymakers no longer believed that containment of Soviet
power in Eastern Europe was enough to guarantee American national security. Now the United
States had to be concerned about communism
globally, especially in emerging Third World
countries. The case of the small country of Vietnam, which won its independence from France
in 1954, would show that localized communist
wars for national liberation could be just as troubling for American foreign policy as the threat of
worldwide Soviet domination.

GRAVE IMPLICATIONS OF THE MILITARY-INDUSTRIAL COMPLEX

From President Eisenhower's Farewell Address (January 17, 1961).

. . . A vital element in keeping the peace is our Military Establishment. Our arms must be mighty, ready for instant action, so that no potential aggressor may be tempted to risk his own destruction.

Our military establishment today bears little relation to that known by any of my predecessors in peacetime, or indeed by the fighting men of World War II and Korea.

Until the latest of our world conflicts, the United States had no armaments industry. American makers of plowshares could, with time and as required, make swords as well. But now we can no longer risk emergency improvisation of national defense; we have been compelled to create a permanent armaments industry of vast proportions. Added to this, 3½ million men and women are directly engaged in the Defense Establishment. We annually spend on military security more than the net income of all United States corporations.

This conjunction of an immense Military Establishment and a large arms industry is new in the American experience. The total influence—economic, political, even spiritual—is felt in every city, every statehouse, every office of the Federal Government. We recognize the imperative need for this development. Yet we must not fail to comprehend its grave implications. Our toil, resources, and livelihood are all involved; so is the very structure of our society.

In the councils of government we must guard against the acquisition of unwarranted influence whether sought or unsought, by the military-industrial complex. The potential for the disastrous rise of misplaced power exists and will persist.

We must never let the weight of this combination endanger our liberties or democratic processes. We should take nothing for granted. Only an alert and knowledgeable citizenry can compel the proper meshing of the huge industrial and military machinery of defense with our peaceful methods and goals so that security and liberty may prosper together.

Source: Public Papers of the Presidents: Eisenhower, 1960–1961. Washington, D.C., 1961. 1038–1040.

The Military-Industrial Complex

When Eisenhower left office in January 1961, he warned the nation of a "military-industrial complex" that already employed 3.5 million Americans and whose concentrated power posed a threat to democratic processes and liberties.

Eisenhower's farewell address showed that he well understood the major transformations in economic and political structures that the cold war had forced on American life. The military-industrial complex that Eisenhower identified had its immediate roots in the business-government partnership of World War II. It entered a second stage in the late 1940s and 1950s, when cold war mobilization and the Korean War led to a major expansion of the military establishment. Defense-related industries and the scientists and engineers they employed entered into a long-term

THE U-2 INCIDENT
Pilot Gary Powers was flying an American U-2 reconnaissance plane, similar to this aircraft, over the Soviet Union in 1960 when the Russians shot him down. The plane's surveillance equipment was so sophisticated that enlargements of photographs showed newspaper headlines from ten miles up. (Wide World)

relationship with the federal government in the name of national security. The Defense Department became practically a state within the state, with its headquarters at the sprawling Pentagon in Arlington, Virginia. In 1968, the Pentagon alone contracted for more than $44 billion of goods and services.

Certain companies did so much of their business with the government that they became almost exclusive clients of the Defense Department. By the mid-1960s, Boeing and General Dynamics received 65 percent of their income from military contracts, Raytheon 60 percent, Lockheed 81 percent, and Republic Aviation 100 percent. Furthermore, the Pentagon tended to award contracts to the largest firms. In 1967, the hundred largest corporations got 65 percent of the government contracts, while the top ten alone received more than 30 percent.

The growth of this military-industrial establishment reflected a dramatic shift in national priorities. As late as 1950, less than a third of the federal budget went to the military. By 1969, the percentage had grown to 56 percent. In dollar amounts, the defense budget grew from $13 billion in 1950 to $47 billion in 1961 and $80 billion in 1972. At the same time, military spending took up a greater percentage of national income as measured by the gross national product. Between 1900 and 1930, except for the two years that the United States fought in World War I, the country spent less than 1 percent of its GNP for military purposes. In the 1930s, defense absorbed only 1.3 percent of the GNP. By the 1960s, the United States regularly devoted close to 10 percent of its GNP to military spending.

The expansion of the military-industrial complex had a direct and ongoing impact on the American people. In 1973, for example, the average New York City resident paid $642 in taxes to support the Pentagon. Channeling money into national security limited the resources available for domestic social needs. Critics of military spending added up the trade-offs—the cost of a subway system for Washington, D.C., equaled the cost of a nuclear aircraft carrier and support ships; the deficit of the Philadelphia school system in 1971 amounted to the cost of a single B-1 bomber; and sixty-six units of low-income housing matched the cost of one Huey helicopter.

The defense buildup also meant jobs, however, and lots of them. In 1966, 17 percent of California's workers were employed in jobs directly generated by defense contracts. In 1971, the Pentagon itself employed 3.8 million workers, with an additional 2.2 million in defense-related private employment. Taking into account the multiplier effect, which measures the indirect benefits of such employment (the additional jobs created to serve and support the defense workers), perhaps as many as one worker in seven owed his or her job to the defense establish-

FIGURE 29.1 NATIONAL DEFENSE AS A PROPORTION OF TOTAL FEDERAL SPENDING, 1940–1970

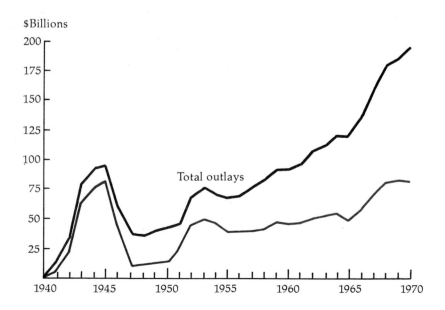

ment. This dependence of individual jobs on heavy defense spending graphically illustrates how the growth of a vast bureaucratic national state, especially one committed to worldwide military responsibilities, affected ordinary lives in the postwar period.

The Limits of Containment

In his inaugural address in January 1961, John F. Kennedy boldly declared that "we shall pay any price, bear any burden, meet any hardship, support any friend, oppose any foe to assure the survival and success of liberty." But in more reflective moods, the young president acknowledged that the United States was "neither omnipotent nor omniscient . . . there cannot be an American solution to every problem." Yet a strongly anticommunist thrust more often than not prevailed with Kennedy, as it did with his successor, Lyndon B. Johnson. The Vietnam War illustrated the limitations of this approach.

Activism Abroad

During the 1960 presidential campaign, Kennedy charged that the Eisenhower administration had permitted the Soviet Union to develop superior nuclear capabilities. Once in office, he found that no such "missile gap" existed. The new president quickly concluded, however, that Eisenhower's strategy of massive retaliation had emphasized nuclear weapons at the expense of conventional military strength. In his first defense message to Congress, Kennedy insisted that the nation develop a diverse arsenal, with weapons "to deter all wars, general or unlimited, nuclear or conventional, large or small." What the United States needed, Kennedy maintained, was the ability to mount a "flexible response," one precisely calibrated to meet actual situations that arose.

Congress quickly acceded to Kennedy's military requests. It boosted the number of combatready army divisions from eleven to sixteen and authorized the construction of ten Polaris submarines and other warships. It intensified the training of special military units—Kennedy suggested the name "Green Berets"—capable of employing "counterinsurgency" tactics against

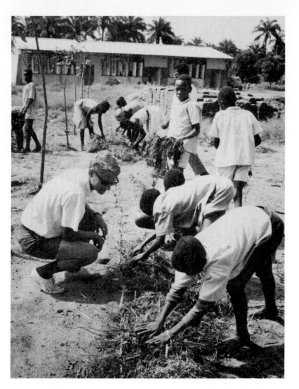

THE PEACE CORPS
In some areas of the world, Peace Corps volunteers, such as this agricultural expert in Dahomey, were known as "Kennedy's children." One idealistic volunteer wrote, "Should it come to it, I had rather give my life trying to help someone than to have to give my life looking down a gun barrel at them." (U.S. Peace Corps)

procommunist guerrillas in the new Third World nations. Overall, Kennedy presided over a major expansion of the military-industrial complex as part of his campaign pledge to get the nation moving again. By 1964, the Kennedy administration had tripled the destructive power of the U.S. nuclear arsenal.

Kennedy also won congressional support for his expanded program of economic aid to foreign countries, of which the Peace Corps was the most popular component. The new Agency for International Development coordinated foreign aid for the Third World, and the Food for Peace program distributed surplus agricultural products to developing nations. In 1961, the president proposed "a ten-year plan for the Americas" called the Alliance for Progress, a partnership between the United States and the

MAP 29.3 THE UNITED STATES AND CUBA, 1961–1962
With Fidel Castro's takeover in Cuba in 1959, American policymakers were confronted with a visible communist stronghold only ninety miles from Florida. In 1961, the United States tried unsuccessfully to overthrow Castro's regime with an invasion launched from Nicaragua. In 1962, a major confrontation with the Soviet Union occurred over Russian missile sites in Cuba. The Soviets removed the missiles after President Kennedy ordered a naval blockade of the island.

republics of Latin America designed to reduce the appeal of communism in that region. Kennedy aides promoted economic growth to stave off the working-class revolution that policymakers feared would result from an unstable economic system. The $100 billion plan was received with cautious optimism south of the border.

An expanded, flexible military and diplomatic force required strong centralized management. Taking the institutional changes of the 1947 National Security Act a step further, Kennedy enhanced the authority of the National Security Council by moving its chief directly into the White House. Reflecting his activist approach to presidential leadership, Kennedy often turned for advice to a small circle of personal aides rather than relying primarily on formal Pentagon

and State Department channels. Such a shift further concentrated foreign policy initiation at the White House.

The nation's strengthened military arsenal and streamlined defense establishment, however, failed to bring Kennedy the universal diplomatic success he had anticipated. Just as Kennedy took office in January 1961, Soviet Premier Nikita Khrushchev publicly described conflicts in Vietnam, Cuba, and elsewhere as "wars of national liberation" that were worthy of Soviet support. Kennedy took Khrushchev's words as a challenge, especially as they applied to Cuba.

Ever since Cuba had won its independence in the Spanish-American War, it had been economically and politically reliant on its powerful neighbor to the north. By 1956, American companies owned 80 percent of Cuba's utilities, 90 percent of its mining operations, and 40 percent of its sugar plantations. On New Year's Day in 1959, Fidel Castro overthrew the unpopular dictatorship of Fulgencio Batista and called for a revolution to reshape Cuban society. American diplomats grew concerned at these social changes, as well as Castro's growing friendliness with the Soviet Union. In early 1961, Kennedy authorized plans originally drawn up by the Eisenhower administration for an invasion by two thousand exiled Cubans to foment an anti-Castro uprising.

The invaders had been trained by the Central Intelligence Agency, but they were ill prepared for their task. After landing at the Bay of Pigs, the hapless forces were crushed by Castro's troops before they could even establish a beachhead. Symptomatic of the inept CIA planning, pilots in Nicaragua who were supposed to provide air cover for the landing forces forgot to set their watches ahead to Cuban time and arrived at the beach an hour too soon. The anticipated rebellion never occurred. The Bay of Pigs fiasco of April 1961 blighted the new administration with an embarrassing failure and cast doubts on Kennedy's activist approach to international affairs.

Although Kennedy devoted much of his attention to developments in the Western Hemisphere, he never lost his preoccupation with the Soviet Union. In June 1961, he met with Khrushchev in Vienna, an encounter that produced only a frank exchange of disagreements. Just days after this meeting, Khrushchev heightened international tensions by deploying soldiers to sever East Berlin from the western sector of the city. In mid-August, the Russians erected the Berlin wall, which still divides the historic German capital, to stop the exodus of East German citizens to the West. Kennedy later visited the Berlin wall, where he invoked the solidarity of the free world by declaring "Ich bin ein Berliner" ("I am a Berliner").

For thirteen days in October 1962, the United States and the Soviet Union came close to war. The Russians had stepped up their aid to the Castro regime after the Bay of Pigs invasion of the previous year. In mid-October, American U-2 aircraft photographed Soviet missile bases under construction in Cuba, complete with missiles that, when assembled, would be able to reach U.S. targets as far as 2,200 miles away. With Cuba just 90 miles from the Florida coast, the threat was too close to ignore.

Kennedy publicly confronted the Soviet Union over their actions. The United States, he declared in a somber televised address, would use its newly enlarged navy to blockade Soviet shipping to Cuba until the missiles were removed. Both the United States and the Soviet Union went on full military alert. On the following Sunday, after one of the most harrowing weeks of the nuclear age, Kennedy and Khrushchev reached an agreement and the Russians removed their missiles from Cuba. To allow Khrushchev to save face, the United States dismantled some outdated missiles in Turkey. "We're eyeball to eyeball," Secretary of State Dean Rusk observed, "and I think the other fellow just blinked."

The cold war tensions raised by the Berlin and Cuban missile crises heightened public support for Kennedy's proposed nationwide system of civil defense shelters. Defense analyst Herman Kahn's popular book, *On Thermonuclear War* (1960), had argued that, with careful civil defense planning, America would only lose between twenty and thirty million people in a nuclear attack. Influenced by Kahn's dark optimism, Kennedy encouraged individual families to build their own backyard bomb shelters. That city dwellers and poor people might not have backyards, or the income to build such shelters, escaped the attention of most policymakers.

This "do-it-yourself" approach to nuclear survival soon got out of control. Several Nevada communities claimed they were ready to shoot invading Californians who sought shelter over the state border. A Catholic priest published an article entitled "Ethics at the Shelter Doorway," which argued, "I doubt that any Catholic moralist would condemn the man who used available violence to repel panicky aggressors plying crowbars at the shelter door." The resulting public furor showed how disturbing "shelter ethics" really were.

After 1963, the backyard fallout shelter craze simply evaporated, as did plans for a comprehensive national shelter program. As the bombs grew larger, the chances of surviving an all-out nuclear attack in a backyard bomb shelter grew more dim. With intercontinental missiles capable

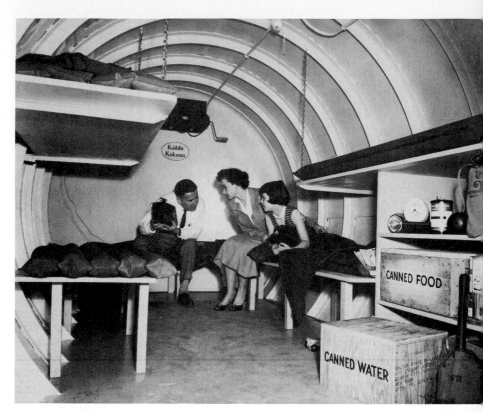

A HOME BOMB SHELTER
The manufacturer of this 1955 "Kiddie Kokoon" claimed that the home bomb shelter would provide three to five days of protection from a hydrogen bomb attack. Studies later showed that children who went through air raid drills at home or in school during the 1950s and early 1960s experienced frequent nightmares, many of which centered on the terror of their own death in a nuclear attack. (Library of Congress)

of reaching their targets a scant thirty minutes after launch, plans for evacuating thousands or millions of people from metropolitan areas seemed exercises in moving them from one place of death to another. Some Americans questioned what kind of a world would await them when they cautiously emerged after weeks or months underground.

Sobered by the Cuban missile crisis and the threat of nuclear annihilation, Kennedy began to seek ways to reduce cold war tensions. In a notable speech at American University in June 1963, he stressed the need to "make the world safe for diversity." Russians and Americans alike, he observed, "inhabit this small planet. We all breathe the same air. We all cherish our children's future. And we are all mortal." Soviet leaders, also chastened by the confrontation over Cuba, were now willing to talk. The two nations agreed to ban the testing of nuclear weapons in the air or in the seas. The test-ban treaty was ratified by the Senate in the fall of 1963.

Kennedy's desire to work out a pattern of peaceful coexistence with the Soviet Union, like Eisenhower's before him, reflected a strand of foreign policy that came to be called "détente." Détente was a different approach from cold war containment. Instead of challenging the Soviet Union, militarily or otherwise, at every corner of the globe, détente accepted the Soviets as an adversary with whom the United States could negotiate and bargain. Coexistence rather than confrontation, and common interests rather than polarities, distinguished détente from the cold war approach of the 1940s and 1950s. But no matter how often American leaders talked about opening channels of communication with the Russians, the obsession with the Soviet military threat to American national security never completely disappeared from U.S. policy. Nor did the Soviet Union moderate its obsession with the threat of the United States to its own security. Throughout the postwar period, both parties have maintained the cold war tensions.

The Vietnam War

Vietnam, which challenged American administrations from Harry Truman's to Richard Nixon's, became a test case of America's cold war policy. Lyndon Johnson echoed the reasoning that justified U.S. involvement in Vietnam in the name of containment:

> In the forties and fifties we took our stand in Europe to protect the freedom of those threatened by aggression. . . . Now, the center of attention has shifted to another part of the world where aggression is on the march and the enslavement of free men is its goal. . . . If we allow the Communists to win in Vietnam, it will become easier and more appetizing for them to take over other countries in other parts of the world. We will have to fight again some place else—at what cost no one knows. That is why it is vitally important to every American family that we stop the Communists in South Vietnam.

The needs and desires of the Vietnamese people hardly entered into this formulation.

The roots of U.S. involvement in Vietnam lay in the instability produced by the decolonization of Southeast Asia after World War II. In Vietnam during the 1940s, a nationalist movement known as the Viet Minh—led by French-educated communist Ho Chi Minh and military strategist Vo Nguyen Giap—demanded independence from France. The French refused to consider the Viet Minh request. Vietnam, the French argued, was "the pillar of the defense of the West in Southeast Asia. . . . If this pillar falls, Singapore, Malaysia, and India will soon fall prey to Mao Tse-tung."

President Truman found such reasoning persuasive. He also wanted to maintain good relations with France, whose support was crucial to the successful operation of the new NATO alliance. Early in 1950, the United States recognized the French-supported government of Bao Dai in Vietnam and began sending supplies to French troops there, a policy maintained by the Eisenhower administration. Meanwhile, Ho Chi Minh and his communist forces stepped up their fight against the French colonial administration. By 1954 the United States had sent more than $2 billion worth of military supplies to the French in Vietnam, paying nearly 80 percent of the cost of continuing the war.

Despite these joint French-U.S. efforts, Viet Minh forces gained strength in northern Vietnam. By the spring of 1954, they had trapped a large French force at the isolated administrative fortress of Dienbienphu. France asked the United States for direct military intervention. Eisenhower refused, and Dienbienphu fell in May 1954, after a fifty-six-day siege.

This dramatic turn of events sent the major parties to the negotiating table. The 1954 Geneva Accords temporarily partitioned Vietnam at the seventeenth parallel, committed France to withdraw its forces from north of that line within ten months, and forbade both North and South Vietnam from entering into any military alliance with an outside power. A final declaration provided that the two partitioned sectors would hold free elections in July 1956 to choose a unified government for the entire nation. The United States was never a party to the agreement. Before the scheduled elections could be held, a pro-western government headed by Ngo Dinh Diem took power in South Vietnam. Diem refused to allow the national elections to take place, mainly because he realized that the popular candidate Ho Chi Minh would easily win in both the north and south. Diem quickly consolidated his power in the south, including a rigged election in which Diem's ballots were printed on red paper, a Vietnamese symbol of good luck, while his opponent's were green, which stood for misfortune.

The Geneva Accords proved only an interlude between two wars, one to rid the country of French colonial control and a second to reunify Vietnam. By January 1955, the United States had replaced France as the dominant power in South Vietnam. American policymakers now asserted that a noncommunist South Vietnam was vital to the security interests of the United States and they charted U.S. policy accordingly. Between 1955 and 1961, the Eisenhower administration sent Diem an average of $200 million a year in aid, mostly military. In addition, approximately 675 American military advisers were stationed in Saigon, the capitol of South Vietnam.

Inheriting the Vietnam situation from the previous administration, President Kennedy initially sought to bolster the faltering regime of Ngo Dinh Diem, whom Vice-President Lyndon

AN IMMINENT COUP IN SOUTH VIETNAM, 1963

Johnson was fond of calling the "George Washington of South Vietnam." Eager to instruct Diem's soldiers in counterinsurgency techniques, Kennedy increased the number of American military advisers to more than fifteen thousand by November 1963. He also sent in economic development specialists to work with Vietnamese peasants to increase agricultural production. Kennedy refused, however, to send American combat troops to assist the South Vietnamese. "In the final analysis," he told a journalist just before his assassination, "it is their war."

The American aid did little good. Diem's political inexperience, combined with his Catholicism in a predominantly Buddhist country, made it impossible for him to create a stable, popular government. He enjoyed much more support from his faraway American backers than he did in his native land. The National Liberation Front (NLF, or Viet Cong), North Vietnam's revolutionary front in the south, made consistent headway against the unpopular Diem regime. These guerrillas blended easily into the local South Vietnamese population. As the situation deteriorated, Diem consistently misled his American allies about South Vietnamese military and social progress.

Matters came to a head in late 1963. Militant Buddhists staged a dramatic series of demonstrations against Diem, including several self-immolations that were recorded by American television crews. Kennedy decided that Diem had to be removed. Ambassador Henry Cabot Lodge, Jr., let it be known in Saigon that the United States would support a military coup that had "a good chance of succeeding." In the fall of 1963, Diem was driven from office and assassinated.

Kennedy's advisers had given little thought to what would follow Diem's ouster. Before they could formulate any plans, Kennedy himself was assassinated and Lyndon Johnson took his place as president. Johnson saw his mission in clear-cut terms. "I am not going to lose Vietnam," he stated emphatically within weeks of becoming president. "I am not going to be the President who saw Southeast Asia go the way China went." A new phase in the Americanization of the war began.

During the 1964 presidential campaign, Johnson declared, "We are not going to send American boys nine or ten thousand miles away from home to do what Asian boys ought to be doing for themselves." Yet plans were already under way for a major escalation of the United States effort, the only way, policymakers agreed, that the South Vietnamese government could prevent a communist takeover. The escalation, which was accomplished during the first several months of 1965, took two forms: the initiation of direct U.S. bombing attacks against North Vietnam and the deployment of American ground troops.

Before escalation could proceed, however, the administration had to have at least tacit congressional support for stepping up the war. Presidential adviser Walt Rostow was one of the first to point out that bombing North Vietnam would

MAP 29.4 THE VIETNAM WAR, 1954–1975
The Vietnam War was a guerrilla war. Fighting was marked by skirmishes and inconclusive encounters rather than decisive battles and major offensives. North Vietnamese supporters of the National Liberation Front filtered into South Vietnam along the Ho Chi Minh trail, which wound through Laos and Cambodia. In the south, the guerrillas followed the formula for revolution promoted by the Chinese leader Mao Zedong and blended into the local population "like fish in the water."

probably require some form of congressional declaration of war. Originally, Johnson had wanted to wait until after the 1964 election to place this potentially controversial request before Congress, but events gave him the opportunity to win such authorization earlier.

During the summer of 1964, American naval forces had supported several South Vietnamese amphibious attacks on the North Vietnamese coast. The North Vietnamese resisted such attacks, and in August, President Johnson told the nation that North Vietnamese torpedo boats had fired on American destroyers in international waters in the Gulf of Tonkin. Johnson asked Congress to authorize him "to take all necessary measures to promote the maintenance of peace and security in Southeast Asia" and to "prevent further aggression." The Gulf of Tonkin resolution passed 88 to 2 in the Senate and 416 to 0 in the House. Only Senators Wayne Morse of Oregon and Ernest Gruening of Alaska opposed the resolution as a "predated declaration of war" that further increased the president's ability to carry out foreign policy without consulting Congress.

Many questions were later raised about the resolution. A draft resolution had been ready for several months awaiting just such an incident. The evidence of a North Vietnamese attack was sketchy at best. As the president admitted soon afterward, "For all I know, our navy was shooting at whales out there." But this trumped-up attack got Johnson what he wanted—the only formal approval of American intervention in Vietnam ever voted by Congress. In Johnson's typically colorful language, he privately compared the resolution to "Grandma's nightshirt—it covered everything."

With congressional support assured and the 1964 election safely won, the Johnson administration began the fateful moves toward total Americanization of the Vietnam War. National security adviser McGeorge Bundy argued that the United States should retaliate against attacks on South Vietnamese military units by bombing a carefully selected set of targets in North Vietnam. Such bombing raids, Bundy reasoned, would cripple the North Vietnamese economy and force the communists to the bargaining table. A special target was the Ho Chi Minh trail, an elaborate network of paths, bridges, and shelters that snaked from North Vietnam through

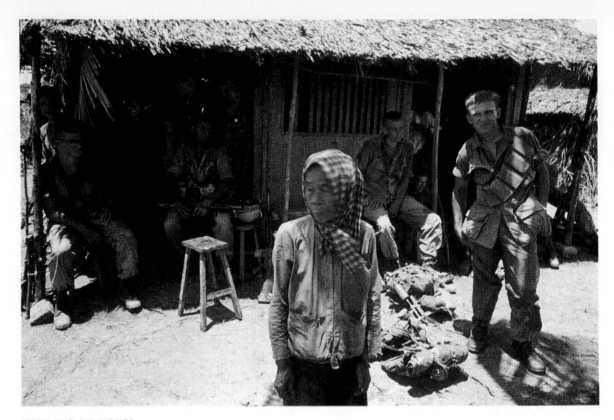

FRIENDS OR FOES?
U.S. Marines often entered South Vietnamese hamlets to search for suspected Vietcong sympathizers and destroy the bunkers where they hid, a process that could inflict heavy damage on the village and sometimes led to civilian deaths. One soldier noted that such behavior hardly won over the local peasantry: "Their homes had been wrecked, their chickens killed, their rice confiscated—and if they weren't pro-Vietcong before we got there, they sure as hell were by the time we left." (© P. J. Griffiths, Magnum)

Cambodia and Laos into South Vietnam. Some twenty thousand North Vietnamese soldiers moved southward along this route each month by 1967, as well as the military hardware and other resources necessary to supply them. Between 1965 and 1968, Operation Rolling Thunder, which got its name from an old Protestant hymn, dropped a million tons of bombs on North Vietnam, eight hundred tons a day for three and a half years. From 1965 to 1973, the United States dropped three times as many bombs on North Vietnam, a country roughly the size of Texas, as had fallen on Europe, Asia, and Africa during World War II.

Much to the amazement of American advisers, the bombing had no effect on the ability of the North Vietnamese to wage war. The flow of troops and supplies to the south continued un-

abated. Instead of destroying enemy morale and bringing the North Vietnamese to the bargaining table, the bombing rekindled North Vietnam's nationalism and intensified its will to fight. American leaders should have learned a lesson from World War II, when extensive bombing of Germany in 1944–1945 had failed to cripple Nazi industrial production and had actually boosted enemy morale. Since North Vietnam had little industry to destroy, the impact of similar bombing on an agricultural society would predictably be even less. The bombing continued nevertheless.

The other major escalation of the American commitment in 1965 was the assignment of American ground troops to combat duty in South Vietnam. Even with the help of numerous American advisers and millions of dollars of supplies, South Vietnamese troops were no longer able to resist the Viet Cong. The first U.S. Marines waded ashore at Da Nang on March 8, 1965, ostensibly to protect the large American air base there. Soon they were patrolling the countryside and skirmishing with the enemy. The American people were not told that a major change in policy had occurred.

During the next three years, the number of U.S. troops in Vietnam grew dramatically. The war increasingly became an American struggle, fought for American aims. More than 75,000 soldiers were fighting there by June 1965, and 190,000 by the end of that year. By 1966, almost 400,000 American soldiers were stationed in Vietnam, 500,000 by 1967, and 540,000 in 1968. In early 1968, the commander of the U.S. forces in Vietnam, General William Westmoreland, asked for 206,000 additional troops, a request that was never fulfilled. Westmoreland's escalating demands confirmed a prediction made by presidential adviser George Ball in 1961. Ball had warned President Kennedy that if American ground toops were committed to Vietnam, there would be 300,000 there within five years. Kennedy had laughed and said, "George, you're cra-

zier than hell." But as Kennedy observed before his death, requests for troops were like having a drink: "The effect wears off, and you have to take another."

The massive commitment of troops and supplies after 1965 brought the United States and South Vietnam no closer to victory. Taking to the extreme Johnson's call "to leave the footprints of America in Vietnam," extensive defoliation and military bombardment destroyed the beautiful country and made it difficult for peasants to practice the agriculture that provided the economic and cultural base of Vietnamese society. After one devastating but not unusual engagement, the commanding U.S. officer claimed, using the logic of the times, "It became necessary to destroy the town in order to save it." Meanwhile, American soldiers and dollars flowed into Saigon and other cities, distorting the local economy and setting off wild, unmanageable inflation.

Why did the American presence in Vietnam have so little effect? The determination of the North Vietnamese and their South Vietnamese sympathizers was a major factor. In the 1940s, Ho Chi Minh had told his French imperialist

JUNGLE WARFARE IN VIETNAM
The horror of losing a buddy in war is plain in the faces of these marines as they try to drag a comrade to safety under fire. Almost two-thirds of the American soldiers who died in action in Vietnam were twenty-one years old or younger. (© Robert Ellison, Black Star)

TIME LINE
PERMANENT MOBILIZATION AND THE COLD WAR

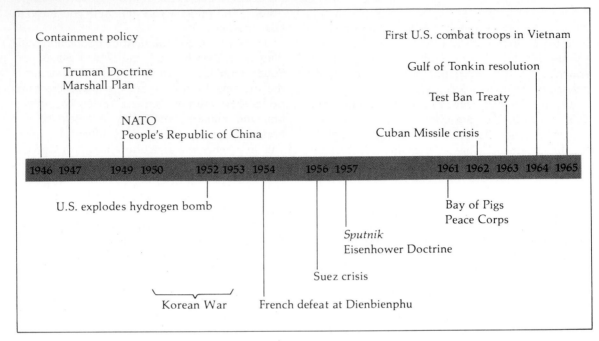

foes, "You can kill ten of my men for every one I kill of yours, but even at those odds, you will lose and I will win." That same strategy held true against the Americans. The Viet Cong were prepared to accept limitless casualties and to fight for as many years as necessary. (Four million Vietnamese on both sides were either killed or wounded in the war, approximately 10 percent of the population.) North Vietnamese strategists astutely realized that the war did not have to be won on the battlefield. They accurately predicted that the United States would be unable to wage an extended war of attrition because American public opinion would eventually limit U.S. participation.

The kind of guerrilla fighting that characterized the Vietnam War also favored the Viet Cong rather than the American ground troops. There were no fronts or actual battles, just skirmishes. A former Marine captain recalled:

> You never knew who was the enemy and who was the friend. They all looked alike. They all dressed alike. They were all Vietnamese. Some of them were Vietcong. Here's a woman of twenty-two or twenty-three. She is pregnant, and she tells an interrogator that her husband works in Danang and isn't a Vietcong. But she watches your men walk down a trail and get killed or wounded by a booby trap. She knows the booby trap is there, but she doesn't warn them. Maybe she planted it herself.

He concluded graphically, "It wasn't like the San Francisco Forty-Niners on one side of the field and the Cincinnati Bengals on the other. The enemy was all around you."

The success of the fighting was measured not in territory gained, but in gruesome "body counts"—the number of enemy soldiers killed. Such casualty figures were sometimes deliberately inflated. As a twenty-four-year old Special Forces captain recalled, "I went out and killed one VC and liberated a prisoner. Next day the major called me in and told me that I'd killed fourteen VC and liberated six prisoners. You want to see the medal?" The pressure of waging war under these conditions drove many soldiers, whose average age was only nineteen, to seek escape with cheap and readily available drugs.

By 1967, despite the glowing reports that were fed to the American public, many administration officials had privately reached more pessimistic conclusions. Pentagon analysts estimated that the North Vietnamese, with only marginal assistance from other communist powers, could keep sending two hundred thousand guerrillas a year into South Vietnam indefinitely. Despite such a prognosis, President Johnson continued to insist that an American victory in Vietnam was vital to U.S. national security and prestige. "If we are driven from the field in Vietnam," he asserted, "then no nation can ever again have the same confidence in American protection." Journalists soon commented that the Johnson administration suffered from a "credibility gap."

Domestic events also forced Johnson and his advisers to reassess their policy. In 1966, the federal deficit stood at $9.8 billion. The deficit jumped to $23 billion in 1967, with the Vietnam War costing the taxpayers $27 billion that year. (The total cost of the war from 1965 to 1973 has been estimated at $120 billion.) Although the war was consuming only 3 percent of the gross national product, compared with 48 percent for World War II and 12 percent for the Korean War, Johnson could no longer hide the enormous expense of the war from the American people. But only in the summer of 1967 did

he ask for a 10 percent surcharge on individual and corporate income, which Congress delayed approving until 1968. By then the inflationary spiral that plagued the American economy throughout the 1970s was already out of control. In addition to the economic dislocations, domestic dissent over the war escalated as the 1968 presidential election neared. Such internal pressures confirmed Ho Chi Minh's prediction that a democratic society could not fight a protracted war of attrition halfway around the world. Time was on North Vietnam's side.

The struggle in Vietnam reflected problems characteristic of every new nation in the postcolonial world—nationalist ambitions, religious and cultural conflicts, economic needs, and political turmoil. In reality, Vietnam was too small to play a significant part in the international balance of power. North Vietnamese communism was intensely regional and nationalistic. Yet the Kennedy and Johnson administrations, and their predecessors, allowed their perception of a worldwide communist threat to control their actions in Vietnam. By 1968, what Lyndon Johnson had once referred to as "a raggedy-ass little fourth-rate country" had brought the world's most powerful military giant to its knees. As in the Korean conflict, the American people were learning that fighting communism was a complicated task.

The end of World War II brought a dramatic shift in American foreign policy, as the United States broke from its isolationist tradition to seek a permanent role in world affairs. The predominant characteristic of this new policy was the cold war with the Soviet Union. Containment originally emerged in response to Soviet pressure on Eastern Europe, but that doctrine was expanded by succeeding administrations to include resistance to communism wherever it appeared. The Korean and Vietnam wars were two outgrowths of the containment doctrine. A cold war mentality shaped U.S. foreign policy throughout the post-World War II era.

Fighting a worldwide battle against communism had strong domestic repercussions. The new importance of foreign affairs enhanced the power of the president. Permanent mobilization concentrated power in the Pentagon and led to the creation of a military-industrial complex dependent on production for war. Growing defense expenditures took up an ever-larger part of the gross national product. Besides paying for defense through taxes and growing deficits, American citizens now lived in a world where fear of nuclear attack became part of daily life and small foreign wars were a constant possibility.

Suggestions for Further Reading

The Origins of the Cold War

The two best overviews are Walter LaFeber, *America, Russia, and the Cold War*, 3rd edition (1976), which takes the story to 1975; and John L. Gaddis, *The United States and the Origins of the Cold War* (1972), which covers the 1940s. Two other excellent studies are Daniel Yergin, *Shattered Peace* (1977), which focuses on the rise of the national security state; and Lloyd Gardner, *Architects of Illusion* (1970), which surveys the policy makers. See also Stephen Ambrose, *Rise to Globalism*, 2nd edition (1980); John W. Spanier, *American Foreign Policy Since World War II*, rev. ed. (1973); and Richard J. Barnet, *The Roots of War* (1972). For perspectives quite critical of American aims, see Joyce and Gabriel Kolko, *The Limits of Power* (1970) and Robert J. Maddox, *The New Left and the Origins of the Cold War* (1977). Martin J. Sherwin, *A World Destroyed* (1975) and Gar Alperowitz, *Atomic Diplomacy* (1965) cover the impact of atomic weapons on policy formulation. Useful for assessing the links between foreign and domestic policy are Robert A. Divine, *Foreign Policy and U.S. Presidential Elections, 1940–1960*, 2 vols. (1974) and Richard Freeland, *The Truman Doctrine and the Origins of McCarthyism* (1972).

The period can also be viewed through individual policy makers. Indispensible are George F. Kennan, *American Diplomacy, 1900–1950* (1952) and *Memoirs, 1925–1950* (1967); and Dean Acheson's modestly titled *Present at the Creation* (1970). Walter Lippmann, *The Cold War* (1947) can be supplemented by Ronald Steel's fine biography, *Walter Lippmann and the American Century* (1980). Adam Ulam presents the Soviet point of view in *The Rivals: America and Russia Since World War II* (1971).

The Cold War in Asia

Akira Iriye, *The Cold War in Asia* (1974) is the best starting point. See also Tang Tsou, *America's Failure in China, 1941–1950* (1963); Kenneth Shewmaker, *Americans and the Chinese Communists* (1971); and Michael Shaller, *The United States and China in the 20th Century* (1979). E. J. Kahn, Jr., *The China Hands* (1975) and Ross Y. Kuen, *The China Lobby in American Politics* (1974) cover the domestic repercussions.

David Rees, *Korea: The Limited War* (1964) is a good introduction, which can be supplemented by Allen S. Whiting, *China Crosses the Yalu* (1960) and Frank Baldwin, ed., *Without Parallel* (1975). Ronald J. Caridi, *The Korean War and American Politics* (1969) covers the Republican response. William Manchester, *American Caesar* (1979) offers an engrossing biography of Douglas MacArthur.

Extending Containment

In addition to LaFeber, *America, Russia, and the Cold War*, the 1950s are well treated in Robert Divine, *Eisenhower and the Cold War* (1981); Ronald Steel, *Pax Americana* (1967); and Blanche Wiesen Cook, *The Declassified Eisenhower* (1981). An excellent book on the CIA is Victor Marchetti and John D. Marks, *The CIA and the Cult of Intelligence* (1974). For developments linking economics, corporations, and the defense industry, see Mira Wilkins, *The Maturing of Multinational Enterprise* (1974); Richard Barnet and Ronald Muller, *Global Reach* (1974); and Paul Hammond, *Organizing for Defense* (1971). On specific policy situations, see Robert Divine, *Blowing in the Wind: The Nuclear Test Ban Debate, 1954–1960* (1978); Robert Stookey, *America and the Arab States* (1975); John Snetsinger, *Truman, the Jewish Role and the Creation of Israel* (1974); and Hugh Thomas, *Suez* (1967). Of interest given his later career are Henry Kissinger, *Nuclear Weapons and Foreign Policy* (1957) and *The Necessity of Choice* (1961).

The Limits of Containment

Godfrey Hodgson, *America in Our Time* (1976) treats the entire postwar period, but the heart of its powerful analysis covers the 1960s. Richard Walton, *Cold War and Counterrevolution* (1972) surveys the foreign policy of the Kennedy administration. Robert Kennedy, *Thirteen Days* (1969) provides a participant's account of the Cuban missile crisis. Richard Barnet, *Intervention and Revolution* (1968) provides the best introduction to United States relations with the Third World. See also John L. S. Girling, *America and the Third World* (1980) and Samuel Baily, *The United States and the Development of South America, 1945–1975* (1977).

Two superb books introduce the Vietnamese conflict and the American role in it: Frances Fitzgerald, *Fire in the Lake* (1972) and Stanley Karnow, *Vietnam: A History* (1983). George Herring, *America's Longest War* (1980) and Alexander Kendrick, *The Wound Within: America in the Vietnam Years, 1945–1974* (1974) also provide overviews. A fascinating source to digest is *The Pentagon Papers* (1971). David Halberstam, *The Best and the Brightest* (1972) gives a deft, and deadly, portrait of the leaders who got the United States into Vietnam. Guenter Lewy offers a controversial defense of the commitment in *America in Vietnam* (1978). James C. Thompson, *Rolling Thunder* (1980) and John Galloway, *The Gulf of Tonkin Resolution* (1970) cover specific topics. Gloria Emerson, *Winners and Losers* (1976) and Michael Herr, *Dispatches* (1977) convey what the war meant to the soldiers who fought it.

THE PHOTOGRAPHIC EYE

Photographs play such an important part in modern life that we rarely stop to think about what they are, what they stand for, or how pervasive they are. How could modern societies exist without photographs on student and employee ID cards, drivers' licenses, and police mug shots? How would consumers decide what to buy without the alluring photographs that accompany modern advertising? How could families keep track of their vacations—and their histories—without albums and shoeboxes full of old photographs? How would people know what their political leaders looked like? We have a much clearer image of such figures as Abraham Lincoln and Eleanor Roosevelt, of whom abundant photographs exist, than of George Washington and Abigail Adams, who lived before the photographic process was developed. No wonder the writer James Agee proclaimed the camera "the central instrument of our time."

Photography is a product of the forces of technological and economic change that industrialization set in motion. The earliest photographs were called *daguerreotypes* (plate 1), after the French inventor Louis J. M. Daguerre, who in 1839 patented the process of transferring an image of light onto a polished mirror surface. By the 1860s, daguerreotypes had been made obsolete by new techniques that allowed multiple copies to be produced from a single negative and printed on paper, rather than glass. In the 1880s, the long exposure time that had been required to record a photographic image was dramatically reduced, enabling the camera to record moving objects. At about the same time, the halftone printing process was developed. This innovation permitted photographs to be reproduced widely in newspapers and magazines. By the

PLATE 1
It was hard work having a daguerreotype taken in the mid-nineteenth century. Subjects had to sit still for nearly thirty seconds while trying to maintain a fairly natural expression (no wonder smiles were rare). In this daguerreotype, Mrs. Kiah Sewall and four of her five children did fine, but the baby moved. (Maine Historical Society)

PLATE 2
In the 1890s, American consumers could buy a Kodak "Brownie" for $25, which included processing. "You press the button, we do the rest" was the Kodak slogan. Such photographs were called "snapshots," a term hunters used to describe shooting from the hip without taking careful aim. (International Museum of Photography at George Eastman House)

PLATE 3
Edward S. Curtis devoted his life to photographing "the vanishing race" of the American Indian. Between 1907 and 1930, he published twenty volumes entitled *The North American Indian,* including this 1925 photogravure of *Francisca Chiwiwi-Islete.* (The Art Institute of Chicago)

1890s, the introduction of flexible rolls of film and gelatine dry plates made photography faster and more convenient. In 1895, a small portable camera called the "Brownie" took photography into homes across the nation (plate 2).

From the outset, photography was linked to family culture. Before the Civil War, the cost of having a picture taken had fallen to less than fifty cents, bringing photographs within the range of ordinary Americans. Photo albums began to appear in parlors alongside the family Bible. In an increasingly mobile and transient society, photographs represented direct and tangible ties with friends and relatives who were absent or dead. Photos mailed to loved ones in distant communities provided a way to keep in touch as family members migrated west. Photographs thus helped maintain family and community cohesion at a time of explosive social and economic change. They still perform this function today.

Photographs have many other purposes as well, and early photographers realized the vast potential of their new medium. For example, photographers in the mid-nineteenth century quickly began to document significant events in American history. Mathew Brady and his associates took about seven thousand photographs of the Civil War; the impact of these pictures was heightened by the novelty of the medium. Later in the century, photographers recorded such milestones as the final link in the first transcontinental railroad and the opening of the Oklahoma frontier to white settlers. Evocative images by W. H. Jackson and Edward S. Curtis documented the vanishing way of life of the Plains Indians (plate 3). Photographs of little-known but spectacularly beautiful places, such as the Yellowstone area and

Yosemite Valley, hastened the creation of the National Park System.

Photography proved especially well suited to awakening the American conscience during the progressive era at the turn of the twentieth century. Although photographs give the illusion of objectivity, they are never neutral; they always present a point of view. One of the first reformers to use photographs to promote social change was Jacob Riis, a Danish immigrant. Riis's book *How the Other Half Lives* (1890), which featured dramatic photographs of the plight of the nation's urban poor, helped pioneer the modern field of photojournalism. Two decades later, Lewis Hine produced what he called "human documents" or "photo-interpretations" on topics such as child labor (plate 4) and immigration, including a series on new arrivals at Ellis Island. In the 1920s, Hine focused on the world of work, including a breathtaking series on the construction of the Empire State Building (plate 5). "If I could tell the story in words," he said, "I wouldn't have to lug a camera." Hine's socially committed photography strongly influenced the documentary photographers who

PLATE 4
Between 1908 and 1921, Lewis Hine took more than five thousand photographs for the National Child Labor Committee. This picture captures a group of breaker boys at the entrance to a Pennsylvania coal shaft in 1910. Breaker boys separated useless slate by hand from the miners' yield of coal. (International Museum of Photography at George Eastman House)

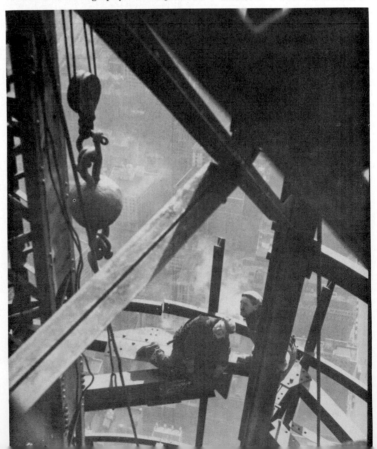

PLATE 5
To capture pictures of the construction of the Empire State Building in New York City, Lewis Hine followed workers up exposed girders, out onto the mooring mast (pictured here), and even had himself suspended in a crane to photograph the final rivet at the top of the 102-story building, then the tallest in the world. Hine published these photographs in *Men at Work* (1932). (International Museum of Photography at George Eastman House)

roamed the country for the Farm Security Administration during the Great Depression. Today, many photographers who cover stories for leading news magazines carry on this tradition.

Although the camera has been used extensively to document the human condition, it also has been an instrument of individual expression, an example of the artist's spiritual and creative control over a machine. Alfred Stieglitz, whose journal *Camera Work* provided a forum for the developing art of photography between 1902 and 1917, epitomized the serious art photographer in European and American culture. The artist Pablo Picasso com- mented admiringly about Stieglitz's photograph *The Steerage* (plate 6), "This is exactly what I have been trying to say in paint."

During the 1920s and 1930s, photography underwent something of a flowering and became a prevalent part of American life and culture. Such photographers as Paul Strand, Berenice Abbott, Edward Weston, Imogen Cunningham, Ansel Adams, and Margaret Bourke-White rose to prominence. Although each of these artists dealt with different types of subject matter—Abbott became known for her images of New York skyscrapers, Cunningham for her photographs of flowers, Adams for his dramatic shots of the American West (plate 7), Bourke-White for her industrial scenes—they all emphasized precise focus, sharp lighting, clarity of subject, and high-quality prints. Their realistic "straight" photography, as it was known, tried to bring out the beauty and significance in the details of everyday life and to focus the viewer's eye on commonplace objects and scenes. Among the many outstanding photographers who furthered their careers with work for the WPA, Walker Evans showed a special appreciation for the humor and the individuality of rural Americans (plate 8).

At the same time, mass-circulation illustrated magazines be-

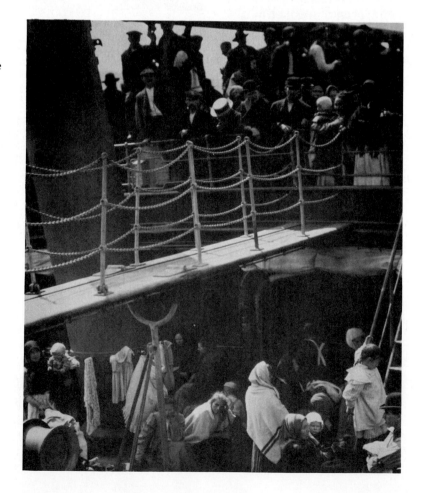

PLATE 6
Alfred Stieglitz was promenading along the first-class deck of the luxury liner *Kaiser Wilhelm II* when he spotted a scene with artistic possibilities. He rushed back to his cabin for his Graflex camera, and snapped *The Steerage* (1907). Stieglitz considered this his finest picture. (The Art Institute of Chicago. Alfred Stieglitz Collection)

PLATE 7
For Ansel Adams, "a great
photograph" has to be "a full
expression of what one feels about
what is being photographed in the
deepest sense and is, thereby, a true
expression of what one feels about
life in its entirety." *Moonrise,
Hernandez, New Mexico* (1941) speaks
for Ansel Adams's deep affinity for
the American West. (The Art
Institute of Chicago. Peabody
Purchase Fund)

PLATE 8
In the photographs of Walker
Evans, one critic observed, "even
the inanimate things, bureau
drawers, pots, tires, bricks, signs,
seem waiting in their own patient
dignity, posing for the picture."
This 1936 photograph is a visual
inventory of these people's daily
lives. (*Roadside Stand near
Birmingham, 1936.* The Art
Institute of Chicago. Gift of Mrs.
James Ward Thorne)

gan to bring new photographs into American homes every week. The most celebrated of these magazines was *Life*, which premiered in 1936. Its first cover featured one of Bourke-White's striking photos of the construction of Fort Peck Dam in Montana (plate 9). As never before, editors relied on pictures to tell news stories.

Pictures were also used for entertainment and escapism. Motion pictures opened a different avenue for photographic expertise and gave people new celebrities to admire—the movie stars. Even "serious" photographers saw movie stars as fascinating subjects. Edward Steichen's early portrait of Greta Garbo (plate 10) is but one example.

By the 1940s, photography had become not only a recog-

nized art, but also one of the dominant elements of American mass communication. Its importance was marked by the establishment of a photography department at the Museum of Modern Art in New York City in 1940 and the formation of the International Museum of Photography in Rochester, New York in 1949.

Since World War II, American photography has evolved in different directions. Human interest photography, exemplified by the highly influential "Family of Man" exhibit that Edward Steichen organized at the Museum of Modern Art in 1955, used photographs as metaphors for the human condition. Other photographers gravitated toward subjects on the fringes of society. At the hands of artists such as

Diane Arbus and Robert Frank, even supposedly "normal" people and scenes seem freakish or bizarre. Arbus's work (plate 11) suggests that something was amiss in the affluent society of the late 1960s and early 1970s. But, unlike the documentary photography of a few decades earlier, it offers no solutions or calls for reform. The problems that Arbus brought to light in her quirky, often disturbing images could not be corrected by progressive legislation; they ran deeper, suggesting something of a spiritual void at the heart of American society. Robert Frank's photographs, generally more somber, showed Americans as a people who had lost their identity to a massive impersonal society. Their work found great acceptance during the soul-

PLATE 9
In late 1936, publisher Henry Luce assigned Margaret Bourke-White to photograph a series of New Deal dams under construction in the Columbia River Basin for the brand new *Life* magazine. Many of the country's best photojournalists worked for *Life* over the next four decades. (*Life* Magazine © 1936 Time, Inc.)

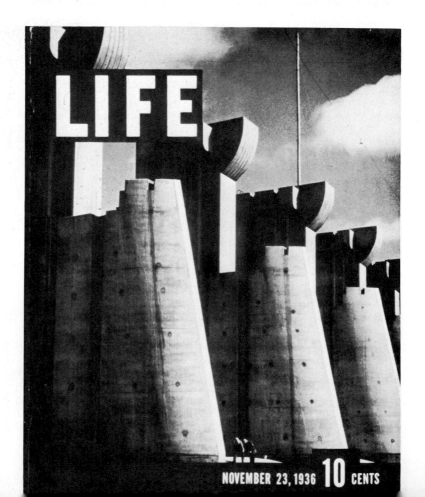

NOVEMBER 23, 1936 10 CENTS

PLATE 11
Diane Arbus was drawn to unconventional subjects, such as transvestites, nudists, carnival freaks, and dwarfs. Most of her subjects look directly into the camera, which makes them look even stranger. The 79-year-old King and 72-year-old Queen that Arbus photographed at a senior citizens' dance in 1970 had never met before. Their names had been picked out of a hat. (© 1970 Estate of Diane Arbus)

PLATE 10
Great photographs have "magic," said Edward Steichen, and his 1928 portrait of actress Greta Garbo certainly does. The movie-going public was fascinated by glamorous stars like Garbo. Monthly fan magazines such as *Photoplay* and *Modern Screen* featured photographs to satisfy the public's insatiable appetite for news about the opulent off-screen lives of Hollywood stars. (International Museum of Photography at George Eastman House. Reprinted with the permission of Joanna T. Steichen)

searching, self-critical years of the Vietnam War and the civil rights movement.

As Americans grappled with difficult social issues in the late 1960s, technological progress brought further advances in photography. One of the most memorable news photos of the twentieth century showed astronauts walking on the moon for the first time, on July 20, 1969. By the 1980s, the two *Voyager* spacecraft were sending back full-color images of Jupiter, Saturn, and Uranus. Photography, which had always recorded scientific phenomena closer to home, was now expanding our knowledge of other worlds.

The capacity for knowledge was also broadened immeasurably by the advent of television, a medium that relied on a special form of camera. Television was developed shortly before World War II, but it did not begin to reach into millions of American homes until the postwar years. The number of photographic images that TV brought to Americans every day became almost limitless.

By the late 1970s and early 1980s, the national storehouse of visual material had grown so vast and powerful that many artists felt no need to create new images. Instead, they began to appropriate existing images and superimpose captions that stimulated advertising slogans or newspaper headlines to comment on American society. Barbara Kruger, one of the leading figures in this movement, placed the word "Perfect" over a young woman's clasped hands (plate 12) and the phrase "Your manias become science" over an atomic cloud. In this way, she commented on issues ranging from the role of women to the threat of nuclear war.

"The images that have virtually unlimited authority in modern society are mainly photographic images," observed critic Susan Sontag in her 1977 discussion of the aesthetic and moral questions raised by modern photography. Berenice Abbott made a similar claim, stating that "the *picture* has almost replaced the *word* as a means of communication." Although such assertions are open to debate, visual images have become an omnipresent fact of American life. As new visual innovations are developed, such as the computer graphics and music videos of the 1980s, photography in all its forms will come to play an even greater role in American society.

PLATE 12
Barbara Kruger's work is both political and feminist. "Is this headless presence the incarnation of 1950s good girl-ness," asked one critic, "or a vignetted image of prayer as [a] ladder to spiritual perfection?" What stands out most in this 1980 photograph is the absolute authority of the word "PERFECT." (*Perfect* [© D. James Dee])

922

30

THE STRUGGLE FOR EQUALITY AND DIVERSITY

The 1960s are often portrayed as a time of social protest and upheaval, a time when things fell apart. Yet this era of questioning and confrontation was not confined to a single decade. From the early 1950s through the mid-1970s, new issues and movements crowded the national agenda. The demand for civil rights gained momentum in the 1950s with early victories against segregation in the South. The youth rebellion and resurgent feminism were also rooted in the supposedly complacent 1950s, and the women's movement made its greatest impact on society in the 1970s.

Why did these demands for political and social change occur when they did? Demographic and cultural shifts were partly responsible. The black exodus from the South made civil rights a national, not a sectional, issue. The baby-boom generation swelled the enrollments of the nation's universities, providing recruits for student protest in the the 1960s. Changes in women's lives, notably their increased access to education and greater participation in the work force, helped spark the revival of feminism.

The civil rights movement was the first protest movement to develop, and the tactics it pioneered—legislative and judicial challenges, nonviolent protests, and mobilization of public opinion—were later adopted by other groups to press their demands. But although legal and political victories raised awareness and expectations, they did not address the underlying structural causes that limited each protesting group's full participation in American society. The next stage—the quest for social and economic equality—proved far more problematic. It was easier to pass a law banning segregated seating on buses in the South than to tackle problems of unemployment, deteriorating housing, and pervasive racism in the nation's cities. It was simpler to pass legislation that guaranteed women equal pay on the job than to change attitudes that still gave women full responsibility for household management and child care even when they worked full-time outside the home.

Even at the height of the protest movements, the people demanding changes in American society were always outnumbered by those who preferred the status quo. The strength of this dominant majority culture was the main reason why the ambitious agendas for social change proposed in this period were never fully realized. Yet these movements for equality and diversity had an impact on American culture. "What started as an identity crisis for Negroes turned out to be an identity crisis for the nation," observed one participant. By the 1970s, society had had its "consciousness raised" (a phrase from the women's movement) about a host of issues and problems that had not been topics of national concern in the immediate postwar period.

The Civil Rights Movement

The postwar transformation of southern agriculture underlay the emergence of the civil rights movement. New Deal agricultural policies and the development of synthetic fibers such as rayon and Dacron after World War II caused cotton acreage in the South to decline from forty-three million acres in 1929 to fewer than fifteen million in 1959. In addition, the postwar mechanization of farming reduced the need for farm labor. As a result, the southern farm population fell from 16.2 million in 1930 to 5.9 million in 1960. This displacement affected both white and black farmers, and both landowners and sharecroppers. Some of the migrants settled in southern cities, where they obtained industrial jobs; many of the rest headed to northern cities, including 3 million blacks, between 1940 and 1960. By 1970, a majority of blacks lived outside the South, mainly in the nation's metropolitan areas. Since northern blacks could vote (unlike their predominantly disenfranchised brethren in the South), this circumstance ensured that civil rights would eventually become a political issue.

The civil rights movement was enormously successful in its early days. By the 1960s, black Americans had won most of the political and legal rights that whites enjoyed. These breakthroughs were especially dramatic in the South, where segregation, the legalized system of separation of the races that had existed since the turn of the century, was dismantled. Between 1963 and 1965, the focus of the movement shifted from the South to the rest of the nation, where problems such as urban poverty and patterns of discrimination in jobs and housing proved harder to eradicate than segregation in the South. Impatience with the lack of progress led to splits in the civil rights movement, rioting in major northern cities, and a growing white backlash. As the civil rights movement struggled to maintain its momentum, other groups, such as Hispanics and native Americans, took up the cry of equal rights on their own behalf.

The Fight for Legal Equality

In August 1955, G. H. Mehta, India's ambassador to the United States, walked into a restaurant at the Houston airport. To his indignant surprise, Mehta was told he could not be served

INTEGRATION IN LITTLE ROCK
Angry crowds taunted the nine black students who tried to register in 1957 at previously all-white Central High School in Little Rock, Arkansas with chants such as "Two-four-six-eight, we ain't gonna integrate." The court-ordered integration proceeded only after President Eisenhower reluctantly mobilized the Arkansas National Guard. (Wide World)

because he had taken a seat in the "whites only" section. This incident, a keen embarrassment to the U.S. government, occurred because a comprehensive system of state and local laws mandated the separation of the races throughout the South.

In most southern states, it was illegal for whites and blacks to eat in the same rooms in restaurants or luncheonettes, use the same waiting rooms or toilet facilities at bus or train stations, or ride in the same taxis. Even drinking fountains were labeled "White" and "Colored." All forms of public transportation were rigidly segregated, either by custom or law. On buses, for example, if whites had filled all the front seats, blacks were obliged to give up seats in the back until every white had a place.

Since the 1930s, black Americans had a growing arsenal of weapons with which to challenge segregation. The federal government had increasingly paid attention to the problems of blacks. It established the Fair Employment Practices Commission in 1941 and, on President Truman's executive order in 1948, desegregated the armed forces. There was some social progress, too. In 1947, Jackie Robinson broke the color barrier in major league baseball. However, Robinson could not always stay in the same hotels or eat in the same restaurants as his teammates on the Brooklyn Dodgers.

Blacks got further ammunition in their fight against discrimination from the Supreme Court. Since the 1940s, the National Association for the Advancement of Colored People (NAACP) had litigated a series of test cases challenging segregation. These suits began to bear fruit in 1944, when the Court declared that blacks could not be denied the right to vote in party primaries. In 1946, it ruled that states could not require segregated seating on interstate buses, and two years later it struck down restrictive residential covenants that forbade the sale of real estate to members of disfavored racial groups.

A major leap forward occurred in 1954. In the case of *Brown v. Board of Education of Topeka*, the Supreme Court ruled that segregated schools violated the Fourteenth Amendment to the Constitution. The decision thus explicitly reversed the doctrine set forth in *Plessy v. Ferguson* (1896) that "separate but equal" facilities did not violate the civil rights of blacks. Speaking for a unanimous court, Chief Justice Earl Warren ruled:

To separate Negro children solely because of their race generates a feeling of inferiority as to their status in the community that may affect their hearts and minds in a way never to be undone. . . . We conclude that in the field of public education the doctrine of "separate but equal" has no place. Separate educational facilities are inherently unequal.

Blacks reacted joyfully. Black parents believed segregation would end immediately and that their children would soon attend integrated—and superior—schools. Black Americans were especially proud that black lawyer Thurgood Marshall, representing the NAACP, had been instrumental in using the white legal system to win such a stunning judicial victory. White reaction, especially in the South, was almost uniformly hostile. President Dwight Eisenhower refused to comment publicly about the decision, other than to acknowledge that it was now the law of the land. In private, he complained that his appointment of Chief Justice Earl Warren was "the biggest damfool mistake I ever made."

Brown v. Board of Education was one of the most far-reaching decisions ever handed down by the Supreme Court. Following its precedent, over the next several years the Supreme Court ruled against segregation in parks, public beaches, golf courses, all forms of interstate and intrastate transportation, and public housing. Yet progress in desegregating schools was frustratingly slow. The Court had declared only that integration should proceed "with all deliberate speed." As many critics later noted, the deliberation was far more evident than the speed. By 1960, less than 1 percent of southern black children attended desegregated schools. Significant school integration did not occur until the 1970s.

The *Brown* decision was so far in advance of prevailing cultural attitudes that it worked as an agent for social change. It forced the federal government to enter, albeit reluctantly, on the side of desegregation. In September 1957, when nine black children tried to enroll at Central High School in Little Rock, Arkansas, Governor Orval Faubus called out the national guard to bar them, despite a court order to the contrary. Every night, national television carried pictures of a white crowd taunting the poised but obviously terrified black students with such chants as "Go back to the jungle." Eisenhower nationalized the Arkansas guard so that integration could proceed. As happened time and again, white extremism provoked a far more sympathetic response from the federal government than would otherwise have occurred.

The magnitude of resistance to school integration deeply discouraged black and sympathetic white southerners who had hoped that the system of Jim Crow segregation would topple in the wake of the *Brown* decision. The realization that more action would be needed fueled the second major stage of the early civil rights movement—nonviolent protest. A spirit of activism had been growing among members of the black community since the 1930s, but the *Brown* decision had a catalytic effect on black aspirations. It encouraged them to think that change was possible.

On December 1, 1955, Rosa Parks, a church leader and member of the NAACP in Montgomery, Alabama, refused to give up her seat on a city bus to a white man. She was promptly arrested and charged with violating a local segregation ordinance. "I felt it was just something I had to do," Parks stated simply. Black activist Eldridge Cleaver put her act of resistance in a broader context: "Somewhere in the universe a gear in the machinery had shifted."

As Montgomery's black community met to discuss the proper response, it turned to the Reverend Martin Luther King, Jr., who had just accepted the post of pastor at Montgomery's Dexter Street Baptist Church. The son of a prominent black minister in Atlanta, King had earned a Ph.D. in theology at Boston University. King embraced the teachings of Mahatma Gandhi, who had organized the brilliant campaigns of noncooperation and passive resistance that ultimately helped India to win its independence from British rule in 1947. Drawing on Gandhian principles, King proposed a massive nonviolent protest to boycott Montgomery's municipal bus system.

For the next 381 days, a united black community formed carpools or walked to work. "My feets is tired, but my soul is rested," said one black woman. Added another, "I'm not walking for myself. I'm walking for my children and my grandchildren." The bus company neared bankruptcy, and downtown stores complained about loss of business. When a federal court ruled that bus segregation was illegal, the city of Montgomery finally complied.

THE ARREST OF ROSA PARKS
Rosa Parks, a forty-two-year-old department store seamstress, is fingerprinted by a Montgomery, Alabama, police officer after being arrested in 1955 for refusing to give her seat on a bus to a white man. The black community organized a 381-day boycott of the Montgomery bus system and eventually won its demand for unsegregated public transportation. (Wide World)

The Montgomery bus boycott catapulted King into national prominence. In 1957, he joined with the Reverend Ralph Abernathy and other members of the southern black clergy to found the Southern Christian Leadership Conference (SCLC), based in Atlanta. Activist organizations such as the SCLC supplanted the NAACP as the main spurs for racial justice.

The next phase of the movement began in Greensboro, North Carolina, on February 1, 1960. Four black college students from North Carolina Agricultural and Technical College—Ezell Blair, Jr., Franklin McCain, Joseph McNeill, and David Richmond—decided to "sit in" at the "whites only" counter of a local Woolworth store. When Blair asked for a cup of coffee, "The waitress looked at me as if I were from outer space." Over the next few days, they were joined by other black students and a few white supporters. The sit-in tactic spread quickly. Within six months, not only the lunch counter in Greensboro but many others throughout the South had been desegregated. By the end of 1960, about 50,000 people had participated in sit-ins or other demonstrations, and 3,600 had gone to jail. The Student Non-Violent Coordinating Committee (SNCC, pronounced "snick"), an off-shoot of the SCLC, coordinated the student sit-ins.

The momentum next switched to the Congress of Racial Equality (CORE), an interracial group founded in 1942. In 1961, CORE organized a "freedom ride" on interstate buses from Washington, D.C., to New Orleans. Black and white freedom riders planned to challenge the segregation of waiting rooms, toilets, and restaurants throughout the deep South. When they got to Anniston, Alabama, club-wielding Ku Klux Klansmen stopped the bus, stoned it, and set it on fire. The freedom riders escaped only moments before the bus exploded. When other riders were beaten mercilessly in Birmingham, Governor John Patterson refused to step in, saying "I cannot guarantee protection for this bunch of rabble rousers."

Such incidents of white extremism were televised on the nightly news, shocking many citizens. Attorney General Robert Kennedy now intervened to protect the freedom riders. Soon the Interstate Commerce Commission ordered the desegregation of all interstate vehicles and terminals. CORE learned the lesson that nonviolent protest could succeed if it provoked vicious white resistance and generated lots of publicity. Only then, it sometimes appeared, would federal authorities act.

The nonviolent phase of the civil rights movement climaxed in August 1963 with a massive March on Washington. Supported by a broad coalition of black organizations, as well as the Protestant National Council of Churches, the National Conference of Catholics for Interracial Justice, the American Jewish Congress, and the AFL-CIO Industrial Union Department, the March on Washington brought more than 250,000 orderly black and white demonstrators—the largest protest assembled up to that time—to the Lincoln Memorial. Martin Luther King, Jr., capped this event with a memorable speech:

I have a dream that one day on the red hills of Georgia sons of former slaves and the sons of former slaveholders will be able to sit down together at the table of brotherhood. I have a dream that one day even the state of Mississippi, a state sweltering with the heat of injustice . . . will be transformed into an oasis of freedom and justice. I have a dream that my four little

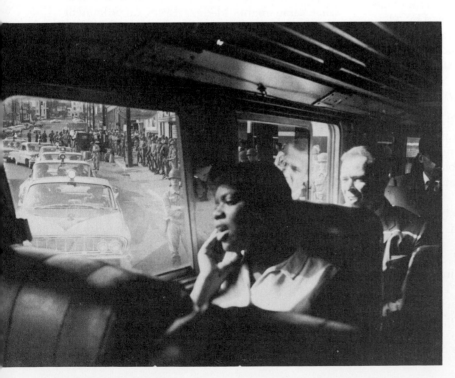

THE FREEDOM RIDERS
Black and white volunteers watch anxiously as they pull into the Montgomery, Alabama, bus station in 1961, while a hostile white crowd gathers outside. Civil rights leader James L. Farmer recalled their determination: "On the bus I noticed . . . boys writing notes and putting them in their pockets, and girls putting them in their brassieres . . . They were writing names and addresses of next of kin. They really had not expected to live beyond that trip. . . ." (© Bruce Davidson, Magnum)

children will one day live in a nation where they will not be judged by the color of their skin but by the content of their character.

He ended with this invocation, "Free at last, free at last, thank God almighty, we are free at last."

King's eloquent speech, and the spectacle of blacks and whites marching solemnly together, did more than any other event to make black protest acceptable to white Americans. The March on Washington epitomized the liberal faith that blacks and whites could work together peacefully to promote racial harmony. It also confirmed King's position, at least in the eyes of the white community, as the leading speaker for the black cause. King's stature rose even higher when he won the Nobel Peace Prize in 1964.

Ironically, as King gained appeal among whites, he lost support in the fragmenting civil rights movement. Students who had risked physical assault to sit in at lunch counters and drugstores were impatient with the gradualism of their elders. Freedom riders who had spent months in harsh southern jails found little relevance in King's commitment to brotherhood and nonviolent change. Activists who had seen fellow workers gunned down by white racists shared the bitterness of one CORE member who said, "I'm sick and tired of going to the funerals of black men who have been murdered by white men." By 1963, the legalistic, nonviolent approach was giving way to demands for immediate action of a more far-reaching nature.

The Federal Response

The accelerating momentum of the civil rights movement had profound implications for the federal government. President Kennedy realized that blacks had helped elect him, but he had dallied on civil rights for fear of alienating conservative white southern supporters in Congress. Events in 1963 pushed the Kennedy administration to take a stronger stand. In Birmingham, Alabama, Martin Luther King, Jr., and the Reverend Fred Shuttlesworth called for demonstrations to protest conditions in what King called "the most segregated city in the United States." In April, thousands of black demonstrators marched toward Birmingham's downtown department stores to picket. They were met by Eugene ("Bull") Connor, the city's commissioner

of public safety, who used snarling dogs, electric cattle prods, and high-pressure fire hoses to break up the crowd; the fire hoses were so strong that they ripped bark from trees and tore bricks from buildings. Television cameras captured the entire scene. "The civil rights movement should thank God for Bull Connor," Kennedy noted. "He's helped it as much as Abraham Lincoln."

President Kennedy, realizing he could no longer straddle the issue, now determined to step up the federal role in civil rights. He went on television in June 1963, to promise major civil rights legislation. Kennedy extemporized at the end of his speech:

We are confronted primarily with a moral issue. It is as old as the scriptures and is as clear as the American Constitution. If an American, because his skin is dark, cannot eat in a restaurant open to the public, if he cannot send his children to the best public school available, if he cannot vote for the public officials who represent him, if, in short, he cannot enjoy the full and free life which all of us want, then who among us would be content to have the color of his skin changed and stand in his place?

For some, Kennedy's speech came too late. That same night, Medgar Evers, a prominent NAACP activist, was shot in the back and killed in Jackson, Mississippi. Kennedy submitted a strong bill to Congress, but even with the killing of Evers, the March on Washington, and the bombing in September of a Birmingham church that killed four black girls, the measure stalled. Two months later, Kennedy was assassinated.

Lyndon Johnson promptly turned passage of civil rights legislation into a memorial to his slain predecessor. The Civil Rights Act, passed in June 1964, was a landmark in the history of American race relations and one of the greatest achievements of the 1960s. Title VII of the act—which outlawed discrimination in public accommodations or employment based on race, religion, national origin, or sex—was its keystone. In addition, the law gave opponents of segregation two powerful new weapons. They could now ask the attorney general to withhold federal funds from any state program, including education, that was not desegregated. They also could appeal discrimination in public accommo-

FANNIE LOU HAMER REGISTERS TO VOTE IN MISSISSIPPI

So then that was in 1962 when the civil rights workers came into this country. Now I didn't know anything about voter registration or nothin' like that, 'cause people had never been told that they could register to vote. . . . So they had a rally. I had gone to church that Sunday, and the minister announced that they were gon' have a mass meeting that Monday night. Well, I didn't know what a mass meeting was, and I was just curious to go to a mass meeting. So I did . . . and they was talkin' about how blacks had a right to register and how they had a right to *vote*. . . . Just listenin' at 'em, I could just see myself votin' people outa office that I know was wrong and didn't do nothin' to help the poor. I said, you know, that's sumpin' I really wanna be involved in, and finally at the end of that rally, I had made up my mind that I was gonna come out there when they said you could go down that Friday [August 31, 1962] to try to register. . . .

He [the registrar] brought a big old book out there, and he gave me the sixteenth section of the Constitution of Mississippi, and that was dealing with de facto laws, and I didn't know nothin' about no de facto laws, didn't know nothin' about any of 'em. I could copy it like it was in the book . . . but after I got through copying it, he told me to give a reasonable interpretation and tell the meaning of that section that I had copied. Well, I flunked out. . . .

Monday, the fourth of December, I went back to Indianola to the circuit clerk's office and I told him who I was and I was there to take that literacy test again.

I said, "Now, you cain't have me fired 'cause I'm already fired, and I won't have to move now, because I'm not livin' in no white man's house." I said, "I'll be here every thirty days until I become a registered voter."

I passed that second test, but it made us become like criminals. We would have to have our lights out before dark. It was cars passing that house all times of the night, driving real slow with guns, and pickups with white mens in it, and they'd pass that house just as slow as they could pass it . . . three guns lined up in the back. . . . Pap couldn't get nothin' to do. . . .

So I started teachin' citizenship class, and I became the supervisor of the citizenship class in this county. So I moved around the county to do citizenship education and later on I become a field secretary for SNCC. . . .

Source: Interview with Fannie Lou Hamer reprinted by permission of the Putnam Publishing Group from *My Soul Is Rested* by Howell Raines. Copyright © 1977 by Howell Raines. 249–250, 252.

---

dations or employment to the Equal Employment Opportunity Commission, which was set up to enforce Title VII.

Despite the enactment of federal civil rights legislation, intense resistance to voting rights for blacks continued in the South, where barely a quarter of blacks were on the voting lists in the early 1960s. SNCC and CORE conducted voter registration drives in 1962–1963, but their workers faced pressure and outright violence for encouraging blacks to register. Reprisals also extended to individual blacks who dared to register.

Black organizations and churches mounted a major registration drive in the summer of 1964. They recruited several thousand volunteers, many from the nation's campuses, to join in "Freedom Summer." Violence struck quickly when three volunteers—James Chaney, a CORE volunteer from Mississippi; Andrew Goodman, a student from New York; and Michael Schwerner, a New York social worker—disappeared from Philadelphia, Mississippi, in June 1964. An investigation was mounted, and Rita Schwerner, Michael's wife, noted, "We all know that this search . . . is because Andrew Goodman and my husband are white. If only Chaney was involved, nothing would have been done." When their bodies were found several weeks later, Goodman and Schwerner had been killed by a single bullet each, while Chaney had been brutally beaten with a chain and then shot several times. Members of the Ku Klux Klan committed the crime, it was later revealed. Fifteen civil rights workers were murdered in the South during Freedom Summer. Only sixteen hundred black voters were registered.

The case for federal action grew stronger in 1965. In February of that year, sheriff's deputies in Marion, Alabama, killed Jimmy Lee Jackson, a black voting-rights advocate, during a voter registration march. Angry black leaders called for a massive protest march from nearby Selma to the state capital, Montgomery, fifty-four miles away. Sheriff's deputies and a mounted posse attacked as soon as the marchers left Selma. The assault took place in broad daylight and was filmed for national television. To add to the nation's shock, Viola Liuzzo, a white woman married to a Detroit union official, was shot and killed by the Ku Klux Klan while ferrying protesters back and forth at the Selma demonstrations. Liuzzo's death and other acts of violence in Selma assured passage of federal voting rights legislation.

The Voting Rights Act of 1965 banned the literacy tests that most southern states had used to prevent blacks from registering to vote. It also placed the entire registration and voting process under direct federal control by authorizing government examiners to register voters in counties where less than 50 percent of the minority residents were on the voting lists. Together with the adoption in 1964 of the Twenty-fourth Amendment to the Constitution, which outlawed the poll tax, the Voting Rights Act made it possible for millions of blacks to register and vote for the first time. Congress extended the Voting Rights Act in 1970, 1975, and 1982.

By the 1970s, the proportion of eligible blacks who were registered in Selma, Alabama, had risen from 2 percent to 60 percent. During the same period, the number of black voters registered in Mississippi rose from twenty-two thousand to three hundred thousand, two-thirds of the black voting-age population there. Nationwide, 20 percent of all blacks were registered in 1960, 39 percent in 1964, and 62 percent in 1971.

Black voters had considerable impact. They triggered the end of the domination of the South by a lily-white Democratic party. In 1965, the former states of the Confederacy had only seventy-two black elected officials; fifteen years later, there were about three thousand. Atlanta and Birmingham had black mayors, Houston had a black chief of police, and candidates who were once ardent segregationists began to court the black vote. By the 1970s, black voters had become an established part of southern politics.

Hartman Turnbow, a black Mississippi farmer who had risked his life to register to vote in a SNCC-sponsored drive during the Freedom Summer of 1964, summed up the momentous changes that had occurred in that decade:

> Anybody had a jus told me 'fore it happened that conditions would make this much change between the white and the black in Holmes County here where I live, why I'da just said, "You're lyin'. It won't happen." I just wouldn't have believed it. I didn't dream of it. I didn't see no way. But it got to workin' just like the citizen-

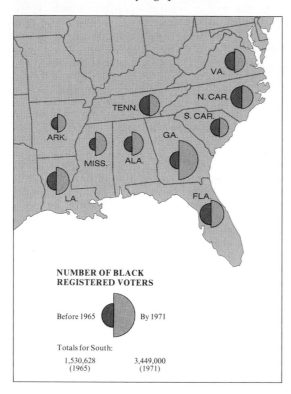

MAP 30.1 BLACK VOTER REGISTRATION IN THE SOUTH
After the passage of the Voting Rights Act of 1965, black registration in the South increased dramatically. These circles are divided to show the number of blacks registered before 1965 (left) and by 1971 (right). States in the deep South, including Mississippi and Alabama, showed the biggest rises.

ship class teacher told us—that if we redish to vote and just stick with it. He says it's gon' be some difficults. He told us that when we started. We was looking for it. He said we gon' have difficults, gon' have troubles, folks gon' lose their homes, folks gon' lose their lives, people gon' lose all their money, and just like he said, all of that happened. He didn't miss it. He hit it kadap on the head, and it's workin' now. It won't never go back where it was.

From Civil Rights to Black Power

Blacks throughout the country, not just in the South, had been energized by the *Brown* decision and federal civil rights legislation. Newly raised expectations led to more demands. Now that the system of legalized segregation had fallen in the South, black leaders concentrated on a more difficult goal—eliminating the institutional, economic, and social structures that made blacks second-class citizens. The civil rights movement now moved from attacking de jure segregation (that is, enforced by law) to de facto segregation (enforced by custom).

Although less flagrant than in the South, northern discrimination was real and pervasive, especially regarding education, housing, and employment opportunities. Although the *Brown* decision outlawed separate but equal schools, it did nothing to change conditions in educational systems where schools were predominantly all-black or all-white because of patterns of residential segregation. In the 1960s, for example, 90 percent of Chicago's black students attended all-black schools. Not until 1973 did federal judges begin to order the desegregation of schools in the North as they had in the South two decades earlier.

As the civil rights movement escalated its demands, it found itself deeply polarized along generational lines. While their elders held back, younger blacks were eager for confrontation and ever faster change. They insisted that they be called blacks or Afro-Americans, not Negroes, a term they judged demeaning because of its historic association with slavery and discrimination.

By the mid-1960s, many young activists even questioned the goal of assimilation into white society itself. Black separatism dated back to the nineteenth century; the Marcus Garvey move-

MARTIN LUTHER KING, JR.
The Reverend Martin Luther King, Jr. (1929–1968) pictured here at a 1957 Prayer Pilgrimage for Freedom in Washington, D.C., was the most eloquent advocate of the black cause in the 1950s and 1960s. By the mid 1960s, his policy of nonviolence was under attack by young black activists. (© Bob Henrique, Magnum).

ment in the 1920s represented its most vibrant twentieth-century appearance to date. In the 1960s, new impetus came from the Nation of Islam, or Black Muslim movement, led by Elijah Muhammad. The Black Muslim ideology was extremely hostile not only to whites but also to traditional civil rights organizations. Forcefully rejecting integration in favor of black nationalism, it stressed black pride, unity, and self-help. Malcolm X, who caustically referred to Martin Luther King's 1963 march as "the farce on Washington," emerged as one of the Black Muslims' most charismatic figures. His autobiography, published after he was gunned down in 1965 by a rival Muslim faction, became one of the decade's most influential books.

The Black Muslims' demand for cultural and political independence appealed to the young veterans of SNCC and CORE. Abandoning the

MALCOLM X ON THE "FARCE ON WASHINGTON"

Not long ago, the black man in America was fed a dose of another form of the weakening, lulling and deluding effects of so-called "integration." It was that "Farce on Washington," I call it. . . .

The morning of the March, any rickety carloads of angry, dusty, sweating small-town Negroes would have gotten lost among the chartered jet planes, railroad cars, and air-conditioned buses. What originally was planned to be an angry riptide one English newspaper aptly described now as "the gentle flood."

Talk about "integrated"! It was like salt and pepper. And, by now, there wasn't a single logistics aspect uncontrolled.

The marchers had been instructed to bring no signs—signs were provided. They had been told to sing one song: "We Shall Overcome." They had been told *how* to arrive, *when*, *where* to ar-

rive, *where* to assemble, when to *start* marching, the *route* to march. First-aid stations were strategically located—even where to *faint*!

Yes, I was there. I observed that circus. Who ever heard of angry revolutionists all harmonizing "We Shall Overcome . . . Suum Day . . ." while tripping and swaying along arm-in-arm with the very people they were supposed to be angrily revolting against? Who ever heard of angry revolutionists swinging their bare feet together with their oppressor in lily-pad park pools, with gospels and guitars and "I Have A Dream" speeches?. . . .

Hollywood couldn't have topped it.

In a subsequent press poll, not one Congressman or Senator with a previous record of opposition to civil rights said he had changed his views. What did anyone expect? How was a one-day "integrated" picnic going to

counter-influence these representatives of prejudice rooted deep in the psyche of the American white man for four hundred years?

The very fact that millions, black and white, believed in this monumental farce is another example of how much this country goes in for the surface glossing over, the escape ruse, surfaces, instead of truly dealing with its deep-rooted problems.

What that March on Washington did do was lull Negroes for a while. But inevitably, the black masses started realizing they had been smoothly hoaxed again by the white man. And, inevitably, the black man's anger rekindled, deeper than ever, and there began bursting out in different cities the "long, hot summer" of 1964, unprecedented racial crises.

Source: Malcolm X (with Alex Haley), *The Autobiography of Malcolm X.* New York: Random House, 1965. 278, 280—281.

---

earlier faith in interracial cooperation, SNCC's Stokely Carmichael coined a new militant slogan, "black power," in 1966. "The only way we gonna stop them white men from whupping us is to take over," he declared. "We been saying freedom for six years and we ain't got nothing. What we gonna start saying is Black Power!" Carmichael's successor at SNCC, H. Rap Brown, was even more rebellious, saying, "America won't come around, so we're going to burn America down" and "Violence is as American as cherry pie." Huey Newton, leader of the militant Black Panthers in California, provocatively insisted that blacks follow the admonition of China's communist leader Mao Zedong that "political power comes through the barrel of a gun."

The black power ideology had important implications for the civil rights movement. Such militancy was confrontational and potentially violent; it rejected Martin Luther King's teachings, especially the goal of integration into white society. There was no longer a question of fine-tuning the system, because the whole system had to be changed. As author James Baldwin asked, "Do I really *want* to be integrated into a burning house?" Within several years of Martin Luther King's "I have a dream" speech, certain elements in the civil rights movement had moved from cooperation with whites to separatism, from nonviolence to armed self-defense, from working within the system to preparing for revolution.

As a result of this growing militancy, most

black organizations went through major identity crises in 1965. By the next year, for all intents and purposes, whites had been kicked out of the civil rights movement. CORE's decision to bar whites from leadership positions symbolized this shift. Whites were told they could not understand what it meant to be black; many whites themselves felt guilty about their own complicity in the institutionalized racism that blacks had experienced.

The new black assertiveness alarmed many other white Americans, however. They had been willing to go along with the moderate reforms of the 1950s and early 1960s, but they balked when blacks started demanding immediate access to higher-paying jobs, better housing in previously white neighborhoods, integrated schools, and increased political power. In 1964, only 34 percent of all whites thought blacks were demanding too much change; by 1966, 84 percent thought so.

More than any other cause, the riots in northern cities between 1964 and 1968 undermined white support for the civil rights movement. Why did the nation's cities explode in violence? The rapid growth of segregated metropolitan areas during the postwar period provided the backdrop. Migration from the country to the city made many black people, especially young adults, painfully aware of their exclusion from the dominant consumer culture. Moreover, they

were angry at white landlords who owned the substandard housing they were forced to live in; at white shopkeepers who made their money from black trade but would not hire black clerks or salespeople; and at all-white unions—especially the building trades—that controlled access to skilled neighborhood jobs. Stimulated by television coverage of southern blacks who banded together to challenge whites and who got results, young urban blacks expressed their grievances with their own brand of "direct action." Their parents and adult neighbors often supported them in spirit. By 1968, riots had occurred in at least seventy-five cities.

The first of the "long hot summers" took place in 1964, when a police shooting of a black criminal suspect in Harlem led to a week of looting and rioting there. The underlying causes, as in many of the later riots, were white control and exploitation of business and real estate in the black community, high black unemployment and poverty, and the volatile issue of police brutality.

Racial turmoil worsened the following summer. A riot in the Watts section of Los Angeles, where 60 percent of the population was on relief, left thirty-four blacks dead and produced the frightening refrain "Burn, baby, burn." Ironically, Watts erupted just five days after President Johnson had hailed passage of the Voting Rights Act of 1965 as the next great step toward racial

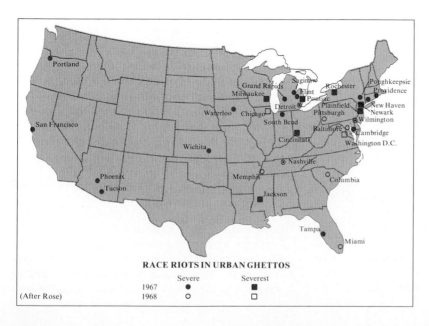

RACE RIOTS IN URBAN GHETTOS

	Severe	Severest
1967	●	■
1968	○	□

(After Rose)

MAP 30.2 RACIAL UNREST IN AMERICA'S CITIES, 1967–1968
The urban riots of 1967 occurred in scattered large urban areas throughout the United States, including the South and West. In 1968, by contrast, rioting broke out only east of the Mississippi River. Major rioting usually did not occur in the same city in two consecutive years.

THE WATTS RIOT
The nation's worst racial disturbance since the Detroit race riot of 1943 began in the Watts section of Los Angeles on August 11, 1965. An altercation broke out when white police officers stopped two blacks for a minor traffic violation. Thirty-four persons died in the Watts riot. (© Michael Alexander, Black Star)

equality. For many young urban blacks, however, the gains of the civil rights movement were often irrelevant to the poverty and economic exploitation that pervaded their daily lives. An exchange between Martin Luther King and a twenty-year-old unemployed black rioter in the smoldering ruins of Watts captured this frustration. "We won!" shouted the young man. How can we have won, King countered, when so many people died, homes were destroyed, and the community lay in ruins? "We won because we made the whole world pay attention to us," the rioter replied. "We made them come."

The riots of 1967 were the most serious of all. Rioting began early in several southern cities, built up in June, and engulfed twenty-two cities in July and August. Large-scale disturbances hit Toledo, Ohio; Grand Rapids, Michigan; Plainfield, New Jersey; and Milwaukee, Wisconsin. Violent riots in Newark and Detroit produced widespread destruction and loss of life. Forty-three people were killed in Detroit alone, and at least a fourth of the city was burned, with $50 million worth of property destroyed. Mayor Jerome Cavanaugh of Detroit compared the devastated city to war-ravaged Berlin in 1945. As

was true of most of the riots, the arson and looting was directed at white-owned property, but little physical violence took place against white people. Almost all the reported sniping turned out to involve wild shooting by the police.

The assassination of Martin Luther King in Memphis on April 4, 1968, by James Earl Ray, a white ex-convict whose motive was unknown, set off a final cataclysm of urban rioting. Major violence broke out in more than forty cities. In Washington, national guardsmen with machine guns protected the Capitol, which was framed against fires from the neighboring ghettoes. In Chicago, where rioting and looting engulfed most of the city's West Side, Mayor Richard J. Daley ordered police to "shoot to kill" suspected snipers.

With King's assassination, the civil rights movement lost the one black leader who still had the capacity to stir the conscience of white America. At the time of his death, he was only thirty-nine years old. During the last years of his life, King had moved toward a more comprehensive view of the structural problems of poverty and racism that blacks faced in contemporary America. In 1967, he confronted the issue of residential segregation in a losing battle for open housing in Chicago. He came out forcefully against the Vietnam War. In 1968, he was planning a poor people's campaign to raise issues of economic injustice and inequality. He had gone to Memphis the day he was shot to support a strike by predominantly black sanitation workers. His premature death robbed the country of a forceful leader in the next stage of the battle.

The 1950s and 1960s brought permanent, indeed revolutionary, changes in American race relations. Jim Crow segregation was overturned in less than a decade, and the passage of significant federal legislation ensured black Americans their basic civil rights. Yet by the time of King's death in 1968, race relations had become polarized. Candidates such as Governor George C. Wallace of Alabama exploited a white backlash against black activism that was by no means confined to the South. By the 1970s, black Americans were too diverse and too divided, both economically and politically, to mount a unified drive for jobs and improved education. Like all Americans, they found that American society provided highly unequal rewards.

The Spreading Demand for Equal Rights

The civil rights movement influenced other groups, such as Hispanics and native Americans, to organize to press their claims. Until 1960, few Hispanic-Americans had participated in politics. Poverty, uncertain legal status, and language barriers kept them politically silent. This situation began to change when the Mexican American Political Association (MAPA) mobilized Hispanics to vote for John F. Kennedy in 1960, providing an important margin of victory in closely contested states such as Texas, New Mexico, and Illinois. In return, several Hispanic-American leaders received prominent appointments in Washington, and federal authorities paid increased attention to their demands.

Younger Hispanics quickly grew impatient with the MAPA, however. More radical and more inclined to celebrate their group's cultural achievements and traditions, the younger leaders pursued increasingly diverse goals. The *barrios*—crowded, neglected slums in Los Angeles

and other California cities—produced the militant Brown Berets, who modeled themselves on Huey Newton's Black Panthers. In 1969, a new term, "Chicano," was coined to replace "Mexican-American." This revolution in consciousness also produced a political party, La Raza Unida ("the united race"), to promote Hispanic interests and candidates in public life.

The founding of La Raza Unida was just one manifestation of a heightened interest in politics and political mobilization. AFL-CIO unions worked to increase Hispanic participation in elections. The civil rights legislation of the 1960s also stimulated Hispanics to get into politics. This strategy paid off with the election of Henry Cisneros as mayor of San Antonio in 1981; Toney Anaya as governor of New Mexico and Louis Montano as mayor of Sante Fe in 1982; and Federico Peña as mayor of Denver in 1983, where Hispanics comprised only 18 percent of the population.

Chicano strategists also pushed for economic objectives. Working in the fields around Delano, California, labor leader Cesar Chavez (shown on page 936) organized the United Farm Workers, the first successful union to represent migrant workers. A 1966 grape pickers' strike and a nationwide boycott of table grapes brought Chavez and his union national publicity. Quietly advocating his cause, Chavez won the support of the AFL-CIO and Senator Robert F. Kennedy of New York. Chavez soon was receiving almost as much media attention as Martin Luther King, Jr.

Puerto Ricans, the second largest component of the nation's Hispanic population, were divided politically. The dream of independence fueled a nationalist movement that occasionally turned to violence; in 1950, a band of nationalist Puerto Rican terrorists made an unsuccessful assassination attempt on President Truman. Most Puerto Ricans, however, favored the militant pursuit of equality and opportunity within the United States. New York City's Herman Badillo, the first Puerto Rican to sit in the U.S. House of Representatives, symbolized their growing political presence.

Cuban refugees comprised the third large group of Hispanics. Nearly half a million people fled Cuba in the wake of Fidel Castro's ascent to power in 1959, creating a refugee community so large and vigorous that it turned Miami into a

CESAR CHAVEZ
Mexican-American labor leader Cesar Chavez addresses a
rally in Guadalupe, California. Chavez won national
attention in 1965 during a strike of migrant farm workers,
most of them Mexican-Americans, against California
grape growers. Drawing on tactics from the civil rights
movement, Chavez called for nonviolent action and
effectively mobilized support from white liberals. (FPG)

cosmopolitan, bilingual city almost overnight.
Although Miami's new Cubans prospered economically, at first they remained dedicated to the
overthrow of Castro and their return to Cuba.
As the Castro regime consolidated its position,
thus foreclosing prospects of returning home,
Cuban-Americans increased their political activity in the United States. They differed from most
other Hispanic voters in being predominantly
middle class, violently anticommunist, and generally conservative.

American Indians also found a model in the
civil rights movement. Like blacks and Hispanics, they proposed a new name for themselves—
native Americans—and organized dramatic
protests and demonstrations to build support
for their cause. Native Americans, who numbered nearly 1.5 million by 1980, had much to
protest. Their unemployment rate, 40 percent in
the 1970s, exceeded that of blacks. They suffered

the worst poverty, the most inadequate housing,
the highest disease rates, and the least access to
education of any group in the United States.

Like other groups in American society, native
Americans organized pressure groups to win
better treatment. As early as World War II, the
National Council of American Indians had lobbied for improvement in Indians' lives. The late
1960s saw the founding of far more radical
groups, such as the American Indian Movement
(AIM), which drew its strength from the third of
the Indian population who lived in the "red
ghettoes" in cities throughout the West.

AIM consciously modeled itself on the activist
black power movement, and for a few years the
tactics of AIM and similar groups attracted considerable public attention. In November 1969,
AIM seized the deserted federal penitentiary on
Alcatraz Island in San Francisco Bay, offering the
government twenty-four dollars worth of trinkets to pay for it. (This was what the white settlers had paid the Indians for Manhattan Island
in 1626.) The Indian occupation of Alcatraz
lasted until the summer of 1971. In November
1972, a thousand protesters occupied the headquarters of the Bureau of Indian Affairs in Washington, D.C., inflicting $2 million of damage on
government records and property. In February
1973, AIM members began a seventy-one day
occupation of the town of Wounded Knee,
South Dakota, the site of the army massacre of
Sioux Indians in 1890. They were protesting the
light sentences given a group of white men convicted of killing a Sioux in 1972. The protesters
took eleven hostages and occupied several buildings to dramatize their cause. But when a gun
battle left one protester dead and another
wounded, the siege collapsed.

Such militant confrontations, designed largely
to capture the interest of the media, did not always increase public support. Therefore, native
Americans also used other methods to advance
their cause. Such books as *Custer Died for Your
Sins* (1969), by Vine Deloria, Jr., a Sioux; N. Scott
Momaday's Pulitzer Prize–winning novel *House
Made of Dawn* (1968); and Dee Brown's best-
selling *Bury My Heart at Wounded Knee* (1971)
increased white empathy for Indian concerns.
Potentially the most far-reaching tactic was the
initiation of lawsuits to reclaim Indian lands illegally taken in violation of federal laws and treaties. Such suits, pitting the Indian claimants

against citizens in states from Maine to Alaska who were currently living on the land, produced economic gains for native Americans and represented a growing public awareness of the injustices they had suffered.

Civil rights, which began as a demand for the rights of black people, also spurred other groups to claim justice and equality. Poor people, led by George Wiley and the National Welfare Rights Organization, organized in the 1960s to demand a larger voice in welfare policy. Calling welfare a right, not a privilege, welfare activists used such tactics as sit-ins at government offices to win better treatment and higher benefits. Homosexual men and women also banded together to protest legal and social restrictions based on sexual preference. The gay liberation movement started with the 1969 "Stonewall riot" in New York City, where patrons of a gay bar in Greenwich Village fought back against police harassment. This assertion of gay pride would probably not have occurred without the example of the civil rights movement. Such increased political activism represents one of the most important legacies of the black demand for equality.

The Challenge of Youth

"There is everywhere protest, revaluation, attack on the Establishment," asserted social critic Paul Goodman at the end of the 1960s. Novelist Norman Mailer agreed. "We're in a time that's divorced from the past," he said. "There's utterly no tradition anymore." The black drive for equality had touched off the challenge to established institutions. Now American youth joined in, mounting colorful and sometimes shocking challenges to authority and traditional social values. Shifts in youth rebellion followed with such bewildering frequency that one anthropologist concluded, "We seem to be producing a new generation every three or four years."

Student Activism

The 1960s witnessed the first active student movement since the 1930s. The idealism of John Kennedy and the New Frontier raised students' expectations of what they and their society could accomplish. The civil rights movement exposed

white youths to the brutality of race relations in the South and taught college students new tactics—marches, sit-ins, and mass confrontations—to use in protests. In addition, the escalation of the Vietnam War in 1965 offered a compelling political cause to rally around.

The depression-scarred generation of the 1930s had been unable to afford higher education, but its children flocked to colleges and universities in the postwar period. In 1940, when only 15 percent of all college-age youth attended college, graduating was a major sign of upward social mobility for members of most ethnic groups and other minorities. By 1960, the year of John Kennedy's election, 40 percent of the college-age population was in college, and by 1963, the year of his assassination, the proportion had reached almost 50 percent.

During the 1950s most students reflected the practical career-oriented values of their society. Business administration was the most popular course of study, and students took little part in politics. Some social critics suggested that students had responded to the repressive atmosphere of McCarthyism by becoming a "silent generation." Yet many young people felt dissatisfied even in the 1950s. A vague awareness of poverty, the black struggle for civil rights and equality, and the looming threat of nuclear war caused some young people to question the materialism of the world. J. D. Salinger's novel *Catcher in the Rye* (1951) became a best-seller because readers identified with Holden Caulfield's quiet revulsion at the thoughtless hypocrisy of his family, neighbors, and schoolmates.

Student dissatisfaction began to coalesce in the early 1960s. In June 1962, forty students from Big Ten and Ivy League universities met at a United Auto Workers conference center in Port Huron, Michigan, to found the Students for a Democratic Society (SDS). Their manifesto, written by Tom Hayden, a University of Michigan student, drew heavily on the writing of C. Wright Mills, a radical Columbia sociologist. It expressed hostility toward bureaucracy, rejected cold war ideology, emphasized community participatory politics, and designated students as the major force for change in society. SDS consciously modeled itself on the activist style pioneered by SNCC, adopting the name "New Left" to distinguish itself from the "Old Left" Communists of the 1930s.

The Free Speech Movement (FSM) at the University of California at Berkeley in 1964 was the first expression of a new student aggressiveness. The university administration announced that political activity would no longer be allowed along a strip of land at the Telegraph Avenue entrance to the campus, where student groups had traditionally distributed leaflets and recruited volunteers. In response, all the major organizations on campus, ranging from SNCC to the conservative Youth for Goldwater, formed a coalition to protest what they considered an abridgment of free speech. They organized a sit-in at the main administration building and won revocation of the ban on political solicitation on campus.

The Free Speech Movement owed a strong debt to the civil rights movement. Berkeley had sent more volunteers to Freedom Summer in Mississippi in 1964 than any other campus, and the students had been radicalized by the experience. Free Speech leader Mario Savio spoke for many of them:

> Last summer I went to Mississippi to join the struggle there for civil rights. This fall I am engaged in another phase of the same struggle, this time in Berkeley. The two battlefields may seem quite different to some observers, but this is not the case. The same rights are at stake in both places—the right to participate as citizens in a democratic society and to struggle against the same enemy. In Mississippi an autocratic and powerful minority rules, through organized violence, to suppress the vast, virtually powerless majority. In California, the privileged minority manipulates the university bureaucracy to suppress the students' political expression.

On a deeper level, Berkeley students had challenged the university because it had grown too big, too impersonal, and too insulated from the major social questions of the day. The largest universities, like the largest corporations, had grown the fastest in the postwar era. Only two campuses had as many as twenty thousand students in 1940. By 1969, thirty-nine had grown at least that large. Many students objected that they were treated as impersonally as a computer punch card. "I am a student," one slogan ran, "Please do not fold, spindle, or mutilate." Emboldened by the Berkeley experience, students at institutions across the country found reasons to protest everything from dress codes to course requirements, tenure decisions, and academic grading systems.

Many students also increasingly felt a deep moral outrage against the Vietnam War. In March 1965, several months after the Berkeley confrontation, President Lyndon Johnson began the major escalation that committed American ground troops to fight in Vietnam. In response, faculty members and student activists at the University of Michigan organized a "teach-in" against the war, where, in marathon sessions, they debated the political, diplomatic, and moral facets of U.S. involvement in Vietnam. This type of forum quickly spread to other universities. Groups such as the Students for a Democratic Society, which at first had focused on grass-roots organizing in the nation's cities, turned their full attention to protesting the Vietnam War. A strong spur to activism was the abolition in January 1966 of automatic student deferments from the draft. Now male students faced conscription to fight in a war many of them considered morally repugnant.

Soon students realized that universities themselves were deeply implicated in the Vietnam War. In certain cases, 60 percent of a university's research budget might come from government contracts, especially from the Defense Department; faculty members might be working on nuclear weapons or counterinsurgency strategies. Students organized to block campus recruitment by the army, the CIA, and the Dow Chemical Company, a special target because it produced the napalm used to burn Vietnamese villages and the chemical called Agent Orange, which defoliated South Vietnam's forests. Students demanded that the Reserve Officer Training Corps (ROTC) be removed from campus because, they argued, the university should not train students for war. Protests against ROTC on campus were central to the major confrontations between students and administrators at Columbia in 1968 and Harvard in 1969. As the president of Hunter College in New York City observed in 1968, "Yesterday's ivory tower has become today's foxhole."

Students also protested the universities' complicity in the problems of the ghettoes that surrounded many urban campuses. Columbia, for example, was a major property owner in Harlem, and university expansion impinged on the surrounding neighborhood. At issue in 1968 was a proposed gymnasium near the Columbia campus. Chanting "Gym Crow Must Go," students tore down the fence at the construction site and took over several Columbia buildings, including the office of President Grayson Kirk. (Photographs of protesters sampling Kirk's cigars and sherry did little to build public support.) At Berkeley, students and administrators clashed in 1969 over a parcel of vacant land near campus that a coalition of students and residents had turned into a "People's Park." When the university asserted its rights to the land, a violent confrontation broke out and an onlooker was killed. At both Columbia and Berkeley, and on other campuses as well, the administration's decision to use city police officers to break up the demonstrations radicalized far more students than had originally supported the protest. In many cases, such turmoil brought academic life to a halt.

Along with challenges to university power and policies, mass demonstrations against the war consumed much of the energy of the student movement in the late 1960s. In November 1969, at least 250,000 people marched on Washington to call for a moratorium against the Vietnam War. The final spurt of student unrest occurred in the spring of 1970. When President Richard M. Nixon ordered an American-backed invasion of Cambodia, student leaders organized a national student strike in protest. Tempers ran especially high at Kent State University outside Cleveland. At a noontime rally on May 4, 1970, panicky National Guardsmen fired into a crowd of students, killing four and wounding eleven. Only two of those killed, Jeffrey Miller and Alison Krause, had been involved in the demonstration; William Shroeder and Sandra Scheur were passing by on their way to class. While campuses were still in shock, word came that two black students had been killed at Jackson State College in Mississippi. More than 450 colleges closed down on strike, and 80 percent of all American college campuses experienced some kind of protest.

In June 1970, a Gallup poll reported that campus unrest was the main issue troubling Americans. But after 1970, the universities basically stayed calm. Students had effectively challenged many aspects of university control over their lives, but their broader attack on American society had been less successful. They returned to the classroom, somewhat cynical, burned out, and no longer ready to change the world.

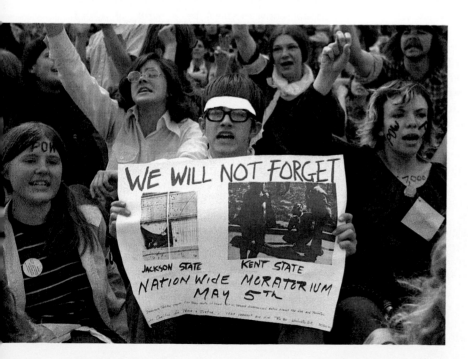

THE KENT STATE KILLINGS
The shooting by National Guardsmen of four students at Kent State University in Ohio on May 4, 1970, set off campus demonstrations and protests throughout the country. The protesters shown here carry a placard memorializing the slain students, as well as the two black students killed soon after at Jackson State College in Mississippi. The president of Columbia University called May 1970 "the most disastrous month . . . in the history of American higher education."
(© Michael Abramson, Black Star)

The Rise of the Counterculture

Together with student activism and protest, new forms of cultural expression emerged among the nation's young. In an amazingly short period of time, youth's clothing and hair styles changed radically. At Berkeley's 1964 Free Speech demonstrations, young men wore coats and ties, women skirts and sweaters. By the time of the antiwar protests, just three or four years later, youth defiantly dressed in a "unisex" fashion that featured ragged blue jeans, tie-dyed T-shirts, beads, and other adornments. Long, unkempt hair symbolized this cultural revolt. The uncomprehending older generation often had a simple response: "Get a haircut."

The forerunners of the "hippies" of the 1960s were members of the Beat Generation of the preceding decade. Given the post-McCarthy climate of conformity, rebellion in the 1950s was far more likely to take artistic than political forms. "Beats" such as poet Allen Ginsberg and writer Jack Kerouac pioneered in articulating the personal alienation that was at the base of much of the rebelliousness of the 1960s. Kerouac's *On the Road* (1957) became the bible of the Beat Generation. Beats popularized beards for men, black tights for women, and sandals for both sexes. They experimented with drugs, and helped revive interest in folk music.

Roots of the cultural rebellion also lay in the active teen culture, which had been developing since the 1920s but flourished in the consumer-oriented 1950s. In 1956, advertisers projected an adolescent market of $9 billion for items including transistor radios (first introduced in 1952), clothes, cars, and records. Such movies as *The Wild One* (1954), starring Marlon Brando, and *Rebel Without a Cause* (1955), featuring James Dean, Natalie Wood, and Sal Mineo, catered to the teen audience. "What are you rebelling against?" a waitress asks Brando in *The Wild One*. "Whattaya got?" he replies.

What really defined the emerging youth generation was its music. Rock and roll sprang forth in the mid-1950s. It developed from white country and western music, black rhythm and blues, and other sources. Elvis Presley became one of the first to popularize this new type of music, and his hit singles "Hound Dog" and "Heartbreak Hotel" sold more than ten million copies in 1956. Adults were appalled. A noted psychiatrist called rock and roll "a communicable disease" and "a cannibalistic and tribalistic kind of music." When Presley appeared on the "Ed Sullivan Show," television cameras showed the teen idol only from the waist up, censoring his skin-tight pants and gyrating pelvis. Young people got the message anyway.

Throughout the 1960s, as English journalist Godfrey Hodgson noted, "popular music coincided uncannily with changing political moods." Folk singer Pete Seeger, free at last from the McCarthy-era blacklist, set the tone for the era's political idealism with such songs as "Where Have All the Flowers Gone?" and Woody Guthrie's "This Land Is Your Land." In 1963, the year of the Birmingham demonstrations and President Kennedy's assassination, Bob Dylan's "Blowin' in the Wind" reflected the impatience of people whose liberalism was turning sour. When folk singers Peter, Paul, and Mary recorded a more melodious version of this song, it sold three hundred thousand copies in two weeks.

Early in 1964, the Beatles, a British band that had honed its sound in the dives of Liverpool, England, and Hamburg, West Germany, burst onto the American scene. Like Elvis Presley eight years earlier, they thrust their way into the national consciousness by a series of appearances on the "Ed Sullivan Show." The Beatles' music, by turns lyrical and driving, was phenomenally successful, spawning a commercial and cultural phenomenon called Beatlemania. The harsher, angrier music of other British groups, notably the Rolling Stones, found a broad audience shortly afterward.

Drugs had almost as important a part as rock music in the youth culture of the 1960s. Drugs were hardly new to the American scene; many jazz musicians in the 1920s and 1930s had used heroin and cocaine to stimulate their creativity, and the Beats had experimented with mind-altering drugs in San Francisco. In the 1960s, however, widespread recreational use of drugs occurred outside artistic and jazz circles.

Marijuana was the preferred drug among college students, but stronger drugs also gained popularity. Lysergic acid diethylamide, popularly known as LSD or "acid," was one of the most potent. First discovered in a Swiss pharmaceutical laboratory in 1938, the hallucinogenic LSD was popularized in California by writer Ken Kesey and his Merry Pranksters, who conducted "acid tests" (public "happenings" where tabs of LSD were distributed) in 1965 and 1966. San Francisco bands such as the Grateful Dead and the Jefferson Airplane, guitarist Jimi Hendrix, and Britain's Pink Floyd developed a style of music known as "acid rock." Even the Beatles, whose early songs had simply stated "I Want to Hold Your Hand" and "Please Please Me," now recorded tunes like "Lucy in the Sky with Diamonds," whose "tangerine trees and marmalade skies" celebrated the new drug-induced consciousness.

For a brief time, adherents of the counterculture—so named because it challenged so many established mores—believed that a new age was dawning, along the lines of the "age of Aquarius" trumpeted in the 1968 Broadway rock musical *Hair*. In 1967, the "world's first Human Be-In" was held at Golden Gate Park in San Francisco. Allen Ginsberg "purified" the site with a Buddhist ritual, political activists embraced "drug freaks," and LSD pioneer Timothy Leary, a former Harvard psychology instructor, urged the twenty thousand people who had gathered to "turn on to the scene, tune in to what is happening, and drop out."

"Tune in, turn on, drop out" and "Make love not war" became catchwords for youthful alienation. By the summer of 1967, San Francisco's Haight-Ashbury, New York's East Village, and similar hippie neighborhoods in other large cities were crowded with young people, as well as swarms of reporters and busloads of tourists who gawked at the so-called flower children. The faith in instant love and peace quickly began to turn sour, however, as dropouts, drifters, and teenage runaways tried to cope with bad drug trips, venereal disease, loneliness, and violence. In 1967, seventeen murders and more than a hundred rapes were reported in Haight-Ashbury alone.

While hippie neighborhoods declined, the appeal of rock music and drugs continued to spread. In August 1969, four hundred thousand young people journeyed to Bethel, New York, to attend the Woodstock Music Festival. Despite torrential rain, people "got high" on music, drugs, and sex. They were treated to one of the finest assemblages of performers ever gathered in one place—Crosby, Stills, Nash, and Young; Santana; Joan Baez; the Who; Sly and the Family Stone; Grace Slick and the Jefferson Airplane; Jimi Hendrix; and others. The successful festival gave its name to the "Woodstock generation" of the late 1960s.

By 1970, the youth culture had revolutionized life-styles and cultural expression. Even as political activism and rebellion waned, their spirit was absorbed and marketed by the consumer

FLOWER CHILDREN
Yale law professor Charles A. Reich celebrated the new freedom of youth in his best-selling book *The Greening of America* (1970). Reich described a new consciousness that had "emerged out of the wasteland of the Corporate State, like flowers pushing up through the concrete pavement. Whatever it touches it beautifies and renews: a freeway entrance is festooned with happy hitchhikers, the sidewalk is decorated with street people, the humorless steps of an official building are given warmth by a group of musicians. And every barrier falls before it." (© Paul Fusco, Magnum)

ANARCHISM
AT THE MOVIES
The movie *Bonnie and Clyde*
(1967), starring Faye Dunaway
and Warren Beatty, became a
cultural phenomenon because its
anarchism, antiheroism, and
violence seemed in keeping with
the mood of the 1960s. Based
loosely on the story of Clyde
Barrow and Bonnie Parker,
famous bank robbers of the 1930s,
the movie builds sympathy for
these appealing criminals, only to
end with their being slain by law
enforcement officials.
(MOMA/Film Stills Archive)

culture. The crowds at Woodstock and other rock festivals revealed the size of the youth market, and corporate entrepreneurs rushed to cash in on it. Advertisers renamed youth the "Pepsi generation." By 1969 rock accounted for two-thirds of the sales of large record companies. The market for expensive stereo systems rose correspondingly.

Forms of alternative expression from the 1960s soon filtered into the dominant culture. *The Village Voice* and *Rolling Stone* outgrew their beginnings as underground publications and became respected pillars of American journalism. Symbols of cultural defiance were co-opted and homogenized by the mass culture. The ragged "bell bottom" blue jeans of the 1960s became the expensive designer jeans of the 1970s. The unkempt hair and beards of male hippies emboldened many middle-aged corporate executives to sport a moustache or allow their hair to cover their ears. The "Afro" hairstyle, once worn only by radical black activists, was now favored by blacks and whites of both sexes who let their hair go natural. Women's fashion picked up the theme of personal liberation with the miniskirt, an innovation that had arrived from England in the mid-1960s.

Popular acceptance of the miniskirt was linked to the new public attitudes about sexuality that characterized the 1960s. As late as 1953, a movie called *The Moon Is Blue* was denied a seal of approval by Hollywood's Production Code Administration because it used words such as "seduce" and "virgin." United Artists released the film anyway. New permissive values soon became commonplace, as expressions that previously had been heard only in locker rooms now entered everyday conversations. By 1968, the film industry devised an "X" rating for films that featured nudity, sex, and explicit language.

Public portrayal and discussion of sexuality changed far more than actual sexual behavior, which had already undergone startling transformations over the course of the twentieth century. In 1948, the book *Sexual Behavior in the American Male*, by biologist Alfred C. Kinsey, had revealed that 85 percent of all American men claimed to have had intercourse before marriage, that half conducted extramarital affairs, and that 10 percent engaged in homosexual activity for at least part of their adult lives. In 1953, Kinsey's *Sexual Behavior in the Human Female* reported that 62 percent of women masturbated, that half had premarital sexual relations, and that a fourth engaged in extramarital affairs. In 1966, William H. Masters and Virginia E. Johnson published *Human Sexual Response*, the product of their detailed, direct laboratory observations of the physiology of arousal and intercourse in men and women. The book became a national best-seller.

The "sexual revolution" of the 1960s eroded some of the inequalities and inhibitions between the sexes. The new availability of contraceptives such as the birth-control pill, first marketed in 1960, and the intrauterine device (IUD) gave women greater control over their reproductive systems. But women still ran more risks, both with their reputations and their bodies, from sexual activity than men did. The new permissive atmosphere of the 1960s and widespread availability of contraception did not necessarily liberate women. Helen Gurley Brown's *Sex and the Single Girl* (1962) promoted swinging sexual freedom for single women at the same time it emphasized emotional and material dependence on men by telling women that their main goal in life should be to snare a husband. As *Ms.* magazine noted pointedly in 1972, "The Sexual Revolution and the Women's Movement are at polar opposites. Women have been liberated only from the right to say 'no'."

The Revival of Feminism

Feminism was a dead issue in 1960. The government had enacted no legislation specifically targeted for women since the Nineteenth Amendment gave them the right to vote in 1920. Such words as "sexism" and "Ms." had not been coined. There were no rape crisis centers or battered women's shelters. Not a single university offered a course in women's studies, and women's sports programs were nonexistent. At least ten thousand women a year lost their lives in illegal back-alley abortions.

All that changed during the next fifteen years. The women's movement rivaled the civil rights movement in the success it achieved in a short period of time. By the mid-1970s, however, feminism had provoked a backlash, and its progress had stalled.

Women's Changing Lives

Social movements do not just spring up when leaders announce a set of demands. Each movement must have a constituency ready to be mobilized. The success of the civil rights movement was linked in part to the massive migration of blacks out of the South, which made race relations a national problem. Student activism had roots in the expansion of collegiate and university enrollments due to the baby boom. Preconditions for feminism lay in the changing social and demographic bases of women's lives.

In 1900, the average woman married by the age of twenty-two and then bore between three and four children, with her last child arriving when she was thirty-two. She had a life expectancy of sixty-two to sixty-six years, and so she could expect to devote most of her adult life to child-rearing By the 1960s and 1970s, women still married at twenty-two, but the birth rate had dropped dramatically, especially since the immediate postwar period. From a peak of 25.3 births per thousand women in 1957, it dropped to 18.0 in 1970 and 15.7 in 1981. Women typically had one or two children, rather than the three or four common at the beginning of the century. Since a woman who survived to age twenty now had a life expectancy of nearly eighty years, she had approximately forty years of adulthood during which she would not be involved primarily in raising children. The dramatic rise in women's participation in the labor force during the postwar years partly reflected this demographic shift.

Women's lives were undergoing other changes as well. More women went to college, and their percentage of the total student body grew. This pattern reversed a decline in the immediate postwar period when the GI Bill gave men a temporary advantage in access to higher education. Many college women had also dropped out of school to marry and raise families at the height of the emphasis on domesticity. By 1960, however, the percentage of women students had climbed to 35 percent, and by 1970 to 41 percent. Women students made up the majority by the 1980s.

Another factor reshaping women's lives was the increase in marital instability represented by rising divorce rates. In 1900, eight per hundred

JOANIE CAUCUS, MODERN WOMAN

The character of Joanie Caucus in Garry Trudeau's popular comic strip, *Doonesbury*, provided a running commentary on women's changing lives in the 1960s and 1970s. Caucus, a former housewife, ran away from her husband and family to a commune and then tried to raise the consciousness of children at the day care center where she worked. Here she applies to law school. After graduation, she became a legislative aid to a female member of Congress, remarried, and had a child in her forties. (DOONESBURY, By Garry Trudeau. Copyright, 1974, G. B. Trudeau. Reprinted with permission of Universal Press Syndicate. All rights reserved.)

FIGURE 30.1 WOMEN AND THE LABOR FORCE, 1800–1980

married couples divorced. This ratio rose slowly through the 1950s and then shot up in the 1960s. By 1965, the divorce rate reached twenty-seven per hundred marriages. By the 1980s, according to census projections, fifty-two marriages per hundred would end in divorce. Women could no longer assume that their marriage would be the most important event of their lives or that it would last until "death do us part."

A corollary to the rise in marital instability was a growth in female-headed households living in poverty. In economic terms, women did not survive divorce as well as men did. Only about a tenth of all divorced women received alimony payments for their own support; about half got child-support payments, which were notoriously hard to enforce. In addition, the segmentation of the work force generally relegated women to low-paying service jobs, so they earned considerably less than men. By 1980, nearly a fifth of all children were being raised by a single mother. Two-thirds of the female-headed households depended on welfare payments, especially from Aid to Families with Dependent Children (AFDC).

These demographic changes have led to a convergence in the patterns of black and white women's lives. Black women have always had a high participation rate in the work force because of their need to contribute to family income. They have also traditionally headed more households on their own. A similar rise in employment and female-headed households has now occurred among white women. Both races have

also seen a dramatic rise in the birth rate of unmarried teenagers, a pattern first observed in the black community in the 1960s. In 1979, more than half the births to black women were to unmarried females.

Black and white women increasingly hold similar jobs, thanks to civil rights agitation that opened white-collar and service jobs to black women. As a result, the pay differential between black and white women has shrunk. While nonwhite women earned only 38 percent of white women's median wages before World War II, they earned 88 percent by 1977. In 1980, however, white and nonwhite women still earned less on the average ($11,703 and $10,915, respectively) than black men ($13,875) and considerably less than white men ($19,720).

As a result of these changes, the traditional view that women will spend their lives at home as wives and mothers has been dramatically undercut. To be female in America now often includes work and marriage, childrearing and a career, or life in a female-headed household. These changing social realities helped foster the revival of feminism in the 1960s.

Two Paths to Feminism

During the 1960s, two independent movements renewed the national interest in women's concerns. The women's rights branch of the new feminism, symbolized by the National Organization for Women (NOW), consisted of older professional women who sought political change by

BARBAROUS RITUALS

Woman Is:

- Kicking strongly in your mother's womb, upon which she is told, "It must be a boy, if it's so active!"

- Being tagged with a *pink* beaded bracelet thirty seconds after you are born, and wrapped in *pink* blankets five minutes thereafter.

- Being confined to the Doll Corner in nursery school when you are really fascinated by Tinker Toys.

- Wanting to wear overalls instead of "frocks."

- Learning to detest the words "dainty" and "cute."

- Being labeled a tomboy when all you wanted to do was climb that tree to look out and see a distance.

- Learning to sit with your legs crossed, even when your feet can't touch the floor yet.

- Hating boys—because they're allowed to do things you want to do but are forbidden to—and being told hating boys is a phase.

- Learning that something you do is "naughty," but when your brother does the same thing, it's "spunky." . . .

- Seeing grownups chuckle when you say you want to be an engineer or doctor when you grow up—and learning to say you want to be a mommy or a nurse, instead.

- Liking math or history a lot and getting hints that boys are turned off by smart girls.

- Finding that almost all jobs open to you pay less for harder work than to men. . . .

- Learning to be *very tactful* if you have men working "under you." More likely, learning to always be working under men.

- Coming home from work—and starting *in* to work: unpack the groceries, fix supper, wash up the dishes, rinse out some laundry, etc., etc. . . .

- Being widowed, or divorced, and trying to get a "good" job—at your age.

- Getting older, getting lonelier, getting ready to die—and knowing it wouldn't have had to be this way, after all.

Source: "Barbarous Rituals," in Robin Morgan, ed., *Sisterhood is Powerful.* New York: Random House, 1970, 179–181, 184, 186–188.

---

working through the system. The women's liberation branch, on the other hand, attracted primarily younger women—recent college graduates who had been active in civil rights, the New Left, and the antiwar movement. These women had a much more radical vision of feminism, one that concentrated on the oppression produced by traditional family and gender roles. They were often quite hostile to men, their separatism mirroring that of black-power advocates. Unlike the traditional women's rights organizations, which were dues-paying, hierarchical groups, the women's liberation movement was looser and mass based, often without any coordination.

Several events set the stage for the development of the women's rights movement. In 1961, President Kennedy established a Presidential Commission on the Status of Women, an attempt to counter criticism about his administration's poor record on women's issues. Eleanor Roosevelt served as honorary head of the commission. The group's report, issued in 1963, documented the employment and educational discrimination faced by women, but its impact extended beyond its rather conservative recommendations. The presidential commission, and the state commissions that were its offshoots, set up a rudimentary network of women in public life who were concerned about feminist issues.

Another event that increased sympathy for feminism was the publication of Betty Friedan's witty *The Feminine Mystique* in 1963. This book, a pointed indictment of the trap of women's suburban domesticity, grew out of Friedan's own experiences as a housewife in the 1950s. Friedan called it "the problem that has no name":

> As she made the beds, shopped for groceries, matched slipcover material, ate peanut butter sandwiches with her children, chauffeured Cub Scouts and Brownies, lay beside her husband at night—she was afraid to ask even of herself the silent question—"Is this all?"

Women responded enthusiastically to her story, especially the white, college-educated middle-class women whose backgrounds resembled the author's. The book sold three million copies, and many more women read excerpts of it in major women's magazines. While *The Feminine Mystique* did not cause the revival of feminism, it became a central text of the new movement, introducing many women to the powerful ideas of modern feminism.

In 1963–1964, the focus shifted toward legislative change. In 1963, on the recommendation of the Presidential Commission on the Status of Women, Congress passed the Equal Pay Act, which directed that men and women be paid the same wages for doing the same job. An event of more far-reaching importance was the passage of the Civil Rights Act of 1964, which had as great an impact on women as it did on blacks and other minorities. The key provision, Title VII, barred discrimination in employment on the basis of race, color, religion, national origin, or sex. The category of sex was added by conservative Representative Howard Smith of Virginia, not out of concern for women's equality—he called it "my little amendment"—but to make the civil rights bill so controversial as to kill it completely. His strategy backfired. Title VII remains a powerful legal tool in the fight against sex discrimination.

Dissatisfaction with the Equal Employment Opportunity Commission's slow implementation of Title VII led to the founding of the National Organization for Women in 1966. This group modeled itself after such black groups as the NAACP: NOW aimed to be a civil rights organization for women. "The purpose of NOW," its statement of purpose declared, "is to take action to bring women into full participation in the mainstream of American society now, exercising all the privileges and responsibilities thereof in truly equal partnership with men." Betty Friedan served as NOW's first president, and its membership grew from a thousand in 1967 to fifteen thousand in 1971. Men made up a fourth of NOW's early membership, and it still ranks as the largest feminist organization in the United States.

Women's liberationists came to feminism by a different path. White women had made up about half the students who went to the South with SNCC in the 1964 Freedom Summer voter-registration project. While in Mississippi, they received conflicting messages. College women developed self-confidence and organizational skills through participation in the project, and they found role models in the black women and older southern white women who had become involved in civil rights through church activities. At the same time, women volunteers were automatically expected to do all the cleaning and cooking at the Freedom Houses where SNCC volunteers lived. "We didn't come down here to work as a maid this summer," one complained, "we came down to work in the field of civil rights."

Given the intensity of their commitment to civil rights, and the lack of a feminist movement as yet to give ideological context to their concerns, Freedom Summer volunteers only tentatively raised their concerns as women. When they did, they compared women's position with that of blacks. "Assumptions of male superiority are as widespread and deeply rooted and every much as crippling to the woman as the assumptions of white superiority are to the Negro," they argued. Such attempts to raise feminist issues were laughed off by both black and white men in the movement. Stokely Carmichael made one of the most pointed retorts: "The only position for women in SNCC is prone."

Black power militancy made white women, like white men, feel less welcome in the civil rights movement after 1966; but when women transferred their energies to student antiwar groups, they found the male-dominated New Left to be just as unsupportive. Once again, women were expected to take notes at meetings, serve coffee, and clean up afterwards, while men did all the intellectual work and monopolized the public-speaking roles. As the New Left focused increasingly on draft resistance as a strategy to oppose the war, women found themselves treated mainly as sex objects. "Girls say yes to guys who say no," went a popular slogan. When women tried to raise feminist issues at conventions, they were shouted off the platform with such jeers as "Move on, little girl, we have more important issues to talk about here than women's liberation." The "little girl" who received this taunt was Shulamith Firestone, whose *The Dialectic of Sex* (1971) was an early bible of the women's movement.

By 1967–1968, groups of radical women

realized that they needed their own movement. The contradictions between the commitment of the New Left to egalitarianism and women's actual treatment by male leaders became so striking that women felt they had no other choice. This process occurred independently in five or six cities. The women's liberation movement went public in 1968 when it staged a protest at the Miss America pageant. The demonstration included a "freedom trash can," into which women were encouraged to throw such symbols of female oppression as false eyelashes, hair curlers, brassieres, and girdles. The media quickly labeled the radical feminists "bra burners." The derisive name stuck, although no brassieres were actually burned.

A technique of more lasting impact was "consciousness raising," group sessions in which women shared common experiences about growing up female. The linkage of women's personal lives with wider societal oppression, summed up by the slogan "The personal is political," was a hallmark of the early radical feminists. As Shulamith Firestone recalled, "Three months of this sort of thing is enough to make a feminist of any woman."

In 1969–1970, the media "discovered" feminism. Media attention brought women's issues to a much broader audience than could ever have been reached by either NOW or the women's liberation collectives. Before 1969, most feminists heard about the movement through word of mouth. After that, the media brought in new converts who broke down the barriers between the two branches of the movement. Feminism's capacity to build a mass base of support was demonstrated on August 26, 1970, when thousands of women throughout the country marched to celebrate the fiftieth anniversary of the Nineteenth Amendment.

Another reason for the blurring of distinctions between women's rights and women's liberation was a growing convergence of interests. Radical women had learned by the early 1970s that some feminist goals could best be accomplished in the political sphere, such as lobbying for child care, equal pay, or abortion reform. In turn, the more traditional political activists developed a much

RUNNING FOR WOMEN'S RIGHTS

Feminists Billie Jean King, (left), Bella Abzug, (with hat), and Betty Friedan, (far right), join runners who carried a torch from Seneca Falls, New York, site of the first women's rights convention in 1848, to Houston for the 1977 National Women's Conference. Funded by Congress in honor of International Women's Year, the conference brought together two thousand delegates and twenty thousand observers who adopted a National Plan of Action for women's rights. (© 1978 Diana Mara Henry)

broader view of women's oppression, including tentative support for divisive issues like lesbian rights and abortion. By 1970, feminists began to think of themselves as part of a broad, growing, and increasingly influential social movement. "It's not a movement," said journalist Sally Kempton, "it's a state of mind." The title of Robin Morgan's best-selling book of that year, *Sisterhood is Powerful,* similarly reflected feminist optimism.

The High Tide of Feminism

Significant progress in the battle for women's equality occurred during the early 1970s. The media had made new terms such as "sexism" and "male chauvinism" part of the national vocabulary. Many colleges across the country started women's studies programs. Former all-male bastions, including Yale, Princeton, and the U.S. Military Academy, admitted woman undergraduates for the first time. *Ms.* magazine was founded in 1972 by Gloria Steinem and other journalists. The proportion of women in graduate and professional schools rose, and more and more women won election to public office. Bella Abzug, Elizabeth Holtzman, Shirley Chisholm, Patricia Schroeder, and Geraldine Ferraro served in Congress; Ella Grasso won election as Connecticut's governor in 1974, and Dixie Lee Ray as Washington's in 1976.

The women's movement achieved passage of significant federal legislation. The Equal Credit Opportunity Act of 1974 prohibited banks and other lenders from discriminating on the basis of sex. Congress authorized child-care deductions for working parents and higher employment benefits for married female federal employees. In many cases, the federal policy on civil rights was simply extended to include women as well as men. Title IX of the Educational Amendments Act of 1972 broadened the coverage of the 1964 Civil Rights Act to include educational institutions; it prohibited colleges and universities that received federal funds from discriminating on the basis of sex. Until a Supreme Court decision undermined it in 1984, Title IX was especially effective in increasing women's access to participation in sports.

The Supreme Court also made several rulings that gave women more control over their repro-

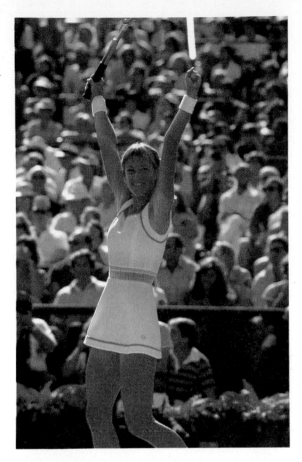

WOMEN IN SPORTS
Tennis star Chris Evert Lloyd shows her joy upon winning her fifth U.S. Open title in 1980. Lloyd symbolized the new opportunities for women in professional sports during the 1970s. Due in large part to Title IX, girls' participation in varsity athletics at the high school level increased 560 percent between 1971 and 1976. (Walter Iooss, Jr./*Sports Illustrated*)

ductive lives. In 1965, the case of *Griswold v. Connecticut* overturned state laws against the sale of contraceptive devices to married women; in 1972, *Baird v. Eisenstadt* extended this protection to single women. In 1973, *Roe v. Wade* struck down Texas and Georgia statutes that allowed abortions only if the mother's life was in danger. According to this controversial decision, states could no longer outlaw abortions during the first trimester, or three months, of pregnancy. The court's reasoning did not address feminist demands for women's control over their bodies. Rather, the justices interpreted abortion as a medical issue, basing their decision on the confidentiality of the doctor-patient relationship. *Roe v. Wade* cemented the liberalization of state abortion laws that began in New York in 1970.

In the 1970s, the women's movement increasingly united around the proposed Equal Rights Amendment to the Constitution (ERA), which stated, "Equality of Rights under the Law shall not be denied or abridged by the United States or any State on the basis of sex." The ERA, first introduced in 1923 by the National Woman's Party, was dusted off by modern feminists after languishing in Congress for almost fifty years. In 1970, the measure passed the House but died in the Senate. In the 1971–1972 session, it passed both houses and was submitted to the states for ratification. Thirty-four states quickly passed the ERA in 1972–1974. Then the momentum stopped. Only Indiana ratified after that point, leaving the amendment three states short of the

necessary three-fourths majority. Most of the states that refused to ratify the ERA were in the South; Illinois also held out, despite spirited campaigns there by ERA supporters. Congress extended the deadline for ratification until June 30, 1982, but the Equal Rights Amendment still fell short.

The fate of the ERA suggested that, by the mid-1970s, much of the momentum of the women's movement had slowed or even stopped. Although 63 percent of women told the Harris poll in 1975 that they favored "efforts to strengthen and change women's status in society," a growing minority of men and women expressed concern over what seemed to be revolutionary changes in women's roles. A new conservatism began to influence political and social life by the mid-1970s, spearheaded by the Moral Majority and other organizations whose mem-

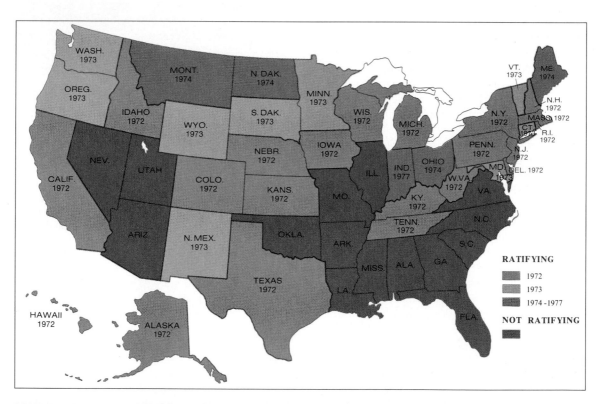

MAP 30.3 STATES RATIFYING THE EQUAL RIGHTS AMENDMENT
The Equal Rights Amendment to the U.S. Constitution quickly won support among the states in 1972 and 1973, but then it stalled. ERAmerica, a coalition of women's groups formed in 1976, lobbied extensively, particularly in Florida, North Carolina, and Illinois, but failed to sway the conservative legislatures in those states. Later efforts to revive the ERA also were unsuccessful.

TIME LINE
THE STRUGGLE FOR EQUALITY AND DIVERSITY

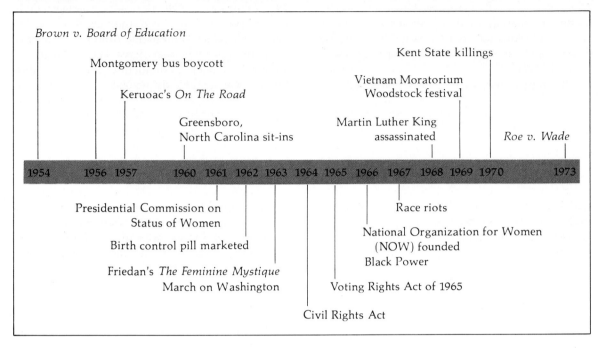

bers belonged largely to fundamentalist religious groups. Especially disturbing to these conservatives were changes in attitudes that seemed to denigrate women who chose to stay home as full-time housewives.

Phyllis Schlafly, long active in conservative causes—she had written *A Choice, Not an Echo*, a best-seller extolling Barry Goldwater in 1963—led the antifeminist backlash. Despite her law degree and active career while raising five children, Schlafly spoke out in behalf of traditional women's roles. She often opened her speeches by saying, "I'd like to thank my husband for letting me be here tonight." She told audiences, "A man's first significant purchase is a diamond for his bride, and the major financial investment of his life is a home for her to live in." Schlafly's Eagle Forum effectively lobbied against the ERA, which it claimed would create an unnatural "unisex society," cause women to be drafted, legalize homosexual marriages, and eliminate separate toilets for men and women. (All these charges are false and have no basis in the language of the amendment.) Anti-ERA lobbyists showed up at state houses with home-baked

bread and apple pies, symbols of their traditional domestic roles. Schlafly's message that women had more to lose than to gain from passage of the ERA found favor among both men and women deeply troubled by the rapid pace of social change.

Like the civil rights movement before it, the women's movement also found that choices were harder, and causes less clear-cut, as the 1970s progressed. The Affirmative Action program, consisting of guidelines instituted by the Labor Department in 1970 to ensure nondiscriminatory hiring through quotas and preferential treatment to blacks and women, was far more controversial than Title VII. "Comparable worth," the doctrine that people with jobs involving similar levels of skill or responsibility, such as secretaries and maintenance workers, should be paid the same wages, was much trickier than the concept of equal pay for equal work.

The legalization of abortion proved so controversial that it sparked a powerful "right to life" movement. Foes of abortion, placing higher value on the rights of the unborn fetus than on the right of the mother to choose whether to terminate her pregnancy, attempted to circumvent and overturn the *Roe v. Wade* decision. In 1976, Representative Henry Hyde of Illinois drafted legislation to deny Medicaid funds to pay for abortions for poor women. The Supreme Court upheld the Hyde amendment in *Harris v. McRae* in 1980.

Although feminism had been forced on the defensive by the mid-1970s, women's lives showed no signs of returning to the values of 1950 or even of 1970. Pervasive changes were here to stay. So, too, were the victories won by blacks, Hispanics, and native Americans, incomplete though they may have been. American society had been permanently altered by this twenty-year struggle for equality.

---

*B*etween 1954 and 1975, social movements challenged the American status quo. The civil rights movement triggered the process, and its attacks on legalized segregation in the South expanded into challenges to institutionalized racism throughout the country. The tactics and ideology developed in the civil rights movement encouraged other groups, including Hispanics, native Americans, poor people, and women, to demand equality as well. Young people also protested, challenging the policies of their universities and American participation in the Vietnam War.

All the protest movements had their roots in structural and demographic changes and shifting cultural values. Black migration from the South because of the transformation of agriculture made civil rights a national, not just a sectional, problem. The postwar baby boom led to a rapid expansion of higher education. More women took jobs outside the home, faced rising divorce rates, and acquired better access to education.

The protest movements followed a similar progression. At first, efforts centered on the political or judicial front. Early successes led to heightened expectations, but the next stage—changing people's attitudes and winning social and economic justice—proved more difficult. The civil rights and women's movements each produced a backlash from those who thought change had gone far enough, but not before lasting alterations had been made in American society.

Suggestions for Further Reading

Godfrey Hodgson, *America in Our Time* (1976), offers the best overview of the entire postwar period. Three strong surveys of the 1960s are Allen J. Matusow, *The Unraveling of America* (1984); William L. O'Neill, *Coming Apart* (1971); and Milton Viorst, *Fire in the Streets* (1979). For additional general material on the period, see Ronald Berman, *America in the Sixties* (1972); Todd Gitlin, *The Whole World Is Watching* (1981); and Peter Joseph's oral history of the decade, *Good Times* (1973).

The Civil Rights Movement

Harvard Sitkoff, *The Struggle for Black Equality* (1981), surveys the period from 1954 to 1980. Richard Kluger, *Simple Justice* (1975), analyzes the Brown decision and its context, while Anthony Lewis, *Portrait of a Decade* (1964), covers southern reaction to the decision. J. Har-

vie Wilkinson III continues the story of the Supreme Court and integration through the 1970s in *From Brown to Bakke* (1979).

Histories of the major civil rights organizations include Clayborne Carson's study of SNCC, *In Struggle* (1981), and August Meier and Elliot Rudwick, *CORE* (1973). Mary Aickin Rothschild, *A Case of Black and White* (1982), describes northern volunteers during the "Freedom Summer." Victor Navasky, *Kennedy Justice* (1971), is extremely critical of President Kennedy's civil rights record; Carl Brauer, *John F. Kennedy and the Second Reconstruction* (1977), provides a more sympathetic view. William Chafe, *Civilities and Civil Rights* (1980), is a superb case study of the impact of civil rights on Greensboro, North Carolina, from the 1950s through the 1970s.

Major texts of the civil rights movement include Stokely Carmichael and Charles Hamilton, *Black Power* (1967); James Baldwin, *The Fire Next Time* (1963); Eldridge Cleaver, *Soul on Ice* (1968); and Malcolm X, with Alex Haley, *The Autobiography of Malcolm X* (1965). Anne Moody, *Coming of Age in Mississippi* (1968), is a moving autobiography; Howell Raines, *My Soul is Rested* (1977), is a fine oral history. Joanne Grant, *Black Protest* (1968), and August Meier and Elliott Rudwick, *Black Protest in the Sixties* (1970), are good anthologies. Martin Luther King tells his story in *Stride Toward Freedom* (1958) and *Why We Can't Wait* (1964). Biographies of King include David Lewis, *King* (1970), and Stephen Oates, *Let the Trumpet Sound* (1982).

Report of the National Advisory Commission on Civil Disorders (1968) analyzes the decade's major race riots. See also Joe R. Feagin and Harlan Hahn, *Ghetto Revolts* (1973), and Robert Fogelson, *Violence as Protest* (1971). Robert Conot, *Rivers of Blood, Years of Darkness* (1968), studies the Watts riot.

Stan Steiner, *La Raza* (1970), and Matt Meier and Feliciano Rivera, *The Chicanos* (1972), document the growing Hispanic political activity. Vine De Loria, Jr., *Behind the Trail of Broken Treaties* (1974) and *Custer Died for Your Sins* (1969), convey the new Indian assertiveness. See also Stan Steiner, *The New Indians* (1968); Helen Hertzberg, *The Search for an American Indian Identity* (1971); and Wilcomb Washburn, *Red Man's Land, White Man's Law* (1971).

The Challenge of Youth

The student activism of the 1960s drew its share of scholarly chroniclers. See Kenneth Keniston, *The Uncommitted* (1965) and *Young Radicals* (1969); Daniel Bell and Irving Kristol, *Confrontation* (1969); Nathan Glazer, *Remembering the Answers* (1970); and Philip Slater, *The Pursuit of Loneliness* (1970). On student revolt, see Seymour Lipset and Sheldon Wolin, eds., *The Berkeley Student Revolt* (1965), and Jerry Avorn, *Up Against the Ivy Wall* (1968). John P. Diggins, *The American Left in the Twentieth Century* (1973), and Irwin Unger, *The Movement: A History of the American New Left* (1974), provide general background; Kirkpatrick Sale, *SDS* (1973), covers one important organization. Lawrence Baskir and William A. Straus, *The Draft, The War, and the Vietnam Generation* (1978), assess who was drafted and why.

Morris Dickstein, *Gates of Eden* (1977), is an excellent account of cultural developments in the 1960s. The standard texts of the counterculture are Theodore Roszak, *The Making of a Counter Culture* (1969), and Charles Reich, *The Greening of America* (1970). Joyce Maynard,

Looking Back (1973), provides a "chronicle of growing up old" in the 1960s. Gerald Howard, ed., *The Sixties* (1982), is a good anthology of the decade's art, politics, and culture. Philip Norman, *Shout! The Beatles in Their Generation* (1981), covers developments in popular music. Joan Didion *Slouching Toward Bethlehem* (1968) and *The White Album* (1979), explore some of the darker sides of the hippie phenomenon.

For background on the Beat Generation of the 1950s, start with Ann Charters, *Kerouac* (1973); Dennis McNally, *Desolate Angel* (1979); and Jane Kramer, *Allen Ginsberg in America* (1969). John Tytell, *Naked Angels* (1976), covers the lives and literature of the Beat Generation. Tom Wolfe's *Electric Kool-Aid Acid Test* (1965) describes the antics of Beat survivors Ken Kesey and his Merry Pranksters in the 1960s.

The Revival of Feminism

Jo Freeman, *The Politics of Women's Liberation* (1975); Barbara Deckard, *The Women's Movement* (1975); and Judith Hole and Ellen Levine, *The Rebirth of Feminism* (1971), chronicle the revival of feminism in the 1960s and 1970s. Gayle Graham Yates, *What Women Want* (1975), concentrates on the movement's ideology, while William Chafe, *Women and Equality* (1977), draws interesting comparisons between feminism and civil rights. Sara Evans, *Personal Politics* (1979), traces the roots of feminism in the civil rights movement and the New Left. Material on the changing demographic aspects of women's lives is found in Alice Kessler-Harris, *Out to Work* (1982); Carl Degler, *At Odds* (1980); and Valerie Kincaid Oppenheimer, *The Female Labor Force in the United States* (1970). Ethel Klein, *Gender Politics* (1984), specifically links demographic change with the revival of feminism. Phyllis Schlafly, *The Power of the Positive Woman* (1978), and Andrea Dworkin, *Right Wing Women* (1983), present the ideas of antifeminist women that gained force in the 1970s.

Betty Friedan, *The Feminine Mystique* (1963), is still powerful. For Friedan's evolving views, see *It Changed My Life* (1976) and *The Second Stage* (1982). Texts of the early women's movement include Robin Morgan, ed., *Sisterhood Is Powerful* (1970); Shulamith Firestone, *The Dialectic of Sex* (1970); Kate Millett, *Sexual Politics* (1970); Germaine Greer, *The Female Eunuch* (1972); and Susan Brownmiller, *Against Our Will* (1975). Sara Ruddick and Pamela Daniels, eds., *Working It Out* (1977), collects the struggles of twenty-three women to find personal and professional fulfillment during a period of rapid change in women's expectations.

31

A PROUD BUT
TROUBLED PEOPLE

At the end of the 1960s, the United States was torn by internal strife and controversy. Much of the domestic unrest stemmed from the Vietnam War. The growing crisis in confidence was increased by an unprecedented scandal at the highest level of the government, culminating in the resignation of President Richard M. Nixon in 1974.

During the decade after Nixon's resignation, the United States faced new challenges in national life. In politics, the New Deal coalition struggled, with less and less success, to maintain a Democratic majority. In the economic sphere, Americans found themselves in a period of declining productivity, limited growth, and runaway inflation, much of it caused by the dramatic rise in imported oil prices that hit like a shock wave after 1973. Inflation abated in the 1980s, but the nation faced an annual federal deficit that approached $200 billion. In foreign policy, following the end of the war in Vietnam, the United States struggled to deal with new challenges such as instability in the Middle East and crises of political authority in Central America. Relations with the Soviet Union remained tense, as both superpowers engaged in an escalating nuclear arms race that threatened the fragile international peace.

While the outlines of economic, political, and international developments are clear, it is harder to generalize about the American people since 1968. The American experience has always been substantially defined not by sameness or consensus, but by elements of difference and diversity—whether by class, race, ethnicity, region, gender, or age. Demographic and social diversity is perhaps the most striking aspect of the American population on the eve of the twenty-first century.

A Time of Troubles

In many ways, the years 1963–1968 had been distinct. The civil rights movement spurred the nation to debate the political issues of the day in terms of morality, justice, fairness, and equality. After 1968, a new set of priorities began to emerge. There was less talk about poverty and civil rights, and more about inflation and law and order. Richard Nixon, who won election as president in 1968 and again in 1972, capitalized on this shifting mood.

1968, a Year of Shocks

The year 1968 ranks as one of the most traumatic in United States history. In Vietnam, it began with the Tet offensive, named for the Vietnamese New Year, on January 31, when a surprise Viet Cong attack struck major installations throughout South Vietnam, including the U.S.

embassy in Saigon. Although the attack was repulsed, the Viet Cong strength mocked American claims that the enemy was being defeated. President Johnson's political stock fell accordingly. Senator Eugene J. McCarthy of Minnesota had already entered the Democratic primaries as an antiwar candidate; in the aftermath of the Tet offensive, he received a stunning 42.2 percent of the vote in the New Hampshire primary in early March. Sensing the vulnerability of the incumbent president, Senator Robert F. Kennedy of New York entered the race several days later. Johnson saw the handwriting on the wall and announced on March 31 that he would not seek reelection. Using the occasion to announce a halt in the bombing of North Vietnam, Johnson vowed to devote his remaining months in office to the search for peace in Vietnam.

Just five days after Johnson's dramatic withdrawal, Martin Luther King, Jr., was assassinated in Memphis, provoking urban riots across the country that left forty-three persons dead. Soon after, a major student confrontation erupted at Columbia University, ending only when police violently removed protesters from the administration buildings they had occupied. Student unrest seemed likely to become a worldwide phenomenon in May, when a massive strike by students and labor unions toppled the French government. Then came the final tragedy. As Robert Kennedy celebrated his victory over Eugene McCarthy in the California primary on June 5, 1968, he was assassinated by Sirhan Sirhan, a young Palestinian who opposed Kennedy's pro-Israel stand. Once again, the nation went through the ritual of burying a Kennedy. A New Yorker captured the mounting sense of frustration and impotence by saying, "I won't vote. Every good man we get they kill."

Disorder and confusion continued to haunt the Democratic party, which was still reeling from Johnson's withdrawal when Kennedy was assassinated. McCarthy proceeded listlessly through the rest of his campaign. Senator George S. McGovern of South Dakota entered the Democratic race in an effort to keep the Kennedy forces together. Meanwhile, Vice-President Hubert H. Humphrey lined up pledges from more traditional Democratic supporters—unions, urban political machines, and state organizations. With Humphrey's growing success, the

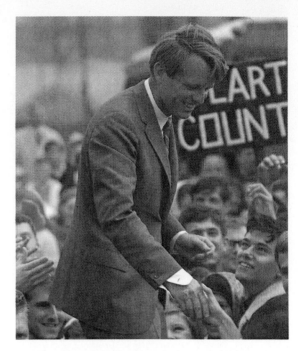

ROBERT F. KENNEDY
Bobby Kennedy inspired strong passions during his 1968 campaign. Followers often tore off his cufflinks as they tried to touch him or shake his hand. Kennedy's assassination in June 1968, coming just two months after Martin Luther King, Jr.'s murder, shocked the nation. (© Steve Shapiro, Black Star)

Democrats suddenly found themselves on the verge of nominating not an antiwar candidate but a public figure closely associated with Johnson's war policies. The stage was set for the Democratic National Convention in Chicago in August.

The Democrats had experienced disastrous conventions in the past, as in the 103-ballot-long meeting in 1924, but the 1968 convention hit a new low. Most of the drama occurred not in the convention amphitheater but in the streets of Chicago. On the night that the candidates were nominated, a battle broke out between the Chicago police and antiwar demonstrators. In what the official report later described as a "police riot," the police dispersed protesters with mace, tear gas, and clubs. While the protesters chanted "The whole world is watching!", the television networks ran film of the riot in the midst of their coverage of the nominating speeches. In one memorable exchange, Senator Abraham Ribicoff of Connecticut interrupted his nominating speech for Senator McGovern to interject, ''With George McGovern we wouldn't have Gestapo tactics on the streets of Chicago.'' The cameras panned to Richard J. Daley, Chicago's old-line Democratic mayor, livid with rage and mouthing obscenities.

Television coverage of the riots was hardly excessive—it consisted of thirty-two minutes on CBS and less than fourteen minutes on NBC—but it cemented an impression of the Democrats as the party of disorder. The Democrats dispiritedly gave the nomination to Hubert Humphrey, who chose Senator Edmund S. Muskie of Maine as his running mate. The convention approved a moderate, proadministration platform.

The Chicago convention reinforced a growing backlash in favor of proponents of ''law and order,'' the catch phrase of the next several years.

Many Americans were fed up with protest and dissent. Governor George C. Wallace of Alabama, a third-party candidate, skillfully exploited the public's growing hostility and anger by making student protests and black riots his campaign issues. He also spoke out against school desegregation and busing. Early polls showed that Wallace would receive as much as 20 percent of the vote, possibly sufficient to deadlock the electoral college and send the election to the House of Representatives.

Richard Nixon, even more than George Wallace, tapped the growing conservative mood of the electorate. After his unsuccessful presidential campaign in 1960 and his failure to be elected governor of California in 1962, Nixon had engineered an amazing political comeback. In 1968 he easily beat back challenges from three governors—Ronald Reagan of California, George

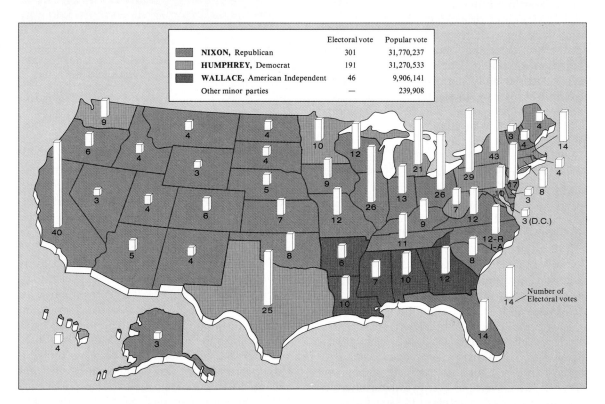

	Electoral vote	Popular vote
NIXON, Republican	301	31,770,237
HUMPHREY, Democrat	191	31,270,533
WALLACE, American Independent	46	9,906,141
Other minor parties	—	239,908

MAP 31.1 Election of 1968

As late as mid-September, third-party candidate George C. Wallace of Alabama had the support of 21 percent of the voters polled, threatening to send the election into the House of Representatives. In the election, however, Wallace received only 13.5 percent of the popular vote, winning five states and showing that the South was no longer solidly Democratic. Republican Richard M. Nixon defeated Hubert H. Humphrey with only 43.4 percent of the popular vote.

Romney of Michigan, and Nelson Rockefeller of New York—to win the Republican nomination. In his campaign, Nixon pledged to represent the "quiet voice" of the "great majority of Americans, the forgotten Americans, the nonshouters, the nondemonstrators." He declared that "The first civil right of every American is to be free from domestic violence."

The election was much closer than might have been expected, considering the Democratic debacle in Chicago. Humphrey rallied in the last weeks of the campaign by disassociating himself from Johnson's war policies. Nixon countered by declaring that he had a "secret plan" to end the war. Nixon received 43.4 percent of the vote and defeated Humphrey by a scant 510,000 votes out of 73 million cast. Wallace finished with 13.5 percent of the popular vote, becoming the most successful third-party candidate since Progressive Robert M. LaFollette in 1924. Nixon's "southern strategy," his carefully crafted inroad into the once solidly Democratic South, gave him an important margin of victory. Yet Nixon owed his election more to the split in the still-potent Democratic coalition than to the emergence of a new Republican majority.

The 1968 election suggested a new mood in the electorate that dominated much of the 1970s. Nixon appealed to what came to be known as the "silent majority," the average voter who was "unblack, unpoor, and unyoung." According to Ben J. Wattenberg and Richard Scammon in their influential book *The Real Majority* (1970), the typical American was not a political science student at Yale but a forty-seven-year-old machinist's wife from Dayton, Ohio:

> To know that the lady in Dayton is afraid to walk the streets alone at night, to know that she has a mixed view about blacks and civil rights because before moving to the suburbs she lived in a neighborhood that became all black, to know that her brother-in-law is a policeman, to know that she does not have the money to move if her new neighborhood deteriorates, to know that she is deeply distressed that her son is going to a community junior college where LSD was found on campus—to know all this is the beginning of contemporary political wisdom.

The images of the first half of 1968 were violent—assassinations, riots, student unrest, and black power. The mood by the time of the election had changed—law and order, distrust of student radicals, and fear of blacks. Nixon's election reflected just one manifestation of a fundamental shift in the political climate. The student protester, the black militant, and the welfare mother were out; the machinist's wife from Dayton was in.

The War at Home

Vietnam, which had long been Lyndon Johnson's war, soon became Richard Nixon's. Fifteen thousand Americans lost their lives in Vietnam during Nixon's presidency. Yet Nixon operated within political parameters that differed fundamentally from Johnson's. Realizing that the public would no longer stand for major sacrifices to win the war in Southeast Asia, Nixon searched for a way out of the Vietnam problem. He dramatically reduced American troop involvement in the ground fighting. When Nixon took office, more than 543,000 American soldiers were serving in Vietnam; by the end of 1970, the number had fallen to 334,000, and two years later it was down to 24,200. American casualties, and the political liabilities they generated, fell correspondingly. At the same time, however, Nixon escalated the American involvement by ordering a massive increase in the bombing raids over North Vietnam and neighboring countries. This expansion of the air war was deliberately downplayed, even hidden from the American public.

Television had much to do with shaping American attitudes toward the war. Vietnam was television's first big war; it brought the fighting directly into the nation's living rooms. The escalation in Vietnam coincided with several trends in news broadcasting, notably the expansion of the nightly network newscast from fifteen minutes to half an hour in 1963. By 1967, CBS and NBC were spending $5 million a year to cover the war from their expanded Saigon bureaus. This investment guaranteed that Vietnam appeared on the news every night. Reporters soon learned that combat footage—what they called "shooting bloody"—had a better chance of airing than reports about pacification or political developments. Every night, the newscasts showed American soldiers steadily advancing in the countryside, while reported body counts suggested staggering Viet Cong losses against minimal U.S. casualties.

The Tet offensive in January 1968 destroyed this complacent picture. Suddenly, television brought home new images—the American embassy in Saigon under siege, with a pistol-wielding staff member peering warily from a window; and the Saigon police chief placing a pistol to the head of a Viet Cong suspect and executing him on the street. About twenty million viewers watched the latter scene, a symbol of the brutality of the war and the corruption and injustice that characterized the regime of Nguyen Van Thieu, the president of South Vietnam from 1967 to 1975.

The Tet offensive set in motion a major shift in American public opinion about the war. Before Tet, a Gallup poll found that 56 percent of the people considered themselves "hawks" (supporters of the war), while only 28 percent identified themselves as "doves" (opponents); women and blacks consistently opposed the war more than did white males. By April 1968, doves outnumbered hawks by 42 to 41 percent. This turnaround did not mean that a majority now supported the peace movement. Many who called themselves doves had concluded that the war was unwinnable and that America ought to cut its losses and get out. They opposed the war on pragmatic, rather than moral, grounds.

At first, Nixon and National Security Adviser Henry Kissinger, a former Harvard government professor, seemed to be extricating the nation from the mire of Vietnam. A new plan called Vietnamization delegated most of the ground fighting to South Vietnamese troops. Vietnamization was a slow process, however, and American policymakers began to consider expanding the war in an attempt to strengthen the faltering South Vietnamese government. In March 1969, Nixon ordered secret bombing raids of neutral Cambodia, through which the North Vietnamese transported supplies and reinforcements. To keep Congress ignorant about these sorties, accurate information about the raids was fed into one Defense Department computer, while fabricated data omitting the Cambodia targets were fed into another computer. The faulty projections from the second computer were made available to Congress. The secret war against Cambodia culminated in an April 30, 1970, "incursion" by American ground forces to destroy enemy troop havens in that neutral country. The Cambodia invasion triggered the campus rioting that led to the Kent State killings. No matter how much the United States escalated its activity, however, the North Vietnamese fought on.

Like Lyndon Johnson, who by 1968 had become so unpopular that his appearance caused protests everywhere except on military bases, Richard Nixon seemed to inspire conflict. Determined to discredit his critics, he denounced student demonstrators as "bums" and stated,

A TELEVISED WAR
This harrowing scene from Saigon during the Tet offensive in 1968 was broadcast on U.S. network news. The NBC bureau chief described the film in a terse telex message: "A VC OFFICER WAS CAPTURED. THE TROOPS BEAT HIM. THEY BRING HIM TO [Brigadier General Nguyen Ngoc] LOAN WHO IS HEAD OF SOUTH VIETNAMESE NATIONAL POLICE. LOAN PULLS OUT HIS PISTOL, FIRES AT THE HEAD OF THE VC, THE VC FALLS, ZOOM ON HIS HEAD, BLOOD SPRAYING OUT. IF HE HAS IT ALL ITS STARTLING STUFF." (Wide World)

VIETNAM VETERAN REMEMBERS

I had been shot. The war had finally caught up with my body. I felt good inside. Finally the war was with me and I had been shot by the enemy. I was getting out of the war and I was going to be a hero. I kept firing my rifle into the tree line and boldly, with my new wound, moved closer to the village, daring them to hit me again. For a moment I felt like running back to the rear with my new million-dollar wound but I decided to keep fighting in the open. A great surge of strength went through me as I yelled for the other men to come out from the trees and join me. I was limping now and the foot was beginning to hurt so much, I finally lay down in almost a kneeling position, still firing into the village, still unable to see anyone. I seemed to be the only one left firing a rifle. Someone came up from behind me, took off my boot and began to bandage my foot. The whole thing was incredibly stupid, we were sitting ducks, but he bandaged my foot and then he took off back into the tree line.

For a few seconds it was silent. I lay down prone and waited for the next bullet to hit me. It was only a matter of time, I thought. I wasn't retreating, I wasn't going back, I was lying right there and blasting everything I had into the pagoda. The rifle was full of sand and it was jamming. I had to pull the bolt back now each time trying to get a round into the chamber. It was impossible and I started to get up and a loud crack went off next to my right ear as a thirty-caliber slug tore through my right shoulder, blasted through my lung, and smashed my spinal cord to pieces.

I felt that everything from my chest down was completely gone. I waited to die. I threw my hand back and felt my legs still there. I couldn't feel them but they were still there. I was still alive. And for some reason I started believing, I started believing I might not die, I might make it out of there and live and feel and go back home again. I could hardly breathe and was taking short little sucks with the one lung I had left. The blood was rolling off my flak jacket from the hole in my shoulder and I couldn't feel the pain in my foot anymore, I couldn't even feel my body. I was frightened to death. I didn't think about praying, all I could feel was cheated.

All I could feel was the worthlessness of dying right here in this place at this moment for nothing.

Source: Ron Kovic, *Born on the Fourth of July.* New York: McGraw Hill, 1976. 221–222.

"North Vietnam cannot defeat or humiliate the United States. Only Americans can do that." Vice-President Spiro T. Agnew followed suit, attacking dissidents as "ideological eunuchs" and "nattering nabobs of negativism," the press as a "tiny and closed fraternity," and Senate opponents of the war as "pampered prodigies." Nixon staunchly insisted that he would not be swayed by the mounting popular protests against the war. When 250,000 protesters marched on Washington in November 1969, the president watched football games on television while barricaded in the White House.

By 1970 dissatisfaction with the war had reached a broader spectrum of American society. Even American troops in Vietnam showed mounting opposition to their mission. They fought on, but many sewed peace symbols on their uniforms. A number of overbearing junior officers were "fragged"—that is, killed or wounded by a fragmentation grenade thrown by their own soldiers. A group called Vietnam Veterans Against the War expressed their profound opposition to the war by turning in their combat medals at mass demonstrations at the U.S. Capitol.

At the same time that Nixon stepped up the bombing raids against North Vietnam, he laid the groundwork for détente with the Soviet Union and China, the two leading communist superpowers. Influenced by the strategy of Henry Kissinger to use China to balance the USSR, Nixon moved away from unconditional support for the nationalist Chinese government on Taiwan. In February 1972, Nixon, long an anticommunist crusader, made a dramatic trip to the People's Republic of China, where he visited the Great Wall and toasted Chinese leaders in

Beijing. (Formal diplomatic relations would be established in 1979.) That May, Nixon made a similar trip to Moscow to sign SALT I, the strategic arms limitations treaty between the United States and the Soviet Union. The two trips were orchestrated to enhance Nixon's presidential stature and to give him considerable television publicity in an election year.

The Democrats would have had a difficult time countering Nixon's public relations coup under any circumstances, but disarray within the party in 1972 made their task even harder. In the aftermath of the 1968 national convention, the party had changed its way of selecting delegates and candidates. The Democrats now pledged to include "minority groups, young people and women in reasonable relationship to their presence in the population." The ratification of the Twenty-Sixth Amendment in 1971, which lowered the national voting age to eighteen, reinforced the impact of this procedural change. Another innovation was the candidate primary, which allowed voters to elect convention delegates directly, rather than have them chosen at party caucuses.

George McGovern reaped the greatest benefit from the new Democratic guidelines. By 1972, the South Dakota senator stood at the head of an army of antiwar activists who blitzed the precinct-level caucuses and won delegate commitments far beyond his voter support. In the past, an alliance of party bosses and union leaders would almost certainly have rejected an upstart candidate like McGovern in favor of a more traditional Democrat such as Hubert Humphrey or Edmund Muskie. But few party leaders qualified as delegates to the nominating convention under the 1972 rules. Typical of the new Democratic look, black leader Jesse Jackson replaced Mayor Richard Daley of Chicago as the head of the Illinois delegation.

McGovern's campaign became an unrelieved disaster. Surprised to learn that his running mate, Senator Thomas F. Eagleton of Missouri, had undergone electro-shock therapy for nervous depression, McGovern first offered him "1,000 percent" support, but then abruptly insisted that he leave the ticket. Sargent Shriver, a brother-in-law of John and Robert Kennedy, was prevailed upon to join the ticket at the last minute. McGovern was far too liberal for many tra-

ditional Democrats, who rejected his ill-defined proposals for welfare reform, did not rally around his antiwar stance, and ignored his charges that the Nixon administration had corruptly abused its power.

Nixon took full advantage of McGovern's weaknesses. Although the president had failed to end the war in Vietnam, his Vietnamization policy had reduced weekly American combat deaths from three hundred in 1968 to almost none in 1972. Just a few days before the election, Henry Kissinger returned from negotiations with the North Vietnamese in Paris and announced, somewhat disingenuously, that "peace is at hand."

Nixon won handily. He received nearly 61 percent of the popular vote and carried every state except Massachusetts and the District of Columbia. The threat of a conservative third-party challenge had been removed the previous May, when George Wallace was shot and paralyzed from the waist down by an assailant in a suburban Maryland shopping mall. McGovern's vote demonstrated large cracks in the traditional Democratic coalition; he received only 18 percent of the southern white Protestant vote and 38 percent of the big-city Catholic vote. Only blacks, Jews, and low-income voters remained loyal to the Democratic cause. Yet Nixon failed to kindle strong Republican loyalties in the electorate. Only 55.7 percent of the voters bothered to go to the polls.

In the aftermath of his landslide victory, Nixon moved to end American involvement in Vietnam. Seeking to break the stalemated negotiations, he initiated the "Christmas bombings." From December 17 to December 30, American planes subjected North Vietnamese civilian and military targets to the most destructive bombing of the entire war. Then, on January 27, 1973, a ceasefire was signed; it differed little from the proposal of the previous October. The Paris Peace Accords promised neither peace nor honor. Basically, they mandated the unilateral withdrawal of American troops in exchange for the return of American prisoners of war held in North Vietnam. For most Americans, that amount of face saving was enough.

The public outpouring of emotion that greeted the six hundred returning prisoners contrasted sharply with public indifference to ordinary Vietnam veterans, who in the following years experienced higher than average divorce, suicide, and unemployment rates, as well as recurring physical and psychological problems called the "post-Vietnam syndrome." For many Vietnam veterans, the war never ended.

The signing of the 1973 Peace Accords did little to resolve the civil war that had raged in Vietnam for almost three decades. Without massive U.S. military and economic aid, and with the continued presence of North Vietnamese soldiers in the south, it was only a matter of time before the South Vietnamese government of General Nguyen Van Thieu fell to the more popular North Vietnamese forces. The inevitable occurred in April 1975, when a North Vietnamese invasion reunited the country. American television viewers watched in horror as desperate South Vietnamese officials and soldiers fought with American embassy personnel for space on the last helicopters that flew out of Saigon before the Viet Cong took over the city, soon renamed Ho Chi Minh City. Strife still engulfs Vietnam and its neighbors Laos, Cambodia, and Thailand. The epitaph that journalist David Halberstam coined for American participation in the war applies to Southeast Asia itself: "No light at the end of the tunnel, only greater darkness."

Watergate

Watergate, the great constitutional crisis of the early 1970s, saw a president manage to avoid impeachment only by resigning from office. Its roots lay in Richard Nixon's secretive style of governing—Henry Kissinger once said Nixon was "the first victim of his own unharmonious nature"—and in his obsession with opposition to the Vietnam War at home. Many of the incidents of secrecy, mistrust, and illegality that Americans later lumped together as "Watergate" grew out of the protest era that preceded them.

The new administration began to stretch the boundaries of the law in the guise of national security just four months into Nixon's first term. In the spring of 1969, the *New York Times* broke the story that the United States had been secretly bombing Cambodia. In retaliation, the White House arranged for the FBI to wiretap illegally—that is, without judicial warrants—several low-level staffers on the National Security Coun-

cil, as well as five newspeople, to investigate the source of the leaks. The source was never found.

The next event to trigger White House paranoia was the leaking of the "Pentagon Papers" to the *New York Times* in June 1971 by Daniel Ellsberg, a former Defense Department analyst who had grown disillusioned with the war. The Pentagon Papers, a classified Defense Department document commissioned in the wake of the Tet offensive, contained so much damaging information about American blunders and misjudgments in the conduct of the war that Defense Secretary Robert S. McNamara had commented in 1968, "You know, they could hang people for what is in there." The Nixon administration unsuccessfully attempted to block publication of the Pentagon Papers, further increasing Ellsberg's stature as a hero to the antiwar movement. In an effort to discredit Ellsberg, White House underlings burglarized his psychiatrist's office to look for damaging information. This attempt also failed.

The Ellsberg break-in was part of a broad response by the administration to the supposed threats presented by domestic dissent to national security. In 1970, White House aide Tom Huston, a former army intelligence officer, drew up an extensive plan for secret domestic counter-intelligence—such as opening mail, tapping phones, and arranging break-ins—that would involve the FBI, CIA, and Justice Department. President Nixon approved the scheme, only to have it blocked by FBI Director J. Edgar Hoover, who refused to cooperate with other government agencies in activities he interpreted as being exclusively within the scope of the FBI. The White House then established a clandestine group of its own. It was headed by G. Gordon Liddy and Howard Hunt and known as the "plumbers" (because they were supposed to plug "leaks" of government information). Other dubious tactics included the use of government agencies such as the Internal Revenue Service to harass opponents of the administration named on an "enemies list" drawn up by aide John Dean.

These secret and questionable activities, supposedly conducted in the name of national security, led to the Watergate scandal. On the evening of June 17, 1972, five men carrying cameras and wiretapping equipment broke into the headquarters of the Democratic National Committee at the Watergate apartment complex in Washington. An alert security guard foiled the break-in, and the burglars were arrested; two other accomplices were apprehended soon after. Two of the accused men had worked as security consultants in the White House; a third held a responsible position on the Committee to Re-Elect the President (CREEP); the remaining four were all from Miami, where they had been involved in CIA-linked anti-Castro activities. Nixon's press secretary, Ronald Ziegler, dismissed the break-in as a "caper," a "third-rate burglary attempt." Nixon himself stated "categorically" that "no one in the White House staff, no one in this administration, presently employed, was involved in this bizarre incident." The cover-up had begun.

On June 23, 1972, six days after the break-in, the president ordered top aide H. R. Haldeman to instruct the CIA to tell the FBI not to probe too deeply into connections between the White House and the burglars. Although Nixon cited the supposed threat to national security, he really feared that the Watergate burglary would lead to an investigation of the dubious fundraising methods and political sabotage—or "dirty tricks"—used by his reelection committee.

The Watergate burglars were convicted and sent to jail. White House counsel John Dean had sought to buy their silence with $400,000 in hush money and hints of presidential pardons. But prodded by the presiding judge, John Sirica, several of the convicted burglars began to talk. A Senate committee launched an investigation. Two reporters on the *Washington Post*, Carl Bernstein and Bob Woodward, kept the story alive. Dean started to get nervous, and in March 1973 he warned Nixon, referring to the cover-up, that "there is a cancer within, close to the presidency, that is growing." On April 30, Nixon accepted the resignations of Haldeman and chief domestic adviser John Ehrlichman. He also fired Dean. In light of mounting evidence that linked the scandal directly to the Oval Office, press secretary Ziegler declared all previous statements on Watergate "inoperative."

In May, a Senate committee chaired by Senator Sam Ervin of North Carolina heard John Dean implicate President Nixon in the cover-up. The most startling revelation came from aide Alexander Butterfield, who revealed that Nixon

had a secret taping system in the White House. "I was hoping you fellows wouldn't ask me about that," Butterfield sheepishly told the committee. Until the tapes, it had been Dean's word against Nixon's; now it might be possible to find out what had actually transpired. The president steadfastly "stonewalled," refusing to release the tapes in the name of executive privilege and national security. When a lower federal court held that he had to give selected tapes to a special prosecutor, Nixon released heavily edited tapes and transcripts whose most frequent phrase seemed to be "expletive deleted." Senate Republican leader Hugh Scott called these edited transcripts "deplorable, disgusting, shabby, immoral." Further damaging Nixon's credibility

NIXON LEAVES THE PRESIDENCY
President Richard M. Nixon frequently posed with his arms outstretched, flashing a "V for Victory" sign. He maintained this stance even on August 9, 1974, as he boarded a helicopter en route to his home in San Clemente, California, minutes after turning over the presidency to Gerald R. Ford. (© Roland Freeman, Magnum)

was a suspicious eighteen-minute gap in the tape of a crucial meeting between Nixon, Haldeman, and Ehrlichman on June 20, 1972, three days after the break-in.

With the evidence becoming increasingly damning, the Watergate affair moved into its final phase in the summer of 1974. The House of Representatives convened impeachment hearings, and on July 30, seven Republicans joined the Democratic majority to vote three articles of impeachment—obstruction of justice, abuse of power, and acting in a way subversive of the Constitution—against Richard Nixon. Two days later, the Supreme Court ruled unanimously that Nixon's claim of executive privilege was insufficient to justify his refusal to turn over the tapes. On August 5, Nixon released the unexpurgated tapes, which contained shocking evidence that he had ordered the cover-up as early as six days after the break-in. In effect, he had been lying to the American people ever since. Senator Barry Goldwater gravely informed the president that Nixon would find no more than fifteen senators willing to defend him. On August 9, 1974, Nixon became the first president to resign from office.

The transfer of power to Vice-President Gerald Ford went remarkably smoothly. (In 1973, Ford had replaced Spiro Agnew, who had resigned after being indicted for allegedly accepting kickbacks on construction contracts while governor of Maryland.) In the wake of the assassinations of John Kennedy, Robert Kennedy, and Martin Luther King, as well as the first resignation of an incumbent vice-president, the idea of substituting leaders no longer seemed quite so unusual to many citizens. The public had greater difficulty a month later in accepting President Ford's "full, free, and absolute" pardon of Nixon on the grounds of sparing the country the agony of rehashing Watergate.

In response to the abuses of the Nixon administration, Congress adopted several reforms to contain the power of what historian Arthur M. Schlesinger, Jr., called "the imperial presidency." The War Powers Act of 1973 required the president to report any use of military force—such as had occurred in Korea, Vietnam, and Cambodia—to Congress within forty-eight hours and directed that hostilities must cease within sixty days unless Congress declared war. The 1974 Congressional Budget and Impoundment Control Act restricted the president's au-

thority to impound federal funds. The Fair Campaign Practices Act of 1974 limited campaign contributions and demanded stricter accounting of campaign expenditures. A strengthened Freedom of Information Act in 1974 gave citizens greater access to the files that the federal government had amassed on them.

In the aftermath of Watergate, twenty-five members of the Nixon administration went to prison, including Nixon's closest advisers, H. R. Haldeman, John Ehrlichman, and Attorney General John Mitchell. Richard Nixon retired to his estate in San Clemente, California. He refused to admit guilt for what had happened, conceding only that Watergate represented an error of judgment.

Lowered Expectations and New Challenges

During the decade after Watergate, some Americans began to suspect that the undisputed world preeminence of the United States since World War II was coming to an end. American economic power in the world market declined as the nation struggled with spiraling inflation, stagnant growth at home, and greater dependence on economic developments abroad. In the wake of Watergate, many citizens became cynical about the federal government and about politicians in general. A sense of growing impotence in foreign policy, foreshadowed by the ambiguities of American involvement in Vietnam, erupted in incidents such as the Iranian hostage crisis of 1979–1981 and the hijacking of a TWA jet by Shiite Muslim terrorists in Lebanon in 1985. In response to disturbing developments on the economic, political, and international fronts, many Americans grappled with the unwelcome idea that perhaps the United States no longer ranked as the world's most powerful country.

Economics, the Environment, and Energy

The American economy at the end of World War II was stronger than that of any other nation. Through the mid-1960s, it achieved a record of steady growth and expansion without inflation or high unemployment. But then the economic picture became clouded. The United States faced

THE COMPUTER REVOLUTION

The first modern computers—that is, information-processing machines capable of storing and manipulating data according to specified programs—appeared in the 1940s. During World War II, engineers and mathematicians at the University of Pennsylvania developed a general-purpose, programmable electronic calculator called ENIAC Electronic Numerator, Integrator, Analyzer and Computer), which could add five thousand ten-digit decimal numbers in one second. It stood eight feet tall, measured eighty feet long, and weighed thirty tons; it used eighteen thousand vacuum tubes for computations. When it performed complex mathematical computations, one scientist noted, ENIAC sounded "like a roomful of ladies knitting." Although ENIAC lacked a central memory and could not store a program, it was the bridge to the modern computer revolution.

By 1947, six computers were under construction, including UNIVAC (Universal Automatic Computer), the first commercial computer system. The word UN-IVAC was synonymous with computer to the general public in the 1950s. UNIVAC was basically a data-processing system that could be tailored to individual customers' needs. In 1951, the U.S. Census Bureau bought the first UNIVAC. Soon CBS-TV signed on, using a UNIVAC to predict the outcome of the 1952 presidential election. At 9 P.M., with only 7 percent of the votes counted, UNIVAC predicted that Dwight D. Eisenhower would sweep the election with 43 states and 438 electoral votes. CBS programmers and network executives, who had expected a closer election, got jittery and altered the program to produce more conservative findings. When the final tally gave 442 electoral votes to Eisenhower, only four votes off the original projection, commentator Edward R. Murrow confessed, "The trouble with machines is people."

Computers are essentially collections of switches, and programs tell the computer which switches to turn on and off. The puzzle that early computer scientists had to solve was how to increase the speed while lowering the cost of this basic operation. Machines like UNIVAC comprised the first generation of computers, which were characterized by their bulky size, dependence on vacuum tubes for computation power, and the use of punch cards for writing programs and analyzing data. Programming such a computer was a laborious process that could take several days because programmers manually had to set thousands of switches in the On or Off position. The fragile vacuum tubes were the weakest part of early computers; the failure of just a few tubes could shut down the entire system. Furthermore, vacuum tubes gave gave off enormous amounts of heat, necessitating noisy and cumbersome air-conditioning units wherever computers operated. Relay switches were also temperamental. After a critical signal relay stopped one early program, scientists finally located the problem—a dead moth trapped in the apparatus, the origin of the term "debugging."

The 1947 invention of the

increasing competition in the world economy, often from West Germany and Japan, which had rebuilt their industrial systems after the war. As a result, American goods were in less demand worldwide. In 1971, the United States had its first balance of trade deficit in almost eighty years. By the 1970s, the U.S. dollar was no longer the strongest currency on the world market. The combination of high prices and low demand stagnated production and produced a condition that came to be called "stagflation." As one Democratic politician defined it, stagflation meant "that all the things that should go up—the stock market, corporate profits, real spend-able income, productivity—go down, and all the things that should go down—unemployment, prices, interest rates—go up." These economic conditions set the tone for much of the 1970s.

One of the most destabilizing influences on the economy of the 1970s was the cost of energy, especially the price of imported oil. The United States consumed almost a third of the world's annual output of petroleum, although it had only 6 percent of the world population. Gasoline fueled American businesses and automobiles; industries that depended on petroleum, ranging from the automobile industry to those that produced such petrochemical by-products as plas-transistor, a development that revolutionized computers and also the whole field of electronics, made possible the second generation of computers. Transistors had the electrical properties of vacuum tubes, but they did not generate heat, burn out, or consume vast quantities of energy. They also were inexpensive to manufacture; a transistor is a semiconductor, and the most plentiful semiconductor is silicon (refined sand). The invention of integrated circuits (IC) in 1958, and greater sophistication in miniaturization, meant that the number of transistors which could be crammed on a silicon chip increased dramatically, with a corresponding increase in computational power. The first 256-bit Random Access Memory (RAM) chip appeared in 1968, soon followed by a 1,024-bit, or 1 K, RAM. By 1971, integrated circuits could contain the entire central processing unit (CPU) of a computer on a single chip called a microprocessor, about the size of the letter "O" on this page. By the mid-1970s, a one-dollar chip provided as much processing power as a computer that had cost a hundred thousand dollars just fifteen years earlier.

Although the microprocessor demonstrated that the technological capability existed to make small computers suitable for home use, industry leaders such as IBM saw no future in such models. Why would anyone want a computer at home? As a result, electronic hobbyists and computer "hackers" led the way in developing the personal computer. In 1974, the magazine *Radio Electronics* published an article on how to build your own computer. In 1975, *Popular Electronics* featured the new Altair 8800 computer, the first personal computer on the market. Its manufacturer, Micro Instrumentation and Telemetry Systems (MITS) in Albuquerque, New Mexico, was swamped with four hundred orders in one afternoon for the $395 kit ($650 assembled). The Altair 8800 had no software. Users had to write their own programs, entering them bit by bit through the toggle switches on the front. The machine had only 256 bytes of memory, too few to do much with the Altair except play with it, which computer hackers happily did.

The big breakthrough came from the upstart Apple Computer Company, the brainchild of Stephen Wozniak and Steven Jobs, two California computer hackers barely in their twenties. After perfecting a machine, they hired a designer who gave their computer a warm beige color and sleek plastic case. A rainbow-colored logo and an imaginative advertising campaign introduced the Apple II to the public in 1977 at a price of $1,195. Apple's annual sales soared from $775,000 in 1977 to almost $1 billion by 1983.

Since the early 1980s, however, the computer industry has entered a period of retrenchment and uncertainty. Industry leaders realized that the market for computers—and the software, games, and other accessories to go with them—was not nearly as huge as it had seemed in the heady days of Apple's early success.

---

tics and nylon, were crucial to the economic structure. The nation's global economic superiority had depended largely on the availability of cheap and abundant energy.

Political and economic developments in the Middle East after 1973 destroyed American complacency regarding energy resources. Oil-rich countries, a group comprised mostly of Arab states, had banded together into an organization called OPEC (Oil and Petroleum Exporting Countries), which began to flex its economic muscle by deliberately raising the price of oil. Between 1973 and 1975 the price of a barrel of oil quadrupled from three to twelve dollars. Because the United States depended heavily on cheap Middle Eastern oil, this price rise, which continued for the rest of the decade, set off a furious inflationary spiral.

Especially disruptive was the OPEC-instituted oil embargo in 1973–1974 in the wake of an Arab-Israeli war. In October 1973, Egyptian and Syrian forces had invaded Israel. They scored stunning military success, partly because Israelis were observing Yom Kippur, the holiest day in Judaism. At first, American policymakers had held back their support of Israel for fear of jeopardizing relations with the oil-producing countries. But the initial attack had been so

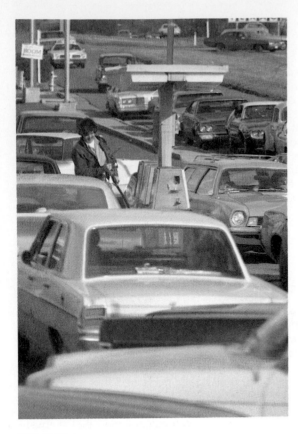

NO GAS
During the energy crisis of 1973–1974, American motorists faced widespread gasoline shortages for the first time since World War II. Although gas was not rationed, gas stations were closed on Sundays, air travel was cut by 10 percent, and a national speed limit of fifty-five miles an hour was imposed. (© Dennis Brack, Black Star)

cheap gasoline. Soon the domestic auto industry was in a recession, as Americans bought cheaper, more fuel-efficient foreign cars.

The energy crisis of the 1970s interacted with an environmental movement that had been building since the late 1960s. Early issues that galvanized public opinion included oil spills, such as one in January 1969 off the coast of Santa Barbara, California; the environmental impact of such projects as the Alaska pipeline, and a proposed airport in the Florida Everglades; and the harmful effects of pollution and smog, much of it produced by auto emissions. The environmental movement registered some early successes— enactment of the Clean Air Act and Water Quality Improvement Act in 1970 and the establishment of the Environmental Protection Agency and the Occupational Safety and Health Administration that same year. In 1971, Congress dropped plans to develop supersonic air transport partly because of environmental concerns.

THREE MILE ISLAND
On March 30, 1979, the Three Mile Island nuclear power plant near Harrisburg, Pennsylvania, came close to suffering a dangerous meltdown of its central core reactor. The accident, caused in part by the failure of safety systems and by human error, helped undermine American faith in nuclear technology, as did the Soviet nuclear disaster at Chernobyl in May 1986. (© Robert Moyer, Black Star).

devastating that the United States reversed its stand and sent enough supplies and military equipment to enable the Israelis to regain most of their lost territory. A ceasefire soon ended the fighting, but the international repercussions were just beginning. In retaliation against the United States, Western Europe, and Japan, which had aided Israel in the Yom Kippur War, OPEC halted all exports.

The United States scrambled to meet its domestic energy needs. The resulting gas shortage forced Americans to curtail their driving or spend long hours in line at the pumps. When they looked for more fuel-efficient cars, the automobile industry had nothing to offer but the "gas guzzlers" that had been built to run on

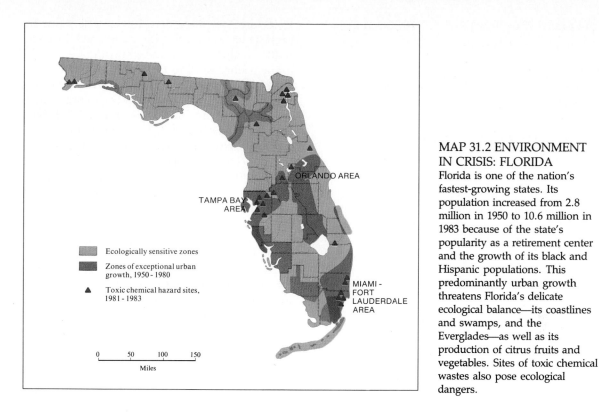

MAP 31.2 ENVIRONMENT IN CRISIS: FLORIDA
Florida is one of the nation's fastest-growing states. Its population increased from 2.8 million in 1950 to 10.6 million in 1983 because of the state's popularity as a retirement center and the growth of its black and Hispanic populations. This predominantly urban growth threatens Florida's delicate ecological balance—its coastlines and swamps, and the Everglades—as well as its production of citrus fruits and vegetables. Sites of toxic chemical wastes also pose ecological dangers.

The environmental movement also raised public awareness of the dangers inherent in the chemicals and petrochemical by-products that had become integral to American consumer goods, including foods, in the postwar period. In 1969, the Agriculture Department banned the use of the pesticide DDT, which, among its many disruptions to the food chain, weakened the shells of birds' eggs. Later in the 1970s, concern shifted to the medical consequences of careless dumping of toxic wastes, by-products of industrial processes. At Love Canal, near Niagara Falls, New York, a housing development had been built over an underground burial site of chemical wastes. Residents noticed that trees turned black and sparks escaped from the pavement; an even graver cause for concern was the abnormally high rate of miscarriages and birth defects reported by Love Canal families. Soon horror stories appeared about other poorly maintained waste-disposal sites across the country. "We just don't know how many potential Love Canals there are," admitted one federal official. "There are ticking time bombs all over."

Another environmental issue, nuclear power,

also produced citizen action. In response to the energy crisis, some politicians and business corporations promoted nuclear power as the solution to America's energy needs. By January 1974, forty-two nuclear power plants were in operation and more than a hundred more had been ordered. Their construction often provoked local protest from citizens concerned about their environmental impact. At a reactor construction site in Seabrook, New Hampshire, the "Clamshell Alliance" staged protests reminiscent of the antiwar demonstrations of the previous decade.

Long-standing public fears about nuclear safety seemed to be confirmed in March 1979. At Three Mile Island, outside Harrisburg, Pennsylvania, a nuclear plant came critically close to a meltdown of its central core reactor, which would have released dangerous levels of radioactive material into the environment. A hundred thousand residents were evacuated as a precaution. The problem was brought under control without a major catastrophe, but a member of the panel that investigated the accident admitted, "We were damn lucky."

Three Mile Island made Americans reassess

the future of nuclear power. Once billed as the solution to all energy needs, the cost overruns, faulty construction, and potential dangers of many nuclear power plants raised grave doubts about their viability. The energy shortage had no easy answer.

Post-Watergate Politics—Failed Leadership

Richard Nixon had hoped to end his two terms as president in 1976 with a triumphant celebration of the nation's two hundredth birthday. But by the time of the bicentennial, Nixon had been forced out of office and many Americans had grown cynical about the political process as a result of Vietnam and Watergate. "Don't vote. It only encourages them," read one bumper sticker during the 1976 presidential campaign. "The lesser of two evils is still evil" another proclaimed.

Gerald Ford, the former congressman from Michigan who had become vice-president after Spiro Agnew's resignation, never established his own legitimacy as president during the two years he held the office. His pardon of Nixon a month after becoming president hurt his credibility as a political leader. Distrust toward politicians spilled onto his choice for vice-president, Nelson A. Rockefeller, the former governor of New York, whose extensive family financial holdings were subjected to lengthy and acrimonious Senate hearings before he finally won confirmation.

Ford's biggest problem as president was the economy, reeling with inflation set in motion by spending for the Vietnam War and worsened by the OPEC price rises. The 1974 inflation rate soared to almost 12 percent. In an attempt to curtail runaway prices, the Federal Reserve tightened the money supply and drove up interest rates. In 1975, the economy entered the deepest downturn since the Great Depression. The government refused to increase spending or cut taxes as the economy contracted. Production declined more than 10 percent, and unemployment afflicted nearly 9 percent of the work force. The 1975 recession temporarily returned the inflation rate to less than 5 percent, but it soon rose again.

In foreign policy, Ford found little scope for presidential leadership. He maintained the continuity of Nixon's initiatives toward détente by asking Henry Kissinger to stay on as secretary of state. Ford kept arms control alive by meeting with Soviet leaders at Vladivostok to begin hammering out details of a hoped-for SALT II (Strategic Arms Limitation) agreement, but little concrete progress occurred. Ford and Kissinger followed Nixon's policy of increasing American support for the shah of Iran, failing to notice that the shah's policy of rapid modernization was provoking bitter opposition among Iran's faithful followers of Islam. The fall of Saigon to the North Vietnamese in 1975 reminded Americans of the failure of the Vietnam policy.

After the paranoia and abuses of the Nixon era, Ford's candor and honesty were a breath of fresh air in political life. But he failed to convince the nation that he had the strength to take charge in times of mounting economic and international problems. "Gerald Ford is an awfully nice man who isn't up to the presidency," *The New Republic* concluded. Governor Ronald Reagan of California almost wrested the 1976 Republican presidential nomination away from him, but Ford staved off this conservative challenge. However, he dumped liberal Vice-President Nelson Rockefeller in favor of hardline conservative Senator Robert J. Dole of Kansas.

Only in the skewed political atmosphere of post-Watergate America could the Democrats have chosen their nominee, James E. Carter, Jr., a former entrepreneur in agricultural commodities (chiefly peanuts) from Plains, Georgia, whose sole political experience had been as governor of that state. "Jimmy Who?" the media scoffed at first, but they soon changed their tune as Carter won delegates in key primaries that gave his candidacy both momentum and credibility. Carter played up his role as a Washington outsider; he pledged to restore morality to government, telling voters, "I will never lie to you." In one of the blandest campaigns in some years, both candidates avoided issues and controversy. Carter and his running mate, Senator Walter F. Mondale of Minnesota—whom Carter picked for his ties to traditional Democratic constituencies such as labor, liberals, blacks, and big-city machines—won the election with 50 percent of the popular vote to Ford's 48 percent.

FIGURE 31.1 INCREASE IN
THE CONSUMER PRICE
INDEX, 1960–1986

Jimmy Carter immediately tried to set a different tone for his administration. On Inauguration Day, he renounced formal wear in favor of a business suit; instead of riding in a limousine, he and his wife, Rosalynn, walked from the Capitol to the White House. Throughout his term, he relied heavily on symbolic gestures—dressing in an informal cardigan sweater for fireside chats to the nation, carrying his own luggage on and off planes, holding town meetings, and staying in the homes of ordinary citizens. Carter's homespun approach soon wore thin as people wondered what substance lay beneath the symbols.

Carter failed to develop an effective style of domestic leadership. His campaign as an outsider had distanced him from traditional sources of power in Washington, and he did little to heal this breach. Shying away from established Democratic leaders, he turned to a group of advisers and friends who had worked with him in Georgia, none of whom had national experience. When his budget director, Bert Lance, was questioned about financial irregularities at his Atlanta bank, the case undercut Carter's pledges to restore integrity and morality in government.

The nemesis of inflation presented the main domestic challenge for the Carter administration. When he took office, the nation was just coming out of the severe 1975 recession. To speed recovery, Carter called for increased spending and lower taxes. When that action provoked renewed inflation, he reversed himself, calling for spending cuts and a delay in the tax reductions. This zigzag fiscal policy did little to build either business or consumer confidence. Unemployment hovered between 6 and 7 percent, and inflation rose from 6.5 percent in 1977 to 12.4 percent in 1980, reaching the level of so-called double-digit inflation. As the Federal Reserve raised rates to counter inflation, interest rates briefly topped 20 percent in 1980, a historic high. A deep recession in 1982 broke the inflationary spiral.

Jimmy Carter had greater success in foreign policy, but even there his efforts often failed to produce the results he had hoped for. A commitment to human rights represented Carter's new direction in foreign affairs. He criticized the suppression of dissent in the Soviet Union—especially as it affected the right of Jewish citizens to emigrate—and withdrew economic and military aid from Argentina, Uruguay, Ethiopia, and other noncommunist countries that violated human rights. He also established an Office of Human Rights within the State Department.

President Carter scored a stunning success in the Middle East, a complex arena of international instability. Relations between Egypt and Israel had remained tense since the 1973 Yom Kippur War. In November 1975, Israel's prime minister, Menachem Begin, moved to break the ice by inviting Egyptian president Anwar Sadat to Israel to discuss the possibility of peace. Sadat came, but the talks stalled. Carter broke the stalemate in 1978 by inviting Begin and Sadat for further negotiations at Camp David, the presidential retreat in the Maryland mountains. Two weeks of discussions and Carter's promise of significant foreign aid persuaded Sadat and Begin to agree on a "framework for peace."

In Latin America, Carter's most important contribution was resolution of the dispute over control of the Panama Canal. Carter negotiated two treaties that acknowledged Panamanian

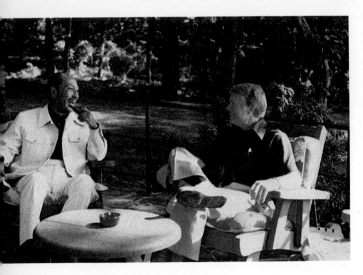

CARTER AND SADAT
President Jimmy Carter's greatest foreign policy
achievement was the personal diplomacy he exerted to
persuade Prime Minister Menachem Begin of Israel and
President Anwar Sadat of Egypt to sign a peace treaty in
1979. Carter, shown here with Sadat, met with the two
leaders both separately and together at Camp David.
(© J. P. Owen, Black Star)

sovereignty over the canal and increased Panama's canal toll revenue. In return, the United
States retained the right to send its ships through
the canal in case of war, even though the canal
itself was declared neutral territory. Despite a conservative outcry that the United States had
given away more than it got, the Senate approved
the treaty.

The most serious foreign problem of the Carter administration occurred in Iran. Early in
1979, a revolution led by a charismatic Muslim
zealot, the Ayatollah Ruhollah Khomeini, seized
power and drove the shah into exile. The United
States lost a strong and secure ally in the Middle
East, and American access to Iran's large oil reserves was jeopardized. Retaliating against a
controversial decision to admit the deposed shah
into the United States for medical treatment,
Muslim students under Khomeini's direction
seized the U.S. embassy in Teheran on November 4, 1979, taking fifty-three American hostages.
American television showed humiliating pictures
of blindfolded hostages at the hands of their
Muslim captors, who demanded that the shah
be returned to Iran for trial and punishment.
The hostages spent 444 days in captivity, win-

ning release at precisely the moment when
Jimmy Carter turned over the presidency to Ronald Reagan on January 20, 1981. The hostages returned home to an ecstatic patriotic welcome, a
reflection of American frustration over their long
ordeal.

While most Americans continued to maintain
patriotically that "We're Number One," the hostage crisis in Iran came to symbolize the loss of
the United States' power to control world affairs.
In many ways, this decline in influence resulted
from the unusual predominance the nation enjoyed after World War II. The return to economic
and political power of Japan and Western Europe, the control of vital oil resources by Middle
Eastern countries, and the industrialization of
part of the Third World had widened the cast
of international actors. Whether future administrations can forge a new U.S. policy to fit a
multipolar world remains to be seen. Many
Americans, however, resisted accepting anything less than the economic and political supremacy of the postwar years.

Social Trends

A new television program heralded the impending change in social mood between the 1960s
and 1970s. "All in the Family," starring Carroll
O'Connor as Archie Bunker and Jean Stapleton
as his long-suffering wife, Edith, premiered in
1969 and soon became one of the most successful television shows of all time. Mirroring the
concerns of the "silent majority" that had elected
Richard Nixon the previous year, Archie Bunker
railed against the social and cultural changes of
the 1960s—women's liberation, welfare mothers,
busing, and sexual permissiveness. The bum-
bling openness with which he expressed his
prejudices, and the smooth way that his family
neutralized his bigotry, brought the major social
issues of the day to prime-time television.

Archie Bunker's conservative rantings against
the social changes of the 1960s reflected the shifting national mood. No issue became more disruptive in the 1970s than that of forced busing of
children to achieve school integration. Although
the Supreme Court had called for desegregation
"with all deliberate speed" in 1954, little had
happened before 1970. In the 1970s, however,
the courts and the Justice Department pushed

for more action, first in the South, which complied, and then increasingly in northern cities, where deeply ingrained patterns of residential segregation produced all-black schools. The flight of white families to the suburbs made urban school systems even more racially imbalanced.

In 1971, the Supreme Court upheld a federal judge's order requiring the Charlotte, North Carolina, school system to use busing to achieve integration—that is, to transport students from their neighborhood schools in order to integrate the citywide school system. Although the Supreme Court in 1974 rejected the idea that suburban schools and city schools had to be combined to achieve racial balance, it made clear that northern cities would have to use busing within city boundaries to integrate their classrooms. These court decisions provoked controversy and violence; buses that transported black students to previously all-white schools were firebombed in Denver and in Pontiac, Michigan.

Some of the worst violence occurred in Boston in 1974–1975. The strongly Irish Catholic working-class neighborhood of South Boston responded to the arrival of black students from Roxbury with mob scenes reminiscent of Little Rock in 1957. Only armed riot police kept South Boston High School open. Many white parents in Boston, and in other cities threatened by court-ordered busing, transferred their children to private schools, increasing the racial imbalance that busing was intended to solve. By the late 1970s, however, the federal courts had backed away from their earlier insistence on busing to achieve racial balance, and local communities redoubled their efforts to preserve neighborhood schools.

Almost as divisive as busing was the implementation of affirmative action quotas to achieve racial and sexual balance. Quota systems were used in such areas as college admissions and employment. Whites, especially white males, soon raised the cry of "reverse discrimination," claiming they had been passed over in favor of less qualified minorities or women. In 1978, a white man named Allen Bakke sued the University of California Medical School at Davis, claiming it had rejected him while admitting minority candidates with lower qualifications. The Supreme Court ruling in *Bakke v. University of California* was inconclusive. By a 5 to 4 margin, the Court proclaimed the illegality of absolute quotas and ordered Bakke admitted to the medical school. At the same time, also by a 5 to 4 margin, it upheld the principle of affirmative action

AN ANTI-BUSING CONFRONTATION IN BOSTON
Tensions over court-ordered busing still ran high in Boston in 1976. When a black lawyer tried to cross the City Hall plaza during an antibusing demonstration, he became another victim of Boston's climate of racial hate and violence. This photograph by Stanley Forman for the *Boston Herald American*, showing protesters trying to impale the man with a flagstaff, won a Pulitzer Prize. (© Stanley Forman—Pulitzer Prize, 1976)

by ruling that racial factors could be considered in making hiring or admission decisions.

Most people, however, regarded the *Bakke* decision as a setback to the growing demands for economic and racial equality that had concerned the nation throughout the 1960s. The public outcries of the 1970s against forced busing and affirmative action formed part of a broader backlash against the social changes of the previous decade. Reflecting new conservatism in the social order, many citizens no longer supported the use of federal power or the political system to encourage further change. One target was feminism. The powerful antiabortion "right to life" movement and the stalled progress of the Equal Rights Amendment suggested the impact of this conservatism.

The mood of the 1970s also featured a retreat from idealism and a growing emphasis on personal fulfillment and enjoyment. It now became fashionable to admit to wanting to make money and be successful. (The 1980s coined the term "yuppies"—standing for "young urban professionals"—to denote these upwardly mobile achievers.) This widespread obsession with lifestyles and personal consumption led journalist Tom Wolfe to label the 1970s the "Me Decade" in an influential 1976 magazine article. In 1978, historian Christopher Lasch derisively called the new orientation the "culture of narcissism" in a widely read book of that title.

Much of the energy of personal liberation went into the fitness craze. Thousands of Americans began riding a ten-speed bicycle or working out on a Nautilus machine in a gym. Jim Fixx's *Complete Book of Running* (1977) spurred the jogging boom. In their fashionable Nike or Adidas running shoes, people tried to keep fit by completing their requisite miles per day. Marathons, once the province of an elite group of long-distance runners, became mass events, with thousands lining up to run the 26.2 mile course.

Americans also sought personal fulfillment through a variety of religious and communal movements that had sprung up in the late 1960s and early 1970s. Some joined encounter sessions—nicknamed "T-groups," for "sensitivity training"—in which they tried to "get in touch with their feelings." Many husbands and wives attended marriage-renewal conferences. Others turned to est (Erhard Seminars Training), Transcendental Meditation (TM), yoga, Zen, Hare Krishna, and Gestalt in a quest for the self. Some parents whose children had joined the Church of Scientology or the Unification Church of the Reverend Sun Myung Moon—whose followers were called "Moonies"—claimed the young people had been brainwashed to give up all their worldly possessions and adopt a rigidly communal life. When hundreds of American followers of the Reverend Jim Jones, a messianic cult leader, ritualistically drank fruit punch laced with cyanide at the "People's Temple" in Guyana in 1978, their mass suicide revealed the excesses of such cults.

The interest in religious cults and aids to inner awareness such as Zen and Transcendental Meditation were part of a major religious revival during the 1970s. Although *Time* magazine had posed the question "Is God Dead?" in a famous 1966 cover, religion in America had been undergoing a revival since the 1950s. Much of this new religious fervor occurred in evangelical Christian denominations, led by such preachers as Billy Graham who learned to use the media to spread the gospel. By the 1970s, seventy million Americans, almost a third of the population, claimed to be "born-again" Christians who had established a direct personal relationship with Jesus Christ. President Jimmy Carter proudly pro-

THE NEW RIGHT
In the 1970s and 1980s, the New Right actively mobilized conservative voters. Two of the movement's most vocal leaders, the Reverend Jerry Falwell and antifeminist crusader Phyllis Schlafly, are shown here at an antiabortion rally in Washington, D.C. (© David Burnett, Contact Press Images)

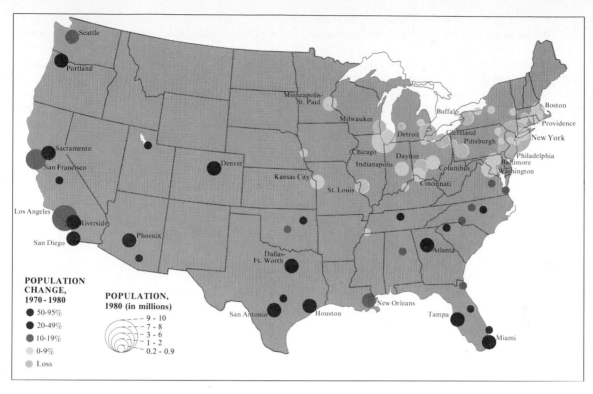

MAP 31.3 THE GROWTH OF THE SUN BELT
While older industrial cities, including New York, Chicago, Philadelphia, and Detroit, lost people in the 1970s, cities in the Sun Belt added to their populations. Between 1970 and 1980, older Sun Belt cities such as Dallas and Los Angeles recorded modest gains—6.8 percent and 4.9 percent, respectively. But booming metropolises registered large increases, among them San Jose, 36.1 percent; Phoenix, 33.7 percent; Houston, 26.1 percent; and San Diego, 24.7 percent.

claimed his born-again status, as did singers Pat Boone and Johnny Cash, former Watergate convicts Jeb Magruder and Charles Colson, and black power activist Eldridge Cleaver.

The religious enthusiasm represented by the evangelical Christians affected national life in concrete ways. Many evangelical groups set up their own school systems, newspapers, and broadcasting networks. The new religious fervor soon entered public life, as leaders such as the Reverend Jerry Falwell, who founded the Moral Majority in 1979, tried to inject their opinions on such sensitive issues as abortion, busing, school prayer, and censorship into political discourse. Yet leaders like Falwell and antifeminist crusader Phyllis Schlafly expressed their ideas with an absolutism and fanaticism that offended other people. "The Moral Majority is neither," read a popular bumper sticker. Nevertheless, the evan-

gelical religious revival and the new conservatism brought the country to the threshold of the 1980s.

Demographic Diversity

A statistical portrait of the United States in the 1970s and 1980s shows that Americans are living longer, having fewer children, divorcing more often, congregating in metropolitan areas, and enjoying better access to education. Most of these shifts had begun to emerge by the 1920s and 1930s, but they accelerated rapidly during the postwar years. These demographic characteristics supply many of the defining features of modern American life.

The 1980 census counted 226,504,825 Americans, an 11.5 percent increase over 1970 and more than twofold jump from the 106 million counted in 1920. The United States has increasingly become an urbanized society. By 1980, three-quarters of the population lived in urban areas (towns of more than 2,500 inhabitants). Since 1950, however, the rate of urbanization has slowed. Urban population increased only 0.1 percent between 1970 and 1980. The fastest-growing cities and metropolitan areas lay in the West, Southwest, and South. During the 1970s, Los Angeles grew 4 percent while older eastern and midwestern cities such as New York and Chicago declined 11 percent.

Major demographic changes in American lives took place during the post-1945 period. The most important trends, all interrelated to some degree, were the increase in the number of women who worked, a decline in the birth rate, the spread of family arrangements other than the traditional nuclear family, an increase in the number of elderly Americans, and broader access to education.

Perhaps the most dramatic social and economic change of the postwar period was the increase in the number of women working outside the home. In 1920, barely a fifth of all women belonged to the labor force; by 1980, more than half did; by the 1990s the figure is projected to reach 75 percent. The largest growth in the number of women who worked—especially married women—occurred during the postwar period. This transformation of women's roles set off a ripple effect throughout the social and economic structure.

The birth rate ranked as one of the demographic indicators most sensitive to social and economic influences. The birth rate in 1980 was only a fourth of what it had been in 1800, barely half of the rate in 1920. The later age at first marriage—22.1 years for women in 1980, 24.6 for men, both up two years from the 1950s—further reinforced the trend toward smaller families.

The declining birthrate affected both the size and the composition of the nation's households. In 1920, the average household consisted of 4.34 persons. By 1960, even during the postwar baby boom, it had shrunk to 3.3. Just twenty years later, the average household had only 2.75 people. Nor did this average household necessarily fit the traditional stereotype of family life—a gainfully employed father, a housemaker mother, and two children. According to the Labor Department, by the late 1970s only 7 percent of the nation's families matched that pattern. The number of unrelated adults living together became so prevalent that the Census Bureau invented a term to describe these new arrangements, POSSLQ ("persons of the opposite sex sharing living quarters"). A popular refrain the next Valentine's Day asked, "Will you be my POSS-L-Q?"

The growing diversity in the nation's households represented one of the most striking demographic developments of the 1970s. Although the nuclear family survived, many Americans chose alternative arrangements for part or all of their lives. The number of people living alone increased 60 percent in the 1970s; single people comprised almost a fourth of the nation's households, putting pressure on the nation's available housing and creating new markets for such consumer services as fast food. Many elderly people, because of increased benefits offered by Social Security, Medicare, and pension and disability funds, maintained their own households well into old age rather than depend on their children. Homosexual men and women set up households of their own.

The rise of single-parent households presented another variation on the traditional family structure. This new life-style resulted from the congruence of several demographic and social trends—women's ability to support themselves through paid employment, the increase in births to unwed mothers, and the rise in the divorce rate. By 1980, almost a fourth of all children under seventeen (17.3 percent of white children, 57.8 percent of black youngsters) lived with one parent—the mother in the overwhelming majority of cases. The percentage of households headed by women grew from 10.2 percent in 1970 to 17.5 percent in 1980. Since the average income of families headed by women amounted to less than half the national average, the preponderance of these households increased the feminization of poverty.

Marital instability, especially the dramatic increase in the divorce rate, contributed heavily to the rise of single-parent households. In 1920, only 1.6 divorces were recorded per one thousand persons; by 1980, the figure had jumped to

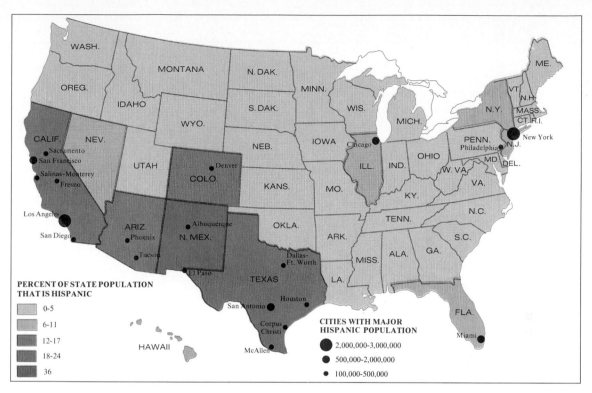

MAP 31.4 AMERICAN HISPANIC POPULATION, 1980
The Hispanic population of the United States is concentrated in California, New York, Texas, Florida, and Illinois, mainly in the major urban areas of those states. In eighteen states, including New Mexico, Arizona, Colorado, California, and Texas, the number of Hispanics exceeds the black population.

5.2. The rate rose most steeply between 1965 and 1975 and then moderated somewhat. Of all the marriages recorded in 1977, however, almost half seemed doomed to end in divorce. Divorce became so common that one commentator called it "almost a necessary initiation into adult relations." A divorce no longer carried the stigma it did in 1962, when it badly damaged the career of Governor Nelson Rockefeller of New York. Americans elected their first divorced president, Ronald Reagan, in 1980.

One of the demographic changes with the most far-reaching consequences was the increasing proportion of people over the age of sixty-five. During the 1970s, this segment of the population grew 20 percent because of the declining birth rate among young people and an increased life expectancy for older Americans. In 1960, for every 100 children under the age of five, there were 81 Americans over sixty-five; by 1980, there were 156. Life expectancy at birth rose from only 54.1 years in 1920 to 73.6 years by 1980. (Women's life expectancy remained consistently several years longer than men's, contributing to an unbalanced ratio between elderly men and women.) Because of the longer life spans, social scientists divided the elderly into two groups—"young old" (ages 65 to 75) and "old old" (75 and up).

In 1981, almost thirty-six million older Americans—approximately 92.5 percent of all those over sixty-five years old—received Social Security payments. The increase in access to Social Security, Medicare, and disability payments meant that workers could retire earlier. In 1980, 28 percent of all men between fifty-eight and sixty-four were not in the labor force, up from 13 percent in 1960. As a result of these cumulative demographic changes, a smaller pool of working Americans underwrote the retirement of a growing population of nonworkers.

Another defining characteristic of the modern age was increased access to education, especially after 1940. Among those aged twenty-five to twenty-nine in 1980, 85.7 percent had completed high school, a jump from 38.1 percent in 1940; in this same age group, the percentage who finished college rose from 5.9 percent in 1940 to 24.3 percent in 1980. Black college enrollment grew more than 250 percent as a result of the civil rights struggle. By the 1980s, however, skyrocketing tuition costs and cutbacks in federal student aid put higher education beyond the reach of even many middle-class families. Still,

Americans generally continued to view a college degree as a step toward personal and professional advancement.

The Reagan Revolution

The post-1968 period had witnessed the slow but steady decline of the New Deal Democratic coalition that dominated politics from Franklin Roosevelt's time to the late 1960s. Although Watergate gave the Democrats a temporary respite, Jimmy Carter's lackluster presidency failed to revitalize the faltering coalition. By the 1980s, the Democratic party no longer had the ability to control the national political system or to set the agenda of significant domestic and foreign issues.

At the same time that the Democrats were

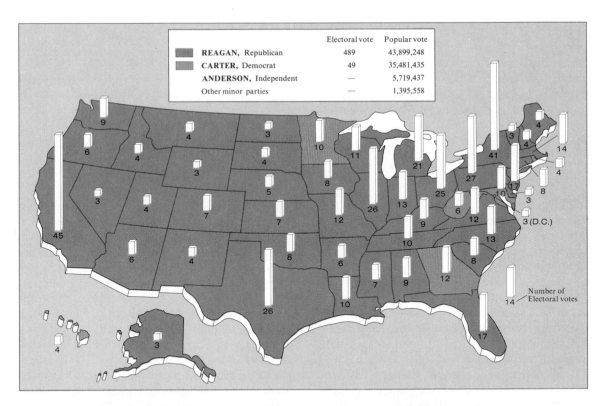

MAP 31.5 ELECTION OF 1980
Ronald Reagan defeated President Jimmy Carter convincingly in the 1980 election, carrying all but five states and the District of Columbia. Even more impressive was that the Republicans won control of the Senate for the first time since 1952 and made gains in the House of Representatives as well. At the age of sixty-nine, Reagan became the oldest person ever elected president.

losing their grip on the electorate, the Republican party was undergoing changes that pointed toward a future of electoral success. The core of the Republican party remained the affluent, upper-middle-class white Protestant voter. But new groups gravitated to the Republicans—southern whites disaffected by big government and civil rights; members of affluent ethnic groups, especially Catholics, who had moved to the suburbs; and young voters who identified themselves as conservatives. Since voting participation is consistently linked to income level, the Republicans benefited from a higher turnout at the polls by their more affluent supporters than did the Democrats, whose party bases lay in the sectors of society (especially the poor and blacks) that were less likely to vote.

Several other factors also sparked the Republican resurgence of the 1980s. Since Republicans had traditionally been the party of the well-to-do and the business community, they had access to financial resources that far outstripped those of the Democrats, whose main support came from the labor movement. This financial superiority enabled the Republicans to excel in direct mailing, fund-raising, and the sophisticated use of television in appealing to voters in the 1970s and 1980s. An additional factor energizing the Republican party was the rise of the New Right, whose social agenda included opposition to abortion, school busing, the Equal Rights Amendment, and the outlawing of prayer in schools. As a southerner and a devout evangelical protestant, Jimmy Carter captured much of this vote in 1976, but by 1980 the New Right was more comfortably ensconced in the Republican party, where its conservative social values formed the basis of the Republican platform. Ronald Reagan parlayed this base of support into a convincing electoral victory in 1980, roundly defeating Carter and Representative John B. Anderson of Illinois, an independent third-party candidate.

Soon after his inauguration, Ronald Reagan seized the chance to redefine the nation's priorities. Ever since Franklin Roosevelt's New Deal, the government had pursued a generally activist approach to social welfare on the assumption that social problems could best be handled by expanding federal action. The election of Ronald

PRESIDENT REAGAN
Ronald Reagan, a former actor, has proved especially adept at mobilizing public support for his policies. Congresswoman Patricia Schroeder of Colorado nicknamed Reagan's administration the "Teflon presidency" because of the tendency for bad news to slip off and leave Reagan's popularity and image unscathed. (© Dennis Brack, Black Star)

Reagan ended this almost fifty-year cycle of activism. "Government is not the solution to our problem," he declared. "Government is the problem." General economic prosperity would better serve the national welfare than government intrusion; freedom, not equality, would be the watchword.

Reagan first moved to reshape the nation's fiscal and tax policies. During his 1980 campaign, he had professed allegiance to the controversial theory of supply-side economics. Instead of increasing demand, Reagan and the supply-siders argued, the government should increase the supply of goods and services offered by the private sector. It could do this by reducing taxes, both for individuals and for businesses, and by balancing the budget. Fewer government regulations, in areas such as pollution control and affirmative action, would enable businesses to expand more productively. A revived economy would eventually yield higher tax revenues, even at lower tax rates.

Reagan won enactment of his economic

A FIRST FOR THE NATION
Geraldine Ferraro, a three-term congresswoman from
New York City, was chosen by Walter F. Mondale to be
his running mate against President Reagan in 1984.
Despite her presence on the ticket, a majority of women
voters supported Reagan. (© Dennis Brack, Black Star)

policy, often called "Reaganomics," from the
Republican-dominated Congress. The 1981 tax
bill was the first since the 1930s that did not produce at least a modest redistribution of income toward those at the lower end of the economic scale.
On the contrary, it favored the wealthy. Deep
cuts in the federal budget, especially for domestic programs, accompanied the tax cut. From
1980 to 1982, according to the Congressional
Budget Office, domestic spending on human resources fell by $101 billion. While congressional
resistance kept some of the more popular social
programs intact, more than half of Reagan's proposed cuts were enacted. The Reagan administration claimed that a "safety net" of welfare
programs would protect the truly needy, but the
net proved inadequate. The Census Bureau reported in 1982 that more than a sixth of all
Americans lived below the poverty line, the
highest proportion since 1965 and a 13 percent
rise over 1980.

The only area of the budget that escaped cuts
was the military, which benefited from Reagan's
commitment to beef up the defense establishment through a five-year, $1.7 trillion military
budget. The allocation of the federal budget
changed accordingly. Military spending in fiscal
1984 comprised 26.8 percent of the budget, up
from 22.6 percent in 1981. Meanwhile, spending
on nonmilitary domestic programs fell from 67.5
percent to 59.5 percent. The rest of the budget
paid the interest on the burgeoning federal debt,
which by 1985 approached $2 trillion.

FIGURE 31.2 THE ESCALATING
FEDERAL DEBT

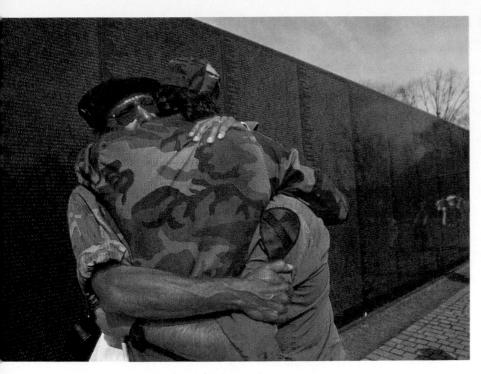

REMEMBERING VIETNAM
When soldiers came home from Vietnam, they received no general homecoming or welcome, no outpouring of support and respect as heroic defenders of freedom abroad. Many returning veterans simply slipped quietly back into the lives they had left behind, with their wounds—both physical and psychic—unhealed. The dedication of the Vietnam Memorial in Washington, D.C., in 1982 marked the beginning of process of reconciliation that is still going on. (© Peter Marlow, Magnum)

The 1982 recession challenged Reaganomics. Unemployment hit 10.7 percent, its highest level since the depression; black and female workers suffered the most. Due to the severe cutbacks in welfare programs, only 45 percent of those who lost their jobs received unemployment compensation, compared with 75 percent at the height of the harsh 1975 recession. The 1982 recession brought the inflation rate down from its high of 12.4 percent in 1980 to 4 percent. (The decline in worldwide energy costs aided the fight against inflation as well.) The tax cuts enacted in 1981 stimulated spending to bring the economy out of the recession. But politicians and economists still debate whether the economic recovery that began after 1982 resulted from Reagan's supply-side theories.

In one area—deregulation, or removing governmental controls on various facets of economic life—Reagan continued a trend begun during the Carter administration, but with several important differences. Carter focused mainly on regulatory agencies that had been created during the late nineteenth and early twentieth centuries. By the 1970s, he and others argued, such restric-

tions no longer served their original purposes but instead restricted competition and raised consumer costs. To rectify this situation, Carter had supported the gradual decontrol of oil and natural gas prices as a spur to domestic production and as a way to encourage conservation during the energy crisis. His administration also oversaw the deregulation of the airline, trucking, and railroad industries, as well as approving the phase-out of deposit interest ceiling rates in 1980.

President Reagan chose different targets for his deregulation efforts. His administration focused especially on agencies created during the 1970s, including the Environmental Protection Agency, the Occupational Safety and Health Administration, and the Consumer Product Safety Commission. It moved to abolish or lessen the impact of government regulations in areas such as the environment, the workplace, health care, and consumer protection, claiming that such regulations were not only inefficient but had impeded productivity because of the high cost of compliance. In addition, the Reagan administration used budget and staff cuts to make

THE AFTERMATH OF NUCLEAR WAR

Defense expenditures under Ronald Reagan brought little security from the fear of nuclear war. Jonathan Schell's The Fate of the Earth *(1982) argued that the only guarantee for surviving a nuclear attack was to prevent it from happening.*

Let us consider, for example, some of the possible ways in which a person in a targeted country might die. He might be incinerated by the fireball or the thermal pulse. He might be lethally irradiated by the initial nuclear radiation. He might be crushed to death or hurled to his death by the blast wave or its debris. He might be lethally irradiated by the local fallout. He might be burned to death in a firestorm. He might be injured by one or another of these effects and then die of his wounds before he was able to make his way out of the devastated zone in which he found himself. He might die of starvation, because the economy had collapsed and no food was being grown or delivered, or because existing local crops had been killed by radiation, or because the local ecosystem had been ruined, or because the ecosphere of the earth as a whole was collapsing. He might die of cold, for lack of heat and clothing, or of exposure, for lack of shelter. He might be killed by people seeking food or shelter that he had obtained. He might die of an illness spread in an epidemic. He might be killed by exposure to the sun if he stayed outside too long following serious ozone depletion. Or he might be killed by any combination of these perils. But while there is almost no end to the ways to die in and after a holocaust, each person has only one life to lose: someone who has been killed by the thermal pulse can't be killed again in an epidemic. Therefore, anyone who wishes to describe a holocaust is always at risk of depicting scenes of devastation that in reality would never take place, because the people in them would already have been killed off in some earlier scene of devastation. . . .

In trying to describe possible consequences of a nuclear holocaust, I have mentioned the limitless complexity of its effects on human society and on the ecosphere—a complexity that sometimes seems to be as great as that of life itself. But if these effects should lead to human extinction, then all the complexity will give way to the utmost simplicity—the simplicity of nothingness. We—the human race—shall cease to be.

Source: Jonathan Schell, *The Fate of the Earth.* New York: Knopf, 1982. 24, 95–96.

---

enforcement of existing regulations more difficult. Reagan further lessened the impact of formerly activist regulatory agencies on economic life by choosing appointees who shared his conservative outlook.

In foreign affairs, Reagan did not break as dramatically from postwar traditions as he had in domestic social policy. He argued that national security would be ensured by a stronger American military presence, coupled with cautious but direct action in the world's trouble spots. Reagan's plan to bring peace to the Middle East never got off the ground and was further complicated by the Israeli invasion of Lebanon in 1982. He sent a contingent of U.S. Marines to Lebanon to keep the peace, but 241 American troops were killed in a car bomb explosion in their Beirut barracks in October 1983. The Reagan administration stoutly proclaimed its intention to halt the spread of subversive communism in Central America. The United States supported a repressive right-wing regime in El Salvador in its fight against leftists, sent extensive military and financial aid to the pro-U.S. "contras" who challenged the communist Sandinista government in Nicaragua, and invaded the tiny Caribbean island of Grenada in 1983 to eliminate a Cuban-supported communist regime thought to threaten the other island states of the region. In 1985, Reagan met with the new leader of the Soviet Union, Mikhail S. Gorbachev, in the first summit meeting between the leaders of the world's two most powerful countries since 1979.

After a string of administrations that ended in discord (Johnson and Vietnam), disgrace (Nixon and Watergate), or frustration (Carter and Iran), many Americans responded warmly to Reagan's revival of the presidency as a tool of national leadership. Reagan restored such confidence in the economy and the presidency that when he asked voters during the 1984 campaign, "Are you better off than you were four years ago?", they answered affirmatively and gave him a landslide victory.

The 1984 Democratic challenger, Walter Mondale, symbolized the New Deal coalition. A protégé of Hubert Humphrey, he had strong ties to unions, blacks, and party leaders. He appealed to many women voters with his groundbreaking selection of Representative Geraldine Ferraro of New York as his running mate. But when the 1984 election thus pitted a popular incumbent Republican president against a New Deal liberal,

the contest was not even close. Reagan received 59 percent of the popular vote, carrying the entire country except Minnesota, Mondale's home state, and the District of Columbia. Reagan did especially well among young (eighteen- to twenty-one-year-old) voters, receiving 62 percent of their support.

Reagan's enormous personal popularity recalled Dwight Eisenhower's appeal in the 1950s and gave the Republicans their greatest strength since the 1920s. However, other Republican candidates in 1984 did not run nearly as well as the president, which allowed the Democrats to maintain control of the House and pick up two seats in the Senate.

The unanswered question clouding all

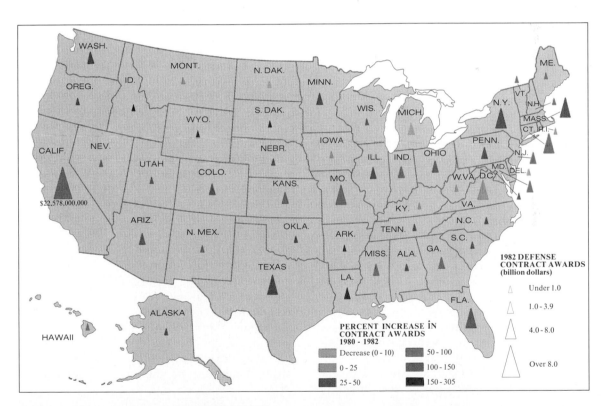

MAP 31.6 THE REAGAN DEFENSE BUILDUP

President Carter began to increase defense spending after its decline in the mid-1970s, but Ronald Reagan increased the buildup dramatically. California continued to be the top recipient of defense dollars. Its $22.5 billion share in 1982 was almost triple the amount received by New York and Texas. High-tech centers such as Connecticut, Massachusetts, and Virginia, as well as states with major defense installations (such as Alaska and Arizona), received defense contracts out of proportion to their population.

TIME LINE
A PROUD BUT TROUBLED PEOPLE

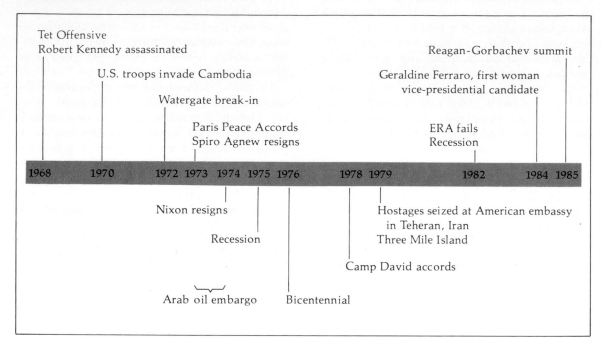

projections for the future was the impact of the increasing federal deficit on politics, government, and the economy. Despite his pledge to balance the budget by 1984, Reagan presided over the largest deficit in American history. From just over $50 billion when he took office in 1981, the deficit rose to an estimated $200 billion annually in 1984. In response, Congress passed the Gramm-Rudman Balanced Budget and Emergency Deficit Reduction Control Act of 1985, which required a balanced budget by 1991. As long as the deficit remained high, budget cutting, not problem solving, would probably assume top priority for the federal government as it approached the twenty-first century.

Despite cries by Ronald Reagan and others for a drastic cut in federal power, such attempts to turn back the clock of history are certain to fail. Perhaps the most far-reaching development of the twentieth century has been the growth of a new bureaucratic order comprised of large-scale national institutions that dominate both public policy and private enterprise. The federal government now plays the predominant role in the nation's economic life, contributing a major share of the nation's gross national product and controlling the growth of the private sector through tax and monetary policies. Although Reagan has changed the priorities of the national government and has attempted to curb its expansion, he has failed to reduce its size or scope. The America of the 1980s and beyond will remain dominated by the modern bureaucratic state.

The year 1968 saw an unprecedented level of domestic unrest, including the assassinations of Martin Luther King, Jr. and Robert F. Kennedy. Richard Nixon was elected president by promising to restore quieter times. However, the nation continued to debate the value of the American involvement in Vietnam, which did not end until the signing of the Paris Peace Accords in January 1973. Meanwhile, the Nixon administration took part in a series of illegal and questionable acts in connection with the president's campaign for reelection in 1972. The resulting Watergate scandal led to Nixon's resignation in 1974.

During the decade after 1974 the United States struggled with economic problems including high inflation, skyrocketing energy costs, and a diminished position in world trade. Many citizens became cynical about national leadership in the wake of Watergate. A new, more conservative social mood limited further progress of the civil rights and women's movements; this mood injected values drawn from evangelical religion into political life. Ronald Reagan capitalized on the changing atmosphere in 1980 by promising a smaller role for the government, a stronger commitment to traditional values, and an end to the burgeoning federal deficit. The one area of the federal budget that continued to grow unabated was defense.

The United States had changed immeasurably from the society it had been in 1900. Longer life spans, a declining birth rate, changing women's roles, greater access to education, and a new diversity in family and living patterns characterized the population. Giant economic and governmental structures further defined the distinctive character of modern American life. On the eve of the twenty-first century, the United States had demonstrably become a modern, post-industrial society.

Suggestions for Further Reading

A Time of Troubles

Two entirely different introductions to the 1968 campaign are provided in Norman Mailer, *Miami and the Siege of Chicago* (1968), and Lewis Chester, Godfrey Hodgson, and Bruce Page, *An American Melodrama* (1970), an account by three British journalists. Kevin Phillips, *The Emerging Republican Majority* (1969), and Richard Scammon and Ben J. Wattenberg, *The Real Majority* (1970), describe the voters whom Richard Nixon tried to reach. See also David Broder, *The Party's Over* (1972); Samuel Lubbell, *The Hidden Crisis in American Politics* (1975), and Frederick G. Dutton, *Changing Sources of Power* (1971). Theodore H. White, *The Making of the President—1972* (1973), covers the Nixon-McGovern contest.

Jonathan Schell, *The Time of Illusion* (1976), offers an insightful discussion of the Nixon administration. It can be supplemented by William Safire, *Before the Fall* (1975); Leonard Silk, *Nixonomics* (1972); and Rowland Evans and Robert Novak, *Nixon in the White House* (1971). Gary Wills, *Nixon Agonistes* (1971), provides a psychological portrait.

Stanley Karnouw, *Vietnam: A History* (1983), carries the story through the fall of Saigon in 1975. Tad Szulc, *The Illusion of Peace* (1978), is a general study of the foreign policy of the Nixon administration, while William Shawcross, *Sideshow: Kissinger, Nixon, and the Destruction of Cambodia* (1979), is strongly critical of one aspect. Robert Jay Lifton, *Home from the War* (1973); Paul Starr, *The Discarded Army* (1973); and Lawrence Baskir and William A. Strauss, *Chance and Circumstance* (1978), discuss the problems of returning Vietnam veterans. Ron Kovic, *Born on the Fourth of July* (1976), is a moving personal memoir.

Schell's *The Time of Illusion* links concern over antiwar protest with the Watergate scandal. Anthony Lukas, *Nightmare: The Underside of the Nixon Years* (1976), and Theodore H. White, *Breach of Faith* (1975), are comprehensive accounts. Also of interest are the two books by the *Washington Post* journalists who broke the story, Carl Bernstein and Bob Woodward, *All the President's Men* (1974) and *The Final Days* (1976). John Dean, *Blind Ambition* (1976), is the best account by a participant; see also H. R. Haldeman, *The Ends of Power* (1978), and Richard M. Nixon, *RN: The Memoirs of Richard Nixon* (1978). Richard M. Cohen and Jules Witcover, *A Heartbeat Away* (1974), describes Spiro Agnew's fall from power. Arthur M. Schlesinger, Jr., *The Imperial Presidency* (1973), analyzes changes in the institution that provided a backdrop for the Watergate affair.

Lowered Expectations and New Challenges

Peter Carroll, *It Seemed Like Nothing Happened* (1982), provides a historian's view of the 1970s. General introductions to economic developments of the decade are in Richard J. Barnet and Ronald E. Muller, *Global Reach* (1974); Richard J. Barnet, *The Lean Years* (1980); Robert

Calleo, *The Imperious Economy* (1982); and Gardner Means et al., *The Roots of Inflation* (1975). John M. Blair, *The Control of Oil* (1976), and J. C. Hurewitz, ed., *Oil, the Arab-Israeli Dispute, and the Industrial World* (1976), treat OPEC developments. Barry Commoner, *The Closing Circle* (1971) and *The Poverty of Power* (1976), and Robert Heilbroner, *An Inquiry into the Human Prospect* (1974), cogently assess the origins of the energy crisis and the prospects for the future. See also Lester C. Thurow, *The Zero-Sum Society* (1980), and Robert Stobaugh and Daniel Yergin, *Energy Future* (1980). Influential books in shaping public awareness of ecology included Paul R. Ehrlich, *The Population Bomb* (1968); E. F. Schumacher, *Small Is Beautiful* (1973); Frances Moore Lappe, *Diet for a Small Planet* (1971); and Philip Slater, *Earthwalk* (1974). On the prospects of nuclear annihilation, see Jonathan Schell's powerful *The Fate of the Earth* (1982).

Much of the material on post-Watergate politics has been provided by journalists rather than historians. Richard Reeves, *A Ford, Not a Lincoln* (1975); J. F. ter Horst, *Gerald Ford and the Future of the Presidency* (1974); and John Osborne, *White House Watch: The Ford Years* (1977), cover the Ford presidency. Jules Witcover, *Marathon* (1977), describes the pursuit of the presidency in 1976, while Theodore H. White, *America in Search of Itself* (1982), looks more broadly at the period between 1954 and 1980. Portraits of the Carter presidency, generally unfavorable, are found in Robert Shogan, *Promises to Keep* (1977); Haynes Johnson, *In the Absense of Power* (1980); and Clark Mollenhoff, *The President Who Failed* (1980). James Wooten, *Dasher* (1978), and Betty Glad, *Jimmy Carter: From Plains to the White House* (1980), are competent biographies. See also Jimmy Carter's own campaign manifesto, *Why Not the Best?* (1975). James Fallow, *National Defense* (1981), is an incisive overview of defense developments.

Carroll's *It Seemed Like Nothing Happened* provides a good introduction to the social trends of the 1970s. Stanley Aronowitz, *False Promises* (1973); Richard Krickus, *Pursuing the American Dream* (1976); and Michael Novak, *The Rise of the Unmeltable Ethnics* (1977), describe the concerns of the white ethnic middle-class. Richard P. Adler, *All in the Family* (1979), is an anthol-

ogy of the controversy surrounding Archie Bunker. Nathan Glazer, *Affirmative Discrimination: Ethnic Inequality and Public Policy* (1975); Thomas Sowell, *Race and Economics* (1975); and Allan P. Sindler, *Bakke, Defunis, and Minority Admissions* (1978), treat the controversial topic of affirmative action.

Tom Wolfe gave the decade its name in "The Me Decade and the Third Great Awakening," *New York Magazine* (August 23, 1976). Influential books included Christopher Lasch, *The Culture of Narcissism: American Life in an Age of Diminishing Expectations* (1978), and Gail Sheehy, *Passages* (1976). Alan Crawford, *Thunder on the Right* (1980), surveys the new conservatism, as does Peter Steinfels, *The Neo-Conservatives* (1979). John Woodridge, *The Evangelicals* (1975), and Marshall Frady, *Billy Graham* (1979), analyze the rise of evangelical religion; James Reston, Jr., *Our Father Who Art in Hell* (1981), tells the story of Reverend Jim Jones and the Guyana tragedy. Carol Felsenthal's biography of Phyllis Schlafly, *The Sweetheart of the Silent Majority* (1981), shows how the Moral Majority identified feminism as a target.

John L. Palmer and Isabel Sawhill, eds., *The Reagan Record* (1984), offers a comprehensive assessment of Reagan's first term in office. Thomas Byrne Edsall, *The New Politics of Inequality* (1984), analyzes the shift in politics and government from the activism of the Democratic years to the new priorities of the 1970s and 1980s. George Gilder, *Wealth and Poverty* (1981), represents the economic views held by many in the Reagan administration. On Reagan himself, see Bill Boyarsky, *Ronald Reagan: His Life and Rise to the Presidency* (1981).

Two books show that statistics can be fun to read, Andrew Hacker, *U/S: A Statistical Portrait* (1983), and Victor Fuchs, *How We Live* (1983). For material on the changing demographic and social base of the American family, see Christopher Lasch, *Haven in a Heartless World* (1977); Mary Jo Bane, *Here to Stay: American Families in the 20th Century* (1976), and Jane Howard, *Families* (1978). Columnist Ellen Goodman comments on changing American life-styles in *Close to Home* (1979). Betty Friedan, *The Second Stage* (1982), proposes a new phase of feminism that looks back to family values.

Declaration of Independence in Congress, July 4, 1776

THE UNANIMOUS DECLARATION
OF THE THIRTEEN
UNITED STATES OF AMERICA

When, in the course of human events, it becomes necessary for one people to dissolve the political bonds which have connected them with another, and to assume, among the powers of the earth, the separate and equal station to which the laws of nature and of nature's God entitle them, a decent respect to the opinions of mankind requires that they should declare the causes which impel them to the separation.

We hold these truths to be self-evident: That all men are created equal; that they are endowed by their Creator with certain unalienable rights; that among these are life, liberty, and the pursuit of happiness; that, to secure these rights, governments are instituted among men, deriving their just powers from the consent of the governed; that whenever any form of government becomes destructive of these ends, it is the right of the people to alter or to abolish it, and to institute new government, laying its foundation on such principles, and organizing its powers in such form, as to them shall seem most likely to effect their safety and happiness. Prudence, indeed, will dictate that governments long established should not be changed for light and transient causes; and accordingly all experience hath shown that mankind are more disposed to suffer, while evils are sufferable, than to right themselves by abolishing the forms to which they are accustomed. But when a long train of abuses and usurpations, pursuing invariably the same object, evinces a design to reduce them under absolute despotism, it is their right, it is their duty, to throw off such government, and to provide new guards for their future security. Such has been the patient sufferance of these colonies; and such is now the necessity which constrains them to alter their former systems of government. The history of the present King of Great Britain is a history of repeated injuries and usurpations, all having in direct object the establishment of an absolute tyranny over these states. To prove this, let facts be submitted to a candid world.

He has refused his assent to laws, the most wholesome and necessary for the public good.

He has forbidden his governors to pass laws of immediate and pressing importance, unless suspended in their operation till his assent should be obtained; and, when so suspended, he has utterly neglected to attend to them.

He has refused to pass other laws for the accommodation of large districts of people, unless those people would relinquish the right of representation in the legislature, a right inestimable to them, and formidable to tyrants only.

He has called together legislative bodies at places unusual, uncomfortable, and distant from the depository of their public records, for the sole purpose of fatiguing them into compliance with his measures.

He has dissolved representative houses repeatedly, for opposing, with manly firmness, his invasions on the rights of the people.

He has refused for a long time, after such dissolutions, to cause others to be elected; whereby the legislative powers, incapable of annihilation, have returned to the people at large for their exercise; the state remaining, in the mean time, exposed to all the dangers of invasions from without and convulsions within.

He has endeavored to prevent the population of these states; for that purpose obstructing the laws for naturalization of foreigners; refusing to pass others to encourage their migration hither, and raising the conditions of new appropriations of lands.

He has obstructed the administration of justice, by refusing his assent to laws for establishing judiciary powers.

He has made judges dependent on his will alone, for the tenure of their offices, and the amount and payment of their salaries.

He has erected a multitude of new offices, and sent hither swarms of officers to harass our people and eat out their substance.

He has kept among us, in times of peace, standing armies, without the consent of our legislatures.

He has affected to render the military independent of, and superior to, the civil power.

He has combined with others to subject us to a jurisdiction foreign to our constitution, and unacknowledged by our laws, giving his assent to their acts of pretended legislation:

For quartering large bodies of armed troops among us;

For protecting them, by a mock trial, from punishment for any murders which they should commit on the inhabitants of these states;

For cutting off our trade with all parts of the world;

For imposing taxes on us without our consent;

I

For depriving us, in many cases, of the benefits of trial by jury;

For transporting us beyond seas, to be tried for pretended offenses;

For abolishing the free system of English laws in a neighboring province, establishing therein an arbitrary government, and enlarging its boundaries, so as to render it at once an example and fit instrument for introducing the same absolute rule into these colonies;

For taking away our charters, abolishing our most valuable laws, and altering fundamentally the forms of our governments.

For suspending our own legislatures, and declaring themselves invested with power to legislate for us in all cases whatsoever.

He has abdicated government here, by declaring us out of his protection and waging war against us.

He has plundered our seas, ravaged our coasts, burned our towns, and destroyed the lives of our people.

He is at this time transporting large armies of foreign mercenaries to complete the works of death, desolation, and tyranny already begun with circumstances of cruelty and perfidy scarcely paralleled in the most barbarous ages, and totally unworthy the head of a civilized nation.

He has constrained our fellow-citizens, taken captive on the high seas, to bear arms against their country, to become the executioners of their friends and brethren, or to fall themselves by their hands.

He has excited domestic insurrection among us, and has endeavored to bring on the inhabitants of our frontiers the merciless Indian savages, whose known rule of warfare is an undistinguished destruction of all ages, sexes, and conditions.

In every stage of these oppressions we have petitioned for redress in the most humble terms; our repeated petitions have been answered only by repeated injury. A prince, whose character is thus marked by every act which may define a tyrant, is unfit to be the ruler of a free people.

Nor have we been wanting in our attentions to our British brethren. We have warned them, from time to time, of attempts by their legislature to extend an unwarrantable jurisdiction over us. We have reminded them of the circumstances of our emigration and settlement here. We have appealed to their native justice and magnanimity; and we have conjured them, by the ties of our common kindred, to disavow these usurpations, which would inevitably interrupt our connections and correspondence. They, too, have been deaf to the voice of justice and of consanguinity. We must, therefore, acquiesce in the necessity which denounces our separation, and hold them, as we hold the rest of mankind, enemies in war, in peace friends.

We, therefore, the representatives of the United States of America, in General Congress assembled, appealing to the Supreme Judge of the world for the rectitude of our intentions, do, in the name and by the authority of the good people of these colonies, solemnly publish and declare, that these United Colonies are, and of right ought to be, FREE AND INDEPENDENT STATES; that they are absolved from all allegiance to the British crown, and that all political connection between them and the state of Great Britain is, and ought to be, totally dissolved; and that, as free and independent states, they have full power to levy war, conclude peace, contract alliances, establish commerce, and do all other acts and things which independent states may of right do. And for the support of this declaration, with a firm reliance on the protection of Divine Providence, we mutually pledge to each other our lives, our fortunes, and our sacred honor.

JOHN HANCOCK

BUTTON GWINNETT
LYMAN HALL
GEO. WALTON
WM. HOOPER
JOSEPH HEWES
JOHN PENN
EDWARD RUTLEDGE
THOS. HEYWARD, JUNR.
THOMAS LYNCH, JUNR.
ARTHUR MIDDLETON
SAMUEL CHASE
WM. PACA
THOS. STONE
CHARLES CARROLL OF CARROLLTON
GEORGE WYTHE
RICHARD HENRY LEE
TH. JEFFERSON
BENJ. HARRISON

THOS. NELSON, JR.
FRANCIS LIGHTFOOT LEE
CARTER BRAXTON
ROBT. MORRIS
BENJAMIN RUSH
BENJA. FRANKLIN
JOHN MORTON
GEO. CLYMER
JAS. SMITH
GEO. TAYLOR
JAMES WILSON
GEO. ROSS
CAESAR RODNEY
GEO. READ
THO. M'KEAN
WM. FLOYD
PHIL. LIVINGSTON
FRANS. LEWIS
LEWIS MORRIS

RICHD. STOCKTON
JNO. WITHERSPOON
FRAS. HOPKINSON
JOHN HART
ABRA. CLARK
JOSIAH BARTLETT
WM. WHIPPLE
SAML. ADAMS
JOHN ADAMS
ROBT. TREAT PAINE
ELBRIDGE GERRY
STEP. HOPKINS
WILLIAM ELLERY
ROGER SHERMAN
SAM'EL. HUNTINGTON
WM. WILLIAMS
OLIVER WOLCOTT
MATTHEW THORNTON

Constitution of the United States of America

PREAMBLE

We the people of the United States, in order to form a more perfect union, establish justice, insure domestic tranquility, provide for the common defense, promote the general welfare, and secure the blessings of liberty to ourselves and our posterity, do ordain and establish this Constitution for the United States of America.

ARTICLE I

Section 1 All legislative powers herein granted shall be vested in a Congress of the United States, which shall consist of a Senate and a House of Representatives.

Section 2 The House of Representatives shall be composed of members chosen every second year by the people of the several States, and the electors in each State shall have the qualifications requisite for electors of the most numerous branch of the State Legislature.

No person shall be a Representative who shall not have attained to the age of twenty-five years, and been seven years a citizen of the United States, and who shall not, when elected, be an inhabitant of that State in which he shall be chosen.

Representatives and direct taxes shall be apportioned among the several States which may be included within this Union, according to their respective numbers, *which shall be determined by adding to the whole number of free persons, including those bound to service for a term of years and excluding Indians not taxed, three-fifths of all other persons.* The actual enumeration shall be made within three years after the first meeting of the Congress of the United States, and within every subsequent term of ten years, in such manner as they shall by law direct. The number of Representatives shall not exceed one for every thirty thousand, but

Note: The Constitution became effective March 4, 1789. Provisions in italic have been changed by constitutional amendment.

each State shall have at least one Representative; *and until such enumeration shall be made, the State of New Hampshire shall be entitled to choose three, Massachusetts eight, Rhode Island and Providence Plantations one, Connecticut five, New York six, New Jersey four, Pennsylvania eight, Delaware one, Maryland six, Virginia ten, North Carolina five, South Carolina five, and Georgia three.*

When vacancies happen in the representation from any State, the Executive authority thereof shall issue writs of election to fill such vacancies.

The House of Representatives shall choose their Speaker and other officers; and shall have the sole power of impeachment.

Section 3 The Senate of the United States shall be composed of two Senators from each State, *chosen by the legislature thereof,* for six years; and each Senator shall have one vote.

Immediately after they shall be assembled in consequence of the first election, they shall be divided as equally as may be into three classes. The seats of the Senators of the first class shall be vacated at the expiration of the second year, of the second class at the expiration of the fourth year, and of the third class at the expiration of the sixth year, so that one-third may be chosen every second year; *and if vacancies happen by resignation or otherwise, during the recess of the legislature of any State, the Executive thereof may make temporary appointments until the next meeting of the legislature, which shall then fill such vacancies.*

No person shall be a Senator who shall not have attained to the age of thirty years, and been nine years a citizen of the United States, and who shall not, when elected, be an inhabitant of that State for which he shall be chosen.

The Vice-President of the United States shall be President of the Senate, but shall have no vote, unless they be equally divided.

The Senate shall choose their other officers, and also a President *pro tempore*, in the absence of the Vice-President, or when he shall exercise the office of President of the United States.

The Senate shall have the sole power to try all impeachments. When sitting for that purpose, they shall be on oath or affirmation. When the President of the

United States is tried, the Chief Justice shall preside; and no person shall be convicted without the concurrence of two-thirds of the members present.

Judgment in cases of impeachment shall not extend further than to removal from the office, and disqualification to hold and enjoy any office of honor, trust or profit under the United States: but the party convicted shall nevertheless be liable and subject to indictment, trial, judgment and punishment, according to law.

Section 4 The times, places and manner of holding elections for Senators and Representatives shall be prescribed in each State by the legislature thereof; but the Congress may at any time by law make or alter such regulations, except as to the places of choosing Senators.

The Congress shall assemble at least once in every year, and such meeting *shall be on the first Monday in December, unless they shall by law appoint a different day.*

Section 5 Each house shall be the judge of the elections, returns and qualifications of its own members, and a majority of each shall constitute a quorum to do business; but a smaller number may adjourn from day to day, and may be authorized to compel the attendance of absent members, in such manner, and under such penalties, as each house may provide.

Each house may determine the rules of its proceedings, punish its members for disorderly behavior, and with the concurrence of two-thirds, expel a member.

Each house shall keep a journal of its proceedings, and from time to time publish the same, excepting such parts as may in their judgment require secrecy; and the yeas and nays of the members of either house on any question shall, at the desire of one-fifth of those present, be entered on the journal.

Neither house, during the session of Congress, shall, without the consent of the other, adjourn for more than three days, nor to any other place than that in which the two houses shall be sitting.

Section 6 The Senators and Representatives shall receive a compensation for their services, to be ascertained by law and paid out of the treasury of the United States. They shall in all cases except treason, felony and breach of the peace be privileged from arrest during their attendance at the session of their respective houses, and in going to and returning from the same; and for any speech or debate in either house, they shall not be questioned in any other place.

No Senator or Representative shall, during the time for which he was elected, be appointed to any civil office under the authority of the United States, which shall have been created, or the emoluments whereof shall have been increased, during such time; and no person holding any office under the United States

shall be a member of either house during his continuance in office.

Section 7 All bills for raising revenue shall originate in the House of Representatives; but the Senate may propose or concur with amendments as on other bills.

Every bill which shall have passed the House of Representatives and the Senate, shall, before it becomes a law, be presented to the President of the United States; if he approve he shall sign it, but if not he shall return it with objections to that house in which it originated, who shall enter the objections at large on their journal, and proceed to reconsider it. If after such reconsideration two-thirds of that house shall agree to pass the bill, it shall be sent, together with the objections, to the other house, by which it shall likewise be reconsidered, and, if approved by two-thirds of that house, it shall become a law. But in all such cases the votes of both houses shall be determined by yeas and nays, and the names of the persons voting for and against the bill shall be entered on the journal of each house respectively. If any bill shall not be returned by the President within ten days (Sundays excepted) after it shall have been presented to him, the same shall be a law, in like manner as if he had signed it, unless the Congress by their adjournment prevent its return, in which case it shall not be a law.

Every order, resolution, or vote to which the concurrence of the Senate and House of Representatives may be necessary (except on a question of adjournment) shall be presented to the President of the United States; and before the same shall take effect, shall be approved by him, or being disapproved by him, shall be repassed by two-thirds of the Senate and House of Representatives, according to the rules and limitations prescribed in the case of a bill.

Section 8 The Congress shall have power:

To lay and collect taxes, duties, imposts, and excises, to pay the debts and provide for the common defense and general welfare of the United States; but all duties, imposts and excises shall be uniform throughout the United States;

To borrow money on the credit of the United States;

To regulate commerce with foreign nations, and among the several States, and with the Indian tribes;

To establish an uniform rule of naturalization, and uniform laws on the subject of bankruptcies throughout the United States;

To coin money, regulate the value thereof, and of foreign coin, and fix the standard of weights and measures;

To provide for the punishment of counterfeiting the securities and current coin of the United States;

To establish post offices and post roads;

To promote the progress of science and useful arts by securing for limited times to authors and inventors the exclusive right to their respective writings and discoveries;

To constitute tribunals inferior to the Supreme Court;

To define and punish piracies and felonies committed on the high seas and offenses against the law of nations;

To declare war, grant letters of marque and reprisal, and make rules concerning captures on land and water;

To raise and support armies, but no appropriation of money to that use shall be for a longer term than two years;

To provide and maintain a navy;

To make rules for the government and regulation of the land and naval forces;

To provide for calling forth the militia to execute the laws of the Union, suppress insurrections, and repel invasions;

To provide for organizing, arming, and disciplining the militia, and for governing such part of them as may be employed in the service of the United States, reserving to the States respectively the appointment of the officers, and the authority of training the militia according to the discipline prescribed by Congress;

To exercise exclusive legislation in all cases whatsoever, over such district (not exceeding ten miles square) as may, by cession of particular States, and the acceptance of Congress, become the seat of government of the United States, and to exercise like authority over all places purchased by the consent of the legislature of the State, in which the same shall be, for erection of forts, magazines, arsenals, dockyards, and other needful buildings;—and

To make all laws which shall be necessary and proper for carrying into execution the foregoing powers; and all other powers vested by this Constitution in the government of the United States, or in any department or officer thereof.

Section 9 *The migration or importation of such persons as any of the States now existing shall think proper to admit shall not be prohibited by the Congress prior to the year 1808; but a tax or duty may be imposed on such importation, not exceeding $10 for each person.*

The privilege of the writ of habeas corpus shall not be suspended, unless when in cases of rebellion or invasion the public safety may require it.

No bill of attainder or ex post facto law shall be passed.

No capitation or other direct tax shall be laid, unless in proportion to the census or enumeration herein before directed to be taken.

No tax or duty shall be laid on articles exported from any State.

No preference shall be given by any regulation of commerce or revenue to the ports of one State over those of another; nor shall vessels bound to, or from, one State be obliged to enter, clear, or pay duties in another.

No money shall be drawn from the treasury, but in consequence of appropriations made by law; and a regular statement and account of the receipts and expenditures of all public money shall be published from time to time.

No title of nobility shall be granted by the United States: and no person holding any office of profit or trust under them, shall, without the consent of the Congress, accept of any present, emolument, office, or title, of any kind whatever, from any king, prince, or foreign state.

Section 10 No State shall enter into any treaty, alliance, or confederation; grant letters of marque and reprisal; coin money; emit bills of credit; make anything but gold and silver coin a tender in payment of debts; pass any bill of attainder, ex post facto law, or law impairing the obligation of contracts, or grant any title of nobility.

No States shall, without the consent of Congress, lay any imposts or duties on imports or exports, except what may be absolutely necessary for executing its inspection laws: and the net produce of all duties and imposts, laid by any State on imports or exports, shall be for the use of the treasury of the United States; and all such laws shall be subject to the revision and control of the Congress.

No State shall, without the consent of Congress, lay any duty of tonnage, keep troops or ships of war in time of peace, enter into any agreement or compact with another State, or with a foreign power, or engage in war, unless actually invaded, or in such imminent danger as will not admit of delay.

ARTICLE II

Section 1 The executive power shall be vested in a President of the United States of America. He shall hold his office during the term of four years, and, together with the Vice-President, chosen for the same term, be elected as follows:

Each State shall appoint, in such manner as the legislature thereof may direct, a number of electors, equal to the whole number of Senators and Representatives to which the State may be entitled in the Congress; but no Senator or Representative, or person holding an office of trust or profit under the United States, shall be appointed an elector.

The electors shall meet in their respective States, and vote by ballot for two persons, of whom one at least shall not be an inhabitant of the same State with themselves. And they shall make a list of all the persons voted for, and of the number of votes for each; which list they shall sign and certify, and transmit sealed to the seat of government of the United States, directed to the President of the Senate. The President of the Senate shall, in the presence of the Senate and House of Representatives, open all the certificates, and the votes shall then be counted. The person having the greatest number of votes shall be the President, if such number be a majority of the whole number of electors appointed; and if there be more than one who have such majority, and have an equal number of votes, then the House of Representatives shall immediately choose by ballot one of them for President; and if no person have a majority, then from the five highest on the list said house shall in like manner choose the President. But in choosing the President the votes shall be taken by States, the representation from each State having one vote; a quorum for this purpose shall consist of a member or members from two-thirds of the States, and a majority of all the States shall be necessary to a choice. In every case, after the choice of the President, the person having the greatest number of votes of the electors shall be the Vice-President. But if there should remain two or more who have equal votes, the Senate shall choose from them by ballot the Vice-President.

The Congress may determine the time of choosing the electors and the day on which they shall give their votes; which day shall be the same throughout the United States.

No person except a natural-born citizen, *or a citizen of the United States at the time of the adoption of this constitution,* shall be eligible to the office of President; neither shall any person be eligible to that office who shall not have attained to the age of thirty-five years, and been fourteen years a resident within the United States.

In case of the removal of the President from office or of his death, resignation, or inability to discharge the powers and duties of the said office, the same shall devolve on the Vice-President, and the Congress may by law provide for the case of removal, death, resignation, or inability, both of the President and Vice-President, declaring what officer shall then act as President, and such officer shall act accordingly, until the disability be removed, or a President shall be elected.

The President shall, at stated times, receive for his services a compensation, which shall neither be increased nor diminished during the period for which he shall have been elected, and he shall not receive within that period any other emolument from the United States, or any of them.

Before he enter on the execution of his office, he shall take the following oath or affirmation:—"I do solemnly swear (or affirm) that I will faithfully execute the office of the President of the United States, and will to the best of my ability preserve, protect and defend the Constitution of the United States."

Section 2   The President shall be commander in chief of the army and navy of the United States, and of the militia of the several States, when called into the actual service of the United States; he may require the opinion, in writing, of the principal officer in each of the executive departments, upon any subject relating to the duties of their respective offices, and he shall have power to grant reprieves and pardons for offenses against the United States, except in cases of impeachment.

He shall have power, by and with the advice and consent of the Senate, to make treaties, provided two-thirds of the Senators present concur; and he shall nominate, and by and with the advice and consent of the Senate, shall appoint ambassadors, other public ministers and consuls, judges of the Supreme Court, and all other officers of the United States, whose appointments are not herein otherwise provided for, and which shall be established by law; but Congress may by law vest the appointment of such inferior officers, as they think proper, in the President alone, in the courts of law, or in the heads of departments.

The President shall have power to fill up all vacancies that may happen during the recess of the Senate, by granting commissions which shall expire at the end of their next session.

Section 3   He shall from time to time give to the Congress information of the state of the Union, and recommend to their consideration such measures as he shall judge necessary and expedient; he may, on extraordinary occasions, convene both houses, or either of them, and in case of disagreement between them, with respect to the time of adjournment, he may adjourn them to such time as he shall think proper; he shall receive ambassadors and other public ministers; he shall take care that the laws be faithfully executed, and shall commission all the officers of the United States.

Section 4   The President, Vice-President and all civil officers of the United States shall be removed from office on impeachment for, and on conviction of, treason, bribery, or other high crimes and misdemeanors.

ARTICLE III

Section 1   The judicial power of the United States shall be vested in one Supreme Court, and in such inferior courts as the Congress may from time to time ordain and establish. The judges, both of the Supreme and inferior courts, shall hold their offices during good behavior, and shall, at stated times, receive for their services a compensation which shall not be diminished during their continuance in office.

Section 2 The judicial power shall extend to all cases, in law and equity, arising under this Constitution, the laws of the United States, and treaties made, or which shall be made, under their authority—to all cases affecting ambassadors, other public ministers and consuls;—to all cases of admiralty and maritime jurisdiction;—to controversies to which the United States shall be a party;—to controversies between two or more States;—*between a State and citizens of another State;*—between citizens of different States;—between citizens of the same State claiming lands under grants of different States, and between a State, or the citizens thereof, and foreign states, citizens or subjects.

In all cases affecting ambassadors, other public ministers and consuls, and those in which a State shall be party, the Supreme Court shall have original jurisdiction. In all the other cases before mentioned, the Supreme Court shall have appellate jurisdiction, both as to law and fact, with such exceptions, and under such regulations, as the Congress shall make.

The trial of all crimes, except in cases of impeachment, shall be by jury; and such trial shall be held in the State where said crimes shall have been committed; but when not committed within any State, the trial shall be at such place or places as the Congress may by law have directed.

Section 3 Treason against the United States shall consist only in levying war against them, or in adhering to their enemies, giving them aid and comfort. No person shall be convicted of treason unless on the testimony of two witnesses to the same overt act, or on confession in open court.

The Congress shall have power to declare the punishment of treason, but no attainder of treason shall work corruption of blood, or forfeiture except during the life of the person attainted.

ARTICLE IV

Section 1 Full faith and credit shall be given in each State to the public acts, records, and judicial proceedings of every other State. And the Congress may by general laws prescribe the manner in which such acts, records, and proceedings shall be proved, and the effect thereof.

Section 2 The citizens of each State shall be entitled to all privileges and immunities of citizens in the several states.

A person charged in any State with treason, felony, or other crime, who shall flee from justice, and be found in another State, shall on demand of the executive authority of the State from which he fled, be delivered up, to be removed to the State having jurisdiction of the crime.

No person held to service or labor in one State, under the laws thereof, escaping into another, shall, in consequence of any law or regulation therein, be discharged from such service or labor, but shall be delivered up on claim of the party to whom such service or labor may be due.

Section 3 New States may be admitted by the Congress into this Union; but no new State shall be formed or erected within the jurisdiction of any other State; nor any State be formed by the junction of two or more States, or parts of States, without the consent of the legislatures of the States concerned as well as of the Congress.

The Congress shall have power to dispose of and make all needful rules and regulations respecting the territory or other property belonging to the United States; and nothing in this Constitution shall be so construed as to prejudice any claims of the United States, or any particular State.

Section 4 The United States shall guarantee to every State in this Union a republican form of government, and shall protect each of them against invasion; and on application of the legislature, or of the executive (when the legislature cannot be convened), against domestic violence.

ARTICLE V

The Congress, whenever two-thirds of both houses shall deem it necessary, shall propose amendments to this Constitution, or, on the application of the legislatures of two-thirds of the several States, shall call a convention for proposing amendments, which, in either case, shall be valid to all intents and purposes, as part of this Constitution, when ratified by the legislatures of three-fourths of the several States, or by conventions in three-fourths thereof, as the one or the other mode of ratification may be proposed by the Congress; provided *that no amendments which may be made prior to the year one thousand eight hundred and eight shall in any manner affect the first and fourth classes in the ninth section of the first article; and* that no State, without its consent, shall be deprived of its equal suffrage in the Senate.

ARTICLE VI

All debts contracted and engagements entered into, before the adoption of this Constitution, shall be as valid against the United States under this Constitution, as under the Confederation.

This Constitution, and the laws of the United States which shall be made in pursuance thereof; and all treaties made, or which shall be made, under the authority of the United States, shall be the supreme law of the land; and the judges in every State shall be bound thereby, anything in the Constitution or laws of any State to the contrary notwithstanding.

The Senators and Representatives before mentioned, and the members of the several State legislatures, and all executive and judicial officers, both of the United States and of the several States, shall be bound by oath or affirmation to support this Constitution; but no religious test shall ever be required as a qualification to any office or public trust under the United States.

ARTICLE VII

The ratification of the conventions of nine States shall be sufficient for the establishment of this Constitution between the States so ratifying the same.

Done in Convention by the unanimous consent of the States present, the seventeenth day of September in the year of our Lord one thousand seven hundred and eighty-seven and of the Independence of the United States of America the twelfth. In witness whereof we have hereunto subscribed our names.

GEORGE WASHINGTON
President and Deputy from Virginia

New Hampshire
JOHN LANGDON
NICHOLAS GILMAN

Massachusetts
NATHANIEL GORHAM
RUFUS KING

Connecticut
WILLIAM S. JOHNSON
ROGER SHERMAN

New York
ALEXANDER HAMILTON

New Jersey
WILLIAM LIVINGSTON
DAVID BREARLEY
WILLIAM PATERSON
JONATHAN DAYTON

Pennsylvania
BENJAMIN FRANKLIN
THOMAS MIFFLIN
ROBERT MORRIS
GEORGE CLYMER
THOMAS FITZSIMONS
JARED INGERSOLL
JAMES WILSON
GOUVERNEUR MORRIS

Delaware
GEORGE READ
GUNNING BEDFORD, JR.
JOHN DICKINSON
RICHARD BASSETT
JACOB BROOM

Maryland
JAMES McHENRY
DANIEL OF ST. THOMAS JENIFER
DANIEL CARROLL

Virginia
JOHN BLAIR
JAMES MADISON, JR.

North Carolina
WILLIAM BLOUNT
RICHARD DOBBS SPRAIGHT
HU WILLIAMSON

South Carolina
J. RUTLEDGE
CHARLES C. PINCKNEY
PIERCE BUTLER

Georgia
WILLIAM FEW
ABRAHAM BALDWIN

Amendments to the Constitution

AMENDMENT I [1791]

Congress shall make no law respecting an establishment of religion, or prohibiting the free exercise thereof; or abridging the freedom of speech, or of the press; or the right of the people peaceably to assemble, and to petition the government for a redress of grievances.

AMENDMENT II [1791]

A well-regulated militia being necessary to the security of a free State, the right of the people to keep and bear arms shall not be infringed.

AMENDMENT III [1791]

No soldier shall, in time of peace, be quartered in any house without the consent of the owner, nor in time of war, but in a manner to be prescribed by law.

AMENDMENT IV [1791]

The right of the people to be secure in their persons, houses, papers, and effects, against unreasonable searches and seizures, shall not be violated, and no warrants shall issue but upon probable cause, supported by oath or affirmation, and particularly describing the place to be searched, and the persons or things to be seized.

AMENDMENT V [1791]

No person shall be held to answer for a capital or otherwise infamous crime, unless on a presentment or indictment of a grand jury, except in cases arising in the land or naval forces, or in the militia, when in actual service in time of war or public danger; nor shall any person be subject for the same offense to be twice put in jeopardy of life or limb; nor shall be compelled

Note: The first ten Amendments are known as the Bill of Rights.

in any criminal case to be a witness against himself, nor be deprived of life, liberty, or property, without due process of law; nor shall private property be taken for public use without just compensation.

AMENDMENT VI [1791]

In all criminal prosecutions, the accused shall enjoy the right to a speedy and public trial, by an impartial jury of the State and district wherein the crime shall have been committed, which district shall have been previously ascertained by law, and to be informed of the nature and cause of the accusation; to be confronted with the witnesses against him; to have compulsory process for obtaining witnesses in his favor, and to have the assistance of counsel for his defense.

AMENDMENT VII [1791]

In suits at common law, where the value in controversy shall exceed twenty dollars, the right of trial by jury shall be preserved, and no fact tried by a jury shall be otherwise reexamined in any court of the United States, than according to the rules of the common law.

AMENDMENT VIII [1791]

Excessive bail shall not be required, nor excessive fines imposed, nor cruel and unusual punishments inflicted.

AMENDMENT IX [1791]

The enumeration in the Constitution, of certain rights, shall not be construed to deny or disparage others retained by the people.

AMENDMENT X [1791]

The powers not delegated to the United States by the Constitution, nor prohibited by it to the States, are reserved to the States respectively, or to the people.

AMENDMENT XI [1798]

The judicial power of the United States shall not be construed to extend to any suit in law or equity, commenced or prosecuted against one of the United States by citizens of another State, or by citizens or subjects of any foreign state.

AMENDMENT XII [1804]

The electors shall meet in their respective States, and vote by ballot for President and Vice-President, one of whom, at least, shall not be an inhabitant of the same State with themselves; they shall name in their ballots the person voted for as President, and in distinct ballots the person voted for as Vice-President, and they shall make distinct lists of all persons voted for as President, and of all persons voted for as Vice-President, and of the number of votes for each, which lists they shall sign and certify, and transmit sealed to the seat of government of the United States, directed to the President of the Senate;—the President of the Senate shall, in the presence of the Senate and House of Representatives, open all the certificates and the votes shall then be counted;—the person having the greatest number of votes for President shall be the President, if such number be a majority of the whole number of electors appointed; and if no person have such majority, then from the persons having the highest numbers not exceeding three on the list of those voted for as President, the House of Representatives shall choose immediately, by ballot, the President. But in choosing the President, the votes shall be taken by States, the representation from each State having one vote; a quorum for this purpose shall consist of a member or members from two-thirds of the States, and a majority of all the States shall be necessary to a choice. And if the House of Representatives shall not choose a President whenever the right of choice shall devolve upon them, before *the fourth day of March* next following, then the Vice-President shall act as President, as in the case of the death or other constitutional disability of the President.

The person having the greatest number of votes as Vice-President shall be the Vice-President, if such number be a majority of the whole number of electors appointed; and if no person have a majority, then from the two highest numbers on the list the Senate shall choose the Vice-President; a quorum for the purpose shall consist of two-thirds of the whole number of Senators, and a majority of the whole number shall be necessary to a choice. But no person constitutionally ineligible to the office of President shall be eligible to that of Vice-President of the United States.

AMENDMENT XIII [1865]

Section 1 Neither slavery nor involuntary servitude, except as a punishment for crime whereof the party shall have been duly convicted, shall exist within the United States, or any place subject to their jurisdiction.

Section 2 Congress shall have power to enforce this article by appropriate legislation.

AMENDMENT XIV [1868]

Section 1 All persons born or naturalized in the United States, and subject to the jurisdiction thereof, are citizens of the United States and of the State wherein they reside. No State shall make or enforce any law which shall abridge the privileges or immunities of citizens of the United States; nor shall any State deprive any person of life, liberty, or property, without due process of law; nor deny to any person within its jurisdiction the equal protection of the laws.

Section 2 Representatives shall be apportioned among the several States according to their respective numbers, counting the whole number of persons in each State, excluding Indians not taxed. But when the right to vote at any election for the choice of Electors for President and Vice-President of the United States, Representatives in Congress, the executive and judicial officers of a State, or the members of the legislature thereof, is denied to any of the male inhabitants of such State, being twenty-one years of age and citizens of the United States, or in any way abridged, except for participation in rebellion, or other crime, the basis of representation therein shall be reduced in the proportion which the number of such male citizens shall bear to the whole number of male citizens twenty-one years of age in such State.

Section 3 No person shall be a Senator or Representative in Congress, or Elector of President and Vice-President, or hold any office, civil or military, under the United States, or under any State, who, having previously taken an oath, as a member of Congress, or as an officer of the United States, or as a member of any State legislature, or as an executive or judicial officer of any State, to support the Constitution of the United States, shall have engaged in insurrection or rebellion against the same, or given aid or comfort to the enemies thereof. Congress may by a vote of two-thirds of each house, remove such disability.

Section 4 The validity of the public debt of the United States, authorized by law, including debts incurred for payment of pensions and bounties for services in suppressing insurrection or rebellion, shall not be questioned. But neither the United States nor any State shall assume or pay any debt or obligation incurred in aid of insurrection or rebellion against the United States, or any claim for the loss of emancipation of any slave; but all such debts, obligations, and claims shall be held illegal and void.

Section 5   The Congress shall have power to enforce, by appropriate legislation, the provisions of this article.

AMENDMENT XV [1870]

Section 1   The right of citizens of the United States to vote shall not be denied or abridged by the United States or by any State on account of race, color, or previous condition of servitude.

Section 2   The Congress shall have power to enforce this article by appropriate legislation.

AMENDMENT XVI [1913]

The Congress shall have power to lay and collect taxes on incomes, from whatever source derived, without apportionment among the several States, and without regard to any census or enumeraion.

AMENDMENT XVII [1913]

Section 1   The Senate of the United States shall be composed of two Senators from each State, elected by the people thereof, for six years; and each Senator shall have one vote. The electors in each State shall have the qualifications requisite for electors of [voters for] the most numerous branch of the State legislatures.

Section 2   When vacancies happen in the representation of any State in the Senate, the executive authority of such State shall issue writs of election to fill such vacancies: Provided that the legislature of any State may empower the executive thereof to make temporary appointments until the people fill the vacancies by election as the legislature may direct.

Section 3   This amendment shall not be so construed as to affect the election or term of any Senator chosen before it becomes valid as part of the Constitution.

AMENDMENT XVIII [1919]

Section 1   After one year from the ratification of this article the manufacture, sale, or transportation of intoxicating liquors within, the importation thereof into, or the exportation thereof from the United States and all territory subject to the jurisdiction thereof, for beverage purposes, is hereby prohibited.

Section 2   The Congress and the several States shall have concurrent power to enforce this article by appropriate legislation.

Section 3   This article shall be inoperative unless it shall have been ratified as an amendment to the Constitution by the legislatures of the several States, as provided by the Constitution, within seven years from the date of the submission thereof to the States by the Congress.

AMENDMENT XIX [1920]

Section 1   The right of citizens of the United States to vote shall not be denied or abridged by the United States or by any State on account of sex.

Section 2   The Congress shall have power to enforce this article by appropriate legislation.

AMENDMENT XX [1933]

Section 1   The terms of the President and Vice-President shall end at noon on the 20th day of January, and the terms of Senators and Representatives at noon on the 3d day of January, of the years in which such terms would have ended if this article had not been ratified; and the terms of their successors shall then begin.

Section 2   The Congress shall assemble at least once in every year, and such meeting shall begin at noon on the 3d day of January, unless they shall by law appoint a different day.

Section 3   If, at the time fixed for the beginning of the term of the President, the President-elect shall have died, the Vice-President-elect shall become President. If a President shall not have been chosen before the time fixed for the beginning of his term, or if the President-elect shall have failed to qualify, then the President-elect shall act as President until a President shall have qualified; and the Congress may by law provide for the case wherein neither a President-elect nor a Vice-President-elect shall have qualified, declaring who shall then act as President, or the manner in which one who is to act shall be selected, and such persons shall act accordingly until a President or Vice-President shall have qualified.

Section 4   The Congress may by law provide for the case of the death of any of the persons from whom the House of Representatives may choose a President whenever the right of choice shall have devolved upon them, and for the case of the death of any of the persons from whom the Senate may choose a Vice-President whenever the right of choice shall have devolved upon them.

Section 5   Sections 1 and 2 shall take effect on the 15th day of October following the ratification of this article.

Section 6   This article shall be inoperative unless it shall have been ratified as an amendment to the Constitution by the legislatures of three-fourths of the several States within seven years from the date of its submission.

AMENDMENT XXI [1933]

Section 1   The eighteenth article of amendment to the Constitution of the United States is hereby repealed.

Section 2   The transportation or importation into any State, Territory, or Possession of the United States for delivery or use therein of intoxicating liquors, in violation of the laws thereof, is hereby prohibited.

Section 3   This article shall be inoperative unless it shall have been ratified as an amendment to the Constitution by conventions in the several States, as provided in the Constitution, within seven years from the date of submission thereof to the States by the Congress.

AMENDMENT XXII [1951]

Section 1   No person shall be elected to the office of President more than twice, and no person who has held the office of President, or acted as President, for more than two years of a term to which some other person was elected President shall be elected to the office of President more than once. But this article shall not apply to any person holding the office of President when this article was proposed by the Congress, and shall not prevent any person who may be holding the office of President, or acting as President, during the term within which this article becomes operative from holding the office of President or acting as President during the remainder of such term.

Section 2   This article shall be inoperative unless it shall have been ratified as an amendment to the Constitution by the legislatures of three-fourths of the several States within seven years from the date of its submission to the States by the Congress.

AMENDMENT XXIII [1961]

Section 1   The District constituting the seat of Government of the United States shall appoint in such manner as the Congress may direct:

A number of electors of President and Vice-President equal to the whole number of Senators and Representatives in Congress to which the District would be entitled if it were a State, but in no event more than the least populous State; they shall be in addition to those appointed by the States, but they shall be considered for the purposes of the election of President and Vice-President, to be electors appointed by a State; and they shall meet in the District and perform such duties as provided by the twelfth article of amendment.

Section 2   The Congress shall have the power to enforce this article by appropriate legislation.

AMENDMENT XXIV [1964]

Section 1   The right of citizens of the United States to vote in any primary or other election for President or Vice-President, for electors for President or Vice-President, or for Senator or Representative in Congress, shall not be denied or abridged by the United States or any State by reason of failure to pay any poll tax or other tax.

Section 2   The Congress shall have the power to enforce this article by appropriate legislation.

AMENDMENT XXV [1967]

Section 1   In case of the removal of the President from office or of his death or resignation, the Vice-President shall become President.

Section 2   Whenever there is a vacancy in the office of the Vice-President, the President shall nominate a Vice-President who shall take office upon confirmation by a majority vote of both houses of Congress.

Section 3   Whenever the President transmits to the President pro tempore of the Senate and the Speaker of the House of Representatives his written declaration that he is unable to discharge the powers and duties of his office, and until he transmits to them a written declaration to the contrary, such powers and duties shall be discharged by the Vice-President as Acting President.

Section 4   Whenever the Vice-President and a majority of either the principal officers of the executive departments or of such other body as Congress may by law provide, transmit to the President pro tempore of the Senate and the Speaker of the House of Representatives their written declaration that the President is unable to discharge the powers and duties of his office, the Vice-President shall immediately assume the powers and duties of the office as Acting President.

Thereafter, when the President transmits to the President pro tempore of the Senate and the Speaker of the House of Representatives his written declaration that no inability exists, he shall resume the powers and duties of his office unless the Vice-President and a majority of either the principal officers of the executive departments[s] or of such other body as Congress may by law provide, transmit within four days to the President pro tempore of the Senate and the Speaker of the House of Representatives their written declaration that

the President is unable to discharge the powers and duties of his office. Thereupon Congress shall decide the issue, assembling within forty-eight hours for that purpose if not in session. If the Congress, within twenty-one days after receipt of the latter written declaration, or, if Congress is not in session, within twenty-one days after Congress is required to assemble, determines by two-thirds vote of both Houses that the President is unable to discharge the powers and duties of his office, the Vice-President shall continue to discharge the same as Acting President; otherwise, the President shall resume the powers and duties of his office.

AMENDMENT XXVI [1971]

Section 1   The right of citizens of the United States, who are eighteen years of age or older, to vote shall not be denied or abridged by the United States or by any State on account of age.

Section 2   The Congress shall have power to enforce this article by appropriate legislation.

Presidential Elections

Year	Candidates	Parties	Percent of Popular Vote	Electoral Vote	Percent Voter Participation
1789	GEORGE WASHINGTON	No party designations	*	69	
	John Adams†			34	
	Other candidates			35	
1792	GEORGE WASHINGTON	No party designations		132	
	John Adams			77	
	George Clinton			50	
	Other candidates			5	
1796	JOHN ADAMS	Federalist		71	
	Thomas Jefferson	Democratic-Republican		68	
	Thomas Pinckney	Federalist		59	
	Aaron Burr	Democratic-Republican		30	
	Other candidates			48	
1800	THOMAS JEFFERSON	Democratic-Republican		73	
	Aaron Burr	Democratic-Republican		73	
	John Adams	Federalist		65	
	Charles C. Pinckney	Federalist		64	
	John Jay	Federalist		1	
1804	THOMAS JEFFERSON	Democratic-Republican		162	
	Charles C. Pinckney	Federalist		14	
1808	JAMES MADISON	Democratic-Republican		122	
	Charles C. Pinckney	Federalist		47	
	George Clinton	Democratic-Republican		6	
1812	JAMES MADISON	Democratic-Republican		128	
	DeWitt Clinton	Federalist		89	
1816	JAMES MONROE	Democratic-Republican		183	
	Rufus King	Federalist		34	
1820	JAMES MONROE	Democratic-Republican		231	
	John Quincy Adams	Independent Republican		1	
1824	JOHN QUINCY ADAMS	Democratic-Republican	30.5	84	26.9
	Andrew Jackson	Democratic-Republican	43.1	99	
	Henry Clay	Democratic-Republican	13.2	37	
	William H. Crawford	Democratic-Republican	13.1	41	

*Prior to 1824, most presidential electors were chosen by state legislators rather than by popular vote.
†Before the Twelfth Amendment was passed in 1804, the electoral college voted for two presidential candidates; the runner-up became the vice-president.

Year	Candidates	Parties	Percent of Popular Vote	Electoral Vote	Percent Voter Participation
1828	ANDREW JACKSON	Democratic	56.0	178	57.6
	John Quincy Adams	National Republican	44.0	83	
1832	ANDREW JACKSON	Democratic	54.5	219	55.4
	Henry Clay	National Republican	37.5	49	
	William Wirt	Anti-Masonic	8.0	7	
	John Floyd	Democratic	‡	11	
1836	MARTIN VAN BUREN	Democratic	50.9	170	57.8
	William H. Harrison	Whig		73	
	Hugh L. White	Whig	49.1	26	
	Daniel Webster	Whig		14	
	W. P. Mangum	Whig		11	
1840	WILLIAM H. HARRISON	Whig	53.1	234	80.2
	Martin Van Buren	Democratic	46.9	60	
1844	JAMES K. POLK	Democratic	49.6	170	78.9
	Henry Clay	Whig	48.1	105	
	James G. Birney	Liberty	2.3		
1848	ZACHARY TAYLOR	Whig	47.4	163	72.7
	Lewis Cass	Democratic	42.5	127	
	Martin Van Buren	Free Soil	10.1		
1852	FRANKLIN PIERCE	Democratic	50.9	254	69.6
	Winfield Scott	Whig	44.1	42	
	John P. Hale	Free Soil	5.0		
1856	JAMES BUCHANAN	Democratic	45.3	174	78.9
	John C. Frémont	Republican	33.1	114	
	Millard Fillmore	American	21.6	8	
1860	ABRAHAM LINCOLN	Republican	39.8	180	81.2
	Stephen A. Douglas	Democratic	29.5	12	
	John C. Breckinridge	Democratic	18.1	72	
	John Bell	Constitutional Union	12.6	39	
1864	ABRAHAM LINCOLN	Republican	55.0	212	73.8
	George B. McClellan	Democratic	45.0	21	
1868	ULYSSES S. GRANT	Republican	52.7	214	78.1
	Horatio Seymour	Democratic	47.3	80	
1872	ULYSSES S. GRANT	Republican	55.6	286	71.3
	Horace Greeley	Democratic	43.9		
1876	RUTHERFORD B. HAYES	Republican	48.0	185	81.8
	Samuel J. Tilden	Democratic	51.0	184	
1880	JAMES A. GARFIELD	Republican	48.5	214	79.4
	Winfield S. Hancock	Democratic	48.1	155	
	James B. Weaver	Greenback-Labor	3.4		
1884	GROVER CLEVELAND	Democratic	48.5	219	77.5
	James G. Blaine	Republican	48.2	182	
1888	BENJAMIN HARRISON	Republican	47.9	233	79.3
	Grover Cleveland	Democratic	48.6	168	

‡Candidates receiving less than 2.5 percent of the popular vote have been omitted. Hence the percentage of popular vote may not total 100 percent.

Year	Candidates	Parties	Percent of Popular Vote	Electoral Vote	Percent Voter Participation
1892	GROVER CLEVELAND	Democratic	46.1	277	74.7
	Benjamin Harrison	Republican	43.0	145	
	James B. Weaver	People's	8.5	22	
1896	WILLIAM McKINLEY	Republican	51.1	271	79.3
	William J. Bryan	Democratic	47.7	176	
1900	WILLIAM McKINLEY	Republican	51.7	292	73.2
	William J. Bryan	Democratic; Populist	45.5	155	
1904	THEODORE ROOSEVELT	Republican	57.4	336	65.2
	Alton B. Parker	Democratic	37.6	140	
	Eugene V. Debs	Socialist	3.0		
1908	WILLIAM H. TAFT	Republican	51.6	321	65.4
	William J. Bryan	Democratic	43.1	162	
	Eugene V. Debs	Socialist	2.8		
1912	WOODROW WILSON	Democratic	41.9	435	58.8
	Theodore Roosevelt	Progressive	27.4	88	
	William H. Taft	Republican	23.2	8	
	Eugene V. Debs	Socialist	6.0		
1916	WOODROW WILSON	Democratic	49.4	277	61.6
	Charles E. Hughes	Republican	46.2	254	
	A. L. Benson	Socialist	3.2		
1920	WARREN G. HARDING	Republican	60.4	404	49.2
	James M. Cox	Democratic	34.2	127	
	Eugene V. Debs	Socialist	3.4		
1924	CALVIN COOLIDGE	Republican	54.0	382	48.9
	John W. Davis	Democratic	28.8	136	
	Robert M. LaFollette	Progressive	16.6	13	
1928	HERBERT C. HOOVER	Republican	58.2	444	56.9
	Alfred E. Smith	Democratic	40.9	87	
1932	FRANKLIN D. ROOSEVELT	Democratic	57.4	472	56.9
	Herbert C. Hoover	Republican	39.7	59	
1936	FRANKLIN D. ROOSEVELT	Democratic	60.8	523	61.0
	Alfred M. Landon	Republican	36.5	8	
1940	FRANKLIN D. ROOSEVELT	Democratic	54.8	449	62.5
	Wendell L. Willkie	Republican	44.8	82	
1944	FRANKLIN D. ROOSEVELT	Democratic	53.5	432	55.9
	Thomas E. Dewey	Republican	46.0	99	
1948	HARRY S TRUMAN	Democratic	49.6	303	53.0
	Thomas E. Dewey	Republican	45.1	189	
1952	DWIGHT D. EISENHOWER	Republican	55.1	442	63.3
	Adlai E. Stevenson	Democratic	44.4	89	
1956	DWIGHT D. EISENHOWER	Republican	57.6	457	60.6
	Adlai E. Stevenson	Democratic	42.1	73	
1960	JOHN F. KENNEDY	Democratic	49.7	303	64.0
	Richard M. Nixon	Republican	49.5	219	
1964	LYNDON B. JOHNSON	Democratic	61.1	486	61.7
	Barry M. Goldwater	Republican	38.5	52	

Year	Candidates	Parties	Percent of Popular Vote	Electoral Vote	Percent Voter Participation
1968	RICHARD M. NIXON	Republican	43.4	301	60.6
	Hubert H. Humphrey	Democratic	42.7	191	
	George C. Wallace	American Independent	13.5	46	
1972	RICHARD M. NIXON	Republican	60.7	520	55.5
	George S. McGovern	Democratic	37.5	17	
1976	JIMMY CARTER	Democratic	50.1	297	54.3
	Gerald R. Ford	Republican	48.0	240	
1980	RONALD REAGAN	Republican	50.7	489	53.0
	Jimmy Carter	Democratic	41.0	49	
	John B. Anderson	Independent	6.6	0	
1984	RONALD REAGAN	Republican	58.4	525	52.9
	Walter F. Mondale	Democratic	41.6	13	

Admission of States into the Union

State	Date of Admission	State	Date of Admission
1. Delaware	December 7, 1787	26. Michigan	January 26, 1837
2. Pennsylvania	December 12, 1787	27. Florida	March 3, 1845
3. New Jersey	December 18, 1787	28. Texas	December 29, 1845
4. Georgia	January 2, 1788	29. Iowa	December 28, 1846
5. Connecticut	January 9, 1788	30. Wisconsin	May 29, 1848
6. Massachusetts	February 6, 1788	31. California	September 9, 1850
7. Maryland	April 28, 1788	32. Minnesota	May 11, 1858
8. South Carolina	May 23, 1788	33. Oregon	February 14, 1859
9. New Hampshire	June 21, 1788	34. Kansas	January 29, 1861
10. Virginia	June 25, 1788	35. West Virginia	June 20, 1863
11. New York	July 26, 1788	36. Nevada	October 31, 1864
12. North Carolina	November 21, 1789	37. Nebraska	March 1, 1867
13. Rhode Island	May 29, 1790	38. Colorado	August 1, 1876
14. Vermont	March 4, 1791	39. North Dakota	November 2, 1889
15. Kentucky	June 1, 1792	40. South Dakota	November 2, 1889
16. Tennessee	June 1, 1796	41. Montana	November 8, 1889
17. Ohio	March 1, 1803	42. Washington	November 11, 1889
18. Louisiana	April 30, 1812	43. Idaho	July 3, 1890
19. Indiana	December 11, 1816	44. Wyoming	July 10, 1890
20. Mississippi	December 10, 1817	45. Utah	January 4, 1896
21. Illinois	December 3, 1818	46. Oklahoma	November 16, 1907
22. Alabama	December 14, 1819	47. New Mexico	January 6, 1912
23. Maine	March 15, 1820	48. Arizona	February 14, 1912
24. Missouri	August 10, 1821	49. Alaska	January 3, 1959
25. Arkansas	June 15, 1836	50. Hawaii	August 21, 1959

Supreme Court Justices

Name	Terms of Service[1]	Appointed by	Name	Terms of Service[1]	Appointed by
John Jay*, N.Y.	1789–1795	Washington	Joseph P. Bradley, N.J.	1870–1892	Grant
James Wilson, Pa.	1789–1798	Washington	Ward Hunt, N.Y.	1873–1882	Grant
John Rutledge, S.C.	1790–1791	Washington	**Morrison R. Waite,** Ohio	1874–1888	Grant
William Cushing, Mass.	1790–1810	Washington	John M. Harlan, Ky.	1877–1911	Hayes
John Blair, Va.	1790–1796	Washington	William B. Woods, Ga.	1881–1887	Hayes
James Iredell, N.C.	1790–1799	Washington	Stanley Matthews, Ohio	1881–1889	Garfield
Thomas Johnson, Md.	1792–1793	Washington	Horace Gray, Mass.	1882–1902	Arthur
William Paterson, N.J.	1793–1806	Washington	Samuel Blatchford, N.Y.	1882–1893	Arthur
John Rutledge, S.C.	1795	Washington	Lucius Q. C. Lamar, Miss.	1888–1893	Cleveland
Samuel Chase, Md.	1796–1811	Washington	**Melville W. Fuller,** Ill.	1888–1910	Cleveland
Oliver Ellsworth, Conn.	1796–1800	Washington	David J. Brewer, Kan.	1890–1910	B. Harrison
Bushrod Washington, Va.	1799–1829	J. Adams	Henry B. Brown, Mich.	1891–1906	B. Harrison
Alfred Moore, N.C.	1800–1804	J. Adams	George Shiras, Jr., Pa.	1892–1903	B. Harrison
John Marshall, Va.	1801–1835	J. Adams	Howell E. Jackson, Tenn.	1893–1895	B. Harrison
William Johnson, S.C.	1804–1834	Jefferson	Edward D. White, La.	1894–1910	Cleveland
Brockholst Livingston, N.Y.	1807–1823	Jefferson	Rufus W. Peckham, N.Y.	1896–1909	Cleveland
Thomas Todd, Ky.	1807–1826	Jefferson	Joseph McKenna, Cal.	1898–1925	McKinley
Gabriel Duvall, Md.	1811–1835	Madison	Oliver W. Holmes, Mass.	1902–1932	T. Roosevelt
Joseph Story, Mass.	1812–1845	Madison	William R. Day, Ohio	1903–1922	T. Roosevelt
Smith Thompson, N.Y.	1823–1843	Monroe	William H. Moody, Mass.	1906–1910	T. Roosevelt
Robert Trimble, Ky.	1826–1828	J. Q. Adams	Horace H. Lurton, Tenn.	1910–1914	Taft
John McLean, Ohio	1830–1861	Jackson	Charles E. Hughes, N.Y.	1910–1916	Taft
Henry Baldwin, Pa.	1830–1844	Jackson	Willis Van Devanter, Wy	1911–1937	Taft
James M. Wayne, Ga.	1835–1867	Jackson	Joseph R. Lamar, Ga.	1911–1916	Taft
Roger B. Taney, Md.	1836–1864	Jackson	**Edward D. White,** La.	1910–1921	Taft
Philip P. Barbour, Va.	1836–1841	Jackson	Mahlon Pitney, N.J.	1912–1922	Taft
John Cartron, Tenn.	1837–1865	Van Buren	James C. McReynolds, Tenn.	1914–1941	Wilson
John McKinley, Ala.	1838–1852	Van Buren	Louis D. Brandeis, Mass.	1916–1939	Wilson
Peter V. Daniel, Va.	1842–1860	Van Buren	John H. Clarke, Ohio	1916–1922	Wilson
Samuel Nelson, N.Y.	1845–1872	Tyler	**William H. Taft,** Conn.	1921–1930	Harding
Levi Woodbury, N.H.	1845–1851	Polk	George Sutherland, Utah	1922–1938	Harding
Robert C. Grier, Pa.	1846–1870	Polk	Pierce Butler, Minn.	1923–1939	Harding
Benjamin R. Curtis, Mass.	1851–1857	Fillmore	Edward T. Sanford, Tenn.	1923–1930	Harding
John A. Campbell, Ala.	1853–1861	Pierce	Harlan F. Stone, N.Y.	1925–1941	Coolidge
Nathan Clifford, Me.	1858–1881	Buchanan	**Charles E. Hughes,** N.Y.	1930–1941	Hoover
Noah H. Swayne, Ohio	1862–1881	Lincoln	Owen J. Roberts, Penn.	1930–1945	Hoover
Samuel F. Miller, Iowa	1862–1890	Lincoln	Benjamin N. Cardozo, N.Y.	1932–1938	Hoover
David Davis, Ill.	1862–1877	Lincoln	Hugo L. Black, Ala.	1937–1971	F. Roosevelt
Stephen J. Field, Cal.	1863–1897	Lincoln	Stanley F. Reed, Ky.	1938–1957	F. Roosevelt
Salmon P. Chase, Ohio	1864–1873	Lincoln	Felix Frankfurter, Mass.	1939–1962	F. Roosevelt
William Strong, Pa.	1870–1880	Grant	William O. Douglas, Conn.	1939–1975	F. Roosevelt

*Chief Justices in bold type

Name	Terms of Service[1]	Appointed by	Name	Terms of Service[1]	Appointed by
Frank Murphy, Mich.	1940–1949	F. Roosevelt	Charles E. Whittaker, Mo.	1957–1962	Eisenhower
Harlan F. Stone, N.Y.	1941–1946	F. Roosevelt	Potter Stewart, Ohio	1958–1981	Eisenhower
James F. Byrnes, S.C.	1941–1942	F. Roosevelt	Byron R. White, Colo.	1962–	Kennedy
Robert H. Jackson, N.Y.	1941–1954	F. Roosevelt	Arthur J. Goldberg, Ill.	1962–1965	Kennedy
Wiley B. Rutledge, Iowa	1943–1949	F. Roosevelt	Abe Fortas, Tenn.	1965–1970	Johnson
Harold H. Burton, Ohio	1945–1958	Truman	Thurgood Marshall, Md.	1967–	Johnson
Frederick M. Vinson, Ky.	1946–1953	Truman	**Warren E. Burger,** Va.	1969–	Nixon
Tom C. Clark, Texas	1949–1967	Truman	Harry A. Blackmun, Minn.	1970–	Nixon
Sherman Minton, Ind.	1949–1956	Truman	Lewis F. Powell, Jr., Va.	1971–	Nixon
Earl Warren, Cal.	1953–1969	Eisenhower	William H. Rehnquist, Ariz.	1971–	Nixon
John Marshall Harlan, N.Y.	1955–1971	Eisenhower	John Paul Stevens, Ill.	1975–	Ford
William J. Brennan, Jr., N.J.	1956–	Eisenhower	Sandra Day O'Connor, Ariz.	1981–	Reagan

A Demographic Profile of the American People

Year	Life Expectancy from Birth White	Life Expectancy from Birth Black	Average Age at First Marriage Male	Average Age at First Marriage Female	Number of Children Under 5 (per 1,000 Women Aged 20–44)	Percent of Women in Paid Employment	Percent of Paid Workers Who Are Female
Industrializing America						
1820					1,295	6.2%	7.3%
1830					1,145	6.4	7.4
1840					1,085	8.4	9.6
1850					923	10.1	10.8
1860					929	9.7	10.2
1870					839	13.7	14.8
1880					822	14.7	15.2
1890			26.1	22.0	716	18.2	17.0
1900	47.6	33.0	25.9	21.9	688	21.2	18.1
1910	50.3	35.6	25.1	21.6	643	24.8	20.0
Modern America						
1920	54.9	45.3	24.6	21.2	604	23.9%	20.4%
1930	61.4	48.1	24.3	21.3	511	24.4	21.9
1940	64.2	53.1	24.3	21.5	429	25.4	24.6
1950	69.1	60.8	22.8	20.3	589	29.1	27.8
1960	70.6	63.6	22.8	20.3	737	34.8	32.3
1970	71.7	65.3	22.5	20.6	530	42.6	36.7
1980	74.4	69.8	23.6	21.8	440	51.1	42.6

SOURCE: *Historical Statistics of the United States, Colonial Times to 1970 (1975).*

American Population

Year	Population	Percent Increase		Year	Population	Percent Increase
Preindustrial America				**Industrializing America**		
1610	350	—		1820	9,638,453	33.1
1620	2,300	557.1		1830	12,866,020	33.5
1630	4,600	100.0		1840	17,069,453	32.7
1640	26,600	478.3		1850	23,191,876	35.9
1650	50,400	90.8		1860	31,443,321	35.6
1660	75,100	49.0		1870	39,818,449	26.6
1670	111,900	49.0		1880	50,155,783	26.0
1680	151,500	35.4		1890	62,947,714	25.5
1690	210,400	38.9		1900	75,994,575	20.7
1700	250,900	19.2		1910	91,972,266	21.0
1710	331,700	32.2				
1720	466,200	40.5				
1730	629,400	35.0		**Modern America**		
1740	905,600	43.9		1920	105,710,620	14.9
1750	1,170,800	29.3		1930	122,775,046	16.1
1760	1,593,600	36.1		1940	131,669,275	7.2
1770	2,148,100	34.8		1950	150,697,361	14.5
1780	2,780,400	29.4		1960	179,323,175	19.0
1790	3,929,214	41.3		1970	203,235,298	13.3
1800	5,308,483	35.1		1980	226,545,805	11.5
1810	7,239,881	36.4		1985	237,839,000	—*

*Percent increase is not calculated until the next census in 1990.
SOURCE: *Historical Statistics of the United States, Colonial Times to 1970* (1975).

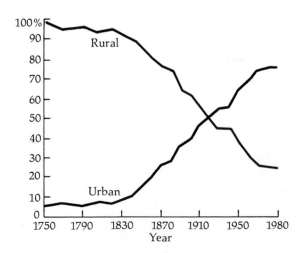

Foreign Origins of the American People

Immigration by Decade

	Industrializing America			Modern America	
Year	Number	Percent of Total Population	Year	Number	Percent of Total Population
1820–1830	151,824	1.6	1921–1930	4,107,209	3.9
1831–1840	599,125	4.6	1931–1940	528,431	0.4
1841–1850	1,713,251	10.0	1941–1950	1,035,039	0.7
1851–1860	2,598,214	11.2	1951–1960	2,515,479	1.6
1861–1870	2,314,824	7.4	1961–1970	3,321,677	1.8
1871–1880	2,812,191	7.1	1971–1980	4,493,000	2.2
1881–1890	5,246,613	10.5	Total	16,000,835	
1891–1900	3,687,546	5.8			
1901–1910	8,795,386	11.6			
1911–1920	5,735,811	6.2			
Total	33,654,785		**1820–1980 Grand total 49,655,620**		

SOURCE: U.S. Bureau of the Census, *Historical Statistics of the United States, Colonial Times to 1970* (1975), Part I, pp. 105–106; U.S. Bureau of the Census, *Statistical Abstract of the United States, 1984* (1983), p. 88.

Regional Origins of Immigrants

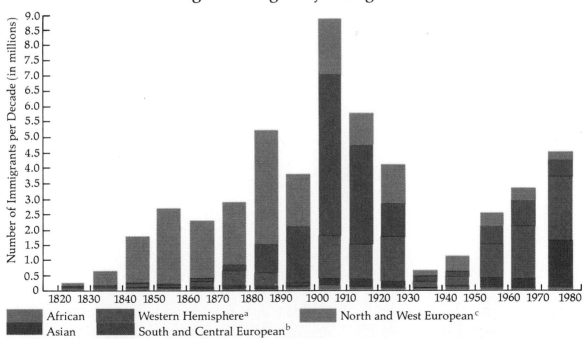

- African
- Asian
- Western Hemisphere[a]
- South and Central European[b]
- North and West European[c]

[a]Canada and all countries in South America and Central America.

[b]Italy, Spain, Portugal, Greece, Germany (Austria included, 1938–1945), Poland, Czechoslovakia (since 1920), Yugoslavia (since 1920), Hungary (since 1861), Austria (since 1861, except 1938–1945), U.S.S.R. (excludes Asian U.S.S.R. between 1931 and 1963), Latvia, Estonia, Lithuania, Finland, Romania, Bulgaria, Turkey (in Europe), and other European countries not classified elsewhere.

[c]Great Britain, Ireland, Norway, Sweden, Denmark, Iceland, Netherlands, Belgium, Luxembourg, Switzerland, France.

SOURCE: Stephan Thernstrom, ed., *Harvard Encyclopedia of American Ethnic Groups* (1980), p. 480; and U.S. Bureau of the Census, *Statistical Abstract of the United States, 1984* (1983), p. 9.

The Aging of the U.S. Population

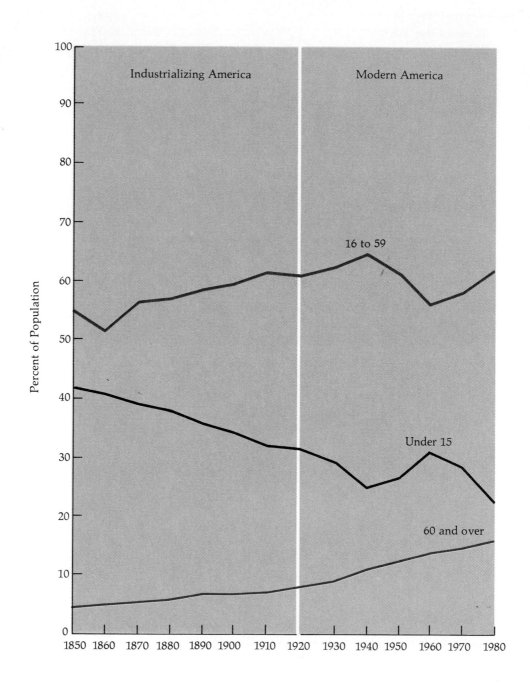

The Labor Force
(thousands of workers)

Year	Agriculture	Mining	Manufacturing	Construction	Trade	Other Services	Total
1810	1,956	11	75	—	—	—	2,330
1840	3,594	32	500	290	350	894	5,660
1850	4,520	102	1,200	410	530	1,488	8,250
1860	5,880	176	1,530	520	890	2,114	11,110
1870	6,790	180	2,470	780	1,310	1,400	12,930
1880	8,920	280	3,290	900	1,930	2,050	17,390
1890	9,960	440	4,390	1,510	2,960	4,060	23,320
1900	11,680	637	5,895	1,665	3,970	5,223	29,070
1910	11,770	1,068	8,332	1,949	5,320	9,041	37,480
1920	10,790	1,180	11,190	1,233	5,845	11,372	41,610
1930	10,560	1,009	9,884	1,988	8,122	17,767	48,830
1940	9,575	925	11,309	1,876	9,328	23,277	56,290
1950	7,870	901	15,648	3,029	12,152	25,870	65,470
1960	5,970	709	17,145	3,640	14,051	37,918	74,060
1970	3,419	664	19,741	4,261	15,234	36,431	79,750

SOURCE: Stanley Lebergott, "Labor Force and Employment, 1800–1960," *Output, Employment, and Productivity in the United States After 1800* (New York: National Bureau of Economic Research, 1966): 118–119. U.S. Bureau of Economic Analysis, *Long-Term Economic Growth, 1860–1970* (Washington, D.C., 1973): 260–263.

Changing Labor Patterns

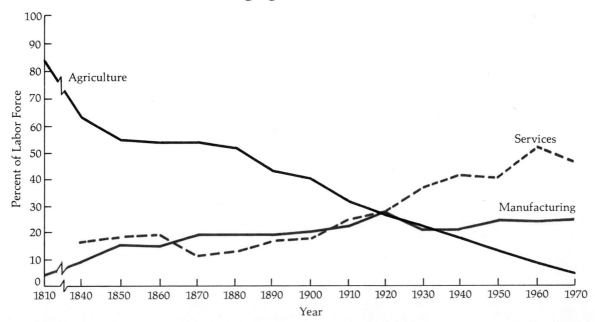

The Growth of the Federal Government

The Federal Government, 1900–1980

EMPLOYEES (millions)				RECEIPTS AND OUTLAYS ($ millions)		
Year	Civilian	Military		Year	Receipts	Outlays
1900	0.23	0.12		1900	567	521
1910	0.38	0.13		1910	676	694
1920	0.65	0.34		1920	6,649	6,358
1930	0.61	0.25		1930	4,058	3,320
1940	1.04	0.45		1940	6,900	9,600
1950	1.96	1.46		1950	40,900	43,100
1960	2.38	2.47		1960	92,500	92,200
1970	2.98	3.06		1970	193,700	196,600
1980	2.87	2.05		1980	520,100	579,600

SOURCE: *Statistical Profile of the United States, 1900–1980.*

Total Federal Debt 1900–1980

INDEX

Page references to illustrations, maps, and their captions appear in *italics*.

Banking and finance: Italian merchant families, 14; Fugger family of Augusburg, Germany, 21; loans to Spain, 21; early English capitalists, 23–24; paper currency issue in Rhode Island, 1715–1750, 87; land banks in colonial period, 87; Currency Act of 1751, 87; Currency Act of 1764, 87, 153; revolutionary war debt, 190–192, 199–200; Hamilton's policies, 209–215; laissez-faire theories and, 213–214; Albert Gallatin and, 231; expansion of banking system, 261–262; merchant capitalism, 261–264; Bank of North America, 262; *McCulloch v. Maryland*, 266; Bank of the United States (First), 212–213, 266; capital formation, early 19th century, 316; Bank of the United States (Second), founded, 354, performance, 362–363, Jackson's veto of, 362–364; Bank of England and Panic of 1837, 337; "Bank War," Jackson's victory in, 362–364; Independent Treasury Act, 367, 430; National Bank acts of 1863 and 1865, 465–466; Legal Tender Act of 1862, 466–467; Civil War financing, 467; Resumption Act of 1875, 507; emergence of investment banking, 527; and role in merger movement, 528; free silver movement, 615–616; 631–633; greenback movement, 631; and the Federal Reserve Act (1913), 672; World War I loans to Allies, 681; Federal Reserve in World War I, 689; international debt status, 689, 714–715; banks in 1920s, 711; Federal Reserve tight money policy, 1920, 712; foreign loans, 1920s, 714; stock market crash, 1929, 738–739, 754, 766; banks in 1930s, 739, 740, 742, 746–747; international economy, 1930s, 741; London Economic Conference, 1933, 804; mortgages, 747, 849–850; New Deal regulations, 749–750; international economy, 1970s, 964–965; Federal Reserve in 1975 recession, 968; *see also* Money supply; Panics and depressions

Bank of England, *see* Banking and finance

Bank of North America, *see* Banking and finance

Bank of the United States, First, *see* Banking and finance

Bank of the United States, Second *see* Banking and finance

Bannister, Thomas, 84

Baptists: middle colonies, 93, 134–135; church-state issue, 260; *see also* Religion

Barbados, *see* West Indies

Barbary states of North Africa, 235

Barbed wire, invented, 594

Bardi family, 14

Barlow, Joel, 257

Barnum, Phineas T., 574

Barrett family of Concord, Mass., 70

Barrow Plantation, 1860–1881, *498*

Barrymore, John, 783

Barrow, Clyde, 942

Barton, Bruce, 711

Barton, Clara, 465

Baruch, Bernard, 748; head of War Industries Board, 690–691

Baseball: 1870–1910, 573; *574;* Black Sox scandal of 1919, 720–721; in 1920s, 720–721; Jackie Robinson, 925; *see also* Leisure

Baseball in Old Chicago, 786

Bates, Ruby, 770–771

Batista, Fulgencio, 905

"Battle Hymn of the Republic" (Howe), 459, 478

Battle of the Bulge, 823–824

Battle of the Wilderness, 475

Bayard, James, 221

Bayard, Nicholas, 68

Bayard, William, 321

Bay of Pigs invasion, 904–905

Beard, Charles A., 203

Beard, Ithamar A., 287

Bear Flag Republic (California), 434–435

Beat Generation, 940

Beatles, 940

Beaulieu, Sarah, on the Civil War home front, 466

Beauregard, P. G. T., 455

Beauvais, France, 8

Beckley, John, 236

Beecher, Catharine, 299, 423, 565; educational reform, 394; on moral education, 395; debate with Angelina Grimké, 395–396

Beecher, Henry Ward, 338, 490, 572, 575

Beecher, Lyman, 300, 343, 344, 387

Beer industry, corporate concentration of, 842

Begin, Menachem, 969

Beiderbecke, Bix, 721

Belcher, Jonathan, 156

Belgium: early iron technology, 518; German invasion, 809

Belknap, William W., 506

Bell, Alexander Graham, 554

Bell, John, in election of 1860, 452

Bellamy, Edward, 648

Belleau Wood, battle of, 687

Bell for Adano (Hersey), 826

Bell Laboratories, 710

Bellow, Saul, 786

Benezet, Anthony, 197

Bennett, James Gordon, 574

Berger, Victor, 695

Bergman, Ingrid, 814

Berkeley, Busby, 783

Berkeley, William, 22, 60, 69; and Bacon's rebellion, 49–51

Berkman, Alexander, 702

Berle, Adolph, 756

Berlin blockade of 1948, 892

Berlin decrees of 1806, 234

Berlin Wall, 905

Bernard, Francis, 155, 164

Bernard, Thomas, 296

Bernays, Edward, 723

Bernstein, Carl, 962

Bessemer converter, 518–519

Bethune, Joanna, 344

Bethune, Mary McLeod, 758

Bettering House, Philadelphia, 127

Beulah (Wilson), 379

Bible Against Slavery (Weld), 387

Bible Society, 300

Bill of Grievances (1906), of the AFL, 658

Bill of Rights, *see* Constitution, U.S.; amendments by number

Billy the Kid (Copland), 785

Bingham, George Caleb, 258

Bird, Caroline, 769; quoted on the Depression, 767

Birmingham, Ala., black protests, 928; killing of black school girls, 928

Birney, James G., 391, 392, 434

Birth control and abortion: in early 19th century, 291–292, 425–426; contraception in WWI, 688; public support for in 1930s, 776; Margaret Sanger and birth control movement, 776; new contraceptives of 1960s, 943; Supreme Court decisions on 949–950; right-to-life movement, 951–952, 972; Hyde amendment to Medicaid, 952; *see also* Birth rate; Families; Women

Birth of a Nation (movie), 729–730

Birth rate: preindustrial Europe, 5–6; Puritan colonists, 42; northern colonies, 92; among slaves, 81–82; by race, *425; see also* Women; Families

Bishop Hill, Ill., *380*

Bishops' War, 29

Bismark, Otto von, 680–681

Black Ball Line, 321, 332

Black Boy (Wright), 818

Black Codes, *see* Blacks, racism and segregation

Black Elk, quoted, 600, 601

Black Hawk, *360;* Black Hawk War, 360

Black Hills, gold rush of 1874, 598

Black, Hugo, 753

Blacklisting, in Hollywood, 867

Black Muslims, 931–932

Black Panthers, 932

Black power movement, emergence of, 931–933; and urban race riots 1964–1968, 933–934; and women, 947

Blacks: in Carolina colony, 43, 83, 102, *104;* as African peoples, on Gold Coast, 76, 103, *104;* in Virginia, 77, 100–105, 132; racism and segregation, 79, 590; in West Indies, 80–81, 104; population, 1776, 83; in Nigeria, 103; in north during colonial period, 197; number of slaves, 1820, 242; number of free, early 19th century, 246; population increase, 1775–1820, 246; mulattoes, 250, 413–414; and African colonization policy, 384–385; population, under slavery, *411;* birth rates among, *425;* in Union Army, 469; migration into northern industry, 1870–1910, 534; in northern cities, 1870–1910, 569; post-Civil War sharecroppers, 602; in the South after reconstruction, 604–606, 607; disenfranchisement, 605; intensification of race hatred, 605–606; soldiers in WWI, *688,* 689; workers in WWI, 692; migration during

About the Authors

JAMES A. HENRETTA is Priscilla Alden Burke Professor of American History at the University of Maryland, College Park. He received his undergraduate education at Swarthmore College and his Ph.D. from Harvard University. Henretta has taught at the University of Sussex, England; Princeton University; UCLA; Boston University; and, as a Fulbright lecturer, in Australia at the University of New England. His publications include *The Evolution of American Society, 1700–1815: An Interdisciplinary Analysis; "Salutary Neglect": Colonial Administration Under the Duke of Newcastle;* and important articles in early American and social history. His present research is in the fields of legal and political history, on a project entitled *Law and the Creation of the Liberal State in America, 1770–1860.*

W. ELLIOT BROWNLEE is Professor of History and Chair of the Department of History at the University of California, Santa Barbara. He is a graduate of Harvard University, received his Ph.D. from the University of Wisconsin, and specializes in U.S. economic history. He has been awarded fellowships by the Haynes Foundation and the Charles Warren Center, Harvard University. He has been a visiting professor at Princeton University. His published works include *Progressivism and Economic Growth: The Wisconsin Income Tax, 1911–1929; Women in the American Economy: A Documentary History, 1675 to 1929; The Essentials of American History* (with R. N. Current, T. H. Williams, and F. Freidel; and *Dynamics of Ascent: A History of the American Economy.* He is currently at work on a history of taxation, *Taxation and Social Choice in America.*

DAVID BRODY is Professor of History at the University of California, Davis. He has taught overseas at the University of Warwick in England, at Moscow State University in the Soviet Union, and at Sydney University in Australia. He is the author of *Steelworkers in America, Labor in Crisis,* and, most recently, *Workers in Industrial America: Essays on the 20th Century Struggle.* He also serves on the editorial board of *Labor History,* as an editor for a series in American working-class history for the University of Illinois Press, and as a chief historical consultant for a series of television dramas about the history of American workers.

SUSAN WARE specializes in twentieth century U.S. history and the history of American women. She received her undergraduate degree from Wellesley College and her Ph.D. from Harvard University. Ware is the author of *Beyond Suffrage: Women in the New Deal; Holding Their Own: American Women in the 1930s,* and the forthcoming *Partner and I: The Public and Private Worlds of Molly Dewson.* She is Assistant Professor in the Department of History at New York University. Previously affiliated with Harvard University, the University of New Hampshire, and Tufts University, she has received grants from the Radcliffe Research Scholars Program and the American Council of Learned Societies. Her current projects include a women's history anthology from 1880 to the present and a collective biography of six prominent women in twentieth century American life.

A Note on the Type

The text of this book was set in 10½/12 Palatino using a film version of the face designed by Hermann Zapf, which was first released in 1950 by Germany's Stempel Foundry. The face is named after Giovanni Battista Palatino, a famous penman of the sixteenth century. In its calligraphic quality, Palatino is reminiscent of the Italian Renaissance type designs, yet with its wide, open letters and unique proportions it still retains a modern feel. Palatino is considered one of the most important typefaces from one of Europe's most influential type designers.

Interior design by Lucy Lesiak Design, Chicago.

Composition by P&M Typesetting, Inc., Waterbury, Connecticut.

Printed and bound by W. A. Krueger Company, New Berlin, Wisconsin.